Frommer's®

Central America

2nd Edition

by Nicholas Gill, Eliot Greenspan,
Charlie O'Malley & Jisel Perilla

WILEY

Wiley Publishing, Inc

Published by:

WILEY PUBLISHING, INC.

111 River St.
Hoboken, NJ 07030-5774

ISBNs 978-0-470-90346-9 (paper); 978-1-118-03351-7 (ebk); 978-1-118-03352-4 (ebk);
978-1-118-03353-1 (ebk)

Editors: Kathleen Warnock, with Andrea Kahn and Jessica Langan-Peck
Production Editor: Jonathan Scott
Cartographer: Elizabeth Puhl
Photo Editor: Richard Fox
Production by Wiley Indianapolis Composition Services
Front cover photo: Altiplano, San Andres Xecul village, Guatemala: young girl passing by the church © SIME / eStock Photo
Back cover photo: Arenal Volcano National Park, Costa Rica © Luis Alberto Aldonza / AGE Fotostock, Inc.

For information on our other products and services or to obtain technical support, please contact our Customer Care Department within the U.S. at 877/762-2974, outside the U.S. at 317/572-3993 or fax 317/572-4002.

Wiley also publishes its books in a variety of electronic formats. Some content that appears in print may not be available in electronic formats.

Manufactured in the United States of America

5 4 3 2 1

CONTENTS

10 PANAMA 650

11 FAST FACTS: CENTRAL AMERICA 725

12 HELPFUL SPANISH PHRASES 731

LIST OF MAPS

ABOUT THE AUTHORS

Writer and photographer **Nicholas Gill** (Honduras) lives in Lima, Peru, and Brooklyn, New York. His work has appeared in publications such as the *New York Times, Los Angeles Times, Conde Nast Traveler, Afar,* and *National Geographic Traveler.* Visit his personal website (www.nicholas-gill.com), or his blog on Latin American food, drinks, and travel (www.new worldreview.com).

Eliot Greenspan (Belize, Costa Rica, Guatemala) is a poet, journalist, musician, and travel writer who took his backpack and typewriter the length of Mesoamerica before settling in Costa Rica in 1992. Since then, he has worked steadily as a travel writer, food critic, free-lance journalist, and translator, and has continued his travels in the region. He is the author of *Frommer's Belize, Frommer's Ecuador, Frommer's Guatemala, Costa Rica For Dummies, Costa Rica Day by Day,* and *The Tico Times Restaurant Guide to Costa Rica,* as well as the chapter on Venezuela in *Frommer's South America.*

Charlie O'Malley (El Salvador, Nicaragua) first became fascinated with Latin America when he watched salsa dancers on a Colombian beach over a decade ago. He has since wrestled with anaconda in Venezuela, rescued turtles in Nicaragua, and been chased by bulls in Ecuador. Based in the Andean Argentine city of Mendoza, he keeps his desire for more adventure in check with lots of good local wine and work on a tourist magazine called *Wine Republic.* With driving skills almost as bad as the locals and an undying penchant for long siestas, he does not think he can ever live in his native Ireland again. He has worked on Frommer's guides to Argentina and South America and contributed to *Frommer's 500 Adventures for Adrenaline Lovers.*

Jisel Perilla (Panama) has written about, lived in, and traveled throughout much of Latin America, where she makes her living as a freelance writer. She currently resides in Bogotá, Colombia, and writes about Latin America for www.latinworld.com and other publications. You can read her personal travel blog at www.anomadlife.wordpress.com. Jisel also is the author of the Colombia chapter in *Frommer's South America.*

HOW TO CONTACT US

In researching this book, we discovered many wonderful places—hotels, restaurants, shops, and more. We're sure you'll find others. Please tell us about them, so we can share the information with your fellow travelers in upcoming editions. If you were disappointed with a recommendation, we'd love to know that, too. Please write to:

Frommer's Central America, 2nd Edition
Wiley Publishing, Inc. • 111 River St. • Hoboken, NJ 07030-5774
frommersfeedback@wiley.com

AN ADDITIONAL NOTE

Please be advised that travel information is subject to change at any time—and this is especially true of prices. We therefore suggest that you write or call ahead for confirmation when making your travel plans. The authors, editors, and publisher cannot be held responsible for the experiences of readers while traveling. Your safety is important to us, however, so we encourage you to stay alert and be aware of your surroundings. Keep a close eye on cameras, purses, and wallets, all favorite targets of thieves and pickpockets.

FROMMER'S STAR RATINGS, ICONS & ABBREVIATIONS

Every hotel, restaurant, and attraction listing in this guide has been ranked for quality, value, service, amenities, and special features using a **star-rating system.** In country, state, and regional guides, we also rate towns and regions to help you narrow down your choices and budget your time accordingly. Hotels and restaurants are rated on a scale of zero (recommended) to three stars (exceptional). Attractions, shopping, nightlife, towns, and regions are rated according to the following scale: zero stars (recommended), one star (highly recommended), two stars (very highly recommended), and three stars (must-see).

In addition to the star-rating system, we also use **seven feature icons** that point you to the great deals, in-the-know advice, and unique experiences that separate travelers from tourists. Throughout the book, look for:

special finds—those places only insiders know about

fun facts—details that make travelers more informed and their trips more fun

kids—best bets for kids and advice for the whole family

special moments—those experiences that memories are made of

overrated—places or experiences not worth your time or money

insider tips—great ways to save time and money

great values—where to get the best deals

The following **abbreviations** are used for credit cards:

AE	American Express	**DISC**	Discover	**V**	Visa
DC	Diners Club	**MC**	MasterCard		

TRAVEL RESOURCES AT FROMMERS.COM

Frommer's travel resources don't end with this guide. Frommer's website, **www.frommers. com,** has travel information on more than 4,000 destinations. We update features regularly, giving you access to the most current trip-planning information and the best airfare, lodging, and car-rental bargains. You can also listen to podcasts, connect with other Frommers. com members through our active-reader forums, share your travel photos, read blogs from guidebook editors and fellow travelers, and much more.

THE BEST OF CENTRAL AMERICA

Whether you're an archaeology buff, an outdoor adventurer, or just someone in search of a good time, Central America presents you with a plethora of diverse travel options. There are so many rainforests to hike, volcanic peaks to climb, and coral reefs to scuba dive, and there's so much colonial splendor to see, that you can't possibly see and do it all in one trip. You can certainly make a good go of it, though. Below are some of our personal favorites to get you started.

THE most UNFORGETTABLE TRAVEL EXPERIENCES

○ **Snorkeling at Shark-Ray Alley & Hol Chan Marine Reserve** (Northern Cayes and Atolls, Belize): These two popular sites are threatened with overcrowding but still live up to their billing. Shark-Ray Alley guarantees a close encounter with schools of stingrays and nurse sharks. The experience provides an adrenaline rush for all but the most nonchalant and veteran divers. Hol Chan Marine Reserve is an excellent snorkeling spot composed of a narrow channel cutting through a coral reef. See chapter 4.

○ **Riding an Inner Tube Through the Caves Branch River Cave System** (Cayo District, Belize): Strap on a battery-powered headlamp, climb into the center of an inner tube, and float through a series of limestone caves, your headlamp illuminating the stalactites and the occasional bat. The entire sensation is eerie and claustrophobic at times, but fun—especially if you go with a small group on a day when the caves are not crowded. See chapter 4.

○ **Watching the Sunrise from the Top of a Pyramid in Tikal** (Guatemala): A visit to Tikal is a remarkable experience, but our favorite way to start a visit here is by catching the sunrise from the top of one of the pyramids. In addition to the ruins and sunrise, the surrounding jungle comes to life with the cries of howler monkeys and the frenzied activity and calls of awakening birds. See chapter 5.

○ **Paying Your Respects to Maximón** (Guatemala): A syncretic saint worshiped by Guatemala's Maya and Catholic alike, Maximón is the bad boy of the religious pantheon. Maximón supposedly responds well to gifts, and has specific tastes, so be sure to bring some rum or a cigar as an offering. Many towns across Guatemala have a carved idol of Maximón, or San Simon, although only a few keep the practice of his daily worship alive. The towns with the most elaborate rituals and traditions include Santiago de Atitlán and Zunil. See chapter 5.

- **Touring the Towns & Villages Around Lake Atitlán** (Guatemala): While Lake Atitlán is exceedingly beautiful, the true charm of the lake is its ability to let you visit a half-dozen or more lakeshore towns via local water-taxi services. The water taxis run regular routes throughout the day, stopping at the villages of Santiago de Atitlán, San Pedro de la Laguna, San Marco, San Antonio Palopó, and more. You can hop on and off the taxis at your whim, and stay as long as you like before heading on to the next place or back home to your hotel. See chapter 5.

- **Exploring the 35km (22 miles) of Winding Mountain Road & Villages of the Rutas de Las Flores** (El Salvador): If you're tight on time, this route offers an excellent sample of what El Salvador has to offer. The route is known for its small towns, each offering something different, from the furniture craftsmen of Nahuizalco, to Juayúa's weekend food-and-craft festival, to the artsy vibe and cool restaurants of Ataco. The route also offers amazing views of thousands of flowering coffee plants and one of the country's highest and longest zip-line canopy tours. See chapter 6.

- **Seeing Suchitoto** (El Salvador): This is one of El Salvador's most beautiful and unique towns and well worth the easy, 1-hour drive north of San Salvador. After a turbulent history during El Salvador's civil war, Suchitoto has reemerged as one of El Salvador's leading international arts and cultural centers, with the country's most luxurious boutique hotels and a famous international arts festival. But despite its international flair, Suchitoto is still a distinctly Salvadoran town, close to the historic town of Cinquera, home to a weekend artisans market, and surrounded by amazing mountain views. See chapter 6.

- **Eating a *Baleada*** (Honduras): The iconic snack food of Honduras, served in stalls and sit-down restaurants all over the country is a folded wheat tortilla stuffed with refried beans, crumbled *queso blanco* (white cheese), sour cream, and occasionally egg, chicken, beef, avocado, onions, or tomatoes. It's so delicious that, after tasting one, you might never want to leave the country. See chapter 7.

- **Seeing the Still-Smoking Flor de Copán Cigar Factory** (Santa Rosa de Copán, Honduras): The Flor de Copán factory is world renowned for its production of fine cigars like the Don Melo line. A tour involves a walk-through of the factory's heady drying and deveining rooms and witnessing the country's most skilled rollers working. Even if you hate smoking, this is a great chance to mingle with real Hondurans, outside the tourist industry. See chapter 7.

- **Visiting Volcán Masaya** (Masaya, Nicaragua): The Spanish called this volcano the "Gates of Hell" and you can understand why when you see its boulder-spitting craters and glowing lava fields. Volcán Masaya is one of the most accessible and scariest live volcanoes in the region—it's also one of the most exciting to see up close. See chapter 8.

- **Turtle-Watching in San Juan del Sur** (San Juan del Sur, Nicaragua): After a spot of sun worshiping on Nicaragua's beaches, come out at night and see one of nature's true wonders—massive turtle hatchings on the beautiful Playa La Flor. The best time to see turtles nesting is August and September. See chapter 8.

- **Gaping at Arenal Volcano/Soaking in Tabacón Hot Springs** (near La Fortuna, Costa Rica): When the skies are clear and the lava is flowing, Arenal Volcano offers a thrilling light show accompanied by an earthshaking rumble that defies description. You can even see the show while soaking in a natural hot spring and having a drink at the swim-up bar at **Tabacón Grand Spa Thermal Resort** (p. 621). If the rushing torrent of volcano-heated spring water isn't therapeutic enough, you can get a massage here, as well. See chapter 9.

○ **Touring the Osa Peninsula** (Southern Costa Rica): This is Costa Rica's most remote and biologically rich region. **Corcovado National Park,** the largest remaining patch of virgin lowland tropical rainforest in Central America, takes up much of the Osa Peninsula. Jaguars, crocodiles, and scarlet macaws all call this place home. Whether you stay in a luxury nature lodge in **Drake Bay** or outside of **Puerto Jiménez,** or camp in the park, you will be surrounded by some of the most lush and intense jungle this country has to offer. See chapter 9.

○ **Hiking Sendero Los Quetzales** (Volcán Barú National Park, Panama): Panama's foremost day hike takes visitors around the northeastern flank of Volcán Barú and through primary and secondary tropical forest and cloud forest that provide a dazzling array of flora and fauna. The trail's namesake resplendent quetzal lives here, too. The trail is mostly downhill from the Cerro Punta side to Boquete, and this is the recommended direction unless you crave a workout. What's unique about this trek is that travelers lodging around Cerro Punta can send their luggage to their next hotel in Boquete, and walk. See chapter 10.

○ **Birding Along Pipeline Road in Soberanía National Park** (Panama): This is the "celebrity" bird-watching trail, famous for the great number of species found here. Some years, Pipeline Road has set the world record for 24-hour bird counts. Even nonbirders can't help getting caught up in the action with so many colorful avians fluttering about, from motmots, trogons, toucans, antbirds, and colorful tanagers, to flycatchers. The farther you go along the rainforest trail, the better your chances are of spotting rare birds. See chapter 10.

○ **Watching the Panama Canal in Action** (Panama): It's one of the modern marvels of the world and pretty incredible when you think that this man-made waterway cut Panama open from the Pacific to the Atlantic. More than 200,000 workers died building this nearly impossible canal; learn more about Canal history at the top-notch Miraflores Visitors Center. See chapter 10.

THE best SMALL TOWNS & VILLAGES

○ **Caye Caulker,** Belize: The official slogan here is "Go Slow." Even going slow, you can walk this small island from end to end in under 20 minutes. The fastest-moving vehicles are bicycles, although lazier souls roam around in golf carts. The town is a small and funky Caribbean beach burg, with a lively mix of restaurants, bars, and tours to keep you busy and interested. See chapter 4.

○ **Flores,** Guatemala: In addition to serving as the gateway to Guatemala's greatest Maya ruin, Tikal, the island town of Flores has ample charms of its own. It's great for walking, and you'll find plenty of restaurants, bars, and small hotels. The town is also loaded with small boats, whose operators are eager to give you a tour of nearby attractions, or simply a sunset cruise on the lake. See chapter 5.

○ **Perquín & Mozote,** El Salvador: Exploring the history and tragedy of the towns of Perquín and Mozote should provide insight into the troubled history of this complex nation. Perquín is a small town in the high eastern mountains, which formed the base of the people's FMLN organization during the civil war. The nearby village of Mozote was the site of one of Latin America's worst modern wartime atrocities; the square and church now feature the well-known Mozote memorial and the names of the townspeople who were killed. See chapter 6.

o **Barra de Santiago,** El Salvador: Santiago is a protected reserve and largely undeveloped fishing village along the country's far western coast. The best thing about the place is its isolation and natural beauty; it's surrounded by wide, nearly deserted, sandy beaches and mangrove-filled estuaries where majestic white egrets glide low over the water. And it sits in front of a miles-long line of volcanoes that seem to rise from the palm-tree-lined estuary shores. You can fish, swim, surf, paddle, spot sea turtles laying their eggs, or just do nothing and enjoy the view. See chapter 6.

o **Miami,** Honduras: Set on a narrow sandbar between the Caribbean and the Los Micos lagoon in Parque Nacional Jeanette Kawas, this Garífuna village, just a small collection of thatched huts, has remained unchanged for a couple of hundred years. Get there while you can though, as development around Tela Bay is a serious threat to this and other communities nearby. See chapter 7.

o **San Juan del Sur,** Nicaragua: This small, colorful fishing village of clapboard houses is slowly morphing into a party town with excellent hotels and restaurants. It sits amid a string of great beaches offering surfing, fishing, sailing, or just glorious idling. See chapter 8.

o **Tortuguero Village** (on the Caribbean coast, Costa Rica): Tortuguero Village is a small collection of wooden shacks on a narrow spit of land between the Caribbean Sea and a maze of jungle canals. It's been called Costa Rica's Venice, but it has more in common with the South American Amazon. As you explore the narrow canals, you'll see a wide variety of herons and other water birds, three types of monkeys, three-toed sloths, and caimans. If you come between June and October, you might be treated to the awe-inspiring spectacle of a green turtle nesting—the small stretch of Tortuguero beach is the last remaining major nesting site of this endangered animal. See chapter 9.

o **Boquete** (Panama): This small town is set amid verdant mountains and is home to some of the world's most unique ecosystems and national parks, such as La Amistad International Park and Volcán Barú National Park. But it's not just about nature in Boquete; here, you'll find some of Panama's best B&Bs, savor some of the world's best coffee, and enjoy a fun dining scene. See chapter 10.

THE best BEACHES

o **Placencia,** Belize: This is the hippest little beach town in Belize. In a Caribbean country lacking in long stretches of beach, Placencia offers nearly 26km (16 miles) of white sand fronting a turquoise sea. You can wander up and down the length of this long beach, or hang out near the little creole village, whose main thoroughfare and directional reference point is a narrow strip of concrete running north to south and known simply as "the sidewalk." See chapter 4.

o **The Balsamo Coast,** El Salvador: Along this 25km (16-mile) strip are some of the country's most beautiful black-sand beaches. The Balsamo Coast is best known for its world-class surfing—the coast is said to be home to the best breaks in all of Central America. See chapter 6.

- **West Bay Beach,** Roatán, Honduras: The crystal-clear water and powdery white sand have led many to call this one of the top beaches in the Caribbean. Don't forget your snorkel gear; the world's second-largest barrier reef is just offshore See chapter 7.

- **The Corn Islands,** Nicaragua: You won't lack company while taking a dip and exploring the coral reefs around these classic Caribbean treasure islands: Spider crabs, parrotfish, and baby barracuda, among others, will dart before your eyes in the pristine blue waters here. See chapter 8.

- **Manuel Antonio,** Costa Rica: The first beach destination to become popular in Costa Rica, Manuel Antonio retains its charms despite burgeoning crowds and mushrooming hotels. The beaches inside the national park are idyllic, and the views from the hills approaching the park are enchanting. This is one of the few remaining habitats for the endangered squirrel monkey. See chapter 9.

- **Isla Bastimentos,** Bocas del Toro, Panama: Cayos Zapatillas, or the "Slippers Islands" (so-called because they resemble footprints), not only fulfill the beach lover's fantasy with their soft sand backed by a tangle of jungle, but also are surrounded by a rich display of coral that attracts hordes of fish, providing good snorkeling. Isla Bastimentos offers terrific beaches with clean sand and blue water. See chapter 10.

THE best OUTDOOR ADVENTURES

- **Scuba Diving or Snorkeling on the Belize Barrier Reef** (Belize): Running the length of the country's coastline, the Belize Barrier Reef is the second-longest continuous barrier reef in the world. You will find some of the best snorkeling opportunities and scuba-diving sites in the world. Whether it's shallow-water snorkeling over multicolored fan and staghorn coral, or scuba diving with whale sharks off of Gladden Spit, the opportunities are nearly endless. See chapter 4.

- **Horseback Riding Through the Cayo District** (Belize): The Cayo District is a perfect area to explore on horseback. Rides can be combined with visits to jungle waterfalls and swimming holes, as well as nearby Maya ruins. **Mountain Equestrian Trails (© 501/669-1124;** www.metbelize.com) has one of the better stables and horse-riding operations in the Cayo District. See chapter 4.

- **Climbing an Active Volcano** (Guatemala): Guatemala's mountainous terrain is predominantly volcanic, and many of these volcanoes are still active. There's nothing as primal as climbing the flanks of an active volcano or peering down into an erupting crater. Both of these experiences are possible on a climb to the summit of **Pacaya** volcano. Once Pacaya has whetted your appetite, there are numerous other volcanoes here to scale, including **Santa María, Tajumulco, Agua,** and **Acatenango.** See chapter 5.

- **Hiking & Swimming in Parque Nacional El Imposible** (El Salvador): Parque Imposible is one of El Salvador's largest, most lush, and richest-in-wildlife national parks, and it's dotted with streams, waterfalls, and natural swimming holes that are perfect for swimming. Tacuba, the small town just outside the park, serves as a great base camp for hiking trips. See chapter 6.

- **Trekking Through La Mosquitia** (Honduras): Rich with wildlife and home to ethnic groups like the Miskito, Pech, Garífuna, and Tawahkas, Central America's largest tract of rainforest is spectacular. Community-based tourism initiatives, run directly in the indigenous villages themselves, can assist in your exploration of the swamps, wetlands, grasslands, lagoons, and beaches here. See chapter 7.

o **Bird-Watching in Honduras:** Trogons, motmots, tanagers, scarlet macaws, boat-billed herons, resplendent quetzals, and toucans are only a small fraction of the avian life you will encounter in places such as Lancetilla, Lago de Yojoa, Pico Bonito, Cerro Azul, and Celaque. Some areas of the country have recorded as many as 400 species. See chapter 7.

o **Kayaking Around Isla Juan Venado** (Nicaragua): Pelicans and herons step over crocodiles, iguanas, and caimans as you paddle through a labyrinth of channels in this mangrove swamp on the Pacific coast, close to León. See chapter 8.

o **Hiking Through Reserva Natural Miraflor** (Nicaragua): Miraflor is a slice of Eden in the northern highlands of Nicaragua. Orchids bloom amid begonias and moss-draped oak trees, while toucans and parakeets hide among the foliage. Hike La Chorrera trail as far as a 60m-high (197-ft.) waterfall, going past ancient caves and prehistoric mounds. See chapter 8.

o **Kayaking Around the Golfo Dulce** (Costa Rica): Slipping through the waters of the Golfo Dulce by kayak gets you intimately in touch with the raw beauty of this under-developed region. Spend several days poking around in mangrove swamps, fishing in estuaries, and watching dolphins frolic. **Escondido Trex** (© **2735-5210;** www.escondidotrex.com) provides multiday custom kayaking trips out of Puerto Jiménez on the Osa Peninsula. See chapter 9.

o **White-Water Rafting & Kayaking the Chiriquí & Chiriquí Viejo Rivers** (Panama): Depending on which section you raft, these two rivers produce serious white water ranging from technical Class 3 to Class 5, some portions of which are so difficult they've been named "Fear" and "Get Out If You Can." There are plenty of tamer floats on Class 2 rivers, such as the Esti, for families and beginners. Virtual solitude, beautiful views, and lush surroundings are part of the tour, too. Contact **Chiriquí River Rafting** (© **720-1505;** www.panama-rafting.com) in Boquete. See chapter 10.

o **Enjoying a Jungle Cruise on Lake Gatún or the Chagres River** (Panama): Kids and adults alike will enjoy this fun adventure on which you're sure to see white-faced capuchin monkeys, caimans, sloths, and dozens of birds. Watch ships make their way to the Miraflores or Gatun locks while a bilingual guide points out tropical flora and fauna in dense, tropical jungle. See chapter 10.

THE most INTRIGUING HISTORICAL SITES

o **Caracol** (Belize): Caracol is the largest known Maya archaeological site in Belize, and one of the great Maya city-states of the Classic era. Deep within the Chiquibil Forest Reserve, the ruins are not nearly as well excavated as Tikal. However, this is part of Caracol's charm. The main pyramid here, Caana or "Sky Palace," stands some 41m (135 ft.) high; it is the tallest Maya building in Belize and still the tallest man-made structure in the country. See p. 132.

o **Tikal** (El Petén, Guatemala): Some say Tikal is the most impressive of all the ancient Maya ceremonial cities. Not only is the site massive and meticulously excavated and restored, but it's in the midst of a lush and lively tropical jungle. The peaks of several temples poke through the rainforest canopy, toucans and parrots fly about, and the loudest noise you'll hear is the guttural call of howler monkeys. In its heyday, the city probably covered as many as 65 sq. km (25 sq. miles) and supported a population of more than 100,000. See p. 206.

o **Joya de Cerén** (outside of San Salvador, El Salvador): Joya de Cerén isn't El Salvador's most visually stunning ruin, but it offers one of Central America's most accurate glimpses into the lives of the region's Maya ancestors, by way of the remains of a Maya village, frozen in time 1,400 years ago when it was buried beneath the ash of a volcanic eruption. Still standing and preserved are the local shaman's house, a community sauna, and private sleeping rooms. See p. 243.

o **Copán** (Honduras): Often referred to as the Paris of the Maya world, these majestic ruins will take you on a dramatic journey through the Maya civilization. The secret to understanding the Copán Ruins is a large square block of carved stone known as the Altar Q, which represents the dynastic lineage of 16 kings whose rule spanned nearly 4 centuries. See p. 362.

o **Huellas de Acahualinca** (Managua, Nicaragua): Six-thousand-year-old footprints of men, women, and children beg the question, were they fleeing a volcanic eruption or just going for a swim? One thing is for sure, the footprints here are some of the oldest pieces of evidence of human activity in Central America. This intriguing site can be visited in a northern suburb of Managua. See p. 457.

o **León** (Nicaragua): This cradle of the revolution has been bombed, besieged, and washed away by hurricanes. Every street corner tells a story, and it's highly recommended that you take a city tour of this fascinating university town with its vibrant murals, tiny plazas, and the biggest cathedral in Central America. Nearby is León Viejo, the original, abandoned colonial city at the feet of its destroyer—Volcán Momotombo. See p. 467.

o **Casco Viejo** (Panama City, Panama): This UNESCO-designated Panama City neighborhood is renowned for its Spanish, Italian, and French-influenced late-18th-century architecture and its narrow streets, bougainvillea-filled plazas, and breezy promenade. But Casco Viejo is also home to some of the country's top historical landmarks, such as La Catedral Metropolitana; the charred remains of the Iglesia de Santo Domingo; Casa Gongora, the best-preserved example of a Spanish colonial home; and the Salon Bolivar, the site of the famous 1826 congress organized by Bolivar to discuss the unification of Colombia, Mexico, and Central America. See p. 671.

THE best MUSEUMS & CHURCHES

o **Old Belize** (Belize City, Belize): Old Belize (© **501/222-4129;** www.oldbelize. com) is part museum, part playground, part beach, and part attraction. There's something for everyone, and plenty for the kids, including a water slide. It's easy to spend several hours, if not a whole day here. See p. 97.

o **Iglesia La Merced** (Antigua, Guatemala): In a city awash in Catholic churches, convents, and monasteries, Iglesia La Merced reigns supreme. The principal procession of the Holy Week celebrations leaves from this church. The ornate baroque facade is bright yellow and white, and the interior is full of art and sculptures. The ruins of the attached convent are also worth a visit. See p. 182.

- **Iglesia de Santo Tomás** (Chichicastenango, Guatemala): Dating from 1540, this modest church serves simultaneously as a place for Catholic worship and ancient Maya rituals. The exterior steps, which possess a perch over the town of Chichicastenango, are believed to represent the 18 months of the Maya calendar. Today, these steps are constantly in use as an altar for Maya prayer and offerings. It was in the attached convent that the oldest known version of the Popol Vuh was discovered. See p. 205.

- **Museo de Arte** (San Salvador, El Salvador): This 2,267-sq.-m (24,400-sq.-ft.), six-room museum of rotating and permanent exhibits offers the visitor an insightful, visual glimpse into the character of the country. Exceptionally interesting is the art of the country's civil war period. Museo de Arte de El Salvador also features the famous towering stone mosaic *Monument to the Revolution*, which depicts a naked man whose outstretched arms are thought to symbolize freedom and liberty. See p. 240.

- **Chiminike** (Tegucigalpa, Honduras): This modish children's museum isn't shy about making sure kids are entertained: a human body room complete with fart sounds, a crawl through an intestinal tract, and a graffiti-prone VW Beetle are all on exhibit. Kids might not realize it, but every quirk is part of the museum's ingenious way to get young people to learn. See p. 339.

- **Antiguo Convento San Francisco** (Granada, Nicaragua): Though the Antiguo Convento San Francisco has a remarkable collection of pre-Columbian statues, it's not the only attraction in this beautiful city. One great way to see all the sites, including the Antiguo Convento, is to take a horse-and-carriage ride through Granada's charming cobbled streets. See p. 483.

- **Miraflores Visitors Center** (Canal Zone, Panama): This top-notch museum is the best land-based platform from which to see the Panama Canal at work. The four-floor museum features an interactive display, a theater, and exhibits providing information about the canal's history and its impact on world trade. Helpful information is provided in English and Spanish, and the museum is well organized and maintained. Best of all are the excellent views of gigantic cargo ships transiting the canal. See p. 692.

THE best SMALL & MODERATELY PRICED HOTELS

- **San Pedro Holiday Hotel** (Ambergris Caye, Belize; ℂ 713/893-3825 in the U.S. and Canada, or 501/226-2014 in Belize; www.sanpedroholiday.com): This brilliantly white three-building complex with purple and pink trim sits in the center of San Pedro town. This was the first hotel on Ambergris Caye when Celi McCorkle opened it over 40 years ago, and still one of the best. Grab a room with an ocean-view balcony. See p. 115.

- **Black Rock Jungle River Lodge** (Cayo District, Belize; ℂ 501/820-4049; www.blackrocklodge.com): Down a long dirt road on the edge of a cliff overlooking the Macal River, this place offers up all the benefits and amenities of a top-notch ecolodge at very reasonable rates. See p. 137.

- **La Casa del Mundo** (Jaibalito, Lake Atitlán, Guatemala; ℂ 502/5218-5332; www.lacasadelmundo.com): Set atop an isolated rocky outcropping jutting into Lake Atitlán, this hotel offers a few rooms with shared bathrooms that are a real steal (even the ones with private bathrooms are a bargain), with stupendous views of the lake. A lakeside fire-heated Jacuzzi and several open-air terraces make this place really special. See p. 197.

o **Casa Mañen** (Quetzaltenango, Guatemala; ✆ 502/7765-0786; www.comeseeit. com): This is my favorite hotel in Quetzaltenango. The rooms are decorated with a range of local arts and craft works, the service is excellent, and the owners are knowledgeable about the various local tour options. The large rooftop terrace offers wonderful panoramic views of the city. See p. 203.

o **Los Almendros de San Lorenzo** (Suchitoto, El Salvador; ✆ 503/2335-1200; www.hotelsalvador.com): This is a rare taste of luxury in a rural mountain village. It's owned by former Paris fashion convention organizer Pascal Lebailly, who spent 17 months with 30 workers transforming a 200-year-old house into an oasis of style. He applied his eye for fashion to create an interior design that's magazine-ready, with a stone pool, glass-enclosed French restaurant, and walls filled with some of El Salvador's best art. You won't find a more romantic or casually elegant hotel in the country. See p. 278.

o **Yamari Savannah Cabañas** (La Mosquitia, Honduras; ✆ 504/443-8009; www. larutamoskitia.com): A solar-powered ecolodge in the wilderness about an hour from Brus Laguna, and you can stay there for just $10 a night. This one is set in one of La Mosquitia's bizarre savannas where you will bird-watch by kayak, inner tube, or traditional cayuco canoe. See p. 438.

o **La Posada Azul** (San Juan del Sur, Nicaragua; ✆ 505/2568-2524; www.laposada azul.com): This delightful boutique hotel will make you feel like you've stepped into a García Márquez novel—its old-school charm is authentic. High ceilings grace wooden interiors and an old-world living room, and a veranda runs the length of the house to a lovely flower garden with a fountain and small pool. See p. 523.

o **Hotel Grano de Oro** (San José, Costa Rica; ✆ 2255-3322; www.hotelgrano deoro.com): San José boasts dozens of old homes that have been converted into hotels, but few offer the plush accommodations or professional service found at the Grano de Oro. All the guest rooms have attractive hardwood furniture, including old-fashioned wardrobes in some rooms. When it's time to relax, you can soak in a hot tub or have a drink in the rooftop lounge while taking in San José's commanding view. See p. 575.

o **Arco Iris Lodge** (Monteverde, Costa Rica; ✆ 2645-5067; www.arcoirislodge. com): This small lodge is right in Santa Elena, and it's by far the best deal in the Monteverde area. The rooms are cozy and immaculate, and the owners are extremely knowledgeable and helpful. See p. 610.

o **The Coffee Estate Inn** (Boquete, Panama; ✆ 720-2211; www.coffeeestateinn. com): Gorgeous views of Volcán Barú, cozy bungalows with full kitchens, and owner-managed, friendly service tailored to your needs are the hallmarks of the Coffee Estate Inn. The bungalows are enveloped in native forest, fruit trees, and flowers that attract myriad birds. The romantic ambience is ideal for honeymooners. See p. 709.

THE best LUXURY HOTELS & ECOLODGES

o **Turtle Inn** (Placencia, Belize; ✆ 800/746-3743 in the U.S. and Canada, or 501/ 824-4912 in Belize; www.turtleinn.com): Building on the experience gained from his Blancaneaux Lodge, and constructing upon the ruins of a hotel destroyed by Hurricane Iris, director Francis Ford Coppola has upped the ante on high-end beach hotels in Belize. The individual villas here are some of the most beautiful and luxurious in Belize. The hotel is set right on an excellent stretch of beach, and the service and dining are top-notch. See p. 146.

- **Chaa Creek** (Cayo District, Belize; ℭ **877/709-8708** in the U.S. and Canada, or 501/824-2037 in Belize; www.chaacreek.com): A pioneer nature lodge in Belize, this collection of cottages was also an innovator in the concept of rustic luxury. Cool terra-cotta tile floors, varnished wood, thatched roofs, and beautiful Guatemalan textiles and handicrafts are elegantly yet simply combined. The property is set on a steep hillside over the lovely Macal River. Service is very friendly and personable, and the lodge provides easy access to a wealth of natural adventures and ancient Maya wonders. See p. 136.

- **Mesón Panza Verde** (Antigua, Guatemala; ℭ **502/7832-2925;** www.panzaverde. com): This elegant and artistic Antigua hotel offers large suites and superb service, and one of the best restaurants in the country. The old building is loaded with artwork and interesting architectural details, and there's a wonderful, mazelike rooftop terrace with panoramic views. See p. 185.

- **Hotel Atitlán** (Panajachel, Guatemala; ℭ **502/7762-1441;** www.hotelatitlan. com): This fabulous hotel is set on the shores of Lake Atitlán, with a stunning view of the lake and its surrounding volcanoes. Beautiful rooms, lush gardens, ample amenities, impeccable service, and a great restaurant make this a complete package. See p. 195.

- **Las Olas Beach House** (Balsamo Coast, El Salvador; ℭ **503/2411-7553**): This upscale adventure resort is perched atop a rocky cliff rising from the Pacific with unrivaled ocean views, a cliff-side infinity pool, and an excellent restaurant. But what really makes this place special are the English-speaking owners and managers who live the life they sell. They will take you surfing, snorkeling, sea kayaking, and off-road motorcycling, as well as on more sedate hiking and horseback-riding tours. See p. 262.

- **The Lodge at Pico Bonito** (La Ceiba, Honduras; ℭ **888/428-0221;** www.pico bonito.com): While you can tour the Parque Nacional Pico Bonito near La Ceiba in a number of ways, few would argue that one of the best is by staying here. This property has its own set of trails, a butterfly farm, a resort-style pool, spa facilities, and a gourmet restaurant. Guided hikes bring you through former cacao fields, across several levels of tropical forest, and to swimming holes and waterfalls that are ideal for taking soaks in. See p. 394.

- **Hotel Plaza Colon** (Granada, Nicaragua; ℭ **505/2552-8489;** www.hotelplaza colon.com): The Plaza Colon hits just the right balance between colonial authenticity and matching the modern traveler's expectations. A wide balcony overlooks the boisterous plaza, and tiled floors lead to an inner balcony that runs around a glorious courtyard and blue mosaic pool. Everything is luxurious and elegant, and the service is prompt and reliable. See p. 486.

- **La Perla** (León, Nicaragua; ℭ **505/2311-3125;** www.laperlaleon.com): La Perla sets a new standard for accommodations in Nicaragua, with impeccable rooms and a palatial interior boasting high ceilings, a spectacular central courtyard, and contemporary Nicaraguan art. See p. 474.

- **Four Seasons Resort Costa Rica** (Papagayo Peninsula, Costa Rica; ℭ **800/819-5053** or 2696-0000; www.fourseasons.com/costarica): This was the first major resort to address the high-end luxury market in Costa Rica. Within its first month,

Michael Jordan and Madonna were notable guests. A beautiful setting, wonderful installations, a world-class golf course, and stellar service continue to make this the current king of the hill in the upscale market. See p. 600.

o **Arenas del Mar** (Manuel Antonio, Costa Rica; ©/fax **2777-2777**; www.arenas delmar.com): With large and ample rooms, excellent service and amenities, a beautiful little spa, and arguably the best beach access and location in Manuel Antonio, this hotel has a lot to offer. See p. 632.

o **The Bristol Panama** (Panama City, Panama; © **265-7844**): This hotel exudes buttoned-up luxury with its conservative decor, but the ambience somehow manages to feel cozy rather than stuffy. The Bristol is known for its bend-over-backward service and fine dining at Las Barandas Restaurant. See p. 678.

o **Canopy Tower** (Soberanía National Park, Panama; © **264-5720**): Birders flock to this ecolodge for its focus on bird-watching and its location in a habitat that's friendly to a wide range of species. The Canopy Tower, a remodeled military radar station in thick jungle, is a cross between a stylish B&B and a scientific research center. The 360-degree observation deck here provides stunning views and a platform with scopes. See p. 699.

THE best LOCAL DINING EXPERIENCES

o **Rojo Lounge** (Ambergris Caye, Belize; © **501/226-4012**): The folks at Azul Resort, an isolated place on Northern Ambergris Caye, serve creative and well-prepared fusion cuisine, in a relaxed, inviting open-air ambience. The menu features some of the more creative fusion items on the island—no mean feat given the competition—and there are also nightly specials. See p. 118.

o **La Ceiba** (San Ignacio, Belize; © **501/820-3350**): Young Belizean chef Sean Kuylen has set up shop at this boutique hotel. His cooking showcases regional cuisine, updated with classical French and fusion touches. See p. 138.

o **Tamarindos** (Guatemala City, Guatemala; © **502/2360-2815**): The chef at this trendy Zona Viva restaurant wows Guatemala City with her eclectic fusion cooking. Tamarindos hits all the right notes. The menu is long and touches many bases, with culinary influences from Asia, Italy, and places in between. Ask about daily specials, as this is where the chef really shines. See p. 174.

o **Kacao** (Guatemala City, Guatemala; © **502/2237-4188** or 2377-4189): This popular restaurant takes Guatemalan cuisine and polishes it up a bit. The cooking is fairly traditional, with signature dishes from around the country, but the service, ambience, and presentation are far more refined than you'll find at almost any other place specializing in Chapin cuisine. Although they do a brisk lunch business, I prefer to come for dinner, when the thatch roof is illuminated by candles and other strategically placed lighting. See p. 174.

o **Alo Nuestro** (San Salvador, El Salvador; © **503/2223-5116**): San Salvador is packed with excellent restaurants offering cuisines from around the world. But Alo Nuestro stands out for its simply delicious food. The restaurant has been open since 1999 and has built a quiet word-of-mouth following among locals and international travelers. The frequently changing menu is a fusion of San Salvador's many ethnic restaurants, with an emphasis on local ingredients. The service is top-notch and the ambience is formal but comfortable. See p. 251.

- **Hacienda San Lucas** (Copán Ruinas, Honduras; ✆ **504/651-4495;** www.hacienda sanlucas.com): On a hill overlooking the Copán valley, this 100-year-old, family-owned hacienda dishes out an authentic Maya Chortí five-course candlelit dinner focusing on fresh, local ingredients. Their tamales, corn chowder, and fire-roasted chicken with *adobo* sauce do not disappoint. See p. 369.

- **El Colibri** (San Juan del Sur, Nicaragua; ✆ **505/8863-8612**): Set within a funky-colored clapboard house with a veranda overlooking a garden, this enchanting restaurant is a piece of art put together from recycled materials. Mosaic-framed mirrors hang between stained-glass lamps and African face masks, while small colored stones hold down your place mats lest the sea breeze carry them away. The international, mostly organic fare, is a work of art, too. See p. 526.

- **La Casita** (Estelí, Nicaragua; ✆ **505/2713-4917**): At this part farmhouse restaurant and part coffeehouse, you can enjoy great local coffee, fresh bread, cheeses, and yogurts in a garden by a beautiful stream with relaxing music in the background. Also on sale are local crafts and herbal medicines. See p. 509.

- **Grano de Oro Restaurant** (San José, Costa Rica; ✆ **2255-3322**): This stylish little hotel has an elegant restaurant serving delicious Continental dishes and decadent desserts. The open-air seating in the lushly planted central courtyard is delightful, especially for lunch. See p. 580.

- **La Pecora Nera** (Puerto Viejo, Costa Rica; ✆ **2750-0490**): I'm not sure that a tiny surfer town on the Caribbean coast of Costa Rica deserves such fine Italian food, but it's got it. Your best bet is go on a culinary roller-coaster ride with a mixed feast of the chef's nightly specials and suggestions. See p. 646.

- **Guari Guari** (Bocas del Toro, Panama; ✆ **6575-5513**): Enjoy the best six-course gourmet dinner in Panama to the murmur of lightly crashing waves in a romantic, reservations-only atmosphere just outside Bocas Town.

THE best MARKETS & SHOPS

- **Nim Po't** (Antigua, Guatemala): A massive indoor space with a soaring ceiling houses this craft-and-textile cooperative warehouse. Textiles, woodcarvings, and ceramic wares from across the country are available. The quality varies greatly, but if you know what to look for, you can find some fine works without having to venture into the farther reaches of rural Guatemala. See p. 184.

- **Diconte Artisans Shop** (Ataco, El Salvador): This five-room shop in the town of Ataco along the Rutas de Las Flores offers whimsical paintings, woodcarvings, and crafts in the surrealistic style of Ataco's two main artists, as well as a room full of colorful textiles made on-site by artisans working five old-style looms. You can also watch the artisans work from the shade of a small gardenside coffee and dessert cafe here. See p. 295.

- **Mercado Central** (San Salvador, El Salvador): Mercado Central near San Salvador's central plaza is the anti-mercado. It's a sprawling, seemingly chaotic warren of shouting vendors, blaring horns, and old women in traditional clothes chopping vegetables in the street. Its biggest attraction is that it's *not* an attraction. Instead, it's the place to visit if you want to see a slice of unfiltered Salvadoran life. See p. 246.

- **Guamilito Market** (San Pedro Sula, Honduras): Products from around the country, as well as El Salvador and Guatemala, fill up hundreds of small stalls at this market.

You'll find everything from hammocks, T-shirts, and Lenca pottery to cigars, Maya figurines, jewelry, coffee, Garífuna coconut carvings, and tortilla stands. See p. 350.

o **Galería Namu** (San José, Costa Rica): This is my favorite gallery and gift shop in downtown San Jose, with an excellent collection of art and craft selections. These folks specialize in finding some of the better and more obscure works done by Costa Rica's indigenous communities. See p. 573.

o **Mercado de Mariscos** (Panama City, Panama): This bustling market is *the* distribution headquarters for fresh seafood from the Pacific and the Caribbean. It's a fascinating place to see the everyday hustle and bustle of a typical Panamanian market and check out the often weird and mysterious seafood selection. You can get some of the best seviche in the city from vendors at the entrance to the market. The **Mercado de Mariscos Restaurant** on the second level serves tasty and authentic seafood dishes. See p. 676.

THE best OF CENTRAL AMERICA ONLINE

Below are some good Internet sources for each country, along with the recommendations on sites that cover the region in general. Each chapter in this book has more country-specific websites.

Country-Specific Sites

o **www.toucantrail.com**: This is an excellent site about Belize geared toward budget travelers, with extensive links and comprehensive information.

o **www.travelbelize.org**: This is the official site of the Belize Tourist Board. It has its fair share of information and links, although you'll probably end up being directed to other sites.

o **www.revuemag.com**: This is an excellent Guatemala-based English-language monthly magazine geared toward tourists and expatriates. The entire magazine, as well as past issues, is available online.

o **www.xelawho.com**: A slightly irreverent English-language magazine produced in Quetzaltenango, Guatemala, and directed at the town's large population of foreign-language students, this site has honest reviews and a wealth of useful information.

o **www.elsalvador.travel**: This great English-language website groups information about El Salvador's attractions into the headings of nature/adventure/culture/the beach. The site also provides a country map outlining El Salvador's 14 departments with demographic information for each.

o **www.letsgohonduras.com**: This is the official site of the Honduras Tourist Board. It has a variety of roundup articles that are good for planning, and lists a decent range of basic information on the major towns, attractions, and national parks in the country.

o **www.intur.gob.ni** and **www.visitanicaragua.com**: The Nicaragua Tourist Board, or NTB, has two sites that are entirely in Spanish, with very limited information but some gorgeous imagery.

o **www.vianica.com**: This independent site about Nicaragua is much more informative than other sites and has data in English on the country, as well as some nifty features such as distance calculators and wildlife lists with photos.

- o **www.ticotimes.net**: The English-language *Tico Times* makes it easy for *norteamericanos* (and other English speakers) to see what's happening in Costa Rica. It features the top story from its weekly print edition, as well as a daily update of news briefs, a business article, regional news, a fishing column, and travel reviews. There's also a link to current currency-exchange rates.

- o **www.panamainfo.com**: This excellent website provides hotel, restaurant, and attraction information, as well as information on retiring, living, and doing business in Panama.

- o **www.visitpanama.com**: The Panamanian Institute of Tourism regularly updates this website, which provides culture, history, and destination-specific information.

Central American Sites

- o **www.latinworld.com**: This is a search engine specializing in Central America, providing information, resource links, and other websites.

- o **www.latinamericabureau.org**: An independent website promoting better awareness of Central America, especially regarding human rights.

- o **www.bbc.co.uk**: The British broadcaster has an excellent world service section that covers in detail past and current affairs in the Americas.

- o **www.oas.org**: The Organization of American States is about the closest you will get to unity in the region. This site is not just for political animals but worth visiting for updates on ongoing issues and up-and-coming cultural events throughout the region.

- o **www.lanic.utexas.edu**: The Latin America Network Information Center is a University of Texas initiative that provides an extensive directory and database. Primarily used for academic research, it also facilitates education programs.

- o **www.newworldreview.com**: An English-language e-zine dedicated to exploring the food and drinks of Central and South America, written by a Frommer's author.

CENTRAL AMERICA IN DEPTH

When you think of Central America, a region that is made up of a jumble of countries along a slim, rugged isthmus connecting the two colossal continents of North and South America, what might first come to mind is the jungle. Add its standing as a tropical dead-end zone to its tumultuous history of war, poverty, crime and corruption, and natural disasters, and it's no wonder the region has often been overlooked as a travel destination. Yet in the past few years, Central America has finally begun to step out of the shade and into the sunlight. As more and more travelers head to the region, it's becoming recognized as a safe and adventurous getaway, one that just happens to have a sorry knack for getting bad press.

Now for some good press: The region has a diverse climate and geography that offers everything from sun-kissed Caribbean islands to lush cloud forests. It also has a rich native-Indian heritage, mixed with a history of Spanish colonialism, both of which have led to a vibrant music-and-art scene that frequently spills out onto the streets in the form of festivals and parades. But perhaps the region's biggest asset is its friendly, kind-hearted people, who may not have much but insist on sharing it with others anyway.

It's also now easier and more comfortable than ever to travel around the region. In the past few years, as millions of visitors have discovered this gem of a destination, airline links have improved drastically and some first-rate ecolodges and mountain refuges have opened up. If you are no longer content with just a pool and beach, and want to climb volcanoes, hike through rainforests, visit towering Maya ruins, take Spanish classes, volunteer, and go scuba diving and surfing—in addition to lounging by some stellar pools and beaches—Central America will not disappoint.

CENTRAL AMERICA IN 2 WEEKS OR MORE

Two weeks will fly by when you're traveling around Central America. Though it is possible to visit three to four countries in this time frame, you will have to sacrifice some amazing places on the way. Below are two suggested itineraries, one visiting the northern four countries and the second touring the southern three. There are, of course, numerous other

Central America in 2 Weeks

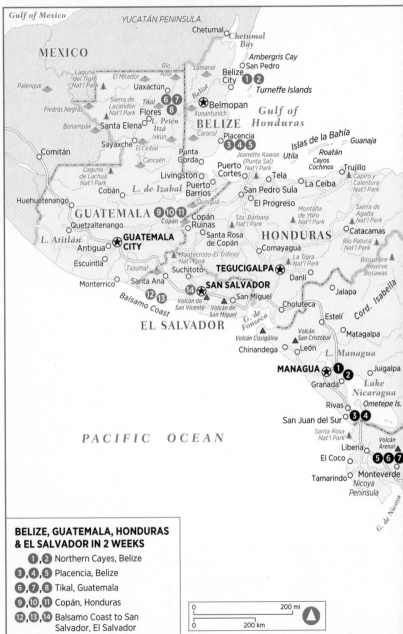

BELIZE, GUATEMALA, HONDURAS & EL SALVADOR IN 2 WEEKS

1,**2** Northern Cayes, Belize

3,**4**,**5** Placencia, Belize

6,**7**,**8** Tikal, Guatemala

9,**10**,**11** Copán, Honduras

12,**13**,**14** Balsamo Coast to San Salvador, El Salvador

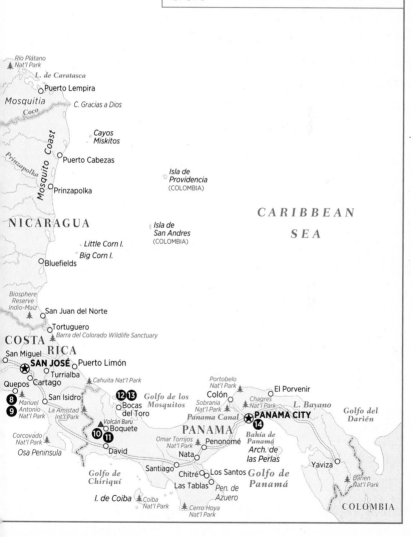

NICARAGUA, COSTA RICA & PANAMA IN 2 WEEKS

①,② Managua & Granada, Nicaragua
③,④ Ometepe Island & San Juan del Sur, Nicaragua
⑤,⑥,⑦ Arenal & Monteverde, Costa Rica
⑧,⑨ Manuel Antonio National Park, Costa Rica
⑩,⑪ The Quetzal Trail, Panama
⑫,⑬,⑭ Bocas del Toro & Panama City, Panama

Isla de Cisne
(HONDURAS)

Río Plátano
Nat'l Park

L. de Caratasca

Puerto Lempira

Mosquitia
Coco
C. Gracias a Dios

Cayos
Miskitos

Puerto Cabezas

Isla de
Providencia
(COLOMBIA)

Prinzapolka
Mosquito Coast
Prinzapolka

CARIBBEAN
SEA

NICARAGUA

Isla de
San Andres
(COLOMBIA)

Little Corn I.
Big Corn I.

Bluefields

Biosphere
Reserve
Indio-Maiz
San Juan del Norte

Tortuguero
Barra del Colorado Wildlife Sanctuary

COSTA RICA
San Miguel
★ **SAN JOSÉ** Puerto Limón
Turrialba
Quepos Cartago
Cahuita Nat'l Park
⑧ *Manuel* San Isidro
⑨ *Antonio*
Nat'l Park *La Amistad*
Int'l Park
Corcovado *Volcán Barú*
Nat'l Park **⑩** Boquete
Osa Peninsula **⑪**
David

Portobelo
Nat'l Park
Colón El Porvenir
⑫⑬ *Golfo de los* *Chagres* *L. Bayano*
Bocas *Mosquitos* *Sobrania* *Nat'l Park*
del Toro *Nat'l Park* ★ **PANAMA CITY**
Panama Canal **⑭** *Golfo del*
PANAMA *Bahía de* *Darién*
Omar Torrijos Penonomé *Panamá*
Nat'l Park *Arch. de*
Nata *las Perlas*

Golfo de
Chiriquí
Santiago
Chitré Los Santos *Golfo de*
Las Tablas *Panamá*
I. de Coiba *Coiba* *Pen. de* Yaviza
Nat'l Park *Azuero*
Cerro Hoya *Darién*
Nat'l Park *Nat'l Park*

COLOMBIA

combinations for tours in the region—you might want to mix and match the suggestions below to create your own itinerary. The following itineraries were also designed with the presumption that you'll be taking private shuttles and taxis. Those on a tighter budget will have to slow right down, to allot more time for traveling between destinations.

BELIZE, GUATEMALA, HONDURAS & EL SALVADOR IN 2 WEEKS

Days 1 & 2: The Northern Cayes, Belize

Arrive in Belize City and head straight for the beach, in this case the pristine Northern Cayes, where you can spend 2 days playing on the water and snorkeling with friendly sharks in Shark-Ray Alley. Be sure to save 1 day for an inland trip to visit the Maya burial cave of Actun Tunichil Muknal. While staying here, enjoy the spectacular oceanfront setting and stellar service at **Victoria House** ★★★ (p. 114).

Days 3, 4 & 5: Placencia, Belize

Head south to the hip little beach town of Placencia. Soak up some rays on this white sandy paradise and feel like a film star by staying at Francis Ford Coppola's **Turtle Inn** ★★★ (p. 146).

Days 6, 7 & 8: The Maya Ruins of Tikal, Guatemala

Tan suitably burnished, it's now time to grab some culture. Take a taxi from Belize and cross the border into Guatemala. Enjoy the awe-inspiring temples of Tikal and then go on a sunset cruise around the island town of Flores. See chapter 5 for hotel recommendations in the area.

Days 9, 10 & 11: Copán, Honduras

The laid-back colonial town of Copán across the border in Honduras offers intriguing ruins regarded as the "Paris of the Maya world," as well as hot springs, a famous cigar factory, **Flor de Copán** ★★ (p. 371), and an excellent boutique resort, the **Hacienda San Lucas** ★★★ (p. 368).

Days 12, 13 & 14: The Balsamo Coast to San Salvador, El Salvador

Round your holiday off with some more beach bliss, this time Pacific side, at El Salvador's Playa los Cóbanas. Here you can go scuba diving around the colorful tropical reef before retiring to the cliff-top **Las Olas Beach House** ★★★ (p. 262). Spend your final day enjoying the magnificent views of the Balsamo Coast from the cliff-side infinity pool, trying not to think of your flight home from San Salvador the next day.

NICARAGUA, COSTA RICA & PANAMA IN 2 WEEKS

Days 1 & 2: Managua to Granada, Nicaragua

Fly into Managua, but don't hang around the capital of Nicaragua—instead, depart for the radiant colonial city of Granada. Sip a rum on the rocks from the gigantic balcony of the **Hotel Plaza Colon** ★★★ (p. 486) overlooking the colorful plaza. Catch a horse and carriage ride through the city's enchanting cobbled streets and take a short boat tour of **Las Isletas** archipelago.

Days 3 & 4: Tour Ometepe Island & Arrive in San Juan del Sur, Nicaragua

Take a day tour of the twin-peak jungle island of Ometepe before transferring to the beach town of San Juan del Sur. Stay at the lovely villa **Posada Azul** ★★ (p. 523) and eat in the garden of **El Colibri** ★★ (p. 526). The following day, catch a water taxi up the coast to some secluded beaches or, if your timing is right, opt for a night excursion to watch the turtle hatching in **Playa La Flor** ★★★ (p. 520).

Days 5, 6 & 7: Arenal & Monteverde, Costa Rica

Get up early to make the journey across the border to Costa Rica, where you can watch molten lava flowing from Arenal Volcano, while safely sitting poolside at the **Tabacón Grand Spa Thermal Resort** ★★★ (p. 621). On your second day, wake up early and take a guided tour of the **Monteverde Cloud Forest Biological Reserve** ★★★ (p. 606). Stop in at the **Hummingbird Gallery** ★ (p. 609) next door to the entrance after your tour. There's great shopping, and the scores of brilliant hummingbirds buzzing around your head at this attraction are always fascinating. Spend the afternoon visiting several of the area's attractions, which might include any combination of the following: the **Butterfly Garden** ★, **Orchid Garden** ★★, **Monteverde Serpentarium** ★, **Frog Pond of Monteverde** ★, the **Bat Jungle,** and the **World of Insects** (p. 608).

Days 8, 9: Manuel Antonio National Park, Costa Rica

Get on the road by noon for your drive to **Manuel Antonio National Park.** Settle into your hotel and head for a **sunset drink** at **Agua Azul** ★ (p. 633), which offers up spectacular views over the rainforest to the sea. The next morning, take a boat tour of the **Damas Island estuary** (p. 630) with Jorge Cruz, and then reward yourself with an afternoon lazing on one of the beautiful beaches inside **Manuel Antonio National Park** ★★ (p. 624). If you can't lie still, be sure to hike the loop trail through the rainforest here and around **Cathedral Point** ★★. Make reservations at the **El Patio Bistro Latino** ★★★ (p. 634) for an intimate and relaxed final dinner in Costa Rica.

Days 10 & 11: The Quetzal Trail, Panama

It's time to cross the border into Panama and make your way to the town of **Cerro Punta.** Send your baggage ahead while you take a 1-day hiking tour around the Barú Volcano through a tropical paradise known as the Quetzal Trail. Keep your eyes peeled for the beautiful but elusive bird of the same name. Catch up with your luggage in Boquete and stay at the **Coffee Estate Inn** ★★★ (p. 709), where you can relax in bungalows surrounded by fruit gardens.

Days 12, 13 & 14: Bocas del Toro to Panama City, Panama

Nearby Boquete is the party-beach town of Bocas del Toro. Here you'll find excellent surfing on crystal-blue Caribbean seas, and you can explore the nearby island utopias known as Cayos Zapatillas. Then retire to your thatched-roof lodge high up in the forest canopy at the **La Loma Jungle Lodge** (p. 717). The next day, transfer to Panama City for your flight home.

CENTRAL AMERICA PAST & PRESENT

The Americas were first populated by humans when Asians crossed the Bering straits into Alaska some 20,000 years ago. These tribes soon fanned southward and funneled into South America through the Central American isthmus. The period around 3000 B.C. saw the arrival of one of the greatest civilizations of the pre-Columbian New World, the Maya culture, which spread its influence from southern Mexico to El Salvador. By A.D. 750, 10 million Maya people lived in elaborate stone cities such as Tikal, Palenque, and Copán. Both savage and sophisticated, the Maya developed hieroglyphics and calendars yet were also fond of human sacrifice to appease the gods. Their empire mysteriously collapsed around A.D. 900. Drought, war, and overpopulation are blamed, but new theories for the civilization's demise appear all the time.

The Spanish came here in 1502 and they brought with them gunpowder, horses, and disease. In return, they discovered a paradise that became a living hell for its own people. By the time the conquistadors stepped off their boats, the great Maya cities had been abandoned and lost in the jungle and the population decimated into small, isolated tribes. These remaining scattered tribes put up some resistance, but were eventually subjugated and enslaved by the conquistadors.

Independence from Spain came in 1821, and the five states that existed then (Guatemala, El Salvador, Honduras, Nicaragua, and Costa Rica) were briefly united in a federation that eventually fell apart in 1838. What happened next—indigenous massacres, military dictatorships, left-wing revolutions, war, utter poverty, and blatant U.S. intervention—meant that the region remained united in misfortune only throughout much of the 19th and 20th centuries.

Peace treaties in the 1990s allowed for a new dawn of democracy in this region. Many ex-combatants from the right and left are now fighting out their differences on congress floors, rather than on city streets. The region is still dreadfully poor, however, and plagued with high unemployment, crime, and rampant corruption, not to mention earthquakes and hurricanes. Development continues at a slow pace. More and more people are abandoning subsistence farming and moving to the cities for low-paid factory jobs. Emigration north is often the only way to break free from the region's poverty, and many families are dependent on remittances from relatives in the United States. Some countries are doing much better than others, Costa Rica and Panama being the best examples. A real-estate and tourism boom there means more jobs but also raises some important questions about the state of the environment. Sustainable and ecofriendly tourism is often seen as Central America's greatest economic hope, and for good reason.

In this section, we'll give you a little bit of background on the history and culture of the countries we cover in this guide. See the individual country chapters for more on both subjects.

Belize

A LOOK AT THE PAST

Before the arrival of the first Europeans, Belize was a major part of the Maya Empire. River and coastal trade routes connected dozens of cities and small towns throughout

MAYA history

Before the arrival of the first Europeans, Mesoamerica was the land of the ancient Maya. Here, mathematicians came up with the concept of zero, astronomers developed a solar calendar accurate to a single day every 6,000 days, and scribes invented an 850-word hieroglyphic vocabulary that scholars consider the world's first advanced writing system. Some of this civilization's practices were less than civil: The Maya built extensive ball courts to play a game called "pok a tok," where the losing team could be executed.

Evidence of human presence in the Maya region dates as far back as the 10th millennium B.C. Maya history is often divided into several distinct periods: **Archaic** (10,000–2000 B.C.), **Pre-Classic** (2000 B.C.–A.D. 250), **Classic** (250–900), and **Post-Classic** (900–1540). Within this timeline, the Classic period itself is often divided into Early, Middle, Late, and Terminal stages. At the height of development, as many as 10 million Maya may have inhabited what are now Guatemala, Belize, Mexico's Yucatán Peninsula, and parts of Honduras and El Salvador. No one knows for sure what led to the decline of the Classic Maya, but somewhere around A.D. 900, their society entered a severe and rapid decline. Famine, warfare, deforestation, and religious prophecy have all been cited as possible causes. See Jared Diamond's bestseller *Collapse* (Penguin, 2005) for more information and speculation.

Unlike the Incas of Peru, the Maya had no centralized ruler. Instead, the civilization consisted of a series of independent city-states, usually ruled by hereditary kings, often at war with one another. The most famous city-state is Tikal, in the northern Petén region, whose massive stone temples are the principal draw for tourists in Guatemala. In A.D. 562, Tikal was defeated in battle by the kingdom of Caracol, in what is now the Cayo District of western Belize.

According to the Popol Vuh, the sacred Maya book of creation myths and predictions, the world as we know it will end on December 21, 2012. While some New Age analysts have dire predictions for the date, more optimistic prognosticators foresee a day of positive human evolution. Hotels around Tikal and other major Maya ceremonial sites are already booking up for this date.

Belize to each other and to major ceremonial and trading cities in Mexico and Guatemala. At the height of development, as many as two million Maya may have inhabited the region that is today known as Belize. No one knows for sure what led to the decline of the Classic Maya, but somewhere around A.D. 900, their society entered a severe and rapid decline. Nevertheless, Belize is somewhat unique in that it had several major ceremonial or trading cities still occupied by Maya when the first Spanish conquistadors arrived.

Christopher Columbus sailed past the Belize coast in 1502, but he never anchored or set foot ashore, and the Spanish never had much success in colonizing Belize. In fact, they met with fierce resistance from the remaining Maya. Part of their problem may have come from Gonzalo Guerrero, a Spanish sailor who was shipwrecked off the coast of Belize and the Yucatán in the early years of the 16th century. Originally pressed into slavery, Guerrero eventually married the daughter of a Maya ruler, and became an important warrior and military advisor in the Maya battles with the Spanish. Though the Spanish led various attacks and attempts at conquest and control of the territory that is present-day Belize, by the mid-1600s, they were forced to abandon all permanent settlements and attempts at colonialism in the country, and began concentrating their efforts on more productive regions around Central and South America and the Caribbean Sea.

The lack of Spanish colonial might left the door wide-open in Belize, and an assortment of pirates, buccaneers, and other unsavory characters were among the first to fill that void and make this their base of operations. These pirates and buccaneers used the Belize coastline and its protected anchorages as hide-outs and bases following attacks on Spanish fleets transporting gold and silver treasures from their more productive colonies.

By the mid–17th century, British loggers were settling along the coast and making their way up the rivers and streams in search of mahogany for shipbuilding and other types of wood for making dyes. Proud and independent, these early settlers called themselves "Baymen" (after the Bay of Honduras). Politically, the Baymen treaded a delicate balance between being faithful British subjects and fiercely independent settlers. A steady stream of Spanish attacks, however, forced the Baymen to seek more and more support from the British. Diplomatic and military give-and-take between Spain and Britain ensued until 1798, when the Baymen won a decisive military victory over a larger Spanish fleet, just off the shores of St. George's Caye. The Battle of St. George's Caye effectively ended all Spanish involvement and claim to Belize, and it solidified Belize's standing within the British Empire.

In 1862, with more or less the same borders it has today, Belize was formally declared the colony of British Honduras. This small colonial outpost became a major source of hardwood and dyewood for the still-expanding British Empire. The forests were exploited, and agriculture was never really encouraged. The British wanted their colony to remain dependent on the mother country, so nearly all the necessities of life were imported.

Throughout the 18th and 19th centuries, African slaves were brought to British Honduras. The slave period was marked by several revolts and uprisings. Black Caribs, today known as Garífuna, migrated here from the Bay Islands of Honduras, although they originally hail from the Caribbean island of St. Vincent. Beginning in the early 1800s, the Garífuna established their own villages along the southern coast.

During the mid–19th century, many Mexican and Guatemalan refugees of the bloody Caste Wars fled across the borders into British Honduras and founded such towns as Corozal and Benque Viejo. Further waves of Guatemalan, Salvadoran, and Honduran refugees, who were fleeing civil wars and right-wing death squads, immigrated to Belize during the 1970s and 1980s.

In the early 1960s, groundwork was laid by the People's United Party (PUP) for granting British Honduras independence. In 1973, the country's name was officially changed to Belize. However, it was not until September 21, 1981, that Belize gained its independence, making it Central America's newest nation. The delay was primarily due to Guatemala's claim on the territory. Fearful of an invasion by Guatemalan forces, the British delayed granting full independence until an agreement could be reached. Although to this day no final agreement has actually been inked, tensions cooled enough to allow for the granting of full sovereignty in 1981. The country is still a member of the Commonwealth.

BELIZE TODAY

Belize is a developing nation, limited by a small economy, a tiny industrial base, a huge trade deficit, and a historical dependence on foreign aid. These problems have been compounded by the British pullout and a universal reduction of international largesse. Sugar and citrus are the principal cash crops, though bananas and seafood exports also help. However, tourism is also an important source of income and jobs, responsible for providing 25% of the nation's jobs and 18% of its GDP.

Belize held its first parliamentary elections in 1984. Since then, power has ping-ponged back and forth between the United Democratic Party (UDP) and the People's United Party (PUP). The former is a more conservative, free-market–oriented party, while the latter champions a more liberal, social-democratic agenda. In the August 1998 elections, PUP won 26 of the 29 parliamentary seats, while the UDP managed to win just 3. However, by 2005 discontent with the PUP over tax increases and money mismanagement had grown widespread and there were even some public demonstrations and disturbances. The UDP pummeled them in 2006 municipal elections, and again in the 2008 national elections, electing Dean Barrow as the country's first black prime minister, and maintaining a strong majority of parliamentary seats.

Thanks to a modest oil find in 2005, crude oil is currently the country's number one export. Tourism is also a promising and important source of income, and this is sure to continue. Increasingly, Belizeans whose fathers and grandfathers were farmers or fishermen find themselves hotel owners, tour guides, waiters, and cleaning personnel.

Guatemala

A LOOK AT THE PAST

Much of Guatemala's early history was lived by the Maya, and they've left ample legacy in words, artifacts, and stone. You'll see the evidence of this legacy all over Guatemala, particularly in the great ceremonial city of Tikal.

While Christopher Columbus never set foot on Guatemala, his oversight did not save the country from Spanish conquest. Conquistador Pedro de Alvarado was sent by Hernán Cortés to Guatemala in 1523. In a ruthless campaign, Alvarado pitted different Maya tribes against each other, and then turned on his unwitting accomplices. According to legend, when Alvarado killed the Ki'che king Tecún Umán at the Battle of Quetzaltenango in 1524, the quetzal (Guatemala's national bird) swooped down into the vast pools of blood and gained its red breast.

By 1525, Alvarado had subdued the western highlands, but the Spanish subsequently met with resistance from many Maya tribes. Multiple invasions of the Petén failed, and the Kekchí in the central highlands held out as well. Unable to control the Kekchí by force, the Spanish allowed a group of Franciscan friars led by Fray Bartolomé de las Casas to attempt the "humane" conversion of the tribe to Christianity. The friars succeeded, the population converted, and the area was given its Spanish name, "Verapaz" or "true peace." A human rights advocate until his death, Las Casas also successfully convinced the Spanish crown to pass the *New Laws* in 1542, awarding some basic protections to the *indígenas*.

During Spanish colonial rule, Guatemala was a Captaincy General, part of the Viceroyalty of New Spain. The Spanish established Guatemala's capital at Ciudad Vieja in 1527, but moved to what is now Antigua (then called Santiago de Guatemala) in 1543 after the old capital was buried in a mudslide from the Volcán de Agua. For 200 years, Antigua was the center of political and religious power of the "Audiencia de Guatemala," including the provinces of Costa Rica, Nicaragua, El Salvador, Honduras, and Chiapas in Mexico. After severe earthquakes ravaged Antigua in 1773, the crown decided to move the capital to safer ground, and chose the site of the ancient city of Kaminal Juyú, today's Guatemala City.

In colonial society, racial divisions were enshrined in law. *Peninsulares,* or Spanish-born Spaniards living in the New World, were at the top of the economic and political pyramid, followed by *criollos* (descendants of Spaniards born in the New World), *mestizos* (of mixed Spanish and Amerindian ancestry), *mulattos* (mixed Spanish and black), Amerindians, *zambos* (mixed Amerindian and black), and blacks. Individuals from the latter three groups were often enslaved outright.

Discontent with the rule of *peninsulares* reached a boiling point in the early 19th century, and a mood of reform swept across New Spain. Most of the fighting took place in Mexico, where a coalition of conservatives and liberals prevailed.

On September 15, 1821, Gabino Gainza, the captain general of Central America, signed the Act of Independence, breaking the region's ties with Spain. By 1840, the Central American Federation had dissolved in civil war, instigated by the conservative dictators who had seized power in most of the nations, such as Rafael Carrera, a charismatic 23-year-old swineherd-turned-highwayman who, in Guatemala in 1838, raised an army, seized control, declared Guatemala independent, and reversed decades of liberal reforms. With the adoption of a constitution in 1851, Carrera became independent Guatemala's first president.

Over the course of the next century, power continued to change hands by military rather than democratic means. Liberal reformers traded off with conservative reactionaries, but one entity saw its influence grow fairly consistently: the United Fruit Company. United Fruit, nicknamed "El Pulpo" (The Octopus) for its sweeping influence, first arrived in Guatemala in 1901, when it purchased a small tract of land to grow bananas. The company built its own port, Puerto Barrios, and after being awarded a railway concession leading inland from the port, had a virtual monopoly on long-distance transportation in the country. United Fruit's rise to prominence coincided with the successive and enduring dictatorships of Manuel José Estrada Cabrera and Jorge Ubico. Collectively, these two men ruled, with great deference to United Fruit Company, from 1898 to 1941.

In 1941, a band of disgruntled military men, joined by students, labor leaders, and liberal political forces, overthrew Ubico, and ushered in a period popularly referred to as "The Ten Years of Spring." Marked by moves to encourage free speech and liberal reforms, this time saw the election of Guatemala's first civilian president of modern times, Juan José Arévalo.

In 1951, Guatemala held its first-ever universal-suffrage election, bringing retired army colonel and political reformer Jacobo Arbenz to power. Confronting a vast gap between rich and poor, Arbenz fought for the passage of the 1952 Agrarian Reform Law, which redistributed thousands of acres of unproductive land to some 100,000 rural families. United Fruit was furious, having lost half its land. In 1954, the CIA, whose director sat on United Fruit's board, sponsored a coup d'état. Guatemala's new government, largely drawn from the ranks of its military, was flown into the capital aboard a U.S. Air Force plane.

The new U.S.-sponsored regime eliminated the reforms of the previous decade, reinstituting rule by and for the *ladino* minority. In the early 1960s, a guerrilla war began between government forces and Marxist rebels, who drew their strength largely from indigenous communities and were headquartered in the highlands.

For the next 30 years, a succession of authoritarian rulers were brought to power by rigged elections or coups d'état. They largely followed the maxim of president and army colonel Arana Osorio, who said, "If it is necessary to turn the country into a cemetery in order to pacify it, I will not hesitate to do so." An estimated 200,000 people died or disappeared during the conflict, most of them indigenous. Death squads killed those suspected of rebel activity. Professors, students, union leaders, and priests were especially prone to attack.

Following the recommendations of the 1987 Central American Peace accords, Guatemalan President Alvaro Arzú negotiated a peace agreement with the URNG (as the united rebel factions were known) in December 1996. The agreement ended the 36-year-old civil war, with the government promising to support a Truth Commission led by the UN Mission to Guatemala, MINUGUA. The constitution was also amended to allow for greater indigenous rights.

Guatemala's situation improved after the end of the war, but great challenges remained. The military still wielded significant power, and did its best to cover up its involvement in the atrocities of the war. In 1998, days after delivering a report on human rights that blamed 80% of the abuses on the military, Catholic Bishop Juan Geradi was bludgeoned to death in his home in Guatemala City. Officials were too afraid of suffering the same fate to investigate the crime.

GUATEMALA TODAY

The Guatemalan economy is still heavily agricultural, based on the production of sugar cane, coffee, and bananas, with tourism and manufacturing playing increasingly important roles.

Despite gradual economic growth since the 1996 peace agreement, the country's war-torn past continues to cast a long shadow on its economy and society. And there's been very little noticeable progress made toward building a better future. The gap between rich and poor is wide. Up to 80% of the population lives below the poverty line, some 54% of young children suffer from malnutrition, and crime continues to be a major problem, with an alarming spike in gang activity. Lawlessness pervades many parts of the country, and impunity reigns nationwide. Vigilante groups, frustrated at the lack of police presence, occasionally take justice into their own hands.

On November 4, 2007, Alvaro Colom of the center-left National Unity for Hope (UNE) party was elected president. However, his administration has had a rocky go of things, with little noticeable progress on the economic and security fronts, and several corruption scandals.

Today, Guatemala struggles to find its footing on the road to recovery. Still, for those intrepid travelers who do visit, you will find a land of great physical beauty, diverse peoples, an abundance of color and craft works, and the almost perfectly preserved cities and streets of the ancient Maya and earliest Spanish settlers.

El Salvador
A LOOK AT THE PAST

El Salvador's earliest residents on record were Paleo-Indian peoples whose history in the country is thought to stretch back 10,000 years and is evidenced by indigenous paintings found near the village of Morazán. The next residents to arrive were the more advanced Olmecs, Mesoamericans who moved into the region around 2000 B.C. The Olmecs held power until roughly 400 B.C., when they were largely replaced by the Maya. The Maya dynasty is responsible for the Classic pyramid ruins such as Tazumal and Casa Blanca—these not only show evidence of contact with other Maya from around what is now Central America but also point to how El Salvador acted as a trading center in the Maya world.

Around the 11th century, the Maya dynasty was replaced by what remains of El Salvador's largest indigenous population, the Nahuat-speaking Pipil, who were part of the nomadic Mexican Nahua tribe and dominated the western part of the country. At the same time, the Lenca tribe, with its own Aztec-based language, settled into and controlled the eastern region of the country, where its descendants remain today. Both the Maya and Lenca dynasties held power until the arrival of the Spanish in 1524 and both waged futile efforts to stop the conquistadors.

When Spaniard Pedro de Alvarado attempted to claim this territory for Spain in 1524, his army was thwarted by Pipil fighters. Alvarado tried again the following year, however, and was able to bring the region under the Spanish flag. Alvarado then named the region El Salvador or "The Savior."

For roughly the next 3 centuries, El Salvador remained under Spanish control. In 1821, El Salvador, along with four other Central American countries, declared its independence from Spain. In 1822, El Salvador decided against joining Mexico and other provinces in a Central American union and had to fight off troops sent to bring the country in line. The country went so far as to request statehood from the United States government. Ultimately, however, El Salvador was able to expel the troops and joined a more equitable union of Central American states, known as the Central American Federation, in 1823.

Things remained relatively calm until 1832, when El Salvador's poor staged the first of what would be numerous uprisings to protest unfair land distribution. Like later uprisings, the 1832 effort resulted in little change. In 1838 the Central American Federation dissolved and El Salvador became an independent country.

During the 19th century, El Salvador's system of land-based oligarchy, presided over by the "14 families" (actually a few dozen), flourished as the coffee industry grew. During that time, the country's much-amended constitution was restructured to give the majority of its 72 legislative seats to landowners. The head of each department was also appointed by the president. The system allowed wealthy coffee-plantation owners to incorporate much of the country's common land into their coffee farms and to maintain a stranglehold over the landless masses.

This obviously didn't sit well with the landless masses, who rose up numerous times to try to force change but were largely powerless against the wealthy elite and their military bidders. One of the largest of these early uprisings, later named "La Matanaza" (The Massacre), took place in 1932 and was led by Farabundo Martí, for whom the people's FMLN organization was later named. It was a failed and brutal uprising, which resulted in the deaths, imprisonment, or deportation of 30,000 indigenous people and government opponents.

Over the next nearly 5 decades, El Salvador's poor suffered under repressive governments that occasionally offered token land reforms, allowing for large-scale armed conflict to be largely avoided. The country did engage, however, in a short 5-day war with Honduras from July 14 to July 18, 1969, over immigration issues, which came to be known as the Soccer War (see p. 30 for more info).

Though the Soccer War quickly became a memory, the anger of El Salvador's poor farmers did not, and by the 1970s, sporadic and violent insurgencies against the government began. The government responded with a largely useless land reform bill in 1976 that did little to improve lives or ease the anger of the *campesinos* (peasant farmers). Some held out hope for improvements when a slightly more moderate group took control in 1979, but that group quickly dissolved under its own political strife and targeting by the military death squads. Many say the final straw came in 1980, with the government's assassination of beloved human rights champion Monseñor Oscar Romero, who was gunned down in the middle of Mass. After four of the country's leading guerilla groups merged into the cohesive and organized Farabundo Martí National Liberation Front, or FMLN, later in 1980, the stage was set for war.

The FMLN staged its first large-scale military offensive on January 10, 1981, in which it gained control over the areas around Chalatenango and Morazán. All ages, including children and the elderly, and both sexes joined in the guerilla movement. The Salvadoran government's response was brutal, particularly at the 2-day, December 1981 Mozote Massacre, when military soldiers executed more than 1,000 men, women, and children in the eastern mountain village of Mozote. The war raged on and off over the next 11 years, with international powers viewing the battle as an ideological struggle between democracy and communism. Cuba supported the guerillas, and the United States—to a total of $7 billion—supported the Salvadoran military government. More than 70,000 people were killed during the war's brutal run, including many who were executed and mutilated by government troops, who then dumped the bodies near town squares in order to warn against terrorism. More than 25% of the country's population was displaced by the war by its end.

By 1991, both sides had had enough of the long stalemate and a spirit of compromise emerged. In 1992, a truce was declared and a peace deal signed. A new constitution was drafted that enacted a number of land reforms and did away with the military death squads in favor of a national civil police; in addition, the FMLN became a legal political party that remains active today. Amnesty for war crimes, of which there were many, was declared in 1993.

EL SALVADOR TODAY

Today, El Salvador continues to struggle. The plight of its *campesinos* and civil war deaths have been replaced by one of Latin America's highest homicide rates, due mainly to the presence of the street gang Mara Salvatrucha, or MS-13. Though MS-13 began on the streets of Los Angeles in the 1980s, heavy deportation of U.S.-based gang members has steadily increased the gang's influence in El Salvador. Continuing government efforts to break up the gang have had small, sporadic impacts, but crime remains a central issue of Salvadoran life.

In 1998, El Salvador was hit by Hurricane Mitch, which killed 374 people, left 55,000 homeless, and stalled the economy. Mitch was followed in 2001 and 2005 by more massive earthquakes that killed over a thousand people, left thousands more homeless, and severely damaged thousands of buildings—many of which remain under repair today, including San Salvador's majestic National Theater.

Since 1992, however, the country's new constitution and cooperation of the two main political parties has allowed El Salvador to remain peaceful. In 2006, former TV sports presenter Tony Saca became president of El Salvador under the conservative ARENA party, and he remains president at press time even though his presidency has witnessed an underperforming economy with high inflation.

Despite rising inflation and other problems, El Salvador's economy grew steadily from the 1990s through to 2007. The percentage of Salvadorans living in poverty was reduced from 66% in 1991 to just over 30% in 2006. Still, many Salvadorans thought the Central America Free Trade Agreement, which the country joined in 2006, caused its economic woes. The 2007 recession in North America had a debilitating effect on El Salvador's export-driven economy, as well as lessening the ever-important remittances from family members working in the States.

The FMLN party subsequently experienced a surprising upswing and won the 2009 presidential elections with its candidate Mauricio Funes, a popular and respected TV journalist. He had toned down his party's left-wing rhetoric, promising to stick with dollarization and keep a friendly distance from Hugo Chavez. The peaceful transfer of power between two old civil war foes was seen as a great advance in Salvadoran democracy.

Since the election, Funes' popularity has proved resilient despite a faltering economy and high crime rate. This can be credited with his centrist approach and refusal to make radical reforms promoted by his core supporters in the FMLN. Moderate initiatives such as free school uniforms and a stand against mining interests have proved popular. He also issued a formal government apology regarding the murder of Archbishop Romero. However stubborn unemployment at 40% and a persistently high poverty rate means Funes may lose the support of his main backer if he is not seen to take a more ambitious approach to El Salvador's economic and social problems.

Honduras

A LOOK AT THE PAST

Prior to the arrival of the Spanish, Honduras was inhabited by the Maya, who drifted down from Mexico and Guatemala to settle in the highlands and valleys throughout the western half of the country. In A.D. 426, they founded the city-state of Copán, considered one of the intellectual capitals of the Maya for its rich architecture and design until, around A.D. 800, the Maya civilization mysteriously began to collapse. While pockets of the Mayas' descendants remained in the region after this collapse, other indigenous groups, such as the Lencas, the Miskito, and the Pech, eventually developed as well.

On July 30, 1502, during his fourth and final voyage to the Americas, Christopher Columbus reached the pine-covered island of Guanaja, becoming the first European to set foot on Honduran soil. Eventually, Columbus would set sail for the northern mainland coast, stopping in Trujillo on August 14 and soon after in Puerto Castilla, where the first Catholic Mass in Honduras took place. The Honduran coast was ignored for several decades until after Hernán Cortés's conquest of the Aztecs, when the Spanish exploration of the mainland began. In 1523, conquistador Gil Gonzáles de Avila reached the Golfo de Fonseca, but was quickly captured by rival Spaniard Cristóbal de Olid a year later, who founded the colony of Triunfo de la Cruz. Olid's soldiers turned on him, though, and he was swiftly executed. Cortés learned of the power struggle and sent trusted Francisco de las Casas to intervene and establish a colony at Trujillo in 1525.

In the 1530s, gold and silver were discovered in the country's western highlands, and an influx of Spaniards quickly arrived on the scene, leading to the founding of the cities of San Pedro de Puerto Caballos, now San Pedro Sula, and Gracias a Dios. In answer to this, a Lenca chief named Lempira unified rival tribes to launch attacks on the Spanish from his fort at Cerquín. The Spanish waged a fierce assault on the fort for more than 6 months, but to no avail. So the Spanish initiated peace talks with Lempira, only to murder him upon his arrival. After his death, resistance from the native groups was slowed and eventually stopped.

The Spanish, now that they were in full control of the territory, proceeded to decimate the native population via enslavement and harsh treatment—they wiped out as much as 95% of the indigenous population within a few decades. To make up for the labor shortage, African slaves were brought in during the 1540s. For the next few centuries, more colonies were founded, and a provincial capital was established in Gracias a Dios, though it was quickly moved to Comayagua. Mining fueled the economy until the collapse of silver prices forced the Spaniards to turn to agricultural endeavors such as tobacco farming and raising cattle.

During the 1600s, the Spanish began looting the riches of the South American continent and sent ships up the Central American coast on their return to Spain. French and English pirates, like the legendary Henry Morgan and John Coxen, began using the Bay Islands as their base for expeditions to plunder these Spanish ships, and they set up semipermanent settlements there. When in 1739 war erupted between England and Spain, the British took control over the islands and established a fort at Port Royal in Roatán. The treaty of Aix-la-Chapelle returned the islands to Spain, though the British reclaimed them during another war in 1779; in 1797, descendants of Carib Indians and African slaves from the Cayman Islands, called the Garífuna, were dumped in Roatán by the British. More waves of Garífuna arrived from the Caymans in the 1830s and began permanent settlements on the islands, as well as along the north coast of the mainland.

In 1821, Honduras declared independence from Spain, along with the Central American territories of Guatemala, El Salvador, Costa Rica, and Nicaragua. After a brief period as part of independent Mexico, it joined the United Provinces of Central America in 1823. Infighting among the provinces brought on the collapse of this federation in 1838, leaving the members to form independent countries. On November 15 of that year, most of current-day Honduras became a separate nation. The Bay Islands gained sovereignty from Britain in 1859.

Over the next 150 years, the country was plagued by political unrest that saw various rebellions, civil wars, coups, rigged elections, invasions, and changes of government. In one of the more unusual events, American William Walker attempted to conquer Central America with his own army but was executed that same year (see the "The Wars of William Walker" box on p. 35 for info).

In the early 19th century, U.S. companies such as the Tela Railroad Company, a subsidiary of United Fruit, now Chiquita, and Standard Fruit, now Dole, established banana plantations along the north coast and held sway over politics in the country. Bananas became the chief product in the country, accounting for as much as 80% of exports in 1929. The bribing of politicians and unjust labor practices marred the industry for much of the 20th century and kept the country from developing its own business elite, which was protested during a 2-month strike by plantation workers in 1954.

In 1956, the country's first military coup took place. A new constitution put the control of the military in the hands of the top general, not in the president, and this began a period of military rule of the country. In 1963, only days before the next election, the military, headed by Colonel López Arellano, seized power and canceled the election. Two years later, he was elected on his own and then served a 6-year term. A year after the next election, he again took control during another military coup. When it was discovered that Arellano took a $1.25-million bribe from the United Brands Fruit Company, previously known as United Fruit, he was removed from office. In his place came General Juan Alberto Melgar Castro, whose reign was rocked by a scandal involving using the military for drug trafficking. Next came General Policarpo Paz García, who would return the country to civilian rule in 1980 with the election of a president and congress.

During the end of the 19th century and much of the 20th century, the two main political parties in Honduras, liberals (who preferred a free-market economy as in the U.S.) and conservatives (who desired an aristocratic-style regime) wrestled power from each other again and again. From 1821 to 1982, the constitution was rewritten an astounding 17 times.

Political conflict was not all internal, however. In 1969, more than 300,000 undocumented Salvadorans were believed to be living in Honduras, and the government and private groups increasingly sought to blame them for the country's economic woes. During a World Cup preliminary match in Tegucigalpa, a disturbance broke out between fans on both sides, followed by a more intense incident during the next game in San Salvador. Salvadorans living in Honduras began to be harassed and even killed, leading to a mass exodus from the country. On June 27, 1969, Honduras broke off diplomatic relations with El Salvador, and on July 14, the Salvadoran air force began an assault on Honduras and took control of the city of Nueva Ocotepeque, marking the start of what would be called the Soccer War. Though the war lasted only 5 days and ended in a stalemate of sorts, in the end, between 60,000 and 130,000 Salvadorans were expelled or fled from Honduras, and more than 2,000 people, mostly Hondurans, were killed. While a peace treaty was signed between the two countries in 1980, even to this day relations between them remain strained.

Civil wars broke out in every country neighboring Honduras in the late 1970s and 1980s. El Salvador, Guatemala, and Nicaragua all saw wide-scale political upheaval, assassinations, and all-out civil unrest. To the surprise of many, Honduras, despite its shaky governments, scandals, and economic problems, escaped major turmoil during this period—the one exception being protests over U.S. military involvement in the country. During the 1980s, the U.S. provided aid to the country, in exchange for using it as a base for counterinsurgency movements (led by the CIA-trained group the Contras) against the Sandinistas in Nicaragua. Student and opposition leaders in Honduras organized massive protests of the U.S. military influence, to which the Honduran military responded by kidnapping and killing protestors. The protests grew, however, and eventually the country was forced to reexamine its policies on U.S. operations in Honduras—especially after it was revealed in 1986 that the Reagan administration had sold arms to Iran to support the anti-Sandinistas in Honduras. In 1988, the military agreement with the U.S. was not renewed and the Nicaraguan Contras ended up leaving the country entirely by 1990, when the Contra war concluded.

During the late 1980s and into the 1990s, struggles to maintain the value of the lempira against the dollar resulted in rapid inflation. Because wages remained the same, many Hondurans simply became poorer than they already were. When Carlos Roberto Flores Facusse became president in 1988, he initiated wide-scale currency reforms and took steps to modernize the economy. Things looked like they were about to change for the better. And then came Hurricane Mitch.

HONDURAS TODAY

In October 1998, the most powerful Atlantic hurricane ever recorded at the time decimated the country. Wind speeds as high as 180 mph caused billions of dollars in damage throughout the country. In the end, more than 6,000 people were killed and more than 1.5 million people were displaced, 70% of roads and bridges were destroyed, 70% of all crops were lost, and entire towns were destroyed by this storm. Relief poured in from the world community, although funds quickly dried up or never materialized (such as $640 million from various European organizations). Though the country has by now recovered greatly from the hurricane, to this day, many economic woes are still blamed on Mitch.

In 2006, Manuel Zelaya Rosales, a rancher from Olancho, was elected president after promises of doubling the police force, reeducating gang members, and lowering petroleum prices. In June 2009 after an attempt to alter the constitution, a move seen by some in the government to be illegal, Zelaya was ousted by the military and then sent into exile. While the world community called for Zelaya to be reinstated, National Congress President Roberto Micheletti stepped in as president. Negotiations with the help of the United States to reinstate Zelaya for the remaining months of his term fell through and in November of that year Porfirio Lobo Sosa of the center-right National Party was elected the country's next president.

One by one, world governments have begun to recognize the new government and the country has begun the long march to repair relations within the country and out, though much work still needs to be done.

Nicaragua

A LOOK AT THE PAST

Evidence of human life in Nicaragua dates back 8,000 years, in the form of shells collected by a tribe called Los Concheros on the Caribbean coast. In the 13th century, the Corotega and Nicarao tribes also settled in the country, when they fled south from Aztec Mexico and found refuge around the country's two great lakes. These same people gave the Spanish a taste of their fighting spirit when the Europeans first landed in 1519. The tribal leaders Nicaroa and Diriangén engaged the conquistador Gonzalez in a brief battle, after which the Spanish retreated.

The Spanish explorer Francisco Hernández de Córdoba first established a permanent colonial foothold in the country in 1524. The tribes were defeated and, despite the occasional rebellion over the next century or so, were eventually subdued and subjugated by the Europeans. Nicaragua became the domain of the Spanish Empire for the next 300 years, with Granada becoming a major merchant city because of its access to the Atlantic. As in other parts of the region, Nicaragua's prosperity led to frequent raids from British, French, and Dutch pirates sailing up the Río San Juan in search of loot and fortune, using the Atlantic coast as their base.

After a period of struggle, Nicaragua won independence from Spain in 1821 along with the rest of Central America. It was briefly a province of Mexico before becoming a part of the short-lived Central America Federation. It emerged as an independent nation in 1838. The English still retained their presence in the Caribbean, controlling the San Juan estuary from the port of Greytown until 1860. In that year, the British signed a treaty surrendering the Caribbean territory to Nicaragua, though in fact the region remained largely autonomous until 1893.

Quick to fill this power gap was America, which influenced Nicaraguan history from the late 1800s on. Nicaragua was of interest to the U.S. because it seemed like a good candidate for a canal between the Atlantic and Pacific. Plans for such a canal are still being considered to this day. When steamship magnate Cornelius Vanderbilt pioneered a land, river, and sea route that saw thousands of North Americans passing up the river San Juan as part of the Californian Gold Rush in the 1850s, the country gained more importance to Americans.

In addition to growing American influence, the 19th century was dominated by a vicious rivalry centered in the cities of Granada and León that continues in some way to this day. During this period, Granada emerged as the establishment capital, favored by landowners and merchants who had little desire for reform. León became the center for liberal bourgeoisie who were inspired by the Enlightenment and the American and French revolutions. Such was their rivalry that a national government was not declared until 1845, and the country was rocked by a civil war that went on intermittently throughout the rest of the century.

The country's political landscape was transformed by another American when mercenary and filibuster William Walker was hired by the León liberals to help in their latest conflict with Granada. His private army of 300 roughnecks won the battle but had no intention of going home. Walker declared himself president in 1855 (with the support of the U.S. government) and instituted policies such as reestablishing slavery and declaring English as the official language. These policies did not go down well, and the Leoneses soon united with the conservatives to defeat Walker at the battle of San Jacinto in 1856. See the box on p. 35 for more info.

A disgraced liberal class then surrendered to 36 years of conservative rule. The fishing village of Managua was declared the country's capital. A nationalist general, José Santos Zelaya, took power in 1893 and marched his troops to the Atlantic coast to lay claim to what until then was Nicaragua's on paper only. The liberal-leaning Zelaya antagonized the Americans by threatening to rival the planned Panama canal with a foreign-financed waterway of his own. He was ousted with the aid of American Marines in 1909. Three years later, a rebellion led by Benjamin Zeledón was crushed by American Marines who basically took over the country. For the next 12 years, there were 10 such uprisings against American-backed, conservative governments. After U.S. interests acquired some of Nicaragua's main businesses, Nicaragua soon found itself in hock to the United States and locked into an agreement where no other country could finance a canal that would interfere with Washington's plans in Panama.

A glimmer of hope came in 1924 when the liberals and conservatives finally agreed to a form of power sharing and the Americans withdrew their military presence. But the pact collapsed when conservative Emilio Chamorro staged a coup d'état and the Constitutional War broke out. Fearing a liberal victory, the U.S. again stepped in and negotiated a settlement that was opposed by one liberal general called Augusto C. Sandino. He held out in the northern highlands despite an American offensive that included the first bombing of a civilian town, Ocotal.

In 1933, the American-trained National Guard was created, led by Anastasio Somoza Garcia. The Americans withdrew, handing power to Juan Bautista Sacasa. Sandino accepted the government's invitation to negotiate but instead was assassinated by the National Guard in 1934 in Managua. The murder was followed by a clampdown by Somoza, who took complete control in 1937.

What followed was 42 years of iron rule by a family dynasty that in the end owned everything worth owning in Nicaragua. The Somoza family became fabulously wealthy and all-powerful. They installed the occasional puppet president and, with the help of the National Guard, rigged elections. When Anastasio Somoza Garcia was assassinated by the poet Rigoberto López Pérez in 1956, he was replaced by his son Luís "Tacho" Somoza Debayle and the regime continued. The only good things to come out of such ravenous, profit-driven rule were public works such as the Pan-American Highway (Carretera Panamericana) and the Lake Apanás hydroelectric plant. There were several attempts on Somoza's life, including an insurrection in 1959 that petered out after 2 weeks.

The Somoza regime showed its gratitude for American patronage in 1961 by allowing its Atlantic coast to be used as the launching pad for the Bay of Pigs operation. In 1963, a new organization called the Frente Sandinista de Liberación Nacional (FSLN) made its presence be known by staging an uprising in the North. Led by the Marxist Carlos Fonseca Amador, the Sandinistas were to prove a thorn in the side of an increasingly repressive regime. Tacho lost an election in 1963 and retired from politics. The new president Renée Schick was soon ousted by Anastasio "Tachito" Somoza in 1967. This younger brother of Tacho proved to be the cruelest and greediest of all the Somozas. He plundered reconstruction funds for the 1972 earthquake disaster and arranged the murder of newspaper editor and critic of the regime, Pedro Joaquin Chamorro, in 1978. On his orders, the national guard massacred hundreds in Masaya and battles broke out in the capital in which the air force bombed its own people. Despite the killing of their leader, Fonseca, in 1976, the Sandinistas gained the upper hand. The town of Matagalpa fell to the FSLN, followed by Estelí, and eventually the capital on July 19, 1979. Somoza fled to Paraguay, where he was eventually killed by a rocket attack in 1980.

The Sandinista revolution brought radical land reform and interventionist economics, policies that made the elite flee to Miami. While the economy collapsed, the poor became educated in hugely popular literacy drives. The new Reagan administration watched with dread what it perceived as a new front in the Cold War. Aid was halted in 1981 and an economic embargo was imposed in 1985, putting the economy into free fall. A new insurgency appeared in the north, this time by a right-wing group called the Contras, financed and trained by the CIA. The Sandinista government had to divert badly needed money toward this new war, as well as impose unpopular policies such as a draft and rationing.

By the end of the 1980s, both sides of this battle were exhausted. The Iran-Contra scandal (p. 30) had dried up support for the counterinsurgents, and the collapse of the Soviet Union was a serious blow to the revolution. A peace accord was proposed by Nicaragua's Central American neighbors (though opposed by the U.S.) and the Sandinistas accepted. Elections were held in 1990, and to the surprise of many, the government lost. A further surprise was a peaceful handover of power with the Sandinistas relinquishing control, but not before a shameful last grab of property and assets.

Violeta Barrios de Chamorro became the president of this new Nicaragua. The widow of the slain editor and leader of a loose coalition known as UNO, Doña Violeta introduced policies aimed at ending the war, reconciling all sides, and kick-starting the economy, with limited success. Meanwhile, the Sandinistas embraced democracy and became the main opposition party, led by veteran Daniel Ortega. Despite strong support, Ortega lost the 1996 election to a corrupt, right-wing politician called Arnoldo Alemán, leader of the Partido Liberal Constitucionalista (PLC). Alemán's tenure was rocked by endless kickback scandals and further tarnished by a disgraceful political pact with Ortega that basically divided power, pushed smaller parties out, and guaranteed immunity from prosecution for both leaders.

When Hurricane Mitch struck in 1998, wreaking havoc across the country and killing thousands, Alemán's appallingly slow reaction sealed his fate as a one-term president. His vice president, Enrique Geyer Bolaños, came to power in 2002, trouncing Ortega with 56% of the vote.

NICARAGUA TODAY

Once in office, Bolaños, acting on his anticorruption campaign pledges, turned on his own party, stripped Alemán of immunity, and had him jailed for 20 years for embezzlement and money laundering. Such justice is a rare thing in Central American politics and Bolaños paid for his crusade by being virtually paralyzed in a congress made up of disaffected and begrudging colleagues, who retaliated by trying to convict him in turn for illegal funding.

In the 2006 election, the Sandinistas were able to capitalize on this infighting and a general downturn in the economy; Ortega won the election with 37% of the popular vote. The initial reaction was a sudden dip in foreign investment, as people feared the country would return to the 1980s-style economy of hyperinflation and debt default. Ortega has, however, softened his Marxist image and declared himself to be market-friendly. Nevertheless, his popularity is low, due to a stalled economy and rising food prices. Both sides of the political spectrum are currently disaffected, with members on the right saying that Ortega has become a crony of Hugo Chavez and members on the left accusing him of selling out. The next elections are due in November 2011, but Ortega has his work cut out for him if he wants to remain in power.

Costa Rica
A LOOK AT THE PAST

Precious little is known of Costa Rica's history before the Spanish conquest. The pre-Columbian Indians who made their home here never developed the large cities or advanced culture that flowered farther north in present-day Guatemala, Belize, and Mexico. However, ancient artifacts indicating a strong sense of aesthetics have been unearthed from scattered excavations around the country. Beautiful gold and jade jewelry, intricately carved grinding stones, and artistically painted terra-cotta objects point to a small but highly skilled population.

In 1502, on his fourth and last voyage to the New World, Christopher Columbus anchored just offshore from present-day Limón. Whether he actually gave the country its name—"the rich coast"—is open to discussion, but the Spaniards never did find much gold or minerals to exploit here.

Despite their small numbers, scattered villages, and tribal differences, the original indigenous inhabitants of Costa Rica fought fiercely against the Spanish, until overcome by superior firepower and European diseases. When the fighting ended, the Spanish conquistadors found very few Indians left to force into servitude. Settlers were thus forced to till their own lands, a situation unheard of in other parts of Latin America. Few pioneers headed this way because they could stake their claims in other parts of the Spanish crown, where large slave workforces were available. Costa Rica was nearly forgotten, as the conquest looked elsewhere for riches to plunder and souls to convert.

The few Spanish settlers that did make a go of it headed for the hills, where they found rich volcanic soil and a climate less oppressive than in the lowlands. Cartago, the colony's first capital, was founded in 1563, but it was not until the 1700s that additional cities were established. In the late 18th century, the first coffee plants were introduced, and Costa Rica had its first major cash crop.

In 1821, Spain granted independence to its colonies in Central America. Costa Rica joined with its neighbors to form the Central American Federation; but in 1838, it withdrew to form a new nation and pursue its own interests. By the mid-1800s, coffee was the country's main export. Free land was given to anyone willing to plant coffee on it, and plantation owners soon grew wealthy and powerful, creating Costa Rica's first elite class.

Until 1890, coffee growers had to transport their coffee either by oxcart to the Pacific port of Puntarenas or by boat down the Río Sarapiquí to the Caribbean. In the 1870s, a progressive president proposed a railway from San José to the Caribbean coast to facilitate the transport of coffee to European markets. It took nearly 20 years for this plan to reach fruition, and more than 4,000 workers lost their lives constructing the railway, which passed through dense jungles and rugged mountains from the Central Valley to the coast. Partway through the project, as funds were dwindling, the second chief engineer, Minor Keith, proposed an idea that not only enhanced his fortunes but changed the course of Central American history. Banana plantations would be planted along the railway right of way (land on either side of the tracks). The export of this crop would help finance the railway, and, in exchange, Keith would get a 99-year lease on 323,750 hectares (800,000 acres) of land with a 20-year tax deferment. The Costa Rican government gave its consent, and in 1878 the first bananas were shipped. In 1899, Keith and a partner formed the United Fruit Company, a

The Wars of William Walker

In 1856, Costa Rica was invaded by William Walker, a soldier of fortune from Tennessee who, with the backing of U.S. President James Buchanan, was attempting to fulfill his grandiose dreams of presiding over a slave state in Central America (before his invasion of Costa Rica, he had invaded Nicaragua and Baja California). The people of Costa Rica, led by their president, Juan Rafael Mora, chased Walker back to Nicaragua. Walker surrendered to a U.S. warship in 1857, but in 1860, he attacked Honduras, claiming to be the president of that country. The Hondurans, who had had enough of Walker's shenanigans, promptly executed him.

business that eventually became the largest landholder in Central America and caused political disputes and wars throughout the region.

In 1889, Costa Rica held what is considered the first free election in Central American history. The opposition candidate won the election, and the control of the government passed from the hands of one political party to those of another without bloodshed or hostilities. Thus, Costa Rica established itself as the region's only true democracy. In 1948, this democratic process was challenged by Rafael Angel Calderón, who had served as the country's president from 1940 to 1944. After losing by a narrow margin, Calderón, who had the backing of the communist labor unions and the Catholic church, refused to concede the country's leadership to the rightfully elected president, Otillio Ulate, and a civil war ensued. Calderón was eventually defeated by José "Pepe" Figueres. In the wake of this crisis, a new constitution was drafted; among other changes, it abolished Costa Rica's army so that such a revolution could never happen again.

In 1994, history seemed to repeat itself—peacefully this time—when José María Figueres took the reins of government from the son of his father's adversary, Rafael Angel Calderón.

COSTA RICA TODAY

Costa Rica has a population of nearly five million, more than half of whom live in the Central Valley and are considered as urban. Some 94% of the population is of Spanish or other European descent, and it is not unusual to see fair-skinned, blond Costa Ricans. This is largely because the indigenous population in place when the first Spaniards arrived was small and was quickly reduced to even more of a minority by wars and disease. There are still some remnant indigenous populations, primarily on reservations around the country; the principal tribes include the Bribri, Cabécar, Boruca, and Guaymí. On the Caribbean coast and in the big cities, there is a substantial population of English-speaking black creoles who came over from the Antilles to work on building the railroad and on the banana plantations. Racial tension isn't palpable, but it exists, perhaps more out of standard ignorance and fear rather than an organized or articulated prejudice.

While interacting with visitors, Ticos are very open and helpful. Time has relative meaning to Ticos. Although most tour companies and other establishments operate efficiently, don't expect punctuality in general.

In a region historically plagued by internal strife and civil wars, Costa Ricans are proud of their peaceful history, political stability, and relatively high level of development. However, this can also translate into arrogance and prejudice toward immigrants from neighboring countries, particularly Nicaraguans, who make up a large percentage of the workforce on the banana and coffee plantations.

Costa Rica is the most technologically advanced and politically stable nation in Central America, and it has the largest middle class. Even the smallest towns have electricity, the water is mostly safe to drink, and the phone system is relatively good and very widespread. Still, the gap between rich and poor has been widening for years. Government, banking, and social institutions are regularly embroiled in scandal. The roads, hospitals, and school systems have been in a slow but steady state of decay for decades. And there are no immediate signs that these matters will improve. Several "Free Zones" and some high-tech investments and production facilities have dramatically changed the face of Costa Rica's economy. Intel, which opened two side-by-side assembly plants in Costa Rica, currently accounts for more than 20% of the country's exports, compared with traditional exports such as **coffee** (3%) and **bananas** (8%). Although Intel and other international companies often trumpet a growing gross domestic product, very little of the profits actually make their way into the Costa Rican economy.

Tourism is the nation's principal source of income, surpassing cattle ranching, textiles, and exports of coffee, pineapples, bananas, and Intel microchips. Over two million tourists visit each year, and more than half the working population is employed in the tourism and service industries. Ticos whose fathers and grandfathers were farmers and ranchers find themselves hotel owners, tour guides, and waiters. Although most have adapted gracefully and regard the industry as a source of new jobs and opportunities for economic advancement, restaurant and hotel staff can seem gruff and uninterested at times, especially in rural areas. An increase in the number of visitors has led to an increase in crime, prostitution, and drug trafficking. Common sense and street savvy are required in San José and in many of the more popular tourist destinations.

The global economic crisis of 2008 to 2009 has hit Costa Rica. Tourism is noticeably down. Still, because credit has historically been so tight, there was no major mortgage or banking crisis in the country. And early signs seem to indicate that Costa Rica has dodged a bullet and should recover nicely.

In 2010, Costa Rica elected its first female president, Laura Chinchilla, who was a vice-president in the Arias administration. Her election should allow for some continuity in the execution of social programs and infrastructure projects.

Panama

A LOOK AT THE PAST

Little is known about the ancient cultures that inhabited Panama before the arrival of the Spanish. The pre-Columbian cultures in this region did not build large cities or develop an advanced culture like the Maya or Incas, and much of what was left behind has been stolen or engulfed in jungle. We know that the most advanced cultures came from central Panama, such as the Monagrillo (2500–1700 B.C.), who were one of the first pre-Columbian societies in the Americas to produce ceramics. Excavation of sites such as Conte, near Natá, have unearthed burial pits with *huacas* (ceremonial figurines) and jewelry, which demonstrates an introduction to metallurgy during the 1st century, as well as trade with Colombia and even Mexico.

The first of many Spanish explorers to reach Panama was Rodrigo de Bastidas, who sailed from Venezuela along Panama's Caribbean coast in 1501 in search of gold. His first mate was Vasco Nuñez de Balboa, who would return later and seal his fate as one of Panama's most important historical figures. A year later, Christopher Columbus, on his fourth and final voyage to the New World, sailed into Bocas del Toro and stopped at various points along the isthmus, one of which he named Puerto Bello, now known as Portobelo.

Meanwhile, Balboa had settled in the Dominican Republic but had racked up huge debts. In 1510, he escaped his creditors by hiding out as a stowaway on a boat bound for Panama. In the years since Columbus's failed attempt, many other Spaniards had tried to colonize the coast, but were thwarted by disease and indigenous raids. Balboa suggested settling at Antigua de Darién, where he became a tough but successful administrator who both subjugated Indians and befriended conquered tribes. Having listened to stories by Indians about another sea, Balboa set out in 1513 with Francisco Pizarro and a band of Indian slaves, and hacked his way through perilous jungle for 25 days until he arrived at the Pacific coast, where he claimed the sea and all its shores for the king of Spain. Balboa was later beheaded by a jealous new governor, Pedro Arias de Avila (Pedrarias the Cruel), on a trumped-up charge of treason.

In 1519, Pedrarias settled a fishing village called Panama, which meant "plenty of fish" in the local language, and resettled Nombre de Dios on the Atlantic to create a passageway for transporting Peruvian gold and riches from the Pacific to Spanish galleons in the Caribbean Sea. The trail was called the Camino Real, or Royal Trail, but later a faster and easier route was established, called the Camino de las Cruces. The land portion of this trail was two-thirds shorter, and met with the Chagres River, which could be sailed out to the Caribbean Sea. This trail can be walked today, and portions of the stone-inlaid path still exist.

By the mid–17th century, dwindling supplies of silver and gold from the Peruvian mines and ongoing pirate attacks precipitated a severe decline in the amount of precious metals being transported to Spain. In 1671, the notorious Welsh buccaneer Henry Morgan sailed up the Chagres River, crossed the isthmus, and overpowered Panama City, sacking the city and leaving it in flames. Those who escaped the attack rebuilt Panama City, 2 years later, at what is now known as Casco Viejo.

Spain finally abandoned the isthmus crossing and Portobelo after the city was attacked by the British Admiral Edward Vernon, and returned to sailing around Cape Horn to reach Peru. Spain granted independence to its Central America colonies in 1821, and Panama was absorbed into "Gran Colombia," a union led by liberator Simón Bolívar that included Colombia, Venezuela, and Ecuador. Panama attempted to split from Colombia three times during the 19th century, but wouldn't be successful until the U.S.-backed attempt in 1903.

Having been a colonial backwater since the pullout of the Spanish in the late 17th century, Panama was restored to prosperity from 1848 to 1869 during the height of the California Gold Rush. Given that crossing from the Atlantic to the Pacific of the U.S. was a long, arduous journey by wagon and prone to Indian attacks and other pitfalls, gold-seekers chose to sail to Panama, cross the Las Cruces trail, and sail on to California. In 1855, an American group of financiers built the Panama Railroad, greatly reducing the travel time between coasts.

Travel time would be reduced even further by the Panama Canal, the history of which dates from 1539, when King Charles I of Spain dispatched a survey team to study the feasibility of a canal (which was deemed impossible). The first real attempt at construction of a canal was begun in 1880 by the French, led by Ferdinand de Lesseps, the charismatic architect of the Suez Canal. De Lesseps had been convinced that a sea-level canal was the only option. Once workers broke ground, however, engineers soon saw the impracticality of a sea-level canal but were unable to convince the stubborn de Lesseps, and for years rumors flew, financial debts mounted, and nearly 20,000 workers perished before the endeavor collapsed. Few had anticipated the enormous challenge presented by the Panamanian jungle, with its mucky swamps, torrential downpours, landslides, floods, and, most debilitating of all, mosquito-borne diseases such as malaria.

Meanwhile, Panama was embroiled in political strife and a nonstop pursuit to separate itself from Colombia. Following the French failure with the canal, the U.S. expressed interest in taking over construction but was rebuffed by the Colombian government. In response, the U.S. backed a growing independence movement in Panama that declared its separation from Colombia on November 3, 1903. The U.S. officially recognized Panama, and sent its battleships to protect the new nation from Colombian troops, who turned back home after a few days.

A French canal engineer on the de Lesseps project, Philippe Bunau-Varilla, a major shareholder of the abandoned canal project, had been given negotiating-envoy status by the Panamanian government for the new U.S.-built canal. His controversial Hay-Bunau-Varilla Treaty gave the U.S. rights that included the use, occupation, and sovereign control of a 16km-wide (10-mile) swath of land across the isthmus, and was entitled to annex more land if necessary to operate the canal. The U.S. would also be allowed to intervene in Panama's affairs.

The French had excavated two-fifths of the canal, built hospitals, and left behind machinery and the operating railway, as well as a sizable workforce of Afro-Caribbeans. For the next 10 years, the U.S., having essentially eradicated tropical disease, pulled off what seemed impossible in terms of engineering: carving out a path through the Continental Divide, constructing an elevated canal system, and making the largest man-made lake in the world.

A stormy political climate ensued in Panama for the following decades. Presidents and other political figures were typically *rabiblancos,* or wealthy, white elites loathed by the generally poor and dark-skinned public. Increasingly, Panamanians were discontented with the U.S. presence and, in particular, its control of the canal. In 1964, several U.S. high-school students in the Canal Zone raised the American flag at their school and ignited protests by Panamanian college students. The protests culminated in the deaths of more than two dozen Panamanians, an event that is now called "Día de los Mártires," or Martyrs Day.

By 1974, the U.S. had begun to consider transferring the canal to Panama. Arias was once again voted into power and after strong-arming the National Guard, he was deposed in a military coup led by Omar Torrijos Herrera, a colonel of the National Guard. Torrijos was an authoritarian leader but a champion of the poor who espoused land redistribution and social programs—a "dictatorship with a heart," as he called it. His most popular achievement came in 1977, with the signing of a treaty with then-president Jimmy Carter that relinquished control of the canal to Panama on December 31, 1999. Also part of the treaty was the closing of U.S. military bases and the U.S. right to intervene only if it perceived a threat against the canal. On July 31, 1981, Torrijos died in a plane accident.

By 1983, the National Guard, renamed the Panamanian Defense Forces (PDF), was controlled by Colonel Manuel Antonio Noriega, and continued to dominate political and everyday life in Panama. Noriega created the so-called Dignity Battalions that aimed to stifle dissent through force, and terrorize anyone who opposed the PDF. For the next 6 years, Noriega kept the Panamanian public in a state of fear, running the country through presidents he had placed in power, killing and torturing his opponents, and involving himself in drug trafficking.

The U.S. imposed tough economic sanctions on Panama that included freezing government assets in U.S. banks, and withholding canal fees, spurning widespread protests against Noriega across Panama City. In 1989, a fresh set of presidential elections pitted the Noriega-picked candidate against Guillermo Endara. When Endara won, Noriega annulled the election amid widespread claims by foreign observers of fraud on the part of the Noriega regime.

With Panama veering out of control, the U.S. began sending troops to bases in the Canal Zone. On December 20, 1989, the U.S. launched Operation Just Cause, led by 25,000 soldiers who pounded the city for 6 days, leaving anywhere from 500 to 7,000 dead, depending on whom you asked. Noriega fled and hid in the offices of the Vatican *nuncio,* where he asked for asylum. He later surrendered and was flown to the U.S., where he was tried, charged, and sentenced to 40 years in prison. The sentence was later reduced and Noriega was due to be released in 2007, but a French extradition request for money laundering meant he remained in a Florida prison at press time. Though Noriega will serve jail time in Panama if he returns, Panamanians are justifiably nervous about his release.

In the wake of Noriega's extradition, Guillermo Endara was sworn in as president of a country racked by instability. In 1994, a former Torrijos associate, Ernesto Pérez Balladares, took over the presidency, instituted sweeping economic reforms, and worked to rebuild Panama's relationship with the U.S., which still had control of the canal. The same year, the constitution was changed to ban the military in Panama.

Balladares was followed by Mireya Moscoso in 1999, the ex-wife of Arias, and Panama's first female president. During her 5 years in power, her approval ratings dropped to less than 30%; she was viewed as incompetent and prone to cronyism and corruption. Moscoso oversaw the handover of the canal. Despite decades of protest against the U.S. presence, many Panamanians in the end expressed ambivalence about the pullout when faced with the economic impact on businesses and the loss of jobs.

PANAMA TODAY

Panama has three million residents, and more than a third of them live in Panama City, Colón, and David. The remaining population is concentrated mostly in small towns and villages in central Panama and the Azuero Peninsula. Officially roughly 70% of the population are *mestizo,* or a mix of Amerindians and Caucasians; 14% are of African descent; 10% are white and other immigrant races; and 6% are Amerindian. About 30% of the population is under the age of 14.

Panamanians no longer indulge in afternoon siestas, but you will notice that things move at a languid pace. Given this and the country's nascent tourism infrastructure, even well-respected tour companies and other tourism establishments can't always be relied on for punctuality.

Panama has a dollarized economy whose major natural resources are its rainforests, beaches, and oceans, making this country an irresistible draw for tourism. Panama's principal source of income is derived from the services sector, including the Panama Canal, the Colón Free Trade Zone, banking, and flagship registry, among other "export" services, all of which account for about three-quarters of the country's GDP.

The withdrawal of U.S. canal workers and military personnel in 2000 had a devastating effect on Panama City's economy, but a growth in the construction sector is currently underway thanks to juicy tax incentives, and skyscrapers seem to shoot up overnight along the city's shoreline. Panama has effectively sold itself as a retirement haven, with its low cost of living, inexpensive land, and dollar-based economy, and many who were once just passing through are putting down stakes in gated communities or taking on new roles as hotel or restaurant owners.

For many years, foreign investors lured by get-rich-quick schemes were snapping up property in a real-estate boom that had many locals grumbling about the soaring value of land; this has slowed down a bit in the last couple of years, but prices have remained high. On the legislative side, the Panamanian government has reformed its tax structure, opened its borders to free trade with key nations like the U.S., and implemented a social security overhaul. Yet money laundering, political corruption, and cocaine transshipment continue to be problems, as is widespread unemployment, with indigenous groups and Colón residents faring the worst. As the nation grows economically, the split between the rich and the poor widens. Today, about 40% of the population is under the poverty level and lacks adequate housing, access to medical care, and proper nutrition.

The current president of Panama is Ricardo Martinelli, a member of the right-leaning Democratic Change Party who has vowed to cut corruption and reduce crime. Martinelli is a former businessman with a degree from the University of Arkansas, and many see his business background as a key to Panama's continued economic development. Reelected with more than 60% of the vote in 2009, many Panamanians are counting on Martinelli to "clean up" Panama and move the country forward.

In 2007, a $5.5-billion expansion of the Panama Canal got underway, a move that ultimately promises to keep the canal relevant. Worldwide tankers have grown too big to fit in the canal, and those ships that can fit must line up for hours to cross. The project is slated for completion in 2014.

A CENTRAL AMERICAN CULTURAL OVERVIEW

Central America's population of 40 million people comes from diverse backgrounds: indigenous, European, African, and West Indian. Because of the history of Spanish influence in this region, *mestizos* (people of both Amerindian and Spanish ancestry) are in the majority. As you head from Panama north, the population of Central America becomes more indigenous. *Mestizos* are in the majority until you reach Guatemala, which has a predominantly Maya culture. Belize also has a population of some 4,000 Mennonites who migrated from Mexico in the 1950s. And along the Atlantic coast, there's a strong African presence that is more West Indian than Latin American in spirit. Most of the communities along this coast are English-speaking.

Though there is much variety, there are some constants in Latin American society. One is an acute wealth gap, with 50% of the population living below the poverty level. The other is a pervasive *machista* attitude. Women are very much still tied to the home, though this attitude is gradually changing and women (especially those in cities) are becoming more independent. Finally, innate racism is unfortunately prevalent in all countries. The lighter your skin, the more educated, sophisticated, and rich you are thought in everyone's eyes.

Most of Central America is also primarily a Roman Catholic society, and family is an integral part of the culture here. Offspring, especially daughters, often remain with their families until they're married and even then multiple generations frequently continue to live in the same house. Most small towns offer little nightlife, since restaurants and shops shutter at dark. Instead, evenings are spent at home or in the town square—nearly every major town in the region is built around a central square that serves as a meeting spot for that community. In most Central American countries, *fútbol*, or soccer, competes with baseball as the leading sport. In countries such as Nicaragua, there is a baseball stadium in even the smallest towns.

One thing you'll find about Central Americans is that they are a warm and outgoing people who are eager to help strangers, at an easygoing pace. Take for granted that any informal meeting will start 30 minutes late. This is not true regarding tourism— tour buses, for example, are expected to leave on time.

Below is a more detailed country-by-country cultural background of this region.

Belize

Belize has a population of some 310,000, roughly half of whom live in one of the six major towns or cities, with the rest in rural areas or small villages. About 45% of the population is considered *mestizo*, descendants of mixed Spanish, Mexican, and/or Maya blood. Making up 30% of the population are the creoles, predominantly black descendants of slaves and British colonists. Belize's three Maya tribes—Yucatec, Mopan, and Kekchi—make up around 10% of the population. The Garífuna constitute about 6.5% of the population, while a mix of whites of British descent, Mennonites, Chinese, and East Indians fill out the rest.

With its tiny population and relative isolation, Belize lacks the vibrant cultural scene found in larger, more cosmopolitan countries. Still, if you poke around, you'll find some respectable local music, literature, art, and architecture to enjoy. For current information about the arts and what might be happening while you're in Belize, contact the **Institute of Creative Arts** (© **501/227-2110**; www.nichbelize.org), which is housed in the Bliss Institute of Performing Arts (p. 104) in Belize City.

Belizean artists range from folk artists and artisans working in a variety of forms, materials, and traditions to modern painters, sculptors, and ceramicists producing representational and abstract works. Out in the western Cayo district, the traditional Maya arts are kept alive by several talented artisans working in carved slate basreliefs. Of these, the García sisters, who run the **Tanah Mayan Art Museum**, a gallery and small museum in the Mountain Pine Ridge area (p. 135), are the prime proponents.

Perhaps the most vibrant place to look for modern art is in southern Belize, where Garífuna painters like Benjamín Nicholas and Pen Cayetano have produced wonderful bodies of work depicting local life in a simple style. Walter Castillo is another excellent modern painter.

Belize doesn't have a strong literary tradition. However, most gift shops and bookstores around the country have a small collection of locally produced short stories, poetry, fiction, and nonfiction. In recent years, there has been a trend to resuscitate and transcribe the traditional Maya and Garífuna tales and folklore, along with the publication of modern pieces of fiction and nonfiction either set in Belize or written by Belizeans. Perhaps the best modern Belizean author is Zee Edgell, and you'll be able to find her works at gift shops around the country.

The most distinctive and popular form of Belizean music you will come across is Punta and Punta Rock. Punta is similar to many Afro-Caribbean and Afro-pop music forms, blending traditional rhythms and drumming patterns with modern electronic

THE Garífuna

Throughout the 18th century, escaped and shipwrecked slaves intermarried and blended in with the native Carib Indian populations on several islands in the Lesser Antilles, but predominantly on St. Vincent. The West Africans were a mixed lot, including members of the Fon, Yoruba, Ewe, and Nago tribes. Over the years, the West African and indigenous elements blended into a new people, known first as Black Caribs and today as Garífuna or Garinagu. The Garífuna have their own language, traditions, history, and rituals, all of which blend elements of the group's two primary cultural sources. African-style drumming with complex rhythmic patterns and call-and-response singing accompany ritual possession ceremonies spoken in a language whose etymological roots are predominantly Arawak.

The Black Caribs were fierce warriors and frequently fought the larger colonial powers to maintain their freedom and independence. In 1796, despite the celebrated leadership of Joseph Chatoyer, the Garífuna were soundly defeated by the British forces, who subsequently shipped several thousand of the survivors off to exile on the island of Roatán, in then–British Honduras. The Garífuna began migrating and eventually settled along the entire coast of what is present-day Honduras, Nicaragua, Guatemala, and Belize. For nearly 2 centuries now, the Garífuna have lived quiet lives of subsistence farming, fishing, and light trading with their neighbors, while steadfastly maintaining their language, heritage, and traditions.

The principal Garífuna settlements in Central America include Punta Gorda, Hopkins Village, and Dangriga, Belize; Livingston, Guatemala; Tela, Trujillo, and La Ceiba, Honduras; and Corn Island, Nicaragua.

instruments (Punta is usually more rootsy and acoustic than Punta Rock, which features electric guitars and keyboards). Pen Cayetano is often credited as being the founder of Punta Rock; you will find his discs for sale throughout Belize, as well as those by his successors Andy Palacio, Peter Flores (aka Titiman), and Chico Ramos. Punta music is usually sung in the Garífuna dialect, although the latest incarnations feature lyrics in English and even Spanish. Dancing to Punta and Punta Rock is sensuous and close, often settling into a firm butt-to-groin grind. Paranda is another modern yet more traditional offshoot of Garífuna music and culture. Featuring acoustic guitars and rhythm ensembles, paranda is a lively, syncopated musical form. Paul "Nabby" Nabor is a popular paranda artist. A similar and rootsy form of contemporary folk music that comes from the Kriol tradition is known as brukdown.

You might want to rent a copy of *The Mosquito Coast* (1986), which was filmed in Belize, though it's set in Honduras. Perhaps the most relevant and readily available film for tourists is *Three Kings of Belize* (Stonetree Records: 2007). Directed by Katia Paradis, this documentary provides an intimate look into the lives of Belizean musicians Paul Nabor, Florencio Mess, and Wilfred Peters. Nabor is a Garífuna singer, songwriter, and guitarist, while Mess plays a traditional Mayan harp, and the recently deceased creole accordionist Mr. Peters was known across Belize as the "King of Brukdown." Out on DVD, you will find *Three Kings of Belize* for sale at bookstores and gift shops all over Belize.

Another good DVD selection is *Sastun* (Create Space: 2009), Guido Verweyen's documentary look into the relationship between Rosita Arvigo and famed Mayan healer Don Elijio Panti. This provides an excellent complement to Arvigo's book *Sastun: My Apprenticeship with a Maya Healer* ★.

Guatemala

Long-lasting Maya and Spanish empires produced an ethnically, linguistically, and economically divided Guatemala. Around half of the population is *mestizo* (known as *ladino* in Guatemala), or Spanish-Amerindian heritage. The other half belongs to one of 23 indigenous Maya groups, each with their own language and customs. The largest is the Ki'che, who live around Lake Atitlán and make up around 10% of the country's population—which totals almost 13 million. Other Maya groups include the Cakchiquel, Tz'utujil, Mam, and Kekchi, and on the Caribbean coast, the Garífuna, descendants of former slaves and Carib Indians.

Racial tensions can be strong between these groups, especially between *ladinos* and the Maya in the cities, and between *ladinos* and Garífuna on the Caribbean coast. Subsurface religious tensions also exist between the vast-majority Catholic population and the fast-growing Evangelical Protestant movement, which draws its greatest support within indigenous communities.

Guatemala's best-known art and craft works are indigenous woven tapestries and clothing. Artisans use natural dyes extracted from the *clavel* and *heraño* flowers, then mix in the crushed bodies of mosquitoes to keep the colors from running. The fabrics are woven on huge looms or simple, portable back-strap looms. Traditional dress for women includes a *huipil* (blouse) and *corte* (skirt), often fastened to the waist with a rope belt. Handicrafts are far from the only art in Guatemala, though. Several top-notch galleries in Guatemala City and Antigua carry a wide range of contemporary local art.

Guatemala's literary tradition dates from pre-Columbian Maya civilization, when Ki'che authors wrote the holy book Popol Vuh. The book traces the history of the Ki'che people beginning with their creation myth, linking the royal family with the gods in order to reaffirm its legitimacy. The book's exact age is unknown; the Spanish first recorded its existence in Chichicastenango in 1701.

Apart from the Popol Vuh, Guatemala's most famous literary works come from Nobel Prize–winning poet, playwright, and ambassador Miguel Ángel Asturias. Considered one of the fathers of magical realism, Asturias authored such works as *El Señor Presidente* (1946), *Viento Fuerte* (1950), and *Hombres de Maíz* (1967).

Literature can't be discussed without mentioning Maya activist Rigoberta Menchú, who won international acclaim with her autobiography, *I, Rigoberta,* published in 1982. Other authors to look out for, in Spanish and occasionally in translation, include the short-story writer Augusto Monterroso, as well as poets Luis Cardoza y Arragon, Otto Rene Castillo, and Humberto Ak'Abal.

In Guatemalan folk music, both *mestizo* and Maya, the marimba is king. *Mestizo* forms reflect their Spanish roots with marimba bands and Spanish-language folk songs influenced by the mariachi and ranchero traditions. Maya music may also feature flute and drum, as with the Ki'che and Cakchiquel, or violins and harps, as with the Kekchi. A favorite contemporary Guatemalan musician is Ricardo Arjona, a rocking songster and lyricist. Songs such as "Ella y El" ("She and He") and "Si el Norte Fuera el Sur" ("If North Were South") are smart works of social and political satire with very catchy melodies.

The Guatemalan film industry is still in its infancy. However, the country has had subtle appearances in mainstream American productions. The 11th season of *Survivor* was filmed at the Maya ruins of Yaxhá, and the tribes were named after ancient cities.

More recently, *Looking for Palladin*, featuring Ben Gazzara and Talia Shire, was shot on location in Antigua. Going back a bit in time, the 1935 film *The New Adventures of Tarzan* was filmed in the rainforests of Guatemala, with the fabulous Atlantic coast waterfalls of Siete Altares playing a feature role.

El Salvador

El Salvador's culture is not a simple one to grasp. This small country is about the size of Massachusetts, with a population of roughly six million—making it the most densely populated Central American nation. It's a place where the beauty of its people stands in stark contrast to the violence of its history. Having suffered through decades of oppression, a bloody civil war, crushing poverty, and horrendous crime, the people of El Salvador have every right to be bitter. But somehow they're not—though the civil war of the 1980s very much remains part of the national psyche, many of the 2.5 million Salvadorans who have migrated to the United States aim to one day return to their beloved El Salvador.

Of El Salvador's roughly six million residents, 90% identify themselves as *mestizo*, or of mixed race. Nine percent identify as white, with most either of Spanish descent or from elsewhere in Europe. Figures vary on the indigenous population and range from 1% to 5%. The majority of El Salvador's indigenous people are descendants of the Pipil, who were part of the nomadic Mexican Nahua tribe that replaced the Maya as El Salvador's dominant population around the 11th century. Today, the greatest concentration of indigenous communities can be found in the southwestern department of Sonsonate, where a few continue to speak the native Nahuat language. A smaller indigenous population descended from the Lenca (Honduras's largest indigenous population) and are found mainly in El Salvador's eastern region. Though more than a third of Salvadorans live in San Salvador, the majority of Salvadorans live in rural areas. The country has a relatively young population, with 36% under the age of 15.

You won't find as obvious a culture here of art, literature, music, or film as you will in nearby Mexico or Guatemala. Rural village markets throughout the country, particularly those in La Palma, do offer traditional arts and crafts called "artesania," though, and the artist Fernando Llort (p. 241) has developed a reputation throughout the world for his art workshop in San Salvador, from which he encourages locals to express themselves through art.

Perhaps the most famous work of literature from here is *La Diáspora*, an award-winning novel by one of El Salvador's leading writers, Horacio Castellanos Moya. It chronicles the struggles of exiles from El Salvador's civil war.

Shopping Tips

International laws prohibit trade in endangered wildlife, so don't buy any plants or animals, even if they're for sale. Do not buy any kind of sea-turtle products (including jewelry); wild birds; lizard, snake, or cat skins; corals; or orchids (except those grown commercially). No matter how unique, beautiful, insignificant, or inexpensive it might seem, your purchase will contribute to the further hunting of endangered species.

At most stores and shops, sales and import taxes have already been figured into the display price, and it is not normal to haggle. You can, however, bargain a price down (within reason) in more informal settings such as city markets.

Native indigenous music, using instruments like the marimba, flute, and drums, was repressed in the early 20th century but has miraculously survived and can be heard today through performers such as Paquito Palaviccini. El Salvador also has its very own take on Colombian *cumbia,* and the country dances to popular musical forms such as salsa, reggaeton, and hip-hop. There is even a form of hybrid Salvadoran rock called *guanarock.*

Arguably the country's most heralded film is the 2004 movie *Film Voces Inocentes,* which tells the story of the Salvadoran civil war through the eyes of an 11-year-old child and is based on the childhood of Salvadoran filmmaker Oscar Torres, who fled El Salvador for the United States in the midst of the war.

Honduras

The vast majority (an estimated 85%–90%) of Honduras's 7.8 million or so people are **mestizos** or *ladinos,* which means they are of mixed American Indian and Spanish descent. The *mestizo* population therefore dominates the country's cities and the economic and political landscape of the country.

There are also eight other major ethnic groups concentrated in various regions around the country, the largest being the **Lenca,** in the southwest, particularly the mountains and valleys near Gracias, and they number around 100,000. The Lencas are descended from Chibcha-speaking Indians who came to Honduras from Colombia and Venezuela several thousand years ago. Nearby in the Copán Valley and along the border with Guatemala, the **Chortí-Maya** is another indigenous group numbering between 4,000 and 5,000. They are descendants of the ancient Maya.

The second-largest ethnic group in the country is the **Garífuna,** descendants of Carib and Arawak Indians who mixed with escaped African slaves and now populate the entire North Coast and the Bay Islands and number around 95,000. The British forcibly transplanted the Garífuna from the Cayman Islands to the island of Roatán in 1787, and from there they moved to other islands and to the mainland. The Garífuna still populate the Bay Islands, though they share the land with the Bay Islanders—another ethnic group descended from pirates and blacks from elsewhere in the Caribbean—and an increasing number of North Americans who are buying property and calling the islands home.

In the department of Yoro in the central highlands, the **Tolupan** inhabit scattered communities isolated among the mountains there. Three other indigenous groups can be found in the La Mosquitia (Mosquito Coast) region of the country. The lack of roads and transportation in this region has allowed the small pockets of **Miskitos, Pech,** and **Tawahkas** to maintain their cultural identities far better than most other indigenous groups in Central America, who have sometimes been engulfed by mainstream society. While the Miskitos are not a straight indigenous group—but rather a cultural mishmash of an unknown tribe, English pirates, and escaped African slaves—the Pech and Tawahkas have remained practically unchanged since preconquest.

Although Honduras has often been overshadowed by the arts emerging from neighboring countries, the country's vibrant and diverse population has led to a number of achievements. Honduras has a thriving folk art scene. Best known are the country's primitivist painters, such as José Antonio Velásquez (1906–83) and Pablo Zelaya Sierra (1896–1933). The Lencas are also known throughout Central America for their pottery and ceramics. Finally, the artisans in Valle del Angeles are prized for their wood and leather work, while the Santa Bárbara area is known for producing excellent junco-palm hats, baskets, and mats.

The country has also been blessed with many gifted writers, including journalist Rafael Heliodoro Valle, poet Juan Ramón Molina, and novelist Ramón Amaya Amador. Medea Benjamin's *Don't Be Afraid, Gringo: A Honduran Woman Speaks from the Heart: The Story of Elvia Alvarado* is the story of a peasant in rural Honduras that's a favorite read of many volunteers and Peace Corps workers. *Banana Cultures: Agriculture, Consumption, and Environmental Change in Honduras and the United States,* by John Soluri, covers the history and growth of Honduras's banana industry, along with the consumer mass market in the United States, while Ramón Amaya Amador's novel *Prisión Verde* gives an unsettling account of life on a banana plantation through the eyes of a worker.

Several well-known writers from abroad have also found inspiration here. William Sydney Porter, aka O. Henry, spent a year or so in Trujillo and Roatán while escaping embezzlement charges in the U.S., after which he coined the term "Banana Republic," and wrote *Cabbages and Kings,* a collection of stories revolving around the fictitious Central American town of Coralio, Anchuria.

Garífuna music has caught on more on the international scene than any other Honduran music. Top albums include Aurelio Martinez's *Garifuna Soul* and Andy Palacios's critically acclaimed *Wátina*. While musicians in both La Ceiba and San Pedro Sula are peddlers of Latin America's ever-present pop, rock, rap, and reggae mix of reggaeton, none has particularly caught on outside of their local followings. Along the North Coast and Bay Islands, the Garífuna have won acclaim for their dance and music, particularly punta, or *bangidy,* an intense dance performed by pairs amid the beats of drums, maracas, and other instruments.

Few notable films have been produced about Honduras. Perhaps the best is *The Mosquito Coast,* the 1986 movie starring Harrison Ford, River Phoenix, and Helen Mirren that was based on the 1982 novel by Paul Theroux. The film focuses on an egotistical inventor, who moves with his wife and children from the U.S. to the north coast of Honduras. They set up their own society in the jungle while battling Christian missionaries, guerillas, and the harsh environment of La Mosquitia.

Nicaragua

Most Nicaraguans refer to themselves as *pinoleros,* in reference to the corn drink *pinol*. This reveals the country's strong rural culture, one in which even the cities' shantytown dwellers are tied to the land. The vast majority of the population of 4.5 million are *mestizo* and 45% work in agriculture, much of it subsistence related. In recent years, there has been a shift to the cities and currently 55% of the population live in an urban area, though. Nicaragua is the poorest country in Central America and the second poorest in the Western Hemisphere, after Haiti. The national poverty rate is 50%, though that rate is often higher in rural areas.

The majority of Nicaraguans are Catholic, though there is a burgeoning minority of evangelicals. Nicaragua is also one of the central places for liberation theology—a third-world take on Catholicism that portrays Jesus as a revolutionary. Traditional Indian beliefs and folklore figures are also very much alive and can be seen on parade at any of the country's famous weekend festivals.

Despite bad blood with the U.S. because of the Contra war in the 1980s, very few ordinary Nicaraguans associate American tourists with that country's foreign policy. Indeed, many have relatives in the U.S. and harbor a wish to get there someday themselves. This friendly attitude toward the U.S. is further highlighted by Nicaragua's obsession with baseball. There is a stadium in every town and the public follows the leagues avidly. Even in the smallest village, you'll find a scruffy pitch with a gang of kids in rags, using wooden planks as bats.

The written word is all-important here—Nicaraguans are famous for being a country of great poets and writers. (Despite this, many poor people have only recently achieved literacy and most Nicaraguans cannot afford a book.) It is a source of great pride that one of the finest poets in Spanish literature, Rubén Darío, hailed from León. *Songs of Life and Hope* is an excellent collection by Darío, or try the anthology *Ruben's Orphans,* translated into English by Marco Morelli.

The Country Under My Skin: A Memoir of Love and War is by one of Nicaragua's best-known writers and poets, Giaconda Belli, and covers her experience as a woman and Sandinista during the revolution. *The Jaguar Smile,* by Salman Rushdie, gives a poetic and humorous account of a trip he made to Nicaragua in 1986 to experience the revolution firsthand. *Blood of Brothers,* by *New York Times* journalist Stephen Kinser, is generally regarded as the best and most evenhanded chronicle of modern Nicaragua.

Poetic folk music is very popular in Nicaragua, and the Mejia brothers are perhaps the country's most famous troubadours. They use the guitar and accordion to sing of love and revolution. Over on the Caribbean coast (where Kenny Rogers is phenomenally popular), old-fashioned country-and-western music rules. Finally, you'll find it hard to avoid the cheerful rhythms of marimba (a wooden xylophone), which play on almost every city plaza.

Most films that are available in English about Nicaragua inevitably dwell on the recent wars. *Under Fire* stars Nick Nolte as a photojournalist covering the Sandinista revolution, uttering the immortal words, "I don't take sides, I take pictures." *Carla's Song* is a gritty and realistic movie about a Glaswegian bus driver taking a Nicaraguan refugee home to her country. *Walker—A True Story* has Ed Harris playing the American filibuster. *The World Is Watching* is an acclaimed documentary about the media coverage of the Contra war, and *The World Stopped Watching* is a just-as-fascinating sequel.

Costa Rica

Costa Rica has a population of some four million, more than half of whom live in the Central Valley and are considered urban. Nearly 96% of the Tico population (Costa Ricans are often referred to as "Ticos") is of Spanish or otherwise European descent, and it is not at all unusual to see fair-skinned and blond Costa Ricans. This is largely because the indigenous population in place when the first Spaniards arrived was small and thereafter was quickly reduced to even more of a minority by wars and disease. There are still some remnant indigenous populations, primarily on reservations around the country; the principal tribes include the Bribri, Cabécar, Boruca, and Guaymí. In addition, on the Caribbean coast and in the big cities, there is a substantial population of English-speaking black creoles who came over from the Antilles to work on the railroad and on the banana plantations. Racial tension isn't palpable, but it exists, perhaps more out of simple ignorance and fear rather than any organized or articulated prejudice.

Roman Catholicism is the official religion of Costa Rica, although freedom to practice any religion is guaranteed by the country's constitution. More than 90% of the population identifies itself as Roman Catholic, yet there are small but visible evangelical Christian, Protestant, and Jewish communities.

A small and provincial country, Costa Rica has culture and arts that are somewhat similarly limited in size and scope. Though Costa Rica's literary output is sparsely translated and little known outside of Costa Rica, there are some notable authors to look out for, especially if you can read in Spanish. **Carlos Luis Fallas's** 1941 tome, *Mamita Yunai,* is a stark look at the impact of the large banana giant United Fruit on the country. More recently, **Fernando Contreras** takes up where his predecessor left off in *Unico Mirando al Mar,* which describes the conditions of the poor, predominantly children, who scavenge Costa Rica's garbage dumps.

Several musical traditions and styles meet and mingle in Costa Rica. The northern Guanacaste region is a hotbed of folk music that is strongly influenced by the marimba (wooden xylophone) traditions of Guatemala and Nicaragua, while also featuring guitars, maracas, and the occasional harp. On the Caribbean coast you can hear traditional calypso sung by descendants of the original black workers brought over to build the railroads and tend the banana plantations. Roving bands play a mix of guitar, banjo, washtub bass, and percussion in the bars and restaurants of Cahuita and Puerto Viejo.

There's also a healthy contemporary music scene. The jazz-fusion trio *Editus* has won two Grammy awards for their work with Panamanian salsa giant (and movie star and tourism minister) **Rubén Blades.** Meanwhile, *Malpaís,* the closest thing Costa Rica has to a supergroup, is a pop-rock outfit that is tearing it up in Costa Rica and around Central America.

Costa Rica has a budding and promising young film industry. Local feature films like *Tropix, Caribe,* and *Passport* are all out on subtitled DVD. In 2008, *El Camino (The Path),* by Costa Rican filmmaker Ishtar Yasin Gutiérrez, was screened at the Berlin Film Festival. In 2009, the film *Del Amor y Otros Demonios (Of Love and Other Demons),* directed by Hilda Hidalgo, based on a novel by Gabriel García Márquez, was released as a Costa Rica/Colombian production.

Panama

There are seven indigenous groups in Panama who, despite foreign influences and modern advancements, have to differing degrees held onto their culture and languages. Ethnic tribes such as the **Kuna,** who live along the central Caribbean coast, are a semiautonomous and insular society that has hardly changed over the past century. However, the eastern Kuna community, near the Darién, has adapted to modern society, wears Western clothing, and practices few native traditions. The **Ngöbe** and **Buglé** are two tribes that are culturally similar and collectively referred to as Guaymí. Ngöbe-Buglés live in the highlands of western Panama (as well as eastern Costa Rica), and are the country's largest indigenous group; many travel nomadically and make their living in coffee production. Eastern Panama is home to two indigenous groups, the **Emberá** and the **Wounaan**—several Emberá communities are close enough to Panama City to be visited for the day. Tiny populations of **Teribe** (also called Naso) and **Bri Bri** live scattered around mainland Bocas del Toro.

People of African descent first came to Panama as slaves of the Spanish during the 16th century, and many escaped into Darién Province, where they settled and became known as *cimarrones.* In and around Portobelo and the eastern Caribbean coast, they call themselves **Congos.** During the 19th century, jobs in canal building and banana plantations lured immigrants from Jamaica, Barbados, and Colombia, who settled along the western Caribbean coast and are commonly referred to as **Afro-Caribbeans** or creoles.

ETIQUETTE tips

Always greet Central Americans with a cheerful *buenos días* in the morning and *buenos tardes* in the afternoon. Excuse yourself from company by saying "permiso." Don't get too hung up on whether you address people formally *(usted)* or informally *(tu* or *vos)*. Most locals make allowances for the fact that you are a foreigner, speaking a strange tongue, and won't get offended by such subtleties. Medical professionals like to be called "Doctora" and it is always wise to address a policeman as "Señor Policia."

Also be careful with your hand gestures. Central Americans use gestures that are often the opposite of what you may be used to. For example, a beckoning index finger is regarded as vulgar. A downward shooing gesture actually means "come here!" The universal finger wag is, however, the same everywhere and can be used in all sorts of situations from haggling to arguments. In addition, Central Americans are not as outwardly affectionate as their South American cousins. Females are sometimes kissed on the cheek, but if in doubt, a handshake will suffice.

Most Central Americans dress in a conservative manner; this is less true for the younger generation, who are more casually fashionable. The torpid weather will compel you to wear light clothes and shorts (and that's perfectly fine in most restaurants and attractions), but be aware that this mode of dress is not acceptable in churches. Also, while most Maya craftspeople are more than happy to see foreigners purchase their goods, for some indigenous people, seeing tourists walking the streets in native garb can be insulting—especially when women unknowingly wear traditional men's clothing, or vice versa. Use caution, and when in doubt, don't model your purchases in any but the most touristy towns or settings until you get home.

One notable book about Panama is *Emperors in the Jungle,* by John Lindsay-Poland, which digs deep into the history of U.S. military involvement in Panama during the past century. *Panama,* by Kevin Buckley, is a gripping read by a former *Newsweek* correspondent who vividly describes the events leading to the overthrow of Manuel Noriega. Another probing insight into the failure of U.S. policy that led to the rise of Noriega and the invasion is *The Noriega Mess: The Drugs, the Canal, and Why America Invaded,* by Luis E. Murillo. *Path Between the Seas: The Creation of the Panama Canal, 1870–1914,* by David McCullough, brings the epic history of the building of the canal to life with McCullough's meticulously researched book.

Ruben Blades may be Panama's current minister of tourism, but he is better known as Panama's best-known salsa singer. He's made dozens of CDs, but you might want to check out *Maestro de la Fania,* his latest creation, and *Lo Mejor vol. 1 and 2,* featuring his greatest hits over his decades-long career.

The Panama Deception is an interesting documentary featuring Elizabeth Montgomery and Abraham Alvarez, among others, that aims to tell the truth about the 1989 invasion of Panama by the U.S. *The Tailor of Panama* (2001) is an excellent spy-thriller staring Pierce Brosnan, Geoffrey Rush, and Jamie Lee Curtis, which centers around the transfer of power of the canal from the Americans to the Panamanian people during the post-Noriega years.

THE LAY OF THE LAND

At 518,000 sq. km (200,000 sq. miles), the seven Central American countries of Belize, Guatemala, Honduras, El Salvador, Nicaragua, Costa Rica, and Panama are squeezed into a narrow landmass (the distance from west to east is a mere 30km/19 miles at the narrowest point of Panama). That's approximately the same surface area as the states of California and New York put together. Yet with 4,500km (2,800 miles) of coastland, numerous mountain ranges, 300 volcanoes, and four tectonic plates crunching into each other, the area is much more of a geological hot spot, with some of the most varied natural diversity in the world.

On one side of the isthmus that is Central America, the muddy swamps and deltas of the Caribbean coast descend onto a narrow shelf of limestone rock that extends several miles out to sea. Here you'll find numerous islands and the second-longest barrier reef in the world, whose rich coral grounds stretch along the coasts of Belize and Honduras. On the other side of the isthmus, the dark Pacific pounds black volcanic beaches up and down the coast, which lead to narrow plains of agricultural land, tropical dry forest, and large freshwater lakes such as Lago de Nicaragua. The Pacific coast is generally less humid, and it's sheltered from the easterly trade winds by a rugged spine of mountains that hold cloud forests and pine valleys.

Earthquakes are common throughout Central America, as are belching, lava-dribbling volcanoes such as **Arenal** in Costa Rica and **Masaya** in Nicaragua. Such a volatile, churning landscape also means the land is dotted with plenty of hot thermal springs and underground cave systems.

Central America's Ecosystems

Central America's **lowland rainforests** are true tropical jungles. Some are deluged with more than 508 centimeters (200 in.) of rainfall per year, and their climate is hot and humid. Trees grow tall and fast, fighting for sunlight in the upper reaches. In fact, life and foliage on the forest floor are surprisingly sparse. The action is typically 30m (98 ft.) up, in the canopy, where long vines stream down, lianas climb up, and bromeliads grow on the branches and trunks of towering hardwood trees. Classic examples of lowland rainforests are found along the **southern Pacific coast** of Costa Rica, the **La Mosquita** region of Honduras, along the **Río Dulce** in Guatemala, and the **Laguna de Perlas** in Nicaragua.

At higher altitudes, you'll find Central America's famed **cloud forests.** Here the steady flow of moist air meets the mountains and creates a nearly constant mist. Epiphytes—plants that live cooperatively on the branches and trunks of other trees—grow abundantly in the cloud forests, where they must extract moisture and nutrients from the air. Because cloud forests are in generally steep, mountainous terrain, the canopy here is lower and less uniform than in lowland rainforests, providing better chances for viewing elusive fauna. The region's most spectacular cloud forests can be experienced at **Monteverde Biological Cloud Forest Reserve** in Costa Rica, **Parque Nacional Celaque** in Honduras, **Reserva Natural Miraflor** in Nicaragua, and the **Chiriqui highlands** of Panama.

At the highest reaches, the cloud forests of this region give way to **elfin forests** and *páramos.* More commonly associated with the South American Andes, a *páramo* is characterized by a variety of tundra-like shrubs and grasses, with a scattering of twisted, windblown trees. Reptiles, rodents, and raptors are the most common residents here. Typical examples of *páramo* can be found at **Chirripó National Park** in **Costa Rica** and parts of the **Guatemalan highlands.**

On the Pacific side of the highlands, you'll still find examples of the otherwise-vanishing **tropical dry forest.** During the long and pronounced dry season (late Nov to late Apr), no rain relieves the unabated heat. To conserve much-needed water, the trees drop their leaves but bloom in a riot of color: purple jacaranda, scarlet *poró,* and brilliant orange flame-of-the-forest are just a few examples. Then, during the rainy season, this deciduous forest is transformed into a lush and verdant landscape. Because the foliage is not that dense, the dry forests are excellent places to view a variety of wildlife, especially howler monkeys and *pizotes* (coati). The best examples of dry forests are found in **Santa Rosa** and **Guanacaste** national parks in Costa Rica and parts of northern Belize.

Along the coasts, primarily where river mouths meet the ocean, you will find extensive **mangrove forests** and **swamps.** Around these seemingly monotonous tangles of roots exists one of the most diverse and rich ecosystems in the region. Bird life includes pelicans, storks, and pink flamingos, and reptiles such as crocodiles and caimans also thrive in this environment.

In any one spot in Central America, temperatures remain relatively constant year-round. However, they vary dramatically according to altitude, from tropically hot and steamy along the coasts to below freezing at the highest elevations.

Flora & Fauna

For millenniums, this land bridge between North and South America served as a migratory thoroughfare and mating ground for species native to the once-separate continents. Perhaps its unique location between both continents explains why the region comprises only .05% of the earth's landmass, yet it is home to 7% of the planet's biodiversity. More than 15,000 identified species of plants, 900 species of birds, 9,000 species of butterflies and moths, and 500 species of mammals, reptiles, and amphibians are found here. And that is just what has been cataloged. The key to this biological richness lies in the many distinct life zones and ecosystems found in Central America. It might all seem like one big mass of green to the untrained eye, but the differences are profound.

All sorts of fish and crustaceans live in the brackish tidal waters off the coast, primarily in the Caribbean but also parts of the Pacific. Caimans and crocodiles cruise the maze of rivers and unmarked canals. There are many snakes, but few are poisonous. Watch out for the tiny coral snake and the bigger barba amarilla. Another creature worth avoiding is the poisonous arrow frog.

Herons, ibises, egrets, and other marsh birds nest and feed along the region's silted banks, as well. Mangrove swamps are often havens for water birds like cormorants, frigate birds, pelicans, and herons. Farther out, both coastal waters are alive with marine life that includes turtles, barracudas, stingrays, marlins, dolphins, and red snappers. Nicaragua boasts the only freshwater shark in the world on Lago de Nicaragua, while the Río San Juan that joins it to the Caribbean is famous for a giant silver fish called a tarpon. Keep an eye out for whales along the Costa Rican coast.

The jungle teems with wildlife, particularly birds. Macaws, parrots, hummingbirds, and toucans are just some of the many reasons Central America is a birder's paradise. The larger birds tend to nest up high in the canopy, while the smaller ones nestle in the underbrush. Count yourself lucky if you catch sight of the beautiful quetzal, Guatemala's national bird, or one of the region's elusive big cats, including jaguars, puma, and ocelots. A little easier to spot are howler monkeys and their simian brethren the spider and squirrel monkeys. Other mammals to look out for on the jungle floor include anteaters, deer, and sloths.

Plant life is very much determined by altitude and climate. The Pacific dry forest is home to hardy species of thorny shrubs that lose their leaves in the high season and burst into flower in April and May. Higher up, the landscape is dominated by pines, oaks, and evergreens. Above 1,600m (5,250 ft.), the flora becomes lusher with orchids, mosses, and ferns all growing abundantly on giant trees.

Searching for Wildlife

Forest animals throughout Central America are predominantly nocturnal. When they are active in the daytime, they are usually elusive. Birds are easier to spot in clearings or secondary forests than they are in primary forests. Unless you have lots of experience in the Tropics, your best hope for enjoying a walk through the jungle lies in employing a trained and knowledgeable guide.

Tips to keep in mind include **listening carefully and keeping quiet**—you're most likely to hear an animal before seeing one. Also, it helps to **bring binoculars and dress appropriately.** You'll have a hard time focusing your binoculars if you're busy swatting mosquitoes. Light, long pants and long-sleeved shirts are your best bet. Comfortable hiking boots are a real boon, except where heavy rubber boots are necessary (a real possibility, if it's been raining). Avoid loud colors; the better you blend in, the better your chances are of spotting wildlife. Finally, **be patient.** The jungle isn't on a schedule. However, your best shots at seeing forest fauna are in the very early-morning and late-afternoon hours.

EATING & DRINKING IN CENTRAL AMERICA

Typical Meals

Rice and beans are the basis of most Central American meals—all. At breakfast, they're called *gallo pinto* and come with everything from eggs to steak to seafood. At lunch or dinner, rice and beans are an integral part of a *casado* (which translates as "married" and is the name for the local version of a blue-plate special). A *casado* usually consists of cabbage-and-tomato salad, fried plantains, and a chicken, fish, or meat dish of some sort. On the Caribbean coast, rice and beans are called *rice 'n' beans,* and are cooked in coconut milk.

However, you don't have to look too far to see that the region boasts an abundant variety of other local dishes, which incorporate unique vegetables, fruit, and grains. Though rice and beans will be on almost all menus, in coastal areas you'll come across an incredible amount of seafood, especially lobster and shrimp. There is a growing controversy around eating lobster, due to overfishing and the danger lobster pickers are put through for very little money. Avoid eating *huevos de paslama* (turtle eggs), since turtles are an endangered species.

In the highlands, you'll find more beef on the menu in the form of *caldos* (stews) served with yucca (manioc root or cassava in English), along with chicken dishes—just don't be too surprised if your chicken comes with the feet still attached. Everywhere you will find corn-based treats like *tamales* (stuffed cornmeal patties wrapped and steamed inside banana leaves), along with *patacones* (fried green plantain chips), often served street-side.

On the whole, you'll find vegetables lacking in the meals you're served throughout Central America—usually nothing more than a little pile of shredded cabbage topped with a slice or two of tomato. For a more satisfying and filling salad, order a *palmito* (hearts of palm salad). The heart (actually the stalk or trunk of these small palms) is first boiled and then chopped into circular pieces and served with other fresh vegetables, with a salad dressing on top. If you want something more than this, you'll have to order a side dish such as *picadillo*, a stew or purée of vegetables with a bit of meat in it.

Central America has a wealth of delicious tropical fruit. The most common are mangoes, papayas, pineapples, melons, and bananas. Other fruit includes *marañón*, which is the fruit of the cashew tree and has orange or yellow glossy skin; *granadilla* or *maracuyá* (passion fruit); *mamón chino*, which Asian travelers will recognize as rambutan; and *carambola* (star fruit).

Fruit is often served as dessert, but there are some other options for sweets. *Queque seco*, literally "dry cake," is the same as pound cake. *Tres leches* cake, on the other hand, is so moist that you almost need to eat it with a spoon. Flan is a custard dessert. It often comes as either *flan de caramelo* (caramel) or *flan de coco* (coconut). Numerous other sweets are available, many of which are made with condensed milk and raw sugar. *Cajetas* are handmade candies, made from sugar and mixes of evaporated, condensed, and powdered milk. They are sold in differing-size bits and chunks at most *pulperías* (general stores) and food stands.

See "Tips on Dining" in the individual country chapters throughout this book for more info.

Beverages

Central America produces some of the best rum in the world, especially Nicaragua and Belize. The best Nicaraguan rum is called **Flor de Caña,** and the best Belize version is **One Barrel. Zacapa Centenario** is generally regarded as the best rum from Guatemala, with **Ron Botrán Añejo** coming a close second. The national alcoholic drink in Panama is called *seco.* Like rum, it is made from sugar cane but has milk and ice added to the mix. The whole region is known for *chicha*, a sweet, fermented corn beverage, and an even stronger variation known as *chicha brava*. *La cususa,* a crude cane liquor that's often combined with a soft drink or tonic, is popular in Nicaragua; a *guaro* is the Costa Rican version of this same drink.

You can find imported wines at reasonable prices in the better restaurants throughout the region. You can usually save money by ordering a Chilean wine over a Californian or European one. Cashew wine is popular in Belize, though you may find it to be too strong and vinegary. *Cerveza* (beer) can be found everywhere, and every country has its most popular native brands.

Popular nonalcoholic drinks include *pinol*, which is toasted, ground corn with water, and *tiste,* a variation made with cocoa beans and corn. Soda in the form of *gaseosa* is everywhere, as are vendors selling small bags of ice-cold mineral water—much more environmentally friendly than bottles. Look out for excellent fruit juices called *liquadas* that can be served with milk or water. Among the more common fruit used in these shakes are mangoes, papayas, blackberries, and pineapples. Order *un fresco con leche sin hielo* (a *fresco* with milk but without ice) if you're avoiding untreated water.

If you're a coffee drinker, you might be disappointed. Most of the best coffee has traditionally been targeted for export, and Central Americans tend to prefer theirs weak and sugary. Better hotels and restaurants are starting to cater to American and European tastes and are serving superior blends. If you want black coffee, ask for *café negro;* if you want it with milk, order *café con leche.* For something different, ask for *agua dulce,* a warm drink made from melted sugar cane and served with either milk or lemon, or straight.

Although water in parts of the region is safe to drink, bottled water is readily available and is a good option if you're worried about an upset stomach. If you like your water without bubbles, request *aqua mineral sin gas,* or *agua en botella.*

Dining Customs

The region's capital cities have the best choices regarding restaurants, with everything from Italian, Brazilian, and Chinese eateries to chains like T.G.I. Friday's. For cheap meals, buffet-style restaurants are very popular, as are street grills on the side of the road. Every country has a different term for these informal types of restaurants, so consult the individual chapters for info.

Outside the region's major tourist destinations, your options get very limited very fast. In fact, many beach destinations are so remote that you have no choice but to eat in the hotel's dining room. Even on the more accessible beaches, the only choices aside from the hotel dining rooms are often cheap local places or overpriced tourist traps serving indifferent meals. At remote jungle lodges, the food is usually served buffet- or family-style and can range from bland to inspired, depending on who's doing the cooking, and turnover is high.

Throughout Central America, people sit down to eat lunch at midday and dinner at 7pm. Some downtown restaurants in big cities are open 24 hours; however, expensive restaurants tend to be open for lunch between 11am and 3pm and for dinner between 6 and 11pm. At even the more expensive restaurants in the region, it's hard to spend more than $50 per person unless you really splurge on drinks.

PLANNING YOUR TRIP TO CENTRAL AMERICA

The country chapters in this guide provide specific information on traveling to and getting around individual Central American countries. In this chapter, we provide you with regionwide tips and general information that will help you plan your trip. For additional help in planning your trip and for more on-the-ground resources in Central America, please see chapter 11, "Fast Facts: Central America," on p. 725.

WHEN TO GO

Central America remains hot throughout the year, unless you spend a night in the chilly highlands. The **rainy season** runs from April to early December, but the region still experiences plenty of sunshine during this period. The **hurricane season** rains down in September to October and can cause flooding everywhere, though it can be particularly bad on the Caribbean coast. The **dry season** runs from Christmas to Easter and this is the tourist peak season. Easter is a particularly good time to go to Central America as the whole region goes crazy for *Semana Santa*. Make sure you book ahead, and expect higher hotel prices during this time of year. The low season means fewer people, lower prices, and you can still have glorious weather. *A drawback:* Some of the region's rugged roads become downright impassable without four-wheel-drive during the rainy season.

Holidays

Latin Americans love a good street party—even ones devoted to celebrating chaste Catholic saints exude a wild exuberance. Christmas is colorful but Easter is the wildest celebration; during Easter week, some countries virtually shut down as the locals head for the beach for a week (be careful of canceled buses during this period). The best place to celebrate Carnaval is in Panama.

Whatever time of year you go, there's bound to be a small town celebrating its patron saint with parades, bullfights, and firecrackers. Many of the region's celebrations have a strong indigenous flavor, and employ folklore and traditional dances to honor things like famous battles or thwarted volcanic eruptions. Below are just some highlights. Consult each individual country chapter for more details on all the revelry.

Calendar of Events

JANUARY

Festival of San Sebastián, Masaya, Nicaragua. Drums, whistles, and chanting reverberate around the streets of Masaya during this festival celebrating Saint Sebastian. The town of Diriamba (30km/19 miles southwest of Masaya) is generally recognized as throwing an even more colorful and authentic parade, too, with a lively mix of pagan satire and colonial pomp. Last 2 weeks in January.

Fiesta de Palmares, Costa Rica. One of the best organized of the country's traditional *fiestas,* the Fiesta de Palmares includes bullfights, a horseback parade *(tope),* and many concerts, carnival rides, and food booths. First 2 weeks in January.

Feria de las Flores y del Café (Flower and Coffee Festival), Boquete, Panama. This festival is one of the grandest celebrations of flowers in the world, drawing thousands of people to Boquete for 10 days. Expect lush flower displays, food stands, live music, amusement rides, handicrafts booths, and hotel rooms booked far in advance. Mid-January.

FEBRUARY

Valentine's Day Cycle Race, Belize. This is Belize's premier road race. Starting in San Ignacio, cyclists pedal to Benque Viejo, turn around, and race all the way back to Belize City. For more information, check out **www.belizecycling.com**. February 14.

Carnaval, Panama. This is Panama's most revered holiday. The largest celebrations take place in Panama City and the Azuero Peninsula, with parades, floats, drinking, costumes, and music. The 4 days preceding Ash Wednesday.

International Permanent Festival of Art and Culture, Suchitoto, El Salvador. This 15-year-old international arts festival was founded by retired but once-world-renowned cinematographer Alejandro Cotto and is one of the country's premier arts events, attracting visual and performing artists from around Latin America and the world. Dates vary in February.

MARCH

Baron Bliss Day, celebrated throughout Belize. While not officially the nation's patron saint, Baron Henry Edward Ernest Victor Bliss is certainly Belize's foremost patron and benefactor. The day is marked with nationwide celebrations. The greatest festivities are held in Belize City, which hosts a regatta, as well as horse and footraces. March 9.

National Orchid Show, San José, Costa Rica. Orchid growers throughout the world gather to show their wares, trade tales and secrets, and admire the hundreds of species on display. Contact the Costa Rican Tourist Board (**www.visitcostarica.com**) for location and dates in 2011 and 2012. Mid-March.

APRIL

Holy Week, celebrated throughout Central America. Religious processions are held in cities and towns throughout Central America during *Semana Santa,* and it is a fantastic time to visit the region. León in Nicaragua throws a particularly colorful event with elaborate sawdust pavement paintings. Antigua in Guatemala is also famous for its celebrations and carpet-lined streets. Holy Week celebrations in Comayagua are one of the biggest festivals in Honduras and feature a week of elaborate processions. Celebrations take place the week before Easter, which sometimes falls in late March rather than April.

Garífuna Day, the Bay Islands and North Coast, Honduras. Dancing, drinking, music, and other cultural activities take place to celebrate the arrival of the Garífuna on Roatán in 1797. April 12.

MAY

Cashew Festival, Crooked Tree Village, Belize. Celebrating the cashew harvest, this weekend festivity features booths selling everything possible under the sun made with this coveted nut, including cashew wine and cashew jelly. Live music and general revelry accompany the celebrations. First weekend in May.

Feria de San Isidro, La Ceiba, Honduras. Hundreds of thousands of revelers flock to this north coast town for the Honduran version of Carnaval. Parades march through the downtown streets, the constant beating of drums is everywhere, and all-night partying occurs on the beaches. The week preceding the third Saturday of May.

JUNE

Festival Corpus Christi, La Villa de Los Santos, Panama. This Panamanian town explodes with activity for a 2-week religious festival known for its elaborate dances led by men in devil masks. Forty days after Easter.

Lobster Festival, Placencia, Belize. You'll get your fill of this crustacean during this extended weekend celebration of the opening of lobster season. In addition to gorging on lobster, you can take in concerts and parties and an arts fair. Check **www. placencia.com** for the latest details. Late June.

Feria Juniana, San Pedro Sula, Honduras. This weeklong festival sees a series of parades and live events celebrating the city's founding. There is a large agricultural fair that attracts thousands, and the week culminates with a huge, colorful parade down the main thoroughfare on June 29. Last week of June.

JULY

Fiestas Julias, Santa Ana, El Salvador. Fiestas Julias, also known as Fiestas Patronal, is a month-long celebration featuring parades, music, and carnival rides honoring Santa Ana's patron saint. Throughout July.

Fiesta of the Virgin of the Sea, Puntarenas, Costa Rica. A regatta of colorfully decorated boats carrying a statue of Puntarenas's patron saint marks this festival. A similar event is held at Playa de Coco. Saturday closest to July 16.

La Fiesta Nacional Indígena de Guatemala, Cobán, Guatemala. This is one of Mesoamerica's greatest celebrations of Maya culture. The city of Cobán features a steady stream of street fairs, concerts, parades, and parties. This is celebrated for 2 solid weeks in late July, sometimes extending into early August.

Festival Patronales de La Virgen de Santa Librada, Las Tablas, Panama. This is famous for its **Festival de la Pollera** on July 22, which showcases the region's most beautiful pollera dresses and elects the "Queen of the Pollera" for that year. July 20 to July 22.

AUGUST

Fiesta de la Virgen de la Asunción, Guatemala. The Virgin of the Assumption is the patron saint of Guatemala City and, by extension, the entire nation. There are celebrations, parades, and small fairs across the country, but the largest celebrations are held in Guatemala City. August 15.

Fiesta of the Virgin of Los Angeles, Cartago, Costa Rica. Each year, Costa Rica's patron saint is celebrated with a massive pilgrimage to the country's only basilica in the former capital city of Cartago, 24km (15 miles) outside of San José. August 2.

Costa Maya Festival, San Pedro, Ambergris Caye, Belize. This is perhaps the largest festival in the country. Drawing participants from the neighboring countries of El Salvador, Mexico, Guatemala, and Honduras, this celebration features a steady stream of live concert performances, street parades, beauty pageants, and water shows and activities. Early August.

SEPTEMBER

Costa Rica's Independence Day, celebrated all over Costa Rica. One of the most distinctive aspects of this festival is the nighttime marching-band parades of children in their school uniforms who play the national anthem on steel xylophones. September 15.

Festival de la Mejorana, Guararé, Panama. This nationally famous folkloric festival features hundreds of dancers, musicians, and singers coming together for a week of events and serious partying. Last week of September.

Belize Independence Day, celebrated throughout Belize. Patriotic parades and official celebrations are mixed with street parties, beauty pageants, and open-air concerts. September 21.

Fiestas Patronales, Masaya, Nicaragua. The handicrafts capital of Nicaragua finds reason to celebrate year-round. The biggest festival date is September 20, though, with the opening of the Fiestas Patronales, weekend parties in different neighborhoods that carry on until December.

OCTOBER

Festival del Cristo Negro (Black Christ Festival), Portobelo, Panama. Thousands of pilgrims come to pay penance and perform other acts of devotion at the Iglesia de San Felipe, home to a wooden black Christ effigy that is paraded around town on this day. October 21.

NOVEMBER

Día de los Muertos (All Saints' Day), Guatemala. The most famous celebration in Guatemala is the "drunken horse race" in the mountain town of Todos Santos. Guatemalans also fly giant, colorful kites to communicate with the dead in the village of Santiago Sacatepéquez. November 1.

Garífuna Settlement Day, Belize, Honduras, Guatemala, Nicaragua. Garífunas from across the Caribbean coast of Central America gather to commemorate their arrival from St. Vincent in 1832. Street parades, religious ceremonies, and dance and drumming performances are all part of the celebrations throughout this zone. November 19.

DECEMBER

Día de la Purísima Concepción, León, Nicaragua. This celebration is known as the *Gritería* (shouting), a type of religious trick or treat. Groups of people walk around, shouting up to households, in order to obtain sweets. The following day is the Día de la Concepción de María, when the whole country goes parade-crazy. December 7.

Quema del Diablo (Burning the Devil), Guatemala. Bonfires fill the streets throughout the country as trash, old furniture, and effigies of Satan are burned in a symbolic ritual cleansing. December 7.

El Tope and Carnaval, San José, Costa Rica. The streets of downtown belong to horses and their riders in a proud recognition of the country's important agricultural heritage. The next day, those same streets are taken over by carnival floats, marching bands, and street dancers. December 26 and 27.

Boxing Day, Belize. While Christmas Day is predominantly for the family in Belize, Boxing Day is a chance to continue the celebration with friends, neighbors, and strangers. Dances, concerts, horse races, and general festivities are put on around the country. December 26.

ENTRY REQUIREMENTS

The passport and visa information in this section is for quick reference; see individual country chapters for complete details for your destination.

Due to concerns about parental abductions, there are special requirements for children visiting many foreign countries, including those in Central America. If you are a lone or single parent or a guardian, you must bring a copy of the child's birth certificate and a notarized consent document from the parent(s). For single parents, a decree of sole custody or a parental death certificate will also do. Ask your airline what's required when you book the ticket; also check the State Department's "Foreign Entry Requirements" page at **http://travel.state.gov**.

BELIZE   No visas are required for citizens of the United States, the European community—including Great Britain and Ireland—South Africa, Australia, or New Zealand. Visitors from these countries do require a current and valid passport.

In 2006, Guatemala entered into an immigration and border-control treaty with El Salvador, Honduras, and Nicaragua. This agreement, which allows free travel between the countries to all nationals of these signatory nations, creates a single 90-day entry visa for foreign visitors. What this means is that if you travel between these four countries, your total stay cannot exceed 90 days without an extension from the immigration authorities in the country you are visiting. If you want to "renew" your Guatemalan visa by exiting the country for 72 hours and then returning on a new tourist visa, it must be to a country not covered in this agreement.

Nationals of certain other countries need a visa or consular permission to enter Belize. For a current list, see the Belize Tourism Board website (**www.travelbelize. org**) or call the nearest Belize consulate or embassy.

GUATEMALA   Citizens of the United States, Canada, Great Britain, all European Union nations, Ireland, Australia, and New Zealand may visit for a maximum of 90 days. No visa is necessary, but you must have a valid passport.

HONDURAS   Citizens of the United States, Canada, Australia, New Zealand, and the European Union require just a passport to enter Honduras and may stay for up to 90 days. The passport must be valid for at least 6 months after the date of entry. Tourist cards, distributed on arriving international flights or at border crossings, are good for stays of up to 90 days. Keep a copy of your tourist card for presentation upon departure from Honduras.

EL SALVADOR   Residents of the United States, Canada, and the United Kingdom do not need visas and can enter the country at the border with a valid passport and the purchase of a $10 30-day tourist card. (Visitors can also ask for a 90-day card when entering the country.) Australia and New Zealand residents require tourist visas, which must be arranged in advance and cost $30.

NICARAGUA   Citizens of the United States, Canada, Australia, New Zealand, and the European Union require just a passport to enter Nicaragua and may stay for up to 90 days. The passport must be valid for at least 6 months after the date of entry.

COSTA RICA   Citizens of the United States, Canada, Great Britain, and most European nations may visit Costa Rica for a maximum of 90 days. No visa is necessary, but you must have a valid passport, which you should carry with you at all times while you're in Costa Rica. Citizens of Australia, Ireland, and New Zealand can enter the country without a visa and stay for 30 days, although once in the country, visitors can apply for an extension.

PANAMA   Panamanian law requires that travelers present a passport valid for at least 3 months, and must either purchase a tourist card at the airport in Panama before clearing customs, or obtain a multiple-entry visa from a Panamanian embassy or consulate before traveling to Panama.

Passport Information

To apply for a passport, residents of the United States can download passport applications from the U.S. State Department website at http://travel.state.gov, or call the **National Passport Agency** at © 202/647-0518.

3

PLANNING YOUR TRIP TO CENTRAL AMERICA

Entry Requirements

Canadian residents should visit www.ppt.gc.ca or call 📞 **800/567-6868.**

British citizens should contact the **United Kingdom Passport Service** at 📞 **0870/521-0410** or on the Web at www.ukpa.gov.uk. Residents of Ireland can call 📞 **01/671-1633** or visit www.irlgov.ie/iveagh.

Australian citizens should contact the **Australian Passport Information Service** at 📞 **131-232,** or visit www.passports.gov.au. Residents of New Zealand should call the **Passports Office** at 📞 **0800/225-050** or 04/474-8100, or log on to www.passports.govt.nz.

For more information on how to obtain a passport, see **"Passports"** in "Fast Facts: Central America," p. 727.

3 Customs

For information about what you can bring with you upon entry, see the "Customs" section in individual country chapters.

WHAT YOU CAN BRING HOME

Every visitor 21 years of age or older may bring in, free of duty, the following: (1) 1 U.S. quart of alcohol; (2) 200 cigarettes, 50 cigars (but not from Cuba), or 3 pounds of smoking tobacco; and (3) $100 worth of gifts. These exemptions are offered to travelers who spend at least 72 hours in the United States and who have not claimed them within the preceding 6 months. It is forbidden to bring into the country almost any meat products (including canned, fresh, and dried meat products such as bouillon or soup mixes). Generally, condiments including vinegars, oils, pickled goods, spices, coffee, tea, and some cheeses and baked goods are permitted. Avoid rice products, as rice can often harbor insects. Bringing fruit and vegetables is prohibited since they may harbor pests or disease. International visitors may carry in or out up to $10,000 in U.S. or foreign currency with no formalities; larger sums must be declared to U.S. Customs on entering or leaving, which includes filing form CM 4790. For details regarding U.S. Customs and Border Protection, consult your nearest U.S. embassy or consulate, or **U.S. Customs** (www.customs.gov).

For specifics on what you can bring back, download the invaluable free pamphlet *Know Before You Go* online at **www.cbp.gov.** (Click on "Travel," and then click on "Know Before You Go! Online Brochure.") Or contact the **U.S. Customs & Border Protection (CBP),** 1300 Pennsylvania Ave. NW, Washington, DC 20229 (📞 **877/287-8667**), and request the pamphlet.

For a clear summary of **Canadian** rules, write for the booklet *I Declare,* issued by the **Canada Border Services Agency** (📞 **800/461-9999** in Canada, or 204/983-3500; www.cbsa-asfc.gc.ca). Canada allows its citizens a C$750 exemption, and you're allowed to bring back duty-free one carton of cigarettes, one can of tobacco, 40 imperial ounces of liquor, and 50 cigars. In addition, you're allowed to mail gifts to Canada valued at less than C$60 a day, provided they're unsolicited and don't contain alcohol or tobacco (write on the package "Unsolicited gift, under $60 value"). All valuables should be declared on the Y-38 form before departure from Canada, including serial numbers of valuables you already own, such as expensive foreign cameras. *Note:* The $750 exemption can be used only once a year and only after an absence of 7 days.

U.K. citizens returning from **a non-E.U. country** have a Customs allowance of 200 cigarettes; 50 cigars; 250 grams of smoking tobacco; 2 liters of still table wine; 1 liter of spirits or strong liqueurs (over 22% volume); 2 liters of fortified wine, sparkling wine, or other liqueurs; 60cc (ml) perfume; 250cc (ml) of toilet water; and £145 worth of all other goods, including gifts and souvenirs. People 16 and under cannot have the tobacco or alcohol allowance. For more information, contact **HM Customs & Excise** at ✆ **0845/010-9000** (from outside the U.K., 020/8929-0152), or consult their website at www.hmce.gov.uk.

The duty-free allowance in **Australia** is A$400 or, for those 17 and under, A$200. Citizens can bring in 250 cigarettes or 250 grams of loose tobacco, and 1.125 milliliters of alcohol. If you're returning with valuables you already own, such as foreign-made cameras, you should file form B263. A helpful brochure available from Australian consulates or Customs offices is *Know Before You Go*. For more information, call the **Australian Customs Service** at ✆ **1300/363-263,** or log on to www.customs.gov.au.

The duty-free allowance for **New Zealand** is NZ$700. Citizens over 17 can bring in 200 cigarettes, 50 cigars, or 250 grams of tobacco (or a mixture of all three if their combined weight doesn't exceed 250g); plus 4.5 liters of wine and beer, or 1.125 liters of liquor. New Zealand currency does not carry import or export restrictions. Fill out a certificate of export, listing the valuables you are taking out of the country; that way, you can bring them back without paying duty. Most questions are answered in a free pamphlet available at New Zealand consulates and Customs offices: *New Zealand Customs Guide for Travellers, Notice no. 4.* For more information, contact **New Zealand Customs,** The Customhouse, 17–21 Whitmore St., Box 2218, Wellington (✆ **04/ 473-6099** or 0800/428-786; www.customs.govt.nz).

GETTING THERE & GETTING AROUND

Getting There

BY PLANE

Every country in Central America now receives international flights, mostly from the U.S. and Mexico. Below is a quick country-by-country glance. See the individual country chapters for more detailed information. For additional help in booking your air travel, please see chapter 11 for "Toll-Free Numbers & Websites," on p. 728.

To Belize

The following carriers offer service to Belize City's **Philip S. W. Goldson International Airport (BZE):**

FROM THE U.S.   American Airlines, Continental, Grupo Taca (via San Salvador), and US Airways.

The only direct flights from Canada are seasonal winter charters. There are no direct flights to Belize from Europe, Australia, or New Zealand

To Guatemala

Most international flights land at **La Aurora International Airport (GUA)** in Guatemala City. A few international and regional airlines fly directly into **Flores Airport (FRS)** near Tikal.

FROM THE U.S. & MEXICO   American Airlines, Continental, Delta, Mexicana, United Airlines, US Airways, and Grupo Taca.

There are no direct flights from Europe, Australia, or New Zealand, but it is easy to get a connection from New York or Miami.

To Honduras

The following carriers fly to San Pedro Sula's **Ramón Villeda Morales International Airport (SAP),** Tegucigalpa's **Toncontín International Airport (TGU),** or **Roatán International Airport (RTB):**

FROM NORTH AMERICA   Air Canada, American, Continental, Delta, United, Taca, and Spirit.

FROM THE U.K. & EUROPE   There are no direct flights, but Delta, Continental, and American Airlines connect through the U.S.

FROM AUSTRALIA & NEW ZEALAND   There are no direct flights, but connections can be made in North American gateway cities.

To El Salvador

The following carriers fly into San Salvador's **Comalapa International Airport (SAL):**

FROM NORTH AMERICA   American, Continental, Delta, and Taca.

FROM THE U.K., EUROPE, AUSTRALIA & NEW ZEALAND   There are no direct overseas flights from the U.K., Australia, or New Zealand. You'll need to fly first into the U.S., with many European flights routing out of Miami and Houston to San Salvador.

To Nicaragua

The following carriers offer service to Managua's **Augusto C Sandino International Airport (MGA):**

FROM THE U.S.   American Airlines, Continental, Delta, United Airlines, Spirit, and Taca.

FROM MEXICO   Aeroméxico.

FROM EUROPE   Iberia (via Miami).

To Costa Rica

International flights land in San José's **Juan Santamaría International Airport (SJO)** and to a lesser extent Liberia's **Daniel Oduber International Airport (LIR);** there are no direct flights from Australia or New Zealand.

FROM THE U.S.   Air Canada, American Airlines, Continental, Delta, Frontier, Grupo Taca, Mexicana, Spirit Air, and US Airways.

FROM EUROPE   Iberia and Martin Air.

To Panama

The following airlines fly into **Tocumen International Airport (PTY)** in Panama City:

FROM THE U.S. & MEXICO   American Airlines, Copa, Delta, Mexicana, and Taca.

FROM THE U.K. & EUROPE   Iberia (via Costa Rica), American Airlines (via Miami), British Airways (via Miami), Continental (via Orlando or Houston), and Delta (via Atlanta).

FROM AUSTRALIA & NEW ZEALAND   Qantas and Air New Zealand (both via Los Angeles).

BY CRUISE SHIP OR FERRY

Luxury cruise liners now sail frequently along the Caribbean and Pacific coast via the Panama Canal, and more and more offer Central American destinations and ports of call. See individual chapters for cruise-ship destinations in each country. Two reputable companies are Miami-based **Seabourn Cruise Line (𝄢 800/929-9391;**

PLANNING YOUR TRIP TO CENTRAL AMERICA

www.seabourn.com) and Californian-based **Princess Cruises** (© 845/075-0031; www.princess.com).

Some key international ferry crossings are between Punta Gorda, Belize, and Puerto Barrios, Guatemala. You can cross into Flores, Guatemala, from Palenque in Mexico. There is a river crossing between San Carlos, Nicaragua, and Los Chiles, Costa Rica.

By Car

It's possible to travel to Central America by car, but it can be difficult. After leaving Mexico, the **Pan-American Highway** (Carretera Panamericana), which is also referred to as the Interamerican Highway, passes through Guatemala, El Salvador, Honduras, Nicaragua, and Costa Rica before reaching Panama. All of these countries can be problematic for travelers for a variety of reasons, including internal violence, crime, corrupt border crossings, and visa formalities. If you decide to undertake this adventure from the U.S., take the **Gulf Coast route** from the border crossing at Brownsville, Texas, because it involves traveling the fewest miles through Mexico.

Anyone driving into Central American countries needs to show a passport; country or international driver's license; proof of vehicle ownership, such as registration card; and proof of insurance. Cars are normally granted 30-day visitation. Many consulates also offer prevalidation of driver's documents, which can quicken the process at the border.

Getting Around

Sometimes, the most frustrating and stressful part of traveling in Central America is getting from point A to point B. The roads are often awful and, though there are plenty of local buses, a lot of them are older and take forever. It is often wise to spring for a private shuttle, especially if you are traveling with other people. (The international bus companies that travel between Central America countries have much better standards.) Because car-rental agencies don't allow cars to be taken across international borders, it's very difficult to drive from country to country. And there is zero train service.

This isn't a blanket statement for all of Central America: In some cases, the buses are modern and well-equipped, and the roads (particularly in El Salvador, parts of Honduras, and Panama), are in pretty decent shape. For our recommendations on the best means of transportation in each country, and details on how to travel by car, bus, and plane, see the individual country chapters.

By Plane

Copa (© 800/359-2672; www.copaair.com) offers the most comprehensive plane service in Central America. The Panama-based airline travels between all the capital cities and is a strategic partner with Continental Airlines. **Grupo Taca** (© 800/400-8222; www.taca.com) also has several routes between Central American countries.

Many countries have commuter airlines offering "puddle jumper" or propeller-airline flights. These flights are not for the fainthearted, as you literally sit right behind the pilots and it can get a little claustrophobic. As you are checking in, the plane's crew will weigh your bags and then weigh you so as not to overload the aircraft—you'll want to pack light.

No matter what flight you book, always reconfirm your flight upon arrival.

By Bus

Though they're a hassle, a bus journey in Central America will likely be one of the lasting memories of your trip. (They're also by far the cheapest way to get around.) Chaotic bus stations, pushy touts, hordes of vendors, and buses packed with people and with livestock will, at the very least, truly allow you to feel that you have left home.

There are different types of buses throughout Central America, and each country may use different terms, but the buses generally fall into the following categories: **Local buses,** otherwise known as "chicken buses," are the cheapest and slowest; they stop frequently and are generally an old, dilapidated American school bus with colorful clientele that may include small farm animals. Many of these buses are intercity or urban buses that service the satellite towns of a particular city. **Expreso buses** are more expensive and faster, but they do not stop (in theory) between cities. They also run much less frequently than the local buses.

Probably the most inconvenient aspect of local bus travel in Central America is that many towns or cities have no central bus stations. In lieu of that, the "stations" are dirty platforms beside busy markets on the city outskirts, where overly enthusiastic touts literally grab tourists' bags and run them to the next departing bus. Many bus lines therefore do not have ticket offices, so you'll have to buy your ticket on the bus.

We discuss which countries have recommendable (and even high-end) bus service, as well as those in which it's not a good idea to get on the bus, in the individual chapters.

International buses run between major cities; these tend to be newer units and more comfortable, although very few are so new or modern as to have bathroom facilities, and they sometimes operate only on weekends and holidays. One advantage is they have their own private terminals so you avoid the chaos of heading to a local market to catch a bus. There are several express bus companies that provide services between Central American countries. **Tica Bus** (© **529/62-626-2880** in Mexico, or 507/314-6385 in Panama; www.ticabus.com) is one of the most reputable and travels from Mexico to Panama. **King Quality** (© **505/228-1454**; www.kingqualityca.com) does not go as far north as Mexico but has a reputation for having more comfortable buses. **Trans Nica** (© **505/277-2104** in Nicaragua) and **Central Line** (© **505/254-5431** in Nicaragua) are two other well-known companies.

If traveling with another person, it is often wise to have one person in charge of luggage while the other secures the bus, tickets, and seats. It is also best to hold onto your bags when boarding and store them above your head where you can see them. Another good tip is when arriving at a terminal (if there is one), check out the departing timetable and book your seat for your departure.

An alternative busing option is **microbuses.** These are small minivans that depart as soon as they fill up with passengers, usually around every 20 minutes. Their main advantage is they depart from city-center locations. However, they can get crowded and are not recommended for long journeys, especially when traveling with luggage.

Pickup trucks are a popular form of public transport in rural areas. Bumpy and uncomfortable, they are often covered in canvas to protect the mostly local passengers from the elements.

Shuttle buses are becoming more and more popular, too. These are privately organized tourist transfers between cities, usually operated by a tour agency or hotel. Much more comfortable and faster than local transport, they are also a lot more expensive.

The Art of Addresses in Central America

Addresses are an inexact science throughout Central America. Larger cities sometimes list building numbers in addresses but not always, and small-town addresses remain a simple set of directions usually mentioning the street, the neighborhood, a nearby landmark, the city, the state (or *"departmento"*), and the country. A typical small-town address might read, "4 Av. Norte, Barrio El Centro across from the cathedral, La Paz, El Salvador." But most of the time, all you'll need is the name of the hotel, restaurant, or attraction to get you where you need to go.

Route numbers are rarely used on road signs in Central America, although there are frequent signs listing the number of kilometers to various towns or cities. Your best bets for on-road directions are billboards and advertisements for hotels. It's always a good idea to know the names of a few hotels at your destination, just in case your specific hotel hasn't put up any billboards or signs. When taking a taxi, always try to have the address of your destination in Spanish so there are no misunderstandings with the driver.

For a sense of distance, to travel south between all capital cities starting at Belize and ending in Panama is approximately 1,400km (870 miles) and would take 4 days of nonstop traveling.

By Taxi

There is no shortage of taxis in all major towns and cities. There are some differences to how they operate. For example, in some countries, taxis have no meter. If this is the case, make sure you agree on a price before climbing in, and ascertain whether the price is per person or for the trip. Sharing with strangers is another frequent occurrence, and you may find yourself waiting while the driver stops along the way to pick up more people. This practice should be avoided at night.

In general, taxis are cheap, but keep in mind that the increasing price of gas is making transportation more expensive throughout the region, so prices quoted in this book are subject to change.

Central America's taxis are usually safe to hail from the street without going to special taxi stations. At night you'll need to call a cab from your hotel or restaurant, as many big-city streets are not safe to walk after dark. Never get into an unmarked car claiming to be a taxi.

By Boat

The Caribbean provides many opportunities to travel by small boat. Small, local water taxis travel to the Bay Islands in Honduras, Caye Caulker in Belize, Bocas del Toro in Panama, and the Corn Islands in Nicaragua. In general, the shorter the ride, the smaller and more uncomfortable the boat will be. Some ferries are rusting hulks, such as the one that carries people, livestock, and cars to Isla Ometepe in Nicaragua. Larger boats, like the ones that cross Lago Nicaragua from Granada to San Carlos, may have first- and second-class seating but that's often on a first-come, first-served basis. First-class passengers generally get a sheltered bench below deck, while second-class passengers get seating on the exposed deck above. A hammock is invaluable on such extended voyages.

The Downside of Renting a Car

Although rental cars no longer bear special license plates (at least in Costa Rica), they are still identifiable to thieves and are frequently targeted. (Nothing is safe in a car in Central America, although parking in guarded parking lots helps.) Transit police also seem to target tourists; never pay money directly to a police officer who stops you for any traffic violation.

Note that boats can be particularly crowded around holiday time, especially Easter week, and common safety precautions should be taken during any trip.

By Car

Renting a car in Central America is no idle proposition. The roads are riddled with potholes, most rural intersections are unmarked, and, for some reason, sitting behind the wheel of a car seems to turn peaceful Central Americans into homicidal maniacs. But unless you want to see the country from the window of a bus or pay exorbitant amounts for private transfers, renting a car might be your best option for independent exploring. (If you don't want to put up with any stress on your vacation, it might be worthwhile springing for a driver, though.)

Before driving off with a rental car, be sure that you inspect the exterior and point out to the rental-company representative every tiny scratch, dent, tear, or any other damage. It's a common practice with many Central American car-rental companies to claim that you owe payment for minor dings and dents that the company finds when you return the car. Also, if you get into an accident, be sure that the rental company doesn't try to bill you for a higher amount than the deductible on your rental contract.

These caveats aren't meant to scare you off from driving in Central America. Thousands of visitors rent cars here every year, and the large majority of them encounter no problems. Just keep your wits about you and guard against car theft and you'll do fine. Also keep in mind that four-wheel-drives are particularly useful in the rainy season (May to mid-Nov) and for navigating the bumpy, poorly paved roads year-round.

Among the major international agencies operating in Central America are **Alamo, Avis, Budget, Hertz, National, Payless,** and **Thrifty.** For a complete list of car-rental agencies and their contact information, see "Toll-Free Numbers & Websites," p. 728, as well as the "Getting Around" sections of country chapters.

Generally speaking, speed limits in the region are about 60 to 90 or 100kmph (37–62 mph) on major roadways and slower on secondary roads. You'll want to stick to this limit, as police speed traps are common, and you don't want a speeding ticket to put a damper on your trip.

It's sometimes cheaper to reserve a car in your home country than to book when you arrive. If you know you'll be renting a car, it's always wise to shop around and reserve it well in advance for the high season because the rental fleet often can't match demand.

Note: Estimated driving times are listed throughout this book, but bear in mind that it might take longer than estimated to reach your destination during the rainy season or if roads have deteriorated.

MONEY & COSTS

High inflation in many Central American countries means the dollar remains strong . . . in some parts of the region. El Salvador has scrapped its own currency and made the U.S. dollar its official currency. The dollar is also the official currency in Panama, although it is used along with the balboa. Belize's currency is pegged to the dollar. Fluctuation in Guatemala tends to be minor, but more pronounced (and unpredictable) in Costa Rica.

Most vendors prefer small bills and exact change. It's almost impossible to find someone who has change for a large bill. Many ATMs give out money in multiples of one or five, so try to request odd denominations of money. For larger sums, try to withdraw in a multiple of 500 instead of 1,000, for instance.

Here's a general idea of what things cost throughout Central America: A taxi from the airport to downtown cities runs $12 to $18; a double room at a budget hotel with private bathroom, $20 to $50; a double room at a moderate hotel, $80 to $120; a double room at an expensive hotel, $150 to $250; a small bottle of water, 50¢; a cup of coffee, $1 to $1.50; admission to most national parks, $10; lunch at a simple restaurant, $3 to $6; and a three-course dinner for one without wine at a fancier restaurant, $15 to $25.

Currency

In many urban and resort areas in Central America, you can use American dollars, even if that's not the local currency. This is not true in more rural areas of Costa Rica, and not true at all in Guatemala. Most major hotels will accept dollars, but smaller restaurants and any taxi that's not an "airport" taxi will probably balk at dollars (unless you're in Panama or El Salvador, where the dollar is the official currency). A list of currencies for all the countries in this guide is below.

Some prices throughout this book, particularly hotel rates, are quoted in U.S. dollars since local currencies can fluctuate. *Note:* Because of high inflation and volatile exchange rates, prices quoted here may vary greatly in accuracy.

BELIZE   The Belize dollar, abbreviated BZ$, is the official currency of Belize. It is pegged to the U.S. dollar at a ratio of 2 Belize dollars to 1 U.S. dollar, or 4 Belize dollars to the U.K. pound. Both currencies are acceptable at almost any business or establishment around the country. Denominations include 50¢ and $1 coins, while notes come in 2, 5, 10, 20, 50, and 100 denominations.

GUATEMALA   The unit of currency in Guatemala is the **quetzal.** In December 2010, there were approximately 8 quetzales to the American dollar, or 12 quetzales to the U.K. pound, but because the quetzal does fluctuate, you can expect this rate to change. There are 1-quetzal coins and paper notes in denominations of 1, 5, 10, 20, 50, and 100 quetzales.

EL SALVADOR   El Salvador uses the **U.S. dollar** as its national currency. Prices in that chapter are quoted in American currency only.

HONDURAS   The Honduran unit of currency is called a **lempira.** It currently hovers at approximately 19 to 1 with the American dollar, and 30 to 1 with the U.K. pound. It comes in paper denominations of 1, 2, 5, 10, 20, 100, and 500 lempiras. There are 100 centavos in a lempira and they come in coin forms of 1, 2, 5, 10, 20, and 50 centavos.

NICARAGUA   The official Nicaraguan currency is the **córdoba** (it is sometimes referred to as a peso). It currently rates at approximately 22 to 1 with the American

CENTRAL AMERICAN CURRENCY CONVERSIONS

	US$1	C$1	UK£1	AUS$1	NZ$1
Belizean dollar	0.50	0.52	0.25	0.52	0.67
Costa Rican colón	0.002	0.002	0.0012	0.002	0.0026
Guatemalan quetzal	0.12	0.13	0.081	0.12	0.16
Honduran lempira	0.054	0.055	0.033	0.054	0.07
Nicaraguan córdoba	0.046	0.047	0.028	0.047	0.061

Note: Panama and El Salvador use the U.S. dollar.

dollar, and 35 to 1 with the U.K. pound. It is made up of 100 **centavos.** Money is denominated in notes of 10, 20, 50, 100, and 500 córdobas. Coins are made of 1 and 5 córdobas and 50 centavos.

COSTA RICA   The unit of currency in Costa Rica is the **colón.** In December 2010, there were approximately 504 colones to the American dollar and 815 colones to the British pound. *Because of this high exchange rate, prices in the Costa Rica chapter are quoted mostly in American currency.* The colón is divided into 100 **céntimos.** Two types of coins are in circulation. The older and larger nickel-alloy coins come in denominations of 10, 25, and 50 céntimos and 1, 2, 5, 10, and 20 colones; and newer, gold-hued 5-, 10-, 25-, 50-, 100-, and 500-colón coins. There are paper notes in denominations of 1,000, 2,000, 5,000, and 10,000 colones.

PANAMA   The unit of currency in Panama is the U.S. dollar, but the Panamanian balboa, which is pegged to the dollar at a 1:1 ratio, also circulates in denominations of 5¢, 10¢, 25¢, and 50¢ coins. (U.S. coins are in circulation as well.) Balboa coins are sized similarly to their U.S. counterparts. Prices in the Panama chapter are quoted in American currency only.

ATMs

The easiest and best way to get cash throughout Central America is from an ATM (automated teller machine). The **Cirrus** (© 800/424-7787; www.mastercard.com) and **PLUS** (© 800/843-7587; www.visa.com) networks work here; look at the back of your bank card to see which network you're on, then call or check online for ATM locations at your destination. Be sure you know your personal identification number (PIN) and daily withdrawal limit before you depart—you'll need a four-digit PIN throughout much of this region. *Note:* Remember that many banks impose a fee every time you use a card at another bank's ATM, and that fee can be higher for international transactions (up to $5 or more) than for domestic ones (where they're rarely more than $2). In addition, the bank from which you withdraw cash may charge its own fee. For international withdrawal fees, ask your bank.

You can also use your credit card to receive cash advances at ATMs. Keep in mind that credit card companies protect themselves from theft by limiting maximum withdrawals outside their home country, so call your credit card company before you leave home. And know that you'll pay interest from the moment of your withdrawal, even if you pay your monthly bills on time.

Credit Cards

Credit cards are another safe way to carry money throughout this region. They provide a convenient record of your expenses, and generally offer relatively good exchange rates. You can also withdraw cash advances from your credit cards at banks or ATMs, if you know your PIN.

Keep in mind that many banks assess a 1% to 3% "transaction fee" on *all* charges you incur abroad (whether you're using the local currency or U.S. dollars).

Visa, MasterCard, American Express, and Diners Club are all commonly accepted in Central America.

IF YOUR WALLET IS LOST OR STOLEN Be sure to tell all of your credit card companies the minute you discover that your wallet has been lost or stolen, and file a report at the nearest police precinct. Your credit card company or insurer may require a police report number or record of the loss. Most credit card companies have an emergency toll-free number to call if your card is lost or stolen; they may be able to wire you a cash advance immediately or deliver an emergency credit card in a day or two. Emergency numbers for each country are listed in the "Money" section of country chapters.

HEALTH
Staying Healthy

For general information about health issues in Central America, log on to the **Centers for Disease Control and Prevention**'s website at **www.cdc.gov/travel**. In addition to the recommendations below, the CDC advises visitors to Central America to protect themselves against hepatitis A and B. Consult your doctor for more information about these vaccinations.

BEFORE YOU GO

It can be hard to find a doctor you can trust when you're in an unfamiliar place. Try to take proper precautions the week before you depart to avoid falling ill while you're away from home. Amid the last-minute frenzy that often precedes a vacation, make an extra effort to eat and sleep well.

Pack prescription medications in their original labeled containers in your carry-on luggage. Also, bring along copies of your prescriptions in case you lose your pills or run out. Carry written prescriptions in generic form, in case a local pharmacist is unfamiliar with the brand name. If you wear contact lenses, pack an extra pair or your glasses.

If you worry about getting sick away from home, you may want to consider **medical travel insurance** (see "Travel Insurance," in chapter 11).

If you suffer from a chronic illness, consult your doctor before your departure. For conditions such as epilepsy, diabetes, or heart problems, wear a **MedicAlert identification tag** (🕽 **888/633-4298;** www.medicalert.org), which will immediately alert doctors to your condition and give them access to your records through MedicAlert's 24-hour hot line.

Contact the **International Association for Medical Assistance to Travelers** (**IAMAT;** 🕽 **716/754-4883,** or 416/652-0137 in Canada; www.iamat.org) for tips on travel and health concerns in the countries you're visiting, and lists of local, English-speaking doctors.

GENERAL AVAILABILITY OF HEALTHCARE

Not surprisingly, most of the region's best hospitals and healthcare centers are in the big cities, but service varies widely. If you do get sick, it's best to contact your home country's consulate or embassy. They all have health departments with staff who can recommend the best English-speaking doctors and hospitals in the area.

COMMON DISEASES & AILMENTS

DIETARY DISTRESS   It's unfortunate, but many travelers to Central America do suffer from some sort of food or waterborne illness. Most of this is just due to tender northern stomachs coming into contact with slightly more aggressive Latin American intestinal flora. Symptoms vary—from minor cases of diarrhea to debilitating flulike illnesses. To minimize your chances of getting sick, always drink bottled or boiled water and avoid ice. In high altitudes, you will need to boil water for several minutes longer before it is safe to drink. If you don't have access to bottled water, you can treat it with iodine or chlorine, with iodine being more effective. You can buy water purification tablets at pharmacies and sporting-goods stores. You should also be careful to avoid raw food, especially meats, fruit, and vegetables. If you peel the fruit yourself, you should be fine.

If you do suffer from diarrhea, it's important to keep yourself hydrated. Many pharmacies sell Pedialyte, which is a mild rehydrating solution. Drinking fruit juices or soft drinks (preferably without caffeine) and eating salted crackers are also good remedies. In extreme cases of diarrhea or intestinal discomfort, it's worth taking a stool sample to a lab for analysis. The results will usually pinpoint the amoebic or parasitic culprit, which can then be readily treated with available over-the-counter medicines.

Typhoid fever is a food- or waterborne illness that occurs throughout Central America (it's caused by salmonella). Long-term travelers should consider a typhoid vaccine before leaving, as the malaria-like symptoms are very unpleasant.

Hepatitis A is another viral infection acquired through water and food (it can also be picked up off infected people), this time attacking the liver. Usually the symptoms of fever, jaundice, and nausea will pass but it can in some cases cause liver damage. There is an effective vaccine that you can take before the trip.

TROPICAL ILLNESSES   **Yellow fever** is no longer a problem in Central America. However, if you are traveling from South America or Africa or another country known to have yellow fever, you will require a vaccination certificate to enter Costa Rica.

Malaria does exist in Central America, especially in rural areas. To protect yourself, wear mosquito repellent with DEET, wear long-sleeved shirts and trousers, and use mosquito nets. You can also take antimalaria drugs before you go; consult your doctor about the pros and cons of such medications. Be sure to ask whether a recommended drug will cause you to be hypersensitive to the sun; it would be a shame to come down here for the beaches and then have to hide under an umbrella the whole time. Because malaria-carrying mosquitoes usually come out at night, you should do as much as possible to avoid being bitten after dark. Also be aware that symptoms such as high fever, chills, and body aches can appear months after your vacation.

Dengue fever, transmitted by an aggressive daytime mosquito, is a risk in tropical environments and densely populated urban areas. As with malaria, the best prevention is to avoid mosquito bites; there is no vaccine available. Dengue is also known as "bone-break fever" because it is usually accompanied by severe body aches. The first infection with dengue fever will make you very sick but should cause no serious damage. However, a second infection with a different strain of the dengue virus can lead to internal hemorrhaging and could be life-threatening. If you are unfortunate enough to get it, take some paracetamol and lots of fluids.

BEES, BUGS & BITES Snakes, **scorpions,** and **spiders** rarely bite without provocation. Keep your eyes open and never walk barefoot. If you're in the jungle or rainforest, be sure to shake your clothes and check your shoes before putting them on. Africanized bees (the notorious "killer bees" of fact and fable) are common in this region, but there is no real danger of being attacked unless you do something silly like stick your hand into a hive. Other than mosquitoes, the most prevalent and annoying biting insect you are likely to encounter, especially along the coast, is sand flies. These tiny biting bugs leave a raised and itchy welt, but otherwise are of no significant danger. They tend to be most active around sunrise and sunset, or on overcast days. Your best protection is to wear light long-sleeved shirts and long pants.

The chances of contracting **rabies** while traveling in Central America are unlikely but not completely impossible. Most infected animals live in rural areas. If you are bitten by an infected dog or bat, wash the wound and get yourself to a hospital as quickly as possible. There is a prevacation vaccine that requires three injections, but you should get it only if you are planning a high-risk activity such as cave exploring. Treatment is effective but must be given promptly.

RIPTIDES Many of the Pacific coast beaches have riptides—strong currents that can drag swimmers out to sea. A riptide occurs when water that has been dumped on the shore by strong waves forms a channel back out to open water. These channels have strong currents. If you get caught in a riptide, you can't escape the current by swimming toward shore. To break free of the current, swim parallel to shore and use the energy of the waves to help you get back to the beach. *Note:* Lifeguards are a rarity in the region.

CRIME & SAFETY

Central America's reputation for gang violence and drug running are not entirely unwarranted. However, such a well-publicized (and sensationalized) crime image will contrast strongly with your experience of the region's friendly, peace-loving people. Travelers rarely experience anything more untoward than being pickpocketed or distracted in some way and relieved of a backpack (and even this is rare). Gun crime is usually confined to the shantytowns and poor barrios and rarely affects tourists. In my experience, the more budget-oriented you are, the more vulnerable you are—a public chicken bus is not as safe as a private shuttle.

Before you depart, check for travel advisories from the **U.S. State Department** (www.travel.state.gov), the **Canadian Department of Foreign Affairs** (www.voyage. gc.ca), the **U.K. Foreign & Commonwealth Office** (www.fco.gov.uk/travel), and the **Australian Department of Foreign Affairs** (www.smartraveller.gov.au).

Once you're in the region, keep some common-sense safety advice in mind: Stay alert and be aware of your surroundings; don't walk down dark, deserted streets; and always keep an eye on your personal belongings. Keep your passport and credit cards on your person (but not stuffed in your back pocket). Theft at airports and bus stations is not unheard of, so be sure to put a lock on your luggage. Rental cars generally stick out, and are easily spotted by thieves (see "By Car" under "Getting Around," earlier in this chapter, for more info).

Public intercity buses are also frequent targets of stealthy thieves. Never check your bags into the hold of a bus if you can avoid it. If this can't be avoided, when the bus makes a stop, keep your eye on what leaves the hold. If you put your bags in an overhead rack, be sure you can see the bags at all times.

See the individual chapters in this book for more specific safety advice.

SPECIALIZED TRAVEL RESOURCES

Travelers with Disabilities

Central America is not well equipped for travelers with disabilities. Where elevators exist, they are often tiny. Many city streets are crowded, narrow, and badly maintained and public buses so frenetic that even able-bodied people have scarcely time to board before the driver roars off. The nature of the terrain means climbing in and out of small buses, boats, and planes, and that will be challenging for travelers with disabilities.

Nevertheless, a disability shouldn't stop anyone from traveling. There are more resources out there than ever before. Some of the best include **MossRehab** (www. mossresourcenet.org), which provides a library of accessible-travel resources online; the **Society for Accessible Travel and Hospitality** (**SATH;** ✆ 212/447-7284; www.sath.org), which offers a wealth of travel resources for all types of disabilities and informed recommendations on destinations, access guides, travel agents, tour operators, vehicle rentals, and companion services; and the **American Foundation for the Blind** (✆ 800/232-5463; www.afb.org), which offers a referral resource for those who are blind or visually impaired that includes information on traveling with Seeing Eye dogs.

For more on organizations that offer resources to travelers with disabilities, go to Frommers.com.

Gay & Lesbian Travelers

Central America is Catholic and conservative. Public displays of same-sex affection are rare and considered somewhat shocking. There are some gay or lesbian bars in the bigger cities but most are rather low-key. Gay and lesbian travelers should choose their hotels with care, and be discreet in most public areas and situations.

Many agencies offer tours and travel itineraries to Central America that are specifically targeted at gay and lesbian travelers. **Above and Beyond Tours** (✆ 800/397-2681; www.abovebeyondtours.com) is the exclusive gay and lesbian tour operator for United Airlines. **Now, Voyager** (✆ 800/255-6951; www.nowvoyager.com) is a well-known San Francisco–based gay-owned and -operated travel service. Another well-known agency is **Olivia Cruises & Resorts** (✆ 800/631-6277; www. olivia.com).

For more gay and lesbian travel resources visit Frommers.com.

Seniors

Although it's not common policy in Central America to offer senior discounts, don't be shy about asking for one anyway. You never know. Always carry some kind of identification, such as a driver's license, that shows your date of birth, especially if you've kept your youthful glow.

Members of **AARP** (formerly known as the American Association of Retired Persons), 601 E St. NW, Washington, DC 20049 (✆ 888/687-2277; www.aarp.org), get discounts on hotels, airfares, and car rentals. AARP offers members a wide range of benefits, including *AARP The Magazine* and a monthly newsletter. Anyone over 50 can join.

Many reliable agencies and organizations target the 50-plus market. Road Scholar (© **800/454-5768;** www.roadscholar.org), formerly known as **Elderhostel,** arranges Costa Rica, Guatemala, Belize, and Panama study programs for those ages 55 and older. **ElderTreks** (© **800/741-7956,** or 416/558-5000 outside North America; www.eldertreks.com) offers small-group tours to Costa Rica, restricted to travelers 50 and older.

Frommers.com offers more information and resources on travel for seniors.

Families

"Children not allowed" is a rare concept in Central America—family values are very important here, so if you're traveling with your whole family, you can expect locals to welcome you with open arms.

A handful of hotels give discounts for children 11 and under, or allow children under 3 or 4 years old to stay free. Discounts for children and the cutoff ages vary according to the hotel, but in general, don't assume that your kids can stay in your room free.

Many hotels also offer rooms equipped with kitchenettes or full kitchen facilities. These can be a real money-saver for those traveling with children. Hotels offering regular, dependable babysitting service are few and far between, however. If you will need babysitting, make sure your hotel offers it before you make your reservation.

To locate Central American accommodations, restaurants, and attractions that are particularly kid-friendly, refer to the "Kids" icon throughout this guide.

Students

Although you won't find discounts at the national parks, most museums and other attractions around Central America offer discounts for students. It pays to ask.

You'd be wise to arm yourself with an **International Student Identity Card (ISIC),** which offers substantial savings on rail passes, plane tickets, and entrance fees. It also provides you with basic health and life insurance and a 24-hour help line. The card is available for $22 from **STA Travel** (© **800/781-4040;** www.sta.com), the biggest student travel agency in the world. If you're no longer a student but are still under 26, you can get an **International Youth Travel Card (IYTC)** for the same price from the same people, which entitles you to some discounts (but not on museum admissions).

Travel CUTS (© **800/667-2887** or 416/614-2887; www.travelcuts.com) offers similar services for both Canadians and U.S. residents. Irish students should turn to **USIT** (© **01/602-1600;** www.usitnow.ie).

Women Travelers

For lack of better phrasing, Central America is a typically "macho" part of the world. Single women can expect a nearly constant stream of catcalls, hisses, whistles, and car horns, especially in big cities. Women should be careful walking alone at night throughout the country.

For general travel resources for women, go to Frommers.com.

Single Travelers

Many people prefer traveling alone. Unfortunately, the solo traveler may have to pay a premium price for the privilege of sleeping alone. On package vacations, single travelers can be hit with a "single supplement" to the base price. To avoid it, you can agree to room with other single travelers on the trip, or you can find a compatible roommate before you go.

GAP Adventures (© 800/708-7761 in North America, or 44/870-999-0144 in the United Kingdom; www.gapadventures.com) is an adventure tour company with a good range of regular and varied tours in Central America. As a policy, they do not charge a single supplement and will try to pair a single traveler with a compatible roommate.

SUSTAINABLE TOURISM

Central America is one of the planet's prime ecotourism destinations. Many of the isolated nature lodges and tour operators around the country are pioneers and dedicated professionals in the ecotourism and sustainable-tourism field. Many other hotels, lodges, and tour operators are simply "green-washing": using the terms "eco" and "sustainable" in their promo materials, but doing little real good in their daily operations. **Responsible Travel** (www.responsibletravel.com) is a great source of sustainable-travel ideas with listings on Central America; the site is run by a spokesperson for ethical tourism in the travel industry. **Sustainable Travel International** (www.sustainabletravelinternational.org) promotes ethical tourism practices, and manages an extensive directory of sustainable properties and tour operators around the region.

Deforestation is the main threat to Central America's fragile ecosystem. Farming has wiped out most of the region's dry tropical rainforests, while logging is a major threat to the cloud forest. Thirty percent of Central America is forest today, which is half of what existed 50 years ago. Such destruction has been devastating to many species, including man himself, in the form of displaced indigenous tribes, and has led to drinking-water shortages, flash flooding, and mudslides.

Fortunately, some countries, particularly Costa Rica, have made great strides toward protecting the region's rich biodiversity. Thirty years ago, it was difficult to find a protected area anywhere in Costa Rica, but now more than 11% of that country is protected within the national park system. Another 10% to 15% of the land enjoys moderately effective preservation as part of private and public reserves, Indian reserves, and wildlife refuges and corridors. Still, Costa Rica's tropical hardwoods continue to be harvested at an alarming rate, often illegally, while other primary forests are clear-cut for short-term agricultural gain. Many experts predict that Costa Rica's unprotected forests will be gone within the early part of this century.

Belize, Guatemala, and Honduras have commendable environmental records, with significant portions of those countries protected. Belize has the best environmental policy, with 40% of the country protected. Although Honduras still has significant forest cover (41%), it is losing 3% year after year; Guatemala is losing 1.7% a year, with 10% of its land classified as highly degraded and 60% at risk.

El Salvador has the worst environmental record in Central America, with only 2% of its original forest left, while Nicaragua is losing 150,000 hectares (370,700 acres) of forest per year. Fifty-seven percent of Panama is covered in forest but the country is losing 6,900 hectares (17,050 acres) a year.

IT'S EASY BEING green

Here are a few simple ways you can help conserve fuel and energy when you travel:

○ Each time you take a flight or drive a car, greenhouse gases release into the atmosphere. You can help neutralize this danger to the planet through "carbon offsetting"—paying someone to invest your money in programs that reduce greenhouse gas emissions by the same amount you've added. Before buying carbon-offset credits, just make sure that you're using a reputable company, one with a proven program that invests in renewable energy. Reliable carbon offset companies include **Carbonfund** (www.carbonfund.org), **TerraPass** (www.terrapass.org), and **Carbon Neutral** (www.carbonneutral.org).

○ Whenever possible, choose non-stop flights; they generally require less fuel than indirect flights that stop and take off again. Try to fly during the day—some scientists estimate that nighttime flights are twice as harmful to the environment. And pack light—each 15 pounds of luggage on a 5,000-mile flight adds up to 50 pounds of carbon dioxide emitted.

○ Where you stay during your travels can have a major environmental impact. To determine the green credentials of a property, ask about trash disposal and recycling, water conservation,

and energy use; also question whether sustainable materials were used in the construction of the property. The website **www.greenhotels.com** recommends green-rated member hotels around the world that fulfill the company's stringent environmental requirements. Also consult **www.environmentallyfriendlyhotels.com** for more green accommodations ratings.

○ At hotels, request that your sheets and towels not be changed daily. (Many hotels already have programs like this in place.) Turn off the lights and air conditioner (or heater) when you leave your room.

○ Use public transport where possible—trains, buses, and even taxis are more energy-efficient forms of transport than driving. Even better is to walk or cycle; you'll produce zero emissions and stay fit and healthy on your travels.

○ If renting a car is necessary, ask the rental agent for a hybrid, or rent the most fuel-efficient car available. You'll use less gas and save money at the tank.

○ Eat at locally owned and operated restaurants that use produce grown in the area. This contributes to the local economy and cuts down on greenhouse gas emissions by supporting restaurants for which the food is not flown or trucked in across long distances.

Though environmental awareness is growing, solving the region's huge environmental problems, including not just deforestation but the effects of overpopulation and industrial pollution, clearly remains an uphill struggle.

Volunteer travel has become increasingly popular among those who want to venture beyond the standard group-tour experience to learn languages, interact with locals, and make a positive difference while on vacation in Central America. Volunteer options are listed under "Special-Interest Trips," below, as well as in this guide's country chapters.

ANIMAL-RIGHTS ISSUES

For information on animal-friendly issues throughout the world, visit **Tread Lightly** (www.treadlightly.org). For information about the ethics of swimming with dolphins, visit the **Whale and Dolphin Conservation Society** (www.wdcs.org).

SPECIAL-INTEREST & ESCORTED TRIPS

Package tours are simply a way to buy the airfare, accommodations, and other elements of your trip (such as car rentals, airport transfers, and sometimes even activities) at the same time and often at discounted prices.

One good source of package deals is the airlines themselves. Most major airlines offer air/land packages, including **American Airlines Vacations** (✆ 800/321-2121; www.aavacations.com), **Delta Vacations** (✆ 800/654-6559; www.deltavacations. com), **Continental Airlines Vacations** (✆ 800/301-3800; www.covacations.com), and **United Vacations** (✆ 888/854-3899; www.unitedvacations.com). Several big **online travel agencies**—Expedia, Travelocity, Orbitz, and Lastminute.com—also do a brisk business in packages.

Travel packages are also listed in the travel section of your local Sunday newspaper. Or check ads in national travel magazines such as *Arthur Frommer's Budget Travel Magazine, Travel + Leisure, National Geographic Traveler,* and *Condé Nast Traveler.*

For more information on package tours and for tips on booking your trip, see Frommers.com.

Escorted Tours

Escorted tours are structured group tours with a group leader. The price usually includes everything from airfare to hotels, meals, tours, admission costs, and local transportation.

Despite the fact that escorted tours require big deposits and predetermine hotels, restaurants, and itineraries, many people derive security and peace of mind from the structure. Escorted tours—whether they're navigated by bus, motorcoach, train, or boat—let travelers sit back and enjoy the trip without having to drive or worry about details. They take you to the maximum number of sights in the minimum amount of time with the least amount of hassle. They're convenient for people with limited mobility, and they can be a great way to make new friends.

On the downside, you'll have little opportunity for serendipitous interactions with locals. The tours can be jampacked with activities, leaving little room for individual sightseeing, whim, or adventure—plus they often focus on the heavily touristy sites, so you miss out on many a lesser-known gem.

Tour Operators Specializing in Central America

Organizing a hassle-free tour in Central America is a challenge. Transport is the main problem, as the roads and public buses are shabby, to say the least. The language barrier is something else to consider when trying to piece together a preplanned itinerary. Often it's best to leave the logistics to the experts. The tour companies below have connections throughout the region, and their staffs can make all of your travel arrangements for you.

o **Adventure Associates** (℃ **02/9389-7466**; www.adventureassociates.com) is the best source in Australia for high-end package tours to Central America.

o **Far Horizons** (℃ **800/552-4575**; www.farhorizons.com) offers cultural and archaeological tours of the region and are the experts if you want to unlock the secrets of the Maya civilization.

o **Imaginative Traveller** (℃ **44/1473-667-337** in the U.K.; www.imaginative-traveller.com) is a good-value operator specializing in budget student, group, and family travel. Their offerings in Belize focus on the entire Mundo Maya, and usually also take in parts of southern Mexico and Guatemala. These trips range in duration from 9 to 31 days.

o **Journey Latin America** (℃ **020/8747-8315**; www.journeylatinamerica.co.uk) is a premier British travel agency offering trips to Central America. The company can arrange airfare and tour packages throughout the region.

o **Ladatco Tours** (℃ **800/327-6162**; www.ladatco.com) has been providing "pampered adventure" since 1966. The company will put together a personalized tour of any country in Central America, including an epic 12-day tour of the region. It also organizes air-only packages.

o **Latin Discover** (℃ **506/2290-4017**; www.latindiscover.com) is a small, high-end operator based in Costa Rica, though it offers tours of the entire region. The company caters to all types of travelers, including honeymooners and independent self-drivers.

o **Tara Tours, Inc.** (℃ **800/327-0080**; www.taratours.com) is one of the most experienced agencies offering package tours to Central America. Tours are personalized based on your interests; some of the specialties include archaeology and spiritual journeys.

o **Tropical Discovery** (℃ **305/593-8687**; www.tropicaldiscovery.com) conducts private and custom-made tours up and down Central America. You can choose between 1-day volcano hiking and 11-day all-inclusive country tours.

o **Via Venture** ★★ (℃ **502/7832-2509**; www.viaventure.com) is a well-run operation specializing in custom-designed itineraries using high-end hotels, as well as an excellent team of guides and ground transport services. They are also strong in the area of adventure tourism and theme vacations. In addition to Guatemala, they run trips and combined itineraries into Belize and Honduras.

Special-Interest Trips

Many outdoor activities can be arranged easily and cheaply upon arrival in Central America. Local operators will have everything you need and can arrange guides and even companions. The quality of tours can vary greatly, and you will find paying a little extra gets you away from the herd. It is strongly advisable to hire knowledgeable guides to get the most out of your visit. See individual chapters throughout this book for specific tour-operator info.

BIRD-WATCHING Resplendent quetzals, tropical kingbirds, social flycatchers, and keel-billed toucans are just some of the many marvelous feathered creatures that inhabit the jungles, savannas, and coastal rocks of Central America. You do not have to venture far from your hotel to catch sight of some creature that will have you fumbling for your camera. Some of the best birding spots are Costa Rica's Parque Nacional Corcovado, Nicaragua's Reserva Natural Miraflor, Belize's Crooked Tree Wildlife Sanctuary, and Panama's Volcán Barú.

HIKING Where to start? At the foot of a cone-shaped volcano or the lake of a rainforest reserve? Central America has numerous hiking possibilities, with its many natural parks, cloud forests, lava fields, and deserted beaches offering a truly breathtaking variety of experiences. If you plan on camping, bring your own gear, as there is little in the way of equipment rental.

DIVING & SNORKELING The Caribbean coast is where the best diving is, particularly around the Bay Islands in Honduras and Caye Caulker in Belize. The Corn Islands are the next big thing in Caribbean coral treasure islands. All the well-known diving zones offer short dives and instructor training. The Pacific is not as popular as the Caribbean because its waters are darker and rougher. You can catch some good dives in places like San Juan del Sur in Nicaragua.

MOUNTAIN BIKING The region's best biking opportunities are in the cooler highland areas, particularly in Guatemala and Costa Rica, as well as Panama and Honduras. There are plenty of outfitters in most cities but be careful that you get a road-worthy bike. Expect poor roads and dangerous drivers. This is definitely a pursuit best suited to the dry season (Nov–Apr).

RIVER RAFTING There is nothing quite like rafting down a fast, tropical river. White-water rafting is becoming more and more popular in a region that has plenty of rivers offering Class 2 to Class 4 rafting. Costa Rica is ahead of everybody else for adventure companies and places. Guatemala and Honduras, as well as Panama, are becoming known for excellent river floating, too.

KAYAKING A little more civilized than river rafting, kayaking is one of the most enriching experiences in Central America. Whether you are paddling on a crater lake or gliding through a Caribbean swamp, kayaking is a great way to break away from the crowd and creep up on some spectacular wildlife. Sea kayaking is popular in Belize and Costa Rica. Las Isletas in Nicaragua is a popular kayaking spot, as is the Chiriquí River in Panama and the Río Cangrejal in Honduras.

SURFING All along the rolling Pacific, you'll find big waves and excellent breaks. It was surfers who first put Nicaragua's San Juan del Sur on the map, and now El Salvador's Punta Roca is also making itself known among wave riders. Costa Rica has the most established surfers' hangouts, particularly around Tamarindo and Jacó, and Parque Nacional Santa Rosa. Don't fancy getting your feet wet? Try volcano surfing in León, Nicaragua—this involves sliding down the side of a black volcano on a waxed surfboard. It's strenuous (especially the walk back up), but great fun.

FISHING Sportfishing is popular all along the Atlantic coast, with lots of marlin, sailfish, tarpon, and snook ready to catch. The Pacific coast also has big-game fishing, with giant dorado and yellowtail tuna. To catch such big fish requires chartering a boat from one of the many outfitters in the region, or you could just do what the locals do and stand in the tide throwing nets at the shoals.

Volunteer Vacations

Here's a list of companies offering educational and volunteer opportunities in Central America; see individual country chapters for specific volunteer options.

Studying the local language in a foreign country is a great learning vacation, and you can find immersion programs in Spanish throughout Central America. Note that there's a fairly wide range of accents throughout the region, with the Guatemalan accent said to be one of the cleanest and easiest Spanish accents to master. Costa Rica's accent is unique and sometimes gets made fun of by other Central America Spanish speakers for their "rr"s. Many of the region's major tourist destinations have Spanish schools, each of which offers the option of living with a local family while you study. Antigua, Guatemala, is particularly known for its Spanish-language classes and homestays, while Estelí in northern Nicaragua is gaining a reputation for such classes. See the boxes on Spanish schools throughout this book for info, or you can prearrange courses and homestays with organizations like **AmeriSpan** (© 0800/879-6640; www.amerispan. com) or **Spanish Abroad** (© 602/778-6791; www.spanishabroad.com). Wherever you decide to study, shop around and examine the options, as some programs are much better organized than others.

- **AmeriSpan** (© 800/879-6640 or 215/751-1100; www.amerispan.com) helps students arrange programs that combine language study, travel, and volunteer opportunities throughout Central America.
- **Amigos de las Américas** (© 800/231-7796 or 713/782-5290; www.amigoslink. org) is always looking for volunteers to promote public health, education, and community development in rural areas of Central America.
- **Earthwatch Institute** (© 800/776-0188 or 978/461-0081; www.earthwatch. org) supports sustainable conservation efforts of the earth's natural resources. The organization can always use volunteers for its research teams in Central America.
- **Habitat for Humanity International** (© 229/924-6935, or check the website for local affiliates; www.habitat.org) needs volunteers to help build affordable housing in more than 79 countries in the world, including most countries in Central America.
- **Spanish Abroad, Inc.** (© 888/722-7623 or 602/778-6791; www.spanishabroad. com) organizes intensive language-study programs throughout Central America.
- **Building New Hope** (© 412/421-1625; www.buildingnewhope.org) is a Philadelphia-based organization always looking for volunteers for its numerous projects, especially in Nicaragua.
- **i-to-i** (© 0800/011-1156; www.i-to-i.org) is a company that specializes in "meaningful travel." It has an extensive range of programs all over the region that are particularly targeted toward gap-year students.
- **Global Volunteers** (© 0800/487-1074; www.globalvolunteers.org) organizes volunteer vacations throughout Central America.
- **Enforex** (© 34091/594-3776; www.enforex.com) is a Madrid-based Spanish-language company that organizes study-abroad programs in several Central American countries.

STAYING CONNECTED

Telephones

Central America's phone systems differ in quality. For example, Costa Rica's system is much more efficient than Nicaragua's. A local call generally costs just a few cents per minute. Calls to cellphones or between competing phone companies can be much more expensive. Public phones are rare, although calling cards are sold in most grocery and general stores. Your hotel is usually your best bet for making calls or sending and receiving faxes, although it may charge exorbitant rates for international faxes.

Your best, cheapest bet for making international calls if you don't have a smartphone that's activated for international calls, or a laptop with Skype, is to head to any Internet cafe with an international calling option (or a Wi-Fi hot spot for your laptop with Skype). These cafes have connections to Skype, Net2Phone, or some other **VoIP service.** International calls can range anywhere from 5¢ to $1 per minute—much cheaper than making direct international calls if you have a really expensive phone plan or are using a phone card. See the "Fast Facts" sections throughout this guide's country chapters for tips on dialing.

Note that a number of establishments like shops and bars in smaller towns throughout this region do not have working land lines—these have been listed wherever possible.

Using a Cellphone

The three letters that define much of the world's wireless capabilities are GSM (Global System for Mobiles), a big, seamless network that makes for easy cross-border cellphone use throughout Central America and dozens of other regions worldwide. In the U.S., T-Mobile, AT&T Wireless, and Cingular use this quasi-universal system; in Canada, Microcell and some Rogers customers are GSM, and all Europeans and most Australians use GSM. Unfortunately, per-minute charges on roaming phone calls can be high—usually $1.50 to $3.50 in this region.

For many, **renting** a phone is a good idea. (Even world phone owners will have to rent new phones if they're traveling to non-GSM regions, such as Japan or Korea.) While you can rent a phone from any number of overseas sites, including kiosks at airports and at car-rental agencies, we suggest renting the phone before you leave home. North Americans can rent one before leaving home from **InTouch USA** (✆ 800/872-7626; www.intouchglobal.com) or **RoadPost** (✆ 888/290-1606 or 905/272-5665; www.roadpost.com). InTouch will also, for free, advise you on whether your existing phone will work overseas; simply call ✆ 703/222-7161 between 9am and 4pm EST, or go to **http://intouchglobal.com/travel.htm.**

Buying a phone can be economically attractive, as many Central American nations have cheap prepaid phone systems. Once you arrive at your destination, stop by a local cellphone shop and get the cheapest package; you'll probably pay less than $100 for a phone and a starter calling card. Local calls may be as low as 10¢ per minute, and in many countries incoming calls are free.

Wilderness adventurers, or those heading to less-developed parts of Central America, might consider renting a **satellite phone** ("satphone"). It's different from a cellphone in that it connects to satellites and works where there's no cellular signal or ground-based tower. You can rent satphones from RoadPost (see above). InTouch USA (see above) offers a wider range but at higher rates. Per-minute call charges can be even cheaper than roaming charges with a regular cellphone, but the phone itself

Where Are You @?

The @ symbol is hard to find on a Latin American keyboard. You must keep your finger on the "Alt" key and then press "6" and "4" on the number pad to the right. If you're still unsuccessful and at an Internet cafe, ask the assistant to help you type an *arroba*.

is more expensive. As of this writing, satphones were outrageously expensive to buy, so don't even think about it.

Internet Access Away From Home

WITHOUT YOUR OWN COMPUTER

It's hard nowadays to find a major city in Central America that *doesn't* have a few cybercafés. Although there's no definitive directory for cybercafés—these are independent businesses, after all—two places to start looking are at **www.cybercaptive.com** and **www.cybercafe.com**.

Aside from formal cybercafés, most **youth hostels** and hotels have at least one computer you can use to log on, and many provide at least 15 minutes free.

WITH YOUR OWN COMPUTER

More and more hotels, cafes, and retailers in Central American cities offer Wi-Fi (wireless fidelity) hot spots. Mac owners have their own networking technology: Apple AirPort. iPass providers (**www.ipass.com**) also give you access to a few hundred wireless hotel lobby setups. To locate other hot spots that provide **free wireless networks,** go to **www.personaltelco.net/index.cgi/WirelessCommunities**. For dial-up access, most business-class hotels throughout Central America offer dataports for laptop modems.

If your computer's not equipped with Wi-Fi (or you're not around an area with a hot spot), bring a **connection kit** of the right power and phone adapters, a spare phone cord, and a spare Ethernet network cable—or find out whether your hotel supplies them to guests.

TIPS ON ACCOMMODATIONS

Upscale travelers can choose from more and more options in Central America. It has taken time, but spurred on by the example and standards of several international chains, service and amenities have been improving across-the-board, particularly in the upscale market. The region's strong suit is still its moderately priced hotels, though. In the $60-to-$125 price range, you'll find comfortable and sometimes outstanding accommodations almost anywhere in the region. However, room size and quality vary quite a bit within this price range, so don't expect the kind of uniformity that you may find at home. Almost all the big hotels have free parking lots, while smaller, budget hotels have street parking.

If you're budget- or bohemian-minded, you can find quite a few good deals for less than $50 a double. ***But beware:*** Budget-oriented lodgings often feature shared bathrooms and either cold-water showers or showers heated by electrical heat-coil units mounted at the shower head, affectionately known as "suicide showers." If your hotel has one, do not adjust it while the water is running. ***Note:*** Air-conditioning is not necessarily a given in many midrange hotels and even some upscale joints. In general, this is not a problem. Cooler nights and a well-placed ceiling fan are often more than enough to keep things pleasant, unless we mention otherwise in the hotel reviews. And although power outages aren't a regular issue (at least in the region's cities) anymore, it is always wise to check out whether your hotel has a backup generator in case things get uncomfortable.

Another welcome hotel trend in the area is the renovation and conversion of old homes into small hotels or B&Bs. Central America is still riding the ecotourism wave, and you'll find small nature-oriented ecolodges throughout the region, too. These lodges offer opportunities to see wildlife (including sloths, monkeys, and hundreds of species of birds) and learn about tropical forests. They range from spartan facilities catering primarily to scientific researchers, to luxury accommodations that are among the finest in the country. Keep in mind that although the nightly room rates at these lodges are often quite moderate, prices start to climb when you throw in transportation (often on chartered planes), guided excursions, and meals. Also, just because you can book a reservation at most of these lodges doesn't mean that they're not remote. Be sure to find out how you get to and from the ecolodge, and what tours and services are included in your stay. Then think long and hard about whether you really want to put up with hot, humid weather (cool and wet in the cloud forests); biting insects; rugged transportation; and strenuous hikes to see wildlife.

A uniquely Central American lodging type you might encounter is the "apartotel." An apartotel is just what it sounds like: an apartment hotel where you'll get a full kitchen and one or two bedrooms, along with daily maid service. A *posada* is a small, usually family-run, hotel, not unlike a B&B.

Wherever you choose to stay, make sure you keep your doors closed or you might have some unwanted hairy visitors. In very rural areas, and even at a high-end ecolodge, closing your doors won't keep out spiders and other insects. They are everywhere. This is the rainforest, and it's *their* domain. Pack a flashlight for those midnight runs to the kitchen, bathroom, or beach. If you're visiting an ecolodge or hotel in any area near the jungle, most accommodations either have screened-in windows or provide mosquito nets. The exceptions are the bare-bones beach shacks along the coast and rustic huts in the jungle.

Hotels listed as "expensive" throughout this book often offer much cheaper rates for travelers booking through their websites. Your best bet throughout this region is negotiating directly with the hotels themselves, especially the smaller hotels. However, be aware that response times might be slower than you'd like, and many of the smaller hotels might have some trouble communicating back and forth in English. Rates quoted throughout the book reflect double occupancy, and differences between low- and high-season rates are noted wherever possible. (Note that there are some bargains to be had during the low or rainy season.)

Also see "Tips on Accommodations" in the country chapters throughout this book for info. For tips on surfing for hotel deals online, visit Frommers.com.

BELIZE

by Eliot Greenspan

B elize proves the cliché that big things come in small packages. This tiny Central American country has the longest continuous barrier reef in the Western Hemisphere; the largest known Classic Maya city, Caracol; and the highest concentration per square mile of the largest new-world cat, the jaguar. It also has one of the most extensive and easily accessible cave systems for amateur and experienced spelunkers alike, as well as a nearly endless supply of some of the world's best snorkeling and scuba-diving opportunities. "You'd betta Belize it!" goes the common local exclamation. The best part about all the world-class attractions and experiences to be found in Belize is that the country's compact size makes it easy to sample a wide range of them in a short period.

4

Belize is the second-youngest nation in the Western Hemisphere, having been granted independence from Britain in 1981. It's also a sparsely populated country, with just over 300,000 citizens and no large cities. Belize is the only country in Central America where English is the official and predominant language.

Originally a major part of the ancient Maya empire, Belize was next settled by pirates and then colonized by the British, using slave labor. The descendants of each of these groups are woven into the historical lore and cultural fabric of modern Belize. Add to the mix the independent Garífuna people, who settled along the remote southern shore in the early part of the 19th century, and the more recent waves of Mexican, Chinese, and East Indian immigrants, and you have an idea of the cultural meld that constitutes this unique Central American country. Belizeans of all cultural stripes tend to get along a lot better and with far fewer outward and untoward shows of racism than citizens of most other nations. This is a small country. The sense of community is strong and, even in the big city, people tend to know their neighbors; and almost everyone is somehow related.

THE REGIONS IN BRIEF

Bordered to the north by Mexico, to the south and west by Guatemala, and to the east by the Caribbean sea, Belize is a small nation, about the size of the state of Massachusetts.

BELIZE CITY   Belize City is a modest-size coastal port city at the mouth of the Belize River. Although it's no longer the official governmental seat, Belize City remains the most important city—culturally, economically, and historically—in the country. It is also Belize's transportation hub, with the only international airport, an active municipal airport, a cruise-ship dock, and all the major bus-line and water-taxi terminals. Belize City has a reputation as a rough and violent urban center, and visitors should exercise caution and stick to the most popular tourist areas of this small city.

THE NORTHERN CAYES & ATOLLS   This is Belize's primary tourist zone. Hundreds of palm-swept offshore islands lie between the coast of the mainland and the protection of the 298km (185-mile) Barrier Reef. This reef offers some of the world's most exciting snorkeling, scuba diving, and fishing. The most developed cayes here, Ambergris Caye and Caye Caulker, have numerous hotels and small resorts, while some of the less developed cayes maintain the feel of fairy-tale desert isles. In addition, there are two open-ocean atolls here, Turneffe Island Atoll and Lighthouse Reef Atoll. For those whose main sport is catching rays, not fish, it should be mentioned that, for the most part, the cayes, and Belize in general, lack wide, sandy beaches. Although the water is as warm and blue as it's touted to be, most of your sunbathing will be on docks, deck chairs, or imported patches of sand fronting a sea wall or sea-grass patch.

THE CAYO DISTRICT & WESTERN BELIZE   This mountainous district near the Guatemalan border has become Belize's second-most-popular destination. Here you'll find some of Belize's most beautiful countryside and most fascinating natural and man-made sights. The limestone mountains of this region are dotted with numerous caves, sinkholes, jagged peaks, underground rivers, and waterfalls. There are clear-flowing aboveground rivers that are excellent for swimming and canoeing, as well as mile after mile of unexplored forest full of wild animals and hundreds of bird species. Adventurers, nature lovers, and bird-watchers will definitely want to spend some time in the Cayo District. This is also where you'll find Belize's largest and most impressive Maya ruins, Caracol.

SOUTHERN BELIZE   Southern Belize encompasses two major districts, Stann Creek and Toledo. The former includes the Cockscomb Basin Wildlife Sanctuary and the coastal towns of Dangriga, Hopkins Village, and Placencia. Placencia boasts what is arguably the country's best beach. Farther south, the Toledo District is Belize's final frontier. The inland hills and jungles are home to numerous Kekchi and Mopan Maya villages. Hidden in these hills are some lesser known and less visited Maya ruins, including Lubaantun and Nim Li Punit. Off the shores of southern Belize lie more cayes and yet another mid-ocean atoll, Glover's Reef Atoll. The cayes down here get far less traffic and attention than those to the north, and they are perfect for anyone looking for all of the same attractions, but fewer crowds.

NORTHERN BELIZE   Anchored on the south by Belize City, this is the country's business and agricultural heartland. Orange Walk Town and Corozal Town are small cities with a strong Spanish feel and influence, having been settled largely by refugees from Mexico's Caste War. The Maya also lived here, and their memories live on at the ruins of Altun Ha, Lamanai, Cerros, and Santa Rita, all in this zone. Toward the western section of this region lies the Río Bravo Conservation Area, a massive tract of virgin forest, sustainable-yield managed forest, and recovering reforestation areas. Northern Belize has some of the country's prime destinations for bird-watchers, including the Shipstern Nature Reserve and Crooked Tree Wildlife Sanctuary.

THE BEST OF BELIZE IN 1 WEEK

The timing is tight, but this itinerary packs a trio of Belize's best destinations into 1 week. It allows for a chance to visit a major Maya ruin, snorkel on the barrier reef, ride an inner tube on an underground river, and relax a bit on the beach.

Day 1: Arrive & Head to Placencia ★★

Arrive into **Belize City** and grab a quick connecting flight to **Placencia.** Spend the afternoon strolling along the beach and the town's famous sidewalk. For dinner, try the tapas and fusion fare served up at **Rumfish y Vino ★★** (p. 148). Head back to the sidewalk after diner, and enjoy a nightcap mingling with locals and tourists alike at the **Barefoot Beach Bar ★** (p. 149).

Day 2: Way Down Upon the Monkey River

Take a tour on the **Monkey River ★** (p. 144), where you're sure to see a rich array of wildlife. In the afternoon you can treat yourself to a spa treatment, get some snorkeling in, or try a seaweed shake. For dinner, head to the **Maya Beach Hotel Bistro ★★★** (p. 148).

Day 3: Cayo Calling

Fly back to Belize City and pick up a rental car for the drive to the **Cayo District ★★**. Stop at the **Belize Zoo ★★** (p. 100) or for a cave tubing adventure en route. Settle into one of the hotels in San Ignacio or one of the lodges located out on the way to Benque Viejo. If there's time, take an afternoon tour to the ruins at **Xunantunich ★★** (p. 132).

Day 4: Climbing Caana

Wake up early and head to the Maya ruins at **Caracol ★★** (p. 132), stopping at the **Río On Pools ★★** and **Río Frío Cave** (p. 133) on your way back to San Ignacio. For dinner, be sure to treat yourself to the creative cuisine offered up by chef Sean Kuylen at **La Ceiba ★★★** (p. 138).

Days 5 & 6: Fly to the Cayes

Head for the cayes. Choose between **Caye Caulker ★★★**, with its intimate funky charm, or **Ambergris Caye ★**, with its wide choice of hotels, resorts, and restaurants. A whole range of activities and adventures await you here. Be sure to try the snorkel trip to **Hol Chan Marine Reserve ★★** and **Shark-Ray Alley ★★** (p. 110). You can also just chill in the sun and sand.

Day 7: Going Home

Return to Belize City in time for your international connection. If you have a chance, stop at the **Belize Tourism Village** (p. 100) to do some last-minute shopping.

PLANNING YOUR TRIP TO BELIZE

Visitor Information

The **Belize Tourism Board,** 64 Regent St. (P.O. Box 325) in Belize City, will mail you a basic information packet. You can order this packet on their website at **www. travelbelize.org**. Alternatively, folks in the United States and Canada can call the

Belize in 1 Week

0 — 20 mi
0 — 20 km

⊛ National Capital
◉ District Capital
⬣ Ancient Ruins

Santa Elena Chetumal
Chetumal Bay
Corozal Town ◉ Sarteneja   MEXICO

MEXICO

COROZAL

Shipstern Lagoon

San José ○ San Estevan ○
Yo Creek ○ **Orange Walk** ◉

Blue Creek
August Pine Ridge ○
Blue Creek Village ○ San Felipe ○
Lamanai ⬣

Maskall ○

⑥ *Ambergris Caye*
San Pedro ○

⑤ *Caye Caulker*

ORANGE WALK

Old Northern Hwy.
New Northern Hwy.

New River

Altun Ha ⬣

Gallon Jug ○

Hill Bank ○ Bermudian Landing Burrell Boom Ladyville ○

BELIZE

Belize City ◉
① ⑦

Hattieville ○

Spanish Lookout ○
Teakettle ○ *Belize River* **Belmopan** ★
③ *Western Hwy.* *Coastal Hwy.*

Northern Lagoon

Turneffe Atoll

Lighthouse Reef Atoll

③ **Xunantunich** ⬣
San Ignacio ◉
⑤ San Antonio ○

Southern Lagoon
Gales Point ○
Mullins River ○

Hummingbird Hwy.

GUATEMALA

MOUNTAIN PINE RIDGE
Middlesex ○

Dangriga ◉

STANN CREEK
Hopkins Village ○

Glover's Reef Atoll

④ CAYO
Caracol ⬣

MAYA MOUNTAINS

Mango Creek ○ Maya Beach ○
Independence (Big Creek) ○ ① Placencia ○
② Monkey River ○

CARIBBEAN SEA

TOLEDO
San Antonio ○ Big Falls ○
Blue Creek ○

Monkey River

Punta Negra

Punta Gorda ◉
Barranco ○

Gulf of Honduras

Sarstoon River *Bahia de Amatique*

Livingston ○

Bahia de Omoa

GUATEMALA Puerto Barrios ○ HONDURAS

① & ② Belize City & Placencia
② Monkey River
③ Cayo/Belize Zoo & Xunantunich
④ Caracol
⑤ & ⑥ Caye Caulker or Ambergris Caye
⑦ Belize City

Belize Tourism Board toll-free at ☎ **800/624-0686.** Travelers from the United Kingdom, Australia, and New Zealand will have to rely primarily on the website, or dial direct to Belize (☎ **501/227-2420**), because the Belize Tourism Board does not have offices or a toll-free number in these countries.

In addition to the official website listed above, you'll be able to find a wealth of Web-based information on Belize with a few clicks of your mouse. Here are a few good places to begin your clicking:

○ **http://lanic.utexas.edu/la/ca/belize**: The University of Texas Latin American Studies Department's database features an extensive list of useful links.

○ **www.belizeforum.com**: These are active and informative forums on living in and traveling around Belize.

○ **www.belizenews.com**: This site provides links to all of Belize's major online news sources, including the online editions of the major newspapers.

○ **www.toucantrail.com**: This is an excellent site geared toward budget travelers, with extensive links and comprehensive information.

TOUR OPERATORS

Local travel agencies are another good source of information. Two in Belize City to try are **Discovery Expeditions,** 5916 Manatee Dr., Buttonwood Bay (☎ **501/223-0748;** www.discoverybelize.com), and **S&L Travel and Tours ★,** 91 N. Front St. (☎ **501/227-7593;** www.sltravelbelize.com). Perhaps the best, personalized travel advice available is that offered up by Katie Valk at **Belize Trips ★★★** (☎ **501/610-1923** or 223-0376; www.belize-trips.com).

Entry Requirements

A current passport, valid through your departure date, is required for entry into Belize. Driver's licenses and birth certificates are not valid travel documents. In some cases you may be asked to show an onward or return plane ticket.

No visas are required for citizens of the United States; the European community, including Great Britain and Ireland; South Africa; Australia; or New Zealand. Nationals of certain other countries do need a visa or consular permission to enter Belize. For a current list, see the Belize Tourism Board website (**www.travelbelize.org**) or call the nearest Belize consulate or embassy.

Tourists are permitted a maximum stay of 30 days. The **Belize Department of Immigration and Nationality** in Belmopan (☎ **501/822-2423**) will sometimes grant an extension of up to 3 months. These extensions are handled on a case-by-case basis and cost BZ$25 for a maximum extension of 3 months.

BELIZEAN EMBASSY LOCATIONS

In the U.S. & Canada: 2535 Massachusetts Ave. NW, Washington, DC 20008 (☎ **202/332-9636;** www.embassyofbelize.org).

In the U.K.: Belize High Commission, 22 Harcourt House, 45 Crawford Place, London, W1H 4LP (☎ **020/7723-3603;** www.belizehighcommission.com).

In Australia: 5/1 Oliver Rd., Roseville NSW (☎ **02/9905-8144**). There is no Belizean embassy or consulate in New Zealand.

Customs

Visitors to Belize may bring with them any and all reasonable goods and belongings for personal use during their stay. Cameras, computers, and electronic equipment, as

TELEPHONE dialing INFO AT A GLANCE

Belize has a standardized seven-digit phone numbering system. There are no city or area codes to dial from within Belize; use the country code, 501 (not to be confused with the area code for the state of Arkansas), only when dialing a Belizean number from outside Belize.

- **To place a call from your home country to Belize,** dial the international access code (011 in the U.S. and Canada, 0011 in Australia, 0170 in New Zealand, 00 in the U.K.), plus the country code (501), plus the seven-digit phone number.

- **To place a local call within Belize,** dial the seven-digit local number.

- **For directory assistance:** Dial ✆ **113** if you're looking for a number inside Belize, and for numbers to all other countries dial ✆ **115** and (for a charge) an operator will connect you to an international directory assistance operator.

- **For operator assistance:** If you need operator assistance in making a call, dial ✆ **115,** whether you're trying to make a local or an international call.

- **Toll-free numbers:** Numbers beginning with 0800 and 800 within Belize are toll-free, but calling a 1-800 number in the States from Belize is not toll-free. In fact, it costs the same as an overseas call.

well as fishing and diving gear for personal use, are permitted duty-free. Customs officials in Belize seldom check arriving tourists' luggage.

Money

The Belize dollar, abbreviated BZ$, is the official currency of Belize. It is pegged to the U.S. dollar at a ratio of 2 Belize dollars to 1 U.S. dollar. Both currencies are acceptable at almost any business or establishment around the country. As long as you have U.S. dollars or U.S. dollar–based traveler's checks, it is unnecessary to change for Belize dollars in advance of your trip. However, travelers from Canada, Europe, Australia, and New Zealand will want to change a sufficient amount of their home currency to U.S. dollars before traveling.

Once you are in Belize, the change you receive will most likely be in Belize dollars, although it is not uncommon for it to be a mix of both currencies. However, do try to have some small-denomination bills for paying taxis, modest meal tabs, and tips.

Tip: Be careful to note whether the price you are being quoted is in Belize or U.S. dollars. Many hotels, restaurants, and tour operators actually quote in U.S. dollars. If in doubt, ask. At a two-to-one ratio, the difference can be substantial.

ATMS   You'll find internationally accessible ATMs in all major cities or towns and tourist destinations, including Belize City, San Pedro, Caye Caulker, Placencia, Punta Gorda, San Ignacio, Belmopan, Dangriga, and Corozal Town. Still, it's wise to bring some spending cash, and charge the rest of your bills. Try not to rely on your ATM card for an emergency cash bailout.

CREDIT CARDS   Most major credit cards are accepted in Belize, although MasterCard and Visa are much more widely accepted than American Express, especially by smaller hotels, restaurants, and tour operators. While there are some exceptions, Diners Club and Discover have made minimal inroads around Belize.

To report lost or stolen credit cards or traveler's checks, call the following numbers: **American Express,** ✆ 1-336/393-1111 collect from Belize; **Diners Club,** ✆ 1-303/799-1504 collect from Belize; **MasterCard,** ✆ 1-636/722-7111 collect from Belize; and **Visa,** ✆ 1-410/581-9994 collect from Belize.

When to Go

PEAK SEASON Belize's high season for tourism runs from late November to late April, which coincides almost perfectly with the chill of winter in the United States, Canada, and Great Britain. The high season is also the dry season. If you want some unadulterated time on a tropical beach and a little less rain during your rainforest experience, this is the time to visit. During this period (and especially around the Christmas and Easter holidays), the tourism industry operates at full tilt—prices are higher, attractions are more crowded, and reservations need to be made in advance.

CLIMATE The weather in Belize is subtropical and generally similar to that of southern Florida. The average daytime temperature on the coast and cayes is around 80°F (27°C), although it can get considerably warmer during the day during the summer months. During the winter months, when northern cold fronts extend their grip south, it can get downright nippy. In fact, from late December to February, "northers" can hit the coastal and caye areas hard, and hang around for between 3 and 5 days, putting a severe crimp in any beach vacation. The best months for guaranteed sun and fun are March through May.

The rainy season runs from June to mid-November, while the hurricane season runs from July to October, with the most active months being August, September, and October. For the most part, the rainy season is characterized by a dependable and short-lived afternoon shower. However, the amount of rainfall varies considerably with the regions. In the south, there may be more than 150 inches of rain per year, while in the north, it rarely rains more than 50 inches per year. Usually there is also a brief dry period in mid-August, known as the *mauger*. If you're skittish about rain and hurricanes, don't come to Belize between late August and mid-October, the height of both the rainy and hurricane seasons.

The Cayo District and other inland destinations tend to be slightly cooler than the coastal and caye destinations, although since there is generally little elevation gain, the differences tend to be slight.

PUBLIC HOLIDAYS Official holidays in Belize include **January 1** (New Year's Day), **March 9** (Baron Bliss Day), Good Friday, Holy Saturday, Easter Sunday, Easter Monday, **May 1** (Labour Day), **May 24** (Commonwealth Day), **September 10** (St. George's Caye Day), **September 21** (Independence Day), **October 12** (Pan American Day), **November 19** (Garífuna Settlement Day), **December 25** (Christmas Day), **December 26** (Boxing Day), and **December 31** (New Year's Eve).

Health Concerns

Staying healthy on a trip to Belize is predominantly a matter of being a little cautious about what you eat and drink, applying sunscreen, and using common sense. See p. 69 in "Planning Your Trip to Central America" for more info on avoiding and treating illness.

COMMON AILMENTS None of the major tropical illnesses is epidemic in Belize, and your chance of contracting any serious tropical disease in the country is slim. Although **malaria** is found in Belize, it's far from epidemic. It is most common along the coastal lowlands, as well as in some of the more remote southern inland communities. Of greater concern may be **dengue fever,** which seems to be most common in lowland urban areas; Belize City and Dangriga have been the hardest hit cities in Belize. See p. 70 in "Planning Your Trip to Central America" for more info on treating and avoiding these diseases.

DIETARY RED FLAGS Even though the water around Belize is generally safe, particularly in most of the popular tourist destinations, and even if you're careful to buy and drink only bottled water, you still may encounter some intestinal difficulties. Most of this is just due to tender northern stomachs coming into contact with slightly more aggressive Latin American intestinal flora.

VACCINATIONS No specific vaccinations are necessary for travel to Belize, although it is recommended that you be up to date on your tetanus, typhoid, and yellow-fever vaccines. It is also a good idea to get a vaccination for hepatitis A and B.

Getting There

BY PLANE

Belize's international airport is Belize City's **Philip S. W. Goldson International Airport** (**BZE;** ℂ **501/225-2045;** www.pgiabelize.com), which is 16km (10 miles) northwest of the city on the Northern Highway. See p. 95 for info on getting from the airport into town or to other destinations in Belize.

FROM NORTH AMERICA **American Airlines, Continental, Delta, Grupo Taca,** and **US Airways** all have regular direct service to Belize from the U.S. Flying time from Miami is just over 2 hours. From Canada, the only direct flights are seasonal winter charters. See chapter 11 for phone numbers and websites.

FROM THE REST OF THE WORLD There are no direct flights to Belize from Europe, Australia, New Zealand, mainland Asia, or Africa. To get to Belize from any of these points of origin, you will have to connect through one of the major U.S. hub cities, used by the airlines mentioned above.

BY BUS

Belize is connected to both Guatemala and Mexico by regular bus service.

Two separate bus lines, **Línea Dorada** (ℂ **502/7926-0070;** www.tikalmayan world.com) and **San Juan Travel** (ℂ **502/7926-0042**), make the run between Belize City and Guatemala's Petén district. Both can be booked in Belize by **Mundo Maya Travels** (ℂ **501/223-0457;** mundomayatravels@yahoo.com). Alternatively, you can take one of the many buses from Belize City (or from San Ignacio) to the Guatemalan border.

Buses (ℂ **501/227-2255**) connect Belize City to Corazal and the Mexican border. The Mexican border town is Chetumal. From here buses leave roughly every half-hour between 5:30am and 7:30pm.

BY BOAT

Fast water taxis connect Belize to Livingston and Puerto Barrios, Guatemala, as well as the Bay Islands of Honduras. These boats arrive at and depart from both Placencia and Punta Gorda. Ask around the docks at either one of these small towns, and you'll be able to find out current schedules and fares.

Getting Around

BY PLANE   Traveling around Belize by commuter airline is common, easy, and relatively economical. Two local commuter airlines serve all the major tourist destinations around Belize. The carriers are **Maya Island Air** (② **501/223-1140;** www.mayaairways.com) and **Tropic Air** (② **800/422-3435** in the U.S. and Canada, or 501/226-2012 in Belize; www.tropicair.com). Both operate out of both the **Philip S. W. Goldson International Airport** (p. 95) and the Belize City **Municipal Airport** (p. 95). In both cases, flights are considerably less expensive into and out of the Municipal Airport.

BY BUS   Belize has an extensive network of commuter buses serving all the major villages and towns, and tourist destinations in the country. However, this system is used primarily by Belizeans. The buses tend to be a bit antiquated, and buyouts and bankruptcies within the industry have left the status of the local bus network in a state of confusion and limbo. See the destination sections for specific details on schedules, and be sure to check in advance, or as soon as you arrive, as schedules do change regularly. Rates run between BZ$4 and BZ$30.

BY CAR   There are only four major roads in Belize: the Northern, Western, Southern, and Hummingbird highways. All are two-lane affairs, and all have speed bumps as they pass through various towns and villages along their way. Belize is only about 113km (70 miles) wide, and around 403km (250 miles) long. Renting a car is an excellent way to see the country. If you are going to the Mountain Pine Ridge area of the Cayo District, you will certainly need a four-wheel-drive vehicle. However, if you're just visiting the major towns and cities like San Ignacio or Placencia, you'll probably be fine in a standard sedan. It's always nice, however, to have the extra clearance and off-road ability of a four-wheel-drive vehicle, particularly during the rainy season (June through mid-Nov).

Among the major international agencies operating in Belize are **Avis, Budget, Hertz,** and **Thrifty;** see the "Toll-Free Numbers & Websites" section in chapter 11 for info. **Crystal Auto Rental ★** (② **800/777-7777** toll-free in Belize; www.crystal-belize.com) is a local company, with an excellent fleet and good prices.

Prices run between BZ$100 and BZ$220 per day for a late-model compact to a compact SUV, including insurance. Most of the rental companies above have a 25-year-old minimum age requirement for renting, although Crystal Auto Rental will rent to 21- to 24-year-olds, but with twice the deductible.

Often included in the price, car-rental insurance runs about BZ$24 to BZ$40 per day with an average deductible of around BZ$1,500, although sometimes for a few extra dollars per day you can get no-fault, no-deductible coverage.

BY TAXI   There's no standardized look or color to taxis in Belize. Many are old, gas-guzzling American models, although newer Japanese sedans are starting to appear. Most taxis are clearly marked in some form or other, usually with a roof ornament. Very few taxis use meters, so be sure to negotiate your fare in advance.

BY BOAT   While it's possible to fly to a few of the outer cayes, most travel between mainland Belize and the cayes and atolls is done by high-speed launch. There are regular water taxis between Belize City and Ambergris Caye and Caye Caulker. Hotels and resorts on the other islands all either have their own boats or can arrange transport for you.

Tips on Accommodations

Belize has no truly large-scale resorts or hotels. While the Radisson and Best Western chains have one property each in Belize City, there are no other chain hotels in Belize. Upscale travelers looking for over-the-top luxury have few options here. True budget hounds will also find slim pickings, especially in the beach and caye destinations. What the country does have is a host of intimate and interesting **small to midsize hotels** and **small resorts.** Most of these are quite comfortable and reasonably priced, although nowhere near as inexpensive as those in neighboring Mexico and Guatemala.

Belize is a noted ecotourism and bird-watching destination, and there are small nature-oriented **ecolodges** across the inland portion of the country. These lodges offer opportunities to see wildlife and learn about tropical forests. They range from spartan facilities catering primarily to scientific researchers to luxury accommodations that are among the finest in the country.

Tips on Dining

Belizean cuisine is a mix of Caribbean, Mexican, African, Spanish, and Maya culinary influences. Belize's strongest suit is its **seafood.** Fresh fish, lobster, shrimp, and conch are widely available, especially at the beach and island destinations. **Rice and beans** are another major staple, served as an accompaniment to almost any main dish. Often the rice and beans are cooked together, with a touch of coconut milk.

There are seasons for lobster and conch. Officially, lobster season runs from July 15 to February 14, while conch is available from October 1 to June 30. Local restaurants and fishery officials have struck a deal to allow lobster to be served in the off season. Supposedly this is lobster caught and frozen during the open season, and not while they are mating in the closed season.

There is an additional 12.5% GST tax, and a 10% service charge is often added to all restaurant bills. Belizeans rarely tip, but that doesn't mean you shouldn't. If the service was particularly good and attentive, you could leave a little extra.

Tips on Shopping

You won't be bowled over by shopping options in Belize, and few people come to Belize specifically to shop. You will find a modest handicraft industry, with different specialties produced by the country's various ethnic communities. The creole populations of the coastal area and outer cayes specialize in coral and shell jewelry, as well as woodcarvings with maritime (dolphins, turtles, and ships) themes. The Belizean Maya population produces replicas of ancient petroglyphs and different modern designs on varying-sized pieces of slate. Finally, the Garífuna peoples of the southern coastal villages are known for their small dolls.

My favorite gift item in Belize is **Marie Sharp's Hot Sauce ★★★**, which comes in several heat gradations, as well as some new flavors. The original blend of habanero peppers, carrots, and vinegar is one of my all-time favorite hot sauces. The company also produces mango chutney and an assortment of pepper jams. You can pick up Marie Sharp products at any supermarket and most gift shops; I recommend you stick to the supermarkets, though, to avoid price gouging. In addition to Marie Sharp's, Lizette's brand of hot sauces is also a good bet.

[Fast FACTS] BELIZE

American Express
American Express Travel Services is represented in Belize by **Belize Global Travel Services Ltd.,** 41 Albert St. (✆ **501/227-7185**), which can issue traveler's checks and replacement cards, and provide other standard services. They are open Monday through Friday from 8am to noon and 1 to 5pm, and on Saturday from 8am to noon. To report lost or stolen Amex credit card or traveler's checks within Belize, call the local number above, or call collect to ✆ **336/393-1111** in the U.S.

Business Hours Banks are generally open Monday through Friday from 8am to 4:30pm. However, in many small towns, villages, and tourist destinations, bank hours may be limited. In very few instances, banks have begun opening on Saturday. Belizean businesses tend to be open Monday through Friday from 8am to noon, and from 1 to 5pm. Some businesses do not close for lunch, and some open on Saturday. Most bars are open until 1 or 2am, although some go later.

Drugstores There are a handful of pharmacies around Belize City, and in most of the major towns and tourist destinations. Perhaps the best-stocked pharmacy in the country can be found at **Belize**

Medical Associates, 5791 St. Thomas Kings Park (✆ **501/223-0303;** www.belizemedical.com) in Belize City.

Embassies & Consulates The **United States Embassy** is in Belmopan on Floral Park Road (✆ **501/822-4011;** http://belize.usembassy.gov). The **British High Commission** is in Belmopan, at Embassy Square (✆ **501/822-2981;** www.ukinbelize.fco.gov.uk). You can contact the **Canadian Honorary Consul** in Belize City at 80 Princess Margaret Dr. (✆ **501/223-1060**). **Australia** and **New Zealand** do not have an embassy or consulate in Belize.

Emergencies In case of any emergency, dial ✆ **90** from anywhere in Belize. This will connect you to the police. In most cases, ✆ **911** will also work.

Hospitals **Belize Medical Associates,** 5791 St. Thomas Kings Park, Belize City (✆ **501/223-0303;** www.belizemedical.com), is a modern, 24-hour private hospital, with emergency care and private practice physicians. The country's main public hospital, the **Karl Heusner Memorial Hospital,** Princess Margaret Drive, Belize City (✆ **501/223-1548**), is open 24 hours and has a wide range of facilities and services.

Language English is the official language of

Belize, and it is almost universally spoken. However, Belize is a very polyglot country, and you are likely to hear Spanish, Patois, and Garífuna.

Newspapers & Magazines Belize has no daily newspaper. There are four primary weeklies: *Amandala,* the *Reporter, Belize Times,* and the *Guardian.* Most come out on Friday, and all are relatively similar in terms of content, although with some differing and usually obvious political leanings. A couple, most notably *Amandala* and the *Reporter,* actually publish twice weekly, and are my favorites.

Police The police in Belize are generally helpful; there is a dedicated tourism police force in Belize City. Dial ✆ **90** or **911** in an emergency. You can also dial ✆ **501/227-2222.**

Post Offices & Mail Most hotels will post a letter for you, and there are post offices in the major towns. It costs BZ$1 to send a letter to the United States, and BZ$1.20 to send a letter to Europe. Postcards to the same destinations cost BZ$.50 and BZ$.60, respectively.

If your postal needs are urgent, or you want to send anything of value, several international courier and express-mail services have offices in Belize City, including **DHL,** 41

Hydes Lane (☎ **501/223-4350**; www.dhl.com); **FedEx,** 1 Mapp St. (☎ **501/224-5221**; www.fedex.com); and **Trans Express,** 41 Albert St. (☎ **501/227-2332**). All can arrange pickup and delivery services to any hotel in town, and sometimes in the different outlying districts.

Safety Belize City has a reputation for being rough and dangerous, especially after dark, and especially in neighborhoods off the beaten path. While things have improved somewhat, the reputation was earned for a reason. Tourist police patrol the busiest tourist areas during the day and early evenings. Still, while most populous downtown areas and tourist attractions are quite safe during the daytime, travelers are strongly advised to not walk around very much at night, except in the best-lit and most popular sections of downtown. Basic common sense and street smarts are to be employed. Don't wear flashy jewelry or wave wads of cash around. Be aware of your surroundings, and avoid any people and places that make you feel uncomfortable.

Outside of Belize City, things get a lot better, but you should still exercise common sense—make sure your valuables are securely stored and don't venture away from major tourist areas by yourself or after dark.

Rental cars generally stick out and they are easily spotted by thieves, who know that such cars are likely to be full of valuables. Don't ever leave anything of value in an unattended parked car.

Taxes There are departure fees of US$39 that must be paid in cash (in either U.S. or Belize dollars) at the international airport upon departure, although sometimes the fees are already included in your airline ticket; the land exit fee is US$19. There is a 9% hotel tax added to all hotel bills, and there is a 12.5% GST tax on all goods and services. A 10% service charge is sometimes added to restaurant bills. Take this into account when deciding how much to tip.

Telephone If you have an unlocked 850/1900MHz GSM phone, **DigiCell** (☎ **501/227-2017**; www.digicell.bz) sells local prepaid SIM chips with a local number. The chip and initial activation costs BZ$50, including BZ$10 of calls. You can buy subsequent minutes on phone cards in a variety of denominations. The SIM chips and calling cards are sold at their office just outside the airport or at one of their many outlets around Belize. Their website also has information on setting up your home phone for roaming in Belize. But be careful, the rates are quite high. Also see p. 80 in "Planning Your Trip to Central America" and the "Telephone Dialing Info at a Glance" box earlier in this chapter for info.

Tipping Most Belizeans don't tip. Many restaurants add a 10% service charge. However, if the service is particularly good, or if the service charge is not included, tipping is appropriate.

BELIZE CITY

Despite a reputation for crime and violence, periodic devastation from passing hurricanes, and the loss of its capital status, Belize City remains the urban heart and soul of Belize. Most visitors treat Belize City merely as a transition point and transportation hub. This is probably what you'll want to do, too. But if you've got a day or two to burn on a layover here, Belize City is a good place to walk around, admire the fleet of working wooden fish sloops, do some craft and souvenir shopping, and stock up on Marie Sharp's Hot Sauce to bring home with you.

Long ago stripped of its status as the country's capital, Belize City remains Belize's business, transportation, and cultural hub. With a population of 71,000, Belize City is surrounded on three sides by water, and at high tide it is nearly swamped. It's a dense warren of narrow streets and canals (the latter being little more than open sewers, and pungent in hot weather), modern stores, dilapidated shacks, and wooden mansions, coexisting in a seemingly chaotic jumble.

Essentials

GETTING THERE

BY PLANE   All international flights into Belize land at the **Philip S. W. Goldson International Airport** (**BZE**; © **501/225-2045**; www.pgiabelize.com), which is located 16km (10 miles) northwest of the city on the Northern Highway.

In the baggage claim area, there's an information booth maintained by the **Belize Tourist Board.** This booth supplies maps and brochures, and will often make a call for you if you need a hotel or car-rental reservation. Inside the international departure terminal is a branch of **Belize Bank** (© **501/225-2107**), open Monday through Friday from 8:30am to 4pm. Across the parking lot, you'll find car-rental and tour-agency desks, open daily from 8am to 9:30pm. A taxi into town will cost BZ$50 to BZ$60.

If you fly in from somewhere else in Belize, you might land at the **Municipal Airport** (**TZA**; no phone), which is on the edge of town. A taxi from here costs just BZ$10. There's no bank or any other services at the municipal airport, although most car-rental agencies can arrange to have a car there for you.

BY BUS   If you arrive in town by bus, you'll probably end up at the main **bus terminal** on West Collet Canal Street. A taxi from the bus station to any hotel in town will cost around BZ$8 to BZ$10.

ORIENTATION

Belize City is surrounded on three sides by water, with Haulover Creek dividing the city in two. The Swing Bridge, near the mouth of Haulover Creek, is the main route between the two halves of the city, as well as the city's principal landmark. At the south end of the bridge is Market Square and the start of Regent Street and Albert Street. This is where you'll find most of Belize City's banks, shops, and offices. To the west and east of these two major roads is a grid of smaller roads lined with dilapidated wooden houses. On the north side of the bridge and to the right is the Fort George area. From the southern side of the city, Cemetery Road heads out of town to the west and becomes the Western Highway, while from the northern side of the city, Freetown Road becomes Haulover Road and then the Northern Highway.

GETTING AROUND

BY TAXI   Taxis are plentiful and relatively inexpensive. A ride anywhere in the city should cost between BZ$6 and BZ$15. If you need to call a cab, ask at your hotel or try **Cinderella Plaza Taxi Stand** (© **501/223-0371**), **Taxi Garage Services** (© **501/227-3031**), or **Majestic Taxi** (© **501/203-4465**).

ON FOOT   Belize City's downtown hub is compact and easy to navigate on foot. However, the city has a rather nasty reputation for being unsafe for visitors, and you'd be wise to stick to the busiest sections of downtown and obvious tourist districts. You can easily walk the entire Fort George neighborhood, as well as the compact business area just south of the Swing Bridge. If you need to venture any farther, take a taxi. Be careful when you walk, as sidewalks are often in bad shape and sometimes quite narrow. And don't walk anywhere at night.

BY BUS   While Belize has an extensive network of bus connections to most cities and rural destinations, there is no metropolitan bus system in Belize City.

4

BELIZE | Belize City

BY CAR   There is little need to drive in Belize City. If you do find yourself driving around Belize City, go slowly, as pedestrians can appear out of nowhere, and pay attention to the general flow of traffic and the many one-way streets. Despite this being a former British colony, cars drive on the right-hand side of the road, and distances are listed in miles. Most rental-car agencies are based at the Philip S. W. Goldson International Airport, although a couple have offices downtown or at the Municipal Airport, and almost all will arrange to deliver and pick up your vehicle at any Belize City hotel. See p. 66 for rental-car agency info.

VISITOR INFORMATION

The **Belize Tourist Board** (© 800/624-0686 toll-free in the U.S. and Canada, or 501/227-2420 in Belize; www.travelbelize.org) has its main office at 64 Regent St., in the heart of the business district of Belize City. If you missed their desk at the airport, they have another information desk here with regional brochures, basic maps, and a score of hotel and tour fliers; the office is open Monday through Friday from 8am to 5pm. Local travel agencies are another good source of information. Two in Belize City to try are **Discovery Expeditions,** 5916 Manatee Dr., Buttonwood Bay (© **501/223-0748;** www.discoverybelize.com), and **S&L Travel and Tours,** 91 N. Front St. (© **501/227-7593;** www.sltravelbelize.com).

FAST FACTS   There are several banks within a few blocks of each other along Regent and Albert streets, just south of the Swing Bridge. The main post office (© **501/227-4917**) is located at 3 N. Front St., across from the Swing Bridge.

   Belize Medical Associates, 5791 St. Thomas Kings Park (© **501/223-0303;** www.belizemedical.com), is a modern, 24-hour private hospital, with emergency care and numerous private practice physicians. The city's main public hospital, the **Karl Heusner Memorial Hospital,** Princess Margaret Drive (© **501/223-1548**), is also open 24 hours and has a wide range of facilities and services.

   Most hotels listed here have either Wi-Fi or a small business center with Internet connections. You can also find Internet cafes scattered around the principal business and tourist districts of Belize City. Rates run between BZ$1 and BZ$8 per hour. Alternatively, **BTL** (© **0800/112-4636;** www.btl.net), the state Internet monopoly, sells prepaid cards in denominations of BZ$10, BZ$25, and BZ$50 for connecting your laptop to the Web via a local phone call. In addition, you can buy a 24-hour period of Wi-Fi access from BTL for BZ$30, which will work at a number of hot spots around the city.

   Most folks rely on their hotel's laundry and dry-cleaning services, although these can be expensive. Alternatively, you can try **Belize Dry Cleaners & Laundromat,** 3 Dolphin St. (© **501/227-3396**).

   For restrooms, head to the little cruise-ship tourist village on Fort Street in the Fort George section of Belize City. (Most hotels and restaurants will let tourists use their facilities, too.)

What to See & Do

There really isn't much reason to take a guided tour of Belize City. The downtown center is compact and lends itself easily to self-directed exploration. There are only a handful of interesting attractions, and all are within easy walking distance of the central Swing Bridge. Below, you'll find reviews of the most interesting attractions, as well as a walking tour of the city.

When cruise ships are in town, you'll find a line of trolley cars and horse-drawn carriages just outside the Belize Tourism Village offering rides around the city. Most of these include a stop, with entrance fee included, to the Museum of Belize (p. 97). If you really need a guided tour of the city, ask at your hotel desk for a recommendation, or call **Belize Horse & Carriage Tours** (✆ **501/602-3048**), **Discovery Expeditions** (✆ **501/223-0748**; www.discoverybelize.com), or **S & L Travel and Tours** (✆ **501/227-7593**; www.sltravelbelize.com). These companies offer a whole range of day trips and combinations to the attractions close to the city and even farther afield.

THE TOP ATTRACTIONS

Belize City is light on attractions. The museums mentioned below are quite quaint and provincial by most international standards, although they are worth a visit if you are spending a day getting to know the city, residents, and local history.

Museum of Belize ★★   Housed in what was once "Her Majesty's Prison," this museum features a collection of historical documents, photographs, currency, stamps, and other artifacts, as well as exhibits of Maya pottery and archaeological finds. Although somewhat small, the collection of Maya ceramic, jade, and both ornamental and functional pieces is worth the price of admission. There are also traveling exhibits, and a room featuring attractively mounted insects from Belize. Just so you won't forget the building's history, a prison cell has been restored to its original condition. The museum takes up the two floors of this historic old brick building. Plan on spending between 1 and 2 hours here.

Gabourel Lane, in front of the Central Bank bldg. ✆ **501/223-4524.** Admission BZ$10, BZ$4 for students, free for children. Mon–Fri 9am–5pm.

Old Belize ★ ☺   This attraction aims at providing a comprehensive experience of the natural, cultural, and political history of Belize, with exhibits re-creating everything from a rainforest to a Maya ceremonial cave, a logging camp, and a Garífuna home. Admission includes a 45-minute guided tour, but you'll probably want to stay longer to explore some exhibits on your own, visit the gift shop, or eat at the restaurant. There's even a pretty decent little beach, with a large water slide and children's playground area, and separate zip-line cable adventure. Plan on spending between 1 and 2 hours here—more if you're going to eat or hang out at the beach. While it's certainly touristy, if you have only a limited amount of time in Belize City, or the country in general, this place does give a good overview.

Mile 5, Western Hwy. ✆ **501/222-4129.** www.oldbelize.com. Admission BZ$30, BZ$15 for children 6–12 for full-access package; BZ$5 adults, BZ$3 children for just the museum. Tues–Sat 8am–4pm; Sun–Mon 10am–4pm.

A Walking Tour

The following walking tour covers both the north and south sides of Belize City, which together comprise the historic downtown center. For most of its length, you'll be either right on the water or just a block or two away. As described, the walking tour should take you anywhere from 2 to 4 hours, depending on how much time you take visiting the various attractions. The only major attraction not right on the route below is the Museum of Belize, although it's only a 4-block detour east from the Swing Bridge. The route laid out on this walking tour is pretty safe during daylight hours, but should not be attempted after dark.

ACCOMMODATIONS ■

Belcove Hotel **19**
Coningsby Inn **23**
The Great House **9**
Hotel Mopan **24**
Radisson Fort George
Hotel and Marina **8**

DINING ◆

Bayman's Tavern **8**
Bird's Isle Restaurant
& Bar **27**
Le Petit Café **12**
Macy's **22**
Nerie's I **3**
Nerie's II **7**
Riverside Tavern **4**
The Smokey Mermaid **9**
Sumathi **5**
Wet Lizard **14**

NIGHTLIFE ●

Bird's Isle Restaurant
& Bar **27**
Club Calypso **2**
Princess Hotel & Casino **2**
Radisson Fort George
Hotel and Marina **8**
Riverside Tavern **4**
Thirsty Thursday's **1**
Tinto & Blanco Wine Bar **9**

CARIBBEAN SEA

Barracks Rd.

Eve St.
Daly
Barracks
Craig St.

University
of Belize

Haulover Creek

Belcan
Bridge

Belchina
Bridge

To
Northern
Highway
and Airport
Freetown Rd.

Belize City
★ Belmopan
B E L I Z E

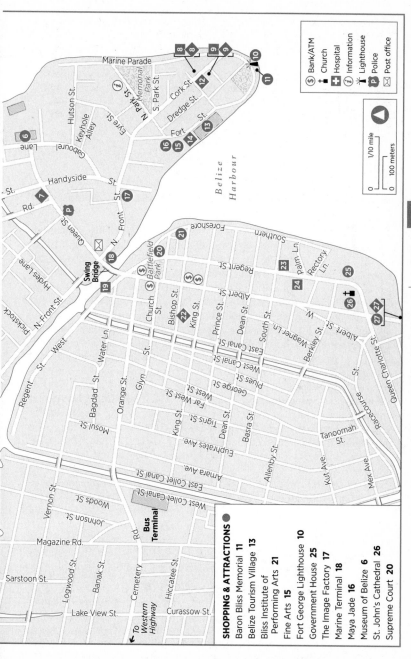

SHOPPING & ATTRACTIONS

Baron Bliss Memorial **11**
Belize Tourism Village **13**
Bliss Institute of
  Performing Arts **21**
Fine Arts **15**
Fort George Lighthouse **10**
Government House **25**
The Image Factory **17**
Marine Terminal **18**
Maya Jade **16**
Museum of Belize **6**
St. John's Cathedral **26**
Supreme Court **20**

4

BELIZE | Belize City

BARON bliss: BOON TO BELIZE

Henry Edward Ernest Victor Bliss, the fourth Baron Bliss of the Kingdom of Portugal, anchored his yacht *Sea King* off of Belize City on January 14, 1926. Within 2 months, the baron would be dead, never having set foot on Belizean soil. Nonetheless, the eccentric Baron Bliss is this tiny country's most beloved benefactor. His time spent anchored in Belize Harbour was enough to convince him to rewrite his will and leave a large chunk of his estate—nearly $2 million at the time—to the country of Belize (then British Honduras). The trust he set up stipulated that the principal could never be touched, and only the interest was to be used. The ongoing bequest has funded numerous public works projects around the country, and today it's hard to miss the baron's legacy. There's the Baron Bliss Memorial, Bliss Institute of Performing Arts, and the Bliss (Fort George) Lighthouse. Every year on March 9, a large regatta is held in Belize Harbour in his honor.

Begin your stroll at the **Fort George Lighthouse** and **Baron Bliss Memorial,** out on the northeastern tip of the city. A small slate stone marks the grave of Henry Edward Ernest Victor Bliss (see "Baron Bliss: Boon to Belize," below). After soaking up the view of the Caribbean and some fresh sea air, head toward downtown on Fort Street. On your left, you'll find the **Belize Tourism Village** (© 501/223-2767), which was built to accommodate the rising tide of cruise-ship passengers. Stop in and shop, or just browse the variety of local and regional arts and crafts.

As you continue, Fort Street becomes North Front Street. Just north of the Belize Tourism Village you'll find **Fine Arts** and the **Image Factory,** by far the two best galleries and fine arts gift shops in the country. Just before reaching the Swing Bridge, you'll find the **Marine Terminal,** where you can pick up water taxis to Ambergris Caye and Caye Caulker.

Now, cross the **Swing Bridge** and head south. On your left is the **Commercial Center.** Wander through the stalls of fresh vegetables, butcher shops, and fish stands. You'll also find some gift shops and souvenir stands here. The **Supreme Court building,** off the small **Battlefield Park** (or Market Sq.) just a block south of the Swing Bridge, is a real prize of English colonial architecture with the city's only clock tower.

Down at the southern end of Regent Street, you'll find the **Government House** and **St. John's Cathedral,** also known by its more official-sounding moniker, the Anglican Cathedral of St. John the Baptist. Both of these buildings were constructed with slave labor in the early 19th century, and they remain the most prominent reminders of the 3 centuries of British colonial presence here. The Government House has been converted into a **House of Culture** (© 501/227-3050), with the mission of encouraging and sponsoring local participation in the arts, music, and dance.

AN ATTRACTION OUTSIDE BELIZE CITY

Founded as part of a last-ditch and improvised effort to keep and care for a host of animals that were being used in a documentary film shoot, the **Belize Zoo ★★**, Western Highway, Mile Marker 29 (© 501/220-8004; www.belizezoo.org), is a national treasure. Gentle paths wind through 12 hectares (30 acres) of land, where the zoo houses more than 125 animals, all native Belizean species, and all orphaned, born at the zoo, rehabilitated, or sent to the Belize Zoo as gifts from other institutions. All the exhibits have informative hand-painted signs accompanying them. It's best to visit early in the morning or close to closing time, when the animals are at their most active and the Belizean sun is at its least oppressive.

The entrance is 180m (600 ft.) in from the Western Highway. Any bus traveling between Belize City and Belmopan or San Ignacio will drop you off at the zoo entrance. Admission is BZ$16 for adults and BZ$8 for children, and the zoo is open daily from 8am to 5pm.

OUTDOOR & WELLNESS ACTIVITIES

Due to the crime, chaos, and often oppressive heat and humidity, you'll probably want to get out of the city, or onto the water, before undertaking anything too strenuous. But if you want to brave the elements, there are a few outdoor activities for you to try in and around Belize City.

FISHING   While most serious fishermen head to one of the cayes or southern Belize destinations, it's possible to line up fishing charters out of Belize City. The marinas at the **Radisson Fort George Hotel & Marina** (✆ 501-223-3333), **Old Belize** (✆ 501-222-4129), and **Princess Hotel & Casino** (✆ 501-223-2670) all have regular sport charter fleets and can arrange a variety of options. You could also check in with the folks at the **Belize River Lodge** (✆ 888/275-4843 in the U.S. and Canada, or 501/225-2002 in Belize; www.belizeriverlodge.com). Expect to pay around US$1,000 to US$1,800 per day for a boat that can accommodate up to four fishermen.

SCUBA DIVING & SNORKELING   The Belize barrier reef lies just off the coast from Belize City. It's a short boat ride to some excellent scuba diving and snorkeling. It is possible to visit any number of excellent sites on day trips from Belize City, including the Blue Hole and Turneffe and Lighthouse atolls. Check in with **Hugh Parkey's Belize Dive Connection** (✆ 888/223-5403 in the U.S. and Canada, or 501/223-5086 in Belize; www.belizediving.com).

SPAS & GYMS   **Best Western Belize Biltmore Plaza** (✆ 800/790-5264 in the U.S. and Canada or 501/223-2302 in Belize; www.belizebiltmore.com) and **Radisson Fort George Hotel & Marina** (p. 102) have small gym facilities and offer basic spa services. However, only the Radisson allows nonguests use of their facilities, with a daily fee of BZ$20.

SWIMMING   Most of the higher-end hotels in Belize City have pools. If yours doesn't, you can head out to the **Cucumber Beach ★** at Old Belize (p. 97). The beach here has both an open-water section and an enclosed, and hence calmer, lagoon. There's also a water slide and children's playground, as well as chaise longues and palm-thatch shade shelters. Admission is BZ$5 for beach access, and BZ$10 for both beach and water-slide privileges. Children are half-price.

SHOPPING

Most shops in the downtown district are open Monday through Saturday from about 8am to 6pm. Some shops close for lunch, while others remain open. Since the cruise ships are such a big market for local merchants, many adjust their hours to specifically coincide with cruise-ship traffic and their particular shore times. By far the largest selection of gift shops and souvenir stands can be found at the **Belize Tourism Village** (8 Fort St.; ✆ 501/223-2767), which is a harborside collection of shops geared toward visiting cruise-ship passengers.

Fine Arts ★★ This is the best gallery and gift shop I've found in Belize. They have a large selection of original artworks in a variety of styles, formats, and sizes. Browse primitivist works by Walter Castillo and Pen Cayetano, alongside more modern abstract pieces, traditional still lifes, and colorful representations of Belize's marine, natural, and human life. 1 Fort St., next to the Belize Tourism Village. *☎* **501/223-7773.** www. fineartsbelize.com.

Maya Jade ★ This place bills itself as a museum and gallery, and while there is a whole room of museum-style displays explaining the history of Mesoamerican Maya jade use and artistry, this is nonetheless predominantly a retail operation. That said, the small selection here includes some very well done necklaces and earrings that you won't find elsewhere. 8 Fort St. *☎* **501/203-1222.**

Where to Stay

Belize City is small, and your options on where to stay are limited. The most picturesque and safest neighborhood by far is the area around the Fort George Lighthouse. You'll find most of the city's best shopping, dining, and accommodations. When getting a price quote from or negotiating with a hotel in Belize, be careful to be clear on whether the price being quoted is in Belize or U.S. dollars.

EXPENSIVE

The Great House ★ This stately colonial-style small hotel is aptly named. Set a block from the water, near the Fort George Lighthouse, this three-story resort and converted mansion was originally built in 1927. All rooms are on either the second or the third floor, and there are no elevators, if that is an issue for you. The rooms on the top floor are my favorites, with high ceilings, wood floors, and a large, shared wraparound veranda. In fact, there are wraparound verandas on both the second and the third floors. While the rooms vary in size, most are very spacious; room no. 1 is one of the largest. Room no. 8 is the smallest room, but it just may have the best view.

13 Cork St. (opposite the Radisson Fort George), Belize City. *☎* **501/223-3400.** Fax 501/223-3444. www.greathousebelize.com. 16 units. BZ$300 double. AE, DISC, MC, V. Free parking. **Amenities:** Restaurant; bar; lounge; concierge; smoke-free rooms. *In room:* A/C, TV, fridge, hair dryer, free Wi-Fi.

Radisson Fort George Hotel & Marina ★★ ☺ This is Belize City's best business-class and luxury hotel. The best rooms here are located in the six-story Club Tower; those on the higher floors have the best views. All are spacious and relatively modern, and feature marble floors and plush furnishings. The Club Tower also has one junior suite on each floor. The Colonial rooms, all of which are nonsmoking, are also large and comfortable. Rooms on the ground floor come with a small private garden terrace, while some of those on the higher floors offer enticing ocean views. The poolside bar here is one of the more popular spots in town, and often features live music. The hotel also features a full-service marina and dive shop, and they've got a comprehensive on-site recycling program.

2 Marine Parade, Belize City. *☎* **800/333-3333** in the U.S., or 501/223-3333 in Belize. Fax 501/227-3820. www.radisson.com. 102 units. BZ$318–BZ$458 double. Rates slightly lower in the off season. AE, DISC, MC, V. Free parking. **Amenities:** 3 restaurants; 2 bars; lounge; babysitting; concierge; well-equipped exercise room; 2 midsize outdoor pools; room service; smoke-free rooms. *In room:* A/C, TV, hair dryer, minibar, free Wi-Fi.

INEXPENSIVE

In addition to the hotel below, you might check out the **Belcove Hotel** (*☎* **501/227-3054;** www.belcove.com), a funky riverside option just north of the Swing Bridge, where doubles range from US$33 to US$52; or **Hotel Mopan** (✆ **501/227-7351;** www.hotelmopan.com; 55 Regent St.), a long-standing and humble little hotel that's a good option in downtown Belize City, where doubles go from US$55 to US$75 (depending on whether you want air-conditioning).

Coningsby Inn 🏄 Housed in a converted old home toward the western end of Regent Street, the rooms here are compact and rather nondescript. Still, they are clean and comfortable. I prefer those on the second floor, although don't choose one of these for the view, which is over an abandoned lot. I would definitely recommend a splurge for one of the air-conditioned rooms. There's a convivial hostel-like vibe to this operation, and the second-floor bar and lounge area is the social hub of the joint.

76 Regent St., Belize City. ✆ **501/227-1566.** Fax 501/227-3726. coningsby_inn@btl.net. 10 units. BZ$100 double without A/C; BZ$120 double with A/C. MC, V. Free street parking. **Amenities:** Bar. *In room:* TV.

NEAR THE AIRPORT

The area around the airport is decidedly undeveloped and of little interest to visitors. Few international flights arrive late enough or leave early enough to necessitate a stay near the airport. Your best bet nearby is the **Belize River Lodge** (✆ **888/275-4843** in the U.S. and Canada, or 501/225-2002 in Belize; www.belizeriverlodge.com), an upscale fishing lodge on the banks of the Belize River, just a few miles from the airport.

Where to Dine

Despite its small size, Belize City has an excellent and varied selection of dining options. While Belizean cuisine and fresh seafood are most common, you can also get excellent Chinese, Indian, and other international fare at restaurants around the city. Note that when the cruise ships are in town, the restaurants in the Fort George area can get extremely crowded, especially for lunch.

MODERATE

In addition to the place listed below, you can get good burgers and bar food at the **Bayman's Tavern** at the Radisson Fort George Hotel (see above). To add some spice to your life, head to **Sumathi** (✆ **501/223-1172**) at 31 Eve St., in the heart of downtown.

Bird's Isle Restaurant & Bar ★ 🏄 BELIZEAN This relaxed restaurant has arguably the best location in the city, seaside on a small island just over a tiny bridge at the far southern end of Regent Street. The main dining hall is a circular wooden deck under a soaring thatch roof. I prefer the open-air seats under shade umbrellas on the wooden deck closer to the water. You can get a range of Belizean staples, fresh seafood, and grilled meats. Portions are hefty. The nightly specials are great deals, especially Wednesdays, with BZ$2.50 burgers. Thursday nights are dedicated to karaoke, while Fridays are turned over to live bands.

Bird's Isle. ✆ **501/207-6500.** Main courses BZ$10–BZ$16; lobster BZ$24. MC, V. Mon–Tues 10:30am–2:30pm; Wed–Sat 10:30am–2:30pm and 5–10pm (Fri–Sat until midnight or later).

Riverside Tavern ★★ INTERNATIONAL One of the most happening spots in Belize City, this large place has both indoor and outdoor seating on a spot overlooking Haulover Creek. The restaurant specializes in hefty steaks and delicious ribs. But you can also get seared tuna, grilled snapper, coconut shrimp, or jerk shrimp. The lunch menu features pizzas, pastas, sandwiches, and rolls. The burgers here—which come in 6-, 10-, and 16-ounce sizes—are rightly famous and served for both lunch and dinner. There are TVs showing sporting events, and at times this place can get quite boisterous.

2 Mapp St. (C) **501/223-5640.** Lunch BZ$15–BZ$40; dinner main courses BZ$24–BZ$60. DISC, MC, V. Mon–Wed 11am–midnight; Thurs–Fri 11am–2am; Sat noon–2am.

The Smokey Mermaid INTERNATIONAL   I love the open-air brick courtyard setting of this semielegant yet relaxed restaurant. There are a couple of raised decks and gazebos and a few fountains, spread out among heavy wooden tables and chairs under broad canvas umbrellas in the shade of large seagrape and mango trees and a wealth of other ferns and flowers. An equally pleasant choice for breakfast, lunch, or dinner, the menu ranges from Jamaican jerk pork to shrimp thermidor to chicken Kiev. I recommend the yuca-crusted catch of the day. The desserts here are excellent, with their signature sweet being the Decadent Ecstasy, a chocolate-coconut pie swimming in ice cream, nuts, and chocolate sauce.

13 Cork St., in the Great House. (C) **501/223-4722.** www.smokymermaid.com. Reservations recommended. Main courses BZ$24–BZ$82. AE, MC, V. Daily 6:30am–10pm.

INEXPENSIVE

In addition to the place listed below, **Nerie's,** which has two locations (124 Freetown Rd., (C) **501/224-5199;** and at the corner of Queen and Daly sts., (C) **501/223-4028;** www.neries.bz), is another simple restaurant specializing in Belizean cuisine, and it's popular with locals. For breakfast, a light bite, or a coffee break, head to **Le Petit Café** ((C) **501/223-3333**) at the Radisson Fort George Hotel. For authentic Belizean cooking and a down-home funky vibe, you can't beat **Macy's** ((C) **501/207-3419**) at 18 Bishop St.

Wet Lizard ★ BELIZEAN   Boasting a prime setting on a second-floor covered deck overlooking the Swing Bridge and Belize City's little harbor, when the cruise ships are in, this raucous restaurant is the most popular spot in town. The menu is simple, with an emphasis on sandwiches, burgers, and American-style bar food. Start things off with some coconut shrimp, conch fritters, or fried calamari, before tackling one of the sandwiches or wraps. You can also get tacos, nachos, fajitas, and burritos, as well as a daily special or two. If you like sweets, save room for the banana chimichanga. The best seats are the small tables and high stools ringing the railing and overlooking the water. Everything is painted in bright colors, and the walls are covered with graffiti and signatures from guests.

1 Fort St. (C) **501/223-5973.** www.thewetlizard.com. Reservations not accepted. Main courses BZ$10–BZ$30. AE, MC, V. Open only when cruise ships are in port.

Belize City After Dark

Belize City is a small, provincial city in an underdeveloped country, so don't expect to find a raging nightlife scene. The most popular nightspots—for both locals and visitors alike—are the bars at the few high-end hotels in town.

PERFORMING ARTS   It's really the luck of the draw as to whether you can catch a concert, theater piece, or dance performance—they are the exception, not the norm. To find out if anything is happening, ask at your hotel, read the local papers, or check in with the **Bliss Institute of Performing Arts** ((C) **501/227-2110**), on Southern Foreshore, between Church and Bishop streets.

THE BAR SCENE   The bar and club scene in Belize City is rather lackluster. The most happening bar in town is the **Riverside Tavern** ★★ (p. 103). This is especially

VOLUNTEER & LEARNING opportunities IN BELIZE

Below are some institutions and organizations that are working on ecology and sustainable development projects.

Cornerstone Foundation ★★ (© 501/678-9909; www.cornerstone foundationbelize.org), based in San Ignacio in the Cayo District, is an excellent and effective nonreligious, nongovernmental peace organization with a variety of volunteer and cultural exchange program opportunities. Programs range from AIDS education to literacy campaigns to renewable resource development and use. Overall, costs are pretty low, and reflect the actual costs of basic food, lodging, and travel in country, with some extra going to support the organization and its work.

International Zoological Expeditions ★★ (© 800/548-5843; www.ize2belize.com) has two research and educational facilities in Belize, on South Water Caye and in Blue Creek Village. IZE organizes and administers a variety of educational and vacation trips to these two stations, for both school groups and individuals. A 10-day program usually costs about US$1,300 to US$1,800.

Maya Research Program at Blue Creek ★ (© 817/831-9011 in the U.S.; www.mayaresearchprogram.org) runs volunteer and educational programs at an ongoing Maya archaeological dig. Two-week sessions allow participants to literally dig in and take part in the excavation of a Maya ruin. The cost is US$1,750 for the 2-week program; discounts are available for longer stays.

Monkey Bay Wildlife Sanctuary ★ (© 501/820-3032; www.monkeybay belize.org) is a private reserve and environmental education center that specializes in hosting study-abroad student groups. They also run their own inhouse educational programs and can arrange a variety of volunteer stays and programs, including homestays with local Belizean families.

Sustainable Harvest International ★★ (© 800/548-5843 in the U.S. and Canada; www.sustainableharvest.org) offers unique programs based on sustainable farming techniques and practices. Their Belize program focuses on organic cacao production in the southern Stann Creek and Toledo districts.

Toledo Institute for Development and Environment ★ (© 501/722-2274; www.tidebelize.org) is a small, grassroots environmental and ecotourism organization working on sustainable development and ecological protection issues in the Toledo District. Contact them directly if you are interested in volunteering.

true on weekends, and whenever there's an important soccer, basketball, or cricket match on. The **Bird's Isle Restaurant & Bar ★** (p. 103) is another lively option, with karaoke on Thursday nights and live music on Fridays. For a casual bar scene, you can also try **Thirsty Thursday's** (© 501/223-1677), out on Newtown Barracks Road. For a somewhat refined place to wet your whistle, head to the **Tinto & Blanco Wine Bar** (© 501/223-4700), a small, dimly lit space on the first floor of the Great House (p. 102), which offers up cocktails, a selection of wines by the glass or bottle, and a small selection of dishes to go along with them.

Travelers and locals alike also tend to frequent the bars at the major hotels and tourist traps. The liveliest are the bars at the **Radisson Fort George Hotel & Marina,** the **Best Western Belize Biltmore Plaza,** and the **Princess Hotel &**

Casino, all of which often have a live band on weekends. Of these, I prefer the **Club Calypso ★** (© **501/223-2670**), an open-air affair built over the water at the Princess Hotel & Casino, although it's sort of a crapshoot as to which bar will be hopping on any given night.

CASINOS For gaming, the **Princess Hotel & Casino** (Newton Barracks King Park, © **888/790-5264** in U.S. and Canada, 501/223-0638 in Belize; www.princess belize.com) is the only game in town, and the casino here is large, modern, and well equipped. While it's not on the scale of Vegas or Atlantic City, the casino is certainly respectable, with enough gaming tables, slots, and other attractions to make most casual gamblers quite happy to drop a few dollars.

Side Trips from Belize City

Given the fact that Belize is so small, it is possible to visit any of the country's major tourist destinations and attractions as a side trip from Belize City. Most are easily reached in less than 2 hours by car, bus, or boat taxi. Other attractions are accessible by short commuter flights. You can visit almost any destination or attraction described in this chapter as a day trip, except for the far southern zone.

Possible destinations for side trips out of Belize City include **Caye Caulker** and **Ambergris Caye,** dive excursions to the nearby reefs, and even the more isolated dive destinations like the **Blue Hole** and the **Lighthouse** and **Turneffe atolls ★★**. **Cave-tubing** excursions are quite popular, and you can also visit the Maya ruins of **Altun Ha, Lamanai, Xunantunich, Cahal Pech,** and even **Caracol** and **Tikal.** All are popularly sold as day tours, often in various mix-and-match combinations.

Most hotels can arrange any of the day trips suggested above. In addition, you can check in with **Discovery Expeditions** (© **501/223-0748;** www.discoverybelize. com) or **S & L Travel and Tours** (© **501/227-7593;** www.sltravelbelize.com). Prices range from about BZ$100 to BZ$300 per person, depending on the tour, means of transportation, and the attraction(s) visited. *Note:* Most of the tours and activities mentioned here and earlier in this chapter are also sold to visiting cruise-ship passengers. When the cruise ships are in town, a cave-tubing adventure, a snorkel trip to Hol Chan Marine Reserve and Shark-Ray Alley, or a visit to either Altun Ha or Lamanai ruins can be a mob scene. If you are organizing your tour or activity with a local operator, mention that you want to avoid the cruise-ship groups, if at all possible.

AMBERGRIS CAYE ★

58km (36 miles) N of Belize City; 64km (40 miles) SE of Corozal Town

Ambergris Caye is Belize's principal sun-and-fun destination. Though Ambergris Caye continues to attract primarily scuba divers and fishermen, it is becoming popular with a wide range of folks who like the slow-paced atmosphere, including an increasing number of snowbirds, expatriates, and retirees. While certainly not akin to big-city traffic, golf carts and automobiles are proliferating and constantly force pedestrians and bicycle riders to the sides of the road. In fact, the ongoing boom has actually led to gridlock. During peak hours, the downtown area of San Pedro is a jumble of golf carts, cars, bicycles, and pedestrians, all moving at a rather slow pace. Development has reached both ends of Ambergris Caye, and steady construction appears destined to fill in the blanks from north to south.

Ambergris Caye is 40km (25 miles) long and only 1km (⅔ mile) wide at its widest point. Long before the British settled Belize, and long before the sun-seeking vacationers and zealous reef divers discovered Ambergris Caye, the Maya were here. In fact, the Maya created Ambergris Caye when they cut a channel through the long, thin peninsula that extended down from what is now Mexico. The channel was cut to facilitate coastal trading and avoid the dangerous barrier reef that begins not too far north of San Pedro.

Despite the fact that much of the island is seasonally flooded mangrove forest, and despite laws prohibiting the cutting of mangroves, developers continue to clear-cut and fill this marginal land. Indiscriminate cutting of the mangroves is having an adverse effect on the nearby barrier reef: Without the mangroves to filter the water and slow the impact of waves, silt is formed and carried out to the reef, where it settles and kills the coral. There is still spectacular diving just off the shore here, but local operators and long-term residents claim to have noticed a difference.

Essentials

GETTING THERE

You've got two options for getting to and from Ambergris Caye: sea or air. The trip is usually beautiful either way. When the weather's rough, it's bumpy both ways, although it's quicker by air, and you're more likely to get wet in the boat.

BY PLANE   There are frequent daily flights between Belize City and **San Pedro Airport** (**SPR;** no phone) on Ambergris Caye. Flights leave from both Philip S. W. Goldson International Airport (p. 95) and Municipal Airport (p. 95) roughly every hour. If you're coming in on an international flight and heading straight for San Pedro, you should book a flight from the international airport. If you're already in Belize City or in transit around the country, it's cheaper to fly from the municipal airport, which is also closer to downtown, and quicker and cheaper to reach by taxi. During the high season, and whenever possible, it's best to have a reservation. However, you can usually just show up at the airport and get a seat on a flight within an hour.

Both **Maya Island Air** (© 501/223-1140 in Belize City, or 226-2435 in San Pedro; www.mayaairways.com) and **Tropic Air** (© 800/422-3435 in the U.S. or Canada, 501/226-2012 in Belize; www.tropicair.com) have 11 flights daily between Goldson International Airport and San Pedro Airport. Flight time is around 15 minutes. These flights actually originate at the Belize City Municipal Airport 10 minutes earlier. When you're ready to leave, flights from San Pedro to Belize City run from 7am to 5pm. Most of these flights stop first at Caye Caulker and then at the international airport before continuing on to the municipal airport. Almost any of the above Tropic Air and Maya Island Air flights can be used to commute between Caye Caulker and San Pedro. Flight duration is just 10 minutes.

Connections to and from all the other major destinations in Belize can be made via the municipal and international airports in Belize City.

 Add It Up: Consider Flying into the Cayes

Because a taxi into Belize City from the international airport costs BZ$50 to BZ$60, and the boat to Ambergris Caye costs BZ$20 to BZ$30, it is only a bit more expensive to fly if you are heading directly to the cayes after arriving on an international flight.

BY BOAT Regularly scheduled boats ply the route between Belize City and Ambergris Caye. All leave from somewhere near the Swing Bridge. Most boats leave directly from the **Marine Terminal,** which is located right on North Front Street just over the Swing Bridge; and the boats are associated with either the **Caye Caulker Water Taxi Association** (✆ 501/223-5752; www.cayecaulkerwatertaxi.com) or **San Pedro Belize Express Water Taxi** (✆ **501/226-3535**). Most are open speedboats with one or two powerful engines. Most carry between 20 and 30 passengers, and make the trip in about 75 minutes. Almost all of these boats drop off and pick up passengers in Caye Caulker on their way. Find out at the Marine Terminal just where and when they stop. The schedule is subject to change, but boats for Ambergris Caye leave the Marine Terminal roughly every 90 minutes beginning at 8am, with the last boat leaving at 4:30pm. The fare is BZ$30 one-way, BZ$60 round-trip between Belize City and Ambergris Caye, and BZ$20 one-way between Caye Caulker and San Pedro. Children travel for half-price.

It is possible to purchase a seat in advance by visiting the Marine Terminal personally. This is a good idea in the high season, although in most cases, you'll need to purchase the ticket in cash upfront. Some Belize City hotels provide this service or can get you a confirmed reservation by phone.

In addition to the Caye Caulker Water Taxi Association, the *Triple J* (✆ 501/223-3464) leaves from Courthouse pier near the Marine Terminal every day at 8 and 10:30am, noon, and 3pm, returning from the Texaco dock on Ambergris Caye at 7 and 9am, and 1 and 3:30pm. The rates for the *Triple J* are similar to those listed above.

GETTING AROUND

The downtown section of San Pedro is easily navigated on foot. Some of the hotels on the northern or southern ends of the island can be quite isolated, however.

Most hotels arrange pickup and drop-off for guests, whether they are arriving or departing by air or sea. Taxis are waiting for all flights that arrive at the airport, and are available for most trips around the island. If your hotel can't call you one, try **Amber Isle Taxi** (✆ **501/226-4060**), **Felix Taxi** (✆ **501/226-2041**), or **Island Taxi** (✆ **501/226-3125**). Fares run between BZ$6 and BZ$20 for most rides.

Golf carts are available for rent from several outlets on the island. Rates run around BZ$120 to BZ$180 per day for a four-seat cart, and BZ$160 to BZ$280 for a six-seat cart. Hourly rates are between BZ$30 and BZ$50. One of the largest and most dependable outfits is **Moncho's Rental** (✆ **501/226-3262**; www.monchosrentals.com). Other dependable options include **Cholo's Golf Cart Rental** (✆ **501/226-2406**) and **Ultimate Cart Rental** (✆ **501/226-3326**; www.ultimaterentalsbelize.com).

I think the best way to get around is on a bicycle. Most hotels have their own bikes, available either free or for a small rental fee. If your hotel doesn't have a bike, call or head to **Joe's Bike Rental** on the south end of Pescador Drive (✆ **501/226-4371**). Rates run around BZ$20 to BZ$30 per day.

Depending on where your hotel is, a water taxi may be your best means for commuting between your accommodations and the restaurants and shops of San Pedro. **Coastal Xpress** (✆ **501/226-2007**; www.coastalxpress.com) runs regularly scheduled launches that cover the length of the island, cruising just offshore from north to south and vice versa. The launches are in radio contact with all the hotels and restaurants, and they stop to pick up and discharge passengers as needed. Rates run around BZ$10 to BZ$50 per person for a jaunt, depending on the length of the ride. Chartered water taxis are also available, and usually charge around BZ$80 to BZ$300, depending on the length of the ride and size of your group.

ORIENTATION

San Pedro (the only town on the island of Ambergris Caye) is just three streets wide. The streets, from seaside to lagoonside, are Barrier Reef Drive (Front St.), Pescador Drive (Middle St.), and Angel Coral Street (Back St.). The airport is at the south end of the busy little downtown. The island stretches both north and south of San Pedro. Less than a mile north of San Pedro there is a small channel, or cut, dividing the island in two. The northern section of the island is much less developed, and is where you will find more of the higher-end isolated resorts. A bridge connects the north and south sections of Ambergris Caye. Pedestrians and bicycles can cross the bridge free, but golf carts and other vehicles must pay a toll of BZ$5 each way.

VISITOR INFORMATION

There's no real tourism information office on Ambergris Caye. Your best source of information will be your hotel desk, or any of the various tour operators around town.

FAST FACTS For the local **police,** dial ✆ **911,** or 501/226-2022; for the **fire department,** dial ✆ **501/226-2372.** In the case of a medical emergency, call the **San Pedro Health Clinic** (✆ **501/226-2536**).

    Atlantic Bank (✆ **501/226-2195**) and **Belize Bank** (✆ **501/226-2450**) are both on Barrier Reef Drive in downtown San Pedro. The **post office** (✆ **501/226-2250**) is on Barrier Reef Drive; it's open Monday through Friday from 8am to noon and from 1 to 5pm. There are plenty of Internet cafes on the island, and most hotels provide connections. One of the best and longest-standing Internet cafes on the island is **Caribbean Connection Internet Café** (✆ **501/226-2573**), at 55 Barrier Reef Dr.

    Most hotels also provide laundry service, but pricing varies widely, so ask first. **Nellie's Laundromat** (✆ **501/226-2454**) is on Pescador Drive toward the south end of town. They charge around BZ$12 per load, and they even offer pickup and delivery service.

What to See & Do

FUN ON & UNDER THE WATER

You should be aware that there really isn't much beach to speak of on Ambergris Caye: There is a narrow strip of sand for much of the length of the island, where the land meets the sea, but even at low tide it isn't wide enough for you to unroll a beach towel on in most places. Many beachfront hotels create their own beaches by building retaining walls and filling them in with sand. You'll find the best of these at the resorts on the northern part of the island, and at Victoria House.

    Likewise, swimming is not what you might expect. For 90m (100 yards) or more out from shore, the bottom is covered with sea grass. In a smart move that prioritizes the environment over tourism, the local and national government have decided to protect the sea grass, which supports a wealth of aquatic life. Beneath the grass is a layer of spongy roots and organic matter topped with a thin layer of white sand. Walking on this spongy sand is somewhat unnerving; there's always the possibility of a sea urchin or stingray lurking, and it's easy to trip and stumble. Swimming is best off the piers, and many of the hotels here have built long piers out into the sea.

FISHING Sportfishing for tarpon, permit, and bonefish is among the best in the world around these cayes and reefs, and over the years a few record catches have been made. If you prefer deep-sea fishing, there's plenty of tuna, dolphin, and marlin to be had beyond the reefs. Outfits that can hook you up (so to speak) include **Fishing San**

Pedro (📞 **501/607-9967**; www.fishingsanpedro.com) and **Go Fish Belize** ★ (📞 **501/226-3121**; www.gofishbelize.com).

Hard-core fishermen might want to check out one of the dedicated fishing lodges, like **El Pescador** ★ (📞 **800/242-2017** in the U.S. and Canada, or 501/226-2398; www.elpescador.com) on Ambergris Caye, or **Turneffe Flats** ★★ (📞 **888/512-8812** in the U.S.; www.tflats.com) out on the Turneffe Island Atoll.

SAILING   The crystal-clear waters, calm seas, and isolated anchorages and snorkeling spots all around Ambergris Caye make this an excellent place to go out for a sail. Your options range from crewed yachts and bareboat charters for multiday adventures, to day cruises and sunset sails. A day cruise, including lunch, drinks, and snorkeling gear, should run between BZ$180 and BZ$300 per person. Most hotels and tour operators around town can hook you up with a day sail or sunset cruise.

SCUBA DIVING & SNORKELING   Just offshore of Ambergris Caye is the longest coral reef in the Western Hemisphere. Snorkeling, scuba diving, and fishing are the main draws here. All are consistently spectacular.

Within a 10- to 20-minute boat ride from the piers lie scores of **world-class dive sites** ★★★, including **Mexico Rocks, Mata Rocks, Tackle Box, Tres Cocos, Esmeralda, Cypress Tunnel,** and **Rocky Point.** A day's diving will almost always feature a mix of steep wall drops and coral caverns and tunnels. You'll see brilliant coral and sponge formations, as well as a wealth of marine life.

There are scores of dive operators in San Pedro, and almost every hotel can arrange a dive trip, either because they have their own dive shop or because they subcontract out. For reliable scuba-diving service and reasonable rates, contact **Amigos del Mar** (📞 **501/226-2706**; amigosdive@btl.net), **Aqua Dives** (📞 **800/641-2994** in the U.S. and Canada, or 501/226-3415; www.aquadives.com), **Ecologic Divers** ★ (📞 **501/226-4118**; www.ecologicdivers.com), or **Patojo's Scuba Center** ★ (📞 **501/226-2283**; patojos@btl.net). Most of these companies, as well as the individual resorts, charge BZ$140 to BZ$220 for a two-tank dive, with equipment rental included. You should be able to get deals on multiday, multidive packages.

THE PERFECT plunge

If you're hesitant to take a tank plunge, don't miss a chance to at least snorkel. There's good snorkeling all along the protected side of the barrier reef, but some of the best is at **Shark-Ray Alley** ★★ and **Hol Chan Marine Reserve** ★★, which are about 6km (3¾ miles) southeast of San Pedro. Shark-Ray Alley provides a nice adrenaline rush for all but the most nonchalant and experienced divers. Here you'll be able to snorkel above and between schools of nurse sharks and stingrays. *Hol chan* is a Mayan term meaning "little channel," which is exactly what you'll find

here—a narrow channel cutting through the shallow coral reef. Some of the more exciting residents of the area are large, green moray eels; stingrays; nurse sharks; and giant grouper. The walls of the channel are popular with divers, and the shallower areas are frequented by snorkelers. Most combination trips to Shark-Ray Alley and Hol Chan Marine Reserve last about 2½ to 3 hours, and cost around BZ$60 to BZ$100. There is a BZ$20 park fee for visiting Hol Chan, which may or may not be included in the price of boat excursions to the reserve.

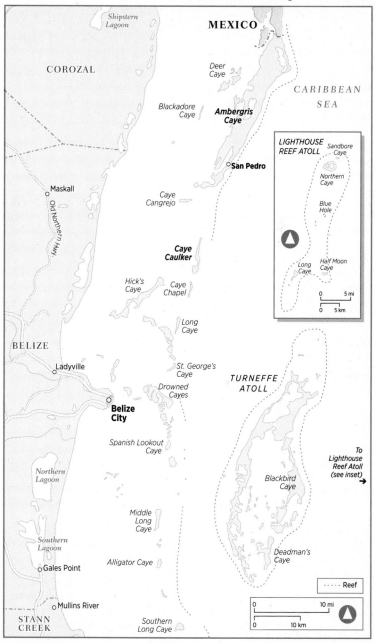

For more adventurous and truly top-rate diving, you'll probably want to head out to the **Turneffe Island Atoll ★★**, **Lighthouse Reef ★★**, and **Blue Hole ★★**. Most of the dive operations on the island offer this trip, or will subcontract it out. You'll definitely want to choose a seaworthy, speedy, and comfortable boat. Most day trips out to Turneffe Island or Lighthouse Reef and Blue Hole run around BZ$320 to BZ$600 per person, including transportation, two or three dives, and tanks and weights, as well as lunch and snacks. All the above-mentioned operators offer day and multiday trips to the outer atoll islands and reefs. Prices average around BZ$600 to BZ$1,000 for a 2-day trip, BZ$800 to BZ$1,500 for a 3-day trip.

Ambergris Caye is also a great place to learn how to dive. In 3 to 4 days, you can get your full open-water certification. These courses run between BZ$650 and BZ$900, including all equipment rentals, class materials, and the processing of your certification, as well as four open-water and reef dives. All of the above-mentioned dive centers, as well as many of the individual resorts here, offer these courses.

There are a host of boats offering snorkeling trips, and most of the above dive operators also offer snorkel trips and equipment rental. Trips to other sites range in price from BZ$30 to BZ$60 for short jaunts to half-day outings, and BZ$100 to BZ$140 for full-day trips. One of the operators who specialize in snorkeling trips here is the very personable Alfonse Graniel and his launch *Li'l Alfonse* (*©* **501/226-3136;** lilalfonse@btl.net). Another good snorkel operator is **Grumpy & Happy** (*©* **501/226-3420;** www.grumpyandhappy.com), a husband-and-wife team that offers private personalized outings. Snorkel gear is available from most of the above operators and at several other sites around town. A full set of mask, fins, and snorkel will usually cost BZ$16 to BZ$30 per person per day.

Tip: Hol Chan and Shark-Ray Alley are extremely popular. If you really want to enjoy them, try to find a boat leaving San Pedro at or before 8am, and head first to Shark-Ray Alley. Most boats dive Hol Chan first, and this is the best way to get a dive with the greatest concentration of nurse sharks and stingrays. By all means, avoid snorkeling or diving these sites at times when the cruise ships are running excursions there. Alternatively, you may want to consider visiting a different snorkeling site, such as Mexico Rocks Coral Gardens, Tres Cocos, or Mata Rocks, where the snorkeling is just as good, if not better, and you're more likely to have the place to yourself.

WINDSURFING, PARASAILING & WATERCRAFT Ambergris Caye is a good place for beginning and intermediate windsurfers. The nearly constant 15- to 20-knot trade winds are perfect for learning on and easy cruising. The protected waters provide some chop, but are generally pretty gentle on beginning board sailors. If you're looking to do some windsurfing, or to try the latest adrenaline boost of kiteboarding, your best bet is to check in with the folks at **Sail Sports Belize** (*©* **501/226-4488;** www.sailsportsbelize.com). Sailboard rentals run around BZ$44 to BZ$54 per hour, or BZ$100 to BZ$140 per day. Kiteboard rentals run BZ$110 for a half-day, and BZ$164 for a full day. Weekly rates are also available. These folks also rent out several types of small sailboats for cruising around close to shore.

Most resort hotels here have their own collection of all or some of the above-mentioned watercraft. Rates run around BZ$40 to BZ$70 per hour for a Hobie Cat, small sailboat, or windsurfer, and BZ$60 to BZ$80 per hour for a jet ski. If not, **Sail Sports Belize** (see above) is your best bet.

FUN ON DRY LAND

BUTTERFLY GARDEN About 7.2km (4½ miles) north of the bridge, **Butterfly Jungle ★** (*©* **501/610-4026;** www.butterflyjungle.org) is a pleasant little attraction with a butterfly breeding program and covered butterfly enclosure. A visit here includes an informative tour and explanation of the butterfly life cycle, as well as a visit to the enclosure, where anywhere from 15 to 30 species may be in flight at any one time. This place is open daily 10am to 5pm, and admission is BZ$20 for adults, free for children 11 and under.

SPAS, YOGA, FITNESS & BODYWORK   While there are no full-scale resort spas or high-end facilities on Ambergris Caye, you can certainly get sore muscles soothed and a wide array of pampering treatments at a series of day spas and independent massage-therapy storefronts. The best of these include the **Art of Touch,** at the entrance to the Sunbreeze Hotel (© **501/226-3357;** www.touchbelize.com), and **Asia Garden Day Spa ★** (© **501/226-4072;** www.asiangardendayspa.com), across from the airstrip. Rates run around BZ$160 to BZ$200 for an hour-long massage.

For a workout, try the modest health club and gym at the **San Pedro Family Fitness Club** (© **501/226-4749;** www.sanpedrofitness.com). These folks also offer aerobic, Pilates, and Tae Bo, and even have a couple of lit tennis courts. This place is a bargain—BZ$30 gets you a full-day pass and access to all facilities.

Finally, if you're in the mood for a good yoga session, you'll want to head just north of the bridge to **Ak'Bol Yoga Retreat ★** (© **501/226-2073;** www.akbol.com), which offers a regular schedule of classes and intensive retreats. They also have rooms and individual cabins, as well as a largely vegetarian restaurant and a small spa.

Shopping

Most of the shopping on Ambergris Caye is typical tourist fare. You'll see tons of T-shirts and tank tops, with dive logos and silk-screen prints of the Blue Hole. Beyond this, the best buy on the island is handmade jewelry sold by local Belizean artisans from makeshift display stands along Barrier Reef Drive. I'd be wary of black coral jewelry, though. Black coral is extremely beautiful, but as with every endangered resource, increased demand just leads to increased harvesting of a slow-growing coral.

Inside Fido's Courtyard at **Belizean Arts ★** (© **501/226-3019**), you'll find the island's best collection of original paintings and crafts. Of special note are the prints and paintings of co-owner Walter Castillo, a Nicaraguan-born artist whose simple, but bold, style captures the Caribbean color and rhythm of Belize.

Another shop at Fido's Courtyard worth checking out is **Ambar ★★** (© **501/226-3101**). The owner and artisan here sells handmade jewelry, with a specialty in amber. The stuff here is a significant cut above the wares you'll find in most other souvenir shops and street stands.

To get your fill of jade, head to the **Ambergris Maya Jade & History Museum,** Barrier Reef Drive (© **501/226-3311**), which has a nice collection of jade artifacts and jewelry, and is really a way to get folks into their retail store.

Where to Stay

IN & AROUND SAN PEDRO

There's a score of hotel options in the heart of San Pedro town. Most are geared toward budget travelers, although a few are quite comfortable and charming. Most of the more upscale resorts are a little bit farther north or south of town.

Very Expensive

The Phoenix ★★★   The stark contemporary architecture here is striking. Most units here are two-bedroom/two-bathroom condo units, although there are a few smaller and a few larger options. All come with full kitchens featuring beautiful granite countertops and stainless steel appliances, a washer and dryer, and large flatscreen televisions in both the living room and the master bedroom. Most have huge balconies that open onto the property's large pool and common area, and the Caribbean sea beyond. The restaurant here, **Red Ginger,** is excellent.

Barrier Reef Dr. (P.O. Box 25), San Pedro, Ambergris Caye. © **877/822-5512** in the U.S. and Canada, or 501/226-2083 in Belize. Fax 501/226-2232. www.thephoenixbelize.com. 30 units. BZ$650–BZ$900 double. Rates lower in the off season, higher during peak periods. AE, MC, V. **Amenities:** Restaurant; bar; concierge; small, contemporary spa and fitness center; 2 outdoor pools; room service. *In room:* A/C, TV/DVD, hair dryer, full kitchen, MP3 docking station, free Wi-Fi.

Victoria House ★★★ 🎁 This elegant and exclusive island retreat features a varied collection of rooms, suites, and villas. Everything is done with a refined sense of style and attention to detail. The resort is set on an expansive piece of land a couple of miles south of San Pedro, with lush tropical gardens and a surprisingly good section of soft white sand fronting it. The plantation rooms and suites are spread through several buildings, and there's a string of individual casitas aligned around a grassy lawn facing the sea. The villas and suites are large, and feature flatscreen televisions and plush furnishings. Some have kitchenettes, and others are duplex units that can be joined or rented separately. Service is attentive yet understated. A full range of tours and activities are offered, and the restaurant here is one of the finest on the island.

Beachfront, 3km (1¾ miles) south of San Pedro (P.O. Box 22, San Pedro), Ambergris Caye. © **800/247-5159** or 713/344-2340 in the U.S., or 501/226-2067 in Belize. www.victoria-house.com. 42 units. BZ$360 double; BZ$596–BZ$624 casita or plantation room; BZ$740–BZ$1,190 suite; BZ$1,190–BZ$2,320 villa. Rates higher during peak weeks, lower in the off season. AE, MC, V. **Amenities:** Restaurant; bar; free bikes; concierge; full-service dive shop; golf cart rental; 2 midsize outdoor pools; watersports equipment rental; free Wi-Fi. *In room:* A/C.

Expensive

The **Blue Tang Inn** (© **866/881-1020** in the U.S. and Canada, or 501/226-2326 in Belize; www.bluetanginn.com) is another good option in this category.

Ramon's Village ★ The handiwork of local son Ramón Núñez, this place is appropriately named, as there is a small-village feel to the collection of thatch-roofed bungalows and suites. At the center of the complex is a small but inviting free-form pool, surrounded by palm trees and flowering plants. Rooms vary in size, and are classified as beachfront, seaside, and garden view, with the beachfront units having the best unobstructed views of the water. All are clean, modern, and comfortable, with colorful-print bedspreads and dark-varnished wood trim. Most have a private or shared balcony with a sitting chair or hammock. There are a few suites, which are larger and provide more room to roam and relax. Room nos. 58 and 61 are large second-floor suites set right near the edge of the sea. Ramon's has one of the longer and prettier beaches to be found in San Pedro.

Coconut Dr. (southern edge of town), San Pedro, Ambergris Caye. © **800/624-4215** in the U.S. and Canada, or 501/226-2067 in Belize. Fax 501/226-2214. www.ramons.com. 61 units. BZ$290–BZ$370 double; BZ$400–BZ$900 suite. Rates slightly higher during peak weeks, lower in the off season. AE, MC, V. **Amenities:** Restaurant; bar; bike and golf cart rental; full-service dive shop; small outdoor pool; room service; watersports equipment rental. *In room:* A/C, hair dryer, no phone.

Sunbreeze ★★ This two-story seafront hotel is built in a horseshoe around a simple garden area, with a small pool at its core. The superior rooms are all spacious, contemporary, and nonsmoking. The standard rooms have small bathrooms, but are otherwise quite acceptable. The five deluxe units feature Jacuzzi tubs and the best views. This hotel is ideally located in the center of town, with its own dive operation and a small arcade of shops. One of the nicest features here is a covered open-air hammock area built over the restaurant and bar. The hotel is directly across from the airstrip, and quite convenient if you are arriving and departing by air.

Coconut Dr. (P.O. Box 14), San Pedro, Ambergris Caye. ℭ **800/688-0191** in the U.S., or 501/226-2191 in Belize. Fax 501/226-2346. www.sunbreeze.net. 42 units. BZ$340 double; BZ$390–BZ$450 deluxe. Rates lower in the off season. AE, MC, V. **Amenities:** Restaurant; bar; bike rental; full-service dive shop; small outdoor pool; room service; smoke-free rooms; watersports equipment rental. *In room:* A/C, TV.

Moderate

In addition to the hotel below, you might want to try **Tides Beach Resort** (Boca del Río Dr., San Pedro; ℭ **501/226-2283;** www.ambergriscaye.com/tides), a three-story oceanfront hotel (from US$85) that's popular with scuba divers and dive groups.

San Pedro Holiday Hotel ★   You can't miss this brilliantly white three-building complex with painted purple-and-pink trim in the center of town. Every room comes with air-conditioning, and most have excellent ocean views and small refrigerators. Get a room on the second floor and you'll have a wonderful balcony—you won't want to leave. Celi McCorkle opened this hotel over 40 years ago, the first on the island, and it's continued to keep pace with the times and tourism boom. This hotel lacks some of the amenities of other options in this price range—there's no swimming pool and not all rooms have televisions—but it makes up for that with its funky island vibe and friendly service.

Barrier Reef Dr. (P.O. Box 61), San Pedro, Ambergris Caye. ℭ **713/893-3825** in the U.S. and Canada, or 501/226-2014 in Belize. Fax 501/226-2295. www.sanpedroholiday.com. 17 units. BZ$220–BZ$250 double; BZ$350 apt. AE, MC, V. **Amenities:** 2 restaurants; bar; bike rental; full-service dive shop; watersports equipment rental. *In room:* A/C, no phone.

Inexpensive

There are quite a few budget options on Ambergris Caye, almost all of them concentrated in the downtown area of San Pedro. True budget hounds should walk around and see who's got the best room for the best price. I list my favorite below.

Ruby's ✦   Most of the rooms at Ruby's overlook the water. The best ones have air-conditioning and a private balcony overlooking the sea. The floors are wooden, the rooms are simply furnished with a couple of beds and little else, and the showers and bathrooms are clean. You can't beat the location at this price in San Pedro. Downstairs you'll find **Ruby's Deli,** which is a good place for breakfast or a casual midday meal. These folks also have a separate hotel on the lagoon side of the island, with clean, spacious, simple rooms at even lower prices. After years of mixed messages, it seems like the owners here have settled on spelling Ruby's with a "y" and not "ie" at the end.

Barrier Reef Dr. (P.O. Box 56), San Pedro, Ambergris Caye. ℭ **501/226-2063.** Fax 501/226-2434. www.ambergriscaye.com/rubys. 21 units. BZ$60–BZ$90 double. MC, V. **Amenities:** Restaurant. *In room:* No phone.

ON NORTH AMBERGRIS CAYE

This is where you'll find most of the larger, more isolated, and more upscale resorts on Ambergris Caye. If you stay here, you will have to rely on your hotel or on the local water taxis to get to and from San Pedro town.

Very Expensive

The individual villas at **Azul Resort** (ℭ **501/226-4012;** www.azulbelize.com) and the boutique **Portino Beach Resort** (ℭ **888/240-1923** in the U.S. and Canada, or 501/678-5096 in Belize; www.portofino.bz) are also good selections.

Captain Morgan's Retreat ★ ☺   Captain Morgan's is a large, lively, and well-equipped resort on a long, lovely section of beach. The rooms are either individual beachfront casitas, or one- or two-bedroom villas set in a series of two- and three-story units. All feature thatch roofs and wood construction, as well as attractive Guatemalan bedspreads and varnished wood furnishings. Every room comes with a private balcony or veranda. I prefer the casitas, which are named after famous pirate captains, for their sense of privacy, although if you want more space and amenities, choose one of the villas, which all come with a fully equipped kitchenette.

Oceanfront, 4.8km (3 miles) north of the cut on northern end of Ambergris Caye. ℂ **888/653-9090** or 307/587-8914 in the U.S., or 501/226-2207 in Belize. Fax 501/226-4171. www.belizevacation.com. 26 units. BZ$398 casita; BZ$498 1-bedroom villa; BZ$840 2-bedroom villa. Rates lower in the off season, higher during peak periods. AE, MC, V. **Amenities:** Restaurant; 2 bars; lounge; complimentary bike use; full-service dive shop; 2 outdoor pools; spa services; watersports equipment rental; free Wi-Fi. *In room:* A/C, minifridge.

Mata Chica ★★★   This boutique resort is hip and chic. Artistic details abound, with an eclectic mix of fabrics, sculptures, ceramics, and paintings from around the world. Every room is a private bungalow or villa, and all can be considered junior suites or better. My favorites are the casitas closest to the ocean, which feature a large sitting area, a king-size bed on a raised platform, and an interior garden shower. Set back, but set high on raised stilts, are two very large villas, and one immense mansion. A large outdoor pool sits in the center of the grounds, and there's another smaller pool, as well as a large outdoor Jacuzzi. There's also a small spa, with a full list of treatments and cures, as well as a full-service tour desk. The hotel also has an excellent restaurant, Mambo.

Oceanfront, northern end of Ambergris Caye. ℂ **501/223-0002** reservations, or 220-5010 at the hotel. Fax 501/220-5012. www.matachica.com. 24 units. BZ$390–BZ$880 double; BZ$1,050–BZ$2,090 villa. Rates include continental breakfast and transfers to and from San Pedro airport. AE, MC, V. **Amenities:** Restaurant; 2 bars; complimentary bike, kayak, and watersports equipment use; 2 outdoor pools; small spa; free Wi-Fi. *In room:* A/C, no phone.

AN ISLAND OF YOUR OWN

Cayo Espanto ★★★   Whether you're a bona fide member of the jet set or you just want to pretend, this is the place for you in Belize. Seven bungalows are spread across this small private island. Each is luxurious and elegantly appointed and set on the ocean's edge. Each comes with a private butler, and all have a private pier jutting out into the ocean. All have wide French doors and windows that open onto private decks and verandas and stunning views. Six of the seven come with a private plunge pool. There's no restaurant or common lounge area here. All meals are served in your villa, or out on your own private deck or dock area. Service is attentive and pampering, and the food is excellent. Cayo Espanto is located just off the western tip of Ambergris Caye.

Cayo Espanto. ℂ **888/666-4282** in the U.S. and Canada. www.aprivateisland.com. 7 units. BZ$2,590–BZ$4,590 double. Rates include 3 meals, all drinks (except wine and champagne), all nonmotorized watersports equipment usage, and transportation to and from San Pedro during daylight hours. Rates slightly higher during peak weeks. AE, MC, V. **Amenities:** Full-service dive operation; small exercise room; 5 small outdoor pools; room service; spa services. *In room:* A/C, TV, hair dryer, minifridge, free Wi-Fi.

Where to Dine

IN & AROUND SAN PEDRO
Expensive

For an elegant dining experience, with fabulous food, setting, and service, it's hard to beat the **Palmilla ★★** (ℂ **501/226-2067**) at the Victoria House (see above).

Blue Water Grill ★★ INTERNATIONAL/ASIAN   This popular place has a broad and extensive menu, as well as a lovely setting overlooking the ocean and piers from the waterfront in the heart of San Pedro. While there's a good selection of pizzas, pastas, and such hearty dishes as grilled beef tenderloin with a creole mustard and black-pepper sauce, or chicken breasts served with fresh herbs, walnuts, and blue cheese, the real reason to come here is for their inspired Asian fare. Start things off with crispy coconut-battered shrimp sticks with a sweet and spicy black-bean dipping sauce. For a main course, I recommend the Japanese spiced grouper with a sesame vinaigrette, or the massive surf and turf. These folks have sushi nights every Tuesday and Thursday. If you come for sushi, be sure to try their spicy scallop hand roll.

At the Sunbreeze hotel, on the waterfront. ✆ **501/226-3347.** www.bluewatergrillbelize.com. Reservations recommended. Main courses BZ$32–BZ$65. AE, MC, V. Daily 7–10:30am, 11:30am–2:30pm, and 6–9:30pm.

Red Ginger ★★ FUSION   Housed in the Phoenix hotel and condo complex, this new restaurant serves up excellent tropical fusion fare in an understatedly elegant room. When the weather permits, you can dine on a patio outside. The long menu offers almost too many temptations. Start with some of the grouper ceviche marinated in mango-lime juice and ginger, or the pulled-pork empanadas. For a main, I recommend the grilled snook with a honey-soy glaze. The nightly chef's tasting menu (BZ$80) is a five-course affair with a variety of choices to meet almost any diner's desire. Lunch is an excellent deal here, and features rotating daily specials.

At the Phoenix hotel, on the waterfront. ✆ **501/226-4623.** www.redgingerbelize.com. Reservations recommended. Main courses BZ$34–BZ$74. AE, MC, V. Wed–Mon 11:30am–2:30pm and 6–9:30pm.

Moderate

Sunset Grill ☺ SEAFOOD/BELIZEAN   Set on a dock over the water on the back side of town, this place serves up excellent local fare and fresh seafood in a convivial, yet relaxed environment. The lunch menu is a bit streamlined, but does include snapper served blackened or with a coconut jerk sauce, although I recommend the fish or shrimp burgers. For dinner, try the Mango Tango Snapper, which is a grilled filet of fresh-caught fish with a spicy mango glaze, and citrus black-bean salsa. A big treat, especially for kids, is the periodic feeding of the massive tarpon who hang around the pier pilings here.

On the lagoon, center of town. ✆ **501/226-2600.** Reservations recommended for dinner. Main courses dinner BZ$35–BZ$65, lunch BZ$16–BZ$34. AE, MC, V. Daily 11am–11pm.

Wild Mangos ★★ INTERNATIONAL/FUSION   Chef Amy Knox has won the Taste of Belize competition twice. The best seats at this down-home open-air joint are those on the outdoor covered wooden deck. The menu is fairly broad and very creative. Start things off with the Tres Amigos, a selection of three different ceviches from their ample menu of creative ceviches. For a main course I like the pan-seared filet of fresh-caught cobia, with a sweet and spicy ancho-honey glaze, or the Conchinita Pibil, a traditional Mayan pork dish slow-cooked in banana leaves. There are often nightly specials, and the desserts are delectable. There's also a somewhat more streamlined lunch menu featuring excellent sandwiches, wraps, tacos, and burritos, as well as salads and other treats.

On the beach, just north of the Sunbreeze Hotel. ✆ **501/226-2859.** Reservations recommended. Main courses dinner BZ$31–BZ$44, lunch BZ$16–BZ$25. AE, MC, V. Mon–Sat noon–3pm and 6–9pm.

Inexpensive

In addition to the places below, **Jambel's Jerk Pit** (✆ 501/226-3515) is right on Barrier Reef Drive. **Ruby's Cafe** and **Celi's Deli,** on the ground floors of Ruby's hotel (p. 115) and the San Pedro Holiday Hotel (p. 115), respectively, are good places to pick up a light meal, and both specialize in fresh-baked breads and pastries, and sandwiches to go.

Other dependable options include **Micky's** (✆ 501/226-2223), which is a popular local joint; **Caramba** (✆ 501/226-4321), which serves a mix of Belizean, Mexican, and Caribbean fare; and **Ali Baba** (✆ 501/226-4042), which specializes in Middle Eastern cuisine. For a seafront seat in the sand, it's hard to beat **Lily's Treasure Chest** (✆ 501/226-2650) or **Estel's Dine By the Sea** (✆ 501/226-2019).

Elvi's Kitchen ★★ BELIZEAN/SEAFOOD/INTERNATIONAL Local legend Elvia Staines began selling burgers out of a takeout window in 1974. Today, Elvi's is arguably the most popular and renowned restaurant on Ambergris Caye, with a word-of-mouth reputation built on the happy bellies of thousands of diners. The restaurant is a thatched, screened-in building with picnic tables, a large flamboyant tree growing up through the roof, and a floor of crushed shells and sand. You can get everything from Belizean stewed chicken to shrimp in watermelon sauce. For lunch, there are still burgers, including traditional beef burgers, although I prefer the shrimp and fish burgers. There's live music every night, with Caribbean night on Thursday, Maya night on Friday, and Mexican night on Saturday. Food specials complement the musical selections.

Pescador Dr., San Pedro. ✆ **501/226-2176.** www.elviskitchen.com. Reservations recommended. Main courses BZ$17–BZ$75; fresh fish, seafood, and lobster priced according to market. AE, MC, V. Mon–Sat 11am–10pm.

ON NORTH AMBERGRIS CAYE

If you're staying in San Pedro or on the southern half of the island, you'll need to take a water taxi. Most of these restaurants will usually be able to arrange this for you, often at a reduced rate from the going fare.

Expensive

In addition to the restaurants reviewed below, you might check out **Mambo** (at Mata Chica, on the northern end of Ambergris Caye; ✆ 501/220-5010), a restaurant with an eclectic menu that touches on a wide range of world cuisines.

Rendezvous Restaurant & Winery ★★ THAI This refined restaurant serves excellent French-influenced Thai cuisine. You'll find Thai classics, such as pad Thai and Larb Nua, and a delicious cold beef salad, right alongside *Cioppini Exotica,* a Mediterranean-inspired seafood stew. There's a relaxed semiformal air to the whole operation, with subdued lighting and cushioned rattan chairs. For a treat, reserve the chef's table, beside the open kitchen, and order up the chef's nightly tasting menu. They vint a few wine varieties right on-site, with imported grape juices. I find these to be pretty immature and thin; you'd do much better to buy an imported bottle off their more traditional wine list.

7km (4½ miles) north of the cut, on the northern section of Ambergris Caye. ✆ **501/226-3426.** Reservations recommended. Main courses BZ$38–BZ$68. MC, V. Wed–Mon noon–2pm and 6–9pm.

Rojo Lounge ★★★ 🎁 FUSION Self-taught chef and owner Jeff Spiegel and his partner Vivian Yu have created an elegant and ultrahip open-air restaurant. There are traditional chairs, as well as couch and plush chair seating, on a broad open deck facing the sea. There's even a table and some bedlike cushions set in a small pool just off the main dining area. It's always wise to try the nightly specials, but whatever you do, don't miss the chorizo, shiitake, and shrimp pot stickers. The guava-glazed baby back ribs are also spectacular. If you're more interested in seafood, there are both crab and grouper cakes, or you could have some homemade conch sausage on a fresh pizza. This place has an extensive wine list, as well as an immense and fabulously stocked bar, and an on-site gourmet market and deli.

At Azul Resort, on the northern section of Ambergris Caye. ✆ **501/226-4012.** www.azulbelize.com. Reservations required. Main courses BZ$36–BZ$68. MC, V. Tues–Sat noon–10pm.

Ambergris Caye After Dark

Ambergris Caye is a popular beach and dive destination, and as such it supports a fairly active nightlife and late-night bar scene. **Wet Willy's** ★ (✆ **501/226-4136**) and the **Tackle Box** (✆ **501/226-4313**), both located off the center of town, occasionally have live music. Another similar option, the **Palapa Bar** ★★ (✆ **501/226-3111;** www.palapabarandgrill.com), is about 1.6km (1 mile) north of the cut on the northern half of the island; this place also sometimes has live music, and boasts a great bar scene both day and night.

Alternatively, you might try one of the beachside bars such as the **Pier Lounge** (✆ **501/226-2002**) at the Spindrift Hotel, which features bingo on Tuesday nights, karaoke on Saturday nights, and the famous "chicken drop," an island version of roulette, at 6pm every Wednesday night. Another popular choice is **Fido's Courtyard** (✆ **501/226-2056**), which has live music every night of the week. For a more chilled-out scene, try the open-air beachfront **La Playa Lounge** (✆ **501/206-2101**).

If you're looking for a dance club and late-night action, your best bets are the two traditional San Pedro discos, **Jaguar's Temple Club** (✆ **501/226-4077**) and **Big Daddy's** (no phone), which are within a stone's throw of each other on Barrier Reef Drive, near the basketball court and the church.

Side Trips from Ambergris Caye

If you've been on the island for a while or want to see more of Belize, a host of tour operators on Ambergris Caye offer excursions to all of the major attractions and destinations around the country, including Altun Ha, Lamanai, Xunantunich, Mountain Pine Ridge, and even Tikal. You can also go cave tubing in the Caves Branch region. Most of these tours involve a flight in a small charter plane.

One of the most popular day trips is to the Maya ruins at Altun Ha. This is also one of the most economical, as it doesn't require a flight. It begins on a powerful boat that will whisk you over to the mainland. You'll take a taxi to the ruins and have lunch before returning to San Pedro. Most operators offering the Altun Ha trip include a lunch stop at Maruba Resort, with the option of adding on a decadent jungle spa treatment. Prices for these trips run around BZ$150 to BZ$300. A similar trip by boat and land is offered to the ruins at Lamanai.

For trips involving a flight, prices range from BZ$250 to BZ$500 per person, depending on the distance traveled and number of activities and attractions crammed into 1 day. Most hotels on the island can book these tours, or you can contact **SEA-duced** (✆ **501/226-2254;** www.seaducedbybelize.com) or **Sea Rious Adventures** (✆ **501/226-4202**).

CAYE CAULKER ★★★

32km (20 miles) N of Belize City; 16km (10 miles) S of Ambergris Caye

While Caye Caulker is no longer the secret hideaway of a few happy hippie backers and chosen cognoscenti, it remains the epitome of a small, isolated, and laid-back Caribbean getaway. Unlike in neighboring San Pedro, you won't find any gridlock traffic here, or be run off the road by cars and golf carts. In fact, golf cart traffic is relatively light, with flip-flops and bicycles fulfilling most of the transportation needs. Let's hope it stays that way. Still, Caye Caulker has begun to experience some of the effects of the boom going on just to the north on Ambergris Caye. There's more development on either end of the island, and the long-neglected northern section of Caye Caulker—across the Split—is starting to be developed.

Essentials

GETTING THERE

As with Ambergris Caye, you've got two options for getting to and from Caye Caulker: sea or air. When the weather's rough it's bumpy both ways, although it's certainly quicker by air, and you're more likely to get wet in the boat.

BY PLANE   Numerous daily flights run between Belize City and **Caye Caulker Airport (CUK;** no phone). Flights leave from both Philip S. W. Goldson International Airport and Municipal Airport roughly every hour. If you're coming in on an international flight and heading straight for Caye Caulker, you should book a flight from the international airport. If you're already in Belize City or in transit around the country, it's cheaper to fly from the municipal airport, which is also closer to downtown.

Both **Maya Island Air** (© **501/223-1140;** www.mayaairways.com) and **Tropic Air** (© **800/422-3435** in the U.S. and Canada, or 501/226-2012 in Belize; www.tropicair.com) have 11 flights daily between Goldson International Airport and Caye Caulker. The flights depart every hour beginning at 7:40am, with the last flight at 5:40pm. Flight time is around 10 minutes. These flights actually originate at the Belize City Municipal Airport 10 minutes earlier. From the municipal airport, the fare should be a bit cheaper. These flights take around 20 minutes, because they stop en route to pick up passengers at the international airport. When you're ready to leave, flights from San Pedro to Belize City run from 7:10am to 5:10pm.

Almost all of the above flights originating in Belize City continue on to San Pedro on Ambergris Caye. Similarly, almost all the return flights originate in San Pedro. The flight between the two islands takes 10 minutes. Connections to and from all the other major destinations in Belize can be made via the municipal and international airports in Belize City.

BY BOAT   Regularly scheduled boats ply the route between Belize City and Caye Caulker. All leave from somewhere near the Swing Bridge, and the majority leave directly from the **Marine Terminal,** which is located right on North Front Street just over the Swing Bridge; the boats are associated with either the **Caye Caulker Water Taxi Association** (© **501/223-5752;** www.cayecaulkerwatertaxi.com) or **San Pedro Belize Express Water Taxi** (© **501/226-3535**). Most are open speedboats with one or two powerful engines, and carry between 20 and 30 passengers, making the trip in about 45 minutes. Almost all of these boats stop to drop off and pick up passengers on St. George's Caye, when there's demand. If you're going to Ambergris or St. George's from Caye Caulker, these boats all continue on and will take you there. Find out on Caye Caulker just where and when they stop. The schedule is subject to

What's in a Name?

The Spanish called this little island "Cayo Hicaco." *Hicaco* is Spanish for the coco plum palm. Some say the name comes from the fact that ships used to be caulked in the calm waters off the backside of this island, hence Caye Caulker. However, a third theory notes that the island appears as Caye Corker on several early British maps. This line of reasoning claims that early sailors and pirates stopped to fill and then "cork" their water bottles with the abundant fresh water found here.

change, but boats for Caye Caulker leave the Marine Terminal roughly every 90 minutes beginning at 8am, with the last boat leaving at 4:30pm. The fare is BZ$20 one-way, BZ$40 round-trip between Belize City and Caye Caulker; and BZ$20 one-way between Caye Caulker and San Pedro.

In addition to the above mentioned companies, the *Triple J* (© 501/223-3464) leaves from Courthouse pier near the Marine Terminal every day at 8 and 10:30am, noon, and 3pm, returning from Caye Caulker at 7:30 and 9:30am, and 1:30 and 4pm. The rates for the *Triple J* are similar to those listed above.

GETTING AROUND

Caye Caulker is small. You can easily walk from one end of the island to the other in around 20 minutes. If you want to cover more ground quickly, a bicycle is your best bet. Many hotels have their own for guests to use free of charge or for a slight rental fee. If not, you can rent a bicycle from one of several stores on Front Street.

While I think it's really unnecessary, you can also rent a golf cart from **Caye Caulker Golf Rentals** (© 501/226-0237), **C & N Golf Carts** (© 501/226-0252), or **Jasmine Cart Rentals** (© 501/206-0212). Rates run around BZ$120 to BZ$180 per day for a four-seat cart.

ORIENTATION

Most boats dock at the pier jutting off Front Street at a spot called Front Bridge—so named because this is the front side of the island facing the reef (east). The town extends north and south from here. As you debark, if you kept walking straight ahead, you'd soon come to the western side of the island and the Back Bridge or dock, where some of the boats dock. Caye Caulker consists of two or three main north-south sand roads, a few cross streets, and numerous paths. The closest street to the water on the east side of the island is Front Street. The next street in is called either Middle Street or Hicaco Avenue, and the next street to the west is called either Back Street or Langosta Avenue. The small Caye Caulker airstrip is on the southern outskirts of town. At the north end of town you'll find the Split or Cut. Much of Caye Caulker is uninhabited. The small town and inhabited sections are quite concentrated.

VISITOR INFORMATION & FAST FACTS

For the local **police,** dial © **911,** or 501/226-2022; for the **fire department,** dial © **501/226-0353.** In case of a medical emergency, call the **Caye Caulker Health Clinic** (© **501/226-0166**).

Atlantic Bank (© **501/226-0207**) is located on Back Street, near the center of the island, and has an ATM that accepts international credit and debit cards. The **post office** (© **501/226-2325**) is also located on Back Street; it's open Monday through Friday from 8am to noon and from 1 to 5pm. There are several **Internet cafes** on the island; just walk along Front Street and find one with an open terminal. I like **Caye Caulker Cyber Café,** which serves drinks—and even has a popular happy hour with reduced rates on drinks and Internet usage. They also have a good book-swap library.

What to See & Do

The main activities on Caye Caulker itself are strolling up and down the sand streets, and swimming and sunbathing off the docks. The most popular spot is at the north end of the island by the **Split ★**. The Split was formed in 1961 when Hurricane Hattie literally split the island in two. Take care when swimming off the docks here. The split is an active channel with regular boat traffic. Also, when the tides are running strong, there's quite a bit of current through the split and it's easy to get dragged along for a few hundred yards or so. If you do get caught in this current, treat it like any riptide: Don't panic, and swim diagonally across the current to get out of it.

Aside from the split, there is not much beach to speak of on the rest of the island. There is a narrow strip of sand for much of the length of the island, where the land meets the sea, but even at low tide it isn't wide enough for you to unroll a beach towel on in most places. In fact, along most of its length this is a small bike and footpath that is probably the busiest thoroughfare on Caye Caulker. Several of the hotels have built long piers out into the sea, with steps down into the water, and swimming is best here.

ON & UNDER THE WATER

KAYAKS & OTHER WATERCRAFT   The calm protected waters just offshore are wonderful for any number of watersports vehicles. Several hotels and tour operators around Caye Caulker have various types of watercraft for guest use, or general rental. Rates run around BZ$20 to BZ$30 per hour for a kayak, BZ$40 to BZ$60 per hour for a Hobie Cat or small sailboat, and BZ$60 to BZ$80 per hour for a jet ski.

KITESURFING & SAILBOARDING   With strong, steady, but not overpowering winds, Caye Caulker is a great place to learn or practice kitesurfing. The folks at **Kitexplorer** (✆ 501/626-4513; www.kitexplorer.com) rent out both kitesurfing and sailboarding equipment. They also offer an intensive 9-hour course in kitesurfing for BZ$740 that is guaranteed to get you up and skimming across the sea.

SAILING   The crystal-clear waters, calm seas, and excellent snorkeling spots around Caye Caulker make this an excellent place to go out for a sail. Unlike on Ambergris Caye, there are no organized bareboat charters available here, but you can go out on any number of different vessels for a half- or full-day sail, a sunset cruise, a moonlight cruise, or a combined sailing and snorkeling adventure. A day cruise, including lunch, drinks, and snorkeling gear, should run between BZ$100 and BZ$240 per person; a half-day tour including drinks, a snack, and snorkeling gear should cost between BZ$70 and BZ$120. Most hotels and tour operators around town can hook you up with an appropriate captain and craft. Or you can head out on the Shark-Ray Alley and Hol Chan tour with **Raggamuffin Tours ★** (✆ 501/226-0348; www.raggamuffintours.com).

SCUBA DIVING & SNORKELING   There's excellent diving and snorkeling close to Caye Caulker. Within a 5- to 20-minute boat ride from the pier lie a couple of world-class dive sites, including **Caye Caulker North Cut, Coral Gardens, Pyramid Flats, Sponge Avenue,** and **Amigos Wreck.** A day's diving here will almost always feature a mix of steep wall drops and coral caverns and tunnels.

Caye Caulker

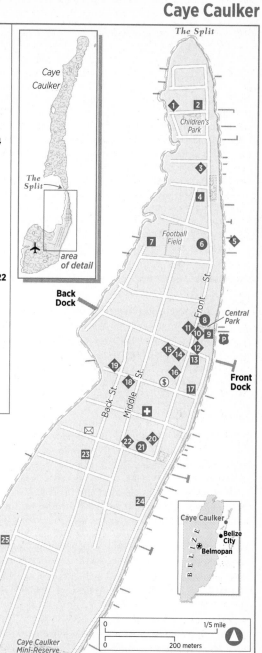

ACCOMMODATIONS■

Caye Reef **2**
De Real Macaw **4**
Iguana Reef **7**
Lazy Iguana
  Bed & Breakfast **25**
Maxhapan Cabins **23**
Popeye's Beach Resort **17**
Seaside Cabanas **13**
Tree Tops Guest House **24**
Yuma's House Belize **9**

DINING◆

Agave **11**
Amor y Café **16**
Don Corleone **3**
Glenda's **19**
Habaneros **14**
Joe's Habanero **20**
Lighthouse Ice Cream
  Parlour **10**
Marin's Restaurant & Bar **22**
Rainbow Grill & Bar **5**
Rose's Grill & Bar **15**
Sand Box Restaurant **12**
Syd's Restaurant & Bar **18**
Wish Willy's **1**

NIGHTLIFE●

Barrier Reef Sports Bar
  & Grill **8**
I&I Bar and Cafe **21**
Oceanside Bar **6**

  $ Bank/ATM
  ✚ Hospital
  P Police
  ✉ Post office

The Split

Caye Caulker

The Split

✈ *area of detail*

Children's Park

Football Field

Front St.

Central Park

Back Dock

Front Dock

Back St.

Middle St.

Airstrip

Caye Caulker Mini-Reserve

Caye Caulker
●Belize City
✱Belmopan
B E L I Z E

| 0 | | 1/5 mile |
| 0 | | 200 meters |

4

BELIZE | Caye Caulker

There are several dependable dive operators on Caye Caulker. Rates are pretty standardized, and you should be able to get deals on multiday, multidive packages. The best dive operations on the island are **Belize Diving Services** ★★ (✆ 501/226-0143; www.belizedivingservice.com) and **Frenchie's Diving** (✆ 501/226-0234; www.frenchiesdivingbelize.com). Both of these operators charge BZ$100 to BZ$180 for a local two-tank dive, with equipment rental running BZ$50 to BZ$60 for a complete package, and BZ$16 to BZ$30 for a mask, snorkel, and fins. All of them also offer a range of certification courses.

For more adventurous diving, you'll probably want to head out to the **Turneffe Island Atoll** ★★, **Lighthouse Reef** ★★, and **Blue Hole.** All of the dive operations on Caye Caulker offer this trip or will subcontract it out. Most day trips out to these dive spots run around BZ$400 to BZ$500 per person, including transportation, two or three dives, tanks, and weights, as well as lunch and snacks.

A host of boats on Caye Caulker offer snorkeling trips, and the above dive operators also offer snorkeling trips and equipment rental. Snorkeling tours range in price from BZ$30 to BZ$60 for short jaunts to half-day outings, and BZ$100 to BZ$180 for full-day trips—a bit more if you want to jump on a trip all the way out to the Blue Hole. A full set of mask, fins, and snorkel will usually cost from BZ$12 to BZ$30 per person per day.

All of the Caye Caulker dive and snorkel operators offer trips to **Shark-Ray Alley** ★★ and **Hol Chan Marine Reserve** ★★. These trips cost between BZ$90 and BZ$280 per person, depending on whether it is a snorkel or scuba dive trip, how long the tour lasts, and whether there is a stop on Ambergris Caye. Many of these include a stop for lunch and a quick walk around town in San Pedro. See p. 110 for more information and a detailed description of Shark-Ray Alley and Hol Chan Marine Reserve.

One of my favorite options for snorkelers is a day cruise to Shark-Ray Alley and Hol Chan with **Raggamuffin Tours** ★ (✆ **501/226-0348;** www.raggamuffintours. com) aboard a classic wooden Belizean sloop. The trip makes three distinct snorkel stops, and includes lunch onboard the boat, snorkeling gear, and the park entrance fee for BZ$90 per person.

FUN ON DRY LAND

Aside from sunbathing, reading, and relaxing, there's little to do on Caye Caulker. However, you could head south of town to the **Caye Caulker Mini-Reserve,** located on the southern outskirts of the town. The term "mini" is certainly fitting. Nevertheless, this local endeavor features a few gentle and well-cleared paths through a small stand of littoral forest. More serious bird-watchers might want to grab a boat and a guide and head to the northern half of the island, where 40 hectares (100 acres) on the northern tip have been declared the **Caye Caulker Forest Reserve.** Over 130 species of resident and migrant birds have been spotted on and around Caye Caulker. No admission fees are charged at either reserve.

EXCURSIONS ON THE MAINLAND

A host of tour operators on Caye Caulker offer excursions to all of the major attractions and destinations around the country, including Altun Ha, Lamanai, Xunantunich, Mountain Pine Ridge, and even Tikal. You can also go cave tubing in the Caves Branch region. Most of these tours involve a flight in a small charter plane.

One of the most popular day trips is to the Maya ruins at Altun Ha. This is also one of the most economical, as it doesn't require a flight. This begins on a powerful boat that will whisk you over to the mainland. You'll then take a taxi to the ruins and have lunch before returning to San Pedro. Most operators offering the Altun Ha trip include a lunch stop at Maruba Resort, with the option of adding on a decadent jungle spa treatment. Prices for these trips run around BZ$140 to BZ$240. A similar trip by boat and land is offered to the ruins at Lamanai.

For trips involving a flight, prices range from BZ$200 to BZ$400 per person, depending on the distance traveled and number of activities and attractions crammed into 1 day. Most hotels on the island can book these tours, or you can contact **Tsunami Adventures** (✆ **501/226-0462;** www.tsunamiadventures.com), a good, all-purpose operator with an extensive list of offerings on and under the water, and all around the cayes and mainland, as well.

Where to Stay

Accommodations on Caye Caulker have improved over the years, but there are still no resorts or real luxury options to be had. In my opinion, this adds to the charm of the place. Budget and midrange lodging options are abundant, and some of these are quite comfortable.

EXPENSIVE

Caye Reef ★★   Fronting the ocean toward the north end of the caye, the two-bedroom, two-bathroom condo units here are fresh, clean and well-equipped. Every unit comes with an ocean-facing balcony, and is decorated with bright Caribbean colors and original local artwork. The rooftop pool, Jacuzzi, and lounge area is a highlight. Cleaning is only once weekly, but that frequency can be increased for a BZ$20 daily fee. Hot water is solar heated and the owners are consciously trying to be sustainable.

Front St. (P.O. Box 31), Caye Caulker. ℂ/fax **501/226-0381** or 610-0240. www.cayereef.com. 6 units. BZ$390 condo; BZ$430 penthouse. Rates slightly higher during peak weeks, lower during the off season. AE, MC, V. **Amenities:** Jacuzzi; outdoor pool. *In room:* A/C, TV, kitchen, free Wi-Fi.

Iguana Reef ★★   This is the closest thing to a resort hotel on Caye Caulker. The spacious rooms are housed in several two-story concrete block structures. All rooms come with air-conditioning, a stocked minibar, and a programmable safe. The deluxe units have a sitting area, a stereo CD player, and a semiprivate veranda. Iguana Reef, which is on the lagoon or back side of the island, has a large and comfortable sandy area for lounging, with a pier leading off this to a nice swimming spot. This is also arguably the best spot on the island to catch a sunset. The hotel also has a very inviting pool.

Back St. (P.O. Box 31), Caye Caulker. ℂ **501/226-0213.** Fax 501/226-0087. www.iguanareeffinn.com. 12 units. BZ$270–BZ$330 double; BZ$750 penthouse. Rates include continental breakfast. Rates slightly higher during peak weeks, lower during the off season. DISC, MC, V. **Amenities:** Restaurant; bar; complimentary kayak use; outdoor pool; free Wi-Fi. *In room:* A/C, stocked minifridge, no phone.

MODERATE

In addition to the place listed below, **Popeye's Beach Resort** (ℂ **501/226-0032;** www.popeyesbeachresort.com) and **Lazy Iguana B & B** (ℂ **501/226-0350;** www. lazyiguana.net) are other good options in this price range.

Seaside Cabanas ★★   This hotel is built in a horseshoe around a small rectangular pool, with a broad wooden deck around it. All the rooms are spacious and painted in lively yellows and reds, and feature modern decorative touches. Four of the rooms come with private rooftop lounge areas with hammocks strung under an open-air thatch roof. These are by far my favorite rooms, but I also like no. 6, a second-floor unit with a small private balcony. There's no restaurant here, but they have a lively bar and an excellent in-house tour operation.

Front St. (P.O. Box 39), Caye Caulker. ℂ **501/226-0498.** Fax 501/226-0125. www.seasidecabanas.com. 17 units. BZ$210–BZ$260 double. Rates slightly higher during peak weeks, lower during the off season. No children 9 and under allowed. AE, MC, V. **Amenities:** Bar; bike rental; outdoor pool; free Wi-Fi. *In room:* A/C, TV/DVD, minifridge, no phone.

INEXPENSIVE

There are scores of budget options on Caye Caulker. I list my favorite and the most dependable choices below. In addition to these, **Yuma's House Belize** (ℂ **501/206-0019;** www.yumashousebelize.com) is a great choice, formerly known as **Tina's Backpacker's Hostel.** This place offers clean, basic rooms, with an oceanfront location and a very lively, hostel-like atmosphere.

De Real Macaw ✦   This place is just north of the center of town, across from a sandy park and the ocean on Front Street. The two "beachfront" rooms are the best rooms, but all are very clean and well kept, with tile floors, tiny television sets, and a front porch or balcony. Most of the rooms come with air-conditioning, but you'll pay more for it. The two-bedroom "condo" and separate beach house both come with a full kitchen, and these folks also rent out fully furnished apartments on a weekly basis, located a little bit away toward the center of town.

Front St., north of Front Bridge, Caye Caulker. ℂ **501/226-0459.** Fax 501/226-0497. www.dereal macaw.biz. 7 units. BZ$50–BZ$110 double without A/C; BZ$120–BZ$140 double with A/C; BZ$240–BZ$260 condo or beach house. Rates lower in the off season. MC, V. *In room:* TV, minifridge, no phone.

Maxhapan Cabins ★   With just three rooms and expansive grounds just outside of the "downtown" hustle and bustle, this place feels like a private oasis. Rooms are housed in two yellow wooden cottages set on raised stilts. The best choice is the individual cabin. Everything is simple, but kept immaculate. There's a communal bar area, as well as a two-story open-air structure meant for chilling out. The owner, Louise, is almost always on hand, providing attentive and personalized service.

Just south of town on 55 Ave. Pueblo Nuevo (P.O. Box 63), Caye Caulker. ℂ **501/226-0118.** maxhapan04@hotmail.com. 3 units. BZ$118 double. MC, V. **Amenities:** Complimentary bike use. *In room:* A/C, minifridge, no phone

Tree Tops Guest House ★ Set just off the ocean in the heart of town, this converted three-story home offers clean, spacious, and cool rooms. There are four rooms on the ground floor. Each comes with tile floors, high ceilings, a standing fan, a cable TV, and a small refrigerator. Two of these share a common bathroom down the hall, but each has a vanity sink in the room itself. However, the best rooms here are the two top-floor suites. Each comes with a king-size bed, cable television, air-conditioning, minifridge, telephone, and private balcony. The Sunset Suite is the best of these, with the largest balcony, and views to both the lagoon and the ocean. If you opt for one of the standard rooms, however, you can still enjoy the view from the rooftop lounge area, which features several hammocks hung under a shade roof.

On the waterfront south of Front Bridge (P.O. Box 29), Caye Caulker. ℂ **501/226-0240.** Fax 501/226-0115. www.treetopsbelize.com. 6 units (4 with private bathroom). BZ$100 double with shared bathroom; BZ$138–BZ$196 double with private bathroom. MC, V. *In room:* TV, minifridge, no phone.

Where to Dine

In addition to the places listed below, **Agave** ★★ (ℂ **501/226-0403**) is an excellent restaurant serving fusion cuisine, and you can't beat the location and ambience of **Rainbow Grill & Bar** (ℂ **501/226-0281**), which is built out over the water.

Also, be sure to stop in at some point at the **Lighthouse Ice Cream Parlour** on Front Street, for a cone or scoop of some fresh, homemade ice cream.

MODERATE

Don Corleone ★★★ ITALIAN/FUSION Contemporary lighting over the bar, combined with slow-turning ceiling fans and polished concrete floors, with heavy wooden tables set with linen tablecloths and fancy flatware, make this the most elegant restaurant on the island. New chef-owner Luca Michelus, from Trieste, via New York, has taken an already established hit and made it better. You can start with an excellent Caesar salad, or try the watermelon salad, with olives and feta cheese. If you don't opt for one of the nightly specials, I recommend the tagliatelle with shrimp and lobster in a pink sauce finished with brandy, although everything is well done. The wine list is varied and fairly priced.

On Front St., north of the center of town. ℂ **501/226-0025.** Reservations recommended during the high season. Pizzas and pastas BZ$22–BZ$34; main courses BZ$28–BZ$50. MC, V. Mon–Sat 5–9:30pm.

Habaneros ★★★ INTERNATIONAL Although the name suggests a Mexican joint, the menu here goes beyond standard Mexican fare. You can get homemade pastas and Thai coconut curries, as well as Brazilian pork. You can also get spicy fajitas made of beef, chicken, or jerk pork. I like to start things off with the Creole Voodoo Cakes, pan-sautéed seafood cakes served with a spicy dipping sauce. The nightly specials tend to be inventive takes on whatever fresh fish and seafood has been caught that day. Heavy wooden tables are spread across the pleasant, open-air, wraparound veranda of this raised-stilt wooden home right on Front Street. There's also indoor seating, but you'll really want to try to grab one of the outdoor spots.

Margaritas and sangria are served by the pitcher, and there's a pretty good wine list for Caye Caulker.

On Front St., near the center of town. ✆ **501/226-0487** or 626-4911. Reservations recommended. Main courses BZ$34–BZ$48. MC, V. Wed–Mon 5:30–10pm.

INEXPENSIVE

Perhaps the best cheap eats on Caye Caulker are the various outdoor grills that set up nightly along Front Street, offering up chicken, shrimp, beef, and lobster (in season) at reasonable rates. In addition, there are several local restaurants serving fresh fish, seafood, and Belizean standards at economical prices. The best of these are **Sand Box Restaurant** (✆ **501/226-0200**), **Syd's Restaurant & Bar** (✆ **501/206-0294**), and **Marin's Restaurant & Bar** (✆ **501/226-0104**). However, my favorite of these local joints is **Rose's Grill & Bar** (✆ **501/226-0407**), on the side street next to Habaneros. For breakfast, head to **Amor y Café** (✆ **501/610-2397**); to check out one of Caye Caulker's most popular spots, head to **Glenda's** (in back of Atlantic Bank; ✆ **501/226-2148**), which specializes in simple Mexican fare. For tasty pizzas, burgers, and Tex-Mex, try **Joe's Habanero ★** (✆ **501/668-8177**), a simple joint with a sand floor, run by the folks behind Habaneros (see above).

Wish Willy's ★ FUSION/SEAFOOD   Serving breakfast, lunch, and dinner out of his own kitchen, Belizean-by-way-of-Chicago chef Maurice Moore has built a reputation for excellent fare in a relaxed open-air yard. Tables are long picnic-style affairs, and you'll often have to share with others. There's no set menu, but it is always built around the freshest ingredients available, simply grilled, or served with an Asian-fusion flare. Conch may come stir-fried in a teriyaki sauce, or in more traditional Belizean-style fritters. And while there are set opening hours, these may be reduced if Maurice's mood or stamina flags.

On the north end of the island, lagoon side, Caye Caulker. ✆ **501/660-7194**. Main courses BZ$10–BZ$18. No credit cards. Daily 7am–9pm (opening hours may vary).

Caye Caulker After Dark

For evening entertainment, you can stargaze, go for a night dive, or have a drink in one of the island's handful of bars. Periodically, one of the bars will crank up the music, and *voilà*—a disco. In general, the scene is so small that most folks will congregate at one or two bars. Which one or two bars are happening might shift from night to night; ask a local or two, and you'll certainly be directed to the current hot spot. My favorite bar is the open-air **I&I Bar and Cafe ★** (✆ **501/625-0344**), which features rustic wooden plank swings for most of its seating. The bar itself takes up the second and third floors of this thatch-roofed wooden structure and is located on a cross street on the southern end of town. Right in the center of town on Front Street, the **Oceanside Bar** (✆ **501/226-0233**) often has either live music or karaoke, and the **Barrier Reef Sports Bar & Grill** (✆ **501/226-0077**) has a good crowd most nights, with everything from trivia contests to sporting events to live music.

Getting Out There: The Outer Atolls

Roughly due east of the northern cayes, out beyond the barrier reef, lie two of Belize's three open ocean atolls, **Turneffe Island Atoll** and **Lighthouse Reef Atoll.** The reef and island rings of tranquillity in the midst of the Caribbean Sea are stunning and pristine places. The outer island atolls are popular destinations for day trips out from Belize City, Ambergris Caye, and Caye Caulker. However, if you really want to experience their unique charms, you should stay at one of the few small lodges located right on the edge of one of them, or on one of the live-aboard dive boats that ply these waters.

EXPLORING THE ATOLLS

Most folks come out here to do one of two things: fish or dive. Some do both. Both activities are world-class. In broad strokes, fishermen should head to Turneffe Island Atoll, while serious divers would probably want to choose Lighthouse Reef Atoll, although there's great diving to be had off Turneffe.

TURNEFFE ISLAND ATOLL ★★   This is the largest of Belize's three ocean atolls, and the largest in the Caribbean Sea. Both the diving and the fishing here are excellent, but the fishing gets a slight nod. The extensive mangrove and saltwater flats are perfect territory for stalking permit, bonefish, snook, and tarpon. Most fishing is done with fly rods, either wading in the flats or from a poled skiff. Turneffe Island Atoll also boasts scores of world-class wall, coral, and sponge garden, and drift dive sites. Most of these sites are located around the southern tip of the atoll. Perhaps the most famous dive site here is the **Elbow ★★★**, a jutting coral point with steep drop-offs, huge sponges, and ample fish life. Another popular site is **Rendezvous Point ★★**, which features several grottoes that divers can swim in and out of, and there's a small modern wreck, the *Sayonara,* sitting in about 9m (30 ft.) of water.

LIGHTHOUSE REEF ATOLL ★★   Boasting nearly 81km (50 miles) of wall and reef diving, including some of the best and most coveted dive sites in all of the Caribbean, this is a true scuba-diving mecca. As the atoll farthest from shore, its waters are incredibly clear and pristine. The central lagoon of this atoll is some 48km (30 miles) long and around 13km (8 miles) wide at its widest point. In the center, you'll find the world-famous **Blue Hole ★★**, a perfectly round mid-atoll sinkhole that plunges straight down to a depth of over 120m (400 ft.). You'll see postcards, photos, and T-shirts all over town showing off aerial views of this perfectly round hole in the ocean. Nearly 300m (1,000 ft.) across, the Blue Hole's eroded limestone karst walls and stalactite formations make this a unique and justifiably popular dive site. However, some of the wall and coral garden dives around the outer edges of the atoll are even better. Of these, **Half Moon Caye Wall ★★** and **North Long Caye Wall ★★** are consistently considered some of the best clear-water coral wall dives in the world.

Water conditions here are amazingly consistent, with an average water temperature of around 80°F (27°C), while visibility on the outer atoll walls and reefs easily averages over 30m (100 ft.).

WHERE TO STAY ON THE OUTER ATOLLS

The lodgings out on the outer atolls are isolated, plush, and pricey. The two main lodges are on Turneffe Island Atoll. Both offer diving and fishing packages, with all transportation, meals, lodging, and activities included. If this is what you're looking for, check out **Turneffe Flats ★★** (✆ **888/512-8812** in the U.S. and Canada; www.tflats.com) or **Turneffe Island Lodge ★★** (✆ **713/236-7739** in the U.S. and Canada; www.turneffelodge.com). If you want to stay here as part of a guided tour, I highly recommend **Island Expeditions ★★** (✆ **800/667-1630** or 604/452-3212 in the U.S. and Canada; www.islandexpeditions.com), who run weeklong adventure excursions here based out of their private tent-camp on Half-Moon Caye.

GETTING THERE   These are remote and isolated destinations. Aside from the lodges, which all offer their own transportation, there is no regularly scheduled transportation here. Private water taxis and charter flights can be arranged.

4

BELIZE

Caye Caulker

Turneffe Island Atoll is a 1½- to 2-hour boat ride from Belize City. The lodges listed above provide their own transportation to and from Belize City as part of their vacation packages.

The quickest and easiest way to get out to these atolls is by helicopter. **Astrum Helicopters** (© **888/278-7864** in the U.S. and Canada, or 501/222-5100 in Belize; www.astrumhelicopters.com) will take you out here for BZ$2,500 in a helicopter that will hold four passengers, and BZ$5,000 in a six-passenger bird.

SAN IGNACIO & THE CAYO DISTRICT ★★

116km (72 miles) W of Belize City; 32km (20 miles) W of Belmopan; 14km (8⅔ miles) E of the Guatemalan border

Western Belize, from the capital city of Belmopan to the Guatemalan border, is a land of rolling hills, dense jungles, abundant waterfalls, clear rivers, extensive caves, and numerous Maya ruins. This region was the heart of the Belizean Maya world, with the major ruins of **Caracol, Xunantunich,** and **El Pilar,** as well as lesser sites like **Cahal Pech.** At the height of the Classic Maya period, there were more residents in this area than in all of modern Belize.

Today, the Cayo District is the heart of Belize's ecotourism industry. There are a host of national parks and protected areas. The pine forests and rainforests here are great for hiking and bird-watching; the rivers are excellent for canoeing, kayaking, and inner-tubing; and the dirt roads are perfect for horseback riding and mountain biking.

The cave systems of the Cayo District were sacred to the ancient Maya, and many of them are open for exploration by novice and experienced spelunkers alike. Some of the more popular underground attractions include **Actun Tunichil Muknal, Barton Creek Cave, Chechem Ha, Crystal Cave,** and the **Río Frío Cave.** Of particular interest is the **Caves Branch River,** which provides the opportunity to float on an inner tube, kayak, or canoe through a series of caves.

Cayo for Short

The name "Cayo" is used to refer to both the Cayo District and the city of San Ignacio.

In the foothills of the mountains close to the Guatemalan border lie the sister towns of Santa Elena and San Ignacio, which are set on either side of the beautiful Macal River. For all intents and purposes, **San Ignacio** is the more important town, both in general terms and particularly for travelers. Just north of town, the Macal and Mopan rivers converge to form the Belize River.

Essentials
GETTING THERE
BY BUS San Ignacio has frequent bus service from Belize City. Buses to San Ignacio leave roughly every half-hour from the main bus station on West Collet Canal Street between 5am and 8pm. Return buses to Belize City leave the main bus station in San Ignacio roughly every half-hour between 4am and 6pm. The fare is BZ$10. The trip takes 2½ hours. Most of the western-bound buses continue on beyond San Ignacio to Benque Viejo and the Guatemalan border. There is no regular direct bus service to the Mountain Pine Ridge area from Belize City.

BY CAR Take the Western Highway from Belize City. It's a straight shot all the way to San Ignacio. You'll come to the small town of Santa Elena first. Across the Macal River lies San Ignacio. If you're heading to San Ignacio and points west, a well-marked detour will lead you through the town of Santa Elena to a Bailey bridge that enters San Ignacio toward the north end of town. The more prominent and impressive Hawksworth Bridge is solely for traffic heading east out of San Ignacio toward Santa Elena, Belmopan, and Belize City.

If you're driving to the Mountain Pine Ridge area, the first turnoff is at Georgeville, around Mile Marker 61. This is the quickest route if you're going deep into the Mountain Pine Ridge area and to Caracol. There's another turnoff in the town of Santa Elena that will take you through Cristo Rey and San Antonio villages, as well as to some of the lodges below. Whichever route you take, the roads merge around Mile Marker 10, where you will come to the entrance to the Mountain Pine Ridge Forest Reserve. A guard will ask you where you are going, and whether you have a reservation, but there is no fee to enter the reserve.

GETTING AROUND

San Ignacio is compact and easily navigated on foot. If you want to visit any of the attractions below, you'll probably have to find transportation. Frequent buses (see above) will take you to the entrances to most of the hotels listed below on Benque Viejo Road, as well as within walking distance of the Xunantunich ruins. Infrequent buses (ask around town or at the bus station; © 501/824-3360) do service the Mountain Pine Ridge area. However, if you don't have your own vehicle, you will probably need to take some taxis or go on organized tours.

You can rent a car from **Cayo Rentals** (© **501/824-2222;** www.cayoautorentals.com) or **Matus Car Rental** (© **501/824-2005;** www.matuscarrental.com). A small four-wheel-drive vehicle here should run you around BZ$120 to BZ$240 per day.

If you need a cab, call the **Cayo Taxi Association** (© **501/824-2196**). Taxi fares around the Cayo District should run you as follows: BZ$6 to BZ$10 around town, BZ$20 between San Ignacio and Bullet Tree Falls, and BZ$50 between San Ignacio and Chaa Creek or duPlooy's. Collective taxis run regularly between downtown San Ignacio and the border at Benque Viejo; the fare is BZ$8 per person.

VISITOR INFORMATION & FAST FACTS

There are several banks right in the heart of downtown San Ignacio: **Atlantic Bank,** at Burns Avenue and Columbus Park (© **501/824-2347**); **Scotiabank,** at Burns Avenue and Riverside Street (© **501/824-4190**); and **Belize Bank,** 16 Burns Ave. (© **501/824-2031**).

To reach the **police,** dial © **911** or 501/824-2022; for the **fire department,** dial © **501/824-2095.** The **San Ignacio Hospital** is on Simpson Street, on the western side of town (© **501/824-2066**). The **post office** (© **501/824-2049**) is on Hudson Street, near the corner of Waight's Avenue.

There are no towns, banks, or general services in the Mountain Pine Ridge, although most hotels in the area do have Internet service.

What to See & Do

The Cayo District is Belize's prime inland tourist destination. There's a lot to see and do in this area, from visiting Maya ruins and caves to a broad range of adventure activities. Most hotels either have their own tour operations or can hook you up with a reputable local operator. In addition, there are several long-standing tour agencies in San Ignacio. Some of the best of these include **Cayo Adventure Tours** (📞 **501/ 824-3246;** www.cayoadventure.com), **Pacz Tours ★★** (📞 **501/824-2477;** www. pacztours.net), and **Yute Expeditions ★** (📞 **501/824-2076;** www.inlandbelize. com). These companies offer nearly all of the options listed in this chapter and more, including multiday tours and adventures.

MAYA RUINS

The Cayo District is in the heart of the Maya highlands, with several major ruins and cave systems used by the ancient residents of this region. The most impressive are **Xunantunich ★★** (on Benque Viejo Rd.) and **Caracol ★★**. Close by, in Guatemala, lies **Tikal ★★★**, perhaps one of the best excavated and most impressive Maya cities in Mesoamerica (see chapter 5).

XUNANTUNICH ★★   Although you may have trouble pronouncing it (say "Zoo-nahn-too-*neetch*"), Xunantunich is an impressive, well-excavated, and easily accessible Maya site. The name translates as "maiden of the rocks." The main pyramid here, El Castillo, rises to 38m (125 ft.) and is clearly visible from the Western Highway as you approach. It's a steep climb, but the view from the top is amazing—don't miss it. You'll be able to make out the twin border towns of Benque Viejo, Belize, and Melchor de Menchos, Guatemala. On the east side of the pyramid, near the top, is a remarkably well-preserved stucco frieze.

Down below in the temple forecourt, archaeologists found three magnificent stelae portraying rulers of the region. These have been moved to the protection of the small, on-site museum, yet the years and ravages of weather have made most of the carvings difficult to decipher. Xunantunich was a thriving Maya city about the same time as Altun Ha, in the Classic Period, about A.D. 600 to 900.

The visitor center at the entrance contains a beautiful scale model of the old city, as well as a replica of the original frieze. Open daily from 8am to 4pm, the site charges an admission of BZ$10. Xunantunich is 10km (6¼ miles) past San Ignacio on the road to Benque Viejo. To reach the ruins, you must cross the Mopan River aboard a tiny hand-cranked car ferry in the village of San José Succotz. After you've crossed the river, it's a short, but dusty and vigorous, uphill walk to the ruins. If you have your own vehicle, you can take it across on the ferry and drive right to the ruins. To get here by bus, take any bus bound for Benque Viejo and get off in San José Succotz.

CARACOL ★★   Caracol (**www.caracol.org**) is the largest known Maya archaeological site in Belize, and one of the great Maya city-states of the Classic era (A.D. 250–950). At one point, Caracol supported a population of over 150,000. Caracol, which means "shell" in Spanish, gets its name from the large number of snail shells found here during early explorations.

Skyscraper

The largest pyramid at Caracol, **Caana** or "Sky Palace," stands some 41m (135 ft.) high, and is the tallest Maya building in Belize, and still the tallest man-made structure in the country.

Caracol has revealed a wealth of informative carved glyphs that have allowed archaeologists to fill in much of the history of this once-powerful city-state. Glyphs here claim Caracol defeated Tikal in A.D. 562 and Naranjo in 631. One of the earliest temples here was built in A.D. 70, and the Caracol royal family has been officially chronicled since 331. The last recorded date on a glyph is 859, and archaeologists conclude that by 1050 Caracol had been completely abandoned.

Caracol is open daily from 8am to 4pm; admission is BZ$15. There's a small visitor center at the entrance, and a guide can sometimes be hired here, although most visitors come with their own guide as part of an organized tour. Caracol is about 81km (50 miles) along a dirt road from the Western Highway. Actually, the final 16km (10 miles) into the park are paved. Plan on the drive taking about 2 hours, or more if the road is in bad shape. A visit to Caracol is often combined with a stop at the **Río On Pools,** or some of the other attractions in the Mountain Pine Ridge area.

WILL NATURAL WONDERS NEVER CEASE?

WATERFALLS   Waterfalls are abundant in this region. Perhaps my favorite is the falls found at the **Río On Pools ★★**. This is a series of falls and pools somewhat reminiscent of Ocho Ríos in Jamaica. There's an entrance hut and parking lot when you enter the area. From here, some concrete steps lead straight down a steep hill to the base of the falls. While the views and swimming are fine at the bottom, it's a strenuous hike back up, and I think you'll find better pools and views by hiking a few minutes upstream. Here you'll find numerous pools and rapids flowing between big rocks. Many of these rocks are perfect for sunbathing. The Río On Pools are around Mile Marker 18½ of the Pine Ridge Road. There's no entrance fee.

You can also visit the **Five Sister Falls ★★**, a lovely series of cascading falls, that divide into five distinct side-by-side cascades just above the riverside beach and bar area of the Five Sisters Lodge. If you are not staying at the lodge, you may visit the falls for BZ$10. The hotel has a little beach area and several natural swimming holes, near the base of the falls. There are also some nature trails you can hike, and a small snack bar, restrooms, and changing facilities. You'll even find a wonderful open-air thatch palapa on the banks of the river strung with hammocks—a compelling spot for an afternoon siesta.

BARTON CREEK CAVE ★   This is one of the area's easier caves to explore. The trip is conducted by canoe, and while there are a few tight squeezes and areas with low ceilings, in general you won't get as wet or claustrophobic here as you will at some of the other caves in Belize. Located beside a small Mennonite community, Barton Creek is navigable for nearly a mile inside the cave. Along the way, by the light of headlamps and strong flashlights, you'll see wonderful natural formations, a large gallery, and numerous Maya artifacts, including several skeletons believed to be the remains of ritual sacrifices.

There's a BZ$10 fee to visit the site, but that doesn't include the canoe trip or transportation. If you drive there yourself, you can hire a canoe that holds two passengers, plus the guide, for around BZ$30 to BZ$40. Tours out of San Ignacio average around BZ$100 to BZ$120 per person, not including the entrance fee. Barton Creek Cave is located just off the Pine Ridge Road, about 6km (3¾ miles) from the Western Highway.

RIO FRIO CAVE   This high vaulted cave is about 180m (600 ft.) long and open at both ends, with a lazy creek flowing through it. There's a path leading through the cave, and several hiking trails through the forests surrounding it. Along the neighboring trails, you will find other caves that you can venture into. However, be careful and be sure to have a good flashlight. To reach the Río Frío Cave, drive the Pine Ridge Road to Douglas Da Silva Village at about Mile Marker 24. Do not follow the turnoff for Caracol, but head into the little village. Here you will see signs for the turnoff to the cave. The cave is about a mile outside the village. There's a small parking area very close to the mouth of the cave and a couple of picnic tables and benches along the river. No admission is charged to visit here.

BUTTERFLIES The **Green Hills Butterfly Ranch & Botanical Collection** (℡ **501/820-4017**; www.green-hills.net) is a lovely project where you'll get to see numerous butterfly species and a range of tropical flora. These folks raise dozens of species of butterflies, and visitors get to see them up close and personal. Located near Mile Marker 8 of the Pine Ridge Road, the ranch offers guided tours (BZ$25) daily, between 8am and 3:30pm. Reservations are recommended.

Just off the main road at Mile Marker 7½ near the village of San José Succotz, **Tropical Wings Nature Center** (℡ **501/823-2265**) similarly features an enclosed butterfly garden with scores of brightly colored and varied species flitting about. There's also a butterfly breeding center, as well as an open-air medicinal plant nature trail. Hummingbird feeders ensure that you'll be buzzed by these frenetic flighty creatures. This place is open daily from 9am to 5pm; admission is BZ$6.

BOTANICAL GARDENS ★★ Next to duPlooy's and run by the same family, the **Belize Botanic Gardens** ★★ (℡ **501/824-3101**; www.belizebotanic.org) is a sprawling collection of local and imported tropical fauna. They have an excellent mix of fruit trees, palms, bromeliads, and bamboos, all well laid out whether you are taking a self-guided or guided tour. The orchid house is not to be missed, with its beautiful collection of orchids and its sculpted waterfall wall. The gardens are open daily from 7am to 5pm. Admission is BZ$10. Guided tours cost BZ$15 per person, including the entrance fee. You can buy a helpful self-guided tour booklet, or take a leisurely horse-and-buggy ride through the lovely gardens.

Located directly between the Chaa Creek and the Macal River Jungle Camp, the **Rainforest Medicine Trail** ★ (℡ **501/824-2037**) is the former Ix Chel Farm, which was set up by Drs. Rosita Arvigo and Greg Shropshire. Rosita studied traditional herbal medicine with Don Elijio Panti, a local Maya medicine man and a folk hero in Belize. The farm boasts a gift shop that features local crafts, T-shirts, and relevant books, including a couple by Arvigo. You'll also find Ix Chel's line of herbal concentrates, salves, and teas called Rainforest Remedies. Self-guided visits to the Medicine Trail, along with a tour of Chaa Creek's Natural History Museum, and a visit to their Blue Morpho Butterfly Breeding project, cost BZ$20. You can easily spend 3 hours visiting all three attractions.

OTHER ADVENTURE ACTIVITIES

HORSEBACK RIDING The terrain here is wonderful for horseback riding. Most horseback tours will take you to one or more of the major attractions in this area, or at least to some quiet swimming hole or isolated waterfall. Most of the hotels here offer horseback tours. Or, you can contact the folks at **Mountain Equestrian Trails** ★ (℡ **501/669-1124**; www.metbelize.com), who have one of the better horse-riding operations in the Cayo District. A half-day trip including lunch costs BZ$122 per person; a full-day trip costs BZ$166.

MOUNTAIN BIKING This region lends itself equally well to mountain biking. The same trails and dirt roads that are used by cars and horses are especially well suited for fat-tire explorations. Most of the hotels in the region have bikes for rent or free for guests. If not, you'll probably have to have them arrange it for you, or contact an agency in San Ignacio.

RIVER TRIPS For much of Belize's history, the rivers were the main highways. The Maya used them for trading, and British loggers used them to move mahogany and logwood. If you're interested, you can explore the Cayo District's two rivers—the Macal and Mopan—by canoe, kayak, and inner tube.

Most tours put in upstream on one of the rivers and then float leisurely downstream. The trip can take anywhere from 1 to 3 hours, depending on how much time you spend paddling, floating, or stopping to hike or swim. All of the local riverside hotels offer this service, as well as a host of operators in San Ignacio. For its part, the Mopan River is more easily accessible in many ways, since Benque Viejo Road borders it in many places. The Mopan is well suited for inflatable kayaks and inner tubes.

In addition to the tour operators listed above, you can contact **David's Adventure Tours** (✆ 501/824-3674). If you want to go inner-tubing, contact the folks at the **Trek Stop** (✆ 501/823-2265; www.thetrekstop.com).

ZIP-LINE CANOPY & CAVE TOURS ★
The folks at **Calico Jack's Village** (✆ 501/820-4078; www.calicojacksvillage.com) have opened up a multiadventure sport attraction in the hills and forests just outside the village of El Progresso. The main attraction here is a zip-line canopy tour, in which you use a climbing harness and pulley system to glide along steel cables from one treetop platform to another. There are a total of six platforms here, connected by five cables. The longest cable is some 427m (1,400 ft.). The roughly hour-long trip costs BZ$110 per person. While here you can also take a guided tour of one of their on-site caves (BZ$90), or hike their jungle trails (BZ$80). Combination packages, with lunch, are available, and they were offering accommodations in the form of cabanas and villas as of December 2010 from US$107 to US$155 per night.

SHOPPING
If you're in the area, stop at the **Tanah Mayan Art Museum ★** (✆ 501/824-3310; daily 8am–5pm), run by the Garcia sisters, some of the premier artisans working in carved slate. While it's a stretch to call their little shop and showroom a museum, you will find a nice collection of the Garcia sisters' carvings, as well as other Maya artifacts and handicrafts. This place is at about Mile Marker 8 of the Cristo Rey Road, about 1.6km (1 mile) before you reach the village of San Antonio. On the other side of the village, you should stop at the **Magaña Zaactunich Art Gallery** (no phone), which carries a range of local craft works and specializes in woodcarvings.

Where to Stay

While San Ignacio is the regional hub and makes a good base, the real attractions in this area are up the rivers and in the forests. Just north of San Ignacio are several lodges set somewhat off the beaten path, where you can canoe down clear rivers, ride horses to Maya ruins, hike jungle trails, and spot scores of birds. Out on the road to Caracol and Mountain Pine Ridge, there are more of these lodges. Except for the true budget traveler, I recommend that you stay at one of these lodges if you can. All offer a wide range of active adventures and tours to all the principal sites in the area.

VERY EXPENSIVE
Blancaneaux Lodge ★★★ This remote ecolodge, owned by Francis Ford Coppola, is set on a steep, pine-forested hillside, overlooking the Privassion River and a series of gentle falls. The individual cabanas here are cozy and intimate. Most of them are "riverfront" units, although a couple are termed "garden view." My favorite are the riverfront "honeymoon" units, which have private plunge pools. Most of the villas are two-bedroom, two-bathroom affairs. The best feature of these is their large, open-air central living area, which flows into a forest- and river-view deck. Villa 7 is Coppola's private villa when he visits, and it features some of the director's photo memorabilia, as well as a painting by his daughter and fellow director Sofia Coppola. You can rent

it whenever he's not around, and it comes with a private plunge pool and a personal butler. The luxurious "Enchanted Cottage" is a short distance from everything else, and has a great view, an infinity pool, and personal butler service, as well.

Mountain Pine Ridge Reserve (P.O. Box B, Central Farm), Cayo District. ℭ **800/746-3743** in the U.S., 501/824-4912 reservations office in Belize, or 824-3878 at the lodge. Fax 501/824-3919. www.blancaneaux. com. 20 units. BZ$560–BZ$1,000 double cabin; BZ$1,080–BZ$1,450 2-bedroom villa; BZ$2,800 Enchanted Cottage. Rates include continental breakfast. Rates lower in the off season, higher during peak weeks. AE, MC, V. Blancaneaux has its own airstrip, and charter flights from Belize City can be arranged. **Amenities:** Restaurant; bar; lounge; bike rental; horse stables; 2 outdoor pools; small spa. *In room:* Free Wi-Fi.

Chaa Creek ★★★   This is the premier lodging choice in this neck of the woods, and one of the best hotels in the country. Much loving care has gone into creating the beautiful grounds and cottages. Located on a high, steep bank over the Macal River, all of the thatched-roof cottages are decorated with local and Guatemalan textiles and handicrafts. Each comes with a quiet porch or balcony area set amid the flowering gardens. My favorite rooms are the large treetop suites, which feature a queen-size bed, a sunken living room area, and a wraparound deck fitted with a sunken Jacuzzi. Canoes and mountain bikes are available, and horseback rides can always be arranged. Over 250 bird species have been spotted within a 8km (5-mile) radius. The guides here are well trained and knowledgeable, and much of the food served is organically grown on the hotel's own farm.

Off the road to Benque Viejo (P.O. Box 53, San Ignacio), Cayo District. ℭ **501/824-2037** reservations office, or 820-4010 at the lodge. Fax 501/824-2501. www.chaacreek.com. 23 units. BZ$540–BZ$700 double; BZ$800–BZ$1,150 suite or villa. Rates include breakfast. AE, MC, V. To reach Chaa Creek, drive 8km (5 miles) west from San Ignacio and watch for the sign on your left. It's another couple of miles down a rough dirt road from the main highway. **Amenities:** Restaurant; bar; lounge; bike rental; concierge; large outdoor pool; smoke-free rooms; small, well-equipped spa; free Wi-Fi. *In room:* No phone.

Ka'ana ★★★   This boutique hotel is stylish and chic. All of the art and furniture on hand are produced within a 40-mile radius of the hotel. If you want all the trappings of a modern luxury hotel, this should be your top choice in the area. Rooms all come with 40-inch plasma televisions, MP3 docking stations, a stocked minibar, and a personal espresso machine. While the rooms are nice enough, you'll definitely want to splurge on the larger, private casitas, which feature small decks in both the front and the back. In addition to the excellent **restaurant** (p. 138), they have a well-stocked wine cellar and cigar bar. This place is a member of the Small Luxury Hotels of the World group. Ka'ana is located about 3km (1¾ miles) southwest of downtown, on the road out to Benque Viejo.

Mile 69¼ on the road to Benque Viejo (P.O. Box 263, San Ignacio), Cayo District. ℭ **877/522-6221** in the U.S. and Canada, or 501/824-0430 reservations office in Belize, or 820-3350 at the hotel. Fax 501/824-2041. www.kaanabelize.com. 15 units. BZ$500 double; BZ$700 casita. AE, MC, V. **Amenities:** Restaurant; bar; lounge; concierge; outdoor pool; room service; smoke-free rooms; small spa. *In room:* A/C, TV, hair dryer, minibar, MP3 docking station, free Wi-Fi.

EXPENSIVE

In addition to the places listed below, the **San Ignacio Resort Hotel ★** (ℭ **800/822-3274** in the U.S. and Canada; www.sanignaciobelize.com) is a plush option right in the town of San Ignacio, while the **Mystic River Resort** (ℭ **501/678-6700;** www. mysticriverbelize.com) is a delightful new lodge made up of individual cabins overlooking the Macal River, and **Five Sisters Lodge** (ℭ **800/447-2931** in the U.S. and Canada; www.fivesisterslodge.com) is a good choice out in Mountain Pine Ridge, at the site of the impressive Five Sisters Falls.

Hidden Valley Inn ★★ This isolated mountain resort has a beautiful setting on over 2,833 hectares (7,000 acres) of private land. The individual bungalows are all plenty roomy, and come with either one queen-size bed or two twin beds, as well as cool red-tile floors, high ceilings, and a working fireplace. Deluxe units feature beautiful claw-foot bathtubs and outdoor waterfall showers. The outdoor pool and Jacuzzi are surrounded by a beautiful slate deck. This is the closest hotel to the Hidden Valley, or Thousand Foot Falls, the tallest waterfall in Belize, a semistrenuous 2-hour hike from the hotel. However, there are actually several other, much more easily accessible, jungle waterfalls and swimming holes right on the property. The property boasts an extensive network of trails, and the bird-watching is excellent. The coffee you're served at breakfast is grown right here, as are many of the vegetables and fruit.

Mountain Pine Ridge (P.O. Box 170, Belmopan), Cayo District. ⓒ **866/443-3364** in the U.S., or 501/822-3320 in Belize. Fax 501/822-3334. www.hiddenvalleyinn.com. 12 units. BZ$390 double; BZ$500 deluxe. Rates slightly lower in the off season, higher during peak periods. MC, V. **Amenities:** Restaurant; bar; lounge; free mountain-bike use; Jacuzzi; small outdoor pool; free Wi-Fi. *In room:* No phone.

Table Rock Camp & Cabañas ★ 📷 This intimate resort is a great choice in the region. Rooms feature high-pitched thatch roofs, plenty of louvered windows for ventilation, cool tile floors, and pretty showers built with smooth, local river stones. Two of the rooms are part of a duplex building, with small private decks off the front. But the Mot Mot cabin here is the top choice, with more space and a spacious private veranda. It's a short hike down to the Macal River, where the lodge keeps several canoes, and has built an open-air octagonal hammock hut, beside a pretty patch of beach. Much of the land is devoted to organic gardens and citrus groves. Meals and service are top-notch.

Mile 5, Cristo Rey Rd. (P.O. Box 179), Cayo District. ⓒ **501/670-4910.** www.tablerockbelize.com. 3 units. BZ$270–BZ$310 double. Rates lower in the off season, higher during peak periods. AE, MC, V. **Amenities:** Restaurant; bar; free bike use; free canoe use; all rooms smoke-free; free Wi-Fi. *In room:* No phone.

MODERATE

The **Cahal Pech Village Resort** (ⓒ **501/824-3740;** www.cahalpech.com), on the outskirts of San Ignacio, is worth considering, as are the riverside options: **Cohune Palms River Cabañas** ★ (ⓒ **501/820-0166** or 609-2738; www.cohunepalms.com), **Clarissa Falls Resort** (ⓒ/fax **501/824-3916;** www.clarissafalls.com), and **Macal River Jungle Camp** (ⓒ **877/709-8708** in the U.S. and Canada, or 501/824-2037 reservations office in Belize; www.belizecamp.com).

Black Rock Jungle River Lodge ★ 📷 So, you *really* want to get away from it all? Well, this is the place. The setting, on a high bluff overlooking the Macal River, is one of the most stunning in the area. The individual cabins here are lovely. The better ones feature large private balconies and fabulous views of the river and/or canyon cliffs. Meals are served in the large open-air dining room and main lodge area, which also has a fabulous view of the river below and forests all around. Much of the fresh produce is organically grown on-site, and electricity is provided by a combination of solar and hydro power sources. Swimming and inner-tubing on the river from the lodge are excellent.

Off the road to Benque Viejo (P.O. Box 48, San Ignacio), Cayo District. ⓒ **501/820-4049** reservations office, or 820-3929 at the lodge. www.blackrocklodge.com. 13 units. BZ$210–BZ$240 double; BZ$300–BZ$360 deluxe. Rates lower in the off season, higher during peak periods. MC, V. If you're driving, take the turnoff for Chaa Creek and duPlooy's, and then follow the signs to Black Rock. **Amenities:** Restaurant. *In room:* No phone.

INEXPENSIVE

There are a host of good budget options in San Ignacio. During the high season, reservations are recommended for the more popular places. At other times, backpackers might prefer to arrive in town early enough to visit a few places, and see which place gives the best bang for the buck. Of the backpacker-geared options, I like the **Hi-Et,** 12 West St. (© **501/824-2828;** thehiet@yahoo.com), with its hostel-like vibe and playful name. For a few more dollars and some more comfort, check out the **Casa Blanca Guest House,** 10 Burns Ave. (©/fax **501/824-2080;** www.casa blancaguesthouse.com).

Midas Tropical Resort ★ ⬩ A short walk from downtown San Ignacio, Midas feels a world away. The round Maya-style cottages have thatch roofs and screen walls, and there are also wood cabins on raised stilts with corrugated roofs. All are comfortable, clean, and spacious, with ceiling fans and plenty of screened windows for ventilation. Some come with air-conditioning and televisions, and you'll pay a little more for the perks. The newer "King deluxe" rooms are the best bets and an excellent value. The hotel has ample grounds with shady trees. The Macal River is only a stroll away down a grassy lane, and you can spend the day lounging on the little beach on the riverbank. If you don't want to swim in the river, these folks offer use of a pool at their in-town sister, Venus Hotel.

Branch Mouth Rd., San Ignacio, Cayo District. To reach Midas, walk north out of town on Savannah Street, which is 1 block east of Burns Ave. The hotel is about .8km (½ mile) from the center of town. © **501/824-3172** or 824-3845. www.midasbelize.com. 13 units. BZ$108–BZ$128 double; BZ$158–BZ$178 King deluxe. MC, V. **Amenities:** Restaurant; free Wi-Fi. *In room:* No phone.

The Trek Stop This rustic little outpost is geared toward backpackers and adventure travelers. The accommodations are spread around a broad garden and backed by dense forest, and range from campsites, to simple cabins, to a couple of newer cabins with private bathrooms. Most of the wooden cabins are small, but they do come with a private little front porch, where you can sit and read. Guests can either eat at the little restaurant here, or cook their own food in the communal kitchen. A wide range of tours and activities are offered, and inner-tubing on the Mopan River is one of their specialties. They also have a 9-hole Frisbee golf course, which is free for guests, and costs BZ$6 per person for visitors.

Benque Viejo Rd., Mile Marker 7½, San José Succotz, Cayo District. © **501/823-2265.** www.thetrek stop.com. 10 units (8 with shared bathroom). BZ$76 double cabin; BZ$48–BZ$56 double with shared bathroom; BZ$10 per person camping. MC, V. **Amenities:** Restaurant; mountain-bike rental; free Wi-Fi. *In room:* No phone.

Where to Dine

EXPENSIVE

La Ceiba ★★★ 🍴 BELIZEAN/FUSION This resort restaurant is one of my favorite restaurants in the country, and a not-to-miss spot if you're staying in the region. Chef Sean Kuylen's shows a deft hand, combining contemporary techniques with local ingredients, many harvested from the organic gardens here. Try the fresh red snapper marinated in herbs and wine and then baked in a salt crust, or the jerk chicken served in a coconut curry stew. I especially like the creative interpretations of Belizean classics, which often show up as daily specials and might feature a version of the seafood stew sere, or a jazzed-up stew beans and rice. However, for lunch you can always find the local pork sausage served in Dukunu—a roasted corn tamale recipe that dates to Maya times—accompanied by a chipotle, guava, and tomato chutney. The wine selection here is excellent, well-priced and expertly stored.

At Ka'ana resort, Mile Marker 69¼ on the road to Benque Viejo. © **501/820-3350.** Reservations recommended. Main courses BZ$24–BZ$66. AE, MC, V. Daily 7am–10pm.

MODERATE

Running W Steak House ★★ STEAK/BELIZEAN   This restaurant is in the San Ignacio Resort Hotel and is affiliated with Belize's largest beef and cattle operation, its namesake. Try the Mayan Steak, marinated strips of tenderloin grilled and served with fresh tortillas. If you want something more traditional, order the 16-ounce porterhouse. There are also fish and chicken dishes, as well as some Belizean standards. The dining room is large and comfortable, with plenty of varnished wood. A few wrought-iron tables line an outdoor patio and make a great place to have lunch with a jungle view, or dinner under the stars.

18 Buena Vista St., in the San Ignacio Resort Hotel. © **501/824-2034.** Reservations recommended. Main courses BZ$20–BZ$60. AE, MC, V. Daily 7am–11pm.

INEXPENSIVE

In addition to Mr. Greedy's (below), **Ko-Ox Han-Nah,** 5 Burns Ave. (© **501/824-3014**), is the place to go for Indian and Pan-Asian food, while **Martha's Restaurant & Pizza House,** 10 West St. (© **501/804-3647**), is a friendly hangout serving local food and pizzas. For inexpensive eats in an outdoor setting, you can try **Hode's Place Bar & Grill** (© **501/804-2522**), on the northern end of town.

Mr. Greedy's Pizzeria ★★ AMERICAN/PIZZA   This place may just serve the best pizza in Belize. Grab a table on a wooden deck fronting the street, or toward the rear of the restaurant where the floor is actually made up of sand. In addition to the pizzas, they serve up a long list of bar food, including excellent burgers, and pasta dishes. For a main dish, I recommend the chicken Parmesan. This place opens early for breakfast, where you can get the day going with a breakfast burrito, or breakfast burger, in addition to more traditional breakfast fare. The bar can get popular at night, and they also offer up free Wi-Fi.

34 Burns Ave. © **501/804-4688.** Main courses BZ$15–BZ$30. MC, V. Daily 6am–midnight.

San Ignacio After Dark

San Ignacio is a sleepy town. Several bars line Burns Avenue in the downtown area, though. I like the relaxed pub vibe at **Mr. Greedy's** ★ (see above). Most nights, but especially on weekends, the most happening spot can be found up the hill at the **Stork Club** (© **501/824-2034**), which is in the San Ignacio Resort Hotel. This place has karaoke on Thursday nights, and live bands often on the weekends. On the north end of town, **Hode's Place Bar & Grill** (© **501/804-2522**) is a massive spot that is popular with locals. They have a tiny casino, as well as a large video arcade, and pool and foosball tables.

If you're the gambling type, you'll want to head to the **Princess Casino** (© **501/824-4099**), which is also in the San Ignacio Resort Hotel. I'd choose this one over the little casino at **Hode's Place** (© **501/804-2522**).

Cave Excursions from the Cayo District

The ancient Maya believed that caves were a mystical portal between the world of the living and the underworld of spirits and the dead. From their earliest days, there is evidence that the Maya made extensive use of caves for ritual purposes, as well as

For the Most Enjoyable Experience at Caves Branch River

The Caves Branch River cave system is a very popular tourist attraction, and it can get crowded, especially in the three caves closest to Jaguar Paw and the public entrance. When the cruise-ship groups are in the caves, it's downright overcrowded. Whatever tour operator you use, try to time it so that you avoid other large groups if possible. I also highly recommend hiking the extra 15 minutes or so upstream to get to the fourth cave. If you choose to do the tour with Ian Anderson's Caves Branch outfit, you are assured of avoiding the crowds. Also, wear plenty of insect repellent, as the mosquitoes can be fierce here (only on the hike—once you're in the caves there are none).

for more mundane and rudimentary things as keeping dry, storing grains, and gathering water. They called this mystical realm **Xibalba.**

Belize is riddled with caves. In almost every explored cave, some evidence of use by the Maya has been uncovered. Fire pits, campsites, burial mounds, and ritual altars have all been found. Numerous pieces of pottery and abundant bones and artifacts have also been encountered. Belize offers many unique and easily accessible opportunities to explore this fascinating world, on foot, by kayak or canoe, or by floating on an inner tube. Don't miss it.

CAVES BRANCH RIVER CAVE SYSTEM ★★★

The Caves Branch River is a gently flowing body of water coming down off the Mountain Pine Ridge. It really should be called a creek in most places. However, what makes the Caves Branch River unique is the fact that it flows in and out of a series of limestone caves that are easily navigable on inner tubes and in kayaks.

There are two major entry points along the river for visits to the Caves Branch caves: One is at **Ian Anderson's Caves Branch ★★** jungle lodge (Mile Marker 41½ Hummingbird Hwy; ✆ **501/822-2800;** www.cavesbranch.com), and the other is just above **Jaguar Paw,** a luxury hotel built on the banks of the river (Mile Marker 37 Western Hwy; ✆ **501/820-2023;** www.jaguarpaw.com). In general terms, travelers looking for more adventurous and gritty trips into the caves should head to Ian Anderson's place; those seeking a gentler tour into the underworld or wanting to sign up for a guided excursion out of any of the country's major tourist centers will inevitably be doing the tour out of the Jaguar Paw entrance.

Most visitors either go directly through Jaguar Paw or use the same section of the river. Either way, you will have to hike upstream to a put-in. Depending on the tour you choose and the amount of hiking you want to do, you will eventually climb into your inner tube and begin a slow float through anywhere from one to four caves. You will be equipped with a headlamp, and little else.

Cave tubing tours cost between BZ$60 and BZ$240, depending on the length of the tour. The most inexpensive way to go is to drive yourself to the government parking area below Jaguar Paw and hire one of the local guides there for around BZ$30 to BZ$50. However, you'll generally get better guides, better service, and better equipment if you go with one of the more established operators.

ACTUN TUNICHIL MUKNAL ★★

Actun Tunichil Muknal means "Cave of the Crystal Sepulcher," and the site was featured in the 1993 National Geographic Explorer film *Journey Through the*

Underworld. This is one of the most adventurous and rewarding caves you can visit in Belize. The trip involves a 45-minute hike through dense forest to the entrance of the cave. A midsize stream flows out of the beautiful entrance. From here you wade, crawl, swim, and scramble, often up to your waist in water. There are some tight squeezes. Inside, you'll come to several ceremonial and sacrificial chambers. Fourteen skeletons and burial sites have been found inside here, as well as numerous pieces of pottery and ceramic shards. There are even two rare slate stelae, believed to have been used by Maya religious and political leaders for ritual bloodletting ceremonies. Many of the skulls, skeletons, and pieces of pottery have been encased in calcium, creating an eerie effect, while others are very well maintained, making it hard to imagine that they are over a thousand years old. Moreover, given its remote location and relatively recent discovery, Actun Tunichil Muknal has been spared much of the serious looting that has plagued many other Maya cave sites. Only licensed guides can take visitors into this cave. Most hotels and tour agencies in the Cayo District can arrange these tours.

PLACENCIA & SOUTHERN BELIZE ★★

242km (150 miles) S of Belize City; 89km (55 miles) NE of Punta Gorda

Southern Belize has only two major towns, **Dangriga** and **Punta Gorda,** and one popular beach village, **Placencia ★★**. For years, this was the least developed region of Belize, but that's changing quickly. Placencia is arguably the hottest and fastest-growing destination in Belize. And the tiny Garífuna settlement of **Hopkins Village ★★** is booming. Both Placencia and Hopkins Village offer some of the longest and finest sand beaches to be found in the country.

Placencia is at the southern tip of a long, narrow peninsula that is separated from the mainland by a similarly narrow lagoon, and boasts nearly 26km (16 miles) of white sand fronting a calm turquoise sea and backed by palm trees. Placencia attracts everyone from backpackers to naturalists to divers to upscale snowbirds.

For years, the village's principal thoroughfare was a thin concrete sidewalk. Once listed in the *Guinness Book of World Records* as the narrowest street in the world, the sidewalk still runs through the heart of the village parallel to the sea. However, the ongoing construction and development boom has made the main road through town (called "the Back Road") actually the town's busiest thoroughfare most days.

Offshore, you'll find some of Belize's most beautiful cayes and its most remote atoll, **Glover's Reef Atoll ★★**. The cayes and barrier reef down here are as spectacular as that found farther north, yet far less developed and crowded. You can literally have an island to yourself down here. Much of the offshore and underwater wonders are protected in reserves, such as the **Southwater Caye Marine Reserve, Glover's Marine Reserve, Sapodilla Cayes Marine Reserve,** and **Laughing Bird Caye National Park.**

Essentials

GETTING THERE

BY PLANE **Maya Island Air** (✆ **501/223-1140** in Belize City, or 501/523-3475 in Placencia; www.mayaairways.com) and **Tropic Air** (✆ **800/422-3435** in the U.S. and Canada, 501/226-2012 in Belize City, or 523-3410 in Placencia; www.tropicair.com)

both have around 10 flights daily between Belize City and Placencia. The first flight leaves at 8:10am and the last flight is at 5pm. Flight time is 35 minutes, with a brief stop in Dangriga. On each airline, there are fewer flights from the Municipal airport.

Flights to and from Punta Gorda on Maya Island Air and Tropic Air stop in **Placencia Airport** (**PLJ;** no phone) to pick up and drop off passengers. On both airlines, flights are sometimes added during the high season or suspended during the low season, so check in advance. Flight time runs between 25 and 50 minutes, depending on whether there is an intermediate stop or two. See "Getting Around," below, for info on getting from the airstrip into town.

BY BUS **James Bus Line** (✆ **501/702-2049**) and **National Transport** (✆ **501/227-2255**) have regular service throughout the day between Belize City and Dangriga, roughly every half-hour between 6:30am and 5:30pm from either the main bus terminal on West Collet Canal Street (National Transport), or the nearby Shell gas station on Cemetery Road (James). The fare is BZ$16. The ride takes about 3 hours. Direct buses leave Dangriga for Placencia daily at 10:30 and 11:30am, and at 4 and 5:15pm. The fare is BZ$10. Buses leave Placencia for Dangriga, with onward connection to Belmopan, San Ignacio, and Belize City, daily at 11am, and 2 and 4:40pm.

However, many independent and bus travelers also reach Placencia via Independence Village and Mango Creek, using the *Hokie Pokie* ferry (✆ **501/523-2376**). This short 15-minute boat ride used to cut a lot of bumpy, dusty miles off the road trip; however, now that the road is paved this is no longer necessary. Still, if you're heading south, this is still the best way to go. The ferry fare is BZ$12. All north- and southbound bus traffic along the Southern Highway stops in Independence Village, near the ferry dock. Ferries between Placencia and Independence Village leave regularly throughout the day, with at least six trips in each direction.

In order to get to Independence Village, you'll need to take any bus heading south to Punta Gorda. **James Bus Line** (✆ **501/207-3937** in Belize City, or 702-2049 in Punta Gorda) and **National Transport** (✆ **501/227-2255**) have service throughout the day between Belize City and Punta Gorda. Buses leave at irregular intervals between 4:30am and 5pm, with at least 15 different buses making the run throughout the day. The one-way fare is BZ$24.

BY CAR From Belize City, head west on Cemetery Road, which becomes the Western Highway. Take this all the way to Belmopan, where you will connect with the Hummingbird Highway heading south. Ten kilometers (6¼ miles) before Dangriga, the Hummingbird Highway connects with the Southern Highway. Take the Southern Highway toward Placencia and Punta Gorda. After 37km (23 miles) on the Southern Highway, turn left onto the road to Riversdale and Placencia. From this turnoff, it's another 32km (20 miles) to Placencia. The drive from Belize City should take around 2½ to 3 hours.

GETTING AROUND

Placencia Village itself is tiny, and you can walk the entire length of the sidewalk, which covers most of the village, in about 10 to 15 minutes. If you need a taxi, call **S & M Taxi** (✆ **501/602-4768**) or **Tuff Gong Taxi** (✆ **501/523-3323**). Fares within the village run BZ$6 for one person, and BZ$3 per person for two or more people. A trip from the airstrip to the village costs BZ$12 for one person, and BZ$6 per person for two or more people.

If you want to rent a car or golf cart while in Placencia, **Barefoot Rentals** (✆ **501/523-3438** or 629-9602; www.barefootrentals.net) is the best option, charging around BZ$120 per day for a golf cart, and between BZ$150 and BZ$180 per day for an SUV.

VISITOR INFORMATION

For most of the peninsula there is only one road. As the road reaches the end of the peninsula and the village of Placencia, it basically dead-ends at the Shell station and some boat docks. Just before this, a dirt spur turns right just beyond the soccer field and heads for a few hundred yards toward the lagoon.

Hotels and resorts are spread all along the length of the Placencia peninsula. To make it easier to understand where a hotel or resort is, the peninsula is broken up into three broad sections: Maya Beach, Seine Bight, and Placencia Village. Maya Beach is the northernmost section of the peninsula, and the hotels and resorts here are quite spread out, with few other services or businesses. More or less anchoring the center of the peninsula is the tiny Garífuna village of Seine Bight. Just to the north and south of Seine Bight village are several other isolated resorts. Down at the southern end of the peninsula is Placencia Village itself.

The helpful **Placencia Information Center** (✆ 501/523-4045; www.placencia. com) is toward the end of the road, in a mini-mall across from the soccer field.

FAST FACTS For the local **police,** dial ✆ 911 or 501/503-3142; you can also reach the **tourist police** at ✆ 501/603-0374. If you need any medical attention, the **Placencia Medical Center** (✆ 501/523-3326) is behind the school in the center of the village.

There's a **Scotiabank** (✆ 501/523-3277) on the main road near the center of the village, as well as an **Atlantic Bank** (✆ 501/523-3431). Scotiabank has an ATM that accepts international cards. There's a **pharmacy** attached to Wallen's Market (✆ 501/523-3346), in the center of the village. The **post office** is above the Fishermen's Co-op, near the start of the sidewalk.

If you need to use the Internet, there's a host of options. If you want Wi-Fi or some food or drink to go along with your surfing, I recommend the **De Tatch** (✆ **501/503-3385**). The **Placencia Office Supply** (✆ **501/523-3205**), which is on the main road and has high-speed connections, is another good option.

What to See & Do in Placencia
ON & UNDER THE WATER

FISHING Fishing around here is some of the best in Belize. There's excellent bonefishing in flats in this area. Anglers can also go for tarpon, permit, and snook, or head offshore for bigger game, including grouper, yellowfin tuna, king mackerel, wahoo, mahimahi, and the occasional sail or marlin. Experienced guides can help you track any of the above fish, and many are taking their guests out fly-fishing for them as well. The folks at **Tarpon Caye Lodge ★** (✆ **501/523-3323;** www.tarponcaye lodge.com) who have a small fishing lodge on the remote Tarpon Caye, and have some of the more experienced fishing guides in town, specializing in fishing for permit and tarpon. You can also try **Trip 'N Travel** (✆ **501/523-3614**), another long-standing local operation with well-regarded guides.

KAYAKING Several hotels and tour operators in town rent out sea kayaks. The waters just off the beach are usually calm and perfect for kayaking. However, the lagoon is probably a better choice, offering up more interesting mangrove terrain and excellent bird-watching opportunities.

If you're looking for a guided tour, the best kayak operator in Placencia is **Toadal Adventures** ★ (✆ **501/523-3207;** www.toadaladventure.com). These folks offer several different multiday kayaking trips, both out on the ocean and on inland rivers. Custom trips can also be designed.

SAILING   The crystal-clear waters, calm seas, and isolated islands surrounding Placencia make this an excellent place to go out for a sail. Your options range from crewed yachts and bareboat charters for multiday adventures to day cruises and sunset sails. A day cruise, including lunch, drinks, and snorkeling gear, should cost between BZ$160 and BZ$300 per person. Most hotels and tour operators around town can arrange a sail or cruise, or you can simply head to the docks, or check in with the folks at **Next Wave Sailing** (✆ **501/661-3744**).

SNORKELING & SCUBA DIVING   There's often decent snorkeling right off the beach, especially if you head north a mile or so. The water's clear and you'll see plenty of fish and bottom life in the sea grass and along the sand bottom.

One of the more popular snorkel excursions is to the nearby **Laughing Bird Caye** (✆ **501/523-3565;** www.laughingbird.org). Just a few miles offshore from Placencia, Laughing Bird Caye is a national park. It's a tiny little island measuring roughly 11×105m (35×350 ft.). There's good snorkeling and swimming offshore, and a beautiful little beach. A host of tour operators take folks here, and then serve a picnic lunch on the beach.

However, if you're serious about diving or snorkeling, you'll want to get out to the **barrier reef** and its dozens of little offshore cayes. It's between 16 and 40km (10–25 miles) out to the reef here, making it a relatively quick and easy boat ride.

The offshore **Gladden Spit** ★★ site is a world-renowned spot to dive with massive whale sharks. Whale shark sightings are fairly common here, right around the full moon, from late March to early July, and to a lesser extent during the months of August through October and December and January.

If you're not staying at a hotel with a dedicated dive operation, check in with the folks at **Avadon Divers** ★★ (✆ **888/509-5617** in the U.S. and Canada, or 501/503-3377 in Belize; www.avadondiversbelize.com) or **Seahorse Dive Shop** ★ (✆ **501/523-3166;** www.belizescuba.com). A snorkeling trip should cost between BZ$60 and BZ$160, depending on the distance traveled and whether lunch is included. Rates for scuba diving run between BZ$120 and BZ$300 for a two-tank dive, also depending on the length of the journey to the dive site and whether gear and lunch are included. Equipment rental should cost from BZ$15 to BZ$30 for a snorkeler, and BZ$30 to BZ$60 for a scuba diver.

GUIDED DAY TRIPS

While the ocean and outlying cayes are the focus of most activities and tours in Placencia, there are a host of other options. The most popular of these include tours to Cockscomb Basin Wildlife Sanctuary, the Maya ruins of Lubaantun and Nim Li Punit, and up the Monkey River. Day trips can run between BZ$100 and BZ$300 per person, depending on the distance traveled and the number of activities offered or sites visited. Almost every tour agency in town offers these trips, or ask at your hotel for a recommended guide or operator.

The most popular "inland" trip offered out of Placencia is up the **Monkey River** ★, and most of it is actually on the water, anyway. About a half-hour boat ride down the coast and through the mangroves, the Monkey River area is rich in wildlife. If you're lucky, you might spot a manatee on your way down. Once traveling up the river, keep

Placencia & Southern Belize

BELIZE

Placencia

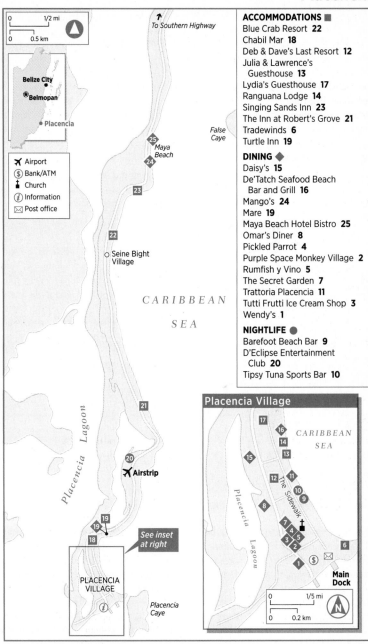

ACCOMMODATIONS ■
Blue Crab Resort **22**
Chabil Mar **18**
Deb & Dave's Last Resort **12**
Julia & Lawrence's
  Guesthouse **13**
Lydia's Guesthouse **17**
Ranguana Lodge **14**
Singing Sands Inn **23**
The Inn at Robert's Grove **21**
Tradewinds **6**
Turtle Inn **19**

DINING ◆
Daisy's **15**
De'Tatch Seafood Beach
  Bar and Grill **16**
Mango's **24**
Mare **19**
Maya Beach Hotel Bistro **25**
Omar's Diner **8**
Pickled Parrot **4**
Purple Space Monkey Village **2**
Rumfish y Vino **5**
The Secret Garden **7**
Trattoria Placencia **11**
Tutti Frutti Ice Cream Shop **3**
Wendy's **1**

NIGHTLIFE ●
Barefoot Beach Bar **9**
D'Eclipse Entertainment
  Club **20**
Tipsy Tuna Sports Bar **10**

4

BELIZE | Placencia & Southern Belize

your eyes peeled for crocodiles, green iguana, wild deer, howler monkeys, and the occasional boa constrictor, as well as scores of bird species. These tours can be done entirely in a motor launch, or may allow you to kayak on the Monkey River portion; I recommend the latter. Most tours include lunch in the quaint little creole fishing village of Monkey River itself, as well as a short hike through a forest trail. Monkey River trips cost between BZ$90 and BZ$120 per person.

Where to Stay

There are a host of accommodations options in and around Placencia. In general, the town's budget hotels and guesthouses are located in the village proper, either just off the sidewalk or around the soccer field. As you head north to the broader and more isolated beaches, prices tend to rise.

VERY EXPENSIVE

In addition to the places listed below, there's the **Chabil Mar** ★★ (✆ 866/417-2377 in the U.S., or 501/523-3606 in Belize; www.chabilmarvillas.com) just north of the village.

The Inn at Robert's Grove ★★★ ☺   This boutique resort boasts two restaurants, three pools, an in-house spa, professional dive and fishing operations, and a tennis court. Rustic red-tile floors, Guatemalan textiles, and Mexican ceramic accents abound. All rooms come with a private balcony, hung with a hammock. Many of the suites come with fully equipped kitchenettes, and all have a large living room and a large balcony. There are six—count 'em, six—Jacuzzis spread around the resort. The rooftop ones are particularly inviting for late-night stargazing and soaking. Guests enjoy unlimited free use of the hotel's sea kayaks, windsurfers, Hobie Cat sailboats, tennis court, and bicycles, as well as free airport transfers. The hotel also owns and manages two small private islands, Ranguana Caye and Robert's Caye. You can take a day trip to these tiny offshore cayes, or spend a night or two in a simple yet comfortable cabin.

Placencia, on the beach north of the airstrip. ✆ **800/565-9757** in the U.S., or 501/523-3565 in Belize. Fax 501/523-3567. www.robertsgrove.com. 52 units. BZ$378–BZ$418 double; BZ$520–BZ$920 suite. Rates lower in the off season, higher during peak weeks. AE, MC, V. **Amenities:** 2 restaurants; 3 bars; lounge; babysitting; concierge; full-service dive shop; exercise room; 3 outdoor pools; room service; small spa; lit outdoor tennis court; complimentary watersports equipment and bike use; free Wi-Fi. *In room:* A/C, TV, hair dryer, minifridge.

Turtle Inn ★★★   This is Francis Ford Coppola's fanciest resort in Central America. You get your choice of a one- or two-bedroom private villa here. Either way you go, you're going to have plenty of space, including a large living room and a spacious bathroom that lets out onto a private interior rock garden, with its own open-air shower whose fixture is a piece of bamboo. Tons of beautiful woodwork and a heavy dose of Asian decor and furnishings dominate the rooms. All of the villas are set on the sand just steps from the beach, but not all have ocean views, hence the price variations. There are two separate pools on the grounds, as well as a small spa and full-service dive operation across the street on the lagoon side of the peninsula.

Placencia Village, on the beach north of the center of the village. ✆ **800/746-3743** in the U.S., or 501/824-4912 central reservation number in Belize, or 523-3244 at the hotel. Fax 501/523-3245. www. turtleinn.com. 25 units. BZ$700–BZ$960 1-bedroom double; BZ$1,080–BZ$1,350 2-bedroom double; BZ$3,700 Coppola Pavilion. Rates include continental breakfast. Rates lower in the off season, higher during peak weeks. AE, MC, V. **Amenities:** 3 restaurants; 2 bars; babysitting; complimentary bikes and kayaks; concierge; full-service dive shop; 2 outdoor pools; room service; watersports equipment rental; free Wi-Fi. *In room:* Hair dryer, minibar.

MODERATE

This is a price range with tons of options. In addition to the hotel listed below, other good choices include **Singing Sands Inn ★** (℗ **888/201-6425** in the U.S. and Canada, or 501/520-8022; www.singingsands.com) on Maya Beach, and **Blue Crab Resort** (℗ **501/523-3544;** www.bluecrabbeach.com), just outside of Seine Bight Village.

Ranguana Lodge 🏷 The five individual cabins at this small family-run hotel are all clean and cozy. In the two older cabins, nearly everything is made of hardwood—walls, floors, ceilings, even the louvered windows. These rooms feature a full kitchenette. The three oceanfront cabins are the newest, and while they are right in front of the sea and have air-conditioning, they are a little smaller and have a little less character. All of the cabins are just steps from the ocean, and all come with a private balcony or porch area.

Placencia Village, on the beach in the center of the village. (℗ **501/523-3112.** Fax 501/523-3451. www.ranguanabelize.com. 5 units. BZ$160–BZ$176 double. Rates include taxes. AE, MC, V. *In room:* TV, minifridge, no phone.

INEXPENSIVE

If the place listed below is full, you can walk around the village and see what's available, or head to **Julia & Lawrence's Guesthouse** (℗ **501/503-3478;** www.juliasrooms.com), **Lydia's Guesthouse** (℗ **501/523-3117;** www.lydiasguesthouse.com), or **Deb and Dave's Last Resort** (℗ **501/523-3207;** debanddave@btl.net), both located just off the sidewalk toward the center of the village.

Tradewinds 🏨 You can't beat the setting of Tradewinds. Perched right on the ocean's edge toward the southern end of the village, the eight individual cabins here are just a few feet from the water. All are comfortable, are roomy, and come with a very inviting porch, hung with a hammock overlooking the waves, where I predict you'll spend most of your time. The less expensive rooms here are set a bit farther back from the sea in a simple triplex building, although each comes with its own little veranda. Everything is painted in lively pastels, and there's a friendly family-like vibe to the whole operation.

Placencia Village, on the beach, south end of the village. (℗ **501/523-3122.** Fax 501/523-3201. www.placencia.com. 9 units. BZ$80–BZ$140 double. Rates slightly lower in the off season, higher during peak weeks. MC, V. *In room:* Minifridge, no phone.

Where to Dine

In addition to the places mentioned below, the main restaurant at the **Inn at Robert's Grove** (see above) is top-notch, as is the Italian restaurant **Mare** at **Turtle Inn** (see above). For simpler Italian fare and homemade pastas in a beachfront setting, try **Trattoria Placencia** (℗ **501/623-3394**), about midway along the sidewalk. Finally, as you wander around town in the heat of the day, be sure to stop in at **Tutti Frutti Ice Cream Shop** for some fresh, homemade ice cream or gelato. Tutti Frutti is on the main road in the Placencia Village Square shopping center, across from the soccer field. **Daisy's,** on the main road near the center of town, also serves up fresh, homemade ice cream, as well as breakfasts, lunches, and dinners.

EXPENSIVE

Maya Beach Hotel Bistro ★★★ FUSION/SEAFOOD This is my favorite restaurant on the Placencia peninsula. There's nothing fancy about the decor or ambience at this open-air beachfront restaurant, but the food and service are top-notch. You can start things off with their trio or *cuatro* of starters. Some of the top choices here are the fish cakes, coconut shrimp and roasted pumpkin, and coconut and green-chili soup. Signature main dishes here include the cacao-dusted pork chop served on a risotto cake, and the nut-encrusted fresh catch served with a papaya-pineapple salsa. The coconut ribs and pork burger are also excellent.

At Maya Beach Hotel, on the Maya Beach. ✆ **501/520-8040.** www.mayabeachhotel.com. Reservations recommended. Main courses BZ$28–BZ$56. AE, MC, V. Tues–Sun 7am–9pm.

MODERATE

In addition to the places below, **Mango's** (✆ **501/600-2040;** www.mangosbelize. com) is a beachside bar and restaurant in Maya Beach. The bar food runs from burgers and shrimp po' boy sandwiches to burritos and quesadillas.

De'Tatch Seafood Beach Bar & Grill ★ BELIZEAN/SEAFOOD This funky open-air beachfront joint is one of the most popular spots in town. Traditional Belizean breakfasts here are hearty and inexpensive. You can get excellent seafood or shrimp burritos or tacos for lunch or dinner. There's an Internet cafe off to one side, and the sea is just steps away. The second-floor open-air deck can get hot in the daytime, but is especially nice on starry nights.

Placencia Village, on the ocean just off the Sea Spray Hotel toward the center of the village. ✆ **501/503-3385.** Reservations not accepted. Breakfast and lunch main courses BZ$6–BZ$16; dinner main courses BZ$12–BZ$36; lobster BZ$34–BZ$50. MC, V. Thurs–Tues 7am–10pm.

Rumfish y Vino ★★ SEAFOOD/FUSION This is the hippest and most sophisticated joint in Placencia. Offering up a wide-ranging menu of fusion fare, bar food, and tapas, this is a great place to come for a long evening of wining and dining. Start off with the succulent conch fritters or some of their homemade fish pâté, and then move on to one of their nightly specials. Standout options include their gourmet mac 'n' cheese, and the Jamaican jerk pork chops. For lunch, I love the fish tacos. The wine list here is unique for Belize, featuring a broad selection of Italian and California wines that they import themselves, and there are also several local beers on tap.

Placencia Village Square, on the main road, across from soccer field. ✆ **501/523-3293.** www.rumfishy vino.com. Reservations recommended. Main courses BZ$14–BZ$27. MC, V. Daily 11am–midnight.

INEXPENSIVE

Other good choices around town include **Omar's Diner** (✆ **501/523-4094**), the **Secret Garden** ★ (✆ **501/523-3420**), **Wendy's** (✆ **501/523-3335**), and the **Purple Space Monkey Village** (✆ **501/523-4094**), all located either on the main road or just off the sidewalk in Placencia Village.

Pickled Parrot ★ INTERNATIONAL This popular place serves up a mix of quality bar food, pizzas, and a nightly range of main dishes and specials. The bulk of the menu is made up of pizzas, burgers, subs, and burritos. Dinner specials range from mango-rum-glazed chicken to lobster curry. There's a relaxed, informal atmosphere at this open-air sand-floored restaurant, and the bar can get rowdy at times, especially after folks have downed a few rounds of Parrot Piss, the bar's signature mixed drink.

Placencia Village. ℭ **501/624-2651.** www.pickledparrotbelize.com. Reservations not accepted. Main courses BZ$10–BZ$30; pizzas BZ$34–BZ$44. V. Mon–Sat noon–9pm.

Placencia After Dark

Two of the most popular spots in town are the **Barefoot Beach Bar ★** (ℭ **501/523-3515**) and the **Tipsy Tuna Sports Bar** (ℭ **501/523-3089**), two neighboring establishments; I prefer the relaxed vibe and outdoor setting of the Barefoot Beach Bar, while the Tipsy Tuna is more of a late-night place, with pool tables and regular live music and karaoke. For late-night action, there's the **D'Eclipse Entertainment Club** (ℭ **501/523-3288**); it's just north of the airstrip so the noise and crowds won't bother residents of the town's hotels and houses.

A Side Trip to Hopkins Village

Hopkins Village is a midsize coastal Garífuna community 53km (33 miles) north of Placencia. It is a picturesque village with colorfully painted raised clapboard houses. It is also my preferred destination for getting a true taste of and some direct contact with this unique culture. This is a great place to wander around talking with children, fishermen, and elderly folks hanging out in front of their homes.

ESSENTIALS

Hopkins Village is set on a long curving swath of beach, which in addition to Placencia is one of the few true beaches in the country. The access road from the Southern Highway heads right into the heart of Hopkins Village. If you continued straight, you'd be in the Caribbean Sea. The village itself spreads out for a few hundred yards in either direction.

Getting There

BY CAR   The turnoff for Hopkins Village is on the Hummingbird Highway, about 13km (8 miles) south of Dangriga. From here, it's 6km (3¾ miles) on a graded gravel road. A few miles farther south on the Southern Highway is the entrance to Sittee River Village; however, you can also enter at Hopkins and head south from there along the coast, as it's really just a small loop.

BY BUS   Only a couple of the buses each day from Dangriga south make the loop through Hopkins Village and Sittee River. The ride takes between 25 and 35 minutes to Hopkins Village, with Sittee River Village just a few miles farther on the route. The fare is BZ$6 each way. Be sure to ask before you get on the bus whether it will drop you off in the village. If not, you will be let off on the Southern Highway, at the entrance to Hopkins, but still some 6.4km (4 miles) away. If this is the case, you will hopefully have arranged pickup with your hotel in advance. Otherwise, you'll have to hitchhike into town.

Getting Around

Hopkins Village itself is tiny and you can easily walk the entire town. If you're staying south of town or want to explore, a bicycle is the preferred means of transportation. Most of the hotels will either lend you a bike or rent you one for a few dollars per day. There are no official taxi services, but if you ask around town or at your hotel, you should be able to hire someone for small trips or excursions.

Visitor Information

Hopkins Village has no banks, or major stores or services. There are, however, a couple of Internet cafes, and you can get gas at the little marina.

WHAT TO SEE & DO

This is a very isolated and underdeveloped area. All the hotels here can help you arrange scuba diving, snorkeling, and fishing outings, as well as tours to attractions such as Cockscomb Basin Wildlife Sanctuary, Sittee River canoeing, Blue Hole National Park, the Mayflower Maya ruins, and cultural tours of Dangriga. One of the better local operators is **Bullfrog Adventures** ★ (© 501/669-0046 or 665-3043; issymcm@yahoo.com), which employs all local, Garífuna guides and boat captains.

If you really want to get a taste of the local culture, sign up for classes at the **Lebeha Drumming Center** ★ (© 501/608-3143; www.lebeha.com), which is on the northern edge of the village. The folks here teach traditional Garífuna drumming and dancing.

WHERE TO STAY

There are several upscale resorts and condo options in Hopkins. My two favorites are **Hamanasi** ★★ (© 877/552-3483 in the U.S. and Canada; www.hamanasi.com) and **Almond Beach Belize & Jaguar Reef Lodge** ★★ (© 866/824-1516 in the U.S. and Canada; www.jaguarreef.com). Both are full-service resorts with in-house dive operations and a host of tour and activity options. In addition to these places, there are also a score of simple guesthouses and small inns. The best of these are **Hopkins Inn** (© 501/523-7283; www.hopkinsinn.com), **Jungle Jeanie's by the Sea** ★ (© 501/523-7047; www.junglebythesea.com), and **Tipple Tree Beya** (©/fax 501/520-7006; www.tippletree.net).

WHERE TO DINE

Even if you're staying at one of the large resorts around here, it's worth heading into town to try a meal at one of the simple, local-run restaurants on the main street. Of these, **King Kassava** (© 501/608-6188), **Iris's Restaurant** (© 501/523-7019), and **Innies Restaurant** (© 501/523-7026) are perennial favorites. All serve excellent fresh seafood, and will usually have some *hudut* (fish cooked in a coconut broth) and other Garífuna dishes on hand. A similar option, which I prefer for its seafront location, is **Laruna Hati** ★ (© 501/661-5753), which is toward the north end of the village. Another excellent beachfront option is the **Driftwood Beach Bar & Pizza Shack** ★ (© 501/667-4872). However, the best restaurant in the village, and one of the best in the country, is **Chef Rob's** ★★★ (© 501/670-0445), run by longtime local legend Rob Pronk.

GUATEMALA

by Eliot Greenspan

A millennium of Maya civilization, 3 centuries of Spanish colonial rule, and nearly 4 decades of guerrilla
war have left Guatemala's economy, politics, crafts,
architecture, languages, and religions with one common trait:
profound variety.

For visitors, the country's charms are nearly as varied as the riotous
colors woven into its famed fabrics. From the Maya ruins of Tikal and the
colonial splendor of Antigua—both exquisitely preserved through the
centuries—to the natural beauty of Lake Atitlán, there are a range of
destinations and attractions here to please just about any type of traveler.
However, Guatemala is also one of the poorest, least developed, and most
violent countries in the region. Nearly 2 decades after the end of a long,
brutal civil war, Guatemala seems perennially poised between starting
along a rising path to prosperity, democracy, and justice, and taking a
precipitous fall into chaos, crime, and continued impunity.

Today, Guatemala struggles to find its footing on the road to recovery. But
that road, like so many in the country, is bumpy, winding, and steep. Still,
for those intrepid travelers who do visit, you will find a land of great
beauty; heartfelt, humble, and diverse peoples; an overabundance of color
and craft works; and the almost perfectly preserved cities and streets of
the ancient Maya and earliest Spanish settlers.

THE REGIONS IN BRIEF

GUATEMALA CITY   Set on a high, broad plateau and surrounded by
volcanic peaks, Guatemala City is the largest city in the country, and the
only one with a contemporary, modern feel. That said, with a population
of more than three million, the city is a sprawling, congested, confusing,
and polluted urban mess. Guatemala City has a small but vibrant arts-
and-nightlife scene, as well as some of the finest hotels and restaurants in
the country. The city sits at an elevation of 1,469m (4,820 ft.) above sea
level, and enjoys moderate temperatures year-round. Home to the country's principal international airport and bus connections to every corner of
the country, Guatemala City serves as a de facto transportation hub for
most, if not all, visitors.

ANTIGUA   This small, picturesque colonial city lies just 40km (25
miles) southwest of Guatemala City. In fact, for a couple hundred years,
it was the nation's capital, until a series of devastating earthquakes and
mudslides forced its evacuation. Like its neighbor and the current capital,

Antigua is also set in a valley surrounded by towering volcanic mountain peaks. However, the Antigua valley is much, much smaller. The entire colonial city is little more than 10 blocks by 10 blocks, with a touch of modern urban sprawl around the edges. The city is one of the most well-preserved examples of a colonial city in the Americas. The colonial core of Antigua is a living museum, with rough cobblestone streets and restored colonial-era buildings, mixed in with a few newer constructions that maintain the colonial style and feel. Combined with this living museum are a host of actual museums, and ruined and restored examples of grand churches, convents, and monasteries. From Antigua, the **Agua** and **Fuego volcanoes** are clearly visible.

LAKE ATITLAN   Lake Atitlán is technically part of the Western Highlands, but for the purposes of this chapter, and in the minds of most travelers, it is a world unto itself. Lake Atitlán is a beautiful mountain lake that is actually the filled-in crater of a massive volcano. It's hard to imagine this, since today, several more volcanoes rise from around the shores and tower over the lake. More than 16km (10 miles) across at its widest point, Lake Atitlán has a series of small villages and a few major towns lining its shores. While roads connect all of these towns (in many cases they are rough dirt and gravel), the main means of transportation between towns and villages is by boat and boat taxi. The main town and gateway to Lake Atitlán is **Panajachel,** which sits on the northern shore of the lake. Other major towns include **Santa Catarina Palopó** and **San Antonio Palopó** to the east of Panajachel, and **Santiago de Atitlán** and **San Pedro La Laguna** across the lake to the south.

THE WESTERN HIGHLANDS   The area to the west and northwest of Guatemala City is widely referred to as the Western Highlands, or Altiplano (the "Highlands" in Spanish). This is the heart of Guatemala's rural Maya population. Following the collapse of the major Maya empires of the Petén and lowland coastal regions, many fled in small groups and family units to Altiplano. Today, the Western Highlands are populated with a patchwork of small, rural farming communities spread around the rough, steep, mountainous region. The towns and cities of **Chichicastenango, Quetzaltenango,** and **Huehuetenango** serve as central market and commercial centers for the smaller surrounding communities. The Western Highlands are home to Guatemala's greatest artisans, and are the best place in the country to purchase arts, crafts, carvings, and textile products. Perhaps the most famous place to buy these goods is the **twice-weekly market** held in Chichicastenango. Those looking for a taste of the real rural Maya Altiplano should visit the village of **Nebaj** and the surrounding area, known as the **Ixil Triangle.**

THE PETEN   The Petén, or El Petén, is Guatemala's largest and least populated province. It occupies the northeastern section of the country, and borders Mexico to the north and Belize to the east. It's an area of lush tropical rainforest, within which lies an immense natural wealth of flora and fauna, as well as many of Mesoamerica's most amazing archaeological treasures. In 1990, the government of Guatemala established the **Maya Biosphere Reserve,** a tract of 1 million hectares (2.5 million acres) that includes most of the Petén province. Moreover, the Maya Biosphere Reserve adjoins the neighboring **Calakmul Biosphere Reserve** in Mexico and the **Río Bravo Conservation Area** in Belize, comprising a joint protected area of more than 2 million hectares (5 million acres).

The only major population centers of note in El Petén are the sister cities of Santa Elena and Flores. In addition to the world-renowned ruins of **Tikal,** visitors to the

Petén can visit the archaeological sites of **Yaxhá, El Ceibal, El Mirador,** and **Uaxactún,** to name just a few.

CENTRAL GUATEMALA   The central section of Guatemala comprises the general area east of Guatemala City, before the Atlantic Lowlands. This is the country's most up-and-coming tourist destination, and includes the **Alta Verapaz** and **Baja Verapaz** regions, as well as **El Oriente,** or the "East." Just over the border in Honduras lie the fabulous Maya ruins of **Copán,** which are often included as a stop on a more complex itinerary through Guatemala. **Las Verapaces** (the plural for the combined Alta Verapaz and Baja Verapaz) is a rich highland region with numerous opportunities to go white-water rafting or cave exploring. It's also home to several of Guatemala's most stunning natural areas, including the pools and waterfalls of **Semuc Champey** and the turquoise splendor of **Lake Lachuá.**

To the south and east of Las Verapaces lies El Oriente. Most visitors come here to visit the town of **Esquipulas.** Housed in the impressive Basílica of Esquipulas is the famous statue the *Black Christ.* Believed to have magical, curative, and wish-giving powers, the church and its Christ attract more than one million pilgrims a year.

ATLANTIC LOWLANDS   The common name for this region is a gross misnomer—Guatemala actually borders the Caribbean Sea. However, most Guatemalan maps, books, and tourist information sources refer to this region as the Atlantic coast or Atlantic lowlands, and the highway is officially known as La Carretera al Atlántico (the Atlantic Hwy.). That quibble aside, this is a beautiful and often neglected part of Guatemala. The region really begins around **Lago Izabal,** the largest freshwater lake in the country. From Lago Izabal, the **Río Dulce (Sweet River)** runs gently down to the sea. Along the way it passes through rich primary forests, several nature reserves, and beautiful steep-walled canyons.

Another primary attraction on the Caribbean coast is the small Garífuna village of **Livingston.** The Garífuna are a unique race born of the intermarriage between escaped slaves and Carib Indians. Livingston, which is known as La Buga in the local Garífuna language, is accessible only by boat. The rainforests around Livingston are great for bird-watching and wildlife viewing.

Located just off the Atlantic Highway are the Maya ruins of **Quiriguá,** which contain some wonderful examples of carved monumental stelae and massive carved rocks.

PACIFIC SLOPE   Below the mountain chains that run the length of Guatemala, from Mexico down to El Salvador, the land gently slopes off and flattens out before meeting the Pacific Ocean. This is a hot, steamy agricultural region with large sugar cane, pineapple, and banana plantations. Spread throughout this agricultural land are several lesser-known Maya and pre-Maya ruins. Of these, **Takalik Abaj** and **Finca El Baúl** are worth a visit by anyone interested in ancient Mesoamerican archaeology. In general, the beaches of Guatemala's Pacific coast have dark sand, rough surf, and little development. Given the length of this coastline, there are few developed beach destinations and resorts. If you expect the same kind of beach experience offered throughout the Caribbean, or even the rest of Central America and Mexico, you will be disappointed. The most popular beach town on the Pacific coast is **Monterrico,** which has a handful of small hotels and resorts. The nearby port towns of **Puerto Quetzal, Iztapa,** and **Puerto San José** have garnered well-deserved reputations as top-notch **sportfishing** centers, with excellent opportunities to land marlin, sailfish, and other deep-sea game fish just offshore.

The Regions in Brief

THE BEST OF GUATEMALA IN 1 WEEK

One week will allow you enough time to visit (and actually enjoy) four of Guatemala's prime destinations. This itinerary takes you to the best of Guatemala, and includes a colonial city, a natural wonder, an extensive traditional market, and the most impressive ancient Maya city in Mesoamerica.

Day 1: Antigua

Once you arrive in Guatemala, head straight to Antigua, check into your hotel, and hit the street. Get familiar with the city by starting out at **Plaza Mayor** ★★ (p. 167) in the center of town. Have a sunset cocktail at **Café Sky** (p. 186), and end the night with dinner at **Hector's** ★★★ (p. 187).

Day 2: The Colonial Core

Start your morning by visiting the major attractions around the city's colonial core. There are almost too many sights, and it may be hard to choose. Your best bet is to sign up for a walking tour with **Antigua Tours** ★★ (p. 180). Many of their tours are led by longtime resident and author Elizabeth Bell.

Spend the afternoon shopping at Antigua's fabulous shops, galleries, and local markets.

Don't miss the opportunity to have dinner, and perhaps listen to a little jazz, at **Mesón Panza Verde** ★★★ (p. 185). Toast your second night in the city with a mix of locals, expats, and tourists at **Café No Sé** ★ (p. 188).

Day 3: Lake Atitlán ★★★

Since this is a relatively tight itinerary, I recommend you stay in or around **Panajachel** ★★★ (p. 189). Spend the day walking around town, and be sure to visit the **Museo Lacustre Atitlán** ★ (p. 191). For a good hike through some beautiful foliage, head to the **Reserva Natural Atitlán** ★★ (p. 191). Splurge for dinner with a meal at **Hotel Atitlán** ★★★ (p. 195).

Day 4: Around the Lake

Set aside the whole day to visit some of the other cities and towns around Lake Atitlán. Sign up for an organized tour, or head down to the docks and climb aboard one of the public boat taxis. You won't have time to visit the more than half-dozen towns and villages around the lake, but you must visit **Santiago de Atitlán** ★★ (p. 191). After that, and as time allows, I recommend a stop in **San Pedro La Laguna** ★ (p. 191), followed by a late-afternoon drink and meal of the varied international fare at **Jarachik** (p. 197).

Day 5: Chichicastenango

Take a day trip to the **market in Chichicastenango** ★★★ (p. 205). Chichicastenango, or Chichi, is a little more than an hour's drive from Panajachel, and all of the local tour agencies and hotel tour desks in Panajachel can arrange a guided tour or simple transfer. Even if you come here just to shop, be sure to take some time to visit the **Iglesia de Santo Tomás** ★★★ (p. 205). You'll get back to Panajachel with plenty of time to enjoy the evening. Head to the **Sunset Café** (p. 198) for a namesake cocktail, and then walk a little way up Calle Santander to **El Bistro** ★ (p. 197) for dinner. End your evening with a drink at the **Circus Bar** ★★ (p. 198).

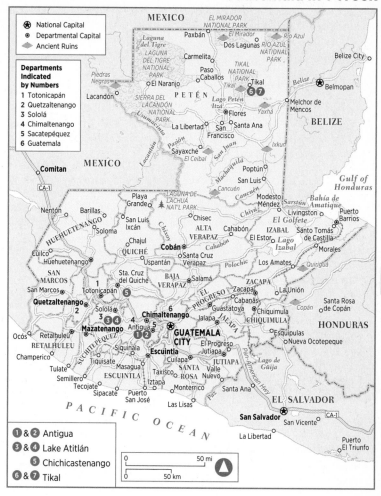

National Capital
Departmental Capital
Ancient Ruins

Departments Indicated by Numbers
1 Totonicapán
2 Quetzaltenango
3 Sololá
4 Chimaltenango
5 Sacatepéquez
6 Guatemala

❶ & ❷ Antigua
❸ & ❹ Lake Atitlán
❺ Chichicastenango
❻ & ❼ Tikal

Note: Chichicastenango's market is open only on Thursday and Sunday. Feel free to swap this day of the itinerary with any of the other 2 days around Lake Atitlán to match the market-day schedule.

Days 6 & 7: Tikal

In my opinion, **Tikal** ★★★ (p. 206) is the most impressive ancient Maya city in Mesoamerica. You'll probably have to leave Panajachel at an ungodly hour to catch your flight, but it'll be worth it. I suggest spending 1 night in the Tikal area, and true Maya buffs will want to stay at one of the hotels at the archaeological site, which will allow you extra hours to explore. Those with a more passing interest can stay in Flores or at one of the hotels on the lake.

Early international flights from Aurora International Airport in Guatemala City are hard to catch if you're flying from Tikal the same date, so you may have to adjust your itinerary to allow an overnight in either Antigua or Guatemala City before your flight home.

PLANNING YOUR TRIP TO GUATEMALA

Visitor Information

The **Guatemalan Tourism Commission (INGUAT),** 7a Av. 1-17, Zona 4, Guatemala City (www.visitguatemala.com), is the principal informational and promotional arm of the Guatemalan government. You can call them toll-free from the United States and Canada at ✆ **800/464-8281,** or directly in Guatemala at ✆ **502/2421-2800.** Once you land in Guatemala, INGUAT has an information booth inside the airport. The booth supplies maps and brochures, and will often make a call for you if you need a last-minute hotel or car-rental reservation. INGUAT also maintains offices or information booths at several of the major tourist destinations around the country.

In addition to INGUAT's official website, you'll be able to find a wealth of Web-based information on Guatemala with a few clicks of your mouse. See "The Best of Central America Online," in chapter 1, for some helpful suggestions on where to begin your online search.

For specific travel-related information, your best bet is to contact one of Guatemala's better travel agencies. Here is a list of some of my favorites:

○ **Clark Tours** (✆ **502/2412-4700;** www.clarktours.com.gt) has been operating for more than 70 years in Guatemala, making it the oldest tour company in the country. They have several offices and are the official representatives of American Express in Guatemala. They offer many tours, including an afternoon in Antigua for around $30 per person; 2- to 4-day archaeology trips starting at around $400 per person; and the 15-day Guatemalan highlights tour that takes in all of the country's major tourist destinations, including Antigua, Lake Atitlán, Chichicastenango, Río Dulce Tikal, and Copán, Honduras, for around $2,000 per person.

○ **Martsam Tour and Travel** ★★ (✆ **866/832-2776** in the U.S. and Canada, or 502/7867-5093 in Guatemala; www.martsam.com) is based on the island of Flores, and these guys are the best operators for Tikal and the Petén, although they also have an office in Antigua and can book tours for the entire country.

○ **Via Venture** ★★ (✆ **502/7832-2509;** www.viaventure.com) is a well-run operation specializing in custom-designed itineraries using the finest high-end hotels in the country, as well as an excellent team of guides and ground transport services. They are also particularly strong in the area of adventure tourism and theme vacations. In addition to Guatemala, these folks run trips and combined itineraries into Belize and Honduras.

Entry Requirements

Citizens of the United States, Canada, Great Britain, all European Union nations, Ireland, Australia, and New Zealand may visit Guatemala for a maximum of 90 days. A current passport, valid through your departure date, is required for entry into Guatemala.

TELEPHONE dialing INFO AT A GLANCE

The country code for Guatemala is 502, which you use only when dialing from outside the country. In this chapter, telephone numbers include this prefix because most businesses' published phone numbers include the prefix.

○ **To place a call from your home country to Guatemala:** Dial the international access code (011 in the U.S. and Canada, 0011 in Australia, 0170 in New Zealand, 00 in the U.K.), plus the country code (502), followed by the eight-digit number. For example, a call from the U.S. to Guatemala would be 011+502+XXXX+XXXX.

○ **To place a call within Guatemala:** There are no area codes inside Guatemala. To make a call, simply dial the eight-digit number.

○ **To place a direct international call from Guatemala:** Dial the international access code (00), plus the country code of the place you are dialing, plus the area code and the local number.

○ To reach an international operator: Dial ✆ 147-120. For directory assistance, call ✆ 2333-1524.

It's possible to extend your tourist visa for an additional 90 days, but the process is slightly tedious. To do so, you must go to the **Immigration Office,** 6a Av. 3-11, Zona 4, Guatemala City (✆ **502/2411-2407**). The process involves presenting several authenticated documents and photocopies. Moreover, these documents will need a lawyer's stamp or a notarization from your embassy. Even though the official fee for an extension is just US$15, the whole process can take as long as a week, and cost between US$20 and US$50.

Guatemala is also part of a 2006 border-control agreement with Honduras, El Salvador, and Nicaragua, allowing travel between the four countries under one tourist card. See p. 226 for info.

GUATEMALAN EMBASSY LOCATIONS

If you need a visa or have other questions about Guatemala, you can contact any of the following Guatemalan embassies or consulates: in the **United States,** 2220 R St. NW, Washington, DC 20008 (✆ **202/745-4952**); in **Canada,** 130 Albert St., Ste. 1010, Ottawa, Ontario K1P 5G4 (✆ **613/233-7237**); and in **Great Britain,** 13 Fawcett St., London, England SW10 9HN (✆ **020/7351-3042**). There are no Guatemalan embassies in Australia or New Zealand, but you could try contacting the embassy in **Japan,** 38 Kowa Building 9F, no. 905, 4-12-24 Nishi Azabu, Tokyo 106-0031 (✆ **81/(03)3400-1830**), or **Taiwan,** 12 Lane 88, Chien Kuo North Road, Section 1, Taipei (✆ **866/2-507-7043**).

Customs

Visitors to Guatemala may bring all reasonable goods and belongings for personal use during their stay. Cameras, computers, and electronic equipment, as well as fishing and diving gear for personal use, are permitted duty-free. Customs officials in Guatemala seldom check arriving tourists' luggage.

Money

The unit of currency in Guatemala is the **quetzal.** In September 2010, there were approximately 8 quetzales to the American dollar, but because the quetzal does fluctuate, you can expect this rate to change.

The quetzal is theoretically divided into 100 **centavos.** However, because of their insignificant value, you will rarely see or have to handle centavos. If you do, there are coins in denominations of 1, 5, 10, 25, and 50 centavos. There are also 1-quetzal coins, which are quite common and handy.

There are paper notes in denominations of 1, 5, 10, 20, 50, 100, and 200 quetzales. This can be a bit of a problem for travelers, since the bill with the largest denomination is worth only around US$25.

If your ATM card doesn't work and you need cash in a hurry, **Western Union** (© 502/2360-1737 in Guatemala; www.westernunion.com) has numerous offices around Guatemala City and in several major towns and cities around the country. It offers secure and rapid money-wire and telegram service, although they charge a hefty commission for the service.

ATMS   ATMs are fairly common throughout Guatemala, particularly in Guatemala City and Antigua, and at most major tourist destinations around the country. You'll find them at almost all banks and most shopping centers. Still, make sure you have some cash at the start of your trip; never let yourself run totally out of spending money, and definitely stock up on funds before heading to any of the more remote destinations in the country. Outside the more popular destinations, it's still best to think of your ATM card as a backup measure, because machines are not nearly as readily available or dependable as you might be accustomed to, and you might encounter compatibility problems.

CREDIT CARDS   MasterCard and Visa are accepted most everywhere. American Express and Diners Club are less common, but still widely accepted. To report a lost or stolen **American Express** card from inside Guatemala, you can call © 336/393-1111 collect in the U.S.; for **MasterCard,** © 1800/999-1480, or call © 636/722-7111 collect in the U.S.; for **Visa,** © 1800/999-0115, or call © 410/581-9994 collect in the U.S.; and for **Diners Club,** call © 502/2338-6801, or call collect to © 303/799-1504.

When to Go

PEAK SEASON & CLIMATE   The tourist high season runs December through March, coinciding with the winter months in most northern countries. It also coincides with Guatemala's dry season. Throughout this season, and especially around the Christmas and Easter holidays, hotels can be booked solid, so be sure to have a reservation, especially in the more popular tourist spots.

In general, the best time of year to visit weather-wise is in December and January, when everything is still green from the rains, but the sky is clear. If you want to avoid the crowds, I recommend traveling during "shoulder" periods, near the end or beginning of the rainy season, when the weather is still pretty good. *Note:* Some of the country's rugged roads become downright impassable without four-wheel-drive during the rainy season (see below).

Guatemala is a tropical country and has distinct wet and dry seasons. However, some regions are rainy all year, and others are very dry and sunny for most of the year. Temperatures vary primarily with elevations, not with seasons: On the coasts it's hot all year, while up in the mountains and highlands, it can be quite cool at night and in the early morning, before the sun heats things up, any time of year. At the highest elevations (3,500–4,000m/11,500–13,100 ft.), frost is common.

Generally, the **rainy season** (or *invierno,* winter) is May through October. The **dry season** (or *verano,* summer) runs from November to April. Even in the rainy season, days often start sunny, with rain falling in the afternoon and evening. The rainforests of the Petén get the heaviest rainfall, and the rainy season here lasts at least until mid-November.

PUBLIC HOLIDAYS   Official holidays in Guatemala include **January 1** (New Year's Day), Thursday and Friday of Holy Week, **June 30** (Armed Forces Day), **July 1** (Day of Celebration), **August 15** (Virgen de la Asunción), **September 15** (Independence Day), **October 20** (Commemoration of the 1944 Revolution), **November 1** (All Saints' Day), **December 24** and **25** (Christmas), and **December 31** (New Year's Eve).

Health Concerns

Guatemala's public healthcare system is overburdened, underfunded, and outdated. Throughout the chapter, I've listed the nearest public hospital and, when available, private hospital or clinic. Still, when you're in Guatemala, your hotel or local embassy will be your best source of information and aid in finding emergency care or a doctor who speaks English. Most state-run hospitals and walk-in clinics around the country have emergency rooms that can treat most conditions. However, I highly recommend that you seek out a specialist recommended by your hotel or embassy if your condition is not life-threatening and can wait for treatment until you reach one of them.

COMMON AILMENTS

Your chance of contracting any serious tropical disease in Guatemala is slim, especially if you stick to the major tourist destinations. However, malaria and dengue fever both exist in Guatemala. **Malaria** is found in rural areas across the country, particularly in the lowlands on both coasts and in the Petén. There is little to no chance of contracting malaria in Guatemala City or Antigua.

Guatemala suffers from periodic outbreaks of **cholera,** a severe intestinal disease whose symptoms include severe diarrhea and vomiting. These outbreaks usually occur in predominantly rural and very impoverished areas. Your chances of contracting it while you're in Guatemala are slight. Other food and waterborne illnesses can mimic the symptoms of cholera and are far more common. These range from simple traveler's diarrhea to salmonella. See p. 69 in chapter 3 for tips on how to treat and avoid such ailments.

No specific vaccines are required for traveling to Guatemala. That said, many doctors recommend vaccines for hepatitis A and B, as well as up-to-date booster shots for tetanus.

Getting There
BY PLANE

Most international flights land at **La Aurora International Airport** (© **502/2321-0000** or 2260-6257; www.dgacguate.com; airport code GUA). A few international and regional airlines fly into **Flores Airport** (FRS) near Tikal. If you're interested only in visiting the Maya ruins at Tikal and touring the Petén, this is a good option. However, most visitors will want to fly in and out of Guatemala City.

BY BUS

Guatemala is connected to Mexico, Belize, El Salvador, and Honduras by regular bus service. If at all possible, it's worth the splurge for a deluxe or express bus. In terms of travel time and convenience, it's always better to get a direct bus rather than one that stops along the way—and you've got a better chance of getting a working restroom in a direct/express or deluxe bus. Some even have television sets showing video movies.

From Mexico, the principal border crossing is at La Mesilla, north of Huehuetenango. From Honduras, the main border crossing is at El Florido, on the route from Copán. From El Salvador, the main border crossing is at San Cristobal, along the Pan-American Highway. And from Belize, the main border crossing is at Melchor de Mencos, in the Petén district.

There are several bus lines with regular daily departures connecting the major capital cities of Central America. **Tica Bus Company** (© **502/2473-1639;** www.ticabus.com) has buses running from Mexico all the way down to Panama, while **Pullmantur** (© **502/2367-4746;** www.pullmantur.com) connects Guatemala with daily service to San Salvador, El Salvador, and Tegucigalpa, Honduras.

Getting Around

BY SHUTTLE   For most of the major destinations, tourist shuttles or a private car and driver are your best means for getting around. There are a couple of major tourist shuttle services in Guatemala, and almost every hotel tour desk and local tour agency can book you a ride to just about any major destination in the country either on a regularly scheduled shuttle or with a private car and driver.

The main tourist shuttle company is **Atitrans ★** (© **502/7832-3371** 24-hr. reservation number; www.atitrans.net) which offers both regularly scheduled departures to most of the major tourist destinations in the country, and private cars or vans with drivers. Or you can contact **Clark Tours,** 7a Av. 14-76, Zona 9, inside Clark Plaza (© **502/2412-4700;** www.clarktours.com.gt); **Maya Expeditions,** 15a Calle "A" 14-07, Zona 10 (© **502/2363-4955;** www.mayaexpeditions.com); **Turansa,** Carretera Roosevelt, Km 15, Zone 11, Super Centro Molino (© **502/2390-5757;** www.turansa.com); or **Via Venture** (© **502/7832-2509;** www.viaventure.com).

Shuttle rates from Guatemala City or Antigua to or from other major destinations run between Q80 and Q400, depending on the destination. A private car or van with driver should cost between Q600 and Q1,600 per day, depending on the size and style of the vehicle and how many passengers are traveling.

BY BUS   This is by far the most economical way to get around Guatemala. Buses are inexpensive and go nearly everywhere in the country. There are two types. **Local buses** are the cheapest and slowest; they stop frequently and are generally very dilapidated. They also tend to be overcrowded, and you are much more likely to be the victim of a robbery on one of these. These buses are commonly referred to as **"chicken buses"** because the rural residents who depend on these buses often have chickens and other livestock as luggage. For all but the most adventurous types, I recommend you avoid these buses.

Express or **deluxe buses** run between Guatemala City and most beach towns and major cities; these tend to be newer units and much more comfortable. They also tend to be direct buses, thus much quicker. Most have working bathrooms, and some have televisions equipped with DVD players showing late-run movies.

BY CAR In general, I don't recommend renting a car in Guatemala. The roads are often dangerous. Guatemalan drivers, particularly bus and truck drivers, have apparently no concern for human life, their own or anybody else's. A brutal Darwinian "survival of the fittest" attitude reigns on Guatemala's roads. Passing on blind curves seems to be the national sport. Pedestrians, horses, dogs, and other obstacles seem to appear out of nowhere. In addition, theft is an issue. I recommend you avoid driving at night at all costs. While rare, there have been armed robberies of tourists and Guatemalans along the highways and back roads of Guatemala, particularly at night.

These caveats aren't meant to entirely scare you off from driving in Guatemala. Thousands of tourists rent cars here every year, and the large majority of them encounter no problems. Renting a car is a good option for independent exploring, and it does provide a lot more freedom and save a lot of time over bus travel. Just keep your wits about you.

Among the agencies operating in Guatemala are **Alamo** (© **502/2362-2701;** www.alamo.com); **Avis** (© **502/2324-9000;** www.avis.com); **Budget** (© **502/2232-7744;** www.budgetguatemala.com.gt); **Dollar** (© **502/2385-1301;** www.dollar.com); **Hertz** (© **502/2470-3737;** www.hertz.com); **National,** 14a Calle 7-57, Zona 9 (© **502/2362-3000;** www.nationalcar.com); and **Thrifty** (© **502/2379-8747;** www.thrifty.com). **Tabarini** (© **502/2331-2643;** www.tabarini.com) is a good local company with offices at 2a Calle A 7-30, Zona 10, as well as at the airport.

Rates run between Q320 and Q960 per day, including unlimited mileage and full insurance.

BY PLANE Guatemala still doesn't have a very extensive network of commuter airlines. The only major destination regularly serviced by commuter traffic is Tikal. **TACA Regional Airline** (© 502/2470-8222; www.taca.com) and **TAG Airlines ★** (© **502/2380-9401;** www.tag.com.gt) both have daily service to Tikal.

Charter aircraft can sometimes be hired to travel to some of the more outlying destinations like Quetzaltenango and Puerto Barrios. If you have a big enough group, or big enough budget, and want to charter a plane, contact **Aero Ruta Maya** (© **502/2418-2700**) or **TAG Airlines** (© **502/2380-9401;** www.tag.com.gt).

Tips on Accommodations

With the exception of a few large business-class hotels in Guatemala City's Zona Viva, Guatemala has no truly large-scale resorts or hotels. What the country does have is a wealth of intimate and interesting **small to midsize hotels** and **resorts.** A few classy luxury boutique hotels are scattered around the country, and are found with abundance in Antigua and around Lake Atitlán. Real budget travelers will find a glut of acceptable and very inexpensive options all across the country.

A hotel is sometimes called a *posada* in Guatemala. As a general rule, a *posada* is a smaller, more humble, and less luxurious option than a hotel. However, there are some very serious exceptions to this rule, particularly in Antigua, where some of the finest accommodations are called *posadas.*

Unless otherwise noted, rates given in this book do not include the 12% IVA and 10% hotel tax. These taxes will add considerably to the cost of your room.

Tips on Dining

With the exception of some regional specialties, the most common and prevalent aspects of Guatemalan cuisine are rather unimpressive. Handmade fresh corn tortillas are the basic staple of Guatemalan cooking. Tortillas, along with refried black beans, are usually served as an accompaniment to some simply grilled meat or chicken. Very few vegetables are typically served at Guatemalan meals.

You will find excellent restaurants serving a wide range of international cuisines in Guatemala City, Antigua, and Panajachel. However, outside the capital and these major tourist destinations, your options get limited very fast.

If you're looking for cheap eats, you'll find them in little restaurants known as *comedores,* which are the equivalent of diners in the United States. At a *comedor,* you'll find a limited and very inexpensive menu featuring some simple steak and chicken dishes, accompanied by rice, refried beans, and fresh tortillas.

Keep in mind that the 12% IVA tax added onto all bills is not a service charge. A tip of at least 10% is expected, and sometimes it is automatically added to your bill.

Tips on Shopping

In many respects, Guatemala City is a great place for shopping, particularly if you're interested in Guatemalan arts and crafts. While it's much more fun and culturally interesting to visit one of the traditional markets, like that in Chichicastenango, you can find just about anything made and sold throughout Guatemala on sale at gift shops in all of the major tourist destinations around the country. Moreover, you can find these arts and crafts in large, expansive markets, as well as in small boutique shops. **Note:** It is illegal to export any pre-Columbian artifacts out of Guatemala.

The best-known crafts are indigenous woven tapestries and clothing. The fabrics are woven on huge looms or simple, portable back-strap looms. Traditional dress for women includes a *huipil* (blouse) and *corte* (skirt), often fastened to the waist with a rope belt. In recent years, mass-produced machine-woven fabrics have begun replacing the more traditional wares. To spot a fake, look for gold or synthetic threads woven into the cloth, and for overly neat stitching on the back.

Other common handicrafts found in gift shops and markets across Guatemala include carved-wood masks and carved stone and jade.

In addition to the arts, crafts, and clothing, Guatemala's **Zacapa rum ★★★** is one of the finest rums in the world. The 23-year-old Zacapa Centenario is as rich and smooth as a fine cognac. Zacapa rums also come in 15- and 25-year aged varieties. You can get Zacapa rum at liquor stores and supermarkets across the country. However, you'll find good prices right at the airport. It's convenient to know you can save that last bit of shopping until the last minute.

[FastFACTS] GUATEMALA

Business Hours Banks are usually open Monday through Friday from 9am to 4pm, although many have begun to offer extended hours. Offices are open Monday through Friday from 8am to 5pm (many close for 1 hr. at lunch). Stores are generally open Monday through Saturday from 9am to 6pm (many close for 1 hr. at

lunch). Stores in modern malls generally stay open until 8 or 9pm and don't close for lunch. Most bars are open until 1 or 2am.

Doctors Contact your embassy for information on doctors in Guatemala, or see "Hospitals," below.

Embassies & Consulates All major consulates and embassies, where

present, are in Guatemala City: **Canada,** 13a Calle 8-44, Zona 10 (*②* **502/2365-1250;** www.canada international.gc.ca); **United Kingdom,** Avenida de la Reforma and 16a Calle, Torre Internacional, Zona 10 (*②* **502/2380-7300;** www. ukinguatemala.fco.gov.uk); and the **United States,** Av. de la Reforma 7-01, Zona 10 (*②* **502/2326-4000;**

http://guatemala.usembassy.gov).

Emergencies In case of any emergency, dial ☎ **1500** from anywhere in Guatemala. This will connect you to **Asistur,** which will have a bilingual operator, who in turn can put you in contact with the police, fire department, or ambulance service, as necessary. Alternatively, you can dial ☎ **110** for the National Police, and ☎ **125** for the Red Cross (Cruz Roja, in Spanish). Moreover, ☎ **911** works as an emergency number from most phones in Guatemala.

Hospitals The country's best hospitals are in Guatemala City. **Hospital Centro Médico,** 6a Av. 3-47, Zona 10 (☎ **502/2279-4949;** www.centromedico.com.gt), is an excellent private hospital, with English-speaking doctors on staff.

Language Spanish is the official language of Guatemala. English is spoken at most tourist hotels, restaurants, and attractions. Outside of the tourist orbit, English is not widely spoken, and some rudimentary Spanish will go a long way. Some 23 Mayan dialects are also widely spoken around the country. In many rural areas, many residents speak their local dialect as their primary language, and a certain segment of the population may speak little or no Spanish.

Mail A post office is called *correo* in Spanish.

Most towns have a main *correo,* usually right near the central square. In addition, most hotels will post letters and postcards for you. It costs around Q7 to send a letter to the U.S. or Europe. Postcards to the same destinations cost Q5). However, it's best to send anything of any value via an established international courier service. **DHL,** 12a Calle 5-12, Zona 10 (☎ **502/2379-1111;** www.dhl.com), and **FedEx,** 14a Calle 3-51, Zona 10 (☎ **1801/00FEDEX** [00-33339]; www.fedex.com), both have offices in Guatemala City, with nationwide coverage for pickup and delivery. DHL also has offices in Antigua and Panajachel.

Newspapers & Magazines *La Prensa Libre* is the country's most highly regarded daily newspaper, with an outstanding investigative reporting staff. The lower-brow *Nuestro Diario* has the highest circulation. There are several other daily papers, including *Siglo XXI.* There are currently no English-language newspapers. The free, monthly, English-language ***Revue Magazine*** (www.revuemag.com) is the most valuable information source for most tourists, with museum, art-gallery, and theater listings. It is widely available at hotels and other tourist haunts around the country.

Police In case of an emergency, dial ☎ **1500** from anywhere in

Guatemala. This will connect you to a bilingual operator at Asistur who can put you in contact with the police, fire department, or ambulance service.

Safety Safety is a serious issue in Guatemala. In Guatemala City, I highly recommend that you stick to the most affluent and touristy sections of town highlighted in this book. Basic common sense and street smarts are to be employed. Don't wear flashy jewelry or wave wads of cash around. Be aware of your surroundings, and avoid any people and places that make you feel uncomfortable. Basically, it is unwise to walk almost anywhere except the most secure and heavily trafficked tourist zones after dark. Rental cars generally stick out and are easily spotted by thieves, who know that such cars are likely to be full of expensive camera equipment, money, and other valuables. Don't ever leave anything of value in an unattended parked car.

Taxes There is a Q240 tax that must be paid upon departure. This is often included in your airline ticket price. Be sure to check in advance. If not, you will have to pay the fee in cash at the airport. There is an additional airport security fee of Q20. A 12% IVA (value added) tax is tacked onto the purchase of all goods and services. An additional 10%

tax, on top of the 12% IVA, is added to all hotel rooms and lodgings.

Tipping While there is a 12% IVA tax on all goods and services, it doesn't count as a tip. In restaurants, a minimum tip of 10% is common and expected. Tip more if the service was exemplary. Taxi drivers do not expect, and are rarely given, a tip.

Toilets Public restrooms are hard to come by in Guatemala. You must usually count on the generosity of some hotel or restaurant, or duck into a museum or other attraction. Although it's rare that a tourist would be denied the use of the facilities, you should always ask first.

Water Drink only bottled water within Guatemala, as waterborne diseases are very common in this country.

GUATEMALA CITY

Guatemala City is the country's capital and largest city. With a population of nearly three million, it's the largest city in Central America. Guatemala City was founded as the country's third capital in 1776, following the destruction of two earlier attempts by natural disasters—earthquakes and mudslides. Christened with the unwieldy name of La Nueva Guatemala de La Asunción de la Valle de la Ermita by Spain's King Charles III, it's most commonly known by its simple abbreviation, Guate. Long before the Spaniards moved their capital here, this was the site of the pre-Classic Maya city of Kaminaljuyú, whose ruins you can visit.

Despite its well-deserved reputation as a sometimes violent and dangerous place, Guatemala City has a lot to offer travelers. The principal commercial and tourist zones are full of fine hotels and excellent restaurants, and the nightlife found in Zona Viva and Cuatro Grados Norte is the best in the country. The city also boasts theaters, art galleries, and several worthwhile museums.

Essentials
GETTING THERE
For more information on arriving in Guatemala City, see "Getting There" in "Planning Your Trip to Guatemala," earlier in this chapter.

BY PLANE All flights into Guatemala City land at **La Aurora International Airport** (© **502/2321-0000** or 2260-6257; www.dgacguate.com; airport code GUA), which is located in Zona 13 on the edge of the city center and about 25km (16 miles) from Antigua. See chapter 3 for details about airlines that service Guatemala City.

There is an **INGUAT** (Guatemalan Tourism Commission; www.visitguatemala. com) information booth inside the airport, which is open to meet all arriving flights.

There are a couple of banks inside the airport that will exchange dollars and some European currencies, and cash traveler's checks. They are usually open whenever there are arriving or departing flights. There's also an ATM near the baggage claim area.

You'll find various shuttle companies offering hotel transfers as you exit either the national or the international terminal. These companies charge between Q30 and Q80 to any hotel in Guatemala City, and between Q50 and Q80 to Antigua. Many of the larger hotels also have regular complimentary airport shuttle buses, which are best to reserve in advance.

If you don't want to wait for the shuttle to fill or sit through various stops before arriving at your hotel, there are always taxis lined up at the airport terminal exits. A taxi downtown will cost around Q40 to Q80.

Avis, Budget, Hertz, National, Tabarini, and **Thrifty** all have car-rental desks at the airport. See "By Car" under "Getting Around," below, for more information.

Breaking the Code

Guatemalan addresses may look confusing, but they're actually easy to understand. All addresses are written beginning with the *avenida* or *calle* that the building, business, or house is on, followed by the nearest cross street and actual building number, written out as a two-number hyphen combination. This is then followed by the zone. For example, the INGUAT Office on 7a Av. 1-17, Zona 4, is located at no. 17, on Avenida 7, near the cross street of 1a Calle in Zona 4. Be very careful, first and foremost, that you're in the correct zone. 7a Av. 1-17, Zona 4; and 7a Av. 1-17, Zona 10, are two radically different addresses.

BY BUS Guatemala's bus system is a mess. Scores of independent companies provide service to just about every nook and cranny in the country. However, there is little rhyme or reason to their terminal locations. If you arrive in town by bus, you may end up at the large, hectic main bus terminal and market area in Zona 4, or at any number of private terminals around the city, often in Zona 1. It's always easy to find a taxi near any of the bus terminals, and I recommend taking one to your final destination in the city (Q40–Q80).

Warning: Guatemalan buses are often the targets of crime, both violent and nonviolent. Do not arrive by bus at night if at all possible, as the bus terminals and surrounding areas are very dangerous at night. If you do, hop in a cab immediately after you arrive.

ORIENTATION

Guatemala City is divided into 21 zones, or *"zonas."* The *zonas* are numbered sequentially in a spiral pattern beginning with Zona 1, the most central and oldest zone in the city. In general, the city is laid out on a standard grid, with *avenidas* (avenues) running roughly north-south, and *calles* (streets) running east-west. Of the 21 zones, there are only a few that you're likely to visit, as they hold the majority of the city's hotels, restaurants, and major attractions.

Zona 1 is the historic center and colonial core of the city. Zonas 9 and 10 are two neighboring upscale neighborhoods where you will find just about all the major hotels, restaurants, shops, travel agencies, and services of note. Zona 10 is commonly referred to as Zona Viva, though only the small section of Zona 10 with the greatest concentration of hotels, restaurants, and shops falls under this category. Zona 4 is a central area, which is home to the INGUAT offices, immigration, the national court system, and a major bus terminal. This is also where you'll find Cuatro Grados Norte, a pedestrian-friendly and safe section of bars, restaurants, shops, and discos. The airport and area around it are Zona 13.

GETTING AROUND

Guatemala City has an extensive network of metropolitan buses, but a vast number of assaults take place on them at all times of day and night. I highly recommend you take a taxi instead.

BY TAXI Taxis are plentiful and relatively inexpensive, and while they're supposed to use meters, many don't. It's always best to ask before taking off whether it will be a metered ride, and, if not, to negotiate the price in advance. A ride anywhere in the city should cost between Q20 and Q80.

If you need to call a cab, ask your hotel or try **Taxi Amarillo Express** (✆ 502/2470-1515; www.amarilloexpress.com), **Taxi Blanco y Azul** (✆ 502/2440-8789), **Taxis 2000** (✆ 502/2433-9984), or **Taxis Las Amaericas** (✆ 502/2362-0583). Taxi Amarillo Express cabs all use meters.

ON FOOT Guatemala City is not very conducive to exploring by foot. The city is spread out, and many of the major attractions are far from one another. Plus, street crime is a problem. It's relatively safe to walk around zonas 1, 4, 9, 10, and 13 by day. However, with few exceptions, you should never walk around Guatemala City at night. Those few exceptions include the most developed parts of Zona 10, or the Zona Viva; and the hip strip of bars and restaurants in Zona 4, known as Cuatro Grados Norte.

BY CAR Driving in Guatemala City falls somewhere between a headache and a nightmare. There is little need to navigate Guatemala City in a car. I highly recommend you take taxis and leave the driving to others. If you do find yourself driving around Guatemala City, go slow, as pedestrians and vehicles can appear out of nowhere. See p. 66 for rental-car info.

VISITOR INFORMATION

The **Guatemalan Tourism Commission** (**INGUAT;** ✆ **502/2421-2800;** www.visitguatemala.com) has its main offices at 7a Av. 1-17, Zona 4. This office is open Monday through Friday from 8am to 4pm, and can provide maps and brochures. More useful for tourists is the booth that they maintain at the airport (✆ **502/2260-6320**), which offers a similar selection of information. They can also make a call for you if you need a hotel or car-rental reservation. This booth is allegedly open for all incoming flights, but may be closed if your flight is very early or late, or too much outside of normal business hours. To get tourist assistance and information from anywhere within Guatemala, dial ✆ **1500.**

Hotel concierges, tour desks, and local travel agencies are another good source of information. There are scores of tour agencies around Guatemala City. I recommend **Clark Tours,** 7a Av. 14-76, Zona 9, inside Clark Plaza (✆ **502/2412-4700;** www.clarktours.com.gt); **Maya Expeditions,** 15a Calle "A" 14-07, Zona 10 (✆ **502/2363-4955;** www.mayaexpeditions.com); and **Turansa,** Carretera Roosevelt, Km 15, Zone 11, Super Centro Molino (✆ **502/2390-5757;** www.turansa.com).

FAST FACTS In case of an **emergency,** call ✆ **1500** or **911.** You can reach the **Cruz Roja (Red Cross)** by dialing ✆ **125.**

Hospital Centro Médico, 6a Av. 3-47, Zona 10 (✆ **502/2279-4949**), is an excellent private hospital, with English-speaking doctors on staff. Alternatively, the **Hospital General San Juan de Dios,** 1a Avenida and 10a Calle, Zona 1 (✆ **502/2220-8396**), is the biggest and best-equipped public hospital in the city.

Clark Tours, Clark Plaza, 7a Av. 14-76, Zona 9 (✆ **502/2412-4700;** www.clarktours.com.gt), is the official representative of American Express Travel Services. They also have desks at the downtown Westin and Marriott hotels.

Internet cafes are ubiquitous in Guatemala City, particularly in the Zona Viva and Zona 1 neighborhoods. Rates run between Q4 and Q12 per hour. Many hotels have either their own Wi-Fi network or an Internet cafe where guests can send and receive e-mail.

The main **post office,** 7a Av. 12-11, Zona 1 (✆ **502/2232-6101**), is a beautiful building. It costs around Q7 to send a letter to the U.S. or Europe. Postcards to the same destinations cost Q5.

What to See & Do

While it's certainly easy to visit all of these attractions on your own by taxi, many travelers like the convenience and built-in guide of an organized city tour. **Clark Tours,** 7a Av. 14-76, Zona 9, inside Clark Plaza (✆ **502/2412-4700;** www.clark tours.com.gt), offers several different city tours. Most of these combine a tour around the principal attractions of Zona 1 and the colonial core with stops at the **Museo Popul Vuh, Museo Ixchel del Traje Indígena,** and one of the city's large markets.

ZONA 1

Catedral Metropolitana (Metropolitan Cathedral) ★★ This stately, blue-domed, earthquake-resistant cathedral was completed in 1868 after 86 years of construction. The neoclassical structure inspires austerity and awe, with its stone floors, colonial paintings, lofty arches, and bursts of gold at its altars. Perhaps the cathedral's most striking feature is the entrance, which is supported by 12 pillars, each of which is inscribed with the names of hundreds of Guatemalans who died or "disappeared" during the civil war. The interior is large and filled with religious icons, carvings, and artworks. You can tour the cathedral in about 20 minutes.

8a Calle and 7a Av., Zona 1. No phone. Free admission. Daily 8am–8pm.

Centro Cultural Miguel Angel Asturias (Miguel Angel Asturias Cultural Center) ★ Set on a hill overlooking downtown and named for Guatemala's most renowned literary figure, this complex houses the National Theater, a chamber theater, and an open-air theater within a modernist structure that almost looks like an ocean liner. Built originally in 1827 among the ruins of the San José military fortress, the complex also contains a military museum, a small art gallery, conference rooms, and three cafeterias.

24a Calle 3-81, Centro Cívico, Zona 1. ✆ **502/2232-4041.** www.teatronacional.com.gt. Free admission. Daily 8am–6pm. Various theater, dance, and concert performances take place at night. Ticket prices vary.

Iglesia La Merced (La Merced Church) ★ Not to be confused with its more famous sister church of the same name in Antigua, this lovely baroque-style building has one of the most ornate facades of any Catholic church in Guatemala City. The interior is quite stunning as well, and features an extensive collection of religious art, sculpture, and relics. Originally built and administered by the order of La Merced, it was taken over by the Jesuits in the early 19th century.

5a Calle and 11a Av., Zona 1. ✆ **502/2232-0631.** Free admission. Daily 6am–6pm.

Iglesia San Francisco (San Francisco Church) ★★ The namesake Francis-can order built this baroque church in the early 19th century. The main altar is an impressive piece of work, at almost 91m (300 ft.) tall and 12m (40 ft.) wide. The church is famous for its woodcarvings, which include its main altar and a couple of beautiful pieces donated by King Charles V of Spain.

13a Calle and 6a Av., Zona 1. ✆ **502/2232-6325.** Free admission. Daily 6am–5pm.

Plaza Mayor ★★ Called the "center of all Guatemala," the Plaza Mayor brings together the great powers of Guatemalan society: the government, the church, the army, and the people. It consists of two large plazas, the Parque del Centenario with its central fountain and the Plaza de las Armas, intended as a military parade ground. The Plaza Mayor was first laid out and designed in 1778, just 2 years after the city

Guatemala City

Museo Nacional de Historia Natural

Museo Nacional de Etnología y Arqueología ①

Museo de los Niños ■

Museo Nacional de Arte Moderno

6a Avenida

5a Avenida

7a Avenida

Diagonal 3

Parque La Aurora

Avenida la Castellana

Mercado de Artesanías ■

Zoo

Boulevard Aeropuerto

1a Calle

Diagonal 12 (Boulevard Liberación)

1a Avenida

La Aurora International Airport ✈

ZONE 9

2a Avenida

Parque Centro América

3a Avenida

4a Avenida

ZONE 13

14a Calle

13a Calle

12a Calle

11a Calle

10a Calle

8a Calle

6a Calle

5a Calle

5

Guatemala City

6a Avenida

5a Avenida

18a Calle

7a Avenida

6a Avenida A

6a Avenida

Plazuela España

Synagogue & Einstein Institute ■

■ Obelisk

Avenida la Reforma ⓘ

7a Avenida

11a Calle

10a Calle

9a Calle

GUATEMALA

Los Próceres Shopping Mall

④

⑫

⑬

⑯

⑭

1a Avenida

⑰

U. S. Embassy

Avenida la Reforma

16a Calle

15a Calle

14a Calle

⑮

ZONE 10

2a Avenida

⑩

13a Calle

⑨

⑧

3a Avenida

⑦

10a Calle

9a Calle

8a Calle

6a Calle

2a Avenida

11

12a Calle

4a Avenida

⑤

11a Calle

⑥

5a Avenida

4a Calle

3a Calle A

6e Avenida

6a Avenida

7a Avenida

13a Calle

Diagonal 6

ZONE 15

4a Calle

3a Calle A

8a Avenida

Universidad Francisco Marroquín ■

0   200 yds

0   200 m

Museo Ixchel del Traje Indígena ③

Museo Popol Vuh

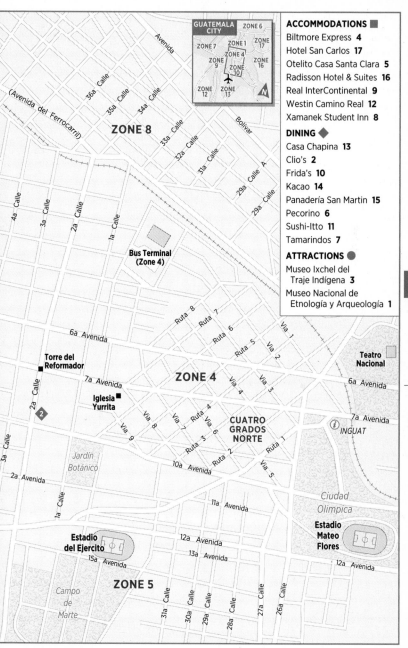

ACCOMMODATIONS ■
Biltmore Express **4**
Hotel San Carlos **17**
Otelito Casa Santa Clara **5**
Radisson Hotel & Suites **16**
Real InterContinental **9**
Westin Camino Real **12**
Xamanek Student Inn **8**

DINING ◆
Casa Chapina **13**
Clio's **2**
Frida's **10**
Kacao **14**
Panadería San Martin **15**
Pecorino **6**
Sushi-Itto **11**
Tamarindos **7**

ATTRACTIONS ●
Museo Ixchel del
  Traje Indígena **3**
Museo Nacional de
  Etnología y Arqueología **1**

was founded. The impressive buildings surrounding the plaza include the Catedral Metropolitana, the Palacio Nacional, and the National Library. Crowds gather here to celebrate holidays, protest, and sell their goods. The makeshift market here is busiest on Sundays, when vendors offer a variety of crafts at reasonable prices, though you might be able to find better deals in the small towns along Lake Atitlán or in Quetzaltenango.

Btw. 6a Calle and 8a Calle, and btw. 5a Av. and 7a Av., Zona 1. No phone. Free admission. Daily 24 hr.

ZONA 10

Museo Ixchel del Traje Indígena (Ixchel Museum of Indigenous Dress) ★★

Ixchel was the Maya goddess of fertility and weaving, and she certainly inspired artistic talent in her people. A collection of textiles from approximately 120 indigenous communities is on display here, providing a good introduction to and history of the crafts travelers are likely to see on their journey across the country. The museum also has two permanent exhibitions of paintings: 61 watercolors of Maya traditional dress from the collection of Carmen de Pettersen, and 48 oil paintings of the Cakchiquel artist Andrés Curruchiche. Three 13-minute videos are shown by request on the second floor. I recommend you ask to see the one on traditional fabrics even before you tour the museum.

Universidad Francisco Marroquín, end of 6a Calle, Zona 10. © **502/2331-3622.** Admission Q40. Mon-Fri 9am–5pm; Sat 9am–1pm.

Zona 13

Museo Nacional de Etnología y Arqueología (National Museum of Ethnology and Archaeology) ★

The National Ethnology and Archaeology Museum houses the most important collection of Maya archaeological artifacts in the country. It traces indigenous history over the centuries and through the present day, using several hundred Maya artifacts to tell the story. (Unfortunately, the only written descriptions are in Spanish.) Exhibits include a room dedicated to Maya technology (paper, and ceramic, shell, and bone tools), as well as a display of indigenous clothing. The highlight of the collection is the jade exhibit, with earrings, bracelets, masks, and an impressive scale model of Tikal.

5a Calle and 7a Av., Finca La Aurora, Local 5, Zona 13. © **502/2475-4010.** www.munae.gob.gt. Admission Q60. Tues–Fri 9am–4pm; Sat 9am–noon and 1:30–4pm.

OUTDOOR & WELLNESS ACTIVITIES

Guatemala City is a hectic, somewhat dangerous, congested urban center, and not a particularly inviting place to pursue most outdoor activities. If you want to exercise or get out into nature, you're best off leaving the city.

BIKING   Though you can forget about riding a bicycle in Guatemala City, several tour companies organize mountain-biking trips in the hills, mountains, and volcanoes outside the city. Contact **Old Town Outfitters ★★** (© 502/5399-0440; www.bikeguatemala.com), which is based in Antigua and can arrange transportation for you to join any of their daily mountain-bike rides.

JOGGING   As is the case with biking, Guatemala City is not very amenable to jogging. There are no public parks or outdoor spaces I can recommend as safe and secure for a foreigner to go jogging, and the busy streets of the secure Zona 10 district are not suitable. If you want to run, try the **Grand Tikal Futura** (© 502/2410-0800; www.grandtikalfutura.com.gt), which has a small outdoor jogging track.

SPAS & GYMS   You can certainly burn some calories or get a nice pampering massage while in Guatemala City. Most of the high-end business hotels in town have some sort of spa or exercise room, which vary widely in terms of quantity and quality. The best-equipped hotel spas I've found include those at the **Real InterContinental** (© 502/2413-4444; www.interconti.com), the **Westin Camino Real** (© 502/2333-3000; www.westin.com), and the **Grand Tikal Futura** (© 502/2410-0800; www.grandtikalfutura.com.gt).

SWIMMING   The tropical daytime heat makes a cooling dip quite inviting. Several of the higher-end hotels in Guatemala City have pools, but none of them will let outside guests use their facilities, even for a fee. If you really want to have access to a swimming pool, check the listing information under "Where to Stay," below, and make sure you choose a hotel with a swimming pool.

TENNIS   The **Westin Camino Real** (© 502/2333-3000; www.westin.com) and the **Grand Tikal Futura** (© 502/2410-0800; www.grandtikalfutura.com.gt) are the only downtown hotels with tennis courts. If you're a die-hard tennis player and must play while in town, you should stay at one of these hotels. There are no other public facilities open to tourists downtown.

SHOPPING

There are two main markets in Guatemala City, the **Mercado Central,** or Central Market, in Zona 1, and **Mercado de Artesanías (Artisans' Market),** in Zona 13. Both are massive and stocked with a wide range of arts, crafts, textiles, and souvenirs available throughout the country. Aside from these, the greatest concentration of shops can be found in the Zona Viva. These shops tend to be higher-end, and you'll often pay a premium price for the same goods available at the markets. However, the markets are often flooded with low-quality items, which are weeded out from the offerings at the higher-end shops.

Carlos Woods Arte Antiguo y Contemporáneo ★★   After several generations of focusing on antiques and classic artwork, this family-run gallery moved into a larger space and began adding contemporary works to their repertoire. The lighting, architecture, and well-thought-out displays make this place feel as much like a museum as a gallery. 10a Av. 5-49, Zona 14. © **502/2366-6883**. www.carloswoodsarte.com.

Colección 21 ★   This is an excellent shop and gallery with a wide range of arts, crafts, textiles, and jewelry of generally high quality. They also have a collection of contemporary paintings, as well as some antiques. 12a Calle 4-65, Zona 14. © **502/2363-0649**. www.coleccion21.com.

Lin Canola ★★   This popular store features a massive selection of Guatemalan cloth and textile products, as well as other arts and crafts items. This is a great place to buy local fabrics in bulk. Originally operated out of the Mercado Central, they now have this downtown outlet, as well as their even newer sister storefront, **In Nola,** in the upscale Zona 10 neighborhood. 5 Calle 9-60, Zona 1. © **502/2253-0138**. www.lin-canola.com.

Mercado Central (Central Market) ★ 🔥   This massive indoor market takes up several floors, covering a square city block in a building just behind the Catedral Metropolitana. This is your best bet for getting good deals on native wares. Offerings range from clothing and textiles to housewares and handicrafts. This market is actually frequented by Guatemalans more than tourists. Be careful of pickpockets. 9a Av. btw. 6a Calle and 8a Calle, Zona 1. No phone.

Sophos ★★ This hip and contemporary bookstore and cafe would fit right into the landscape in Seattle, New York, or Paris. They carry a wide selection of titles in Spanish and English, and feature rotating art exhibits and regular workshops, performances, readings, and book signings. Av. La Reforma 13-89, Zona 10. © **502/2419-7070**. www.sophosenlinea.com.

Where to Stay

In Zona 11, the **Grand Tikal Futura** ★★, Calzada Roosevelt 22-43, Zona 11 (© **502/2410-0800;** www.grandtikalfutura.com.gt), is a well-equipped modern option, well suited for those having a rental car dropped off before driving out to Antigua or the Western Highlands.

ZONAS 9, 10, 13 & ENVIRONS

These side-by-side zones contain the greatest concentration of hotels, restaurants, bars, and shops in the city, and heavy police presence makes them relatively safe for strolling and exploring on foot. Most of the hotels here are high-end business-class affairs, but there are actually options to fit all budgets.

Very Expensive

In addition to the hotel listed below, the **Westin Camino Real** ★★, 14a Calle and Avenida La Reforma, Zona 10 (© **800/228-3000** in the U.S. and Canada, or 502/2333-3000 in Guatemala; www.westin.com), is an excellent high-end hotel.

Real InterContinental ★★★ This is my favorite of the high-end, business-class hotels in this area. The rooms, facilities, and service are a notch above those of the competition, though most of the hotels in this class do a very good job. Rooms are spacious and in great condition, and all are carpeted and feature firm beds and 25-inch flatscreen televisions. Rooms on the InterClub floors have separate check-in desks, butler services, and a private lounge with regularly replenished snacks, free continental breakfast, and daily complimentary cocktail hour. There's an attractive pool area with a large Jacuzzi nearby. The hotel is situated on a busy corner in the Zona Viva, with scores of good restaurants, bars, and shops just steps away.

14a Calle 2-51, Zona 10. © **502/2413-4444.** Fax 502/2413-4445. www.interconti.com. 239 units. Q880–Q1,440 ($110–$180) double; Q1,840–Q2,400 ($230–$300) junior suite. AE, DISC, MC, V. Free valet parking. Amenities: 2 restaurants; 2 bars; babysitting; Jacuzzi; well-equipped gym and spa; pool; room service; smoke-free rooms. In room: A/C, TV, hair dryer, minibar, Wi-Fi.

Expensive

In addition to the hotel listed below, the **Biltmore Express** ★★, 1a Av. 12-46, Zona 10 (© **502/2410-5000;** www.biltmoreexpress.com.gt), is a comfortable business-class option, while **Otelito Casa Santa Clara** ★★, 12a Calle 4-51, Zona 10 (©/fax **502/2339-1811;** www.otelito.com), is a hip, intimate boutique choice.

Radisson Hotel & Suites ★★ This is another excellent and well-located business-class hotel in Zona 10. The rooms are all large and well appointed, with contemporary decor and all the amenities you might expect. All rooms should really be classified as suites, or at the very least junior suites. Each has a large sitting area, dry bar, and kitchenette. The service here is excellent. Separate floors are reserved for single women travelers, families, or those involved in the adoption process. There's a small sushi bar and restaurant just off the lobby, in addition to their more typical restaurant serving international fare.

1a Av. 12-46, Zona 10. © **800/333-3333** in the U.S. and Canada, or 502/2421-5151 in Guatemala. Fax 502/2332-9772. www.radisson.com. 115 units. Q720–Q1,200 ($90–$150) double. AE, DC, MC, V. Free parking. Amenities: 2 restaurants; bar; babysitting; small gym; Jacuzzi; room service; sauna; smoke-free rooms; free Wi-Fi. In room: A/C, TV/DVD, hair dryer, kitchenette, minibar.

Moderate

Hotel San Carlos 🎁 Right on the busy Avenida La Reforma, this charming three-story hotel features a Tudor exterior that's a little out of place in this Central American country. The British influence is apparent in the rooms, which feature antique furniture or knockoffs. My favorite rooms have plenty of space and varnished wood floors. This place it is good for a lodging at this price in terms of amenities and comfort. The San Carlos has a small lap pool in a pretty garden area.

Av. La Reforma 7-89, Zona 10. ℂ **502/2247-3000.** Fax 502/2247-3050. www.hsancarlos.com. 23 units. Q720 ($90) double; Q1,000–Q1,400 ($125–$175) suite. Rates include full breakfast and complimentary airport transfers. AE, DC, MC, V. Free parking. Amenities: Restaurant; bar; lounge; pool; room service; free Wi-Fi. In room: TV, hair dryer.

Inexpensive

With the opening of **Xamanek Student Inn,** 13 Calle 3-57, Zona 10 (ℂ **502/2360-8345;** www.mayaworld.net), backpackers finally have an excellent option in the heart of the Zona Viva.

ZONA 1

While this area is convenient for visiting the city's colonial-era attractions, it is much less secure and tourist-friendly than the *zonas* listed above. If you stay here, be particularly careful after dark. Take a taxi, even for short trips.

Moderate

Hotel Royal Palace ★ 🎁 This is the most atmospheric option in the Old Town. From the crystal chandeliers in the grand lobby to the well-maintained rooms, this classic hotel maintains all the charm and ambience of a bygone era. The rooms are large and stylish, some with carpeting and others with antique tile floors. My favorite rooms are those with balconies overlooking the street, where you can watch the daily parade from the comfort of your own room. (The trade-off for this great people-watching is more street noise.)

6a Av. 12-66, Zona 1. ℂ **502/2416-4400.** Fax 502/2416-4314. www.hotelroyalpalace.com. 76 units. Q440 ($55) double; Q520 ($65) junior suite. Rates include full breakfast. AE, DISC, MC, V. Free parking. **Amenities:** Restaurant; bar; concierge; gym; room service; sauna. *In room:* TV, hair dryer.

Inexpensive

In addition to the place listed below, **Hotel Colonial,** 7a Av. 14-19, Zona 1 (ℂ **502/2232-6722;** www.hotelcolonial.net), is another good choice.

Posada Belén ★ 🍴 If you're looking for a charming, family-run bed-and-breakfast at a very reasonable price, this should be your first choice in Zona 1. The converted colonial-era home that houses this hotel was built in 1873, and features a lush and beautiful interior garden. Rooms are decorated with rustic wood furniture, checkerboard tile floors, and local arts and crafts. The hotel is set on a short transited street, so its rooms are quieter than many of the downtown options. This place has an extensive collection of Maya artifacts and colonial-era art and carvings. The owners and their in-house guides and drivers are very friendly and knowledgeable.

13a Calle A10-30, Zona 1. ℂ **866/864-8283** in the U.S. and Canada, or 502/2253-6178 in Guatemala. Fax 502/2251-3478. www.posadabelen.com. 11 units. Q392 ($49) double. AE, DC, DISC, MC, V. Free parking. **Amenities:** Restaurant; lounge; room service; Wi-Fi. *In room:* No phone.

ZONA 13 (NEAR THE AIRPORT)

Given the fact that hotels in zonas 9 and 10 are less than 10 minutes away from the airport by taxi, there's no real advantage to staying near the airport. You'll enjoy much better access to restaurants, bars, and shopping if you stay at any of the hotels listed above. Still, if you want the option, the **Crowne Plaza ★**, Avenida Las Ameritas 9-08, Zona 13 (✆ **502/2422-5050**; www.crowneplaza.com), should be your top high-end choice, while **Dos Lunas Guest House,** 21a Calle 10-92, Zona 13 (✆ **502/2332-5691;** www.hoteldoslunas.com), is good for those watching their budgets.

Where to Dine

As with the hotels, the best and most varied selection of restaurants in Guatemala City is to be found in zonas 9 and 10. Likewise, there are some good restaurants in Zona 1, particularly for lunch, as the area can be a little sketchy at night. One excellent exception is the 2-square-block pedestrian mall area of Zona 4 known as **Cuatro Grados Norte,** which is full of bars, restaurants, shops, and art galleries.

ZONAS 9 & 10

In addition to the places listed below, the restaurant at the boutique hotel **Otelito Casa Santa Clara,** 12a Calle 4-51, Zona 10 (✆ **502/2339-1811**), and **Jake's,** 17a Calle 10-40, Zona 10 (✆ **502/2368-0351**), are two excellent, upscale fusion restaurants with many local fans. For French food, try **Clio's,** 4a Av. 12-59, Plaza Fontabella, Zona 10 (✆ **502/2336-6948;** www.cliosbistro.com), and for sushi try **Sushi-Itto,** 4a Av. 16-01, Zona 10 (✆ **502/2368-0181;** www.sushi-itto.com.gt). Refined Italian food can be found at **Pecorino,** 11a Calle 3-36, Zona 10 (✆ **502/2360-3035;** www.ristorantepecorino.com), while **Casa Chapina,** 1a Av. 13–42, Zona 10 (✆ **502/2337-0143**), serves good traditional Guatemalan fare in a cozy ambience. And, for margaritas and Mexican cuisine, try **Frida's,** 3a Av. 14-60, Zona 10 (✆ **502/2367-1611**).

Very Expensive

Tamarindos ★★★ 🎬 INTERNATIONAL/FUSION This restaurant offers a perfect blend of creative and artful cooking, accompanied by attentive service and a very attractive ambience. Inside you'll find several different dining rooms, each with its own decor. The menu is long and eclectic, running the gamut from steak with a chili poblano sauce to moo shu duck. Italy and Asia are the dominant culinary influences, as seen in everything from sushi to risotto, but there are some traditional Continental dishes, as well as nightly specials, on the menu as well. Save room for dessert; their molten *bomba de chocolate* (chocolate bomb) is superb.

11a Calle 2-19A, Zona 10. ✆ **502/2360-2815.** www.tamarindos.com.gt. Reservations recommended. Main courses Q68–Q282. AE, DC, MC, V. Mon–Sat 12:30–4pm and 7:30–10:30pm.

Expensive

Kacao ★★ 🎬 GUATEMALAN This elegant restaurant is *the* place to come for traditional Guatemalan cooking prepared and presented with style and flare. Various regional specialties include *pepian,* chicken in a pumpkinseed-and-tomato sauce from the Western Highlands, and *tapado,* spicy Caribbean seafood soup in coconut milk. The silky black-bean soup is finished off in a clay bowl and baked in the oven. There are a host of steak, poultry, and seafood options. For dessert, try the fried apple rings served with a vanilla-rum sauce. The restaurant decor is as traditional as the menu. Waiters wear traditional Maya garb, and the tablecloths are old *huipiles.*

2a Av. 13-44, Zona 10. ✆ **502/2237-4188** or 2377-4189. Reservations recommended. Main courses Q44–Q176. AE, DC, MC, V. Daily noon–4pm and 6–11pm.

Inexpensive

Panadería San Martín 🍴 CAFE/BAKERY   Set on a busy corner in the heart of the Zona Viva, this place is busy throughout the day. Folks come here for breakfast, lunch, or a coffee break, and the San Martin handles them all well. Breakfasts are excellent, and you can't beat the lunch special of soup alongside a half-sandwich and a half-salad for Q50. These folks have a bakery on premises, and a wide selection of sweets and gourmet coffees. The indoor seating is a bit too sterile for me, with its high-backed booths and Formica tables. I prefer to grab a seat in the shady outdoor patio or on the front veranda.

13a Calle 1-62, Zona 10. ✆ **502/2420-9916.** www.sanmartinbakery.com. Reservations not accepted. Main courses Q30–Q48. AE, DC, MC, V. Daily 6am–8:30pm.

ZONA 1

For a taste of Spanish food that fits in perfectly with the Spanish colonial charms of the Old City, try **Restaurante Altuna,** 5a Av. 12-31, Zona 1 (✆ **502/2251-7185;** www.restaurantealtuna.com).

Inexpensive

Arrin Cuan ★ ☺ GUATEMALAN   This is my favorite restaurant in Zona 1. The main dining room features wood tables crammed around the edges of a small interior garden. The menu is heavy on Guatemalan classics, with such regional dishes as *kac ik,* a filling turkey soup from the Alta Verapaz. If you want to sample something really exotic, order the *tepezquintle,* a large rodent served grilled over hot charcoal. This place has a children's play area, and plenty of free parking in a guarded lot across the street. They also have a branch in the Zona Viva at 16a Calle 4-32, Zona 10 (✆ **502/2366-2660**), but I prefer this original site. A marimba band plays most days during lunch and dinner.

5a Av. 3-27, Zona 1. ✆ **502/2238-0242.** www.arrincuan.com. Main courses Q50–Q80. AE, DC, MC, V. Daily 7am–10pm.

Guatemala City After Dark

Guatemala City is a large, metropolitan city. However, its after-dark pleasures are somewhat limited. Part of this is due to the dangerous nature of much of the city, especially after dark. Many of the late-night offerings are confined to a couple of centralized "safe" areas, which gives the scene a little bit of an apartheid feel.

For visitors and locals alike, there are two main after-dark destinations—the Zona Viva and Cuatro Grados Norte. Both offer a broad range of bars, restaurants, and clubs in a compact area that's safe and pedestrian-friendly.

Your best bet for finding out what's going on is to ask your hotel concierge, or pick up a copy of the free monthly ***Revue Magazine*** (www.revuemag.com), which is widely available at hotels and other tourist haunts around the country. If you can read Spanish, ***Recrearte*** (www.revistarecrearte.com) is another good source of information, with local listings for theater, concerts, and art galleries.

BARS & PUBS   For a mellow scene and a cozy place to catch a game or shoot some pool, head to **Cheers,** 13a Calle 0-40, Zona 10 (✆ **502/2368-2089**). Another bar popular with tourists and expatriates is **William Shakespeare Pub,** 13a Calle and 1a Avenida, Torre Santa Clara II, Zona 10 (✆ **502/2331-2641**). To mingle with some Guatemalans, try heading to **Rattle 'N' Hum,** 4a Av. 16-11, Zona 10 (✆ **502/2366-6524**).

In Cuatro Grados Norte, I like **Del Paseo** (✆ 502/2385-9046) and **Kloster** (✆ **502/2334-3882**) for drinks and socializing, and **Trovajazz** (✆ **502/2334-1241**) as a place to catch some live music. The entire area is suited to a bar-crawl or scouting stroll, where you can choose which place most suits your fancy.

Most bars don't charge a cover unless there's a live act, in which case the cover is anywhere from Q10 to Q80. Discos and dance clubs often have a cover of between Q15 and Q40.

DANCE CLUBS   Perhaps the best dance club in town is **Kahlua** ★, 1a Av. 15-06, Zona 10 (✆ **502/2333-7468**), a large complex with a hip young crowd and music and decor to match.

THE PERFORMING ARTS   The greatest number of high-quality performances take place at the **Centro Cultural Miguel Angel Asturias** ★★, 24a Calle 3-81, Centro Cívico, Zona 1 (✆ **502/2232-4041**; www.teatronacional.com.gt), which features the country's largest, most modern, and most impressive theater. Offerings range from local and visiting ballet companies and symphonies to theater and modern dance.

Another principal venue for the performing arts is the theater at the **Instituto Guatemalteco Americano** ★ (**IGA;** ✆ **502/2422-5555**; www.iga.edu), which is located at Ruta 1, 4-05, Zona 4, on the outskirts of Cuatro Grados Norte. These folks maintain a steady schedule of events that range from children's and traditional theater to art film cycles and dance performances. Check out their website for current event schedules.

Side Trips from Guatemala City

Several side trips out of Guatemala City are possible, ranging from day trips and tours to multiday excursions. I recommend you take any of these trips as part of an organized tour. All the major hotels have tour desks that can arrange these for you. Alternatively, you can contact **Clark Tours,** 7a Av. 14-76, Zona 9, inside Clark Plaza (✆ **502/2412-4700**; www.clarktours.com.gt), or **Maya Expeditions,** 15a Calle "A" 14-07, Zona 10 (✆ **502/2363-4955**; www.mayaexpeditions.com).

TOP TOURS & EXCURSIONS

Antigua ★★★   The fabulous colonial city of Antigua is just 45 minutes away from Guatemala City by car or bus. All of the local tour companies offer half- and full-day tours to Antigua. I definitely recommend you sign up for a full-day tour if possible. Antigua is *that* beautiful, and there is *that* much to see. Half-day tours cost Q240 to Q400, including lunch and entrance fees to all attractions. Full-day tours cost Q400 to Q640, including lunch. For more information on Antigua, see below.

Chichicastenango on Market Day ★★★   If you're in Guatemala City with a free Thursday or Sunday, you'll want to take a day trip to the fabulous market in Chichicastenango. These tours also hit Panajachel and Lake Atitlán on the way back, so you get to kill two or more birds with one stone. This is a full-day tour, with a fair amount of travel time, but it's worth it. These tours cost between Q360 and Q720, and include lunch. For more information on Chichicastenango and its market, see later in this chapter.

Tikal ★★★   Perhaps the most popular day tour out of Guatemala City is to the amazing Maya ruins of Tikal. These tours generally involve a very-early-morning flight and even earlier hotel pickup. The tours give you a good, full day in Tikal. However, if you've got the time, I seriously recommend you add at least a 1-night extension to

VOLUNTEER & LEARNING opportunities
IN GUATEMALA

There are plenty of options for active, adventure, special-interest, or theme vacations to Guatemala. Popular themes and activities include bird-watching, Maya archaeology, cave explorations, and mountain biking. In many cases, you may want to add on a specific theme tour or partake in some adventure activity as an a la carte option within the broader scope of your trip to Guatemala. However, some of you may want to build your entire itinerary around a specific theme or activity.

o **Art Workshops in Guatemala** (℡ 612/825-0747 in the U.S. and Canada; www.artguat.org) offers many creative opportunities, including nearly every genre of writing, plastic arts, and even yoga. While there are opportunities to try your hand at Maya weaving, that class watches the real experts at work and visits the markets where their works are sold. Ten-day tours run around Q14,360 to Q15,960 per person, plus airfare, depending on the workshop.

o **Entre Mundos** (℡ 502/7761-2179; www.entremundos.org), which is based in Quetzaltenango, functions as a bridge between a host of nongovernmental organizations and community projects. They specifically work to connect foreign volunteers with appropriate community, social, health, and educational projects.

o **Habitat for Humanity International** (℡ 502/7763-5308 in Guatemala; www.habitatguate. org) has several chapters in Guatemala and sometimes runs organized Global Village programs here. Their Global Village trips are large, group-escorted trips that include work on a Habitat for Humanity building project, as well as other cultural and educational experiences. The costs range from Q9,600 to Q16,000, not including airfare, for a 9- to 14-day program.

o **Jim Cline Photo Tours** (℡ 877/350-1314 in the U.S. and Canada; www.jimcline.com) is guided by a professional photographer who teaches participants to see Guatemala through the camera lens. The 10-day "Living Maya" tour, limited to nine people, focuses on colonial architecture, markets, villages, the natural beauty of Lake Atitlán, and the Maya people. Cost is around Q28,600 per person, plus airfare.

the tour. These tours run around Q2,400 to Q2,800, including round-trip airfare, park entrance fee, and a guide. Budget an additional Q400 to Q1,200 per person per day for multiday excursions, depending on the level of accommodations chosen. For more information on Tikal, see later in this chapter.

ANTIGUA ★★★

40km (25 miles) SW of Guatemala City; 108km (67 miles) SE of Chichicastenango; 80km (50 miles) SE of Panajachel

Antigua is a gem, an enchanting blend of restored colonial-era architecture and rugged cobblestone streets, peppered with ruins and brimming with all the amenities a traveler could want—beautiful boutique hotels, fine restaurants, and plenty of shopping and activity options. Antigua sits in a small valley surrounded by towering volcanoes, which are clearly visible over the red-tile roofs and church bell towers that dominate the small city's skyline.

Antigua was Guatemala's capital from 1543 to 1776. It was founded after mudslides and flooding destroyed the country's first capital, in what is today Ciudad Vieja, in 1541. Originally christened La Muy Noble y Muy Leal Ciudad de Santiago de los Caballeros de Goathemala (the Very Noble and Very Loyal City of Santiago of the Knights of Guatemala), it was for centuries perhaps the New World's finest city. Antigua flourished throughout the 17th and 18th centuries, pouring the massive wealth generated by the Spanish conquest into the construction of churches, government buildings, universities, convents and monasteries, private homes, and military garrisons.

After an earthquake in 1773 destroyed most of the city, the government was relocated to Guatemala City. There was great resistance to the move, and in 1777, the government instituted a law making it illegal to live in Antigua. Eventually, the city was almost entirely abandoned and stayed that way until the 20th century. In 1944, Antigua was declared a National Monument by the Government of Guatemala, and in 1979, UNESCO named it a World Heritage Site.

Antigua has the most elaborate and stunning **Holy Week celebrations** ★★★ in Guatemala, and perhaps even the Americas. During Holy Week, the streets are decorated with intricate and beautiful *alfombras* (rugs) made of colored sawdust and flower petals. A steady stream of religious processions parade through the streets and over these *alfombras,* which are quickly replaced with new ones.

Essentials

GETTING THERE

BY PLANE   The nearest airport to Antigua is **La Aurora International Airport** (✆ **502/2321-0000** or 2260-6257; www.dgacguate.com; airport code GUA) in Guatemala City. Since Antigua is so close to Guatemala City, many visitors book their first and last nights—and often a few more—in Antigua. Once you've made it through Customs, you can be settled into your hotel in Antigua in less than an hour, if you don't hit too much traffic.

BY SHUTTLE   The most common way to get to and from Antigua is on a minivan shuttle. Several companies operate regular minivan shuttles between Antigua and most major tourist destinations, including the airport, downtown Guatemala City, Lake Atitlán, and Chichicastenango. If you're coming to Antigua directly from the airport, you'll usually find several shuttles waiting, just after clearing Customs. All charge between Q50 and Q80 per person. Some will leave as soon as they are full, while others leave on fixed schedules.

If you're already in Guatemala City, or arriving from any other destination, ask your hotel or any tour agency about booking a shuttle to Antigua. Alternatively, you can book directly with one of the shuttle companies, like **Atitrans** (✆ **502/7832-3371;** www.atitrans.net).

Rates between Antigua and other popular destinations run around Q160 for Panajachel, Q160 for Chichicastenango, and Q640 for Flores/Tikal.

BY TAXI   A taxi is the fastest and easiest way to get from the airport or Guatemala City to Antigua. A taxi should cost between Q200 and Q320. Expect to pay the higher rate, maybe even a little more, after dark.

BY BUS   Buses from Guatemala City to Antigua leave from the El Trebol intersection in Zona 8. Buses leave every 15 minutes or so, usually as they fill up, between 5:30am and 7pm. The fare is Q8 for the 1-hour ride. The main bus terminal in Antigua is at the end of 4a Calle Poniente, next to the Municipal Market. Buses leaving Antigua for Guatemala City follow roughly the same schedule. Safety is a serious concern on these buses, and I recommend you take a taxi or shuttle.

BY CAR   The best route to Antigua from Guatemala City is to take the Calzada Roosevelt out of town. The Calzada Roosevelt heads northwest out of Guatemala City, through Zona 11 (passing right in front of the Tikal Futura Hotel), before turning into the Pan-American Highway (CA-1). Take this and exit at San Lucas. From here you'll take the well-paved, windy highway (RN10) into Antigua. The ride takes about 40 to 45 minutes with no traffic.

GETTING AROUND

ON FOOT   Antigua is walkable, and cars and taxis are unnecessary to explore the colonial core of the city. The entire downtown section of Antigua, which is where most attractions are, extends less than 10 blocks in any direction from the Plaza Mayor. However, watch your step—several hundred years and a few serious earthquakes have made Antigua's streets and sidewalks treacherous in places.

BY TAXI   Taxis and tuk tuks are plentiful in Antigua. A ride anywhere in the city should cost between Q20 and Q30. Some of the taxis in Antigua use meters, but if the one you get into doesn't, be sure to negotiate a firm price beforehand. If you need to call a cab, ask your hotel, or try **Taxis Antigua** (✆ 502/7832-2360).

BY CAR   While you won't need a car to explore Antigua, you may want one for a trip to Chichicastenango, Lake Atitlán, or other nearby towns. In Antigua, try **Tabarini,** 6a Av. Sur, #22 (✆ 502/7832-8107; www.tabarini.com).

VISITOR INFORMATION

The Guatemala Tourism Commission, **INGUAT,** 2a Calle Oriente, #11 (✆ 502/7832-3782; www.visitguatemala.com), has a bilingual staff, and offers regional brochures, basic maps, and a score of hotel and tour fliers. The office is open Monday through Friday 8am to 5pm, and Saturday and Sunday 9am to 5pm.

Local travel agencies and hotel tour desks are another good source of information. There are numerous travel agencies all over town. Some of the best include **Lax Travel Antigua** ★, 3a Calle Poniente, #12 (✆ 502/7832-1621); **Sin Fronteras** ★, 5a Av. Norte, #15A (✆ 502/7720-4400; www.sinfront.com); **Rainbow Travel Center** ★, 7a Av. Sur, #8 (✆ 502/7931-7878; www.rainbowtravelcenter.com); and **Via Venture** ★★, 2a Calle Oriente, #22 (✆ 502/7832-2509; www.viaventure.com).

FAST FACTS   Several banks have branches right on the Plaza Mayor or within a 2-block radius, including **Banco Industrial,** 5a Av. Sur, #4 (✆ 502/2420-3000); and **Banco Reformador,** 4a Calle Poniente, #1A (✆ 502/7832-4876). All of these have ATMs, will change money, and will make cash advances against a credit card. The best hospital in Antigua is **Hospital Privado Hermano Pedro,** Av. La Recolección, #4 (✆ 502/7832-1190), a modern 24-hour private hospital offering a wide range of services, including emergency and trauma units.

There are scores of *farmacias* around Antigua, and you can probably find one simply by walking around. **Farmacia Fénix,** 6a Calle Poniente, #35 (✆ 502/7832-5337), offers free delivery and has several outlets.

There are a host of Internet cafes around Antigua, and a growing number of hotels and restaurants are offering Wi-Fi. **Conexiones,** 4a Calle Oriente, #14 (✆ **502/7832-3768;** www.conexion.com), or the **Funkey Monkey,** 5a Av. Sur, #6 (✆ **502/7832-7181**), are two good bets.

The main Antigua police station is at the Palacio de los Capitanes Generales (✆ **502/7832-2266**), on Plaza Mayor. The **tourism police** (✆ **502/7832-7290**) is a division of the larger police force with bilingual officers trained specifically to deal with tourists. Their office is around the corner on 4a Av. Norte, and is open 24 hours.

What to See & Do

Antigua is a fabulous city for a leisurely stroll, and along the way you can visit a museum or do some shopping. There are also a number of tour agencies in town, and most hotels have a tour desk. All of these offer a standard city tour, as well as visits to volcanoes, Chichicastenango market, Lake Atitlán, and 1-day and multiday trips to Tikal.

The best city tours are the walking tours offered by **Antigua Tours ★★** (✆ **502/7832-5821;** www.antiguatours.net). They offer a wide range of tour and hotel booking options, but are best known for their walking tours with longtime resident and author Elizabeth Bell, whose books about Antigua include *Antigua Guatemala: The City and Its Heritage* (Antigua Tours, 2005). The 3-hour tour (conducted by Bell) leaves Tuesday, Wednesday, Friday, and Saturday at 9:30am and with another experienced guide on Monday and Thursday at 2pm and costs $20. On days when Bell is not available, other well-trained and personable guides lead the tour. These folks have an office on the west side of the main plaza, next to the Café Condesa, and another next to the Casa Santo Domingo.

MAJOR ATTRACTIONS

The **Plaza Mayor ★★** is the central axis of all Antigua. In colonial times, this was the city's main market and meeting area. Today, it's a great place to grab a shady seat and watch the parade of life pass before you. The current park was built in the 20th century, and covers a city block with towering trees, well-tended gardens, pathways lined with sturdy benches, and a beautiful fountain at its core.

The most distinguishing architectural feature north of Plaza Mayor—even more so than the Convento de las Capuchinas and the Iglesia La Merced (see below)—is the **Arco de Santa Catalina (Santa Catalina Arch).** This arch spans 5a Av. Norte, about 3 blocks north of the Plaza Mayor. It was built in the mid–17th century to allow nuns to pass from one part of the Santa Catalina Convent to the other without being seen. In the 19th century, a clock was added to a cupola atop the center point. Today, 5a Av. Norte is often called Calle del Arco.

Casa del Tejido Antiguo ★ This museum will tell you everything you ever wanted to know about textiles. It has a sizable collection of typical clothing from various regions of Guatemala. The exhibits of colorful, vintage *cortes* and *huipiles* are complemented by ample information on how they're woven, the history of the process, and the broader cultural significance of Maya cloth. Informative placards explain the exhibits, but guided tours in English and Spanish are available and recommended if you're deeply interested in the subject.

1a Calle Poniente, #51, btw. Ruínas Recolección and San Jerónimo. ✆ **502/7832-3169.** Admission Q5. Mon–Sat 9am–4pm.

Antigua

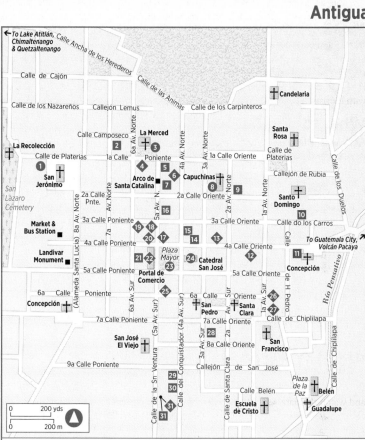

←To Lake Atitlán, Chimaltenango & Quetzaltenango

Calle Ancha de los Herederos

Calle de Cajón

Calle de las Ánimas

Calle de los Nazareños

Callejón Lemus

Calle de los Carpinteros

Candelaria

Calle Camposeco

La Merced **3**

2

Santa Rosa

La Recolección

Calle de Platerías

1a Calle Poniente

6a Av. Norte

4a Av. Norte

3a Av. Norte

1a Calle Oriente

Calle de Platerías

4

5

Callejón de Rubia

San Jerónimo

Arco de Santa Catalina **7**

Capuchinas **6**

8

2a Av. Norte

9

Santo Domingo

San Lázaro Cemetery

2a Calle Pnte.

3a Av. Norte

2a Calle Oriente

1a Av. Norte

10

Calle de los Duelos

Market & Bus Station

3a Calle Poniente

16

3a Calle Oriente

Calle de los Carros

To Guatemala City, Volcán Pacaya ↗

8a Av. Norte

19 **18**

15

Landívar Monument

4a Calle Poniente

20 **17**

14

13

4a Calle Oriente

12

Calle de H. Pedro

11

Concepción

Alameda Santa Lucía

5a Calle Poniente

21 **22**

Plaza Mayor

24 Catedral San José

5a Calle Oriente

Río Pensativo

23

Portal de Comercio

Concepción

6a Calle Poniente

25

6a Calle Oriente

San Pedro

Santa Clara

26

7a Calle Poniente

6a Av. Sur

5a Av. Sur

4a Av. Sur

7a Calle Oriente

2a Av. Sur

1a Av. Sur

27

Calle de Chiplilapa

San José El Viejo

28

3a Av. Sur

8a Calle Oriente

San Francisco

9a Calle Poniente

Calle del Conquistador (4a Av. Sur)

Callejón de San José

Calle de Chiplilapa

Calle de Sn Ventura

29

30

Calle de Santa Clara

Calle Belén

Plaza de la Paz

Belén

31

31

Escuela de Cristo

Guadalupe

0 — 200 yds
0 — 200 m

5 | GUATEMALA | Antigua

ACCOMMODATIONS ■

Black Cat Hostel **21**
Casa Azul **15**
Casa Concepción **11**
Casa Encantada **29**
Casa Ovalle **9**
Casa Santo Domingo **10**
The Cloister **7**
Hotel Posada de Don Rodrigo **16**
Hotel Posada La Merced **2**
Mesón Panza Verde **31**
Posada Asjemenou **5**
Posada del Angel **30**
Palacio de Doña Leonor **14**
Posada San Pedro **28**

DINING ◆

Café Condesa **22**
Café Mediterraneo **25**
Café Sky **27**
Doña Luisa Xicoteneatl **13**
El Sabor del Tiempo **18**
El Sereno **6**
Hector's **4**
La Fonda de la Calle Real **17, 19, 20**
Mesón Panza Verde **31**
Nokiate **26**
Welten **12**

ATTRACTIONS ●

Casa del Tejido Antiguo **1**
Catedral San José **24**
Convento de las Capuchinas **8**
Iglesia La Merced **3**
Plaza Mayor **23**

MEXICO

Tikal○

BELIZE

Livingston○
L. Izabal

Lake Atitlán

HOND.

Antigua ●★Guatemala City

EL SAL.

Catedral San José ★   Vowing to learn from the destruction of the cathedral during the earthquakes of 1583, the city began construction of a new, more complex, and supposedly stronger cathedral in 1669. The structure, completed in 1680, contained seven entrances, five naves, 78 arches, 18 chapels, a main sacristy, and a main chamber. Unfortunately, seismology tends to repeat itself, and that cathedral was leveled in the great earthquake of 1773. You can visit the ruins from the south gate on 5a Calle Oeste. The entire structure was rebuilt in the 19th century (the sacrarium is the only piece used from the original). The interior is not notably impressive, but houses a statue of Christ carved by Quirio Cataño, famous for carving the "Black Christ" of Esquipulas.

4a Av. Norte, on the east side of Plaza Mayor. No phone. Admission Q10 to visit the ruins; free for the main cathedral. Daily 9am–5pm.

Convento de las Capuchinas ★★   The Capuchins are a Roman Catholic order who seek sanctification through a life of work, privation, and continual penitence. Unlike other convents of old, the Convento de las Capuchinas did not require women to donate a dowry to join, though in Antigua that egalitarian outlook kept their ranks at fewer than 28 nuns. Completed in 1736, the impressive convent was abandoned after an earthquake in 1773 scared the nuns to safer ground. Fortunately, the damage was relatively minor, and the well-preserved courtyards, gardens, bathing halls, and nuns' private cells are now open to the public. Mannequins occupy some of those cells, demonstrating cloistered life. The roof is a great spot to take in a good view of the city.

2a Av. Norte and 2a Calle Oriente. © **502/7832-0743.** Admission Q40, Q20 students and children 11 and under. Daily 9am–5pm.

Iglesia La Merced ★★★   This church's central plaza is one of the most important launching points for processions during Holy Week. Built in a baroque style and adorned with stucco pilasters, it's also one of the best restored and preserved in the city. Architect Juan de Dios began work on the building in 1749, and completed it in 1767. The facade of the yellow temple is adorned with amazing detail, and several impressive paintings can be found inside, including the well-known work "Jesus Nazareno."

1a Calle Poniente and 6a Av. Norte. No phone. Free admission to the church; Q5 to visit the convent ruins. Daily 9am–6pm.

Spanish & Other Educational Classes

There are a host of Spanish-language schools in Antigua. Most offer small group or individual immersion-style classes between 4 and 5 hours daily, as well as various other activities and guided trips and tours. Most offer the option of a homestay with a local family, or a booking at any one of many hotels around the city. The schools I recommend include **Academia de Español Antigüeña,** 1a Calle Poniente, #10 (© **502/7832-7241;** www.spanishacademyantiguena.com); **Academia de Español Guatemala** ★, 7a. Av. Norrte # 63 (© **502/7832-5057;** www.acad.conexion.com); **Centro Lingüístico Maya** ★, 5a Calle Poniente, #20 (© **502/7832-0656;** www.clmaya.com); and **Escuela de Español San José el Viejo** ★★, 5a Av. Sur, #34 (© **502/7832-3028;** www.sanjoseelviejo.com).

Rates run Q1,000 to Q2,400 per week including classes, excursions, homestay, and airport transfers.

SEMANA SANTA (Holy Week)

The Christian **Semana Santa** ★★★ celebrations in Antigua are an extravagant mix of religious fervor, civic pride, and artistic achievement. Throughout the week there are a score of Masses, vigils (*velaciones*), and public processions. The processions can vary in size, and are often made up of hundreds of worshipers, who include men in regal purple robes, women in white linens and lace, and ubiquitous incense carriers. Other processions feature men in white hooded costumes (whose style was later borrowed by the Ku Klux Klan), women in somber black dresses (as if in mourning), and the occasional horseback-riding members. Most carry large floats (*andas*) with sculptures of Jesus Christ, Mary Magdalene, and other saints.

Some of the *andas* are enormous (as much as 3 tons) and require as many as 100 men to carry them on their shoulders. Individual processions can last for many hours, and you'll notice a complex choreography used to keep the shoulders and legs of those carrying them fresh.

Although the celebrations officially begin on Ash Wednesday, the real spectacle begins on Palm Sunday and peaks on Good Friday. Throughout the week, elements of the Passion, Crucifixion, and Resurrection are reenacted and celebrated. The sheer scope of the celebrations is hard to describe. The smell of incense and a thick smoke often hang heavy over the whole city.

If you plan on coming during Semana Santa, book your room well in advance, as much as a year or more in some of the more popular hotels here. The real score during Holy Week is rooms overlooking some of the streets on the processional routes. Of the hotels listed below, **Hotel Posada de Don Rodrigo** and **Posada del Doña Leonor** both have choice second-floor rooms with balconies fronting one or more of the processional routes. ***Warning:*** Be careful as you enjoy the Semana Santa celebrations. Pickpockets and petty thieves thrive in the crowded streets. Leave your money and valuables in your hotel safe.

If you want to do volunteer work in the area, check in with **Proyecto Mosaico** ★, 3a Av. Norte, #3 (✆/fax **502/5817-6660;** www.promosaico.org), an organization that formed in the wake of Hurricane Mitch and works as a clearinghouse to connect volunteers with worthy projects and organizations around Guatemala.

SHOPPING

Antigua is probably the best city for shopping in Central America. Options range from high-end jewelry and clothing stores to fine-art galleries and open-air street vendors selling local crafts and textiles. There are shops to fit all budgets and tastes.

In general, prices are higher in Antigua than anywhere else in Guatemala. The higher-end stores have set prices, and rarely budge on them. However, the handicraft and souvenir outlets, as well as the larger markets and street vendors, will all bargain.

Casa de Artes ★★   If you're looking for the best, this is it—but you'll pay for it. This is probably the art and handicraft shop with the highest-end selection. Different rooms are dedicated to woodcarvings, traditional textiles, ceramics, jewelry, and paintings. Open Monday to Saturday 9am to 1pm and 2:30 to 6:30pm, and by appointment. 4a Av. Sur, #11. ✆ **502/7832-0792**. www.casadeartes.com.gt.

If you're planning to head to the large and hectic markets—whether here, in Chichicastenango, or around the country—to bargain and shop, it's good to get an idea of what to look for before you dive in. I recommend visiting **Casa de Artes** or **Nim Po't** before setting out in search of any arts, crafts, or textiles. The folks at Casa de Artes carry high-end pieces, and their staff is very knowledgeable, so you can learn the difference between a quality piece of work and something that's mass-produced. Be sure to ask where the different styles are from, and see if any specific town or region strikes your fancy.

Doña María Gordillo ★ This place, which traces its origins to 1874, is an institution, and justifiably so. A glass counter filled with a wide range of homemade sweets—made from marzipan, shredded coconut, dulce de leche, and candied fruit—runs the length of the storefront. Open daily 10:30am to 2pm and 3 to 7pm. 4a Calle Oriente, #11. © **502/7832-0403**.

Jades S.A. These folks are pioneers of Guatemala's jade industry, and their main factory is a museum of their history and dedication to quality production. Wares range from jewelry and replica masks to gift items and sculptures. It's open daily from 9am to 6:30pm. 4a Calle Oriente, #34. © **502/7832-3841**. www.jademaya.com.

Joyería del Angel ★★ 🎁 Custom-made one-of-a-kind pieces are the forte of this place. Though many of the pieces are quite expensive, there are some more moderately priced works, as well as the occasional sale items. It's open daily from 9am to 6pm. 4a Calle Oriente, #5A. © **502/7832-3189**. www.delangel.com.

Mercado de Artesanías y Compañía de Jesús ★ This clean and modern facility was built to give a semipermanent home to the many street vendors who had set up shop around Antigua. It features a tightly packed maze of small souvenir stands selling standard, mass-produced fare aimed at the unsuspecting tourist market. However, there are a few vendors selling quality wares, but you'll have to know your stuff and sift through a lot of junk to get to anything good. It's open daily from 8am to 7pm. 4a Calle Poniente. © **502/7832-5599**. www.munideantigua.com.

Nim Po't ★★★ 🔥 This large indoor market works as a sort of consignment warehouse for local craft and textile cooperatives selling arts, crafts, and textiles from around Guatemala. The prices here are very fair, but the quality of the merchandise varies greatly. Still, you can find excellent *huipiles* and carved masks. It's open daily from 9am to 9pm. 5a Av. Norte, #29. © **502/7832-2681**. www.nimpot.com.

Wer ★★ 🎁 Owned by local artist Alejandro Wer, this converted 250-year-old home houses a massive collection of contemporary Guatemalan art by more than 100 artists in several of its rooms. It's open daily from 9am to 5:30pm. 4a Calle Oriente, #27. © **502/7832-7161**.

Where to Stay

Whether you're looking for a budget room in which to plop down your backpack or a top-notch luxury inn in which to kick up your feet, your choices are endless.

VERY EXPENSIVE

In addition to the places listed below, you can't go wrong at either **Palacio de Doña Leonor** ★★ (© 502/7832-2281; www.palaciodeleonor.com), housed in the old home of Pedro de Alvarado's daughter Leonor, or **Posada del Angel** ★★ (© 502/7832-0260; www.posadadelangel.com), which has hosted a fair number of dignitaries and stars over the years.

Casa Santo Domingo ★★ 🎁 This grandiose hotel lives up to the hype. The hotel is a tourist attraction in and of itself, spread over massive grounds that include the colonial-era ruins of an old convent, a working chapel, several museum-quality display areas, and a large amphitheater. The rooms are all top-notch, with comfortable beds, stately decor, and a host of amenities. Most have working fireplaces, and the best have balconies with volcano and sunset views. Even if you're not staying here, be sure to visit the Casa Santo Domingo, particularly around sunset—there is a sunset terrace with a perfect view of the nightly setting behind Volcán de Agua. Stick around for a drink or dinner as night falls, and the whole place is transformed into a candlelit fantasy.

3a Calle Oriente, #28. © **502/7820-1220.** Fax 502/7820-1221. www.casasantodomingo.com.gt. 129 units. Q1,680 ($210) double; Q3,560 ($445) suite. AE, DC, MC, V. Free parking. Amenities: Restaurant; bar; Jacuzzi; large outdoor pool; room service; sauna. In room: TV, hair dryer, minibar.

Mesón Panza Verde ★★★ 🎁 Although this place is not nearly as massive in scale, I find it as captivating and special as the Casa Santo Domingo. The standard rooms are acceptable, with small private garden terraces. However, the rest of the rooms, which are all suites, are the reason this place is so wonderful. All are spacious and beautifully decorated, with an eclectic mix of furnishings, artwork, and design touches from Guatemala and around the world. My favorite rooms are nos. 9 and 10, which are ground-floor suites with private garden patios and huge bathrooms. The **restaurant** (see review below) is one of the best in Antigua. There's also a small lap pool, an art gallery, and a wonderful rooftop terrace.

5a Av. Sur, #19. © **502/7832-2925.** www.panzaverde.com. 12 units. Q800 ($100) double; Q1,320–Q1,520 ($165–$190) suite; Q2,000 ($250) master suite. Rates include full breakfast and taxes. Rates lower in the off season and for extended stays, higher during peak periods. AE, DC, MC, V. Free parking. Amenities: Restaurant; bar; small lap pool; free Wi-Fi. In room: TV.

EXPENSIVE

Other good options in this price range include **Casa Concepción** ★ (© 502/7832-5821; www.hotelcasaconcepcion.com), a pretty, well-run boutique bed-and-breakfast; the **Cloister** ★ (© 502/7832-0712; www.thecloister.com); and **Hotel Posada de Don Rodrigo** ★ (© 502/7832-0387; www.hotelposadadedonrodrigo.com).

Casa Encantada ★★ 🎁 Although most rooms at this refined boutique B&B are rather compact, what they lack in size they make up for in comfort and style. The best room here is the large, rooftop suite, which has plenty of space and a private Jacuzzi. However, my favorite room is no. 7, which is tucked in the back of the hotel and reached by a rock walkway over a small pool. At night this pathway is lit with candles and is quite romantic. Breakfast is served on the delightful open-air rooftop, with great views of the red-tile roofs and the surrounding hills and volcanoes.

9a Calle Poniente Esquina, #1. © **866/837-8900** toll-free in the U.S. and Canada, or 502/7832-7903 in Guatemala. www.casaencantada-antigua.com. 10 units. Q760–Q1,240 ($95–$155) double; Q1,520–Q2,200

($190–$275) suite. Rates include full breakfast. These are weekend rack rates; rates lower midweek and off season, higher during peak periods. AE, DC, MC, V. Parking nearby. Amenities: Bar; small pool; free Wi-Fi. In room: TV, hair dryer, minibar.

MODERATE

In addition to the places listed below, **Casa Ovalle** (✆ 502/7832-3031; www.hotelcasaovalle.com) is another excellent, intimate bed-and-breakfast housed in a converted home.

Casa Azul ★   Unlike the other hotels in Antigua, this place has a modern and eclectic style, with an array of furniture styles from Art Deco to contemporary. The rooms all have very high ceilings, especially those on the second floor. My favorite room in the house is no. 8, a second-floor corner unit with lots of space and great views over the rooftops of Antigua. Casa Azul is very well located, just a half-block from the Plaza Mayor. There's no restaurant here, but breakfast is served, and a host of restaurants are located nearby.

4a Av. Norte, #5. ✆ **502/7832-0961.** Fax 502/7832-0944. www.guatemalainns.com/hotels/antigua/casa_azul.php. 14 units. Q722 ($90) double. Rates include breakfast. Rates lower in the off season, higher during peak periods. AE, DC, MC, V. Parking nearby. Amenities: Jacuzzi; small outdoor pool; sauna. In room: TV.

INEXPENSIVE

There are a host of cut-rate backpacker hotels and hostels around town, or you could also try **Posada San Pedro** (✆/fax **502/7832-3594;** www.posadasanpedro.net) or **Posada Asjemenou** (✆ **502/7832-2670**). Of the hostels, I recommend the **Black Cat Hostel** (✆ **502/7832-1229;** www.blackcathostels.net).

Hotel Posada La Merced ☺   This economical option is located right near La Merced church. The rooms are spread around a sprawling, converted colonial-style home, and all open onto one of two central courtyard areas. The rooms are simple, clean, and homey. A modest amount of local artwork and neo-colonial wooden furniture livens up the rooms. There are a couple of apartments with kitchenettes for longer stays, and two-bedroom/one-bathroom "suites" that are good for families. There's also a large communal kitchen for all of the guests to use. The owner and staff here are quite personable and helpful.

7a Av. Norte, #43. ✆ **502/7832-3197** or 7832-3301. www.posadalamercedantigua.com. 23 units. Q320–Q480 ($40–$60) double. Rates lower in the off season, higher during peak periods. Rates include taxes. AE, DC, MC, V. Parking nearby. Amenities: Free Wi-Fi. In room: No phone.

Where to Dine

Matching Antigua's abundance of top-notch hotels, boutique inns, and B&Bs, the city has a wide range of excellent dining options. In addition to the places listed below, **Café Mediterráneo,** 6a Calle Poniente, #6A (✆ 502/7832-7180), and **El Sabor del Tiempo,** 3a Calle Poniente and Calle del Arco (✆ **502/7832-0516**), are both excellent Italian restaurants. **Nokiate,** 1a Av. Sur, #7 (✆ **502/7832-9239**), serves sushi and Pan-Asian treats. For a view, you can't beat the rooftop terrace dining at **Café Sky,** 1a Av. Sur, #15 (✆ **502/7832-7300**).

EXPENSIVE

Other long-standing and dependable high-end dining options in town include **El Sereno** ★, 4a Av. Norte, #16 (✆ **502/7832-0501**), and **Welten** ★★, 4a Calle Oriente, #21 (✆ **502/7832-4335**). Both feature excellent international and Continental fare in elegant and refined settings.

Mesón Panza Verde ★★★ 🏛 INTERNATIONAL/FUSION   This is perenni-ally one of the top restaurants in Antigua, for good reason. The ambience is fabulous, the service professional and attentive, and the food superb. Chef Christophe Pache blends traditional French techniques and training with a wide range of world influ-ences. Tables are spread around several open-air terraces, assorted rooms, and nooks; my favorite seats are poolside under a vaulted stone roof. Enjoy live jazz Wednesday to Friday nights, and Sunday during brunch. This place has an extensive and reason-ably priced wine list, as well as some good top-shelf cognacs, tequilas, rums, and single-malt whiskeys.

5a Av. Sur, #19. 🕻 **502/7832-1745.** www.panzaverde.com. Reservations recommended. Main courses Q80–Q160. AE, DC, MC, V. Mon–Sat noon–3pm and 7–10pm; Sun 10am–4pm and 7–10pm.

MODERATE

Hector's ★★★ 🏛 INTERNATIONAL   Almost always bustling, this tiny new restaurant serves excellent bistro-style fare in a cozy, amiable space. There are only six or so tables and a few chairs at a small bar, which fronts the open kitchen. There are always daily specials, a pasta option, and some regular favorites, like beef bour-guignon. I recommend the seared duck breast served over a potato-and-carrot gratin, with some balsamic roasted grapes along for the ride. There's no sign here, and owner/chef Hector Castro says the place really doesn't have an official name, but you'll be able to find it, right across from the La Merced Church.

1a Calle Poniente, #9A. 🕻 **502/7832-9867.** Main courses Q55–Q135. AE, MC, V. Daily 12:30–10pm.

La Fonda de la Calle Real ★ GUATEMALAN   This is *the* place to come in Antigua for authentic Guatemalan cuisine, but don't expect a quiet, laid-back joint. It's become so popular, in fact, that they now have three branches in town—all within a block of one another. The menu features a range of classic Guatemalan dishes from *pepian,* a spicy chicken dish, to *kac ik,* a filling turkey soup from the Cobán region. All of the branches do a good job of re-creating a sense of colonial ambience with wood furniture and tall-backed chairs. I like the second-floor seating at the original outlet listed below, but the location at 3a Calle Poniente, #7, is much more spacious.

5a Av. Norte, #12. 🕻 **502/7832-0507.** www.lafondadelacallereal.com. Main courses Q75–Q125. AE, DC, MC, V. Mon–Thurs 8am–10pm; Fri–Sat 8am–11pm; Sun 8am–9pm.

INEXPENSIVE

Similar to the place listed below in terms of offerings, **Doña Luisa Xicoteneatl** (🕻 **502/7832-2578;** 4a Calle Oriente, #12) is a simple restaurant and bakery, and one of the original, and still going strong, backpacker hangouts in town.

Café Condesa 🍴 INTERNATIONAL   Located just off the central park, this place is a great choice for breakfast, coffee, or a light lunch. The sandwiches are very creative and come on homemade bread. I like the vegetarian La Tara, with homemade herb garlic cheese and tomato pistou. You can also opt for one of several quiche options or a large salad, and finish with one of the fresh pies or desserts. Sundays feature an all-you-can-eat brunch. Even when this place is packed, which it often is, the service is extremely fast. The restaurant is tucked in the back of a small collection of shops, inside the Casa del Conde.

5a Av. Norte, #4. 🕻 **502/7832-0038.** Breakfast Q30–Q50; salads and sandwiches Q32–Q50; dessert Q16–Q22. AE, DC, MC, V. Sun–Thurs 7am–8pm; Fri–Sat 7am–9pm.

ANTIGUA AFTER DARK

You'll find plenty of bars and clubs in Antigua, but overall, the nightlife scene is pretty mellow. In fact, by city ordinance, all bars and clubs must shut down by 1am. Adaptive as always, what follows are several nightly "private" after-hours parties, which are safe for tourists to attend. The parties shift around, and you'll almost certainly be handed a flier "inviting" you to one if you are still hanging around any of the bars in Antigua as the witching hour approaches.

My favorite bar in town is **Café No Sé ★**, 1a Av. Sur, #11C, between 5a Calle and 6a Calle (no phone; www.cafenose.com) a laid-back, boho joint with occasional live music. Nice rowdy bars popular with tourists and locals alike include the nearly neighboring Reilly's, 5a Av. Norte, #31 (✆ **502/7832-1327**), and Frida's, 5a Av. Norte, #29 (✆ **502/7832-1296**), as well as Monoloco, 5a Av. Sur, #6 (✆ **502/7832-4235**).

For dancing, you'll want to try **La Casbah**, 5a Av. Norte, #30 (✆ **502/7832-4235**); **Café 2000**, 6a Av. Norte, #2 (✆ **502/7832-2981**); or La Sala, 6a Calle Poniente, #9 (✆ **502/7882-4237**).

OUTDOOR ACTIVITIES & SIDE TRIPS FROM ANTIGUA

Most visitors come to Antigua for the history, culture, dining, and shopping, but outdoor enthusiasts will find there's something here for them too. If you're looking for adventure, your best bet is to contact **Old Town Outfitters ★★** (✆ **502/5399-0440**; www.adventureguatemala.com), who offer a range of mountain biking, hiking, and other activities around Antigua and the country.

Volcán Pacaya ★★ About 1½ hours from Antigua is the country's most popular volcano destination, **Volcán Pacaya.** Rising to 2,552m (8,370 ft.), Pacaya is in a near constant state of eruption. Tours tend to leave either very early in the morning or around 1pm. I recommend the later tours, especially in the dry season, as you may get to see some of the lava glowing red against the night sky. More likely you'll be treated to the sight, sound, and smell of volcanic gases and steam.

Most ascents of Volcán Pacaya begin at San Francisco de Sales, where you must pay the Q30 national park entrance fee. From here you'll hike for about 1½ hours to reach the base of the crater's rim, where the steep hiking trail gives way to a solid slope of loose debris made of lava rocks and ash. This final stretch is a steep and arduous scramble, with loose footings and many small rock slides—don't climb directly behind anyone else in your group. On the way down, more adventurous and athletic hikers can "ski" down.

Those who make it to the summit will encounter an otherworldly scene of smoke and gas, with the occasional volcanic belch. Some of the rocks will be very hot to the touch. Very infrequently, Pacaya will let loose with a spectacular eruption. When the skies are clear, the views are amazing.

Sturdy, closed-toe hiking shoes or boots are necessary. You'll also want to bring water, a warm sweat shirt, and (depending on the forecast) rain gear. Finally, if you're coming on one of the later tours, be sure to either bring a flashlight or make sure your tour agency provides one. Before you go, get current safety information, in terms of both volcanic and criminal activity, from your tour agency, INGUAT, or the Antigua tourism police. It's sometimes possible to camp here, which is your best chance of seeing the nighttime lava show. If this interests you, many of the tour agencies listed above also offer camping options.

Tour prices range between Q80 and Q320 depending on the size of your group and whether lunch and the national park entrance are included.

PANAJACHEL & LAKE ATITLAN ★★★

115km (71 miles) W of Guatemala City; 37km (23 miles) S of Chichicastenango; 80km (50 miles) NW of Antigua

Aldous Huxley famously claimed that **Lake Atitlán ★★★** was "the most beautiful lake in the world," and that Italy's Lake Como paled in comparison. Formed thousands of years ago in the crater of a massive volcano, Lake Atitlán is more than 16km (10 miles) across at its widest point. It sits at nearly 1.6km (1 mile) high in altitude, and is surrounded on all sides by steep verdant hills, picturesque Maya villages, and massive volcanoes with striking pointed cones. The views from the lakeshore, the hillsides above the lake, and the boats plying its waters are all stunning, and seemingly endlessly varied, as the light and cloud cover shift constantly throughout the day.

The shores of Lake Atitlán are populated with a series of small villages and a few larger towns connected by rugged roads and frequent boat traffic. Panajachel is the gateway to Lake Atitlán. It's the largest city on the lake's shore and the most easily accessible by car and bus from the rest of Guatemala.

Essentials

GETTING THERE

BY SHUTTLE Panajachel is connected to Guatemala City, Antigua, and Chichicastenango by regular tourist shuttle buses. These range from minivans to standard buses. Fares between Panajachel and Guatemala City run around Q80 to Q200; between Panajachel and either Antigua or Chichicastenango is about Q40 to Q160. Any hotel tour desk or local tour agency can book you one of these shuttles, or you can contact **Atitrans** (𝄢 **502/7832-3371**; www.atitrans.net) or **Turansa** (𝄢 **502/ 5651-2284**; www.turansa.com). *Warning:* Almost all of the shuttles from Guatemala City to Panajachel stop first in Antigua, where there is often a wait and/or switch of vehicle.

BY CAR To drive to Panajachel and other cities along the lake, take the **Pan-American Highway** (CA-1) to the junction at Los Encuentros. A few miles north of Los Encuentros is the turnoff to Sololá. In Sololá, follow the signs and flow of traffic to the road to Panajachel. The drive takes around 2½ hours from Guatemala City.

GETTING AROUND

Panajachel is compact, so it's fairly easy to walk anywhere in town. In fact, most people spend most of their time walking up and down the long strip that is Calle Santander. If you need a taxi or tuk tuk, they are plentiful and can almost always be flagged down anywhere in town.

If you want to rent a motorcycle, scooter, or bicycle, ask at your hotel or at any of the many tour agencies around town.

BY BOAT Panajachel is connected to all the towns and villages ringing the lake by regular boat-taxi service. There are two separate dock areas. The docks below the end of Calle Santander are used by boats heading east around the lake, as well as those going directly to Santiago de Atitlán. The docks at the end of Calle del Embarcadero are used by the boats heading west around the lake, as well as those going directly to San Pedro La Laguna.

There are several types of boats providing service around the lake. The least expensive boats are large and slow, and follow a regular schedule. However, smaller, faster boat taxis leave throughout the day—some by regular schedule, others as they fill up—and are definitely worth the few extra dollars. The slower boat taxis take about an hour to go from Panajachel to either San Pedro La Laguna or Santiago de Atitlán. The smaller, faster boats cut that time in half.

The boats operate from around 5am to 6pm. However, if you're coming back to Panajachel from any of the villages across the lake, you should try to grab a boat by around 4pm, as service after that becomes less frequent and less reliable. Schedules change according to demand, but you should never have to wait more than a half-hour to find a boat heading in your direction.

Boat taxis, their captains, and street touts almost always try to gouge tourists. There is a de facto difference between what locals pay and what tourists pay, and it's often hard to get a firm sense of what the official rates are or should be. Always ask your hotel or the INGUAT office about current fares before heading to the docks, and then try to be polite but firm in sticking to those guidelines.

In general, a small, fast boat taxi between Panajachel and San Pedro La Laguna or Santiago de Atitlán should cost around Q25 each way; between San Pedro and Santiago, or between San Pedro and San Marcos, about Q15. The slow water taxi between Panajachel and either San Pedro or Santiago should cost Q20. **Note:** Pay only for the leg of the ride you are actually taking. There is absolutely no reason to reserve a return trip in advance, and you run the risk of not meeting up with that specific boat or captain at the appointed time and losing your fare.

If you don't want to wait for a taxi and you've got a small group together, or if you'd prefer a private ride, you can always hire an entire boat that will hold up to 10 to 12 people. These boats charge around Q150 to Q300 for a trip to any of the towns around the lakeshore. The higher fares are for those towns farthest away from Panajachel.

ORIENTATION

Panajachel sits on the north shore of Lake Atitlán. As you enter Panajachel from the Pan-American Highway (Carretera Panamericana) and Sololá, you'll be on Calle Principal (also known as Calle Real), which continues on around the lake toward Santa Catarina Palopó. Soon after you enter Panajachel, you'll come to a major intersection at Calle Santander. The actual center of the town, called the Old Town, or Ciudad Vieja, is about 3 blocks from this intersection and about 10 or so blocks from the lakeshore. By far the majority of the action in Panajachel is centered on Calle Santander, which runs from this intersection directly toward the lake, where it dead-ends. The sidewalks are crowded with street vendors and are such a jumble that most people walk in the center of the street, making way, as necessary, for the sporadic traffic.

VISITOR INFORMATION

There's an **INGUAT** (Guatemala Tourism Commission) office (© **502/7762-1392**) on Calle Santander 1-87, in the Centro Comercial San Rafael. It's open Monday through Friday from 9am to 5pm. They can give you a map of Panajachel and the Lake Atitlán area, and help you with hotel reservations and figuring out the current bus and boat-taxi schedules.

FAST FACTS There are a host of banks on Calle Principal and around the Old Town, including **Banco de Comercio, Banco Industrial,** and **Banco G&T.** There

GUATEMALA | Panajachel & Lake Atitlan

are also scores of Internet cafes around Panajachel, both in the Old Town and along Calle Santander. The **post office** is at the corner of Calle Santander and Calle 15 de Febrero. The nearest hospital is the **Hospital Nacional Sololá** (✆ **502/7762-4121**) in Sololá, although in a pinch you can contact the small **Centro de Salud Panajachel** (✆ **502/7762-1258**).

What to See & Do
IN PANAJACHEL

The principal activities in Panajachel are strolling along Calle Santander and the lakeshore, shopping, and hanging out in one of the cafes, bars, or restaurants.

The main **Catholic church,** in the heart of the Old Town, dates from 1567, and was restored in 1962. The old stone facade looks almost whitewashed, and the diminutive plaza in front of the church is a major meeting place for locals.

Museo Lacustre Atitlán ★ ☺ A series of excellent and informative displays explains the geology and geography behind the formation of the lake. One of my favorite displays is the three-dimensional scale model of the lake and its surrounding mountains and volcanoes. The museum also showcases a collection of ceramic pieces discovered in the area, many of which were brought up from the depths of the lake by scuba divers. Plan on spending about a half-hour to 45 minutes here.

At the Posada Don Rodrigo. At the south end of Calle Santander, Zona 2. ✆ **502/7762-2326.** Admission Q40, free for children 11 and under. Mon–Fri 8am–6pm; Sat–Sun 8am–7pm.

Reserva Natural Atitlán ★ A couple of nature trails, a butterfly garden, and botanical gardens are the offerings at this reserve. The trails pass through some areas of dense forest, and feature a few high-hanging bridges to get you up into the canopy. You'll certainly see a range of tropical bird species, and if you're lucky you may see a monkey or two. The reserve has a visitor center, restaurant, and small section of private beach. There's also a zip-line canopy tour here.

In the San Buenaventura valley, just down the road from the Hotel Atitlán (see below), about .4km (¼ mile) before Panajachel, on the road in from Sololá. ✆ **502/7762-2565.** www.atitlanreserva.com. Admission Q44, Q25 students and children 11 and under, including a guided tour through the butterfly garden and breeding exhibit; Q188 canopy tour. Daily 8am–5pm.

AROUND THE LAKE

There are perhaps a dozen or more small towns and villages set on the shores around the lake. The two most significant towns are **San Pedro La Laguna ★** and **Santiago de Atitlán ★★**, both pretty much south across the lake from Panajachel. Other towns of note and interest to visitors include **San Marcos La Laguna, Santa Cruz La Laguna, Santa Catarina Palopó,** and **San Antonio Palopó.** Almost all of these towns are more popularly known by their abbreviated names of San Pedro, Santiago, San Marcos, and so on.

San Pedro is probably the most popular of these towns. It features a host of language schools and budget hotels, and has earned a reputation as a hippie and backpacker haven.

Santiago ★★ is a picturesque Tz'utujil town with a distinct character and fiercely independent streak. Santiago de Atitlán was the site of a horrible massacre during the civil war and one of the first villages to organize against the paramilitary and military forces. The Santiago de Atitlán *huipil* and men's pants are unique and highly prized by foreigners buying indigenous textiles. The cult of Maximón (see the box, below) is very strong in Santiago, and as soon as you step off any boat here, you'll be met with offers

MAXIMÓN: DON'T FORGET TO BRING HIM A GIFT!

The Maya introduction to Catholicism often came with the threat of immolation, hanging, or beheading, and they soon rationalized that this new religion could easily be superimposed on their own. When they saw the statue of Mary crushing a snake under her foot, they prayed to Gukumatz, the creator snake god.

The Maya also brought their own saint to their brand of Catholicism. Maximón (pronounced "Mashimon") was a pre-Columbian Maya god of the underworld known as Maam, or Grandfather. The modern name is a blend of Maam and his other name, San Simon. Maximón symbolizes male sexual virility and brings rain to fertilize the earth. He's known as the saint of gamblers and drunkards, and is thought to give wealth and worldly success to his followers.

Despite the Catholic church's attempt to demonize the dark-skinned Maximón by equating him with Judas, he is still found in churches, shops, and homes across Guatemala. He is now depicted as a 20th-century mustached man wearing a black suit, red tie, and wide-brimmed hat, and is represented in life-size wood statues, small dolls, or pictures on votive candles. He's given offerings of tobacco, alcohol, Coca-Cola, and a tropical plant with orange-red berries.

Maximón's feast day is October 28. On this day, and on the Wednesday of Holy Week, he's carried through the streets on the shoulders of his followers. In some villages he's hung from the main church's cross at the end of the ceremony. Maximón's more scandalous side forces most followers to keep him out of public view for the rest of the year, for fear that his famed sexual desires may run amok. He is kept in the house—and sometimes the outhouse—with his whereabouts changing regularly. In most towns with strong Maximón traditions (including Santiago de Atitlán and Zunil), locals will bring you to see him for a small tip. If you go, be sure to bring a cigar or some rum to leave in offering. In most cases, you'll have to pay a small fee for each photo you take.

from local kids and touts to take you to see him. You'll definitely want to visit Maximón, but don't feel obligated to go along with the first person who approaches you.

San Marcos ★ and **Santa Cruz** ★ are two small communities on the northwestern shores of Lake Atitlán. Both are set on hillsides above the lakeshore. However, each has a selection of small hotels spread along the water's edge. For some reason, these two towns have developed as hot spots for yoga retreats and holistic getaways, with several hotels in each town catering to this niche. The most popular and long-standing yoga retreats and meditation centers in the area are **Las Pirámides del Ka** (© 502/5205-7151; www.laspiramidesdelka.com) and **Villa Sumaya** (© 502/4026-1390; www.villasumaya.com).

Santa Catarina Palopó and **San Antonio Palopó** are two Kaquichel Maya towns on the northeastern shore of the lake connected to Panajachel by a well-paved road. **Santa Catarina** is particularly well known for its distinctive *huipil* of dark blues and greens with intricate embroidery. The brilliantly whitewashed church in San Antonio is especially pretty, with an enviable perch and fantastic view over Lake Atitlán.

SPANISH CLASSES

There are several Spanish schools in Panajachel. The best include **Jardín de América Spanish School** ★ (© 502/7762-2637; www.jardindeamerica.com)

Lake Atitlán

and the **Spanish School Jabel Tinamit** (✆ **502/7762-6056;** www.jabeltinamit. com). Rates are around Q1,000 to Q1,600 per week, and include 4 hours of class per day and a homestay with a local family.

OUTDOOR ACTIVITIES

In addition to the attractions above, Panajachel and Lake Atitlán are good bases for active adventures. Most hotels have a tour desk that can arrange any of the activities below, and then some. Or you can book through **Hunab Kú Travel & Adventure** (✆ **502/7762-6060;** www.hunabkutours.com) or **Atitrans** (✆ **502/7762-0146;** www.atitrans.com), both with offices on Calle Santander.

In addition to the activities listed below, you might ask around and try your hand at fishing on the lake, or sign up for a mountain bike tour. For something completely different, head underwater with **ATI Divers** (✆ **502/5706-4117;** www.laiguana perdida.com), which offers daily scuba dive tours.

BOATING   **Boat tours** ★★ on the lake are one of the most popular activities in Panajachel. All the hotel tour desks and tour agencies in town offer organized tours, most of which depart from Panajachel in the morning and make stops in San Pedro La Laguna, Santiago de Atitlán, and San Antonio Palopó. The tours generally last

The beautiful countryside and volcanic peaks around Lake Atitlán are quite enticing to climbers and hikers. However, due to the current security situation, poverty, and a history of violence, it's often not safe for tourists to be on isolated trails or back roads. It's best to sign up for a guided tour if you want to scale a volcano or hike to one of the nearby villages or lookouts.

around 5 to 6 hours. Most cost between Q50 and Q120, which gets you the guaranteed boat ride and an hour to 90-minute layover in each town. You can also sign on for a more elaborate tour that includes a bilingual guide and lunch. These generally run between Q240 and Q480 per person.

HIKING   At 3,020m (9,900 ft.), **Volcán San Pedro** towers over and behind the town. The trail is generally wide and well maintained, and the round-trip hike should take between 5 and 6 hours. Tour desks all over town offer guided hikes to the summit for around Q40 to Q120 per person. Other hikes around San Pedro head to **Cerro de la Cruz,** a beautiful hilltop with great views, and to **La Nariz del Indio (Indian's Nose),** another lookout spot that allegedly looks like a Maya profile from afar.

HORSEBACK RIDING & MOUNTAIN BIKING   The countryside here is beautiful and horseback and mountain bike tours can be set up by any hotel tour desk or tour agency. In Santiago de Atitlán, longtime residents **Jim and Nancy Matison** (✆ **502/5811-5516** or 5742-8975; wildwestgua@yahoo.com) offer a range of rides, including a full-day tour with lunch for Q480 per person, and shorter rides for Q160 per person per hour, plus Q60 per hour for the guide.

KAYAKING & CANOEING   You can rent canoes and kayaks from a variety of hotels and operators in most towns around the lake. Just ask around. Rates run around Q10 per hour and Q30 to Q40 per day. If you're in good shape, you can paddle to one of the nearby towns or villages. Remember that the winds and chop tend to kick up in the afternoon.

SWIMMING   The lakeshore along the front of Panajachel is filled with public beaches. You'll often find local kids and, to a lesser extent, tourists swimming here. However, I think the boat and foot traffic and pollution make it unappealing. If you want to swim in the lake, I recommend heading to the beach at the Reserva Natural Atitlán (see above) or in front of one of the smaller villages.

Shopping

Calle Santander and the road ringing the lakeshore are crammed with street vendors selling all sorts of Guatemalan handicrafts, from clothing and other textile products to stone and woodcarvings and leather goods. There are also a fair number of stalls selling handmade jewelry and trinkets, but these are relatively run-of-the-mill works that have no real connection to the land or its people.

The nearby towns of **Santiago de Atitlán, Santa Catarina Palopó,** and **Sololá** have deep and highly developed arts, crafts, and textile traditions. It's worth taking a trip to one or all of these towns to shop for the local wares. In addition, Panajachel makes a perfect base for visiting nearby **Chichicastenango** (p. 205) on market day. All of the tour operators in town offer day trips to Chichi on Thursdays and Sundays.

Note: It's become common practice to take old *huipiles* and dip them into a large dye vat of either blue or ocher. This gives the *huipil* an interesting look, but it's very far from traditional, and often serves to mask an inferior piece of work.

Where to Stay

IN PANAJACHEL
Very Expensive

Hotel Atitlán ★★★ 🗝️ Beautiful and luxurious rooms, fabulous grounds, impeccable service, and an excellent restaurant make this the top choice in Panajachel. The hotel is jampacked with colonial-era and local art, sculpture, and religious iconography. The rooms are all distinct and come with a private balcony or gardenfront patio. Ask for a third-floor room to get the best lake and volcano views. The extensive botanical gardens and aviary are true treasures, and the lakeview pool and infinity-edge Jacuzzi may make it hard for you to get up the impetus to tour the lake, towns, and markets just off the hotel's grounds.

Finca San Buenaventura. ℰ **502/7762-1441** or 7762-2060 reservations office. Fax 502/7762-0048. www.hotelatitlan.com. 62 units. Q960 ($120) double; Q1,600 ($200) junior suite; Q2,000 ($250) master suite. AE, DC, MC, V. **Amenities:** Restaurant; bar; lounge; babysitting; concierge; Jacuzzi; outdoor pool; room service; all rooms smoke-free; small spa w/sauna; unlit outdoor tennis court; free Wi-Fi. *In room:* TV, hair dryer.

Expensive

Posada Don Rodrigo ★ 😊 This lakefront property at the end of Calle Santander is a great choice in the heart of Panajachel. The sprawling grounds, tasteful rooms, fabulous terrace views, and in-house attractions set it apart from the competition. The standard rooms feature dark, colonial decor with heavy wood furniture, stucco walls, and a fireplace. The lakefront rooms are a bit more spacious and worth the modest splurge, which gets you a small private balcony and shared lawn. The pool, with a big spiral slide, and a very well-done museum (**Museo Lacustre Atitlán,** above) make this an excellent choice for families.

At the south end of Calle Santander, Zona 2. ℰ **502/7762-2326** or 7832-9858. www.hotelposada dedonrodrigo.com. 39 units. Q800–Q880 ($100–$110) double. Rates include full breakfast. AE, DC, MC, V. **Amenities:** Restaurant; bar; lounge; babysitting; outdoor pool; room service; free Wi-Fi. *In room:* TV, no phone.

Moderate

Other good midrange options include **Hostal Real Santander** (ℰ **502/7762-2915;** necos@itelgua.com) and **Hotel Regis** (ℰ **502/7762-1149;** www.hotelregis atitlan.com).

Hotel Dos Mundos ★ 🌿 Not as stylish or fancy as the Don Rodrigo (above), this is still an excellent option right on Calle Santander. The rooms, as well as the pool and gardens, are set back off the main drag. All the rooms are spacious and well kept. I prefer room nos. 11 through 23, which front the pool and garden area and share a veranda. The other rooms are a bit closer to the street, though not so close that noise is a problem. The hotel has a popular Italian restaurant, **Linterna,** as well as a separate cafe and bar.

Calle Santander 4-72, Zona 2. ℰ **502/7762-2078** or 7762-2140. Fax 502/7762-0127. www.hoteldos mundos.com. 22 units. Q560 ($70) double. AE, DC, MC, V. **Amenities:** Restaurant; bar; cafe; outdoor pool; room service. *In room:* TV.

Inexpensive

Hotel Primavera 🍴 This small hotel is a step above the score of budget options on Calle Santander. Most of the rooms are on the second floor and feature bay windows that overlook the street. The rooms are relatively small and standard, but they are kept immaculate. I like no. 9, which has a private staircase and balcony, and is set back from the busy street.

Calle Santander. ✆ **502/7762-2052.** Fax 502/7762-0171. www.primaveratitlan.com. 10 units. Q320–Q400 ($40–$50) double. AE, DC, MC, V. **Amenities:** Restaurant. *In room:* TV, no phone.

Where to Stay Around the Lake

IN SAN PEDRO LA LAGUNA

Another well-located option in this small town is **Casa Elena** (7a Av. 8-61, Zona 2; ✆ **502/5980-4400**).

Hotelito Amanacer/Sak'cari ★ 🍴 The second-floor rooms, with a shared veranda overlooking the lake, are your best bet at this semimodern hotel. Only three of the rooms have queen-size beds, so be sure to request one of these if you're traveling as a couple. The hotel also has a large, clean steam bath, and offers the use of kayaks for free. The name is a little redundant since "amanacer" and "sak'cari" mean sunrise in Spanish and Tz'utujil, respectively.

7a Av. 2-10, Zona 2. ✆ **502/7721-8096** or 2475-1802. www.hotelsakcari.com. 16 units. Q256 ($32) double. AE, DC, MC, V. **Amenities:** Free Wi-Fi. *In room:* No phone.

IN SANTIAGO DE ATITLAN

Located even farther outside of the town center, **Posada de Santiago** (✆ **502/7721-7366;** www.posadadesantiago.com) is another pretty lakeside hotel.

Bambú Hotel & Restaurant ★ 🍴 This is my favorite hotel in Santiago de Atitlán. Rooms include two bungalows with private patios overlooking the lake and those in the two-story building a bit farther back. Both options are spacious and cozy with warm earth tones and pretty artwork. The hotel has a pool and an excellent Nuevo Spanish-influenced restaurant with lake and volcano views. The town is just a 15-minute walk or short cab ride away, and any of the boat taxis from Panajachel or San Pedro will drop you off at the hotel's private dock.

Carretera San Lucas Tolimán, Km 16. ✆ **502/7721-7332.** Fax 502/7721-7333. www.ecobambu.com. 11 units. Q520–Q600 ($65–$75) double. Rates include continental breakfast and taxes. AE, DC, MC, V. **Amenities:** Restaurant; bar; midsize outdoor pool; sauna. *In room:* No phone.

IN OTHER VILLAGES

Casa Palopó ★★★ This small, artsy hotel exudes elegance. Most of the rooms have king-size beds, large bathrooms with Mexican majolica sinks, and large terraces with gorgeous views. There's a private villa above the main building with two gorgeous master suites, a Jacuzzi, a full kitchen, dining and living rooms, and a private infinity-edge pool. The villa also comes with a personal butler and cook. Back down at the hotel, the **restaurant** is worth a visit even if you're not a guest here, and the pool with wood gazebo is a good place to unwind.

Carretera a San Antonio Palopó, Km 6.8, Santa Catarina Palopó. ✆ **502/7762-2270.** Fax 502/7762-2721. www.casapalopo.com. 9 units. Q1,344–Q1,648 ($168–$206) double; Q1,760–Q2,104 ($220–$263) suite; Q7,440 ($930) villa. Rates higher during peak periods, lower during the off season. AE, DC, MC, V. No children 14 and under allowed. **Amenities:** Restaurant; bar; concierge; small gym and spa services; small outdoor pool; room service; free Wi-Fi. *In room:* Minibar.

La Casa del Mundo ★ 🛏 This hotel sits at the top of several steep flights of steps on a rocky outcropping that juts into the lake. The rooms' distinctive decor mixes local arts and crafts with a European sense of style. Every room has a view of the lake, and a few have private balconies with lake and volcano views. There are several open-air tiled terraces spread around the grounds, all with great views. On one of these terraces, near the water, is the hotel's wood-fired hot tub, located to allow you to alternate between the hot tub and the cool lake. You can also rent kayaks.

Jaibalito. ℂ **502/5218-5332** or 5204-5558. www.lacasadelmundo.com. 16 units, 10 with private bathroom. Q288 ($36) double shared bathroom; Q512–Q632 ($64–$79) double with private bathroom. Rates slightly higher during peak periods. Rates include taxes. No credit cards. **Amenities:** Restaurant; bar; Jacuzzi; Wi-Fi (Q25/$3.15 per hour). *In room:* No phone.

Villa Sumaya ★★ 🛏 If you're looking for spiritual and physical rejuvenation, this is the place for you. The individual cabins are beautifully done with tile floors, cotton comforters, local crafts, and a large veranda with several chairs and a hammock. All rooms face the lake, with the towering silhouettes of volcanoes in the background. The hotel's **Blue Tiger Temple** is a wonderful wood-floored yoga and meditation room that often attracts visiting instructors and retreat guests, and there's always a massage therapist on call. There's a good beach for swimming, and the grounds are lush with tropical flowers.

Santa Cruz La Laguna. ℂ **502/4026-1390** or 4026-1455. www.villasumaya.com. 15 units. Q520–Q880 ($65–$110) double. AE, DC, MC, V. **Amenities:** Restaurant; bar; babysitting; Jacuzzi; pool; sauna. *In room:* No phone.

Where to Dine

Panajachel is the only town here with a real dining scene and variety of restaurants. In most cases, at the other towns and villages, you'll probably be eating mostly at your hotel or *posada*. San Pedro is a slight exception to that rule. In San Pedro, do try the laid-back atmosphere and mostly vegetarian cooking offered at **Zoola ★** (ℂ 502/ 5847-4857) and the varied international fare at **Jarachik** (ℂ **502/5958-9417**).

Back in Pana, in addition to the places listed below, **Guajimbo's** (ℂ **502/7762-0063**) is a popular Uruguayan-style steakhouse that often has live music; **Las Chinitas** (ℂ **502/7762-2612**) is the town's most popular Asian restaurant, with a mix of Chinese, Thai, and Indian options. For a casual meal, try **Deli Jasmín,** Calle Santander (ℂ **502/7762-2586**). For something fancier, head to **Hotel Atitlán** (see above), and for something simpler, try one of the lakefront restaurants spread over the hill above the main boat docks.

MODERATE

El Bistro ★ ITALIAN This place serves excellent pastas and entrees in a convivial open-air setting. While there's some indoor seating, the best tables are found in a covered courtyard just off Calle Santander lined with plants, palms, and bamboo. Homemade fettuccine is available with more than 15 different sauces, and other pasta options include lasagna and cannelloni. For something heartier, opt for grilled fish, chicken parmigiana, or steak pizzaola. When you order, the waiter will ask if you want your pasta "al dente" or "normal." "Normal" would be overcooked for most people accustomed to good Italian cooking.

Southern end of Calle Santander. ℂ **502/7762-0508.** Reservations recommended. Pasta Q50–Q60; main courses Q50–Q80. AE, DC, MC, V. Tues–Sun 7:30am–10pm; Mon noon–10pm.

Sunset Café GUATEMALAN/MEXICAN   As the name suggests, sunset is a good time to come here. The wonderful view makes the standard Mexican fare more memorable. I like the *fajitas de pescado* (fish fajitas) and *enchiladas verdes* (chicken enchiladas in a green tomatillo sauce). There's live music here most nights, so grab a drink, a plate of nachos, and a seat under the tree (heavily hung with orchids and bromeliads) that grows through the thatch roof.

Calle Santander and Calle del Lago. ℂ **502/7762-0003.** Reservations recommended for large groups. Main courses Q40–Q100. AE, DC, MC, V. Daily 11am–midnight.

INEXPENSIVE

Café Bombay ★ 🍴 INDIAN/VEGETARIAN   The name of this place indicates that they dish out Indian cuisine, which you will find here, but you'll also get everything vegetarian from pad Thai and tacos to lasagna and falafel. In addition, excellent sandwiches, soups, and smoothies are served, as well as vegan fare. The atmosphere is casual, and on a nice day you can grab a seat on one of the umbrella-covered tables just off Calle Santander.

Calle Santander. ℂ **502/7762-0611.** Reservations not accepted. Main courses Q50–Q75; sandwiches Q20–Q40. No credit cards. Wed–Mon 11am–10pm.

Lake Atitlán After Dark

Panajachel has a fairly active nightlife. For nearly 20 years, my favorite place has been the **Circus Bar ★★** (ℂ **502/7762-2056**), which has a relaxed vibe, simple menu, and decor to match the joint's name. They also frequently have live music. Circus Bar is located in what's considered Panajachel's mini–Zona Viva. Of the bars on Calle Santander, I like the **Pana Rock Café** (ℂ **502/7762-2194;** www.panarockcafe. com), which is a takeoff on the Hard Rock chain.

For loud and late-night dancing, try **Rumba Disco,** Calle Principal (ℂ **502/7762-1015**); **El Aleph,** Avenida Los Arboles (ℂ **502/7762-0192**); or **El Chapiteau Discoteque,** Avenida Los Arboles (ℂ **502/7762-0374**).

Over in San Pedro, you'll find **El Barrio ★** (ℂ **502/5577-2601**), the **Alegre Pub ★** (ℂ **502/7721-8100;** www.thealegrepub.com), and the **Buddha ★★** (www.thebuddhaguatemala.com), which often features live music.

All of the above nightlife picks are located on the winding street connecting the two main docks in town, known locally as "Gringo Alley."

QUETZALTENANGO & THE WESTERN HIGHLANDS ★

201km (125 miles) NW of Guatemala City; 90km (56 miles) S of Huehuetenango

The rugged geography of Guatemala's Western Highlands is a patchwork of volcanic mountains and lakes populated by small, and often isolated, villages of the country's many Maya people. Some of the primary tribes who call this area home include the Ki'che, Mam, Kekchi, Tz'utujil, Ixil, Kaqchiquel, and Jacaltec. Most still practice small-scale plot farming on *milpas,* which are predominantly sown with corn. Locals live on a mix of subsistence farming and bartering. Aside from the food they grow, they also produce intricately designed and brightly colored woven textiles. In Spanish, the Western Highlands are called the Altiplano.

The highland burg of **Quetzaltenango** is the largest city and commercial hub in the Altiplano, and the second-largest city in Guatemala, with a population of more than 300,000. This was and still is a principal center of the Maya Ki'che of Guatemala—and many locals still refer to the city by its Ki'che name **Xelajú.** In fact, most people simply call the place **Xela** (pronounced "*Sheh*-la"). Xelajú is close to the site where Ki'che King Tecún Umán was killed in battle against the Spanish conquistador Pedro de Alvarado. Following Tecún Umán's defeat in 1524, the city was renamed Quetzaltenango, or "place of the Quetzal," which is what Alvarado's Nahuatl mercenaries called it.

Thanks to the presence of a large national university and scores of language schools and foreign volunteer programs, there's a college-town vibe to the city, and you'll find several good coffee shops and used bookstores in Xela, and even a couple of art-movie houses. You'll also find more nightlife here than anywhere else in the country outside of Guatemala City.

Quetzaltenango makes an excellent base for visiting a host of nearby towns and attractions, including **hot springs,** small villages with impressive **markets and churches,** and towering **volcanoes** waiting to be hiked.

Essentials
GETTING THERE
BY BUS   Several bus lines provide regular service in comfortable modern buses throughout the day between Xela and Guatemala City. **Líneas Dorada** (✆ **502/2415-8900** in Guatemala City, or 7767-5198 in Xela) has express buses leaving from 16a Calle and 10 Avenida, Zona 1, in Guatemala City, at 7am and 3pm. The return buses leave Xela from 12 Avenida and 5a Calle, Zona 3, at 4:30am and 3:30pm.

Transportes Galgos (✆ **502/2253-4868** in Guatemala City, or 7761-2248 in Xela) has buses leaving Guatemala City for Xela at 8:30am and 2:30 and 5pm. The return buses leave Xela from Calle Rodolfo Robles 17-43, Zona 1, at 4 and 8:30am, and at 12:30pm.

The trip on either bus line takes about 4 to 5 hours. The fare is around Q55 to Q75 each way.

BY CAR   To drive to Quetzaltenango, take the **Pan-American Highway** (CA-1) north out of Guatemala City. At Cuatro Caminos, take the turnoff for Quetzaltenango, which lies 13km (8 miles) to the southwest, after the small city of Salcajá. The trip takes about 4 hours from Guatemala City. Quetzaltenango is also connected to the southern Pacific Coast Highway, which visitors would use to go down to Retalhuleu and the Pacific beaches.

GETTING AROUND
Taxis and tuk tuks are plentiful in Xela. You can always find one around Parque Centro America. Fares around town should run between Q15 and Q30. If you can't flag one down, have your hotel call one for you, or call **Taxi Blanco y Azul** (✆ **502/7763-2285**) or **Mario López** (✆ **502/4884-7950**). If you want to rent a car for the day, or longer, contact **Tabarini** (✆ **502/7763-0418;** www.tabarini.com). Rates run around Q360 to Q720 per day, depending on the size and style of the vehicle.

ORIENTATION
The long, narrow **Parque Centro América** is the central hub of Xela. You'll find most of the hotels, restaurants, language schools, and offices, and the main Catholic church, either right on this central plaza or within a few blocks. You can see the massive cone of the Santa Maria Volcano 3,677m (12,064 ft.) towering over the southern horizon from almost anywhere in town. Xela sits at 2,334m (7,657 ft.) above sea level.

The climate here is relatively cool, and sometimes damp, particularly May through mid-November. Be sure to have a light jacket or sweater for the evenings.

VISITOR INFORMATION

There's an **INGUAT** office (© **502/7761-4931**) fronting the Parque Centro America in the Edificio Casa de la Cultura. They can provide you with a city map and basic information on tours and attractions in and around Xela.

FAST FACTS **Banco de Occidente, Banrural,** and **Banco Industrial** all have branches right on Parque Centro America, and there are dozens of other bank branches around town. Since this is a university and language-school city, you'll also find an abundance of **Internet cafes** in Xela.

In the event of a medical emergency, the **Hospital La Democracia,** 13a Av. 6-51, Zona 3 (© **502/7763-6671**), is a well-equipped, modern hospital. You might also try **Hospital Privado Quetzaltenango,** Calle Rodolfo Robles 23-51, Zona 1 (© **502/7761-4381**), a well-equipped private hospital. To reach the **National Police** dial © **502/7765-4987.** However, for most tourist needs, whether it be for information or an emergency, you should call **Asistur** (© **1500**), which is a toll-free call. The main **post office** (© **502/7761-7608**) is about 4 blocks west of the central park at 4a Calle 15-07, Zona 1.

What to See & Do

It won't take you long to visit Quetzaltenango's principal attractions. The **Parque Centro América** ★, with its open-air gazebo, is the town's focal point. On the southeastern side of the park you'll find the **Catedral Metropolitano de los Altos,** which is actually two churches. Fronting the park is the ornate facade of the **Catedral del Espíritu Santo** ★, which is all that remains of the city's original 16th-century baroque church. Behind this facade is the more modern, and much larger, **Catedral de la Diócesis de los Altos,** which was inaugurated in 1899.

On the south side of the park sits the **Casa de la Cultura,** 7th Calle 11-09, Zona 1 (© **502/7761-6031**), a large building that houses the INGUAT offices and the **Museo de Historia Natural** (© **502/7761-6031,** ext. 123), which, in my opinion, can be missed. It gets a fair amount of press in the local tourist propaganda, and is housed in the popular Casa de la Cultura, next to the INGUAT office. Should you decide to visit the exhibits, which include dinosaur bones, Maya artifacts, and a room dedicated to the marimba (a large wooden xylophone and the bands that play it), the museum is open Monday through Saturday from 8am to noon and 2 to 6pm. Admission is Q6.

North of the park and town center is the **Teatro Municipal (Municipal Theater)** ★, 14a Avenida and 1a Calle (© **502/7761-2218**), a wonderfully restored theater built between 1884 and 1908. The theater hosted its first concert in 1903 and is still functioning today. It's worthwhile to catch a show if there's one while you're in town. Just across from the Teatro Municipal is the equally well-restored **Teatro Roma,** 14a Av. A (© **502/7761-4950**), the city's first cinema. While they no longer show movies here, they do have occasional performances, which are worth a visit.

Tours, Treks & Attractions Around Quetzaltenango

While there is little to see in Xela itself, there are a host of tour and activity options within easy reach of the town. All of the hotels and tour agencies listed in this section can arrange any of the tours or excursions listed below.

The best agencies in Xela include **Adrenalina Tours ★** (© **502/7761-4509;** www.adrenalinatours.com), which has its offices in the Pasaje Enriquez building just off Parque Centro America; **Altiplano's Tours** (© **502/7766-9614;** www.altiplanos. com.gt); and **Quetzal Trekkers ★★**, Casa Argentina at 12a Diagonal, 8-37, Zona 1 (© **502/7765-5895;** www.quetzaltrekkers.com). In addition to the hikes and treks mentioned below, you can also sign on for a 6-day trip through **Nebaj** and **Todos Santos Chuchumatán;** a 3-day hike from **Xela** to **Lake Atitlán;** and a 2-day trek to the summit of **Tajumulco** volcano, at 4,220m (13,845 ft.), the highest point in all of Central America.

ZUNIL & FUENTES GEORGINAS

Zunil ★ is a picturesque little town on the shores of the Salamá River and is surrounded by verdant agricultural fields. It has a beautiful whitewashed church and narrow, cobblestone streets that wind up the hills from the river. Zunil is famous for its worship of **Maximón** (p. 192), who is known as San Simon here in Zunil. San Simon is housed in different local homes at different times, and you can ask anyone in town where to find him. A small tip is expected for taking you to see the saint's statue. Monday is market day in Zunil, and while small, it's still a colorful and vibrant market.

Quetzaltenango offers a number of Spanish schools, most with immersion-style lessons, small classes, excursions, and homestay accommodations with a local family. The best are **Casa Xelajú**, Callejón 15 D, 13-02, Zona 1 (© 502/7761-5954; www.casaxelaju.com); **Celas Maya Spanish School**, 6a Calle 14-55, Zona 1 (© 502/7761-4342; www.celasmaya.edu.gt); **Proyecto Lingüístico Quezalteco** ★, 5a Calle 2-40, Zona 1 (© 502/7765-2140; www.plqe.org); **Ulew Tinimit Spanish School** ★, 4a Calle 15-23, Zona 1 (© 502/7763-0516; www.spanishguatemala.org); and **Utatlán Spanish School**, 12a Av. 4-32, Zona 1 (© 502/7763-0446; www.utatlan.com). Rates run between Q1,200 and Q1,600 per week, including homestay, most meals, and some organized excursions.

Hot springs can be found in several places on the way to Zunil, including Los Vahos, El Recreo, and Los Cirilos, but they all pale in comparison to **Las Fuentes Georginas** ★ (© 502/5704-2959), a hot springs complex just beyond Zunil. The large pool here is set in rock and surrounded by steep hills. The hottest water is found closest to the hillside, and gets cooler as you move farther away. As of this writing, Las Fuentes Georginas was closed for reconstruction, following a massive mudslide that filled the main pool. However, the hot springs are expected to reopen by the time this book hits the stands. Traditionally, Las Fuentes Georginas is open daily from 8am to 6:30pm. Admission is Q50 for foreigners, with a reduced rate for nationals. A package price, including round-trip transportation, runs Q75. Parking is an extra Q10 if you come in your own car.

Zunil is located 9km (5½ miles) south of Xela on the road to Retalhuleu and the Pacific coast. Las Fuentes Georginas is another 8km (5 miles) beyond Zunil up a beautiful, winding road that heads into the mountains. A taxi from Xela to the hot springs should charge around Q100 each way. The fare is a bit less if you're going only to Zunil. Alternatively, **Adrenalina Tours** (see above) runs a twice-daily shuttle to Las Fuentes Georginas, leaving Xela at 8am and 2pm, and returning at noon and 6pm. The cost is Q40.

VOLCAN SANTA MARIA ★★

The skyline south of Quetzaltenango is dominated by the 3,677m (12,064-ft.) **Volcán Santa María.** All of the tour agencies listed above lead hikes to the summit, and most leave Xela before dawn for the town of Llanos del Pinal. From here it takes between 3 and 4 hours of strenuous hiking to reach the summit. On a clear day, you can see as far as Mexico. You can also see a host of other Guatemalan volcanoes, including Tajumulco, Siete Orejas, and Acatenango, as well as the volcanoes surrounding Lake Atitlán and the volcanoes Fuego and Agua just outside of Antigua. The best view here, however, is of the crater of Santa María's very active sister volcano, **Santiaguito.** Santiaguito is in an almost constant state of eruption, belching out gases, volcanic ash, and molten lava. Guided tours run between Q80 and Q240 per person, depending on group size. During the dry season, it's possible to camp near the summit, which is worth it for the amazing sunrise and sunset views.

SAN ANDRES XECUL

The ornate church here is definitely worth a visit. Try to come in the afternoon, when the sun hits the church's facade, as it's much harder to get a good photo in the morning, when the sun is behind the church. Up the hill from the main church is a much smaller church worth a visit for two reasons. First, the high perch here offers a wonderful view of the main church and town. Second, this church and the plot of land beside it are still actively used for Maya ritual prayers and ceremonies, and you can almost always find local Maya worshiping here. San Andrés Xecul is 9km (5½ miles) from Xela, just beyond Salcajá, and off the road to Cuatro Caminos.

SAN FRANCISCO EL ALTO

While Chichicastenango's market gets most of the press and acclaim, insiders know that **San Francisco El Alto's Friday market ★★** is the largest traditional market in Guatemala. As in Chichi, San Francisco's central plaza is taken over on market day and packed with merchants from all over the highlands. However, far fewer tourists come here. Instead, large wholesalers and local barterers are the principal buyers. The goods are far more geared to everyday Guatemalans, and you'll have to hunt to find the textiles and arts and crafts. Animal activists should be aware that part of the market here is reserved for live animals—everything from dogs and cats to pigs and chickens. You'll also see caged birds and the occasional captured monkey. San Francisco El Alto is 17km (11 miles) from Xela beyond Cuatro Caminos on the way to Huehuetenango.

SHOPPING

The shopping scene is rather uninspired in Xela, but because of the large university and language-school presence here, there are several good used bookstores in town, with selections of both English- and Spanish-language books. **Vrisa Bookshop,** 15a Av. 3-64, Zona 1 (© **502/7761-3237**), and **North & South Bookstore,** 8a Calle and 15 Av. 13-77, Zona 1 (© **502/7761-0589**), are both good choices. For Guatemalan textiles or craft work, head to the Friday market at San Francisco El Alto (see above).

Where to Stay

MODERATE

If you want amenities that include a pool and Jacuzzi, try **Hotel Bonifaz** (© **502/7761-2959;** www.quetzalnet.com/bonifaz), at 4a Calle 10-50, Zona 1.

Casa Mañen ★★ 🎒 The immaculately restored building that houses this B&B might be pushing 200 years, but it's still my top choice in Xela. The rooms feature thick, antique terra-cotta floors, hand-woven wool blankets and rugs, firm and comfy beds, and a wealth of local art and craft works for decoration; most have working fireplaces. I prefer the second- and third-floor rooms, which are above the street and away from the action. The hotel's terrace offers great views of the city.

9a Av. 4-11, Zona 1. © **502/7765-0786.** Fax 502/7765-0678. www.comeseeit.com. 8 units. Q400–Q520 ($50–$65) double; Q560–Q800 ($70–$100) suite. Rates include full breakfast. AE, DC, MC, V. *In room:* TV.

INEXPENSIVE

In this category, **Hotel Modelo,** 14a Av. A 2-31, Zona 1 (© **502/7761-2529**), is another good choice. Backpackers and real budget hounds should head to the **Black Cat,** 13 Av. 3-33, Zona 1 (© **502/7761-2091;** www.blackcathostels.net).

Casa Doña Mercedes 🍴 There are tons of budget options in Xela, but I prefer this joint. The converted old home is just 2 blocks from the Parque Centro America. The rooms are cheerful and immaculate, there's a shared kitchen, and the service is friendly and efficient.

6a Calle and 14a Av. 13-42, Zona 1. ✆ **502/7765-4687** or 5687-3305. www.hostalcasadonamercedes. com. 9 units. Q184 ($23) double with shared bathroom; Q296 ($37) double with private bathroom. Rates include taxes. V (with 10% surcharge). **Amenities:** Free Wi-Fi. *In room:* No phone.

Where to Dine

It's hard to beat the views from **El Balcón de Enríquez,** 4a Calle 12-33, Zona 1 (✆ **502/7765-2296**), which I like for breakfast or a light meal. Other options for a light meal or simple coffeehouse include **Café La Luna ★,** 8a Av. 4-11 (✆ **502/ 7761-2242**), with its hodgepodge of antiques; **Casa Antigua,** 12a Av. 3-26, Zona 1 (✆ **502/7765-8048**), or **Café Bavaria,** 5a Calle 13-14, Zona 1 (✆ **502/7763- 1855**), which has a wonderful Sunday brunch featuring live jazz. For good Indian and vegetarian fare, head to **Sabor de la India ★,** 2a Calle and 15a Av. A 19, Zona 1 (✆ **502/7765-2555**); for ribs, steaks, and excellent Tex-Mex fare, grab a table at **Restaurante y Cantina Dos Tejanos,** 4a Calle 12-33, Zona 1 (✆ **502/7765- 4360**); and for excellent pizzas and pastas, try **Trattoria La Genovese da Alfredo,** 14 Av. A, 3-38, Zona 1 (✆ **502/5915-3231**).

El Pasaje Mediterráneo ★★ TAPAS/INTERNATIONAL Tables are spread over several floors, in various nooks and crannies, in this hip restaurant inside the Pasaje Enriquez, a local landmark filled with shops and restaurants. Most of the menu is made up of a range of tapas, although they aren't strictly traditional Spanish-style tapas. You will find dishes with Greek and French, as well as Spanish influences. Don't miss the eggplant rolls with goat cheese and a sun-dried tomato tapenade. Larger combo plates are also available.

4a Calle 12-33, Zona 1, inside El Pasaje Enriquez. ✆ **502/5515-6724.** Reservations recommended. Tapas Q35-Q80. AE, DC, MC, V. Daily 11am-3pm and 5:30-11pm.

Royal Paris ★ FRENCH/INTERNATIONAL This restaurant has the reputation of being the fanciest dining option in town, but the pretense and prices are mellow enough to attract a good share of the local student crowd. Channel the fancy French restaurant by ordering a pork chop in an apple-and-cream sauce, or go the bistro route for lunch with one of the excellent sandwiches, made on a homemade baguette or whole-wheat bread. Live music is featured here most weekend nights.

14a Av. A 3-06, Zona 1, 2nd floor. ✆ **502/7761-1942.** www.royalparis-quetzaltenango.blogspot.com. Reservations recommended. Main courses Q50-Q100. AE, DC, MC, V. Tues-Sun noon-11pm; Mon 6-10pm.

Xela After Dark

Xela has a very active nightlife. Many start things off at the very popular **Salon Tecún ★** (✆ **502/7761-2350**) in the interior passageway of the Enríquez building, fronting the Parque Centro América. The long wooden tables with bench seating fill up most nights with a mix of locals and language students. A better option is **El Balcón de Enríquez ★★** (✆ **502/7765-2296**), which is in the same building but has second-floor outdoor seating that overlooks the park below.

Several bars and discos are concentrated within 2 blocks around 14a Av. A, which is known as Xela's Zona Viva (Live Zone). This is the place to come if you want to

Quetzaltenango & the Western Highlands

GUATEMALA

barhop. Popular dance clubs include **La Parranda,** 6a Calle and 14a Avenida, Zona 1 (no phone), and **Zona Kokoloko's,** 15a Avenida and 4a Calle (*©* **502/5904-9028**).

For a mellower vibe, try **Pool And Beer,** 12a Av. 10-21, Zona 1; **La Fonda del Che,** 15a Av. 7-43, Zona 1; or **El Cuartito,** 13a Av. 7-09, Zona 1. A couple of informal cinemas cater to Xela's student population, showing DVDs on a large flatscreen TV or projected onto a screen. **Blue Angel Video Cafe,** 7a Calle 15-79, Zona 1 (*©* **502/7761-7815**), is the longest running, and features two screening rooms. Films are shown at 8pm and cost Q10. Ask around town, or pick up a copy of the free weekly *Xela Who* (www.xelawho.com) to find the current schedule.

A Side Trip: Chichicastenango

Santo Tomás de Chichicastenango is a small, highland city with perhaps the most impressive—certainly the most famous—open-air market in Guatemala. Although the twice-weekly market and the city have adapted to the flood of tourists, they both maintain a sense of tradition and the indelible mark of Maya culture that stretches back for millenniums. The city center is made of narrow, cobblestone streets, and just outside the center, the landscape is one of deep ravines and sparsely populated hillsides. The large main plaza is Chichi's central hub. This is ground zero of the market, and where you'll find the city's main church, and municipal office buildings. Almost all of the hotels, restaurants, banks, shops, and other services can be found within a 4- or 5-block radius of the central plaza.

GETTING THERE   Your best bet for getting to Chichi is with a shuttle company, or as part of an organized tour. All of the tour agencies in Xela, Antigua, Panajachel, and Guatemala City can arrange this. You don't really need a tour guide, and a simple shuttle is probably the best way to go. Full-day tours cost between Q340 and Q675, and may include lunch.

THE MARKET ★★★   Thursday and Sunday are market days in Chichi, and on these days, the city is a mad orgy of sights, sounds, and smells. Maya craft sellers from across the highlands set up makeshift booths around the central plaza, spilling over onto sidewalks, the church steps, and up various side streets. A broad selection of Guatemalan handicrafts is available, including carved-wood masks and religious figures, ceramic wares, and an immense selection of the country's amazing native textiles. In addition to the craft works, vendors sell fruit, vegetables, flowers, medicinal herbs, and more. *Note:* While a discerning shopper can find quality goods in Chichicastenango's market, much of what is offered is now machine-made and geared toward the mass tourist market. Despite the seeming chaos, there's actually a historical order to the setup, with vendors selling certain products in specific areas that have been designated for as long as anyone can remember. In fact, while tourists might think the entire market is geared toward them, the market is actually the central meeting place for intervillage trade and commerce among the various highland Maya.

Vendors begin arriving in Chichi the afternoon before market day, and set up throughout the evening and into the early morning. The best time to shop is either very early, before the tour buses from Guatemala City and Lake Atitlán begin arriving, or in the afternoon, after everyone's cleared out.

THE IGLESIA DE SANTO TOMAS ★★   This church was built by Dominican priests more than 450 years ago on top of an ancient Maya worship site. It remains the heart and soul of Chichicastenango and—to this day—is used as much for traditional

Quetzaltenango & the Western Highlands

Maya ceremonial purposes as it is for Catholic Mass. Local Maya can almost always be found on the steps leading up to the church, burning copal incense and candles, and offering prayer. Each of the 18 steps represents one of the months in the Maya calendar. Rather than the expected pews, you'll find makeshift shrines and altars spread out on the floor with pine needles and candles. It was in the church's convent that the oldest known copy of the ancient **Popol Vuh** text was discovered.

The church is on the southeast corner of the main plaza. *Note:* Out of respect, the front door of the church is informally reserved for locals and high church officials. Visitors are encouraged to use the side door.

TIKAL & EL PETEN ★★

548km (341 miles) NE of Guatemala City; 65km (40 miles) N of Flores; 100km (62 miles) NW of the Belize border

Occupying the entire northeastern section of Guatemala, the Petén is Guatemala's largest and least populated province. Most of the Petén is forest—thick tropical rainforest. It is a lush and wild landscape that contains some of Mesoamerica's richest archaeological treasures. The Petén Province is home to perhaps the most impressive and best preserved of the ancient Maya ceremonial cities, **Tikal.** It is also home to numerous other lesser, and less excavated, sites. In addition, the area is a rich and rewarding destination for bird-watchers and ecotourists.

Tikal is the greatest of the surviving Classic Maya cities. It is estimated that Tikal once supported a population of about 100,000 people. Archaeologists have identified over 3,000 structures, and in its heyday the city probably covered as much as 65 sq. km (25 sq. miles). Tikal is far more extensively excavated than any ruins in Belize, and unlike the grand cities and excavations in Mexico, Tikal rises out of dense jungle. The pyramids here are some of the most perfect examples of ceremonial architecture in the Maya world. Standing atop Temple IV, you are high above the rainforest canopy. The peaks of several temples poke through the dense vegetation. Toucans and parrots fly about, and the loudest noise you'll hear is the guttural call of howler monkeys.

Flores is the unofficial capital of the Petén region of Guatemala. Seen from the air, Flores appears almost perfectly round. This quiet town, with its colonial-style buildings and cobblestone streets, is one of the most fascinating in Guatemala. Though most people spend time here only en route to or from the Tikal ruins, Flores is well worth exploring for a day or two. A walk around the circumference of the island presents a sort of Venetian experience. Buildings come right down to the water's edge, and dugout canoes, kayaks, and motor launches sit at makeshift docks all around the island.

Essentials
GETTING THERE
BY PLANE TACA Regional Airline (© 502/2470-8222; www.taca.com) has two daily flights to Flores Airport (FRS) from La Aurora International Airport in Guatemala City. Flights depart at 6:30am and 6pm, with return flights at 8:05am and 7:35pm. **TAG Airlines** (© 502/2380-9401; www.tag.com.gt) has one daily flight departing at 6:30am and returning from Flores at 4:30pm. The flight takes around 50 minutes, and fares range from Q1,200 to Q1,920 each way.

The Flores airport is on the road to Tikal, about 2.4km (1½ miles) east of Santa Elena. A taxi from the airport into Santa Elena or Flores should cost you around Q25.

Collective taxis and minivans to Tikal are usually waiting at the airport (if not you'll have to head into Santa Elena or Flores first). These charge around Q50 per person each way. A private taxi can be hired for the drive for around Q400.

BY BUS There are several companies operating first-class buses to and from Guatemala City. **ADN** (© **502/2251-0610** in Guatemala City, or 7924-8131 in Santa Elena; www.adnautobusesdelnorte.com) and **Línea Dorada** (© **502/2232-5506** in Guatemala City, or 7926-0070 in Santa Elena; www.tikalmayanworld.com) both operate out of the main bus terminal in Santa Elena, located about 8 blocks south of downtown along 6a Avenida. The trip to Guatemala City takes about 8 to 10 hours, and first-class fares run around Q190 to Q280. If you arrive by bus, you'll have to arrange a taxi, collective taxi, or minivan ride out to Tikal. Línea Dorado also has service to and from Belize City.

BY CAR To drive to Tikal from Guatemala City, you must first drive to Santa Elena. The best and fastest route is via Río Dulce. Take the **Carretera al Atlántico** (CA-9) out of Guatemala City to La Ruidosa crossroads at Km 245. From here it's 34km (21 miles) north on **Hwy. CA-13** to Río Dulce and another 180km (112 miles) from Río Dulce to Santa Elena. From Santa Elena, you'll need to drive 32km (20 miles) to the crossroads at Ixlú (El Cruce), and turn north toward Tikal, which is 65km (40 miles) away. The route and turnoffs are all well marked, and the drive should take about 8 hours.

Warning: It's strongly advised that you do not drive at night. It's a sad fact that armed groups occasionally set up roadblocks along these isolated, yet frequently trafficked, roads. While this is a rare occurrence, it's better to be safe than sorry.

BY ORGANIZED TOUR Organized day trips leave daily for Tikal from Guatemala City and Antigua. Costs for these all-inclusive trips are approximately Q2,000 to Q2,800 per person including round-trip airfare, ground transportation, park entrance fees, a guide, and lunch. These tours generally leave at around 5am and get back to Guatemala City or Antigua at around 6pm. Budget an additional Q400 to Q1,200 per person per day for multiday excursions, depending on the level of accommodations chosen. In Guatemala City, call **Clark Tours** (© **502/2412-4700;** www.clarktours. com.gt) or **Via Venture ★★** (© **502/7832-2509;** www.viaventure.com).

GETTING AROUND

BY TAXI OR MINIVAN If you don't have a car, the best way to get around this area is by minivan. Most are unmarked—the only prominent company is **San Juan Travel** (© **502/5847-4738**). Minivans from Flores and Santa Elena to Tikal leave roughly every hour between 5 and 10am, and less frequently thereafter. These minivans leave from Tikal for the return trip roughly every hour from noon to 6pm. Every hotel in Flores and Santa Elena can arrange a minivan pickup for you. The trip usually takes an hour and costs around Q50 to Q60 per person each way. You can buy a round-trip fare at a slight savings; however, this commits you to a specific minivan company, and I've found I prefer paying a little extra to have more flexibility in grabbing my return ride when I'm ready to leave. You'll find vans waiting to collect passengers in the main parking lot at the ruins.

A private cab (which is usually a minivan) from Tikal to Santa Elena/Flores will run around Q350 to Q450 each way. Between Tikal and El Remate, the fare is about Q150 to Q200. Be sure to bargain, as the first price you are quoted is almost certainly above the going rate and subject to some negotiation.

BY CAR   There are several local car-rental agencies at the airport. Of these, a good choice is **Tabarini Rent A Car** (© **502/7926-0253;** www.tabarini.com). All rent small jeeps and SUVs. Do get a four-wheel-drive vehicle; even though you may never need the traction or off-road ability, the extra clearance will come in handy. Rates run from Q350 to Q450 per day.

ORIENTATION

Tikal National Park is located 65km (40 miles) north of the sister towns of Flores and Santa Elena. There is no village or town inside Tikal National Park. There is an entrance booth 18km (11 miles) south of the ruins. After paying your entrance fee and driving in, you will come to the large central parking area and visitor center. This is where you will find the two museums, gift shops, a collection of simple restaurants, and the four hotels mentioned later. The ruins themselves are about a 15- to 20-minute walk through the forest from the trail entrance here.

Flores is a picturesque little town built on an island in the middle of Lake Petén Itzá. A narrow causeway connects Flores to Santa Elena. The name Flores is often used to denote both towns. Since accommodations options are so limited near the ruins, a majority of travelers end up staying in Flores or Santa Elena.

About midway between Flores and Santa Elena, you'll find El Remate, a village on the eastern shores of Lake Petén Itzá that is a popular spot to stay while visiting Tikal. El Remate is much more tranquil and pristine than Flores or Santa Elena. Currently, a handful of budget lodgings can be found in the tiny village here, while more upscale options are on the lakeshore heading north out of the village.

VISITOR INFORMATION

There is an information booth run by the Guatemalan Tourist Board, **INGUAT** (© **502/7926-0533;** www.visitguatemala.com), at the Flores airport, and another one in downtown Flores (© **502/5116-3182**) on Avenida Flores, on the north side of the Central Park. Both can help provide basic maps to the region and ruins, as well as brochures for local hotels and tour agencies.

FAST FACTS   There are no banks, ATMs, medical facilities, laundromats, or other major services available at Tikal National Park. There is a small post office, however, for mailing off postcards and letters.

You'll find several banks in downtown Santa Elena. Most have ATMs, and many of these will work with your debit or credit card. There are also a couple of ATMs on the island of Flores. Check with your home bank and the PLUS or Cirrus systems in advance to confirm. All will exchange money. Most of the hotels and restaurants in Flores and Santa Elena will also exchange dollars for quetzales, although they may give you a slightly less favorable rate than you would get at a bank.

The **Flores post office** is on the Avenida Barrios, 1 block south of the Parque Central, or Central Park, which is in front of the church. **Santa Elena's post office** is on Calle 4 and Avenida 7. To contact the **local police,** dial © **502/7926-1365.**

Exploring Tikal

Tikal is one of the largest Maya cities ever uncovered and the most spectacular ruins in Guatemala. The ruins of Tikal are set in the middle of a vast jungle through which you must hike from temple to temple. The many miles of trails through the park provide numerous opportunities to spot toucans and parrots and such wild animals as coatimundis, spider monkeys, howler monkeys, and deer. Together, the ruins and the

Tikal

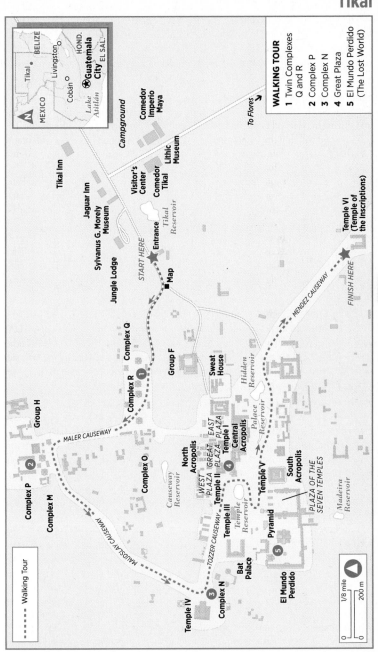

abundance of wildlife make a trip to Tikal an absolute must for anyone interested in Maya history, bird-watching, or wildlife viewing.

Tikal was a massive ceremonial metropolis. At its height, Tikal may have covered as much as 65 sq. km (25 sq. miles). So far, archaeologists have mapped about 3,000 constructions, 10,000 earlier foundations beneath surviving structures, 250 stone monuments (stelae and altars), and thousands of art objects found in tombs and cached offerings. There is evidence of continuous construction at Tikal from 200 B.C. to the 9th century A.D., with some suggestion of occupation as early as 600 B.C. The Maya reached their zenith in art and architecture during the Classic Period, which began about A.D. 250 and ended abruptly about 900, when for some reason Tikal and all other major Maya centers were abandoned. Most of the visible structures at Tikal date from the Late Classic Period, from 600 to 900.

No one's sure just what role Tikal played in the history of the Maya: Was it mostly a ceremonial center for priests, artisans, and the elite? Or was it a city of industry and commerce as well? In the 16 sq. km (6 sq. miles) of Tikal that have been mapped and excavated, only a few of the buildings were domestic structures; most were temples, palaces, ceremonial platforms, and shrines.

Tikal National Park is open daily from 6am to 6pm. Admission, which must be paid at the entrance gate, is Q150 per person, per day. If you'd like to stay in the park until 8pm (for sunset and nocturnal wildlife viewing), get your admission ticket stamped at the office behind the Stelae Museum. If you arrive after 3pm, your admission is good for the following day as well. The best times to visit the ruins are in early morning and late afternoon, which are the least crowded and coolest times of day.

Tikal is such an immense site that you really need several days to see it thoroughly. But you can visit many of the greatest temples and palaces in 1 day. To do it properly, as a first-time visitor, you should probably hire a guide. Guides are available at the visitor center and charge around Q80 to Q160 for a half-tour of the ruins. In addition, most hotels and all tour agencies in the region offer guided tours.

A WALKING TOUR

To orient yourself, begin your tour of Tikal at the visitor center and neighboring Stelae Museum. Here you'll find some informative exhibits and relics, as well as an impressive relief map of the site. See "The Museums," below, for more information on the Stelae Museum.

A full tour of Tikal will require an extensive amount of walking, as much as 10km (6 miles). The itinerary described here will take you to most of the major temples and plazas, and can be accomplished in about 3 to 4 hours. If your time is really limited, you should follow the signs and head straight to the Great Plaza. If you have the time, consider this route:

Walking along the road that goes west from the entrance area toward the ruins, turn right at the first intersection to get to **twin complexes Q** and **R.** Seven of these twin complexes are known at Tikal, but their exact purpose is still a mystery. Each complex has two pyramids facing east and west. At the north is an unroofed enclosure entered by a vaulted doorway and containing a single stele and altar; at the south is a small palace-like structure. Of the two pyramids here, one has been restored and one has been left as it was found, and the latter will give you an idea of just how overgrown and ensconced in the jungle these structures had become.

At the end of the Twin Complexes is a wide road called the **Maler Causeway.** Turn right (north) onto this causeway to get to **Complex P,** another twin complex, a

15-minute walk. Some restoration has been done at Complex P, but the most interesting points are the replicas of a stele (no. 20) and altar (no. 8) in the north enclosure. Look for the beautiful glyphs next to the carving of a warrior on the stele, all in very good condition. The altar shows a captive bound to a carved-stone altar, his hands tied behind his back—a common scene in carvings at Tikal.

From Complex P, head south on the **Maudslay Causeway** to **Complex N,** which is the site of **Temple IV, the Temple of the Two-Headed Serpent ★★★**. Finished around A.D. 740, Temple IV is the tallest structure in Tikal—64m (210 ft.) from the base of its platform to the top. The first glimpse you get of the temple from the Maudslay Causeway is awesome; most of the temple has not been restored, and all but the temple proper (the enclosure) and its roof comb are covered in foliage. The stairway is occluded by earth and roots, but there is a system of steep stairways (rough-hewed wooden ladders set against the steep sides of the pyramid) to the top of the temple. The view of the setting and layout of Tikal—and all of the Great Plaza—is magnificent. From the platform of the temple, you can see in all directions and get an idea of the extent of the Petén jungle, an ocean of lush greenery. **Temple III (Temple of the Great Priest)** is in the foreground to the east; **temples I** and **II** are farther on at the Great Plaza. To the right of these are the **South Acropolis** and **Temple V.**

Temple IV and all the other temples at Tikal are built on this plan: A pyramid is built first, and on top of it is built a platform; the temple proper rests on this platform and is composed of one to three rooms, usually long and narrow and not for habitation but rather for priestly rites.

From Temple IV, walk east along the **Tozzer Causeway** to get to the **Great Plaza,** about a 10-minute walk. Along the way you'll pass the twin-pyramid Complex N, the **Bat Palace,** and Temple III. Take a look at the altar and stele in the complex's northern enclosure—two of the finest monuments at Tikal—and also the altar in front of Temple III, showing the head of a deity resting on a plate. By the way, the crisscross pattern shown here represents a woven mat, a symbol of authority to the Maya.

THE GREAT PLAZA ★★★

Entering the Great Plaza from the Tozzer Causeway, you'll be struck by the towering stone structure that is Temple II, seen from the back. It measures 38m (125 ft.) tall now, although it is thought to have been 42m (138 ft.) high when the roof comb was intact. Also called the Temple of the Masks, from a large face carved in the roof comb, the temple dates from about A.D. 700. Walk around this temple to enter the plaza proper.

Directly across from Temple II you'll see Temple I (Temple of the Great Jaguar), perhaps the most striking structure in Tikal. Standing 44m (144 ft.) tall, the temple proper has three narrow rooms with high corbeled vaults (the Maya "arch") and carved wooden lintels made of zapote wood, which is rot-resistant. One of the lintels has been removed for preservation in the Guatemala National Museum of Archaeology and Ethnology in Guatemala City. The whole structure is made of limestone, as are

Beat the Crowds

Tikal fills up with tour buses most days, with the hours between 10am and 2pm being the busiest period. I prefer visiting the Great Plaza either before or after the main crowds have left. Feel free to reverse the order of this walking tour if it will help you avoid the masses.

most others at Tikal. It was within this pyramid that one of the richest tombs in Tikal was discovered, believed to be the tomb of Tikal ruler Hasaw Chan K'awil. When archaeologists uncovered it in 1962, they found the former ruler's skeleton surrounded by some 180 pieces of jade, 90 bone artifacts carved with hieroglyphic inscriptions, numerous pearls, and objects in alabaster and shell. *Note:* Tourists can no longer scale temples I or III. However, those in need of serious cardio workouts will get their fill climbing some of the other temples.

The **North Acropolis** (north side of the Great Plaza) is a maze of structures from various periods covering an area of 8 hectares (20 acres). Standing today 9m (30 ft.) above the limestone bedrock, it contains vestiges of more than a hundred different constructions dating from 200 B.C. to A.D. 800. At the front-center of the acropolis (at the top of the stairs up from the Great Plaza) is a temple numbered **5D-33.** Although much of the 8th-century temple was destroyed during the excavations to get to the Early Classic Period temple (A.D. 300) underneath, it's still a fascinating building. Toward the rear of it is a tunnel leading to the stairway of the **Early Classic** temple, embellished with two 3m-high (10-ft.) plaster polychrome masks of a god—don't miss these.

Directly across the plaza from the North Acropolis is the **Central Acropolis,** which covers about 1.6 hectares (4 acres). It's a maze of courtyards and palaces on several levels, all connected by an intricate system of passageways. Some of the palaces had five floors, connected by exterior stairways, and each floor had as many as nine rooms arranged like a maze.

Before you leave the Great Plaza, be sure to examine some of the 70 beautiful stelae and altars right in the plaza. You can see the full development of Maya art in them, for they date from the Early Classic period right through to the Late Classic period. There are three major stylistic groups: the stelae with wraparound carving on the front and sides with text on the back; those with a figure carved on the front and text in glyphs on the back; and those with a simple carved figure on the front, text in hieroglyphs on the sides, and a plain back. The oldest stele is no. 29 (now in the Tikal Museum—see "The Museums," below), dating from A.D. 292; the most recent is no. 11 in the Great Plaza, dating from A.D. 869.

If you head south from the Temple II, you will come to the area known as **El Mundo Perdido (The Lost World).** This plaza contains the **Great Pyramid,** which stands 34m (112 ft.) high and is the oldest excavated building in Tikal. This pyramid is one of the most popular spots for watching the sunset. If you've timed it right, you might be able to hang out here and watch the show; otherwise, make a mental note to get your bearings and come back later, if possible. Directly east of the Great Pyramid is the **Plaza of the Seven Temples,** which dates to the Late Classic period. Bordering this plaza on the east side is an unexcavated pyramid, and behind this is Temple V. This entire area is known as the **South Acropolis.** You can climb Temple V, but be forewarned, the climb, both up and down a very steep and rather rickety wooden stairway, is somewhat harrowing. The view from above is beautiful. However, the steep pitch of the pyramid's original stairway is almost as scary as the climb.

If you cross through the South Acropolis to the east and then turn north in the general direction of the Great Plaza, you will come to the East Plaza. From here you can walk southeast on the Mendez Causeway to **Temple VI (Temple of the Inscriptions),** which contains a nearly illegible line of hieroglyphics that are the most extensive in Tikal. It's worth coming out this way just for the chance to spot some wild animals, which seem to be fairly common in this remote corner of the park.

Tikal is a magical and mystical place. Many claim that this magic and mystique is heightened only around sunrise and sunset. Sunsets are easier to catch and a more dependable show. Sunrises tend to be more a case of the sun eventually burning through the morning mist than of any impressive orb emerging. However, afternoons can often be clear, especially during the dry season, allowing for excellent sunset viewing from the tops of the main temples here. In either case, much of the attraction can be found all around you, as the bird and animal life of the jungle are much more active around sunrise and sunset. If you're staying right at the ruins, your chances are better of catching either or both of these occasions.

If you're not staying inside the national park, minivans and collective taxis leave Flores and El Remate early enough to get you to the Tikal entrance gate at 6am when it opens. This will generally enable you to get to the top of one of the main temples by 6:30am, which is usually still early enough to catch the sun burning through the mist just over the rainforest canopy.

If you plan on staying for sunset, be absolutely positive that your return transportation will wait for you. The park officially closes at 6pm. Depending on the season, the sun will set below the treetops anywhere between 5 and 6pm, allowing just enough time to watch the spectacle and get out of the park in time.

Tip: If you're planning on catching either the sunrise or the sunset, it's a very good idea to bring along a flashlight, just in case.

THE MUSEUMS

The most formal museum here has been officially christened the **Sylvanus G. Morely Museum,** but is also known as the **Tikal** or **Ceramic Museum.** This museum contains a good collection of pottery, mosaic masks, incense burners, etched bone, and stelae that are chronologically displayed—beginning with Pre-Classic objects on up to Late Classic pieces. Also on exhibit are a number of jade pendants, beads, and earplugs, as well as the famous **stele no. 31,** which has all four sides carved. Another fine attraction here is the reconstruction of the tomb of Hasaw Chan K'awil, who was also known as Ah Cacao, or "Lord Chocolate." The museum is by the Jungle Lodge and Jaguar Inn.

The second museum is known as the **Lithic** or **Stelae Museum** and is in the large visitor center, which is on your left as you arrive at the parking area coming from Flores. This spacious display area contains a superb collection of stelae from around the ruins. Just outside the front door of the museum is the scaled relief map (mentioned above) that will give you an excellent perspective on the relationships between the different ruins here at Tikal. Both museums are open daily from 8am to 5pm, and Q80 will get you into both.

Tip: Visit the museums only if you have extra time, or a very specific interest in either the stelae or the ceramic works. The ruins themselves are far more interesting.

Other Area Attractions & Ruins

Flores is a wonderful town to explore by walking. The whole island is only about 5 blocks wide in any direction. At the center is a small central park or plaza, anchored by the town's Catholic church. Be sure to take a peek inside to check out the

SEEING THE forest FROM THE TREES

beautiful stained-glass windows. One of the most popular things to do in Flores is take a **tour of the lake ★**. You will be inundated with offers for boat tours. Ask at your hotel or one of the local tour agencies, or talk to the numerous freelancers approaching you on the street. Be sure to inspect the craft beforehand, if possible, and make sure you feel comfortable with its lake-worthiness. Also, make sure your guide is bilingual. These tours last anywhere from 1 to 3 hours, and usually include stops at La Guitarra Island (Guitar Island), which features a picnic and swimming area, as well as at the mostly unexcavated ruins of Tayasal. Here, be sure to climb **El Mirador ★**, a lakeside pyramid that offers a fabulous view of Flores. Many of these tours also stop at the small **Petencito Zoo** and **ARCAS** (www.arcasguatemala.com), a conservation organization and animal rehabilitation center that has some interpretive trails and displays of rescued animals either in recuperation or unable to be released. These tours cost between Q80 and Q160 per person, depending on the length of the tour and the size of your group. Don't be afraid to bargain. Entrance to the zoo is an extra Q20.

You can also **explore the lake** on your own in a kayak or canoe. While you can do this out of Flores, I find the lakeshore near El Remate a better place to take out a kayak or canoe. Rates run around Q15 per hour. To find a worthy craft, ask at your hotel or at one of the local tour agencies. Be careful paddling around the lake; when the winds pick up, especially in the afternoons, it can get quite choppy and challenging.

A host of local tour operators here can arrange any number of tours and activities in the area, as well as guided tours to Tikal and the ruins listed below. The best of these are **Martsam Travel ★★** (© 866/832-2776 in the U.S. and Canada, or 502/7867-5093 in Guatemala; www.martsam.com) and **San Juan Travel** (© **502/5847-4738**).

YAXHA & OTHER REGIONAL RUINS

Thanks to the publicity bestowed on this site by the TV show *Survivor: Guatemala,* **Yaxhá** is now one of the prime archaeological sites to visit in Guatemala. In fact, this is the third-largest Maya ceremonial city in Guatemala—behind Tikal and El Mirador. Be sure to climb **Temple 216 ★★★**, located in the East Acropolis. This is the tallest structure here, and provides excellent views of lakes Yaxhá and Sacnab, as well as the surrounding rainforests. The sunsets here rival those in Tikal. Yaxhá is one of the few Maya cities to retain its traditional Maya name, which translates as "green waters." You can combine a visit to Yaxhá with a trip to the ruins of **Topoxté,** which are located on a small island in Lake Yaxhá. This small yet intriguing site is thought to have been a residential city for local elites. However, it was also a fortified city, where Maya warriors put up a valiant defense against Spanish forces. *Note:* You'll probably be warned, and see the signs, but just in case, do not swim in Lake Yaxhá, as it is home to a robust population of crocodiles.

Many organized tours here also include a stop at the nearby minor ruins of Nakum, which are currently being excavated. However, this makes for a long day. The turnoff for the 11km (7-mile) dirt road into the site is located about 32km (20 miles) east of Ixlú, or El Cruce. The admission grants you access to Yaxhá, Topoxté, and Nakum. If you want to stay at Yaxhá, camping is allowed at a well-tended campsite down by the lakeshore.

Another popular site is **El Ceibal ★**, which offers one of the most scenic routes along the way. To reach El Ceibal, you first head the 64km (40 miles) from Flores to Sayaxché, which is a good-size town for El Petén (it even has a few basic hotels). From Sayaxché, you must hire a boat to carry you 18km (11 miles) up the Río de la Pasión. El Ceibal is a Late Classic–era ruin known for having the only circular temple in all of El Petén. There are also several well-preserved stelae arranged around one small temple structure on the central plaza, as well as a ball court. Your best bet for visiting El Ceibal is to book the excursion with one of the tour agencies in Flores or Santa Elena. Full-day trips run around Q600 to Q800. Overnight trips can also be arranged, combining a visit to El Ceibal to even more obscure Maya sites like Aguateca and Petexbatún. If you want to stay in this area, check out **Chiminos Island Lodge ★** (✆ 502/2335-3506; www.chiminosisland.com), which has six rustic yet luxurious cabins in the rainforest on a small island in the waters of the Petexbatún Lagoon.

Finally, truly adventurous travelers can book a multiday jungle trek to **El Mirador ★★**, the largest Maya ceremonial city in Guatemala. Barely excavated, El Mirador features the tallest pyramidal structure in the known Maya world, La Danta, which reaches some 79m (260 ft.) in height. The trip here involves at least 5 days of hiking and jungle camping. **Martsam Travel ★★** (✆ 866/832-2776 in the U.S. and Canada, or 502/7867-5093 in Guatemala; www.martsam.com) is the best operator to contact for one of these trips.

SPANISH CLASSES

Eco Escuela de Español ★ (✆ 502/5940-1235; www.ecoescuelaespanol.org) runs a community-based language-school program in the small village of San Andrés, on the shore of Lake Petén Itzá. The program costs just Q1,200 per week, including lodging and three meals daily with a local family, as well as 4 hours of daily class time, usually one-on-one. The setting allows for intensive language instruction, as well as many chances to really interact with the local culture and natural surroundings.

If you want to stick closer to the action in town, check in with the **Dos Mundos Spanish Academy** (✆ 502/5830-2060; www.flores-spanish.com), which offers a wide range of course and accommodations options.

Where to Stay

Since accommodations in Tikal are limited, most travelers either choose to (or must) overnight in the sister cities of Flores and Santa Elena. Still, this is not necessarily such a bad thing. There's a lot more to do and see in Flores and Santa Elena, and a far wider range of hotels and restaurants to choose from. Still, unless you have more than 2 days to spend exploring the region, I recommend staying near the ruins, as it allows you to enter early and stay late. It also allows you to avoid the Great Plaza and North Acropolis during the peak period of the day, when they are swarmed with day-trippers.

AT THE RUINS

In addition to the place listed below, the other hotels near the ruins are the **Jaguar Inn** (𝄐 **502/7926-0002;** www.jaguartikal.com) and **Tikal Inn** (𝄐 **502/7861-2444;** www.tikalinn.com). Alternatively, you can set up a tent on some concrete pads near the parking lot, under an open-air thatch palapa roof. The camping area has shared shower and toilet facilities, and a communal cooking area. The **campground** (no phone) charges Q80 for the privilege of putting up a tent and using the facilities. You can also rent hammocks and pitch them under open-air palapas for an additional Q40. *Tip:* If you plan on sleeping in a hammock, or taking an afternoon siesta, you should try to get a mosquito net that fits over the hammock. Most of the places that rent and sell hammocks in this area have these nets.

Jungle Lodge ★   Also known as Posada de la Selva, this is the biggest and most comfortable hotel right at the park. However, at times there can be a cattle-car feel to the operation. The majority of the rooms, and the best rooms, are housed in duplex bungalows, with high ceilings, white-tile floors, two double beds with mosquito netting, and a ceiling fan. Each has its own little porch with a couple of chairs. Two junior suites feature king-size beds, a large Jacuzzi-style tub (but without jets), and private patios in both the front and the back of the room. There are 12 older rooms with polished cement floors and shared bathroom facilities. It's hot and steamy here in the jungle, so you'll appreciate the hotel's pool, which is built on a rise and shaped like a Maya pyramid.

Tikal village, Petén. 𝄐 **502/7861-0447** or 2476-8775. Fax 502/2476-0294. www.junglelodgetikal.com. 50 units (40 with private bathroom). Q1,200 (US$150) bungalow; Q320 (US$40) double with shared bathroom. MC, V. **Amenities:** Restaurant; bar; small outdoor pool. *In room:* No phone.

IN FLORES & SANTA ELENA

In addition to the places below, **Hotel Petén** (𝄐/fax **502/7867-5203;** www.hoteles depeten.com), in Flores, and **Hotel Casa Elena de las Flores** (𝄐 **502/7926-2235;** www.casaelenadelasflores.com), in Santa Elena, are good budget choices.

Hotel Santana ★   This is a great choice if you're looking to snag a lakefront room with a balcony and a view, all at a good price. Most of the rooms here fit the criteria I just mentioned. Still, be sure you get a lakeview room, and not one of the less desirable interior affairs. The rooms are all cool, clean, and fairly spacious, and a cut above the rest of the options on the island in this price range. The open-air dining room is a great place to enjoy the lakeside setting as well. There's a small kidney-shaped pool, with a built-in waterfall and swim-up bar.

Calle 30 de Junio, Flores, Petén. 𝄐/fax **502/7867-5123** or 7867-5193. www.santanapeten.com. 35 units. Q320–Q480 (US$40–US$60) double. AE, MC, V. **Amenities:** Restaurant; outdoor pool; free Wi-Fi. *In room:* A/C, TV.

La Casona del Lago ★★   This is the most luxurious hotel in the Flores area. Located right on the shores of the lake, with excellent views of its waters and picturesque island city, the three-story building is built in an L-shape, around a central pool and Jacuzzi area. Rooms are spacious, with two double beds, white-tile floors, a couple of chairs, and a separate desk area, and they feature a host of modern amenities,

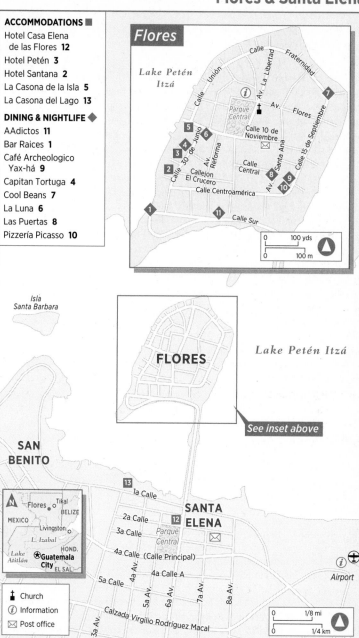

ACCOMMODATIONS ■

Hotel Casa Elena
 de las Flores **12**
Hotel Petén **3**
Hotel Santana **2**
La Casona de la Isla **5**
La Casona del Lago **13**

DINING & NIGHTLIFE ◆

AAdictos **11**
Bar Raices **1**
Café Archeologico
 Yax-há **9**
Capitan Tortuga **4**
Cool Beans **7**
La Luna **6**
Las Puertas **8**
Pizzería Picasso **10**

Flores

*Lake Petén
Itzá*

Calle Unión

Calle

Fraternidad

Av. La Libertad

Parque
Central

Av. Flores

Calle 15 de Septiembre

Calle 10 de
Noviembre

Av. Santa Ana

Calle 30 de Junio

Av. Reforma

Calle
Central

Callejon
El Crucero

Calle Centroamérica

Av. Santa Ana

Calle Sur

0   100 yds
0   100 m

*Isla
Santa Barbara*

FLORES

Lake Petén Itzá

See inset above

**SAN
BENITO**

Flores • Tikal
BELIZE
MEXICO
Livingston
L. Izabal
HOND.
Lake
Atitlán ⊛ **Guatemala
City** EL SAL.

1a Calle

2a Calle
3a Calle
Parque
Central
4a Calle (Calle Principal)
4a Calle A
5a Calle

**SANTA
ELENA**

13
12
4a Av.
5a Av.
6a Av.
7a Av.
8a Av.

Calzada Virgilio Rodríguez Macal

3a Av.

✝ Church
ⓘ Information
✉ Post office

Airport

0   1/8 mi
0   1/4 km

5

GUATEMALA | Tikal & El Peten

including 21-inch televisions. Don't confuse this with **La Casona de la Isla,** which is on Flores, and part of the same small chain of hotels.

Calle Litoral, Zona 1, Santa Elena, Flores, Petén. ✆/fax **502/7952**-8700**.** www.hotelesdepeten.com. 32 units. Q704–Q784 ($88–$98) double. Rates include full breakfast and taxes. AE, DC, MC, V. **Amenities:** Restaurant; outdoor pool; Jacuzzi; free Wi-Fi. *In room:* A/C, TV, hair dryer.

IN EL REMATE

La Casa de Don David Hotel (✆ **502/7928-8469;** www.lacasadedondavid.com) is another long-standing popular place in this area, with great service and a friendly vibe.

La Lancha Resort ★★   Owned by Francis Ford Coppola, the main lodge has a commanding view of the lake and features a soaring, open-air A-frame thatch roof oriented toward the view. Below the lodge is a kidney-shaped pool. A steep trail leads down to the shore of the lake, where you'll find a swimming area and some canoes and kayaks. The rooms are all duplex bungalows. The six "lakeview" units are quite spacious, while the "jungleview" rooms are more compact. All are tastefully and artistically decorated and very comfortable. All feature a shared wooden veranda, and you can probably figure out the view from the room names.

Lago Petén Itzá, Petén. ✆ **800/746-3743** in the U.S., or ✆/fax 502/7928-8331 in Guatemala. www. lalanchavillage.com. 10 units. Q1,680–Q2,240 (US$210–US$280) double. Rates lower in the off season, higher during peak periods. AE, MC, V. **Amenities:** Restaurant; bar; bike rental; outdoor pool. *In room:* A/C, minifridge, no phone, free Wi-Fi.

La Mansión del Pájaro Serpiente ★ 🏚   Set off the main road to Tikal, on a hillside overlooking the lake, this place has both standard and deluxe bungalows, beautiful gardens, and a friendly atmosphere. The bungalows feature beautiful stone and woodworking details, with local textile and crafts filling out the decor. The deluxe rooms feature televisions and air-conditioning. The free-form pool is set amid lush gardens, and almost feels like a natural pond in the jungle. The open-air restaurant has a great view of the lake and specializes in local cuisine. The owners raise peacocks, and there are always several wandering around here.

El Remate, Petén. ✆/fax **502/7926-8498** or 5702-9434. 11 units. Q360 ($45) double; Q440 ($55) deluxe double. No credit cards. **Amenities:** Restaurant; outdoor pool. *In room:* No phone.

Where to Dine

Most folks who stay near the ruins take all their meals at their hotel. If you're looking for variety or staying at the campsite, there are several little restaurants (*comedores*) between the main camping area and parking lot and the gate at the beginning of the road to Flores. Within the area of the ruins, you'll find picnic tables beneath shelters and itinerant soft drink peddlers, but no snack stands. If you want to spend all day at the ruins without having to walk back to the parking area for lunch, take sandwiches. Most of the hotels here and in Flores, as well as the *comedores,* will make you a bag lunch to take into the park.

There are tons of places to eat around Flores and Santa Elena. Most are simple affairs serving local and Mexican cuisine, and geared toward locals and the backpacker crowd. Most of the hotels listed above have decent restaurants, too.

In addition to the places below, **Pizzeria Picasso,** Calle 15 de Septiembre, across from El Tucán (✆ **502/7867-5198**), serves pretty good wood-oven pizza and a variety of pastas, while **Café Archeologico Yaxhá,** Calle 15 de Septiembre (✆ **502/5830-2060;** www.cafeyaxha.com), is a relaxed and welcoming new place that serves local fare, including dishes based on pre-Columbian recipes and ingredients, as well as coffee drinks and fresh fruit smoothies.

Capitán Tortuga ★ INTERNATIONAL   This popular restaurant has a long and wide-ranging menu. You can get everything from pizzas to barbecue ribs to vegetarian shish kabobs. They also have a wide range of coffee and espresso drinks, as well as ice creams and freshly baked desserts. The large main dining room sits under a high thatch room. However, I prefer the tables on the small outdoor patio that fronts the lake, or in the second-floor, open-air dining room reached from a stairway out back.

Calle 30 de Junio, next to La Casona de la Isla, Flores. © **502/7867-5089.** Main courses Q32–Q120. AE, MC, V. Daily 11:30am–11pm.

La Luna ★★ ◼ INTERNATIONAL   This hip little restaurant is the most creative and refined option in Flores. The menu ranges from steak in pepper sauce to lobster tails, with a host of fish and chicken—and even some vegetarian—options in between. There are three separate dining areas, and all are artistically decorated. My favorite room features a faux ceiba tree in the center and a wild sculpture on one wall made of wood and mirrors.

Calle 30 de Junio, across from La Casona de la Isla, Flores. © **502/7867-5443.** Main courses Q40–Q130. MC, V. Mon–Sat noon–11pm.

Flores & Santa Elena After Dark

Most folks simply frequent the bar at their hotel, or stick around after dinner at one of the local restaurants. There are several bars along Calle Sur fronting the lake just over the bridge as you enter Flores. Of these, **AAdictos** (no phone) is one of the liveliest. For a view of the lake and a happening party scene, you can head to **Bar Raices** (© 5521-1843), at the far western end of Calle Sur. Another good option, near the center of the island, is **Las Puertas** ★ (© 7867-5242), which plays a mix of house and chill dance tunes in a hip little space, and sometimes features live music; it's at the corner of Calle Centroamérica and Avenida Santa Ana. Finally, for a mellow scene, try **Cool Beans** ★ (© 5571-9240; Calle 15 de Septiembre), a popular place for tourists and itinerant backpackers, with a convivial, laid-back vibe; free Wi-Fi; plenty of board games; and a view of the lake to boot.

For those staying at one of the hotels out by the ruins, the best nighttime activity is to visit the ruins by moonlight. Those staying here can have their admission ticket validated to allow them to roam the park until 8pm, and in some cases even later, depending on the disposition of the guards. If the moon is waxing, full, or just beyond full, you're in for a real treat (just ask around beforehand about safety issues).

6 EL SALVADOR

by Charlie O'Malley

I t was only a matter of time before El Salvador established itself as a captivating place to visit. Those dark, Pacific shores, with perfect waves and cone-shaped volcanoes rising out of lush coffee farms, could not be kept secret forever.

Stories of charming rural villages and moss-covered Maya ruins attracted curious adventurers not deterred by this small country's dark history of bloody civil war and ongoing problems with gang violence. A recent tourism boom saw outdated preconceptions come crashing down, and in their place beautiful boutique hotels going up.

El Salvador is a great place to explore. Its beaches offer miles of deserted shores and friendly fishing villages, along with some of Central America's best surf spots. Two national parks offer lush semitropical jungle, high cloud forests, waterfalls, rivers, and a plethora of birds and plant life. The capital city of San Salvador offers high-end hotels, restaurants, and nightclubs that would be at home in any of the world's major cities. And the country's small villages offer tiny town squares filled with people whose renowned kindness to one another and visitors is in sharp contrast to the nation's violent but ancient history.

As well as having many treasures, El Salvador is an easy country to move around in, with everything within a few hours' distance on mostly well-paved roads. It is also one of the cheapest countries in the region, with delightful bargains to be found for handicrafts, hotels, and tours.

REGIONS IN BRIEF

El Salvador is Central America's smallest country—it's roughly the size of Massachusetts—and the most densely populated country in the region, with a population of roughly six million. It's the only Central American country without a Caribbean coast; it's bordered by Guatemala to the north, Honduras to the east, and Nicaragua to the south. In addition to the bustling, modern capital of San Salvador, the country includes dozens of charming rural villages that are starting to cater to tourism, 307km (191 miles) of Pacific coast, and a number of national parks that highlight the country's landscape of steep volcanoes and mountains. The country has distinct rainy and dry seasons and a hot, tropical climate that varies more by altitude than by time of year.

SAN SALVADOR & ENVIRONS San Salvador is El Salvador's capital and the second-largest city in Central America. Its 568 sq. km (220 sq.

miles) are home to 1.6 million residents and the majority of the nation's wealth. Many travelers consider the city to be either an oasis of modern luxury or a gaudy mix of smog and fast food. They're both right. San Salvador does offer many high-end, international restaurants, hotels, and designer shops that would be at home in the world's grandest cities. But Pizza Hut and KFC do seem to be on every corner, bus emissions choke the streets, and all that new luxury collides with the poverty you'll see on the faces of children hustling for change at streetlights. It's a city suffering from the growing pains of transformation. But no matter what your opinion of San Salvador is, it is worth a visit if you have the time. Highlights include a historic downtown containing the nation's iconic buildings, the country's two most important art museums, and hidden gems such as watching the city's lights come alive at dusk from high above in Planes de Los Renderos. Since it's centrally located along El Salvador's two main highways, and most of the country's attractions are less than a couple of hours away, it can be a good base from which to explore the rest of the country.

WEST & NORTHWEST EL SALVADOR   The west's main attractions are the Ruta de las Flores and Parque Nacional El Imposible. The **Ruta de las Flores** is a wonderful 36km (22-mile) drive along a scenic mountain highway winding through thousands of acres of coffee fields and Salvadoran villages featuring weekend artisan and food festivals. **Parque Nacional El Imposible** is a huge national park in the far west offering hours of hiking through lush jungles, across streams, and beside picturesque waterfalls. Beside the park is the small village of Tacuba, which serves as a good base camp for park visits. In the northwest, you'll find **Santa Ana,** the second-largest city in the country, with a roster of visitor-friendly colonial sites, and **Parque Montecristo,** a cloud forest preserve that shares a border with Guatemala and Honduras. During rainy season, Montecristo is one of the greenest and most lush environments in the country. The nation's western region also offers the stunning blue waters of **Lago de Coatepeque** and the challenging volcano hikes of **Parque Nacional Los Volcanes.**

NORTH & CENTRAL EL SALVADOR   North of San Salvador are the villages of Suchitoto, La Palma, and El Pital. **Suchitoto** is a beautiful mountain village that offers some of the best views and history in the entire country. **La Palma** is another standout town, which is well known as a center of art (particularly for its town murals). And in the far north is **El Pital,** which is the country's highest point at 2,730m (8,957 ft.) above sea level. You can also shop for some of El Salvador's most artistically crafted hammocks in the village of **Concepción de Quezaltepeque,** also known as the City of Hammocks, where nearly the entire town and multiple generations of craftsmen have dedicated themselves to the art of hammock making.

THE COASTS   El Salvador's 307km-long (191-mile) Pacific coast is one of the highlights of the country. The coast stretches from the turtle breeding grounds, deserted beaches, and mangrove-filled estuary of **Barra de Santiago,** then goes past Central America's largest Pacific reef in **Playa Los Cóbanos** and the unique boutique hotels and great surfing of the **Balsamo Coast,** before finally reaching the wealthy playgrounds of **Costa del Sol** and **Tamarindo.** In between are dozens of small fishing and beach communities to discover.

THE EAST   The eastern part of the country is best known for the tragic history of war experienced here (for more on this, see the box on p. 317). In **Perquín,** you'll find a small war museum showcasing the left's efforts during El Salvador's 12-year civil war. In the town of **Mozote** are memorials to the more than 1,000 innocents

While planning your trip, keep in mind that many of El Salvador's largest cities are far from attractive tourist centers. Though San Salvador offers a level of luxury you won't find elsewhere in the country, El Salvador's second-tier cities, particularly Sonsonate and San Miguel, have both congestion and crime without many modern luxuries. You might stop in both cities to stock up on supplies or catch a long-distance bus, but with better hotels and restaurants usually available just a short trip away, you don't have to base yourself in either place.

who were systematically executed over 2 horrific days in December 1981 by members of the Salvadoran army.

THE BEST OF EL SALVADOR IN 1 WEEK

So much to choose from, so little time. El Salvador is a tiny country but it is packed with outdoor and cultural treasures. You could easily spend weeks exploring its attractions. But if you have only 7 days, the itinerary below can offer you a little taste of the country. My advice is to rent a car if you truly want to see the countryside. Car rental is cheap and the roads are well paved, and it gives you the opportunity to stay in those little, out-of-the-way lodges that dot the countryside, especially along the Ruta de los Flores.

This itinerary does not head east simply because the largest number of interesting villages and natural areas in El Salvador are clustered in the west. But the east offers some excellent attractions, such as Perquín's **Museo de la Revolución** (p. 320), the historic **Mozote monument** (p. 321), and the undeveloped and charming **Isla de Montecristo ★★** (p. 268).

Day 1: Arrive in San Salvador ★

San Salvador is El Salvador's center of luxury, with the kind of high-end, international restaurants, shopping, and hotels you won't find elsewhere in the country. So take some time to soak up its modern amenities before heading out into El Salvador's more rural areas. Try to arrive in the morning so that you can settle into your hotel and then taxi over to El Centro. In the city center, you can spend a couple of hours viewing El Salvador's iconic **Catedral Metropolitana ★** (p. 240), **Teatro Nacional ★** (p. 240), and huge street market **Mercado Central ★** (where you can perhaps grab lunch; p. 246). Then bus or cab over to the other side of town to spend the afternoon in the Zona Rosa and Colonia San Benito neighborhoods, where you can visit the **Museo de Arte ★★★** (p. 240) and **Museo Nacional de Antropología Dr. David J. Guzman ★★** (p. 240). Afterward, stop by the **Mercado Nacional de Artesanias ★★** (p. 246) or stroll the shops of the **Boulevard del Hipódromo** (p. 254), where you can enjoy a great dinner in one of the area's ethnic restaurants. If you have the energy, continue on to the nightclubs and lounges of the **Multiplaza Mall** (p. 246) or just head back to the hotel to rest up for a trip to Suchitoto the next day.

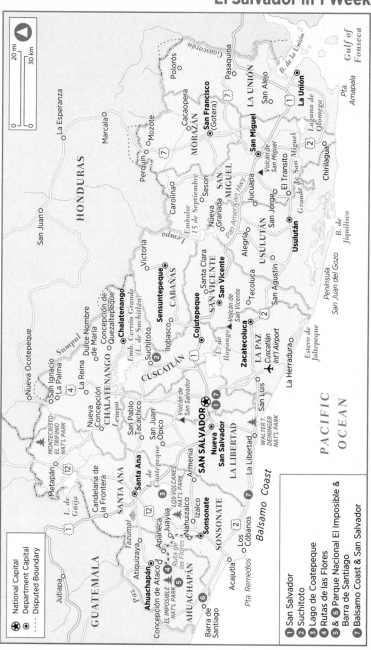

National Capital
Department Capital
Disputed Boundary

1 San Salvador
2 Suchitoto
3 Lago de Coatepeque
4 Rutas de las Flores
5 & 6 Parque Nacional El Imposible &
   Barra de Santiago
7 Balsamo Coast & San Salvador

Day 2: Suchitoto ★★★

Today, you'll head to **Suchitoto** (p. 271), 47km (29 miles) north of San Salvador, and one of El Salvador's most charming towns. A much-disputed territory during the civil war, this town has remade itself into a premier cultural destination, with some of El Salvador's best art galleries and boutique hotels, along with a rich history and abundant natural beauty. You can spend the day simply enjoying the vibe, taking in the weekend artisans' market, or going on a daylong history or nature tour.

Day 3: Lago de Coatepeque ★★

Get up early for the 2½-hour trip due west through Santa Ana or San Salvador to **Lago de Coatepeque** ★★ (p. 308). Coatepeque offers 23 sq. km (9 sq. miles) of pristine, recreational waters in a nearly perfectly round crater lake 740m (2,428 ft.) above sea level. The nation's rich and famous have their mansions along its shores. Each night a spectacular sun sets behind the lush walls of the crater rim, and visitors can spend the day swimming, fishing, riding watercrafts, or soaking in the views.

Day 4: Rutas de las Flores ★★

The Rutas de las Flores is a collection of beautiful little towns along a 35km (22-mile) stretch of winding mountain road, located about 1½ hours south of Lago de Coatepeque. You can do the route in 1 day if you stop first in **Nahuizalco** (p. 289) to check out the furniture, **Juayúa** (p. 291) to see the black Christ, and **Ataco** ★★★ (p. 294) to see some cool art you won't find elsewhere in El Salvador. End the day in a coffee farm lodge close to Ataco (p. 296).

Days 5 & 6: Parque Nacional El Imposible ★★ & Barra de Santiago ★★★

Various daylong adventures to **Parque Imposible** (p. 300), a huge, lush national park with one of the country's largest and most diverse wildlife collections and lush, mountainous hiking terrain, are run out of the nearby base camp of Tacuba. The next day, head 1 hour south to **Barra de Santiago** (p. 264) along El Salvador's Balsamo Coast to spend the night.

Day 7: Balsamo Coast to San Salvador

Barra de Santiago is a tiny fishing village and protected nature area with a mangrove-filled estuary on one side and the Pacific Ocean on the other. You can fish, swim, and surf its deserted beaches, watch giant sea turtles lay their eggs in season, and bird-watch in the estuary. It's a great place to relax before returning home—the airport is an easy 2- to 2½-hour drive past the beautiful beaches and small villages of this coast.

PLANNING YOUR TRIP TO EL SALVADOR

Visitor Information

El Salvador has a helpful national tourism organization, **CORSATUR,** which features a useful website (**www.elsalvador.travel**), a central office in San Salvador, and offices

CORSATUR offices

San Salvador: Edificio Carbonel 1, Colonia Roma, Alameda Dr. Manuel Enrique Araujo and Pasaje Carbonel, San Salvador (✆ **503/2243-7835;** www.elsalvador.travel; Mon–Fri 8am–5pm). The office offers local and national maps and brochures, and tourism official Claudia Argumedo speaks English.

Puerto La Libertad: Km 34.5 Carretera de Literal, Puerta de La Libertad, La Libertad, El Salvador (✆ **503/2346-1634;** cat.lalibertad@gmail.com; Mon–Fri 8am–5pm, Sat–Sun 8am–4pm).

Salcoatitán: Km 82 Carretera CA-8, Salcoatitán, Departamento de Sonsonate (✆ **503/2401-8675;** cat.rutasdelasflores@gmail.com; Mon–Fri 8am–4pm, Sat–Sun 9am–1pm). This is the main tourist office for the Ruta de las Flores, and it is located 300m (984 ft.) north of Salcoatitán in front of the gas station Larin. No one in this office speaks English, but they offer some English-speaking hotel and attraction brochures.

Suchitoto: Calle San Martin, Barrio El Centro, Suchitoto, Custcatlán, El Salvador (✆ **503/2335-1835;** cat.suchitoto@gmail.com; Mon–Fri 8am–5pm, Sat–Sun 8am–4pm). Ask for Manuel Selada.

La Palma: 1a Calle Pte, La Palma, Departmento La Palma, El Salvador (✆ **503/2335-9076;** cat.lapalma@gmail.com; Mon–Fri 8am–4pm, Sat–Sun 9am–1pm). This small office close to the town square has friendly staff and lots of literature on the area.

in Suchitoto in the north, Nahuizalco on the Rutas de Las Flores, and Puerto de La Libertad along the Balsamo Coast; see the box "CORSATUR Offices," below, for specific info. Alternatively, you can always head to the local city hall, called the Alcaldía, where you'll find the occasional English-speaking employee who can help you out. It's best to do as much research as possible before arriving in El Salvador because most towns don't have tourism offices or English-speaking tourism officials. However, there are many small hotels with English-speaking owners who will gladly give information on the area.

Other valuable tourism organizations include the following:

SalvaNatura (33 Av. Sur 640, Colonia Flor Blanca, San Salvador; ✆ **503/2279-1515;** www.salvanatura.org) administers and provides information for Parque Imposible and Parque Nacional Los Volcanes. It's open Monday to Friday from 8am to noon and 2 to 5pm.

Institute Salvadoreño de Turismo (**ISTU;** 719 Calle Rubén Darío, btw. 9a and 11a Av. Sur, San Salvador; ✆ **503/2222-8000;** www.istu.gob.sv) provides information about El Salvador's parks and has a great website. It's open Monday to Friday from 7:30am to 3:30pm.

Ministerio de Medio Ambiente y Recursos Naturales (Km 5.5 Carretera a Santa Tecla, Calle and Colonia Las Mercedes, Building MARN No. 2, San Salvador; ✆ **503/2267-6276;** www.marn.gob.sv), is the organization you have to call to enter Parque Montecristo.

Concultura (19 Av. Norte and Calle Guadalupe; ✆ **503/2510-5320;** www.presidencia.gob.sv) is the nation's premier arts organization and offers a website with a nationwide arts calendar.

Planning Your Trip to El Salvador

EL SALVADOR

Don't let the name "Turicentro," or "Tourist Center," fool you. You'll see signs for these outdated parks near towns, lakes, and mountains around El Salvador, but they are nothing special. Though some have pools and small restaurants, or *comedores,* they're usually decades-old parks with cement picnic tables and chairs painted in 1970s colors with a few cinder block cabins. There's nothing necessarily wrong with these places—the Turicentros at Lago Ilopango and Costa del Sol, for instance, are enjoyable enough, provide lake and beach access, and are popular with locals. Just don't expect anything fancy. Turicentros are open daily 8am to 4pm and cost 80¢ to enter. They are run by the **Instituto Salvadoreño de Turismo** (ISTU; 719 Calle Rubén Darío, btw. 9a and 11a Av. Sur; ℂ **503/2222-8000;** www.istu.gob.sv).

TOUR OPERATORS

Eco Mayan Tours ★★ (Paseo General Escalón 3658, Colonia Escalón, San Salvador; ℂ **503/2298-2844;** www.ecomayantours.com) is one of the country's largest tour companies, with nationwide tours, travel services, and a helpful English-language website. **Gringo Tours** (Calle Francisco Morazán #27; ℂ **503/2327-2351;** www.elgringosuchitoto.com) is run by American Robert Broz and based in Suchitoto, offering custom-made itineraries for the entire country. **Akwaterra Tours** (San Salvador; ℂ **503/2263-2211;** www.akwaterra.com) will arrange tours all over the country and a stay at the agency-owned coffee lodge in Juayua on the Ruta de las Flores. **Nahuat Tours** (ℂ **503/7874-8402;** www.nahuatours.com) is based in Santa Ana and arranges adventure tourism excursions around the country.

Entry Requirements

Residents of the United States, Canada, and the United Kingdom do not need visas and can enter the country at the border with a presentation of a valid passport and the purchase of a $10 30-day tourist card. (Visitors can also ask for a 90-day card when entering the country.) Australia and New Zealand residents require tourist visas, which must be arranged in advance and cost $30.

El Salvador is part of a 2006 border control agreement with Honduras, Guatemala, and Nicaragua, allowing travel between the four countries under one tourist card. The number of days of your tourist card is determined at the first of the four countries entered.

SALVADORAN EMBASSY LOCATIONS

In the U.S.: 2308 California St., NW, Washington, DC 20008 (ℂ **202/265-9671;** fax 202/232-3763; www.elsalvador.org).

In Canada: 209 Kent St., Ottawa, Ontario, K2P 1Z8 (ℂ **613/238-2939;** fax 613/238-6940).

In the U.K.: Mayfair House, 8 Dorset Sq., Marylebone, London, NWI 6PU (ℂ **0207/224-9800;** fax 0207/224-9878).

In Australia: Consulate only: Level three, 499 St. Kilda Rd., Melbourne, VIC 3004 (ℂ **03/9867-4400;** fax 03/9867-4455; cherrera@rree.gob.sv).

CUSTOMS

Visitors to El Salvador can bring in no more than 200 cigarettes or 50 cigars, 2 liters of alcohol, and gifts worth up to $500. As with most countries, there are heavy restrictions on the import and export of plants, animals, vegetables, and fruit.

Money

The unit of currency in El Salvador is the **U.S. dollar.** The country made the switch from its native colón in 2001. The U.S. dollar is dispensed in all the normal denominations, but small-town *tiendas* (stores) rarely have change for a $20, so get small bills whenever you can. ATMs, known as *cajeros automáticos,* can be found in all major cities but are hard to come by in rural towns. Even when a smaller town has an ATM, it may not accept your card—stock up on cash when you can.

Bank machines accept most major card networks such as Cirrus, PLUS, Visa, and MasterCard. I've had the best luck with a PLUS card at Scotiabank ATMs. Credit cards are accepted mainly only in the larger hotels, restaurants, and shops. Sometimes you get lucky in the most unexpected places, but generally small shops or restaurants in villages are *solo efectivo,* or cash only. Those that accept credit cards usually take American Express, Diners Club, Visa, and MasterCard.

Money Talk

Widely used local slang for a quarter is a *"cora."*

You can forget about traveler's checks. Almost no one outside of large San Salvador hotels accepts these anymore. If you feel more comfortable carrying traveler's checks, you can exchange them for currency at most banks or American Express offices (see p. 232 for locations).

The costs of basics in El Salvador are cheap with San Salvador slightly more expensive than the rest of the country. You'll spend $6 or more for long cab rides and $5.50 for most fast-food purchases in the capital. Outside of San Salvador, however, all costs are considerably lower. A 10- to 15-minute taxi ride in La Palma is $3 and *pupusas* (the national dish) cost 25¢ each in smaller towns. Hotels and restaurants are much cheaper than comparable places in the United States or the U.K., and some real bargains are to be had off the beaten track.

When to Go

PEAK SEASON   El Salvador's peak seasons are "Semana Santa," or Holy Week, which precedes Easter Sunday, the month of August, and mid-December through Christmas. Prices during these times can be higher, but not always. Some hotels actually run specials to keep up with the competition; it just depends on how busy the hotel thinks it will be. Either way, you need to book any decent hotel well in advance during these times or you won't get a room.

CLIMATE   The country has two distinct seasons in terms of weather. The first is **dry season,** which runs from November to April. The second is **rainy season,** which runs from May to October. Since there is little temperature variation between these seasons, the question of which season is best for travel is not a simple one. The short answer would be November, when the rains have stopped but the landscape has not yet dried out. However, both seasons have something to recommend them. In dry season, the country's predominantly dirt secondary roads are easier to navigate—

some roads are impassible without a four-wheel-drive during rainy season—and, well, it's not raining. In rainy season, on the other hand, El Salvador's environment is at its most lush and alive. Rainy season also doesn't necessarily mean all-day downpours: the country's highest elevations do receive daily rain and are often covered in a misty fog, but rainy season in the lower elevations can mean little more than daily afternoon showers.

Temperatures throughout El Salvador vary more according to elevation than season. The beaches and San Salvador can get up into the high 80s°F (low 30s°C) year-round, with even higher heat waves in the summer, while the coldest mountains can fall to near freezing, with averages of 54° to 73°F (12°–23°C) year-round. The coldest month is December and the hottest month is May.

PUBLIC HOLIDAYS Public holidays in El Salvador include New Year's Day (Jan 1), Semana Santa (Holy Thursday through Easter Sunday), Labor Day (May 1), the Festival of El Salvador (Aug 1–6, though the rest of Aug remains a busy vacation season), Independence Day (Sept 15), Día de la Raza (Oct 12), All Souls' Day (Nov 2), and Christmas celebrations (Dec 24, 25, and 31).

Health Concerns

COMMON AILMENTS The most common travel ailments in El Salvador are diarrhea and food-borne stomach upset. To stay healthy, be sure to drink only bottled water and ice you know to be purified, and stick to established restaurants. Dengue fever, known as "broken bones disease," is also on the rise in El Salvador. There is a low risk of malaria in El Salvador, centered mainly in rural areas of high immigration near the Guatemalan border. See p. 69 in "Planning Your Trip to Central America" for more info on how to prevent and treat common ailments.

VACCINATIONS The only vaccination necessary to enter El Salvador is for yellow fever, which is required only for persons 6 months or older coming from high-risk tropical areas. Those traveling from the U.S. and Europe do not need the vaccination, and the World Health Organization does not recommend it. However, it's a good idea to be up on all your shots, as many diseases that are all but wiped out in other parts of the world still exist in El Salvador. The CDC recommends getting shots for hepatitis A and B, typhoid, measles, rubella, mumps, rabies, and tetanus. It's best to consult a travel clinic 4 weeks prior to travel to check your vaccination history and discuss your itinerary.

Getting There

BY PLANE

El Salvador's only international airport is Comalapa International Airport or **Cuscatlán International Airport** (**SAL;** ✆ **503/2366-2520;** www.cepa.gob.sv/aies/index.php), 44km (27 miles) south of San Salvador. It is a major 17-gate international hub with daily flights from the United States, Canada, Europe, and South America. **Cuscatlán** also serves as the main hub for primary Central and South American carrier Grupo Taca. The airport serves more than two million passengers per year, and includes numerous rental-car companies, hotel information booths, duty-free shops, and restaurants.

FROM NORTH AMERICA American, Continental, Delta, and Taca offer flights to the United States. **American** flies out of Miami, Los Angeles, and Dallas/Fort Worth. **Continental** flies to and from Houston and Newark. **Delta Airlines** flies out of Atlanta. **Taca Airlines** stops in Chicago, Dallas/Fort Worth, Houston, Los Angeles, Miami, New York, and Washington, D.C. TACA, Delta, Continental, and **Northwest** offer flights from Canada to San Salvador, too. See chapter 11, "Fast Facts: Central America," for airline info.

FROM THE UNITED KINGDOM, AUSTRALIA & NEW ZEALAND There are no direct overseas flights from the U.K., Australia, or New Zealand. You'll need to fly first into the United States—many European flights route out of Miami or Houston to San Salvador.

BY BUS

Central America's major luxury bus carrier, **Tica Bus** (✆ **503/2243-9764;** www.ticabus.com), offers air-conditioned buses from San Salvador to Nicaragua, Honduras, Guatemala, Mexico, Costa Rica, and Panama, ranging from $17 each way to Guatemala and $80 each way to Panama. Tica arrives into San Salvador's **San Benito Terminal** (Blvd. el Hipódromo, Local #301, Colonia San Benito; ✆ **503/2243-9764**).

The bus company **King Quality** (✆ **503/2271-1361;** www.kingqualityca.com), which also features modern, air-conditioned buses, travels from San Salvador to Guatemalan cities such as Antigua and Guatemala City, as well as San José, Costa Rica. Prices range from $33 to $62. King Quality buses arrive into San Salvador's **Puerto Bus Terminal** (Alameda Juan Pablo II at 19a Av. Norte; ✆ **503/2222-2158**).

Finally, the company **Pullmantur** (✆ **503/2243-1300;** www.pullmantur.com) offers $35-to-$59 trips from Guatemala City to the Hotel Sheraton Presidente in San Salvador (Av. La Revolución, Colonia San Benito; ✆ **800/325-3535**).

Getting Around

BY BUS

El Salvador is an easy and fun country to see by bus. There are few places in this small nation that cannot be reached by one of El Salvador's many decades-old, brightly painted, former elementary-school buses. Most city buses are 25¢ to 35¢ with few, if any, rides within the country costing more than $2. Salvador's larger cities have dedicated bus depots, but in smaller villages, the buses often come and go directly from the main square. In small towns and along many slow-moving roads, you can also hail buses as you would a taxi by waving your arm.

 Older Is Better

Stick to the older buses in El Salvador. You might be tempted to hop on one of the country's newer, more modern-looking buses, but these rides rarely have air-conditioning, they cram just as many people on, and because they have bucket rather than bench seats, you'll have even less room than in the older buses. Fortunately, most buses are of the ancient variety. They regularly get fixed up, painted wild colors, decorated with religious symbols, and put back in service. Granted, these buses are packed, hot, bumpy, and stop frequently, but they will get you where you need to go, in style and more comfortably.

Tips on Driving in El Salvador

- *"Alto"* means stop.
- Many small towns have a **one-way system** around the central plaza, so keep right as you enter each town.
- Lines of **traffic cones** will occasionally block your way. These are speed checks and you just weave through them.
- Make sure you get a *"Tarjeta de Circulacion"* (vehicle registration) from your car-rental company and double-check that it is not out-of-date.
- **Do not drive at night** in order to minimize your risk of robbery.
- When visiting larger cities, it's best to **leave your car parked in your hotel parking lot** and just take buses and cabs.

Buses in El Salvador are also mobile markets and charities. Be prepared for vendors to hop aboard at each stop to sell fruit, bottled water, and *dulces* (candies). You'll likely encounter brightly dressed clowns who solicit for various charities, as well. Though riding a bus in El Salvador is an excellent way to get to know the country's people and culture, don't detour away from the main tourist routes mentioned in this book, and avoid nighttime bus travel or you'll risk encountering some safety issues. Also, when you're carrying luggage, it is doubtless less hassle to just hail a cab or hire a car.

BY CAR

El Salvador is one of the easiest countries in Central America to see by car, since it boasts newly constructed, well-paved, and well-marked highways running the length of the country from east to west and north to south. Hwy. CA-1, also known as the Pan-American Highway or "Carretera Panamericana," is the nation's main artery traveling from the western Guatemalan border through San Salvador to the eastern Honduran border. Hwy. CA-2 runs the same direction along the coast and is intersected by three major north-south highways running the length of the country. Once you get off the main roads, however, things get a little different. The secondary roads are not usually paved. So even in dry season, it's best to rent a truck. In rainy season, I recommend renting a four-wheel-drive as some roads are not passable with regular vehicles.

Keep your eyes peeled while driving anywhere: El Salvador's roads are filled with old jalopies moving at half the posted speed, motorcycles puttering along on the shoulder, farmers walking with carts that stick a few feet into the road, and pedestrians just inches from the lane.

See the destination sections below for info on **renting cars** throughout the country.

BY FERRY

There is regular ferry service across Lago Suchitlán to Suchitoto (p. 272), and ferries ply the waters around La Unión, but additional ferry service is nonexistent.

BY TAXI

Taxis are prevalent in the country's bigger cities and are usually easy to catch around each city's main square—they're safe to hail on the street, except at night, when you should have your hotel call you one. Smaller cities usually don't offer taxis but many feature small moto-taxis (called *tuk tuks*), which are basically red, canvas-covered, three-wheeled motorcycles. Tuk tuks are often much cheaper than regular taxis—sometimes as little as 25¢ for a few blocks—and you get the added bonus of wind in your hair.

Tips on Accommodations

El Salvador's hotels vary widely in quality, style, and price. San Salvador's larger hotels are mainly multinational chains that follow internationally accepted standards for service and amenities, but most hotels outside the capital are individually owned (which means you'll find some true gems and some real stinkers). There are also a few international and national chain hotels scattered around the country, but generally most small-town hotels are going to be simple cinder-block or stucco buildings with medium to smallish rooms, minimal decoration, and old furniture. Most are comfortable, with friendly, helpful on-site owners. Just don't expect everything to be shiny and new.

Rates range from more than $125 for a luxury room in San Salvador to $14 for a simple, comfortable room in a small mountain town. The bigger the town, the higher the price. And an 18% tax, which is included in the prices quoted in this chapter, is applied to all hotel rooms. Rooms aren't necessarily more expensive during Holy Week, Christmas, and early August. Sometimes they are cheaper. But they definitely book solid, so make your reservations for these weeks well in advance. Single travelers can often get a discounted rate on a double room (known as *tarifa sencilla*), and checkout times are usually midday or as late as 1pm.

Tips on Dining

Outside of the high-end, international restaurants of San Salvador, Salvadoran dining can get a bit repetitive, with most small-town restaurants offering roughly the same combo of cooked fish, meat, or chicken with rice and salad. Occasionally, a restaurant owner throws in an Argentine sausage or a veggie dish. But for the most part, you'll be offered just plain-ish meat with a starch and greens. There are a few highlights, however. The first is El Salvador's national dish, the *pupusa*. Styles vary but generally *pupusas* are corn tortillas filled with pork and cheese and grilled warm and brown. They're usually served with a side of hot sauce and a tasty *curtido,* which is like a slightly spicy coleslaw, and sell for 25¢ to $1.50 each. You'll find them everywhere and two to four make a meal. You'll also want to try El Salvador's *refrescos/liquados,* which

TELEPHONE dialing INFO AT A GLANCE

The country code for El Salvador is **503**, which you use only when dialing from outside the country. Telephone numbers in this chapter include this prefix because most businesses' published phone numbers include the prefix.

To place a call from your home country to El Salvador, dial the international access code (011 in the U.S. and Canada, 0011 in Australia, 0170 in New Zealand,

00 in the U.K.), plus the country code (503), plus the eight-digit phone number.

To place a call within El Salvador, simply dial the eight-digit number beginning with 2 for land lines and 7 for cellphones.

To place a direct international call from El Salvador, dial **00** for international access, plus the country code to the nation you are calling, followed by the area code and local phone number.

are a combination of fruit, ice, and water or milk. (My favorite's a banana, milk, and honey concoction.)

If you have a strong stomach, you might want to give one of the country's many *comedores*, which are small, often family-run restaurants, usually with a mom or grandmother in the kitchen serving *pupusas* and a few items based on whatever is available that week. And if you've had your fill of traditional cuisine, a world-class collection of Asian, Brazilian, Italian, Peruvian, and other cuisines is available in San Salvador.

The country's 13% dining tax is normally included in the menu price with an additional 10% tip added to most bills. Check your tab before tipping.

Tips on Shopping

As with dining, there is a world of difference between shopping in San Salvador and shopping in the rest of the country. San Salvador offers nearly everything you could want or need and is filled with high-end malls and expensive designer shops. But the smaller towns often offer only small *tiendas*—one-room food stores with a few necessities—street markets, and small variety stores.

Weekends tend to see town squares turned into markets offering everything from arts and crafts to cheap calculators. Most Salvadoran markets also sell traditional artesania—a broad term for El Salvador's various textile, wood, and art crafts, which often take the form of wooden crosses, decorative boxes, or natural wood surfaces painted in the unique style of the country's most famous artist, Fernando Llort (p. 241).

[FastFACTS] EL SALVADOR

American Express American Express traveler's checks can be exchanged at most banks, but few businesses in El Salvador accept them. American Express offices are located in San Salvador (Anna's Travel, 3ra Calle Poniente 3737, btw. 71 and 73 Av. Norte, ✆ **503/2209-8800;** or Servi-Viajes, Paseo General Escalón 3508 No. 4, ✆ **503/2298-6868**), in San Miguel (Anna's Travel, 8 Calle Poniente 815, Roosevelt Bario San Filipe, San Miguel; ✆ **503/2661-8282**), and in Santa Ana (Anna's Travel, 2 Calle Poniente and 4 Av. Norte No. 4, Santa Ana; ✆ **503/2447-1574**).

Business Hours Most banks and Casa de la Cultura community centers are open Monday through Friday 8:30am to 5pm and 8:30am to noon or 1pm on Saturdays. Some banks and Casas de las Culturas have extended Saturday hours. Business offices follow a similar schedule but are closed Saturdays and Sundays. Also note that many national tourist sites such as Tazumal and Joya de Cerén are open Sundays but closed Mondays.

Small-town shops often close for an hour or two around midday, and smaller village restaurants close around 6pm. San Salvador's restaurants close between 8 and 11pm, with nightclubs staying open until the wee hours.

Embassies & Consulates The **U.S. Embassy** in San Salvador is at Urbanización Santa Elena, Antiguo Cuscatlán (✆ **503/2278-4444;** http://san salvador.usembassy.gov). The **Canadian Embassy** is at Centro Financiero Gigante, Alameda Roosevelt and 63 Av. Sur, lobby 2, location 6 (✆ **503/2279-4655**). **Australia** has no embassy or consulate, but has an agreement allowing the Canadian embassy to assist Australian citizens. The **United Kingdom** has a consulate at 17 Calle

Poniente 320 (© **503/2281-5555;** gchippendale@gibson.com.sv). The U.K. embassy in Guatemala City, Guatemala (16 Calle 0-55, Zone 10, Edificio Porre Internaciónal, level 11; © **502/2367-5425;** http://ukinguatemala.fco.gov.uk/en, handles visa and passport issues for residents of the United Kingdom traveling in El Salvador. **New Zealand** does not have a consulate or embassy in El Salvador. Kiwis need to contact the New Zealand embassy in Mexico City (Jamie Balmes 8, 4th floor, Los Morales, Polanco, Mexico, D.F. 11510; © **5255/5283-9460;** jorge.arguelles@nzte.govt.nz) for assistance.

Emergencies Emergencies from anywhere in the country can be handled by calling © **911.** Some towns also have local numbers for tourist police, fire, and other agencies. Those numbers are listed below wherever applicable.

Hospitals The nation's premier private hospital is **Hospital de Diagnóstico and Emergencias Colonia Escalón** (21a Calle Poniente and 2a Diagnol 429, Urbanización. La Esperanza Paseo del General Escalón, San Salvador; © **503/2506-2000**). If you have a serious medical issue but are not ready or willing to leave the country, this is the place you need to go. Public hospitals, which are not recommended, are scattered throughout the country and can get you

patched up well enough for transport home or to San Salvador. A complete list of El Salvador's public hospitals with contact information can be found at **www.mspas.gob.sv**.

Language Spanish is the official language of El Salvador. Few Salvadorans outside of San Salvador's hotels speak English, so it's a good idea to learn a few words and to bring a Spanish phrase book with you.

Maps Maps are exceedingly hard to come by in El Salvador. The main CORSATUR office in San Salvador (p. 238) offers large, colorful, tourism-style country and San Salvador maps. But few small towns offer street maps. Most towns are easy to find off the main highways and are walkable once you arrive.

Newspapers & Magazines *El Diario de Hoy* and *La Prensa* are El Salvador's most readily available newspapers. *El Diario* considers itself to be the country's paper, while *La Prensa* seems to have a more international perspective. Both are written in Spanish. The best English-language magazine you'll find in El Salvador is the Guatemala-based *Revue Magazine,* which offers travel, culture, and business features concerning Central America.

Police Police and other emergency agencies can be reached throughout the

country by calling © **911.** A few towns also have designated tourist police offices with additional phone numbers. Those numbers are listed below.

Post Offices & Mail Most towns in El Salvador have post offices marked by a blue sign reading CORREOS. Offices are open Monday through Friday from 8am to 5pm in larger cities and 7am to noon and 2 to 5pm in small towns. To mail a standard letter from El Salvador to the United States costs around 65¢, and 85¢ to Europe and Australia. For a list of post office addresses and phone numbers, visit **www.correos.gob.sv** and click on "Correos de El Salvador."

Taxes All hotels charge an 18% tax. Restaurants charge 13% on the total cost of the bill, and often sneak in an automatic 10% for service—check your bill carefully to avoid overtipping. See "By Plane," earlier in this chapter, for info on the country's airport departure tax.

Tipping A 10% tip is automatically added to most restaurant checks, and taxi drivers don't expect a tip. No hard standard exists for bellhops, but $1 per bag will keep you in their good graces. Also, many tour guides work entirely for tips, with a $2 minimum expected for anytime up to an hour. After that, it's up to you to compensate for exceptional service.

SAN SALVADOR ★

When Mayor-elect Norman Quijano announced in 2010 he was going to clean up San Salvador, nobody believed him. El Salvador's capital is a typical Central American city that suffers from pollution and heavy traffic, and there is a great divide between the rich and the poor, which means there are some unsafe, crime-ridden neighborhoods. Volcanoes and hills surround a bowl-shaped city with the finer neighborhoods sitting on the slopes and the historical center being one giant market with ugly stalls blocking the sidewalks. Earthquake damage has taken its toll on older buildings, and the city—which is Central America's second-most-populated behind Guatemala City—lacks any grand vistas. Instead of pretty architecture, San Salvador seems to have the highest concentration of fast-food restaurants in the world; Burger King, Wendy's, and Pizza Hut are on practically every corner. Yet the mayor has kept his promise; the streets are piece by piece being cleared and there is an air of revitalization in the air.

San Salvador is a frenetic, modern, international city in which travelers will find examples of the best and the worst of Central America. On the plus side, the nation's capital offers one of region's most diverse collections of international restaurants. You can sample fusion, Italian, Asian, Brazilian, and other cuisines at restaurants with top-notch service and, at least by North American and European standards, reasonable prices. You can also lay your head on the fluffy pillows of high-end luxury hotels such as Hilton, Sheraton, and InterContinental Real, and shop at an international collection of designer stores in sparkling new malls such as the Multiplaza and Gran Via. In addition, the city boasts a world-class art museum, a historic center (El Centro), a nearby international airport, and beach resorts within 1 hour's drive. It's a city with a lot going for it.

If you have limited time in El Salvador, my advice is to skip San Salvador and base yourself in laid-back Suchitoto or on a nearby beach resort. Like many big cities, San Salvador takes a while to seduce a newcomer, so if you do have the time, by all means linger and experience the heart of Salvadoran urban culture.

Essentials

GETTING THERE

BY PLANE   El Salvador International Airport, also known as Comalapa or **Cuscatlán International Airport** (SAL; ✆ **503/2366-2520;** www.cepa.gob.sv/aies/index.php) is 44km (27 miles) and a roughly 45-minute drive from San Salvador. Cuscatlán International is serviced by major North American carriers such as **American, Delta,** and **Continental,** as well as Latin American carriers **Copa** and **Mexicana.** It's also a major hub for **Taca** airlines with direct flights to major American cities. See chapter 11, "Fast Facts: Central America," for airline info.

To get to the capital from the airport, take bus no. 138, which costs $1.75. Alternatively, you can arrange transportation with your hotel or pay $25 for one of the taxis waiting by the airport exit.

BY BUS   There are three main bus terminals in the city servicing different sectors of the country, plus the small, private terminals of the plusher international bus companies. The public stations are chaotic and busy. Some lines have different categories. *Directo* is a misnomer as these buses usually stop everywhere, much like the *ordinarios. Especial* generally has A/C, comfy seats, TV, and many fewer stops.

Terminal de Oriente (Final de Av. Peralta and Blvd. del Ejército; ② **503/2271-4171**) is 4km (2½ miles) from the city center and serves the east and north of the country. You can catch bus no. 29 or 52 from Boulevard de los Heroes, but the drop-off is at a busy roundabout that you must cross by a pedestrian walkway and likewise if you are going into the city. It is much more convenient to catch a taxi. Buses here leave for the Honduran border (3 hr.) as well as San Miguel (2½ hr.) and Suchitoto (1½ hr.).

Terminal de Occidente (Blvd. Venezuela, Colonia Roma; ② **503/2223-5609**) is closer to the city center, 1.5km (1 mile) southwest of Parque Cuscatlán. It serves the west of the country, including the southwestern coast and most of the Guatemalan border crossings. Main destinations include Joya de Cerén (1¼ hr.), La Libertad (1 hr.), Lago de Coatepeque (40 min.), Los Cóbanos (2 hr.), Santa Ana (1½ hr.), and Sonsonate (1½ hr.).

Terminal del Sur, also known as Terminal San Marco (Carretera a Aeropuerto; no phone) is 5km (3 miles) south of the city and serves the south and southeast of the country. Bus no. 26 goes to and from the city center. The station's main destinations are Costa del Sol (2½ hr.), Zacatecoluca (1½ hr.), and Usulután (2½ hr.).

You can take **Tica Bus** (② **503/2243-9764;** www.ticabus.com), which is one of Central America's largest and most luxurious carriers with destinations throughout Central America, from the **San Carlos Terminal** (Calle Conception No. 121 at the San Salvador Hotel; ② **503/2243-9764**) and **San Benito Terminal** (Blvd. del Hipódromo; ② **503/2243-9764**). **King Quality/Comfort Lines** (② **503/2271-3330**) has two terminals: **Terminal Puerto Bus,** 3a Calle Poniente and Alameda San Juan Pablio II; and **Zona Rosa,** Boulevard de Hipódromo and Avenida La Revolución. **Pullmantur** (② **503/2243-1300;** www.pullmantur.com) operates from the Hotel Sheraton Presidente, Avenida La Revolución, Zona Rosa.

ORIENTATION

San Salvador is Central America's largest city in terms of size, sprawling 570 sq. km (220 sq. miles) east from the base of Volcán San Salvador. The three main tourist zones are **El Centro** in the east, and the **Escalón** neighborhood and Boulevard del Hipódromo in **Zona Rosa** in the west. All three neighborhoods are connected by the city's main east-west highway, known as **Alameda Franklin Delano Roosevelt,** east of the **Plaza de Las Américas** and **Paseo General Escalón** west of the plaza. El Centro includes the city's traditional square, national cathedral, and theater, and is a crowded, urban area. It's safe during the day, but best not visited at night. Zona Rosa and Escalón are more upscale residential neighborhoods, and offer some of San Salvador's top restaurants, nightclubs, and shops. Adjacent to Zona Rosa to the west, you'll find the Colonia San Benito neighborhood, home to the **Museo Nacional de Antropología Dr. David J. Guzman** and **Museo de Arte.** It's not a good idea to stray too far from these three areas without local knowledge or a guide.

Though most of your travel in San Salvador will be east-west along Roosevelt/Escalón, the city also has a couple of key north-south routes. The main north-south route through the El Centro section is known as Avenida España north of Plaza Barrios and Avenida Cuscatlán south of the Plaza. Avenida Norte, which becomes the Boulevard de Los Heroes, splits the middle of the city; to travel south to the Zona Rosa and Colonia San Benito neighborhoods from the Paseo General Escalón, follow Avenida Manuel E Araujo to Boulevard del Hipódromo.

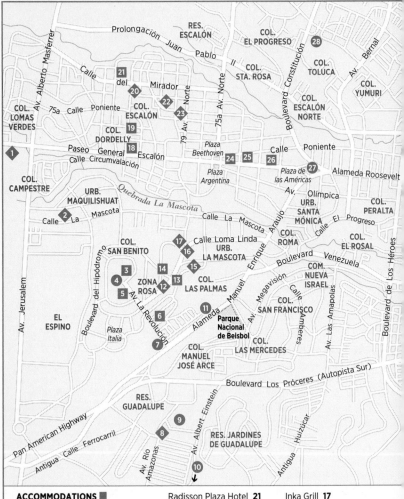

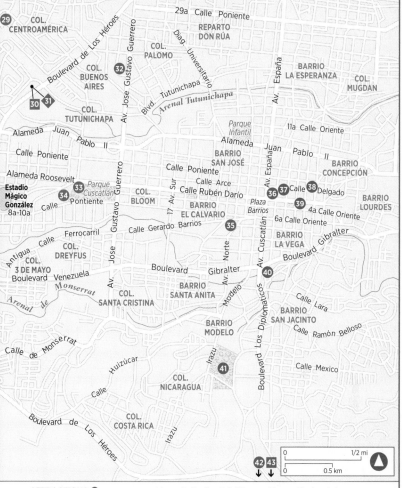

Getting Around

BY BUS   Buses rule the road in San Salvador and are a great way to see the city, since they stop frequently and go just about everywhere. Bus no. 30b is the line you'll most need to remember. The 30b will take you from Metrocentro (Blvd. de Los Héreos and Calle Sisimiles) across town to Zona Rosa and within walking distance of the city's two major museums. Most intercity buses can be taken from in front of the Metrocentro mall. To travel across the city from El Centro, take bus no. 101 to the Plaza de Las Americas, where you can hop on no. 30b.

Most buses cost 25¢ to 35¢ and run between 5am and 7:30pm daily, with less frequent service on Sundays. The CORSATUR tourist office (see "Visitor Information," below) can provide additional bus route information.

BY TAXI   You might want to consider using a cab instead of the bus, depending on how far you're traveling—it costs only about $4 to take a cab many places in the city. Exact fares range depending on your negotiating skills, the driver, and whether the cab has a meter. If you speak Spanish, you'll get the best deal by finding a cab without a meter and negotiating a price before getting into the cab. If the taxi has a meter, demand at least an estimate of the cost before agreeing to the trip.

San Salvador has numerous taxicab companies, any of which can be safely hailed on the street during daytime as long as you use a traditional-looking taxi (yellow with a little taxi sign on top).

BY CAR   Getting around by rental car is a great way to see El Salvador and a horrible way to see San Salvador. The city's roads are packed and not well marked. A wrong turn can also send you into a neighborhood you'd rather not visit or into the midst of a street market. Since taxis are relatively inexpensive and easy to grab, and local buses are cheap and numerous, I recommend leaving your rental at your hotel or renting a car on your way out of the city.

San Salvador offers plenty of local and international rental agencies. **Avis** (© 503/2339-9268), **Budget** (airport office © 503/2339-9942; city office © 503/2264-3888), **Hertz** (© 503/2339-8004), **Thrifty** (© 503/2339-9947), **Alamo** (© 503/2367-8000), and **National** (© 503/2367-8001) all have airport and downtown San Salvador locations. Locally, **Brothers Rent A Car** (Centro Commercial Feria Rosa Bldg. H, local 208, in front of Casa Presidencial; © 503/2218-1856) offers the best deals. Rates range from $40 to $150 a day with taxes and insurance.

ON FOOT   Both of San Salvador's main tourist centers, El Centro and Zona Rosa, are highly walkable. It's in between those neighborhoods where you'll need transportation. El Centro's attractions are centered around the main square Plaza Barrios, and most of Zona Rosa's sights are along walkable Boulevard del Hipódromo. The city's major museums in the Colonia San Benito neighborhood are also within walking distance of each other.

VISITOR INFORMATION

San Salvador's national tourism bureau (CORSATUR) office is located at Alameda Dr. Manuel Enrique Araujo, Pasaje and Building Carbonel No. 2, Colonia Roma (© **503/2243-7835;** www.elsalvador.travel), and is open Monday through Friday 8am to noon and 1 to 5pm. The airport also offers a tourism office (© **503/2339-9454**) with English-speaking staff that's open Monday through Friday from 7am to 6pm.

FAST FACTS   San Salvador offers a plentiful supply of the nation's major banks, and ATMs here accept most common international cards. The best and safest locations are in the city's many malls. Bank hours generally run from 9am to 4pm Monday to Friday, with a half-day on Saturday from 9am to noon. A **Banco Cuscatlan** (🕿 **503/2212-2000**) is in the Galarias Escalón mall along Paseo General Escalón. **Banco de America Central** (🕿 **503/2254-9980**) is also located on Paseo General Escalón. On Boulevard de los Heroes there is a **Banco Cuscatlan** (🕿 **503/2212-2000,** ext. 4205) on the intersection with Avenida Izalco and a **Scotiabank** (🕿 **503/2260-9038**) located in Metro Sur mall. In the city center you'll find a **Banco Cuscatlán** on Avenida Cuscatlán and a **Scotiabank** on 2a Calle Poniente. Most of the above banks will cash traveler's checks.

Farmacia Super Medco, Avenida La Revolución and Boulevard Hipódromo, Zona Rosa (🕿 **503/2243-3599**), is open 24 hours with an all-night service window on Boulevard Hipódromo. **Farmacia Rowalt,** Avenida Los Sisimiles and Avenida Sierra Nevada, close to Boulevard de los Heroes (🕿 **503/2261-0515**), also dispenses 24/7 and delivers from 8am to 5pm. Just ring the doorbell if it appears closed. In the city center try **Farmacia Principal,** Calle Delgado 227 (🕿 **503/2222-8093**), open daily 8:30am to 8pm.

Ambulances can be reached directly at 🕿 **503/2222-5155** and the **fire department** is at 🕿 **503/2555-7300. Police** can be contacted at 🕿 **503/2261-0630.** The general emergency number is 🕿 **911.**

The best medical care is at the modern **Hospítal de Diagnóstico Escalón** (99 Av. Norte, Plaza Villavicencio; 🕿 **503/2264-4422**). **Hospital de Diagnóstico,** Calle 21 Pte and 2a Diagonal, Boulevard de los Heroes (🕿 **503/2226-8878**), is a well-respected and good-value private clinic.

Correos Central, 15 Calle Poniente and 19 Av. Norte, Centro Gobierno, El Centro (🕿 **503/2555-7600**), is the main post office and is open weekdays 7:30am to 5pm and Saturday 8am to noon. There is a another **Correos** outlet located on the second floor of the Metrocentro, open weekdays 8am to 7pm and Saturday 8am to noon. **DHL** (🕿 **503/2264-2708**) has an office on Avenida Alberto Masferrer Norte. It is open weekdays 8am to 5pm and Saturday 8am to noon.

There are plenty of Internet cafes in the city center yet very few in the upscale residential zones like Colonia Escalón. Most offer Internet calls and CD burning. Charges vary from $1 to $2 an hour. **Cyber Café Genus,** Av. Izalco 102-A, Boulevard de los Heroes (🕿 **503/2226-5221**), is open weekdays 9am to 11pm and Saturday 10am to 8pm. **PC Station,** Metro Sur, Boulevard de los Heroes (🕿 **503/2257-5791**), is another option in the same area. It is open Monday to Saturday 7am to 10pm and Sunday 9am to 7pm. In the city center go to **Ciber Shack,** 2a Av. Sur and 4a Calle Ote. (no phone). Open Monday to Saturday 7:30am to 6:30pm.

There are no **public toilets** in the city except in the shopping malls. Ask nicely in any restaurant and you'll have no problems.

Festivals

The **Festival of El Salvador** in early August marks a nearly countrywide vacation during which everyone who can heads to their vacation spot of choice. Schools and businesses close so that communities can host parades, celebrations, and religious processions honoring Jesus Christ ("El Salvador") as the patron saint of the country. The largest celebrations are here in the nation's capital.

What to See & Do

THE TOP ATTRACTIONS

Catedral Metropolitana ★   El Salvador's national cathedral is not as stunning as some famous European cathedrals, but it is steeped in Salvadoran history and offers an example of the nation's adopted artistic style. Historically, the church was the site of deadly massacres prior to the country's civil war, and great celebrations after the 1992 peace accords. The church has been damaged and rebuilt three times and is considered a symbol of the nation's rebirth from tragedy. Today the cathedral features a huge mural by El Salvador's most revered living artist, Fernando Llort. As the aesthetics here are somewhat secondary to the history, read up a bit before you go to know what you are looking at.

Av. Cuscatlán and 2a Calle Oriente at Plaza Barrios. No phone. Free admission. Daily 8am–noon and 2–4pm.

Museo de Arte ★★★   The Museo de Arte is one of San Salvador's must-sees. The 2,267-sq.-m (24,400-sq.-ft.) museum includes six rooms of rotating exhibits and a permanent collection that helps newcomers get a sense of the country. One of the highlights is the art from the 1980-to-1992 civil war period, which clearly but subtly demonstrates the desperation of the time. In front of the museum is the towering stone mosaic Monument to the Revolution, which depicts a naked man whose outstretched arms are thought to symbolize freedom and liberty. You'll need 1 to 3 hours to explore the museum, and English-language tours are free for parties of 10 or more and $40 total for parties of 1 to 9. Call or e-mail (**educacion@marte.org.sv**) 24 hours in advance to schedule an English-language tour. The museum also has an attractive restaurant called **Punto Café.**

Final Av. La Revolución, Colonia San Benito. ℃ **503/2243-6099.** www.marte.org.sv. Admission $1.50 adults, 50¢ students, free for children 7 and under. Tues–Sun 10am–6pm.

Museo Nacional de Antropología Dr. David J. Guzman ★★   San Salvador's anthropology museum is the city's other must-see, but only if you speak Spanish or can arrange an English-speaking tour. The ancient tools, weapons, pottery, and ceramic artifacts on exhibit here offer an intriguing glimpse into the lives of El Salvador's indigenous community and explain the evolution of agriculture and early trade in the country. However, signs are in Spanish only. Since the museum is only a 10-minute walk from the art museum, it's still worth a quick look if you can't arrange an English-language tour and are in the area. An English-speaking tour guide is available at the front desk or at the number below.

Av. La Revolucíon, Colonia San Benito. ℃ **503/2243-3927.** www.munaelsalvador.com. Admission $3, $5 to bring in camera or video equipment. Tues–Sun 9am–5pm.

Teatro Nacional ★   The 2001 earthquake deprived San Salvador of its most treasured cultural institute for almost 8 years. Now that it's newly renovated and reopened, you can visit its splendid salons on day visits or enjoy its weekend performances of theater, opera, and classical music. Built between 1911 and 1917, the Teatro Nacional is considered one of Central America's oldest theaters and one of El Salvador's grandest buildings. The French Renaissance structure has 10 large columns across the front and a grand European interior of high ceilings, big chandeliers, and an opulent, multistory theater.

2 Av. Sur and Calle Delgado, 1 block east of Plaza Barrios. ℃ **503/2222-8760.** $3 admission. Wed–Sun 8am–4pm.

REMEMBERING MONSEÑOR romero

Monseñor **Oscar Arnulfo Romero,** commonly referred to as Monseñor Romero, is arguably El Salvador's most revered native son. He was born in 1917, and at age 20 he went to Rome to study at Gregorian University and begin his career in the priesthood. He returned to El Salvador at 26, and spent the next 20 years as a priest in San Miguel. In 1966, he became secretary of the Episcopal Conference and editor of the archdiocese's newspaper, *Orientación.* In 1975 he was appointed archbishop of the Diocese of Santiago de Maria and was promoted to Archbishop of San Salvador in 1977. Romero was not at first considered to be a revolutionary, and his appointment disappointed some of the country's more progressive religious leaders.

Less than a month after his appointment as archbishop, Romero was deeply affected by the assassination of his personal friend Rutilio Grande, who had been organizing for the nation's poor.

Romero took up Grande's mantle and became an outspoken critic of government repression, injustice, and El Salvador's death squads. He also criticized Jimmy Carter and Pope John Paul II for their governments' support of the Salvadoran military.

On March 24, 1980, following a sermon in which he was reported to have called on El Salvador's government soldiers to end their repressive tactics, Romero was shot and killed. His funeral in front of the country's national cathedral drew more than a quarter of a million mourners and was itself the site of gunfire and bomb blasts. The **chapel** where Romero was shot (Calle Toluca, Colonia Miramonte beside Hospital La Divinia Providencia; ✆ **503/2260-0520**) remains open and has a plaque marking the tragedy. Across the street, Romero's living quarters have been preserved as a museum with his personal effects and photos of the crime scene and funeral.

OTHER ATTRACTIONS

Centro Monseñor Romero ★   This center tells the story and displays the images and personal items of the six Jesuit priests, their housekeeper, and the housekeeper's daughter who were brutally murdered in the university rectory November 16, 1989, in the midst of El Salvador's bloody civil war. The murders made international headlines and demonstrated the war's high level of personal violence. Considering that El Salvador is a country with a complex and occasionally disturbing history, the 30 minutes you'll need to tour this one-room center are worth it to have a broader understanding of the country and its people.

Universidad Centroamericano José Siméon Cañas. ✆ **503/2210-6600,** ext. 422. Free admission. Mon-Fri 8am–noon and 2–6pm; Sat 8–11:30am.

El Arbol de Dios   Arbol de Dios is the gallery and nonprofit office of El Salvador's most revered living artist, Fernando Llort, who founded an art movement in the small mountain town of La Palma in 1972 by teaching locals to use available materials to create art about their lives. His colorful style, which is filled with natural and religious references, has since swept the country and can be found in hundreds of shops and at the National Cathedral. The gallery is small and requires less than 30 minutes to take in. But if you want to see a few of the original pieces of art that inspired thousands of copies, this is the place. If you're not that into art or Llort, it may not be worth the trip.

Av. Masferrer Norte, Colonia Lomas Verdes. © **503/2263-9206.** Free admission. Mon–Fri 8am–5pm.

Hospital La Divinia Provedencia ★ It was at the altar of this small hospital chapel in the midst of mass on March 24, 1980, that one of El Salvador's most revered citizens, Monseñor Oscar Arnulfo Romero, was gunned down in front of his parishioners. Today the church remains a working chapel with pictures of Romero and a small plaque marking the place where he was killed. Across the street, Monseñor Romero's living quarters are now a museum displaying his personal items with photos of the crime scene and the thousands who flocked to his funeral in front of the national cathedral. If you're at all interested in the details of El Salvador's civil war, this is worth a visit.

Calle Toluca, Colonia Miramonte. © **503/2260-0520.** Free admission. Mon–Sat 9am–noon and 2–4pm.

Iglesia El Rosario ★★ 🎒 This is one of the most visually interesting churches in San Salvador, and well worth the 5-minute walk off the main square. El Rosario's concrete, half-moon, bunker-like appearance is a bit bizarre and unchurchlike from the outside, but inside visitors are greeted by lines of colored light streaming in from abstract stained glass running up the height of its two curved walls. Abstract metalworks form the altar and run the length of a third wall. The Stations of the Cross are represented by spare concrete-and-metal art pieces and are showcased in a low-ceilinged area, which is lit by natural light filtered through small squares of colored glass.

4a Calle Oriente and 6a Av. Sur. No phone. Free admission. Daily 6:30am–noon and 2–7pm.

Jardín Botánico La Laguna 🌿 Unless you're really into plants and flowers, you shouldn't make the trip here. La Laguna is a beautiful and lush 3-hectare (7½-acre) park inside an extinct volcano crater with winding paths through hundreds of species of plants and flowers from around the world. The park, which you can explore in 30 minutes, offers an open-air cafeteria beside a small pond and numerous secluded nooks and crannies to escape the heat. The only problem is that the garden is in the midst of a busy factory district, so you'll need to dodge trucks and walk through less than savory surroundings to get to the entrance. If La Laguna were in the city center, it would be a real gem, but I can't say it's worth a special trip.

Universidad Centroamericano José Siméon Cañas, Antigua Cuscatlán. © **503/2243-2012.** Admission $1. Tues–Sun 9am–5:30pm.

Monumento a la Memoria y la Verdad ★ The Monument to Memory and Truth is an 85m (279-ft.) black granite wall displaying the names of the 25,000 victims of the civil unrest, political repression, and war of the 1970s and 1980s. It is a stern reminder of just how much this country has suffered and is all the more powerful as you realize how recently these horrendous events took place. The long list gives force to the brutal statistics of a dark period.

Northern side of Parque Cuscatlán. No phone. Free admission. Daily 6am–6pm.

Museo de Arte Popular *Sorpresas* (literally meaning surprises) are miniature clay models of Salvadorans as they go about their daily business. Meticulously detailed, they are extremely popular and one of the country's signature handicrafts. This museum celebrates the skill and craftsmanship that goes into each piece with an excellent collection of hundreds of pieces. The doctor, the housewife, and the departing emigrant are just some of the characters created with humor and skill. The town of Llobasco is the best known source of such lovely creations.

Av. San Jose 125, 7 blocks northwest of Blvd. de los Heroes. © **503/2274-5154.** Admission $1. Tues–Fri 10am–5pm; Sat 10am–6pm.

Museo de la Palabra y La Imagen   Black-and-white portraits evoke the left-wing upheavals of the 20th century in three exhibition rooms in a museum dedicated to the writers and activists of that era. The studio of an illegal radio station is re-created in homage to the FMLN-backed broadcaster *Radio Venceremos*. Themes such as famous Salvadoran feminists and events of the 1930s are put on show, as well as books and documents. TV war footage is available to view in a small cinema. The museum also holds a small bookshop.

27 Av. Norte, 3 blocks east of Blvd. de los Heroes. © **503/2275-4870.** www.museo.com.sv. Admission $2. Mon–Fri 8am–noon and 2–5pm; Sat 8am–noon.

Parque Zoológico Nacional ☺   This leafy 7-hectare (17-acre) zoo south of the city center is a hugely popular weekend spot for San Salvador families. Here you'll find winding, shady paths, and numerous small lagoons inhabited by roughly 400 animals and 125 species including such crowd pleasers as lions, elephants, alligators, and a huge selection of birds.

Final Calle Modelo. © **503/2270-0828.** Admission 60¢. Wed–Sun 9am–4pm.

Plaza de Las Américas ♨   Plaza de Las Americas is a large, grassy traffic circle in the midst of a busy intersection containing the much-photographed Monumento Salvador del Mundo, or Monument to the Savior of the World. The monument includes a tall, four-sided concrete base with crosses on each side topped with a statue of Christ standing on top of the world. It's fine as statues go, but there's no parking and it's a bit tricky crossing numerous lanes of traffic to reach the circle. So unless you're a photography buff searching for the perfect shot, you might want to just take in the view from a bus window.

Alameda Franklin Delano Roosevelt. No phone. Free admission. Daily 24 hr.

Tin Marín Museo de los Nínos ☺   This interactive children's museum and learning center boasts 24 exhibits giving kids fun, hands-on learning in the areas of culture, the environment, health, and technology. Little ones can dress up like doctors in a pretend operating room, put on plays in the theater, walk inside a volcano, and make child-size houses more environmentally friendly.

6 and 10 Calle Poniente, btw. Parque Cuscatlán and Gimnacio Nacional, Colonia Flor Blanca. © **503/2271-5147.** Admission $2. Tues–Fri 9am–5pm; Sat–Sun 10am–6pm.

NEARBY ATTRACTIONS

Joya de Cerén ★★   While not as visually grand as the nearby Tazumal ruins (p. 306), Joya de Cerén offers one of Central America's best glimpses into the daily lives of the region's Maya ancestors. Discovered in 1976, this UNESCO World Heritage Site comprises the remains of a Maya community frozen in time 1,400 years ago when it was buried beneath the ash of a volcanic eruption. The archaeological park requires about 1 hour to explore and includes a Spanish-language-only museum and the partial remains of the village's buildings, including a shaman's house, a community sauna, and bedrooms with sleeping platforms. Only parts of the buildings remain, so you'll need a little imagination to appreciate what you are seeing. But you won't

STAYING safe

"But isn't it dangerous there?" you'll hear your friends saying when telling them of your upcoming trip. The short answer is no, El Salvador is, in fact, a safe country to travel in. However, it does have its issues and dangers, and they should still be taken into account when moving around the country. The street gang Mara Salvatrucha, which has members throughout the country, is considered to be among the most violent in the world, and El Salvador has one of the planet's highest homicide rates—14 a day in 2010. Street and bus robberies in bad neighborhoods are also not uncommon—it's foolish to deny that these conditions exist. But if you follow a few simple rules, you should have a safe and enjoyable trip.

Among the most important things to consider when traveling in El Salvador is not to stray too far off the travelers' path without knowledge of the area or a guide. Neighborhoods can change quickly and it's often difficult to distinguish between safe and unsafe areas by appearance alone. Some of the leafier, residential neighborhoods immediately outside larger cities are among the most prone to robbery. The main tourist areas of the bigger cities, however, are usually filled with people and are among the most heavily patrolled.

Small-town squares are also usually filled with locals into the evening and are among the safest places you're likely to visit. Don't be spooked by the presence of heavily armed police and private security guarding many of the country's banks, businesses, and tourist areas: El Salvador has a turbulent history and the seemingly ominous presence of armed guards—even in small towns—has simply become part of the culture. Heavy firepower does not mean an area is particularly dangerous.

Avoid traveling between towns or walking away from main squares at night; if you must venture out, always take a cab at night in bigger cities. It's also a good idea not to hike in rural, isolated areas without a guide.

Don't carry or display items of obvious value such as jewelry or expensive cameras; if you don't look like you have anything worth stealing, you're less likely to be robbed. Get in the habit of looping an arm or leg through the strap of your bag when you sit in a restaurant or bus depot, and don't leave bags unattended even for a moment. Simply being aware of what is around you helps: If someplace doesn't feel safe, it probably isn't. Just walk away.

Perhaps the most important safety tip, stressed to me by many Salvadoran friends and provided as standard advice by government agencies, is to give up your valuables if robbed. El Salvador's criminals are known to turn quickly violent when resisted. So if you're confronted, don't try to reason and don't bargain for your laptop.

find ruins anywhere else in the country that are so well preserved, making this definitely worth seeing.

Km 35 Carretera a San Juan Opica. No phone. $3 adults, free for children 4 and under. Tues–Sun 9am–4pm. At press time, the park offered only 1 English-speaking guide; call ahead (✆ **503/2401-5782**) to schedule a tour. Bus: 108 from San Salvador.

Lago Ilopango ♥ Ilopango is El Salvador's largest and deepest lake and offers a pleasant afternoon break from the city heat. But unless you are on a prearranged scuba-diving trip, Ilopango is overrated as a major attraction. You're better off heading

56km (35 miles) east to Lago de Coatepeque, which has more pristine surroundings, better restaurants, and more activities. But if you just want to get out of the city for a few hours, the 100-sq.-km (39-sq.-mile) Lago Ilopango is an easy 16km (10-mile) drive from the city, and its tourist center, called Parque Acuático Apulo, offers a handful of inexpensive, gazebo-style restaurants with lake views, a big pool, and $10 per 30-minute boat tours. You can swim in the lake but the park features only a small, uncomfortable, pebble-filled beach.

Ilopango, which reaches a depth of 250m (820 ft.), is a popular diving spot and El Salvador's top diving tour company. **El Salvador Divers** (✆ **503/2264-0961; call in advance to arrange a trip**) has a lakeside dive facility with dive equipment, boats, and overnight facilities.

Canton Dalores Apulo, Ilopango. ✆ **503/299-5430.** Admission 80¢. Daily 8am–4pm. Bus: 15.

Los Planes de Renderos ★★ 🎒
Heading up to Los Planes de Renderos to watch the lights of San Salvador come alive on a Sunday night is one of the city's most underrated joys. Planes de Renderos is a small community about a 20-minute bus ride from San Salvador, with a large overlook offering sweeping views of the city and surrounding mountains. The village also features numerous small shops and *pupusarias.* Though you can venture up to Renderos any night, Sunday is when you'll find Salvadoran families enjoying a festival-like atmosphere with music, dancers, and street vendors. At dusk, everyone who can fit lines up along Renderos's overlook to watch the lights of San Salvador in the valley below slowly create a sea of lights while the largely unpopulated surrounding mountains fade to black. It's a beautiful sight. A lot of the crowd then heads over to **Pupusaria Señor Pico,** which is across the street from the overlook and offers tasty snacks and partial views from an upstairs balcony.

Bus: 30 to Planes Los Renderos. Bring extra cash, as the last bus back leaves at 7pm and taxis are $8.

Parque Archeologío San Andrés
If you have time for a third ruin, you'll enjoy your visit here. Otherwise, stick to Tazumal and Joya de Cerén. San Andrés is the partially excavated main plaza of a Maya community that was active between A.D. 600 and 900 and ruled over this Valle de Zapotitlán. The site was excavated in 1977 and today consists of a roughly 9m-tall (30-ft.) pyramid—which may have housed royal tombs—and other partially excavated structures. There's also a Spanish-language museum featuring a 1.5×4.5m (5×15-ft.) topographical country map and a large-scale model of the site. San Andrés offers some beautiful long-range views but doesn't stir the imagination like Cerén or offer Tazumal's exemplary architecture. The ruins require less than 30 minutes to explore.

Km 32 Carretera a Santa Ana. ✆ **503/2319-3220** or 2235-9453. Admission $3. Tues–Sun 9am–4pm. Bus: 201 from San Salvador to San Andrés.

Volcán San Salvador
Volcán San Salvador is an iconic part of the capital, since it looms over the landscape west of the city. The main volcano complex, which peaks at 1,960m (6,430 ft.), was formed after an eruption roughly 70,000 years ago with smaller volcanic activity forming secondary peaks and craters such as Volcán San Salvador's most visited spot, the Boquerón or "big mouth" crater, which is 500m (1,640 ft.) deep and more than 1km (⅔ mile) wide. There have been no violent eruptions on Volcán San Salvador in 800 years, but, say experts, even the slightest eruption could have catastrophic effects on the densely populated city. If you decide to explore the complex, don't do so without a guide, as the volcano's proximity to San Salvador makes it a prime robbery area.

Tour companies, such as Eco Mayan Tours (☎ **503/2298-2844**), can arrange transportation and guided tours here starting at $25 per person.

Shopping

San Salvador offers the best upscale shopping in El Salvador, with most high-end shops centered in four large, modern malls (see below). The city's Zona Rosa section along the **Boulevard del Hipódromo** is lined with smaller independent shops and the small **Basilea shopping center** (Blvd. del Hipódromo; ☎ **503/2279-0833**), which features small boutiques and jewelry stores.

San Salvador's largest but least upscale of those malls is **Metrocentro** (Blvd. de Los Héroes and Calle Sisimiles), across the street from the InterContinental Real Hotel. Metrocentro has a few designer shops, but it's better for basics. More upscale is the **Galerías Escalón** (Paseo General Escalón, no. 3700; ☎ **503/2245-0800**), which is a mall with designer shops, chic restaurants, and a multiscreen cinema in the midst of the exclusive Escalón residential neighborhood. And about 20 minutes from Metrocentro are the Multiplaza and Gran Via malls. The **Multiplaza Mall** (Calle El Pedregal and Carretera Panamericana a Santa Ana, Antigua Cuscatlán; ☎ **503/2248-9800**) is the city's most upscale mall, with designer shops such as Zara clothing, a multiscreen cinema, and a wing offering some of the city's best nightclubs and lounges. About a block from Multiplaza is the **La Gran Via Mall** (Carretera Panamericana a Santa Ana and Calle, Chiltiupan, Antigua Cuscatlán; ☎ **503/2273-8111**), which is smaller than Multiplaza but centered around a large, inviting outdoor courtyard with upscale designer shops, a multiscreen cinema, and restaurants with outdoor seating. If you have time to visit only one of these malls, Gran Via is the best place to eat and people-watch on its central outdoor plaza, Multiplaza has the best nightlife, and Escalón is the place to go for small boutiques.

MARKETS

Mercado Central (Central Market) ★ Go here if you want to see a decidedly unfiltered and urban Salvadoran market. This isn't a tourist-centric, hammock-filled pedestrian plaza. The Central Market is a sprawling, seemingly chaotic mercado of blaring horns, shouting vendors, and old women in traditional clothes chopping vegetables and wrangling live chickens. The main attraction at this multiblock indoor and outdoor market is that it is not designed for tourists: It's just *the* place locals go to buy everything from their dinner to electronic gadgets.

6a Calle Oriente, btw. Calle del Cementerio and Av. 29 de Agosto, El Centro. (Walk 3 blocks west and 2 blocks south of Plaza Barrios.) No phone. Daily 7:30am to around 6pm.

Mercado Ex-Cuartel Though smaller, calmer, and more tourist-friendly than the nearby Mercado Central, the indoor Mercado Ex-Cuartel is filled with tourist kitsch, the same textile bags you'll see in most Central American markets, and lots of unremarkable women's shoes. There is some original art for sale, along with a smallish collection of decorative boxes and crosses. But if you want a souvenir representative of El Salvador and its artisans, you're better off going to Mercado Nacional de Artesanias or buying in one of El Salvador's small village markets.

8a Av. Sur and Calle Delgado, El Centro. (Walk 1 block north and 3 blocks east of the National Cathedral.) No phone. Free admission. Daily 9am–6pm.

Mercado Nacional de Artesanias ★★ The lack of locals, the paved parking lot, and wave after wave of buses stopping directly in front tell you that this is San

Salvador's most touristy marketplace. But despite the lack of local flavor, the quality of the art and crafts is high and the prices aren't bad. The market includes long rows of vendors selling unique hammocks, textiles, ceramics, and decorative crafts from artisans around El Salvador. A midsize textile bag will run you $8 and a large, well-crafted hammock should cost approximately $26. You could wait to buy directly from a craftsman in a village market, but you can also buy here knowing that the quality is high and the price is surprisingly fair.

Alemeda Dr. Manuel Enrique Araujo, Colonia San Benito. © **503/2224-0747.** Daily 9am–6pm.

Where to Stay

San Salvador is an oasis of international style and service in El Salvador. The Hilton Princess, Sheraton Presidente, and the InterContinental Real are the most luxurious of the city's international chains and live up to the high standards of those brand names. Local hotel Las Palmas is my favorite place to stay in town. But all of the hotels listed below are comfortable and have something, be it price, location, or service, to recommend them. The Zona Rosa neighborhood—which includes the Hilton Princess and Las Palmas hotels—is among the city's safest and most tourist-friendly places to stay.

VERY EXPENSIVE

Hilton Princess ★★   It's a close call, but the Hilton Princess wins the title of San Salvador's most luxurious business hotel. What sets this 11-story chain hotel in the heart of tourist-friendly Zona Rosa apart are its detailed, European castle-style interior and after-work amenities. Although all of San Salvador's high-end business hotels offer what you need to work, the Hilton goes further by easing the stress of commerce with perks such as a huge Jacuzzi and larger-than-average exercise room. From the rich leather and dark woods of **Churchill's Bar** to the hotel's European murals and statuary, the Hilton also exudes old-world charm and luxury. If your visit is primarily business and you enjoy conducting it in luxury, this is the place to stay.

Av. Magnolias and Blvd. del Hipódromo, Zona Rosa. © **800/321-3232** or 503/2268-4545. Fax 503/2268-4500. www.sansalvador.hilton.com. 204 units. $130–$176 standard; $205–$235 executive level; $368 and up suite. AE, DC, DISC, MC, V. **Amenities:** Restaurant; 2 bars; $14 airport transfers; concierge; executive level; health club w/Jacuzzi and sauna; outdoor pool; room service; 2 floors smoke-free. *In room:* A/C, TV, hair dryer, minibar, Wi-Fi.

InterContinental Real ★   The InterContinental Real is a high-end, international chain and solid business hotel, but it's a slightly less appealing option overall than the Hilton Princess or the Sheraton. It's in the city's main commercial district, which, though good for business travelers, isn't tourist-friendly; the pool and gym are also small and not overly inviting. On the plus side, the InterContinental is across the street from El Salvador's biggest shopping mall, Metrocentro, and offers the hippest **restaurants** (p. 251) and **lounges** of the big three.

Calle Sisimiles and Blvd. de Los Hereos, Colonia Miramonte. © **503/2211-3333.** Fax 503/2211-4444. www.ichotelsgroup.com. 234 units. $105–$134 standard double; $152–$170 executive double; $413 and up suite. Rates include continental breakfast. AE, DC, DISC, MC, V. **Amenities:** 3 restaurants; bar; $15 airport transfers; babysitting; concierge; executive level; heath club & spa w/sauna; small outdoor pool; room service; 181 smoke-free rooms. *In room:* A/C, TV, hair dryer, high-speed Internet, minibar.

Radisson Plaza Hotel ★★   On the slope of Colonia Escalón, overlooking the city, the Radisson is a large, modern six-story building with a bird-filled tree garden at one end. Its main attraction is a grand patio overlooking a big, no-nonsense pool. The rooms are ample with cream walls, carpeted floors, and small, marble-top writing desks, and the bathrooms come with all the modern conveniences you'd expect from a five-star hotel. Everything is new, immaculate, and well maintained. Some rooms have marvelous views of the city and volcano. The huge dining area has a circular island counter serving hearty breakfasts, and it adjoins the outside patio. Inside there is a smaller, cozy bar and restaurant adjacent to the expansive lobby. A big, well-equipped gym faces the pool and a spa is hidden away in the basement. The staff is gracious, and hiccups such as a broken coffeemaker were resolved in minutes. All your luxury needs are catered to. On the downside, the breakfasts are expensive and there is no free Internet service. There is an exorbitant charge to use the computers in the business center or Wi-Fi in your room. Look out for weekend and family deals.

89 Av. Norte and 11 Calle Poniente, Colonia Escalón. ⓒ **800/395-7046** or 503/2257-0700. Fax 503/2257-0710. www.radisson.com/sansalvadores. 126 units. From $129 standard double; $250 junior suite; $400 master suite. AE, DC, MC, V. Free parking. **Amenities:** 2 restaurants; bar; $15 airport transfers; babysitting; business center, concierge; executive level; heath club & spa w/sauna; outdoor pool; room service; Wi-Fi. *In room:* A/C, TV, hair dryer, high-speed Internet, minibar.

Sheraton Presidente ★★ Sheraton Presidente is an excellent high-end business hotel with all the amenities you'll need to get your work done, but it's also a slightly better place to stay than the Hilton Princess for those combining business and pleasure. That's because the Sheraton offers a huge pool and is a short walk to the city's two major museums and the shop-filled Boulevard del Hipódromo. The large outdoor pool includes a small waterfall to drown out city noise and is next to an outdoor putting green (rare in El Salvador). The interior of this four-story hotel is what you would expect of a high-end chain but nothing more; rooms are of average size with nondescript, corporate decor. The hotel is often near capacity, so book early and request a room on the back side to get pool views and less noise.

Av. La Revolución, Zona Rosa. ⓒ **800/325-3535** or 503/2283-4000. Fax 503/2283-4070. www.sheraton.com/sansalvador. 225 units. $125 standard double; $211 executive-level double; $411 and up suite. Executive rates include buffet breakfast. AE, DC, DISC, MC, V. **Amenities:** 2 restaurants; bar; $15 airport transfers; concierge; health club & spa w/sauna; huge outdoor pool; room service; 120 smoke-free rooms. *In room:* A/C, TV, kitchens or kitchenettes (in suites), hair dryer, minibar, Wi-Fi.

EXPENSIVE

Quality Hotel Real Aeropuerto ★ ☺ This Quality Hotel is a bit pricey but much nicer than you would expect of an airport hotel—it's a viable option even if you aren't leaving early in the morning. Just 5 minutes from the Comalapa International Airport and an easy 35-minute drive from downtown, this three-story hotel offers such non-airport touches as an Xbox video game console, a pool with poolside **bar** and Jacuzzi, and an upscale **restaurant.** All the necessary business amenities are also available. The rooms are standard chain size and nondescript, but a few offer pool views. If you want the amenities of the posh city hotels, but the peace and quiet of the suburbs, this is your place.

Km 40.5 Carretera al Aeropuerto, La Paz. ⓒ **877/424-6423** or 503/2366-0000. Fax 503/2366-0001. www.qualityinn.com. 149 units. $141-$182 double. Rates include buffet breakfast. AE, DC, DISC, MC, V. **Amenities:** Restaurant; bar; free airport transfers; babysitting; exercise room; Jacuzzi; outdoor pool; room service; 50 smoke-free rooms. *In room:* A/C, TV, fridge (in some), hair dryer, minibar (in some), Wi-Fi.

Suites Las Palmas ★★★ 🛏 Las Palmas is the best and hippest nonbusiness hotel for the money in the city. This modern, seven-story hotel is within walking distance to Zona Rosa's best restaurants and shops; offers big, modern suites with kitchens for the price of other hotels' basic rooms; and boasts unusual designs and amenities. The pool, Jacuzzi, and sleek Asian-fusion **restaurant** are all set on the rooftop and feature amazing views, as does the exercise room, which includes a wall of glass overlooking the city. The suites are large with king- or queen-size beds, often with kitchens and couches. Suite amenities and prices vary greatly, so pin down what you're getting when making your reservation; request upper-floor rooms, which have balconies and views. Though Las Palmas's name doesn't carry the cachet of the international chains, it's every bit as luxurious and a better deal.

Blvd. del Hipódromo, Zona Rosa. ℰ **503/2250-0800.** Fax 503/2250-0888. www.hotelsuiteslas palmas.com.sv. 47 units. $69–$90 standard double; $89–$119 deluxe double; $119–$139 presidential suite. Some rates include breakfast. AE, DC, DISC, MC, V. **Amenities:** Restaurant; bar; $15 airport transfers; small exercise room; Jacuzzi; rooftop pool; room service; 8 smoke-free rooms. *In room:* A/C, TV, full kitchens or kitchenettes (in some), Wi-Fi.

MODERATE

Hotel Villa Florencia Zona Rosa   A yellow corner building adorned with flowers hides a small, modern hotel with an excellent location. The furnishings are a mix of old and new with comfy sofas in the small lobby and a gilded balustrade overlooking a stone tiled patio, which acts as an open breakfast area in the morning. There's a patio, and computers you can use in the lobby. High ceilings and big beds adorn the good-size rooms with TV and telephone. No. 7 has the best view. The staff is friendly but doesn't speak English. Price and location make this hotel an excellent choice.

Calle Las Palmas 262, corner of Av. La Revolución, Zona Rosa. ℰ **503/2257-0236.** www.hotelvilla florencia.com. 14 units. $65 double. Rates include continental breakfast. AE, DC, MC, V. **Amenities:** $25 airport transfers. *In room:* A/C, TV, Wi-Fi.

Hotel Villa Serena San Benito ★★   It's bare-bones, but the San Benito is one of the best moderate options in San Salvador. The hotel opened in 2006 and offers huge, sunny suites and rooms, has spotless facilities, and, like the nearby Sheraton Presidente, is within walking distance of the city's two major museums and Boulevard del Hipódromo's shopping and restaurant district. The large, airy suites feature big kitchens with modern appliances and separate lounging areas. The staff is also incredibly friendly. On the downside, the hotel doesn't have a pool or restaurant. San Benito is the best choice for those who prefer a great location and a good deal over amenities.

Calle Cicunvalación, No. 46, Zona Rosa. ℰ **503/2237-7979.** 34 units. $62–$73 double. Rates include continental breakfast. AE, DC, DISC, MC, V. **Amenities:** $23 airport transfers; smoke-free rooms. *In room:* A/C, TV, full kitchens (in suites), Wi-Fi.

La Posada del Angel   If you want a home away from home, you can't go wrong with this cozy little guesthouse. Two angels hang over the reception area and two angels act as hosts to meet your every need. Mother and daughter Ana and Racquel are the proud English-speaking owners of a modern, light-filled suburban-style home. Every room is different but well appointed with carved headboards and wrought-iron lamps. No. 3 is the largest, with ample bathroom and tiled floors. There is a lush garden out back with communal gallery and dining area. The owners go out of their way to make you feel at home and are a fountain of information regarding nearby restaurants and things to do in the city.

85a Av. Norte 321, Colonia Escalón. ℰ **503/2237-7171.** 10 units. From $55 double. Rates include continental breakfast. AE, DC, MC, V. Free parking. **Amenities:** $25 airport transfers; communal kitchen. *In room:* A/C, TV, Wi-Fi.

La Posada del Rey Primero   This handsome residential home has an airy, colonial feel with high ceilings, stucco walls, and wrought-iron furniture. Jungle paintings hang on green and orange walls in a handsome lobby and dining area. The rooms are big, with modern flourishes such as air-conditioning and TVs. Big, firm beds are complemented by solid carved furniture. There is a courtyard out back with a small, unfortunately empty pool surrounded by plants and clay urns. Pleasant communal areas with comfy seats and lots of reading material look out over the courtyard. The rooms on the second floor are larger and best for views and light.

Calle Dordelly #4425, Colonia Escalón. ✆ **503/2264-5245.** www.posadadelreyprimero.com. 12 units. $53–$64 double. Rates include continental breakfast. AE, DC, MC, V. **Amenities:** $25 airport transfers. *In room:* A/C, TV, full kitchens (in suites), Wi-Fi.

Mariscal Hotel & Suites   The Mariscal is pricier than the other two options in Escalón (see below), but also a bit more upscale. It features 18 big rooms and suites that aren't necessarily any better than the area's other two hotels, but with matching linens and modern furniture sets, it does feel a bit fancier. The one- and two-room suites are large, with couches, dining tables, and well-appointed kitchens. Suites vary in quality, so request a suite with a modern kitchen: Suite no. 1 is the best, with a big bathroom and two televisions. Mariscal is also on a heavily trafficked road, so make sure to request a room farthest from the street when you book.

Paseo General Escalón, No. 3658, Colonia Escalón. ✆ **503/2283-0220.** Fax 503/2223-5889. 18 units. $65 double; $80 suite. Rates include continental breakfast. AE, DC, DISC, MC, V. **Amenities:** $20 airport transfers; room service; all rooms smoke-free. *In room:* A/C, TV, hair dryer, kitchens (in suites), Wi-Fi.

INEXPENSIVE

Hotel Plaza Antigua ★ 🍴   Plaza Antigua is an excellent, low-priced option in a great location. It isn't going to blow you away with its decor or amenities, but it's in one of San Salvador's nicest neighborhoods, Escalón, and steps from the swanky Galerías Escalón mall. The two-story hotel is situated around a courtyard with a small pool. Rooms are of average size—all can be viewed on the hotel's website—with nicely tiled bathrooms. Request room no. 5, which is the quietest and catches the afternoon breeze. Given Plaza Antigua's location, they could probably charge more if they decorated a bit.

1a Calle Poniente, No. 3844, Colonia Escalón (behind Galerías Escalón). ✆ **503/2223-9900.** Fax 503/2224-5952. hotelplazaantigua@gmail.com.com. 15 units. $45–$55 double. Rates include continental breakfast. AE, DC, DISC, MC, V. **Amenities:** Restaurant; $35 airport transfer; small outdoor pool; room service; 3 smoke-free rooms. *In room:* A/C, TV, no phone, Wi-Fi.

Villa Castagnola Hotel   Villa Castagnola is an excellent option for comfortable, affordable accommodations in the Escalón neighborhood, though it's about half the size of the Plaza Antigua. With only six rooms, Castagnola is as quiet a hotel as you will find in San Salvador. On-site husband-and-wife managers, Raul and Tatiana Nunes, offer a high level of personal service and will help you arrange area tours. The rooms are also larger than you would expect, and there's a pleasant, upstairs, open-air seating area with views of Volcán de San Salvador. The best room is no. 1, which has two sleeping areas and a big bathroom.

1a Calle Poniente and 73 Av. Norte, No. 3807, Colonia Escalón. ✆ **503/2275-4314** or 2275-4315. Fax 503/2211-6482. www.hotelvillacastagnola.com. 6 units. $45–$65 double. Rates include continental breakfast. AE, DC, DISC, MC, V. **Amenities:** Restaurant; $25 airport transfers; room service. *In room:* A/C, TV, fridge, Wi-Fi.

Where to Dine

San Salvador offers a world-class array of ethnic restaurants ranging from Asian to Peruvian. And one of the best places to sample those culinary offerings is the Boulevard del Hipódromo in the tourist-friendly Zona Rosa district. This stroll-friendly street on the city's west side offers a cluster of restaurants within just a few blocks. A few trusted Zona Rosa favorites are listed below, but since the city's restaurant scene is growing rapidly, you might want to take a stroll along the Boulevard to find your own favorite spot.

EXPENSIVE

Fiasca Do Brasil Rodizio & Grill ★★ BRAZILIAN   It's all about the meat. Fiasca is one of San Salvador's few Rodizio restaurants, which means they keep the *carne* coming. Rodizio is an all-you-can-eat Brazilian style of dining in which waiters bring huge skewers of meat or fish to your table and slice the cuts onto your plate. Fiasca specializes in the *picaña* or top rump cut, which many Brazilians consider to be beef's finest. And at Fiasco you don't wait long for your second helping, as the restaurant maintains a ratio of 18 servers to a maximum 92 diners. Fiasca Do Brasil is the principal restaurant of the luxury InterContinental Real hotel and offers a unique, high-end dining experience for a reasonable price. As a result, the place is often packed and reservations are required. Ask for one of the raised booths along each wall, which are off the busy main dining floor.

Calle Sisimiles and Blvd. de Los Hereos. ⓒ **503/2211-3333.** Reservations required. Rodizio dining $25. AE, DC, DISC, MC, V. Daily 6–10:30am, noon–3pm, and 7–11pm.

Hunan ★ CHINESE   After 10 years in a packed restaurant market, Hunan is still the place to go for Chinese. A bit plain and strip-mall-looking from the outside, Hunan's one-room, 250-person seating area is a lesson in Chinese interior design, with intricately carved wooded chairs and embroidered red velvet seats, enormous wall murals, and dozens of porcelain vases with flowers for sale filling up the huge space. But it's Hunan's unique "Pato Peking"–style cuisine, which is a particularly spicy and hearty variety of Chinese cooking, that keeps the diners coming back. Standout dishes include shrimp with tofu in a lobster salsa and duck with black mushrooms and oyster sauce. Hunan's service is also seamless.

Paseo Escalón, No. 4999, Colonia Escalón. ⓒ **503/2263-9911.** Main courses $18–$26. AE, DC, DISC, MC, V. Mon–Thurs noon–3pm and 6–10pm; Fri–Sat noon–3pm and 6–11pm; Sun noon–4pm and 6–9pm.

MODERATE

Alo Nuestro ★★★ FUSION   It's so good, they don't need to advertise. For almost 10 years, this restaurant has built a quiet, word-of-mouth following as one of the best restaurants in the Zona Rosa section of town. What draws the crowds is that Alo Nuestro fuses the best of San Salvador's international dining options into a single restaurant that uses local ingredients. The result is such tasty dishes as crispy sea bass sautéed in asparagus, mushrooms, and sweet corn with a light soy ginger sauce. Another treat is the garlic-spinach stuffed sautéed chicken breast with a blue cheese wine sauce and squash. Unique weekly specials such as sautéed tilapia over *loroco* (a local flowering green) crepes with basil sauce keep things fresh. The interior is small but spacious, with ample space between the tables, and there's a large, romantically lit outdoor deck with a view of the nearby mountains. The restaurant is also surprisingly affordable, with most entrees costing under $20.

Calle La Reforma, No. 225, Zona Rosa. ✆ **503/2223-5116.** Reservations recommended. Main courses $12–$20. AE, DC, DISC, MC, V. Mon–Thurs noon–2:30pm and 7–10:30pm; Fri noon–2:30pm and 7–11pm; Sat 7–11pm.

El Charrúa GRILL   In front of a palm-lined roundabout in a pleasant residential zone, El Charrúa provides every possible option for the confirmed carnivore. Beef, goat, rabbit, suckling pig, and lamb are just some of the many sizzling delights prepared on a grill in front of the bar. Uruguayan *asado* is a marathon barbecue where a procession of meat keeps coming, including sausage, chicken, and every cut of the cow. The restaurant also does a decent ceviche. The decor includes red brick, flowerpots, and an Indian mural—a reference to the Charrúa tribe the restaurant is dedicated to.

Plaza Israel, Colonia Escalón. ✆ **503/2263-3128.** Main courses $6–$12. AE, DC, MC, V. Tues–Sun 8am–11pm; Mon 4pm–midnight.

Inka Grill ★ PERUVIAN   The Inka Grill is a rare taste of the Andes in El Salvador. Dark woods, deep oranges, rich detail, and interesting Inca-inspired art greet diners as they enter this Peruvian oasis a few blocks off the Zona Rosa dining district. The dishes are pure Peruvian, with plates such as the *ronda criolla, chicharrones* or deep-fried rinds of chicken and pig with artichoke hearts, yucca, and sweet potato, or the appetizer of Peruvian *tamales de choclo* (corn tamales) with an onion salsa. Inka Grill is part of a seven-restaurant chain with locations in Costa Rica, Guatemala, the United States, and a second San Salvador location at the Gran Via mall. This spot near Zona Rosa is the better of the two because it is more secluded and tranquil, and offers a more uniquely Peruvian ambience.

79 Av. Sur and Pasaje A, Zona Rosa (a few blocks off Blvd. del Hipódromo). ✆ **503/2230-6060.** Main courses $9.95–$20. AE, DC, DISC, MC, V. Sun–Wed 2–10pm; Thurs–Sat 2–11pm.

La Hola SUSHI   Japan and El Salvador collide in spectacular fashion at this large street-corner restaurant in the Zona Rosa. La Hola is a big, rickety arrangement of multifloored dining areas and patios partitioned with bamboo walls and frond-trimmed roofs. Fairy lights and star lanterns clash in a tacky arrangement of nautical decor and tropical flare. You cannot fault the food, however. The menu is as large as the prawns it offers, and the sushi list includes ample platters of sashimi and Japanese-style ceviche. Lobster, crab, paella, and octopus will sate the appetite of any seafood lovers, and there is pasta and pizza and even fondue for those who fancy something down-to-earth. Generous portions of sake will oil the vocal chords for a spot of karaoke later on the big screen in the corner. It's a strange but filling experience.

Blvd. del Hipódromo 230, Zona Rosa. ✆ **503/2233-6865.** Main courses $6–$12. AE, DC, MC, V. Mon–Sat 11am–2am; Sun 11am–midnight.

La Ventana INTERNATIONAL   This is an inviting, bar-style restaurant with dark tones of wood, brick, and olive green walls. Modern art sculptures and photo exhibition stands look a little out of place amid a counter bar dispensing German beers. The menu is global, with everything from curry *wurst* to Hungarian goulash. There are also Mexican, French, and Italian dishes on the extensive menu. Delicious lentil soup followed by vegetable-stuffed crepes proved very filling. The drinks list includes 41 different cocktails and a variety of wines including *liebfraumilch*. Located on a leafy street in front of a small plaza, it has a small, shady courtyard out back with seats.

85 Av. Norte 510 and 9 Calle Poniente, Plaza Palestina, Colonia Escalón. ℂ **503/2263-3188.** Main courses $6–$12. AE, DC, MC, V. Tues–Sun 8am–11pm; Mon 4pm–midnight.

Tre Tratelli Pasta Café & Restorante ★★ ☺ ITALIAN   The alluring aroma of Italian herbs, garlic, and tomatoes envelops you in this casual, midpriced Italian restaurant in the heart of Zona Rosa's dining district. The ambience is laid-back but busy, with a semiopen kitchen. The two main dining areas, minimally decorated with Italian advertising art, give off the feel of a friendly neighborhood Italian joint, so the sophisticated menu, fusing Italian cooking with lighter California fare, may surprise you. You'll definitely want to try the *canelone modi de mar,* which is rolled pasta stuffed with fish, shrimp, salmon, zucchini, and red peppers in a cream sauce with mussels and asparagus, or the Mediterranean-style seviche with shrimp, calamari, olive oil, capers, tomato, onions, and garlic. Tre Tratelli's food and service are superior to its midlevel price.

Blvd. del Hipódromo, No. 307, Zona Rosa. ℂ **503/2223-0838.** Reservations required for groups larger than 10. Main courses $8–$16. AE, DC, DISC, MC, V. Daily 11am–11pm.

INEXPENSIVE

Kalpataru ★★ 🍴 VEGETARIAN   If you're thinking vegetarian in San Salvador, think Kalpataru. For 22 years, this restaurant and holistic health center has lived up to its mission statement to serve 100% vegetarian in a friendly environment. A few minutes from the city's main restaurant district, Kalpataru is worth the taxi ride for its large selection of $1.30 vegetarian *pupusas* and a tasty but affordable lunch buffet. Kalpataru also offers vegetarian tamales, veggie soups, and veggie pizza. The two-story restaurant includes a meditation center and library with books, CDs, and natural healing products.

Calle La Mascota, No. 928, Urbanización Maquilishuat. ℂ **503/2263-1204.** Lunch buffet $8.80; main courses $1.30–$5.50. AE, DC, DISC, MC, V. Mon–Sat noon–8pm (lunch buffet noon–3pm); Sat breakfast buffet 7–11am.

La Cantata del Café ★★★ 🍴 SALVADORAN   The vibe is great, the food is better, and the prices are ridiculously low. This little seven-table joint on the corner near the entrance to José Simeón Cañas University doesn't look like much from the outside, but don't let that fool you. A young and friendly staff presides over the artistic space, which boasts local art on the walls, live music in the corner, and a shelf of interesting books to read while sipping one of La Cantata's 30 hot and cold coffee drinks. The laid-back vibe is reason enough to hang out here, but the food—despite the low price—is delicious. Sandwiches, salads, pizza, and pastas all hover around $3. A huge portion of penne pasta with chicken comes piping hot with a rich, spicy sauce, big chunks of chicken, and a side of tasty garlic bread. Add a beer and bottled water and the bill still barely reaches five bucks. La Cantata might be one of the tastiest meals you'll have in San Salvador.

Calle Mediterranio, No. 26, Colonia Jardines de Guadalupe (1 block from the entrance to José Simeón Central American University). ℂ **503/2243-9425.** Main courses $2.50–$3.25. No credit cards. Mon–Sat 8:30am–8pm.

Las Cofradias SALVADORAN   This is a great introduction to local food and recipes. A corner counter is piled high with black pots holding soups, corn dishes, and juices that the locals serve to themselves before joining their friends at simple picnic tables. Las Cofradias is as traditional as you'll get with a dazzling array of local criolla

SPANISH classes IN EL SALVADOR

Salvadorans are famously friendly, patient, and genuinely pleased when visitors attempt to speak their language. But that doesn't mean your high-school Spanish isn't painful to listen to. So if you're going to be spending some time here, you might as well brush up on the native tongue. Luckily, numerous short-term, affordable language programs are available throughout the country.

In San Salvador, you'll find the **Mélida Anaya Montes Spanish School**—part of El Salvador's human justice organization **Centro de Intercambio y Solidaridad** (**CIS**; Av. Bolivar 103, Colonia Libertad, San Salvador; ✆ **503/2226-5362;** www.cis-elsalvador.org)—which offers one- to four-person classes taught by Salvadoran teachers, homestays with local families, and a strong emphasis on social justice in El Salvador. Students participate in 4-hour daily classes and can also participate in a program introducing them to El Salvador's political progressive organizations, communities, and political parties. Classes begin on

Mondays year-round and cost $223, plus a $25 registration fee, per week, including food and lodging. Classes on their own are $100 per week.

The lakeside hostel **Amacuilco** (Calle Principal, Lago de Coatepeque, Santa Ana; ✆ **503/7822-4051;** amacuilco hostal@hotmail.com), by beautiful Lago de Coatepeque, offers a 5-day, 20-hour Spanish course including food, lodging, and kayak rentals for $120. El Salvador's **SalvaSpan language school** (5a Calle Poniente, btw. 4 and 6 Av. Sur No. 15, Santa Ana; ✆ **503/7051-4171** in El Salvador, or 413/374-0159 in the U.S.; www.salvaspan.com) offers language classes at a place of your choosing—for instance, if you want to take 2 days of classes in Suchitoto, 2 days in Playa Sunzal, and 2 days in Ataco, the SalvaSpan teachers can accommodate you. Classes are $175 to $200 per week for 5 days of 4 hours per day, one-on-one instruction. Homestays can be arranged in San Salvador and Santa Ana for an additional $125 to $150.

dishes such as corn tamales, plantain, and sweet tortillas. *Tradicion del Campo* is a hearty mixture of beans, yucca, and beef. The excellent buffet is served at night only but offers 60 different Salvadoran dishes. Lunchtime is from the more limited menu. The decor is a little soulless with plain walls and barred windows, but there is lots of light. It is easy to miss the entrance door and the steps upstairs but the security guard will point the way. In an adjoining room there is a small craft store with a limited stock of ceramics and silverware.

85 Av. Norte 643, Colonia Escalón (1 block from Radisson). ✆ **503/2264-6148.** Main courses $2.50–$5; buffet $8.50 No credit cards. Sun–Thurs noon–3pm and 5–10pm; Fri–Sat noon–3pm and 5–11pm.

San Salvador After Dark

San Salvador offers an excellent array of high-end lounges, dance clubs, and a few laid-back bars. The city's current hot spot is the strip of nightclubs and lounges in the **Multiplaza Mall.** Don't let the word "mall" fool you: On weekends this two-story nightlife strip is packed with San Salvador's stylish young elites. Multiplaza's offerings are modern and upscale, and you'll need to dress your best. **Boulevard del Hipódromo** is San Salvador's other happening nightlife spot, anchored by a major dance club and numerous smaller bars and lounges. As with Multiplaza, you can take a cab to Boulevard del Hipódromo and then barhop by foot the rest of the night. A few independent spots, such as **La Luna Casa de Arte,** are scattered around the city. But some San Salvador neighborhoods can be dangerous at night, so unless you're with a local, it's best to stick to the better-known spots. Also avoid the "private" clubs suggested by cabdrivers.

THEATER, DANCE & CLASSICAL MUSIC

San Salvador's performing arts scene lags a bit behind its nightlife, but national and international performances can be found. The most glamorous spot for the performing arts is the newly renovated **Teatro Nacional,** 2 Av. Sur and Calle Delgado, 1 block east of Plaza Barrios (© **503/2222-5689**). The next best place to see art performances in San Salvador is the **Teatro Presidente** (Final Av. La Revolución; © **503/2243-3407**), located beside the Museo de Arte. The city's downtown **Casa de la Cultura** (Primera Calle Poniente, No. 822; © **503/2221-2016**) also has a small space with year-round performances and art exhibits.

The country's premier dance school, **La Escuela Nacional de Danza** (1 Calle Poniente, No. 1233; © **503/2221-0972**), performs often in the Teatro Presidente and around the country. You can also find a nationwide arts calendar on the website of El Salvador's main arts organization, **Concultura** (© **503/2510-5320;** www.presidencia.gob.sv).

DANCE CLUBS

Envy ★★   This two-level, flatscreen-TV-filled dance club in the Multiplaza mall is considered San Salvador's most exclusive spot, with three VIP lounges and expensive annual memberships required for Salvadorans to enter. Foreigners pay $15 to dance under the stars of a retractable roof and get down to the sounds of an international cadre of DJs. This place has a great vibe and the dance floor is always packed, but dress to impress as the door policy is pretty strict. Multiplaza mall, Calle El Pedregal and Carretera Panamericana a Santa Ana. © **503/2243-2576.**

Stanza 6 ★   Next door to Envy is the much smaller, slightly more chill Stanza 6 lounge. It also has a $10 cover, DJs, and an exclusive, international club feel. But it's more intimate, with one level and couches for postdance conversations. Multiplaza mall, Calle El Pedregal and Carretera Panamericana a Santa Ana. © **503/2243-7153.**

LIVE MUSIC & BARS

Café de la T ★★   This atmospheric, bohemian bar exudes the revolution and left-wing sentiment. Abstract paintings hang on the walls next to Zapatista posters and campesino portraits. Its decor is a mismatch of crude murals, sagging sofas, butt-filled ashtrays, and crumbling walls, but it certainly has atmosphere. A small bar sits in the corner of a large L-shaped space with two large fans hovering overhead. The clientele are a healthy mix of locals and expats; they come to watch movies on Wednesday and Thursday evenings (7:30pm) and dance to salsa on a Friday night (cover charge $2). Great coffee is served—*la T* in the title being a play on *latte*—but you'll also find an abundance of rum and beer. Calle San Antonio Abad 2233. © **503/2225-2090.** Mon-Thurs 10am-10pm; Fri-Sat 10am-2am.

La Luna Casa de Arte ★★★ ⬛   Off the Boulevard de Los Héroes, about a 10-minute taxi ride from that street's many nightlife spots, La Luna is worth the trip. This popular travelers' spot features live music ranging from 1980s metal to merengue and whatever other unique performances it can scrounge up. It's now well known among *extranjeros* or foreigners, but I've been there a bunch of times and it still somehow feels like a special find. Calle Berlín, Urbanización Buenos Aires off the Blvd. de los Héreos. © **503/2260-2921.**

Zanzibar ★   Zanzibar is a big, fun, open-air bar overlooking Boulevard del Hipódromo. This is a great place to warm up your night. It's loud, friendly, and unpretentious. Local promoters also often stage DJ and live music events on the adjacent patio. Blvd. del Hipódromo, Zona Rosa. © **503/2279-0833.**

THE PACIFIC COAST

A coastal road twists and turns around tiny bays and inlets at the center of El Salvador's Pacific coast, before receding into long stretches of endless waves to the west and east. The rocky cliffs of the Balsamo Coast overlook jet-black crescent shores that are pounded by some of the best surf waves in Central America. This is the center of El Salvador's beach scene, where the emphasis is on good surfing and seafood. Tiny lodges sit amid ramshackle villages with very little infrastructure and only the occasional high-class resort. Farther west and east the coastal road disappears and the long desolate shores hide such gems as the Barra de Santiago and Bahía Jihuilisco.

The Balsamo Coast ★★

The Balsamo Coast, the winding 25km (16 miles) of surf, sand, and cliff-side beaches stretching from Puerto La Libertad to just past Playa Zonte, is one of the highlights of El Salvador. Along this strip are some of the country's most beautiful black-sand beaches and traveler-friendly villages. The Balsamo Coast is currently best known, however, for its world-class **surfing**—the coast is said to be home to the best breaks in all of Central America. The point break in the little village of Playa Sunzal is an excellent place to learn to surf, as the big waves are more than a half a kilometer (⅓ mile) off the beach, with smaller, lesson-friendly waves closer to shore. The Balsamo Coast's other famous break, Punta Roca in La Libertad, is an internationally renowned surf spot best left to the experts.

The Balsamo Coast offers plenty for the nonsurfer to do, as well; hiking, fishing, swimming, and horseback riding are all within reach, and the coast is just a 1-hour drive to the shops, restaurants, and nightclubs of San Salvador.

Beginning in the port city of La Libertad and traveling west, the main villages of the Balsamo Coast are Playa Tunco, Playa Sunzal, and Playa El Zonte. (And in between these four towns are signs pointing to smaller oceanfront and fishermen's villages that are waiting to be explored.) **Playa Tunco** is the most developed and interesting of the main villages because it has beachfront restaurants, unique hotels, and Internet cafes, along with a coastline that's great for surfers and swimmers. **Playa Sunzal** is a tiny village about a half-mile farther west, with a famous surf break, a few backpacker surf hostels, and a handful of *pupusarias*. **Playa El Zonte,** the farthest west of the Balsamo Coast's developed villages, is a half-mile stretch of hotels and restaurants fronting a beach that's also a good spot for swimmers and surfers. The region's main town, **La Libertad,** is a crowded, hectic oceanfront city best known for its long fisherman's pier. Other than its Punta Roca surf break and the pier, La Libertad doesn't have much to offer. It also has a reputation for being among the country's most dangerous cities; though it's safe to visit the pier or sightsee in town during daylight hours, there's no reason to stay overnight in La Libertad.

Essentials

GETTING THERE

BY BUS   From San Salvador, take the frequent **bus no. 102** to Puerto La Libertad. The trip costs 55¢ and takes 1 hour. From La Libertad you'll catch **bus no. 192**, which travels the length of the Balsamo Coast past Playa El Zonte. It takes 30 minutes and costs 45¢. **Bus no. 80** travels between La Libertad and Playa Sunzal, takes 30 minutes, and costs 25¢. Both bus nos. 192 and 80 will stop wherever you request along the main road. Simply tell the driver which town you'd like to visit and they'll let you off at the right spot. Most towns are a direct 5- to 10-minute walk toward the water from the main road.

BY CAR   From San Salvador, follow **Hwy. CA-4** for 45 minutes to 1 hour to La Libertad, where you'll turn right at the ocean and follow coastal **Hwy. CA-2** west along the Balsamo Coast. Each town is well marked and a short drive off CA-2.

ORIENTATION

The heart of the Balsamo Coast stretches approximately 25km (16 miles) from La Libertad to just past Playa El Zonte along the winding but well-paved coastal Hwy. CA-2. The region is dotted with fishing villages, rocky and sandy beaches, and cliff-filled alcoves. La Libertad is the largest city here, with ample grocery stores, ATMs, and a post office. Playa Tunco is the second-most-developed town, with a number of beachfront hotels, restaurants, surf shops, and Internet cafes.

GETTING AROUND

To get around this coast by bus, simply walk to any spot along the main highway CA-2 and hail one of the many no. 192 buses that travel in both directions about every 10 minutes; these will drop you off anywhere along the main road and cost between 25¢ and 45¢, depending on where you are going.

It's easy to drive around this area on your own: The main road linking all towns, Coastal Hwy. CA-2, is well maintained and the entrances to all the coastal towns are well marked.

The Balsamo Coast also has a number of local taxi drivers who can take you from La Libertad to Playa Sunzal for a negotiable $5 and from La Libertad to Playa Zonte for around $10. Call **Ricardo** (© 503/7277-3699) or **Fausto** (© 503/7741-2571) for a lift.

VISITOR INFORMATION

The region's national **tourism office** is in Puerto La Libertad (at Km 34.5 Carretera Literal, 90m/300 ft. from the Shell gas station; © 503/2346-1898). It's open daily from 8am to 5pm.

Most of the Balsamo Coast's banks, ATMs, and pharmacies are in La Libertad along 2a Calle Poniente in the center of town. Since La Libertad can be a bit hectic and has a reputation for high crime, it's better to use the ATM and buy your groceries and gas at the large, modern shopping center 1km (⅔ mile) east of town along the coastal road. The shopping center is a 10-minute walk from the La Libertad pier and includes a grocery store and four ATMs that accept a variety of North America bank cards. A Shell gas station is across the street.

La Libertad's **tourist police** can be reached at © **503/2346-1893; ambulance** service can be called at © **503/2335-3049;** and the **fire department** number is © **503/2243-2054.** La Libertad's **post office** is located along 2a Calle Oriente, directly north of the pier.

La Libertad

Puerto La Libertad is a crowded, hardscrabble, oceanfront city 32km (20 miles) south of San Salvador. Despite improvements to the city center, many travelers stop here only to catch buses to the rest of the coast, stock up on supplies, or visit the fisherman's pier and newly refurbished *malecon*. Surfers also flock here from around the world to surf the renowned Punta Roca surf break just outside of town.

La Libertad has a reputation for high crime, but it's perfectly safe to visit the fisherman's pier or stock up on essentials during the day. Since many superior hotels are within a short drive or bus ride, and it's not safe to walk around at night, I don't recommend staying here overnight. If you must, the nicest nearby hotel is **Hotel Punta Roca** (4a Calle Poniente and 5a Av. Sur, Puerto La Libertad, La Libertad; ✆ **503/2335-3261;** www.puntaroca.com.sv). Rooms are $50 a night. It has a sister hotel with the same name that's just outside the city and a little more expensive at $58 for a double.

The long pier and its nearby market are La Libertad's main attractions. Past the market, toward the end of the pier, you can watch as fisherman haul in their morning catch and send it down the pier to market. Just feet from the pier, you can also see local surfers riding the waves and, in the distance, the famous surf of the Punta Roca break. The pier is open daily from 6am to 7pm, but nearby, guarded parking is 75¢ a day.

Banks, ATMs, pharmacies, and grocery stores are on the road just north of the oceanfront; a shopping center is 1km (⅔ mile) east along from the pier.

Playa San Diego

This is a long, wide beach 4km (2½ miles) east of La Libertad. It has some private residential houses and a cluster of restaurants at one end where you'll find a river estuary popular with bathers. Two coastal roads run parallel with the beach. On one you'll find **Restaurante Costa Brava,** Calle a Playa San Diego (✆ **503/2345-5698**), 200m (656 ft.) from the beach. The restaurant is nothing special in itself, but it does have a nice pool, safer than the nearby ocean and cleaner than the estuary. Day-trippers can use the pool free as long as they spend more than $5 in the restaurant. Needless to say, it gets packed on weekends. There are also three very basic rooms to rent for $30 each.

Playa San Blas

This private beach offers more seclusion and security than nearby places, without being too exclusive or elitist. It is not the best for surfing, but its long, dark shore makes for a relaxing day of sunbathing. There are two excellent hotels that allow day-trippers to come and go. The gated entrance is at Km 39.5 on the main coastal road.

Sol Bohemio This small, multicolored establishment has a lovely setting amid dense foliage, a small pool, and a lush lawn you could play golf on if you had room enough to swing. Blue exterior walls hold up a palm-thatched roof and hide stylish rooms with attractive, traditional tiles, yellow walls, and bright bedcovers. Only one room has A/C; the others can get stuffy despite fans. The lodge's main attraction is the hammock-adorned garden and shady communal areas.

Playa San Blas. ✆ **503/2338-5158.** www.solbohemio.com. 3 units. $25 double. AE, DC, MC, V. Free parking. **Amenities:** Restaurant; bar. *In room:* A/C (in 1 unit), fan, TV.

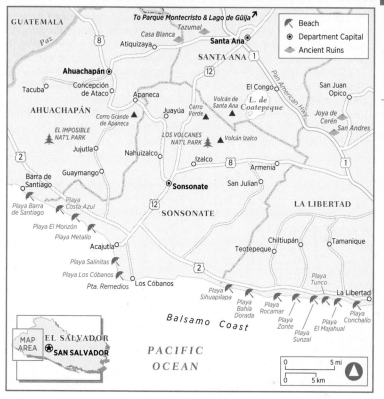

Beach
Department Capital
Ancient Ruins

To Parque Montecristo & Lago de Güija

Tazumal
Casa Blanca
Atiquizaya · Santa Ana ·
SANTA ANA

Ahuachapán ·

Tacuba · Concepción
de Ataco · Apaneca
AHUACHAPÁN Cerro Grande Juayúa Cerro
de Apaneca Verde

EL IMPOSIBLE
NAT'L PARK

Volcán de
Santa Ana L. de
Coatepeque

El Congo · San Juan
Opico ·

Joya de
Cerén
San Andres

Jujutla · Nahuizalco ·

LOS VOLCANES
NAT'L PARK Volcán Izalco

Izalco

Armenia ·

Barra de Guaymango ·
Santiago
·

Playa Barra
de Santiago

Playa
Costa Azul

Sonsonate San Julian ·

SONSONATE

LA LIBERTAD

Playa El Monzón

Playa Metalío
Acajutla ·

Chiltiupán ·
Teotepeque ·

Tamanique ·

Playa Salinitas
Playa Los Cóbanos
Pta. Remedios Los Cóbanos

Playa
Sihuapilapa

Playa
Tunco

La Libertad ·

Balsamo Coast

Playa
Bahía Playa
Dorada Rocamar Playa
Conchalio
Playa Playa
Zonte El Majahual
Playa
Sunzal

MAP
AREA EL SALVADOR
· SAN SALVADOR

PACIFIC
OCEAN

0   5 mi
0   5 km

Playa Tunco ★

Playa Tunco, 7.5km (4⅔ miles) west of La Libertad, is the Balsamo coast's most visitor-friendly location and a "must stop" along this coast. Visitors and Salvadorans alike flock here on weekends to enjoy the waves, black-sand beaches, laid-back vibe, tasty seafood restaurants, and new and unique hotels. Tunco has something to offer most travelers.

Tunco consists of a main road ending on the beach and a side road with beachfront hotels. Numerous small restaurants, hotels, Internet cafes, and a couple of surf shops offering lessons are all tightly packed into this roughly 1km-long (⅔-mile) area. The beach is long with black sand and large rock formations just offshore. The surf at Tunco and nearby Sunzal can get big, but there's usually a small, near-shore break that can accommodate beginner surfers and swimmers.

Opportunities for outdoor tours abound; for instance, nearby **Las Olas Beach House** (see below) offers hiking, kayak, surfing, horseback riding, and off-road motorcycle tours. But my favorite activity here is spending evenings on the second-story, thatched-hut deck of Erika's beachfront restaurant (see below), watching the sun go down behind the surfers. That's paradise.

Sink or Swim

You should swim at your own risk all along the western Pacific coast of El Salvador. There are few public lifeguards and most beachfront hotels don't provide them. So if the waves are big, you're not a great swimmer, or it feels like there's too strong a current, you probably shouldn't go in. There are even a number of river mouths meeting the ocean where the current can be particularly overpowering; don't swim in these locations. However, the protected Tamarindo area offers the calmest waters in the country, and when the waves are small along Playa Tunco, Playa Sunzal, or Barra de Santiago, you should have no problem. Just keep in mind there is often no one around to save you if you do encounter any issues.

To get here, take bus no. 192 from La Libertad and get off near Km 42 at the main Tunco entrance, which is marked by a large sign advertising the area's many hotels and restaurants. The town center is a 5-minute walk from there.

WHERE TO STAY

One of the great things about Playa Tunco is that it has accommodations to please everyone. The town offers everything from a $3-a-night campground that's just 44m (144 ft.) from the ocean to a magical retreat with a sweat lodge and cave bar.

Hotel y Restaurante Tekuaní Kal ★★ 📖 This unusual, artistic, Maya-inspired boutique beachfront hotel is worth every penny of its slightly higher rates. Tekuaní Kal, a few hundred yards off Tunco's main road, is unique—it's perhaps best known for its large, whimsical, Maya-inspired cement sculptures that are scattered around the garden-like property. Rounding out the Maya feel is a newly constructed cave bar and a Maya sweat lodge that hosts weekly traditional purification ceremonies led by a local. The property winds down a rocky cliff to the beach and includes a small infinity pool and waterfall. Rooms are of average size with interesting Maya art; room nos. 1 through 4 have the best ocean views. Service is excellent, with a friendly staff and an English-speaking on-site owner.

Km 42 Carretera Literal. 🕾 **503/2389-6388.** www.tekuanikal.com. 6 units. $84 double. Rates include breakfast. AE, DC, DISC, MC, V. **Amenities:** Restaurant; small infinity pool and larger swimming pool; room service; sauna. *In room:* A/C, TV, no phone, Wi-Fi.

La Guitara Hotel and Bar La Guitara is the newest, most modern, low-priced option on the Tunco block and can't be beat for the money. The hotel has nine attached and semiattached cabins (adjoining one other) with private bathrooms and patios with hammocks. The large grassy property is on the beach and offers a big pool, Ping-Pong and pool tables, and a bar. Tunco offers many low-priced options, but what sets La Guitara apart are its modern, efficient, air-conditioned cabins. Papaya's Lodge (see below) is still the best place in town to meet other travelers, but La Guitara is the place to go if you already have travel companions and want a more tranquil experience and nicer rooms.

Km 42 Carretera Literal. 🕾 **503/2389-6398.** info@surfingeltunco.com. 9 units. $30 double. No credit cards. **Amenities:** Bar; Internet (free in lobby); pool. *In room:* A/C (in 5 rooms), no phone.

Papaya's Lodge 🏄 Papaya's is Tunco's best-known hostel and one of its best low-cost options. In the middle of the action on Tunco's main street and just a short distance from the ocean, Papaya's is a laid-back, family-friendly surf hostel with eight rooms, including three with private bathrooms. Payapa's also features a fully stocked kitchen open to guests, a breezy upstairs deck, and a gazebo with hammocks over a small river that runs through the area. Since this is a hostel, don't expect a palace, but you'd be hard-pressed to find a more welcoming and well-maintained place to spend a few surf- and hammock-filled days. The hostel is beside an Internet cafe and surf shop that offers board rentals and bilingual surf lessons.

Km 42 Carretera Literal. ☏ **503/2389-6231.** www.papayalodge.com. 8 units, 5 with shared bathroom. $12–$14. No credit cards. **Amenities:** Kitchen; surfboard rental. *In room:* Fan, no phone.

Roca Sunzal ☺   Roca Sunzal is a good midrange, beachfront option for those who prefer a hotel over a hostel. Across the street from Papaya's Lodge, the 16-room Roca Sunzal offers an open-air, oceanview **restaurant** and a central courtyard with a nice-size pool. Roca Sunzal is also one of Tunco's more family-friendly hotels, so there are often lots of kids running around. The rooms are in a two-story, U-shaped building around the pool, so only a few rooms offer beach views. Room no. 13 is the largest of the oceanview rooms, with the best view.

Km 42 Carretera Literal. ☏ **503/2389-6126.** Fax 503/2389-6190. www.rocasunzal.com. 16 units. $48–$60 double Mon–Fri; $58–$70 double Fri–Sun; $120–$140 suite. AE, MC, V. **Amenities:** Restaurant; pool; $8–$10 room service; surfboard rental. *In room:* A/C, fan, TV (in some), kitchen and fridge (in some).

Tortuga Surf Club 🏌   This attractive, functional building is right on the beach with a wood-framed patio and large balcony upstairs leading to four large, bright rooms. Tile floors, tall ceilings, and immaculate fittings look over a small pool and beach deck. Some high stools sit along a counter looking into an open kitchen, and there is a row of surfboards available to guests. There is also a small Internet cafe and gift store, as well as a surf store, and guides are available with four-wheel-drives to do tours of the area and nearby beaches.

El Tunco Access Rd. ☏ **503/7888-6225** or 2298-2986. www.elsalvadorsurfer.com. 4 units. $25 double with shared bathroom; $45 double with A/C and private bathroom. AE, DC, MC, V. Free parking. **Amenities:** Restaurant; bar; Internet cafe. *In room:* A/C, fan.

WHERE TO DINE

On the beach at the end of Tunco's main street are two restaurants, **Restaurante Erika** (☏ **503/2389-6054**) and **La Bocana Restaurante** (☏ **503/2389-6238**). It's easy to confuse the two, as both offer similar two-story deck seating overlooking the ocean and menus with delicious fish entrees ranging from $7 to $10. The distinguishing factor is that Erika's is more of a locals' joint while La Bocana attracts more out-of-towners. Whichever you choose, aim to grab a seat on one of their decks at sunset, since the views are amazing.

The full-service restaurants at **Tekuaní Kal** (☏ **503/2389-6388**) and **Las Olas** (☏ **503/2411-7553**) also offer great views and fresh seafood entrees, as well as a chance to see these two great hotels without the cost of a room.

PLAYA TUNCO AFTER DARK

Playa Tunco is one of the few small towns in El Salvador to have a nightlife scene, and it's centered around **Roots Campground,** off the town's main road. Each Saturday, Roots sponsors a live music or DJ party on its huge, grassy beachfront. The cover charge depends on the event, but it's usually a good time.

Tucked against a rock cliff along a dark, narrow shore, **Casa de Mar** (© 503/2389-6284; www.casademarhotel.com) is the most upscale, luxury boutique hotel on the Balsamo Coast (btw. Playas El Tunco and El Suzal at Km 43.5). Five buildings sit at different levels, with terraced gardens and small waterfalls surrounding a wooden decked pool. There are 10 suites in all, each with its own style but all sharing luxurious fittings and colorful decor. They all have ample space including dining and living areas. Overlooking it all is an excellent restaurant called **Café Sunzal,** which specializes in creative Asian-Salvadoran fare such as curry shrimp laced with coconut and bacon. This really is a gorgeous property, though the beach is black sand and a dark rocky shore. Rooms start at $110, including breakfast.

Playa Sunzal

Playa Sunzal is a tiny community next to Tunco (and 9km/5½ miles west of La Libertad), which features a couple of surf hostels, a few *pupusarias* along the main highway, and a rocky point break that's made the village famous among surfers. You can reach Sunzal from the highway or by taking a 10-minute stroll along the beach to the right from Tunco and turning inland at an opening in the retaining wall just before the point break. Follow the path and turn right at your first opportunity. There are a couple of hostels on this path, and *pupusarias* are on the highway ahead and to the left.

WHERE TO STAY & DINE

Las Olas Beach House ★★★   Located 2km (1¼ miles) west of Sunzal's beach, Las Olas has stunningly beautiful cliff-top vistas and is *the* place to stay in the area if you want an adventurous but upscale vacation. The property has an infinity pool and a huge saltwater pool at the bottom of the cliff on which it's perched—from here, you get great views of the Sunzal point break and the rocky coast. The sizable rooms have a Caribbean-Hawaiian surfer vibe, with lots of shells and colorful fabrics in the decor. But the real attraction is the hotel's adventure offerings. Las Olas's manager and two on-site owners speak English and are adept at taking guests on surfing tours to the best spots in the country, heading up motocross tours through off-road mountain trails, and conducting kayaking, snorkeling, horseback riding, and hiking tours. These folks know what they're doing and enjoy outdoor experiences as much as their guests. The 3- to 4-hour tours are $25 to $40.

Las Olas's **restaurant** is decidedly upscale and serves delicious seafood dishes such as mahimahi and a fresh-as-it-comes seafood chowder.

Km 45 Carretera Literal. © **503/2411-7553.** javierlasolas@yahoo.com. 5 units. $70 double with shared bathroom; $125 double with private bathroom. Rates include breakfast. AE, DC, DISC, MC, V. **Amenities:** Restaurant; airport transfers ($35); 2 pools; sports equipment rental w/tours or lessons. *In room:* A/C, no phone.

Playa Zonte

Playa Zonte is a beautiful 1km (⅔-mile) stretch of sandy and rocky beach 19km (12 miles) west of La Libertad. Many travelers break into Tunco-versus-Zonte camps, with Zonte siders preferring that beach town for its less-developed and more laid-back vibe. Surfers like its strong beach break, and nonsurfers can enjoy its sandier beaches, depending on the tides.

To get to Playa Zonte, follow coastal highway CA-2 west from La Libertad to approximately Km 53 and look for the La Casa de Frida sign. Turn left there. Coming from the west, look for a sign on your left reading INTERVIDA EL SALVADOR with an image of the earth. Turn right there. The main road into Zonte has two entrances and is like a giant circular driveway leading to the hotel area. So you can take either entrance and get to the same place.

WHERE TO STAY & DINE

Zonte offers a small collection of laid-back beachfront hostels and restaurants. One of the best places to stay is the well-known **La Casa de Frida** (Km 53.5 Carretera Literal No. 7, Playa Zonte; ✆ **503/2252-2949;** www.lacasadefrida.com). The many portraits of Mexican artist Frida Kahlo hanging by the entrance confirm that you've found your way to this friendly three-room hostel. Each room has four beds, and it runs $10 per bed or costs $20 per person to have the room to yourself. The hostel is on the beach and its small **restaurant** is one of the best in town. If Frida's is booked, try the nearby five-room **Olas Permanentes hostel** (Km 53 Carretera Literal, Playa El Zonte; ✆ **503/2510-7621;** www.olaspermanentes.com). This family- and surfer-friendly hostel offers private rooms with private bathrooms for $25 and surfboard rentals for $12. **Horizonte Surf Resort,** Playa Zonte (✆ **503/2323-0099;** www.horizontesurfresort.com) is another oasis of calm amid what is a ramshackle neighborhood. Some rooms are little more than tarted-up cells, except for a six-bed suite with large windows, a wooden floor, and a split-level layout. What makes the place is its lovely pool and garden area surrounded by lawn and palm trees. Doubles start at $30. **Esencia Nativa ★**, Playa Zonte (✆ **503/2302-6258;** www.esencianativa.com), is a laid-back collection of five colorful rooms, a garden, a pool, and a communal lounge piled high with books, games, magazines, and hammocks. It's a perfect surfer's hangout with restaurant, surf school, and board rental. Doubles with A/C start at $25.

In addition to the restaurant at La Casa de Frida, the **Costa Brava Restaurante** (Km 53.5 Carretera Literal, Playa El Zonte, a 5-min. walk west from Frida's; ✆ **503/2302-6068**) offers a big fish and meat menu for $6 to $12, with oceanview seating.

Playa Los Cóbanos

Playa Los Cóbanos is a tiny, not very attractive fishing village about an hour's drive west of La Libertad, which lacks any decent hotels and restaurants. The Los Cóbanos area, however, happens to be home to two of the country's best all-inclusive resorts.

ESSENTIALS

GETTING THERE   From Sonsonate, take **bus no. 26,** which stops directly in Playa Los Cóbanos.

When driving from the east, follow coast highway CA-2 to Hwy. CA-12, where you will turn south toward the ocean and follow the signs to Los Cóbanos. The road dead-ends in the town center 8km (5 miles) after leaving the highway. From Sonsonate, take Hwy. CA-12 and follow the signs.

ORIENTATION & GETTING AROUND   The road off the main highway to Playa Los Cóbanos dead-ends into Cóbanos's 2-block-long, beachfront town center. Both Decameron and Los Veraneras are within a few minutes' drive.

BARRA DE SANTIAGO & LA COCOTERA
resort ★★★

A long finger of land packed with coconut trees is lapped by an estuary on one side and the roaring Pacific on the other. Barra de Santiago is, bar none, one of the most beautiful spots in El Salvador and where you'll find the country's top beach hotel. **La Cocotera ★★★** (✆ **503/2245-3691;** www.lacocotera resort.com) offers a rare taste of international style in a remote and beautiful part of the country. This six-room, semi-all-inclusive ecoresort features three modern, two-level cabins, each with two huge rooms, luxurious Asian-inspired bathrooms, and large flatscreen TVs. The hotel property stretches from the bay to the beach, meaning you have water on both sides. It includes a restaurant, bar, and pool dotted with custom-built furniture. The best rooms are the three upstairs units with soaring ceilings, king-size beds, and waterview balconies. The downstairs rooms have two twin beds with pullouts to sleep four. Rates start at $129 for a double.

Barra de Santiago is in the far west of the country where the dark beaches stretch out for miles. It is a 2-hour drive (76km/47 miles) from San Salvador and offers little infrastructure. You'll need to make advanced reservations and prearrange transportation in the area, as it requires a few twists and turns to get to this undeveloped corner of the country.

WHERE TO STAY

Las Veraneras Resort ★★ ☺ Veraneras is one of El Salvador's most enjoyable and affordable luxury resorts and is home to one of the country's few public golf courses. The resort's biggest draw is its 7,000-yard, 18-hole rolling but open course. Veraneras also has plenty for nongolfers to do, like lounging by one of the pools, taking an ocean swim from the sandy beach club, playing tennis, or letting the kids enjoy the large children's play area. The individual, one-story villas are modern and spare but comfortable, with separate living rooms, full kitchens, and shady patios. The resort also features some English-speaking staff and can arrange tours around the country. Veraneras more than delivers on its affordable $59, two adults with a child base rate. Because of all its amenities, Veraneras is a great place to base your El Salvador vacation.

Km 88.5 Carretera a Los Cóbanos. ✆ **503/2420-5000** or 2247-9191. www.veranerasresort.com. 60 units. $59–$159 villa. AE, DC, DISC, MC, V. **Amenities:** 2 restaurants; 2 snack bars; airport transfers ($30); bikes; children's play area w/pool; exercise room; golf course; 3 pools; room service; Wi-Fi in common areas. *In room:* A/C, TV, kitchen or kitchenette.

Royal Decameron Salinitas If you like all-inclusives, you won't be disappointed here. Decameron is El Salvador's largest all-inclusive resort and offers all the grandeur and amenities that a large, multinational chain can offer. Four chlorinated pools and a huge saltwater pool stretching into the Pacific are scattered around the sprawling, lush property. Rooms, which are large and colorfully decorated, sleep up to four and are located in four multistory buildings with balconies around the property. A cadre of international, all-you-can-eat-and-drink bars and restaurants keep guests full and happy. The generally bilingual staff organizes on-property activities and can arrange tours for an extra charge to El Salvador's Maya ruins, along with windsurfing, scuba diving, and kayaking trips.

Km 79 Carretera a Acaljutla. ✆ **503/2429-9000.** www.decameron.com. 552 units. $118–$158 double Apr–June; $138–$178 double Sept–Oct. Rates include all food and drink. AE, DC, DISC, MC, V. **Amenities:** 5 restaurants; 4 bars; airport transfers ($23); babysitting; exercise room; 5 pools; room service; spa, Jacuzzi, and sauna; free watersports equipment; Wi-Fi in common areas. *In room:* A/C, TV, fridge.

EASTERN PACIFIC COAST

66km (41 miles) SE of San Salvador

In contrast to the Balsamo Coast, the eastern Pacific coast is less developed and has no scenic coastal road winding around tiny coves, yet it does have its charms. A flat expanse of desolate beaches is broken up by the occasional fishing village, estuary, and mangrove swamp. Some of those beaches fill up with partying locals on weekends and holidays, especially around the strip known as Costa del Sol. The high walls on this long peninsula hide high-end resorts and luxury beach homes. Farther east there is lots of virgin territory to explore, such as **Bahía de Jiquilisco, Isla Montecristo,** and **Isla Meanguera,** but little infrastructure—it's best to see these with a tour company. Surfers flock to **Playa El Cuco** while sun worshipers swear by the just-discovered **Playa El Espino.** The uninteresting port town of La Unión in the far east is the country's biggest port and gateway to the rocky, tropical islands of the Golfo de Fonseca, a hot and humid pirate bay shared with Honduras and Nicaragua.

Costa del Sol

Costa del Sol's reputation is better than its reality. This stretch of highway southeast of San Salvador, with the Pacific on one side and a beautiful bay on the other, is known as the beach getaway for El Salvador's wealthy elite. If you're invited to one of the locals' large beach houses, no doubt you'll have a blast. But for the average traveler, the region is hard to get a handle on. Huge walls block the beach from the region's homes, and Costa del Sol offers no central area of activity. There's no charming cluster of interesting restaurants or shops, and most visitors check into their hotel, hang out on their hotel beach, and eat in their hotel restaurant during their stay.

That said, Costa del Sol can be an excellent beach day trip, as it's only 25 minutes from the airport and 45 minutes from San Salvador, with public beach access at the local tourist center. Costa del Sol's beaches are also huge, sandier, and, when the waters are calm, better for swimming than the rockier beaches to the west. The area even offers a gorgeous bay with an international cadre of yachts bobbing in its protected waters, where regular folks can rent some watercraft. It's definitely possible to have a great time here, especially if you're looking for a packaged resort experience.

ESSENTIALS
Getting There
BY BUS   From San Salvador, take **bus no. 133** toward Zacatecoluca. Ask to be let off at the road to Costa del Sol. From there, wait for **bus no. 19,** which will drop you off in front of your hotel along Costa del Sol's main road.

BY CAR   From San Salvador, follow **Hwy. CA-2** east to Km 43 and look for the detour south toward Costa del Sol. Follow the signs and, as there is no Costa del Sol town center, look for the kilometer markers that match the address of your hotel.

GETTING AROUND

The best way to navigate Costa del Sol is by foot along the beach. You can also catch **bus no. 193** anywhere along Costa del Sol's main road, which runs regularly throughout the day. Many of the hotels and homes block access to the non-paying public though you can find an entrance near the Hotel Haydee Mar at Playa los Blancos (Km 64) or at the end of the peninsula.

WHAT TO SEE & DO

Boating in the bay and swimming or sunbathing on the beaches are the main attractions here—most people just enjoy whatever their hotel has to offer during their visit to the area. But Costa del Sol does have a few places outside of the hotels worth checking out, including **Aqua Fun** (Km 75.5 Blvd. Costa del Sol; ✆ **503/2305-5294**), a laid-back bar and restaurant on the bay with a big pool, pool table, bay views, and $70-per-hour motorized watercraft rental. It's a good place to take a break from the beach. If you just want to visit for the day, head to Costa del Sol's **Turicentro** (Km 63.5 Blvd. Costa del Sol; ✆ **503/2338-2050**). This is one of the country's better tourist centers with beach access, a nice pool, changing rooms, picnic tables, and a restaurant. Admission is 80¢ and the center is open daily from 7am to 4pm.

WHERE TO STAY

Bahía del Sol Hotel 🖐 Bahía del Sol is a reasonably priced and enjoyable enough place to stay, but it's a bit overhyped. It's developed a megaresort reputation because it *is* the place to be if you want to dock your yacht, take a $1,200-per-day deep-sea fishing excursion, or play blackjack. Its biggest draws are its small casino and marina. But for the average traveler, it's just a slightly-above-average resort, albeit one with some ocean and bayfront rooms and town houses with outdoor Jacuzzis. Most of the rooms, however, are average size, with nondescript decor, and are situated away from the water and the good views.

Km 78 Blvd. Costa del Sol. ✆ **503/2327-0300** or 2510-7200. www.bahiadelsolelsalvador.com. 55 units. $138–$147 double; $300 large suite. Rates include breakfast, lunch, and dinner. AE, DC, DISC, MC, V. **Amenities:** 2 restaurants; 2 bars; exercise room; room service; Wi-Fi in lobby and some common areas. *In room:* A/C, TV, full kitchens (in suite).

Comfort Inn ★★ ☺ Despite its chain hotel status and low-end reputation, the Comfort Inn might be Costa del Sol's best hotel. This six-story, beachfront hotel was built in 2006 with all of the money and technology an international chain can afford—which means everything is newly updated and looks great. All the rooms have balconies with beautiful, long-range Pacific views, and the grounds include two huge pools—one of which is the largest I've seen in El Salvador—a poolside bar, an open-air restaurant, and a wide, sandy beach. The rooms are at least as large as you'll find in other El Salvador hotels, and the bathrooms are larger and more modern. Three large suites are also available on the top floor. Room service is a bit slow and a load of laundry is a ridiculous $13, but the decent room rates compensate for this.

Km 75.5 Blvd. Costa del Sol. ✆ **877/424-6423** or 503/2325-7500. www.hoteleselsalvador.com. 63 units. $165 double; $236 suite. Rates include 3 meals. AE, DC, DISC, MC, V. **Amenities:** Restaurant; bar; 2 pools; room service; smoke-free rooms; Wi-Fi in lobby. *In room:* A/C, TV.

Estero y Mar ★ ☺ Just as the name applies, this midsize resort is surrounded by "estuary and sea." Shops, bars, restaurants, gardens, and pools are spread across a small peninsula just west of Costa del Sol (*note:* it is not on the main strip) and only 30 minutes from San Salvador airport. This is a conventional resort with a jungle feel

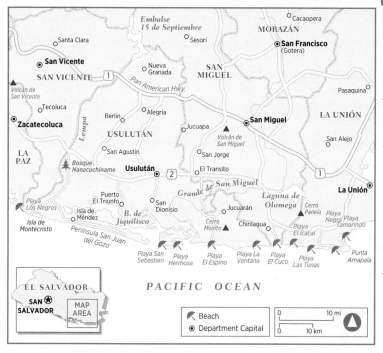

as there are mangrove swamps and waterways nearby. Don't expect tranquil nature, however, as guests and local day-trippers take full advantage of the fleet of beach buggies and jet skis available for rent. Be aware that access is down a dirt track that runs parallel to the beach, so bring good directions or, better still, arrange for the hotel to pick you up.

Playa El Pimental, San Luis Talpa. © **503/2270-1172.** www.esteroymar.com. 30 units. $63–$88 double. AE, DC, DISC, MC, V. Free parking. **Amenities:** 2 restaurants; 2 bars; Internet computer in lobby; 3 pools; soccer court; volleyball court; small zoo; Wi-Fi. *In room:* A/C, TV.

WHERE TO DINE

Most visitors stick to their hotel restaurants, but Costa del Sol also has two independent restaurants worth trying.

Acajutla Seafood Restaurant ★★ (Km 73.5 Blvd. Costa del Sol; © **503/2338-0397**) is on the bay side of the main road and has great views and bay breezes. Its three-page seafood menu offers exquisitely prepared dishes such as mixed grilled lobster and crab with butter and garlic sauce. Main courses start at $12. **Mar y Sol** ★ (Km 75.5 Blvd. Costa del Sol; © **503/2301-8250**) is a comfortable, laid-back, and inexpensive place to have a simple meal and a cold beer, and take in the beautiful view of the bay. The restaurant is located along Costa del Sol's main road and offers a covered, open-air deck with bench seating overlooking the estuary. Main courses start at $4.

Isla de Montecristo ★★

Isla de Montecristo, 80km (50 miles) southeast of San Salvador, is a gorgeous, largely undeveloped 2.5-sq.-km (1-sq.-mile) island, situated where the large Río Lempa empties into the Pacific. The tiny island is home to acres of fruit trees, a few farming communities, and hundreds of nesting birds. Most visitors come to the island by dugout canoe or small motorboat to spend a couple of days hiking, fishing, or just swinging in a hammock along the river.

The best way to get to the island is to travel to the nearby community of La Pita and catch a boat there across to the island. This 30-minute canoe journey is half the fun of the trip, since you'll spot birds flying low and fish skimming the surface of the water along the way. It takes a bit of effort, especially by bus, to get to La Pita itself, so it's best to call one of the hostels mentioned below to arrange lodging and transportation.

ESSENTIALS
Getting There
BY BUS   From San Salvador, take **bus no. 302** toward Usulután and tell the driver to let you off at San Nicolás Lempa near the Texaco Station. Buses leave from there for the 13km (8-mile) journey to La Pita daily at 5am and 2pm and return at 5:30am and 3pm.

BY CAR   Follow **Hwy. CA-2** to Km 87 and turn at the Texaco station; then follow the road until it dead-ends in La Pita.

ORIENTATION & GETTING AROUND
Isla de Montecristo is a small, undeveloped island with family farms and one tiny town center with two hostels and a restaurant, which serves as the port where visitors arrive and depart. You can walk across the island from the river to the Pacific along unmarked trails in about 30 minutes—there are no buses or taxis on the island. The island has no shops other than a single *tienda,* so you'll need to head to San Salvador or Puerto La Libertad for services like banks, hospitals, and Internet access.

WHAT TO SEE & DO
Isla de Montecristo is home to a wide variety of birds, including majestic white egrets, which, seemingly on cue, pose for near-perfect photos as they glide low over the calm estuary waters here. Locals can take you on tours in dugout canoes to places where you can spot other bird life, along with the area's unique, 15-centimeter-long (6-in.) jumping fish, which skim along the surface near shore. Or you can simply stroll around the island. Note that the currents on the Pacific side can be strong, so swimming in the ocean is not recommended.

WHERE TO STAY & DINE
The island offers two thatched-roof hostels with beds and hammocks and one restaurant that will cook you fish and *pupusas.* **Hostal Juan Lobo** (© **503/2634-6387;** no credit cards) has four huts with cement sleeping pads topped by mattresses and a large open-air gazebo with hammocks. Hammocks are $3 a night and two- to three-person cabins are $10 a night. Much nicer, however, is **Cabanas y Rancho Brisas del Mar** (© **503/2367-2107;** no credit cards), which offers two rustic but comfortable two-bed-plus hammock cabins with patios right on the

 Avoid Puerto El Triunfo

You must pass through this town to get to Bahía de Jiquilisco but try not to linger. It has a reputation for high crime and gang violence.

In between Isla de Montecristo and the beaches to its east is the huge **Bahía de Jiquilisco.** This largely undeveloped inlet offers untouched natural beauty with dozens of mangrove-lined channels to paddle, islands to explore, great views, and beautiful ocean and bay beaches. The bay is also a major stop along the way for 87 types of migratory birds and a nesting ground for sea turtles. It remains one of the coast's most untouched and naturally beautiful areas. The only problems are that the easiest way to get here is by passing through the dangerous and seedy little village of Puerto El Triunfo, and there is little tourism infrastructure immediately around the bay. As a result, Jiquilisco is best explored with a tour company such as **Eco Mayan Tours** (Paseo General Escalón 3658, Colonia Escalón, San Salvador; ✆ **503/2298-2844;** www. ecomayantours.com), which can provide transportation and the equipment necessary to explore the bay.

river for $15 a night. Brisas del Mar also has the island's only open-air, riverside restaurant. Both hostels provide round-trip boat transportation from La Pita for $20 per person and offer 1- to 2-hour estuary tours for $5 to $10 per person. Prices can often be negotiated down.

Back on the mainland in La Pita is **Hostal Lempa Mar** (✆ **503/2310-9901** or 7787-5824; no credit cards), which features small but comfortable three-person, $25-per-night cabins and a riverside restaurant. The hostel will take you to the island for $10 per person each way.

PLAYA EL ESPINO

A wide, gorgeous beach that is splendidly isolated on weekdays and alive with beachgoers on weekends, Playa El Espino is gaining a reputation as one of El Salvador's best places to throw down a towel and enjoy the sun, sea, and sand. Access used to be difficult but now a newly paved road means you can get there easily by bus or car from the main town of Usulután. New hotels are popping up all the time, the best of which are listed below.

Hotel Real Oasis Espino (Playa El Espino; ✆ **503/2270-2798** or 7856-3445; www.realoasisespino.com.sv) is plain and a little soulless. Its main attraction is its wide-open beachside location and good-size pool with tiny circular island and mini footbridge. There is a thatched, rancho-style dining area with hammocks and deck chairs and smaller thatched picnic spots you can hire by the day. Look out for greatvalue all-inclusive packages such as 2 nights and 4 days for $110 per person. **La Estancia de Don San Luis** (Calle a Arcos, 1,300m/4,250 ft. west of school, Playa Espino; ✆ **505/2270-1851;** www.playaespino.com) is an open property that sits right on the beach and consists of low, white bungalow rooms, thatched picnic areas, green lawns, and a picket fence. The facilities are modern and basic, with bright, clean rooms and tiny bathrooms. A good pool and friendly owners make for a laidback, casual break. Double rooms cost $50.

PLAYA EL CUCO

First impressions may not be so good when you see a ramshackle gathering of food huts and shacks. Keep going and it opens up into a vast plain of sand with a distant shore that goes on for miles. El Cuco is a medium-size fishing village that also

Tired of the beach? Take the morning off from sunbathing to visit the 1,243m-high (4,078-ft.) Volcán de Conchagua Volcán just south of La Unión. Ride to the top in a four-wheel-drive and you'll find a mirador with incredible views of the entire Golfo de Fonseca, La Unión port, the islands, and the coasts of Honduras and Nicaragua. On its slopes is a pleasant little village of the same name, worth checking out for its 17th-century church, leafy plaza, and laid-back vibe.

functions as a popular Salvadoran beach getaway. Swimmers often share the ocean with small boats heading out for the day, and the beach is lined with tables there for drying the fishermen's morning catches, as well as thatched-roof covered restaurants catering to Salvadorans enjoying the weekend. If you want to step off the normal tourist path for a couple of days, this is a great place to go. Three kilometers (1¾ miles) west, you reach Playa La Flores, reputedly one of the best places to surf in the country and with none of the crowds associated with the Balsamo coast.

To get there take **bus no. 385** from San Miguel or drive east along Hwy. CA-2 and follow the signs.

WHERE TO STAY

El Cuco offers small, nonluxury hotels such as **Hotel Vina del Mar** (Calle al Esterito, 100m/328 ft. off the main square; ✆ **503/2619-9122;** $40 with air-conditioning, $20 without air-conditioning), as well as the more luxurious **Hotel Pacific Paradise** (500m/1,640 ft. before Esterón, Intipucá; ✆ **503/2502-2791;** www.hotelpacificparadise.com), which has a couple of pools and big, two-bedroom bungalows for $120 per night. **Las Flores Surf Club,** Playa El Cuco (✆ **503/2619-9065;** www.lasfloresresort.com), offers a seven-room, all-inclusive, four-star slice of luxury, with the prices to match. Three- and 4-night single-occupancy, nonsurfing packages begin at $1,150 for two or $790 per person; the surf packages cost a few hundred dollars more. But you get what you pay for—the grounds are set on a beautiful, and private, beach cove; the rooms are enormous and boast a modern, Asian-inspired decor; and the staff caters to your every need.

OTHER BEACHES

Farther east, you'll find the calm waters and uncrowded beaches of **Playa Tamarindo.** Tamarindo is nestled into a cove near the end of El Salvador's coast, which makes its ocean waters some of the calmest and best for swimming in the country. The area is also known for quality deep-sea fishing and its inhabited islands 1 hour off the coast. Tamarindo hotels, such as **Hotel Tropico Inn** (La Metaza, Playa El Tamarindo, La Unión; ✆ **503/2649-5082**), aren't cheap at about $75 a night. But the area is lush and tropical, and you'll likely be the only international traveler around.

Nearby is one of El Salvador's hidden gems—**Playa Maculis.** This 1.5km-long (1-mile) crescent-shaped beach is very private, with few houses and lots of trees. At either end two rocky points jut out into the sea. This protects the waters from the lateral current that can be so dangerous on the Salvadoran coast. Neither are there any rocks along the shore so it is perfect for swimming. A few feet away from the tide, you'll find **Los Caracoles** (✆ **503/2335-1200;** www.hotelsalvador.com), a breezy four-bedroom house with a lovely round pool surrounded by wooden deck and a bar within arm's reach. Owned by the same proprietor who runs the famous Los Almendros de San Lorenzo in Suchitoto, this lovely little beach house is a little piece of paradise. The house can be rented for $220 a night, a bargain considering that it sleeps eight and comes with a housekeeper/cook.

GOLFO DE FONSECA

Now you have reached the limits of this part of the coast, a gorgeous bay with post-card-pretty islands, fishing villages, and dark, volcanic beaches. Once a pirate hide-out—there is an enduring legend that Sir Francis Drake buried his stolen loot here—the inlet is now shared with Honduras and Nicaragua and has very little tourist infrastructure. El Salvador has sovereignty over just a handful of islands, the most important of which is Isla Meanguera. Here there are no roads nor cars and everybody travels by boat. There is one public boat a day from La Unión so to get around is very difficult unless you prearrange everything with your hotel or go with a tour company, such as **La Ruta del Zapamiche** (© **503/2228-1525;** www.larutadel zapamiche.com) or **Nicarao Tours** (© **503/2228-1525**). Another option is to hire a fisherman to take you out from the nearby beaches of El Tamarindo or Maculis. **Hotel La Joya del Golfo,** Isla Meanguera (© **503/2648-0072;** www.hotellajoya delgolfo.com), is a three-story hacienda-style house located on the shoreline with a handsome wooden deck and private pier. One of its four large rooms costs $79.

SUCHITOTO & NORTH CENTRAL EL SALVADOR

North Central El Salvador is dominated by **Lago de Suchitlán,** a serene man-made lake that is now the home of more than 200 species of migrating birds. It is presided over by the pretty village of Suchitoto, undoubtedly a jewel in the crown of El Salvador's attractions. A short ride from San Salvador, this former-rebel-town-turned-arts-center is a preferred base of operations for visitors who wish to explore the surrounding hills and volcanoes and learn more about the country's wartime history and artistic heritage. From the lake the hills rise dramatically toward the Honduran border, leading to the country's highest peak, **Cerro El Pital.** Nestled in those hills are laid-back villages and handicraft centers such as **Concepción de Quezalte-peque** and **La Palma.** Forests, waterfalls, and former rebel camps are just a few of the attractions that are explored by many as they make their way north to the Honduran border at the frontier towns of **Citala** and **El Poy.**

SUCHITOTO ★

Guatemala has Antigua. Nicaragua has Granada, and El Salvador has Suchitoto. Its laid-back, cobbled streets, low colonial town houses, and gorgeous church are a few of the sights that make this little town worth a visit. Incredible views of the surrounding countryside, a central location, and a thriving arts scene may coax you into choosing it as a base for your travels.

Suchitoto was a volatile and fought-over territory during El Salvador's civil war, and many battles unfolded on the nearby mountain and former guerrilla stronghold of Cerro Guazapa. But it has recovered and remade itself into one of El Salvador's premier scenic and arts destinations. With a mix of international arts, upscale boutique hotels, natural beauty, and famously friendly people, it's now a place where you might plan on coming for a day but end up staying for a week.

This small, walkable town and surrounding area offer camera-ready mountain views, and a charming main square filled on weekends with locals and visitors enjoying the weekly market. The town has also become an international arts center, with the opening of galleries by an array of international owners and renovation of Suchitoto's Teatro Las Ruinas, which hosts an annual international arts festival. Over the past few years, some of El Salvador's finest boutique hotels, including the exquisitely designed Los Almendros and Las Puertas on the main square, have made the town a destination, too.

When you learn of all the opportunities for day trips, such as boat rides on the country's largest man-made lake, **Lago Suchitlán,** and tours to the historic village of **Cinquera,** Suchitoto should be on your list of El Salvador "musts."

Essentials

GETTING THERE

BY BUS   From San Salvador, take **bus no. 129** from **Terminal de Oriente** (Final de Av. Peralta and Blvd. del Ejército, San Salvador; ✆ **503/2271-4171**). Buses leave every 15 minutes, cost 80¢, and arrive in 1 hour and 45 minutes. Buses stop 1½ blocks from the main square.

BY CAR   If you're driving from San Salvador, follow the **Pan-American Highway** (Carretera Panamericana) past Lago Ilopango until you see the sign for San Martin. Take the San Martin exit and follow it to the Plaza Central, where you will find signs leading you the remaining 28km (17 miles) to Suchitoto.

ORIENTATION & GETTING AROUND

Most of what you'll want to see in Suchitoto is within a 5-minute walk of the central plaza, Parque Centenario. The town is small and walkable, and its streets are quiet and largely traffic free. Avenida 15 de Septiembre runs north-south in front of the plaza and 2A Calle Oriente runs east-west by the plaza, becoming 2a Calle Poniente west of the plaza. Lago Suchitlán is an easy 30-minute stroll out of town along Avenida 15 de Septiembre but a tough 45-minute climb back.

A ferry also transports cars and people across Lago Suchitlán to the north daily from roughly 7am to 5pm, for $7 per car and $2 per person. To get to the launching area, turn left just before the Turistico Puerto San Juan tourist center and follow the dirt road down to the lake.

VISITOR INFORMATION

Visitor information is easy to come by in Suchitoto. For the formal scoop, head to the **tourist office** (Av. Francisco Morazán, 2 blocks off the main square; ✆ **503/2335-1782**), open daily from 8am to noon and 1 to 4pm. The office has an English-speaking staff that can offer tips on Suchitoto's attractions and hands out town maps. For a locals' perspective, sit with a cup of coffee on the porch of **Artex Café** (✆ **503/2335-1440**) on the southeast corner of the square. Eventually you'll be joined by an assortment of expats, business owners, and other characters who come here to use the Internet, enjoy a pastry, or pass the time.

TOUR OPERATORS

English-speaking tour guide **Rene Barbón** (✆ **503/2335-1679** or 7118-1999; vistacongasuchi@yahoo.com) is based at the **Lupita del Portal** cafe on the plaza

ACCOMMODATIONS ■
El Tejado Hotel y
    Restaurante **9**
Hostel Rinconcito
    del Gringo **2**
Hotel Villa Balanza
    La Barranca **4**
La Posada del Sol **18**
La Posada de Suchitoto **3**
La Puertas de Suchitoto **16**

Los Almendros de
    San Lorenzo **7**
Posada Alta Vista **12**

DINING ◆
El Harlequín Café **11**
El Necio **17**
Las Puertas **15**
Los Almendros **6**
Rinconcito del Gringo **1**

ATTRACTIONS ●
Iglesia Santa Lucia **13**
La Casa del Escultor **10**
Lago Suchitlan **8**
Los Tercios **19**
Museo de Obras Maestras
    de la Pintura Nacional **5**
Teatro de las Ruinas **5**
This is My Land Artisans
    Market **14**

and offers an array of tours that provide an excellent sense of the region's history and natural beauty. Rene's most popular outing is a 6-hour trip that involves hiking in the 3,921-hectare (9,690-acre) Parque Ecológio de Cinquera and visiting the historic civil war village of Cinquera. The tour also includes a 1½-hour presentation by Cinquera resident Don Pablo, translated by Rene, who gives a firsthand account of the gruesome realities of the civil war. Other tours include a 3-hour hike to a nearby waterfall, horseback riding, and nighttime animal-watching tours, as well as a 5-hour flat-water canoe paddling tour. Tours range from $15 to $30.

Eco Tourism La Mora (© **503/2323-6874;** www.ecoturismolamora.es.tl) offers Spanish-only hiking and horseback tours to nearby Volcán Guazapa, also known as Cerro Guazapa. This 1,435m (4,700-ft.) mountain is home to 200 plant species and 27 types of birds, as well as many types of butterflies and reptiles. According to some, you can still spot small bomb craters left over from the war here. Two- to 5-hour tours cost $16 to $40.

Gringo Tours (Calle Francisco Morazán #27; ✆ **503/2327-2351;** www.elgringo suchitoto.com) is run by local restaurant owner and American expat Robert Broz. He is more than happy to give you the lowdown on the town, in addition to offering fascinating tours that specialize in the archaeological heritage and civil war history of the area, including a tour of Cinquera. Tours start at $50 for a half-day for a group of one to four. Robert can also organize accommodations and custom-built itineraries.

In town, you can take a 2-hour **Historic Building Walking Tour** via the Suchitoto tourist office (Av. Francisco Morazán; ✆ **503/2335-1782**). The tour consists of visits to 32 historic Suchitoto buildings, including the former homes of three presidents and a former convent now serving as an arts center. The tour can be booked with 24 hours' notice, and costs $10 for 1 to 5 people, $15 for 5 to 20.

FAST FACTS   Suchitoto has two ATMs, one on the southeastern square and the other a half-block north on Avenida 15 de Septiembre. **Farmacia Santa Lucía** (✆ **503/2335-1063**) is just off the square at Avenida 5 de Noviembre and Francisco Morazán. The Police Station (✆ **503/2335-1141**) is located close to the town square, on Avenida 15 de Septiembre and 4 Calle Pte. For health emergencies, head to **Hospital Nacional de Suchitoto** (Av. José María Pérez Fernández; ✆ **503/2335-1062**). The **post office** (✆ **503/2304-0104**) is near the corner of Avenida 15 de Septiembre and 2a Calle Oriente.

What to See & Do

Suchitoto is known as much for its mountain scenery and artsy vibe as for its formal attractions. You could spend the morning savoring an Argentine feast prepared by a local sculptor and the afternoon listening to the sounds of thousands of migrating birds on the county's largest man-made lake. You can hike waterfalls and learn of the horrible realities of El Salvador's civil war. Or you can just sit and enjoy the square and colorful weekend artisans' market. For some more structured options, though, you may want to consider a guided tour (see above).

In addition to the attractions below, there's also small art museum, the **Casa Museo de Alejandro Cotto,** Calle al Lago (✆ **503/2335-1140**), in town, though its hours are so irregular, it can't be considered an official tourist site.

Iglesia Santa Lucia ★   Santa Lucia church is one of El Salvador's premier examples of colonial architecture and is undergoing a much anticipated restoration. Its brilliant white facade, set against a green mountain backdrop, is one of the first things visitors see upon arrival, and its dark, rich wood interior packs some serious history. It took 9 years to build and was completed in 1853. Above its six-columned atrium is a small clock, topped by a silver plate donated by a grateful bride. The altar is made of elaborately carved wood, and 36 tall wood beams run down the sides of the long, narrow church. Santa Lucia also features numerous life-size statues encased in glass and a small, pen-and-ink drawing of a crying Jesus. It doesn't match the grandeur of Santa Ana's Gothic cathedral (p. 305), but it's one of the country's more beautiful and traditional churches and makes for a peaceful and serene break from the heat.

Parque Centenario, btw. Calle San Marco and 2a Calle Oriente. No phone. Free admission. Daily 8am–noon and 1-6pm.

If you're anywhere near Suchitoto in February, stop by the **International Permanent Festival of Art and Culture ★★**. This annual, month-long international performance and art festival was founded by renowned cinematographer and Suchitoto resident Don Alejandro Cotto almost 20 years ago, and it continues to attract visual and performance artists from around the world. The festival is held each weekend in February, with free performances in the recently renovated Teatro de Las Ruinas, one of Suchitoto's oldest buildings.

La Casa del Escultor ★★   The Argentine sculptor Miguel Martino is one of numerous artists who are currently reinventing Suchitoto as an international arts center—but he's the only one who also happens to be a mean cook. In addition to his fine woodworking art, Miguel is well known for his Sunday-afternoon Argentine feasts, which take place at his gallery, La Casa del Escultor, 2 blocks off the main square. From noon to 4:30pm each Sunday, Miguel prepares huge quantities of Argentine beef and vegetables on a wood-burning grill inside his studio and gallery for 30 to 35 people, who must call ahead to reserve a spot. He then closes the doors and everyone proceeds to drink Argentine wine and talk art or whatever comes up. Plates include five kinds of meats or five types of veggies.

2a Av. Sur, 26-A. ℂ **503/2335-1836.** Free admission. Food $9–$15. Gallery hours Sat–Sun 9am–5pm. Meals Sun noon–4:30pm.

Los Tercios ★   Even Suchitoto's waterfalls look like art. Los Tercios, a stunning waterfall and small swimming hole located an easy 1.5km (1-mile) stroll out of town, has foot-wide slices of vertical rock jutting out along the face of its 9m (30-ft.) waterfall. The unique shape of the rocks here is thought to have resulted from rapidly cooling ancient magma. Though water flows over the falls only from May to December, Los Tercios is worth a visit year-round, since the unique rock formations are the main attraction. Be prepared to climb down a few rocks to get a good look. Vendors often come here to sell *pupusas* and drinks on the weekends, so refreshments should be on hand after your climb. Though the falls are relatively easy to reach, it is wise to go accompanied by a guide or local as there have been some isolated reports of robberies on the trail.

1.5km (1 mile) southeast of the main square. Free admission. Walk out of town along Av. 5 de Noviembre and turn left onto Calle a Cinquera just before Noviembre ends. Follow Calle a Cinquera to just past the chain-link fence on the left. Turn left through the gate btw. the chain-link fence and a small building. Walk straight and look for a path to your right, which will take you to the falls.

Museo de Obras Maestras de la Pintura Nacional   The Teatro de Las Ruinas (see below) contains this small gallery of Salvadoran art, including 31 abstract, Impressionist, and realist, post-1950 paintings created by Salvadoran artists—including Suchitoto's own single-name artist "Chaney," as well as Negra Alvarez and Augusto Crespin. Also included in the gallery is a traditional Greek-style bust of the Suchitoto arts promoter and once-world-famous cinematographer Alejandro Cotto. You can visit the gallery year-round by calling and making an appointment.

2 a Calle Poniente and 4a Av. Norte. ℂ **503/2335-1909.** Admission $1. Tues–Thurs 8am–noon; Fri–Sun 9am–noon and 1–5pm.

Teatro de las Ruinas   As the name implies, this corner theater was a pile of ruins for many years until a renovation led by the filmmaker Alejandro Cotto transformed it into the cultural focal point of what is now a town that has a strong cultural scene. Grey granite arches lead to salons with high, coved ceilings and chandeliers. The lobby holds an art gallery with some of the country's best artists on display, including Salvador Llort and Armando Solis. Farther inside, you'll find a 300-seat theater with white pillared walls and plastic chairs. Here there are performances of opera, plays, and orchestras, and it is especially alive during the International Permanent Festival of Art and Culture in February and March.

Southeastern corner of Parque San Martin. No phone. Art gallery admission free. Concert tickets $1–$10. Mon–Fri 10am–4pm and during theater performances.

Outdoor Activities

Lago Suchitlán ★★   Just a short bus ride out of town is the 135-sq.-km (52-sq.-mile), man-made Lago Suchitlán, from where you can take a cooling, scenic boat ride to **La Isla de Los Pájaros (Island of the Birds)** and listen to the calls of thousands of migrating birds. Lago Suchitlán was created in 1973 when the government dammed Río Lempa to produce electrical power, and now serves as a fishing hole for local communities and a stop for migrating birds. Surrounding the lake are the **Puerto San Juan** tourist center, a large open-air restaurant, and stands for craft vendors.

Covered tourist boats are just to the left of the tourist center and offer 45-minute to 1-hour, $25 lake tours including stops at La Isla de Los Pájaros. Also available are $12, 30-minute tours that don't include a stop at the island. At press time a local operator was setting up an "**Aqua Canopy**" with plans to zip thrill seekers out over the water to an island. Ask at the tourist center for more information.

Turicentro, Lago Suchitlán. ⓒ **503/2335-1957.** Admission 50¢, 25¢ children 6 and under. Daily 7am–7pm. Take the white minibus with SUCHITOTO written on the side from the center of town.

Parque Ecológio de Cinquera and the Village of Cinquera ★★   Parque Ecológio de Cinquera is a 3,921-hectare (9,690-acre) preserve and forest 1 hour from Suchitoto. It's not as grand as Parque Imposible (p. 300) or Montecristo (p. 312), but it has a small waterfall and a few trails, and is worth a walk in the woods when paired with the historic village of Cinquera a few minutes from the park entrance.

The tiny village of Cinquera was a stronghold of guerrilla resistance during the civil war, and numerous buildings, including the church, have been preserved to show bomb and bullet damage inflicted by government troops. The town square also displays the tail of a downed army helicopter and a mural depicting the history of the war and the image of the brutally executed 15-year-old girl who was the town's first martyr. A separate mural depicts the two ninth-grade boys whose call to arms is said to have sparked the guerrilla resistance in the region. Spanish-language tours of the town are available through **La Asociación de Reconstrucción y Desarrollo Municipal,** or ARDM (Main Sq. 1 block from the Alcaldía; ⓒ **503/2389-5732;** ardmcqr@yahoo.es). Or ask around town for Spanish-speaking Cinquera resident Don Pablo, who can provide a unique firsthand and sadly brutal account of the war.

To get here, take bus no. 482 from Suchitoto, which leaves Suchitoto daily at 9:15am and 1:30pm. It returns from Cinquera only once a day, at 1pm. The trip takes 1 hour and costs 80¢. It is a rough road and should not be attempted in an ordinary rental car.

No phone. Park admission $5. Daily 8am–5pm. Bus: 482.

Celebrating in Suchitito at the Corn Festival

Every August the **Festival de Maiz** celebrates everything there is to do with corn. Church processions, harvest blessings, and food fairs are all part of a celebration that reaches back to pre-Columbian times. There is also a festival king and queen elected to head the party.

Shopping

Galería de Pascal   This small gallery is owned by Pascal Lebailly, a former Paris fashion convention producer and owner of the exquisitely decorated Los Almendros hotel (p. 278). Lebailly has applied that same sense of fashion and design in choosing the Salvadoran and Central American art on display and for sale. The gallery also includes a small gift shop offering Salvadoran coffee, ceramics, hammocks, and handbags, among other items. 4a Calle Poniente, No. 2b. ℂ **503/2335-1008.** Mon–Fri 10am–6pm; Sat–Sun 9am–6pm.

This Is My Land Artisans Market ★★   It's not the biggest or most diverse mercado in El Salvador, but it's definitely one of the most enjoyable. Each Saturday and Sunday, the Association of Artisans and Artists of Suchitoto sets up shop on the town square with offerings of Salvadoran crafts and traditional cuisine. Colorful paintings, textiles, and, of course, the Salvadoran food staple, *pupusas,* are in plentiful supply. But the real reason to visit the weekend market is just to enjoy the vibe. There's no better place to watch local families mingle and chat well into the night, listen to local music, and soak in the town's beautiful mountain setting. Parque Centenario. ℂ **503/2335-1782.** Free admission. Fri-Sun 9am-7pm.

Where to Stay
EXPENSIVE

La Posada de Suchitoto ★   La Posada is a few more blocks off the square than Suchitoto's other high-end hotels, but the pool, lake view, and slightly lower price are worth the 5-minute walk. The 12-room La Posada offers a traditional hacienda-style atmosphere with an attentive staff in colonial garb and a large lakeview **restaurant** with tasty, reasonably priced fare. La Posada is a bit older than the other two pricey hotels, so the rooms and amenities aren't shiny and new. But the character, casual atmosphere, and well-trained staff help balance things out. You'll want to book early to reserve one of the hotel's six lakeview rooms.

Final 4a, Calle Poniente. ℂ **503/2335-1064.** Fax 503/2335-1164. www.laposada.com.sv. 12 units. $73 double; $89 lakeview double. Rates include full breakfast. AE, DISC, MC, V. **Amenities:** Restaurant; pool; room service; Wi-Fi in common areas. *In room:* A/C, fan, TV.

Las Puertas de Suchitoto ★★   Though it's not as luxurious as Los Almendros, you can't beat Las Puertas in terms of its view and location. Also renovated within the past few years, Las Puertas is on Suchitoto's charming central plaza facing the church. Each of its six large upstairs rooms features custom-designed wood furniture and private balconies, which are perfect places to watch the sun rise over the mountains and light up the towers of Iglesia Santa Lucia. All of the rooms are in a single row on the second floor so no room is better than another. The hotel also features a large balcony overlooking Volcán Quazapa and a good **restaurant.**

2a Av. Norte and Av. 15 de Septiembre. ℰ **503/2393-9200.** www.laspuertassuchitoto.com. 6 units. From $82 double. Rates include full breakfast. AE, DC, DISC, MC, V. **Amenities:** Restaurant; bar; bike rental ($6.50 per day); room service; 2 smoke-free rooms. *In room:* A/C, TV, Wi-Fi.

Los Almendros de San Lorenzo ★★★   This is one of the most luxurious independent hotels in El Salvador. Owner and former fashion producer Pascal Lebailly required nearly a year and a half and 30 workers to fully renovate the 200-year-old colonial house that is now his six-room hotel. Each large room is individually decorated in a modern hacienda style with iron bathroom accents and lighting designed specifically for the hotel. A glass-enclosed **French restaurant** sits above the figure-eight-shaped stone pool, and a small, comfortable **bar** sits beside a central courtyard with fountain. But what makes Los Almendros special is the eye for detail with which Pascal chose the art, furniture, and overall tone. The whole effect is like staying overnight in an interior design show. In 2010, the owner added two suites that can accommodate four adults in luxury, with lake views as an added bonus.

4a Calle Poniente, No. 2b. ℰ **503/2335-1200.** www.hotelsalvador.com. 8 units. $85–$110 double; $135 suite. Rates include full breakfast. AE, DC, DISC, MC, V. **Amenities:** Restaurant; bar; airport transfers ($80); pool; all rooms smoke-free. *In room:* A/C, TV.

MODERATE

El Tejado Hotel y Restaurante ★★   This is the best moderately priced option in town. Though El Tejado's viewless rooms are nothing to e-mail home about, they're comfortable and decently sized, with high ceilings and inviting, hacienda-style tiled front patios. What makes Tejado stand out is the price, which is up to $30 less than the three higher-end options in town. Tejado also offers a cool, leafy atmosphere; a large open-air **restaurant** with great lake views; and a big, inviting pool. And since it's only a few blocks off the main square, it's a perfect place for those who adhere to the old "who spends time in their room anyway?" style of travel. If you can't get a room, you can still use Tejado's pool for $3.35 a day.

3a Av. Norte, No. 58. ℰ **503/2335-1769.** Fax 503/2335-1970. www.gaesuchitoto.com/eltejado/tejado contactoeng.htm. 9 units. $50–$55 double; $85 5-person suite. Rates include full breakfast. AE, DC, DISC, MC, V. **Amenities:** Restaurant; pool; room service; Wi-Fi in common areas. *In room:* A/C, TV, no phone.

Posada del Sol   One thing you don't lack here is space. This cream-colored town house holds an ample living room and courtyard out back that overlooks the town and has nice views of the surrounding mountains. The pool is big, as is the garden with hammocks, mango trees, and coconut trees. The rooms are clean, if a little old-fashioned, with dark-wood furnishings and mirrored wardrobes. Bathrooms are small but immaculate. The hotel is a family-run affair and though it might do with sprucing up, it is still a great bargain considering the space and amenities.

2a Av. Sur 39. ℰ **503/2335-1546.** 6 units. $35–$60 double. No credit cards. **Amenities:** Restaurant; pool. *In room:* A/C, TV, no phone.

INEXPENSIVE

Hostel Rinconcito del Gringo   A few bare, basic rooms and one dorm are below a casual restaurant of the same name. This is an extreme budget option with little in the way of amenities, though there is a cozy communal area with TV, wood trunk, coffee table, and sofa. The main advantage of staying here (besides stretching your dollars) is the excellent Salvadoran and Mexican food upstairs; there's also your American-Salvadoran host, the gregarious Robert Broz, a fountain of information on the area and an excellent guide who enjoys showing guests and diners the secret delights of the town, including a somewhat eye-opening nightlife tour. The restaurant itself is small, colorful, and casual, with open walls and a sunny atmosphere. It serves great shakes and giant quesadillas.

Calle Francisco Morazán #27, 1.5 blocks west of the Market and City Hall. (✆ **503/2327-2351.** www.elgringosuchitoto.com. 3 units. $10 double. No credit cards. Free parking. **Amenities:** Restaurant. In room: Fan, no phone.

Hotel Villa Balanza La Barranca ★★ 🍴 This is without doubt the best deal I could find in Suchitoto: a charming stand-alone house on the crest of the hill with marvelous views of the lake. The lobby is a sitting room that leads to a little garden with patches of lawn and a wrought-iron gate. Three small rooms lie adjacent, one a small chapel. Upstairs are the best rooms, as the view from them is spectacular from a wraparound balcony overlooking the lake. However, these two rooms have a shared bathroom; the ground-level rooms have private bathrooms. The rooms are small but immaculate, with carved headboards, tiled floors, and tiny wardrobes. The bathrooms are clean and colorful, with nice touches like painted vines and flowers along the walls, giving it a cozy, down-to-earth feel. The only drawback is the short but steep walk into town. **Note:** The hotel should not be confused with the owner's restaurant of the same name, located several blocks uphill. If no one is around when you arrive, you must go to the restaurant to find the owner.

North end of 6a Av. Norte. (✆ **503/2335-1408** or 2269-3687. www.villabalanzarestaurante.com. 5 units. $20 double with shared bathroom; $25 double with private bathroom. AE, DC, DISC, MC, V. Free parking. **Amenities:** Computer w/Internet; communal kitchen; Wi-Fi. In room: Fan, TV, no phone.

Posada Alta Vista ★ It's bare-bones, but affordable, modern, and right off the square. Don't look to Alta Vista for much in terms of amenities, but a clean, comfortable, air-conditioned room with a rooftop deck less than 45m (148 ft.) from the main square for roughly $20 a night is just about as good a deal as you're going to find. Alta Vista's only downside is that at press time the showers were cold water only. Hotel operators say hot showers are on the way, however. Make sure to request an upstairs front room with a balcony, as those rooms are superior.

Av. 15 de Septiembre, Casa 8, just off Parque Centenario. (✆ **503/2335-1645.** Fax 503/2335-1590. www.posadaaltavista.com. 8 units. $25 double. V. **Amenities:** Free coffee in lobby; all rooms smoke-free. In room: A/C, fan, TV, no phone.

Where to Dine

Like El Salvador in general, Suchitoto is a town reinventing itself after a long, difficult history. New restaurants seem to be popping up every year. Listed below are just a few of the established choices, but the main square and side streets also offer a plethora of *comedores* and *pupusarias* that are worth checking out.

El Harlequin Café ★★ 🍴 ☺ SALVADORAN El Harlequin is the kind of funky place we all hope to find when traveling. Hidden behind a little sign and metal door on a quiet street a couple of blocks off the main square is this romantic hideaway, filled with candlelight, jazzy music, interesting art, and tasty food. The menu is simple but offers a lot to choose from, including comfort food such as a tuna salad, chicken and rice, and cream soups; there's even a children's menu. Combine the food with the artsy feel and intimate lighting, and El Harlequin stands out as a great place to pass a quiet evening over a bottle of wine.

3a Av. Norte, No. 26. ℂ **503/2325-5890.** Main courses $3.50–$8. AE, DC, MC, V. Sun–Mon and Wed–Thurs 10am–10pm; Fri–Sat 10am–midnight.

Las Puertas ★ SALVADORAN   Las Puertas offers a mix of first-class service and delicious food at reasonable prices, along with great people-watching. The service is formal and elegant, the chef is imported from San Salvador, and the kitchen is new and high-tech. The result is delicious dishes such as ravioli with shrimp and vegetables. The restaurant's dining room is an open, upscale space with a soaring ceiling and windows overlooking the square. Reservations aren't required, but call ahead for outside seating or one of the two windowfront tables.

2a Av. Norte and Av. 15 de Septiembre. ℂ **503/2393-9200.** Main courses $11–$13. AE, DC, DISC, MC, V. Daily 7am–9pm.

Los Almendros ★★★ FRENCH   Eat at least one meal here while you're in town. The food is delicious, the setting is elegant, and the price is a lot lower than you would expect. French owner Pascal Lebailly has used his well-honed eye for design in creating this casual but upscale, glass-enclosed French restaurant that overlooks Los Almendros's romantically lit pool. With French chef Hérvey Laurent applying his *Cordon Bleu* skills to dishes such as chargrilled salmon with lime and butter, Los Almendros is likely to serve one of your better meals in El Salvador. The restaurant also uses local ingredients and serves Salvadoran coffee.

4a Calle Poniente, No. 2b. ℂ **503/2335-1200.** Main courses $5.50–$14. AE, DC, DISC, MC, V. Daily 7:30am–9pm.

Restaurante La Villa Balanza ★★ SALVADORAN   Here the decor is as piled high as the food portions. Fishing nets, indigenous sandals, an old radio, clothes irons, and sewing machines make up a local history collection as eclectic as the food. Tacos are piled high with guacamole, mashed beans, and cheese. Corn tortillas accompany excellent salads and fish. There are also more conventional chicken and beef dishes, as well as ceviche and giant prawns. Located in front of the quiet, bushy plaza Parque San Martin, the property is a delightful, rambling arrangement of open patio, picnic tables, chunky roof tiles, plants. and sculptures with old relics from the war on display such as a 340-kilogram (748 lb.)bomb. *La balanza* means *scale*, with reference to the sculpture of a weighing scale with a pile of tortillas against a bomb.

Northwest corner of Parque San Martin. ℂ **503/2335-1408.** Lunch special $2.50; main courses $5–$12. AE, DC, DISC, MC, V. Tues–Sun 10am–9pm.

Rinconcito del Gringo ★★ 🎁 SALVADORAN/MEXICAN   A·shake here is a meal in itself and one portion of quesadillas will feed an army. There are excellent vegetarian options as well as seafood tacos and burritos. The walls are adorned with local art, and tables with colorful tablecloths. Located in a quiet part of town, this is a relaxed and casual family restaurant with a friendly English-speaking owner.

Calle Francisco Morazán #27, 1½ blocks west of the Market and City Hall. ℂ **503/2327-2351**. www.elgringosuchitoto.com. Main courses $3.50–$6. No credit cards. Mon–Fri 8am–9pm; Sat–Sun 8am–9:30pm.

Suchitoto After Dark

El Necio ★★   Amiable bartenders and posters calling for peace and revolution set the tone for this laid-back, lefty dive joint. In fact, the walls are covered with more than enough images of Ché, John Lennon, and a virtual history of leftist icons to keep your mind occupied whenever you're not busy listening to the occasional live music or deep in conversation with one of the friendly locals or travelers who come here to chat over ice-cold Pilseners. 4a Av. Sur (by 4a Calle Ote). © **503/2335-1708.** Daily 6pm–midnight (or later). No credit cards.

CONCEPCION DE QUEZALTEPEQUE

30km (19 miles) N of Suchitoto; 77km (48 miles) N of San Salvador

Concepción de Quezaltepeque, known as the City of Hammocks, is a tiny village tucked into El Salvador's northern central mountains, where generations of artisans have devoted their lives to making midday naps more enjoyable. Nearly the entire town is involved in hammock production and sales. Some locals weave intricate tapestries that hang from the sides of the hammocks on sale here; others twist individual threads into thin ropes that are eventually crafted into colorful *hamacas* sold in villages around the country.

Quezaltepeque is made up of only a few small streets, on which are gathered a group of hammock shops, surrounding a town square, so don't expect to spend more than a couple of hours here. And since you can buy Quezaltepeque-made hammocks around the country, the shopping is not actually the best part of visiting this town. The most enjoyable thing to do is to chat up a hammock shop owner and ask to see where and how their hammocks are made. With a little charm and a good grasp of Spanish, you might convince someone to show you the ropes, so to speak. Most craftsmen display their work on weekends, but the best time to ask owners for a behind-the-scenes peek is Tuesday and Wednesday when things aren't so busy.

Essentials

GETTING THERE & GETTING AROUND

From Suchitoto, take **bus no. 129;** the trip lasts 1½ hours. From San Salvador, take **bus no. 126,** which takes about 2½ hours. Both trips will cost you less than $2.

From San Salvador, drive north out of the city along **Hwy. CA-4,** from which you will turn west onto **Carretera Longitudinal del Norte** toward Chalatenango. Follow this road until you turn north toward Chalatenango and spot signs to Quezaltepeque.

Most of Quezaltepeque hammock shops and *comedores* are clustered within a few blocks of the square, so the best way to see the town is on foot.

VISITOR INFORMATION

There are no hotels, large restaurants, ATMs, or Internet cafes in town, so there isn't much visitor information to be had. But if you speak Spanish, you can stop by the **Casa de la Cultura** (Barrio El Central on the main square; © **503/2331-2242**) to learn more about the town's history. The nearby city of Chalatenango, which you will pass coming and going to Quezaltepeque, has ATMs, fast-food restaurants, and grocery stores.

What to See & Do

The primary activity here is strolling around looking for deals on hammocks crafted by artisans who have dedicated their lives to the art form. But you'll have an even better time if you can get a peek behind the scenes. I can't guarantee it will happen, but if you call Spanish-speaking hammock artisan **Missal Goldames** (© **503/2331-2001**) in

VOLUNTEER opportunities IN EL SALVADOR

If you enjoy mixing a little humanitarian work in with your volcano hiking and village visiting, El Salvador offers a plethora of volunteer activities from building homes and schools to teaching English. Below are the best options:

Habitat for Humanity (Colonia General Arce, Calle Jorge Domingue 4-H; *C* **503/2298-5253;** informacion@ habitatelsalvador.org.sv) began building earthquake-resistant homes here in 1992 after the end of the war and now has six offices and ongoing projects throughout the country. There's plenty to do, including the construction of new communities in Santa Ana and San Vicente. Habitat requires a minimum 5-day commitment and a $45-per-day fee for room and board, orientation, and transportation. You'll need to register 3 to 6 months in advance of your trip.

If you like working with your hands, you can also check in with **Seeds of Learning** (**SOL;** 585 Fifth St. W., Sonoma, CA 95476; *C* **707/939-0471**), which builds schools in rural El Salvador. SOL volunteers work side by side with local community members to build schools, so volunteers really get to know the people they are helping. SOL, which has been working in El Salvador since 1999, requires a 10-day commitment, and the program costs $1,200, including lodging at a basic hotel or retreat center, food, transportation, and excursions.

Scholarships are available for volunteers under 30 years of age.

English-language skills are also increasingly important to Salvadorans, and the country has numerous English teaching opportunities. **Global Crossroad** (415 E. Airport Fwy., Ste. 365, Irving, TX 75062; *C* **866/387-7816;** www.globalcrossroad.com) offers 1- to 12-week teaching programs in San Salvador, Sonsonate, and Santa Ana, beginning at $899 for food, housing, and transportation from the airport upon arrival. Volunteers stay with host families and teach primarily children. Global Crossroad also offers short-term volunteer opportunities teaching computer skills, taking care of orphan children, and helping to maintain communities.

Travelers willing to make a longer teaching commitment should check out El Salvador–based **Centro de Intercambio y Solidaridad,** or CIS (Av. Bolivar 103, Colonia Libertad, San Salvador; *C* **503/ 2226-5362;** www.cis-elsalvador.org). CIS was formed after the signing of the peace accords to help promote solidarity among the Salvadoran people and cultural exchange with other countries. Volunteers pay only a $100 registration fee and $70 per week for room and board with a local family, and volunteers receive half-price ($50) Spanish classes. A 10-week commitment is required, though. Other CIS volunteer opportunities are available as needs arise.

advance, he might just give you a tour around town. You can also stop by his shop along the main road, 1 block short of the square on the right.

If you don't see any hammocks you like along the main street, ask someone for *otras tiendas de hamaca* and, if you're lucky, they will point you to a friend's house where some are for sale.

Where to Stay & Dine

Quezaltepeque has no hotels and requires only a couple of hours to explore, so there isn't a big reason to stay overnight. If you do, your best option is the new and luxurious

Chalate Country Club (see below), 10 minutes outside Quezaltepeque. I don't recommend staying in Chalatenango. It's crowded, unattractive, and hard to navigate, and has no recommendable lodgings.

Food options in Quezaltepeque are limited to a few informal *pupusarias* near the hammock shops. If you want a more substantial meal, call the restaurant **Teresa de Leon** (1 block off the main street; ✆ **503/2331-2381**) 1 day in advance, as it's open only upon request. It serves *comidas tipicas* (rice and beans with beef and chicken variations) and a main course costs $3.50. You can also head to Chalatenango for fast food or, for the best option in the region, try the restaurant at the Chalate Country Club hotel.

Chalate Country Club ★★ 🏨 ☺   Chalate is an oasis of luxury that's worth the money if you plan to stay in the area for a few days. Opened in April 2007, this 14-room hotel offers large rooms, modern bathrooms, and grassy and tree-filled private grounds to explore, two children's pools, and a playground. Parents can lounge by six adult pools or shoot pool on two tables. And the restaurant is a cut above rural El Salvador's normal "roasted meat with rice and salad" menu. Continental cuisine, such as a tasty chicken breast wrapped in bacon and surf and turf, is $10 to $13. The kids' menu ranges from $3.50 to $4.75. There's no bus to the hotel, so you'll need to take a $7, 15-minute taxi ride from Quezaltepeque or Chalatenango.

The hotel did not include Wi-Fi at press time, but I was assured it would be installed. The property is also adding a large, upscale housing development, whose owners will be part of a members-only club that will use the property's facilities.

Km 63.5 Carretera a Chalatenango, San Rafael, Chalatenango. ✆ **503/2354-7620.** www.chalate countryclub.com. 14 units. $45 double. AE, DC, MC, V. **Amenities:** Restaurant; 2 children's pools and playground; health club w/exercise machines and 2 saunas; 6 outdoor adult pools; room service; tennis courts. *In room:* A/C, TV.

LA PALMA & EL PITAL ★

84km (52 miles) N of San Salvador; 50km (31 miles) W of Chalatenango

A thin, rectangular-shaped town is wedged along a mountainside. At first glance, La Palma seems like any small, scruffy mountain town high up near the Honduran border. Yet look closer, and you'll see that its telegraph poles are painted with bird and flower motifs. The small plaza wall has colorful renditions of armadillos and anteaters, and murals bearing chickens and snakes dot the town. La Palma is in fact the unlikely center of a famous art movement and is the former home of El Salvador's most revered living artist, **Fernando Llort.** Today, visitors come from around the world to snap photos of the dozens of Llort-style murals decorating the town's walls and browse its many artisans' shops. Llort moved to La Palma in 1972 and taught the townspeople to create art using available materials to reflect their lives. The resulting works are filled with color, geometric designs, and natural and religious symbols. Llort eventually left La Palma but the artists he inspired continue to create works on display in the galleries and on the buildings along La Palma's two main roads.

Despite its remote location and small size, La Palma has numerous restaurants and a couple of nice hotels. La Palma is also an excellent jumping-off point for hikes up nearby El Pital mountain, which is the highest point in El Salvador and summits on the border with Honduras.

Essentials

GETTING THERE

BY BUS From Chalatenango, hop on **bus no. 125** and ask the driver to let you off at Amayo, where you can catch **bus no. 119** to the center of La Palma. The trip takes about 1 hour and 15 minutes. You can reach Chalatenango in just over 2 hours from San Salvador on bus no. 125.

BY CAR La Palma is just off **Hwy. CA-4,** which is the country's main north-south highway. Just drive north a little less than 1 hour from Chalatenango and about 1½ hours from San Salvador and follow the signs. If you reach the Honduran border, you've gone a few miles too far.

ORIENTATION & GETTING AROUND

Like many of El Salvador's rural towns, La Palma is small enough to walk just about everywhere. There are only two main avenues that you can walk end to end in about 10 minutes. But if you're feeling lazy, La Palma offers many three-wheeled moto-taxis that will take you anywhere along those two streets for 25¢. You can also easily catch a $3 moto-taxi that'll take you 10 minutes outside town to the luxurious Entre Pinos resort or small village of San Ignacio.

VISITOR INFORMATION & FAST FACTS

The tourist information office is known as **El Centro Atención Turistica La Palma** (℃ 503/2335-9076; cat.lapalma.corsatur@gmail.com) and is on the north-eastern corner of the central plaza. The staff is friendly and helpful, but speaks limited English. Opening hours are Monday to Friday 8am to 4pm and Saturday to Sunday 9am to 1pm. There's a **Banco Cuscatlán** (℃ 503/2305-8331) with an ATM just off the main square.

WHAT TO SEE & DO

The main thing to do in La Palma is viewing building murals and shopping for arts and crafts in the galleries along the town's two main roads. Keep in mind that the galleries seem to have a lot of the same style of artwork you'll see in every shop in the country. A trained eye would probably be able to tell the difference, but I couldn't. Though you can pick up a small kitschy souvenir for under $10, some of the better framed pieces can be $40 or more. Since the art is actually fairly expensive, you might just want to bring your camera and take some shots of the beautiful murals—I consider these to be the best art in town.

OUTDOOR ACTIVITIES

La Palma's other attraction is its close proximity to El Salvador's highest point, **El Pital.** El Pital is 30 minutes outside of La Palma, rises 2,730m (8,957 ft.) above sea level, and offers an easy 1½-hour each-way hike to the top up a winding fire road. Only the last 20 minutes get a bit steep, and all along the way are great views. The last stretch to the summit is privately owned, and a family monitors the road. So if two guys come stumbling out of the woods, demanding money, don't sweat it: They own the place. The usual fee is $5 to $8 but you can sometimes get by for half that depending on your charm and guide.

Just before the summit, ask your guide to show you the four-story-high meteor that hit the mountain long before anyone can remember. Risk takers can climb on top of the meteor by walking across a small tree bridging a 12m (40-ft.) drop. At El Pital's summit, you'll find a small, white monument marking the border with Honduras and

BORDER crossing: EL SALVADOR TO HONDURAS

There is no charge to leave El Salvador at El Poy but there is a **$3 tax** to enter Honduras. The Salvadoran immigration office is open 24 hours but its Honduran counterpart is open only from 4am to 10pm. Bus no. 119 passes through La Palma every half-hour, stopping at 7pm. It takes 30 minutes and costs 50¢. The bus stops 100m (328 ft.) before the border and El Poy immigration office. There are onward connections to Nueva Coatepeque and Copán Ruinas via La Entrada.

a radio tower with a guard and vicious-looking dog behind a fence. Like many remote locations in El Salvador, it's not wise to hike up here alone. Your hotel can arrange a guide. To get here by bus, take a moto-taxi from La Palma for $3 to San Ignacio, where you will catch the no. 509 bus toward Las Pilas. After about 30 minutes, get off at Río Chiquito and have the driver point you in the right direction.

Shopping

Artesanias Kemuel ★   This is the best stand-alone shop in town for Llortian-style arts and crafts. The store offers lots of uniquely painted wood crosses that stand out in a town full of painted wood crosses, and it even sells a rare collection of framed Llort-style works on simple white paper. Artesanias's unique collection might be the result of an inside connection, of course—the store's owner and principal artist, Vitelio Jonathan Contreras, is Llort's nephew by marriage The art pieces and larger crosses cost $25 to $75. It's open daily from 8am to 6:30pm. Calle Principal, Barrio El Centro. ℂ **503/2352-1289.** viteliocontreras@yahoo.com.mx.   •

Mercadito Artesanal   This market across from the La Estancia Restaurante is a bit smaller than Placita, with just 10 vendors spread around a small courtyard, and it's a bit heavy on the laminated wood art and wood bracelets you'll see in every other mercado in Latin America. But if you look hard, you can find some genuine pieces of interesting, original, locally created art. The market also has a decent amount of women's clothing with simple Llort-esque designs. Textile bags run around $6 and small, painted decorative chairs run $10 before haggling. The market also has a small *comedor*. It's open daily from 9am to 7pm. Calle Gerardo Varrios, Barrio El Central, in front of the La Estancia Restaurante. No phone.

Placita Artesanal La Palma ★   Placita is the best market in town to search for original arts and crafts. It's bigger than Mercadito and seems to offer fewer mass-produced items and more locally produced crafts. I spoke with numerous vendors here and they were immediately able to give me the actual names and stories of the artists who produced many of the picture frames, wood boxes, and painted crosses on sale. It's open daily from 8am to 6pm. Barrio El Centro across from La Iglesia Catolica. No phone.

Where to Stay   •

In addition to the following hotel options, you might consider the **El Pital Highland Hotel** (ℂ **503/2259-0602;** www.elpital.com.sv), which is on the fire road at the start of any hike to El Pital. It offers a restaurant and four-person rooms for $110, two-person rooms for $70, and three-person cabins for $90.

Entre Pinos Resort ★★★ ☺   This upscale, mountain-lodge-style hotel was built in 1998 and is spread over 45 hectares (110 acres). It offers comfortable, midsize rooms and enough amenities to keep the family busy for days. Guests can hike or ride on horseback over private dirt roads and trails, play tennis, swim, soak in the big Jacuzzi, and play soccer on a full-size field. Kids tired of all that outdoor activity should like the video arcade. Though the hotel has a remote location, the English-speaking staff can easily arrange tours to the rest of the country, as well as to the Copán ruins in Honduras and El Pital. Entre Pinos is not exactly on par with the corporate megaresorts you'll find in other countries, but it is among El Salvador's best hotels, and serves as a great base for any longer El Salvador vacation.

Km 87.5 Carretera Troncal del Norte, San Ignacio. ☏ **503/2335-9312.** Fax 503/2278-2811. www.entrepinosresortandspa.com. 57 units. $75–$94 double; $125 5-person cabins. AE, DC, MC, V. **Amenities:** 3 restaurants; free airport transfers; bikes; health club & spa w/Jacuzzi; 2 pools; room service; 10 smoke-free rooms; tennis courts; Wi-Fi. *In room:* A/C, fan, TV, fridge, hair dryer.

Hotel La Palma ★★ ✦   La Palma is the best affordable hotel choice in town. It's rustic and simple but offers a cool, garden-like setting; a range of room options; great service; and a big **restaurant** with outdoor seating. The proprietor, Salvador, has owned the place for over 30 years and is happy to use the basic English he's picked up to provide information or arrange trips to El Pital. All 32 rooms are simply decorated and of average size but are comfortable. Rooms are spread throughout the leafy, hillside property, which winds down to a wide, rocky riverbed. When you book, request room no. 26. It's the newest room and offers the best view. If that's booked, ask for one of the rooms in the new building on the hill.

Barrio El Tránsito, La Palma. ☏ **503/2335-9012.** www.hotellapalma.com.sv. 32 units. $28 double. No credit cards. **Amenities:** Restaurant; babysitting ($6 per day); room service. *In room:* No phone, Wi-Fi.

Paseo del Pital ★ ☺   This hotel looks like an average motel with an L-shaped building surrounding a small parking lot right in the center of town. Recent refurbishments mean it is actually a good choice, especially if you get a back room overlooking the huge pool and water slide. The chalet-style rooms are a little bland but very clean, are quite big, and have lots of light. The bathrooms are faultless and the back balcony has a great view of the surrounding hills. The conference room looks like a very old university lecture room with student chairs included, and in general the decor is a hodgepodge of styles and garish colors. Still, it is the pool that makes it, and non-guests can gain day access for a very reasonable $2.

Barrio el Central. ☏ **2305 9344.** 9 units (3 family size, accommodating 7). $25 double. No credit cards.

Posada de Reyes ★ 🎁   Just a few miles past Entre Pinos and La Palma is the tiny village of San Ignacio. It's a pleasant Salvadoran village, with a white church beside a small public square. There's no particular reason to visit, except to catch a bus to El Pital and to stay at the unusually comfortable Posada de Reyes Hotel. This 14-room, three-story hotel was built in 2005 and offers uniquely spectacular views, big rooms, a well-maintained and inviting pool—which is unique among small, independently owned El Salvador hotels—and a lush, flower-filled landscape. It looks average from the outside but is modern, spacious, and comfortable on the inside. And at $25 to $35, it's almost as cheap as Hotel La Palma. Request room no. 15, which has windows on two sides and a balcony. A short moto-taxi ride will get you here from La Palma or you can take bus no. 119.

1 block north of the Alcaldía, Barrio El Centro. ℭ **503/2335-9318.** www.hotelposadadereyes.com. 15 rooms. $20–$35 double. No credit cards. Pets permitted. **Amenities:** Restaurant; pool; Wi-Fi in lobby. *In room:* A/C, TV, fridge, no phone.

Where to Dine

You'll need some hot coffee while you wander the wet streets of La Palma. **Café d Café,** Calle Gerarado Barrios 40 (ℭ **503/2335-9190**), makes the best cup I could find and is a bright, pleasant place with pastoral murals adorning the walls. It is on the left as you enter the town from the south at the V-junction just before the plaza. **Soni's Cake Panaderia y Pasteleria,** 2a Av. Sur (ℭ **503/258-0125**), has a great selection of pastries, though the decor is a little soulless.

Del Pueblo Restaurante y Artesanias ★★ 🍴 SALVADORAN   If you want protein, this is the place to come. The scent of spicy, simmering beef is the first thing you'll notice as you enter this two-room restaurant, which features one of the town's most interesting abstract murals on its front wall. The specialty of the house is the 170-gram (6-oz.) beef and sausage combo with salad, rice, cheese, and beans; it's delicious. The other items are variations on the same meat, sausage, and chicken theme. Breakfast is a traditional serving of eggs, beans, cheese, and platano. Wine and beer are also available. Locals consider Del Pueblo to be among La Palma's finest restaurants.

Calle Principle, No. 70, Barrio El Centro. ℭ **503/2305-8504.** Main courses $1.25–$4.95; breakfast $2–$3.25. No credit cards. Daily 7am–8pm.

Restaurante Los Pinares ★★ LATIN AMERICAN/SALVADORAN   Los Pinares, the main restaurant at the Entre Pinos Resort (see above), is worth the few dollars for a moto-taxi ride from La Palma. The restaurant has covered, open-air seating beside an outdoor pool and a large vegetarian, meat, fish, and pasta menu with unique items such as roasted boar and Jalapeño steak. But the best choices might be the mixed salad, which is twice the size and features twice the variety of ingredients as the average Salvadoran restaurant salad, or the creamy spaghetti with chicken, which has just the right amount of spicy kick. Wine, beer, spirits, and a children's menu are also available. Prices here are two to three times those of the restaurants in La Palma, but the food and service match the added cost.

Km 87.5 Carretera Troncal del Norte, San Ignacio. ℭ **503/2335-9312.** Main courses $9–$23; breakfast $2–$4.60. AE, DC, MC, V. Mon–Thurs 7am–8pm; Fri–Sun 7am–9pm.

Restaurante y Pupusaria La Palma ★ SALVADORAN   It's cheap, it's tasty, and the portions are huge—perhaps that's why this is *the* place where locals eat in town. Pupusaria La Palma is also one of the seemingly few buildings in town that's not covered in murals (its facade is instead covered in tree trunks). There are actually no decorations at all here, just one room with bench seating and pictures of the entrees on the wall. The menu is as simple as the decor; highlights include items such as roasted and fried shrimp, and chicken served with rice or fries, tortillas, and a salad. The $1.90 burritos and tacos are a good bet, but the *hamburgesas* are not too tasty.

Calle Central, across the street from Telecom Internet. ℭ **503/2334-9063.** Main courses $3.75–$6.50. No credit cards. Daily 8am–8pm.

RUTA DE LAS FLORES ★★★

Hwy. CA-8, Km 72 to Km 107, starts 68km (42 miles) W of San Salvador

The Ruta de las Flores, or Route of the Flowers, is a collection of five unique mountain villages along a winding, 35km (22-mile) scenic stretch of Hwy. CA-8 in the heart of El Salvador's coffee country. The route is known for the beauty of its flowering coffee plants and unique arts, crafts, and furniture markets, and highlights include the village of Nahuizalco and its handcrafted furniture; Salcoatitán, with two of the route's more interesting restaurants; and Juayúa, which features the region's largest food and artisan festival, as well as a renowned black Christ statue. The route also includes the towns of Apaneca, known for its zip-line canopy tour, and Ataco, which is filled with some of the country's most unique art.

The towns along this route are a few kilometers apart, well marked, and only a short distance off the main highway. The highway itself also offers a few interesting hotels and restaurants. Though all five towns can be seen in one long day or two, you might want to schedule a few days to properly take in the vibe of one of the country's most scenic and culturally unique regions.

Essentials

GETTING THERE

The first stop on the Ruta de las Flores, Nahuizalco, is 5km (3 miles) from Sonsonate and 68km (42 miles) from San Salvador. To get there from San Salvador, take **bus no. 205** to Sonsonate followed by **bus no. 249, 23,** or **53d.** Bus nos. 249 and 23 stop about 1km (⅔ mile) from the center of Nahuizalco but continue into the heart of each of the other villages. Bus no. 53d travels only between Sonsonate and Nahuizalco.

Each of the buses mentioned runs daily from roughly 5am to 6pm and costs between 25¢ and $1. The no. 205 bus from San Salvador runs about every 30 minutes, while the local buses come along about every 10 minutes.

It's easy to drive this route: All of the towns along the way are just a few minutes off main Hwy. CA-8 and are very well marked.

GETTING AROUND

Bus nos. 249 and 23 will take you from just outside Nahuizalco to each of the route's small towns. Once in each town, you'll be able to walk to whatever you'd like to see, except for the few hotels and restaurants that are scattered along the main highway. Las Rutas does not offer any taxis, but taxi driver **Israel Rodriguez** (② 503/7734-7598) in Sonsonate can take you from Sonsonate to Las Rutas and from town to town along the route for $15 to $25. Juayúa also offers three-wheeled moto-taxis, which you'll find along the square and which will take you anywhere in Juayúa for less than $1.

Visitor Information

A national tourist office branch is located at Km 82 Carretera CA-8, Salcoatitán (② 503/2401-8675; cat.rutasdelasflores@gmail.com). Tourist office staff speak only Spanish, but offer some bilingual pamphlets and brochures about the area. Office hours are Monday to Friday from 8am to 4pm and Saturday and Sunday from 9am to 1pm.

FAST FACTS Make sure you stock up on cash in Juayúa, which is the only town along the Ruta de las Flores with a bank machine. Most vendors and restaurants

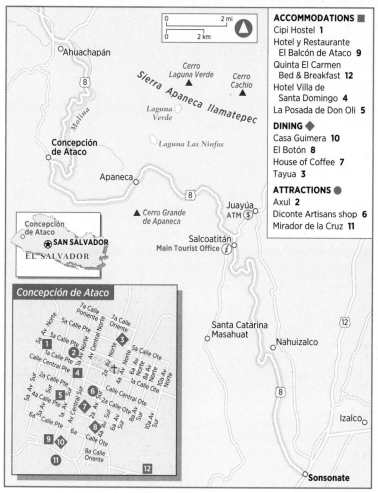

ACCOMMODATIONS ■
Cipi Hostel **1**
Hotel y Restaurante
  El Balcón de Ataco **9**
Quinta El Carmen
  Bed & Breakfast **12**
Hotel Villa de
  Santa Domingo **4**
La Posada de Don Oli **5**

DINING ◆
Casa Guimera **10**
El Botón **8**
House of Coffee **7**
Tayua **3**

ATTRACTIONS ●
Axul **2**
Diconte Artisans shop **6**
Mirador de la Cruz **11**

accept only cash in all five Ruta de las Flores towns. Internet access is available in Juayúa at **Nautilus Cyber** (Calle Merceditas Cáceres and 2a Av. Norte; ✆ **503/2452-2343**) and in Ataco at **Cyber Nautica** (2a Calle Poniente, No. 5, Barrio Santa Lucia; ✆ **503/2450-5719**). Small pharmacies are located in Juayúa near the main square.

Nahuizalco

Nahuizalco is the first stop on the Ruta de las Flores and offers one of the country's best furniture and wood craft markets. Unlike most Salvadoran markets, which sell Fernando Llort–inspired arts and crafts, Nahuizalco's market, along the town's main road every weekend, is known for its unique wicker and wood furniture creations.

SONSONATE: PREPPING FOR LA RUTA DE LAS FLORES

Sonsonate (65km/40 miles west of San Salvador) is mentioned here only because it is the largest city before the Ruta de las Flores and you'll likely either bus through or catch a connecting bus from here in order to reach the Ruta de las Flores. Sonsonate is not a city you should visit for fun. It's crowded and not that attractive. But it can be a good place to stock up on cash at the HSBC Bank or groceries at the large La Dispensa de Don Juan grocery store, both on the main square.

If you find yourself with a few hours here while you're waiting for a bus, Sonsonate does have one redeeming quality—**Parque Acuático Atecozol.** This is a huge water park about 10 minutes (about a $5 taxi ride) out of the city with lots of shady garden-like places to relax, a poolside restaurant, a kids' pool, and the biggest public pool with a water slide I've seen in El Salvador. The park is open daily from 8am to 4pm and admission is 80¢.

The quaint hotels of the Ruta de las Flores are only a few miles away, so you should really drive on there, but if you have to stay in Sonsonate, try the **Plaza Hotel** (9a Calle Oriente, Barrio El Angel, btw. Av. Nortes 8a and 10a; ✆ **503/2451-6628**; hotelplaza_sonsonate@yahoo.com). Rooms are $35 to $45 and the hotel features a pool and Internet access.

Many of the wares sold at the weekend market can be found during the week in the shops also lining the main road. One of the best is **Arte y Mueble,** or Art and Furniture (✆ **503/2453-0125**). The shop's furniture is handcrafted by owner Jose Luis, whose creations are a mix of spare, modern lines and sturdier, dark-wood, nature-inspired designs. The store, which can arrange shipping around the world, is open Tuesday through Sunday from 10am to 5pm. Another shop worth checking out is **Artesanias Cassal** (✆ **503/2453-0939**; open daily 8am–6pm), which offers interesting wooden masks, jewelry, and art. Finally, about half a block before Nahuizalco's church and square, on the right, is a building with a large, open door, allowing passersby to watch artisans handcraft furniture.

Nahuizalco is 72km (45 miles) west of San Salvador and is well marked off the main highway. A main road leads into town and terminates at Nahuizalco's small cathedral and square. The square offers a fountain, a few shady seating spots, and an English-language plaque that lists a short town history. Note that one of Nahuizalco's well-known attractions, the "candlelight market," no longer exists, at least in its old form. Vendors added electric light bulbs to this market a few years ago and now sell mostly family necessities, so it's not really worth visiting.

Salcoatitán

The second town along the Ruta de las Flores is also the route's smallest village. Though Salcoatitán is pleasant enough, there's no compelling reason to stop; it takes about 30 seconds to drive through town, and Nahuizalco and Juayúa's weekend markets are larger and more interesting. About 2 blocks before Salcoatitán is one of the route's more interesting restaurants, Los Patios.

Los Patios (Calle Principal, 2 blocks east of Salcoatitán; ✆ **503/2401-8590**) is an upscale, modern hacienda-style eatery. The restaurant's mountainview patio overlooks thousands of coffee beans laid out to dry and the machinery used to process them. Los Patios is a bit pricier than other area eateries at roughly $12 an entree, but the food and ambience are worth the price. The restaurant's owner is also an abstract Salvadoran sculptor who displays and sells her works from a gallery beside the restaurant.

Juayúa

Next up is the Ruta de las Flores's largest, most bustling town, offering the region's longest-running weekend food and artisan festival, as well as mountain and coffee plantation tours. Juayúa (pronounced *Hooyou-uh*) is a good place to base your Ruta de las Flores stay, as it is roughly in the middle of the route and boasts hotels, restaurants, supermarkets, and bank machines in addition to its attractions.

Each Saturday and Sunday, the large main plaza fills with locals and travelers enjoying daylong live music, dozens of artisan vendors, and a dozen or so food vendors who, for more than a decade, have been frying everything from *pupusas* to chicken tenders. It's a fun, family-friendly atmosphere worth planning your Ruta de las Flores trip around.

Juayúa is perhaps best known for its "black Christ" statue, which sits above the altar of the **Iglesia de Cristo Negro** cathedral on the main square. Visually, the black Christ looks just like a regular Christ statue painted black. But the concept of the black Christ dates back hundreds of years and is revered throughout Central America via annual black Christ celebrations, including a Juayúa festival each January 6 to January 15. La Iglesia is open daily from 6am to noon and 2 to 6pm, and admission is free.

Guided tours based out of Juayúa take hikers through coffee plantations, past towering waterfalls—including the well-known Los Chorros de la Calera—and up to natural hot springs and geysers. Bring a bathing suit, and prepare to get muddy (the mud at the hot springs is supposed to be good for the skin). Tours usually leave early in the morning, range from 5 to 7 hours, and cost $7 to $20. For tour information, visit **Hotel Anáhuac** (1a Calle Poniente and 5a Av. Norte; ✆ **503/2469-2401**).

WHERE TO STAY IN JUAYUA

Casa Mazeta Hostal　This yellow-and-brown corner house is both a funky lodge and an atmospheric hostel. It has only four rooms, one of which is a dorm. With its communal kitchen, TV room, and big garden, Casa Mazeta is geared for the young, independent traveler who is not afraid to do his or her own laundry in a huge laundry room—or you can pay somebody to do it for $3 a bag. High ceilings, dark-wood furnishings, traditional tiled floors, and arty fixtures like pewter relief doors make this place stand out from the average hostel. One small room out the back even has its own powerful fountain. It might not be as spick-and-span as the Hotel Anáhuac 4 blocks away but it has character and a great price. Useful touches are the large lockers in the dorm that will hold a backpack, and a secure garage.

1a Calle Ote at 2a Av. Norte. ✆ **503/2406-3403.** hostalcasamazeta@gmail.com. 4 units. $20 double. No credit cards. Free parking. **Amenities:** TV room; laundry service; Wi-Fi. *In room:* TV, fan.

Hotel Anáhuac ★★ ✦　This well-designed corner house offers a laid-back, hostel-style environment with a classy, boutique hotel touch. It has six shared and superbly decorated private rooms and a communal kitchen. Bright yellow walls and hip, artistic murals set the tone, with an overgrown garden courtyard decked out with wood sculptures and hammocks. The rooms are medium size, brightly lit, with skylights in the bathrooms and excellent local art from a particular artist. I stayed in the sculptor room and wanted to take several pieces with me. All the rooms open out onto the courtyard and overall the hotel has a cozy, earthy feel. There is a lobby computer for guests to use. The young owners, Cesar and Janne, are warm and welcoming and speak prefect English; they have lots of information about the route and surrounding areas and can organize tours.

1a Calle Poniente and 5a Av. Norte. ✆ **503/2469-2401.** www.hotelanahuac.com. 6 units. 2 dorms sleep 6, at $7 per person; $25 double with private bathroom. AE, DC, MC, V. Free parking. **Amenities:** Communal kitchen, living room w/TV; laundry service; Wi-Fi. *In room:* Fan, no phone.

Hotel y Restaurante El Mirador   Rooms here are basic but comfortable and efficient, with brightly colored walls and private bathrooms. All have tiled floors and face out onto a courtyard. Overall, the hotel is clean and comfortable, and it is just off the main square—you can't miss its bright blue-and-yellow facade. Perhaps Mirador's best features are its friendly staff and its airy, top-floor, glass-enclosed sitting and dining areas, which have incredible views of the surrounding countryside and distant volcanoes. There's also a computer in the lobby that guests can use, and they will book tours for you.

4a Calle Poniente on the left just as you enter town. ✆ **503/2452-2432.** www.elmiradorjuayua.com. 19 units. $28 double. AE, DC, DISC, MC, V. Free parking. **Amenities:** Restaurant; laundry service; Wi-Fi. *In room:* TV, fan.

Posada El Encanto   With its brick and cream-colored walls, this small hotel looks like a well-to-do residential home done in the faux colonial style. It certainly has a neat suburban feel, with tiled floors and white walls that lead to a tiny garden out back. The rooms are a decent size with solid dark-wood furniture and wardrobes and not a white plastic garden chair in sight. The eight rooms have private bathrooms and everything is well done and maintained. I'd still pip for Hotel Anáhuac for charm, character, and value, but if you want comfort and security, El Encanto is a decent, if bland, second choice. The hotel is 6 blocks east of the main plaza on the road to Santa Ana. Don't confuse it with the same-name establishment on the opposite side of the road (a sprawling restaurant, event venue, and pool area). They have the same owners but the restaurant and some other facilities. are open only on weekends. Hotel guests do have access to the pool.

✆ **503/2452-2187.** www.hotelelencanto.com. 8 units. $50 double; $32 single. Rates include breakfast. No credit cards. Free parking. **Amenities:** Pool; Wi-Fi. *In room:* A/C (in 3 rooms), fan, TV.

WHERE TO DINE IN JUAYUA

Among the better places to eat in Juayúa is **Restaurante R&R** (2 blocks off the main square at Calle Merceditas Cáceres, No. 1–2; ✆ **503/2452-2083**). English-speaking Salvadoran chef Carlos Cáceres has created a little Louisiana-style steakhouse in the midst of the Salvadoran mountains, and the menu features spicy takes on Tequila, Texas, and New Orleans–style steaks. The Texas steak is amazing. A veggie plate is also available and most items are $3.50 to $10. **Parque Restaurante La Colina** (Km 82 Carretera a Juayúa; ✆ **503/2452-2916**) is outside the town but worth the visit as it offers excellent—and hard to find—fajitas, along with other Mexican dishes and a host of grilled fish and meat dishes. Most entrees are $4.50 to $9.50. Besides R&R, Juayúa lacks a decent upscale restaurant in the center with good food and atmosphere.

A lovely little find is **Tienda San José** (2a Calle Pte; ✆ **503/2479-2349**), on the northeastern corner of the main plaza. It looks like just a shop piled high with toiletries until you turn left as you enter and find an old-world salon with pre-revolution decoration (pick which revolution) and sunflower-themed knickknacks. It's dark, it's grotty, but it has a cluttered charm and more important an excellent window table overlooking the color and chaos of the plaza outside. Popular with locals, the menu offers ribs, ribs, and more ribs, with some rice and salad added for variety. I could not fault it. Main courses range from $3 to $5 and it is open Monday to Friday 8:30am to 11pm and Saturday to Sunday 8:30am to midnight.

El Cadejo (Av. Daniel Cordon Norte and 1a Calle Ote.; ℓ **503/7352-7470**) is a funky, garage-style bar and restaurant that spills out onto the street Thursday to Sunday from 3pm to late. Live music, theater, and poetry make this colorful venue the bohemian center of Juayúa, and the restrooms are certainly the most interesting I have seen in a long time, with luminous figurines running across the cubicles. The bar is decorated with local art but don't criticize too loudly, as the barman is probably one of the painters. He'll serve you snacks and occasionally hard-to-get sushi. If you are here to drink, try the raspberry mojitos.

Apaneca

Continuing down CA-8 to Km 91, you'll find the village of Apaneca, which is surrounded by hills of flowering coffee plants and has become best known in the past couple of years for its high-wire, zip-line canopy tour. Information about Apaneca can be found at the local **Casa de la Cultura** (Av. 15 de Abril Sur and Calle Francisco Manendez Oriente, Barrio San Pedro; ℓ **503/2433-0163**).

Apaneca Canopy Tours (Av. 15 de Abril and Calle Central; ℓ **503/2433-0554**), which has an office in the center of town, offers 1-hour and 1½-hour zip-line tours, in which participants zip on steel cables hundreds of feet off the ground, over lush forests and a nearby coffee plantation. The company offers 13 cables that are roughly 1,800m (5,900 ft.) above sea level; its longest cable stretches 280m (919 ft.) and the highest is 125m (410 ft.) off the ground. During April and May, or coffee flowering season, thousands of white coffee flowers cover the fields below the tour, and in January and February, or harvest season, the flowers are replaced by bright red berries. Year-round, tour participants can see all the way to Guatemala's active Pacaya Volcano from the highest perch. Also included in the tour is a half-hour walk through a local coffee plantation during which an English-speaking guide explains the elements of the coffee plant and the growing process. The canopy tour even includes some locally grown brew to cap off your experience.

Tours are $30, and leave from the tour office Tuesday to Sunday at 9:30am, 11:30am, 3pm, and 7pm from June to October, and 7 days a week the rest of the year. It's best to make an appointment in advance, but you can also just show up at the times stated above to see if you can get a spot. Off-road **motorcycle** and **bicycling tours** can also be arranged through Apaneca Canopy Tours.

WHERE TO STAY

Hotel y Restaurante Las Cabañas This lovely 15-cabin hotel is owned by the same artist owner as Salcoatilán's Los Patios restaurant (see above), and she has applied her artistic eye for detail to create a lush, secluded garden setting dotted with individual cabins with shady front patios, and sculpture around the grounds. The cabins are simple, without an overarching design theme except bold colors and log wood trimmings. They are slightly larger than average and very comfortable. Las Cabañas is on Hwy. CA-8 and just a few blocks' walk from the Apaneca town center. Its hillside location affords lovely views of the green valley below, and the excellent **restaurant** has a handsome interior with wide, arched windows. It serves Salvadoran

Just 4km (2½ miles) before Ataco as you drive north from Apanecam, you will come across a slice of Eden known as **Entre Nubes** (Km 94; ℭ **503/2452-9643;** www.entrenubescafe.com). This garden restaurant (the name means "amidst the clouds") makes a perfect coffee stop while you're immersing yourself in the glories of Salvadoran nature. The owner's son, Daniel, is a trained agronomist and speaks perfect English. He's more than willing to give you a 20-minute walking tour of the 1.6-hectare (4-acre) hillside property. Paths covered with freshly cut cypress leaves lead you through lines of tall hardwood trees known as *gravileo* that shade coffee plants and big blue explosions of hortensia. You can pick fruit from orange, lemon, and mandarin trees and, if you are a city slicker, see where exactly avocados and plantains come from. You can do as the hummingbirds do and sip nectar from a yellow bell-like flower known as *thumbergia,* all the while listening to Daniel's enthusiastic and enlightening explanation of the life cycle of each plant, animal, and insect around you, including the cocoons that lie in the armpits of *ceiba* trees that transform into monarch butterflies. At the end of the tour, your host will give a homegrown coffee tasting and demonstration, in the midst of the garden fountains, hammocks, and abundant flowers. Entre Nubes is open every day from 8am to 6:30pm. Meals cost between $3.50 and $8 and all credit cards are accepted. Tours are free, but call ahead if you are in a large group. The roadside restaurant is on the right-hand side just after the Autogas station as you go north toward Ataco.

and international food with the focus on quality imported beef and homegrown vegetables and fruit.

Km 91 Hwy. CA-8, Apaneca. ℭ **503/2433-0500.** www.cabanasapaneca.com. 15 units. $52 double. Rates include breakfast. AE, DC, DISC, MC, V. **Amenities:** Restaurant. *In room:* Fan, TV, no phone.

Santa Leticia Mountain Resort ★ Situated 2km (1¼ miles) south of Apaneca, Santa Leticia Mountain Resort is a luxurious 19-room hotel and a 230-acre coffee plantation. A large log-cabin facade with a wooden porch leads to an atmospheric **restaurant** with funky-colored rooms out back and eight stand-alone bungalows. Rooms are spacious and cheerful, with multicolored fabrics, wrought-iron beds, and small, private bathrooms. The rooms open out onto a charming gallery with spindly tree-trunk pillars and roof rafters. Two solar-powered pools are center stage and the restaurant boasts all glass walls and a stone fireplace. The bungalows are larger and more private, with shaded porch areas and hammocks. You can take a tour of a nearby coffee farm, and there is a fascinating collection of pre-Columbian relics, including 2,000-year-old stone sculptures, located throughout the property.

Km 86.5 Hwy. CA-8, just outside Apaneca. ℭ **503/2433-0357** or 2298-2986. www.hotelsantaleticia. com. 19 units. $58 double; $68 cabin. AE, DC, DISC, MC, V. **Amenities:** Restaurant; children's playground; 2 pools. *In room:* Fan, TV.

Ataco ★★★

Ataco is my favorite stop along the Ruta de las Flores—it boasts an artistic style and vibe you really won't find anywhere else in the country.

The first things you may notice are the unique, fantastical murals of surreal animals with big eyes and wild hair on some of the town's buildings. These murals set the tone for the town and are the work of young married artists Cristina Pineda and Alvaro Orellana. Their designs, also available on wood, ceramic, and traditional canvas in Ataco's shops, are unlike artwork you'll see anywhere else in El Salvador. The couple's main gallery is called **Axul** (1a Calle Poniente and 1a Av. Norte, No. 5; © 503/2450-5030) and is just off the main square. The shop is marked by a mural on the outside and offers the couple's signature surreal style in various formats. You can chat with Pineda and Orellana and watch other artists at work in the back of the shop daily from 9am to 6pm.

Another of Ataco's attractions is the **Diconte artisans shop** (2 Av. Norte and Calle Central Oriente, No. 8; © 503/2450-5030; ring the doorbell to enter the shop on weekdays), which is part art shop, part textile mill, and part dessert bistro. Diconte offers five rooms of woodcarvings, paintings, and other crafts in the unique Ataco style, as well as a room of colorful textiles made on-site by artisans working five old-style looms. Visitors can watch the textile artisans at work from Diconte's garden-style dessert and coffee shop.

If you want to take a break from art shopping, hike up to the town's **Mirador de la Cruz.** The Mirador is a mountain overlook a 15-minute hike from the main square. To get there, walk 5 blocks south from the church along 2a Av. Norte, which becomes 2a Av. Sur after crossing Calle Central. Continue walking until the road bends to the right. At the bend is a Catholic church, behind which are steps to the overlook. At the end of the steps, turn right, walk through an opening in the fence, and follow the trail to the cross that marks the top of the hill. The hike up to the top is steep but paved, and you'll be rewarded with a great view, some benches to relax on, and a small plaque with information (in English) about Ataco.

WHERE TO STAY & DINE

Ataco booms on the weekends with locals coming from the capital and Sonsonate. For this reason, many hotels and restaurants are open on weekends only. **Hotel Villa de Santa Domingo** (1 Av. Norte, No. 6, in front of the Casa de la Cultura; © 503/ 2450-5242) is a good midrange choice, offering an 11-room hacienda-style hotel around a main courtyard with a small restaurant and comfortable $25-to-$35 rooms. On Friday and Saturday only, you can also stay at the well-known, but slightly over-rated—they have scaled back operations in recent years and service seems a bit lackluster now—**La Posada de Don Oli** (1a Av. Sur, No. 6; © 503/2450-5155). This half–private home/half-hotel offers a **restaurant** and three standard rooms situated around a courtyard, for $28. Ask for one of the upstairs rooms with a balcony for the best deal.

Cipi Hostel This is the best budget option in town. In fact, it is the only option in town if it is a Tuesday and you cannot manage the steep hill (or price) at El Balcón, which is the only other hotel open on weekdays in the town center. What Cipi's lacks in amenities is more than made up for by space, by cleanliness, and by Elena, the young, helpful, English-speaking owner. The garden is big and somewhat muddy, but if you can mange the steppingstones, they will bring you to a low, back garden building with seven colorful, airy rooms, four of which have basic but private bathrooms. A chorus of roosters will wake you in the morning, as will the thud of fruit falling on the rooftop. The owner also conducts walking tours of a nearby coffee farm with a 3-hour excursion costing $7 per person.

BO Sta. Lucia 1 Calle Poniente, No. 14. *C* **503/226-32324.** www.travellerspoint.com. 7 units. $25 double; $18 single. No credit cards. **Amenities:** Kitchen. *In room:* No phone.

Hotel y Restaurante El Balcón de Ataco ★   El Balcón is Ataco's only luxury option that stays open all week. The price just might be worth it, as this small six-room hotel is perched on the side of a hill high above town, with balconies offering long-range views of the town and surrounding mountains. The rooms have a modern feel; they're also unusually sunny and offer the convenience of in-room Wi-Fi. There's a full-service **restaurant** on-site, as well. If you don't want to experience a laid-back hostel vibe and prefer a few more amenities, you should stay here over Cipi Hostel.

8a Calle Oriente and Calle el Naranjito. *C* **503/2450-5171.** elbalcondeataco@gmail.com. 6 units. $35–$45. Rates include full breakfast. AE, DC, DISC, MC, V. **Amenities:** Restaurant. *In room:* TV, no phone, Wi-Fi.

Quinta El Carmen Bed & Breakfast ★   This low, red-brick villa, just outside the town, is surrounded by lush gardens and makes for a luxurious and interesting stay, not least because it has an adjacent coffee farm. Large rattan armchairs sit on a tiled patio that leads to well-appointed rooms with white walls and dark wooden rafters. A red carpet adorns an inviting living room next to an elegant dining room with indigenous handicrafts and textiles hanging on walls and sitting on shelf spaces. The rooms are ample, with lots of light and adjoining bathrooms and well-equipped kitchenettes. The **restaurant** serves standard fare such as burgers and *pupusas* and, of course, excellent coffee. Coffee tours are available and there are even land lots for sales if you would like a second home in the middle of a coffee farm. The entrance is on the right as you travel north to Ahuachapán and is a 15-minute walk from the town plaza.

Km 97, Ataco. *C* **503/2243-0304.** www.elcarmenestate.com. 4 units. $62 double; $93 suite. Rates include breakfast. AE, DC, DISC, MC, V. *In room:* TV, no phone, Wi-Fi.

WHERE TO DINE IN ATACO

One big reason Ataco is my top Ruta de las Flores pick is its unique restaurants. However, like the hotels, many restaurants and bars are open only on weekends. The ones listed below are open all week.

Casa Guimera ★ SPANISH   This low, cream-colored building used to be the well-respected Hostal Alepac before the owner fell in love and ran off with a Dutch backpacker. Now it has been reincarnated as one of the finest dining experiences in Ataco, a little two-roomed Spanish eatery with hundreds of tiny photos of satisfied customers lining the walls while a model of a Spanish galleon sails overhead and a grandfather clock ticks in the corner. Time passes quickly here as you work through delicious 8-ounce steaks, a variety of tapas, and a selection of wines from the vineyards of faraway La Rioja. Montse, the Spanish owner, is in attendance and speaks decent English. This cozy place is next to the white-domed chapel known as Iglesia El Calvara, 3 blocks west from the town entrance. There's a play area for kids, as well as a gift shop.

Secunda Av. Sur Final. *C* **503/2406-6312.** www.casaguimera.webs.tl. Main courses $7–$10. No credit cards. Tues–Fri 10am–9pm; Sat 8am–10pm; Sun 8am–5pm.

El Botón ★ FRENCH   This charming little French restaurant features a rare–in–El Salvador find of quiche and crepes, along with empanadas, coffee, and beer. The decor could be described as whimsical with a corner counter that also functions as a multicolored button display. Primary-colored furniture and flower-decorated shelves complete the picture. El Botón is certainly one of the most distinctive restaurants in El Salvador and comes alive on Saturday night with live music.

2a Av. Sur, No. 19. ℂ **503/2450-5066.** Main courses $7–$10. AE, DC, MC, V. Wed–Mon 10am–8pm; Sat 8am–11pm.

The House of Coffee ★ CAFE   *Rustic* is an adjective I'm guilty of overusing when describing establishments in rural El Salvador; however, it is *not* a term I can use here. With its slate gray walls, arty black-and-white photos, and dark leather seating, the House of Coffee is an island of style in a rugged, rural hamlet. Its moniker is to be taken seriously, with the focus of this hip cafe firmly on just that—*café*: where it comes from, what it is, and what they do to it. The Escalon family has been growing coffee since the 1880s, and this store is like a showroom for their passion. A glass partition with heaped beans inside overlooks a pleasant courtyard, in the corner of which is a stainless steel coffee roaster that produces 20 varieties of coffee, including Borgonna and Ristretto. The Café Pacamara recently won the Oscar of coffee awards known as "The Cup of Excellence." Besides hot coffee, cold coffee, and frozen cappuccinos, the menu also offers waffles, crepes, brownies, and crème brûlée. If you don't make it to Ataco, you can still get an upscale coffee fix in San Salvador, as there is a sister establishment at Plaza Futuro in front of the Crowne Plaza.

Av. Central 13. ℂ **503/2450 5353.** thoc@hotmail.el. Snacks $2.50. AE, DC, MC, V. Tues–Sun 9am–7pm.

Tayua SALVADORAN   The menu is small but surprising, with sandwiches, salads, and pasta. Standout items include the El Democratico sandwich, with mushrooms and Gruyère cheese on a baguette, and the El Variado—perhaps El Salvador's tastiest sandwich—with black forest ham, salami, and Gouda cheese on a baguette. Salads, pastas, and sandwiches range from $4 to $8. The place has a cool Asian-style decor.

Av. Central Norte, No. 31. No phone. Main courses $7–$10. AE, DC, MC, V. Sun–Fri 10am–8pm; Sat 8am–11pm.

WHERE TO STAY OUTSIDE ATACO

El Jardín de Celeste ★   The best value and most beautifully situated stay along the CA-8 highway is this small, 10-cabin hotel and restaurant 4km (2½ miles) east of Ataco. This beautiful complex is part lodge, part plant nursery and is set up like a secret garden, with log-style cabins spread among winding, flower-filled paths. The three- to five-person cabins have front porches with hammocks, barbecue grills, and, depending on the cabin, kitchens, dining rooms, and living rooms. All are simply furnished with white walls, tiled floors, and the occasional painting or textile. The suite is especially nice, with a fine four-poster bed draped in lace curtains. Flowers adorn every corner, including a handsome restaurant with carved doors, old elaborate pillars, nice wood furnishings, and an international menu.

Km 94 btw. Apaneca and Ataco. ℂ **503/2433-0277** or 2433-0281. www.eljardindeceleste.com. 10 units. $40–$63 cabin. AE, DC, DISC, MC, V. Free parking. **Amenities:** Restaurant. *In room:* TV, no phone.

Hotel Alicante ☺   Hotel Alicante is unbeatable when it comes to amenities. It offers a big Jacuzzi and sauna, an exercise room, and massage service, along with an outdoor pool, all spread out through a property of lush lawns, trees, and flower beds. A series of cabins and larger guesthouses feature tin roofs, varnished log walls, and rock pillars. The rooms are plain but cheerful (each has two double beds) and the two cabins on the property have compact kitchens and living areas, as well as private patios. It's excellent for families, with a playground and an elaborate circular pool with island bridge and waterfall. There is also a rather large, alpine-style **restaurant.**

Though it has nice views, the hotel is close to the highway and lacks a little of the tranquillity you'll find in other lodges in the area.

Km 93.3 Carretera CA-8, btw. Juayúa and Ataco. ℭ **503/2433-0572.** www.alicanteapaneca.com. 28 units. $70 double; $150 cabin. Rates include breakfast. AE, DC, DISC, MC, V. Free parking. **Amenities:** Restaurant; gym; Jacuzzi; pool; spa. *In room:* TV, fan, no phone.

Las Flores de Eloisa   Lovely little cabins set amid lush gardens seem to be the main theme with hotels in the area. It is no surprise, then, when you find out that Las Flores de Eloisa belongs to the same family as El Jardín de Celeste (see above). You have a plant nursery acting as the grounds, hiding several cabins with simple and attractive furnishings. The bungalows have lots of space with two separate rooms, bathrooms, and solid beds. The property also operates a garden **cafe** serving lunch and dinner.

Km 92.5, btw. Apaneca and Ataco. ℭ **503/2433-0415** or 2433-0277. www.eljardindeceleste.com. 7 units. $30 cabin. AE, DC, DISC, MC, V. Free parking. **Amenities:** Restaurant. *In room:* TV, no phone.

Ahuachapán

Like Sonsonate, Ahuachapán (44km/27 miles west of Sonsonate and 16km/10 miles off the route's main CA-8 highway) is technically part of the Ruta de las Flores, but as the busy capital of this department, it is more a place to grab some cash or check your e-mail before heading elsewhere. Ahuachapán is, however, known for its high level of geothermal activity, and visitors can tour nearby Los Ausoles, a gathering of gurgling, steaming pits of superheated mud and water, as well as check out the inside of a nearby power plant that transforms that subterranean heat into electricity. **Eco Mayan Tours** (Paseo General Escalón 3658, Colonia Escalón, San Salvador; ℭ **503/2298-2844;** www.ecomayantours.com) provides tours to the pits—including a chance to roast corn on the cob over them—and a tour of the plant. Tours are $30 from Ahuachapán or $75 to and from San Salvador.

Unlike in Sonsonate, there are also some sights to see in town. **Plaza Concordia** (3a Calle Poniente, btw. Av. Menendez and 4a Norte) is the more pleasant of the city's two plazas, which are just 5 blocks apart on the main street, Avenida Menendez. Concordia Plaza is home to Ahuachapán's main cathedral, **Nuestra Señora La Asunción,** which is known for its interesting stained-glass windows (I don't think they're that spectacular). The other main church in town, **Iglesia El Calvario,** is 5 blocks down from the Plaza Concordia on Avenida Menendez, and sports a similarly spartan exterior to the Nuestra Señora.

Most buses arrive and depart town from a crowded section of 10a Calle Oriente, a few minutes' moto-taxi ride from Plaza Concordia. A **Scotiabank** is at Avenida Menendez and 4 Calle Poniente, and there's Internet access at **Ciber Café Cetcomp** (2a Av. Sur at 1a Calle Poniente; ℭ **503/2413-3753**).

PARQUE NACIONAL EL IMPOSIBLE ★★ & TACUBA

If the mists clear, you can see all the way to Guatemala from the lookout points above El Salvador's most splendid park with the most wonderful name. Parque Nacional El Imposible has some unbelievable beauty and makes a brave attempt at making up for all the lost nature the rest of the country has suffered. Green, rugged hills hold gurgling streams, fern-lined waterfalls, moss-draped caves, and Maya petroglyphs.

Abundant with bird life and animal life, old coffee farms have become forests again, and fragrant flowers and pink mushrooms border the park's trails and eight rivers. Only 2 hours west of the capital, the park has two official entrances on its southern and western borders, though you might find it more convenient to enter by the northern back door through the sleepy town of Tacuba, at the extreme end of the Ruta de las Flores circuit.

Tacuba

60km (37 miles) W of Sonsonate; 100km (62 miles) W of San Salvador

Tacuba is a small town in far-western El Salvador that hugs the edge of the 3,278-hectare (8,100-acre) Parque Nacional El Imposible and serves as base camp for treks into the park. In addition to boasting great views of the mountains and volcanoes and a pretty central plaza, Tacuba has enough *tiendas* to keep you stocked up on food and drink and happy after a long day's hike. This area had very few tourists until recently, and it's still slowly developing its infrastructure. Currently, there are no banks or ATMs and only two viable lodging options, so plan your accommodations in advance and bring all the cash you'll need.

Essentials

GETTING THERE & GETTING AROUND

Buses coming to Tacuba from around El Salvador go into nearby Ahuachapán, from where you can catch **bus no. 264** or one of the many buses with TACUBA written across the top. The trip takes 40 minutes and costs 60¢. You'll be dropped off a couple of blocks from Tacuba's town square. From San Salvador to Ahuachapán, take **bus no. 202** (2¼ hr., $1.10); from Santa Ana to Ahuachapán, take **bus no. 210** (1¼ hr., 50¢); and from Sonsonate to Ahuachapán, take bus no. 249 (2 hr., $1).

From San Salvador, you can drive the **Pan-American Highway** (Carretera Panamericana) in the north or **CA-8** along the Ruta de las Flores in the south to the town of Ahuachapán. In Ahuachapán, look for Parque Concordia and the white church there, where you'll see a sign directing you onto the road for Tacuba. The drive from Ahuachapán takes about 30 minutes.

Tacuba is a very small town, and nearly everything is within a short walk of the main square.

VISITOR INFORMATION

Tacuba does not have a tourist office, so the best source of information is local English-speaking guide **Manolo Gonzales** (𝄞 **503/2417-4268;** www.imposible tours.com)—he's one of the best in the whole region. If you speak Spanish, information is also available at Tacuba's **Casa de la Cultura** (1a Calle Oriente and Av. España, 1 block south of the Alcaldía; 𝄞 **503/2417-4453**).

FAST FACTS   Tacuba has no banks or ATMs, so bring cash. But Tacuba's main street, Avenida Cuscatlán Sur, south of the square, offers a few small *tiendas* and shops with signs reading CIBER, where there are a few Internet-access computer stations.

Since there is no official northern entrance to the park, it's easiest to go with Tacuba's well-known, English-speaking guide Manolo Gonzales. Manolo is the owner of **Imposible Tours** (Av. Cuscatlán near Calle 10, Tacuba; 𝄞 **503/2417-4268;** www.imposibletours.com) and the son of the owners of Hostal de Mama y Papa (see below). Manolo offers 6- to 8-hour day and night tours into the park for $20 per person, including the entrance fee. His most popular tour is an 8-hour waterfall tour, which involves hiking for hours deep into the jungle and jumping from waterfalls ranging from 2 to 12m (6½–39 ft.) in height. On this tour, you'll have to jump or be lowered down the highest waterfall, in addition to taking part in hours of rigorous hiking. **Note:** If you're out of shape or afraid of heights, the tour may not be for you.

Manolo offers an easier $20 coffee plantation and hot springs tour in which you witness the entire coffee cultivation process from field to factory, or bean to cup, and then head into the mountains to spend the afternoon soaking in hot springs. There's also a 2-day bicycle tour in which participants are driven to the highest point in the park and ride bicycles down through the jungle all the way to the Pacific Ocean. The rock-bottom $55 cost includes round-trip transportation from Tacuba, dinner and drinks at the beach, breakfast, lunch, and a kayak tour, along with stops at some towns along the Ruta de las Flores. Other tours include a night animal-watching tour and a tour in which you're driven to the park's highest point before hiking down to a natural swimming pool. Try to call at least 2 days in advance to schedule tours.

Exploring Parque Nacional el Imposible ★★

Parque Imposible is one of El Salvador's most lush and most diverse forests and should be a definite stop for nature lovers. The 3,278-hectare (8,100-acre) park derives its name from its challenging terrain and once-dangerous gorge, which for years claimed the lives of men and mules who traversed the area transporting coffee crops to the south. The animals had to be blindfolded so terrifying was the crossing, with a narrow ridge and a drop of 3,000m (9,840 ft.) on either side. A bridge was built over the gorge in the 1960s and celebrated with a plaque declaring *May 1968—No Longer Impossible.* The forest was declared a national park in 1989. Today, the park is home to more than 400 types of trees, 275 species of birds, and hundreds of species of butterflies. Pumas, wild pigs, and 100 types of mammals, many on the endangered species list, make their home in the park along with more than 50 kinds of reptiles and amphibians. In addition to ample opportunities to spot wildlife, visitors can easily spend days hiking trails through the thick forests, swimming in the natural pools, and jumping off the waterfalls here.

Park admission is $6 per person. All visitors must first register with park administrator **SalvaNatura** (33 Av. Sur, No. 640, Colonia Flor Blanca, San Salvador; ⓒ **503/2279-1515;** www.salvanatura.org) to secure a guide and get permission to enter the park. SalvaNatura also offers $10-per-day Spanish-language guides and $40 day trips from San Salvador including transportation, a Spanish-speaking guide, and entrance fee.

The official park entrance is on the park's south side near the community of San Benito. To enter from the south, beginning in Sonsonate, catch bus no. 24-HAS to Cara Sucia. In Cara Sucia, you can catch a $1 pickup ride for the remaining 45 minutes to the park. The pickups leave Cara Sucia at 6:30am, 8am, 10am, 12:30pm, and 2:30pm. They leave the park to return to Cara Sucia at 7am, 9am, 11am, noon, and 2pm. You can also make the drive yourself, but the road is very bumpy and requires a four-wheel-drive or truck with good ground clearance. There is a new entrance farther west at San Francisco Menendez, the turnoff for which is 5km (3 miles) west of Cara Sucia.

Centro de Visitantes Mixtepe Located 100m (328 ft.) inside the San Benito entrance, this old wooden house has been restored and turned into a simple museum and solar-powered interpretation center. The colorful rooms hold the park's administration office and are where you go to pick up your guide to show you around the park. There are some display cases explaining the park's different facets, as well as a very bare-bones gift store and bookshop. A lookout gives you a sense of place with the Pacific and Guatemala in the distance. It is not necessarily a place you want to hang around too long, as all the interesting stuff is outside in the forest, though you will be thankful for the restrooms.

San Benito Entrance, Parque Nacional El Imposible. No phone. www.salvanatura.org. Free admission.

TRAILS WITHIN PARQUE IMPOSIBLE

Guides are obligatory and will be assigned to you at the visitor center. The three main trails are not too difficult and it is possible to switch and combine. A $10 tip per group to the guide is customary, as guides receive no salary. The easiest trek is to **Mirador El Mulo,** a lookout point with lovely views of the Río Guayapa valley. The 1km (.6-mile) trail is signposted with displays explaining the local flora and fauna. You will pass a river source and the old coffee plantations now replaced by forest. Farther past Mirador Mulo there is another viewing point called **Mirador Madre Cacao.** The trail then drops drastically toward a beautiful river pool called **Los Enganches,** approximately 3.5km (2.2 miles) from the trail start. Back up the hill on the trail that passed Mirador Madre Cacao, the path continues upriver for 1km (⅔ mile) until you reach a waterfall and pool. Here you'll find a carved stone known as **Piedra Sellada,** adorned with Mayan script that dates from A.D. 1500. The trail to **Cerro El León** is the most ambitious, with a steep 4km (2½-mile) hike to the park's tallest mountain at 1,113m (3,561 ft.). The trail leaves from the visitor center and descends into a jungle gorge before emerging on the other side through a dense forest to the peak, which needless to say has some beautiful panoramic views.

Where to Stay & Dine in Tacuba

Hostal de Mama y Papa ★   This small, well-known hostel lives up to its reputation as the place to stay in Tacuba. The setting is lush and garden-like, with a few hillside rooms offering patios and views. Numerous animals run around the place and there's an actual Mama and Papa tending to the property who'll make you feel right at home. (Mama also runs the hostel's **restaurant** about 91m/300 ft. down the road.) As with many of the country's small, independent hotels, don't expect state-of-the-art rooms or fancy decor. The rooms are average size and the bathrooms are merely functional. But the vibe is friendly and you'll get to hang out with the English-speaking guide Manolo (see "Exploring Parque Nacional El Imposible," above), who lives here. Note that the guest rooms have no locks, but the owners can lock valuables in the office.

Av. Cuscatlán near Calle 10. ✆ **503/2417-4268.** 5 units. $6 per bed in dorms; $15 per person private rooms. No credit cards. **Amenities:** Restaurant nearby; kitchen. *In room:* Fan upon request, no phone.

Hostal y Restaurante Miraflores   A low red-brick building with green doors and an arched entrance leads to a lush courtyard surrounded by five basic rooms. The rooms are clean but the shared bathroom could do with a scrub. *Note:* There is no hot water. Small and humble, the Miraflores should be your third choice if the other two hotels listed here do not work out. It does have a pretty good **restaurant** with a varied menu, including Chinese, Mexican, and Italian.

2a Av. Norte at 7a Calle Ote. ✆ **503/2417-4746.** miraflores@hotmail.com. 5 units. $23–$29 double. No credit cards. **Amenities:** Restaurant; kitchen. *In room:* Fan, no phone.

Las Cabañas de Tacuba Hotel y Restaurante   Las Cabañas is where you should stay if Mama y Papa's is already booked. It's certainly nice enough, but not as handy as a base camp for trips into Parque Imposible; hotel staff will even tell you to go to Mama y Papa's for any info about the park. Though the property consists of just a few rooms contained in pretty nondescript buildings, the grassy grounds of the hotel are pleasant and there's a big pool (which was being repaired at press time) and an open-air **restaurant.** The rooms are nothing special in terms of size or ambience, though the newer "cabins" beside the pool are the best value.

1a Calle Poniente, roughly 90m (300 ft.) down the hill from the Alcaldía, Barrio San Nicolás. © **503/2417-4332.** 12 units. $35–$45 double. Rates include full breakfast. V. **Amenities:** Restaurant; pool. In room: Fan, TV.

Where to Stay in Parque El Imposible

In addition to the ecolodge below, Parque Nacional El Imposible offers three camp-sites for $4 per night. Facilities are basic with no showers, though there is a river close by that you can bathe in without using soap or shampoo.

El Imposible Eco Lodge ★★   Five six-person cabins are just 800m (2,625 ft.) from the park entrance at San Benito, on the southern fringes of the park. Set on the side of a hill, the cabins are basic, A-frame wooden structures, but they are large and handsome, with all-wood walls and private verandas with easy chairs and ham-mocks. Inside they are spacious, with room for one double bed and four bunks. As they are quite spread out, they offer lots of privacy. On the top of the hill is a restau-rant called **Ixcanal** with red-brick walls and wood trimmings, serving simple regional dishes. There's also a small rock-lined pool with natural spring water. The lodge also functions as a research center for the NGO SalvaNatura and is solar-powered, with an organic compost waste system.

Caserio San Miguelito, San Benito. © **503/2411-5484** or 7700-4699. www.elimposible-ecolodge.com. 5 units. $30 double; $55 cabin. No credit cards. **Amenities:** Restaurant; pool. In room: Fan, no phone.

SANTA ANA & NORTHWESTERN EL SALVADOR

64km (40 miles) W of San Salvador

Though El Salvador's charms aren't normally found in its crowded, hectic cities, Santa Ana's unique Gothic cathedral, ornate theater, and easy access to the country's most significant Maya ruin make it a place worth visiting.

Santa Ana, an easy, 40-minute drive west of San Salvador, is the country's second-largest city, with approximately 275,000 residents. Yet Santa Ana avoids the sprawling nature of San Salvador because most of its attractions are centered around the city's leafy main square, known as **Parque Libertad.** The city's main in-town attractions are its large, neo-Gothic cathedral and ornate and brightly painted theater. Both are among the county's more architecturally interesting landmarks. The plaza itself also offers a glimpse into old and new El Salvador, with young, mohawk-sporting skate punks in stylish clothes mingling with older women in traditional dress.

Perhaps the best reason to visit Santa Ana is that El Salvador's most important Maya ruin, Tazumal, is only a 13km (8-mile) bus ride away. Santa Ana also offers the modern conveniences of bank machines, Internet outlets, and a super grocery store. Though it was once the county's most prosperous town, it now has some unsafe

ACCOMMODATIONS ■
Hotel Libertad **5**
Hotel Sahara **1**
Tolteka Plaza **4**

DINING ◆
Lover's Steak House **2**
Restaurante La Pampa
Argentina **3**

ATTRACTIONS ●
Centro de Arte
Occidental **9**
El Teatro Nacional
de Santa Ana **6**
La Catedral de la Señora
de Santa Ana **7**
Museo Regional
del Occidente **10**
Palacio Municipal **8**

neighborhoods. The tourist-filled main plaza and its immediate surroundings are safe and well patrolled, however.

Essentials

GETTING THERE

BY BUS From San Salvador, take **bus no. 201** to Santa Ana's Metrocentro terminal (at 10a Av. Sur; no phone). The trip takes about 1½ hours and costs $1 to $1.50.

Buses to and from Metapán (p. 312) leave from Santa Ana's Metrocentro terminal. **Bus no. 218** to Tazumal leaves from the corner of 4a Av. Sur and 9a Calle Poniente. Lago de Coatepeque (p. 308) can be reached via **bus no. 209** from either the Metrocentro terminal or in front of La Universidad Catolica de Occidente. All these buses leave approximately every 20 minutes, and rates start as low as 35¢.

BY CAR   Simply follow the signs on your 1-hour drive west from San Salvador along the well-paved and well-marked **Pan-American Highway,** and you'll reach Santa Ana.

ORIENTATION

Santa Ana is a large city but is easily navigated, as most everything you need is on or near Parque Libertad (the center of the city). The main east-west thoroughfare near the central plaza is Calle Libertad Poniente, which becomes Libertad Oriente east of Parque Libertad. And the main north-south route is Avenida Independencia Sur, which becomes Independencia Norte north of the plaza. The character of the surrounding neighborhoods around Parque Libertad can change quickly, especially after dark, so don't wander too far off the main plaza.

GETTING AROUND

BY BUS   The only bus you'll likely take while in Santa Ana will be bus no. 51, which runs every 5 minutes from 8am to 10pm daily from the main square to the Metrocentro mall. The main terminal at 10a Av. Sur is crowded and the buses there often take a while to depart. Rates within the city run 25¢.

BY TAXI   Taxis are easily found on or near Parque Libertad and cost $4 to $6 to most parts of Santa Ana. Taxis are not easy to find off the main square, so you'll need to ask your hotel or restaurant to call you a cab in other areas of town; always take a taxi at night, even if it's just for a few blocks.

BY CAR   As in San Salvador, it's best to park your car immediately upon arrival. Many of Santa Ana's streets are poorly marked, so it's easy to get lost. And the character of Santa Ana's neighborhoods can change abruptly, so you don't want to take too many wrong turns. Off-street parking is recommended.

ON FOOT   Most everything you'll want to see is on Parque Libertad or within a couple of blocks of the square. You'll need a taxi to reach a few of the better hotels and restaurants, but otherwise you can walk to almost everything.

VISITOR INFORMATION

Santa Ana does not have a tourist office, so your best source of tourist information will be your hotel staff or an English-language tour guide provided by a company such as **Nahuat Tours** (© **503/7874-8402;** www.nahuatours.com). If you speak Spanish, Santa Ana's **Casa de la Cultura** (2a Calle Poniente; © **503/2447-0084**) can also provide information.

FAST FACTS   Scotiabank is 1 block off the Parque Libertad behind the Municipal Palace at the corner of Calle Libertad and 2a Av. Norte. The bank has two external ATMs. Internet access can be found at **SGD/Soluciones Graficas Digitales** (Calle Libertad Poniente; © **503/2447-2750**), which is upstairs in a small shopping center on the southeast corner of the square.

Santa Ana's post office is 4 blocks south of the square at 7a Calle Poniente, No. 30, near the corner of 7a Calle Poniente and Avenida Independencia Sur (© **503/2441-0084**). The city's main hospital, **Hospital Nacional Regional San Juan de Dios,** is at Final 13 Av. Sur, No. 1 (© **503/2447-9037**). An outlet of El Salvador's supercenter grocery store **La Dispensa de Don Juan,** which offers just about everything you won't find in smaller towns, is on Parque Libertad's southeast corner.

Festivals

If you are in Santa Ana in July, check out the **"Fiestas Julias"** or the July Festival. This month-long celebration involves parades, carnival rides, and music and is also known as Fiesta Patronal, since it honors the city's patron saint.

What to See & Do

Santa Ana's main attractions are its Gothic-style cathedral, old-world-style theater, and the Maya ruins of Tazumal. Many also visit to stock up on supplies at the city's modern grocery store before heading to the Parque Montecristo (p. 312).

Santa Ana's primary in-town attraction, **La Cathedral de la Señora de Santa Ana** (1a Av. Norte, Parque Libertad; ✆ **503/2447-7215;** free admission; Mon–Sat 6:30am–noon and 2–5:30pm, Sun 7am–noon and 2–5:30pm), offers a more elaborate, European, neo-Gothic style than El Salvador's traditional white Spanish colonial churches. The cathedral, built between 1906 and 1913, features an exterior with lots of old-world-style nooks, crannies, and arches with bell towers on each side. The interior has grand columns and a beautiful marble altar.

El Teatro Nacional de Santa Ana (Parque Libertad; ✆ **503/2447-6268**) is not only one of El Salvador's most attractive buildings, but also likely its most lime green. The odd and nearly fluorescent exterior color is the first thing you'll notice about this theater, which opened in 1910 and features a grand balcony overlooking the square. Inside you'll find an ornate, old-world lobby leading to the grand, three-story theater, complete with elaborate molding and ceiling portraits of long-dead artists. Two rows of balconies line the walls and an intricate tile floor fronts that stage. The theater is open Monday to Friday from 8am to noon and 2 to 6pm, as well as Saturdays 8am to noon, with art performances and exhibits held year-round. Call the theater for performance dates and times. Shows cost 50¢ to $3 or you can just take a look inside for a 50¢ admission fee.

The **Centro de Arte Occidental** (✆ **503/2447-6045**), opposite the Santa Ana theater, once housed an art museum, but now primarily offers arts classes to local children. You can poke around the mildly interesting building for free if you ask at the front desk. Two blocks southwest of the square, in the city's old Banco Central de Reserva building, is the **Museo Regional del Occidente** (Av. Independencia Sur, No. 8; ✆ **503/2441-1215**), with rotating exhibits covering the natural, social, and economic development of the western region, including a permanent, in-depth history of the country's currency. Admission is $1 and the museum is open Tuesday through Saturday from 9am to noon and 1 to 5pm.

Also on the square is the **Palacio Municipal,** which is Santa Ana's town hall and is usually filled with folks standing in line to do all the things one does at city hall. Though there's not much to see here overall, the palace's courtyard is surprisingly inviting and serves as a respite of peace and quiet from Santa Ana's more hectic main square. You can peek in for free from 8am to noon and 2 to 6pm Monday through Saturday. Another building into which you can peek, depending on your charm and language skills, is the **Casino Santaneco.** This private club across from the national theater features a swank, restored interior that's not open to the public but can be glimpsed if you convince the guy at the front door to let you in.

OUTSIDE SANTA ANA

Parque Arqueológico Casa Blanca ♟ Casa Blanca is a smaller Maya site worth seeing mostly because it's a 5-minute taxi ride from Tazumal. Casa Blanca is basically a leafy park with a Spanish-language museum and a winding, 15-minute trail passing a few grassy mounds; one slightly excavated, two-story mound with exposed stone steps; and the park's main attraction, a 9m-tall (30-ft.), partially excavated Maya pyramid. Casa Blanca isn't worth traveling all the way from Santa Ana to see, but if you're in the area, you might want to stop by.

Km 74.5 on the bypass at the east entrance to Chalchuapa. ℂ **503/2408-4641.** Admission $3 adults. Tues–Sun 9am–4:30pm. Bus: 210 from Santa Ana or 218 from Santa Ana to Tazumal.

Sitio Archeologico Tazumal ★★★   If you had to choose only one ruin to visit in El Salvador, this should be it. Tazumal is the county's most visually interesting and fully excavated set of Maya ruins. Located 13km (8 miles) from Santa Ana, Tazumal, which means "the place where the victims were burned" in the early Ki'che language, is the remains of a Maya community that inhabited the area from A.D. 100 to 1200. It's believed that Tazumal functioned as an important trading center, and much of the site remains unearthed. Most of the construction here is believed to have taken place from A.D. 400 to 680, so there are signs of a definite Teotihuacan influence (the Mexican site reached its peak during the same period) in many structures.

On view are 10 sq. km (3¾ sq. miles) of ruins, including a fully excavated Maya temple pyramid, ball court, and other structures considered to be classic examples of Maya architecture and similar to those found in other parts of Central America. The park also contains numerous other structures that archaeologists are leaving covered until proper funding and care can be ensured; in addition, officials are returning the main pyramid to its natural state via the removal of a cement shell that was once thought protective but later deemed unnecessary. Visitors are no longer allowed to climb any structures due to damage from the 2001 earthquake.

The site also includes a small museum with a number of artifacts that indicate that this society was in contact with other Central American Maya communities. Though it's much smaller than better-known ruins in Guatemala or Honduras, and requires only about 45 minutes to explore, Tazumal's importance to El Salvador's history and its Maya architecture make it worth the drive. Most tour companies such as the local company **Nahua Tours** (ℂ **503/7874-8402**) and the larger **Eco Mayan Tours** (ℂ **503/ 2298-2844;** www.ecomayantours.com) make stops here.

Entrance on Calle Tazumal in Chalchuapa. ℂ **503/2444-0010.** Admission $3 adults, free for children 4 and under. Tues–Sun 9am–4pm. Bus: 218 from Santa Ana stops 547m (1,800 ft.) from the entrance.

Shopping

Though Santa Ana doesn't have any small shops worth mentioning, it does have a large, modern shopping mall called **Metrocentro** (ℂ **503/2440-6277**). It's on Final Avenida Independencia Sur and is open daily from 9am to 9pm.

Where to Stay

Hotel Libertad ★ 🍴   If you don't need anything fancy, stay here. Hotel Libertad is as bare-bones as it gets. There's no hot water, no Internet, and no restaurant. But it's safe, clean, and just 1 block off Parque Libertad—which means it's minutes away from the cathedral, theater, restaurants, and most of what you'll need in Santa Ana. Because Parque Libertad is Santa Ana's tourist center, the area is also safe and well patrolled by police. The hotel will not exactly grace the pages of interior design magazines, but it's well maintained and the staff will go out of their way to meet your demands. When booking a room, ask for room no. 15 or 16, both of which are upstairs and farthest away from the lobby.

4a Calle Oriente, No. 2, 1 block north of the square (near the corner of Calle Oriente and 1a Av. Norte). ✆ **503/2441-2358.** 12 units. $12–$20 double. No credit cards. *In room:* Fan, TV, no phone.

Hotel Sahara ★ ✋ Despite its 50-year reputation as Santa Ana's grand hotel, Sahara really isn't that grand. Hotel Tolteka Plaza offers more amenities and Hotel Libertad is a lot cheaper. But when you combine location and comfort, Sahara ekes out a victory. It's 5 blocks from Parque Libertad, offers the convenience of a full-service **restaurant** and Wi-Fi, and has a rooftop deck. The rooms are of average size and the bathrooms even smaller; request room no. 204, which is the biggest, or room no. 215, which offers the most peace and quiet. The area between the hotel and the main square bustles with a street market during the day but can be dangerous at night. Always have the front desk call you a cab after dark.

3a Calle Poniente, btw. Av. Sur and Av. José Matías Delgado. ✆ **503/2447-8865.** Fax 503/2447-0456. hotel_sahara@yahoo.com. 30 units. $44–$58 double. Rates include full breakfast. AE, DC, DISC, MC, V. **Amenities:** Restaurant. *In room:* A/C, TV, Wi-Fi.

Tolteka Plaza ★ Tolteka is Santa Ana's most modern and luxurious hotel option. The rooms are larger than you might expect, and the hotel offers a rare-outside-San-Salvador hot water heating system (rather than the usual electronic shower heads). There's also an inviting courtyard pool, Wi-Fi, and a full-service restaurant. The hotel is just a short taxi ride or long walk to the Metrocentro bus terminal, which also means it's about a 10-minute cab ride to Parque Libertad. As part of a national hotel chain, the Tolteka also has a rather corporate feel, with no unique charm and no interesting decor. When booking, try to reserve room no. 101, 106, 201, 219, or 220, as they overlook the pool and are farthest from street noise. The English-speaking staff can arrange tours or a taxi to Parque Libertad.

Av. Independencia Sur. ✆ **503/2487-1000.** Fax 503/2479-0868. www.hoteleselsalvador.com/hotel tolteka. 50 units. $59–$71. AE, DC, DISC, MC, V. **Amenities:** Restaurant; bar; pool; room service; smoke-free rooms; Wi-Fi in lobby. *In room:* A/C, TV, hair dryer.

Where to Dine

Lover's Steak House ★★ ☺ STEAK Lover's Steak House is nearly as tasty as its rival La Pampa, but with a more casual, family-friendly atmosphere. Bench seating and beer-brand advertising set the laid-back tone of this 18-year-old restaurant. The English and Spanish menu is larger than La Pampa's and includes North American comfort food such as chicken wings, hamburgers, and a club sandwich. Portions are also larger, with bigger baked potatoes and lots of vegetables. Since Lover's and La Pampa are about evenly priced and both require a taxi ride, your choice depends on your mood. If you want an upscale, romantic dinner, head to La Pampa. If you have a talkative group, have a few kids, or just want a casual vibe, Lover's is the better choice.

4a Av. Sur and 17 Calle Poniente. ✆ **503/2440-5717.** Reservations required for groups of 10 or more. Main courses $9–$22. AE, DC, DISC, MC, V. Sun–Thurs 11am–10pm; Fri–Sat 11am–11pm.

Restaurante La Pampa Argentina ★★★ STEAK/ARGENTINE La Pampa steakhouse is by far Santa Ana's finest restaurant, and it serves what is likely to be one of the tastiest steaks you'll have in El Salvador. The restaurant is styled after and shares a menu with the well-known San Salvador steakhouse of the same name. You'll need a taxi and a few minutes to get here, but it's worth the trip. The modern, hacienda-style interior is elegant but comfortable, with tables far enough apart to allow for quiet conversation. Upstairs seating overlooks the main dining room and includes two small outdoor terraces. The service is outstanding and on par with that at San Salvador's finest restaurants, with Spanish-speaking waiters able to explain the intricacies of the steaks and cuts. The menu offers 15 steak and sausage options along with fish and chicken dishes, but the specialty of the house is the 224-gram (8-oz.) *entraña,* or skirt-cut steak. Every large steak platter is served with salad, vegetables, potatoes, and a delicious beef consommé.

25 Calle Poniente, btw. 10a and 12a Av. Sur. ⓒ **503/2406-1001.** Reservations recommended. Main courses $10–$25. AE, DC, DISC, MC, V. Mon–Thurs 11am–3pm and 6–10pm; Fri–Sun 11:30am–11:30pm.

LAGO DE COATEPEQUE ★★

18km (11 miles) S of Santa Ana; 56km (35 miles) W of San Salvador

Lago de Coatepeque, an almost perfectly round crater lake 740m (2,428 ft.) above sea level, makes for one of El Salvador's most beautiful and enjoyable getaways. The lake is a short drive from Santa Ana, which means it's an easy day trip from that town—but it's worth staying a couple of days to enjoy all its attractions; the 23-sq.-km (9-sq.-mile) pristine lake is ideal for swimming, fishing, riding watercraft, and soaking in beautiful views.

Lago Coatepeque was formed thousands of years ago by the eruption of the nearby ancient volcano, the Coatepeque Caldera. Today, the lake's rich blue waters and lush, tree-filled crater walls serve as a weekend getaway for El Salvador's rich and famous, whose mansions line the shore. Luckily, those rich and famous folks left a roughly 500m (1,640-ft.) section open to the public, which is now filled with restaurants and hotels offering tours, watercraft rentals, and fishing piers. There's little lake access other than through these hotels or restaurants, but most allow single-day use of their piers for a small fee. Perhaps the highlight of any visit is the sunsets: Each evening, visitors line the hotel piers with cameras ready to capture classic and captivating photos of the sun dipping below the crater walls.

Essentials
GETTING THERE
BY BUS   From Santa Ana (p. 302), take bus **no. 209** or **220.** From San Salvador (p. 234), take **bus no. 201.** Tell the driver you want to go to Lago Coatepeque and he'll let you off anywhere you wish along the lake's strip of hotels and restaurants. The ride from Santa Ana takes a little less than 1 hour; the ride takes an hour and a half from San Salvador.

BY CAR   From San Salvador, travel west and from Santa Ana travel east along the well-paved **Pan-American Highway** and follow the well-marked signs to the lake. After reaching the lake area, you'll drive slowly down a winding dirt road along the crater wall to the water. Lago Coatepeque includes only one small section of hotels, so if you get lost, just say, "Los Hoteles?" and locals will point you in the right direction.

ORIENTATION & GETTING AROUND
The majority of Lago Coatepeque's hotels and restaurants are along a single, approximately 500m (1,640-ft.) stretch of the lake. A dirt road rings the lake and is lined with

a nearly unbroken stretch of high, cement walls hiding the lake houses of the nation's wealthy.

The best way to get around this area is on foot; the hotels and restaurants are within walking distance of one another, and some great views can be had by taking a long stroll around the lake. If you are driving, keep in mind that the dirt road around the lake is rocky and best navigated by truck or four-wheel-drive.

You'll need to call a taxi, such as the local company **Taxi Leo** (© **503/2502-2495**), in advance to take you to Santa Ana or the region's other attractions, since taxis can't be hailed on the street.

VISITOR INFORMATION

Lago Coatepeque doesn't have a visitor center, so your best source of information will be hotel staff or tour companies such as Santa Ana–based, bilingual, **Nahua Tours** (© **503/7874-8402**). The closest **national tourist office** is along the Ruta de las Flores 1km (⅔ mile) east of the town of Nahuizalco (Km 71, Nahuizalco; © **503/2453-1082;** Mon–Fri 8am–5pm, Sat–Sun 8am–4pm). You can also call the national tourist office in San Salvador (© **503/2243-7835**) for info.

There are no bank machines, Internet cafes, or large stores in the area.

What to See & Do

Lago de Coatepeque is primarily a place to lounge by the water, take a swim, or just enjoy the view. For day-trippers, the best deal is the $2-per-day fee to use the pier and $4-per-hour kayak rental offered at Hostal Amacuilco (see below). Or stop by Restaurante Las Palmeras (see below), which offers $70-per-hour motorized watercraft rental and 30-minute to 3-hour lake tours for $25 to $80.

Where to Stay

Lago de Coatepeque can be a great place to base your exploration of this part of the country, because the archaeological sites of Tazumal, San Andres, and Joya de Cerén, as well as the hiking trails and vistas of Parque Nacional Los Volcanes, are all within 1 hour's drive. Below are your best accommodations options.

Hostal Amacuilco ★ 🍴   If you like a laid-back hostel vibe, you'll love Amacuilco. Amacuilco offers nearly everything you'll find at Villa Serena and Torremolinos, only cheaper and with less formality. This small (just five rooms), family-friendly hostel sits right on the water and has a lakeview restaurant, a pier, and the most garden-like setting of all the lake's hotels. Its rooms—including two private rooms every bit as pleasant as those at Torremolinos—are spread among leafy grounds and include a dorm room directly over the water with great views. Amacuilco also offers guests free kayak use and Internet access, as well as a comfortable lounge area with TV. Like most hostels, Amacuilco isn't perfect and could use some paint here and there. But it's cheap, friendly, and offers all the necessities you'll find at the lake's more expensive hotels. A 5-day Spanish course, including food and lodging, is also available for $120.

Calle Principal. © **503/7822-4051.** amacuilcohostal@hotmail.com. 5 units. $23–$30 private rooms; $7 per bed in dorm rooms; $4 camping. No credit cards. **Amenities:** Restaurant; dune buggy rental; Internet in lobby; free kayak rental; room service. *In room:* A/C (in some), fan.

Hotel Torremolinos   Torremolinos is kind of like the resort in the movie *Dirty Dancing*—it has the look and feel of a grand 1950s-era Catskills hotel. Unfortunately, the '50s were a long time ago and, today, this once-grand hotel remains charming but dated. The rooms seem to have been decorated 20 years ago with whatever mismatching items were lying around, the bathrooms aren't attractive, and there's no Internet. On the plus side, the hotel's lakefront property offers cozy gardens, lounge areas with wrought-iron tables and chairs, two pools, and a two-story pier restaurant over the water with nice breezes and great views. Torremolinos is also less expensive than Villa Serena, and its **restaurant** offers the tastiest food on the lake. So if you prefer character over modern amenities and new furniture, Torremolinos is your place.

Calle Principal. ☏ **503/2441-6037.** www.torremolinoslagocoatepeque.com. 16 units. $32–$47 2–4 beds per room. Rates include continental breakfast. AE, DC, DISC, MC, V. **Amenities:** Restaurant; bar; laundry service; pool; smoke-free rooms, watersports rentals. *In room:* A/C, fan, TV (in some), fridge (in some).

Hotel Villa Serena ★ Opened in 2007, Villa Serena is Lago Coatepeque's most modern and expensive option, so it should be your choice if you prefer fancy amenities like Wi-Fi and solar-powered, piping hot showers. The hotel boasts five modern, adequate-size rooms with sparkling tiled bathrooms, as well as a comfortable seating and hammock area with lake views. There's no restaurant, but breakfast is included and nearby restaurants can deliver. The hotel fills up quickly on weekends, so book in advance; try to ask for room no. 4, which offers the best view. Note that Villa Serena's $25-per-hour kayak rental and $25-per-day charge for nonguests to use the pier are overpriced; nearby Hostal Amacuilco rents kayaks for $4 per hour and nonguests use its facilities for $2 per day.

Calle Principal. ☏ **503/2260-7544.** www.hotelvillaserena.com.sv. 5 units. $73 double. Rates include breakfast. AE, DC, MC, V. **Amenities:** Airport transfers ($15); all rooms smoke-free; spa, watersports rental. *In room:* A/C, fan.

Where to Dine

Restaurante Barde La Rioja ★★ SALVADORAN This restaurant inside the Hotel Torremolinos (see above) has the best service, food, and ambience on the lake—though the hotel might be a bit dated, its restaurant has kept pace with its grand reputation. Torremolinos offers two large seating areas; you can choose between a main hall with arched columns overlooking the hotel grounds and lake, and a two-story pier sitting high off the water with great views and afternoon breezes. The specialties of the house are the tasty cream-of-crab soup and lake fish stuffed with shrimp. As with many fine Central American restaurants, diners get a tiny sample appetizer to nibble before the main entree. Prices are slightly lower than those of the area's other two large restaurants. The main dining room features live music Sunday afternoons from 1 to 5pm.

Calle Principal. ☏ **503/2441-6037.** Main courses $4.50–$12; breakfast $3.50–$4. AE, DC, DISC, MC, V. Daily 8am–9pm.

Restaurante Las Palmeras SALVADORAN ☺ Palmeras is a great place to hang out during the day and have a snack or cold beer, (but when it's time for dinner, head to the Restaurante Barde La Rioja, above). This restaurant is the lake's newest and flashiest, featuring dining spaces under a thatched hut and on a bamboo-style pier. You can't go wrong with the chicken sandwich with fries, the garlic shrimp appetizer, or Caesar salad. Though the dinner menu is extensive, with more than 20 fish, beef, and chicken dishes, and the management maintains a family-friendly atmosphere, the entrees are a bit expensive and not as tasty as those at Barde La Rioja.

Calle Principal. ☏ **503/7248-5727.** Main courses $8–$20. AE, DC, MC, V. Daily 7am–9pm.

Restaurante Rancho Alegre SALVADORAN   Alegre is Palmeras's older, slightly run-down but less expensive, and every bit as tasty, neighbor. The two restaurants have nearly identical fish, beef, and chicken dishes, and are both situated on piers over the water. But Alegre is not as flashy as Palmeras and its pier has begun to show signs of age. (Renovations were underway at press time.) This appears to be the restaurant of choice for Salvadorans, though, no doubt because the locals are drawn by the cheap, delicious cuisine. Menu highlights include a delicious $5 Salvadoran breakfast of eggs, beans, cheese, and platano. The restaurant offers rooms for rent as well, but they aren't recommended.

Calle Principal, by Las Palmeras. ⓒ **503/2441-6071.** www.restauranteranchoalegresv.com. Main courses $6–$15. V. Daily 9am–8pm.

A Side Trip to Parque Nacional Los Volcanes ★★

Parque Nacional Los Volcanes is the informal name given to the 4,500 hectares (11,120 acres) of private and public lands 8km (5 miles) southwest of Lago de Coatepeque, which are home to the steep and barren **Volcán Izalco,** the highest volcano in El Salvador, the recently active **Volcán de Santa Ana,** and the green hills of Cerro Verde.

The park, known officially as Parque Nacional Cerro Verde, is centered around a parking lot near the top of Cerro Verde Mountain, from which visitors set off on challenging 4-hour round-trip hikes to both Volcán Santa Ana and Volcán de Izalco. An easy 35-minute hike near the summit of Cerro Verde also begins and ends at the parking lot. If you love to hike, this park offers some of the most interesting and convenient treks in the country.

Volcán Santa Ana is the third-highest point in the nation and one of its most active volcanoes; in October 2005 an eruption here killed two people, disrupted numerous villages, and spewed huge volcanic boulders up to a mile away. The eruption closed the volcano to hikers for 3 years, but officials reopened the mountain in 2008. The 4-hour hike to the 2,381m (7,812-ft.) summit is strenuous, but visitors will be rewarded with stunning views of Lago de Coatepeque. The climb is difficult and you'll need to be in shape, but it's the easier of the park's two major hikes.

Volcán de Izalco is the park's most visually dramatic volcano and challenging climb, requiring a nearly 3-hour scramble up a steep, rocky, and barren moonscape to the 1,952m (6,404-ft.) summit. Izaco is also one of Central America's youngest volcanoes—it formed in 1770 and erupted almost continuously until 1966. The eruptions were said to be so violent that they could be seen by sailors at sea; hence, the volcano was nicknamed the "Lighthouse of the Pacific." Today, the summit is a nearly perfect cone and its spare, blackish landscape stands in sharp contrast to the lushness of the surrounding hills.

Climbing Izalco is only for those in good physical shape. And no matter how physically fit you are, you can't do both climbs in 1 day. All hikes in the park must be led by a guide, and guided hikes with a minimum of three people leave the parking lot only once daily, at 11am.

ESSENTIALS

GETTING THERE & GETTING AROUND   From Santa Ana, take **bus no. 248,** which stops at the park entrance near the parking lot. Buses leave Santa Ana at 8:30am Tuesday through Thursday and 7:30am Friday through Sunday. They return daily at 3pm. From San Salvador, take a bus directly to Santa Ana (see p. 303 for info) and then follow the directions above, or get off short of Santa Ana in El Congo and ask the driver to direct you to the spot where you can catch the no. 248 bus to the park.

If you're driving from San Salvador, follow **Hwy. CA-8** to the exit for El Congo. After exiting, turn right at the gas station. Follow that road until you turn left at the sign for Cerro Verde. The road will dead-end into the Cerro Verde parking lot. From Santa Ana, follow **Hwy. CA-1** to the exit for Lake Coatepeque. Almost immediately after exiting, turn left onto Hwy. CA-8. Follow this road until you turn right at the sign for Cerro Verde, after which point the road will dead-end into the park's lot.

VISITOR INFORMATION   Park information is available from park administrator **SalvaNatura** (33 Av. Sur 640, Colonia Flor Blanca, San Salvador; ✆ **503/2279-1515;** www.salvanatura.org). The park is open daily 8am to 5pm, but you'll need to arrive before 11am to secure a guide to hike one of the volcanoes; groups meet at the small building in the parking lot that says CASETA DE GUIAS. Admission is $1 and the guides work for tips. A small *comedor* serving *pupusas,* roasted chicken, and rice is located in the far corner of the parking lot.

WHERE TO STAY NEARBY

Lago de Coatepeque and Santa Ana are both less than 30km (19 miles) away, so you can easily base your trip to Parque Nacional Los Volcanes out of one of those two areas. But, if you want to stay overnight so that you can hike both volcanoes, the best option is nearby Campo Bello, which offers little white igloo-looking cabins, a camping area, and great views of Volcán de Izalco. SalvaNatura (see above) also offers cabins and rooms just off Cerro Verde's parking lot.

Cabañas Campo Bello ★★ 🎒   Just 20 minutes from the Parque Nacional Los Volcanes, Campo Bello stands out as the most surreal but stunning accommodations choice in the area—seven small white cement igloos with differently colored, brightly painted doors dot the property, which is backed by a near eye-level view of Volcán de Izalco's rim. Each spare but comfortable igloo features two small bedrooms and a bathroom. Igloo no. 1 offers the best view of the volcano. One-bedroom cabins and tent campsites are also available, and Campo Bello provides tips-only guided tours of both volcanoes from the hotel property.

To get to Campo Bello, veer right at the Campo Bello sign off the main road toward the Cerro Verde parking lot. You'll then need a four-wheel-drive during rainy season or a high-ground-clearance truck the rest of the year to drive the remaining 15 minutes to the hotel. You can also take the no. 248 bus here; simply tell the driver to let you off at the road for Campo Bello.

At the entrance to Parque Nacional Cerro Verde. ✆ **503/7729-3712** or 2271-0853. Fax 503/2222-1861. www.campobello.com.sv. 14 units. $25 for 2-person cabins; $40 for 4-person igloo cabins. No credit cards. Amenities: Barbecue pits; volcano tours. In room: No phone.

METAPAN & PARQUE MONTECRISTO

46km (29 miles) N of Santa Ana

Most travelers view Metapán as a scruffy town on the highway to and from the northwestern border with Guatemala. However, take the time to descend into its historical center and you'll be surprised as its sordid modernity along the main road transforms into a quaint set of streets, low-rise colonial buildings, and a picturesque church. A 300-year-old ceiba tree stands in the middle of a fine plaza, and the restored town hall (*alcaldía*) boasts two giant jaguar statues (symbols of local indigenous strength and resilience), as well as railings made from rifle barrels captured in a 1903 war with Guatemala. The town's most unique feature is a two-story whitewashed building with a gallery running the length of the plaza; nothing unusual there, until you ascend the steps to a restaurant upstairs and discover a full-size soccer pitch with spectator stands out back—apparently the place to be on a Friday night as the proud locals (known as *Metapánecos*) defend their 2010 national champion title. Besides its authentic small-town appeal, Metapán does not have much in the way of accommodations or restaurants (for the moment). It is, however, the gateway to the beautiful Parque Montecristo cloud forest and to the relatively unexplored but gorgeous Lago de Güija.

Essentials

GETTING THERE & GETTING AROUND   Buses to and from Metapán connect at Santa Ana's Metrocentro terminal with onward connections to San Salvador. The town's rudimentary bus depot is next to the Hotel San José on the main highway and entrance into the town center, which is a 5-minute walk downhill. Here you can catch local buses every 30 minutes to the Guatemalan border crossing at Anguiatú or a twice-daily bus to the Honduran border at Citalá, which is a rough-and-tumble 3-hour drive but with memorable mountain scenery.

The entrance to Parque Montecristo is approximately 16km (10 miles) and a 40-minute drive north of Metapán. Buses don't run to the park, so arrange transportation at the bus depot next door to Hotel San Jose (see "Where to Stay," below), where you'll find numerous pickup trucks waiting to take you to the park. A 1-day round-trip pickup ride is about $55. **Note:** There is no point attempting this without a park permit acquired in San Salvador.

To get to Lago de Güija from Metapán, take **bus no. 235,** which leaves about every 10 minutes from the terminal next to the Hotel San Jose (see "Where to Stay," below). Tell the driver "Lago de Güija" and you'll get off about 5 blocks from the lake, beside a small, bright-blue building and a sign reading PLAYA TURISTA with an arrow pointing to a road on the right. Follow that road to the lake.

If you're driving, turn left out of the Hotel San Jose and drive past the bus terminal on your left for about 10 minutes until you see the PLAYA TURISTA sign. Turn right and follow the road to the water. The pickups that take travelers to Parque Montecristo also run the route to the lake for $10 each way. A good local car-rental company specializing in SUVs is **V&M,** Carretera Internaciónal Km 110 (© **503/2402-1330** or 7883-1498; e-mail: tadeo2009@yahoo.com).

VISITOR INFO & FAST FACTS   Metapán Tourism Office (© **503/2402-3123;** metapanturistico@hotmail.com) is on the southwestern corner of the plaza and is open Tuesday through Saturday 8am to 5pm and Sunday 8am to midday. The staff has limited English but is enthusiastic and will help book accommodations and transport in the area. There's a **Scotiabank** (© **503/2402-0039**) at Avenida Ignacio Gomez, with a 24-hour ATM. The **Hospital Nacional Metapán Arturo Morales** (© **503/2442-0184**) is on Carr Principal, 400m (1,312 ft.) south of the town's entrance. For Internet access, head to **Ciber Café** (© **503/2442-4029**) on 2 Av. Sur.

What to See & Do
EXPLORING PARQUE MONTECRISTO

Parque Nacional de Montecristo is a 1,972-hectare (4,873-acre) protected reserve tucked high in El Salvador's mountains, bordering Honduras and Guatemala. (The park's highest point, known as **Punto Trifinio,** actually extends into Honduras and Guatemala and reaches 2,400m/7,874 ft.) It features some of the country's most lush forests and most diverse flora and fauna, including dozens of orchid species and rare birds like toucans, quetzals, and striped owls. Wild pigs, spider monkeys, coyotes, and other wildlife also inhabit the park but aren't so easily spotted.

The best time to visit is right after rainy season when the park is at its most lush. Year-round, though, the region's high humidity and low-hanging clouds give the park its mystical cloud forest feel and maintain its perpetually cool, damp environment, which hovers between 42° and 64°F (6°–18°C). The thick canopy provided by the towering laurel and oak forests also provides the dark cover necessary for an array of orchids, mosses, lichens, and ferns to thrive here. The garden, **De Cien Anos,** offers Montecristo's best orchid viewing and is an hour's drive (on bumpy gravel road) from the park entrance. This garden, which is 1,798m (5,900 ft.) above sea level, is open daily from 8am to noon and 1:30 to 3pm. Montecristo also offers a historic hacienda-style house and a museum with an odd collection of objects ranging from a 3.5m-tall (11-ft.) model of a lookout tower to various animal skulls, along with info about the park's fauna. The museum is open daily from 8am to 3pm.

Los Planes and Montecristo's higher-altitude cloud forests are open November 1 through April 30 from 7am to 3pm daily. Those areas are closed May 1 through October 31 to foster breeding. The rest of the park, including the museum, is open year-round. All visitors must receive prior permission to enter the park from Montecristo's administrative offices at the **Ministerio de Medio Ambiente y Recursos Naturales** (Km 5.5 Carretera a Santa Tecla, Calle and Colonia Las Mercedes, Bldg. MARN No. 2, San Salvador; © 503/2267-6276; www.marn.gob.sv). Hiking without a guide is prohibited beyond the immediate camping and cabin areas, since the trails are not well marked and it's easy to get lost in the haze of the cloud forest.

The park rents cooking burners, gas stoves, and outdoor barbecue grills for $35 per night and camping sites for $3 to $6 per night. Dorm beds in an old colonial house near the park entrance with a big, shady front porch are $10 per night. To reserve a room, call the **Ministerio de Medio Ambiente y Recursos Naturales** (© 503/2267-6276) or the park's main tour guide **Carlos Gutierres Mejiá** (© 503/7201-7557). Carlos speaks Spanish only but can reserve sleeping space, lead guided hikes, or arrange transportation from the park entrance to its higher altitudes.

EXPLORING LAGO DE GÜIJA

Also nearby Metapán is the stunningly beautiful **Lago de Güija** ★ and the marshlands of **Lagunas de Metapán.** The deep blue Lago de Güija is a 45-sq.-km (17-sq.-mile) lake straddling the Salvadoran and Guatemalan borders whose shores are lined with largely undeveloped fishing villages and whose waters are dotted with islands where pre-Columbian artifacts were uncovered nearly 85 years ago. The lake's main attractions are its unspoiled beauty and lack of tourist infrastructure. You won't find any info kiosks here. You can just wander the shore until you find a local fisherman who'll take you out on the lake, where you can soak in outstanding views of the surrounding inactive lakeside volcanoes.

RESERVA ecológica EL LIMO

Can't make it to Montecristo National Park because of timing or lack of permits? **Reserva Ecológica El Limo** makes for an excellent Plan B as it has 14 hectares (35 acres) of lush, rolling hills traversed by rivers, weirs, and waterfalls and is surrounded by mountains, coffee plantations, and cane fields. It is 4km (2½ miles) north of Metapán on a rough, mountainous road that requires a sturdy 4×4 and some expert driving. Besides its rural allure, the private reserve also has three very well-appointed cottages to rent and a 1,400m (4,600-ft.) canopy line for those who prefer to fly rather than hike. The attractive and well-designed cottages are a bargain as they cost $55, sleep five and have gorgeous views. A half-day of canopy costs $30 including transport to and from Metapán. To book and arrange transfers, contact the owner Siegfredo (© **053/ 2442-0149;** www.canopyvillalimon.com) or pop into the tourist office on Metapán's main plaza. The owner can provide secure parking in town if you do not wish to brave the mucky road by car.

If you need to make more concrete plans, call local Spanish-speaking fisherman and tourist boat owner **Pedro San Doval** (© **503/2483-9949**) in advance to arrange a tour for about $25 per hour. **La Perla** (© **503/2415-6490**) can set up a boat trip across the border for lunch in a small Guatemalan village for about the same cost.

Where to Stay

The most convenient place to stay in Metapán if you're heading to Parque Montecristo is **Hotel San Jose** (Carretera Internaciónal 113; © **503/2442-0056**). This somewhat down-at-heel hotel is across the street from a small bus terminal and the collection of pickup trucks that take you to the park. It's also within a block of a couple of sandwich shops and next door to the large Supermercado de Todo, where you can stock up on supplies before heading out on any hikes. The 27-room Hotel San Jose is the only high-rise hotel in Metapán, and costs from $35 to $47 for an average-size room with balcony. The decor is dated and a little depressing, and it has little in the way of amenities; but unfortunately it is the only viable option in town, and it is at least clean and safe with secure parking.

By far the best, most accessible place to stay in the area is **Restaurante y Cabanas La Perla** (Canton Las Piedras, Caserio, Azacualpa; © **503/2415-6490** or 310/880-9782 in the U.S.; www.laperladeazacualpa.com), which is right on Lake Güija, about 20 minutes outside Metapán. This small, four-room hotel offers gorgeous views of the lake, pedal boats for rent, and a boat that will take you across the lake for lunch in a small Guatemalan village. La Perla features large modern rooms with two queen-size beds for only $35 per night, a big pool with a poolside **bar,** and a **restaurant** with Salvadoran classics and American dishes ranging from $5 to $7.50. The rooms also feature rooftop decks overlooking the water. The hotel provides free round-trip transportation from Metapán with advance reservations. If you don't mind adding 20 minutes to your ride to Montecristo or want to spend a few days on the lake, you should stay here.

Where to Dine

Even if you just plan a quick circuit of Metapán plaza before continuing on your way, it is worth your time to stop for a coffee at **Balompie Café** (3ra. Av. Norte, Local 17, second floor; ✆ 053/2402-3567), considering that it has a beautiful arched colonial facade on one side and a full-size soccer pitch on the other. You can have one eye on a local game and the other on the pretty plaza while enjoying standard fare such as chicken, pasta, and beef. The restaurant is open Wednesday to Sunday from 10am to 1pm. The same building runs the length of the plaza and has several casual cafes and *pupusarias,* but for the moment the town lacks any choice in fine dining.

At **Parque Acuático Apuzunga** (Km 100 Carretera de Santa Ana; ✆ **503/2440-5130;** www.apuzunga.com) you can canopy the river, raft the river, fish the river, and then eat the fish from the same river. This is a sprawling garden restaurant, fish farm, rafting outfitter, and pool complex 12km (7½ miles) south of Metapán. The rancho-style restaurant has a riverside setting and spacious gardens with open-air dining areas interrupted occasionally by thrill seekers gliding by on a cable. It specializes in a local fish known as tilapia, which is farmed on-site and served with salad and rice. The owner, Jesus Sanabria Zamora, is a gregarious host who will take you on a tour of the property he is very proud of. Look for the entrance signs approximately 8km (5 miles) south of Metapán, on the right as you travel north. It is open every day from 7am to 6pm.

EASTERN EL SALVADOR

Alegría: 49km (30 miles) W of San Miguel. Perquín: 53km (33 miles) N of San Miguel. San Miguel: 138km (86 miles) E of San Salvador. San Vicente: 56km (35 miles) E of San Salvador.

Eastern El Salvador might seem less action-packed than the attraction-filled west, but its rural charm and civil war history make this less-visited corner of El Salvador well worth the trip. Highlights include the charming, cool mountainside village of Alegría; the historic town of Perquín, which has the country's most definitive collection of FARC war relics; and the tragic village of Mozote, whose people suffered one of modern Latin America's worst wartime atrocities. Although this is also one of the poorest sections of the country, you'll find the residents of the east to perhaps be the friendliest of your trip.

Alegría ★

Located 1,200m (3,937 ft.) above sea level, high up in coffee country, the charming little town of Alegría offers some of the best views in the nation, as well as great hiking trails and a friendly, vibrant community. Late into the evening, the town's small, recently renovated square teems with multigenerational families chatting with neighbors, kids playing, and teenagers hanging with friends. The small tourism kiosk and the mayor's office, both of which are on the main square, can arrange coffee plantation tours, hikes to a nearby crater lake, and info on the town's more than 150 beautiful flower displays. Situated conveniently between Perquín and San Salvador, Alegría is an easy stop off the main tourist trail.

ESSENTIALS
Getting There & Getting Around

From San Miguel, catch any bus toward San Salvador and tell the driver to let you off in Triunfo. There you'll catch a minibus to the city of Santiago de Maria, where you

Exactly how El Salvador's 12-year civil war got started depends on whom you ask. More specifically, it depends on where that person falls on El Salvador's socioeconomic scale. Some on the upper end will tell you the war was caused by senseless terrorism by those who had no right or cause. Some on the lower end of the pay scale see the war as a courageous people's struggle. But, generally speaking, the war began because El Salvador's *campesinos,* or peasant farmers, got tired of living as, well, *campesinos.*

By the late 1970s, these *campesinos* had struggled for decades without much progress despite occasional and tepid reforms passed by El Salvador's right-wing military government and land-based oligarchy, and calling for war began to seem like the best way to call for change. Add to the mix yet another failed government reform in 1976, the 1980 government assassination of the beloved human rights leader Monseñor Oscar Romero, and the organization in 1980 of four left-wing people's groups into the formidable **Farabundo Martí National Liberation Front (FMLN),** and the stage for war was set. Some had hope that war could be avoided when a group of slightly more moderate government agents took control of the government and nationalized some aspects of the economy in 1979 and 1980. But those moderates didn't go far enough and were themselves soon targets of the country's right-wing military death squads.

The FMLN launched its first major offensive against the Salvadoran military in 1981 and successfully gained control of areas around Chalatenango and Morazán. The Salvadoran military's response—with the help of the U.S. government, which spent $7 billion trying to defeat the organization—was fierce and lasting. The war raged on and off for the next 12 years until both sides had had enough. The atrocities of the right, including individual assassinations and the 1981 **Mozote Massacre** (see p. 27 for info), have been well documented since. A peace deal was signed in 1992, most war crimes were legally forgiven, and the FMLN agreed to halt its military operations and become a political party. In 2009, the unthinkable happened when the FMLN candidate Mauricio Funes won the presidency, a sign that these one-time revolutionaries had finally entered the political fold.

can take one of a steady steam of buses the final 4km (2½ miles) to Alegría. A steady stream of buses also run daily between Alegría and nearby Maria de Santiago, where you can make connections to the rest of the country.

When driving from San Salvador in the west or San Miguel in the east, follow **CA-1,** also known as the Pan-American Highway (Carretera Panamericana), and get off at the sign for Santiago de Maria. Follow the signs the remaining 4km (2½ miles) to Alegría.

Alegría is a very walkable town; its tourism office, Internet cafe, restaurants, and hotels are all within a few blocks of its town square.

Visitor Information

Tourist information in Spanish is available in a small tourist kiosk just off the main square (no phone; Tues–Sun 8am–4pm).

FAST FACTS Alegría has no banks, ATMs, or post office, but all of these can be found in nearby Santiago de Maria. A pharmacy is 1 block from the square across from the church. Internet access is available daily from 8am to 9pm for $1 an hour in a cafe behind the main tourist kiosk; call ☎ **503/2628-1159** for info. Alegría's tourist police can be reached at ☎ **503/2628-1016** and ambulance service is at ☎ **503/2611-1332.**

What to See & Do

Alegría's main draws are its cool mountain climate, amazing views, and friendly vibe. The town is also known for its dozens of houses with unique flower displays. The mayor's office (in the main square; ☎ **503/2628-1001**) can arrange visits. **Alegría tours** (☎ **503/2611-1497**), owned by English-speaking Saul Tercios, also offers $15, 2-hour to half-day tours of area coffee farms, a nearby crater lake, and historic sites within Alegría.

Where to Stay

Cabaña La Estancia de Daniel   An orange wall, topped with chunky terra-cotta tiles and bearing plaques of famous townsfolk, surrounds a lovely, if a little cramped, garden property with five cabin-style accommodations. Tables and hammocks adorn some quiet nooks and crannies inside this family-run property which is 1 block west of the main plaza. The rooms are smallish but nicely decorated with volcanic flagstones and small shuttered windows. Each cabin sleeps a family of four and though the property is a little too cluttered, it is the tropical garden that makes it unique with orchids, coffee bushes, and a fragrant white flower known as *galanderias*. The main drawback is lack of a view but this is still an excellent budget option with a convenient location.

Calle Manuel Enrique Aruayo and 2a Av. Sur. ☎ **503/2628-1030.** fredypostecapa@yahoo.com. 5 units. $20 double; $25 cabin sleeps 2 adults and 2 children. No credit cards. Private parking. **Amenities:** Wi-Fi. *In room:* TV.

Casa de Huespedes La Palma 🌶   This hotel is older and a bit less updated than the Cartagena (see below), but it's comfortable, affordable, and right on the square. The hotel is hidden behind a flower-filled patio, but when you find the front door and ring the bell, you'll be greeted by hotel staff and two friendly dogs who'll settle you into their comfortable, family-style hotel immediately. The three big rooms here are plain, with almost nothing on the walls, but they are larger than most and, at $10 per person for a room in the center of town, they're a great deal.

Calle Pedro T Mortiño on the town square. ☎ **503/2628-1012.** 3 units. $20 double. No credit cards. *In room:* TV.

Hostal y Café Entre Piedras ★ 🌶   Located in a stone-walled property on the southeastern corner of the plaza, Entre Piedras may not look like much from the outside, but when you enter, you'll find a spacious, well-built house with lots of white walls and dark wood features. Built by a German immigrant in the 1960s, the structure has stood the test of time and offers handsome, spacious rooms with high cedar-wood rafters and solid furniture and beds. It also operates as a cafe and has a homey feel. The all-stone courtyard is shaded by orange and mandarin trees and there is a small pool at the back. This is a great value place to stay and its cool tidiness is in stark contrast to the cluttered charm of Casa de Huespedes La Palma across the plaza.

2a Av. Sur and Pje Gimaldi. ☎ **503/2313-2812.** www.hostalentrepiedras.com. 4 units; 1 dorm sleeps 4. $32 double; $16 single; $10 dorm bed. No credit cards. **Amenities:** Cafe; bar; pool; TV room.

Vivero y Restaurante Cartagena ★   Cartagena isn't the cheapest property in town, but it's Alegría's best hotel. The hotel is a 10-minute walk from the main square

If you are traveling along the Pan-American Highway east of San Salvador, try to take a short detour into San Vicente to have a look at the town's much-photographed clock tower. The five-story white cement tower in the middle of the town square is quite beautiful, with a kind of Dr. Seuss whimsy about it. It is $1 to climb to the top, where you can get some lovely views. From San Salvador, you can take bus no. 116 to the center of town. If you're driving, San Vicente is just a few miles off the Pan-American Highway (Carretera Panamericana) and is well marked.

but its flower-filled setting and mountainside views are worth the added trip. The hotel's eight cabins are plain but boast inviting front patios and larger-than-average sleeping areas. Cabin nos. 3, 4, and 5 are perched on the edge of the mountain and offer amazing views. The cabins fill up in August, December, and around Easter so reserve well in advance during these times. The hotel also has a restaurant and sells plants and locally produced crafts. The walk to the hotel is all downhill but it's a tough hike back up; you can ask the hotel to arrange transportation back to the square.

Final Barrio El Calvario. (ℂ 503/2628-2362 or 2628-1131. cral1966@hotmail.com. 8 units. $50–$80 cabin. No credit cards. **Amenities:** Restaurant. *In room:* No phone.

Where to Dine

La Fonda de Alegría ★ SALVADORAN   La Fonda boasts Alegría's largest and most interesting menu. Just down the hill from the square en route to the Cartagena hotel, this restaurant offers a twist on basic Salvadoran cuisine with items such as a 4-ounce steak with Argentine sausage, avocado, and baby onions, and an Argentine sausage plate with refried beans. The English- and Spanish-language menu also features traditional *pupusas*, tacos, and hamburgers. La Fonda doesn't offer much in the way of views, but its open-air seating catches the mountain breezes just right.

Av. Gólgata. (ℂ 503/2628-1010. Main courses $4.25–$9. No credit cards. Daily 9am–9pm.

Restaurante El Portal SALVADORAN   Though not as diverse in its offerings as La Fonda, El Portal does offer an ample menu and is right on the square. This 10-table, casual restaurant serves unique items such as Indian-spiced chicken with rice and salad and more traditional fare like steak dishes. It also has two big windows allowing for prime town-square people-watching. But possibly best of all is that El Portal has a working cappuccino machine. In a country with thousands of acres of coffee plants, you'd think there would be cappuccino on every corner. They're actually a rarity, so the frothy blends whipped up here are a real find.

Av. Pedro T Mortiño on the square. (ℂ 503/2628-1144. Main courses $4.50–$9. No credit cards. Daily 9am–9pm.

Perquín ★★

Perquín, tucked high in El Salvador's northeast mountains near the Guatemalan border, sheds light on El Salvador's tragic civil war. This town was the headquarters for the FMLN in this part of the country during the war and is today best known for its **Museo de la Revolución Salvadoreña,** which displays artifacts and tells the story of the revolutionary guerrilla movement's efforts during the war. In addition,

Perquín has a tourist-friendly square, a couple of small artisans' shops, and a cool mountain climate that make it a nice stop.

ESSENTIALS

GETTING THERE From San Miguel, take bus **no. 332C** roughly 53km (33 miles) to Perquín; the bus stops right in the town square. If you're driving from San Miguel, take highway **CA-7** into Perquín.

ORIENTATION Perquín is a small, walkable town with a tiny but attractive village square. Most of what you'll want or need is within a few blocks of the center, and the Museo de la Revolución is a 5-minute walk from the center.

GETTING AROUND Though you can walk to Perquín's attractions, you'll need to arrange a microbus or pickup truck at Perquín's tourist office (Colonia 10 Enero; ☎ 503/2680-4086) to take you 8km (5 miles) to Mozote. Also, Perquín's best hotel, the Lenca Montana, is 1.5km (1 mile) south of the square.

VISITOR INFORMATION & FAST FACTS Perquín's **tourist information office** (Colonia 10 Enero; ☎ 503/2680-4086) is open daily from 8am to 4:40pm. There are no banks or ATMs in Perquín. The **post office** (☎ 503/2675-1054) is on the main square opposite the church. Internet is available for $1 per hour at **Servicomputer** (Calle Principal; ☎ 503/2680-4353) and a **pharmacy** is 1 block east of the square across the street from the church.

WHAT TO SEE & DO

El Mirador at Cerro de Perquín Across the street and a 10-minute hike uphill from the Museo de la Revolución (see below) is this lookout point, which is set in an area of the forest that once housed guerrilla camps. There's not much to see here today, since there's nothing obvious remaining from the guerrilla days on the hike. But the Mirador offers a great view and a little exercise.

Av. Los Heroes, Barrio La Paz (across the street from the museum). No phone. Admission 50¢. Daily 8am–4pm.

Museo de la Revolución Salvadoreña ★★ This museum is the main reason travelers come to Perquín. The small, four-room edifice offers illuminating photos and Spanish-language histories of guerrilla martyrs, including those of the war's many female soldiers, and displays civil war weaponry and equipment along with posters of inspirational slogans used during the war. Big rocket launchers, large chunks of a downed army helicopter, and even an old Ford sedan and Peugeot are displayed. One of the more interesting exhibits is the preserved studio of revolutionary Radio Venceremos. Near the station are the remains of a crater from an army bomb that barely missed its mark. Some museum displays include small English-language explanations, and guides are available for a small tip. You shouldn't leave town without visiting this proud piece of the people's history.

Av. Los Heroes, Barrio La Paz. ☎ **503/7942-3721** or 2634-7984. 5-min. walk northwest of the square. Admission $1.20. Daily 8am–4pm.

WHERE TO STAY & DINE

Within Perquín's town center, you'll find small *comedores* offering *pupusas* and simple roasted chicken or beef. The best are **La Cocina de Mama Toya y Mama Juana** (Carretera a Perquín, a few blocks south of the square; ☎ **503/2680-4045**) and **La Cocina de La Abuela** (Carretera a Perquín, a few blocks south of the square; no phone). Mama Juana is on the left as you enter Perquín and offers the cheapest eats

Most travelers have some awareness of El Salvador's bloody 12-year civil war, which ended with the signing of peace accords in 1992, and are curious to better understand the war and its aftermath. But be judicious with that curiosity. El Salvador's civil war was exceedingly violent, often included torture, and took place in a relatively small area. Because of El Salvador's high population density, very few Salvadorans of a certain age failed to be personally affected by it. I learned the hard way not to casually ask too many questions about those times. Salvadorans are renowned for their friendly nature and will tell you about the war if asked. But, almost inevitably, their stories will include the loss or torture of a wife, a child, or a father. The war is not a taboo subject, but these are horrific memories that should not be casually unearthed. It's better to ask questions of educators or Salvadorans you know well.

at $2 for a roasted chicken and rice dinner. Mama Juana's also has some not-so-attractive rooms for $6 per night. Across the street from Mama Juana's is La Cocina de La Abuela, or "kitchen of the grandmother," which is open Saturdays and Sundays from 7am to 9pm and offers 35¢ *pupusas* and grilled steak for $4.50 to $7.50.

The best restaurant in the area, is 1.5km (1 mile) south of town in the **Hotel de Montaña** (Km 205.5 Carretera a Perquín, Morazán; ✆ **503/2680-4046** or 2680-4080). The hotel restaurant has a large English-language menu with tasty chicken, fish, and meat items from $5.80 to $8.80, including a delicious chicken dish with cheese and mushrooms, rice, and salad for $6. The restaurant also has outdoor seating with great views.

Perkín Lenca Hotel de Montaña ★★ 🎁 Montaña is the best place to stay in the Perquín area. Located 1.5km (1 mile) south of town, this modern, cabin-style hotel sits on a steep mountainside just off the main road and offers modern rooms, a full-service restaurant, and great views. English-speaking hotel owner, informal El Salvador historian, and American native Ronald Brenneman came to the area to assist refugees during the civil war, fell in love with the country, and decided to stay. The hotel's seven cabins were built in 2000 and the 10 rooms were constructed in 2006. The best deals are the rooms at $30 per night for two people. The rooms aren't big but have a modern, rustic feel, and are at the top of the mountain with comfortable patios offering high-altitude views. Some of the profits from the hotel go toward funding a grammar school that Brenneman's foundation recently opened in the area.

Km 205.5 Carretera a Perquín. ✆ **503/2680-4046** or 2680-4080. www.perkinlenca.com. 17 units. $50–$110 cabin; $20–$30 2-bed room; $60 4-bed room. Rates include full breakfast. AE, DC, DISC, MC, V. **Amenities:** Restaurant; room service. *In room:* Fan, Wi-Fi.

Mozote ★★

Mozote is a small village 8km (5 miles) south of Perquín where the Salvadoran army executed more than 1,000 townspeople on December 11 and 12, 1981. Members of the army rounded up and separated the town's residents into groups of men, women, and children and then executed each group in and around the square and church. The burning of town buildings followed. The massacre is considered one of the worst in modern Latin American history and drew criticism from around the world. The

As the country's third-largest city, San Miguel offers neither the sophistication of big-city San Salvador nor the charms of El Salvador's small villages. There is little point in visiting here as it doesn't offer anything you can't find in greater supply elsewhere. Since the town does have a large bus terminal with departures around the country, you may very well find yourself transferring through here, especially if you want to get to Perquín in the north. If you find yourself in San Miguel with a few hours to kill, there is an interesting regional museum to visit. **Museo Regional de Oriente** on 8a Av. Sur and Calle Oriente (© **503/ 2660-1275**). Admission is $1 and it is open Monday through Saturday 9am to noon and 1 to 5pm. If you do need to spend the night, the **Comfort Inn,** Final

Alameda Roosevelt and Carratera a La Unión (© **877/424-6423;** www.comfort inn.com), is your best option. It has a pool, an exercise room, Wi-Fi, and a small restaurant and bar, and is a short cab ride from the square. It's also across the street from the large, modern **Metrocentro Mall.** Rooms start at $65 for a double. To get to San Miguel, the San Salvador bus no. 301 stops along the Pan-American Highway (Carretera Panamericana) and takes approximately 2 hours and 45 minutes west to San Miguel. If driving from San Salvador, head 2½ hours east along Hwy. CA-1, also known as the Pan-American Highway, and follow the signs. You can avoid the city center by taking the bypass road known as Final Alameda Roosevelt.

---

tragedy was recognized by a United Nations truth commission in 1992 after many of the bodies were excavated at the site. Today, the names of the children killed are inscribed in a shrine in the church garden, and the famous Mozote memorial—a metal silhouette of a family holding hands—sits in the town square beside squares of wood inscribed with the names of those who died. Stopping in town to view the memorial here is necessary if you want to fully grasp the tragedy of the country's civil war.

To get to Mozote from Perquín, you'll need to arrange a pickup or microbus with Perquín's tourist office (Colonia 10 Enero; © **503/2680-4086**). If you're driving, turn off the main road south of Perquín at the sign BIENVENIDOS A ARAMBALA. Follow the road for 1.5km (1 mile) and veer right at a fork in the road. Follow it for another 1.5km (1 mile) and turn left at the intersection, then go 2 blocks and turn right at the MONUMENTO EL MOZOTE sign and follow more signs to the town square.

HONDURAS

by Nicholas Gill

Honduras has been unjustly overshadowed by its neighbors for decades. For some time, divers have passed over Honduras to go to Belize, nature and beach lovers have headed for Costa Rica, and culture and history buffs have gone to Guatemala and Mexico. This is beginning to change, as more and more visitors are coming to realize that all of these can be found in Honduras, and that, even though large crowds and over-development threaten other Central American countries, Honduras is still practically untouched, with more cloud forests and unexplored tracts of wilderness than anywhere else in the region.

Much of it may still be taken up by banana cultivation, but few other countries in the world today can lay claim to such obvious natural beauty. About the size of Tennessee, Honduras is home to 20 national parks, a couple of biosphere reserves, and nearly 100 other protected ecological areas. The cultural diversity here is also notable. The country has almost eight million people, mostly *mestizos* (mixed descendants of the Spanish and Amerindians), as well as another 10% made up of eight main indigenous groups: the Lencas, the Chortís, the Tolupan, the Garífunas, the Miskitos, the Pech, the Tawahkas, and the Bay Islanders.

Adventure has been woven into the fabric of this country over the past 400 years. Christopher Columbus set foot on the Bay Islands and the North Shore on his fourth and final voyage to the Americas in 1502, but that may be the most boring tale. Consider that the country's history involves pirates raiding gold from Spanish ships and hiding the booty in caves on the Bay Islands, archaeologists searching for Maya ruins and crystal skulls, and a North American named William Walker launching a raid on the country with his own small army. Throw in conquistadors, indigenous warriors, multinational fruit corporations, whale sharks, and indigenous land rights and you have one of the most exciting environments on the planet.

Until recently, Honduras's tourist infrastructure has been limited, but things are slowly coming together, even with the political troubles that 2009 brought. Visitors can expect more variety, better hotels, and a greater range of wild and wonderful tours and attractions than before. With newly expanded ports, cruise landings on the Bay Islands have exploded. Luxury ecolodges near La Ceiba can now compete with anywhere else in Central America, and beach resorts are set to turn Tela Bay into the next Cancun. The Maya ruins of Copán are luring more and more visitors. Even La Mosquitia, traditionally one of the least accessible places in the Americas, is turning to community-based tours and excelling at them.

THE REGIONS IN BRIEF

Covering 111,369 sq. km (43,000 sq. miles), Honduras is the second-largest country in Central America (Nicaragua is the largest) and the only one without volcanoes. It borders the Caribbean Sea, Pacific Ocean, Guatemala, Nicaragua, and El Salvador and is only a short ferry ride from Belize. Like points on a compass, the country can be divided into four major geographical sections: the lush forests and coastline to the north, the impenetrable jungles of La Mosquitia to the east, the mountains and pine forests of the western and central parts of the country, and the dry, dusty south. Forty percent of Honduras is made up of rainforests, while the coasts comprise nearly 966km (600 miles) of beaches.

THE SOUTH The country's 100km (62-mile) Pacific coast separates Honduras from El Salvador in the west and Nicaragua in the east, and marks the western boundary of the southern region, which extends up to the sprawling capital of **Tegucigalpa** (called Tegus by locals). Tegucigalpa is the cultural center of the country and home to excellent museums, great restaurants and markets, and a smattering of luxury hotels. Just outside town, you will find small craft villages and one of the best national parks in the country, the **Parque Nacional La Tigra.**

THE WEST Mountains, cowboys, Maya ancestors, ancient ruins, cloud forests, Catholic festivals, and the largest lake in the country all join together to create western Honduras, one of the most diverse regions of the country. From the economic hub of the country, **San Pedro Sula,** you'll move southward across the fertile Sula valley to the Maya ruins of **Copán,** passing the bird-watching hot spot of **Lago de Yojoa,** the one-time capital of Central America, **Gracias,** the cigar and coffee center of **Santa Rosa de Copán,** and the colonial town of **Comayagua.**

THE NORTH COAST The North Coast is an ecodream of lush tropical forests, 805km (500 miles) of empty white-sand beaches, fruit farms, and enough adrenaline-pumping sports to keep you busy for months. Near La Ceiba, the country's official capital of ecotourism, you'll find the **Cuero y Salado Wildlife Refuge,** white water on the **Río Cangrejal,** the waterfalls and hiking trails of **Pico Bonito National Park,** and easy access to the Bay Islands and the Cayos Cochinos. **Tela,** with even more natural attractions, like the **Lancetilla Botanical Garden** and **Los Micos Lagoon,** is set to become the site of a major beach project that could soon drastically change this laid-back banana town. Elsewhere in the region, you'll find friendly Garífuna villages and the once-happening beachfront and Spanish fort in **Trujillo.**

THE BAY ISLANDS Stilted island houses, turquoise water, Garífuna settlements, and some of the best diving on earth make the Bay Islands one of the country's leading attractions. While you'll find a number of cruise ports and luxury resorts on **Roatán** and hostels and cheap restaurants on the backpacker paradise that is **Utila,** these two islands still retain their laid-back charm. The least visited of the three Bay Islands, **Guanaja,** is practically untouched.

LA MOSQUITIA This largest tract of wilderness in Central America is often called a mini-Amazon. The region is as wild as they come and is made up of indigenous tribes, rarely visited biological reserves, and tiny coastal communities where electricity is a rare luxury. Tour groups are increasingly exploring the **Río Plátano Biosphere Reserve** via rafting trips, though they are facing competition from new community-based ecotourism projects.

THE BEST OF HONDURAS IN 1 WEEK

This itinerary will take you to the major attractions in the country, from the Maya ruins of Copán, to the mangroves and tropical forests of the North Coast, to the turquoise waters of the Bay Islands. It covers a little bit of everything. If you are less concerned about beaches and diving, opt to change your time in the Bay Islands for a quick fly-in-and-out trip to La Mosquitia, or to spend more time exploring the Copán Ruínas area. Alternatively, you may be content to spend your entire trip lying on the beach or diving in Roatán or Utila, rather than heading inland at all. (Though San Pedro Sula is the country's largest international airport, it's possible to take an international flight directly to Tegucigalpa, Roatán, or La Ceiba too).

Days 1 & 2: Arrive in San Pedro Sula & Head to Copán ★★★

Upon landing in San Pedro Sula, head to the town of **Copán Ruínas ★★★** (p. 360) and spend your first day exploring. The next morning, wake up early to tour the Maya ruins of Copán before the crowds arrive, along with **Las Sepulturas ★** (p. 364). Have lunch at **Hacienda San Lucas ★★★** (p. 368)—or save it for dinner—and then take the afternoon and evening to explore the markets, **Museo Regional de Arqueología Maya ★** (p. 365), or bars in town.

Days 3 & 4: From Santa Rosa de Copán to Tela ★★

From Copán, travel into the mountains to check out the **Flor de Copán cigar factory ★★** (p. 371) in Santa Rosa de Copán, stopping at the Maya ruins of **El Puente ★** (p. 366) on the way. Then travel **La Ruta Lenca ★★★** (p. 376), stopping in small villages and exploring colonial churches, before settling into your hotel in **Gracias** (p. 372), the capital of the department of Lempira.

Wake up early the next morning for your best chance at seeing the elusive quetzal and other wildlife during your hike through **Parque Nacional Montaña de Celaque ★★★** (p. 378). Afterward, head to **Tela** on the coast to check into the **Hotel Telamar ★★★** (p. 384), once the home of United Fruit executives and now a five-star resort.

Days 5 & 6: See More Attractions Around Tela or Journey to La Ceiba ★

Check out **Jardín Botánico Lancetilla ★★** (p. 383), the world's second-largest botanical garden, or to take a boat tour in **Parque Nacional Jeanette Kawas** or **Punta Sal ★★★** (p. 383), where you can spot howler monkeys, jaguars, and hundreds of species of birds.

Or head a few hours up the coast to **La Ceiba,** perhaps to check into the **Lodge at Pico Bonito ★★★** (p. 394) in Pico Bonito National Park. You can easily spend 2 days here hiking, rafting, or on zip-line tours. Day-trip options abound, too, including snorkeling **Cayos Cochinos ★★★** (p. 397), one of the most unspoiled coral reefs in the country, or visiting the Garífuna village of **Chachauate ★** (p. 398).

Honduras in 1 Week

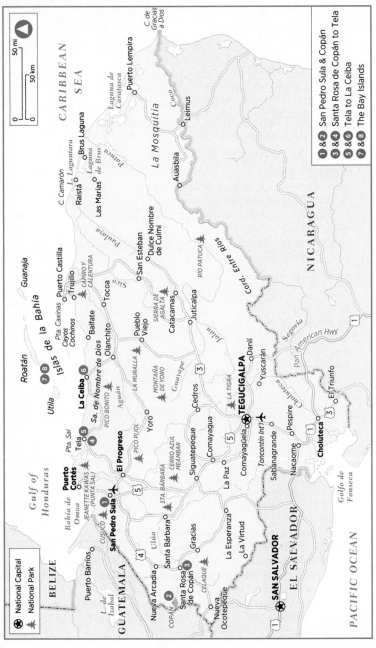

National Capital
National Park

0 — 50 mi
0 — 50 km

1 & 2 San Pedro Sula & Copán
3 & 4 Santa Rosa de Copán to Tela
5 & 6 Tela to La Ceiba
7 & 8 The Bay Islands

TELEPHONE dialing INFO AT A GLANCE

The country code for Honduras is **504,** which you use only when dialing from outside the country. Telephone numbers in this chapter include this prefix because most businesses' published phone numbers include the prefix.

○ To place a call from your home country to Honduras: Dial the international access code (**011** in the U.S. and Canada, **0011** in Australia, **0170** in New Zealand, **00** in the U.K.) plus the country code (504), followed by the number in Honduras. For example, a call from the United States to Tegucigalpa would be 011+ 504+000+0000.

○ To place a call within Honduras: All you have to do is dial the number.

○ To place a direct international call from Honduras: Dial **193** for an international operator. Dial the country code of the destination you are calling, plus the area code and the local number.

Days 7 & 8: The Bay Islands ★★★

From La Ceiba, catch a ferry or plane for a short trip to Roatán, the most developed of the Bay Islands. Here you can explore West End Beach and dive on the world's second-largest barrier reef. In addition, you can head to **Anthony's Key** ★★ (p. 411) to swim with dolphins, take part in zip-line canopy tours in **Gumbalimba Park** ★ (p. 412), or visit the Garífuna communities on the east end of the island.

On day 8, transfer to the San Pedro Sula airport to make your flight out of the country.

PLANNING YOUR TRIP TO HONDURAS

Visitor Information

You'll find a municipal or regional tourism office in nearly every city throughout the country, often in small booths in central parks and squares; these are generally open Monday to Friday from 8am to 4pm, often with a 1-hour break at noon. The **Instituto Hondureño de Turismo (IHT),** or the National Tourism Institute, does not have offices abroad, but promotes the country through their website: www.letsgo honduras.com. Additional websites of interest include these:

○ **www.bayislandsvoice.com**: A monthly newsmagazine covering the history, art, culture, dining, development, and social issues of Roatán, Utila, and Guanaja.

○ **www.hondurasthisweek.com**: This English-language newspaper given out in tourist towns and big cities all over Honduras has an online edition with weekly features, videos, podcasts, weather reports, and news.

○ **www.hondurastips.honduras.com**: An excellent full online and print guidebook to the major tourism destinations in Honduras, with information and maps that are updated seasonally by the Institute of Tourism.

- **www.larutamoskitia.com**: The definitive site for exploring La Mosquitia. Questions about when to go, how to get there, what to do, and what you will see are answered in detail. The site is run by a nonprofit community-based tour agency that offers multiday tours throughout the region and arranges day tours from individual communities.
- **www.sidewalkmystic.com**: An independent online planning guide to Honduras, with descriptions of highlights, travelogues, hotel and restaurant listings, and other how-to information.

TOUR OPERATORS

While many international tour operators run tours to Honduras, they are almost always contracted out through local operators such as those mentioned below. Booking directly will save you a bundle. Most are based in La Ceiba, but have offices in other parts of the country as well.

- **Garífuna Tours ★★** (© 504/440-3252; www.garifunatours.com) is one of the most complete and well-respected operations in the country. While they specialize in daylong adventure trips to the national parks along the North Coast near La Ceiba and Tela, they also run package tours to the Bay Islands, La Mosquitia, and Copán.
- **La Mosquitia Eco Aventuras ★★** (© 504/414-5798; www.honduras.com/moskitia) is run by internationally known naturalist Jorge Salaverri. They offer everything from 10- to 14-day rafting trips in the Río Plátano Biosphere Reserve and explorations in even more remote parts of La Mosquitia to day hikes in national parks along the North Coast.
- **Roatán Charters ★** (© 800/282-8932; www.roatan.com) is a one-stop shop for almost any tour, regional flight, or hotel in Honduras or Belize, though they focus mostly on the Bay Islands.
- **Jungle River Tours** (© 504/440-1268; www.jungleriverlodge.com) is a budget operator that focuses on adventure activities such as rafting, kayaking, and hiking in select destinations along the North Coast.
- **La Ruta Moskitia ★★★** (© 504/406-6782; www.larutamoskitia.com) is a grass-roots tourism initiative that arranges a wide variety of day tours and guided 4- to 9-day excursions with cultural groups in La Mosquitia.

Entry Requirements

Citizens of the United States, Canada, Great Britain, South Africa, New Zealand, and Australia require valid passports to enter Honduras as tourists. Citizens of any of these countries conducting business or enrolled in formal educational programs in Honduras also require visas. Tourist cards, distributed on arriving international flights or at border crossings, are good for stays of up to 90 days. Keep a copy of your tourist card for presentation upon departure from Honduras. (If you lose it, you'll have to pay a small fine.) You can extend your visa, once, for another 90 days at any immigration office for $20.

Honduras is part of a 2006 border control agreement with El Salvador, Guatemala, and Nicaragua allowing travel between the four countries under one tourist card. The number of days of your tourist card is determined at the first of the four countries entered.

Honduras still has a long way to go in terms of attracting wellness travelers, especially compared to neighbors like Costa Rica. Still, there are a few decent wellness retreats and some new projects on the horizon. The mountains in the west, once the land of the Mayas, are the center of spiritual and wellness tourism in the country. **Hacienda San Lucas** near Copán (p. 368) often holds comprehensive yoga and spiritual cleansing retreats led by internationally renowned names in the field, while the Gracias area is becoming more and more known for its hot springs. On the **Bay Islands,** several resorts have spas, though the ranges of treatments and services offered are nowhere near those featured in nearby Caribbean island resorts.

HONDURAN EMBASSY LOCATIONS

In the U.S.: 3007 Tilden St., NW, Ste. 4M, Washington, DC 20008 (© **202/966-7702;** www.hondurasemb.org).

In Canada: 151 Slater St., Ste. 805, Ottawa, ON, K1P-5H3 (© **613/233-8900;** www.embassyhonduras.ca).

In the U.K.: 115 Gloucester Place, London, W1U 6JT (© **020/7486-4880;** honduras.embassy-uk.co.uk).

In Australia: Level 7, 19–31 Pitt St., Sydney NSW 2000; P.O. Box H6, Australia Square NSW 2000 (© **02/9247-1730**).

Customs

Any travel-related merchandise brought into Honduras, such as personal effects or clothing, is not taxed. Visitors entering Honduras may also bring in no more than 400 cigarettes, 500 grams of pipe tobacco, or 50 cigars, and 2.5 liters of alcoholic beverages per adult.

Money

The unit of currency in Honduras is the **lempira.** The value of the lempira has held steady around the current exchange rate of about 19 lempira to the U.S. dollar, which is the rate used for prices listed in this book. Bills come in denominations of 1, 2, 5, 10, 20, 50, 100, 200, and 500. There are no lempira coins. **Note:** American dollars are commonly accepted in the Bay Islands, particularly at hotels—as a result, some reviews in that section list rates only in U.S. dollars.

Dollars, pounds, and euros can be exchanged in banks and many hotels, as well as with unofficial street money-changers found in parks, airports, and border crossings. ATMs are the most common way to exchange money, and most cities here have multiple banks with ATMs, many of them operating 24 hours. **BAC, Unibanc,** and **Banco Atlántida** are the most reliable and are compatible with a variety of networks, including Cirrus, PLUS, Visa, and MasterCard. Honduran banks do not usually charge a fee to use their ATMs, but your own institution might charge you for foreign purchases or withdrawals, so check before you go. You'll find ATMs in banks, grocery stores, gas stations, and pharmacies.

Traveler's checks are becoming less and less common, yet are still used occasionally and can be exchanged at most banks in the country, though a 2% fee is often charged. Visa and MasterCard are widely accepted throughout Honduras, and American Express and Diners Club are becoming increasingly common, although 12% surcharges are normal.

7 | When to Go

High tourist season in Honduras is during national holidays and the dry season, running roughly from January to June. Rain can occur anytime during the year, and flooding in the highlands can completely shut down roads and transportation at any time. For the Bay Islands, you should book well in advance during Semana Santa (Easter week) and Christmas/New Year's. The best months for spotting whale sharks are March and April, when rates also tend to go up. In La Mosquitia, the drier months (Feb–May and Aug–Nov) are easiest for travel; it stays nicer year-round in the Bay Islands.

Honduras lies completely within the Tropics. Temperatures range from hot and humid on the Caribbean coast (75°–93°F/24°–34°C), to mild and even cool in highland areas (61°–68°F/16°–20°C), to hot and dry along the southern Pacific coast (82°–90°F/28°–32°C). Seasonally, temperatures don't vary drastically and the change mostly relates to elevation. The amount of precipitation does vary, though. May to November is typically considered the rainy season for the interior, while September to January brings the rains for the North Coast, Bay Islands, and La Mosquitia. Hurricane season runs from August to November, although most, not all, hurricanes are a minor inconvenience.

Honduras's national holidays are New Year's Day (Jan 1), Maundy Thursday (Mar 20), Good Friday (Mar 21), Americas Day (Apr 14), Labor Day/May Day (May 1), Independence Day (Sept 15), Morazán Day (Oct 3), Christopher Columbus Day (Oct 12), Army Day (Oct 21), and Christmas Day (Dec 25).

Health Concerns

Few visitors to Honduras experience anything other than run-of-the-mill traveler's diarrhea in reaction to unfamiliar foods and any microorganisms in them, although outbreaks of cholera and hepatitis do occur. Honduras's tap water should be avoided. Mosquito-borne illnesses such as **malaria** and **dengue fever** also occur, especially during the rainy season, when mosquitoes are most prevalent. See p. 69 in "Planning Your Trip to Central America" for more info.

Hepatitis A, polio, tetanus, smallpox, and typhoid shots are recommended (but not required) for visitors planning to be in contact with local residents on an extended basis. A hepatitis B shot is suggested, but not required. Malaria and yellow fever are rare, yet if you intend on visiting extremely remote areas in La Mosquitia, you may want to discuss with your doctor your options for prevention.

Getting There
BY PLANE

Honduras has four international airports, in San Pedro Sula (p. 346), Tegucigalpa (p. 335), Roatán (p. 405), and La Ceiba (p. 387).

There are nonstop flights and connections from the United States and Canada to every international airport, although the most frequent flights land in San Pedro Sula's

Ramón Villeda Morales International Airport (SAP) and Tegucigalpa's **Toncontín International Airport (TGU)**. The major carriers are **American, Continental, Delta, TACA,** and **Spirit.** There are daily nonstop flights from Miami, Atlanta, Houston, Ft. Lauderdale, and Newark (seasonally) to San Pedro Sula and/or Tegucigalpa. There are also nonstop flights to Roatán (Bay Islands) on Thursdays, Saturdays and/or Sundays with Continental (Houston), Delta (Atlanta), and TACA (Miami and Houston). See chapter 11, "Fast Facts: Central America," for airline phone numbers and websites.

There are no direct flights between the U.K. or Europe and Honduras. Delta, Continental, and American Airlines fly between Europe and Honduras through transfer points in the United States.

From Australia and New Zealand, your best bet for getting to Honduras is by connecting in a North American gateway such as Los Angeles or Houston, and then taking any of the airlines listed under "Getting There" in the "Essentials" section of each region.

BY CRUISE SHIP & FERRY

Getting to Honduras by cruise ship is becoming increasingly popular. Cruise dockings in Roatán—to either the recently expanded port at Dixon's Cove or the new fenced-off part of the island at Mahogany Bay—have exploded in recent years. At present, the only cruise ship dock is at Coxen Hole in Roatán, which serves **Carnival** (© **888/227-6482;** www.carnival.com), **Royal Caribbean** (© **866/562-7625;** www.royalcaribbean.com), **Princess** (© **800/774-6237;** www.princesscruises.com), and **Norwegian** (© **866/234-7350;** www.ncl.com) cruise lines.

From Puerto Cortés there is ferry service to Big Creek/Mango Creek and Placencia, Belize, with the **D-Express** (© **504/991-0778;** www.belizeferry.com) on Mondays at 11:30am, returning Fridays at 9:30am. The trip takes 4 hours and costs L1,000.

BY BUS

Bus travel to and from other Central American countries is quite common with long-term travelers, but it might be too slow for you if you're visiting the region for a short time. The most popular bus operator in the region is **Tica Bus** (16a Calle and Av. 5; © **504/220-0579;** www.ticabus.com), which has daily departures from Tegucigalpa to San Salvador (6½ hr. away), Managua (7–8 hr. away), and Guatemala City (14 hr. away) that continue as far as Mexico and Panama. **Hedman Alas** (13a Calle and Av. 11; © **504/237-7143;** www.hedmanalas.com) offers daily service from Copán to Antigua and Guatemala City. There are many less direct routes to the El Salvador, Guatemala, and Nicaragua borders via slow, crowded chicken buses that rarely cost more than a dollar or two. If you are on a budget or just traveling a short distance, these aren't a bad choice, but if you have less time, stick to a reputable express company—prices anywhere in the region rarely top L95 per hour of travel.

Getting Around

Apart from the coasts and between San Pedro and the capital of Tegucigalpa, highways and paved roads in the country are severely lacking, even to national parks and tourist attractions. In and around La Mosquitia and to/from the Bay Islands, transportation by water or air is your only option for getting around.

BY PLANE

While the country's regional air carriers are more expensive than transportation by road or ferry, they are still relatively reasonably priced and can shave a day or two off your travel times within Honduras. The country has three domestic airlines: the regional TACA airline **Isleña** (© **504/441-3190;** www.flyislena.com), **Aerolíneas Sosa** (© **504/550-6545;** www.aerolineasosahn.com), and **CM Airlines** (© **504/ 668-0068;** www.cmairlines.com). Each has regular flights to/from select destinations in the country, including San Pedro Sula, Tegucigalpa, La Ceiba, Roatán, Guanaja, Utila, Puerto Lempira, and Brus Laguna. **Sami Airlines** (© **504/442-2565** in La Ceiba, or 433-8031 in Brus Laguna) has charter flights in four-person planes to La Ceiba and destinations in La Mosquitia such as Ahuas, Palacios, Belén, Brus Laguna, and Puerto Lempira. **Bay Island Airways** (© **303/242-8004** in the U.S., or 9858-8819 in Roatán; www.bayislandairways.com) offers transport around the Bay Islands via small seaplanes. See the destination sections below for more info.

BY FERRY

There is regular ferry service from the North Coast of Honduras to the Bay Islands. The *Galaxy Wave* (© **504/445-1795**) travels daily from La Ceiba to Roatán at 9:30am and 4:30pm, and from Roatán and La Ceiba at 7:30am and 2pm for a cost of L500. The *Utila Princess* (© **504/425-3390**) travels daily between La Ceiba and Utila at 9:30am and 4pm, and from Utila to La Ceiba at 6:20am and 2pm for a cost of L400. **Island Tours** (© **504/434-3421**) has an irregular service from Trujillo to Guanaja on Sundays and Thursdays at 4pm, and from Guanaja to Trujillo on Mondays and Fridays at 9am, for a cost of L750.

BY BUS

There are hundreds of bus companies in Honduras, most operating out of dirt lots and offering travel only to nearby destinations. Routes between major cities often have the fastest service and are a cheap and easy way to get from place to place. Buses to more offbeat destinations are usually slower and more crowded. There are two luxury bus companies popular with foreign travelers that travel to major cities: **Hedman Alas** (© **504/237-7143;** www.hedmanalas.com) has frequent service between San Pedro Sula, Tegucigalpa, Tela, La Ceiba, and Copán. **Viana Clase de Oro** (© **504/225-6584**) has five first-class buses journeying daily between Tegucigalpa and San Pedro Sula that continue on to La Ceiba. You can expect to pay roughly L38 to L76 per hour of bus travel on a luxury service. For local buses, you might pay a 10th of that.

BY CAR

Car and motorcycle rentals are available at most major airports from multinational companies such as Avis, Payless, Hertz, and Budget, as well as local companies. (See chapter 11, "Fast Facts: Central America," for info.) The highways along the North Coast, between San Pedro Sula and Tegucigalpa, and between San Pedro Sula and Copán, are the best in the country. Elsewhere, roads are partially paved or unpaved and are frequently flooded or impassable during the rainy season.

BY TAXI

In Tegucigalpa and some of the country's other major destinations or cities, taxis are supposed to have and use meters, although this isn't always the case. In more rural areas, taxis almost never have meters.

Tips on Accommodations

Accommodations in Honduras range from full-scale resort complexes and luxury hotels aimed at business travelers to small guesthouses, bed-and-breakfasts, and rooms rented out of someone's house. Price ranges listed in hotel write-ups reflect low to high season, though apart from the Bay Islands, most hotels do not have high-season rates.

High tourist season in Honduras is during national holidays and the dry season, running roughly from January to June, depending on what part of the country you're visiting. There is a 4% tourism tax added to all hotel rates, in addition to the 12% standard tax.

Tips on Dining

Honduras is not known for its cuisine. It does not have the creative culinary background and diverse regional plates that some Latin American countries like Mexico or Peru have. Yet, if you look around and even go off the beaten track, there are some absolute gems. The national dish of Honduras is the *plato típico,* an array of beef, plantains, beans, marinated cabbage, sour cream, and tortillas. *Anafres,* a refried-black-bean and cheese fondue served in a clay pot accompanied by tortilla chips, is a favorite appetizer. Like tacos in Mexico or *pupusas* in El Salvador, the *baleada*—a folded wheat-flour tortilla filled with beans, crumbled cheese, and sour cream, and sometimes beef, chicken, or pork—is a snack food found everywhere. In the highlands, *chuletas de cerdo,* or pork chops, are on most restaurant menus, as are steaks and other beef dishes. On the North Coast and the Bay Islands, Garífuna restaurants, or *champas,* which are thatched-roof wooden shacks often on stilts, are well known for their *tapado,* a seafood stew made with sweet potatoes, malanga, yucca, and plantains. Other popular stews are made with coconut milk and served with cassava bread.

A 10% service fee is often tacked onto bills at high-end restaurants; otherwise, it's customary to leave a 10% tip.

Tips on Shopping

While large air-conditioned shopping malls with international chains can be found in large cities like San Pedro Sula and Tegucigalpa, the best shopping for souvenirs in Honduras is often found on the street or in small artisan markets. Common items from the **western** and **southern** parts of the country include cigars, coffee, woven baskets, jade jewelry, leather goods, Lenca pottery, embroidery, and woodcarvings. **Copán** is the unrivaled center for arts and craft shopping, with a dozen small markets and many small shops and street vendors. The **Guamilito Market** in San Pedro Sula has items from all over the country, as do the artisan shops in **Valle de Angeles.** On the **Bay Islands,** Garífuna paintings and textiles, woodcarvings, straw baskets, hats, wind chimes, and carved coconuts can be found in souvenir shops in Utila and Roatán. When cruise ships are docked at Coxen Hole, there are usually small stands selling handicrafts from around the country, though prices tend to be high. In **La Mosquitia,** woodcarvings, textiles, and jewelry can be purchased, in most cases directly, from villagers.

American Express

American Express is represented in Honduras by **BAC** in Tegucigalpa at Boulevard Suyapa, Fte. (📞 **800/327-1267**). The office is open Monday to Friday from 9am to 4pm and Saturday 9am to noon.

Business Hours

Banks are open Monday to Friday from 8:30am to 4:30pm, and on Saturday from 9am to noon. General business hours are Monday through Friday from 9am to 5pm, although most restaurants and shops stay open to at least 8pm and are open daily.

Doctors

Many doctors in Honduras, especially in San Pedro Sula and Tegucigalpa, speak basic English. For a list of English-speaking doctors, call your embassy.

Embassies & Consulates

The **U.S. Embassy** is in Tegucigalpa, at Avenida La Paz (📞 **504/236-9320**; http://honduras. usembassy.gov). The **Canadian Embassy** in Tegucigalpa is at Edif. Finaciero Banexpo Local #3, Col Payaqui, Boulevar San Juan Bosco (📞 **504/232-4551**; www.embassy honduras.ca). The **British Consulate** can be found in Tegucigalpa at Colonia Reforms 2402 (📞 **504/237-6577**; reforma@cascomark. com). There are no Australian or New Zealand

embassies or consulates in Honduras.

Emergencies

For a police emergency, call 📞 **199.** For fire, call 📞 **198.** To call an ambulance, dial 📞 **195.**

Hospitals

The best hospitals and medical centers in Honduras are in San Pedro Sula and Tegucigalpa, and for any serious treatment it would be preferable to transfer to either city. The cost of medicine and treatment can be expensive, but most hospitals and pharmacies accept credit cards.

The best hospital in Tegucigalpa is the **Honduras Medical Center** on Avenida Juan Lindo (📞 **504/216-1201**); in San Pedro, try **Hospital Centro Médico Betesda** at 11a Av. NO and 11a Calle NO (📞 **504/516-0900**).

Language

Spanish is the main language in Honduras, but most people on the Bay Islands speak English. The Native languages of Lenca, Miskito, and Garífuna are also spoken in some regions.

Post Offices & Mail

Honduras has no stamp-vending machines or mailboxes, so you'll have to head to the post office to send a postcard, or ask your hotel if they can do it for you. A letter sent via regular mail to the U.S. will arrive in 5 to 10 days; the cost, at press time, is L30

for a letter and L20 for a postcard. Most post offices are open Monday to Friday from 8am to 5pm, and Saturday 8am to noon. DHL and FedEx have offices in major cities such as Tegucigalpa, San Pedro Sula, and La Ceiba.

Safety

San Pedro Sula, La Ceiba, and especially Tegucigalpa have crime problems similar to most other major Latin American cities. Most crime involves petty theft, although violent crime is not unheard of. Visitors should take measures against being pickpocketed, especially in crowded areas and at night, and they should not leave valuables in a parked vehicle due to frequent break-ins.

Taxes

Honduras levies a steep 12% **sales tax,** called ISV (Impuesto de Servicios), on all goods and services except medicine. There is a 4% tourism tax added to all hotel rates, tours, and car rentals in addition to the 12% ISV, although small hotels and community-based tour operators may not add the tax, especially if you can pay in cash. Many high-end hotels and restaurants also add a 10% service charge, which is meant to take care of tipping.

There is an international departure tax of approximately $34, payable in cash only in U.S. dollars or

Honduran lempiras, from any of the country's international airports. The departure tax on all domestic flights is approximately $1.50, and is payable only in U.S. dollars or lempiras.

Telephone See the box "Telephone Dialing Info at a Glance," earlier in this chapter, along with p. 327 in "Planning Your Trip to Central America," for info.

Tipping Diners should leave a 10% to 15% tip in restaurants, although some high-end restaurants automatically include gratuity. In hotels, tipping is left to the guest's discretion. There's no need to tip taxi drivers.

TEGUCIGALPA

241km (150 miles) S of San Pedro Sula; 86km (53 miles) S of Comayagua

Many travelers would rather not try to pronounce the name of the capital of Honduras, let alone visit it. (It's pronounced "Te-*goo*-si-*gal*-pa.") Whatever horror stories you have heard about Central American capitals, don't take them too seriously. While it isn't a favorite tourist destination like Copán, La Ceiba, or the Bay Islands, "Tegus," as Hondurans call it, is a fairly pleasant place if you can get past the smog, shantytowns, and traffic. While it was long believed that the name was a Nahuatl word meaning "silver mountain," that is not likely not the case. That story was probably made up to lure miners and settlers to the city in the mid-1500s. The meaning of the name is more clearly defined as "place of colored stones." The city sits snugly in a valley at about 1,000m (3,280 ft.), sheltering it from the sweltering heat that plagues San Pedro Sula and La Ceiba. There are several great museums and churches within the colonial center, a great clump of cloud forest nearby, and the largest cathedral in the country, a revered pilgrimage site, is only minutes from the center.

The city was founded on September 29, 1578, but it wasn't until 1880 that the capital was moved here from Comayagua by President Marco Aurelio Soto. In 1938, the city of Comayagüela was incorporated into Tegucigalpa and nearly doubled the size, which today stands at over one million inhabitants. The city is no longer the economic center of the country (that is San Pedro), but, as the capital of Honduras, it's still an important area for commerce and politics.

Essentials
GETTING THERE

Although most international travelers fly into the larger and more modern San Pedro Sula Airport, Tegucigalpa's **Toncontín International Airport** (**TGU;** ☎ **504/234-2402**) does have a few international routes. **American Airlines** (☎ **504/220-7585**), **Continental Airlines** (☎ **504/550-7124**), **Delta** (☎ **800/791-1000**), and **TACA** (☎ **504/221-6495**) all land here from North American destinations.

Regional airlines serving the capital are **Isleña Airlines** (☎ **504/236-8778;** www.flyislena.com), **Aerolíneas Sosa** (☎ **504/443-2519**), and **CM Airlines** (☎ **504/234-1886;** www.cmairlines.com). There are direct flights to Roatán, La Ceiba, and San Pedro, while other destinations connect in La Ceiba.

Toncontín has just one ATM, a craft shop, a call center, and a small cafe. The airport is 6km (3¾ miles) south of the center on the highway to Choluteca. A taxi to downtown will be about L200 to L240. Alternatively, you can catch a northbound bus or *collectivo* (shared) taxi to the center of town for L20 right outside the main airport gates—just listen for the touts shouting, "Te-goose!"

Tegucigalpa doesn't have a main bus terminal; most of the companies have terminals within a few blocks of each other in the Comayagüela section of town. Because this neighborhood isn't safe, use caution getting there and do not leave your baggage unattended. **Hedman Alas** (13a Calle and Av. 11; ✆ **504/237-7143**) has luxury service four times a day to San Pedro Sula (3½–4 hr.; L535), where connections can then be made to Copán, Tela, or La Ceiba. **Viana Clase de Oro** (Blvd. FFAA at the ESSO station; ✆ **504/225-6584**; L600) has five first-class buses daily to San Pedro Sula that continue to La Ceiba from 6:30am to 6pm.

Other options for getting to San Pedro include the operator **Saenz** (Centro Commercial Perisur; ✆ **504/233-4229**; L456), which has regular and first-class, non-stop service six times a day to the capital, along with **El Rey Express** (Banco Central; ✆ **504/237-8561**; L418), which stops in Comayagua as well as San Pedro. For La Ceiba (7 hr. away; L475), try the operator **Cristina** (✆ **504/441-2028**), which has five daily departures between 5:30am and 3:30pm.

Travelers crossing the El Salvador and Nicaragua borders have several options. To get to El Amatillo (3½ hr.; L140), on the El Salvador border, you have to catch one of the buses leaving from the Mercado Mayoreo, southwest of Comayagüela on the highway to Olancho. For the Nicaraguan border at El Paraíso (2 hr.; L120) via Danlí, try **Discua Litena** (Mercado Jacaleapa; ✆ **504/230-0470**), which leaves every hour from 6:30am to 7:30pm.

If you're traveling elsewhere in Central America, your best choice is **Tica Bus** (16a Calle and Av. 5; ✆ **504/220-0579**; www.ticabus.com), a company that has daily departures to San Salvador (6½ hr.; L950), Managua (7–8 hr.; L1,045), and Guatemala City (14 hr.; L1,140) and journeys as far as Mexico and Panama.

ORIENTATION

Tegus is one of the few colonial cities in Central America that does not follow a typical Spanish layout with a grid of streets surrounding a central square, mostly because of the uneven surface of the city. The colonial center of the city is more of a narrow strip on a central grid of about 7×20 blocks, and there are several squares—the largest is **Parque Morazán,** or the Parque Central. The city's pedestrian-only street, **Calle Peatonal,** leads west from this square, and other main streets and avenues run into or parallel to it. Most of the city's museums, churches, and artisan shops can be found within 6 blocks of Parque Central, too. The commercial center of the city and where you will find the best hotels, restaurants, and shops is **Colonia Palmira,** on the north side of the fast-food-lined Boulevard Morazán. West of the Río Choluteca, a river that divides the city, and southwest of the center is the neighborhood of **Comayagüela,** where most of the city's bus terminals can be found; this is a poorer, less safe part of town.

GETTING AROUND

Much of Tegucigalpa can be explored on foot. The colonial center and Colonia Palmira are all safe and secure during the day, though you should stick to taxicabs at night and never travel alone, just to be sure.

Taxis are cheap, plentiful, and far safer for getting between neighborhoods than walking or taking the city's public buses. Traveling within the center is usually less than L40 via cab. You can also take *colectivo* taxis for about half the price.

Most city buses run from the south or west and journey through Comayagüela before heading north and east out of the city. You'll probably use the no. 21 Tiloarque–La Sosa bus, which has stops at the Mercado Mayoreo and throughout downtown, or

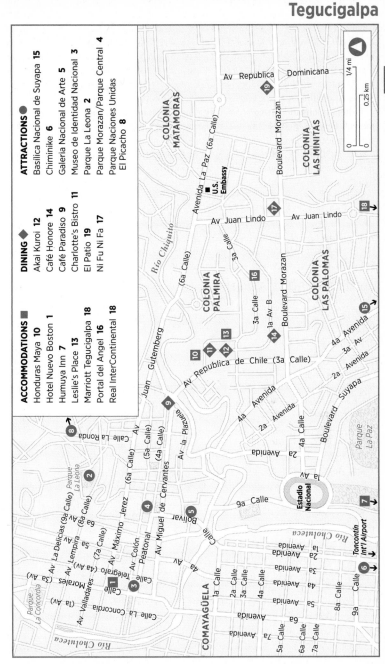

ACCOMMODATIONS ■
Honduras Maya **10**
Hotel Nuevo Boston **1**
Humuya Inn **7**
Leslie's Place **13**
Marriott Tegucigalpa **18**
Portal del Angel **16**
Real InterContinental **18**

DINING ◆
Akai Kuroi **12**
Café Honore **14**
Café Paradiso **9**
Charlotte's Bistro **11**
El Patio **19**
Ni Fu Ni Fa **17**

ATTRACTIONS ●
Basílica Nacional de Suyapa **15**
Chiminike **6**
Galeria Nacional de Arte **5**
Museo de Identidad Nacional **3**
Parque La Leona **2**
Parque Morazan/Parque Central **4**
Parque Naciones Unidas
El Picacho **8**

the no. 32, which stops at the National University, the most. It'll cost only about L10 to get anywhere in town. Or you might want to simply take cabs instead of busing it around town, because of safety issues.

Tegucigalpa is right on one of the best highways in the country, CA 5, which ends 241km (150 miles) away in San Pedro Sula, passing Lago de Yojoa, Siguatepe, and Comayagua en route. CA 5 also heads south to Choluteca, where you can connect with CA 1, or the Pan-American Highway (Carretera Panamericana), which runs to El Salvador, Nicaragua, and beyond. The CA 11-A road to Copán is a jaw-dropping route through the mountains, which is windy, mostly unpaved, and sometimes impassable due to rain. Many drivers prefer to head back toward San Pedro Sula and catch highway CA 4.

If you're heading to the North Coast, you have two options: One is to go back to San Pedro Sula, and the other is an unpredictable route through the wild Olancho region that is prone to highway robberies and poor roads. Most choose the prior.

Car-rental agencies can be found the airport and in town. Companies include **Advance** (beside the Institute of Tourism, Col. San Carlos; ☎ **504/235-9528**; www.advancerentacar.com), **Avis** (Edificio Marinakys at Blvd. Suyapa; ☎ **504/239-5712**; www.avis.com), **Payless** (Edificio Saenz at Blvd. Europea; ☎ **504/245-7054**; www.www.paylesscar.com), and **Hertz** (Centro Comercio Villa Real; ☎ **504/235-8582**; www.hertz.com).

VISITOR INFORMATION

The **Instituto Hondureño de Turismo** (Av. Cruz and Calle Mexico; ☎ **504/220-1600**; www.letsgohonduras.com) has friendly English-speaking staff who can provide general information and give you their excellent bilingual guide, *Honduras Tips*. It's open Monday to Friday from 7:30am to 4:30pm.

FAST FACTS   Most banks and ATMs are either downtown or along Boulevard Morazán, as well as the malls. **BAC** (Blvd. Morazán and Av. Cruz) exchanges traveler's checks and has a 24-hour ATM, as does **Banco Atlántida** on Parque Central. There's an official currency exchange booth at the airport; less official operations are on Calle Peatonal and in the Parque Morazán.

Honduras Medical Center (Av. Juan Lindo; ☎ **504/216-1201**), one of the country's top hospitals, is open 24 hours, as is **Clinica Viera** (across from the Alcadia; ☎ **504/237-3156**).

Hondutel, 1 block off Parque Central at Avenida Colón and Calle El Telégrafo, offers international calls, although you can find cheap call service at any of the cyber-cafés in the colonial center.

The main **police** office is at 5a Avenida and Avenida Lempira; police can be reached by dialing ☎ **504/779-0476** or 199.

The downtown **post office** is at Avenida Barahona and Calle El Telégrafo. There are also a **DHL** (☎ **504/220-1800**) and **Mailboxes, Etc.** (☎ **504/232-3184**) on Boulevard Morazán.

Safety note: Tegucigalpa as a whole is not a safe city. Parts, such as the center of town and Boulevard Morazán, are fine for strolling during the day, but don't flash any valuables like jewelry, cameras, or fancy electronics. In other areas, especially in Comayagüela and around the bus terminals, walk with extreme caution and try to avoid walking alone. At night, always take taxis wherever you go.

What to See & Do
ATTRACTIONS IN TOWN

Parque Morazán or **Parque Central ★★** is the epicenter of all activity in the city's colonial center, and most museums and churches can be found within a few blocks of it. In addition to the park's attractions listed below, it's worth seeing the baroque **Cathedral,** on the eastern edge of the park, which was built between 1765 and 1782 and honors Saint Michael (San Miguel) the Archangel, Tegucigalpa's patron saint. **Iglesia de Nuestra Señora de los Dolores,** a few blocks northwest of the park, was built in 1732, and features an attractive selection of religious art such as reliefs of the Stations of the Cross, along with a carved altar. The big plaza fronting the church is often packed with artisan stalls and food vendors. Other churches such as **Parroquia San Francisco,** the oldest church in the city (it was built in 1592), and **Iglesia la Merced,** beside the Galeria Nacional de Arte, are worth a peek when open (hours vary).

Chiminike ★★ ☺ This fun, funky children's museum is all about interactivity. Exhibits like a grocery store and construction site have been designed to get kids to learn about the world without their knowing it. Most fun is the room dedicated to El Cuerpo Humano, or the human body room, where there's a giant Operator game, a crawl-through intestinal tract, and the chance to make fart noises. Also in the museum is a giant volcano that produces "lava," a bubble room, a VW Beetle that encourages finger-paint graffiti, and a room tilted at a 22-degree angle.

Blvd. Fuerzas Armadas de Honduras, 7km (4⅓ miles) south of the center. ✆ **504/291-0339.** www.chiminike.com. Admission L50. Tues-Fri 9am-noon and 2-5pm; Sat-Sun 10am-1pm and 2-5pm.

Galeria Nacional de Arte ★★ The most important art museum in the country, the Galeria Nacional de Arte is housed beside Iglesia la Merced in a building that dates from 1694, and that in its past lives was a convent and home to the Universidad Nacional. The exhibits, in both English and Spanish, are displayed chronologically according to when they were created. The exhibits begin with rock art and petroglyphs from pre-Maya civilizations, and then move into stone and ceramic art from the Mayas and other indigenous groups. The colonial period is widely represented with oil paintings, gold and silver objects, sculptures, and religious art. The modern era has hundreds of excellent pieces from internationally known Honduran painters like Pablo Zelaya Sierra and José Antonio Velásquez.

Plaza de la Merced. ✆ **504/237-9884.** Admission L50. Mon-Sat 9am-4pm; Sun 9am-1pm.

Museo de Identidad Nacional ★★ This brilliant museum opened in 2006 in the former Palace of Ministries. It features some big-name art exhibitions from around Latin America and also displays the history of the country from its Pre-Columbian beginnings to modern times via charts, photos, documents, scale models, art, and artifacts like the femur and tibia of a giant sloth. Their latest addition is *Virtual Copán,* an animated film shown four times a day that takes you through a virtual tour of the Maya ruins and explains how they were built.

Av. Barahona and Calle El Telégrafo. ✆ **504/238-7412.** www.min.hn. Admission L50. Tues-Sat 9am-5pm; Sun 10am-4pm.

Parque Naciones Unidas El Picacho ☺ This new park about 6km (3¾ miles) from the center of town is home to the huge concrete statue of Christ, *Cristo del*

Picacho, that watches over the city. The main reason to come here is for the views of the capital and the surrounding mountains. But there's also a small zoo with animals from around the country, like monkeys, snakes, macaws, and iguanas, as well as a taxidermy collection that, in my opinion, is located too close to the living creatures. Buses to here leave from behind Iglesia Los Dolores (see above).

Entrance 5km (3 miles) north of downtown. Admission L20. Daily 8am–5pm.

ATTRACTIONS OUTSIDE TOWN

The serene, 18th-century Spanish mining town of **Santa Lucia,** about 30 minutes outside Tegucigalpa, is a favorite weekend retreat for the residents of Tegucigalpa. There are artisan shops, outdoor cafes, an 18th-century church with Spanish oil paintings, and a few nice lodges, including the **Hotel Santa Lucía Resort (✆ 504/ 779-0540;** www.hotelsantaluciaresort.com). Doubles range from L475 to L950. To get here from Tegucigalpa, take any San Juancito–bound bus and ask to be let off at the turnoff from town, 2km (1¼ miles) from the center.

The colonial mountain village of **Valle de Angeles ★** is 22km (14 miles) east of Tegucigalpa, just 8km (5 miles) past Santa Lucía. Though it's nearly empty during the week, it's packed full during the weekends with day-trippers from Tegucigalpa. It's far more touristy than Santa Lucía, but in a good way. The town has been virtually restored to its 16th-century glory. Many of the streets are pedestrian-only and are lined with *artesenía* shops that sell goods from all over the country, like woodcarvings, wicker baskets, hand-carved furniture, paintings, Lenca pottery, dolls, and even a leather factory and outlet. Items cost quite a bit less than in Tegucigalpa. From Tegucigalpa (45 min. away) you can catch a bus from the corner of Avenida Próceres and Avenida República Dominicana.

The **Basílica Nacional de Suyapa ★★** (no phone; www.virgendesuyapa.hn) is the largest cathedral in the country, but is perhaps better known for being the discovery site of a tiny cedar statue of the Virgin Mary. This statue, discovered in 1747, is famous throughout Honduras for its healing powers. The Virgin has long been the patron saint of the country and in 1982 was named by papal decree as the patron saint of all of Central America. The permanent home of the statue is the nearby Iglesia de Suyapa, but the statue is brought to this Gothic cathedral, built in 1954, for special events like the Feria de la Virgen de Suyapa. The cathedral's grounds are open to visitors daily, but the basilica itself is open only during Mass and holidays. You can take a taxi to Suyapa, 7km (4⅓ miles) south of the center on Boulevard Suyapa, from Parque La Merced; a standard taxi should cost about L55 to L95.

Every February 3 and the week surrounding that date is **La Feria de la Virgen de Suyapa,** a time for celebration of the iconic statue throughout Tegucigalpa and the whole country. The processions and festivities in Tegucigalpa are centered around the Basílica de Suyapa.

OUTDOOR ACTIVITIES

Tegucigalpa is far from a major golfing destination, but it does have a small, 9-hole course, considered one of the best in the country. The **Villa Elena Country Club (✆ 504/224-0400;** www.villaelena.synthasite.com) is 9km (5⅔ miles) north of the capital on the road to San Pedro Sula, and in a new residential and ecological reserve area. There's also a Mexican restaurant, a bar, and tennis courts.

For the best views of the city, hike up the steep **Paseo La Leona** of Barrio Buenos Aires, which features a small, grassy area with benches, a playground, and a small cafe. There are a few interesting colonial mansions bordering the park, though all are private residences. If you want to save your strength, you can take a taxi there and walk back down to the center. (Just avoid doing so after dark.)

Shopping

If you can't make it out to **Valle de Angeles,** which offers wares for quite a bit cheaper than in the city, for souvenir shopping (p. 340), head to any of the artisan stalls by the Iglesia Los Dolores and along Avenida Miguel de Cervantes, just before the bridge to Colonia Palmira. Or check out **Megaplaza Mall,** on Avenida Juan Pablo II near the Marriott Hotel, which has all the chain shops and restaurants that you would expect in a big North American mall.

Where to Stay
VERY EXPENSIVE

Marriott Tegucigalpa ☺ While it's a small step down from the Real InterContinental next door, the Tegucigalpa Marriott—formerly the Crowne Plaza—is more or less what you would expect from the international chain: It's big, with lots of facilities, a nice pool, a few good restaurants, and a great complimentary breakfast buffet, but otherwise it's nothing you haven't seen before. Like the Real InterContinental, it is out of the way of most attractions, unless chain restaurants and an air-conditioned mall are on your itinerary.

Av. Roble, beside Multiplaza Mall. ✆ **504/232-0033.** Fax 504/235-7700. www.marriott.com. 153 units. L3,020 double; L3,500 executive room. Rates include breakfast. AE, DC, MC, V. **Amenities:** Restaurant; bar; fitness center; pool; spa. *In room:* A/C, TV, hair dryer, minibar, Wi-Fi (additional charge).

Portal del Angel ★★★ Some laughed when the idea of a luxurious boutique hotel in Tegucigalpa was being floated, but Portal del Angel has been up and running for a decade now. Why? Because it has style. It's both hip and elegant at the same time. Marble pillars and wrought-iron balconies are paired with tropical plants, and floors say tropical opulence in every way. Rooms are better yet, with lots of space, good lighting from large windows, parquet and caoba floors, and locally made hand-carved chests and furniture. The bar closes at 10pm, but that's late enough for a fine Honduran cigar and glass from their decent wine list. It's in the Zona Viva neighborhood, within a block from top restaurants and bars.

Av. República del Perú 2115, Colonia Palmira. ✆ **504/239-6538.** www.portaldelangel.com. 23 units. L2,470 double; L3,800 suite. MC, V. **Amenities:** Restaurant; bar; pool. *In room:* A/C, TV.

Real InterContinental ★★ The guiding principle behind this hotel, the top lodging in the city, is to make guests feel like they aren't even in Tegucigalpa. Upon entering, you are transported to a world of marble floors and pillars, vaulted ceilings, Moorish arches, shaded lounges, and tropical plants in all the right places. Rooms have flatscreen TVs with "on demand" video, clock/radios with MP3 connections, and an earthy decor, punctuated by tasteful jungle-themed art. Executive suites have computers with flatscreen monitors, cordless phones, and fax machines. The downside, especially if you are here to sightsee, is that you are well away from the center, albeit in an up-and-coming area with chain restaurants and a mall.

Av. Roble, next to Multiplaza Mall. ✆ **504/290-2700.** Fax 504/231-2828. www.ichotelsgroup.com. 157 units. L2,565 double; L5,130 suite. AE, DC, MC, V. **Amenities:** Restaurant; bar; fitness center; pool. *In room:* A/C, TV, hair dryer, minibar, Wi-Fi (additional charge).

EXPENSIVE

Honduras Maya ★   Standing proudly on the top of the hill in what could be considered the best location in Colonia Palmira, the 10-story Honduras Maya hotel and convention center is a favorite of business travelers and tourists. Much of the hotel has been renovated in the past few years, which has helped revive it. Don't worry, though; the Mayan designs on the boxy facade are still there. The rooms, comparable to the Marriott and Real InterContinental, have all been given a face-lift as well. Corner rooms have windows on two sides and the best views, which on clear days at sundown show the city in a beautiful glow. There are several restaurants and bars, plus a few shops and an attached casino.

3a Calle and Av. Republica de Chile, Colonia Palmira. 🕐 **504/280-5000.** www.hotelhondurasmaya. com. 163 units. L2,470 double. Rates include breakfast. AE, MC, V. **Amenities:** 2 restaurants; bar; gym; pool; tennis courts; travel agency. *In room:* A/C, TV, minibar, Wi-Fi.

Humuya Inn ★★ 🛍   First-rate service and a well-maintained property are what make this underrecognized hotel great. Rooms and common areas are painted brightly and have high wood-beam ceilings and tile floors. Indigenous art is sprinkled throughout, lending the hotel a personal touch that some of the larger and more expensive chain hotels lack. Rooms are clean and decently sized, and have the same amenities of hotels that charge twice the price. The hotel is in a residential area, about 10 minutes from the city center; in my opinion, this is actually a plus, since it helps keep your stay quiet.

Colonia Humuya 1150. 🕐 **504/239-2206.** Fax 504/239-5099. www.humuyainn.com. 12 units. L1,140 double; L1,710 suite. MC, V. **Amenities:** Restaurant; laundry service. *In room:* A/C, TV, fridge (suites only), hair dryer, Wi-Fi.

MODERATE

Leslie's Place ★   What's that tiny bed-and-breakfast doing tucked in between the Honduras Maya and other high-rise hotels on top of the hill in Colonia Palmira? It's serving as a welcome change, that's what. This bright-yellow private-home-turned-inn is one of the better budget places in the area. Though they're not as impressive as those at the nearby, more expensive resorts, rooms are spacious and breezy, with tile floors and matching wood furniture. There's a pleasant breakfast-and-lunch area beside the property's garden.

Calzada San Martin 452, Colonia Palmira. 🕐 **504/220-5325.** Fax 504/220-7492. www.dormir.com. 20 units. L1,254 double with fan; L1,450 double with A/C. Rates include breakfast. MC, V. **Amenities:** Restaurant. *In room:* A/C, fan, TV, Wi-Fi.

INEXPENSIVE

Hotel Nuevo Boston   One of the few acceptable budget places to stay in the city center, the American-owned Nuevo Boston is just a few steps from the Iglesia Los Dolores (p. 339). The rooms surround two small courtyards and are pretty basic; there aren't even TVs. Rooms facing the street are bigger and have balconies. Reliable hot water and clean private bathrooms are available, though, which is about all you can hope for in this price range.

Maximo Jeréz 321, downtown. 🕐 **504/237-9411.** 6 units. L340 double. No credit cards. *In room:* Fan.

Where to Dine
EXPENSIVE

Akai Kuroi ★ JAPANESE   This trendy, new Japanese and sushi restaurant, in Colonia Palmira and not far from the Honduras Maya, may be pricey, but it's for a good reason. The rolls, sashimi, and teppanyaki are all beautifully prepared and the service is outstanding. Since this is one of the city's more decidedly upscale dining spots, on most evenings you'll find a group of beautiful young people drinking and sharing a sushi boat here.

Av. Republica de Peru beside Hotel San Martín, Colonia Palmira. (©) **504/208-4435.** Main courses L190-L475. AE, MC, V. Mon-Sat noon-11pm; Sun noon-7pm.

Charlotte's Bistro ★ INTERNATIONAL Though Charlotte's is across the street from the Villa Real shopping plaza and very much in the center of Tegucigalpa, blink and you might think you stumbled into a Parisian cafe. The restaurant, tucked into a leafy colonial house, is one of the more romantic options in town and more elegant than nearby trendier restaurants, like Akai Kuroi. The food is eclectic, ranging from French and Italian to Thai, Indian, and Honduran. There's also a coffee bar selling cakes and pastries where you can stop by for a snack or linger after your meal.

3a Calle and Av. Republica de Chile, Colonia Palmira. (©) **504/238-1803.** Main courses L130-L265. MC, V. Mon-Wed noon-10pm; Thurs-Sat noon-11pm.

El Patio ★★ HONDURAN In operation for 3 decades, El Patio is legendary in the capital for its Honduran cuisine. The rustic atmosphere, complete with a brick patio and open grill, seems to have struck a chord with the populace and has attracted everyone from priests and presidents to famous Honduran musicians. Grilled meats and chicken are the specialty and are all served with french fries, plantains, or onion rings. There's also *anafres* (refried-bean and cheese fondue in a clay pot), surf and turf, *chuleta de cerdo* (pork chops), and a large *pinchos* menu, consisting of small meat plates with kebabed chicken, beef, pork, shrimp, or chorizo all prepared in a dozen ways.

Near the end of Blvd. Morazán, Colonia Palmira. (©) **504/221-4141.** Main courses L150-L265. MC, V. Daily 11am-11pm.

Ni Fu Ni Fa ARGENTINE This Argentine-style steakhouse is one of the current "it" spots in Colonia Palmira. Thick slabs of beef—mostly high-quality imported cuts, including multiperson combination platters with chorizo, pork, ribs, and steak—are the modus operandi here. There's also a nice salad bar, full bar, and selection of Argentine wine. A second location recently opened in the Barrio Los Andes section of San Pedro.

Mall El Dorado at Blvd. Morazán, Colonia Palmira. (©) **504/221-2056.** Main courses L130-L340. AE, MC, V. Daily 11am-11pm.

MODERATE

Café Honore ★ DELI Café Honore, a small, airy eatery with just a handful of tables on a busy restaurant strip in Colonia Palmira, is best known for gourmet sandwiches that most locals dream of being able to eat daily. Only high-quality meats and cheeses, which are sold on the deli side of the restaurant, and freshly baked breads are used. Try the El Josefredo with serrano ham and Manchego cheese, or the Turkey and Cranberry. There's also a nice array of soups, including tasty corn chowder, Peruvian ceviche, carpaccio, a global wine list, Blood Mary specials, and Putomayo music collections often playing.

Av. Republica de Argentina 1941, Colonia Palmira. (©) **504/239-7566.** Main courses L75-L150. MC, V. Daily noon-10pm.

INEXPENSIVE

On the patio in front of Iglesia Los Dolores (p. 339), as well as other locations around the city center, there are food stalls set up selling some of the tastiest dishes for the cheapest prices. You'll find Honduran *baleadas,* Salvadoran *pupusas,* grilled chicken and beef kabobs, and the occasional intestine. As always with street food, stick to the cleaner stalls and the ones the locals are going to. Credit cards aren't accepted, and most meals cost between L10 and L60.

Café Paradiso ★ CAFE   This is a true cafe in every sense of the word. Not only is it a perfect place for coffee, tea, and snacks like ham-and-cheese croissants, but it serves as a hub of local art and culture. In addition to boasting a small bookstore and free Wi-Fi, the cafe shows indie movies every Tuesday, hosts poetry readings on Thursdays, and features acoustic music acts on the weekends. Located in an aged colonial building with wrought-iron windows, the Paradiso also has more Spanish flair than most other places in the center. For anyone who's antiestablishment or looking to tune into the local art scene, it's paradise.

Av. Miguel Paz Barahona 1351, center of town. ℂ **504/237-0337.** Main courses L55–L110. No credit cards. Mon–Sat 10am–10pm.

Rincon Mexicano MEXICAN   If you want to find a meal between museum visits and prefer to avoid the fast-food chains that dominate downtown, this small eatery with a maze of simple dining rooms is a good choice. Tortas, tacos, and chicken mole are all worth their weight in Aztec gold, while the cheap-as-chips margaritas are hard to avoid.

Av. Colón and Calle El Telégrafo, Downtown. ℂ **504/222-8368.** Main courses L70–L140. AE, MC, V. Mon–Sat noon–midnight.

Tegulcigapa After Dark

The most elegant way to spend an evening in the capital is to head to a highbrow performance downtown at the spectacular Teatro Nacional Manuel Bonilla (Av. Barahona at Parque Herrera; ℂ **504/222-4366**), modeled after the Plaza Athenée in Paris. On select nights you will find opera, dance, and concerts featuring some of the best performers in the country. You can ask at the box office or check the local newspapers for dates and prices.

There are several casinos in Tegucigalpa hotels, though the only one that's any good is the **Casino Royale** at the Honduras Maya (p. 342). They have table games like blackjack, roulette, and baccarat, as well as a small section of slot machines. Bring an ID to get in and don't even think about wearing shorts—it's a dressy nightlife spot.

Most of the city's bars and clubs are in Colonia Palmira along Boulevard Morazán, and most have covers of about L100. Try **Kabballah Lounge** (in front of the Naciones Unidas/United Nations; www.kabbalahlounge.com), a sleek bar and lounge attracting a mix of 20- and 30-somethings. This is the most gay-friendly bar in town. If you are staying at one of the more upscale hotels, ask your concierge to put you on the guest list. Also, don't count out **Sabor Cubana** (Av. República de Argentina 1933) in Colonia Palmira for salsa dancing. For a pub atmosphere, try **Salt & Pepper** (Calle Castaño Sur; ℂ **504/235-7738**) or **Fine London Pub** (Av. Republica de Peru across from Hotel Honduras Maya; ℂ **504/238-1446**). If you'd like to catch a movie, the best theater is the **Cinemark** (ℂ **504/231-2044;** www.cinemarkca. com) at the Multiplaza Mall on Avenida Juan Pablo II.

A Side Trip to Parque Nacional La Tigra ★

This 238-sq.-km (92-sq.-mile) cloud forest park, the first protected area in the country, is only 22km (14 miles) from Tegucigalpa. Named a national park in 1982, La Tigra had been nearly destroyed by loggers and the El Rosario Mining Company until the government stepped in, although much of what is left is secondary growth. Remnants of mine shafts and buildings can still be found in the park, although they should be avoided in most instances.

Most who visit the park are after one thing: birds. More than 350 species have been identified in the park, which is second in the country to Lago de Yojoa. Rare species such as the resplendent quetzal, wine-throated hummingbird, and rufous-browed wren, are seen by a lucky few, as are mammals such as pumas, agoutis, and armadillos. Plant life includes pine forests, bromeliads, orchids, ferns, lichens, and mushrooms.

There are eight good hiking trails through the park, as well as two entrances. At the first entrance, at Jutiapa, there's a small **visitor center** (© **504/238-6269;** www.amitigra.org) with a few cabins and a small new ecolodge with rooms that rent for L475 per person. Most hiking trails begin from this first entrance; these trails are used by the majority of visitors and are in good condition. The **Sendero Principal,** the main route through the park that extends 6km (3¾ miles) from one end to the other, follows what was once the main road for the miners, and has been allowed to deteriorate into a more natural state. Almost all other trails branch off from this one, including the **Sendero la Cascada,** a trail that reaches a small waterfall (it's best visited Oct–Feb, when the water is more visible) after 2km (1¼ miles). It connects to the **Sendero la Mina,** or the mine trail, several kilometers from the other end of the park. **Sendero las Plancitos,** an 8km (5-mile) loop from the Sendero Principal, is the longest, toughest, and least-used trail in the park and your best chance at spotting wildlife.

The second entrance, at the western end of the park, is at the **El Rosario Mining Company headquarters,** 3km (1¾ miles) above the town of San Juancito. There's a small ecolodge, **Cabaña Mirador El Rosario** (© **504/987-5835**), run by a German couple not far from the entrance. A double runs L475. Camping is not allowed in the park, but there is a small campground (L100 per person) near the Jutiapa entrance with fire pits and toilets.

Unless you are going with a tour company or have your own car, access to the park is not easy. To get to Jutiapa by bus, you need to catch an El Hatillo–bound bus (the trip takes 1½ hr., and buses run daily every 45 min. beginning at 6am) from the Dippsa station, at Avenida Jeréz and Avenida Plazuela. Let the driver know you are going to the park and he'll drop you about 2km (1¼ miles) from the entrance at Los Planes, the closest you can get. For the western entrance, take a San Juancito–bound bus (the trip takes 1½ hr., and buses leave daily at 3pm) from Mercado San Pablo. From San Juancito, you must walk or hitch a ride the 3km (1¾ miles) uphill to El Rosario.

Grayline Tours (www.graylinemundomaya.com) runs 6-hour tours from Tegucigalpa on a regular basis and includes lunch and a guided hike on a short trail from Jutiapa. The cost is $90. **Amitigra** (© **504/232-6771;** www.amitigra.org), a nonprofit ecological foundation in Tegucigalpa, controls access to the park and can make arrangements for staying overnight in the visitor center. The park is open daily from 8am to 5pm. Admission is L190 per adult, and L95 per child.

WESTERN HONDURAS

The western part of Honduras is a land far removed from the country's beach mindset—it's a place where cowboys share the streets with cars and where orchids grow amid plentiful pine forests. For many, this is the real Honduras, and it technically also includes the must-see ruins of Copán; Santa Rosa de Copán, one of the centers of the country's cigar production; and Gracias, Central America's first capital and the gateway to the cloud forests of Parque Nacional Montaña de Celaque—all of which are covered separately below.

Your first foray into the West will most often be the pulsating capital of San Pedro Sula. While it lies in the corner of the region, you almost always have to come through this vibrant, cluttered city to get anywhere here. As you travel farther away from San Pedro Sula, the population thins out substantially, the mountains grow taller, and the fog and mist thicken. Even deeper into the mountains are numerous Lenca villages such as La Campa, which have remained practically unchanged for centuries.

San Pedro Sula

San Pedro Sula, the loud, brash, economic transportation hub of Honduras (241km/150 miles north of Tegucigalpa) often serves to introduce visitors to the western part of the country, if not the country as a whole, although many high-tail it out of here almost immediately after arriving. There is little of interest to passing tourists other than a few good hotels, westernized malls, North American chain restaurants, a handful of good markets, a couple of museums, and some upscale clubs. The chaotic, sometimes dangerous center lacks much charm and the city's wealthy cling to the suburbs on the outskirts and surrounding hillsides.

The city was founded on June 27, 1536, by Don Pedro de Alvarado and was originally named Villa de San Pedro de Puerto Caballos, although it was quickly renamed San Pedro "Sula," from the Usula word that means "Valley of Birds." The town was intended to be a point of transfer of goods from Nicaragua, El Salvador, and Guatemala onto the coast at Puerto Cortés. However, pirate attacks nearly destroyed that mission, and the town was practically deserted by the 19th century. It remained a rural backwater until the 1920s, when the United Fruit Company set up shop to expand their banana plantations; the population exploded from about 10,000 to 100,000 in just a few years. Much of the country's industry and exportation still revolves around the city, the second largest in the country.

ESSENTIALS
Getting There

Ramón Villeda Morales International Airport, sometimes just called **San Pedro Sula International Airport** (**SAP**), sits 15km (9⅓ miles) east of the city on the road to La Ceiba. It is the country's busiest airport and offers the most international connections. Continental, American Airlines, Delta, TACA, and Spirit fly here directly from points in the U.S. such as Miami, Houston, Atlanta, New York, Los Angeles, and Fort Lauderdale. Regional airlines serving San Pedro include **Isleña Airlines** (© 504/552-8322; www.flyislena.com), **Aerolíneas Sosa** (© 504/550-6545; www.aerolineasosahn.com), and **CM Airlines** (© 504/668-0068; www.cmairlines. com); these airlines fly to Tegucigalpa, La Ceiba, Roatán, Puerto Lempira, and other Central American destinations such as San Salvador, San José, Guatemala City, and Managua.

ACCOMMODATIONS ■

Casa del Arbol **6**

Crowne Plaza **5**

Gran Hotel Sula **7**

Hilton Princess
San Pedro Sula **13**

Metrotel Express **10**

Real InterContinental
San Pedro Sula **15**

Tamarindo Hostel **2**

DINING ◆

Arte Marianos **12**

Café Skandia **7**

Deriva Enoteca **1**

El Portal de las Carnes **14**

Plaza Tipico Coracts **9**

Restaurante Don Udo's **3**

ATTRACTIONS ●

Museo de Arqueología
e Historia de San
Pedro Sula **8**

Museo de la Naturaleza **4**

Parque Central **11**

A taxi from the airport to the center of town should run about L190 to L230. There's also a **Hedman-Alas** (☏ **504/553-1361;** www.hedmanalas.com) bus terminal at the airport, with buses that run three times a day to La Ceiba or six times a day to Copán or Tegucigalpa.

All roads lead to San Pedro. It is the transportation hub of the country and almost always a necessary point of transfer between any two long-distance points. The best highway in the country and one of the best in Central America—CA 5—traverses the distance between San Pedro Sula and Tegucigalpa and passes through Lago de Yojoa, Siguatepe, and Comayagua along the way. It can be extremely crowded (semi trucks use this road to haul goods from one coast to the other) and accidents can drag traffic to a screeching halt, yet if things move smoothly you can make the 241km (150-mile) trip in under 4 hours on this road.

If you're coming to San Pedro Sula from Tela, La Ceiba, or the North Coast, take **CA 13.** If you're driving here from Copán, you have a straight shot on **CA 11** to the town of La Entrada, where you will continue on **CA 4** to downtown.

Most major North American car-rental agencies, such as **Avis** (☏ **504/668-3164;** www.avis.com), **Budget** (☏ **504/668-3179;** www.budget.com.hn), **Hertz**

(☏ **504/668-3156;** www.hertz.com), and **Thrifty** (☏ **504/668-3154;** www.thrifty.com) have a counter at the San Pedro airport and an office in town.

For years there was only talk of a main bus terminal, but when that talk turned to action, few bus companies actually moved there, and remained scattered across the city. In 2008, after much ado, all bus companies finally moved into the new terminal. The new station, the **Terminal Metropolitana de Autobuses,** is 5km (3 miles) south of town, on CA 5 toward Tegucigalpa. Hedman Alas (7 and 8 Av., 3 Calle NO; ☏ **504/553-1361;** www.hedmanalas.com) is the best bus line in Honduras and the most useful for tourists who are sticking to the country's main destinations. It has mostly nonstop, first-class service several times per day to the San Pedro airport (20 min. away), Tela (1½ hr. away), La Ceiba (3 hr. away), Trujillo (6 hr. away), Copán Ruínas (3 hr. away), Comayagua (3½ hr. away), and Tegucigalpa (4½ hr. away). The company also offers connecting service in Copán to Guatemala City and Antigua, Guatemala.

Other companies that travel from San Pedro Sula to Tegucigalpa include **Saenz** (☏ **504/553-4969**), which has regular and first-class, nonstop service six times a day to the capital, **El Rey Express** (☏ **504/550-8950;** www.reyexpress.net), and **Viana** (Av. Circunvalación; ☏ **504/556-9261**), which offers Clase Oro/Gold Class service to Tegucigalpa, as well as La Ceiba.

To reach Gracias, try **Gracianos** (☏ **504/656-1403**) at the main terminal, which has departures until 2pm for the 4½-hour ride that passes through Santa Rosa de Copán and La Entrada. To reach Tela, try **Tela Express** (9 Av. 9 and 10 Calle; ☏ **504/550-8355**) with five daily departures. If you're heading to La Ceiba and Trujillo, check out **Cotuc** (☏ **504/520-1597**), which has five daily trips from the main terminal.

To reach Managua or Guatemala City, your best choice is **TICA** (☏ **504/556-5149**), which runs buses daily at 5am from the main terminal. Buses first stop in Tegucigalpa before heading out of the country.

Orientation

The dividing marker for San Pedro Sula is **Avenida Circunvalación,** a large boulevard that encircles the downtown area, with Parque Central at its center. Many amenities, like gas stations, restaurants, and malls, can be found radiating off this avenue. The center of town is laid out in a standard grid divided by four quadrants: northeast, southeast, northwest, and southwest. Avenues lead from north to south; streets, from east to west. The area on the western side of Circunvalación is where you will find the City Mall, Multiplaza Mall, several top hotels, and nearly all of the best restaurants and nightspots.

Getting Around

Apart from a few of the major hotels, almost every site of interest to the typical traveler sits within the circular Circunvalación and can be reached on foot. Some areas can be dangerous, through, and robberies have occurred, so it is best to take taxis, especially during the night. Rides in the center will rarely run over L35.

Visitor Information

There's no official visitor center in San Pedro Sula, but you can check out the private tour office **Servicios Culturales y Turísticos** (Calle 4a, btw. Av. 3a and 4a; ☏ **504/552-4048**) for maps and information.

FAST FACTS **Banco Atlántida** (✆ **504/558-1580**) on Parque Central exchanges traveler's checks, gives cash advances on credit cards, and has an ATM. There are also ATMs in every mall, most of the large hotels, some gas stations, and scattered about downtown in 24-hour booths. There's a black-market currency exchange at Parque Central, but rates are no different from those of the money-changers in storefronts and at the airport.

You can contact your embassy for a list of doctors in San Pedro or try **Centro Médico Betesda** (Av. 11a NO and Calle 11a NO; ✆ **504/516-0900**), which is open daily 24 hours for emergencies and has consultations from 9 to 11am and 3 to 6pm.

Within a few blocks of Parque Central, there are a dozen small Internet cafes charging less than L20 per hour that also have net phones for international calls and software for downloading digital photos. Or try the local telephone company **Hondutel,** at Avenida 4a SO and 4a Calle SO, where you can make long-distance calls for a few lempira a minute. There's also a cybercafé at the airport, but prices there are four times as expensive.

The **Tourist Police** (Av. 12a NO and Calle 1a; ✆ **504/550-3472**) take calls daily, for 24 hours.

The **post office** is at Avenida 3a SO and Calle 9a SO Correos. You can send packages from here, but a safer and more efficient way is through **DHL** (Circunvalación at Brigada No. 105; ✆ **504/550-1000**) or **FedEx** (Calle 17 and Av. 10 SO No. 56).

WHAT TO SEE & DO

Parque Central (Central Park) is the heart of San Pedro and is located smack in the middle of town at 1 Calle and 3 Avenida. Most of the city's attractions, as well as restaurants and shops, are clustered around this park. Though the park lacks the charm of colonial centers in Tegucigalpa and Comayagua, it's still the most identifiable landmark (apart from the giant Coca-Cola sign on one of the hillsides) and most popular meeting place in the city. The **Cathedral** at the 3 Avenida side of the park, built in 1949, doesn't have the history or elegance of some of the country's better-known churches; nevertheless, it is worth a peek (it's open only during Mass) in this attraction-starved city.

Museo de Arqueología e Historia de San Pedro Sula (Museum of Anthropology and History of San Pedro Sula) ★ Only a few blocks from Central Park, this must-see museum walks you through the history of the Sula Valley and Honduras from pre-Columbian times, during colonial rule, and into the modern era. Most of the artifacts, which have labels in English and Spanish, were found in the area. There's a bookstore and handicraft shop inside with hard-to-find books on the Mayas, Honduran history, and handmade crafts from indigenous tribes.

3a Av. and 4a Calle NO. ✆ **504/557-1496.** Admission L40. Mon–Sat 9am–4pm; Sun 9am–3pm.

Museo de la Naturaleza (The Nature Museum) This regional natural history museum details the plant life and wildlife of the Sula Valley and the rest of the country through the art of taxidermy, bones, diagrams, and extensive charts and labels. It's worth a look if you have a particular interest in biology or have time to kill in San Pedro, but otherwise is skippable.

Calle 1 and Av. 12a NO. ✆ **504/557-6598.** Admission L20. Mon–Sat 8am–noon and 1–4pm.

PARQUE nacional EL CUSUCO

While it is difficult to reach and not nearly as majestic as **Parque Nacional Montaña de Celaque** (p. 378), **El Cusuco** ★★ is well worth the time and effort if you're in the San Pedro Sula area for a few days. Set in the Merendón Mountain Range—45km (28 miles) away from the city—the park is dominated by lush, unspoiled cloud forest and some of the most diverse avian life of any national park in the country. If you arrive early, you have the chance to spot quetzals (they're easiest to spot Apr–June), toucans, parrots, and even a few mammals. There are two trails from the visitor center, Quetzal and Las Minas, that take no more than a few hours to explore. You can usually hire a guide from the visitor center for L90. Admission is L285, and the park is open daily from 8am to 4:30pm. Your best option for staying overnight here is in one of the cabins in Buenos Aires run by **Fundación Ecologista HR Pastor** (Av. 12a NO and Calle 1a; ℂ 504/557-6598). Cabins run L230 per person and must be reserved in advance.

SHOPPING

The sprawling **Guamilito Market** ★ between 8 and 9 Avenida and 6 and 7 Calles NO has products from around the country, as well as El Salvador and Guatemala, which fill up literally hundreds of small stalls. You'll find everything from hammocks, T-shirts, and pottery to cigars, Maya figurines, jewelry, coffee, and Garífuna coconut carvings. Expect to bargain and never accept the first price. Of special note is the small section of women who make tortillas not far from the food stalls—even if you don't buy anything, the market is worth a visit to see these women at work. The market is open daily from 10am to 5pm.

For high-quality handcrafted leather handbags and purses, try **Danilo's** (Av. 18 SO and Calle 9; ℂ 504/552-0656; www.danilos.com). **Maymo Art Gallery** (2 Calle SO and 7 Av. No. 24; ℂ 504/553-0318) exhibits and sells paintings from Honduran artists, such as Benigno Gomez, Roque Zelaya, and Maury Flores.

The best malls in Honduras can be found in San Pedro. **City Mall** (Circunvalación and Carr; no phone), opened in late 2005, is home to more than 200 shops, a Cinemark movie theater, seven banks, and almost 30 restaurants.

WHERE TO STAY
Very Expensive

Crowne Plaza ★★ 🍴 This former Holiday Inn was completely gutted before being reopened as a Crowne Plaza. The result is well worth the effort. They have a fine location a couple of blocks from the central park right on one of the city's main thoroughfares, though the recent additions—with a sushi bar, new Peruvian chef, sleek bar area, lounges for executive travelers, casino, and an outdoor pool—give you little need to leave. The rooms are quite nice and comparable to what you will find in the Hilton and InterContinental. Deep red walls, beige carpet, MP3 docking stations, and LCD TVs set a not-overly-luxurious but comfortable contemporary tone.

1 Calle and Av. 11 NO, Barrio Guamilito. ℂ 504/550-8080. www.crowneplaza.com/sanpedrosula. 125 units. L1,880 double. AE, MC, V. Free parking. **Amenities:** Restaurant; bar; fitness center; pool; Wi-Fi. *In room:* A/C, TV, MP3 docking station.

Hilton Princess San Pedro Sula ★ ☺ Although the Hilton is 2km (1¼ miles) from the city center, it's just a banana's toss away from the Zona Viva and its nearby malls. The boxy yet elegant Republican-style building has all the amenities you would expect from a Hilton: a small sofa and seating area, 250-thread-count sheets, Crabtree and Evelyn soaps, and HBO. There's also a decent but overpriced restaurant, an English pub, and a pool area that could easily fit in on any Caribbean beach. It's a small step down from the Real InterContinental.

10 Calle and Av. Circunvalación SO. ℂ **504/556-9600.** Fax 504/556-9595. www.sanpedrosula.hilton. com. 124 units. L2,870 double; L3,820 suite. AE, DC, MC, V. **Amenities:** Restaurant; bar; pool. *In room:* A/C, TV, hair dryer, minibar, Wi-Fi.

Real InterContinental San Pedro Sula ★★ The best thing about this hotel is that it doesn't feel like it's in the city. The tropical plant–lined driveway and posh marble entryway give the impression of a resort atmosphere that is only further encouraged by the umbrellas, chaise longues, turquoise pool, and waiters strolling around with rum-based drinks with little umbrellas sticking out of them. The rooms and services are what you would expect from a Real InterContinental: bright, luxurious, comfortable, clean, and modern. Most of the hotel was remodeled in the past 5 years, so for the time being, it still has a leg up on the nearby Hilton Princess. They missed out on adding some personal touches like local art, however, except in the beautiful **Vertigo bar.**

Colonia Hernandez and Blvd. de Sur. ℂ **504/545-2500.** 142 standard rooms, 7 suites. L2,641 double; L7,200 suite. AE, DC, MC, V. **Amenities:** Restaurant; bar; pool. *In room:* A/C, TV, hair dryer, minibar, Wi-Fi.

Expensive

Casa del Arbol ★ 💼 From the moment you walk into this boutique hotel, you'll feel like you've set foot in a cozy hospital—the cleanliness is that noticeable. The rooms and bathrooms are quite clean, but otherwise standard with grayish walls, tile floors, and patterned bedspreads. There's also a small desk and a tiny balcony that you can barely plant two feet on. The hotel is built around a big leafy tree, which gives it somewhat of a tropical vibe and adds some character that every other hotel in the city misses.

6 Av., btw. 2 and 3 Calle NO. ℂ **504/504-1616.** www.hotelcasadelarbol.com. 13 units. L1,500 double. Rates include breakfast. AE, MC, V. **Amenities:** Restaurant; bar. *In room:* A/C, TV.

Gran Hotel Sula While the lack of significant renovations has caused the Gran Hotel to become not as grand as it once was, its rooms are decently sized and its amenities are almost comparable to the Hilton or Real InterContinental, including flatscreen TVs. Many of the rooms have balconies overlooking neighboring Parque Central; the lower levels can get a bit noisy, so opt for one of the higher levels or a room in the back facing the pool. Their 24-hour **Skandia coffee shop/diner** and **Granada restaurant** (with an excellent Sun brunch) make it hard to leave the hotel, but if you do, almost everything is just a few steps away.

Parque Central. ℂ **504/552-9999.** www.hotelsula.hn. 117 units. L1,520 double; L2,000 suite. AE, MC, V. **Amenities:** Restaurant; bar; coffee shop; gym; pool. *In room:* TV, kitchenette (in suites), Wi-Fi.

Moderate

Metrotel Express ★ Formerly the Microtel Inn and Suites, this hotel is all about location. If you plan to head out to the Bay Islands or elsewhere in the country and not spend much time in town, this is a midrange oasis of calm and convenience by the airport. The rooms are reminiscent of a North American cookie-cutter chain hotel like a Days Inn, yet haven't been worn in. **Larson's Restaurant,** their American diner, isn't half bad; it serves all-day breakfast and is a much better option than the fast food over at the airport. Nice bonuses include a little pool area and helpful staff who can arrange trips to Lago de Yojoa or Tela.

Km 4 Blvd. al Aeropuerto. ℃ 504/559-0300. www.hotelhonduras.com. 60 units. L1,140 double. Rates include breakfast. AE, MC, V. **Amenities:** Restaurant; bar; high-speed Internet in business center; pool. *In room:* TV, Wi-Fi.

Inexpensive

Tamarindo Hostel ★ The Tamarindo is the unequivocal home of the almost-nonexistent San Pedro backpacker scene. Accommodations are divided between dorm-style rooms and private rooms, all with their own bathroom and hot-water showers. Funky painted walls with Honduran art, graffiti, tapestries, and whatever else fits with Tamarindo's eclectic and cool vibe keep the decor interesting. The rooms and setting are not glamorous by any means. It's kind of like staying over at a group of college students' off-campus house. There are loads of extras like a community room with a TV and DVD collection, two terraces with hammocks, free use of the kitchen, and even a small pool.

9 Calle NO and 11 Av. No. 1015, Barrio Los Andes. ℃ 504/557-0123. www.tamarindohostel.com. 3 dorm rooms, 3 private rooms. L200 per person dorm; L850 private room. MC, V. **Amenities:** Pool. *In room:* A/C, Wi-Fi.

WHERE TO DINE
Expensive

Arte Marianos ★★ 🍴 HONDURAN/SEAFOOD   On a gastronomic level, Arte Marianos is perhaps the most important restaurant in San Pedro. Their specialty is high-quality—and prices to go with it—Honduran coastal and Garífuna specialties like conch ceviche, grilled and steamed fish platters, and tapado, a type of a seafood stew made with coconut milk. There's a large wine list and a handful of grilled meat dishes. Every table is set with a side of coconut bread. The often-crowded restaurant is in a cheery, converted nautical-themed house in the Zona Viva neighborhood with porthole-style windows.

9a Calle SO and 15a Av. SO, Zona Viva. ℃ 504/552-5492. Main courses L300–L600. AE, DC, MC, V. Daily 11am–10pm.

Deriva Enoteca SOUTH AMERICAN   This hip wine bar in a residential neighborhood just north of the plaza across from the Hostel Tamarindo is one of the newest additions to San Pedro's culinary scene. Chilean and Argentine wines and Peruvian Piscos, available both as carry out and from their restaurant, are the focus of the loungelike setup sporting white drapes, Spanish tiles, a few open-air tables, and plenty of vegetation. Their menu, a mix of Peruvian and Italian fare, focuses on dishes such as meats and seafood that go well with wine.

9 Calle NO and Av. 11a NO, Barrio Los Andes. ℃ 504/516-1012. Main courses L190–L380. AE, MC, V. Mon–Sat 10am–9:30pm.

El Portal de las Carnes STEAK   It's safe to say that El Portal de las Carnes is the best Uruguayan steakhouse in Honduras. That may sound like an understatement, but there are several of them spread around the country. Brochettes, ribs, sirloin, filet mignon, and national and imported beef of every other sort are paired with seviches and seafood. This upscale yet rustic eatery is popular among the business crowd.

10 Calle and 15 Av., Barrio Suyapa. ⓒ **504/552-6137.** www.relportal.com. Main courses L152–L300. AE, MC, V. Mon–Sat 11:30am–2pm and 5–10pm.

Restaurante Don Udo's ★ INTERNATIONAL This often crowded Dutch-owned restaurant has been a staple on San Pedro's restaurant scene for decades. The colonial ambience at this first location attracts San Pedro's upper crust, who come for a decent variety of international dishes like pastas, steaks, seafood, and sandwiches. Their set lunch menus, usually three courses, are a great value. They have one of the more rounded wine lists in San Pedro, with bottles from Argentina, Chile, and Italy. Their outdoor patio occasionally has live music.

13 Av. NO and 7a Calle NO. ⓒ **504/553-3106.** Reservations recommended. Main courses L170–L420. AE, MC, V. Mon–Sat 11:30am–2pm and 6–11pm; Sun 10am–2pm.

Moderate

Restaurante Vicente ★★ ITALIAN This restaurant has been open since 1962 and so, as with the owners' other restaurant next door, Pizzeria Italia, it's definitely an institution in town. It's more formal than the pizzeria, and doles out standard Italian fare such as pastas, risottos, calzones, and wine—it's a menu that has changed very little, and it probably never will, since folks keep coming back.

Av. 7 and Calle 1 NO. ⓒ **504/552-1335.** Main courses L90–L275. MC, V. Daily 11am–10pm.

Inexpensive

Café Skandia INTERNATIONAL This 24-hour cafe and diner is the most reliable restaurant near Parque Central. In the Gran Hotel Sula (p. 351), it serves hearty Honduran breakfasts, *baleadas,* and roast chicken, as well as North American items like burgers, onion rings, milkshakes, and apple pie a la mode.

1a Calle NO at Parque Central. ⓒ **504/552-9999.** Main courses L55–L150. MC, V. Daily 24 hr.

Plaza Típica Coracts ★★★ HONDURAN A quick bite in San Pedro doesn't have to be limited to Popeye's and Burger King. This large, covered, open-air food court just north of the plaza is the city's street-food mecca with 20 or so stalls serving regional dishes from provinces such as Colón, Yoro, Cortés, and Atlantída, along with Guatemalan, Salvadoran, and Mexican fare. Standards are higher than for normal street fare, so the food, for the most part, is safe to eat.

Av. 3a NO and Calle 3a NO. No phone. Main courses L55–L100. No credit cards. Daily 8am–5pm.

SAN PEDRO SULA AFTER DARK

While the consensus has always been that La Ceiba has the best nightlife in Honduras, San Pedro isn't far behind and it's catching up fast. To start the night off right, head to **Beer Bar** (third floor of the City Mall; ⓒ **504/580-1343;** Tues–Sat 2pm–midnight, Sun 2–7pm), where you can find a vast assortment of beers, both bottle and tap, from across Latin America, Europe, and the U.S. **Le Loft** (8a Calle SO and Circunvalación; Mon–Sat 5pm–2am), in the Zona Viva, which opened in 2008, is one of the hottest new spots. The two-level bar and lounge with DJs spinning house and techno isn't as obnoxious or stuffy as some of the other places, has no cover, and dishes out American-style pub food until late.

Along the Circunvalación and in the Zona Viva, at Av. 15a and 16a SO between calles 7a and 11a SO in Barrio Suyapa, are the majority of the city's many bars, lounges, and clubs. The **Cube** (8a Calle SO and Av. 16; Thurs–Sat 9pm–3am) attracts mostly young people intent on spending most of the night on a crowded dance floor.

If slinging back gin and tonics and playing roulette or blackjack are more your thing, check out **Casino Copán** in Hotel Copantl (Blvd. del Sur; ☏ **504/556-7108**; www.copantl.com).

Lago de Yojoa ★

Although it is right on CA 5 between the big tourist sites of San Pedro Sula and Tegucigalpa, few travelers do more than see this breathtaking lake from their bus window. Covering 89 sq. km (34 sq. miles), at 700m (2,300 ft.) above sea level, and surrounded by misty pine-covered mountains, coffee fincas, and two national parks, this is the largest natural lake in the country and is one of Central America's most overlooked natural attractions. There are several great hotels and guesthouses in settings so tranquil, not to mention dozens of fish restaurants with awe-inspiring views, that it is mind-boggling that the place isn't swarming with busloads of tourists like Lake Atitlán in Guatemala. Not that this is a bad thing. The serenity is the chief reason most visitors come here. One group of travelers has long visited Yojoa: birders. These intense, dedicated enthusiasts come from around the world on birding tours in the hopes of spotting the rare and vast number of species in Yojoa. Nearly 400 species have been identified on the lake and on its shores, making it one of the preeminent birding destinations in a country known for birding. If you left your binoculars and avian identification charts at home, there are still plenty of ways to enjoy the setting, from renting a rowboat, to hiking in either of the two cloud forests, touring a Lenca archaeological site, or visiting the country's only microbrewery.

ESSENTIALS

You'll need to have your own car to explore the more remote corners of the lake, as there aren't taxis in town. The country's major highway, CA 5, runs between San Pedro Sula and Tegucigalpa and passes right beside the eastern edge of the lake and the town of La Guama, from where you can easily take Hwy. 54 to the north and Peña Blanca. You can also get to or from San Pedro directly via the windy Hwy. 54, though this takes a bit longer at about 2 hours. Any Tegucigalpa-bound bus that's coming from San Pedro will let you off at La Guama and vice versa; the ride from San Pedro Sula (L150–L250) takes 3 hours. Minibuses regularly ply the route between here and La Guama and Peña Blanca, as do taxis (L20).

CA 5 parallels the eastern edge of the lake, where most restaurants and hotels can be found, as well as the small town of La Guama and Parque Nacional Cerro Azul Meámbar. On the north side of the lake, you will find the town of Peña Blanca, which is the largest town surrounding the lake and where small markets, a few banks, and cybercafés can be found. It is still a rather secluded place to base yourself, and the Parque Eco-Archeological de Los Naranjos is here as well. On the western side of the lake is Parque Nacional Montaña de Santa Barbara.

Most of the parks in this area are self-guided, so you can easily hire locals to guide you at any of the entrances. The **D&D Brewery** (☏ **504/994-9719;** www.dd-brewery.com) runs a variety of organized tours in the region, though.

WHAT TO SEE & DO

Parque Eco-Archeological de Los Naranjos ★ This small Lenca site on the northern edge of the lake is a far better ecopark than an archaeological one. Just a few mounds and piles of stones can be found at the site, which dates back to approximately 700 B.C. More exciting are the 6km (3¾ miles) of stone paths and dirt trails that weave through much of the complex, including a hanging bridge. This is one of

Volunteer Opportunities in Parque Nacional Cerro Azul Meámbar

The Christian NGO **Proyecto Aldea Global/Project Global Village** (© 504/239-8400; www.paghonduras.org) has been in charge of managing Parque Nacional Cerro Azul Meámbar since 1992. Conserving the natural environment, providing sustainable development for the rural communities that live in the buffer zone around Cerro Azul, and helping jump-start ecotourism projects are just part of the work they do in and around the park. Groups and individuals are encouraged to contact the nonprofit organization if interested in lending a helping hand to one of their numerous projects in the area.

the best spots for bird-watching around the lake, and there's even a small tower for birders near the mounds. A small museum and visitor center with information on finds at the site and general background of the Lencas graces the entrance and parking area. To get here from La Guama or Peña Blanca, you can catch a minibus to El Jaral on Hwy. 54, which should drop you off on the main drag, if not right at the park.

3km (1¾ miles) from the town of Peña Blanca, El Jaral. © **504/650-0004.** Admission L100. Daily 8am–4pm.

Parque Nacional Cerro Azul Meámbar ★★   The majestically misty mountains along the eastern side of the lake make up this 478-sq.-km (185-sq.-mile) park. The base of the park comprises coffee plantations and tropical forests, which turn to pine forest that then turns to cloud forests as the mountain climbs to a height of 2,047m (6,715 ft.). The park is a significant supplier of water to the surrounding communities and contributes more than 70% of the water to Lago de Yojoa. The isolation of the park means that wildlife here is flourishing. Several hundred bird species including keel-billed toucans and resplendent quetzals, as well as more than 50 species of mammals, such as peccaries, tapirs, monkeys, pumas, and jaguars, can be found inside the park. Plus there are loads of orchids, an elfin forest, and a handful of waterfalls.

From the visitor center near Los Pinos, there's access to three main hiking trails, ranging from 1 to 8km (.7 to 5 miles) in length. There are several other trails into the park from surrounding communities as well.

Like many of the cloud forests in Honduras, this one is nearly impossible to reach, even though it has six entrances. Public transportation to the park is nonexistent and you need a 4WD to go on your own. The main entrance is at the town of Los Pinos. To get to there, take the marked turnoff at La Guama from CA 5 and continue up the steep, bumpy road for about 15 minutes until you reach Santa Elena and then follow the signs until you reach Los Pinos and the visitor center. Beside the visitor center there are nine excellent **cabins** ★★ (© **504/608-5510;** L850) with private bathrooms and electricity that were built in 2008 that sleep up to three, as well as two dorm-style cabins (L160 per person). If you want the best chance of seeing wildlife, then spending the night in these cabins and waking up before dawn when the birds and animals are most active is highly recommended.

Turnoff at La Guama for Los Pinos. © **504/239-8392.** www.paghonduras.org/ecology.html. Admission L20. Daily 8am–6pm.

Parque Nacional Montaña de Santa Barbara   This cloud forest park on the western side of Lago de Yojoa is dominated by the second-highest peak in the country, Santa Barbara, sometimes called El Maroncho. The mountain is as pristine as they come and visitors here are rewarded with some of the biggest biodiversity in the country. Orchids, more than 400 species of birds like trogons, toucans, and wood-peckers, as well as butterflies, fungi, spider monkeys, anteaters, and jaguars, can all be spotted. There is no infrastructure in the park whatsoever, but there are a few unmarked trails that can reach the 2,744m (9,000-ft.) summit, over about a 2- or 3-days' walk. You can ask around for a guide in the villages of El Playón, Los Andes, or San Luis Planes, which border the park, for approximately L200 per day. The park can be reached by catching a bus from Peña Blanca to any of the towns that border the park, or on a guided hike or bird-watching tour through D&D brewery.

Free admission. For information, try the Santa Barbara tourist office at ✆ **504/643-2338.**

Pulhapanazak Falls ★★   Pulhapanazak is the awe-inspiring waterfall that adorns tourist brochures and posters you see pretty much everywhere. The 43m-high (141-ft.) waterfall on the Río Amapá crashes down to a rocky base and radiates a heavy mist from the moist tropical air. Occasionally you can catch a glimpse of a scarlet macaw or toucan in the trees around the falls. There's a pretty park with a cafeteria and picnic tables above the falls, as well as a few swimming holes. Guides, usually local kids who hang around outside the park, can take you into a small cave behind the waterfall for a small tip. It's a slippery and often muddy path down to the base, so be extra careful.

It's easiest to reach Pulhapanazak on a guided tour, since getting here by bus is time-consuming and complicated. (By public transportation you must catch a San Pedro–headed bus from Peña Blanca and then, after about 10km/6 miles, get off at San Buenaventura. From here you must catch a taxi westward 45 min. or so up a bumpy dirt road to the entrance.)

Admission L20. Daily 6am–6pm.

OUTDOOR ACTIVITIES

Bass fishing, which once attracted fishermen from around the world until the stocks were severely depleted, is slowly making a comeback in the lake; there are lots of opportunities to sail too. **Honduyate Marina** (right on CA 5; ✆ **504/608-3726**) is the best operator to use for getting out on the water. They rent out sailboats and fish-ing boats, and give tours on an old ferry. Another option is to head to the **D&D Brewery** (see below) and rent a rowboat for about L55 per day.

Hummingbirds, orioles, motmots, cuckoos, tanagers, oropendolas, toucans, and even the occasional resplendent quetzal are among the nearly 400 birds that have been recorded around the lake. Brit Malcolm Glasgow, **D&D Brewery's** on-site ornithologist (✆ **504/994-9719**), is the best known guide in the area and has near encyclopedic knowledge of the Yojoa's avian life. He leads half-day trips to the best birding spots on the lake via rowboat, at a charge of L225 per person, as well as trips to Santa Bárbara National Park for L600 per person, including transport. Minimum two people; prices drop for larger groups.

WHERE TO STAY

D&D Bed and Breakfast ★★★   Run by American expat and bluegrass musician Robert Dale, who also operates the attached D&D microbrewery, this quirky little compound is set on one of the most beautiful areas of the lake. The easygoing setup and service give the impression that you're staying at a friend's house. Standard rooms in the lodge are quite simple and a bit cramped—they just barely fit a bed and bathroom—but the overall value is good for the price, and the atmosphere is excellent. The cabins, one of which has a Jacuzzi, are much more spacious, are newer, and have small porches with hammocks. As an added bonus, all water used at D&D—including the sinks and showers—is purified as part of the beer-making process. Also, Dale is as knowledgeable on travel and the history of the region as anyone and is a good source of info for things to do and planning the next stage of your trip. D&D can also arrange bird-watching and trips to the national parks, and hook you up with a rowboat for exploring the lake.

3.7km (2⅓ miles) past Peña Blanca, El Mochito. ☎ **504/9994-9719.** www.dd-brewery.com. 4 standard rooms, 5 cabins. L230 double; L500 cabin. Rates include breakfast. No credit cards. **Amenities:** Restaurant; bar; brewery; laundry; pool. *In room:* Fan.

El Cortijo del Lago   American John Chater, who has lived in Honduras for decades—and was once an editor for a rival guidebook company—and his wife, Marta, have built this small lodge on a beautiful strip of the lake between La Guana and Peña Blanca. There is not much going on in the way of decor, but the rooms are spacious and clean, and they have electric showers in the bathroom. The rooms are on a hill so the big windows, particularly in the rooms on the second floor, look down onto the lake and the mountains beyond. The hotel has a couple of boats for excursions on the lake, and they work closely with Cerro Azul and Los Pinos and can help arrange tours and transportation to the park.

2km (1¼ miles) from La Guama on Hwy. 54. ☎ **504/608-5527.** www.elcortijodellago.com. 4 units. L600 double. MC, V. **Amenities:** Restaurant; bar. *In room:* A/C, fan, purified water.

La Posada del Lago   Right on CA 5, this upscale yacht club, which is also known as the Honduyate, is by far the fanciest place to sleep on the lake. All of the enormous rooms are bright and clean, and come with little extras like DVD players and sitting areas; most important, all rooms boast amazing lakeside views. The property also has a few small cabins nearby, which are older and far more rustic. The lodge and **Chalet de Lago restaurant** are a favorite of wealthy vacationing Hondurans and locals alike—this is very much the lake's social hub. You can also book charter boats here.

Km 161 of Hwy. CA 5. ☎ **504/608-3726.** www.honduyatemarina.com. 5 rooms, 4 cabins. L1,690 double; L2,090 suite; L285 cabin. Rates include breakfast. AE, MC, V. **Amenities:** Restaurant; bar; pool. *In room:* A/C, fan, TV/DVD, Wi-Fi.

WHERE TO DINE

In addition to D&D Brewery, a string of 30 or so seafood restaurants rest along highway CA 5 on the edge of the lake. All are open-air eateries serving more or less the same menu. You get to pick your fish, usually tilapia, and the preparation, such as *frito* (fried) or *a la plancha* (grilled). It's served whole (with the head and fins) and accompanied by lime and fried plantain chips. Main courses run L75 to L150, and the restaurants are generally open daily 10am to 8pm.

D&D Brewery ★★★ INTERNATIONAL   When American expat Robert Dale discovered he couldn't get a decent pint in Honduras, he decided to brew his own. Thus the D&D Brewery became the first and only microbrewery in the country. Using hops imported from Stowmarket in England, the tiny brewery pumps out stouts, ales, lagers, and even mango beers, as well as their own sodas flavored with mango, apricot, and raspberry. Locally picked blueberries are used to make blueberry soda and the restaurant's famous blueberry pancakes. The rest of the menu is a mix of American and Honduran staples like omelets, soups, burgers, and *anafres* (black-bean and cheese fondue, served with chips). Dale occasionally will bust out his guitar and supply bluegrass music to accompany your meal.

3.8km (2⅓ miles) past Peña Blanca. ✆ **504/994-9719.** www.dd-brewery.com. Main courses L76–L152. No credit cards. Daily 10am–8pm.

Comayagua

For more than 3 centuries Comayagua, which is 71km (44 miles) south of Lago de Yojoa, was the capital of Honduras, until the capital was moved to Tegucigalpa in 1880. The city was founded in 1537 by the Spanish explorer Alonso de Cáceres, and it has, without a doubt, the strongest colonial history in the country. Traces of the city's past can still be seen in the architecture of the palaces, churches, and squares—slowly being restored—in the city center. For much of the year, the town is empty, with a trickle of visitors, but during Semana Santa (Holy Week), the city comes alive for the most passionate religious celebration in the country.

ESSENTIALS

Comayagua is a few blocks northeast of the highway, CA 5, which runs between Tegucigalpa (1½ hr. away) and San Pedro Sula (3½ hr. away). **El Rey Express** (✆ **504/237-8561;** www.reyexpress.net) runs hourly to both San Pedro (L200) and Tegucigalpa (L50). **Transportes Rivera** (1a Av. SO and 2a Calle SO; ✆ **504/772-1208;** L200) runs to San Pedro hourly from 5am to 4pm. To get to Lago de Yojoa, get on any San Pedro–bound bus and ask to be let off at La Guama. Buses stop and can be picked up at the Texaco gas station toward the turnoff to the highway.

Anywhere in the center of Comayagua can be reached on foot. The town follows a standard grid, surrounding the Parque Central. Nearly all churches, museums, and restaurants can be found within a few blocks of the square. In the Parque Central, there's a small **Tourist Center** (✆ **504/772-2080;**) with maps and brochures.

Banco Atlántida (1a Calle NO and 2a Calle NO) will exchange traveler's checks and has an ATM. To make long-distance calls, head to **Hondutel** (1a Av. NE and Calle 5a NO). Internet cafes are scattered all around the center.

WHAT TO SEE & DO

Nearly the entire colonial center of town—churches, historic buildings, squares, and cobblestone streets—was recently revived after a major, multiyear renovation funded by the Spanish Cooperation Agency. In addition to the attractions below, you might stop to check out the exterior of the colonial churches **Nuestra Señora de la Caridad** (7a Calle NO and 3a Av. NO) and **Iglesia y Convento de San Francisco** (Av. 1a NE and 7a Calle NO) by the Parque Central. Though the **Caxa Real** (1a Av. NE and 6a Calle NO, near Plaza de San Francisco), the country's first tax-collection house, has been more or less destroyed by fires and earthquakes over the years, you can see its stone facade.

Catedral de Santa María ★★ The towering white cathedral on the north end of Parque Central, also known as La Iglesia de la Inmaculada Concepción, is considered by many to be the most beautiful cathedral in all of Honduras. Construction began on it in the late 17th century and was completed on December 8, 1711. Four of the original 16 hand-carved wood and gold-plated altars still survive. The clock in the church tower is one of the oldest in the world and the oldest in the Americas. Built around 1100 for the Alhambra in Granada, the clock was given to the town as

Semana Santa in Comayagua

Semana Santa (Holy Week) ★★★ is a huge deal in Comayagua. From Palm Sunday to Easter Sunday, the city is flooded with visitors, pilgrims, day-trippers, and everyone else who wants to experience the most passionate religious celebration in Honduras. Processions and festivities occur every day in and around the city's colonial churches and plazas.

Good Friday is when you will see *alfombras,* colorful sawdust carpets, laid out to be trampled on during the solemn Via Crucis Procession, in which a volunteer carries a cross on his back through the streets beginning at 10:30am. If you plan on staying in the city during Semana Santa, be sure to book your hotel as much as 6 months in advance.

a gift from King Phillip III and originally was placed in the Iglesia La Merced before being moved here.

Southeast corner of Parque Central. Free admission. Mon–Fri 9:30am–noon and 2–5pm; Sun during Mass.

Iglesia La Merced   Just 4 blocks south of Catedral de Santa María and fronting a small plaza of its own, Iglesia La Merced is the oldest church in Comayagua and one of the oldest in Central America. It was built in 1550, though an earthquake in 1774 destroyed one of the belfries and caused extensive damage. Inside are several paintings that date from the 16th century.

1a Av. NE and 1 Calle NO. Free admission. Daily 7am–8pm.

Museo Colonial de Arte Religioso   This museum is in a building that dates back to 1558 and was home to the first university in Central America, though a major fire has kept it closed since April 2009. The collection, most of which was saved, is from Comayagua's colonial churches, which were once virtual storehouses of valuable art. You'll see chalices, sculptures, paintings, and historical documents such as Honduran general Francisco Morazán's marriage certificate. The latest reports have the museum reopening in mid-2011.

Av. 2a de Julio and 3a Calle NO. ✆ **504/772-0169.** Admission L40. Mon–Sat 9am–noon and 2–4:30pm.

Museo Regional de Arqueología   Formerly a presidential mansion and the site of the National Congress of Honduras, this newly renovated museum surrounding a grassy courtyard is home to the most comprehensive collection of Lenca artifacts. Most pieces on display are from archaeological sites within the valley and region surrounding Comayagua. Artifacts include textiles, pottery, stone carving, tools for grinding corn, and even petroglyphs; a few small rooms are also devoted to exhibits on national Honduran culture. There's a small craft store in the back.

6a Calle NO and Av. 20 de Julio. ✆ **504/772-0386.** Admission L20. Tues–Sun 8am–4:30pm.

WHERE TO STAY

Hotel Casa Grande ★★ 🎒   This small bed-and-breakfast, hidden away on an unassuming street a few blocks from the square, is one of the most atmospheric hotels in western Honduras. Chances are that when the city of Comayagua finishes its renovation and more tourists start arriving here, you'll hear much more about this colonial building cum bed-and-breakfast. Stone and *azulejo* tile walls and lots of tropical plants augment the lobby and halls, while wood floors and hand-carved wood furniture give the rooms a splash of personality.

7a NO Abajo, Comayagua. ✆ **504/772-0772.** Fax 504/772-0441. www.hotelcolonialcasagrande.com. 10 units. L952 double. Rates include breakfast. MC, V. **Amenities:** High-speed Internet in lobby; laundry service. *In room:* A/C, fan, TV.

Hotel Santa Maria   Right on the highway, this modern hotel lacks the charms of the cozy Hotel Casa Grande, but in regard to comfort and amenities, nothing compares to it in Comayagua. Rooms are clean, and have the look and amenities of a Holiday Inn. There are conference facilities and well-manicured gardens, but the best reason to stay here is the big, refreshing swimming pool.

Km 82 on CA 5. ✆ **504/772-7672.** Fax 504/772-7719. 28 units. L1,560 double. MC, V. **Amenities:** Restaurant; bar; pool. *In room:* A/C, TV, Wi-Fi.

WHERE TO DINE

Cactus Restaurant MEXICAN   On a busy corner across from Iglesia La Merced, this Mexican restaurant is a welcome addition to the Comayagua dining scene. Standard Mexican fare like tacos, gringas, quesadillas, and nachos, plus a few beef and shrimp plates, taste great and are cheap. Tables are indoors with A/C or outside on a patio, and both are graced by Mexican decor and music.

Parque La Merced. No phone. Main courses L55–L150. MC, V. Wed–Mon 11am–10pm.

Villa Real ★ HONDURAN/INTERNATIONAL   Just behind the cathedral, this elegant restaurant makes good use of its colonial structure and flower-filled courtyard. Various rooms are filled with period furniture and art, which you are more than welcome to explore before or after your meal. Hearty Honduran *tipicos*—steak, rice, beans, tortillas, white cheese, and avocado—are standard fare here, as are *chuletas de cerdo* (pork chops) and grilled seafood.

Behind the cathedral, Parque Central. ✆ **504/772-0101.** Main courses L100–L250. MC, V. Daily 11am–11pm.

COPÁN RUINAS ★★★ & COPÁN TOWN ★★

64km (40 miles) W of La Entrada; 12km (7½ miles) S of the Guatemalan border

Not far from the Guatemalan border lies Copán, one of the most spectacular Maya ceremonial cities of Mesoamerica. The town, 1km (⅔ mile) from the archaeological site, is a small, picturesque city with rough cobblestone streets and a buzzing central plaza that's the heart and soul of the place. It is reminiscent of a more compact version of Cusco, Peru, although tourism is growing here at an equally impressive rate. For example, in the 1970s, there were just a couple of small hotels mostly visited by archaeologists. Now there are more than 70. Copán is surrounded by beautiful forests with waterfalls, hot springs, and excellent bird-watching and adventure tourism possibilities.

Essentials
GETTING THERE

If you're driving to Copán from San Pedro Sula, you have a pretty much straight shot on **CA 4** to La Entrada, where you can continue on **CA 11** to Copán, a 2½-hour drive.

To get to and from Tegucigalpa is much trickier. From Copán, there is a beautiful route through the mountains to Gracias from La Entrada on **CA 11-A,** but the road is windy, mostly unpaved, and sometimes impassable due to rain. Many drivers prefer to head back toward San Pedro Sula and catch **Hwy. 20** or **CA 5** south for the 3½-hour drive to the capital.

Copán Ruínas

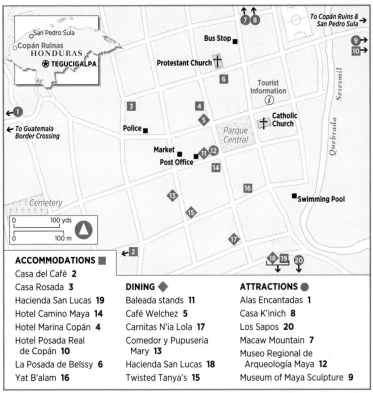

ACCOMMODATIONS ■

Casa del Café **2**
Casa Rosada **3**
Hacienda San Lucas **19**
Hotel Camino Maya **14**
Hotel Marina Copán **4**
Hotel Posada Real
  de Copán **10**
La Posada de Belssy **6**
Yat B'alam **16**

DINING ◆

Baleada stands **11**
Café Welchez **5**
Carnitas N'ia Lola **17**
Comedor y Pupuseria
  Mary **13**
Hacienda San Lucas **18**
Twisted Tanya's **15**

ATTRACTIONS ●

Alas Encantadas **1**
Casa K'inich **8**
Los Sapos **20**
Macaw Mountain **7**
Museo Regional de
  Arqueología Maya **12**
Museum of Maya Sculpture **9**

Hedman Alas (© **504/651-4037** in Copán Ruínas, or 651-4037 in San Pedro Sula; www.hedmanalas.com) offers five daily trips to San Pedro Sula with connections to La Ceiba, Tela, and Tegucigalpa. They also run buses to Guatemala City daily at 1:30 and 6pm. The fare is L874 each way and takes about 5 hours. **Copán Connections** (© **504/651-4182**), below Twisted Tanya's, can arrange private buses and transportation to Antigua, Tikal, La Ceiba, Tegucigalpa, and the Bay Islands. Prices vary depending on the number of people. Local buses run from the dirt lot across the bridge at the entrance to town and head to La Entrada, 2 hours away, where riders can then transfer for Gracias, Santa Rosa de Copán, San Pedro Sula, or several other villages in the region.

ORIENTATION

It may be confusing, but the actual Maya ruins here are called Copán, while the little town is officially known as Copán Ruínas. Most folks refer to it generically as Copán or make the appropriate distinction when necessary. The town is compact, and everything of importance is within a 4-block radius of the central plaza. No official street names are actually used, and directions are given in relation to the central plaza or some other known landmark.

Crossing the Border

Crossing the border at El Florido on your way to Guatemala City or Antigua is relatively easy and the crossing is open 24 hours a day, so the long waits and crowds that the point was once known for have diminished significantly. Be prepared to pay the L20 departure tax (although some travelers have been asked for more) leaving Honduras and a L25 fee to enter Guatemala. Both sides accept lempira and quetzales, Guatemala's national currency, although money-changers are everywhere. If you're driving a rental car, be sure to have all your papers in order and clear the trip with the rental-car agency in advance.

GETTING AROUND

You can easily walk anywhere in Copán Ruínas, including from town to the archaeological site. However, if you need a taxi, they are plentiful and inexpensive. Most of the taxis are small motor taxis or tuk tuks, which circulate around town and gather on the north and south sides of the central plaza. If you can't find one, call **Cooperativo Multicomer** (© 504/651-4054) or **Lulo** (© 504/961-7823). A taxi ride between town and the archaeological site should cost L20 to L40 per person.

VISITOR INFORMATION & FAST FACTS

Banco Atlántida and **BAC** both front the central plaza and are fast and safe places to exchange money or use an ATM. To contact the local **police,** dial © 504/651-4060. The **post office** (© 504/651-4447) is just west of the Copán Museum. There are a half-dozen Internet cafes around town; most charge around L20 to L40 per hour. For medical emergencies, ask your hotel, or call Dr. Boqui at the **Clínica Handal** (© 504/651-4408). **Hondutel,** half a block south of the central plaza, and **La Casa de Todo,** 1 block from the park (© 504/651-4689) are the best places for international phone calls.

What to See & Do

COPAN ★★★

Copán is one of the grandest and most magnificently preserved of all Maya ceremonial cities. Surrounded by thick jungle and set beside the gentle Copán River, the ruins are famous for their raw stone-carved hieroglyphics, the massive stelae, and the impressive Hieroglyphic Stairway. Your visit here should include the extensive archaeological ruins, recently excavated tunnels, and Museum of Maya Sculpture.

The current area around Copán has been inhabited since at least 1400 B.C., and some of the earlier discoveries here show Olmec influences. The Great Sun Lord Quetzal Macaw, who ruled from A.D. 426 to 435, was the first of 16 consecutive kings who saw the rise and fall of this Classic Maya city. Some of Copán's great kings included Smoke Jaguar, 18 Rabbit, and Smoke Shell. The history of these kings is meticulously carved into the stones at the ruins.

Copán was famously "discovered" in 1839 and bought for just $50 by the adventurer John L. Stephens, who documented the story in his wonderful book, *Incidents of Travel in Central America, Chiapas and Yucatán* (1841). The book is beautifully illustrated by Stephens's companion Frederick Catherwood.

Visitor Information

The entrance to the Copán archaeological site is along a well-marked highway about a half-mile from the town of Copán Ruínas. The visitor center and ticket booth are at one end of the parking lot; the Museum of Maya Sculpture is at the other. The Copán Guides Association has a booth at the entrance to the parking area. Here, you can hire a bilingual guide for a 2-hour tour of the site, which includes the Sepulturas, for L950, no matter the size of your group. These guides are extremely knowledge-able, and are highly recommended to hire for your first visit. They aren't necessary to tour the museum, as the signs are in English, or the tunnels, which are so short that the guide isn't necessarily of much value.

Admission to the archaeological site, which includes the main Copán ruins and the Sepulturas, is L285. Admission does not include a guide. Visits to the tunnels and Museum of Maya Sculpture are extra.

Museum of Maya Sculpture ★★

Considering that the ruins get more and more crowded as the day goes on, I recommend that you visit the new Museum of Maya Sculpture after seeing the ruins. The museum is across from the entrance to the archaeological park, a few hundred yards from the small visitor center where you pay your entrance fee. This large, two-story structure was built to protect some of Copán's more impressive pieces from the elements. Inside you'll see beautifully displayed and well-documented examples of a broad range of stone carvings and hieroglyphics. At the center of the museum is a full-scale replica of the Rosalia Temple, which lies well-preserved inside the core of Temple 16 (which you'll see later at the ruins). The museum also contains the reconstructed original facade of one of the site's ball courts. Admission to the museum is L95.

The Ruins ★★★

The ruins are at the end of a relatively short path from the museum exit. I recommend starting at the western plaza of Temple 16. As you face Temple 16, the Acropolis will be to your left. A trail and steps lead around the back, where you can enjoy a view over the Copán River to the surrounding mountains. Follow the path to the Patio of the Jaguars, where you'll find the entrances to the Rosalia and Jaguar tunnels. Continue on over the top of the Acropolis and the Temple of Inscriptions, and then down into the Great Plaza, where Copán's greatest hieroglyphic treasures were found.

The Temple of Inscriptions anchors the south end of the Great Plaza. To its east is the Hieroglyphic Stairway. This stairway, built by King Smoke Shell, rises up some 64 steps, each of which is carved or faced with hieroglyphs, telling the history of Copán's kings and their line of succession. To those literate in the language, the stairs once read as a giant book. Today, many of the carved stairs have fallen or faded, but enough remain to give a sense of the scale of this amazing achievement. The stairway is currently under cover, which makes it difficult to see. The lighting is poor, especially on cloudy days, but the trade-off in terms of preservation makes this necessary.

At the foot of the Hieroglyphic Stairway, and all around the Great Plaza, are examples of Copán's carved stelae. Many of these are carved on all four sides with detailed depictions of rulers, animals, and mythic beasts, as well as glyphs that tell their stories. Some of the stelae are originals, while others are replicas.

Las Sepulturas ★

Located about 2km (1¼ miles) from the Great Plaza, Las Sepulturas is believed to have been a major residential neighborhood reserved for Copán's elite. The site gives you a sense of what the day-to-day living arrangements of an upper-crust Maya may

Copán Archaeological Site

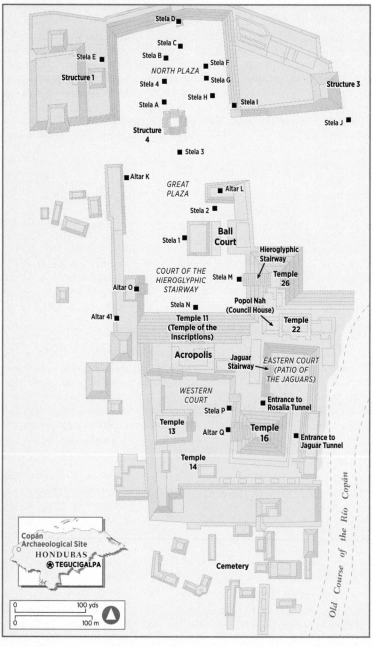

Stela D

Stela C

Stela E

Stela B

Stela F

Structure 1

NORTH PLAZA

Stela G

Structure 3

Stela 4

Stela H

Stela A

Stela I

Structure 4

Stela J

Stela 3

Altar K

GREAT PLAZA

Altar L

Stela 2

Stela 1

Ball Court

Hieroglyphic Stairway

COURT OF THE HIEROGLYPHIC STAIRWAY

Stela M

Temple 26

Popol Nah (Council House)

Altar O

Stela N

Temple 22

Altar 41

Temple 11 (Temple of the Inscriptions)

Acropolis

Jaguar Stairway

EASTERN COURT (PATIO OF THE JAGUARS)

WESTERN COURT

Stela P

Entrance to Rosalia Tunnel

Temple 13

Altar Q

Temple 16

Entrance to Jaguar Tunnel

Temple 14

Old Course of the Río Copán

Copán Archaeological Site

HONDURAS

⊛ **TEGUCIGALPA**

Cemetery

0   100 yds
0   100 m

have been like. Las Sepulturas was once connected to the Great Plaza by a broad, well-worn causeway (which has been identified by NASA with digital satellite imaging), but today it's reached via a gentle path through lush forests with excellent bird- and animal-watching opportunities.

The Rosalia & Jaguar Tunnels ★

Opened to the public in 1999, these two tunnels give visitors a firsthand look at the historical layering technique of the Maya builders, who would construct subsequent temples around and over existing ones, no matter how beautiful and intricate the original. Entrance to the two tunnels is an extra L190 above the general admission, though these are well-lit modern excavations and not tunnels left by the ancient Maya, so it's a tossup as to whether it's really worth the extra money. However, the tunnels are fascinating and do give you a further sense of the massive scale of the archaeological undertaking.

ATTRACTIONS IN & AROUND TOWN

Alas Encantadas   This is a small butterfly garden and breeding project with loads of winged creatures, exhibits illustrating the various stages of metamorphosis, and a botanical garden with more than 200 species of orchids.

300m (984 ft.) outside of town on the road to the Guatemalan border. ✆ **504/651-4133.** Admission L115 adults, L45 children. Daily 8am–4:30pm.

Café Welchez Coffee Plantation ★★   Finca Santa Isabel is where the Café Welchez brand of shade-grown coffee is produced. The tour, which leaves by bus from Copán, begins in the mountain nursery and takes you through the entire processing method, with the occasional chance to spot birds and butterflies in the surrounding rainforest.

Outside Copán. ✆ **504/651-4200.** www.cafehonduras.com. Tours are given daily with Yaragua Tours (✆ **504/651-4147;** www.yaragua.com) and cost L475 per person, including transportation.

Casa K'inich ☺   The Casa K'inich, or the Maya Children's Museum, moved from its small spot on the north side of the square to a hill overlooking the city of Copán Ruinas. It won't take much of your time, but it's worth a look for the interactive and educational exhibits that teach kids (and adults) how to count and add in different Mayan dialects and how to play the ancient ballgame of the Maya.

Fuerte Cabañas. ✆ **504/651-4105.** www.asociacioncopan.org. Free admission. Mon–Sat 8am–noon and 1–4pm.

Los Sapos   The small ceremonial site of Los Sapos, across the river from Copán, is believed to be tied to ancient Maya birthing and fertility practices. This is a small and minimally excavated site. You can see some stone carvings of *sapos*, or frogs, and the carved figure of a pregnant woman. In addition, the site features the exposed foundations of a few large structures. Several tour agencies in town offer horseback-riding tours that include a visit here.

5km (3 miles) from Copán Ruínas, on the grounds of Hacienda San Lucas. ✆ **504/651-4495.** Admission L40. Daily 9am–5pm.

Macaw Mountain ★ ☺   Macaw Mountain is one of the newer attractions in Copán Ruínas and features an extensive collection of tropical birds, primarily parrots and macaws, and some local raptors. The way the birds are displayed makes this place special. (The enclosures are quite large and well done, and you can even walk through some of them.) This attraction is spread out over a lush setting of a tropical

LA ENTRADA & THE ruins OF EL PUENTE

If you're planning on exploring western Honduras, you'll likely be stopping at La Entrada at one point. This town serves as a junction of CA 4 and CA 11, so it is lined with buses that lead to Copán (2 hr. away), San Pedro Sula (1½ hr. away), Santa Rosa (1½ hr. away), and lesser-known villages in the region.

La Entrada is a dusty, uninteresting town that would serve as nothing more than a transport hub if it weren't for the Maya ruins of **El Puente ★**, which are just 10km (6¼ miles) away. This is the second-most-important archaeological park in Honduras after Copán, although you wouldn't know it by the number of visitors. Unless your visit parallels that of a tour bus, you'll likely have the entire site to yourself. The majority of the buildings on the site, opened in 1994, date from the Late Classic Period between the 6th and 9th centuries. Of the more than 200 buildings in the park, only 9 have been excavated. The centerpiece is a medium-size pyramid set on a wide grassy plaza that's lined with a few other buildings that have been cleared from the encroaching jungle. There's a small visitor center and museum at the entrance, about 1km (⅔ mile) from the ruins.

To get to the El Puente archaeological site, you will need to hire a taxi, which costs L230 round-trip from La Entrada. Admission is L55 and the park is open daily from 8am to 4pm. Or you can go on a guided tour, through Hotel El San Carlos (see below).

You can visit El Puente as a day trip, but if you'd like to stay overnight, **Hotel El San Carlos** (junction of CA 4 and CA 11; ✆ **504/661-2228;** www.hotelelsan carlos.com; L600 double) is the only decent place in the area. Just a few meters from the junction, this 45-unit hotel isn't half bad. There's a pool where you can listen to the squawks of their two macaws, clean rooms with cable TV, and a restaurant that's the best in town.

forest and coffee plantation, with a beautiful river and well-designed trails. There's an excellent riverside restaurant and a separate coffee shop with home-roasted beans.

4.8km (3 miles) west of the central plaza up a dirt road. ✆ **504/651-4245.** www.macawmountain.com. Admission L200. Daily 9am–5pm.

Museo Regional de Arqueología Maya ★   Also known simply as the Copán Museum, this museum holds a small collection of pottery and artifacts from the ruins, as well as a series of interpretive and explanatory displays. Perhaps the most interesting exhibit here is the complete burial niche of an ancient Copán scribe. If you're going to the ruins and the museum there, there's no need to visit this place. However, if you're hanging around town, it will take you only about 30 to 45 minutes to tour all the exhibits.

West side of Parque Central. No phone. Admission L40. Daily 9am–5pm.

Outdoor Activities

If you want to go bird-watching, take a horseback ride, soak in a nearby hot spring, explore some caves, or tube on the Copán River, contact local tour agencies **McTours** (✆ **504/ 651-4453;** www.mctours-honduras.com), **Yaragua** (✆ **504/651-4147;** www.yaragua. com), or **Xukpi** (✆ **504/651-4435;** www.xukpitourscopan.com).

Hot Springs & Health Retreats

The **Luna Jaguar Spa Resort** (☎ 504/651-4746; www.ipercorsidiicaro.com/php/luna_ing.php) is a luxury spa where a simple hot springs facility once stood. There's a pool you can bathe in for L60 admission, though the real reason to make the trek all the way here (24km/15 miles) is to enter the **Acropolis** (L200) across a hanging suspension bridge over the river. It has a somewhat Disney-esque feel to it with statues and stellae, sort of like a small Xcaret (the Cancun aeco-archaeological park). Once you cross the bridge into the Mayan netherworld, you enter a place of lush rainforest intersected by stone paths and gurgling streams that cross in and around dozens of small steaming pools of varying temperatures with waterfalls trickling in and out of them. *Collectivos* there cost L40 and the last one is at 4pm. From their office in their hotel (see above) in town, they offer packages that provide transportation to the spa.

Spa Ixchel (☎ 504/651-4114; www.spaixchelhonduras.com) 8km (5 miles) south of Copán at Hacienda San Isidro, a coffee finca, offers mud baths, skin treatments, meditation sessions, massages, and Maya Temascal treatments.

Shopping

The streets of Copán Ruínas are brimming with simple souvenir shops selling T-shirts, jade carvings, hammocks, masks, cigars, and Guatemalan crafts and textiles. There are several good markets scattered within a couple of blocks of the square with independent vendors that haul their crafts in from the surrounding villages. The best are **Pabellon Maya** (☎ 504/643-2833), beside the ATM on the plaza, and **Casa del Sol ★** (☎ 504/651-3559), just off the plaza.

La Casa de Todo, 1 block downhill from the Banco de Occidente corner of the central plaza (☎ 504/651-4185), is an excellent gift shop with unique local crafts, a coffee shop, an Internet cafe, and a simple restaurant serving Guatemalan fare; they even have a couple of rooms for overnight stays or can do your laundry. **Casa del Jade** (www.casavillamil.com), 1 block north of the plaza, is part of a Guatemalan chain that sells a wide variety of jewelry and collectibles that contain the Maya's preferred stone. The boutique gift shops beneath the hotel **Yat B'alam** on Calle la Independencia have one of the most unique and upscale selections of Honduran-made crafts, accessories, and home furnishings.

Where to Stay
EXPENSIVE

Casa Rosada ★★   Elegance and romance are two words that come to mind when trying to describe this charming, new Spanish colonial–style inn with just a few rooms. They don't overdo anything. Hand-carved wooden mirror frames and hand-woven accent rugs have been chosen with care. Rooms feature brick floors, 300-thread-count sheets, Honduran art on the walls—there's a small gallery downstairs—and big windows with views of the town and surrounding mountains. The bathrooms are the finest in Copán, with a shower featuring dual shower heads and speakers so you can listen to the radio while bathing. There's even a bidet.

2 blocks NW of the park. © **504/651-4321.** www.lacasarosada.com. 5 units. L1,655 double. Rates include breakfast. MC, V. **Amenities:** Cafe. *In room:* A/C, TV, DVD player, hair dryer, Wi-Fi.

Hacienda San Lucas ★★★ 📷
This is my favorite hotel in the area, set on a hillside across the river from and overlooking the Copán archaeological site. The rustic elegance of the rooms is a throwback to its former life as a farm and ranch, as are the high wood-beam and plank ceilings. The large rooms are outfitted with two queen-size beds, a large shared veranda with hammocks, and a beautiful stone shower. The hotel **restaurant** has excellent meals, and they have a yoga platform overlooking the river and ruins. The hotel abuts the Los Sapos ruins, and has several excellent hiking trails on its grounds. Sunsets are observed from a long lawn off of the main lodge building.

5km (3 miles) south of Copán Ruínas on the road to Los Sapos ruins. © **504/651-4495** or 651-4495. www.haciendasanlucas.com. 8 units. L615 double. Rates include full breakfast. AE, MC, V. **Amenities:** Restaurant; bar.

Hotel Marina Copán ★★
The best hotel in Copán Ruínas proper spans an entire city block facing the central plaza. The rooms are all tastefully decorated and come with large TVs, while the suites have tons of space and other nice touches, such as a Jacuzzi, a kitchenette, and a view. My favorite is no. 331, a third-floor corner suite with a large balcony and a great view of town. Many of the standard rooms come with a balcony, so it's worth requesting one when you make a reservation. There's a pool in the center of the hotel and plenty of areas to relax among plants and fountains.

Parque Central. © **877/893-9131** in the U.S. and Canada, or 504/651-4070 in Copán Ruínas. Fax 504/651-4477. www.hotelmarinacopan.com. 52 units. L1,980 double; L3,950–L5,510 suite. Rates lower in the off season, higher during peak periods. AE, MC, V. **Amenities:** Restaurant; bar; small gym w/ sauna; laundry service; midsize pool; room service. *In room:* A/C, TV, Wi-Fi.

Hotel Posada Real de Copán ★★
What it lacks in proximity to the center it makes up for via its one-of-a-kind views—the Posada Real, the largest hotel in the area, overlooks the hills and vegetation of the Copán valley. This hotel, more than any other in Western Honduras, is a resort. It even has its own helipad! The vast property, etched out of the dense jungle, surrounds a central courtyard that houses a pool. The rooms are a bit on the plain side, with reddish tile floors, gold or orange walls, wood furniture, and little else in the way of decor. The hotel is a hit with conferences, weddings, meetings, conventions, and most other large events.

1km (⅔ mile) from town near the archaeological site. © **504/651-4480.** Fax 504/651-4497. www.posadarealdecopan.com. 80 units. AE, MC, V. L1,615 double. **Amenities:** Restaurant; bar; helipad; laundry service; pool; shuttle service. *In room:* A/C, fan, TV.

MODERATE

Casa del Café ★
This house-turned-bed-and-breakfast, a few blocks outside the center of town, has a good view of the Copán valley and the mountains of neighboring Guatemala. The rooms are all cheery, bright, and comfortable. Those occupying the higher ground are a little older and smaller, but they have the aforementioned view from their shared veranda. The newer rooms have exposed beam ceilings and beautiful

mosaic tile sinks, with a veranda that lets out onto a small garden. The owners are extremely knowledgeable about the area, and they also rent out a few fully equipped apartments nearby.

1 block south and 4 blocks west of the central plaza. ☏ **504/651-4620.** Fax 504/651-4623. www. casadecafecopan.com. 10 units. L1,045 double. Rates include full breakfast. AE, MC, V. **Amenities:** Laundry service. *In room:* No phone.

Hotel Camino Maya ☺   The Camino Maya occupies prime corner space on the central plaza, so it competes with the Hotel Plaza Copán for the title of best-located moderate hotel. The lower level is home to the lobby and the Xibalba bar, run by Twisted Tanya's (see below), and Elisa's restaurant, while the second level holds the guest rooms. These rooms aren't terrible, but the floral bedspreads, tacky wallpaper and curtains, and mismatching wood and metal furniture could use a makeover. The hotel beats the Plaza Copán in extras, though. As space in the center of Copán is limited, the hotel's recreation area, with two pools, extensive gardens, hammocks strung from trees, two restaurants, and short trails, is a huge plus of staying here. Nonguests can use this recreation area, 4 blocks from the hotel, for L40 a day.

Southeast corner of Parque Central. ☏ **504/651-4518.** Fax 504/651-4517. www.caminomayahotel.com. 23 units. L1,350 double. Rates include breakfast. MC, V. **Amenities:** Restaurant; bar; pool. *In room:* A/C, fan, TV, fridge.

Yat B'alam ★★ 🍴   This absolutely charming independent hotel is one of the best values in western Honduras. I'm hesitant to call it a boutique hotel for fear that the price will go up; it's currently an absolute steal. If it were located in Antigua, just a few hours across the border, it would cost three times as much. The ground floor is laid out like a cobblestone colonial street lined with craft shops and a cafe. There are just a handful of rooms, all on the second level, with tiled floors, dark-wood contemporary furniture, and deep red decor. The triples have particularly high ceilings, and rooms near the street have the best views. Common areas with couches are sprinkled throughout, and boast good views as well.

Calle la Independencia. ☏ **504/651-4338.** Fax 504/651-3517. www.yatbalam.com. 6 units. L1,235 double. MC, V. **Amenities:** Cafe; laundry service. *In room:* A/C, fan, TV, fridge, Wi-Fi.

INEXPENSIVE

La Posada de Belssy   If you need a clean, no-frills room but have outgrown sleeping in backpacker dorms, cross your fingers that La Posada de Belssy isn't full. They have a cool rooftop lounge that's always full of other travelers chatting about their Central American exploits, but few other amenities.

1 block north of the plaza. ☏ **504/651-4680.** www.laposadadebelssy.com. 8 units. L300 double. No credit cards. *In room:* TV, fan.

Where to Dine
EXPENSIVE

Hacienda San Lucas ★★★ INTERNATIONAL/HONDURAN   The in-house restaurant at this lovely hotel is probably the best in Copán, and certainly the most atmospheric. Meals are served in an open-air patio in front of the old hacienda building. The five-course candlelit dinners are one of the finest culinary experiences in Honduras, with the choice of main courses including the house specialty of fire-roasted chicken with *adobo* sauce, a mole based on the herbs, spices, and nuts used by the ancient Maya. Lunches are more casual and range from homemade tamales to a salad-and-sandwich combination. The dinner hours listed below are for seatings;

you can then stay and enjoy the meal, which can take a couple hours. A taxi from town should run you L50 to L75 each way.

5km (3 miles) south of Copán Ruínas on the road to Los Sapos ruins. ⓒ **504/651-4495.** www.hacienda sanlucas.com. Reservations necessary. Lunch L150–L300; prix-fixe dinner L475. AE, MC, V. Daily 8:30am–3pm and 7–8:30pm.

Twisted Tanya's ★★ INTERNATIONAL   Part upscale fusion restaurant and part itinerant party central, this place mixes together elegance and extravagance in equal doses. The lovely open-air, second-floor corner dining room has white muslin curtains and fancy table settings. Their theory is "If it is in the market, it's on the menu," and the menu changes daily, and may include anything from homemade curries with coconut rice to salmon in a Jack Daniel's glaze. There are always a couple of vegetarian items to choose from. Twisted Tanya's offers a L418 prix-fixe menu of soup or salad, entree, and dessert. An early-bird backpacker special will get you soup, pasta, and dessert for just L114. The desserts here are all homemade, decadent, and deservedly renowned. Their popular two-for-one happy hour is from 4 to 6pm.

1 block south and 1 block west of the central plaza. ⓒ **504/651-4182.** www.twistedtanya.com. Reservations recommended. Main courses L115–L285. AE, MC, V. Mon–Sat 2–10pm.

MODERATE

Café Welchez INTERNATIONAL   Café Welchez's setting at the corner of the central plaza gives this small-room cafe one of the best views in town. While it is a bit pricey compared with Copán's other restaurants, the food is decent, especially for a light meal, and it's a nice, quiet place to rest your feet and read a book. Try their *ticucos a la crema,* a corn tamale with red beans slathered in a creamy sauce. Quiche, sandwiches, local coffees, ice coffees and drinks, and coconut flan round out the menu.

Central plaza. ⓒ **504/651-4070.** Main courses L60–L200. MC, V. Daily 7am–10pm.

Carnitas N'ia Lola ★★ ☺ HONDURAN   Grilled meats are the specialty of this two-level restaurant on the edge of town. N'ia's is one of the most popular restaurants in Copán, partly because of the delicious food and partly because of the waitresses who carry drinks and dishes from the kitchen on their heads. Brochettes, typical dishes, tacos, and steaks are all good. *Anafre,* a bean fondue eaten with tortilla chips, is served in place of bread. Happy hour is 6:30 to 8:30pm.

2 blocks south of the central plaza. ⓒ **504/651-4196.** Main courses L120–L300. MC, V. Daily 7am–10pm.

INEXPENSIVE

Comedor y Pupuseria Mary ★★ SALVADORAN/HONDURAN   The central focus of the cuisine here is the *pupusas,* a type of corn pancake filled with chicken, meat, beans, or cheese that comes from neighboring El Salvador. There are nearly a dozen variations that range from an unbelievable L10 to L15. Just a couple will get you full. The restaurant is open early and has typical breakfasts, set tipico lunches, and nightly dinner specials.

½ block south of the market. No phone. Main courses L10–L100. No credit cards. Daily 7am–10pm.

For a Quick, Cheap Bite: *Baleada* Stands

At night in front of the Hondutel office just off the square, several *baleada* carts and other food stands are set up.

The *baleadas* are simple—just a corn tortilla with refried beans and fresh cream—and cheap (L10).

Copán Ruínas After Dark

Copán Ruínas is a relatively quiet town. Aside from the hotel and restaurant bars (of which Twisted Tanya's is always a good call), the most happening spot seems to be **Café Xibalba** (inside the Camino Maya hotel; ☏ **504/651-4182**). In addition, you might try the **Tunkul Bar** (1½ blocks west of the central plaza; ☏ **504/651-4410**), or head to the **Sapo Rojo** (1 block form the park) for a more relaxed vibe. **Wine Barcito** (Calle Independencia, 1 block south of Parque Central; no phone), in a tiny room beside the Pabellon Maya souvenir shop, is tops for wine. **Papa Chango's** (down the hill from the center and near the Hedman-Alas bus station; no phone) is the only real spot for a very late night, as a noise ordinance in the center forces restaurants and bars in Copán to close by midnight.

SANTA ROSA DE COPÁN

45km (28 miles) to Gracias; 110km (68 miles) to Copán

Santa Rosa is the commercial and administrative hub of western Honduras, and, though it isn't overflowing with tourist sights, it makes a good base for exploring elsewhere in the department of Lempira. The town has long been known for growing high-quality tobacco, and this crop has played an important part in the town's history. The La Real Factoria del Tabaco was established here by the Spanish in 1765, and it led to considerable wealth for the city. Today the city still boasts a number of pretty, *azulejo*-covered colonial buildings that were built by the Spanish, and tobacco remains an important part of the economy.

Essentials

From San Pedro Sula, take CA 4 to La Entrada and head south on CA 11-A; the trip takes about 2½ hours. To drive to or from Copán, you must also go through La Entrada, and transfer to Hwy. 11.

The city's bus terminal sits in a lot on the main road about 1.5km (1 mile) from the center. Direct buses make the 3-hour trip to San Pedro Sula about four times per day; tickets cost L80. To get to Copán Ruínas, you can either take a 3-hour direct bus (L40) or transfer after 1½ hours to La Entrada (L20) for a Copán bus (L20). Buses also make the 1¼-hour trip to Gracias (L30) and the 2½-hour trip to the Guatemalan border at Aguas Caliente (L75). All buses leave when they're full, not according to a set schedule.

There are two sections of Santa Rosa. The first is the colonial core of the city, which centers on the top of a hill that includes Parque Central and the Centro Historico. The other lines the highway about 1km (⅔ mile) from the center, and is where you'll find the bus terminal, the cigar factory, and many poorly constructed residences. Taxis can shuttle you between the center and the highway for about L20.

The tourist office (☏ **504/662-2234**) is in a round building smack in the middle of Parque Central and doubles as a cybercafé. It's open Monday to Saturday from 8am to noon and 1:30 to 6pm.

Banco Atlántida (south side of Parque Central) has a 24-hour ATM and will exchange traveler's checks. The **tourist office** (☏ **504/662-2234**) is in a round building smack in the middle of Parque Central and doubles as a **cybercafé** (Mon–Sat 8am–noon and 1:30–6pm).

What to See & Do

Just entering the **Flor de Copán Cigar Factory ★★** (4 blocks east of the bus terminal, Barrio Miraflores; ✆ **504/662-0111;** admission L40; daily 10am–2pm) building is intoxicating—the scent of tobacco is in the air as you enter the premises. During your tour, you'll get a fascinating look into a full-fledged, working Honduras cigar maker. Highlights include peeks at warehouses full of drying tobacco leaves, as well as rooms of workers deveining the leaves, shaping the tobacco, rolling the cigars, and finally packing the final product for export.

Although you can't buy cigars at the Flor de Copán cigar factory, you can purchase them from the distributor **Tabacos Hondureños S.A. ★★** (Centanario 168; ✆ **504/662-0111**), which has a small shop right in town a block from the park. Several large humidors stock a wide selection of cigar boxes from the Santa Rosa de Copán factory, which produces a variety of labels. Prices are significantly cheaper than they are outside of the country. A few handicrafts and regional products can also be found here and in the small shops around Parque Central.

The tour company **Lenca Land Trails** (✆ **504/662-1128**) arranges tours into nearby Lenca villages and to bird-watching and other destinations in the region.

While this celebration isn't as large as the **Semana Santa (Holy Week)** celebrations in Comayagua, the 7 days before Easter are still quite a spectacle in Santa Rosa de Copán. Six traditional processions reenact the Easter story and begin on Holy Thursday.

Where to Stay & Dine

Hotel Elvir ★ (Centanario and Av. 3a NO; ✆ **504/662-0103;** www.hotelelvir.com; 43 units; L750 double, L2,090 suite) has been open since 1955, but you wouldn't guess it, since it's undergone several renovations and remodels. The standard rooms are spacious but a bit bland; the two suites are considerably nicer and larger, and have Jacuzzis. Still, the services are the best in the city, and the facilities—including a rooftop pool with great views and a delightful open-air colonial courtyard—are first-rate. Owner Max Elvir is one of the staunchest promoters of tourism in western Honduras.

While it lacks the colonial style of Hotel Elvir and is a bit more out-of-the-way from the center, the modern, 50-unit **Casa Real ★** (Calle 2a and 3a NO; ✆ **504/662-0801;** fax 504/662-0802; www.hotelcasarealsrc.com; L1,149 double) has by far the best setup in Santa Rosa. Their grassy courtyard is centered around a pleasant open-air restaurant, **Casa Romero,** and a pool area that seems straight out of a Roatán resort. The rooms are, sadly, much plainer than the beautiful property, with clean tile floors but shoddy furnishings and decor.

At Avenida 1a SE, **Flamingo's ★★** (main courses L95–L285) is the classiest restaurant in Santa Rosa and where the tobacco bigwigs dine when they're in town. The menu is mostly international, with a few coastal Honduran staples like conch soup and *pescado al ajillo* (fish in garlic sauce). Grilled meats, pastas, and salads are also served.

The tiny cafe and coffee shop **Ten Nepel** (L10–L40), beside Hotel Elvir, is good for java, juice, or a quick snack. There are a couple of tables in an elegant setting, and highlights on the menu include granitas, espresso, and bagels.

GRACIAS

45km (28 miles) to Santa Rosa de Copán; 155km (96 miles) to Copán

You wouldn't know it just by looking at it, but this sleepy town was once the Spanish capital of Central America. After its founding in 1536, it was named Gracias a Dios, after founder Captain Juan de Chavez, a Spanish conquistador, who spent many long days combing the mountains for flat land: "Gracias a Dios que hemos hallado tierra llana" ("Thank God that we found flat land") were reportedly his first words. In 1544, Gracias became home to the Spanish Royal courthouse and was given jurisdiction over a territory covering the area between Mexico and Panama, but that didn't last long. Four years later, the court moved to Antigua, Guatemala, and little else was heard about Gracias for many years.

Essentials

GETTING THERE
From San Pedro Sula (4 hr. away) or Copán (3 hr. away), take CA 4 to La Entrada, and then head south on CA 11-A until you hit Gracias. The bus terminal is a dusty lot across the street from the market. Direct buses make the 5-hour drive from San Pedro Sula about five times per day; the ride costs L100. To get here from Copán Ruínas, you must first take a 2-hour bus ride to La Entrada (L40) and then transfer to a Copán bus for another 2-hour ride. Buses head to a few other nearby destinations too.

ORIENTATION & GETTING AROUND
Gracias comprises a small grid of streets that sits on a dash of flat land in the most mountainous part of Honduras, at the foot of the pine-covered Montaña de Celaque. Roads leading to the city are only partially paved, which is why getting there often requires going through San Pedro Sula, even if you're coming from Tegucigalpa.

Apart from its surrounding sites, most of the attractions in Gracias can be seen on foot. The colonial core of the city is concentrated around a small grid of streets less than 10 blocks long. To get to Celaque or to the hot springs, you will need to take a taxi, which can be found near the market or the park. Alternatively, you can visit on a guided tour; see "Parque Nacional Montaña de Celaque," later in this chapter, for info.

VISITOR INFORMATION
Gracias lacks an ATM, but **Banco de Occidente** at the Parque Central will exchange currency and traveler's checks. There are a few small cybercafés around the park and most are quite slow. For international phone calls, head to **Hondutel,** 1 block from the park, beside the post office. The **tourist office** is in a small kiosk in the middle of the park. It's open Monday to Friday from 8am to noon and 2 to 5pm, as well as Saturday from 8 to 11:30am.

What to See & Do

The **Parque Central,** a small tree-filled square surrounded by colonial buildings, is the most active spot in town and recently completed a major renovation. **La Iglesia de San Marcos,** on the southern side of the park, was built in the late 1800s. Beside it you can find the remnants of the **Audiencia de los Confines,** now the home of the parish priest. One block to the north is **Las Mercedes,** the most attractive of the three colonial churches in the city. The facade dates from 1610.

Balneario Aguas Termales ★ ☺ After a day of hiking the steep hills of Celaque, there's nowhere better to turn than this naturally steamy pool of thermal water. The Balneario hot springs complex sits hidden on a hill submerged in pine woods outside of town. There are several pools ranging from 92° to 96°F (33°–36°C), which attract a steady stream of visitors and locals. It's most crowded on nights and weekends, and particularly family-friendly (there are even changing rooms here, a rarity in the country). There's a small cafe and bar near the pools. You can buy oranges, which are believed to give skin a healthy glow, from vendors working the site.

6.5km (4 miles) south of Gracias. Admission L30. Daily 8am–8pm.

Casa Galeano & Jardín Botánico ★   Once the home of a wealthy colonial family, this restored colonial house from the 1840s has become one of the best museums in western Honduras outside of Copán. Colonial artifacts, models of villages, old photographs, murals, and pre-Columbian tools are paired with a brilliant folk-art collection of masks and other items created by the region's indigenous cultures. There are rotating art exhibitions, mostly from unknown regional artists. In the rear of the building is a botanical garden. The collection of plants here, begun by the Galeanos, is one of the oldest botanical gardens in Central America. It's quite small, but the assortment of native species is good.

In front of Iglesia San Marcos. Admission L30. Daily 9am–6pm.

El Fuerte de San Cristóbal   This small fort, perched atop a hill just a short walk from the Parque Central above Hotel Guancascos, boasts the best views of Gracias. Apart from the tomb of one-time Honduras (1841–42) and El Salvador (1847–52) President Juan Lindo and a few Spanish cannons, there is little of cultural interest here, however.

4 blocks west of Parque Central, above Hotel Guancascos. Free admission. Daily 8am–4pm.

Termas del Río   This new hot springs facility owned and operated by the Posada de Don Juan is at Km 7 on the road to Santa Rosa. There are two elegant-looking pools of different temperatures, one of which is quite large, as well as changing facilities. If you are turned off by the number of people using the public facilities, these more modern and private springs are probably for you. Reservations are needed to visit.

Km 7 on the road to Santa Rosa. ✆ **504/656-1304.** josearmando_morales@yahoo.com. Admission L100. Daily 7am–9pm.

SHOPPING

Aside from the gift shops at Guancascos and Posada de Don Juan, there's no better place in town to shop than **Lorendiana** (Calle Principal, 2 blocks south of the Mercado Municipal; ✆ **504/656-1058**). By browsing the wares on sale at this one-room co-op, you'll get a real feel for the bounty of Lempira's forests. You'll find rows and rows of jars of preserves, hot sauces, dulce de leche, candy, dried fruit, tortillas, and handicrafts, all at good prices.

Where to Stay

Guancascos ★   What sets this hotel apart from others in Gracias is the view. Since it's located on an old coffee farm on the hillside below San Cristóbal Fort, guests can see the city's entire grid of streets, colonial churches, and terra-cotta roof tiles from the porch chairs of the top-level rooms. All rooms have wood floors, simple furniture, and regional accents like handicrafts and paintings. The Dutch owner makes sure the gardens are full of flowering shrubs and trees, which attract a loyal following of hummingbirds and butterflies, and is a wealth of information on the area—the owner can easily set up guided tours to Parque Nacional Celaque. The open-air **restaurant** here doubles as a common area.

Below Fuerte de San Cristóbal. ✆ **504/656-1219.** www.guancascos.com. 11 units. L475 double. MC, V. **Amenities:** Restaurant; high-speed Internet in lobby. *In room:* TV.

Posada de Don Juan ★★★ 🏆 Major renovations—which have thankfully not destroyed the colonial charm—went into this hotel in 2008, and it has now, with a huge annex, more than doubled in size, and added a full restaurant and bar, a beautiful courtyard pool, an array of luxury rooms, and a conference room. Even the smaller older rooms, which surround a cobblestone courtyard that doubles as a parking lot, have gotten a face-lift with fresh new decor even though the prices have stayed the same. If the older rooms are nice, the new rooms are a thing of beauty. With earthy tones fitting for Gracias, dark hardwood furniture, high-beamed ceilings, and everything from the light fixtures to the door handles being expertly picked, these are by far the best in town. In addition, the hotel has built its own private hot spring facilities on the road to Santa Rosa, Termas del Río, which is open to the public and can be included in package stays at the hotel.

1 block from the park. ℭ **504/656-1020.** www.posadadedonjuanhotel.com. 42 units. L855–L1,235 double. AE, MC, V. **Amenities:** Restaurant; bar; Jacuzzi; pool. *In room:* A/C, fan, TV, purified water, Wi-Fi.

Villas del Agua Caliente ☺ This series of rustic cabins is strewn on a hillside a few hundred feet from Balneario Aguas Termales (see above). It's a bit isolated, so if you don't have a car, getting in and out can be problematic. Some of the bungalows have several bedrooms and could sleep a decent-size family, while others are smaller, yet still spacious. Simple handmade wood furniture, Lenca decor, and wall hangings define the otherwise bland rooms.

At Balneario Aguas Termales. ℭ **504/608-5370.** 16 units. L300 double. Rates include breakfast. No credit cards. **Amenities:** Restaurant; bar. *In room:* TV, fan.

Where to Dine

Guancascos ★ INTERNATIONAL/HONDURAN The food is only part of the allure of this restaurant in the Guancascos hotel (see above)—the elevated view is the main attraction. The small gift shop, which stocks helpful information on sites and activities in the area, means the restaurant serves as something of a visitor center too. The good food ranges from local staples like *baleadas* and Honduran breakfasts to German-style artisan breads and fresh juices.

Below Fuerte de San Cristóbal. ℭ **504/656-1219.** www.guancascos.com. Main courses L57–L190. MC, V. Daily 7am–10pm.

Meson de Don Juan ★ HONDURAN This hotel restaurant expanded in 2008 to become the largest restaurant in town. It's very modern, with a mix of contemporary and rustic furniture, and features a flatscreen TV near the bar. They make a mean *chuleta de cerdo* (pork chop) with plantains, but the seafood dishes (tilapia especially), steaks, burgers and sandwiches, pastas, and full Honduran breakfasts are also quite good. There are even a few vegetarian entrees.

Inside Posada de Don Juan. ℭ **504/656-1020.** www.posadadedonjuanhotel.com. Main courses L76–L228. AE, MC, V. Daily 6am–10pm.

Rinconcito Graciano ★★★ HONDURAN "We dreamers are in a world of our own," said Lizeth Perdomo, owner and chef of Rinconcito Graciano who is actively involved in tourism and historic preservation in the area. Her approach is nothing less than extraordinary: Rescue traditional Lencan recipes—some of them passed down from her mother and grandmother—and use mostly organic produce from local farmers. Few of the dishes, which are served in locally made clay pottery, can be found in restaurants elsewhere in the country. Here you'll find *ticucos* (a tamal with legumes, beans, and loroco), *chorocos* (tamal recipe from San Manuel de Colohete), and *lengua de res* (tongue). There are a wide variety of vegetarian dishes as well.

2 blocks south of the Municipal market on Av. San Sebastion. © **504/656-1171.** Main courses L75–L150. No credit cards. Daily 11am–9pm.

Side Trips from Gracias

LA RUTA LENCA ★★★

La Ruta Lenca, or the Lenca Route, is a grass-roots tourism initiative to help bring tourism revenue to the small villages south of Gracias and give tourists insight into a little-known indigenous group, the Lencas. The cultural group was derived from Chibcha-speaking Indians who came from Colombia and Venezuela more than 3,000 years ago. They number around 100,000 in Honduras and 40,000 or so in El Salvador and are known throughout the country for their earthenware pottery, and several towns also have small craft cooperatives. The best times to visit any Lenca villages are during Sunday markets and *Guancascos,* annual gatherings between two villages to celebrate peace. La Ruta Lenca passes through the mountain villages of La Campa, Belén Gualcho, San Manuel de Colohete, San Sebastián, Corquín, and Mohaga, among others. This string of rural towns that dot this part of the country features adobe houses, corn and bean fields, the occasional museum and colonial church, and beautiful mountain views. During the rainy season (Apr–Nov), the hills and trees are a vibrant green and the scent of flowering plants wafts though the air.

The association of guides **Colosuca** (© **504/656-0627** or 222-2124, ext. 502; www.colosuca.com), based in Gracias and Santa Rosa, offers tours for L200 to L300 per group of one to five to Lenca villages and offers the opportunity to combine trips with activities such as colonial architecture, mountain biking, hiking, bird-watching, and horseback-riding tours. The guides are all locally trained and many are actively involved in cultural preservation.

LA CAMPA ★★

La Campa is the first town you reach when leaving Gracias, just 16km (10 miles) away on a well-paved road. The village is quite small, just a few hundred residents that live in a cluster of adobe houses with tile roofs scattered on a few hills. The centerpiece of town is Iglesia de San Matías, built in 1690 and restored in 1938, which sits at the lowest point in the village with the houses sort of hovering around it. The sheer white facade backed by the rocky cliffs is a site to behold. The church is only officially opened for mass, though you can usually find someone to open it for a small tip. The interior is quite plain apart from one faded oil painting and a beautiful carved-wood altar. The price for photos inside the church is L30 each—yikes!

Ceramics are a big part of life in Lenca villages. La Campa is best known for massive urns made by hand—perfectly cylindrical—that are called *cántaros.* You can see a few examples in front of the municipal building. Several artisan workshops in town, such as **Alfarería Lenca** and the home of **Doña Desideria Pérez,** are open to visitors and have small shops where you can buy the signature Lenca bowls, plates, wind chimes, and vases. The people in the workshops love visitors and are eager to explain their work process. High on the hill near the road in is the **Centro de Interpretación de Alfarería Lenca** or **La Escuelona** (daily 8am–4:30pm; admission L30), set in a colonial building with many examples of Lenca pottery with explanations and details on historical significance.

As far as facilities go on La Ruta Lenca, La Campa is the most advanced, with a municipal building across from the church that contains a small tourist office and several small hotels such as **Hostal J.B.** (© **504/551-3772;** hostal_jb@yahoo.com; L200 double) and the new **Hotel Bellavista** (© **504/625-4770;** similar prices). You can inquire at either Hostal J.B. or the tourist office regarding guided hikes and rides on horseback in the area that visit caves, canyons, and nearby villages such as **Cruz Alta,** famous for its *tejado de pino,* a type of basketry made with pine needles.

If you don't have time to push farther into the hills, a stop here that can be done rather quickly from Gracias is recommended. To get to La Campa, there is one daily bus from Gracias (L20) at noon that continues to San Marcos de Caiquín and San Manuel de Colohete, and the return stops in La Campa between 6:15 and 6:45am.

SAN MARCOS DE CAIQUIN

Continuing from La Campa, the road gets a little less smooth and it winds up about 6km (3¾ miles) over the hills to a fork. If you stick to the right, you will reach San Manuel de Colohete, while to the right is this small adobe village amid the pines. There are just a few simple *comedores* (simple restaurants) and *pulperias* (grocery stores) in the quiet village, as well as a small church, built in 1750, that was renovated in recent years. Several family homes will rent out rooms to visitors for a small price.

SAN MANUEL DE COLOHETE

A bumpy 14km (8⅔ miles) from La Campa, 1½ hours from Gracias, sits San Manuel de Colohete, one of the favorite stops on any tour of La Ruta Lenca. The town itself is the largest in the area, though that isn't saying much. There are just a few narrow, twisting streets on a flat piece of land with a small grassy square on the far end. The locals don't see many visitors and are still surprised when one shows up, though they are quite friendly if you need any help.

Of all the colonial churches along La Ruta Lenca, San Manuel de Colohete's is the one you should not miss. The intricately carved white facade that dates back to 1721 was recently renovated, and at last check they were still working on the roof and back end of the church on the outside. To get inside, you must be here on Sunday; otherwise, no one can open up the doors. Inside are several frescoes that date back 400 years and an ornate wooden altar. The best time to visit is on the 1st and 15th of every month when San Manuel hosts a lively outdoor market (6am–noon) where people from the surrounding villages come to sell their produce and general knickknacks.

SAN SEBASTIAN

The road gets even worse past San Manuel de Colohete and ends in San Sebastián except for an almost impenetrable road to Belén Gualcho. There is talk of paving the road in the near future that would complete a full circuit around Parque Nacional Celaque. For now, though, the few that make it here will find another charming colonial village, much like the others with an impressive church and small square, but with far fewer visitors. There are a few *very* basic *comedores* and simple *hospedajes* (lodgings) in town.

BELEN GUALCHO

Better reached from Santa Rosa de Copán than Gracias, Belén Gualcho is best known for its Sunday-morning market. Get here early, as the market tends to dissipate by 11am. This one is set high—1,600m (5,250 ft.)—on the mountain and features one of the most ornate cathedrals anywhere along La Ruta Lenca. Some argue that the three domes and mountain setting rank it above the church in San Manuel de Colohete. There are a couple of basic hotels and *comedores* that fill up on weekends with marketgoers, as well as a Hondutel and cybercafé. There is access into Celaque just outside of town. You can even return via the Gracias trail. The route tends to be confusing, so you will need a guide (contact Colosuca-Celaque Tours or ask around in town), but the full hike up can be done in about a half-day. Other hikes can lead you to San Sebastián (5–8 hr.) or to the Santa Maria de Gualcho waterfall (5–6 hr. round-trip) past the village of El Paraíso. There are two daily buses (L50) here from Santa Rosa de Copán at around 3am and 8am for the 2- to 3-hour ride, with service doubling on Sundays.

PARQUE NACIONAL MONTAÑA DE CELAQUE ★★★

Meaning "box of water" in the Lenca dialect, Celaque is one of the largest tracts of cloud forest remaining in Central America and one of the most unspoiled national parks in the country. Its 11 rivers supply villages as far away as El Salvador with fresh water. Nearly 50 species of mammals, several hundred species of birds, and a few dozen types of reptiles have been identified in the park. Celaque's pine forests hide rare wildlife such as resplendent quetzals, ocelots, jaguars, monkeys, and pumas, but consider yourself lucky to catch a glimpse of just one of these, as the dense mist and fog often obscure views.

The only way to see the park is by hiking a pretty steep ascent, and the often wet and muddy trails make it difficult for those who aren't physically fit. From the visitor center, on the Gracias side, there is one main trail leading uphill that branches off into several other trails. (A few well-placed signs and ribbons mark where the trails break off.) The shortest trail takes about 2 to 3 hours, and lets you off at a small outlook where the Santa Lucia waterfall can be seen from afar. A more difficult hike is the 2,383m (7,818-ft.) climb up Cerro El Gallo, which winds for about 3 or 4 hours through spider monkey stamping grounds before reaching the top. Hardest of all is a hike to the top of Cerro de las Minas, the tallest peak in Honduras at 2,849m (9,347 ft.); it requires at least 2 days.

There are a few small campsites on the El Gallo and Las Minas trails, and you can also bunk at the **visitor center** (no phone; at the forest's edge by Río Arcagual) for L50. The park is easily reached by car from Gracias, which is 9km (5⅔ miles) away, although tours often leave from Santa Rosa and other towns that surround the park. From Gracias, you can also take a moto-taxi for about L100 to the end of the road, which is a 30-minute or so walk to the visitor center. Guides are not required, but recommended. Walter Murcia, who runs **Puma Trail Tours** (© **504/656-1113;** waltermurcia@hotmail.com), is the most respected guide in the area. Other guides can be arranged in Gracias at **Guancascos** (see above) or through **Colosuca** (see above). Admission to the park is L50.

THE NORTH COAST ★

Everywhere you look in the north-coast region of Honduras, the tourism infrastructure is thriving and playing off of the region's healthy cultural and environmental diversity. Garífuna villages and *mestizo* cities live side by side with a growing number of American retiree communities, and ecotourism is on the verge of a major eruption—swanky new jungle lodges are being erected on former chocolate plantations and hiking trails are carving their way through national parks like Pico Bonito.

Zip-line tours are now as common as *pan de coco,* kayaking and canoe tours can be had in every mangrove-forested lagoon, and serious birders are descending upon the region like migrating herons. Up and down the coast, major beach projects are also in the works; the most significant could possibly turn Tela Bay into the next Cancun.

Though it seems like the North Coast is finally getting its moment in the spotlight, this part of the country is steeped in history. Spanish explorers and conquistadors first entered the country here, and colonial-era forts still guard the coast from would-be pirate attacks. The Garífuna, an ethnic group descended from Carib Indians and West African slaves, arrived along this coast at the end of the 18th century. And the presence of Dole and Chiquita here made this town an important part of the country's history as a banana republic.

Omoa

Omoa is about as laid-back a place as you will find. Gentle breezes from the Merendón mountain range, the backdrop of the town, swoop down across the jungle-clad coastline and leave the hustle and bustle of Puerto Cortés far behind. This sleepy beach community takes more of an easygoing, Belizean vibe, and the atmosphere has more of a beach and tourist scene than in neighboring Puerto Cortés. While San Pedro residents and foreigners are increasingly flocking here to build vacation homes, mostly outside of town, the crowds are minimal and on most days you will have the town almost to yourself. History buffs take note: Omoa is home to one of the most important colonial-era forts in the Caribbean, **Fortaleza de San Fernando,** which recently finished an extensive renovation.

The town's main attraction is undoubtedly the **Fortaleza de San Fernando de Omoa** (admission L40; Mon–Fri 8am–4pm, Sat–Sun 9am–5pm), in the center of the town. It is one of the architectural highlights of Honduras and a gem of a colonial fort, the largest in Central America. Slaves—both Indians and Africans—supplied the labor for much of the construction, which began in 1759 and never technically finished. It was designed to ward off pirate attacks from such buccaneers as Peg Leg and Black Diego, who were after the silver shipments from the Tegucigalpa mines headed to Spain. A 2-year reconstruction was completed at the end of 2008 and the national monument is looking better than ever. There is a small site museum in one of the outer buildings with a collection of artifacts like cannons, guns, scale models, and photos. Guides are available at the entrance for a negotiable fee, about L40 to L60 per tour.

For beachgoers, the **public beach** beside the pier in town is so-so. The water is clear and shallow; however, debris from the rivers on both sides of it can be an issue. The community has done a good job of keeping the beach and water clean in recent years, though, so expect improvements. About a 45-minute walk, or 2 to 3km (1½ miles) down the highway from the entrance to town, you can hike to a river with a nice swimming hole and waterfall. The trail is a bit difficult to spot, so just ask anyone for directions to *"la cascada."*

ESSENTIALS

Omoa is 18km (11 miles) west of Puerto Cortés and 35km (22 miles) from the Guatemalan border at Tegucigalpa. Buses for Cortés (L20), from where you can transfer to San Pedro Sula, depart from a small terminal on Calle 3a every 20 to 30 minutes during daylight hours. If you're headed to the border, go to the highway and flag down any passing bus to Corinto, where you can stamp out of the country and then continue on. Chances are others will be waiting too. If you have a group together, Roli's Place (© 504/658-9082) can organize transfers to Puerto Barrios in Guatemala or to La Ceiba to connect to the ferries for the Bay Islands.

From Puerto Cortés there is ferry service to Big Creek/Mango Creek and Placencia, Belize, with the **D-Express** (© 504/991-0778; www.belizeferry.com; L1,000) on Mondays at 11:30am, returning Fridays at 9:30am. The trip takes 4 hours and returns Fridays at 9:30am.

Nearly everything in Omoa is compact and sits on a 2km (1¼-mile) stretch of road between the highway and the beach, with the fort about at the halfway point. There is no ATM here, though Banco de Occidente on the highway exchanges traveler's checks and will exchange currency. There are two cybercafés in town that have international phone calls.

WHERE TO STAY & DINE

The new guy in town, **Coco Bay** ★ (© 504/658-9007; L1,150 double), is a 5-minute walk to the beach and set up in halves: One half is a single level of rooms, while the other half holds the parking lot (parking spots face the rooms), flower gardens, pool and lounge area, and restaurant. Floors are white tile and walls are pastel colors.

For years **Roli's Place** (© 504/658-9082; L240 doubles; L100 dorms) has been the backpacker hangout of Omoa and the unofficial tourist center. You can find out what to do in town, find a bus schedule, pick up a map, and surf the Web. Oh, and you can get a bed. The Swiss hosts have built air-conditioned cabins in recent years, though the budget crowd sticks to the dorm rooms, hammocks, and campsites, which are significantly cheaper.

In the hotel of the same name right beside the pier, **Flamingo's** (main courses L60–L140) serves a little bit of everything in their big open-air *champa*: shrimp or fish, whether grilled, fried, steamed, or in garlic sauce, is the most popular choice.

Restaurante Fisherman's ★★ (main courses L100–L250), on the beachfront, serves huge plates, as in "if you can finish one, call me and I will be your manager for eating competitions" kind of big. The menu is similar to those of the others along the beachfront, with a mix of Honduran staples and seafood dishes like *Sopa Marinera* or fresh fish either breaded or grilled. The entrees come with a pile of plantain chips, salad, and beans that can barely fit on the plate.

Tela ★★

By 2012, you probably won't be able to recognize Tela, a beachside town 87km (54 miles) east of San Pedro Sula. A major government tourism initiative, with help from the World Bank, has promised to turn Tela Bay into one of the most important beach destinations in Central America. There have been plenty of delays and setbacks, but it looks like within a couple of years there will likely be several four- and five-star megaresorts, an 18-hole designer golf course, and a marina operating. Controversy has been swirling around the project, though, as opposition groups claim that a Cancun-like resort would completely wipe out the already fragile ecosystem at the city's Laguna de los Micos and do little for the Garífuna communities there. These groups may have run out of luck, though. Ground has already been broken for one of the resorts, roads are being expanded, and 20 new bilingual tourist police have already been trained and hired.

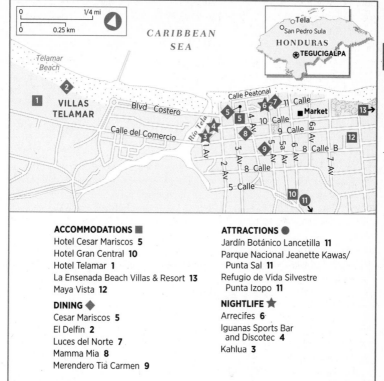

ACCOMMODATIONS ■
Hotel Cesar Mariscos **5**
Hotel Gran Central **10**
Hotel Telamar **1**
La Ensenada Beach Villas & Resort **13**
Maya Vista **12**

DINING ◆
Cesar Mariscos **5**
El Delfin **2**
Luces del Norte **7**
Mamma Mia **8**
Merendero Tia Carmen **9**

ATTRACTIONS ●
Jardín Botánico Lancetilla **11**
Parque Nacional Jeanette Kawas/
  Punta Sal **11**
Refugio de Vida Silvestre
  Punta Izopo **11**

NIGHTLIFE ★
Arrecifes **6**
Iguanas Sports Bar
  and Discotec **4**
Kahlua **3**

The conquistador Cristobal de Olid founded Tela on May 3, 1524, the day of the Holy Cross, and gave it the name Triunfo de la Cruz. The abbreviation of the name, T. de la +, would eventually lead to the shortened name of Tela. In the early 1800s, the Garífunas began to arrive here from Roatán and set up communities all over Tela Bay, many of which are still around. Toward the end of the century, the municipality began to form around the banana plantations of the Tela Railroad Company, a subsidiary of the United Fruit Company, which owned the Chiquita brand. The company monopolized city politics until they moved their offices to La Lima in 1976.

Today, as tourism has taken hold of the city, its days as a banana republic are a thing of the past. While the skeletal remains of the Tela Railroad and United Fruit offices are gathering dust, the employee homes have been turned into one of the country's best resorts, the Hotel Telamar.

ESSENTIALS
Getting There
Tela sits on CA 13 halfway between San Pedro Sula and La Ceiba, each a little more than an hour away depending on traffic. Any bus between La Ceiba and San Pedro

Sula will make a stop at Tela. For San Pedro (L60), try **Tela Express** (2a Av. NE just past the train tracks; ✆ **504/550-8355**), with five daily departures making the 1½-hour trip. For La Ceiba (L40) or Trujillo (L120), catch a **Cotuc bus** (at the Dippsa gas station on the highway; ✆ **504/441-2199**) or head to the minibus terminal at 9a Calle NE.

Orientation

The city of Tela sits on the southernmost point of Tela Bay; Parque Nacional Punta Izopa and Parque Nacional Jeannette Kawas/Punta Sal flank each side of it and are connected by unpaved roads that are sometimes impassable when it rains. The city center, Tela Vieja, is compact, with a small grid of streets hugging the coast. The Río Tela splits the town into two, with Tela Vieja on the east and Tela Nueva—home of the Hotel Telamar and the old Tela Railroad buildings—on the west bank.

Getting Around

Anywhere in the city of Tela can be reached on foot, but to reach most of the surrounding attractions, you will need some form of motorized transport. Your own **car** is the best method if you wish to explore the national parks and coast on your own. There are no car-rental agencies in Tela, so you'll have to head to the airports in La Ceiba (p. 387) or San Pedro Sula (p. 346). **Taxis** are best for getting to Lancetilla, the surrounding beaches, and Garífuna villages along the coast, but most drivers won't make the long trips to the national parks. A ride in town should cost no more than L20. **Minibuses and pickups** ply the highway and coastal roads, though they are infrequent. Most cost only L10.

Visitor Information & Fast Facts

For tourist information, try the **Tela Chamber of Commerce** (www.telahonduras. com) or **PROLANSATE** (Edificio Kwawas at Calle del Comercio; ✆ **504/448-2042;** www.prolansate.org), which has brochures, maps, and information regarding the national parks in the area.

All amenities can be found in Tela Vieja. The most convenient bank, **Banco Atlántida** (4a Av. NE and 9a Calle NE), has an ATM and exchanges traveler's checks. You can make international calls at **Hondutel** (4a Av. NE and 7a Calle NE) or at most of the Internet cafes near Parque Central. The **Tourist Police** (✆ **504/448-0253;** daily 24 hr.) can be found at 11a Calle NE and 4a Av. NE.

WHAT TO SEE & DO

Moving west from Tela along the coast, you will encounter the Garífuna communities of Triunfo de la Cruz, Tornabé, San Juan, La Ensenada, Río Tinto, and lastly Miami. The farther you get from Tela, the more traditional the villages become. **Miami ★★★**, which sits on a sandbar between the ocean and the Los Micos lagoon in **Parque Nacional Jeanette Kawas/Punta Sal,** is the most interesting. Literally unchanged for 200 years, the village is composed of thatched huts without electricity or running water. Local boatmen can paddle you out on dugout canoes or take you out on motorized boats into the lagoon. Once you reach the town, you can lounge on the empty white-sand beach there or munch on fresh seafood from the informal restaurants the locals set up for tourists.

You can get to Miami with your own car, but the village is more commonly visited on tours (L550 per person) to the national park with **Garífuna Tours** (✆ **504/448-2904;** www.garifunatours.com). The standard L55 park admission fee applies to entering the village.

Jardín Botánico Lancetilla ★★ Lancetilla, the second-largest tropical botanical garden in the world, was established in 1926 by American botanist William Popenoe, who was hired by United Fruit to research varieties of bananas and figure out how to treat diseases found in the plantations. Popenoe was a curious fellow, and quickly began to import plants and fruit from around the world to Lancetilla, including the African Palm, which has long been one of the most important cash crops in the country. United Fruit continued Popenoe's work for years after he left. The Honduran government, which took control in 1974, continues the research today at the garden. The 1,680-hectare (4,150-acre) park has more than 1,200 species of plants such as palms, fruit trees, and hardwoods, along with poisonous and medicinal varieties that are superbly labeled and organized. From the visitor center, which is about 2km (1¼ miles) from the highway, you walk through a bamboo forest to the arboretum that makes up the most visited section of the park. Here you will find Popenoe's house and a small graveyard where his wife, Dorothy, is buried. Guides lead groups on hour-long tours of the arboretum for L95. Trails delve deeper into the reserve, which includes significant tracts of primary and secondary tropical and subtropical humid forests.

Botany is not the only science of interest. Ornithology is a big deal here, too. Nearly 400 species of birds have been recorded in Lancetilla, as well as numerous butterflies and reptiles. Bird tours leave at dawn in the hopes of spotting trogons, tanagers, orioles, motmots, and toucans, among others. Call Lancetilla a few days ahead of time to arrange a tour, for L300 per group. There's a small cafeteria and a few basic cabins with air-conditioning and private bathrooms near the visitor center (L380 per night), but they're occasionally filled with researchers.

5km (3 miles) north of Tela. ✆ **504/448-1740.** Admission L115. Daily 7:30am–3pm.

Parque Nacional Jeanette Kawas/Punta Sal ★★★ Parque Nacional Punta Sal was renamed after the Honduran activist and president of Prolansate, Jeanette Kawas Fernández, who was killed after establishing the park amid controversy from business groups who claimed the land. Few will argue, though, about the amazing biodiversity in the 782-sq.-km (302-sq.-mile) park. Wildlife found here includes marine turtles, dolphins, manatees, caimans, migratory birds (which are easiest to spot Nov–Feb), ocelots, peccaries, monkeys, and many others.

On the western end of the Bay of Tela, the park is divided into two parts: the lagoon and the peninsula. Acting as a barrier for Tela Bay from the *nortes,* strong winds that blow in the winter months, the peninsula is a triple threat of postcard-perfect beaches, pristine coral reefs, and lush green jungle—dolphins and howler monkeys are regularly seen during the snorkel tours. Micos Lagoon is separated by a small sandbar from the ocean and surrounded by numerous canals that weave through mangrove forests where hundreds of bird and animal species can be seen.

Nearly every tour operator in Tela, including **Garífuna Tours** (✆ **504/448-2904;** www.garifunatours.com), leads almost-daily tours to either the peninsula or the lagoon. You can also hire a boat in Miami, though prices are similar and will not include transportation from Tela.

West End of Tela Bay, Miami. No phone. Admission L55; tours L500–L550 per person depending on group size. Daily 8am–6pm.

Refugio de Vida Silvestre Punta Izopo ★ Twelve kilometers (7½ sq. miles) from Tela on the eastern end of Tela bay, Punta Izopa has a similar ecosystem to

The **Mango C@fe** (① 504/448-0338; www.mangocafe.net) has the only Spanish school in town with 20 hours of one-on-one introductory classes per week for L2,700. Intermediate and advanced classes, as well as discounts at the affiliated **Hotel Mango** (Av. Panama and the Río Tela; ① 504/448-0338), are also available.

7

The North Coast

HONDURAS

Jeanette Kawas, yet is far less visited. Here the Platáno and Hicaque rivers empty into the ocean in a maze of canals and lagoons sheltered by mangroves. The diverse bionetwork harbors caimans, manatees, turtles, monkeys, and a long list of avian life. The reserve is best explored by kayak. **Garífuna Tours** (① 504/448-2904; www. garifunatours.com) and most other Tela tour operators regularly lead trips here using sit-on-top kayaks. The cost is about L475 to L570 per person. You can also recruit boatmen in Triunfo de la Cruz (just west of the park), though you will need to get a group together to make it worthwhile.

BEACHES

A dozen kilometers (7½ miles) or so of white-sand beaches backed by lazy palm trees stretch around Tela Bay. The best beach in the city proper is in front of the Hotel Telamar (below), west of the Río Tela, which is open to the public and has beach chairs and umbrellas for rent (L25). In Tela Vieja, the beachside boardwalk has a few restaurants, bars, and craft vendors, though the beach is often dirty and it's not safe to leave your valuables. On the eastern end of the bay about a 20- to 30-minute walk from the city along the beach, the La Ensenada Beach Villas and Resort is fronted by the clearest water and calmest ocean of anywhere on the bay. Decent beaches can also be found outside the city, though, in the Garífuna villages like Tornabé and Miami.

SHOPPING

There are a few souvenir shops around Tela Vieja. The best is **Casa del Sol,** a chain that is in the Hotel Cesar Mariscos (see below). For jewelry and crafts, try the vendors who line up on the boardwalk and also near the El Delfin restaurant and the beach at the Villas Telamar. A special buy is the coconut bars and *pan de coco,* or coconut bread, that roving Garífuna women sell from baskets carried on their head.

WHERE TO STAY
Expensive

Hotel Telamar ★★★ ☺   The Telamar is easily one of the best, most unique accommodations in the country and exactly the kind of place that is going to set Tela apart from places like Cancun, Mexico, and the Papagayo peninsula in Costa Rica in the years to come. This one-time gated community of houses for the executives of the Tela Railroad Company has been renovated to become a full-scale village-style resort. Guest accommodations are in either the neighborhood of pastel-colored one- to four-bedroom stilted villas or the new main buildings. Rooms in the newer, more modern hotel section face the ocean or the pool, while the remodeled villas face either the ocean or the gardens. Kids will delight in their 90m-long (295-ft.) swimming pool with a slide, along with the bridges, children's play area, and a second, smaller pool.

Even when the lineup of megaresorts opens in this region in 2012, it will be hard to match the history and character here.

1km (⅔ mile) west of town, Tela Nueva. ⓒ **504/269-4414.** Fax 504/448-2984. www.hoteltelamar.com. 210 units. From L2,410 double; from L5,400 villa. AE, MC, V. **Amenities:** 3 restaurants; 3 bars; golf course; pool; tennis court. *In room:* A/C, TV, hair dryer, kitchen (in villa), Wi-Fi.

La Ensenada Beach Villas and Resort ★★ Appearing out of nowhere in 2008, this midsize condo resort has transformed the far eastern end of Tela Bay. Set on a stretch of beach with clear turquoise water, the hotel is practically by itself; amid the palm trees, private pier, and passing boats. There is a massive pool area just off the beach that is the hub of all activity, with several bars and restaurants, sort of like the Villas Telamar, as well as a thatched-roof swim-up or walk-in bar in the middle of the water. The rooms are back from the beach and lack ocean views, although they do front another pool that lacks all the bells and whistles of the other. The rooms are condo style with separate bedrooms with private bathrooms, kitchens, and living areas.

3km (1¾ miles) east of Tela center. ⓒ **504/557-9562.** www.laensenadatela.com. 94 units. L2,280 double. AE, MC, V. Free parking. **Amenities:** Restaurant; bars; pool. *In room:* A/C, TV, hair dryer, kitchen, Wi-Fi.

Moderate

Hotel Cesar Mariscos A small step up from the nearby Hotel Sherwood, this hotel is next door on the Tela beachfront. It's owned by Caribe Expeditions, a tour operator that runs trips to Punta Sal, and was built in 1996 above the well-known restaurant of the same name. Cheery rooms with tile floors and lots of light look out onto their small infinity pool and the beach. Opt for the rooms with private balconies. The property also has one five-person apartment with a small kitchen.

Calle Peatonal and Av. Uruguay. ⓒ **504/448-2083.** www.hotelcesarmariscos.com. 20 units. L1,330 double; L2,090 apt. Rates include continental breakfast. MC, V. **Amenities:** Restaurant; bar; pool. *In room:* A/C, TV.

Inexpensive

Hotel Gran Central ★★ 📷 This completely restored building, just 2 blocks from Parque Central, is one of the best architectural transformations on the North Coast. What was once a dilapidated building now has a tropical urban feel with high ceilings, black-and-white tiled floors, and potted plants everywhere. Rooms have wood shutters, palm trees painted on the walls, high ceilings, and private terraces. If they replaced the worn furniture—especially the couches—with more modern pieces, they could quadruple the rate.

Av. Honduras. ⓒ **504/448-1099.** www.hotelgrancentral.com. 8 units. L950 double; L1,500 apt. AE, DC, MC, V. **Amenities:** Restaurant; bar. *In room:* A/C, fan, TV.

Maya Vista ★ Maya Vista's French-Canadian owners have created a tiny paradise of sorts in the city, just a block from the Río Hiland where it meets with the Caribbean. Quiet and relaxing, with tall leafy trees that are woven through the design of the whole building, the property is suggestive of a treehouse. A rooftop lookout tower and several thatched roof terraces with hammocks allow for expansive views all the way to Punta Izopo. Rooms with one to three beds are decorated with murals of Maya designs and beach themes; I recommend opting for one of the slightly more expensive rooms with balconies. The owners will create meal and accommodations packages on request.

8a Calle NE and 9a Av. NE. ⓒ **504/448-1497.** www.mayavista.com. 9 units. L855–L1,140 double. AE, MC, V. **Amenities:** Restaurant; bar. *In room:* A/C, TV, fridge (in some).

WHERE TO DINE
Moderate

El Delfin ★ INTERNATIONAL   This thatched-roof beach palapa in front of the Telamar supplies the beach chairs and sometimes the music for the cleanest and most prime piece of sand in Tela. During the day it's filled with hungry beachgoers who come for sandwiches, burgers, grilled seafood, and shrimp every which way. Toward sundown, the bar heats up and margaritas, mojitos, and Cuba libres can be spotted at every table. There's occasionally live music.

1km (⅔ mile) west of town, Tela Nueva. ℂ **504/269-4414.** Main courses L115–L270. MC, V. Daily 7am–11pm.

Cesar Mariscos ★ SEAFOOD   All activity on Tela's small beachfront boardwalk, including children selling *pan de coco,* revolves around this restaurant, which is considered the best in town. Tables are set in the indoor dining room, under the boardwalk canopy, or under the umbrellas on the sidewalk. While they have beef on the menu, seafood is the specialty. The shrimp in garlic sauce is one of the best on the North Coast, while the grilled fish, lobster, and seafood stew are tasty too.

Calle Peatonal and Av. Uruguay. ℂ **504/448-2083.** Main courses L95–L305. MC, V. Daily 7am–10pm.

Luces del Norte SEAFOOD   Between the park and the beach, this simple seafood restaurant, with a concrete floor and livened up with plants, is a local favorite. Red snapper is one of their many specialties and it's served up fried, grilled, steamed, or in a number of sauces. The menu is large and branches out beyond Honduran seafood into Chinese rice dishes, pastas, and breakfast. The kitchen is small so the food tends to take a while if there is a crowd. Bring bug spray; the mosquitoes tend to be nasty in this part of town.

1 block north of the park. No phone. Main courses L120–L200. MC, V. Daily 8am–9pm.

Inexpensive

Mamma Mia ★ ITALIAN   This is a favorite expat hangout for the sports and music videos on the TV, cheap meals, and Internet cafe and call center across the little courtyard. Pizza and southern Italian fare and a few Garífuna dishes are quite good, and the prices are among the lowest in town. Occasionally, Garífuna cultural performances are presented.

1 block west of the park. ℂ **504/448-4301.** Main courses L60–L140. MC, V. Daily noon–9pm.

Merendero Tia Carmen HONDURAN   This small, informal eatery is the best spot for typical Honduran dishes, especially their delicious *baleadas,* a tortilla stuffed with beans, cheese, and anything else you have your heart set on. There are also tacos, *liquados,* fresh fruit juices, and coffee.

Calle 8 and Av. 4. No phone. Main courses L38–L95. No credit cards. Daily 7am–8pm.

TELA AFTER DARK

The sidewalk tables at **Arrecifes** (no phone) on the boardwalk just past Cesar Mariscos attract an upscale young crowd who come for cheap mixed drinks and beer. The bar at **El Delfin restaurant** (see above) gets busy on the weekends when there is occasionally live music; the **Hotel Telamar** property also boasts a small bar and disco. A smattering of discos are in town, but all are a bit seedy. The most popular are **Iguanas Sports Bar and Discotec** (10a Calle NE and 2a Av. NE; no phone) and **Kahlua** (10a Calle NE and 2a Av. NE; no phone), next door to each other in the Zona Viva. Covers on Fridays and Saturdays are L100.

La Ceiba ★

La Ceiba, the third-largest city in Honduras and the capital of the department of Atlántida, is named after a huge Ceiba tree on the coast that was once a community meeting place. Recently, the city (97km/60 miles east of Tela) has become known as the country's ecotourism headquarters. The city itself, established a little more than 100 years ago, is sort of thrown together and dirty, its beaches are polluted, and it doesn't hold much of interest. It works best as a base to explore the countless remarkable attractions that are within a short drive, such as Class 4 white-water rapids, hiking trails through several stunning national parks, a wildlife refuge with caimans and manatees, vast empty beaches, sprawling pineapple plantations, and much more. And it's the jumping-off point for the Bay Islands, by both ferry and plane, and the Cayos Cochinos. Whether you like the gritty town or not, you must come through La Ceiba if you want to experience the finest natural wonders in Honduras.

ESSENTIALS
Getting There

La Ceiba's **Golosón International Airport** (**LCE;** ✆ **504/443-3925**) is 12km (7½ miles) west of the city on the road to Tela. The only international airline that lands at the airport is **Skyservice** (seasonal to Toronto; ✆ **800/701-9448**). If you are flying to or from the Bay Islands, you can try domestic airlines such as **Isleña** (✆ **504/441-3354;** www.flyislena.com), **Aerolineas Sosa** (✆ **504/443-1399;** www.aerolineasosahn.com), or **Lanhsa Airlines** (✆ **504/442-1283;** www.lanhsa.com), as all offer daily flights. There are ATMs, a few small shops and snack bars, money-exchange services, an Internet cafe, and car-rental counters in the terminal. A 10- to 15-minute taxi ride from Golosón International to the center of town should cost about L115.

From La Ceiba, there are two high-speed ferries that run twice a day to Roatán and Utila from the Muelle de Cabotaje, 5km (3 miles) east of La Ceiba. For Roatán, the *Galaxy Wave* (✆ **504/443-463;** Safeways_Galaxy@yahoo.com) departs La Ceiba at 9:30am and 4:30pm, returning at 7am and 2pm from the terminal at Dixon's Cove. The one-way price is L500 and the ferry has room for 360 people, air-conditioning, a sun deck, and a small snack shop.

The *Utila Princess II* (✆ **504/425-3390**) makes the hour-long trip back and forth between the Municipal Pier Utila. The ship, which is about one-third the size of the *Galaxy Wave,* departs La Ceiba at 9:30am and 4pm, returning at 6:20am and 2pm. The price is L400 each way.

Yachts from around the Caribbean stop in La Ceiba and occasionally will take on passengers for a fee or in exchange for work. If you are looking for a ride or need a place to anchor, the **Lagoon Marina** (✆ **504/440-0614;** www.lagoonmarinalaceiba.com) is your best bet. There are 25 slips for boats up to 36m (118 ft.) in length, as well as a nice pool area, bar, and apartments for rent by the month (L14,250).

La Ceiba straddles CA 13 on the North Coast about halfway between San Pedro Sula and Trujillo. There aren't as many big car-rental companies in the city as there are in San Pedro or Tegucigalpa, but there are a few. Apart from **Avis** (CA 13 at La Ceiba; ✆ **504/441-2802;** www.avis.com.hn), most rental companies have counters at the airport, including local companies **Advance** (✆ **504/441-1105;** www.advancerentacar.com) and **Ace** (✆ **504/441-2929;** www.acerentacar.com).

Two luxury bus companies, Hedman Alas and Viana Express, have their own terminals in town. **Hedman Alas's terminal** (✆ **504/441-2199;** www.hedmanalas.com)

La Ceiba

ACCOMMODATIONS ■
Hotel Olas del Mar **1**
La Aurora **12**
Quinta Real **4**

DINING ◆
Chef Guity's **3**
Expatriates Bar & Grill **10**
La Palapa **5**
Playa Taty's **6**
Pupuseria Universitaria **2**
Ricardo's **9**

ATTRACTIONS ●
Museo de Mariposas **11**
Parque Nacional
  Pico Bonito **13**
Refugio Nacional de Vida
  Silvestre Cuero y Salado **13**

NIGHTLIFE ★
Hibou **8**
La Palapa **5**
Mango Tango **7**

is on the main highway east of town toward Trujillo, beside the Supermercado Ceibeño #4. Their four daily buses (5:15am–5:30pm) make the 1½-hour trip to Tela (L325) before making the 3½-hour trip to San Pedro Sula (L420), where connections can be made to Copán and Tegucigalpa. **Viana** (✆ **504/441-2330**), whose terminal is just west of the main bus terminal near the Esso gas station, has similar service.

All other bus companies operate out of the **Main terminal** (Mercado San José, Blvd. 15 de Septiembre) about 2km (1¼ miles) west of the center. **Diana** (✆ **504/441-6460**) has nine daily departures for San Pedro Sula between 6am and 5:30pm. For the 7-hour ride to Tegucigalpa, **Cristina** (✆ **504/441-2028;** L475) has five daily departures between 5:30am and 3:30pm. For the 3-hour trip to Trujillo (L100), try **Cotuc** (✆ **504/441-2199**), which runs from 8am to 6pm.

Orientation

The city of La Ceiba is sandwiched between the imposing green mountains of Pico Bonito National Park and the Caribbean Sea. Much of the town straddles the highway, CA 13, although urban sprawl is heading in every direction. A handful of estuaries split the town into several sections, with the center surrounding the wide, shady

Parque Central. Two main avenues, San Isidro and 14 de Julio, run parallel to the beach. The mostly Garífuna neighborhood, Barrio La Isla, to the northeast of the park along the beach, is where you will find the Zona Viva, quite a few hotels, restaurants, and tour operators.

Getting Around

Almost everything of interest within the city sits within a 10-block radius of the Parque Central, so getting around on two legs is easy. But buses are a cheap and useful way to get around to outlying areas. You can easily flag down any of the frequent buses on the main highway, going in the direction you are headed, either toward Tela or Trujillo, for less than L20 for short distances. A **taxi** anywhere in the center should run no more than L40, while trips to the airport or the ferry terminal are three or four times more.

Visitor Information

There's a **visitor center** (📞 **504/440-1562**) on the first floor of the Banco de Occidente building on Parque Central; it's open Monday to Friday from 8am to 4pm. There's another office (📞 **504/440-3044**) at Avenida San Isidro and 8a Calle with more brochures and maps.

FAST FACTS Banco Atlántida (Av. San Isidro and 6a Calle) and **BAC** (Av. San Isidro and 5a Calle) in the center of town have 24-hour ATMs and will exchange traveler's checks. Both have locations at the Megaplaza Mall too.

The hospital **Eurohonduras** (1a Calle and the beach; 📞 **504/443-0244**) is open 24 hours. To reach the police, call 📞 **504/441-0860,** daily 24 hours.

There are four or five **Internet cafes** within 2 blocks of the park with high-speed service for less than L30 per hour. They also provide cheap international calls. **Hondutel** (Av. Rosa and 6a Calle) also offers local and international calls.

The **post office** is at Avenida Morazán and 14a Calle.

FESTIVALS

More than 200,000 visitors from around Honduras and Central America descend upon La Ceiba during **La Feria San Isidro,** or Carnaval week, which takes place every May and culminates on the third Saturday of the month. While the celebration of the city's patron saint, San Isidro, is the motive, the festival has far less of a religious theme than that in Comayagua. Here it's more of a big party where live music, dancing, parades, an endless lineup of food and T-shirt vendors, and intoxication take place each night in a different part of town. The last night is the most intense, with horses, floats, and costumed dancers parading down Avenida San Isidro. It's not as organized as Carnaval in Río or Mardi Gras, but it's a spectacle to behold nonetheless. Reserve hotel rooms months in advance.

WHAT TO SEE & DO

In addition to the attractions below, there are several Garífuna communities within a short drive of the city that make for a quick and inexpensive trip. The most interesting is **Sambo Creek,** 21km (13 miles) east, which is a peaceful retreat from the grime and noise of La Ceiba. Some travelers prefer to base themselves here, as it boasts several nice hotels, such as **Hotel Canadien** (📞 **504/440-2099;** www.hotelcanadien. com; L950 double), as well as a clean beach and several excellent traditional Garífuna seafood restaurants. Boatmen can even arrange trips to the Cayos Cochinos if you get a group together.

Garífuna Tours (☏ 504/440-3252; www.garifunatours.com) or **Omega Tours** (☏ **504/440-0334;** www.omegatours.info) are two good operators who can set you up with trips to Garífuna villages and to the attractions below.

Museo de Mariposas ☺   This private 93-sq.-m (1,000-sq.-ft.) museum exhibits more than 14,000 butterflies, moths, and insects from more than 100 countries, although more than 9,000 are from Honduras. Highlights include blue-tipped damselflies, flying cockroaches, walking sticks, and black tarantula wasps. Specimens are displayed in glass cases that cover the walls, and guided tours point out the largest, smallest, most colorful, heaviest, and most unusual. Other exhibits include butterfly traps, information posters, night collecting setups, and a 25-minute video on insects (available in English or Spanish).

Casa G-12, 3 blocks south of Hotel La Quinta, Colonia El Sauce. ☏ **504/442-2874.** www.honduras butterfly.com. Admission L50. Mon–Sat 8am–5pm.

Parque Nacional Pico Bonito ★★★   Named after a jagged green 2,436m (7,990-ft.) mountain south of La Ceiba, Pico Bonito national park is central to La Ceiba's ecofuture. Along with holding one of the top nature lodges in the world, the more-than-100,000-hectare (24,700-acre) park ranges in altitude from sea level to more than 2,000m (6,600 ft.), which results in seven different ecosystems and an extremely high level of biodiversity. While much of the park is off-limits and remains unexplored, there are large tracts of nearly virgin rainforest, cloud forest, waterfalls, rivers, and crystalline pools to explore. Bird life includes more than 400 bird species, such as toucans, trogons, motmots, and hummingbirds, while mammals spotted here include jaguars, ocelots, tapirs, pumas, deer, and white-faced and spider monkeys, as well as hundreds of species of reptiles, amphibians, and butterflies.

There are several entrances into Pico Bonito and a few different ways to see the park; fortunately, access is getting easier. The most common entry point is through **Pico Bonito Lodge.** It used to be that you had to be a guest to access their trails; however, guided tours (L570 per person) for nonguests have recently been established that include lunch at the lodge. Their private trails have the best infrastructure and contain several bird-watching towers, well-marked stone paths, and a swimming hole on the Coloradito River. You must make reservations in advance with the lodge.

In the town of El Pino, 19km (12 miles) west of La Ceiba, next door to the lodge and just past the Quebrada Seca Bridge, there is another entrance, which most tour operators in La Ceiba use. Here you will find the 2.5km (1.5-mile) **Zacate River Trail,** which passes a few nice swimming holes and ends at the Cascada Zacate. The **El Pino Tourist Committee** (☏ 504/386-9878) arranges guided hikes on the trail for L500 per person including the L120 park admission fee. Alternatively, just hop on any Tela or San Pedro Sula–bound bus and ask to be let off at El Pino.

On the Río Cangrejal side of the park, there is a trail entrance near the town of **Las Mangas.** There is just one main trail that shouldn't take more than 2 to 3 hours each way. It begins with a hanging bridge over the river and extends to the 60m (200-ft.) Cascada El Bejuco, as well as a couple of smaller waterfalls.

The nonprofit community organization **Guaruma** (☏ 504/406-6782; www. guaruma.org) has two different guided hikes in the park, led by trained young locals: the 2-hour (L60 per person) **Guaruma trail** and the 4-hour (L120 per person) **La Muralla trail.** Reservations should be made in advance. **Jungle River Tours** (☏ 504/440-1268; www.jungleriverlodge.com) also runs guided hikes that include a night at Jungle River Lodge (see "Where to Stay," below).

Refugio Nacional de Vida Silvestre Cuero y Salado ★★★ Three rivers, the Cuero, Salado, and San Juan, feed this massive estuary that is one of the most important natural reserves in Honduras. Wildlife is abundant and with a little luck you will see a decent selection of birds and mammals. There are almost 200 species of birds in the reserve, as well as sloths, ocelots, jaguars, otters, howler and white-faced monkeys, iguanas, caimans, and elusive West Indian manatee.

Since the reserve is nearly impossible to find on your own, even if you're a seasoned guidebook writer, the best way to explore the canals and mangrove forests is by boat from the visitor center in Salado Barra. Two-hour motorboat tours leave regularly from this visitor center, although some longer tours, on which you have a much better chance of encountering manatees, are also available. Going with a tour operator such as **Garífuna Tours** (see above) or **Omega Tours** (see above) is a much easier way to see the park and far cheaper in most instances; it usually costs L760 to L950. If you are going on your own, you will have to fork over money for admission plus the entire cost for the boat and guide, rather than splitting it. Considering that wildlife-watching is best done at dawn, you might want to stay the night at the visitor center's dorm lodging (L135) or pitch a tent (L55) on the premises of the park.

30km (19 miles) west of La Ceiba. ✆ **504/443-0329.** Rail journey L190. Admission L189, guide L125, and 2-hr. boat tour L275. Daily 6:30am–6pm.

OUTDOOR ACTIVITIES
Beaches
The beaches in La Ceiba city are polluted and possibly even dangerous to your health and physical well-being. If you must, try the beach in front of Quinta Real (see below), which is the most manicured, although the water is still putrid. A much better beach is Playa de Perú, a couple of kilometers (just over a mile) east of the Muelle de Cabotaje, or at Sambo Creek, 21km (13 miles) east of the center.

Canopy Tours
There are two zip-line canopy tours near La Ceiba, in which participants are strapped to a long metal line and propelled by gravity at high speeds from platform to platform over the jungle. The tours are the closest the average person can get to swinging on a vine like Tarzan through the jungle. **Jungle River Tours** (✆ **504/440-1268;** www.jungleriverlodge.com) offers a tour that runs over the Río Cangrejal in Pico Bonito National Park. The exhilarating 2½- to 3-hour excursion unfolds over a total of eight high wires, the longest being 198m (650 ft.). The trip costs L665 and includes a free night at the Jungle River Lodge, but not transport—that runs an additional L40 to L150. The other canopy tour is in **Sambo Creek,** 21km (13 miles) east of La Ceiba on the road to Trujillo; look for the signs along the highway. The zip lines are about a 30-minute horseback ride through thick rainforest from the tour office. The 13 different cables end at a small waterfall and swimming hole fed by thermal springs. Departures are at 9am and 2pm. This tour is operated by **Turaser** (✆ **504/ 429-0509;** www.hondurasroatantravel.com) out of the Palma Real Resort; it costs L855.

Horseback Riding
While horseback riding is more common in the mountains of the western half of Honduras, tours are increasing in popularity along the North Coast. **Omega Tours** (✆ **504/440-0334;** www.omegatours.info) has several different rides. Day trips include a ride along the beach (6 hr.) near the Río Bonito and another ride (4–8 hr.)

on a dry riverbed in the buffer zone of Pico Bonito National Park, leading to the village of La Colorada, to a Petroglyph rock, and/or the small Maya ruins of Chibcha. All trips (L760–L1,425) include a free night in their lodge. They also offer multiple day trips on the Río Sico and to the Río Blanca Valley.

White-Water Rafting & Kayaking ★★

The Río Cangrejal, cutting its way through Pico Bonito National Park, offers some of the best white-water rafting and kayaking anywhere in Central America. Plus, it is only 45 minutes from La Ceiba. The river is populated by Class 2 to 5 rapids, which pass through lush green forests, beside waterfalls, and over—sometimes into—massive granite boulders. Trips begin with a short hike to the drop-in site and last 2½ to 7 hours, depending on the sections of the river you sign up for.

Nearly every tour operator in La Ceiba does some kind of rafting or kayaking trip on the Río Cangrejal, as well as on the Río San Juan toward Tela. Prices are significantly cheaper than those for a rafting trip in North America or Europe, ranging from L665 to L1,140. **Jungle River Tours** (☎ **504/440-1268;** www.jungleriverlodge. com) and **Omega Tours** (☎ **504/440-0334;** www.omegatours.info) throw in free nights in their lodges (see "Where to Stay," below) with their tour, while **Garífuna Tours** (☎ **504/440-3252;** www.garifunatours.com) offers package deals that combine rafting trips with other activities around La Ceiba. All trips with these operators include lunch, transport to and from La Ceiba, experienced guides, and quality safety equipment.

At Cacao Lagoon east of La Ceiba past the village of Roma, **La Moskitia Ecoaventuras** (☎ **504/550-2124;** www.lamoskitiaecoaventuras.com) offers kayaking trips. The lagoon is a twisting maze of mangroves where sightings of howler monkeys, bats, kingfishers, herons, and other wildlife are frequent. The 5- to 6-hour trip includes a relaxing visit to a sheltered beach.

SHOPPING

The best place for a wide selection of handicrafts, including Garífuna dolls, Lenca pottery, tribal textiles and jewelry, and other assorted items from around the region and country, is the **Rain Forest Souvenir shop** (Av. La Bastilla; ☎ **504/443-2917**). **Souvenir El Buen Amigo** (☎ **504/414-5504**) has a variety of handicrafts and regional items at its two locations, beside Expatriates Restaurant in Barrio El Iman and on Avenida 14 de Julio, downtown. **Piq' Art Gallery** (Av. Morazán beside Farmacia Kielsa; ☎ **504/440-4041;** www.piqartgallery.com) sells paintings from Honduran artists as well as assorted crafts and furniture.

The **Mall Megaplaza,** at Avenida Morazán and 22a Calle (no phone), is home to North American chain stores, fast-food restaurants, a movie theater, an Internet cafe, and a few banks. Visiting this mall makes for a completely un-Honduran experience, but there is air-conditioning. It's open daily from 10am to 9pm.

Even if you don't buy anything, it's worth the effort to just walk through La Ceiba's main rambling **street market** ★ to check out the mouthwatering fruit and vegetables on display. If you look hard enough, you'll find a *baleada* stand or two. For stuff like CDs, DVDs, shoes, sunglasses, beach towels, or crafts, look no further. The market is on 6a Calle and Avenida 14 de Julio, and is open Monday to Saturday from 6am to 5pm, and Sunday from 6am to noon.

WHERE TO STAY
Expensive
Quinta Real ★★ ☺   Quinta Real is a resort in the heart of the city fronting the beach. If you're looking for a true beach resort, this isn't it. The beach here is polluted and filthy, although they at least try to give the impression of cleanliness. It's best to stick by their glitzy, yet kid-friendly, pool area, where you can still look out onto the ocean. Don't get this hotel confused with the Palma Real, which is 22km (14 miles) to the east. Unlike that quiet oasis, this hotel is carved out of the otherwise rough-and-tumble Zona Viva, and surrounded by raucous bars and restaurants. It manages to be an oasis of sorts, however, by keeping clean, modern, and exclusive. Tiled floors, light wood furniture, and your average beach decor fill out the clean, modern rooms. Suites feature an extra sitting room. It's not the Ritz, but it's the classiest thing in La Ceiba proper.

Av. 15 de Sept. and Av. Victor Hugo, Zona Viva. ✆ **504/440-3311.** Fax 504/440-3315. www.quintareal hotel.com. 81 units. L1,560 double; L3,420 suite. AE, MC, V. **Amenities:** Restaurant; bar; laundry service; pool. *In room:* TV, hair dryer, Wi-Fi.

Moderate
La Aurora   The big square glass La Aurora is right on the highway not far from hordes of fast-food chains and gas stations, which makes it especially convenient if you intend on exploring destinations outside the city. Little differentiates the hotel from a standard Holiday Inn just off a highway exit in the United States. It even smells the same, down to the chlorine from the pool that wafts through the halls. Rooms are bland, but the beds are comfortable, the floors are clean, and there's even a small couch in most.

Carretera La Ceiba-Tela. ✆ **504/440-2060.** 45 units. L880 double. MC, V. **Amenities:** Jacuzzi; pool. *In room:* A/C, TV, minibar, Wi-Fi.

Inexpensive
Hotel Olas del Mar ★ 🛍   This beachfront hotel in the center, just across the bridge to the Zona Viva, is one of the most overlooked in the city and is left out of most guidebooks. It's hard to see why. The rooms are basic but clean, the outside hallways have a few nice lounge areas, and the view is the same as from the Quinta Real. The beds are a bit stiff and the rooms are bare-bones plain, but compared to similarly priced hotels in the area, it's a steal. Did I mention they have a nice big sun deck facing the beach that's a nice place to kick off your sandals and relax?

Av. 14 de Julio and 1 Calle, Zona Viva. ✆ **504/440-1857.** Fax 504/443-3681. www.hotelolasdelmar.com. 19 units. L600 double. MC, V. **Amenities:** Restaurant; karaoke bar. *In room:* A/C, TV.

HOTELS OUTSIDE LA CEIBA
Very Expensive
Las Cascadas ★★   Las Cascadas is far more chic and luxurious than the lodge at Pico Bonito, yet it doesn't feel pretentious at all. Located beside a waterfall and

several small creeks that run into the Río Cangrejal, it couldn't have a more dramatic setting. The two suites and two cabins are constructed of polished river stone, wood, and thatched roofs and all include screened-in porches overlooking the waterfall, stone showers, and a queen-size mahogany canopy bed and one or two single beds. The suites are attached to the lodge, while the cabins are separate. The Bejuco cabin adds a Bali-style outdoor shower, while the River House adds a kitchen. All rooms are all-inclusive, which includes beer and wine. *Note:* This lodge does not allow young children as guests.

Km 8.8 Carretera La Ceiba-Yaruca. © **877/271-6407** in the U.S., or 504/9805-2200. www.lascascadas lodge.com. 4 units. L3,135 per person based on double occupancy. Rates include meals, drinks, and airport transfers. AE, MC, V. **Amenities:** Restaurant; bar; high-speed Internet in lobby; Jacuzzi; satellite phone; pool. *In room:* A/C, fan, hair dryer.

The Lodge at Pico Bonito ★★★ 🖻   When you arrive at Pico Bonito, you'll be greeted by a tuxedoed staff member who'll hand you a tropical drink with a little umbrella. It only gets better from there. The Lodge at Pico Bonito is the only luxury ecolodge in Honduras, and the luxury shows: The 21 posh cabins are adorned with rattan furniture and wood floors, small porches dissected by lazy hammocks, and chic, modern bathrooms decorated with Mexican tiles. The cabins are connected to the main lodge via a raised wooden walkway that runs through cacao and coffee trees. Pico Bonito purposely lacks cable TV and Wi-Fi, but does have quieter amenities rarely found in ecolodges, such as warm showers, in-room massage services, and gourmet dining in its insanely overpriced yet still amazing Mesoamerican-themed **restaurant.**

The lodge is set at the foot of 2,400m (7,900-ft.) Pico Bonito, and boasts a 98,800-hectare (189,000-acre) area of pristine cloud and rainforest, which is home to crocodiles, spider monkeys, tapirs, and jaguars. Two hundred acres of the property are the buffer area of Pico Bonito National Park. A private butterfly sanctuary and serpentarium are on the grounds, and the lodge runs a number of guided hiking and other adventure tours.

La Ceiba, Atlántida, CP 31101. © **888/428-0221** or 504/440-0388. www.picobonito.com. 21 units. L3,420 standard cabin; L4,845 superior cabin. AE, MC, V. **Amenities:** Restaurant; bar; high-speed Internet in lobby; pool. *In room:* A/C, fan.

Expensive

Palma Real Beach Resort ★   The Palma Real, the only true beach resort on La Ceiba's Caribbean coast, is 22km (14 miles) east of the city on the road to Trujillo just past Sambo Creek. This sprawling residential and entertainment complex is on a beautiful stretch of sand, seemingly in the middle of nowhere, and has a massive pool that stretches across almost the entire property. The facilities, which are also used by the residents of the 150 villas in the complex, include a small water park (the **Water Jungle,** with a wave pool, a lazy river, and a few slides), **Hola Ola Theater** (with nightly shows and live music), the **Caña Brava Restaurant** (with buffet meals), several a la carte restaurants, and the **Guiffitti Disco.** The rooms are exactly what you would expect: clean tile floors, clunky wood furniture, and unadventurous bedspreads and decor. Packaged deals attract plenty of Canadians, Hondurans, and Salvadorans.

Km 20 Carretera La Ceiba-Trujillo. © **504/429-0501.** Fax 504/429-0505. www.grupopalmareal.com. 160 units. L2,280 double. AE, MC, V. **Amenities:** Restaurant; bar; disco/theater; pool; tennis courts. *In room:* A/C, TV, hair dryer, Wi-Fi.

Moderate

Casa Cangrejal ★   This small, Canadian-owned B&B is beautifully constructed of river stones and wood, giving it the feel of a medieval castle. Numerous artful touches grace the building, such as bright orange or green walls and blue bedspreads, a crab design in a common-room floor, a man-made pond, and a few stone patios with funky wooden chairs that are great for bird-watching. The amenities are basic and you won't find a TV here, though they do have Wi-Fi, but if you're looking for a real retreat that takes you away from the norm in both setting and architecture, Casa Cangrejal is a gem.

Río Cangrejal road. ✆ **504/408-2760.** www.casacangrejal.com. 4 units. L1,710 double. Rates include breakfast. No credit cards. *In room:* Wi-Fi.

Inexpensive

Jungle River Lodge   This small lodge beside the Río Cangrejal in Pico Bonito National Park is owned by Jungle River Tours and is most often used in conjunction with one of their tours, usually for free. The lodge itself is constructed of all natural materials and completely submerged in the jungle. Rooms, which are a mix of dorms and some doubles with and without bathrooms, are smallish and basic, but for the price and the convenience, they can't be beat.

Km 8.8 Carretera La Ceiba-Yaruca. ✆ **504/440-1268.** Fax 504/440-1268. www.jungleriverlodge.com. 7 units. L190 dorm; L330 double without bathroom; L455 double with bathroom. AE, MC, V. **Amenities:** Restaurant; bar. *In room:* Fan.

WHERE TO DINE
Moderate

Expatriates Bar & Grill ★ CONTINENTAL   Expatriates is a big-time hangout for the English-speaking crowd in La Ceiba. The charcoal grill pumps out goodies similar to those at any respectable North American grill, like steaks, fish, shrimp, and chicken breasts. Spicy chicken wings, nachos, and even vegetarian dishes are a welcome retreat for homesick snowbirds. The *chuletas* (pork chops) are served with beans and rice and are mouthwatering. Flatscreen TVs offer the best access in La Ceiba to any North American sporting event. A decent selection of Honduran cigars, a full bar, plenty of tropical cocktails, and free Wi-Fi are added bonuses. A *champa*-style thatched roof is the ceiling of the second-level **restaurant,** and they have an uncovered section great for stargazing.

Calle 12, Colonia El Naranjal. ✆ **504/440-1131.** Main courses L95–L265. MC, V. Mon–Fri 3:30–11:30pm; Sat–Sun 11am–late.

La Palapa INTERNATIONAL   This rambunctious palapa behind the Quinta Real (p. 393) is one of the most happening spots in town for food and drinks. It's better known for drinking than eating, though they have a fairly large menu and the place isn't nearly as grimy as some other restaurants in town. The food is modeled after a Mexican grill, and is heavy on lots of finger foods as well as platters of chorizo and grilled meat, steaks, tacos, nachos, fish, and pasta. Service tends to be slow. There are DJs or live music on the weekends.

Calle 1, by Hotel Quinta Real, Zona Viva. ✆ **504/443-3844.** Main courses L95–L300. MC, V. Daily 11am–late.

Playa Taty's ★★ INTERNATIONAL   This rustic beachfront *champa* in the Zona Viva dishes up some of the highest-quality, most eclectic menu items around. There's a variety of steaks and seafood combo platters served with salad and garlic mashed potatoes, plus sandwiches, jambalaya, shrimp étouffée, and coconut shrimp. The grilled grouper with lime cream is delicious on its own but enters heavenly territory when paired with a piña colada or glass of sangria.

On the beachfront, 1 block east of Hotel Quinta Real, Zona Viva. © **504/440-1314.** Main courses L165–L300. MC, V. Wed–Sat 11am–11pm; Sun 11am–8pm.

Ricardo's ★★ INTERNATIONAL   Well known throughout the North Coast, Ricardo's has been attracting fruit company execs, wealthy Hondurans, politicians, and everyone else who would like a touch of class for years. As the framed awards on the walls will let you know, this spot has even been named the best restaurant in Central America on several occasions. Start your meal with the best salad bar in La Ceiba. For an entree, you can choose among great pasta and soup dishes, along with beef filet and grilled or steamed fish in a number of hearty, citrusy, or spicy sauces. For dessert, sink your taste buds into a *pastel de tres leches,* or three-milk cake. Dining is either in the air-conditioned dining room or on the outdoor patio, both of which have an equally formal atmosphere.

Av. 14 de Julio and Calle 10a, Zona Mazpan. © **504/443-0468.** Main courses L133–L342. AE, MC, V. Mon–Sat 11am–1:30pm and 5:30–10pm.

Inexpensive

Chef Guity's ★ HONDURAN   Hidden away on a shady piece of beach in the Zona Viva, sandwiched between the bridge and the Quinta Real, this *champa,* a traditional elevated thatched beach hut, is renowned for its Garífuna seafood specialties. Views and breezes from the ocean add to the pleasure of dining at this rustic two-level restaurant, though it is the food that sets it apart. The seviche (raw seafood marinated in lime juice), makes for a good choice of appetizer. Grilled kingfish, seafood stews, *caracols* (snails), steaks, and chicken round out the entree options, all of which attract a loyal following of mostly locals.

On the beachfront, west of the Quinta Real, Zona Viva. No phone. Main courses L75–L190. No credit cards. Mon–Sat 11am–10pm.

Pupuseria Universitaria SALVADORAN   *Pupusas* are the Salvadoran equivalent of the Honduras *baleada.* Both are simple snack foods that use more or less the same ingredients. The bigger-than-normal *pupusas* here are filled with either *chicharrón* (fried pork) and cheese or just plain cheese, wrapped in a doughy corn tortilla, and served with hot sauce. Other classic Salvadoran items are on the menu as well. On weekends the tables fill up with a preclub crowd that comes here to snack and drink.

1a Calle and Av. 14 de Julio, Zona Viva. © **504/440-1070.** Main courses L50–L150. No credit cards. Daily 11am–9pm.

LA CEIBA AFTER DARK

La Ceiba is known for its nightlife, though hot spots rise and fall. Most clubs are open from Wednesday or Thursday to Saturday, from the afternoon until the early morning, and covers are generally L40 to L100. The most upscale place in town, and your best chance at encountering another visitor, is **Hibou** ★★ (© **504/440-1700**), a multipart club on the beach at Avenida Bonilla. The indoor part is a full-on disco with a raised dance floor, several bars, and DJs blasting the latest Top 40 reggaeton and rock tracks, while the outdoor section is a more atmospheric, thatched-roof beach bar with occasional live music. **La Palapa** (© **504/443-3844**), behind the Quinta Real, is popular with visitors and upscale Hondurans who want to eat and drink with a group of friends but don't want to stand in a crowded disco. There's occasionally live music.

Volunteer Opportunities in Northern Honduras

The North Coast of Honduras, centering around La Ceiba, is one of the most active volunteering centers in Central America. Dozens of organizations have offices in the city and help arrange projects for anyone willing to lend a helping hand. Two standouts are **Guaruma** (© 504/406-6782; www.guaruma.org), a Honduras-based nonprofit that helps promote environmental awareness and conservation in the Río Cangrejal watershed on the eastern edge of Pico Bonito National Park, and **Children of the Light** (© 504/3304-1414; www.thechildren ofthelight.org), a Christian organization that has built a school and has organized other community outreach projects for street children in the region.

There is a cluster of discos and grungy multilevel bars in the Zona Viva on Calle 1a, like **Mango Tango** (no phone), that can be good for a drink or two, though the crowd varies depending on the night. Others can be quite dangerous; I recommend sticking with the more upscale clubs.

Cayos Cochinos ★★★

When skies are clear, you can see the Cayos Cochinos, or Hog Islands, off the North Coast of Honduras—that's how close to the mainland they are. Thirty kilometers (19 miles) northeast of La Ceiba, these two small islands, 13 coral cayes, and a few tiny sandbars—almost all privately owned—are as close to paradise as one could imagine. The two main islands, Cayo Menor and Cayo Mayor/Grande, are home to just one luxury ecoresort, a few private homes, a research station, and one small Garífuna community. That's it. If isolation is what you want, then look no further.

The coral reefs surrounding the islands are some of the most undisturbed on the Mesoamerican Barrier Reef System and were designated as a Marine Protected Area in 1993 and a Marine Natural Monument in 2003. No commercial fishing is allowed in the 489-sq.-km (189-sq.-mile) reserve, and rules are strictly enforced, which has allowed the reefs and the fish that live on it to flourish. Wildlife on the land—which is also protected—includes pink boa constrictors, iguanas, sea turtles, and tropical birds, among other amphibians and reptiles. Legend has it that the Hog Islands were so named because pirates left hogs there for a convenient food supply during their travels.

ESSENTIALS
Getting There & Getting Around

The Cayos Cochinos can be reached by boat, usually via a day trip from La Ceiba. The trip takes approximately 1 to 1½ hours, depending on the tide. The easiest way to get there is either by staying at the one hotel, the Plantation Beach Resort, that provides transportation, or by visiting on a tour with **Garífuna Tours** (© 504/440-3252; www.garifunatours.com) in La Ceiba, which runs daily snorkel tours to the cayes, including a stop for lunch at Chachauate. Tours run L650 per person.

It is also possible to reach the cayes from the towns of Sambo Creek and Nueva Armenia by hiring a local boatman or fisherman, but you must get a small group together to make it affordable. One such boatman who runs trips is **Omar Acosta** (© 504/408-1666; L665 per person). Dive boats frequently come on day trips from Roatán, while yachts from around the Caribbean moor here as well.

There is a L190 fee (L95 when you come with a tour operator) upon entering the Cayos Cochinos, to be paid at the Fundación Cayos Cochinos research station on Cayo Menor.

WHAT TO SEE & DO

Tiny **Chachauate Cay** ★ is home to the only permanent settlement in the Cayos Cochinos. The Garífuna village has no running water or electricity, and the only bathrooms are in communal outhouses. The thatched houses are home to just a few dozen families that eke out a living from fishing and tourism. There are a couple of small eateries serving fried fish and plantains, plus a few craft stands that are set up informally when a tour boat arrives. Locals rent out their homes to visitors for around L100 per night.

The mountainous **Cayo Grande** is home to several good **hiking trails** through the lush jungle, beginning right at Plantation Beach resort and running to the highest points of the island—from where on a clear day you can see miles in every direction. At the highest point, 140m (459 ft.), there is a small lighthouse.

The turquoise waters and unspoiled coral reef around the Cayos Cochinos are an ideal spot for underwater exploring, so much so that many prefer diving and snorkeling here to the Bay Islands. There are more than 60 dive sites scattered around the reserve, and many others that have yet to be named. Within the walls, drifts, small wrecks, and sea mounds, you'll find sponges, grunts, sea fans, sea whips, grouper, lobsters, sea urchins, and parrotfish. Less common are manta rays, bottlenose dolphins, whale sharks, and hawksbill turtles. Most dive resorts in the Bay Islands will lead day trips here, but the only dive operation based in the Cayos Cochinos is at the Plantation Beach Resort (see below).

WHERE TO STAY

Plantation Beach Resort ★★   Located on Cochino Menor, this upscale resort is as removed from the modern world as a beach resort can get and still manage to be comfortable. Electricity is the biggest amenity, and that's a good thing—there's nothing to distract you from soaking in the beautiful surroundings. The lodge—set on 4 hectares (10 acres) of virgin forest—was built of stone and mahogany native to the tiny island. Rooms vary in size, but the quality is roughly the same throughout, with tile or wood floors punctuating a rustic yet cozy setup. Plantation has one of the better dive operations in the country and offers PADI certification courses. Transportation to the resort is not included with a stay, but the hotel will arrange pickup from San Pedro Sula or La Ceiba. Their small restaurant is *the* hangout in town for visiting yachties who moor near the hotel.

Cochino Menor. ✆ **866/751-0147.** www.plantationbeachresort.com. 12 units. L1,900 double; L14,250 all-inclusive weekly fee, including diving; L12,350 all-inclusive weekly fee without diving. V. **Amenities:** Restaurant; bar; watersports equipment. *In room:* Fan.

Trujillo

The coastal city of Trujillo, long a beach retreat for the people of San Pedro Sula and Tegucigalpa, has yet to fully recover from the 1998 devastation of Hurricane Mitch. It's not that the place is a mess, but rather that visitors haven't been flocking here. The beaches are in good shape and the airport has been repaired, but there aren't any flights. Trujillo seems to have completely missed the rampant progress going on in places like La Ceiba, 165km (103 miles) west.

Trujillo has borne witness to many of the most significant events in Central American history. On August 14, 1502, Christopher Columbus set foot on the American mainland here for the first time on his fourth and final voyage. The first Catholic Mass on the continent soon followed. In 1860 the North American William Walker, after having previously taken over Nicaragua with a small army and a failed attempt to invade Costa Rica, conquered the fort of Trujillo. After 5 days of fighting with British and Honduran forces, however, Walker surrendered and was executed by Honduran authorities. In the early 1800s, Trujillo was one of the first places on the mainland where Garífuna settlers—after they were dumped on Roatán by the British—began to build communities. The Garífuna influence is still strong along the coast of Trujillo Bay to this day.

ESSENTIALS
Getting There
CA 13, which begins at El Progreso outside of San Pedro Sula, runs parallel to the coast all the way to Trujillo, first stopping in Tela and La Ceiba. Two more scenic roads run through the interior of the country through Olancho, highways 39 and 23, but neither is well paved and both are often impassable during heavy rain. The **bus** terminal for Cotuc (📞 **504/444-2181**) buses is in Barrio Cristales, although they also stop at the Texaco gas station toward the entrance to town, about 1km (⅔ mile) from the center. Cotuc buses travel daily to La Ceiba (3 hr. away; L100), Tela (4½ hr. away; L150), and San Pedro Sula (6 hr. away; L200). Cotraipbal also runs buses to these destinations, which depart from the terminal next to the Texaco station, almost every other hour.

ORIENTATION
The colonial center of Trujillo is built on a hill beside the town's fort, high up from the bay, and surrounded by green mountains. A few roads lead down to the beach below the center, where there is a string of seafood shacks and the Garífuna neighborhood of Cristales. A dirt road runs west along the coastline to the Garífuna communities of Santa Fe and Guadalupe. The unused airport, 1km (⅔ mile) away from Trujillo's center, is on the eastbound road outside of town. Puerto Castilla Trujillo's deepwater port, is 8km (5 miles) east across the bay.

Getting Around
Trujillo's center is easily navigable by foot, even when you factor in having to walk up and down the hill to the beach below. The bus terminal and many of the town's hotels will need to be reached by taxi, however. Local buses run sporadically to Santa Fe to the west, leaving from the old cemetery. More frequent buses head east to Puerto Castilla from the Texaco terminal.

Visitor Information & Fast Facts
For tourist information, see the **Trujillo Honduras Pages** (www.trujillohonduras. com). **Banco Atlántida** on the Parque Central has a 24-hour ATM and will exchange traveler's checks. Internet access can be found at a number of small shops near the park or at **Casa Kiwi** (see "Where to Stay," below). You can make long-distance phone calls at **Hondutel,** 1 block south of the park.

WHAT TO SEE & DO
Cementerio Viejo ★ Now that the weeds have been pulled and the site is renovated, the gates of this old cemetery in the center of town have been unlocked and opened to the public. Many of the graves are more than 300 years old. The most

significant is the grave of William Walker, the American adventurer who launched several invasions of Central American nations and was shot by a firing squad in Trujillo in 1860. His grim end is noted on his epitaph with the word "fusilado."

6 blocks southeast of Parque Central. No phone. Free admission. Daily dawn–dusk.

Fortaleza de Santa Barbara ★★   Imposing its iron fist from its elevated point in the center of town is the Fortaleza de Santa Barbara, a Spanish colonial fortress that was erected to help defend Trujillo Bay from pirate attacks. The 17th-century fort was reportedly much bigger centuries ago and extended down to the beachfront. Today you will find a vast outline of stone walls with moss growing through the cracks and a couple of small buildings. A row of iron cannons point out toward the water below and, if you've drunk plenty of *guifitty* (a Garífuna moonshine), incoming buccaneers. There is a small museum within the fortress with a collection of colonial items, muskets, pirate relics, naval memorabilia, and Garífuna masks.

Northeast corner of Parque Central. No phone. Admission L95. Daily 8am–noon and 1–4pm.

Museo Rufino Galan   This idiosyncratic little museum is closer to a junk heap than an official museum. The barely standing wood building, a few blocks from the square, is filled with piles of pre-Columbian artifacts, alleged pirate relics, books, chests, farm equipment, old tools, and anything else that is good at collecting dust. There's even a pet spider monkey tied up outside. You may have to ask around for the owner, as the museum doesn't follow any set hours.

Calle 18 de Mayo and Río Cristales. No phone. Admission L50. Hours vary.

Parque Nacional Capiro y Calentura   The 1,235m (4,050-ft.) mountain that stands behind Trujillo is the setting for this 4,500-hectare (11,120-acre) national park. There is little infrastructure to the park and hikers rarely come this way. Those that do are rewarded with vibrant bird life, including macaws, the occasional howler monkey, and several distinct zones of tropical forest. The entrance to the park is via a dirt path south of town, and the park office is staffed on rare occasions. It takes about 3 hours to reach the top of the peak, where there is a small radar station. For the best bird-watching, set out before dawn.

3km (1¾ miles) south of Parque Central. Admission L60. Daily 8am–4pm.

Refugio de Vida Silvestre Guaimoreto   Similar to Cuero y Salado and the Laguna de los Micos on the North Coast, Guaioreto, 5km (3 miles) east of Trujillo, is a large lagoon surrounded by mangrove forest, intersected with canals, and home to abundant wildlife. Migratory birds flock here from November to February. Due to the lack of tourists in Trujillo, there aren't any tour operators that arrange trips here anymore; therefore, you must go to the lagoon and negotiate with a local fisherman for a canoe or boat ride (roughly L300 per 2 hr.). **Casa Kiwi** (*©* **504/434-3050;** www.casakiwi.com) sometimes will arrange trips here as well.

5km (3 miles) east of Trujillo. *©* **504/434-4294.** Free admission.

OUTDOOR ACTIVITIES

The main reason most visitors trek all the way out to Trujillo is for its **beaches.** Wide golden sands, gentle breezes, very few waves, and even fewer beachgoers make them seem like deserted islands. The best places to enjoy the sun are in front of the *chambas* below the fort, where you can borrow a beach chair, or near the airport and the Hotel Christopher Columbus (see "Where to Stay," below). Emptier beaches can be found hidden below the road in the small coves that stretch for 19km (12 miles) to the west of town.

To the west of Trujillo, down a potholed dirt road, is a string of Garífuna fishing villages. All are home to a few thatched seafood shacks, a basic *hospedaje* or two, *punta* music flowing through the air, and serene beaches with rarely a soul in sight. **Santa Fe,** 12km (7½ miles) from Trujillo, is my favorite stop because of its legendary **Comedor Caballero** ★★ (no phone), aka Pete's Place, a traditional Garífuna restaurant on the beach with some of the best seafood on the North Coast. A bit farther and even more difficult to reach are the villages and beaches of **San Antonio** and **Guadeloupe.** Buses leave from the Cementerio Viejo in the center of town to these villages several times per day.

SHOPPING

Small artisan shops can be found around Parque Central and toward the beach. The best is **Artesma Garífuna** (☎ 504/434-3583) in Barrio Cristales, which sells beach gear, coconut carvings, drums, and an array of little knickknacks. The gift shop **Made in Honduras** (☎ 504/839-2768; www.hondurastreasures.com) is across the road from the airport in a purple-and-turquoise wooden house. The 100%-fair-trade handicrafts range from tree-bark paintings, coffee, jewelry, and nativity scenes from La Mosquitia, Olancho, and the North Coast. Displays in the store describe how most items were made, by which family, and from where.

WHERE TO STAY
Moderate

Casa Alemania ★★ 🏄 Friendly owners German Gunter and his Honduran wife, Paula, both trained massage therapists, run this beachfront Trujillo inn between town and the airport, which has somehow managed to stay under the radar though it has been open since 2004. Gunter will get you anything you need to make your stay worthwhile, including German food and beer. Polished hardwood floors and trim are matched with soft white linens and big windows that face the beach (take any of the three rooms on the second level for the best views). The larger rooms add a small kitchenette with sink and minifridge. If you are on a budget, they will do their best to accommodate you with dorm-style beds or a camping space that has shower access and electricity.

Beachfront btw. the center and airport. ☎ **504/434-4466.** 10 units. L580 doubles; L750 larger rooms. MC, V. Free parking. **Amenities:** Restaurant; bar; massage/spa services. *In room:* A/C, fan, TV, DVD player, minifridge.

Hotel Christopher Columbus ☺ The Hotel Christopher Columbus has seen better days. It was once billed as one of the top hotels on the North Coast, but then Hurricane Mitch scared off all the customers. Now it is starving for guests. They keep the lime-green paint fresh, but the place is nearly always empty and it's beginning to show its age. Rooms are outdated, almost to the point of being cool again—they call to mind a 1950s-style roadside motel, with retro furniture and spots of Astro Turf on the terrace. Still, the full-scale resort, on one of the best stretches of beach in town, is a decent stay, and the friendly and upbeat staff helps you overlook any failings. The pool area isn't bad, and they have a small dock, kayaks, and snorkel equipment for guests to use.

1km (⅔ mile) east of Parque Central, beside the airport. ☎ **504/434-4966.** Fax 504/434-4971. 52 units. L1,200 double. AE, MC, V. **Amenities:** Restaurant; bar; tennis courts; watersports equipment. *In room:* A/C, TV.

Tranquility Bay ★ 🏷 New Canadian owners are breathing new life into Tranquility Bay's five 150-sq.-m (1,615-sq.-ft.) seaside cabins tucked away down a forested hill near the beach, a few miles west of town. Each cabin has a terra-cotta roof, a porch with a couple of chairs, walls decked out in cheery yellow paint, and a few splashes of Honduran decor. Cabins are clean and a decent overall value. There's a big, inviting pool close to the beach, and they have a small creek that runs through the property. If you don't have your own transport, access to town can be an issue.

3km (1¾ miles) west of town. ℃ **504/928-2095.** www.tranquilitybayhonduras.com. 5 units. L1,045 double. No credit cards. **Amenities:** Restaurant; bar. *In room:* Fan.

Inexpensive

Casa Kiwi ★★ 🎁 Six kilometers (3¾ miles) east of Trujillo on the road to Puerto Castilla, a New Zealand woman has set up Casa Kiwi, Trujillo's best backpacker hangout. The quickly expanding compound is on a quiet stretch of beach with little other civilization around. The rooms, all available at bargain prices, are in your choice of dorms, private rooms, or cabins. While the dorms are clean and the cabins are more private, the middle rooms are the best overall value. Apart from Casa Kiwi's standalone **bar** and **restaurant,** there are lots of little extras like a pool table and bike and snorkeling rentals. This place also hosts the occasional weekend bonfire party and arranges tours.

6km (3¾ miles) from Trujillo on the road to Puerto Castilla. ℃ **504/434-3050.** www.casakiwi.com. L700 *cabaña;* L180 double; L100 dorm. No credit cards. **Amenities:** Restaurant; bar; Internet cafe. *In room:* A/C (in *cabañas*), fan.

WHERE TO DINE

Coco's Bar & Grill HONDURAN/INTERNATIONAL On the beach beside Hotel Christopher Columbus, this *champa* has been recently renovated with thin white curtains hanging from the thatched roof and white leather lounge chairs to give a South Beach element to a city not normally known for its panache. The food varies from tasty Honduran seafood to so-so international comfort food: four types of ceviche, shrimp scampi, fried fish, nachos, and hamburgers.

Beachfront beside Hotel Christopher Columbus. L100–L160. MC, V. Daily noon–9pm; open later on weekends.

Merendero del Centro HONDURAN This bustling *tipico* restaurant is good for quick and simple but filling Honduran breakfasts of beans, corn tortillas, eggs, and ham. They're best known for their *baleadas* and dirt-cheap lunch specials. Plastic tables and kids running around add some authenticity, if nothing else.

3a Calle. No phone. Main courses L55–L110. No credit cards. Daily 6am–8pm.

Playa Dorado ★★ ☺ HONDURAN Of the several *champas* on the beach below the fort (any of which are the most atmospheric places to eat in town), Playa Dorado is the best. The owners will let you pick your fish, priced by size, and choose how you want it prepared. Their *camarones al ajillo,* shrimp sautéed with garlic and lime and served with a big plate of french fries, has my mouth watering as I type. There are a few beef items on the menu, but considering that you are on the beach, I'd stick with seafood.

On the beachfront below the fort. No phone. Main courses L75–L225. No credit cards. Daily 11am–9pm.

TRUJILLO AFTER DARK

Rogue's Gallery, sometimes called Jerry's, in the concrete, tin-roofed building near the beach *champas,* is good for a sunset cocktail or beer. **Truxillo Disco,** at the edge of a bluff facing the sea, is the most popular disco in town. Don't show up before 10pm or you'll be alone. There's no cover.

THE BAY ISLANDS ★★★

Las Islas de la Bahía, or the Bay Islands, are best known for their clear Caribbean waters and their pristine coral reef—the second largest in the world. The three main islands of Roatán, Utila, and Guanaja, along with Barbareta and 60 or so other tiny cayes, have long been one of the major dive destinations in the world. Although they are no longer the cheapest places to get dive certification, prices remain considerably cheaper than anywhere else in the Caribbean, and package deals for divers are vast. All-inclusive tours that include lodging, food, dives, airfare, and lots of extras can be had by any visitor seeking a deal.

The cultural makeup of the islands has been a tumultuous one. The first pre-Columbian settlers were likely related to the Pech Indians on the mainland, and a few small archaeological sites are still scattered among the surrounding hills. Christopher Columbus is believed to be the first European to find the islands, when he anchored in Guanaja in July 1502. In the following decades, Spanish ships came to take native slaves and set up *encomiendas*, where, in exchange for Christianization, the indigenous people were forced to pay tribute and labor to the Spanish Crown. As the Spanish began to loot the New World of its gold and transport the riches across the Caribbean back to Spain, the islands became a hide-out for French and English raiding boats. Pirates such as Henry Morgan and John Coxen began to frequent the islands for the next 2 centuries, although they left little trace. War broke out between England and Spain in 1739, and the British took control of the islands and set up forts at Port Royal in Roatán. The islands were returned to Spain in the treaty of Aix-la-Chapelle in 1748, taken back by the British during another war in 1779, and then left uninhabited after Spanish attacks in 1782. In 1797, a few thousand Garífuna, descendants of Carib Indians and African slaves from the Cayman Islands, were dumped at Punta Gorda in Roatán by the British, and many settled there while others headed for the mainland. In the 1830s, a new wave of white and black settlers came from the Caymans and set up the main towns that remain population centers today. The British government claimed control over the islands during this time, and although Honduran sovereignty of the islands was recognized in 1859, many of the islanders continued to see themselves as a part of the British Empire.

Today, the Bay Islands are at a major turning point in their history. Fishing, which has been the lifeblood of the islanders for several centuries, is quickly being replaced by tourism as the most important trade. Luxury home developments targeting North Americans are creeping onto every island, and slews of Latino workers from the mainland are attracted by the high standards of living and available work, while the native Afro-Caribbean population is getting pushed to the fringes of the islands. Entire chunks of land, such as the West End of Roatán, are being snapped up by developers, and hotels and resorts are replacing the islands' once-traditional stilted wood houses. The influx of cruise ships on Roatán has already added adventure parks and tour buses, and there's talk of more ports and bigger ships, but for the time being, the Bay Islands are still serene Caribbean hide-outs, where English is the mother tongue and the American dollar is the main currency.

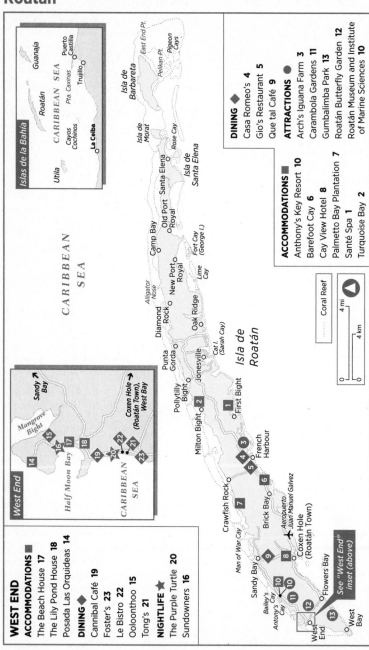

Islas de la Bahía

Guanaja
Puerto Castilla
Pta. Caxinas
Trujillo

CARIBBEAN SEA

Utila
Cayos Cochinos
La Ceiba

Roatán

DINING ◆
Casa Romeo's **4**
Gio's Restaurant **5**
Que tal Café **9**

ATTRACTIONS ●
Arch's Iguana Farm **3**
Carambola Gardens **11**
Gumbalimba Park **13**
Roatán Butterfly Garden **12**
Roatán Museum and Institute of Marine Sciences **10**

ACCOMMODATIONS ■
Anthony's Key Resort **10**
Barefoot Cay **6**
Cay View Hotel **8**
Palmetto Bay Plantation **7**
Santé Spa **1**
Turquoise Bay **2**

East End Pt.
Pigeon Cays
Pelikan Pt.

Isla de Barbareta

Isla de Morat
Rose Cay
Santa Elena
Old Port Royal
Isla de Santa Elena

CARIBBEAN SEA

Camp Bay

Alligator Nose
Fort Cay (George I.)
New Port Royal
Lime Cay

Diamond Rock
Oak Ridge

Punta Gorda
Jonesville
Cat I. (Sarah Cay)
Isla de Roatán

Pollytilly Bight
Milton Bight
First Bight

Mangrove Bight
Sandy Bay

West End

Half Moon Bay
Coxen Hole (Roatán Town), West Bay

CARIBBEAN SEA

French Harbour

Crawfish Rock
Brick Bay
Aeropuerto Juan Manuel Galvez
Man of War Cay

Coxen Hole (Roatán Town)

Sandy Bay
Bailey's Cay
Antony's Cay
Flowers Bay
See "West End" inset (above)
West End
West Bay

Coral Reef

4 mi
4 km

WEST END
ACCOMMODATIONS ■
The Beach House **17**
The Lily Pond House **18**
Posada Las Orquideas **14**

DINING ◆
Cannibal Café **19**
Foster's **23**
Le Bistro **22**
Ooloonthoo **15**
Tong's **21**

NIGHTLIFE ★
The Purple Turtle **20**
Sundowners **16**

Ouch! Watch Out for Sand Flies

One thing the Bay Islands do not lack is sand flies, sometimes called no-see-ums. These pesky little gnatlike creatures, one-third the size of mosquitoes, bite and leave annoying little red bumps that you cannot help but scratch. While some of the major resorts send their staff out to rake the sand, which kills sand fly eggs, on most of the islands you just have to deal with them, especially on Utila, where they are particularly fierce. There is no best repellent for these nasty buggers. Some recommend Cactus Juice Sun Cream or coconut oil, while others feel just regular bug spray works best.

High season is almost year-round here and it can be especially difficult to find rooms during holiday weeks. Things slow down from January to February and during the hurricane season in September and November, and prices will drop significantly.

Roatán ★★★

Roatán, 29km (18 miles) east of Utila, is the largest, most developed, and most visited of the Bay Islands. The real estate market has been hot in recent years, but is now closer to spewing lava as once-quiet beach communities become full-scale resorts or second homes for North Americans, who are flocking here like barracudas and snapping up every inch of available land. The cruise season is also expanding rapidly—Royal Caribbean and Carnival cruises alone have invested a combined $80 million in increasing the capacity. When a cruise ship is docked at Coxen Hole, look out: The island will be crawling with craft markets and tour buses, and the best beaches like West Bay become crowded with sun worshipers.

Much of the new development is on the west side of the island, where tourism is concentrated, while Garífuna communities dominate the eastern half. If you look in the right places, you can still see the Bay Islands of yesteryear. Many of the island's hills remain undeveloped enough to be covered in tropical oak, evergreen palms, and gumbo-limbo trees, and just one (partly paved, partly potholed) road runs the length of the island. Diving and snorkeling remain the most popular activities on the island, but other options are growing. Now you can also zip-line across the jungle-clad hills, take a submarine hundreds of feet into the ocean, or take an aerial real estate tour.

ESSENTIALS
Getting There

While most tourists come from La Ceiba via ferry or flight, an increasing number of international travelers fly directly into Roatán's Juan Manuel Gálvez International Airport, sometimes called simply **Roatán International Airport** (**RTB**; ⓒ **504/ 445-1088**). It's 3km (1¾ miles) from Coxen Hole on the highway to French Harbour. Continental, Delta, American Airlines, and Taca fly here directly between points in the U.S. such as Houston, Newark, Atlanta, and Miami. See p. 728 in chapter 11 for airline phone numbers and websites. If you are flying out of Roatán to an international destination, don't forget you will have to pay the $34 departure tax at the airport.

If you are flying to or from La Ceiba, Tegucigalpa, or San Pedro Sula, you are limited to domestic airlines. **Isleña** (ⓒ **504/445-1918;** www.flyislena.com), **Aerolineas Sosa** (ⓒ **504/445-1154**), and **CM Airlines** (ⓒ **504/234-1886;**

www.cmairlines.com) all offer daily flights. **Bay Island Airways** (ℂ **504/946-5665** in the U.S., or 504/933-6077; www.bayislandairways.com) offers interisland transport via small seaplanes from the West End. Prices range from $220 for two people to the Cayos Cochinos to $360 for two people to Guanaja. **Roatán Air Services** (ℂ **504/455-6879;** www.roatanair.com), based in Coxen Hole, also runs charter flights to Guanaja, Utila, and the Cayos Cochinos in their three-passenger Cessna 172 and a six-passenger Aero Commander 560. Similarly, they'll run aerial photography and real estate tours ($160 for 30 min.).

Most tourists will take a taxi from the airport, which should run under L400 ($20) to anywhere on the island. If you walk out of the airport to the highway, you can also catch one of the frequent buses (L20–L40/$1–$2) that run during the day.

Roatán's superferry, the ***Galaxy Wave*** (ℂ **504/445-1798** or 443-4630; Safeways_ Galaxy@yahoo.com), zooms passengers from the ferry terminal at Dixon's Cove in Roatán to La Ceiba at 7am and 2pm, and returns at 9:30am and 4:30pm. The price is L420 ($22) each way, and the ferry has room for 360 people and offers air-conditioned rooms, a sun deck, and a small snack shop. It looks like a monster compared to Utila's small ferry and is much more stable; however, folks with weak stomachs might end up feeling sick by the time they step off the ship, particularly during the choppier afternoon trips. From the ferry terminal, you can catch a taxi, rent a car, or catch a bus simply by walking out to the main road.

A **catamaran service** (ℂ **504/3346-2600;** vfine@hotmail.com; L1,040/$55) sometimes operates for the 4-hour ride between Roatán and Utila on the 39-foot *Nina Elisabeth II,* though it departs only when there are sufficient passengers.

Cruise-ship dockings in Roatán have exploded in recent years. Carnival and Royal Caribbean are the biggest players, though Norwegian, Premier, Sun Cruises, Radisson, Wind Star, Commodore, and Regal also make port calls on a less frequent basis.

Orientation

Roatán sits 56km (35 miles) from La Ceiba on the North Coast of Honduras, and in between Utila and Guanaja. The 64km-long (40-mile) and no more than 4km-wide (2½-mile) island has a mountainous center that is covered in lush, green jungle. One main highway zigzags from one end of the island to the other, hitting every major settlement along the way. Coxen Hole, in the center of the island, is home to the majority of the population and is the Roatán transportation hub.

Getting Around

During daylight hours, buses and minibuses ply back and forth from one end of the island to the other on Roatán's one main road for a fare of L20 to L40 ($1–$2) per person, depending on how far you travel. Most buses will travel only east or west from Coxen Hole to one end of the island.

With a decent highway that runs much of the length of the island, driving in Roatán is a pleasant way to explore and reach some of the more remote sites. Several rental-car agencies have stands at the airport, including **Caribbean Rent a Car** (ℂ **504/455-6950;** www.caribbeanroatan.com) and **Avis** (ℂ **504/445-1568;** www.avis.com.hn). Prices range from about L850 to L1,511 ($45–$80) per day.

Taxi stands are located in every major tourist center, and waiting taxis sit outside most of the island's largest resorts. Prices are relatively high compared with those on the mainland. A ride from the airport or Coxen Hole to the West End will run about L400 ($20) per person. After 6pm, when the buses stop running, fares go up. *Colectivo* taxis, which pick up other passengers, are a cheaper option.

Water-taxi service runs daily from 9am to 9pm and is a convenient way to get between West End and West Bay. Just flag down a passing boat at any dock and one should stop. The fare is L30 ($1.50) during the day, L38 ($2) in the evening. You can rent motorized **scooters** at stands across the island. **Captain Van's Rentals ★★** (✆ **504/403-8751;** www.captainvans.com), on the West End and in West Bay, is the most popular and accessible operator for visitors. The cost is about L740 ($39) per day.

Visitor Information & Fast Facts

The **Roatán Marine Park Office** (Half Moon Bay, West End; ✆ **504/445-4206;** www.roatanmarinepark.com) has dive maps, some equipment, and information on saving the reef and natural sites in the Bay Islands. You can also buy a L190 ($10) Roatán dive tag/bracelet here.

Almost every hotel on the island has a **dive center** or can give you special rates with one. Dive packages and certification courses attract a majority of travelers to Roatán, where rates are some of the lowest in the world, at less than $40 per dive. Most of the large hotels, such as the Mayan Princess (p. 417), have ATMs, and there are a few stand-alones scattered about in the West End and elsewhere. All other banks can be found in Coxen Hole or French Harbour. You can exchange traveler's checks at BANFAA, located in the airport.

You can find cybercafés and calling centers scattered about the major tourist centers, but these computers tend to be slow. Most hotels now have Wi-Fi or a computer with Internet access for guests to use.

The majority of hospitals can be found in Coxen Hole, although many travelers prefer **Anthony's Key Medical Clinic** (✆ **504/445-1003**) in Sandy Bay.

COXEN HOLE

Coxen Hole, the largest city and capital of the department of the Bay Islands, isn't the idyllic beach paradise that you might expect to find in Roatán. It's more of a, well, hole. Whether you like it or not, though, chances are you are going to pass through the city, which is home to the airport and the ferry and cruise terminal, and functions as a transportation hub for buses and taxis. Apart from a few small hotels and restaurants, there isn't much in the way of tourist amenities—you're probably better off basing yourself in another part of Roatán.

One of the highlights of visiting this part of Roatán is **Yaba Ding Ding** (Bonilla Building on the waterfront; no phone; www.yabadingding.com; Mon–Sat 9am–5pm), which is one of the best craft shops in Honduras. Named after the local slang for pre-Columbian artifacts, the store stocks excellent Lenca pottery, straw baskets and weavings from the highlands, and Garífuna art.

Where to Stay

Cay View Hotel Of the handful of budget, crumbling hotels that sit near the water by the ferry dock at Coxen Hole, the Cay View is probably the best. With 19 rooms, it's the largest. Rooms aren't pretty and are quite worn, but there's air-conditioning, cable TV, and a decent Honduran restaurant and bar overlooking the water. It's a handy spot to keep in mind only if you arrive to the island too late to drive to a different part of Roatán, and just want a cheap place to stay for a night.

Oceanfront, Coxen Hole. ✆ **504/445-0269.** 19 units. L475 ($25) double. No credit cards. **Amenities:** Restaurant; bar. *In room:* A/C, TV.

FRENCH HARBOUR

French Harbour was once better known as the home of one of the largest fishing fleets in the Western Caribbean, but is quickly becoming engulfed by the onslaught of tourism and residential developments aimed at foreigners. While the compact town and port hold most of the town's population, the area as a whole is more spread out and self-contained than the West End and West Bay. Most of the hotels are fairly isolated and have their own private beaches, dive centers, and restaurants, so most visitors find little reason to leave their individual compounds or venture into town. A **Megaplaza Mall,** the first on the islands, with dozens of chain restaurants and stores, opened in late 2009 on the highway.

WHAT TO SEE & DO

Arch's Iguana Farm   Several thousand iguanas inhabit this property in French Key, just east of French Harbour, toward Fantasy Island. There are four different species on the farm, all native to the Bay Islands, and they are absolutely everywhere. Watch when you walk: They are literally falling out of the trees and out of the bushes. There's also a small pool with sea turtles and tropical fish. The place is overall fairly basic and an interesting excursion; however, the treatment of the coati, white-faced monkey, and spider monkey makes it a place for those with any sort of a conscience to avoid.

French Key, just east of French Harbour. ✆ **504/975-7442.** Admission L100. Daily 8am–3:30pm.

Where to Stay

Barefoot Cay ★ ☺   A small walk-on barge travels the 100m (328 ft.) back and forth from the main island and the 1.6-hectare (4-acre) island of Barefoot Cay, a new-ish resort area on the south shore of Roatán. Apart from the marina, which attracts yachties from around the Caribbean, the property has just four bungalows, a couple of villas, and a loft-style hotel. The spacious bungalows and villas have full kitchens and patios, as well as Balinese showers, which are partially open-air. The lofts are a single room with a kitchen and patio, while the loft suites add a second bedroom. The pool area—with its adjacent two-level *cabaña*—is the social center of the property and a decent place to grab a meal or drink, or to soak in a 360-degree view of the cay. On the waterfront, there's an 260m-long (863-ft.) dock and a thatched-roof palapa with a lowered platform, which grants easy access for kayakers who want to circle the cay or snorkelers who want to explore the reef that's just offshore.

Btw. French Harbour and Brick Bay. ✆ **504/455-6235.** Fax 504/455-6304. www.barefootcay.com. 9 units. L3,705 ($195) lofts; L7,315 ($385) loft suites; L6,100 ($320) bungalows; L10,355 ($545) villas. Dive and all-inclusive packages are also available. MC, V. **Amenities:** Restaurant; bar; pool; spa services; watersports equipment. *In room:* A/C, fan, TV/DVD, fridge, kitchen, Wi-Fi.

Palmetto Bay Plantation ★★★   Isolated on a stretch of Roatán's loneliest shore, this hotel has given the island one of its first tastes of the worldly exotic, with the Balinese-style ecofriendly beach houses. Their villas vary slightly, but all can sleep at least four. Some have two bedrooms, while others have three. A few lack A/C (there's a decent breeze here so you don't necessarily need it), while a few lack an ocean view. Their best room, the Coconut Grove Cottage, has a private plunge pool and sits right on the beach. Each of the bungalows has high ceilings, hardwood floors, and a full kitchen. The property is spectacular through and through. The infinity pool fronts a glass-and-wood pyramid that holds the restaurant and bar. The whole place

TOP SCUBA diving SITES IN ROATÁN

Roatán is nothing less than a diving paradise. There are more than 130 dive sites scattered around the island and, in just 1 day of diving, you can experience the full range of dives from coral reefs, canyons, and walls to wrecks and tunnels. The waters are crystal clear, and the reef, part of the second-largest barrier reef in the world, runs just offshore. Many of the best dive sites are right off the dock or within a 5-minute boat ride. Following is a list of the best dive sites:

- **Mary's Place ★★★**: Mary's Place near Sarah Cay is one of the most legendary dive sites around the island. Here you crawl through volcanic tunnels, crevices, and canyons around a reef plateau that has vertical walls that drop as much as 36m (118 ft.). You'll encounter black groupers, feather black coral, gorgonians, large bearded fire worms, and barrel sponges.

- **Four Sponges ★**: This dive site in Sandy Bay is one of the most complete, and is the best for beginning divers. The site is defined by its different levels of reef that range from 3 to 36m (10–118 ft.), allowing for the opportunity to encounter a wide range of sea life, like electric-blue chromis, barracuda, toadfish, yellow jawfish, scorpionfish, and sponges.

- ***Prince Albert* Wreck**: Since it sank back in 1985 near the Coco View Resort, the 50m (165-ft.) ship *Prince Albert* has attracted more soft coral growth than any other wreck on the island. There's also a sunken DC-3 plane that you can explore nearby.

- **Calvin's Crack**: This Jonesville dive site is defined by the huge—Calvin must have been a big guy—crevice ranging from 9 to 24m (30–80 ft.) in depth that runs through the reef. Brain, leaf, and black coral; sponges; gorgonians; rainbow parrotfish; fan leaf algae; and the occasional sea horse can often be sighted along the walls of the crevice.

- **Spooky Channel ★★**: The Spooky Channel (sometimes called Wayne's Place), on the northwest shore near Sandy Bay, is, well, spooky. The floor, ranging from 6 to 27m (20–90 ft.), is lined with sea whips and crabs, and cleaner shrimp crawl about on the abundant coral formations.

- ***El Aguila* Wreck**: *El Aguila* is a 656m (200-ft.) cargo ship that sank in 1997 by Anthony's Key Resort and was later split in three by Hurricane Mitch. It sits 100m (328 ft.) below the surface of Sandy Bay. Green Moray and garden eels can be found in varying spots around the wreck, as can large grouper, blue parrotfish, glassy sweepers, nudibranches, and anemones.

feels and is rather isolated, so you have the entire beautiful beach all to yourself and the others at the resort. The atmosphere is polished, but it doesn't lack charm.

North of French Harbour. ✆ **504/9991-0811.** www.palmettobayplantation.com. 27 units. L4,275 ($225) per villa; add L1,045 ($55) adult/L665 ($35) child per day for all-inclusive. Weekly rates available. MC, V. **Amenities:** Restaurant; bar; airport transfers; Jacuzzi; pool; Wi-Fi. *In room:* A/C, kitchen.

Santé Spa ★ 🎁   This wellness facility and B&B on a cay near Parrot Tree Plantation is one of the best little accommodations on the island. Without road access, there's little noise apart from the wind in the palms and crashing surf. Accommodations are in either two rooms in the main building, or a small cottage near the lagoon. Decor and amenities are simple yet cozy and charming. Prices include use of the spa facilities, a morning yoga session, and continental breakfast.

East of French Harbour. ✆ **504/408-5156.** www.santewellnesscenter.com. 3 units. L2,185 ($115) double. MC, V. **Amenities:** Pool; spa. *In room:* A/C ($10 surcharge per day), fan, high-speed Internet, minibar.

Turquoise Bay ★   Quietly, Turquoise Bay has grown a loyal following of returning customers. The resort is quite secluded on the north side of the island, about 15 minutes east of French Harbour. It's not flashy or overly luxurious and it isn't going to really "wow" you like Palmetto Bay, but overall the ambience is pleasant and the price is good. The spacious contemporary rooms—set in four-unit bungalows—are decorated with splashes of African flair. Each has a different bright color scheme, but all are done up quite nicely, the tile floors and bathrooms are clean, and rooms have oceanview balconies. There's a pool and a National Geographic dive center on the property.

Milton Bight. ✆ **504/413-2229.** www.turquoisebayresort.com. 26 units. L2,430 ($128) double. MC, V. **Amenities:** Restaurant; bar; airport transfers; pool. *In room:* A/C, TV.

Where to Dine

Casa Romeo's ITALIAN   Romeo's, set in the hotel of the same name, has been a Honduras institution since 1976, and many of the recipes have been passed down since the 1940s from Romeo's father Don Di, who owned the famous Maxim's in La Ceiba and later the Buccaneer Inn on Roatán. The menu ranges from Italian standards like *penne alla carbonara* to thick cuts of beef and seafood that are prepared every which way from *fra diavolo* (in spicy tomato sauce) to breaded and grilled. My favorite item is the conch chowder. The restaurant is on the edge of the harbor and makes good use of the view.

Main St. ✆ **504/455-5854.** Main courses L152–L285 ($8–$15). AE, MC, V. Mon–Sat 10am–2:30pm and 5–10pm.

Gio's Restaurant ★ SEAFOOD   Few dare to utter the name Gio's without mentioning king crab, and for good reason: People have been flocking to this restaurant since it opened several decades ago for its special king crab *al ajillo* (in garlic sauce). Other seafood dishes and even steaks are finely executed and cater to finicky international tourists. There are two separate dining rooms; one is open-air on the dock, while the other sits inside with the air-conditioning blasting. All seats have inviting views of the harbor, and make for ideal spots for relaxing with a drink in your hand for the rest of the day.

Under the El Faro Inn, Main St. ✆ **504/455-5214.** Main courses L190–L250 ($10–$20). MC, V. Mon–Sat 10am–2pm and 5–10pm.

SANDY BAY

Sandy Bay is a tranquil town on the North Coast that has become a popular stop on many cruise-ship tours, which come to experience the cultural highlights of the islands. Standout attractions here include the Roatán Museum and Institute of Marine Sciences, and a dolphin encounter. Note that while the beaches in the reserve are stunning and surrounded by some of the most dramatic coral formations in Roatán, the beaches in town are murky and scruffy.

For scuba diving and snorkeling, try Sandy Bay's most popular resort, **Anthony's Key Resort** (see "Where to Stay & Dine" below).

What to See & Do

Carambola Gardens   These tropical gardens, across from Anthony's Key Resort, have a nice collection of native plants of the Bay Islands; this is also a good spot on Roatán to check out rare iguanas and parrots. You can spend a couple of hours here easily, just taking in the views of reefs below and strolling around the trails and hiking to the top of "Carambola Mountain." Kids might not enjoy this as much as some of the older visitors. On cruise ship days the serenity can be lost.

Sandy Bay. ✆ **504/445-3117.** www.carambolagardens.com. Daily 8am–5pm. Admission L120 ($6).

Dolphin Encounter ★★ ☺   On Bailey's Key, which is part of Anthony's Key Resort, the famous Bottlenose Dolphin Encounter program offers visitors the chance to interact with these wonderful creatures. Open-water dives, snorkel programs, and beach encounters are the most common option, and allow for physical interaction with dolphins. More involved are the training programs where you can work with the staff at the Roatán Institute for Marine Sciences in 1- or 2-day sessions. There's also a dolphin show every day except Wednesday at 4pm.

Kids can get in on the dolphin action, too: Every summer Anthony's Key Resort and the Institute of Marine Sciences offer **Dolphin Scuba camps** ($850 per camper) where children can learn about dolphins and even swim and interact with them. They get to practice their scuba diving and snorkeling, as well as learn about the ecosystem and cultures of Roatán. Think of it as an exotic summer camp.

Bailey's Key, Roatán Institute for Marine Sciences, Sandy Bay. ✆ **504/445-3008.** www.anthonyskey.com. L1,180 ($62) for the Dolphin Encounter; L2,600 ($136) for a dolphin dive; L100 ($5) dolphin show.

Roatán Museum and Institute of Marine Sciences ★   The Institute of Marine Sciences is the island's main research center and is host to technical lectures and serious research, but it's also a place where visitors can learn about the ecology of the Bay Islands through captivating exhibits. Displays feature fish, reptiles, birds, plants, and other examples of island life, and there are exhibits on the history and culture of the area. The facility is part of the 13-sq.-km (5-sq.-mile) Sandy Bay marine reserve.

Roatán Institute for Marine Sciences, Sandy Bay. ✆ **504/445-3008.** Admission L100. Daily 8am–5pm.

Where to Stay & Dine

Anthony's Key Resort ★★   For 4 decades, Anthony's Key Resort has been one of the leading dive and leisure destinations in the Bay Islands. If you are looking for a hotel that will completely transport you to another world, this is it. The vast complex is submerged in mangrove and palm forests and is reminiscent of an island village where frequent water taxis shuffle you back and forth from place to place. The property is set partly on two small cayes and partly on the north shore of the island near Sandy Bay. There are 56 single-unit wooden bungalows, 10 of them on the hill on the main island, with the rest on the key. Bailey's Key, just west of the main key, is home to the best beach on the property and a Dolphin Encounter lagoon. Also on the grounds are the Institute of Marine Sciences and Roatán Museum, which guests can enjoy free.

Garífuna Day, on April 12 each year, commemorates the arrival of the Garífuna on Roatán in 1797, and celebrations are held all along the North Coast of the country and the Bay Islands. Hundreds of thousands of people revel in the streets, march in parades, and party on the beaches for much of the night, so get ready to party if you're in town then.

Anthony's Key Resort, Sandy Bay. ☏ **954/929-0090.** www.anthonyskey.com. 56 units. From L9,100 ($480) per person for a 4-night dive package with 3 daily meals and activities. MC, V. **Amenities:** Restaurant; bar; laundry service; pool; watersports equipment. *In room:* A/C (in some), fan.

Que tal Café ★ CONTINENTAL   One of the favorite restaurants on the island, for those who have been away, has moved from Coxen Hole to Sandy Bay in the Lawson's Rock Beach Club. They are big on breakfast here, plus their sandwiches and fresh-baked cookies are pretty good, but the gossip tends to be fairly tasty too.

Lawson's Rock Beach Club, Sandy Bay. ☏ **504/445-3295.** MC, V. Main courses L133-L260 ($7-$14). Mon-Fri 8am-3pm; Sat 8am-2:30pm; Sun 9am-noon.

WEST END

West End, so-called because it is on the west end of Roatán, is the tourist center of the island and is home to the most hotels, restaurants, bars, dive shops, tour operators, and general tourist amenities. From the highway, the town hugs the road and the beach in both directions for just a mile or two. The town itself is quite small and has a sort of thrown-together feel to it, since buildings are scattered about with no apparent order. Prices tend to be cheaper here than in the West Bay, thus attracting plenty of backpackers and die-hard divers, although it is still more upscale than all of Utila.

Essentials

The West End can be reached by bus from Coxen Hole for L40 ($2), by a water taxi for L30 to L38 ($1.50–$2) from West Bay, or by a regular taxi from anywhere on the island. There is a taxi stand near the entrance to the highway where a few cabs (which charge L400/$21 to Coxen Hole) are usually waiting.

If you want to explore the island for a day or two, a great option is to rent a mountain bike, scooter, or motorcycle. **Captain Van's** (☏ **504/403-8751;** www.captainvans.com) has locations in both the West End, on Main Street near the Baptist Church, and the West Bay Mall. Prices begin at L171 ($9) per day for a bike and L740 ($39) per day for a scooter.

What to See & Do

Gumbalimba Park ★ ☺   Gumbalimba is a good place to come if you have just 1 day in Roatán and want to experience as much as you can, which is why the place is often packed when a cruise ship is in town. It's kind of a one-stop adventure shop. There's a zip-line section, a large stretch of beach with clear kayaks, SNUBA, snorkel gear, and a pool, and even a small cave with cheesy replica pirates and exhibits that describe their historical relationship with the Bay Islands. Their main attraction, though, is their nature trail that runs through an area of very dense jungle and is filled with rare tropical plants and flowers native to the region, as well as a hanging rope bridge over a small lake, cages of macaws and other parrots, and a small island that's home to a few monkeys.

On the West Bay Rd. btw. West End and West Bay. ⓒ **504/445-1033.** www.gumbalimbapark.com. Admission L320 ($17); L1,045 ($55) for park admission and zip-line package. Daily 9am–4pm.

Roatán Butterfly Garden Try to spare a few hours for a visit to Roatán's butterfly garden. Tours are self-guided through the 278-sq.-m (3,000-sq.-ft.) walkthrough enclosure, and they give you a small chart to identify the 30 or so rare butterfly species and tropical plants. Separate from the butterflies are a few cages of birds native to Honduras, such as aracaris and toucans.

Near the entrance to the highway, West End. ⓒ **504/445-4481.** www.roatanbutterfly.com. Admission L140 ($7). Sun–Fri 9am–5pm.

Outdoor Activities

West End beaches are smallish and not as nice as those in the West Bay (just a quick ferry ride away), but there are a few spots where the water is just as clear as anywhere on the island. Half Moon Beach is probably the best option.

If you don't dive, snorkel, or even swim but still want to experience the undersea world of the Bay Islands, you have a few options. The **Roatán Institute of Deep Sea Exploration** (no phone; www.stanleysubmarines.com) offers 3,280 to 6,560m (1,000–2,000-ft.) dives and shark dives in a submarine. The small vehicles have room for just one pilot and two passengers. **Underwater Paradise** (ⓒ 504/445-6465) has semisubmarine glass-bottom boat tours three times a day from the Half Moon Bay Resort for L380 ($20) adults or L190 ($10) children, and the **Coral Explorer** (ⓒ **504/455-5379**) has a similar tour from West Bay.

For another unique perspective on the island, **Bay Island Airways** (ⓒ **303/242-8004** in the U.S., 9858-8819 or 9858-8824 in Honduras; www.bayislandairways. com) offers a variety of ways to view the island from the air. They have aerial real estate tours (L6,840/$360 per hour for two), trips to the Pigeon Keys (L10,000/$520 for a 3-hr. tour for two), and simple sightseeing and photography tours (L2,300/$120 for a 15-min. flight).

The waters surrounding Roatán are full of Pelagic species like tuna, wahoo, mahimahi, blue and white marlin, shark, and king mackerel. **Early Bird Fishing Charters** (ⓒ **504/445-3019**; www.earlybirdfishingcharters.com), a member of the conservation-minded Fisherman's Association of Roatán, leads frequent excursions from the West End to waters all around the island. Prices begin at L7,600/$400) for a half-day tour with one to four people. Pescado Roatán (ⓒ **504/9930-6139;** www. pescadoroatan.com) specializes in fly, flats, and remote deep sea trips, all using new boats and top-of-the-line equipment.

Shopping

All shops in Roatán are on Main Street in the West End, but most are little stores selling a mishmash of things. One standout store is **Wave Gallery** (ⓒ **504/445-4303**), in a bright yellow house on the beach, which is worth a browse for its paintings, jewelry, and crafts made by Honduran artists. The **Roatán Marine Park Office** (Half Moon Bay, West End; ⓒ **504/445-4206;** www.roatanmarinepark. com) has dive maps, some equipment, and information on saving the reef and natural sites in the Bay Islands. You can also buy a L190 ($10) Roatán dive tag/bracelet here.

DIVING operators IN ROATÁN

Dive packages and certification courses attract countless travelers to Roatán, where rates are less than $40 per dive. Prices are not as cheap as Utila or Guanaja, though they are not far off. Here are a few recommended dive schools, listed by location:

French Harbour

o **Coco View Resort** (✆ 504/911-7371; www.cocoviewresort.com)

o **Fantasy Island Resort** (✆ 504/455-7499; www.fantasyislandresort.com)

Sandy Bay

o **Anthony's Key Resort** ★ (✆ 954/929-0090; www.anthonyskey.com)

West End

o **Coconut Tree Divers** (✆ 504/445-4081; www.coconuttreedivers.com)

o **Reef Gliders** (✆ 504/403-8243; www.reefgliders.com)

o **Native Sons** (✆ 504/445-4003; www.nativesonsroatan.com)

o **Sueno del Mar Dive Center** (✆ 800/298-9009 [U.S.]; www.suenodelmar.com)

West Bay

o **Bananarama Dive Resort** (✆ 504/445-5005; www.bananaramadive.com)

o **Octopus Dive School** ★ (✆ 504/403-8071; www.roatan-octopusdiveschool.com)

Where to Stay

The Beach House ★ This bright yellow wooden house in the heart of Half Moon Bay, just beside Sundowner's Bar, has grown a loyal following for the friendly staff and nice Caribbean view from each room. The hotel lacks the frills and dive services of many resorts here, though three of the four rooms sleep four people, so this is a good family choice. Each room has its own personality and shape, though one adds a full kitchen and another a private deck.

Half Moon Bay, West End. ✆ **504/445-4260.** www.roatanonline.com/beach_house. 4 units. L2,850 ($150) double. No credit cards. **Amenities:** Laundry service. *In room:* A/C, TV w/DVD, fridge.

The Lily Pond House ★★ 🛍 This charming little house, just off the main road near Half Moon Bay, is set amid a lush garden and trees, making it just as attractive for the birds and butterflies as those who are looking for something different from the typical dive resorts that make up many of the accommodations in Roatán. The honeymoon suite is the largest of the four rooms, although the rooms don't really differ that much in size or amenities. All are quite spacious, with wood floors and canopy beds. Plus they have private entrances, en suite bathrooms, and porches, so you can keep your privacy. They also hold yoga classes on the rooftop garden three times a week.

Half Moon Bay, West End. ✆ **504/403-8204.** 4 units. L1,800 ($95). No credit cards. **Amenities:** Breakfast room; airport transfers; laundry service. *In room:* A/C, TV w/DVD, fridge, Wi-Fi.

Posada Las Orquideas � Posada Las Orquideas sits in front of Mangrove Bight, where there isn't a beach, but there is a dock and a wharf with beach chairs, and the town beaches are just a 10-minute walk away. The three-level building opened in 2006 and the rooms still seem new with their shiny wood floors and wicker furniture. There's a balcony in every room with a table and hammock where you can watch the boats pass by below. It's good value for the price.

To the right from the highway, West End. ✆ **504/445-4387.** www.posadalasorquideas.com. 18 units. From L1,330 ($70) double low season and L1,520 ($80) double high season (July–Sept and Dec–Apr). A/C is an additional L285 ($15). AE, MC, V. **Amenities:** High-speed Internet (free in lobby). *In room:* A/C, fridge, kitchen (in some).

Where to Dine

Cannibal Café ★ ☺ MEXICAN   This wildly popular restaurant and bar in front of the Sea Breeze Inn is always a great choice for a snack or drink. It's set in a rustic wooden shack, and serves the sorts of standard Americanized Mexican fare like burritos and nachos that appeal to hungry divers. Get a margarita to wash your meal down and you'll fit right in at this party spot.

Main St., West End. ✆ **504/445-4026.** L76–L152 ($4–$8). No credit cards. Mon–Sat 10:30am–10pm.

Foster's ★ INTERNATIONAL   Foster's is in a stilted house in the middle of the ocean connected to the shore by a few-hundred-foot dock. You can't get a better sea view than the one from here, which is why this is the spot in town for a sunset meal or drink. Burgers, chicken wings, coconut shrimp, seafood, and steaks make up most of the menu. It can get boisterous on weekends, when there's a DJ or live band.

On a dock over the water off of Main St., West End. ✆ **503/403-8005.** Fax 503/403-8789. www.fostersroatan.com. Main courses L133–L380 ($7–$20). AE, MC, V. Mon–Sat 10:30am–midnight.

Le Bistro ASIAN   This Southeast Asian–inspired restaurant is one of the more adventurous in the West End. Much of the menu is composed of Vietnamese treats like *acras* (fritters), egg rolls, spring rolls, and won tons that come served with your choice of fillings such as shrimp, grouper, pork, chicken, or vegetables. They also have beef hot pots, *Mixao* (chicken and shrimp over noodles in a ginger sauce), and combo platters. The restaurant is quite rustic, wedged between a closed dive shop and another store, and seems as if it were imported from a Saigon market.

Main St., West End. ✆ **504/403-8854.** Main courses L114–L209 ($6–$11). No credit cards. Daily 6–9pm.

Ooloonthoo ★★ INDIAN   Ooloonthoo is probably the best restaurant in Roatán. Canadian chef Paul James and his Indian wife have done such a good job of giving this restaurant an authentic Indian coastal feel, you might just think you're in Goa while dining here. The decor is simple, with little touches like background Indian music, silk saris draped across the ceiling, and banana leaves strewn on the tables, all adding to the "am I still in Honduras?" ambience. Curries made from scratch dominate the menu, such as the Rogan Josh or pork vindaloo, while other highlights include tandoori Cornish game hen and *murgh masala,* a mild northern Indian chicken dish.

To the right from the highway to Half Moon Bay, West End. ✆ **504/403-8866.** www.ooloonthoo.com. L95–L380 ($5–$20). MC, V. May–Nov Mon–Fri 6–9pm; Dec–Apr Sun–Fri 6–9pm.

Tong's ★ THAI   One of the more romantic settings on the West End, Tong's offers both an indoor dining room and an intimate outdoor patio and pier with tables that sit right out over the water. Thai staples are all worth trying: pad thai, tom yam, or any of their three curries (panang, green, or red).

Main St., West End. ✆ **504/9682-4288.** Main courses L230–L340 ($12–$18). MC, V. Tues–Sun noon–2:30pm and 5:30–9:30pm.

West End After Dark

There are dozens of watering holes to choose from on the West End, and they fill up almost every night from sunset until the early morning. Thatched-roof beach bar **Sundowners** ★ is one of the West End's main hangouts. Its prime spot on one of the best sections of beach in town draws lots of walk-ups, as do the specials on beer, mixed drinks, and the 4-to-7pm happy hour. Try the Monkey Lala, a frozen blend of Kahlúa, ice cream, coconut, and vodka. The **Purple Turtle,** basically a wooden patio that runs between the street and the water, is beloved for the cheap drinks. On weekend nights the crowd spills out into the street.

WEST BAY

About 2km (1¼ miles) southwest of the West End sits a 1.5km (1-mile) stretch of powdery white sand, set against the mellow tides of a perfectly turquoise sea. This is West Bay, the finest beach in all of Honduras and one of the top beaches in all of the Caribbean. If your idea of a good vacation is to lounge around in the sand and sun with a continuous rotation of tropical drinks being brought your way, look no further. The focus here is less on diving—although diving is still a big deal—than general beachgoing activity. When you decide to move from your palm-fringed slumber, you can ride jet skis, take a boat tour, or browse the souvenir stands sprinkled across the beach. If you want to snorkel, you can rent gear almost anywhere and walk a few feet into the water to spot all sorts of colorful fish swimming around a good tract of coral reef.

Almost the entire beach is chockablock with hotels and condos, the majority of which have no more than a few dozen rooms. Although the town lacks other tourist amenities like restaurants, that's changing—West Bay has so many new tourist projects in the works that it sometimes feels more like a construction site than a resort area. When a cruise ship is in town, the place can get downright crowded, but for much of the week, West Bay is still an idyllic resort.

What to See & Do

The 1.5km (1-mile) **West Bay Beach** ★★★ is the main attraction here and one of the region's best. The water resembles an aquarium of sorts, since you can see down to the bottom and watch brightly colored marine life pass you by. Many of the resorts have beach chairs and umbrellas set up in the sand, although you may need to pay a fee and get a wristband to use them. Apart from snorkeling, you can rent Wave Runners or go parasailing, ride a paddle boat, or water-ski.

Where to Stay

Infinity Bay Spa & Resort ★★   Similar to the Mayan Princess, though it intends to become more luxurious when it is finished, Infinity Bay is another new condo/resort complex that opened in late 2007. Here, studios and one-, two-, and three-bedroom condos are set in three-level villas facing the pool or West Bay beach. All rooms are very modern with stainless steel appliances, flatscreen TVs, tiled floors, and contemporary furniture and decor. Highlights are their long dock that extends far into the water, poolside bar, and beachfront restaurant.

West Bay, Roatán. ✆ **504/445-5016.** Fax 504/445-5062. www.infinitybay.com. 145 units. L2,375 ($125) oceanview studio in the low season and L2,850 ($150) the rest of the year; from L4,560 ($240) 2-bedroom; from L7,125 ($375) 3-bedroom. MC, V. **Amenities:** Restaurant; bar; airport transfers. *In room:* A/C, TV, fan, full kitchens in nonstudios, Wi-Fi.

Mayan Princess ★★ ☺ The Mayan Princess is one of the top accommodations in Honduras. The posh units are privately owned and rented out by the hotel management. The one-bedroom and two-bedroom condos still feel like the tile has just been laid and the wicker furniture has never been sat in. They have full kitchens, a dining area, living rooms, and a patio or balcony that faces the ocean or sprawling pool area that runs almost the length of the complex and is bordered by tropical gardens that are interwoven with waterfalls and walkways. The oceanfront side of the property is the best in the West Bay because of the primo beach chairs and umbrellas and the good bit of shade that covers their beach bar and restaurant, one of the best all-around dining options in the West Bay.

West Bay, Roatán. ☎ **504/445-5050.** Fax 504/445-5065. www.mayanprincess.com. 60 units. From L3,135 ($165) for a poolside room on weekdays and L3,590 ($189) on weekends. MC, V. **Amenities:** Restaurant; bar; laundry service; pool; watersports equipment; Wi-Fi. *In room:* A/C, fan, TV, kitchen.

West Bay B&B ★ 🍴 Considering that the back end of the much-more-expensive Infinity Bay is as far from the beach as this small, owner-run bed-and-breakfast, this might be the best deal on the Bay Islands. There are five rooms with varying number of beds and one two-room condo. Some rooms can sleep up to six. The rooms feel a bit bare, but are nicely decorated, and the common room is quite comfortable with a big couch, Internet cafe, and DVD collection.

West Bay, Roatán. ☎ **504/445-5080.** www.westbaybedandbreakfast.com. 6 units. L1,310–L1,880 ($69–$99) double, including breakfast; L1,880 ($99) condo. MC, V. **Amenities:** Restaurant; laundry; Wi-Fi. *In room:* A/C, TV, minifridge.

Where to Dine

Beach Club San Simon ★★ INTERNATIONAL San Simon isn't just a restaurant, but a place to enjoy the beach. Many come from other parts of the island and spend the day here, renting out their beachside cabanas or lounge chairs. The main dining area is under their elegant beachfront palapa. They're known for their rotisserie chicken that uses an old Venetian recipe. The rest of the menu jumps around quite a bit: pastas, filet mignon, grilled fish and lobster, and enchiladas. It fills up on cruise-ship days and is occasionally closed for private parties.

West Bay Mall, West Bay. ☎ **504/445-5035.** www.thebeachclubroatan.com. Main courses L75–L230 ($4–$12). AE, MC, V. Daily 10am–10pm.

Mangiamo ★★ DELI This small deli and gourmet food market in the West Bay Mall is a place where you can grab a quick fresh-ground coffee from Olancho or a fancy sandwich—hot pastrami to basil cashew chicken. Their breakfast menu is my favorite on the island: eggs Benedict, breakfast burritos, stacks of pancakes, and egg sandwiches with pancake buns. Wine and beer to stock your fridge with can be purchased here, too.

West Bay Mall, West Bay. ☎ **504/445-5035.** www.roatandeli.com. Main courses L75–L230 ($4–$12). AE, MC, V. Mon–Sat 8:30am–5pm.

Pizzeria Il Pomodoro/Buffalo Steakhouse INTERNATIONAL These are actually two restaurants near the Paradise Beach Club, which share the same kitchen and are separated by a partial wall. Regardless of which restaurant you dine in, you can order from both menus. The pizzeria menu offers pastas, lasagnas, and wood-fired pizzas, while the steakhouse offers beef imported from the U.S. in the form of T-bones, rib-eyes, and New York strips. To make things more complicated, they have an attached gelateria, Angelo's, which serves dessert. Since the West Bay has few other dining options that aren't overpriced resort restaurants, the multifaceted talents of this über restaurant come as a relief.

Paradise Beach Club, West Bay. ☎ **505/403-8066.** Main courses L133–L342 ($7–$18). AE, MC, V. Daily noon–midnight.

Utila ★★

Utila has only one main settlement, called East Harbour, or simply Utila town. Although it is the smallest of the three main Bay Islands and the nearest to the mainland (at 29km/18 miles west of Roatán), Utila is still the wildest and most untouched. Islanders, many of them the descendants of pirates and Garífunas, are eager to casually chat with anyone about the weather or local news. Some may even tell you that Captain Morgan's lost booty from his raid on Panama in 1671 is still hidden in the surrounding hills.

Apart from a few chic dive resorts, almost the entire population of Utila is clustered together along one stretch of coast, while the other 80% or so is made up of mangroves and wetlands. Many have called this island a backpacker's paradise because of the cheap accommodations, the restaurants, the bar scene that rages well into the night almost every night, and the sandy-bottom rates for dive certification—once considered the lowest in the world. It is less polished than nearby Roatán, but beach resorts are slowly starting to carve their way out of the mangroves. Even the certification costs are roughly on par with those in Roatán these days. Chances are that it is going to be a good while before a dirt-cheap dorm bed in a rickety old house goes out of style in Utila, though.

ESSENTIALS
Getting There

Currently only one small airline makes the 20-minute trip between Utila and La Ceiba, with connections to Tegucigalpa and San Pedro Sula. **Aerolineas Sosa** (☎ **504/443-2519;** www.aerolineasosahn.com) makes the trip twice a day Monday to Saturday and three times on Sunday. Taxis (L40–L60/$2–$3 per person) await flights for the 10-minute trip.

The *Utila Princess II* (☎ **504/425-3390**) makes the hour-long trip back and forth between the Municipal pier Utila and the Muelle de Cabotaje dock in La Ceiba. The ferry departs Utila daily at 6:20am and 2pm, and returns to La Ceiba at 9:30am and 4pm. Ticket booths are located on both piers. The price is L373 ($20) each way. A **catamaran service** (☎ **504/3346-2600;** vfine@hotmail.com; L1,040/$55) now operates for the 4-hour ride between Roatán and Utila on the 39-foot *Nina Elisabeth II.* There is no set schedule, but the boat attempts to run on a daily basis in the high season.

Orientation & Getting Around

The crescent-shaped East Harbour on the eastern end of Utila is where 90% of the population lives. The Municipal Pier marks the center of town; Main Street, the main road on the island, runs perpendicular about 1km (⅔ mile) in each direction. To the left is Sandy Bay and to the right is a small peninsula that ends at the bridge that connects to Bando Beach. With a few exceptions, almost all hotels and tourist amenities can be found within 1km (⅔ mile) of the pier. Another road, Cola de Mico or Monkey Tail Road, branches off Main Street up over Pumpkin Hill, eventually leading to the airport and the north side of the island.

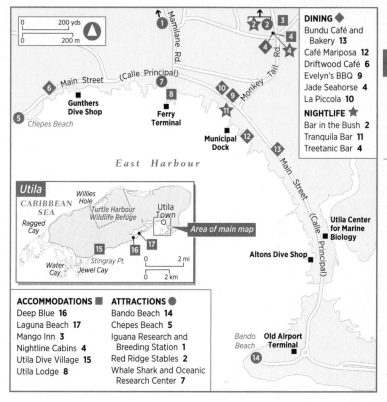

DINING ◆
Bundu Café and
  Bakery **13**
Café Mariposa **12**
Driftwood Café **6**
Evelyn's BBQ **9**
Jade Seahorse **4**
La Piccola **10**

NIGHTLIFE ★
Bar in the Bush **2**
Tranquila Bar **11**
Treetanic Bar **4**

ACCOMMODATIONS ■
Deep Blue **16**
Laguna Beach **17**
Mango Inn **3**
Nightline Cabins **4**
Utila Dive Village **15**
Utila Lodge **8**

ATTRACTIONS ●
Bando Beach **14**
Chepes Beach **5**
Iguana Research and
  Breeding Station **1**
Red Ridge Stables **2**
Whale Shark and Oceanic
  Research Center **7**

There are few cars on Utila, let alone taxis. Considering that almost everywhere is within walking distance or reached over water, the only time you really need a taxi or a car is to get back and forth from the airport. Golf carts, scooters, and bicycles, which are available for rent, are the most common vehicle-assisted ways to get around the island. Visit **Lance Bodden Rentals** (✆ **504/425-3245**) behind BGA bank to make arrangements. Discounts are given for long-term rentals.

Visitor Information
There are two banks in East Harbour, both within a hummingbird's flight of the pier. **Banco BGA** (✆ **504/425-4117**) and **Banco Atlántida** (✆ **504/425-3374**) exchange traveler's checks and have an ATM. **Mango Tree House,** on Main Street just to the left from the pier, is the island's most reliable Internet cafe and can also make international phone calls. **Hondutel,** beside the Bay Island College of Diving, also makes international calls.

WHAT TO SEE & DO
Iguana Research and Breeding Station ☺ The small nonprofit German-run station is a learning center for those interested in not only iguanas, but also the tortoises, snakes, frogs, spiders, fish, and other animal life found on the Bay Islands.

Many live species can be found in aquariums, terrariums, and outdoor breeding cages; and your admission includes a tour where kids can walk into—if they dare—some of the enclosures. This is one of the few places in the world where you can catch a glimpse of the spiny tail or swamp iguana, a species endemic to Utila and in danger of extinction because of the islanders' love of eating them and the destruction of the mangroves. Longer tours to the Bat Caves, Pumpkin Hill, and the mangrove forests are also available, as well as volunteer opportunities.

Follow Mamilane road until you see the signs for the turnoff. ℂ **504/425-3946.** www.utila-iguana.de. Admission L40 ($2). Mon, Wed, and Fri 2–5pm.

Whale Shark and Oceanic Research Center ★★ The whale shark, the largest fish in the world, is frequently seen in Utilan waters, and the island is a hot spot for whale shark research. This small organization is focused on protecting these creatures and the coral reefs by collecting data with the help of divers and operators, educating the public, and hosting and participating in major studies. The good news for visitors to Utila is that they have a full line of courses and tours. Their 4-hour whale shark encounter and research trips include a short background lecture on whale shark ecology, the use of snorkel gear, and the possibility of seeing whale sharks up close in the water. They also offer PADI specialty courses such as AWARE fish ID and Coral Reef Conservation courses and underwater photography. Volunteers are often needed to help with whale shark research and development of the program.

Main St., in front of the Bay Islands College of Diving. ℂ **504/425-3760.** www.wsorc.com. Free admission. Daily 8am–7pm.

Outdoor Activities

While Utila isn't known for its beaches like other places in Honduras, it does have a few decent options for sunbathers and swimmers. There are several good beaches within walking distance of town. **Bando Beach** (ℂ **504/425-3137**), just past the bridge from the Point, is privately owned and you must pay a small admission (L40/$2) to get in. There's a small beach bar that also rents snorkel gear and kayaks. **Chepes Beach** to the west of Sandy Bay is the main public beach. They are constantly at work there to improve the infrastructure.

The small, uninhabited **Water Cay** is similar to many of the beaches you'll find in the Cayos Cochinos: It's made of a cluster of palm trees circled by a white sandy beach and turquoise water. Charters and dive trips often stop here for lunch or weekend barbecues and parties. The first weekend of August, it is host to the largest party in Utila, the Sun Jam festival (see below). A few hotels and several shops in town, including **Utila Water Sports** (ℂ **504/425-3264;** www.utilawatersports.com) rent sit-on-top kayaks to explore the channels, lagoons, and mangroves around the island.

Located on the road to the airport, **Red Ridge Stables** (ℂ **504/390-4812**) offers horseback-riding treks to the inner jungle, Pumpkin Hill Beach, the freshwater caves, and other destinations on the island that aren't submerged completely in swamp and mangroves. Trips run L665 ($35) for a 2-hour ride.

For 1 night every August, partygoers from around Honduras descend upon the tiny 1.2-hectare (3-acre) island Water Cay off Utila for the raucous **Sun Jam festival** (www.sunjamutila.com; L760/$40), where top DJs from around the region pump electronic music to a lively and often intoxicated crowd.

With prices hovering around L4,750 ($250) for a PADI 4-day Open Water Certification, it's no wonder that **scuba divers** from around the world descend on the small island. Almost any certification or course can be taken from a number of dive

TOP FIVE SCUBA diving SITES IN UTILA

- **CJ's Drop Off:** Near Turtle Harbour on the north side of the island, these dramatic coral cliffs sink about 5m (16 ft.) to 100m (328 ft.)—one of the biggest vertical drops in the entire Caribbean. The walls are teeming with sea life. There's a chance to see stingrays, moray eels, and hawksbill turtles.

- *Halliburton:* Sunk by divers, for divers. This large wreck, submerged under 30m (100 ft.) of water, is covered in brightly colored sponges and coral, including fireworms found on the deck. Moray eels are often seen around the hull of the ship, while groupers and barracudas can be seen all around it.

- **Stingray Point** ★: Two reef walls sprinkled with canyons and topped by a coral garden come together at this site on the western end of the island. Spotted eagle rays and stingrays can often be found in the sandy channels here. Large sea fans and soft coral plumes are particularly copious in the area.

- **The Maze:** This north-side site is defined by the wide canyon and a significant wall drop (40m/130 ft.). Elkhorn coral and star coral are matched in beauty by the variety of plant life such as sea fans and rope sponges. The famous Willy's Hole, filled with glassy sweepers, is also found here.

- **Black Hills** ★★: Black Hills, a large seamount with steep drop-offs, is about 1.5km (1 mile) off the south shore of Utila and home to a vibrant array of sea life such as hawksbill turtles, queen angelfish, thousands of blue and yellowtail wrasse, horse-eye jacks, sea horses, and spadefish. Sea fans, whips, and gorgonians and other sea plants litter the site.

shops. There are roughly 90 permanent mooring buoys around the island, giving access to the reefs, wrecks, walls, and tunnels that frequently line the pages of top diving magazines. Most whale shark sightings occur in March and April.

The dive shops on Utila are second to none in Honduras. On Main Street in East Harbour, dive instructors seem to outnumber people five to one. Competition is fierce and the operators can be catty at times, but standards tend to be relatively high. Some operators to try include these: **Alton's Dive Center** (✆ **504/425-3704;** www.diveinutila.com); **Bay Islands College of Diving** ★ (✆ **504/425-3291;** www.diveutila.com); **Captain Morgan's Dive Shop** (✆ **504/425-3349;** www.divingutila.com); **Deep Blue Divers** (✆ **504/425-3211;** www.deepblueutila.com); **Utila Dive Center** ★ (✆ **504/425-3350;** www.utiladivecenter.com); and **Utila Water Sports** (✆ **504/425-3264;** www.utilawatersports.com).

WHERE TO STAY
Expensive

Deep Blue ★ This award-winning PADI Resort is, like all other upscale accommodations in Utila, west of Sandy Bay and reached only by boat. The 10 deluxe rooms, all in one main building, are clean and contemporary without being overly posh. They have hardwood floors, handmade wood furniture, and pleasant, blue bedspreads and curtains, and feature art provided by Gunter Kordovsky, who runs Gunter's Driftwood gallery in town. Deep Blue, which has three great dive sites just off its shores, has long been one of the most respected dive operators on the island, and many of the guests here take advantage of all-inclusive dive packages. The resort is also heavily involved in the study of whale sharks, through their Whale Shark and Oceanic Research Center (see above for info).

West of Sandy Bay. ⓒ **504/425-2015.** Fax 504/425-3211. www.deepblueutila.com. 10 units. 1-week dive packages from L22,800 ($1,200) in high season. Rates include dives and 3 daily meals. MC, V. **Amenities:** Restaurant; bar; Internet in lobby; watersports equipment. *In room:* A/C, fan, fridge, Wi-Fi.

Laguna Beach ★ This 5.5-hectare (14-acre) luxury property, one of the few on the island, is just across the lagoon from Sandy Bay, and is reached only by boat. Apart from one two-bedroom beach cabin, accommodations are in single- or double-room bungalows that sit on stilts on the mangrove-shrouded waterfront. The medium-size bungalows were constructed using pine native to the island, and boast small porches over the water. The rooms are quite rustic, with simple furniture and no TVs, but there are other surprising extras like a weekly beach barbecue and a whale shark–shaped pool. The property has a very communal atmosphere, and contact with other guests is common. Plus, there's an astounding nine boats, including a luxury yacht (the *Utila Aggressor*) that is available for excursions and cocktail parties. Their diving equipment is among the best on the island, and most who visit the resort come here on some sort of dive package.

Located west of Sandy Bay. ⓒ **504/425-3239.** www.utila.com. 20 units. L2,660 ($140) low season double; 7-night all-inclusive dive packages start at L22,700 ($1,195) per person. MC, V. **Amenities:** Restaurant; bar; bikes; high-speed Internet (free, in lobby); laundry; pool. *In room:* A/C, fan.

Utopia Village ★★ Utopia Village is a type of accommodations that's somewhat new to Utila—a stylish boutique resort. It was created by a group of seven friends from the U.S., Canada, and the U.K. who have combined their individual talents to create this upscale hotel on the island. Rooms are spread out in several buildings and adorned with hardwood floors, contemporary furniture, and a decor that swings between Caribbean and Balinese. The overall feel of the beachfront property is hip and a tad New Age, but they don't go overboard and the result is more than pleasant. There's a meditation/yoga garden, a lounge where you can watch movies, and a pool table. One downside, or upside, of staying here is that the resort is a few miles from town and you can get back and forth only by a 20-minute boat ride.

On the western end of the island. ⓒ **504/3344-9387.** www.utopiautila.com. 19 units. Diving, fishing, and spa packages, rates range from $1,458–$1,541 for 7 nights, depending on package during high season; Minimum 4-night stay required. Children under 11 stay free in room with adult in summer season, pay 50% in high season. MC, V. **Amenities:** Bar; Internet in lobby; spa. *In room:* A/C, fan, fridge, Wi-Fi.

Moderate

Nightline Cabins ★★ 📖 If Peter Pan came to Utila, this is where the boy wonder would stay. The Nightline Cabins are among the most unique accommodations in Honduras (or Central America, for that matter). Every inch of the property is covered in some sort of whimsical decor or piece of art, mostly from flea market purchases in Los Angeles and markets in Central America. Each room is a wonderland of design, utilizing bright colors and mosaics and uncharacteristic layouts. Bathrooms have quirky details like curved glass walls and seashell soap trays. At night, the leafy trees and walkways that punctuate the property are lit up, guiding guests to the on-site **Jade Seahorse** restaurant (see "Where to Dine," below) and **Treetanic Bar** (see "Utila After Dark," below).

Calle Cola de Mico. ✆ **504/425-3270.** www.jadeseahorse.com. 6 units. L1,370 ($72) double; L950 ($50) single. MC, V. **Amenities:** Restaurant; bar. *In room:* A/C, Wi-Fi.

Utila Lodge ★★ Sometimes just called the Lodge, this small hotel spread out on stilts over East Harbour has been a staple on the Utila dive scene for a few decades. The worn cabins, built of island pine, are situated over the water, and all have screened-in porches where you can relax in a hammock and watch the sun sink into the harbor. Accommodations are not luxurious by any means, but are clean and comfortable, and have all the modern amenities that the high-end resorts on the west end of the island do. At the end of their huge dock (in fact, the entire resort is a dock of sorts), there's a Jacuzzi, which is a perfect place to end the day after a few dives. Many who stay here come in conjunction with the associated Bay Islands College of Diving that sits next door. As a result, the lodge offers facilities to the entire dive community of Utila, including a 24-hour trauma center equipped with the island's only hyperbaric recompression chamber.

West of the Municipal pier. ✆ **504/425-3143.** www.utilalodge.com. 8 units. L3,020 ($159) double Aug to mid-Jan; L3,600 ($189) double mid-Jan to May. 7-night dive packages start at L18,000 ($949) per person, including 3 daily meals, dives and equipment, airport transfers, and a bottle of wine. MC, V. **Amenities:** Restaurant; bar; Jacuzzi; watersports equipment. *In room:* A/C, fan, TV, Wi-Fi.

Inexpensive
Mango Inn ★★ 🍴 ☺ In the budget-to-midrange category, the Mango Inn, tucked away on a busy corner on Cola de Mico road, is without question the best option on the island. There are a variety of rooms spread around the leafy property, many of them facing the large pool area. The deluxe cabins have high ceilings, huge tiled showers, a small sitting room, and a porch, while the less expensive rooms all have similar amenities but are slightly smaller and older. Last but far from least, the huge Mango Cottage, next door to the hotel, comes with a full kitchen and family room, a screened veranda, two bedrooms, and fresh modern decor. Dive packages with two daily dives begin at L11,570 ($609) and are available via the Utila dive center, which has the same owners.

Calle Cola de Mico. ✆ **504/425-3335.** Fax 504/425-3327. www.mango-inn.com. 16 units. L855 ($45) double mid-Dec to mid-Aug and L1,045 ($55) mid-Aug to mid-Dec; L1,710-L2,090 ($90-$110) deluxe cabins; L2,470-L2,945 ($130-$155) Mango Cottage. MC, V. **Amenities:** Restaurant; bar; pool. *In room:* A/C, fan, TV.

WHERE TO DINE
Moderate
Café Mariposa INTERNATIONAL This eye-catching yellow restaurant is the first thing you'll see when you arrive at the Municipal Pier. Because of its elevated position, sticking out onto the harbor, there's probably not a better view of the water than from here. The menu is pricier than that of most of the restaurants in town—which isn't saying much—but it's worth the minor splurge for a decent meal. There's an eclectic menu of salads, grilled dishes, and seafood. Happy hour is from 5 to 7pm, just in time for sunset, and there's free Wi-Fi. Occasionally they sell walk-up ceviche, pizza by the slice, and *licuados* from the street too.

East of the Municipal pier. ✆ **504/425-2979.** Main courses L95-L190 ($5-$10). No credit cards. Wed-Sat 5-10pm; Sun 9am-noon.

Evelyn's BBQ ★ INTERNATIONAL   From the slow, chatty waiters to the Bob Marley and Jamaica memorabilia on the walls, this place exudes a definite island vibe. The barbecue dishes, mostly made on the street-side charcoal grill, like blackened mahimahi, grilled shrimp, and steaks, are well worth the price. When it rains, this creaky wooden building's street-side porch is the best place to watch the parade of tourists running through the mud, trying not to get wet.

West of the Municipal pier by Monkey Tail Rd. No phone. Main courses L95–L230 ($5–$12). MC, V. Daily noon–10pm.

La Piccola ITALIAN   Sometimes called Kate's Italian restaurant, La Piccola is an Italian restaurant that's actually run by Italians, and without question, it is the most elegant restaurant offering on Utila. Dining rooms are set around a candlelight patio and a leafy garden. Impressively, this restaurant suits any budget. They offer cheaper dishes aimed at budget travelers—a must on this island—like spaghetti and pesto, along with less backpackerish dishes like filet mignon. There's even a decent wine list with bottles from South America and Europe.

West of the Municipal pier, on Calle Principal. ✆ **504/425-3746.** Main courses L95–L290 ($5–$15). No credit cards. Wed–Sun 5–10pm.

Inexpensive

Bundu Café and Bakery INTERNATIONAL/BREAKFAST   Open for breakfast, lunch, and dinner, the Bundu is a top choice for hungry divers looking for a carbolicious meal. Crepes, banana pancakes, and omelets are top breakfast items, while half-pound burgers, chicken salad and avocado wraps, and pizzas make up the lunch and dinner menus. A big plus is the huge book exchange here, the largest on the island, as well as the free Wi-Fi and full bar.

East of the Municipal pier, on Calle Principal. ✆ **504/425-3557.** Main courses L60–L120 ($3–$6). No credit cards. Thurs–Mon 6am–10pm.

Driftwood Café ★★ INTERNATIONAL   This restaurant reaching over the water in Sandy Bay claims home-style Texas cooking as their line of attack, but the menu is more eclectic and well-rounded. Beer-battered fish and chips, barbecue ribs and chicken, T-bone steaks, and one hell of a fish stick are all on offer. Sundays mean smoked brisket, along with a daylong happy hour. To start the night off right, try their Chilled Monkey Balls, a potent shot made with homemade Kahlúa.

Calle Principal, east of Chepes Beach, Sandy Bay. ✆ **504/425-3366.** Main courses L75–L190 ($4–$10). No credit cards. Daily 8am–9:30pm.

Jade Seahorse ★ CARIBBEAN/INTERNATIONAL   This restaurant, set on the ground floor of the Nightline Cabins (see above), looks like your grandfather's toolshed after eating peyote. In keeping with the whimsical theme of the hotel, the restaurant is cluttered with woodcarvings, mosaics, ship wreckage, and whatever else can be hung on a wood beam. Thankfully, the food is not as off-the-wall, but dishes like their West Indian vegetarian chili or any of the seafood entrees slathered in coconut, citrus, or other creative sauces *are* delicious.

Calle Cola de Mico. ✆ **504/425-3270.** www.jadeseahorse.com. Main courses L95–L171 ($5–$9). No credit cards. Daily 6–10pm.

UTILA AFTER DARK

On any given night of the week, East Harbour in Utila is one of the most happening spots in Honduras. The scene is fueled by the dive crowd that often hits the bottle after stepping off the boat and has a dozen happy hours to choose from. The night starts early and ends late. Apart from the spots listed below, most restaurants and a smattering of smaller watering holes make for lively places to grab a Monkey La-la or frosty beer.

Bar in the Bush is the place to go on Wednesdays and Fridays, when everywhere else in town closes and the party moves up Cola de Mico road to this late-night bar. On any given night, you'll see DJs spinning the latest reggaeton and dance tracks to an already-toasted crowd. **Tranquila Bar ★** is where the party usually starts for the night. Set on a wooden dock over a water bar just west of the pier on Main Street, the dive boats often pull right beside the bar when they are done for the day to pull off their flippers and replenish everyone's fluids. Happy hour is from 3 to 7pm. **Treetanic Bar ★** is fashioned after a shipwreck and set high in a cluster of mango trees at the Jade Seahorse (see above), easily making for the most surreal setting in town. The nightly happy hour from 5 to 6pm has a loyal following of dive instructors and expats.

Guanaja ★

It's a funny little place, Guanaja. In many ways, it's the forgotten Bay Island. Christopher Columbus landed here on July 30, 1502, during his fourth and final voyage to the Americas, but he didn't stay long. Over the next few centuries the island became a favorite pirate hide-out and was visited by everyone from Henry Morgan and Blackbeard to the Barbarossa brothers. Today, most locals base themselves around the small key Bonacca Cay, while the main island remains practically untouched. The islanders, an amalgamation of culture if there ever was one, jump back and forth between Caribbean English and Spanish, and everyone seems to be related.

Time is told in hurricanes by the roughly 10,000 residents. In 1998, Hurricane Mitch's 285kmph (185-mph) winds blew over the island's once-dominant pine trees and knocked many of the stilted houses right off their stilts. Especially hard hit was Mangrove Bight, on the eastern end of the island, which was all but wiped off the map. A decade later, while nearby Roatán and Utila are experiencing rampant development, Guanaja has seen very little. Hotels and restaurants close on a frequent basis, but then are bought by someone else and reopened. It's a constant cycle. There is frequent talk of large luxury resorts opening here, but so far little action. Some development is occurring on the West End, mostly because North Americans and wealthy Hondurans are building vacation homes there, but for now Guanaja remains one of the most unspoiled islands in the Caribbean.

ESSENTIALS
Getting There
Guanaja's airstrip sits in the middle of the main island, across from Bonacca, beside a mangrove-lined canal. This is one of the most no-frills airports you will ever see, down to the baggage claim area, which is on the docks—bags are unloaded via rolling carts that come right from the plane. Once you have your luggage, you will need a boat transfer to your hotel (which should be able to arrange a boat for you), or a water taxi to Bonacca (water taxis wait for arriving planes).

Just one airline makes the 30-minute trip on an almost daily basis between Guanaja and La Ceiba, with connections to Tegucigalpa and San Pedro Sula. **Aerolineas Sosa** (© **504/453-4359;** www.aerolineasosahn.com) makes the trip daily at 10am and 4pm. Air taxi service **Lanhsa Airlines** (© **504/442-1283;** www.lanhsa.com) also makes trips to and from La Ceiba. **Guanaja Air** (© **901/507-5297** in the U.S.; www.guanajaair.com) is a charter option and is the only operation based on Guanaja. They charge L3,705 ($195) per person each way (two-person minimum). Passengers can buy tickets at any of the airline offices on Bonacca, right near the taxi dock. (You can't buy a ticket at Guanaja's airport.)

Unlike Roatán and Utila, Guanaja lacks regular ferry service from the mainland. In 2007 a very slow, no-frills ferry service on the *Bimini Breeze* began between Trujillo and Guanaja, running twice a week—from Trujillo on Tuesdays and Sundays at 4pm and from Guanaja on Mondays and Fridays at 9am—though at press time it wasn't running. You can buy tickets directly on the boat for L650 ($34), or call © **504/987-0875** for reservations.

Orientation

Guanaja lies approximately 70km (43 miles) from the North Coast of Honduras and just 12km (7½ miles) east of Roatán. It is the tallest of the Bay Islands and is almost completely covered by hills. The western tip is cut off from the rest of the island by a small canal, "the Cut," running just beside the airport. Bonacca town, the center of nearly all services and the most populated part of the island, isn't actually on the main island, but is off a small cay just off the south coast. There are no roads except one small stretch that runs a few kilometers between the settlements of Savannah and Mangrove Bights, on the eastern end of the island.

Getting Around

Even though regular **water taxi** service prices are high, because of the cost of fuel, water taxis are one of the best ways to get around the island. Standard prices are listed at the airport and on the ferry dock at Bonacca town. You can generally flag down a taxi while waiting on any dock. There is one regular **ferry** service from Bonacca to Savannah Bight on the *Sava*, which runs back and forth several times a day. This is by far the cheapest way to get around the island (L20/$1 each way). Apart from the occasional shop that sells basic supplies, almost all facilities of any kind can be found in Bonacca town. The town's only cybercafé is on the main street turning left from the ferry dock, as is the bank **Banco Atlántida** (© **504/453-4262**), which exchanges currency and traveler's checks, and several small pharmacies. For phone service, make a right from the docks to the **Hondutel** office (© **504/455-1389**).

WHAT TO SEE & DO

Bonacca town ★★★, a short ride from the main island, is the most populous part of Guanaja and one of the most unique communities in the Bay Islands and the Caribbean. It's also known as Bonacca Cay and by locals as, simply, the Cay. Though the vibe remains refreshingly laid-back, there's a desire to clean up and begin attracting more tourists to what many call jokingly the "Venice of Honduras."

The population in Bonacca is mostly made up of settlers from the Cayman Islands who came in the 1830s, with a growing number of Latinos from the mainland and a scattering of expats. Apart from the many stilted pastel houses that branch out all across the water and line the canals, there are three small guesthouses, a couple of churches, and a handful of shops and tiny restaurants. The town is divided into small clusters with silly nicknames like firetown, honkytown, funkytown, and Vietnam. But perhaps because of its overall small size, Bonacca is an extremely tightly knit—and gossipy—place. If you're walking from one end to the other, someone on the other end will likely have already heard about you by the time you arrive.

OUTDOOR ACTIVITIES

Bonefishing is a popular activity in Guanaja and can be done just offshore all around the island. A world record for largest bonefish was set here not long ago. Every hotel

TOP SCUBA diving SITES IN GUANAJA

- **Mestizo Reef:** The life-size statue of Christopher Columbus at this site was erected in 2006 in honor of the 500-year anniversary of Columbus discovering Guanaja. There's also a statue of Lenca hero Lempira, Spanish cannons, vases, and 16th-century relics.

- **Vertigo:** The drastic drop-off—from 11m (36 ft.) to almost 48m (157 ft.)—on this section of the barrier wall is teeming with life. Black-and-white crinoids can be spotted here, along with deep-water gorgonians, barrel sponges, grouper, and trumpetfish.

- **Don Enrique Wreck:** This classic Guanaja dive centers on a sunken shrimp boat at about 27m (90 ft.) of water, although the mast stands upward to about 15m (50 ft.) below the surface. Lots of colorful fish circle the site and spotted eagle rays are frequently seen.

- **Jado Trader Wreck:** This is one of Guanaja's most visited sites and one of the most-talked-about wrecks in the Caribbean. The sunken freighter sits in 33m (110 ft.) of water on a sandy shelf beside a barrier wall. It's a deep descent, even for advanced divers, but the rewards—morays, grouper, yellowtail, and the occasional hammerhead shark—are well worth it.

can offer a trip. Deep-sea charters frequently troll for marlin, tuna, wahoo, mahimahi, mackerel, and barracuda. **Coral Bay** (☎ 866/266-7974; www.coralbay.ca) has bonefishing, fly-fishing, and deep-sea charters around the island for around L4,750 ($250) for a half-day charter. **Fly Fish Guanaja** (☎ 970/708-0626; www.flyfish guanaja.com) has all-inclusive 7-day saltwater fly-fishing trips based out of their private lodge on one of the cayes, including round-trip airfare, for L57,000 ($3,000).

Being the most mountainous of the Bay Islands does have its advantages. Several kilometers of **hiking trails** can be found crisscrossing the tiny island, mostly from the northern side. The **Big Gully Waterfall** is a short hike from Michael's Rock on the north side of the island, through fields of avocado, coco plums, and banana trees. The falls have a small pool at the bottom, but it isn't very deep unless there's a good rain the day before. From the falls you can continue to the highest point on the island at 408m (1,340 ft.). As with everywhere else in the Bay Islands, tourism in Guanaja is oriented toward **diving.** Every resort on Guanaja has dive masters and boats and offers packages for divers by the week and sometimes month. The reef here isn't affected by the island runoff like in Utila and Roatán, but some damage has occurred from pollution from Bonacca and Savannah Bight. Still, Guanaja's reef is in pretty good shape and sees very few divers compared with the other islands. Every resort on the island has its own dive outfit and offers accommodations and dive packages. Diving without a room is generally more expensive and costs about L760 to L950 ($40–$50). Both **Nautilus** (☎ 952/953-4124; www.usdivetravel. com) and **Coral Bay** (☎ 866/266-7974; www.coralbay.ca) offer dive packages and dives without accommodations.

California-based operator **Half Moon Bay Kayak CO** (☎ 650/773-6101 in the U.S.; www.hmbkayak.com) runs 8-day sea-kayaking trips in Guanaja based at Graham's

Place for L34,200 ($1,800) per person, not including airfare. Trips are led by Doug Connor, who has operated Caribbean Kayak Adventures in Guanaja since 1998, and use a motorized support boat so kayakers can return to the lodge each night and start from a new location the following day. **West Peak Inn** (see below) also runs trips that begin and end at their cabins, though they camp on beaches the rest of the week.

If Caribbean crowds turn you off, but you still want crystal-clear water and coral reefs, Guanaja is the place for you. Miles of white beaches are backed by untouched lush green hills. The best beaches are at the northern side of the island near **Michael's Rock** or at the **West End** near the West Peak resort. Smaller strips of sand can be found elsewhere, including on the cayes that are sprinkled off the southern coast out from Savannah Bight.

WHERE TO STAY
Expensive

Villa at Dunbar Rock ★★ Few hotels can lay claim to a setting so dramatic— this chic white house sits on Dunbar's Rock, a picturesque location off Sandy Bay that also happens to have caused much controversy—city officials sold this rock, a local landmark, to a hotel developer and were chased off Bonacca Cay as a result. The property resembles something better suited for the island of Capri or a Dalí painting than the Caribbean backwater. The four guest rooms are clean, but fairly sparse and basic with wood furniture, tile floors, and fans. Apart from the small deck that leads to the dock and a small garden, you are mostly limited to the inside of the hotel (which boasts an honor bar and dining room) and a few balconies.

Sandy Bay, Guanaja. ✆ **952/953-4124.** www.villaondunbarrock.com. 4 units. L22,750 ($1,197) per person, per week, which includes transport, meals, diving, and fishing. No credit cards. **Amenities:** Dining room; laundry service. *In room:* Fan, no phone.

MODERATE

Coral Bay Dive Resort ★ This small collection of seaside-facing cabins on the hillside across from Bonacca Cay is set back on a corner of the main island between the airport and Sandy Bay, tucked away among stilted houses and empty green hills. The private stretch of beach is accompanied by a small waterfall and trickling stream that runs throughout the property and provides an elegant soundtrack for sleep. The 12 large and airy wood cabins are clean and cozy, with satellite TVs, modern tiled bathrooms, and electric showers. There's a dive master on-site and they have a decent kayak to use if desired. Seven-night packages (L19,152/$1,008 per person) include island tours, hikes, sunset cruise, diving, bone and deep-sea fishing, horseback riding, and a day trip to Bonacca.

South side of the main island. ✆ **866/266-7974.** www.coralbay.ca. 12 units. Cabins L3,040 ($160) a night for divers and L2,736 ($144) for nondivers during high season and holidays. Rates include 3 daily meals and airport transfers. MC, V. **Amenities:** Dining room; bar; pool. *In room:* A/C (in some), satellite TV, fridge.

Island House   This small wooden hotel on the northwestern side of the island is owned and operated by Bo Bush, a local islander descended from English pirates, and his family. Bush has a wealth of knowledge about the island and even gives informal barhops and tours of Bonacca. The property has one main house and two small guesthouses, all set into the pine-covered hillside. Rooms have Spanish tile floors, simple wooden furniture, and balconies, as well as fans and satellite TV. There's good snorkeling and diving right off the beach and you're free to use the hotel's kayaks to paddle around nearby Michael's Rock. The dock bar is a good gathering place for the few locals who live on this side of the island.

Michael's Rock, Guanaja. ✆ **504/991-0913.** Fax 504/453-4146. www.bosislandhouse.com. 5 units. L1,425 ($75) double. Rates include 3 meals, welcome cocktail, and airport transfers. 7-day dive packages from L13,300 ($700). MC, V. **Amenities:** Restaurant; bar; high-speed Internet (free in lobby). *In room:* Satellite TV.

West Peak Inn   The Inn is on the northwestern tip of Guanaja, right on 4km (2½ miles) of pristine turquoise water and white sands. The property is quite small and laid-back—if you like lots of noise and people, this isn't the place. The handful of wood buildings forms a small compound with a dock, restaurant, and storage rooms, along with the four solar-powered cabins. All have private bathrooms—the water doesn't get warm until the afternoon, though—and screened-in patios. They're all just off the beach, one of the best in all of Guanaja. There are a few trails through the banana, mango, and pineapple plantations that run up the hillsides for you to explore, plus you can use their sit-on-top kayaks, snorkels, and fishing gear if diving isn't your thing. They'll also run weeklong kayaking trips that begin and end at the hotel—you'll camp on beaches the rest of the time.

West End, Guanaja. ✆ **504/3377-6114,** or 831/786-0406 in the U.S. www.vena.com/wpi. 4 units. L3,500 ($190) double. Rates include 3 daily meals, snorkel gear, dock fishing, and airport transfers. Children's discount available. AE, MC, V when booked through a travel agent. **Amenities:** Restaurant; bar. *In room:* Fan.

Inexpensive

Hotel Miller   There are three small guesthouses on Guanaja and other informal rooms for rent, but Hotel Miller is by far the best and the only one that actually attempts to appear like a working hotel. The two-story house sits smack-dab in the middle of Bonacca town, a few minutes from the taxi dock. For the Bay Islands, the place is far from idyllic—it resembles Grandma's house with its lace curtains and collection of beat-up Victorian furniture, rooms are dingy and worn, there's no ocean view, and not much light comes in from the small windows. Still, the place is clean and the price is the best you will find in Guanaja. For those on very tight budgets, ask about the even cheaper rooms without TV or air-conditioning.

Bonacca town, Guanaja. ✆ **504/453-4527.** Fax 504/453-4202. 29 units. L600 ($32) double. No credit cards. **Amenities:** Dining room; Internet; laundry service. *In room:* A/C (in some), satellite TV, no phone.

WHERE TO DINE

Graham's Place ★ SEAFOOD   On a small cay a short taxi ride away from Bonacca or Savannah Bight, Graham's Place is by far the most attractive restaurant in Guanaja, primarily because of its sweeping views of the main island, and it's also a major party location. The menu at the thatched-roof, open-air restaurant is defined by whatever's fresh in the cooler, usually fish caught that day. It also features sandwiches, chicken, and meat dishes, along with a long list of tropical drinks and beers. The dock area where the restaurant resides functions as an aquarium of sorts, since there's a small pen keeping the tropical fish, stingrays, and sea turtles—bought so they wouldn't be eaten by the locals—from swimming away. The owner, Graham, who hails from the Cayman Islands, also has a few apartments for rent.

Graham's Cay, Guanaja. ✆ **305/407-1568.** www.grahamsplacehonduras.com. Main courses L135-L300 ($7-$15). No credit cards. Daily 7am-10pm.

Manati GERMAN   This German-run eatery in Sandy Bay is one of the best all-around restaurants anywhere on the island. They serve mostly German specialties like weiner schnitzel and even German beer, as well as grilled fish and typical island plates based on the latest catch. The place fills up on the weekends.

Sandy Bay, Guanaja. ✆ **504/408-9830.** www.manati-hn.com. Main courses L115-L350 ($6-$18). No credit cards. Tues-Sun noon-10pm (hours vary).

Mexi Treats MEXICAN   The only Mexican or remotely Latin place on Guanaja is this favorite of hungry divers, who often stop here to refuel with lunch, and other tourists staying on the island. It's the only true fast-food joint in the area, with a menu of *chilaquiles, baleadas,* nachos, burritos, and burgers.

Bonacca. ✆ **504/453-4170.** Main courses L55-L110 ($3-$6). No credit cards. Mon-Fri 8am-1:30pm and 6-9:30pm; Sat-Sun 6am-10pm.

LA MOSQUITIA

La Mosquitia is the largest tract of virgin tropical rainforest in Central America and the Northern Hemisphere; it's a mini-Amazon of sorts. While it covers the entire northeastern part of the country, the region is only sparsely populated with villages of indigenous groups like the Pech, Tawahka, Garífuna, and Miskitos, as well as mainland Mestizos. The region has five natural reserves: the Río Plátano Biosphere Reserve, the Tawahka Anthropological Reserve, the Patuca National Park, the Cruta Caratasca Wildlife Refuge, and the Rus Rus Biological Reserve. Many of the zones are practically untouched and packed with rare wildlife of every sort. Yet there is not a luxury ecolodge in sight. Apart from a few ingenious tour companies, the region is almost unexplored and just waiting for a tourism boom. If you are looking for an adventure or a place well off the beaten path, you've got it.

This region was inhabited as far back as 1000 B.C. by Chibcha-speaking Indians who migrated here from South America, which over time divided into separate indigenous groups such as the Pechs and Tawahka. Christopher Columbus, the first European to visit, stopped briefly on his fourth voyage in 1502. Spanish missionaries were the first to explore the region, though it took them nearly a century of rebellion from the tribes to establish any sort of permanent settlement. (It didn't help that pirates frequently raided Spanish ships laden with riches from South America, which deterred further settlements.) Government control over the region has been loose at best; it wasn't until the 1950s that any sort of formal governance began to take shape here, but at times lawlessness still reigns supreme, simply because the region is too big and sparse to properly patrol.

While the tourist infrastructure is slowly improving, it is still relatively small and in many cases all but nonexistent. Phones are rare, which makes hotel reservations nearly impossible to make, though there is always a room somewhere even if it means a hammock in a family's hut. Transportation between each village can take a day of waiting until a boat or plane fills up. Still, most of the towns are within the confines of the **Río Plátano Biosphere Reserve** or a short distance from it, so tours—either set up in advance with **La Ruta Moskitia** (www.larutamoskitia.com) or a less formal one in the spur of the moment—are quite easy. Most visitors, unless on a multiday tour, will base themselves in Las Marías, Raista/Belén, or Brus Laguna and take day tours from there. Apart from Puerto Lempira, which is on the far corner of La Mosquitia and reached by plane, all towns are within a 30-minute to 6-hour boat ride from one another.

Essentials

GETTING THERE

Aerolineas Sosa (☎ 504/445-1154; www.aerolineassosa.com) flies to Brus Laguna three times per week, leaving at 10am and returning at 11am. Sosa also flies to Puerto Lempira from Monday to Friday at 8am, returning at 11am. Flights are often canceled due to weather and lack of passengers. **Sami Airlines** (☎ 504/442-2565 in La Ceiba, or 433-8031 in Brus Laguna) occasionally flies from La Ceiba to Brus Laguna or Belén. The runway at Palacios, which was once the main access point in the region, is currently closed due to lack of repair. From each airstrip you should have no problem walking to town.

Along the North Coast of Honduras, irregular cargo boat service links the coast of La Mosquitia to the rest of the country. The docks at **Puerto Castilla** are the best place to get the next boat, which generally leaves at least once per week. It is possible to make it to La Mosquitia by bus, although if your plan is to go during the rainy season (Oct–Jan), don't expect this to work. From Tocoa, just south of Trujillo, you can catch a pickup truck, or *paila,* to Batalla leaving from the Municipal Market daily between 7 and 11am. The ride is 4 to 5 hours and costs L400. In Batalla, there will be boats waiting to take you the additional 1- to 2-hour journey to Palacios, Raista, and Belén for roughly L200.

GETTING AROUND

Traveling independently in La Mosquitia isn't cheap or easy—it's much easier to get around here with a tour operator. Though options are still extremely limited and you should always expect to wait around a few days here and there, your best method of independent transport is by water. Along the coast you can almost always find a boat to take you from one community to the next. Often the locals expect tourists to hire a local boatman for a private boat and will stay mum on information on when the next boat leaves. Since regular schedules aren't posted, you just have to cross your fingers and hope you speak to the right person. There is direct boat service, priced per boat, between most major destinations, as follows: Palacios to Raista/Belén (L800; 1½ hr.), Raista/Belén to Las Marias (L3,000; 5 hr.), Raista/Belén to Brus Laguna (L1,500; 2 hr.), and Brus Laguna to Las Marias (L3,500; 6 hr.). If your Spanish is good, ask around at the docks for *colectivo* boats, which are considerably cheaper.

Sami Airlines (☎ 504/442-2565 in La Ceiba, or 433-8031 in Brus Laguna) can get you from one town to the next via four-person planes. They have offices in Ahuas, Palacios, Belén, Brus Laguna, and Puerto Lempira. Air-taxi service **Lanhsa Airlines** (☎ 504/442-1283; www.lanhsa.com) also makes trips between La Ceiba and Puerto Lempira.

TOUR OPERATORS

If you have a limited amount of time or a set schedule for traveling in La Mosquitia, a trip with a tour operator is your only choice. Most have several tours available that will combine multiday rafting trips down the Río Plátano or Río Patuca, visits to indigenous villages, wildlife-watching, hiking, and stays at private campgrounds and lodges. They make use of planes and have arrangements with local transportation organizations to make sure your trip moves smoothly. Trips can last from 3 days to several weeks. Some operators to try include the following:

- **La Ruta Moskitia** ★★ (℗ **504/443-1276;** www.larutamoskitia.com), a 100% community-owned and -operated tourism initiative, offers both day trips from Raista, Belén, and Brus Laguna, and multiday tours through the region that have been applauded by the international media. Both land- and air-based tours are available. They list upcoming tours you can join on their website (thus reducing the price by being in a group) and offer tips to help plan an independent trip. Check their website for news and updates in the region.

- **La Moskitia Ecoaventuras** ★ (℗ **504/440-2124;** www.lamoskitiaecoaventuras. com) has 8- to 12-day rafting expeditions on the Tawahka Asangni Biosphere Reserve and custom bird-watching tours throughout La Mosquitia.

- **Omega Tours** (℗ **504/440-0334;** www.omegatours.info) has a wide variety of tours from La Ceiba to La Mosquitia, including 8- to 12-day trips on the Río Patuca, a 13-day trip on the Río Plátano, and many shorter trips to see petroglyphs and isolated villages.

Western La Mosquitia

BATALLA

While it has always played second fiddle to nearby Palacios on the other side of Bacalar Lagoon, safety concerns and lack of tour opportunities have finally put this lively Garífuna village on the radar. They have been developing their own tourism programs with the help of La Ruta Moskitia and given a much-needed infusion of culture to this frontier area of La Mosquitia. Apart from hammocks strung in rustic family huts, there are no accommodations. Most visitors opt to stay in Palacios or head deeper into the region, while hanging out here for the day. The town is quite small, just a cluster of houses and huts on a sandy bank.

Outside of watching the local women make casaba bread, there are two tours the community has set up for travelers, which can be arranged on arrival, though it is better to set them up ahead with La Ruta Moskitia. The first is a 2-hour cultural activity that takes place in the evening, in which the 20-odd-member village folkloric dance and drum group perform **Garífuna songs and dances,** followed by a traditional Garífuna meal (generally seafood soup and coconut and ginger bread).

The second, a **boat tour** in Laguna Bacalar, has long been the most popular tour out of Palacios, where it can be arranged as well, though the guides tend to be more enthusiastic from Batalla. You'll travel by motorized canoe through canals through the mangrove forests that line the edges of the lagoon while looking for birds, monkeys (howler and white-faced), and the endangered Caribbean manatee.

By road, you can reach Batalla from the town of Tocoa by *paila,* or pickup truck (L500). Trucks leave from the municipal market in Tocoa (not far from Trujillo) at around 7am to noon for the 5-hour ride, though if you want to continue on to Raista/ Belén, you will want to get on the first truck. From Batalla you can catch the *colectivo* boat for the 1- or 2-hour ride—depending on water levels—to Palacios (L250), where boat service to other parts of La Mosquitia can be found.

PALACIOS

The mixed *mestizo* and Miskito town of Palacios, the second-largest settlement in La Mosquitia, sits on the opposite side of the Bacalar lagoon from Batalla and is no longer the access point for travel in La Mosquitia because there is no longer a landing strip and partly because of safety concerns. Drug runners coming from South America often hang out here, and it's becoming known for lawlessness.

There are a few basic hotels in Palacios such as **Hotel Moskitia** (📞 **504/978-7397;** L400 double), which has a small restaurant and 10 rooms with private bathrooms, fans, and TVs. Slightly larger and more rustic **Hotel Río Tinto** (📞 **504/966-6465;** L150), on the waterfront, has 15 rooms with private bathrooms and a simple *comedor.*

Most arrive here from Tocoa via Batalla (see above) in the morning and catch the connecting *colectivo* boat to Raista/Belén (2½ hr.; L200). It is also possible to hire an *expreso* boat—ask around for Dona Anna Marmol to set something up—to take you to Raista/Belén (1½ hr.; L800).

A service between Palacios and Brus Laguna began in late 2008 and at press time was still up and running and hopefully will continue service. The boat, the *Miss Liseth,* owned and operated by Miguel Guzman (📞 **504/9762-5846;** L400), departs Brus Laguna at 2:30am on Monday, Wednesday, and Friday and arrives at 5am. The boat departs for the return to Brus Laguna at 4pm and arrives at 7pm.

Laguna de Ibans
PLAPLAYA
This Garífuna village at the western edge of the Laguna de Ibans and the Caribbean is best known for creating the Sea Turtle Conservation Project, which protects the green, loggerhead, and leatherback turtles that nest on the nearby beaches every year. Tours for the beaches depart during the evenings from February to September to help spot egg-laying turtles and nests. There are just a few very basic accommodations and *comedores,* all in family homes, in Plaplaya.

As in Batalla (see above), if you have a group together you can arrange a Garífuna cultural night with a traditional meal. More unique to Plaplaya, though, is a seasonal grass-roots conservation project. From April to July, the village becomes involved with the **Sea Turtle Conservation Project ★★**. With the help of volunteers, everyone joins together to help protect the loggerhead and leatherback turtles that nest on Plaplaya's beaches annually. Duties involve collecting the eggs, which hatch 3 months later, and reburying them in a protected sanctuary before poachers and animals get to them. Ask in town for Dona Patrocinia for more information.

The boat between Raista/Belén and Palacios will stop in Plaplaya, though be sure to tell the boat driver ahead of time. Pickup trucks also drive to Raista/Belén on occasion.

RAISTA/BELEN ★★
These two connected Miskito towns sit on a thin strip of land between the Laguna de Ibas and the Caribbean. If it wasn't for the grassy airstrip, often used for soccer games or grazing horses, you wouldn't realize you had left one town and entered the next. Flowering bushes and fruit trees decorate the colored little plank-board houses with neat little yards. They are carved out of the fields, mangroves, and forests and connected by a web of footpaths and one sandy road that runs parallel to the beach. Raista is slightly more compact and has a greater concentration of trees and shade than Belén. A growing number of tour options, proximity to Las Marias, a steady number of incoming flights, and better boat traffic have recently made these tiny villages a center of tourism in La Mosquitia, though facilities are still quite rustic. Electricity runs only part of the day and via personal generators at some houses at

other times. There are just a few basic *comedores* and little shops with basic supplies, all of which are run out of family homes.

Getting There & Getting Around

To hire a boatman to take you elsewhere in La Mosquitia, ask the Bodden family in Raista at Raista Ecolodge or Mario Miller in Belén at Pawanka Beach Cabins. Prices, while they fluctuate often depending on gas prices, were, at last check, as listed here: Raista/Belén to Palacios (1½ hr.), L800; to Las Marias (5 hr.), L4,000 round-trip with a 3-day wait; and to Brus Laguna (2 hr.), L1,500, from one to four people. A *colectivo* **boat** (2 hr.; L250) leaves almost daily from Río Plátano, a small town where the river meets the ocean, to Brus Laguna. You'll have to catch an early-morning pickup from the main road in Raista/Belén or walk for 2 hours to get to Río Plátano for the departure. Speak with Melissa Boden at Raista Ecolodge for details.

Sami Airlines (© **504/433-8031** in Brus Laguna) has sporadic flights to and from Belén to Brus Laguna, La Ceiba, and elsewhere in La Mosquitia. When there are enough passengers, a plane comes. It's as simple as that. The Sami airline office sits right off the runway in Belén.

What to See & Do

While they are rarely used except for walking by the locals, the seemingly endless, sand dollar–rich, wide, white sand **beaches** that run nearly the entire coast of La Mosquitia are one of the country's overlooked gems. Sand flies and mosquitoes are a slight concern, though they are not as bad as on the Bay Islands.

The most popular tour, especially for those not going to Las Marias, is to hire a boatman to take you to explore the wildlife-infested **creeks of Parú, Ilbila,** and **Banaka** (L1,500; for up to three people), where there are good opportunities to spot birds, deer, paca, and monkeys. In the evenings a favorite excursion is to go **crocodile spotting** (L600; for up to three people) in the small canals and mangroves near Belén. You'll likely spot plenty of bird life too during the 1- to 2-hour trip.

As in nearby Garífuna villages, Raista/Belén loves to put on a show for visitors who ask for the cultural activity ahead of time. During the night, a local women's group performs a series of **traditional Miskito songs and dances** (L850 per group), passed down for generations. A traditional dinner is also served.

A basic 4- to 5-hour **jungle survival course** (L600; for up to three people) can be taken from Raista as well. A local guide will teach you how to find food and water, identify medicinal plants and teach you their uses, and show you how to find your way in the jungle.

For all activities, contact Melissa Bodden at Raista Ecolodge, Mario Miller at Pawanka Beach Cabanas, or La Ruta Moskitia before arrival. Prices are dependent on the number of participants.

Where to Stay & Dine

Built in 2006 and run by the friendly Bodden family, which spearheads tourism in Raista, the **Raista Ecolodge ★★** (© **504/408-4986;** www.larutamoskitia.com; L360 double) has eight cabins and is the number-one choice for passing tour groups. Built in a traditional style on stilts with wood plank floors and walls and a thatched roof, the spacious rooms have been covered in screen in the open spaces to keep the bugs out, though every bed (a single and a double in every room) is still topped with a mosquito net. The cold-water bathrooms are shared, but the toilets are modern and kept clean. The excellent kitchen will prepare all meals for you (L50–L65 per meal).

Mario Miller's **Pawanka Beach Cabañas** (✆ **504/433-8150;** www.larutamoskitia. com; L360 double) are a 10-minute walk past the airstrip bordering the beach near a small wetland area—you need to cross a creaky wooden bridge to get on the property. The three-stilted *cabañas* a stone's throw from the Caribbean are the best accommodations in Belén. The rooms are of similar quality to those at the Raista Ecolodge, with beds with comfortable mattresses and mosquito nets, shared modern bathrooms, and no electricity. Basic meals (L50–L65) are served out of the kitchen.

Reserva de la Bíosfera del Río Plátano ★★★

This is one of the most astounding natural reserves in the world. The Río Plátano Biosphere Reserve, named a UNESCO World Heritage Site in 1980, is home to more than 525,000 hectares (1.3 million acres) of wetlands, beaches, pine savannas, tropical forests, and rivers. Here indigenous communities of the Pech and Miskito live much the way they have for hundreds of years. The reserve is home to some of the highest levels of biodiversity anywhere in the world, and nearly 400 species of birds have been recorded here, including great green and scarlet macaws, harpy eagles, jabirus, toucans, kingfishers, the aplomado falcon, and numerous migratory species. The lagoons and rivers are home to manatees, southern river otters, caimans, and several rare species of sea turtle. On land, you'll find Baird's tapirs, jaguars, giant anteaters, spider monkeys, white-tailed deer, and white-lipped peccaries, among others. While a tourism infrastructure is lacking and there isn't even a visitor center or park admission fee, community-based ecotourism programs are growing in Las Marias and Raista/Belén.

It's easiest to visit the reserve via a guided tour, though coming on your own is not unrealistic. The easiest way is to make your way to Las Marias or Brus Laguna, both inside the northern end of the park, where you can find lodging and arrange for tours deeper into the wilderness. To get the most out of the reserve and increase your chances to see wildlife, a rafting trip down the Río Plátano with La Moskitia Ecoaventuras is a must. The best time to visit is during the dry seasons, which run from February to May and from August to November. The rainy season, from November to January, can make travel here difficult. Regardless of when you come, it's almost certain you'll encounter a short downpour.

LAS MARIAS ★★

Las Marias is, traditionally, a Pech community on the Río Plátano, near the highlands of the rainforest. It is the village farthest into the Biosphere Reserve from the coast and the base for most to explore the reserve. Community-based tourism programs, with the help of international NGOs, have trained more than 150 workers in tourism (124 secondary guides, 24 primary guides, and 7 naturalists) out of 106 Pech and Moskito families. A variety of tours exploring the wilderness, hikes to nearby peaks, wildlife-watching, and community-based programs and basic tourist facilities have helped make Las Marias one of the most successful cultural and natural conservation projects in Latin America.

One boat landing near several guesthouses, a couple of churches, a small *pulperia,* and a school clustered together in a general area mixed with patches of wilderness are often considered the village of Las Marias. That is half true. The term *village* is applied quite loosely here. There is not exactly a center of town, but rather clusters of thatched-roof wooden houses scattered along both sides of the sloping banks of the Río Plátano for several kilometers.

Las Marias is most easily reached by motorboat from Raista/Belén or Brus Laguna, though it can be reached by rafting downriver from Olancho. The price isn't cheap: L4,000 round-trip per boat for the 5- or 6-hour ride from Raista with a 3-day wait. The price is fixed, so there is no use bargaining.

What to See & Do

Over the past few years the community has been developing numerous new tours and hiking routes, all the while training guides and naturalists. They have become highly organized, as you will come to find out. Upon your arrival you will be approached by the *sacaguia,* a head guide elected every 6 months to be the "go to" person for visiting groups and assigning guides. He will handle the money, arrange your tours and walk you through them, and answer any questions you might have. For every tour you book, the *sacaguia* will get a small coordination fee (L100) from the group. He'll also ask for a small donation for repairs and trail maintenance. It is not obligatory, but a L50-to-L100 donation is a nice gesture and definitely appreciated. Prices per tour depend on the number of guides required—which get a per-day fee—multiplied by the number of guides. Primary guides receive L250 per day, while secondary guides receive L150 per day. At the end a small tip, 10% or so, is suggested. Keep in mind that these prices are per group and are going toward a community that has chosen to preserve the wilderness around them rather than tear it down.

The most popular tour is the **Pipante canoe ride to the Walpaulban Sirpi petroglyphs** (two to three guides). The 1-day excursion involves traveling upriver from Las Marias for 1 to 2 hours to the famous ancient petroglyphs carved into rocks right in the Río Plátano. A second set of petroglyphs, **Walpaulban Tara,** can also be visited on a 2-day trip (three guides) that has a similar itinerary as Walpaulban Sirpi, which you will also see, but includes spending the night in a small *hospedaje* at the start of the trail.

There are several good hikes offered here: the 3-day round-trip hike (three guides plus canoe) to the jagged point of **Pico Dama,** the 2-day hike (two guides) to **Pico Baltimore,** the 1-day hike (one guide) to **Pico de Zapote,** and the 2-day hike (three guides plus canoe) to **Cerro Mico,** which doesn't face any steep inclines, though it does cover a mix of flat and rolling terrain and is set mostly in thick jungle. There's also the **Village Trail loop** (L250), which you can easily do on your own if you just want to walk and have no desire to learn about medicinal plants. The entire circuit should only take a couple of hours.

Where to Stay

There are a half-dozen simple guesthouses in Las Marias, though the majority of visitors stay at the two on the river next to the boat landing. **Doña Rutilla** is the only place in town with a generator and a public telephone and can accommodate the greatest number of visitors—20—in her six-stilted, thatched-roof cabins. Each room has several beds, with comfortable mattresses and mosquito nets. The toilet, like all others in town, is an outhouse with bucket flush. Meals can be prepared for a small fee. **Doña Justa** next door is quite similar, though the rooms are a bit bigger, have porches with hammocks, and overlook a nice flower garden. If either of these is full, you can follow the village trail to reach another three small guesthouses with similar facilities. Rooms run from L80 to L120 per person.

Brus Laguna

Brus Laguna—the inland body of water, not the town—is the second-largest lagoon in La Mosquitia. It was originally named Brewer's Lagoon, after the pirate "Bloody

Brewer," who used the inlet as his hide-out. The lagoon is unique in that during the rainy season it is filled with fresh water as the Sigre, Twas, and Patuca rivers collectively flow into it, but is filled with salt water the rest of the year.

BRUS LAGUNA

Brus Laguna is a genuine frontier town, mostly Moskito, where horses outnumber cars in the small grid of dirt streets and is surrounded by a sea of swamp, mangroves, and savanna. The town clusters around a few blocks close to the covered main pier, but urban sprawl has added a smattering of houses and cattle ranches as far as 5km (3 miles) out into the wilderness. Electricity runs only from 9am to noon and 6 to 9pm, though several shops and hotels have generators.

The small **general store,** at the corner just up from the pier, is your one-stop shop for almost anything. Basic supplies, airline tickets, hotel information, simple meds, snacks, fishing tackle, money exchange, and transportation information are all found here. There is a **Hondutel** on the main street where you can make international phone calls. A small shop beside Hotel Ciudad Blanca is the best **cybercafé** in town, and they can do international phone calls as well.

Getting There

Brus Laguna's small airstrip sits a few kilometers from the town center. Just follow the main drag straight through the fields and ranches. You can buy tickets for either airline at the general store just up from the pier on the right. The owner will also give you a lift to the airstrip for L50. **Aerolineas Sosa** (www.aerolineassosa.com) flies to Brus Laguna three times per week from La Ceiba, leaving at 10am and returning at 11am. **Sami Airlines** (© 504/433-8031 in Brus Laguna) has several flights a week to Raista/Belén and La Ceiba, as well as on occasion to Puerto Lempira and Ahuas.

Expreso **boats** can be hired to go to Raista/Belén (2 hr.; L1,500; one to four people) and Las Marias (5–6 hr.; L5,000 and the boat will wait up to 3 days for your return) There is also a *colectivo* boat (2 hr.; L250) that leaves almost daily from Brus Laguna to Barra Platano, a small town where the river meets the ocean, where you can walk for 2 hours or hitch a ride to Raista/Belén. There is also a boat service between Palacios and Brus Laguna on the *Miss Liseth,* owned and operated by **Miguel Guzman** (© 504/9762-5846; L400). The boat departs from Brus Laguna at 2:30am (yes, that time is correct!) on Monday, Wednesday, and Friday and arrives at 5am. It departs for the return trip at 4pm and arrives at 7pm.

What to See & Do

History buffs will appreciate a visit to the English fort on **Cannon Island.** In the 18th century the island was used as a base to launch naval raids and to help defend the lagoon against the Spanish. Ask any boatman in town or contact La Ruta Moskitia to arrange a trip (L250–L300) here.

While cultural and wildlife tours are on the rise, **fishing** has always been the game in Brus Laguna. The abundance of snook, tarpon (sometimes as large as 200 lb.), and grouper have attracted elite fisherman from all over the world to Brus Laguna. **Team Marin Fishin** (© 504/9987-0875; www.teammarinhondurasfishing.com) runs the most frequent and serious tours (all-inclusive) in the lagoon, which includes fishing, all meals, round-trip airline tickets from La Ceiba, a local guide in La Ceiba, a local English-speaking fishing guide for all fishing excursions, boat transport, and airport transfers. Tours start at $889 per person, based on double occupancy, for a 3-night/4-day excursion.

Every other tour in Brus Laguna can be set up with **La Ruta Moskitia** (www. larutamoskitia.com) or with Dorcas Wood (© **504/443-8009**) at the Yamari Savannah Cabañas. One of the more relaxed options is to explore the creeks and lagoons deep in the Pine Savannah by **kayak or rubber inner tube.** You can also ride through the Savannah on **horseback.**

Where to Stay & Dine

Hotel Ciudad Blanca ★ (© **504/433-8029;** L500 double) is the most modern and impressive hotel in Brus Laguna, which isn't saying much. Rooms have private bathrooms with reliable hot-water showers, A/C, and TVs.

Still one of the better accommodations in Brus Laguna, **Hotel La Estancia** (© **504/433-8043;** L350 double) is just left of the pier. Bedspreads and decor, as well as the entire front facade, could use a face-lift, but the property is kept clean and a generator will keep that A/C pumping all day long.

The **Yamari Savannah Cabañas** ★★ (© **504/443-8009;** www.larutamoskitia. com; L200 per person) sit about an hour from town in an isolated setting in the heart of the pine savannah on the bank of a small canal. There are just three *cabañas*, featuring mosquito netting and solar lighting. Owners Dorcas and Macoy Wood set up nighttime crocodile excursions, horseback riding, fishing, and other activities. Transportation to the property is not included in the price and runs about L200 to L250 per group each way.

Dining in Brus Laguna is limited to just a few options, such as **Mapak Almuk** ★ (main courses L50–L100) on the main street, where they give you the options for the day based on what they have fresh or frozen. Breakfast is a straightforward Catracho breakfast with rice, beans, plantains, cheese, and tortillas. The other meals are similar, but add fried chicken, fried fish, or beef. **Merendero Emilia** (main courses L50), across the street, is slightly cheaper, though you get what you pay for. Fried chicken is sometimes all they have.

NICARAGUA

by Charlie O'Malley

L ush jungle islands, turquoise Caribbean shores, and green lagoons with volcanoes in the background all beckon from Nicaragua. Besides such splendid natural beauty, you're also guaranteed peace and tranquillity in Central America's largest and safest country. It is hard to believe that Nicaragua's recent history has been one of war, rebellion, earthquakes, volcanic eruptions, and devastating hurricanes as its people and landscape evoke pure *alegria* (happiness).

This land of poetry and poverty, murals and martyrs, is located on the lower elbow joint of the Central American isthmus. Honduras borders it to the north and Costa Rica to the south. Its landscape varies greatly from the volcanic lowlands along the Pacific to the impenetrable swampland of its Caribbean coast, with misty mountain highlands in between. It is dominated by two large lakes that are in turn dominated by volcanic peaks towering above the waterline. It is a land of coffee, tobacco, and banana plantations. Despite its being the second-poorest nation in the Western Hemisphere, its people are proud, educated, and passionate about literature and art. It is the birthplace of Rubén Darío—a giant of Spanish poetry—and the location of a vibrant art scene based around the primitive paintings of the Solentiname Archipelago.

If you're after fun and adventure, you can surf the rum-and-sunshine town of San Juan del Sur or hike the jungle paradise of Miraflor nature reserve; or choose between visiting the misty mountain retreats of the Northern Highlands versus the white, deserted beaches of the Caribbean Corn Islands. But people are not just coming here to kick back, but also to give back. The country has a profusion of volunteering opportunities, from helping street kids in Granada to rehabilitating wildlife on Ometepe Island. Wherever and however you decide to visit the country, know that Nicaragua's fascinating history and character will surely make an impression on you—as will those glorious views from your hammock.

THE REGIONS IN BRIEF

The vast majority of Nicaraguans live and work in the **Pacific Lowlands** on the west coast of the country, and this is where you will probably be spending much of your time. In this part of the country, lofty volcanoes tower along hot dusty plains that run from the northern highlands and around two major lakes as far as the Pacific coastline and Costa Rica. At its center is the strange, elusive capital city of **Managua** on the shore of

Lago Xolotlán, also known as Lago de Managua. Technically, the Northwest, Granada and Masaya, and the Southwest all fall within this larger region, but I've divided up this section within this chapter according to these three smaller subregions.

THE NORTHWEST   The university city of **León** oozes history, with its countless churches and museums and the largest cathedral in Central America. Here you can surf dark Pacific shores or climb darker volcanic slopes. The fertile volcanic soil and two distinct seasons here mean this low-lying area is the country's most agriculturally productive region, though much of it is also dry jungle bush.

GRANADA & MASAYA   León's colonial rival, **Granada,** is on the great, dominating lake of Cocibolca, also known as Lago de Nicaragua. The old merchant city is an architectural marvel and easily the most beautiful spot in Nicaragua. It is also close to many of Nicaragua's best attractions, such as handicraft mecca **Masaya** and the satellite artisan villages known as **Pueblos Blancas. Volcán Masaya** is the most accessible and frightening field of craters and red-hot lava, while **Volcán Mombacho** boasts great hiking. The huge crater lake **Laguna de Apoyo** is a refreshing dip and peaceful shoreside retreat.

THE SOUTHWEST   Nicaragua's southwestern shore is littered with numerous beach towns, the most interesting of which is **San Juan del Sur,** close to the Costa Rican border. This colorful clapboard village lies amid a string of beautiful beaches offering great surfing, fishing, and lounging. To the south is **Reserva La Flor,** the scene of spectacular nighttime turtle hatching.

LAGO DE NICARAGUA   The wide, expansive Lago de Nicaragua is surrounded by volcanic peaks and is home to hundreds of islands, including the cone-shaped twin peaks of **Isla de Ometepe,** a serene jungle island with excellent trekking, horse riding, and beaches. Farther south is the rainbow-colored artists' colony **Archipelago de Solentiname.** Lake Nicaragua is also the only freshwater lake with sharks. The Río San Juan connects it to the Caribbean, and the lake's eastern shore is tantalizingly close to the Pacific coast. The truly adventurous can take the pirate route from here down the jungle river of San Juan to the old Spanish fort of **El Castillo.**

THE CARIBBEAN   The Caribbean coast and its huge interior cover half of Nicaragua, and this region comprises the widest lowland plain in Central America. It is also the most sparsely populated part of Nicaragua and in many ways seems like a different country. It's far from hospitable, especially to the north. Swampy, tropical rainforest is punctuated by lagoons, deltas, and muddy river mouths. Though it may not be as hot as the western side of the country, it is very wet and humid.

Twenty-three rivers run from the central highlands as far as the Atlantic coast. The Río Coco in the north is the longest and forms part of the Honduran border. The Río San Juan to the south forms the boundary with Costa Rica and makes for an epic journey from **Lago Nicaragua.** The people are different, too, with a number of indigenous tribes (predominantly Miskito) mixed with Afro-Caribbeans and descendants of English buccaneers. They speak both Spanish and patois English and mostly live off fishing, along with a little lumbering and tourism.

The most important towns are the rusty ports of **Bluefields** and **Puertas Cabezas.** The former is becoming important from a tourism point of view. The gritty town of Bluefields can be reached only by river or air but is the gateway to the beautiful **Pearl Lagoon** and the sandy, desert islands of the **Pearl Cays.** It is also the jumping-off point to reach two Nicaraguan jewels—the **Corn Islands,** 80km (50 miles) off the coast and surrounded by perfect white beaches and coral reef amid turquoise waters.

THE NORTH-CENTRAL REGION North of Lago Xolotlán (Lago Managua), the ground gradually rises into the steep mountain highlands of Northern Nicaragua, pushing as far as the country's highest mountain, the 2,438m (8,000-ft.) **Pico Mogotón** at the Honduran border. Here the temperature is cooler and the landscape picturesque. River valleys run through pine-covered hills and cloud forests of hardwood. Waterfalls, orchids, and numerous birds vie for your attention in important nature reserves such as **Miraflor.** This region is also very fertile in parts and agriculturally important, producing Nicaragua's black gold, aka coffee, as well as tobacco and livestock. Apanás Dam here is an important source of electricity for the entire country.

In the far north, you'll find numerous small towns in a rugged interior—the two most important are **Estelí** and **Matagalpa.** This is cowboy country, home to a tough and resilient people who can be hospitable and aloof at the same time, but are always fascinating. It is one of the least visited parts of the country but offers excellent trekking and nature watching, as well as lodgings in lush mountain retreats and fair-trade coffee plantations.

THE BEST OF NICARAGUA IN 1 WEEK

Frankly, it is impossible to visit everywhere in the country in 1 week, especially when you experience the country's awful bumpy roads and decrepit public transport system. And you probably won't want to leave most towns after just a bit of time spent there—with the possible exception of Managua. Below is a sweeping tour of the country that leaves out some amazing places, such as León and the Northern Highlands. You might want to expand your trip by another week so as to see the rest of the country. In order to follow this itinerary, you'll have to get around on private transport shuttles or taxis. If you are on a tight budget and plan on using public transport, you'll need more time to get around.

Days 1 & 2: Arrive in Managua & Head to Granada ★★★

Fly into Managua, but don't hang around the capital too long. More beautiful places beckon, like the radiant colonial city of **Granada,** 2 hours south. Head there, and settle into the **Hotel Plaza Colon ★★★** (p. 486) to relax and perhaps sip a rum on the rocks from the balcony overlooking the colorful plaza. The next morning, catch a horse-and-carriage ride through the city's cobbled streets and down to the lakeshore, where you can take a boat tour of **Las Isletas** archipelago (see p. 492 for tips on how to see the islands in a less touristy manner).

Days 3 & 4: Tour Isla de Ometepe ★★ & Arrive in San Juan del Sur ★

Arrange for a tour company to pick you up at your hotel and take you to the town of **San Jorge,** where you can catch a boat across to the twin-peak jungle island of **Ometepe.** You won't have time to climb its volcanic peaks, but a 4WD will take you on a coastal tour of this island of howler monkeys, pre-Columbian carved stones, and mud-bathing farm animals.

Return to San Jorge in the early evening and head back to the beach town of **San Juan del Sur.** Stay at the lovely villa known as **La Posada Azul ★★**

Nicaragua in 1 Week

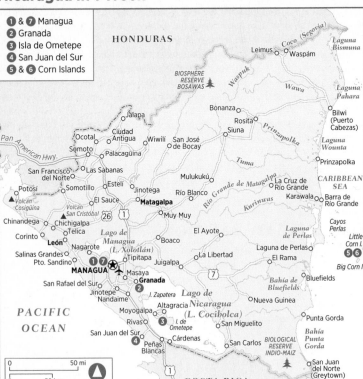

① & ⑦ Managua
② Granada
③ Isla de Ometepe
④ San Juan del Sur
⑤ & ⑥ Corn Islands

HONDURAS

Leimus   Coco (Segovia)   Laguna
              Waspám   Bismuna

BIOSPHERE
RESERVE
BOSAWAS

Waspuk   Wawa   Laguna
                          Pahara

Jalapa   Bonanza
          Rosita   Bilwi
Ocotal   Siuna   (Puerto
Ciudad   Wiwilí San José Prinzapolka Cabezas)
Antigua   de Bocay
Somoto Palacagüina   Laguna
                                 Wounta
San Francisco Las Sabanas   Mulukukú   La Cruz de Prinzapolka
del Norte   Río Grande
Potosí Somotillo Estelí Jinotega Río Blanco Río Grande de Matagalpa Karawala CARIBBEAN
Volcán   El Sauce Matagalpa   Kurinwas Barra de SEA
Cosigüina Volcán ②⑥ ① Muy Muy   Río Grande
Chinandega San Cristóbal   Río Grande de Matagalpa Cayos
         Chichigalpa   El Ayote   Perlas
Corinto Telica Lago de Boaco   Little
León   Managua   Laguna   Corn I.
Nagarote (L. Xolotlán)   de Perlas ⑤⑥
Salinas Grandes Tipitapa Juigalpa La Libertad Laguna de Perlas
Pto. Sandino MANAGUA Masaya   El Rama Big Corn I.
San Rafael del Sur ①⑦ Granada   Bluefields
Jinotepe   ②   I. Zapatera Lago de   Bahía de
Nandaime   Altagracia Nicaragua Nueva Guinea Bluefields
Moyogalpa   (L. Cocibolca)
PACIFIC   Rivas I. de   San Miguelito Punta Gorda
OCEAN   San Juan del Sur Ometepe   Bahía
              Peñas Cárdenas San Carlos BIOLOGICAL Punta
              Blancas   RESERVE Gorda
                              INDIO-MAIZ San Juan
0   50 mi   del Norte
                          COSTA RICA (Greytown)
0   50 km

(p. 523) and eat in the garden of **El Colibrí** ★★ (p. 526). The following day, catch a water taxi up the coast to some beautiful, secluded beaches or, depending on the time of year, take a night excursion to watch the spectacular turtle hatching in **Playa La Flor** ★★★ (p. 520).

Days 5 & 6: The Corn Islands ★★

Catch a taxi back to Managua for the midday flight to these Caribbean treasure islands. Soak up the sunset on bleach-white **Picnic Beach** ★★★ before retiring to a rustic restaurant on stilts amid turquoise waters called **Anastasia's on the Sea** ★ (p. 549). Stay at the **Casa Canada** ★★ (p. 548) and enjoy its gorgeous pool before snorkeling the pink coral beach of **Sally Peaches** (p. 546).

Day 7: Managua

Head back to Managua, and give the capital a second look if you have time. Take a tour of its ghost-downtown, the **Zona Monumental.** Visit the tomb of poet Rubén Darío and peer into the majestic ruins of the city's old cathedral. Have time for dinner? Enjoy French cuisine at the city's top restaurant, **La Marseillaise** (p. 463), and shop for some last-minute gifts of rum and cigars.

PLANNING YOUR TRIP TO NICARAGUA

Visitor Information

The **Instituto Nicaraguense de Turismo,** or INTUR, has offices in all the country's main cities, though some are better than others and only a few have English-speaking staff. The ministry's two websites, **www.intur.gob.ni** and **www.visitanicaragua.com**, are written entirely in Spanish, with very limited information, but have some gorgeous images. INTUR's main office is 1 block south and 1 block west of the Hotel Crowne Plaza in Managua (🕿 **505/2222-6610**). Here you will find a pretty good selection of maps and guides.

For other travel-related info, try the following websites:

○ **www.nicaragua.com**: This is a slick, well-presented site with good English-language articles and overviews of the main regions. It is, however, limited regarding hotel information, since it primarily functions as a booking service.

○ **www.vianica.com**: This is an excellent website with information on the entire country—it goes further than most travel sites by giving out actual phone numbers and websites of hotels and restaurants.

○ **www.nicaliving.com**: Nicaliving is a website by and about expats living in Nicaragua. Though the information can be a little hit-and-miss, it's worth checking out for its blogs, to see what the issues of the day are.

TOUR OPERATORS

You might also contact the below travel agencies that specialize in trips to Nicaragua:

○ **Tours Nicaragua ★★**, Centro Richardson, next to Banco Central de Nicaragua, Managua (🕿 **505/2265-3095**; www.toursnicaragua.com), specializes in private tours with highly qualified guides. Itineraries are custom-designed and can include nature trips to the Solentiname Archipelago, adventure tours on Ometepe Island, or beach holidays on the Pacific coast.

○ **Nicaragua Adventures ★**, Calle La Calzada, 2½ blocks east of Parque Central, Granada (🕿 **505/2552-8461**; www.nica-adventures.com), runs 1-day to 5-day package tours, including one called "3 Seas" that whisks you from the Caribbean Corn Islands to Lago de Nicaragua to the Pacific coast.

○ **Vapues Tours,** on the northern side of Iglesia El Laborio, León (🕿 **505/2315-4099**; www.vapues.com), is a more conventional tour company that organizes a variety of group excursions, including day tours to Volcán Mombacho and city tours of León and Managua.

○ **Explore Nicaragua Tours,** 30m (98 ft.) west of Iglesia Las Palmas, Managua (🕿 **505/2250-1534**; www.explorenicaraguatours.com.ni), is a clearinghouse for tours all over the country, including coffee farms in Matagalpa. They also arrange flights, car rentals, and hotel reservations.

Entry Requirements

Citizens of the United States, Canada, Australia and New Zealand, and the European Union require just a passport to enter Nicaragua and may stay for up to 90 days. The passport must be valid for at least 6 months after the date of entry. Visas can be extended at the Office of Immigration in Managua for $12 a month. The office,

TELEPHONE dialing INFO AT A GLANCE

The country code for Nicaragua is 505, which you use only when dialing from outside the country. Telephone numbers include this prefix because most businesses' published phone numbers include the prefix.

- **To place a call from your home country to Nicaragua:** Dial the international access code (011 in the U.S., 0011 in Australia, 0170 in New Zealand, 00 in the U.K.) plus the country code (505), the city or region's area code, and the local number.
- **To make long-distance calls within Nicaragua:** Dial a 0 before the eight-digit number.

- **To place an international call from Nicaragua:** Add 00 before the country code.
- Dial Ⓒ **113** for **directory assistance.** Dial Ⓒ **110** for **long-distance assistance.** Dial Ⓒ **116** to make **collect calls** to the U.S., U.K., Australia, and Canada. Dial Ⓒ **118** for **police** help, dial Ⓒ **115 06 120** to report a fire, and Ⓒ **128** for the Red Cross.
- **New Numbers:** In 2009, all Nicaraguan telephone numbers increased from seven to eight digits with the addition of the number "2" before all fixed lines and the number "8" before all cellphone numbers.

called the **Dirección General de Migración y Extranjería** (Ⓒ **505/2244-3989**), is located 2½ blocks north of the Tenderi stoplights.

Nicaragua is part of a 2006 border-control agreement with Honduras, Guatemala, and El Salvador, allowing travel between the four countries under one tourist card. The number of days of your tourist card is determined at the first of the four countries entered.

When leaving Nicaragua, you must pay a C700 ($33) airport tax, which must be paid in cash in either U.S. dollars or Nicaraguan córdobas. (This is sometimes included in the price of your airline ticket.) There is also a tourist entry fee of C100 ($4.65) that must be paid upon arrival into the country. In theory, you may also be asked for an onward ticket and proof of sufficient funds, but this rarely happens.

NICARAGUAN EMBASSY-CONSULATE LOCATIONS

For countries not listed below, consult **www.ni.embassyinformation.com**.

In the U.S. & Canada: 1627 New Hampshire Ave., NW, Washington, DC 20009 (Ⓒ **202/939-6570;** fax 202/939-6545).

In the U.K.: Ste. 31, Vicarage House, 58–60 Kensington Church St., London W8 4DP (Ⓒ **020/7938-23733;** fax 020/7937-0952; www.nicaragua.embassyhome page.com).

In New Zealand: 50 Clonbern Rd., Remuera (Ⓒ **64/9/373-7599;** fax 64/9/373-7646; c.tremewan@auckland.ac.nz).

Customs

There are taxes on all brand-new electronic, alcohol, and other luxury goods that are not obviously personal objects. Items such as drugs and weapons are prohibited, but also be careful not to carry fruit and vegetables.

Money

The official Nicaraguan currency is the **córdoba** (it is sometimes referred to as a peso). It is made up of 100 **centavos.** Money is denominated in notes of 10, 20, 50, 100, and 500 córdobas. Coins are made of 1 and 5 córdobas and 50 centavos. At press time, the exchange rate was 21.5 córdobas to the American dollar. It's often difficult to find change for 100-córdoba notes and next to impossible to change the princely sum that is a 500-córdoba note (a bank is your best bet for doing so).

Córdobas are pretty much useless outside Nicaragua and should be exchanged before you leave. Prices in this chapter are quoted in córdobas with the symbol C, and American dollars ($), since U.S. dollars are widely accepted. Because of high inflation and volatile exchange rates, prices quoted may vary greatly in accuracy.

Sales tax in Nicaragua is known as **IGV** (Impuesto General de Valor) and allows for an extra charge of 15% on all goods. Always check menus, hotel rates, and price lists to see if it's included in the quoted price.

CURRENCY EXCHANGE   U.S. dollars are widely accepted in Nicaragua and can be used to pay taxis, hotels, restaurants, and stores. Do keep some córdobas on hand because you might run into spots where you'll need them. You can convert your currency in hotels, at *casas de cambio* (money-exchange houses), at some banks, and at Managua International Airport. It is difficult to change traveler's checks outside the capital; see p. 503 for locations of currency exchange houses there.

ATMS   ATMs are now commonplace, even in far-flung places like the Corn Islands. There are plenty in the main cities, such as Managua, Granada, and León (try gas stations and shopping malls). Don't bet on finding any off the beaten path. Typically, ATMs are connected to **Cirrus (© 800/424-7787)** or **PLUS (© 800/843-7587)** networks. Many ATMs also accept Visa and MasterCard.

CREDIT CARDS   Visa, American Express, MasterCard, and Diners Club are the commonly accepted cards. Credit cards are accepted at most hotels and restaurants except the very cheapest ones. You cannot use credit cards in taxis or at most attractions (museums, parks, and so on).

When to Go

PEAK SEASON   The tourist season runs from December to April, culminating in Easter celebrations (early Apr).

CLIMATE   Like most of Central America, Nicaragua's climate is tropical and the year is split between summer (Dec–Apr) and winter (May–Nov), though the temperature is consistent throughout the year, ranging from 54° to 82°F (12°–28°C). The main seasonal difference involves rainfall; the rainy season falls between May and October, with hurricanes buffeting the coast in September and October. Generally speaking, the Caribbean side of the country receives a lot more rainfall than the Pacific side. Altitude is also a factor with the weather—the highlands have a more springlike climate compared to the hotter and more humid lowlands and coastal areas.

PUBLIC HOLIDAYS   Public holidays include New Year's Day (Jan 1); Easter Week (Thurs, Fri, Sat before Easter Sunday), Labor Day (May 1), and Christmas Day (Dec 25). Liberation Day (July 19) celebrates victory over the Somoza regime, while the Battle of San Jacinto (Sept 14) rejoices the ending of William Walker's tyranny in 1856. Independence Day (Sept 15) is followed by Día de los Muertos (Nov 2), or the Day of the Dead, which is the Latin American version of All Souls' Day. Feast of the Immaculate Conception (Dec 8) is also known as La Purisma.

Health Concerns

Contaminated water and food, as well as mosquitoes, are the usual sources of discomfort in Nicaragua. Always be careful about what you eat and insist on bottled water. As for those pesky mosquitoes, a good repellent with DEET should be enough to see off bugs that bear unwanted gifts such as dengue fever and malaria. Go to **www.cdc.gov** for more specific info on malaria hot spots (relegated to rural areas in Nicaragua), and also see p. 69 in chapter 3 for info.

Getting There

BY PLANE

Augusto C. Sandino International Airport (MGA; ✆ 505/2233-1624; www. eaai.com.ni), is 11km (7 miles) east of Managua and is the country's main airport. Here you'll find direct flights from Miami, Houston, Dallas, Mexico City, San Salvador, Panama City, and San José. **American Airlines** (✆ 800/433-7300 in the U.S., or 505/2255-9090 in Managua; www.aa.com) flies twice a day from Miami. **Continental Airlines** (✆ 505/2278-7033 in Managua; www.continental.com) operates one evening flight from Houston. **Delta** (✆ 505/2254-8130 in Managua; www.delta.com) has a daily flight to Atlanta. **Spirit Airlines** (✆ 505/2233-2884 in Managua; www.spiritair.com) operates a daily flight to Fort Lauderdale.

Copa (✆ 505/2267-0045 in Managua; www.copaair.com) has connections all over Central America, particularly Guatemala, Panama, San José, and San Salvador. **Aeroméxico** (✆ 800/226-0294 in the U.S., or 505/2266-6997 in Managua; www.aeromexico.com) flies four times a week to Mexico City. **TACA** (✆ 505/2276-9982 in Managua; www.taca.com) operates flights from Miami, Panama, and San Salvador. **Iberia** (✆ 800/772-4642; www.iberia.com) flies once a day to Miami with onward connections to Europe.

BY BUS

There are a handful of established international bus companies that trundle up and down the Central American isthmus. All have separate stations and offices in Barrio Martha Quezada in Managua, and some have offices in León, Rivas, and Granada where you can also alight. **Tica Bus,** 2 blocks east of the Antiguo Cine Dorado, Barrio Bolonia (✆ 505/2222-6094 or 2222-3031; www.ticabus.com), is the best-known operator, with intercity routes going as far as Mexico City. The bus from Honduras leaves Tegucigalpa daily at 9:15am, takes 8 hours, and costs $23. The bus from San José in Costa Rica leaves daily at 3am, takes 7 hours, and costs $23. They also operate a route from San Salvador, leaving from the Hotel San Carlos at 3am and arriving in Managua 9 hours later. The cost is $35.

King Quality, Calle 27 de Mayo, in front of Plaza Inter (✆ 505/2228-1454; www.king-qualityca.com), has a reputation for being more comfortable, and provides meals. Their service from Honduras leaves at 6am and 2pm and costs $42. The Costa Rica service leaves San José at 3pm, takes 8 hours, and costs $42. The bus from San Salvador leaves at 3:30am, 5:30am, and 11:30am. It takes 12 hours and costs $51.

Trans Nica, 300m (984 ft.) north of Rotonda Metrocentro and 50m (164 ft.) east (✆ 505/2277-2104 or 270-3133; www.transnica.com), serves El Salvador, Costa Rica, and Honduras. Their bus from Costa Rica departs from San José at 4:30am, 5:30am, and 9am. It takes 9 hours and costs $23. **Central Line,** next to King Quality (✆ 505/2254-5431), goes south to San José in Costa Rica. It leaves Costa Rica at 4:30am and takes 9 hours. The cost is $20. For departure times from Managua, see "Getting There" in the "Managua" section on p. 450.

For those on a strict budget who are in no hurry and don't mind the discomfort of jumping off and changing buses at the border, getting around by a "chicken bus" (see "Getting Around," below, for info) is another option. The two main crossings on the Honduran border are Guasale and El Espino. These buses arrive in and depart from Managua at **Mercado Israel Lewites,** also known as **Bóer** (📞 **505/2265-2152**), and **Mercado Mayoreo** (📞 **505/2233-4729**). The main crossing into Costa Rica is Peñas Blancas. Buses arrive and depart from **Mercado Roberto Huembes** (no phone). It is very important that you get two stamps—exit and entrance stamps—from the corresponding immigration office on either side, or you may have problems entering or leaving at the border.

BY CRUISE SHIP/FERRY

San Juan del Sur is now a well-established stop-off for luxury cruise liners plying the Caribbean and Pacific coast via the Panama Canal. Two companies that make this trip are Miami-based **Seabourn Cruise Line** (www.seabourn.com) and California-based **Princess Cruises** (www.princess.com).

Getting Around

Getting around Nicaragua is very often taxing. Decrepit roads and a chaotic public transport system mean you may have to shell out for an expensive taxi or shuttle ride between cities if you don't fancy taking a crowded local bus. Fortunately, everything is relatively close and the only real epic journeys are taken if you want to explore the interior highlands or get to the Caribbean by land and sea.

BY PLANE

At the end of Managua's airport terminal, there is a tiny departure lounge that accommodates Nicaragua's domestic airline operator. **La Costeña** (📞 **505/2263-2142;** www.lacostena.com.ni) provides "puddle jumper" planes that carry people and packages to Puerto Cabezas, San Carlos, Bluefields, and the Corn Islands. For more information, see the destination sections throughout this chapter.

BY BUS

Have you ever wondered where those old yellow school buses go after being decommissioned from carrying North American children? They go south. The potholed roads of Nicaragua are full of trundling **"chicken buses,"** or old school buses, which riders (some of whom *do* carry livestock) can hop on and hop off of at multiple destinations, making for a very slow ride.

The country also has small express vans that are faster than chicken buses, but—since they still allow as many folks as possible to pile on along the way—they can get very crowded and uncomfortable on long journeys.

Some better-quality bus companies do exist, but in general traveling by bus is a colorful yet exhausting and sometimes intimidating business. For exact arrival and departure points in each city, and for the names of bus companies, check "Getting There" and "Getting Around" info in each town detailed below.

BY TAXI & SHUTTLE BUS

Taking taxis or shuttle buses is an increasingly popular way of getting around the country. Small, private companies, which are usually connected to a travel agency or hotel, will pick you up at your airport or hotel and transfer you to your next destination. It is particularly popular for those traveling between the main tourist destinations—Granada, San Juan del Sur, Managua, and León. The price depends on whether you are lucky enough to have somebody else sharing the ride, but will never be less than C570 ($27) between destinations. Two reputable companies are **Tierra Tour** (⑦ **505/2552-8723;** www.tierratour.com) and **Paxeos** (⑦ **505/2552-8291;** www.paxeos.com). See "By Taxi" under "Managua," later in this chapter, for info on taking taxis within the city.

BY CAR

Nicaragua used to be described as a country of oxen and Mercedes Benzes, but now it is more like a country of old school buses and SUVs. In general, the roads are very bad and you will be doing yourself a big favor if you spring for a four-wheel-drive. One good thing about driving here is that there is very little traffic. The Northern Highlands is the most beautiful area for touring by car.

Car rentals are generally cheap, but it is wise to shop around. Make sure you get unlimited mileage or are aware of the charge per kilometer if you go over. A car costs C288 to C1,727 ($13–$80) per day, and more if you require a 4WD. The best-known company is **Hertz** (⑦ **505/2266-8400** in the InterContinental Hotel, or 2222-2320 in the airport; www.hertz.com). **Lugo Rent-a-Car** (⑦ **505/2266-4477**) and **Dorado Rent-a-Car** (⑦ **505/2278-1825**) are both located at Rotonda El Dorado in Managua. **Alamo** has a desk in the international airport (⑦ **505/2277-4477;** www.alamonicaragua.com) and offices in Granada and San Juan del Sur. **Budget,** 1 block south of Estatua Montaya (⑦ **505/2255-9000;** www.budget.com.ni) and **Avis,** ½ block south of Estatua Montaya (⑦ **505/2268-1838;** www.avis.com.ni), are two other good options. Note that many towns (such as Masaya) lack rental-car outlets, so if you are intent on touring the country by car, it is probably best that you do so from Managua or Granada.

Tips on Accommodations

Hotels in Nicaragua are improving all the time, but lower your expectations the farther you get away from the capital or tourist centers like Granada and San Juan del Sur. Even in increasingly popular destinations like the Corn Islands and Isla de Ometepe, luxury hotels are still in short supply. In general, though, the country does offer great variety in terms of accommodations, from exclusive resorts on the Pacific coast to authentic Spanish colonial houses in Granada. The Northern Highlands and the lake islands offer rustic working farms with lots of personality but little in the way of amenities. Most prices for hotels below are in U.S. currency only, since most don't quote their rates in córdobas. Most hotels quote their rates excluding the 15% tax (so remember to factor that in).

Tips on Dining

Nicaragua isn't exactly a culinary destination, but Managua has the best choices regarding restaurants, with Granada a distant second. León and San Juan del Sur are beginning to get some very good high-end eateries, as well. In general, buffet-style restaurants, called *comedores,* are very popular, as are street grills (*fritangas*) on the side of the road. Every town has a Mercado Municipal, with ultracheap food stalls. Corn, rice, and beans dominate most menus but you'll also come across an incredible amount of seafood, especially lobster and shrimp.

In Nicaragua, prices on menus in most restaurants exclude a 15% tax and a 10% service charge. These are automatically added to your bill at the end.

Tips on Shopping

Nicaragua is handicraft heaven. **Masaya,** 29km (18 miles) south of Managua, is the center of the handicraft scene in the country. Here you'll find everything from cotton hammocks, woodcarvings, rocking chairs, textile arts, leather work, and ceramics. The Monimbó neighborhood in Masaya is famous for leather work, woodwork, embroidery, and toys. Every town and city has a central market where you will find similar goods, as well. The Solentiname Islands are famous for primitive art, and Managua has many art galleries that display such work.

[FastFACTS] NICARAGUA

American Express
American Express is at the Viajes Atlántida office, 1 block east of Rotonda El Gueguense, Managua (© **505/2266-4050**). It is open Monday to Friday from 9am to 5pm.

Business Hours Banks are generally open weekdays from 8:30am to 4pm and some are open on Saturday mornings. Shopping hours are weekdays from 8am to midday and 2 to 5pm and Saturday 8am to noon. Shopping centers are open daily from 10am to 8pm.

Embassies All embassies are in Managua, as follows: **United States,** Carr Sur Km 4.5 (© **505/2266-6012,** or 266-6038 after hours); **Canada,** De los Pipitos, Calle Nogal No. 25, Bolonia (© **505/2268-0433** or 268-3323), and the **United Kingdom,** on Carretera Masaya, Los Robles (© **505/2278-0014** or 2278-0887). **Australia** and **New Zealand** do not have an embassy or consulate in Nicaragua.

Emergencies The following emergency numbers are valid throughout

Nicaragua. For an ambulance, call © **128;** in case of fire, call © **115;** for police assistance, call © **118.**

Hospitals The best hospital in Managua is the **Hospital Bautista,** 1km (⅔ mile) east of the Inter-Continental Hotel (© **505/2249-7070** or 2249-7277); some staff members are English-speaking.

Language Nicaragua's official language is Spanish, but a form of creole English is also frequently used along the Caribbean coast and the Corn Islands.

Maps It is hard to produce reliable maps of towns and cities that have no street names yet, but Intur makes a good effort at it. *Guía Mananic* is one good country map that can be purchased at most bookstores in the country.

Newspapers & Magazines Major local papers are *El Nuevo Diario* (center-left) and *La Prensa* (conservative). *La Tribuna* is the country's main business paper and *El Mercurio* is the most popular tabloid.

Post Offices & Mail Post offices are generally open Monday through Friday from 8am to 6pm and Saturday from 8am to 1pm. Airmail postage for a letter weighing 7 ounces or less from Nicaragua to North America is 60¢, and $1 to Europe. Mail takes on average between 7 and 10 days to get to the U.S. and Europe.

Safety Crime in Nicaragua is reportedly on the increase, but it's by no means as bad as in other Central America countries. Travelers should be especially alert to pickpockets and purse snatching on the streets and on buses in Managua. Always keep your belongings in sight while dining or drinking, and expect street kids to ask for money or food. A different safety concern, but worth noting, is the strong Pacific currents and lack of lifeguards. Be aware of this while enjoying the beach.

Taxes Nicaragua's value-added tax (IGV) is 15% and is generally added on after the bill, especially in the finer restaurants. If you're ever unsure about a price, ask if the bill includes *el impuesto* (the tax). See "Entry Requirements," earlier in this chapter, for info on the airport departure tax.

Telephone & Fax Public phones take either phone cards (sold at kiosks on the street) or coins. Local calls cost 20 centavos or about 5¢ to start, and charge more the longer you talk. ENITEL is the name of the biggest phone company, though it is still often referred to as TELCOR. You will find an ENITEL office in all major cities and towns. There are telephone booths on many corners, but you may have difficulty finding one that accepts change (it's easier to find ones that work with calling cards).

See "Telephone Dialing Info at a Glance," earlier in this chapter.

Tipping A 10% tip is expected at cafes and restaurants. This is often added to the bill automatically, even though the waiter or waitress may never see it. If you are worried your tip is not getting into the right hands, give a little extra to the waiter directly. You are not obliged to pay the automatic tip if the service was bad.

MANAGUA

Managua is a strange place. It has an eerie ghost-downtown surrounded by anonymous neighborhoods pockmarked with volcanic craters and crisscrossed with streets that lack character as well as names. Amid this are sprawling markets, slick malls, chaotic bus terminals, tacky theme bars, and boisterous dance clubs. The city is a frustrating, bewildering place and easily the least-accessible, hardest-to-negotiate, and toughest-to-discover capital city in Central America.

If the city seems like one big accident, that's because it is. Originally it was a proud indigenous fishing village on the shores of Lago Xolotlán—proud enough to fend off the somewhat surprised and vengeful Spanish. But the small village found itself the country's capital when León and Granada reached a compromise to end their vicious 19th-century rivalry and chose Managua. It's been rough going since. A devastating earthquake in 1931 caused havoc, as did a fire several years later. The city experienced a brief boom in the 1950s and 1960s and for a while was one of the region's most advanced metropolises. All that changed on December 23, 1972, when another earthquake hit, and 8 sq. km (3 sq. miles) of the city were flattened and 10,000 people killed. Revolution followed and the city was bombed by its own leaders. The rich elite fled to Miami and the city stagnated under the Sandinistas. It is only in recent years that Managua has finally begun to emerge from the rubble.

Once you figure out how to negotiate and get around this peculiar city of 1.5 million souls, you'll see that it has a lot to offer. Despite the chaos and heat, it is, after all, the cultural, political, economic, and academic engine of the country. You also can't avoid Managua, as all international flights land here. Whether you stay or not, it is up to you. Stay long enough and you can dance on volcanic rims, eat in tropical courtyards, listen to poetic folklore, experience a vibrant art scene, peek into crumbling cathedrals, and, ultimately, understand Nicaragua all the more.

Essentials
GETTING THERE
By Plane
The small, modern **Augusto C. Sandino International Airport** (**MGA**; ☎ **505/ 2233-1624;** www.eaai.com.ni), is 11km (7 miles) east of Managua. A taxi from the

Managua

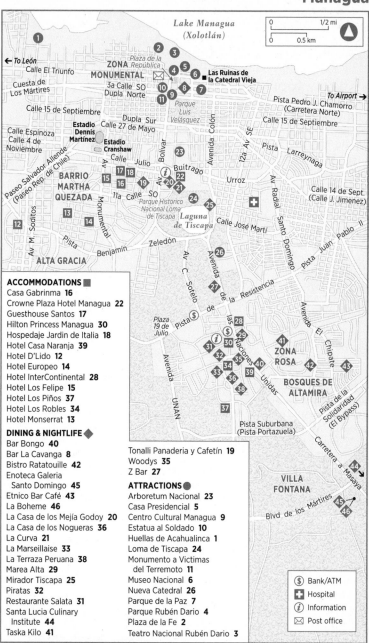

Lake Managua
(Xolotlán)

0   1/2 mi
0   0.5 km

← To León

To Airport →

ACCOMMODATIONS ■
Casa Gabrinma **16**
Crowne Plaza Hotel Managua **22**
Guesthouse Santos **17**
Hilton Princess Managua **30**
Hospedaje Jardin de Italia **18**
Hotel Casa Naranja **39**
Hotel D'Lido **12**
Hotel Europeo **14**
Hotel InterContinental **28**
Hotel Los Felipe **15**
Hotel Los Piños **37**
Hotel Los Robles **34**
Hotel Monserrat **13**

DINING & NIGHTLIFE ◆
Bar Bongo **40**
Bar La Cavanga **8**
Bistro Ratatouille **42**
Enoteca Galeria
  Santo Domingo **45**
Etnico Bar Café **43**
La Boheme **46**
La Casa de los Mejía Godoy **20**
La Casa de los Nogueras **36**
La Curva **21**
La Marseillaise **33**
La Terraza Peruana **38**
Marea Alta **29**
Mirador Tiscapa **25**
Piratas **32**
Restaurante Salata **31**
Santa Lucia Culinary
  Institute **44**
Taska Kilo **41**

Tonalli Panaderia y Cafetín **19**
Woodys **35**
Z Bar **27**

ATTRACTIONS ●
Arboretum Nacional **23**
Casa Presidencial **5**
Centro Cultural Managua **9**
Estatua al Soldado **10**
Huellas de Acahualinca **1**
Loma de Tiscapa **24**
Monumento a Victimas
  del Terremoto **11**
Museo Nacional **6**
Nueva Catedral **26**
Parque de la Paz **7**
Parque Rubén Dario **4**
Plaza de la Fe **2**
Teatro Nacional Rubén Dario **3**

$ Bank/ATM
✚ Hospital
ⓘ Information
✉ Post office

8

NICARAGUA | Managua

airport to the city center costs C400 ($19), though you can save some money by walking across the roadway in front and hailing an ordinary city cab, which should cost about half that. Always negotiate before jumping in. If you are hauling lots of luggage, especially in the midday sun, it is easier and safer to just grab an official airport taxi. Frequent city-bound buses pass in front of the airport, but again you must cross the busy street to hail one, as none enters the airport grounds. (See "Getting There," on p. 446, for info on arriving in the country by plane.)

BY INTERNATIONAL BUS   Managua has no central bus station, and each international bus company has its own departure points in Barrio Martha Quezada. **Tica Bus,** 2 blocks east of the Antiguo Cine Dorado (© **505/2222-6094** or 2222-3031; www.ticabus.com), has the most intercity routes and goes as far as Mexico City. The bus to Honduras leaves for Tegucigalpa daily at 5am, takes 8 hours, and costs C460 ($21). The bus to San José in Costa Rica leaves daily at 6am, 7am, and noon; takes 9 hours; and costs C460 ($21). Tica Bus also operates a route to San Salvador, leaving at 5am and arriving in San Salvador 12 hours later. The cost is C700 ($33).

   King Quality/Cruceros del Golfo, opposite Tica Bus (© **505/2228-1454;** www.kingqualityca.com), has a reputation for being more comfortable and also provides meals. The Honduras bus departs daily at 3:30am and 11:30am, takes 8 hours, and costs C820 ($38). The bus to San José in Costa Rica leaves daily at 1:30am, takes 9 hours, and costs C860 ($40). The bus to El Salvador leaves at 3:30am, 5:30am, and 11:30am and arrives in San Salvador 12 hours later. The cost is C600 ($28).

   Trans Nica, 483km (300 miles) north of Rotonda Metrocentro (© **505/2277-2104;** www.transnica.com), services El Salvador and Costa Rica. Their bus to Costa Rica departs at 5:30am, 7am, 10am, and 3pm. It takes 9 hours and costs C400 ($19). The San Salvador bus leaves at 5am and 12:30pm, costs C1,000 ($47), and takes 12 hours. **Central Line,** next to King Quality (© **505/2254-5431**), goes south to San José in Costa Rica, leaving at 4:30am and costing C400 ($19). For departure times to Managua from Honduras, Costa Rica, and El Salvador, see "Getting There" on p. 61 in chapter 3.

BY DOMESTIC BUS   To travel from Managua to other Nicaraguan cities, you must first get your head around the multiple stations and markets and meeting points that dot each city, each serving as a transport hub for a particular direction.

   Mercado Roberto Huembes (no phone) serves the south, primarily Masaya, Granada, Rivas, San Juan del Sur, and the Costa Rican border. It is in the southeast of the city, on Pista Portezuelo, halfway between Rotonda Centroamérica and Semaforos de Rubenia. A taxi to this terminal should not cost more than C120 ($5.60). Huembes is the biggest and busiest terminal in the city. Make sure you get off at the bus stop side of the market, known as *parada de los buses.* Be aware that you will be swamped by locals as soon as you get out of your taxi, and it is normal for them to grab your stuff and run to whatever bus they want to put you on. Always check that the one you get put on truly is the next one leaving or the *expreso* (an express service with fewer stops), by asking around.

   Buses to the north and east depart from **Mercado Mayoreo** (© **505/2233-4729**) in the far eastern fringes of the city, on Avenida de Circunvalación Mercado Mayor. Here you can get buses to Estelí, Matagalpa, Jinotega, and San Carlos. A taxi to the market should not cost more than C160 ($7.45) from the city center, or you can take the urban bus *Ruta 102* from Barrio Martha Quezada. **Expresos del Norte** (© **505/2233-4729**) is one of the better bus companies with a punctual schedule and good-condition *expreso* buses that service the northern part of the country.

Mercado Israel Lewites (✆ **505/2265-2152**), sometimes referred to as El Bóer, takes you west and northwest to León, Chinandega, and the Honduran border. This chaotic place is located in the western outskirts of the city on Avenida Heroes de Batahola, 1km (⅔ mile) south of the American embassy. A taxi to the market should not cost more than C100 ($4.65) from the city center.

The **UCA** is the city's biggest university and also a convenient spot to jump on an express minibus or microbus to Masaya and Granada. It is located 1 block from the Rotonda Metro Centro. Microbuses depart when full (every 20 min. or so), from 6am to 9pm.

Orientation

Managua is less a city and more a collection of bland neighborhoods bundled together, separated occasionally by strips of marsh and wasteland. Be prepared to get lost and confused. No matter where you choose to stay, you will have to get around by taxi to see the highlights, because it is so spread out.

The former downtown area hugs the southern shore of Lake Xolotlán and is now known as the **Zona Monumental.** It sits beside the lakefront in the northwest quadrant of the city. Directly south is the city's hilltop **Laguna Tiscapa,** and between them is the area with the famous La Pyramide hotel and the Plaza Shopping Mall. To the east is the budget hotel neighborhood known as **Barrio Martha Quezada.** South of the Laguna Tiscapa the area becomes more upscale and modern. Here begins the **Microcentro,** with its five-star hotels and nightlife district—known as the **Zona Rosa.** Managua's best and safest market, Mercado Roberto Huembes, lies 2km (1¼ miles) east of the Microcentro. The city's more upscale neighborhoods are known as **Los Robles, Altamira, Bolonia,** and **San Juan.** Farther south you'll find the upscale mall **Galerias Santo Domingo** and the restaurant zone known as **Zona Viva.**

The **Pan-American Highway (Carretera Panamericana)** crosses Managua in a horseshoe shape and is known as Carretera Masaya on its southeast approach and Carretera Norte in the northeast. The cloud-billowing Masaya volcano appears on the right as you drive south out of the city.

Street Maps   If you plan on hanging around Managua, you're going to need a good map. The government organization **INETER** (✆ **505/2249-2746;** www.ineter. gob.ni) produces the best street map of Managua (it's the best city map of any for Nicaragua, for that matter). Maps can be purchased at their main office opposite the Hospital Metrópoli Xolotlán and cost C80 ($3.70). The tourism board **Intur** (✆ **505/2222-6610;** www.visit-nicaragua.com) also provides free maps, but these seem to only feature the establishments that are advertised; see "Visitor Information," below, for locations. The main office is located 1 block south and 1 block west of the Crowne Plaza hotel.

Getting Around

BY BUS   Though Managua's *urbano* bus system is cheap and frequent, it has a woeful reputation for pickpockets and robberies, and well-dressed foreigners are said to be especially targeted. In general, if you stick to the city center and take buses during daylight hours, you should be okay. The buses can also be very overcrowded during rush hour as they are the only form of public city transportation. Buses come along every 10 minutes and charge a fare of C7 (35¢).

You can get on the bus only at designated bus stops. Following are the most convenient routes: **Urbano 109** travels from Plaza de la República to Mercado Roberto Huembes, passing by Plaza Inter. **Urbano 110** goes from Mercado Israel Lewites (Bóer) to Mercado Mayoreo, passing La UCA, Metrocentro, Rotonda de Centroamérica, Mercado Huembes, and Mercado Iván Montenegro. **Urbano 116** starts at the Montoya statue and passes Plaza Inter and Mercado Oriental before ending at Rotonda Bello Horizonte. **Urbano 118** goes from Parque Las Piedrecitas to Mercado Mayoreo, passing Mercado Israel Lewites (Bóer), Rotonda El Gueguense, Plaza Inter, and Mercado Oriental. **Urbano 119** travels from Lindavista to Mercado Huembes, passing Rotonda El Gueguense and la UCA.

BY TAXI   Don't worry—cabs will honk at you before you even see them. Cab sharing is common, and strangers often share a ride (this is a dangerous practice at night). Offer the taxi driver extra cash if you want to travel alone. Taxis are not metered, so you need to agree on a price before boarding and make sure you determine whether the amount quoted is per person or for the group. Fares go up 50% after dark. Because of Managua's puzzling address system, you will find yourself overdependent on drivers to get you around. Get the address of your hotel in Spanish, and carry it with you. Most hotels will recommend their own favored taxi companies, but many may charge a premium rate. Hotel taxis generally do not pick up strangers on the way to your destination. If you do find a good, reliable taxi driver (and there are many), take his telephone number. Many will gladly show you around the city for a flat day rate of approximately C1,000 ($47).

BY CAR   Driving in Managua is like getting lost in a huge bowl of noodle soup—the streets are that messy and intertwined. That said, traffic is pretty light and the roads in the city center are in fairly good condition. Just be warned, even with the most advanced GPS system you will still get lost. You should get a car in the city only if you intend on staying here or plan a tour of the country. See p. 729 for car-rental-agency info.

ON FOOT   Unless you are a marathon walker, do not mind the heat, and are in absolutely no rush, don't plan on getting around Managua on foot. This city is frustrating for walkers as it is so spread out; in addition, the streets lack charm and, even worse, names. What may hurt the most are the frequent missing manhole covers. If you do insist on getting by on foot, keep your eyes peeled or you might risk serious injury.

VISITOR INFORMATION

Intur has its main city office 1 block south and 1 block west of the **Crowne Plaza Hotel** (© **505/2222-6610;** www.visit-nicaragua.com). It is open daily from 8am to 1pm. There's also an office at the airport (© **505/2263-3176**), which is open Monday to Friday 8am to 9pm and Saturday and Sunday 8am to 5pm.

FAST FACTS   ATMs are located outside most banks, in malls and service stations, and at the airport. Most banks will also change dollars to córdobas. There are bank branches all over the city, in particular around Plaza España (also known as Rotonda El Gueguense), along with casual street changers (known as coyotes) who actually give better rates and a faster service with no passport required. **Banpro,** Edificio Malaga, Plaza España (© **505/2266-0069**), and **Bancentro,** 1 block south of Rotonda El Gueguense (© **505/2268-5013**), are two conveniently located banks.

The grandly titled main post office, **Palacio de Correos** (© **505/2222-2048;** www.correos.gob.ni), is 2 blocks west of the Plaza de la Republica in the former Enitel building. Here you'll also find an excellent philatelist store.

WHERE THE STREETS HAVE NO name: GETTING AROUND IN MANAGUA

Managua is a city that has no street names or numbers, that uses as reference points landmarks that don't exist anymore, and that insists on using a unit of measurement (the *vara*) not recognized anywhere else. The city also doesn't use the fundamental cardinal points north, east, or west (south is okay, though). To make it worse, some places have two names (which is perhaps better than having none at all). It is a wonder people get anywhere!

And yet somehow they do. Once you master the old indigenous-colonial positioning system, you can appreciate its convoluted logic. Here are some tips on how to "address" the problem and stop yourself or your taxi driver from driving around in circles and going up the bend.

Landmarks are all-important, whether one exists or not. Most addresses start with a well-known building, roundabout, or monument, followed by how many blocks or *varas* in whatever direction. (A

vara is an old Spanish unit of measurement that equals .8m/31 in.)

North is *al lago* (toward the lake). East is *arriba* (referring to the rising sun). West is *abajo* (referring to the setting sun). And south is *al sur.* A typical example of an address using these terms looks like this: Donde fue la Vicky, 4c al lago, 30 vrs arriba. This translates as "From where Vicky was, 4 blocks north and 20 varas east." Incidentally, Vicky used to be a bar, now long closed.

Other important words to remember are *cuadra* (block, often abbreviated as "c"), *al frente* (in front of), and *contiguo a* (beside). *Casa esquinera* means the corner house.

The above rules apply to most Nicaraguan cities and towns, with slight differences such as in Granada, where *al lago* means east. Because of its size, Managua is definitely the most difficult and cryptic town to get around, though.

Farmacia 24 Horas, 150m (492 ft.) east of Rotonda Bello Horizonte (☏ 505/2240-06233), is good for any late-night pharmacy emergencies. **Farmacia 5 Estrellas,** 3½ blocks north of Semafor El Colonial (☏ 505/2248-8026), is an option closer to the center.

Hospital Vivian Pellas, Carretera Masaya Km 9.7 (☏ 505/2255-6900; www.metropolitano.com.ni), is the city's most modern (it was built in 2004) and best-equipped hospital. **Hospital Bautista,** 2 blocks south of Casa RMA, Barrio Largaespada (☏ 505/2249-7070), also has a good reputation.

The main headquarters of the **Policia Nacional** (☏ 505/2277-4130) are in the Edificio Faustino Ruiz, Plaza del Sol. For **emergencies,** dial ☏ 118.

Internet cafes are all around the city, but if you have trouble finding one, just head to any of the malls that dot the city. **iMac Center,** 1 block east and ½ block south of the Semáforo UCA (☏ 505/2270-5918), offers cheap Internet for C30 ($1.40) an hour. It is open daily from 8am to 8pm. **Cyber City,** in front of UCA (☏ 505/2604-7416), is another good place, as is the modern and comfortable **Cyber,** on the ground floor of Plaza Inter. They both charge C40 ($1.85) an hour and are open daily 10am to 10pm.

There are no **public restrooms** except in malls. Restaurants should allow you to use their bathrooms if you ask nicely. If you find yourself needing a restroom while in the Zona Monumental, head to the Centro Cultural Managua. There are public bathrooms on the second floor.

What to See & Do
DOWNTOWN
Even the most ramshackle cities usually have a dynamic downtown area. Not, however, Managua. The city's center (**Zona Monumental**) was destroyed by a powerful earthquake in 1972, and the whole area has been left largely untouched and put aside, as its name implies, for monuments of the past and the occasional government building. It is a dilapidated, decrepit zone with many poor squatters and empty buildings. Yet it is worth an early-morning stroll around to see what remains and to learn the stories behind each building. At night it is best avoided. Its center is the **Plaza de la Revolución,** otherwise known as the Plaza de la Republica, depending on your political point of view. The most interesting thing to see here is **Las Ruinas de la Catedral Vieja,** a half-block east of the plaza—it's a poetic testament to the tragic history of Nicaragua. Completed in 1929, this cathedral survived several earthquakes until the big one in 1972 made it too dangerous to enter. Much of it still stands, and you can peer into its shell-like structure and spy beautiful frescoes and statues.

Palacio Nacional de la Cultura is just south of the old cathedral and was once the National Congress. It was here that Sandinista rebels instigated a hostage siege in 1978 that ended with the release of political prisoners. Now it is the beautifully restored site of the **Museo Nacional** (© **505/2222-2905**). The museum has an extensive collection of pre-Columbian pottery and statues, and is situated in the same building as the National Library. There is a marvelous revolutionary mural above the main staircase that leads up to the library. The museum is open from 8am to 5pm daily. Admission is C40 ($1.85).

The **Casa Presidencial** sits opposite the Palacio Nacional. Completed in 1999, this president's office created a controversy as loud as its colors because of its exorbitant cost. The current Sandinista president Ortega refuses to work from such an opulent building and has threatened to turn it into a giant children's kindergarten. Just south of the plaza is the **Centro Cultural Managua** (© **505/2222-5291**). This used to be Managua's main hotel, the Gran Hotel, until the 1972 earthquake toppled the uppermost floors. Now all that remains are two stories of exhibition rooms and concert halls. It's open from 9am to 4:30pm Monday to Saturday, with later openings for shows. Murals decorate the entire building and an arts-and-crafts fair is held here the first Saturday of every month. The building is free to enter, though there may be an admission price for any special exhibitions and performances.

On the lake side of the Plaza de La Republica, in **Parque Rubén Darío,** you'll find a stark white statue dedicated to Nicaragua's greatest poet, Rubén Darío. Continue your literary-themed walk by next strolling through **Plaza de la Cultura República de Guatemala.** This is dedicated to the Guatemalan writer and 1967 Nobel winner Miguel Angel Asturias Rosales. His book *El Presidente* is one of Latin America's greatest portraits of a tyrant.

The **Teatro Nacional Rubén Darío** ★ (© **505/2266-3630;** www.tnruben dario.gob.ni) was built in 1969 and is one of the few buildings to survive the 1972 earthquake. It's a beautiful structure and the cultural heart of Managua. The 1,200-person auditorium hosts plays, dance performances, and even the occasional fashion show. Performances can be sporadic, but its daytime opening hours are Monday to Friday from 10am to 6pm and Saturday to Sunday from 10am to 3pm. It is where Nicaragua's great come to rub shoulders, but don't let that turn you off. Tickets are very affordable. The theater is 1 block north of the Plaza de la Republica, in front of the **Malecón,** Managua's lakeside promenade, which features food stalls and great views of the breezy Lake Xolotlán in the distance. (Note that the water is unsuitable for bathing.)

Just west of the theater is **Plaza de la Fe (Faith Plaza),** ex-president Alemán's concrete homage to Pope John Paul II. That president was later discovered to have stolen from the state's coffers, but perhaps he thought his papal extravagance might buy him a place in heaven anyway.

Three blocks south on Avenida Bolivar is the **Estatua al Soldado,** otherwise known as *El Guerrillero sin Nombre* (the Unknown Guerrilla). This is a large, muscular paramilitary statue, with a pickax in one hand and an AK-47 in another. It is an important city landmark, but 3 blocks east you'll find something a little more conciliatory and bipartisan. The **Parque de la Paz** ★ is a lighthouse growing out of a buried mound of weapons and tanks—a symbolic proclamation by ex-president Violeta Chamorro that the Contra war was over. The nearby shantytown and general poverty are reminders that this country has some problems to solve yet.

One final, poignant statue to see downtown is the **Monumento a Victimas del Terremoto,** a memorial to those who died in the earthquake of 1972. It is located in front of the **Cancilleria,** where the Iglesia de San Antonio used to stand. If you want a simple explanation about why this city is so fragmented and just plain ugly, see this portrait of a man standing amid the wreckage of his home, and read its moving poem by Pedro Rafael Gutierrez called "Requiem for a Dead City."

SIGHTS OUTSIDE ZONA MONUMENTAL

Arboretum Nacional ☺   In this small, sunny forest, you'll find a collection of 200 of Nicaragua's native flora. The arboretum is worth a visit for anyone craving greenery in this ungreen city. Still, it must be said, some plants look better than others. It is especially worth visiting in March when Nicaragua's national flower, the *sacuanoche,* comes into fragrant bloom. The red flower of the national tree, the *malinche,* blossoms here from May to August.

Av. Bolivar, Barrio Martha Quezada. ✆ **505/2222-2558.** Admission C5 (25¢). Mon–Fri 8am–5pm.

Huellas de Acahualinca ★   Situated 2km (1¼ miles) north of the Telcor building on the way to the lake, this remarkable site displays 6,000-year-old footprints of men, women, and children forming a line along what is suspected to have been a riverbed. The question is, were they fleeing a volcanic eruption or just going for a swim? It is perhaps one of the oldest pieces of evidence of human activity in Central America. The site now has a simple museum showcasing the footprints.

Catch a taxi here and ask the driver to wait for you, as the area is isolated and a little dangerous. A two-way taxi ride should not cost more than C200 ($9.30) from the Metrocentro. The more adventurous can dress down and catch bus no. 112 in front of Plaza de la Republica or no. 102 on Calle Colon in Barrio Martha Quezada.

Acahualinca, El Cauce. ✆ **505/2266-5774.** Admission C40 ($1.85). Mon–Fri 8am–5pm.

Loma de Tiscapa   A statue of Sandino stands on this high point close to the center. Also known as Parque Historico, the Loma de Tiscapa was once the site of Somoza's presidential palace, and it now offers a blustery view of the city and the Tilcapa volcanic lagoon. The lake is now polluted but you can do a canopy tour across it to the crater if you are feeling really courageous (and don't mind risking drowning in sewer water). The zip-line platform from which you launch yourself is open Monday to Saturday from 8am to 4:30pm and costs C230 ($11). Other historical sites in the area include Las Masmorras, a notorious Somoza jail now closed to the public, and the old site of the American Embassy, destroyed in the 1972 earthquake.

Western end of Calle José Martí, 1km (⅔ mile) north of Nueva Catedral. No phone.

Nueva Catedral   From the outside, this church looks like it was designed by a vengeful atheist architect. Inside, the atmosphere is a little more serene and Zen-like, but it's still hard to figure out whether you are in a Soviet nuclear reactor or an Islamic prison. Commissioned by Catholic philanthropist and Domino's Pizza founder Tom Monaghan, the building's one abiding characteristic is the multitude of onion-shaped domes that make up the roof. Described by one visitor as "the worst church in the world," it has a disquieting feel, not improved by its isolated location alongside squatter shacks and a barbed-wire perimeter fence. The end effect is so bad, it's almost good.

South of Tiscapa, on the Carretera Masaya. ⓒ **505/2278-4232.** Free admission. Mass is celebrated Tues–Sat at noon and 6pm, Sun 11am–6pm.

Shopping
MARKETS
Mercado Roberto Huembes ★, both a market and a significant transit stop for the city's chicken buses and intercity expresses, is chaotic, colorful, and overwhelming. It is also the most tourist-friendly and accessible of all the big markets in Managua. You'll find everything from fruit to hubcaps here. Its arts and crafts stalls are just as good as anything you'll get in Masaya, and it's also a great place to find local music CDs. The market is open daily from 7:30am to 5pm, and is located 4km (2½ miles) southeast of the Zona Monumental on Pista Portezuelo.

There are other major markets dotted around the city's suburbs, most notably **Israel Lewites** (also known as **Bóer**), where you can catch an express bus to Rivas and San Juan del Sur. It is 3km (1¾ miles) southwest of the Zona Monumental on Avenida Heroes de Batahola and sells everything from cheap toys to fresh fruit. It is open daily from roughly dawn to dusk. One market to avoid, unless you are with a savvy local guide, is the sprawling **Mercado Oriental,** 2km (1¼ miles) east of Plaza de la Revolución. It's huge and offers unique items, but it's also not safe to go on your own.

Much more civilized is **Mama Delfina,** 1 block north of Enitel Villa Fontana (ⓒ **505/2267-8288**). Here you'll find a pleasant minimarket of gorgeous handicrafts from all over the country and a coffee shop upstairs where you can cool off and rest. It is open daily from 8am to 7pm.

MALLS
Okay, perhaps visiting a shopping mall is not an authentic Latin American experience, but believe it or not, the mall is here to stay and Nicas have taken to the indoor, air-conditioned nightmare as heartily as the world in general has. Some of Managua's best restaurants are situated in or beside a mall, and many of the city's malls differ in size, quality, and authenticity. So allow yourself the guilty pleasure if you need to, and run those last-minute errands under one roof. Just be careful which mall you choose. **Metrocentro,** in front of Rotonda Rubén Darío (ⓒ **505/2271-9450;** www.gruporoble.com), is the usual gamut of designer labels and screaming babies and is best avoided unless you have a penchant for giving your money to rich multinationals while in a poor country that needs it more.

Plaza Inter, in front of Hotel Crowne Plaza, Managua (✆ **505/2222-2613;** www.plazaintermall.com.ni), is a little more down-to-earth, but still filled with lots of foreign stores and goods. The **Centro Comercial de Managua,** Colonia Centroamérica, in front of Colegio Salvador Mendieta (✆ **505/2277-3762**), is an open selection of fashion stores, bookshops, banks, Internet cafes, and one post office. It is 1 block north of the National Cathedral. My favorite mall is **Galerias Santa Domingo** (✆ **505/2276-5080**), an upmarket collection of stores and open-air restaurants, which is a 10-minute taxi ride southeast of the city center.

Where to Stay

Lodgings of varying quality are spread all over the city, and what zone you choose to stay in will have a big effect on your first and lasting impressions of Managua. The **Microcentro** is a concrete jungle, but it's where the best five-star accommodations can be found. On the opposite end of the scale, **Barrio Martha Quezada** is where all the budget hotels and hostels are clustered. With its handful of Internet cafes and bars, the whole zone has earned the name Gringolandia, but I find it to be rather abandoned and uninviting in general, especially at night. It is relatively safe, though the barrio to the east has a reputation for being dangerous; if you are careful, you will be fine. It is the central district where all the backpackers and budget travelers go. Here you'll find a cluster of hostels and *hospedajes* (budget accommodations) where quality varies wildly, the Crowne Plaza being an upscale exception. One advantage Barrio Martha Quezada has is that the international bus companies, such as Tica Bus, pass through here.

Ultra budgeters should try **Casa Gabrinma** (✆ **505/2222-6650**), 1 block south and half a block east of Tica Bus. Though it might not look like much from the outside, once you get inside, it improves, with a nice inner courtyard and five basic, clean rooms. Rates start at $10. **Hospedaje Jardín de Italia** (✆ **505/2222-7967**), 1 block north of Shannon Pub, is another good budget choice, with clean rooms and private bathrooms. Rates start at $20.

It must be said, though, that if you really want to enjoy Managua, you should spend a bit more and stay in one of the more upscale districts such as Bolonia and Los Robles. It is here you will find some of the nicest hotels and restaurants.

THE MICROCENTRO

Hilton Princess   A short, sun-blasted stroll from the InterContinental, the Hilton Princess is a smaller version of its more expansive neighbor. The style could best be described as mock classical, with its wood paneling and marble floors somewhat betrayed by low ceilings, garish carpets, and piped-in elevator music. Everything is immaculate and the rooms are big, gorgeous, and comfortable. The rooms are bathed in light and have huge beds, a small business desk, a handy coffeemaker, and an ironing board tucked away in the wardrobe. The bathrooms come in that ubiquitous cream color that all top hotels seem to prefer, with a wash basin that's separate from the small bathtub and shower. Staff members are very efficient and quick to resolve the occasional mishap.

2 blocks from InterContinental Hotel on Carretera Masaya, Microcentro. ✆ **505/2255-5777.** Fax 505/2270-5710. www.managua.hilton.com. 107 units. From $179–$214 double. AE, DC, MC, V. **Amenities:** Bistro and bar; concierge; fitness room; laundry/valet service; pool; room service. *In room:* A/C, cable TV, hair dryer, Internet, minibar.

Hotel Casa Naranja ★ 📷   Casa Naranja has character *and* comfort. This boutique hotel is hidden behind lots of greenery on a quiet residential street close to the commercial district. The decor is warm, inviting, and very tropical. Attractive terra-cotta tiles complement the genuine antique furniture set around a gorgeous colorful garden. The rooms are a good size, with feather-stuffed mattresses and lots of light. There are rooms for the allergy-prone and some are even wheelchair accessible—a novelty in Nicaragua. All in all you can't do much better if chain hotels are not your style but you still like your luxuries.

Km 4.5 Carretera Masaya, Microcentro. ✆ **305/396-2214** in the U.S., or 505/2277-3403. www.hotel casanaranja.com. 9 units. From $100 double; from $115 suite. Rates include breakfast. AE, DC, MC, V. **Amenities:** Bar; airport pickup; concierge; laundry and dry cleaning; room service. *In room:* A/C, cable TV, hair dryer, Wi-Fi.

Hotel InterContinental ★★   If you want five-star convenience in the center of the city, the InterContinental is hard to beat. The hotel's lobby makes a good first impression, with a large, attractive space with brick domed ceilings, cream-colored pillars, and fine art on the wide corridor walls. The decor throughout is muted and modern. Rooms are expansive and soundproof, with king-size beds, flatscreen TVs, wide and accommodating safes, and an all-important in-room coffeemaker. The moderate-size bathrooms have good shower heads and mirrored wardrobes. The mostly business clientele enjoy the on-site international **restaurant** and the mall across the street. It is one of the few places you can buy the export-only El Padron cigars; ask at the back bar. My only complaint is that the hotel charges a high commission for any currency-exchange transactions.

South of Metrocentro Mall on Carretera Masaya, Microcentro. ✆ **800/444-0022** in the U.S., or 505/2278-4545. Fax 505/2278-6300. www.ichotelsgroup.com. 164 units. From $139 double; from $246 suite. AE, DC, MC, V. **Amenities:** Cocktail lounge and restaurant; airport shuttle (C100/$4.65 one-way); concierge; health and fitness center; laundry service; outdoor pool; room service. *In room:* A/C, cable TV, hair dryer, minibar.

LOS ROBLES & SAN JUAN

Hotel Los Piños ★   This is one of the more tasteful and elegant small hotels I've found in Managua, with lots of space and light and beautiful interiors. From the outside it looks like a modern, yellow and brown building located on a leafy suburban street close to the Zona Rosa. Inside you'll find grand windows, tall ceilings, dark wood floors, and lovely art. Black leather seating contrasts with wicker rocking chairs in the many communal spaces upstairs and down. The family photos on the mantelpiece add a personal touch. Rooms are big with white tile floors and elegant matching furniture that includes wood and wrought-iron bed heads. One of its best features is the good-size garden with a generous pool surrounded by hammocks and foliage.

Calle San Juan 314, 1 block south and ½ block east of Gimnasio Hercules, Reparto San Juan. ✆ **505/2270-0761.** www.hotelospinos.com. 15 units. From $75 double. Rates include breakfast. AE, DC, MC, V. **Amenities:** Pool. *In room:* Cable TV, Internet and computer stations.

Hotel Los Robles   Though Casa Naranja pays a little bit more attention to detail, Los Robles comes a close second in the expensive boutique-hotel category. Attractive ironwork and heavy, dark-wood antiques adorn this colonial house with a hacienda-style front. All of this leads to a beautiful leafy garden with splashes of bright flowers and a trickling fountain. The rooms are big and airy, with hand-crocheted bedspreads. The bathrooms are more than adequate and have all-important high-pressure hot showers. Lake Managua is only several blocks away and it's a short stroll to some of Managua's best restaurants and bars. All in all, staying in Los Robles feels like staying in the house of a rich aunt who happens to also do a great breakfast buffet. They'll also give you free use of a cellphone for your stay.

30m (98 ft.) south of Restaurante La Marseillaise, Los Robles. ☏ **505/2267-3008.** Fax 505/2270-1074. www.hotellosrobles.com. 14 units. From $98 double. Rates include breakfast. AE, DC, MC, V. **Amenities:** Breakfast room; laundry and dry cleaning; room service; Wi-Fi in business center. *In room:* Cable TV, hair dryer.

ALTA GRACIA AND BOLONIA

Hotel D'Lido ✦   On a quiet residential street, Hotel D'Lido doesn't particularly stand out from the other homes in this quiet neighborhood. Its rooms are simple but spacious, though the furniture could do with a revamp and the bedspreads are a little too bright for my taste. Nevertheless, D'Lido is a reliable hotel that has been operating since the 1970s. It's also a good budget option, especially when you consider the inviting pool out back along with the thatched-roof veranda and courtyard. It's a 15-minute drive from the center of town. They'll also pick you up from the airport for $20.

Carretera Sur Km 3 (2½ blocks south of Centro Toyota Autonica), Altagracia. ☏ **505/2266-8965.** www. hoteldlido.com. 32 units. From $40 double; from $51 triple; from $61 quadruple. Rates include breakfast. AE, DC, MC, V. **Amenities:** Pool. *In room:* Cable TV, Internet and computer stations (in some rooms).

Hotel Europeo ✦ ☺   This is a pleasant, good-value hotel on a suburban street a 5-minute taxi ride from the Microcenter. Tidy, elegant rooms overlook a tropical courtyard with a nice pool and an **open-air restaurant** serving delicious lobster. Bathrooms are small with an enclosed shower and somewhat noisy air vents. Despite nice touches such as the art hanging on the walls and attractive wooden ceilings, the decor could stand a little sprucing up. Still, it makes for a relaxing stay and serves as a great escape when you tire of touring the city.

60m (197 ft.) west of Canal 2, Bolonia. ☏ **505/2268-2130.** Fax 505/2268-5999. www.hoteleuropeo. com.ni. 35 units. From $79 double; from $93 triple. Rates include breakfast. AE, MC, V. **Amenities:** Bar and grill; laundry service; pool. *In room:* A/C, cable TV, high-speed Internet.

Hotel Montserrat   Contemporary meets colonial with a Nicaraguan twist is how to best describe the Hotel Montserrat. Open since 1990, it is family-run and very much retains a homey feel, with pastel-colored walls and local crafts scattered around. The building, however, is new, so you can enjoy its old-world aesthetic with all the modern advantages. There are times things don't go as smoothly as they should—on my last visit, there was no hot water sporadically, for example—but in general this is a comfortable hotel in a nice residential zone close to the city center. There is a relaxing **restaurant** serving an eclectic mix of Thai, Middle Eastern, and Nicaraguan cuisine on-site, too.

1 block west and half a block north of Optica Vision, Bolonia. ☏ **866/978-6260** in the U.S., or 505/2266-5060. www.hotelmontserrat.com. 15 units. From $63 double; from $80 triple. Rates include breakfast. AE, MC, V. **Amenities:** Restaurant; bar; airport transfer ($25); laundry service. *In room:* A/C, cable TV, fridge, Wi-Fi.

BARRIO MARTHA QUEZADA

Crowne Plaza Hotel Managua ★★   The Crowne Plaza is Managua's most famous hotel and a prominent city landmark; it's shaped like a giant white pyramid. Howard Hughes turned it into his home in the '70s when he had plans to transform the Corn Islands into the new Las Vegas. The earthquake soon put a stop to that, and his plane was the first one out of Managua after disaster struck. Formerly known as the InterContinental, the Crowne Plaza has had an extreme makeover and is very different from the basic hotel that journalists used to hunker down in to cover the war. Today, you'll find luxurious rooms with lots of light, color, and spacious bathrooms. The large pool is one of the best in the city.

Octavo Calle Suroeste 101, Barrio Martha Quezada. ℂ **505/2228-3530.** www.ichotelsgroup.com. 60 units. From $90 standard double; from $135 suite. AE, DC, MC, V. **Amenities:** Restaurant; airport shuttle ($20); concierge; gym; laundry and dry cleaning; outdoor pool; spa. *In room:* Cable TV, high-speed Internet, minibar.

Guesthouse Santos   This is the *mochileros* (backpackers') favorite place to bunk down for a couple of days and exchange war stories. A large funky courtyard is surrounded by multicolored rooms, some of which have private bathrooms. Try to get a mattress upstairs as there is more of a breeze up there. Though everything could use a good scrub, the many folks who stay here don't seem to care; this is the best place in town to meet others traveling around Central America.

1 block north and 1½ blocks west of Tica Bus, Barrio Martha Quezada. ℂ **505/2222-3713.** 12 units, 2 with private bathroom (including 2 large dorms). From $6 dorm; $14–$17 double; from $24 triple. AE, DC, MC, V. **Amenities:** Restaurant; bar; laundry facilities. *In room:* Fan, high-speed Internet, no phone.

Hotel Los Felipe   This is the best budget hotel in the Martha Quezada area. The small rooms have low beds and garish bedcovers, but are quiet, bright, and simply furnished. Some have tiny private bathrooms. There is a swimming pool in a leafy courtyard with a palm-thatched dining area. The **restaurant** offers good Nicaraguan fare. Some rooms are quite crammed with bunk beds that hold four people; others are less crowded. All have a psychedelic color scheme that extends out onto the white-railed street entrance, which sports a blue wall and funky wooden sign.

1½ blocks west of Tica Bus, Barrio Martha Quezada. ℂ **505/2222-6501.** www.hotellosfelipe.com.ni. 28 units, 5 with private bathrooms. From $20 double with fan; $30 double with A/C. AE, MC, V. **Amenities:** Internet kiosk; minigym; laundry service; pool. *In room:* A/C (in some), fan, cable TV.

NEAR THE AIRPORT

Best Western Las Mercedes   The chalet-style rooms are somewhat simple and identical, but perfectly adequate. The hotel's main attraction is a nice pool with loungers surrounded by a tropical garden of palm trees and plants. Because of its location, the Best Western makes a good stopover if you don't plan on hanging around Managua or a good first port of call if you want to rest and freshen up before you venture farther into the city. Despite its conventional feel, the hotel has made forward-thinking efforts regarding renewable energy, such as using solar panels to heat water. That said, that hot water can be a little unreliable and in general the hotel could be a little cleaner. There is a rather soulless restaurant here that is convenient if you find yourself delayed in the airport. They'll also shuttle you to the airport for free.

In front of Aeropuerto Internacional de Managua, Km 10.5 Carretera Norte. ℂ **800/2528-1234** in the U.S., or 505/2255-9910. www.lasmercedes.com.ni. 174 units. $85 double. AE, DC, MC, V. **Amenities:** Restaurant; bar; gym; laundry and dry-cleaning services; 2 swimming pools; room service; Wi-Fi. *In room:* A/C, cable TV, hair dryer.

Where to Dine

Don't let the city's shabby appearance fool you. When it comes to food, Managua offers everything. If you are finally beginning to tire of *gallo pinto* (rice and beans, and its variations), the capital offers many restaurants that serve much more than rice and beans. You will find Asian, French, and Italian eateries around the city, but mostly in the better-off neighborhoods or the shopping malls. This is the only place in the country where you can order fondue, Peruvian, or sushi. For the more budget-conscious there is no shortage of street outlets and roadside grills (called *fritangas*), especially in the Martha Quezada area and the Rotonda Bello Horizonte. Trendy restaurants open and close all the time or just change addresses, so don't be afraid to ask a local where to go for the latest gourmet spots. **Galeria Santa Domingo mall** has a lively roof terrace with a collection of outdoor restaurants that are full of diners in the evening. The prices quoted are the average of the main-course options.

LOS ROBLES

La Casa de los Nogueras ★ MEDITERRANEAN   This restaurant was often named when I asked knowledgeable locals for recommendations, and when I got there, I was not disappointed. La Casa de los Nogueras exudes sophistication, and the Mediterranean-style food matches the decor in exquisite taste and presentation. It's in an authentic colonial-style villa on a residential street, decorated with religious paintings hanging beneath high ceilings and set amid antique furniture with a beautiful garden. Try the breaded cutlets on a bed of corn purée with mint sauce. Popular with the business elite, it can be a little formal.

Av. Principal No. 17, Los Robles. ✆ **505/2278-2506.** Main courses C384 ($20). AE, DC, MC, V. Daily noon–3pm and 7–10pm.

La Marseillaise FRENCH/INTERNATIONAL   La Marseillaise is a culinary institution in Managua, one of the first to offer gourmet cuisine since before the war. The building itself is a work of art, with a beautifully manicured lawn and sculpted hedge leading to an arched door and villa-style house. Inside, pieces of fine art adorn the walls, as Nicaragua's beautiful people dine on delicious filets of fish and meat in rich sauces. The desserts are alone worth a visit. The restaurant is on a suburban street in Los Robles—just look for all the sparkling SUVs parked outside and you'll know you have arrived.

Calle Principal, #4 (4 blocks north of Enitel Villa Fontana), Los Robles. ✆ **505/2227-0224.** AE, DC, MC, V. Main courses C500 ($23). Daily noon–3pm and 6–10pm.

Taska Kiko SPANISH   You might find yourself rubbing elbows with ambassadors and ex-guerrillas at this tapas house, a favorite for power lunches between the country's great and good. The food is great and good, too, with enough platters of octopus, crab, and goat cheese to fuel a run for the presidency. You'll also find some of the best paella in town here (the owners are Spanish). The building itself is large, open-air, with a dry frond roof sitting on a wooden framework.

1 block east of Monte de los Olivos, Los Robles. ✆ **505/2270-1569.** Main courses C170 ($7.90). AE, DC, MC, V. Mon–Sat 11:30am–10pm.

THE ZONA VIVA

La Boheme MEDITERRANEAN/FUSION   This restaurant is in the upscale mall known as Galerias Santo Domingo. Its decor, however, is very much Old World, with granite walls and arched galleries. Everything is beautifully lit by candles and backlights, lending a romantic vibe. There is a large circular alcove in the corner and more conventional seating up front. Some dishes are works of art that border on kitsch, like the chicken and potato purée in the shape of a chick (it is delicious, though). The wine list is particularly good, with labels from all over the world, including selections from France and Italy.

Galerías Santo Domingo, Módulo 3B, Zona Viva. ✆ **505/2276-5288.** Main courses C250 ($12). AE, DC, MC, V. Daily noon–midnight.

THE MICROCENTRO

La Terraza Peruana ★ 🎁 PERUVIAN   If you want real ceviche washed down with a real pisco sour, La Terraza is the place to go. This is a laid-back restaurant with a great ambience too. Small stone picnic tables sit within a tropical veranda covered in terra-cotta tiles, in the center of which is a trickling fountain. The staff is prompt and serves with a smile. In addition to ceviche, the menu offers kabobs, beef stew, pasta, and fish. Try the olive oil—it was the best I had in Nicaragua. A small bar serves cocktails.

80m (262 ft.) north of the Pasteleria Sampson, Microcentro. © **505/2278-0031.** Main courses C150 ($7). AE, DC, MC, V. Daily noon–11pm.

THE ZONA ROSA

Marea Alta SEAFOOD One of the best seafood joints in town is also the infamous location of a kidnapping. The U.S. ambassador was taken from here at the height of the revolution. Now it appears as a rather nondescript corner restaurant with blue walls and a front patio lined with palm trees. The fish motif hints at the marvelous prawns and paella cooking in the kitchen.

1 block south of Hotel Seminole. © **505/2270-2459.** Main courses C250 ($12). AE, DC, MC, V. Daily noon–midnight.

Restaurante Salata MIDDLE EASTERN Falafel, shawarma, and kabobs are what this restaurant does best, and it is one of the most genuine Middle Eastern eateries in town, with a great location close to the Zona Rosa. The decor is modern and minimal, with white walls and hardwood seating. You cannot miss the huge brown canopy outside. It's worth a visit for something different.

Southern corner of Hotel Seminole. © **505/2270-2542.** Main courses C250 ($12). AE, DC, MC, V. Mon–Sat 11:30am–10pm.

BARRIO QUEZADA

Tonalli Panadería y Cafetin 👫 BAKERY The bright mural outside this bakery, which displays the female symbol intertwined with pre-Columbian motifs, gives you the hint that Tonalli is something more than just a shop dispensing delicious bread and pastry. In addition to being a great place to stop for a hearty breakfast or strong afternoon coffee, Tonalli is also a woman's cooperative and is active in promoting health and social issues. The cafe is set in a simple orange cottage with terra-cotta tiling, and has a lovely garden courtyard with seating.

2½ blocks from Cine Cabrera, Barrio Martha Quezada. © **505/2222-2678.** Breakfast starts at C150 ($7). AE, DC, MC, V. Mon–Fri 7am–7pm; Sat 7am–3pm.

ALTAMIRA

Bistro Ratatouille 📷 FRENCH BAKERY This is the best-kept secret in town and a slice of French charm in the sweltering tropics. Bistro Ratatouille is an unassuming little cafe sitting amid a row of stores, but the food is excellent with homemade quiche and *crem boullé* (crème brûlée) topping the list. Owner Laurence specializes in sweets such as apple and cranberry fruit pies and even produces her own ice cream. The multicolored furniture only adds to the charm. The Bistro Ratatouille makes a welcome retreat for a midmorning treat.

In front of Iglesia San Agustin, Altamira. © **505/2270-9865.** Snacks start at C150 ($7). AE, DC, MC, V. Mon–Fri 10am–3:30pm.

CITY OUTSKIRTS

Intermezzo del Bosque NICARAGUAN On a forested hillside overlooking the city and lake, wrought-iron furniture sits on a circular platform with a breathtaking view. Behind this platform is a large wooden dome-shaped dining area that calls to mind an indigenous village hall. The menu comprises well-presented seafood and grilled meat dishes. The lobster, on a bed of pasta in white sauce, is particularly good. There is live music, with traditional costume and dance performances on weekends. It might get a little too touristy, but you won't care when you take in the view—this place manages to make Managua look beautiful, which is no small achievement.

5km (3 miles) south of Colegio Centroamérica. ✆ **505/2271-1428.** www.intermezzodelbosque.com. Main courses C384 ($18). AE, DC, MC, V. Tues–Fri 5–11pm; Sat–Sun 12:30–11pm.

Santa Lucia Culinary Institute ★★★ NICARAGUAN/INTERNATIONAL
This is a "must" for all foodies. There aren't many restaurants that can boast five different kitchens, a grill house, a coffee bar, a cocktail bar, and an in-house bakery. Run by Nicaragua's own celebrity chef Nelson Porta, this excellent eatery doubles as a culinary school and has one of the best wine lists in the country. On the menu, you'll find a great variety of international and local dishes, such as smoked salmon carpaccio, tortilla soup, and lobster cooked in lemon and wine.

At the entrance to the Las Colinas neighborhood. ✆ **505/2276-2651.** Main courses C250 ($12). AE, DC, MC, V. Daily noon–3pm and 6–11pm.

Managua After Dark

The capital is undoubtedly the best place in the country if you are a night owl, want to catch some live music, or want to show off your dancing skills. You'll find drinking holes all over the city, but it is best to stick to certain areas that are safer. **Zona Rosa** is the disco strip. It stretches along the Carretera Masaya from the new cathedral to the Rotunda Centroamérica and beyond. Here you'll find an ever-changing string of pubs, clubs, and restaurants that come and go with alarming frequency. You'll also find a cluster of bars in front of the Hotel Crown Plaza. Another popular nightlife spot is the **Zona Viva,** around the Galerias Santo Domingo shopping mall. For up-to-date listings on what's going on around town, check *Esta Semana,* an entertainment listings supplement in the newspaper *El Nuevo Diario,* or go to the website **www.bacanalnica.com**.

LIVE MUSIC

Look hard enough and you'll find live music performances all over the city. I've listed the best and most established venues below, but if mariachis light your fire, you should also go for a stroll around the **Rotonda Bello Horizonte.** This busy roundabout, surrounded by fast-food restaurants and cheap eateries, is very much a local hangout, and is the favored circuit for groups of baritone mariachis and wandering troubadours doing their thing *con gusto.* **Bar La Cavanga** ★, near the Centro Cultural Managua (✆ **505/2228-1098**), is a 1950s-style bar resurrected from the ruins of the old Gran Hotel. Here you'll get some real culture in the form of jazz and folk music, and listen to it surrounded by pictures of old Managua. **La Casa de los Mejía Godoy** ★★, 1 block east of Crowne Plaza (✆ **505/2270-4928**), is the city's most famous live music venue. Here you'll find the renowned musical brothers Enrique and Carlos Mejía Godoy performing what has become the soundtrack to the country's revolution and the heartbeat of a culture that revels in songs and storytelling. **Mirador Tiscapa,** Bo Largaespada Paseo Tiscapa, Managua (✆ **505/2222-3452**), is an open-air restaurant overlooking the Tiscapa crater lake with a large dance floor offering live performances of salsa, merengue, and rumba on Saturday nights.

THE BAR SCENE

Bar Bongó (✆ **505/2277-4375**) is one of the livelier spots in the Zona Rosa district, with Cuban food and live music on weekends. It is 3 blocks south of the Metrocenter. **Enoteca Galerías Santo Domingo** (✆ **505/2276-5113**) is a busy wine bar in the shopping mall of the same name that attracts a well-polished clientele, especially on weekends. **Etnico Bar Café,** Planes de Altamira (ⓒ **505/2270-6164**), is a moodily lit bar with some world music going on in the background. **Woodys,** 40m (131 ft.) south of Hotel Seminole (ⓒ **505/2278-2751**), is a popular "after office" drinks place with a pavement terrace. They specialize in chicken wings and *chichilados* (a spicy beer version of a bloody mary). **Z-Bar,** Antiguo Rest Los Gauchos (ⓒ **505/2278-1735**), has an open-air bar with a dance floor churning out good old-fashioned rock 'n' roll. **La Curva** (no phone) is on a corner behind the pyramid-shaped Crowne Plaza. This beach-style bar with bamboo walls and frond roof looks somewhat out of place amid the downtown traffic and nighttime corner hookers. It is heaving, however, on Friday nights with crowds dancing to salsa, merengue, and cumbria. Saturdays are a little more sedate, with '70s and '80s rock and pop. Its open plan with no walls also means it's a good spot for some early-evening people-watching. It is open Monday to Saturday 5pm to midnight. **Piratas,** 1 block south of Hotel Seminole (ⓒ **505/2278-3817**), is a funky theme bar in the heart of the Zona Rosa and a slick establishment of dark woods, pirate murals, anarchic graffiti, and black leather furniture. The wraparound veranda on this corner location means you get to ogle all the passing traffic while feeding on pub grub and cocktails. It can get noisy, however, and the service is slow.

NIGHTCLUBS

El Chaman in the Metrocentro Mall (ⓒ **505/2278-6111**) is a young and popular dance club with the most ridiculous American Indian–themed decor. Yet it has been around for quite a while now and keeps packing visitors and locals into its smoke-filled corridors to listen to rock and techno. The cover charge is C200 ($9.30). **El Quetzal ★**, Rotonda Centroamérica, in front of Registros Publicos (ⓒ **505/2277-0890**), is an old-school salsa and cumbia dance hall. You'll be the only tourist there but that's fine, as long as you can shimmy like the rest of the mixed, raucous crowd. The cover charge is C200 ($9.30).

XS, Zona Rosa (ⓒ **505/2277-3086**), is your typical glittery nightclub with mirrors to admire yourself in (and others) as you punch the air to techno. The cover charge is C200 ($9.30). It is located in front of T.G.I. Friday's on Carretera Masaya. **Hipa Hipa ★**, Plaza Coconut Grove (ⓒ **505/2278-2812**), attracts a wealthy, trendy college-age crowd that take to its three boisterous dance floors to groove to salsa, merengue, and techno. It's famed for attracting *fresas,* or strawberries, as Managua's *It girls* are affectionately known. The cover charge is C200 ($9.30). The doormen are notoriously selective, so dress up and pout. **O.M.,** Carretera Masaya, across from T.G.I. Friday's (no phone), is where to go if you like being treated like a rock star and charged accordingly. The cover charge is C200 ($9.30).

Island Taste ★★, 2 blocks east of Siemens, Km 6, Carretera Norte (no phone), is a lot more down-to-earth and a is famous hangout for Caribbean exiles in the capital. The friendly crowd gets down to proper roots-style Caribbean tunes. **Moods,** Zona Viva, Galerías Santo Domingo (ⓒ **505/2276-5276**), plays disco, house, and electro in a somewhat sterile but boisterous disco-bar. The cover charge is C200 ($9.30). **Club Hollywood,** Zona Rosa, Edificio Delta (ⓒ **505/2267-0263**), is arguably Managua's most exclusive nightclub, so dress sharp. The cover charge is C200 ($9.30).

A Side Trip to Pochomil Beach

Pochomil is a pleasant Pacific beach a 90-minute drive from the city that's popular with weekenders. The sand is dark with seashells and the waves are large and relentless. The fishermen standing in the water casting nets add to the local, laid-back feel. The beach's "center" is a basic strip of down-at-the-heel restaurants selling seafood, soda, and beer. Accommodations options are limited and the beach is all but deserted on weekdays except during Easter celebrations. It's the most convenient escape from the scorching capital and your quickest route to a hammock if you have just arrived or are just about to leave the country. Note that there is a perennial problem with telephone service in the village.

WHERE TO STAY

Vistamar ★ 📷 ☺   This hotel has the best and most luxurious accommodations on the beach. Pink clapboard chalets are surrounded by a circle of palm trees and a white picket fence; at the center are two inviting, kidney-shaped pools and a small bar thatched with palm fronds and adorned with flowers. The bungalows are split into two good-size rooms with large fans overhead and tiled floors leading to a floor-length window facing the beach. This opens out onto a sunset veranda with rocking chairs and hammocks. The overall mood is light and beachlike, with ceramic lamps and delightful shell-inlaid tile work in the smallish bathrooms. Everything is immaculate and well maintained.

Pochomil Beach. ✆ **505/2265-0431.** Fax 505/2265-8099. www.vistamarhotel.com. 43 units. From $130 double. AE, DC, MC, V. **Amenities:** Restaurant; bar; babysitting service; kids' club; Internet in lobby; pool. *In room:* A/C, cable TV.

LEÓN & THE VOLCANIC LOWLANDS

This historic university city was once the nation's capital. It lost the title in 1852, but has been at the forefront of Nicaraguan politics ever since and was a focal point during the Sandinista revolution. The Somoza regime met rebellion with bombings and persecution and at one point torched the central market. A failed uprising in 1978 was the beginning of the end for the dictatorship, and the city was liberated soon after.

León is a city with character and with a story to tell. It has countless churches, museums, and the largest cathedral in Central America, along with narrow cobbled streets that lead to tiny parks and provocative murals. It is also the birthplace of Nicaragua's greatest hero, the poet Rubén Darío, and nearby is an ancient abandoned colonial city called *León Viejo*. If you are going to take only one guided city tour in Nicaragua, you should do so in León.

It makes a great base for seeing the northwest region of the country. Within striking distance are the dark sandy strands of Poneloya and las Peñitas beaches, as well as the wildlife reserve of Isla Juan Venado, which offers a mangrove sanctuary for nesting turtles. Ten smoking volcanoes stand like sentries from Lago Managua to the Gulf of Fonseca. They stand over the hot lowlands of which historic León, the thriving agro-city Chinandega, and the port Corinto are the most important towns. Those volcanoes may appear ominous, but they provide rich soil—making the area an agricultural powerhouse and the most populated part of the country. If you come to hike the area's many volcanoes, walk or surf its dark Pacific strands, watch turtles nesting, or indulge yourself in León, the cradle of the revolution, you will be joining a swell of visitors who are building the tourism industry here.

Essentials

GETTING THERE

BY BUS   León's **bus station,** 6a Calle NE (© **505/2311-3909**), is 1km (⅔ mile) northeast of the center. Managua is 75 minutes away by microbus and costs C23 ($1.05); buses depart a few times daily. Estelí is 3½ hours away and costs C81 ($3.75); there are two buses a day, at 5am and 3pm. Chinandega is a half-hour away and costs C20 (95¢). The trip there takes 1½ hours by ordinary bus and 45 minutes by microbus. There are also connections to Corinto (1½ hr.) and Matagalpa (3 hr.) costing C22 ($1) and C80 ($3.70), respectively.

BY TAXI-SHUTTLE   **Tierra Tour,** 1½ blocks north of Iglesia La Merced (© **505/ 2315-4278;** www.tierratour.com), organizes transfers to Managua and farther afield. Their shuttle service leaves daily for Granada at 4pm. Price depends on the size of your group, but their schedules are flexible and they can drop you off right at your hotel.

Orientation

León's street system is numerical. The junction of Avenida Central and Calle Central Rubén Darío forms an axis at the northeast corner of Parque Central. Streets going north or south are called **calles** and ascend numerically, as do **avenidas** that go west and east of Avenida Central System. Generally speaking, this numbering system is ignored by locals; when giving directions, they will almost always describe a location in terms of landmarks. The main market called Mercado Central is situated behind the cathedral. The old indigenous town of Subtiava is now a western suburb.

GETTING AROUND

León is good for strolling around—it's perhaps easiest to discover its many historic buildings on foot. To get to outlying areas, you can take local buses or *ruleteros* (pickup trucks with canvas covers), which leave from Mercado Central and the bus terminal (see "By Bus," above). Fares cost C6 (30¢). Note that the roads around the city are in terrible condition, and it is not uncommon to see children filling potholes with dirt in exchange for coins from passing motorists. Taxis are easy to catch on any corner and fares start at C10 (45¢).

VISITOR INFORMATION

The **Intur office,** 2a Av. NO (© **505/2311-3682**), is open Monday through Friday from 8am to 12:30pm and 2 to 5pm. They have an excellent map of the city and the staff members are very helpful, though they speak little English. Another Intur **Tourist Information Office** (© **505/2311-3992**) has opened just north of the cathedral, and here you may be lucky to find some North American volunteers to help you out with maps and directions.

FAST FACTS   There are three ATMs 1 block east of the cathedral; banks to try with ATMs are **Credomatic,** 1a Calle NE (© **505/2311-7247;** www.bac.net), and **Bancentro,** which is 20m (66 ft.) south of Parque La Merced (© **505/2311-0911**).

The area's largest hospital is **Hospital San Vicente** (© **505/2311-6990**), past the bus station.

One efficient Internet outlet is **Compuservice,** in front of Policlinica la Fraternidad (no phone). It is fast, reliable, and open Monday to Saturday from 8am to 9:30pm and Sunday from 9am to 6pm. **Club en Conexion** (no phone), 3 blocks north and

León & the Volcanic Lowlands

NICARAGUA

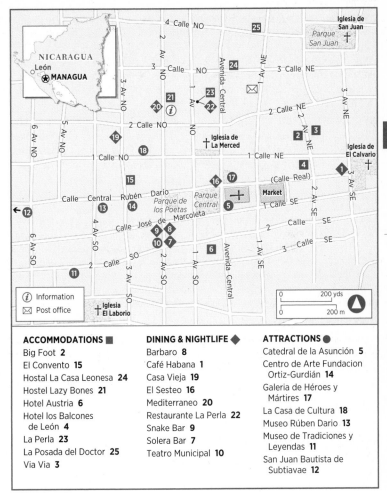

ACCOMMODATIONS ■

Big Foot **2**
El Convento **15**
Hostal La Casa Leonesa **24**
Hostel Lazy Bones **21**
Hotel Austria **6**
Hotel los Balcones
  de León **4**
La Perla **23**
La Posada del Doctor **25**
Via Via **3**

DINING & NIGHTLIFE ◆

Barbaro **8**
Café Habana **1**
Casa Vieja **19**
El Sesteo **16**
Mediterraneo **20**
Restaurante La Perla **22**
Snake Bar **9**
Solera Bar **7**
Teatro Municipal **10**

ATTRACTIONS ●

Catedral de la Asunción **5**
Centro de Arte Fundacion
  Ortiz-Gurdián **14**
Galeria de Héroes y
  Mártires **17**
La Casa de Cultura **18**
Museo Rúben Dario **13**
Museo de Tradiciones y
  Leyendas **11**
San Juan Bautista de
  Subtiavae **12**

a half-block east of the cathedral, offers Internet access, along with air-conditioning, and is open Monday to Friday from 7:30am to 9:30pm and Saturday 7:30am to 7pm. They both charge an hourly rate of C20 (95¢).

Go to **Farmacia Lopez,** Calle Rubén Darío, for pharmacy needs (no phone).

The main post office, **Correos de Nicaragua** (© 505/2311-2102), is 3 blocks north of the cathedral. You'll find public phones outside the Enitel office on the northwest corner of the Parque Central.

TOUR OPERATORS

Vapues, on the north side of Iglesia El Laborio (© 505/2315-4099; www.vapues. com), is one of the city's main tour operators, organizing everything from flights to

festivals IN LEÓN

Día de la Purísima Concepción takes place on December 7 and is known for *Griteria* (shouting), a type of religious trick or treat. Groups of people walk around, shouting up at any households that display a shrine and declaring their happiness over Mary's conception. Next it's sweets and treats all around. The following day is the Dia de la Concepción de Maria, when the whole country goes parade-crazy.

Semana Santa (Easter, late Mar or early Apr) is a big occasion in Nicaragua, and León is famous for its colorful celebrations. Along with the usual religious parades and street parties with lots of food and drink, artists create elaborate pictures on the ground using colored sawdust. The depictions are beautiful, but get swept away at the end of the festival. Semana Santa is also a week when everybody heads for the beaches of Poneloya and Las Peñitas for some rum and sunshine.

La Griteria Chiquita is a variation on the more famous *Griteria* in December and a holiday that's unique to León. It happens on August 14, the anniversary of a 1947 eruption from nearby Cerro Negro that threatened to destroy the city. A local priest initiated a "shouting" and stopped the volcano in its tracks, and this is now celebrated with parades and other festivities.

Día de la Virgen de Merced celebrations start on September 23, when revelers run through the street dressed up as one big spitting bull. The next day, the town's people parade sans costume through the streets in honor of the city's saint.

---

hotel reservations. **Tierra Tour,** 1½ blocks north of Iglesia La Merced (© **505/2315-4278;** www.tierratour.com), organizes tours of the area and transfers to Managua and farther afield. **Surf Tours Nicaragua** (© **505/8440-4123;** www.surftours nicaragua.com) specializes in surfing tours of the north Pacific coast and offers 7-day packages with accommodations included.

Quetzaltrekkers ★, 1½ blocks east of Iglesia La Recollección (© **505/2311-6695;** www.quetzaltrekkers.com), is an agency with a difference. It is run by volunteers and all profits go to helping street kids in León. They conduct volcanic hiking tours to Momotombo and Cerro Negro, among others.

Julio Tours ★, a half-block north of the cathedral (© **505/2311-1927** or 8625-4467; www.juliotoursnicaragua.com.ni), is operated by Julio Pineda, an excellent English-speaking city guide who specializes in historical and cultural tours of the city.

WHAT TO SEE & DO

Cathedral de la Asunción ★★★   The Catedral de la Asunción, which took 100 years to build and is the biggest church in Central America, dominates the town center and is a must-see. Three architectural styles grace its magnificent proportions—colonial, neoclassical, and baroque. The original building was destroyed by rampaging Englishman William Dampier in 1685, and one statue of a black Christ still bears the hack wounds of a pirate's sword. The cathedral acts as a kind of pantheon to some of Nicaragua's most famous national figures. You'll find the Tomb of Rubén Darío, guarded by a weeping lion. Inquire at Intur for a tour of the church's atmospheric Gothic roof. With its lichen-stained cupolas and buttresses, it's a great photo opportunity, and of course there is a good view of the surrounding city and countryside.

Central Plaza. No phone. Admission C40 ($1.85). Mon-Sat 8am-noon and 2-4pm.

Centro de Arte Fundación Ortiz-Gurdian ★★ If you're getting a little tired of fading murals, make your way to this lovely and extensive gallery, the best art collection in the country. Two beautifully restored town houses hold a dazzling selection of paintings and sculptures ranging from 16th-century Cuzco School portraits to modern Nicaraguan installations. You'll also find some surprises, like works by Rembrandt, Picasso, and Miró.

1 block west of Parque Rubén Darío. No phone. www.fundacionortizgurdian.org. Admission C12 (55¢), free on Sun. Tues-Sat 10:30am-6:30pm; Sun 11am-7pm.

Galeria de Héroes y Mártires ★★ This is a homegrown photographic exhibition celebrating León's fallen revolutionary figures. It celebrates those who stood and fell against the Somoza regime, and is run by their mothers. It is a humble and humbling site with the faces of Nicaragua's fallen youth in the '70s and '80s looking you in the eye. There's a craft shop on-site if you feel like buying a revolutionary souvenir. Ask for the curator, Madre Cony, to show you around.

1a Calle NE. No phone. Suggested admission C20 (95¢). Mon-Fri 8am-5pm; Sat 8am-noon.

La Casa de Cultura ★ This quaint, colonial building with an imposing wooden balcony is a hive of activity for culture and education. There is a rotating art exhibition of local and international artists, often with a biting social commentary. You can also take dance, music, and art classes and there is always a chessboard available to challenge the local Kasparov. See the "Spanish Classes in León" box, below, for information on language classes and homestay immersions here.

1a Calle NE. ✆ **505/2311-2116.** Free admission; fees for classes. Mon-Fri 8am-noon and 2-6pm.

Museo de Tradiciones y Leyendas ☺ This is one of León's quirkiest and most interesting museums, housing a collection of handcrafted figurines that celebrates Nicaragua's rich heritage of legends and characters. Its founder, Señora Toruña, has re-created such colorful folk figures as the Pig Witch and the Golden Crab. Kids should particularly enjoy this museum.

2a Calle SO. No phone. Admission C70 ($3.25). Tues-Sat 8am-noon and 2-5pm; Sun 8am-noon.

Museo Rubén Darío Born in 1867, Darío is Latin America's greatest poet and a pioneer of 19th-century modernism. Here you can visit his childhood home—a neat and simple adobe-style house. There are copies of the Paris magazine he produced, as well as correspondence from when he was ambassador to Argentina and Spain.

Spanish Classes in León

Leon Spanish Language School is in **La Casa de Cultura, Parque de la Mercad,** 1½ blocks west of Casa de Cultura, Antenor Sandino Hernandez (✆ **505/ 8865-3579** or 311-2116; www.spanish nicaragualeon.net), and offers a variety of Spanish classes and homestays. **Dariana Spanish School,** half a block west of Iglesia El Calvario (✆ **505/2311- 1235;** www.metropolitana-ss.com), organizes one-on-one classes and immersion courses.

The **Maribio Volcanoes** are a 60km (37-mile) line of black cones and smoldering craters. There are 21 volcanoes and they are within striking distance of León. They afford several 1-day excursions of vigorous mountain climbing rewarded with spectacular views. It is always wise to go with a local guide or tour operator, as some of the slopes can be treacherous and access across private land difficult to negotiate on your own.

Momotombo is one of the most challenging (and can also be visited in 1 day from Managua). Rising 1,280m (4,200 ft.) in a perfect cone shape, it is the country's most famous volcano. Its upper half is made up of loose shale, which makes it hard to conquer. The volcano has erupted 14 times in the past 500 years, and the geothermal plant on its slopes provides a quarter of Nicaragua's electricity. The lower slopes are made up of dry tropical forest and hold wildlife such as iguanas, parrots, and butterflies. It has a lake known as Laguna Monte Escalante. It takes 8 hours up and down and is best done with a local tour company, though you can get there independently by hiking beyond the ruins of León Viejo and going north along the highway. Here you enter through the power plant, but access is often denied.

Cerro Negro is a more popular volcano hike and a little easier. That is not to say it is less exciting. This 675m-high (2,215-ft.) volcano may not look as impressive as its sister cones, but it is one of the most active in the country and constantly belches noxious fumes. It takes 3 hours to go up and down, but go early to avoid the midday heat, as there is absolutely no shade. The slopes are increasingly popular for a spot of volcano board surfing (see "Outdoor Activities," below) on the way down,

which is great fun. Any of León's tour operators can arrange this, but make sure you have proper protective gear. To get there independently, you must jump on a bus and go east to the town of Lechecuago. Here you will find a poorly maintained trail that takes you to the top.

Volcán Telica is one of Nicaragua's most active and is constantly throwing ash over the town of Telica. Active since 1527, the 1,061m-high (3,480-ft.) cone last erupted in January 2007. It holds a 9,000-hectare (22,240-acre) dry-forest reserve on its slopes and makes for a good 7-hour round-trip trek. There are two ways to approach it. One is from Telica on the road to a community known as La Quimera. The other is from Santa Clara, the town next to the Hervidores de San Jacinto, where you can pick up a guide to show you the way.

San Cristobal is the highest and most handsome at 1,745m (5,725 ft.) with an almost perfect symmetrical shape. It is also one of the most active and challenging to climb. Here you'll definitely need a guide as the access roads are complicated and ever-changing. A guide can be easily found in the town of Chichigalpa, and a horse too. Hotel Los Balcones offers hiking trips from León that include a stay on a coffee farm on the volcano's slopes. Avoid going from November to March, when the summit can be extremely windy. It is an 8-hour round-trip.

Note: None of these volcano hikes is a walk in the park, especially when the wind is up. Bring plenty of water, and be prepared for a workout. It is best to go in the rainy season as the summer months can be sweltering and uncomfortable, especially when farmers burn their fields from March to May.

You'll also find a collection of original copies of his books filled with the poetry that inspired the Nicaraguan people with words such as, "If one's nation is small, one makes it large through dreams."

Calle Central, 3 blocks west of plaza. No phone. Free admission, but donations are welcome. Tues–Fri 8:30am–noon and 2–5pm; Sat 9am–noon.

OTHER SIGHTS

León has countless churches and plazas to explore, as well as buildings and murals of historical significance. **Iglesia de la Recoleccion,** 1a Av. NE, is a gorgeous church with carved stone vines around a pillared facade. The baroque construction has a well-preserved and imposing bell tower. **Iglesia de El Calvario** is on a small hill overlooking Calle Central Rubén Darío. Its twin red-brick bell towers guard a neoclassical facade, and inside you'll find two marvelous statues of the Good Thief and the Bad Thief. Colorful panels depict biblical scenes, while slim wooden columns hold decorative motifs. **La Iglesia y Convento de San Francisco,** located in front of the Museo Rubén Darío (see above), has two gorgeous altars and a pretty, tree-shaded courtyard to the side. **San Juan Bautista de Subtiava ★** is 1km (⅔ mile) west of the central plaza in the old indigenous quarter of Subtavia and is León's oldest intact church.

One-and-a-half blocks from the city's cathedral is **Iglesia La Merced.** Constructed in 1762 by the Mercederian order, it's a fine example of baroque and neoclassical design. It faces a small park and has an attractive bell tower, with nice views. **Iglesia San Juan,** 3a Av. SE, is in an atmospheric part of town amid adobe houses. The church was built in 1625. If you continue farther north, 1 block from its east side, you'll come across León's old abandoned train station.

Every Saturday, the tidy and open **Parque Central ★**, on the northern side of 1 Calle SE, holds a community fiesta called Tertulia Leonesa, with live music and lots of food and drink. It starts in the afternoon and goes on until midnight. Many worthwhile attractions radiate from the park. **Colegio La Asuncion,** 1a Calle SO, was the first theological college in Nicaragua. **Palacio Episcopal,** 1a Calle SE, is an attractive colonial building, as is the **Colegio de San Ramón,** 1a Calle SE. The **Mausoleo de los Héroes y Mártires** is within a small plaza bordered by a fascinating mural detailing the revolution. **Casa de Obrero,** 2a Av. NO, is where poet Rigoberto López Pérez assassinated the dictator Anastasio Somoza Garcia while dressed as a waiter. There is a plaque outside the house celebrating the event as the "beginning of the end." You can take another trip down revolutionary road at the **Old Jail,** 4a Calle SO, which was the site of a significant skirmish between rebels and the National Guard. It is now a remembrance garden.

Outdoor Activities

KAYAKING   The nature reserve **Isla Juan Venado ★★** is an intriguing stretch of mangrove swamp with abundant wildlife. It makes for a perfect spot of paddling. The reserve is situated 30 minutes west near the beach town of Las Peñitas. Beach hostel **Barca de Oro** (✆ **505/2231-7275;** www.barcadeoro.com) rents out kayaks and surfboards.

VOLCANO SURFING   Yes, you read correctly. Hurtling down the side of a live, black volcanic mound has become the latest craze in Nicaragua, and the place to do it is just outside León city on the 40-degree slope of Cerro Negro. The people at **Big Foot Hostel** (✆ **505/8917-8832;** www.bigfootnicaragua.com) were the pioneers, and they run daily excursions up to the belching mountain and back, for about C400

($19). Tour agency **Vapues** (℃ **505/2315-4099;** www.vapues.com) also runs daily excursions for the same price. Whoever you go with, make sure you have the proper equipment—jumpsuit, goggles, gloves, and kneepads—because volcano surfing is very exciting and a little dangerous. It takes less than an hour to reach the volcano's base by truck, followed by a 45-minute slog up to the rim.

TREKKING The nearby volcanoes Momotombo and Cerro Negro (see the "Volcano Hopping from León" box, above, for details) are the most popular trekking excursions. **Quetzaltrekkers,** 1½ blocks east of Iglesia La Recollección (℃ **505/2311-6695;** www.quetzaltrekkers.com), specializes in treks to both places, as does **Big Foot** (see above; ℃ **505/8917-8832;** www.bigfootnicaragua.com).

8 Where to Stay

Accommodations in León are improving all the time, and there are plenty of places to choose from in the city center, many with atmospheric courtyards and relaxing hammocks. All hotels listed below are within walking distance of the central plaza and cathedral.

EXPENSIVE

El Convento ★ This luxury hotel certainly lives up to its name—it was reconstructed from the ruins of a convent established in 1639. Its low, cream-colored walls are next to a church, so you may feel like you're entering a religious order when you arrive. There is nothing monastic about its interior. It has one of the most elaborate courtyards of any hotel in the country—immense, with sculpted hedges encircling a fountain. A blue-pillared gallery surrounds the central patio, leading to sumptuous rooms with polished tile floors, king-size beds, and antique furniture. The ballroom, an immense space with elegant chandeliers, and the art gallery (which boasts an expansive lobby, high raftered ceilings, and baroque woodcarvings), are both worth peeking into. Overall, this hotel is atmospheric and very seductive, though nearby La Perla trumps it in terms of customer service.

3 Av. NO, by Iglesia San Francisco. ℃ **505/2311-7053.** Fax 505/2311-7067. www.elconventonicaragua. com. 32 units. From $112 double; from $140 triple; from $160 suite. Rates include breakfast. AE, DC, MC, V. **Amenities:** Restaurant; coffee shop; laundry service; room service. *In room:* A/C, cable TV, Internet.

La Perla ★★★ Elegant and spacious, La Perla is a jewel. This colonial mansion has been restored with great attention to detail by its two American owners. Its glittering white facade leads to a palatial interior of high ceilings and contemporary Nicaraguan art. In addition to a spectacular central courtyard, there is a smaller courtyard farther back, with a blue-tiled pool. Rooms vary in size; the presidential suite is the biggest, with sweeping dimensions, a giant half-poster bed, a grandiose wardrobe with elaborate woodcarvings, and huge double doors that open out onto two small balconies. The standard rooms are much more compact, but still impeccably decorated, with soft carpets and flatscreen TVs. At the front of the hotel is one of León's best restaurants, the **Terrace,** while the **Canal Bar** is a good stop for a drink. The staff is bilingual and superfriendly.

1 Av. NO, 1 block north of Iglesia La Merced. ℃ **505/2311-3125.** Fax 505/2311-2279. www.laperlaleon. com. 15 units. From $120 double; from $138 suite; from $178 presidential suite. Rates include breakfast. AE, MC, V. **Amenities:** Restaurant; bar; pool. *In room:* A/C, cable TV, minibar, Wi-Fi.

MODERATE

Hostal la Casa Leonesa This hostel is slightly more dated and ramshackle than some of the others in price range, but this one has a central courtyard that holds a small pool. The rooms are average size with frumpy bedding and old-fashioned furnishings. The main sitting room is elegant and authentic, with dark, polished rocking chairs and tiling. The bathrooms are tiny but immaculate, although everything here could do with sprucing up.

3 blocks north of cathedral and ½ block east. © **505/2311-0551.** www.casaleonesa.com. 9 units. From $55 double. Rates include breakfast. AE, DC, MC, V. **Amenities:** Laundry service; small pool. *In room:* A/C, cable TV, Wi-Fi.

Hotel Austria ☺ This is a modern, medium-size hotel that lacks somewhat in character but has a good location and decent service. The rooms are large and some have balconies that overlook an attractive courtyard with a lawn. The decor is modern with pine and wicker furniture and loud scarlet-and-green bedcovers. The rooms could do with a little more light, but the bathrooms are large and well maintained. In general, it is a clean establishment and family-friendly.

2 Calle SO, 1 block southwest of the cathedral. © **505/2311-1206.** Fax 505/2311-1368. www.hotelaustria. com.ni. 35 units. From $60 standard double; from $72 minisuite double; from $100 junior suite triple. AE, MC, V. **Amenities:** Restaurant; high-speed Internet (fee); laundry service. *In room:* A/C, cable TV.

Hotel Los Balcones de León ⚑ Los Balcones has a delightful, lived-in, colonial feel. A lush courtyard with lots of flowerpots, plants, and ornaments leads to a handsome wooden stairway and big communal balcony with colorful seating. (Be warned that the balcony can be rather noisy, as it overlooks a busy street.) The rooms vary greatly but the best are upstairs and have inviting wrought-iron bed frames resting on varnished floorboards. The rooms downstairs are not as nice and lack good light; all rooms come with well-equipped bathrooms.

Corner of 1 Calle NE and 2 Av. NE. © **505/2311-0250.** Fax 505/2311-0233. www.hotelbalcones.com. 20 units. From $59 double; from $71 triple; from $77 quadruple. Rates include breakfast. AE, DC, MC, V. **Amenities:** Restaurant; bar; airport transfer; Internet in lobby; laundry service. *In room:* A/C, cable TV.

La Posada del Doctor 🛏 This hotel has struck a nice balance between local charm and modern expectations. The garden patio is spacious and attractive, with fountains gracing a small, verdant lawn. The gallery has an old-world charm; it is so crammed with rocking chairs, antique chests, and art that you may feel like you have stepped into a cozy sepia photo. A wood-paneled, open-air dining area with steep lean-to roof adds a modern touch, and the colorful assortment of bric-a-brac gives the hotel a playful atmosphere. Smallish rooms surround the courtyard and they have sunny furnishings and sturdy beds. There is a communal kitchen. All in all, it's a pleasant mix between a modern Leónese home and a B&B.

20m (66 ft.) west of Parque San Martin. © **505/2311-4343.** www.laposadadeldoctor.com. 11 units. From $45 double with no A/C; $65 double with A/C. Rates include breakfast. AE, DC, MC, V. **Amenities:** Kitchen; laundry service. *In room:* A/C, cable TV, Wi-Fi.

INEXPENSIVE

In addition to the spots below, another hostel in León making a name for itself is **Big Foot** (© **505/8636-7041;** www.bigfootnicaragua.com). Australian and Dutch owned, it has established itself as the expert on volcano surfing (see above) on the nearby Cerro Negro. The hostel is a half-block from the Servicio Guardian, in front of Via Via hostel (see below). Dorm beds cost $6 and private rooms $13 per night.

Hostel Lazy Bones This huge open-air backpacker's hostel seems to have struck a nice balance between privacy and gregariousness with 11 stable-style private rooms, three of which have their own bathrooms, along with two big cavernous dorm rooms.

These all run the length of a very long courtyard, which functions as part lawn, part bar, part pool, and part pool hall, and is decorated with the usual funky motifs that are the rage in hostels the world over.

2 Av. NO, 2½ blocks from the Parque de los Poetas. ☎ **505/2311-3472.** www.lazybonesleon.com. 13 units. From $8 dorm; from $19 double with shared bathroom; from $28 double with private bathroom. AE, DC, MC, V. **Amenities:** Bar; laundry; pool. *In room:* No phone.

Via Via Part hostel, part cafe, and part meeting point, Via Via is a backpacker's favorite, with dorms and three private rooms with shared bathrooms facing a lush courtyard. The rooms have recently been decorated and now come with fans and mosquito nets. The courtyard has a lovely atmosphere, particularly in the evenings and on weekends when there's live music. An in-house travel agency provides interesting tours such as art workshops and cooking classes with locals. The inexpensive **restaurant** offers hearty meals, including decent vegetarian options. Via Via is part of a global network of hostels and cafes and a great place to hook up with fellow travelers if you're traveling alone.

2 Av. NE, 50m (164 ft.) south of the Servicio Agrícola Gurdián. ☎ **505/2311-6142.** www.viaviacafe.com. 1 dorm with 14 beds and 3 private rooms. From $5 dorm; from $15 double. AE, MC, V. **Amenities:** Restaurant; laundry service. *In room:* Fan, no phone.

Where to Dine

Down-to-earth León has equally down-to-earth food. Because of its sizable student population, most restaurants serve *comida tipica*, cheap traditional fare, as well as ubiquitous burgers and pizzas. It might be some time before the city's restaurants earn culinary accolades, yet slowly but surely gourmet centers are beginning to pop up. Wherever you go, you'll usually get character in the form of high ceilings, tiled floors, and a courtyard.

EXPENSIVE

Restaurante La Perla ★★ INTERNATIONAL/NICARAGUAN Here you'll find perhaps the finest dining in all of León. Part of La Perla hotel, this restaurant's elegant white facade and tall enchanting ceilings are enough to give you an appetite for Nicaraguan and international cuisine. Paintings by some of the country's greatest artists hang on the walls and the large salon is framed by handsome mahogany doors and large windows overlooking the front courtyard and street. On the menu are Caesar salad, filet mignon, and fresh crab picked on the same day from the nearby Poneloya beach. The pâté platter is delicious, as is the smoked salmon. The restaurant has one of the finest wine lists in the country. The gracious owners and excellent hosts Mark and Jim are often on hand to share a joke or story. Finish the evening with a coffee from beans grown by the owners on the side of a volcano or a cocktail in the adjoining bar. Eating here makes for a very memorable experience.

1 Av. NO, 1½ blocks north of Iglesia La Merced. ☎ **505/2311-3125.** www.laperlaleon.com. Main courses C342–C570 ($16–$27). AE, DC, MC, V. Daily noon–3pm and 7–11pm.

MODERATE

In addition to the restaurants reviewed below, **Casa Vieja,** 1½ blocks north of Iglesia San Francisco (☎ **505/2311-3701**), attracts a mixed crowd and has a laid-back, bohemian feel. It also has an attractive bar that serves pub grub; a snack here should not cost more than C160 ($7.45). **Café Habana,** on Calle Central and Rubén Darío (no phone), is a small bar and restaurant run by a Cuban expat. It has a friendly atmosphere and serves great steak and mojitos. A main course should cost no more than C200 ($9.30). Note, though, that service can be slow.

Mediterraneo ★ 🍴 INTERNATIONAL   This is a colorful, relaxing restaurant with bossa nova humming in the background and well-dressed waiters serving well-heeled diners. Though there's an interior dining area, the courtyard is where the action is. At night, it's an elegant sight, with black-and-white tiled floor, backlit palm fronds, and artwork on the sunflower-yellow walls. The menu is extensive, offering everything from beef stroganoff to pizza to pasta. Delicious complimentary tomato-and-garlic tapas get the ball rolling.

2 Av. NO, 1 block north of La Casa de Cultura. ✆ **505/8895-9392.** Reservations recommended on weekends. Main courses C200–C300 ($9.30–$14). No credit cards. Tues–Sun noon–11pm.

INEXPENSIVE

El Sesteo CAFE   This large, airy corner cafe sits on the main plaza with huge doorways looking out onto all the action passing by. Big fans whirl high up in the ceilings, and old photos of León's movers and shakers adorn the walls, while people sit at large wooden tables set on old-fashioned tiles. The menu is nothing special, offering meat and seafood in hearty portions. It is a good stop for a *liquado* and a sandwich, though if you fancy something different, try the *chancho con yucca* (fried pork with yucca and cabbage).

Corner of Av. Central and Parque Central. ✆ **505/2311-5327.** Main courses C160–C200 ($7.45–$9.30). No credit cards. Daily 7am–10pm.

León After Dark

With all these students in town, the nightlife is anything but sleepy and goes on all week. **Teatro Municipal,** 2 Calle SO and 2 Av. SO (✆ **505/2311-1788**), is the best venue for live performances of theater and music. In recent years a handful of bars and restaurants have sprung up close to the theater south of Parque de Los Poetas. **Solera Bar,** 2 Calle SO and 2 Av. SO (no phone), has a cozy, welcoming decor with old doors and dark rafters above a courtyard with a mural of a village scene. It attracts a well-to-do clientele and has live music Tuesday through Saturday. It is open from 9am to 2am daily. Nearby is **Snake Bar,** Calle José de Marcaleta and 2 Av. SO (✆ **505/2311-5921**), a green, corner town house with a roadhouse feel and a long bar popular with students. It's open from 11am to 3am every day and has live music on Tuesdays and Wednesdays. **Barbaro,** Calle José de Marcaleta and 2 Av. SO (✆ **505/2315-2901**), has a touch more class, with whitewashed walls, wooden lintels, and terra-cotta tiled floors. There is lots of space and light in this L-shaped salon with Nicaraguan art on the walls and quaint barn doors. It is open daily from 8am to midnight, closing a little later on weekends.

Side Trips Around León
LEON VIEJO

León was founded in 1524 by Francisco Hernández de Córdoba in the foothills of Volcán Momotombo. The volcano proved to be a volatile neighbor, and after a series of earthquakes and an eruption in 1610, the Spanish were forced to move 30km (19 miles) east and reestablish the city where it now stands. The old city lay lost and covered in ash until it was rediscovered in 1967. Excavations have revealed a fascinating site, including the headless corpse of Hernández de Córdoba beside the remains of his executioner, Pedrarias Dávila. The founding Spaniard was punished for insubordination. **León Viejo,** a neat collection of brick walls and pillar stumps, is now a UNESCO World Heritage Site, with spectacular views from the surrounding hills. It makes for a great day trip and can be organized by most travel agencies in León city. If you would prefer to go on your own, catch a bus to La Paz Centro 3km (1¾ miles) east of the city. There you catch another bus to Puerto Momotombo 15km (9⅓ miles) away. Be aware that the last bus returns from the ruins at 3pm. **Vapues Tours** and **Grayline Tours** conduct tours of the ruins. On-site there is a small **Visitor Center** (no phone), and local English-speaking guides will take you around for a small fee. Admission is C2 (10¢), C25 ($1.15) if you bring a camera, and C50 (2.30¢) if you bring a video camera. The ruins are open daily from 8am to 5pm.

ISLA JUAN VENADO WILDLIFE RESERVE ★

Have you ever wanted to see a mangrove warbler? Perhaps that's not on everybody's list of things to see, but this small yellow bird can be found only in mangrove swamps, and there's one on the Pacific coast west of León, just south of Las Peñitas. Isla Juan Venado is a 21-sq.-km (8-sq.-mile) wetland reserve that you can explore by boat or kayak. You'll find pelicans and herons stepping over crocodiles, iguanas, and caimans in a labyrinth of channels and waterways. This is also an important turtle nesting site, where thousands of turtles hatch. Tours can be arranged with operators in the city (p. 469) or you can go on your own and hire a boat in Las Peñitas village. There is an entrance fee of C40 ($1.85).

PONELOYA & LAS PEÑITAS BEACHES

20km (12 miles) west of León

A 20km (12-mile) drive from León, down a freshly paved road, are two beautiful beaches known as Poneloya and Las Peñitas. Popular with Leóneses escaping the city heat during the weekend, these dark-sand beaches are deserted on weekdays, though they're growing increasingly popular with surfers. *Beware:* The dark waves here are big and the currents strong. There is no lifeguard and drownings are frequent, especially during the high season (around Easter week).

ESSENTIALS

Buses leave every half-hour from the Mercadito Subtiava, 12 blocks west of the city center; jump on any of the urban buses that ring the city and they will eventually pass by the market. Incredibly, the big old school buses to the beach are sometimes faster than taxis, as the latter drive very slowly in order to avoid the huge potholes. The last bus returns to the city at 6:40pm and costs C20 (95¢).

WHERE TO STAY ON THE BEACH

The best hotels are on the southern strand of Las Peñitas. **Barca de Oro Las Peñitas** (✆ **505/2317-0275;** www.barcadeoro.com) won't win any architectural awards, but its location is perfect, right on the beach at the northern end of Isla Juan Venado, the mangrove and lagoon reserve famous for its turtle nesting. The decor is basic, with plastic seating and multicolored tablecloths everywhere, but you get a mosquito net with your bed and incredible sunset views. Doubles start at $20. **Hotel Suyapa Beach,** Las Peñitas (✆ **505/8885-8345;** www.suyapabeach.com), is modern, clean, and family-run. There is an open-walled seafood restaurant out front on the beach and a pleasant pool area with sun loungers in the hotel garden. The rooms are simple and medium size with spotless bathrooms. The small, modern lobby has colorful wicker chairs but is somewhat lacking in ambience and decoration. Rooms start at $35.

GRANADA ★★★ & THE MASAYA REGION

50km (31 miles) S of Managua; 150km (93 miles) SE of León

History clings to every chunky terra-cotta tile that drapes this town's multicolored one-story cottages and town houses. Granada is a living, breathing museum to the opulence of the old Spanish Empire. Among its highlights are a luminous cathedral, which stands in front of one of the country's most vibrant squares, and its pretty cobbled streets, which run down to the dark shores of **Lake Cocibocha** (also known as Lago de Nicaragua). Granada is a delightful surprise in contrast to the mediocre shabbiness of Managua.

Its perfectly preserved beauty is all the more surprising considering its history of violence and plunder. Back in the 16th and 17th centuries, the city was pillaged by pirates and buccaneers, and in the 19th, razed by the despot William Walker. The American tyrant went so far as to plant a sign in its ruins declaring: "HERE WAS GRANADA." The words, and the man, soon died, but the city lived on. Originally a Chorotega Indian settlement called Xalteva, the city was founded in 1524 by Francisco Fernandez de Córdoba. It is Nicaragua's oldest city and sits at the foot of the Volcán Mombacho. Its access to the Caribbean via the Río San Juan allowed it to become a rich city of Spanish merchants and landowners. British and French pirates raided it several times in the 17th century, the most famous being Henry Morgan and William Dampier. They looted and burned each time yet the city always managed to resurrect itself. Granada blooms with colonial, neoclassical, and Italian architecture. It is, and was, the conservative bastion of Nicaragua and was capital of the country several times as it pursued a sometimes vicious tug of war for control with the more liberal León in the north.

Today, Granada is a prosperous, conservative city, benefiting from a surge in tourism and property development. Tourists have replaced pirates and the only rumpus these days is caused by the squawking flock of jackdaws that swarm through the trees in its central plaza. It has some of the country's best hotels and restaurants and is an ideal base from which to explore the rest of the country. Nearby are the archipelago of islands Las Isletas, the handicrafts center Masaya, and the towns of Pueblos Blancos, as well as excursions to Volcán Mombacho and Laguna de Apoyo.

Essentials

GETTING THERE

BY BUS   Buses leave from Managua for Granada from in front of the university campus UCA (2 blocks west of the Metrocenter) daily every 15 minutes, starting at 5:50am and ending at 8pm. The journey takes 1 hour and costs C15 (70¢). You can also catch a regular Granada-bound bus from Mercado R. Huembes in Managua, starting at 5:25am and terminating at 9:30pm. There are several bus terminals in Granada, depending on where you are going or where you are coming from. **COGRAN** (no phone) is 1½ blocks south of the plaza's southwest corner and is used by *expresos* en route to Managua. The trip takes 1 hour and costs C15 (70¢). Buses leave every 15 minutes, starting at 4am and ending at 7pm. The service ends at 6pm on Saturday and Sunday. Buses also leave from the Central Plaza every 15 minutes from 5:30am to 7pm and cost C16 (75¢). **Parque Sandino** is another departure point. It is on the north side of the city close to the old railway station. All buses pass by the entrance road to Masaya.

The southbound bus to Rivas from Granada leaves from the **Shell Palmira,** on the south side of the city, beside the Palé superstore. The trip takes 2 hours and costs C25 ($1.15). The first departure is at 5:45am and the last at 2:45pm. If you want a direct bus to Masaya, you must go to the bus stop behind **Palé,** although most Managua-bound buses will drop you off close to the town. The journey takes 45 minutes and costs C8 (35¢).

International bus companies have their own individual dropping-off and departure points, all along Avenida Arrellano on the west side of the city. **Tica Bus** (✆ 505/2552-4301) is a half-block south of the old hospital. The Panama-bound bus leaves at 7am but it is advisable to get there at 6:15am. **TransNica** (✆ 505/2552-6619) is 3 blocks south of the old hospital, on the corner of Calle Xalteva. There are three departures for Costa Rica, at 6:30, 8, and 11am (arrive early to get a seat). The ride takes 7 hours and costs $46 round-trip, $23 one-way.

BY SHUTTLE/TAXI   **Paxeos,** beside the cathedral on the southeast corner of Parque Colón (✆ 505/2552-8291; www.paxeos.com), organizes private and shared transfers to and from Managua airport and other locations such as San Jorge (where you catch the ferry to Isla de Ometepe). The trip to Managua costs between C363 ($17) and C860 ($40) depending on group size.

BY BOAT   The port is at the east end of Calle La Calzada. Boats leave from here on Monday and Thursday for the 4-hour trip (C80/$3.70) to Alta Gracia on Isla de Ometepe (a faster ferry leaves from nearby San Jorge). The boat continues on to San Carlos, stopping at Morrito and San Miguelito on the northern shore of Lago de Nicaragua. The entire trip takes 14 hours and costs C240 ($11), returning on Tuesday and Friday. There are no cabins or sleeping accommodations on the boat, and it can be quite uncomfortable, especially if there are rough seas and many people.

You can also get to Ometepe from **Granada** on a 4-hour voyage that leaves twice a week. The *Mozorola* leaves every Wednesday and Saturday at 11am and docks at Altagracia on the island. It returns every Tuesday and Friday at 11am. The fare is C20 (95¢).

Orientation

Everything revolves around the central plaza (known as Parque Central or Parque Colón), and the sunlit cathedral that overlooks it will be your first and lasting

---

Granada's International Poetry Festival

Granada's annual poetry festival is an international favorite. Flower-decked floats traverse the city with a team of bards from different countries reciting their works in multiple languages while musicians, dancers, street performers, and 12-foot puppets known as *fantoches* add a heady air of carnival and celebration. The festival takes place on the third week of February. For exact schedules check out the festival website at **www.festivalpoesia nicaragua.com**.

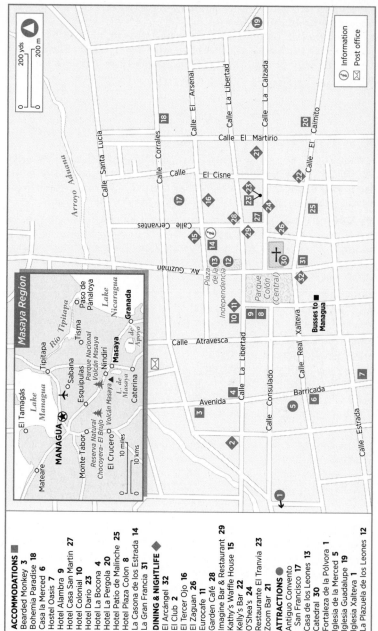

Masaya Region

El Tamagás · Lake Managua · Tipitapa
Mateare · Sabana · Esquipulas · Tisma
MANAGUA · Monte Tabor · Reserva Natural Chocoyera-El Brujo · El Crucero · Volcán Masaya
Parque Nacional Volcán Masaya · Nindirí · Paso de Panaloya · Lake Nicaragua
Caterina · L. de Masaya · Masaya · L. de Apoyo · **Granada**

ACCOMMODATIONS ■
Bearded Monkey **3**
Bohemia Paradise **18**
Casa la Merced **6**
Hostel Oasis **7**
Hotel Alambra **9**
Hotel Casa San Martin **27**
Hotel Colonial **10**
Hotel Darío **23**
Hotel La Bocona **4**
Hotel La Pergola **20**
Hotel Patio de Malinche **25**
Hotel Plaza Colon **8**
La Casona de los Estrada **14**
La Gran Francia **31**

DINING & NIGHTLIFE ◆
El Arcángel **32**
El Club **2**
El Tercer Ojo **16**
El Záguan **26**
Eurocafe **11**
Garden Café **28**
Imagine Bar & Restaurant **29**
Kathy's Waffle House **15**
Kelly's Bar **22**
O'Shea's **24**
Restaurante El Tranvia **23**
Zoom Bar **21**

ATTRACTIONS ●
Antiguo Convento
San Francisco **17**
Casa de los Leones **13**
Catedral **30**
Fortaleza de la Pólvora **1**
Iglesia de la Merced **5**
Iglesia Guadalupe **19**
Iglesia Xalteva **1**
La Plazuela de los Leones **12**

ⓘ Information
⊠ Post office

8

NICARAGUA | Granada & the Masaya Region

impression of the city. The best hotels are around this lively tree-lined plaza. Calle Calzada runs along the northern side of the cathedral in an easterly direction toward the lake and the dock. This street is partially pedestrianized and is where you'll find many of the city's best restaurants and cafes, along with some hotels. Calle Atravesada is a narrow, busy, commercial street, running north and south, 1 block west of the plaza. Volcán Mombacho rises to the south, and the easterly lake has a scruffy waterfront and departure point for Las Isletas, known as Complejo Turístico Cocibolca.

GETTING AROUND

You can easily explore central Granada on foot, though you may want to jump on one of the horse-drawn carriages at the main plaza in order to feel like royalty as you are trotted through the streets. A half-hour ride should cost no more than C95 ($4.40); always agree on a price before getting onboard.

BY BICYCLE   Bicycles are for rent at **Bearded Monkey,** Calle 14 de Septiembre (© **505/2552-4028**); **Bicicleteria** (no phone), a half-block south of the park; and **De Tour,** 150m (492 ft.) east of the Alcaldía (© **505/2552-0155**). A bike rental for the day should not cost more than C190 ($8.85), including water and a map.

BY CAR   You don't really need a car to explore Granada itself, but having one will help if you're planning excursions in the surrounding area. Car rentals cost approximately C800 ($37) a day. **Alamo** (© **505/2552-2877**) has an office in the Hotel Colonial, 20m (66 ft.) west of the plaza's northwest corner. **Budget** (© **505/2552-2323;** budgetgr@hotmail.com) is located at the Shell Guapinol station on the road to Managua. **Avis** (© **505/8467-4780;** reservations@avis.com.ni) is on Calle La Calzada in the city center.

BY TAXI   Taxis can be found on the southern side of the square. Fares start at C15 (70¢).

VISITOR INFORMATION

Intur, Calle El Arsenal (© **505/2552-6858**), is 1 block from the cathedral and a half-block behind the Casa de Leones. It is open Monday to Friday from 8am to noon and 2 to 5pm. Here you will find a good map detailing all the city's historic buildings. The website **www.granada.com.ni** gives an excellent pictorial display of the city, but little else.

TOUR OPERATORS   **Vapues Tours,** in the blue house next to the cathedral (© **505/2552-8291;** www.vapues.com), is one of the city's main agencies, and it organizes everything from transfers to flights to local tours. **Tierra Tour,** Calle la Calzada, 2 blocks east of the cathedral (© **505/2552-8723;** www.tierratour.com), organizes excursions to Masaya and Ometepe Island, as well as kayaking excursions on Lago de Nicaragua and canopy tours. **Eco Expedition Tours,** Calle la Calzada, 3½ blocks east of the cathedral (© **505/2552-8103**), organizes regular boat tours of Las Isletas that cost approximately C300 ($14) and can also arrange transfers. **Oro Travel,** Calle Coral (© **505/2552-8103;** www.orotravel.com), is a multilingual operation that can provide help with just about every excursion in the area. **Zapatera Tours,** Calle Palmira and La Cancha (© **505/8842-2587;** www.zapateratours.com), offers 1-day tours to the little-visited Zapatera archipelago. Prices start at $40 per person per day with an overnight option of camping on the islands. The owner, Kevin, also offers a mountain bike tour around Mombacho and Masaya and volcano climbs.

FAST FACTS ATMs are at **Banpro,** Calle Atravesada, in front of Teatro González (📞 **505/2552-2723**), and **Bancentro,** farther down Calle Atravesada (📞 **505/ 2552-6555**). There are also machines at Esso Garage on the main road and at Lacayo Supermarket on Calle Real Xalteva.

Banco de América Central on the plaza (📞 **505/2552-3355**) changes traveler's checks and gives cash advances on Visa and MasterCard with no commission. You will also find many street money-changers in this area who generally give a good rate and are trustworthy.

Internet access costs approximately C26 ($1.20) per hour and there are plenty of cybercafés dotted around the city. Try **Café E-mail** on Avenida Guzman near Parque Central (no phone). They also have a space located in the Casa de los Leones (no phone). Both are open daily from 7am to 10pm. **Inter Café** on Calle la Libertad (no phone), also near Parque Central, is open from 8am to 9pm Monday to Saturday. Granada has embraced wireless technology with enthusiasm and you'll find Wi-Fi in most of the city's upscale hotels and cafes.

The main **post office** is on Calle Atravesada opposite Cine Karawala (no phone) and is open Monday to Friday 8am to noon and 1 to 5pm, Saturday 8am to noon.

What to See & Do

A visit to **Antiguo Convento San Francisco ★★★** (📞 **505/552-5535**) should be at the top of your sightseeing list. This navy blue structure was built in 1529 and destroyed by pirate Henry Morgan in 1679 and by William Walker in 1856. It has risen from the ashes several times and acted as a barracks, a university, and now a museum. As well as being a beautiful building, with galleries and courtyards, it houses a remarkable collection of pre-Columbian statues with zoomorphic forms of birds and jaguars found on Zapatera Island. The museum is 2 blocks north and 1 block east of the main cathedral. It is open Monday to Friday from 8:30am to 5:30pm and Saturday to Sunday from 9am to 4pm. Admission is C38 ($1.75).

Nearby is the **Casa de los Leones,** Calle Guzman and El Arsenal (📞 **505/2552-6437;** free admission), a historic building with a neoclassical facade. It is now a cultural space, housing exhibition rooms, a library, bookshop, cafe, and concert hall. It's open daily 7am to 6pm and is situated on the majestic, pillar-lined walkway that's called **La Plazuela de los Leones.** This walkway runs along the northeastern corner of the city's epicenter—**Parque Colón** (also known as Parque Central) ★—a lively square that's crammed with stalls, food vendors, musicians, and horse-drawn carriages that carry visitors around the city. The city square holds the city's main landmark, the magnificent, luminous orange **Catedral** on Calle Guzman and La Calzada. Despite the stunning exterior, the church's interior is simple and somewhat disappointing; it was built in the 20th century on the ruins of a previous church. It is open daily from 7am to 8pm. Admission is free.

If you cross the park and walk east on Calle Real Xalteva for 2 blocks, you'll come across the **Iglesia de La Merced ★★**, Real Xalteva and 14 de Septiembre. This is considered Granada's most beautiful church, and its baroque facade and intricate interiors have inspired poets, while withstanding a tumultuous history of pirate attacks and civil war skirmishes. The bell tower offers great views of the city but is often not open (ask the caretaker, if you can find him). The church has irregular opening hours but it is always best to go early. Admission is free.

Six blocks farther west on Calle Xalteva is the **Fortaleza de la Pólvora,** a fort built in 1748 to guard munitions and ward off pirates. Its medieval structure was used as a jail during the Somoza dictatorship. It is now a military museum and makes for an interesting visit—you can climb one of its five small towers. It has no fixed opening hours, but you should be able to get in during the day.

Be sure to check out the rest of the city's churches, especially the dark and atmospheric **Iglesia Guadalupe** on the eastern side of the city, 4 blocks from the Parque Colón on Calle la Calzada. On the other side of town you'll find **Iglesia Xalteva,** 5 blocks west of the central plaza on Calle Xalteva. The high, arched walls were built by the Spanish to separate them from the local architecture. Continue west on Xalteva, and you'll reach the town cemetery, an elaborate *necrolandia* with some grandiose tombs, including a fair attempt at the Magdalena de Paris. On the eastern side of the city at the end of Calle La Calzada are the gray shores of **Lago Cocibolca.** Here you'll find Granada's version of a waterfront walk, known as **Complejo Turístico Cocibolca.** Though the lake provides some magnificent panoramic views, the shore is sadly neglected and litter-strewn. You'll pass it on the way to the departure point for tour boats going to Las Isletas.

Outdoor Activities

CANOPY TOURING   The slopes of **Reserva Natural Volcán Mombacho** offer some spectacular opportunities to glide through the jungle. **Canopy Tours Mombacho** (📞 505/2267-8256) has a 16-platform course close to the park entrance. **Hacienda Cutirre** has a 17-platform canopy system on the eastern face of the volcano. Trips there can be arranged through **Mombotour** (📞 505/2552-4548; www.mombotour.com). See Reserva Natural Volcán Mombacho, below, for more details.

HIKING   **Reserva Natural Volcán Mombacho** has some of the best-maintained trails in the country. Numerous travel operators offer 1-day excursions here or you can take a short bus ride to the park entrance. It is possible to hike from the city to the huge crater lake, **Laguna de Apoyo** (p. 495), a popular watering hole holding abundant wildlife within its rim. **Volcán Masaya National Park** (p. 499) offers a jaw-dropping look into the gates of hell and is possible to see in a day excursion from the city.

HORSEBACK RIDING   Blue Mountain (📞 505/2552-5323; www.bluemountainnicaragua.com) is a ranch outside the city where you can also lodge and do wildlife excursions. Rates start at C700 ($33).

KAYAKING   **Laguna de Apoyo** has several launching pads for those who like to paddle around. You can rent kayaks from lakeside lodgings **San Simian Eco Resort** (📞 505/8813-6866) or the **Monkey Hut** (📞 505/8887-3546). More interesting to explore are the chain of islands called Las Isletas in Lago de Nicaragua. Here there are some bird-filled waterways and an interesting island fort called El Fortin. **Mombotour,** Calle Atravesada, next to BDF (*©* **261/8552-4548;** www.mombotour.com), offers the local experts for this.

Shopping

The **Mercado Municipal** (open daily 6am–6pm) is a busy, sprawling hive of activity 1 block south of the central plaza. Here you'll find everything from soap to sombreros, but it is dark, dingy, and slightly claustrophobic. Shopaholics should take a morning and visit the nearby handicrafts mecca of Masaya (p. 496). **Galeria Istmo,** Calle Atravesada, in front of Bancentro (*©* **505/2552-4678**), offers the best in Nicaraguan art and design. **Casa Natal,** 1½ blocks east of Calle El Caimito (no phone), sells handicrafts from all over Nicaragua, including woodcarvings from Solentiname and black ceramics from Jinotega. **Casa de Antiguedades,** 1 block north of Calle Arsenal (*©* **505/2874-2034;** haroldsandino@hotmail.com), is a treasure-trove of antiques and is great for a morning browse. **Doña Elba Cigar Factory,** 1 block west of Iglesia Xalteva (*©* **505/8860-6715**), is a small operation producing 3,000 *puros* a day. At this factory, located in the family's home, you can learn to roll your own while sitting at an elaborate dining table engraved with a picture of the Last Supper. The factory also produces cedar gift boxes with inset pictures of Granada cathedral. The factory is open from 7am to 7pm. For English- and Spanish-language books and magazines check out the **Maverick Reading & Smoothie Lounge,** 1 block west of Casa de los Leones on Calle El Arsenal (*©* **505/2552-4120**).

Where to Stay

Granada has the best selection of colonial-style hotels in all of Nicaragua. Even the most humble *hospedaje* will have an atmospheric courtyard and gallery with rocking chairs beneath arched pillars. That said, the rooms themselves may strike you as small, with tiny bathrooms and dangerously steep stairs, especially if you have had one *cerveza* too many late at night. The high prices (remember most hotels quote prices without 15% tax) do not often reflect quality or good service, so shop around before you decide.

EXPENSIVE

Hotel Dario ★★   Hotel Dario's wedding cake facade is a little over-the-top, but magnificent. The two-story arrangement of white and green classical ornamentation leads to a lobby with intricate tiling and handsome wood panels. An elegant inner gallery of varnished pillars surrounds a courtyard with garden paths and a central fountain. Ornate flowerpots sit on white bowling-pin walls. The rooms have tall doors, wooden floors, and wrought-iron beds. Some are smallish; the best have

---

> ### Knead to Know
>
> One of Granada's most inspiring ventures is a massage parlor called **Seeing Hands,** located in the **Euro Cafe** on the northwest corner of the central plaza (*©* **505/2552-2146**). Blind locals who have been trained in the art of massage will give you a very relaxing hour on the slab for only $13, and you can even read a book from the in-house bookstore while you get massaged.

balconies with views of Mombacho. There is a small pool and tiny gym, but the best features are the lovely seating areas with giant fans overhead, adding to the feeling you are in an atmospheric period drama. The Dario is one of the best quality places in town, reliable and unforgettable. It is located on the main pedestrian street with lots of restaurants, including its own, called the **Tranvía.** There is also a charming in-house cafe called **El Chocolate.**

Calle La Calzada. ✆ **505/2552-3400.** www.hoteldario.com. 22 units. From $100 double. AE, DC, MC, V. Airport pickup $35. **Amenities:** Bar; laundry service; pool; Wi-Fi. *In room:* A/C, cable TV, Internet.

Hotel La Bocona ★★★   Everything about La Bocona is regal. This beautifully restored colonial complex has six huge rooms surrounding three courtyards, one of which has a lovely turquoise pool. Chandeliers hang over four-poster beds and period furniture. You'll feel like royalty in this palatial property 2 blocks from the main plaza. The Danish owner has remained true to the original architecture, with no walls knocked down, while converting it into a five-star establishment. For this reason, the spacious, modern bathrooms are across the courtyard (and you can get there in comfort, with slippers and robes provided). The street outside can be noisy at night, but there are plenty of nooks and crannies to escape to, including a top-notch spa, the **Cocoberry.** The hotel's name (the *little mouth*) is inspired by a colonial stone mailbox outside—the first in Granada.

Calle La Libertad, 2 blocks west of Parque Central. www.hotellabocona.com. 6 units. $100–$165 double. AE, DC, MC, V. **Amenities:** Airport pickup ($35); laundry service; pool; spa; Wi-Fi. *In room:* A/C.

Hotel Patio de Malinche 🍴 ☺   This hotel's attractive but humble entrance belies a magnificent colonial complex with two courtyards, one with a spectacular pool. A tastefully decorated two-story building with whitewashed walls and arched wooden doorways surrounds the main courtyard. This courtyard leads to large, airy rooms done up in muted tones with the occasional splash of color, like a scarlet bedspread or hand-woven tablecloth. Rocking chairs and hammocks are placed in strategic locations throughout, making for an abundance of great places to rest. It might lack the artful details of other historic hotels in the city, but the Patio de Malinche has a bright, welcoming atmosphere that makes up for it.

Calle El Caimito, by Calle El Cisne. ✆ **505/2552-2235.** www.patiodelmalinche.com. 15 units. From $82 double; from $96 triple. Rates include breakfast. AE, DC, MC, V. **Amenities:** Bar; airport pickup ($35); laundry service; pool; Wi-Fi. *In room:* A/C, cable TV, Internet.

Hotel Plaza Colon ★★★ 📷   The one abiding memory I have of this beautiful hotel is sipping rum on its wide, polished balcony, while overlooking the boisterous plaza, filled with tourists and vendors working to the rhythm of merengue. The sumptuous decor hits the right balance between colonial authenticity and the modern traveler's expectations. Rooms have modern amenities such as cable TV, but also come with grand built-in wardrobes and luxurious king-size beds. Exquisite tiled floors lead to an inner balcony that runs around a glorious courtyard and pool. Everything is lustrous and elegant and the service is prompt and reliable. Make sure to get the staff to adjust the air-conditioning to silent mode and be prepared for a dawn chorus of jackdaws outside. Adjoining the genteel lobby is an excellent wine store.

Calle Consulado, by Parque Colón. ✆ **505/2552-8489.** Fax 505/2552-8505. www.hotelplazacolon. com. 27 units. From $114 double; from $195 suite. Rates include breakfast. AE, DC, MC, V. **Amenities:** Wine bar; Internet in lobby; pool. *In room:* A/C, cable TV, minibar.

La Gran Francia ★★ 📷   Staying at la Gran Francia feels like residing in a museum—a beautiful, well-located, and courtly museum. Impeccably done religious paintings hang on the walls and a wooden monk greets you at the bottom of the stairs. The Spanish-tiled steps lead to an upper gallery surrounding a long courtyard with a small pool below. The rooms are grand in every sense. An ample, inviting bed is surrounded by considerable space, punctuated with stout furniture and a small balcony overlooking a busy side street. In the good-size bathrooms, original ironwork faucets hang over hand-painted wash basins displaying old-fashioned street scenes. My only criticism is that the staff is very much like the sculptures—wooden and unresponsive. Across the street is the hotel's **restaurant,** which boasts a mellow, inviting bar where guests can enjoy a free welcome drink after checking in.

Southeast corner of Parque Central and Calle El Caimito. ⓒ **505/2552-6000.** Fax 505/2552-6001. www.lagranfrancia.com. 21 units. From $125 double; from $140 triple; from $137 suite. Rates include breakfast. AE, MC, V. **Amenities:** Restaurant; bar; laundry service; pool; room service. In room: A/C, cable TV, Internet, minibar.

MODERATE

Bohemian Paradise ★★ 🐟 *Buena, bonita, barata* (lovely, gorgeous, and cheap) is how you would describe this intimate guesthouse. The Bohemian Paradise is bright, modern, and a little plain. It may not look like much from the outside—a mustard-colored street cottage—but once you enter, there's a pleasant arrangement of comfortable rooms. Sizes vary; the king suite is the largest and most magnificent. It has a Jacuzzi surrounded by tall windows and an open-air shower. There is a lovely private balcony in the king suite with a view of the lake. Out back is a long, narrow garden with a fountain and plants. The co-owner Lucy is English-speaking and friendly, making it more of a homestay than a hotel. Price-wise it beats everybody.

Calle Corrales, 1½ blocks east of Antiguo Convento San Francisco. ⓒ **505/2552-0286.** www.seecentral america.com. 5 units. From $35 queen double; $80 king double. AE, DC, MC, V. **Amenities:** Internet in lobby. *In room:* A/C, cable TV.

Hotel Alhambra The grand old dame of Granada, the Hotel Alhambra is an example of just how a luxury hotel used to be. Here you'll find a purpose-built hotel with all the creature comforts as well as a flamboyant nod to Granada's colonial past. The elaborate facade of pillars, arches, cornices, and pink relief leads to an atmospheric lobby with an old-world feel. Marble floors are bordered by intricate Spanish tiles amid antique furniture and big, old lamps. There's the mandatory lush courtyard out back and an ample round pool. The front rooms with balcony are the best appointed, and all have chunky period beds, colorful quilted bedding, and heavy, sagging drapes. Some rooms could do with a little sprucing up, but in general everything is quite clean and well maintained. Its location right in front of the Central Plaza means you are right in the thick of it.

Northwest corner of Central Plaza. ⓒ **505/2552-4488.** www.hotelalhambra.com.ni. 60 units. From $85 double. AE, DC, MC, V. **Amenities:** Restaurant; Internet cafe; laundry; pool; room service. *In room:* A/C, cable TV, minibar, Wi-Fi.

Hotel Casa San Martin Quaint, authentic, and reasonably priced, the simple and unassuming exterior of the Casa San Martin gives way to elegant rooms that surround a small courtyard with an inviting gallery of wicker rocking chairs, multicolored tables, and ceramic urns. The decor is simple with hardwood floors, wrought-iron beds, and vintage lamps. The rooms are large, but a little dark. The central location on the main pedestrian street can be a little noisy and some rooms are too close to the kitchen.

Calle La Calzada, 1 block east of Central Plaza. ⓒ **505/2552-6185.** www.hcasasanmartin.com. 8 units. From $55 double. AE, DC, MC, V. **Amenities:** Laundry. *In room:* A/C.

Hotel Colonial ★ 🎁　As you approach this midsize hotel and note its attractive, navy blue facade and row of international flags, you might think it is just another conventional lodging. Yes, it is, but it's conventionally done Granada style. The reception area is a spectacle of green walls and Corinthian pillars holding up an intricate ceiling of classic moldings. Balustrades of marble are graced with giant Grecian urns holding potted plants. The courtyard, with a pool and mosaic-covered island bar, is just as lavish. The hotel's rainbow colors run into the rooms themselves, which are big with beautiful four-poster beds and polished floors. The suites have giant corner Jacuzzis tucked beneath green tiled archways. It is all rather over-the-top, but refreshingly different for anyone used to the muted gray and beige tones that seem to plague the modern chain hotel. This hotel has character as well as a friendly, professional, bilingual staff.

Calle La Libertad, 25m (82 ft.) west of Parque Central. ✆ **505/2552-7581.** Fax 505/2552-7299. www. hotelcolonialgranada.com. 37 units. From $75 double. AE, DC, MC, V. **Amenities:** Restaurant; pool. *In room:* A/C, cable TV, Wi-Fi.

Hotel La Pergola 🎁　La Pergola gets its name from a roof terrace with a view of the cathedral and Mombacho. It is not a bad place to end an evening and plan your itinerary while gazing over the rooftops. Cream-colored walls are fringed with colorful tiles and shaded by heavy eaves and simple arches. Rosebushes and swinging chairs adorn a spacious gallery that leads to large, simple rooms. This is the best-value colonial-style lodging I found, though I must warn you, there are problems with the hot water.

Calle El Caimito, 3 blocks east of Central Plaza. ✆ **505/2552-4221.** www.lapergola.com.ni. 11 units. From $48 double. AE, DC, MC, V. Free parking. **Amenities:** Bar; room service. *In room:* A/C, Wi-Fi.

La Casona de los Estrada ★　A stay at this boutique property ensures that you'll have a classic Granada experience. You'll feel like one of the old aristocracy as you walk through its wide entrance hall graced with a huge gilded mirror, and into the large open courtyard filled with plants and flowers. The rooms are handsome with high wooden ceilings and tiled floors. Some are much bigger than others—ask what is available at check-in. The bathrooms are smallish, but spotless, and everything is well maintained. This place manages to make you feel like you're staying at an enormous palace when there are only six rooms, some of which overlook the garden and one of which has a private courtyard. There's a friendly, attentive staff.

Calle El Arsenal, by the Antiguo Convento San Francisco. ✆ **505/2552-7393.** www.casonalosestrada. com. 6 units. From $50 double. Rates include breakfast. AE, DC, MC, V. **Amenities:** Bar; airport transfers ($35); room service. *In room:* A/C, cable TV.

INEXPENSIVE

Bearded Monkey　The Bearded Monkey is the most popular and funky *mochilero* hangout in Granada. With its huge bulletin board, free movies, book exchange, music library, and many hammocks, it's a backpacker's paradise. The cafe bar is a good meeting point. There's a dartboard to help break the ice and bikes to rent if you wish to explore. The old colonial building holds both dorms and private rooms, some of which have no windows and all of which have shared bathrooms. A mosquito net will come in handy here, as will bug spray. The owners also operate the Monkey Hut in Laguna de Apoyo (p. 496).

Av. 14 de Septiembre and Costado. ✆ **505/2552-4028.** www.thebeardedmonkey.com. 10 units (including 3 large dorms). From $6 dorm; $14–$17 double; from $24 triple; $22–$36 suite. AE, DC, MC, V. **Amenities:** Restaurant; bar; high-speed Internet in lobby; laundry facilities. *In room:* No phone.

Hostel Oasis ★★ 🔥 This hostel has nary a multicolored barn door or funky mosaic-tiled bathroom in sight. The Oasis breaks the mold by offering the sort of stylish facilities you'd expect in a more expensive B&B, except here guests sleep in dorms and can use the kitchen. Its main asset is its great pool in a back courtyard surrounded by stone-clad columns holding up a gallery of balconies and doorways. There is also a pleasant garden courtyard with lounge chairs. The dorms are basic but not too claustrophobic, though the bunk beds might be too short for lankier visitors. The private rooms are small and functional, all the furniture matches, the TV works, and everything is immaculate. Some have their own bathrooms. The Oasis is for the more discerning *mochilero* who wants a little luxury without paying too high a price.

Calle Estrada and Av. Barricada. ℂ **505/2552-8006.** www.nicaraguahostel.com. 21 units. From $8 dorm; from $13 private room. AE, DC, MC, V. **Amenities:** Cafe; high-speed Internet in lobby; laundry service; pool. *In room:* A/C (extra charge), fan, cable TV (extra charge).

Where to Dine

Most restaurants are on the pedestrian street Calle La Calzada or 2 blocks north of it, close to Antiguo Convento San Francisco. Recent years have seen an explosion of gourmet options with foreign-owned eateries competing with the locals and often winning, as they have more variety. However, if you want a true Granada snack experience, try the delicious *chancho con yucca* (pork served on banana leaf) from a stall on the plaza; served with tropical marimba music in the background, it's at least as good as waffles or smoothies and a mite more genuine.

EXPENSIVE

El Arcángel Restaurant ★★ INTERNATIONAL Not everybody can afford to stay at one of Granada's most opulent hotels, La Gran Francia, but most can round up $14 to dine at its elegant restaurant. Decor-wise, it is truly *de Granada,* with obligatory tropical courtyard, high ceilings, and antique trappings. What makes El Arcángel stand out is its menu. The food is modern, eclectic, and adventurous. Who could resist whiskey-slathered steak or snapper cooked in banana and brown sugar? Treat yourself.

Southeast corner of Central Plaza. ℂ **505/2552-6000.** www.lagranfrancia.com. Main courses from C280 ($13). AE, DC, MC, V. Daily 11am–11pm.

El Tercer Ojo ★ ASIAN FUSION El Tercer Ojo is an exotic haven of Far Eastern delights. The interior is a visual feast, with purple silk cushions and curtains and a golden Buddha watching from the liquor shelf. A small bar with Parisian prints leads to a pleasant courtyard adorned with artwork and masks. The menu is extensive and includes Asian staples such as Thai chicken and shrimp with Vietnamese curry. There are a variety of tapas, shish kabob, and fish dishes. This laid-back and intimate restaurant also has a pretty good international wine list with offerings from Argentina, Italy, Spain, France, and Chile.

Calle El Arsenal, on the corner of Antiguo Convento San Francisco. ℂ **505/2552-6451.** Main courses from C200 ($9.30). AE, DC, MC, V. Daily 11am–11pm.

Restaurante El Tranvía ★★ INTERNATIONAL/SEAFOOD This old-fashioned restaurant is tucked inside the roomy Hotel Dario. Its large white salon, with giant doors looking out onto Calle La Calzada and old black-and-white photos on the wall, makes for an elegant and cool setting. The menu is very much concentrated on seafood, with lobster from the Corn Islands featured. The shrimp *al Diablo* is a spicy mix of shrimp with pepper, tomatoes, and ginger. It also comes in a curry sauce or a

VOLUNTEERING opportunities IN NICARAGUA

Nicaragua has always attracted an unconventional tourist, starting with the pirates and Californian gold prospectors centuries ago. A new breed of visitor appeared after the Sandinista revolution—thousands of *internacionalistas* intent on joining the great leap forward and helping the country's poor and impoverished (the less than committed were wittily referred to as Sandalistas). Those idealists have morphed into ordinary people doing amazing things, and Nicaragua is a hot spot for volunteering opportunities in Central America. Below is a list of the more established volunteer organizations offered in the country, but just scratch the surface, and you'll find many more. If you are serious about taking up a good cause, you need to commit considerable time (at least a month) and have basic Spanish skills to get the most from your experience.

GRANADA

Building New Hope (www.building newhope.org) is a Pittsburgh-based nonprofit organization that runs a learning center for underprivileged kids, among many other projects in Granada. The volunteer organizer is Donna Tabor and she can be contacted through their website. Tax-deductible donations are also welcome.

Hogar Madre Albertina (© 505/2552-7661) is a girls' orphanage that needs money and volunteers. Desperate to get rid of an old laptop? You can donate yours here, as well as donate your time by teaching a computer class. The orphanage is 2 blocks north of Colegio Padre Misieri.

La Esperanza Granada (© 505/2552-7044; www.la-esperanza-granada.org) helps educate locals in rural areas as well as offering much-needed healthcare. They provide cheap accommodations and can organize homestays if you're looking for total cultural and language immersion. Their office is in Hospedaje Central, 1½ blocks east of the central plaza.

SAN JUAN DEL SUR

San Juan del Sur Biblioteca Movil (janem101@aol.com) is sponsored by the Hester J. Hodgdon Libraries for All Program. Teachers and donations are needed, as well as Spanish books, which can be sent to the library's U.S. depository at 1716 del Norte Blvd.,

---

sauce of scotch and mushrooms mixed with coconut milk. The wine list is decent. The dining experience here is definitely romantic—you may get serenaded by some wandering musicians during your meal. The waiters are dressed formally but wear a smile.

Calle La Calzada (150m/492 ft.) northeast from the cathedral. © **505/2552-3400.** www.hoteldario. com/tranviaeng.htm. Main courses C300–C400 ($14–$19). AE, DC, MC, V. Daily noon–10pm.

MODERATE

El Zaguan STEAKHOUSE   This modern restaurant may lack the exotic charm of other establishments but it is undoubtedly the best place for steak in town. The redbrick bar and walls are split by a curved wicker partition and the tablecloths come with a tartan design. It's the open-flame grill that will attract your attention, draped as it is with slabs of beef. Some dishes come complete with a minigrill that sits beside you on the table, sizzling with sausage and ribs. The service is excellent and the experience is often accompanied by serenading mariachis.

Street behind cathedral. No phone. Main courses C180 ($8.35). AE, DC, MC, V. Daily noon–3pm and 6–11pm.

Loveland, CO 80538, or dropped off when you visit.

The **Newton-San Juan del Sur Sister City Project** (www.newtonsanjuan.org) is a Massachusetts-based nonprofit organization that sends teams of doctors, dentists, and builders to San Juan. Visit their website or e-mail local representative Rosa Elena Bello at **rosaebel@ibw.com.ni**.

MATAGALPA

Habitat for Humanity (📞 505/2772-6121; www.habitatnicaragua.org.ni) is a Christian organization that builds housing for the poor in an effort to "change Nicaragua house by house." They have projects all over the country, including León and Bluefields. Their Matagalpa branch is 2 blocks east of the Deportiva Brigadista.

Centro Girasol (📞 505/2772-6030) is a community center that can hook you up with different organizations that need volunteers, such as indigenous rights campaigners **Movimento Comunal** and **Comunidad Indígena.** Their offices are in the yellow building at the bridge, as you enter the city from Managua.

OMETEPE

Nuestro Pequeños Hermanos (www.nph.org) operates an orphanage in San Lázaro that offers volunteer programs on the island and in other parts of Central America.

La Suerte Biological Teaching Station (www.lasuerte.org) is dedicated to protecting rainforests and wildlife. They offer teaching opportunities to students and professors and accommodate educational groups with the goal of "Bridging the Americas."

Bainbridge-Ometepe Sisters Island Association (www.bosia.org) does countless good works on the island, including promoting fair-trade coffee, creating schools, offering scholarships, and improving water systems.

MANAGUA

Si a la Vida (www.asalv.org) works with troubled kids and expands their opportunities through education, sports, and art. They seek volunteers with experience in healthcare, construction, and agriculture. They also operate a retreat on Ometepe Island.

Eurocafe CAFE   This busy coffeehouse/bookstore is on the northeastern corner of the central plaza and has a hip, traveler vibe with a relaxing courtyard out back and a Ping-Pong table in the corner of the garden. The bookstore is small and to the side, with a limited selection of paperbacks that start at $10. The real attraction here is a mug of steaming Nicaraguan coffee and delicious homemade Italian ice cream and pastries.

Esquina Noreoeste del Parque Cenral, Granada. 📞 **505/2552-2146.** www.eurocafenica.com. Snacks C150 ($7). AE, DC, MC, V. Daily 7:30am–9pm.

Garden Café 📷 CAFE   When a Californian and a Nicaraguan met in a Managua university to study international relations, they took their course work literally and decided to get hitched. The result is one of Granada's coolest cafes with the brightest, healthiest menu. Here you'll find a leafy respite with a courtyard that could only be described as 60 sq. m (645 sq. ft.) of sumptuous jungle. Excellent smoothies, well-presented salads, and elaborate sandwiches sate thirst and hunger. Some of the best coffee in town goes well with the muffins and lemon cake. The large hammock often provokes good-humored arguments among diners over whose turn it is to take it.

Calle La Libertad, 1 block east of Plaza. 📞 **505/2552-8582.** Snacks C80 ($3.70). Mon–Sat 7am–3pm.

Imagine Bar and Restaurant INTERNATIONAL   This cozy, corner town house has an appealing menu that offers platters of squash that look like art, or warm brie served with roasted garlic, or succulent lamb chops with chimichurri sauce. Owner Kevin Cohen will gladly give you a quick tour of the open kitchen out back with the hottest grill in town, fired up by lava rocks from Masaya volcano. As well as having some homegrown veggie options, Mr. Cohen has mastered a dessert made from mangos from his own farm. The mango bread, drenched in ice cream and chocolate syrup, wins raves from the clientele. The owner is an accomplished guitarist who often jams with the live-music bands that play Tuesday, Thursday, Friday, and Saturday. Kevin is also a licensed boat operator, specializing in taking people to the islands of Zapatera.

Calle La Libertad and Calle Cervantes. ⓒ **505/2552-4672.** www.imaginerestaurantbar.com. Main courses C180 ($8.35). AE, DC, MC, V. Sun–Wed 5–10pm; Thurs–Sat 5pm–1am.

Kathy's Waffle House CAFE   Kathy's seems to be the breakfast spot for foreigners in Granada, though the occasional local drops by to enjoy menu items such as massive Belgian waffles in a variety of delicious syrups. French toast and full egg breakfasts are also on the menu, as well as very decent milkshakes and smoothies. Diners sit on an elevated patio in front of the beautiful Convento San Francisco—it's a perfect spot to start your day and plot out your itinerary.

Calle El Arsenal, ½ block west of the Antiguo Convento San Francisco. No phone. Snacks from C100 ($4.65). AE, MC, V. Daily 7am–2pm.

Granada After Dark

The more upscale bars and nightclubs in town are west of the central plaza, while the more down-at-heel local joints are on the lakeshore close to the Complejo Turístico. Here there is a strip of bars and nightclubs, the best of which are **Pantera** (no phone) and **Cesars** (ⓒ **505/2552-7241**). Be warned, however, that wandering this part of town at night is for the young, adventurous, and even foolish. If you do fancy a night by the lake, dress down and make sure you get a taxi back, as the walk into the city is through a notoriously crime-ridden spot.

El Club, Calle La Libertad and Avenida Barricada Granada (ⓒ **505/2552-7376;** www.elclub-nicaragua.com), is young, trendy, and cool. A well-appointed disco bar up front leads to a designer-style courtyard of pebbled walkways, backlit palm trees, and purposely worn furniture. **Zoom Bar,** La Calzada, 3 blocks from Parque Colón (ⓒ **505/8643-5855;** http://nicaraguarestaurant.typepad.com/zoombargranada/home_page), is a good place to go for huge burgers and sports. **O'Shea's** (ⓒ **505/8454 1140**) is a small Irish bar on the pedestrian street La Calzada and is alive with late-night revelers enjoying fish and chips, baked potatoes, and chicken curry. The owner is a Dubliner called Tom who runs the long, narrow bar with efficient ease. The pub quiz on Wednesdays is very popular. **Kelly's Bar,** La Sirena and El Caimito (ⓒ **505/8825-1078**), is another popular bar, sometimes heaving with beer-soaked gringos and locals at 3pm. It's the type of place where the TV sits on beer crates and you have to shout to be heard, but it is a happening spot with live music on weekends.

Side Trips from Granada
LAS ISLETAS
Trailing away from Granada's southern waterfront is the 354-island archipelago known as Las Isletas, formed by a volcanic eruption from nearby Mombacho over 10,000 years ago. These tiny jungle islands are parts of the mountain blown into the

lake during a massive eruption. They are now lush mounds that host mini–monkey sanctuaries, humble *campesino* huts and lavish mansions, and attractions such as an island cemetery and an old Spanish fort called **Fortín San Pablo.** It is a popular day trip, and boats leave frequently from the southern end of the **Complejo Turístico Cocibolca** (the lakeshore tourist area). You can go there on your own by taking a taxi or walking a half-hour south along the shore of the Centro Turístico until you reach a building with small pontoons and boats that leave as soon as they fill up. Or take a tour with any of the travel operators in the city center (p. 482).

I found the conventional tour of the islands to be a disappointment. Every rock seemed to be sporting a real estate sign and the motorboats scared away all wildlife. The quality of restaurants in the touristy parts of the islands leaves a lot to be desired, with limited menus and outhouse restrooms (bring your own toilet paper).

The true way to enjoy the islands, and avoid the hordes, is to get up early and go farther out in a kayak or private boat. Aquatic birds such as egrets, herons, and cranes can be spotted in the early morning or evening, as well as kingfishers and cormorants. You soon realize that the islands are individual communities, each with a school, a cemetery, restaurants, and bars on individual mounds of basalt topped with tall ceiba trees and mango orchards. Though wealthy weekenders have started buying up their own private slices of paradise (usually on the north side of the archipelago), the vast majority of the islanders are poor and survive on fishing *guapote* and *mojarra* from the dark waters on the south side. This is by far the most interesting part to see. Conventional agencies offer short, unsatisfactory tours of the islands. For something more thorough, try agencies such as **Mombotour** (p. 495). If you'd like to stay on the islands, the best place is the new, plush **Jicaro Lodge ★★** (© **505/2552-6353;** www.jicarolodge.com), an upscale island getaway with a matching price of $480 for a double room in the high season.

PARQUE NACIONAL ARCHIPIELAGO ZAPATERA

A separate archipelago from Las Isletas, known as **Archipiélago Zapatera,** lies 2 hours away from Granada and is famous for its pre-Columbian stone carvings (a spectacular collection of which can be seen in the Convento San Francisco; see p. 483). There are 11 islands in total, the largest of which is **Isla Zapatera,** a dormant volcano covered in both tropical dry and wet forest. Rising to 625m (2,050 ft.), the island boasts lots of wildlife, a crater lake, and more than 20 archaeological sites that date back as far as 500 B.C. The vast range of zoomorphic statues,.many of which have been shipped to the mainland and as far off as the Smithsonian Institute, reveal that the island was once an important religious site.

There is still plenty left behind to see, and indeed there is much more thought to be buried underneath that the government cannot afford to dig out. One of the most interesting places is **Zonzapote,** which seems to have been part of an amphitheater or a temple belonging to the Chorotega tribe. There are some great hiking opportunities on the island, including a trek to **Banderas Hill** and a more arduous climb to the island's highest point, **Cerro Grande,** also known as **Zapatera Hill.** The view is spectacular with Ometepe Island in the distance. There is a small settlement of people in Sonzapote, ex-refugees from the Contra war, among whom you can find a guide to take you around.

Isla el Muerto is a small island to the north. Its moniker, "Death Island," might deter you from visiting, but a little fearlessness will pay off, and you can see some of the most spectacular rock drawings in the country. They are laid out on a huge slab of stone measuring 100×25m (328×82 ft.) on the island's summit. The location is believed to be a burial site, thus the name.

It is wise to visit the islands with a reputable tour agency such as **Oro Travel** or **Tours Nicaragua** (p. 443), the latter of which provides a National Museum archaeologist as a guide to explain the island's many wonders. Otherwise, the archipelago, 40km (25 miles) south of Granada, can take an hour or more by *panga* (open motorboat).

There is a public boat service from Puerto Asese (℡ **505/2552-2269**) or you can hire a private boat for between $100 and $150 round-trip. If you do decide to visit independently, remember this is a national park and a ranger may ask you for your permit from MARENA, which you can get only in San Salvador. A guide is obligatory to hike the island and there are no stores, though there are a few very rough, basic lodges and restaurants.

RESERVA NATURAL VOLCAN MOMBACHO ★★

Look south from your hotel balcony and you'll see a mountain with a wide, blunted summit. Look closer and you'll realize that the summit is in fact the jagged crater of a huge volcano that blew its top 10,000 years ago. Volcán Mombacho is still active, though it has been 500 years since its last significant eruption knocked its side wall out and drained its lake, sweeping away an Indian village called Nandaime in the process.

Hidden in its high, dark cloud forest are red-eyed frogs, howler monkeys, orchids, a dazzling array of butterflies, and a species of salamander unique to the mountain. In all, there are 119 types of birds, 60 species of animals, 10 varieties of amphibians, 28 species of reptiles, and an amazing 30,000 different insects, only 300 of which have been documented and identified. Its lower slopes have given way to coffee plantations and ranches, but its upper reaches are now a protected reserve, with some of the best-maintained nature trails in the country. One such trail is called **Sendero el Crater,** a 1.6km (1-mile) track around the volcano's 1,345m-high (4,413-ft.) rim, during which you'll have ample chances to take in the forest-lined interior and its numerous mammals, birds, and types of flora. During this hike, you will also pass fascinating fumaroles—ground vents blasting hot, sulfurous air. More serious hikers should try **Sendero la Puma,** a more arduous trek that is twice as long and involves climbing to some lookout points with fantastic views. It takes 3 hours to complete. The volcano has five craters, three of which are covered in vegetation. The summits can be quite cloudy, but usually clear in the early afternoon, offering great views of Granada and Las Isletas. To see the most of the abundant wildlife, it is recommended you stay overnight at the research center and trek in the early morning. Day-trippers usually have to suffice with the abundant flora of the cloud forest, including ferns and bromeliads.

The reserve is managed by an NGO called **Fundación Cocibolca** (℡ **505/2552-5858;** www.mombacho.org) and is open from Tuesday to Sunday, though Tuesday and Wednesday are normally reserved for organized groups. Admission is C200 ($9.30). The most convenient way to visit the reserve is through the numerous travel operators in town that offer 1-day excursions; see p. 482 for info. If you wish to go there independently, jump on a Rivas or Nandaime bus and alight at Empalme el Guanacaste. It is then a half-hour walk uphill to the park entrance. Once you pay the entrance fee, an old army truck leaves every 2 hours to take you up to the foundation's Biological Station 6km (3¾ miles) away. Here they offer mountain-lodge-style accommodations if you wish to spend the night on the side of an active volcano. There is also an interesting model of the volcano explaining its evolution. If you have your own transport (4WD only), there is an extra charge of C300 ($14) per vehicle to enter the reserve.

In addition to great hiking, the slopes of Mombacho offer some spectacular canopy runs. **Canopy Tours Mombacho** (© 261/8888-2566) is close to the reserve entrance. This 16-platform course is 1,700m (5,577 ft.) long, and many tour operators include it in their 1-day tour of the reserve. Here you sweep over coffee plantations and tall trees before enjoying a drink on a viewing platform at the end of the ride. The company is not part of the park management, but they pick you up in the same area as the park truck, so you have to enter the park. There is also a spectacular 17-platform canopy system at **Hacienda Cutirre ★** on the eastern face of the volcano. This is a little more hard-core and challenging but no less exhilarating. The fact that it was designed by the inventor of the sport means you're in for a heart-stopping ride, including a vertical descent on a rappel line at the end. The site is difficult to access independently and best arranged with travel operators and canopy specialists **Mombotour** (© 261/2552-4548; www.mombotour.com). A day trip costs C800 ($37).

RESERVA SILVESTRE PRIVADA DOMITILA

Thirty-five kilometers (22 miles) south of Granada, on the lakeshore, there is a private reserve with one of the best, and few, examples of lowland tropical dry forest in the country. Wildcats and howler monkeys prowl this rustic property, and because it is so small there is a good chance of catching sight of them. Also ready to pose for any photographers are a vast array of birds, butterflies, and mammals. There is a basic lodge offering full board accommodations for a somewhat pricey $65 per person, but it is worth it if you want to spend time in such a beautiful place. The property can be explored on horseback and the owners organize sailing trips to the nearby Zapatera Archipelago, just offshore (see above). Day-trippers are charged $5 admission, and it's an additional $10 to $40 for a guide to show you around. The foliage can get a little bare in the summer, so it is best to visit in the rainy season, from November to January. The reserve can be reached only by 4WD and it is best arranged with the reserve's agent **Amigo Tours** in the Hotel Colonial (© 261/2552-4080), or you should contact the reserve owner Maria José Mejía directly at Casa Dr. Francisco Barbarena in Granada city (© 261/2552-4548; www.domitila.org).

LAGUNA DE APOYO

Directly west of Granada is a huge, pristine volcano lake known as Laguna de Apoyo. This dark-blue body of water is 200m (656 ft.) deep and set in a lush, forest-covered circular valley with nature trails, small villages, and the occasional ministerial mansion. The crater is alive with animals, including white-faced monkeys, butterflies, toucans, and hummingbirds. The Volcán Apoyo is very much dormant, though it is known to tremor occasionally and the lake holds some underwater thermal vents. Because of the lake's isolated habitat, it contains several unique species of fish. There are a handful of restaurants and lodges on the lakeshore, but to truly appreciate the lake's sweeping grandeur, it is best to view it from the rim above, especially from the several miradors you come across while touring the Pueblos Blancos (see the "Masaya" section, below).

Getting There

It's a 20-minute drive from Granada to Laguna de Apoyo, and a C300 ($14) taxi ride is the most convenient way of getting there. Alternatively, you can arrange the trip via the hostel **Bearded Monkey** (see earlier in this chapter) or its sister lodge, the

Monkey Hut (see below). Don't think about driving on your own; once you get off the highway from Granada, the road is a beautifully brick-paved lane—an anomaly in a country with such bad roads. But the perfect paving stops after just a few minutes, and the rest of the way makes for very difficult driving.

Another way of getting to the lake is to simply walk from Granada. A dirt road from the city cemetery's northeast corner heads west until you reach a crossroads just below the crater's lip. You must then turn right and cross a field to get a view of the lake. The trek takes approximately 3 hours there and back.

Where to Stay

There are several hotels and lodges along the lakeshore, many with wooden piers for swimmers and kayakers. **Crater's Edge,** Laguna de Apoyo (© **505/8895-3202;** www.craters-edge.com), is a modern, one-story red-brick building with a broad roof and lots of light. Several levels of patios accommodate deck chairs and hammocks affording lovely views of the lake. It's affiliated with Hostel Oasis in Granada, and there's a daily shuttle bus that leaves every day at 10am and 4pm to the sister property; it costs C100 ($4.65) and takes 30 minutes. Doubles range from $22 to $44. The **Monkey Hut,** Laguna de Apoyo, 100m (328 ft.) from the bottom of the hill (© **505/8887-3546;** www.thebeardedmonkey.com/monkeyhut.htm), is the sister lodge to the Bearded Monkey in Granada but has a lot more class. This property's wide, terraced garden, filled with comfy sun loungers, leads down to the shore. Guests stay in a handsome wooden cottage with dorms or a separate cabana. Double rooms start at $23. **Norome Villas ★**, on the eastern shore of Laguna de Apoyo (© **505/8883-9093;** www.noromevillas.com), is a large, self-contained resort that is easily the most luxurious lodging on the lake. Nicely tiled floors lead to orange Caribbean-style villas. There is a gorgeous pool and spectacular lakeside restaurant and bar. Doubles start at $65.

MASAYA

89km (55 miles) from Granada

Welcome to Masaya—Nicaragua's capital of shopping. In a country that is a treasure-trove of quality handicrafts, Masaya is the industrious nucleus, churning out an endless array of tempting souvenirs such as intricate pottery, handsome woodcarvings, sturdy leather goods, and beautiful hand-woven hammocks. This restless city of 100,000 creative souls is spread along a hot plain and up a gentle slope to the Masaya crater lake, with the smoldering Volcán Masaya in the distance. Though it was first explored by the Spanish in the 16th century, the city was not founded until 1819. It has a fiery history of rebellion and resistance to whoever tried to impose their will, be it a volcano, filibusterer, American Marine, or dictator. What was left of the city's colonial heritage was shattered by a series of earthquakes in 2000, yet it retains a colorful and vibrant character.

Most visitors experience Masaya as a 1-day shopping trip from the capital or Granada, and many never venture beyond the Gothic, palm-lined walls of Masaya's block-size Old Market (Mercado Viejo). That's a pity, as the city has more to offer than what you can stuff in your suitcase. In addition to its beautiful waterfront promenade and an old fort, the nearby Volcán Masaya is the most accessible active crater in the country and the most terrifying and exciting to visit. In the surrounding table-top mountains are a string of villages known as the **Pueblos Blancos,** each with its own niche in hand-honed craftsmanship. Masaya is also famous for throwing a good street party, with festivals running throughout the year featuring such colorful participants as 3.6m-tall (12-ft.) women on stilts, costumed dogs, and "headless" priests. Arrive at the right time, in fact, and you might never want to leave the party.

Essentials

GETTING THERE

BY BUS   From Managua, take any southbound bus from the Mercado Huembes. You'll be dropped off at Masaya's **Mercado Municipal,** on the western side of the city. The journey takes 1 hour and costs C20 (95¢). Another departure point in Managua is the **UCA** (p. 505), from where microbuses leave every 20 minutes, dropping passengers off at **Parque San Miguel,** 1 block east of the Mercado Viejo. The ride is 45 minutes and costs C20 (95¢).

From Granada take any Managua-bound bus from **COGRAN,** 1½ blocks southwest of the plaza, or one of the Masaya *expresos* that leave from behind the **Palé Supermarket.** The journey takes 45 minutes and costs C20 (95¢), and passengers are dropped off at Masaya's Mercado Municipal. The Mercado is also the main departure point when you are leaving Masaya.

BY TAXI/SHUTTLE   **Paxeos,** beside the cathedral in Granada (© **505/2552-8291;** www.paxeos.com), can organize private and shared transfers to and from Masaya. The trip to Granada costs between C570 and C860 ($17–$40), depending on group size.

GETTING AROUND

A car is not necessary in the city but definitely is worthwhile if you want to explore the surrounding area. **Budget** (© **505/2522-5788**) has an office at Km 28, Carretera Masaya. **Hotel Ivania's** (p. 500) is the only place in town that rents out cars. Alternatively, you might hire a taxi for the day so you can sit back, relax, and not get lost. A car and driver for the day in this area should cost approximately C1,100 ($51).

VISITOR INFORMATION

Intur (© **505/2522-7615**) is inside the Mercado Viejo and offers good maps and information regarding workshops in the surrounding area. It is open Monday to Friday from 8am to 12:30pm and 1:30 to 5pm, and on Saturday from 8am to 12:30pm.

FAST FACTS   There are plenty of ATMs conveniently located within the Mercado Viejo (Old Market). **Banpro** (© **505/2522-7366**) is on the southwestern corner of the market, as is **Bancentro** (© **505/2522-4337**). **Banco de América Central** changes traveler's checks and is located 1 block north of the market. You will also find many street money-changers in this area.

There are several Internet cafes on the south side of the park. **Cablenet Café** is opposite the Hotel Regis and is open daily from 8am to 10pm, except Sundays, when it closes at 3pm. The main **hospital** (© **505/2522-2778**) is on the main road to Granada. The city's **police station** (© **505/2522-4222**) is a half-block north of the old market. A post office is inside the Mercado Viejo, as is a DHL counter.

What to See & Do

ATTRACTIONS IN MASAYA

Mercado Nacionál de Artesanía ★★, also known as the Mercado Viejo, is the biggest attraction in town. This entire block is a hive of stalls and cultural activity and is the showcase market for the country's handicrafts industry. Built in 1891, it was

FESTIVALS IN masaya

The Masaya calendar is so chock-full of parades and street parties, you have to wonder how the locals ever get around to weaving the hammocks or making the rocking chairs they're so famous for selling. The city's festivals are a rich mix of indigenous, religious, and colonial customs, and all the parties here are very much a family affair, with each household bringing its own particular flavor to the celebrations. Below is a month-by-month listing of the best festivals.

January: Drums, whistles, and chanting reverberate around the streets of Masaya during the **Festival of San Sebastian,** particularly in the barrio of Monimbó. Sticks clatter as a battle is staged before the eventual reconciliation, when crowds shout "Viva San Sebastian!" Though Masaya's celebrations are good, the town of Diriamba (30km/19 miles southwest of Masaya) is generally recognized as throwing the most colorful and authentic San Sebastian parade in the country, with a lively mix of pagan satire and colonial pomp.

The festival takes place on January 19, 20, and 21.

February: Every dog gets its day during the 3 weeks before Easter Sunday. Locals spill out onto the city streets with their pets dolled up in elaborate costumes for the **Festival of San Lázaro.** They are giving thanks to the patron saint of pets for keeping their little loved ones in good health. The canine fashion parade gathers first at the Santa Maria Magdalena church on Plaza Monimbó and then parades from there.

March/April: The whole country goes crazy for Easter, and Masaya is no different during Semana Santa celebrations.

May: The Santiago crater in Volcán Masaya National Park burst into life in 1852 and threatened to engulf the city until it was stopped in its tracks by **La Señora de la Asunción.** This miracle is celebrated on May 20, by people swamping the streets and exchanging crosses made from platted palm leaves.

destroyed during the revolution and restored in 1997. It is easy to stay several hours within its stone walls and browse the many stalls selling everything from cotton hammocks to colorful art. Here you'll also find conventional stores, cafes, ATMs, and the tourist office. The market is 1 block east of the central plaza, also known as Parque 17 de Octubre. It's open daily from 8am to 7pm.

Museo y Galería Héroes y Mártires (inside the town hall, Alcaldía, 1½ blocks north of the central park; no phone) is a small museum dedicated to those who fought the Somoza regime. Among its exhibits of photos and guns is an unexploded napalm bomb. The museum is open Monday to Friday from 8am to 5pm. Admission is free but donations are welcome. **El Malecón ★** is the breezy city promenade 6 blocks west of the central plaza. It sits high above the waterline but affords great views and has several cafes. This waterfront comes alive with people whenever there is a game at the nearby baseball stadium. It's a great place to visit on a horse-drawn carriage ride.

The **Catedral de la Asunción** (on the main plaza; no phone) is also worth a visit. Damaged by the 2000 earthquake, the early-19th-century baroque church is undergoing restoration but can still be entered during services; admission is free. **Iglesia de San Jerónimo** (5 blocks north of the central plaza; no phone) is a plainer church but affords a great view from its bell tower. Admission is 50¢.

June: During the month of June, the Pueblo Blancos of San Juan de Oriente, Diriá, and Diriomo throw the most bizarre processions as part of the buildup to the fiestas patronales, with dancing warriors reenacting battles by beating each other over the head with bulls' penises. Another village, called Masatepe, has a much more civilized horse parade on the first Sunday of the month.

September: September 20 is the kickoff for the **Fiestas Patronales** (patron saint celebrations), or weekend parties in different neighborhoods that go on until December. Mock battles take place as well as folk dances. Boisterous groups go from door to door in costumes, shimmying to cheerful and uplifting marimba music.

October: The fantastical Masayan creature called the *chancha bruja* (witch pig) comes to life during the **Fiesta de los Aguisotes (Bad Omen Festival),** as well as other folk-tale ghouls such as the *arre chavalo* (headless priest). During **Fiesta de Toro Venado,** Masayans take on the guise of public figures and ridicule them through song, dance, and processions. Both parties take place on the last weekend of October, on Friday and Sunday, respectively.

November: During the **Folkloric Festival,** Masaya celebrates its handicrafts heritage, with artisanal stalls appearing all around the city. It's held the last week of November.

December: The **Procesión de San Jerónimo** is the big one, the final blowout of the Fiestas Patronales (Christmas celebrations). On the first Sunday of the month, Saint Jerónimo (the city's patron saint) is paraded through streets crammed with flower bearers and dancers. Traditional stomping routines are also performed. Early on Christmas Day, all the town's children spill out onto the street with pots, pans, and fireworks—anything that makes noise—calling everybody to church.

ATTRACTIONS OUTSIDE MASAYA

Coyotepe Fort 🖸   Coyotepe fort held political prisoners and was used by the National Guard to mortar-bomb the city during the 1980s revolution. It was also the location of the heroic last stand by national hero Benjamín Zeledón against U.S Marines in 1912. Now it is a quieter place, with Boy Scouts conducting tours of the facility and its dungeons. Whitewashed battlements and squat, yellow-domed towers overlook the city and lakes and afford a pleasant visit that belies this structure's dark history. The fort is a 1km (⅔-mile) hike north of the old train station but I recommend taking a taxi, as it is a fairly hard stroll.

Carretera Masaya Km 1. No phone. C19 (90¢). Daily 8am–5pm.

Volcán Masaya National Park ★★★   Volcán Masaya is not a cone-shaped volcano but rather a low, gaping wound of smoking craters and glowing lava. The whole effect is so frightening that the Spanish took to calling this volcano the "gates of hell" and the Chorotegas tribe christened it the "mountain that burns" and made human sacrifices in the hope that doing so might avert more eruptions. It is the most accessible live volcano in Nicaragua, because a road leads directly to its chasm. This park is at once intriguing and terrifying, especially when you learn that in 2000 the volcano hurled a large boulder that destroyed a nearby car in the parking lot. In the same lot today, the attendants advise you to park facing downhill so as to make a quick getaway—very reassuring.

The park consists of several volcanoes and craters and is easy to explore, with a system of hiking trails, many of which can be done on your own. The self-guided trail **Sendero los Coyotes** is a 6km (3.7-mile) walk from the visitor center and runs through lava pits to a lake. The **Santiago Crater** is home to a curious species of parakeets that seem immune to the pit's noxious fumes; the crater is best viewed from the parking lot at the edge. **El Comalito** is a small, smoking hillock and **Tzinan-canostoc** is a series of lava tunnels. Both can be visited only with a guide along the Coyote trek. On some treks you may have to change direction because of the fumes, and you'll need to get a gas mask to see the lava holes up close. Most travel operators offer 1-day excursions to the park from Managua, Granada, or Masaya. To get there independently, you must travel 6km (3¾ miles) north of Masaya on the main highway.

You can get a good map and brochure, and there's a nature museum, at the visitor center, about 2km (1¼ miles) from the main entrance. Buy your tour tickets at the visitor center before you rendezvous with your guide at the crater.

Carretera Masaya Km 6. © **505/2552-5415.** Daily 9am–4:45pm. Admission C77 ($3.60).

Shopping

Any shopping excursion in Masaya should include a stop at the Mercado Viejo (see "What to See & Do" above), but there are other shopping outlets around the city. **Mercado Municipal Ernesto Fernández** is a bigger, more chaotic, and somewhat crammed market with cheap restaurants and butcher stalls, as well as a good selection of handicrafts and leather ware. Goods are also slightly cheaper than at the Mercado Viejo. The market is adjacent to the main bus terminal and a few blocks from the Mercado Viejo. It is open daily from 8am to 7pm.

You'll find hammocks everywhere in Masaya, but if you'd prefer to see their place of origin, check out the *fabricas de hamacas* (hammock workshops) in Barrio San Juan, 2 blocks east of the Malecón and 1 block north of the Old Hospital. One good stand-alone hammock shop to try is **Los Tapices de Luis,** a store specializing in hammocks and wall hangings.

If you want to see more arts and crafts workshops, walk 1km (⅔ mile) south of the central plaza to the indigenous barrio of **Monimbó.** Here you'll find a cottage industry of shoemakers, basket weavers, saddle makers, and woodcarvers. Ask in the central tourist office for information or just knock on some doors when you get there. If you want to go farther afield, head to the workshops of the Pueblos Blancos (see "A Side Trip to the Pueblos Blancos," below).

WHERE TO STAY & DINE

Considering its many attractions and shopping possibilities, Masaya should have more and better hotels. Unfortunately, the town is usually visited as a day trip, with people staying in Granada or Managua. Thus, there's a dearth of decent inns.

Hotel Ivania's, 3½ blocks from the Iglesia El Calvario (© **505/2522-5825;** www.hotelivanias.com), is one of the town's better establishments, with a helpful, attentive staff (a rare thing in Nicaragua), as well as a convenient location and a restaurant. The decor is dated and slightly idiosyncratic—the hotel's facade is an attractive pink color with stone carved window frames, but inside it gets rather dark and garish. The rooms are small and the bathrooms smaller, but the hotel does have an all-important backup generator. Rates start at $65 for a double.

Hotel Maderas Inn, half a block east of Iglesia San Jerónimo (© **505/2522-5825**), is a small family-run property tucked inside a modern yellow house. It has a good location and a friendly staff. The decor is plain, except for the hammocks on the roof terrace—they're a great place to relax. Doubles start at $21.

A Side Trip to the Pueblos Blancos ★

A scattering of isolated "white villages," or Pueblos Blancos, sits in the hills south of Masaya, and make for a great 1-day excursion by car or bus from Masaya, or from Managua or Granada. These villages got their name from their simple Spanish-style churches and occasional white *casitas,* with colorful doors and windows. Each individual town is known for producing a signature handicraft, be it ceramic wind chimes or bamboo furniture, so shopping is the main draw here.

Any trip to the Pueblos Blancos should start with a journey up the **Catarina Mirador,** a spectacular lookout point on the rim of Laguna de Apoyo crater lake. Here you can make believe you can see all of Nicaragua, with Granada and Masaya at your feet and the twin peaks of Ometepe Island in the distance on Lago de Nicaragua. The town is famous for its basket making and lush, tropical nurseries. The mirador is behind the village church and can be easily approached on foot; if you are driving, you'll have to pay an admission of C20 (95¢).

Catarina Mirador was apparently the favored hangout of the military leader Augusto C. Sandino, and it's where he dreamed about and plotted Nicaragua's liberation. He was born in the nearby village of **Niquinohomo,** 3.2km (2 miles) away, where a bronze statue now stands. Close to the northwest corner of the town plaza is Sandino's childhood home, which is now a small museum and library. The town also has a charming colonial church called **Parroquia Santa Ana** that is reputedly 320 years old. Both the museum and the church have erratic opening hours, but if you ask around you should eventually find somebody with info and a key.

Several miles east and southeast is the village of **San Juan de Oriente.** Pottery is the specialty, and if you ask at any store they should allow you to take a look at their backyard workshops with kilns. Continue south and you'll reach the twin villages of **Diriá** and **Diriomo,** which face each other on the highway. Diriá has a good hilltop view and some trails from here lead down to the shore of Laguna de Apoyo. Diriomo is famous for its black magic and *brujas* (witches) who will read your fortune, or at least give you the right directions back to Masaya.

To visit **Masatepe,** you must double back and follow the road northwest. This sleepy village is the country's rocking chair capital and is known for its excellent mahogany and wicker carpentry. Stop for lunch at **Mi Teruño Masatepino** (© **505/8887-4949**), a charming open-air eatery just south of the town on the highway close to Pio XII. Continue west and you'll reach the largest of the Pueblos Blancos, **San Marcos,** a thriving university town with a pretty town plaza.

To return to Masaya, you can take the northern road through la Concepción or backtrack east to Catarina. (This is also the road to Granada and Managua.) Though it's easiest to see the pueblos by rental car, frequent buses do shuttle around the region, albeit at a slow pace, and they do not pass through every town. Buses leave daily from Mercado Municipal in Masaya, Mercado Huembes in Managua, and 1 block south of Granada's market. *Expreso* buses pass through the Pueblos Blancos every 40 minutes Monday through Friday, but less so on weekends. The Intur office in Masaya (p. 482) offers good maps of the region.

NORTH-CENTRAL NICARAGUA

Deep, fertile valleys drift upward into misty skies, hiding humble homesteads, patchy jungle, and tumbling waterfalls. North-central Nicaragua is mysterious, charming, and relatively unknown. It is also very chilly. Here the lush landscape of the highlands makes for a cool, refreshing climate that'll come as a welcome relief if you've just arrived from the hot coast.

Though this is cowboy country today—a land of hardy farmers with easy smiles and humble hospitality—the region hasn't always been so peaceful. This tough, beautiful land was a war zone for much of the 20th century. It was here that General Sandino battled American Marines, part of a war for power with the U.S. in which the mountain town of Ocotal became the first city in history to be attacked from the air in 1931. After an American-backed president came to power in 1937, things were calm here until the rise of the Sandinistas in the 1970s and their march on Managua from the north. Contras in the 1980s then wreaked havoc until a 1990s peace treaty allowed farmers to work their fields of tobacco, coffee, and vegetables once again without a rifle slung over their shoulders. Then complete disaster struck in the form of Hurricane Mitch in 1998. The devastating storm most affected the north of the country, wiping away entire towns.

This part of Nicaragua is calm again, and the only clouds are those real ones that roll down the mountain and envelop you. The north has proved itself to be an enduring beauty. Commerce has returned in the form of abundant harvests and swarming street vendors. Ecotourists come to trek in the pristine jungle. Agro-tourism has a great future in the form of coffee-farm and tobacco-factory tours. Whether you're watching old ladies roll cigars in Estelí or exploring rural retreats near Matagalpa, this part of Nicaragua cannot fail to attract and enchant you.

Estelí

Estelí is sometimes called the "Diamond of the Segovias." Such a sobriquet might be a little exaggerated, but Estelí *is* set on a broad, flat valley, surrounded by peaceful villages, and is a glorious sight in the sun. Its cathedral and shady plaza make for a pleasant stroll, and you can easily spend a day or two here taking in its revolutionary murals, shopping for excellent handicrafts, and perhaps visiting one of the cigar factories or coffee farms in the area. Its several universities means it has a youthful, vibrant population, and its location as the last main town before the Honduran border means many travelers stop off here for a taste of the highlands.

A Sandinista stronghold, Estelí was heavily bombed by the Somoza regime, adding credence to its other, less appealing, nickname—the "River of Blood." Hurricane Mitch left its mark too—the usually dry Río Estelí became a massive torrent that gouged its way through the city's hinterland, taking people and houses with it. The town has now settled back into a peaceful farming lifestyle. It's currently a city of 110,000 and an important agricultural center for tobacco, wheat, cattle, and cheese. It's also the closest town to the spectacular Miraflor Nature Reserve, the waterfall Salto Estanzuela, and the Tisey reserve, and is the biggest Nicaraguan city before the Honduran border.

ESSENTIALS
Getting There
BY BUS   The city's market bus station is known as **COTRAN Sur,** 15 blocks south of Parque Central (© **505/2713-6162**), and it serves major cities such as Managua,

León, and Matagalpa. There are hourly buses for the capital that take 3 hours and cost C60 ($2.80). The last bus for Estelí from Managua is at 5:45pm. Matagalpa-bound buses leave from Estelí every 30 minutes, with the last bus leaving at 4:20pm. This trip takes 2 hours and costs C40 ($1.85). There are only two services a day between León and Estelí. These buses leave León at 6:30am and 3pm and Estelí at 6:45 and 3:10pm. The journey takes 3 hours and costs C60 ($2.80).

There are also numerous microbuses that serve these routes regularly.

BY CAR   To drive from Managua, you must take the airport road east to Tipitapa and then go north via Sebaco. The road then forks with Matagalpa northeast and Estelí northwest. **Budget Rent a Car** (℃ 505/2713-2584; Estelí@budeget.com. ni) is located 20m (66 ft.) south of the Monumento Centenario on the Panamericana. **Dollar Rent A Car** (℃ 505/2713-3060) is on the Panamericana at Km 1140.

Orientation & Getting Around

The city center is between the Río Estelí and the Pan-American Highway and is easily explored on foot. The commercial heart is around the intersecting streets of Calle Transversal and Avenida Principal (also know as Av. Central). There is a street-numbering system based around this axis, but it is typically ignored. Most everything is a few blocks from the Plaza or Texaco station.

Visitor Information

There's a small **Intur,** a half-block south of Parque Central on Avenida Central (℃ 505/2713-6799), but it's pretty useless. It is open Monday to Friday from 7am to 2pm. Many of the city's Spanish schools are good sources of information concerning where to go in the area, as well. **Agencia de Viajes Aries** (℃ 505/2713-3369) is a conventional agency offering transport bookings and tours of the area. It is 1 block west and half a block south of the ENITEL building on Avenida Principal. **Hospedaje Luna,** 1 block north behind the cathedral (℃ 505/8441-8466; www.cafeluzy luna.com) is a great source of local information, and the English owner will even help organize tours such as seeing the town's murals or visiting the thriving cigar factories.

FAST FACTS   There are three banks on the corner 1 block west and 1 block south of the plaza, one of which is **Bancentro,** 2½ blocks south of the plaza on Avenida Principal (℃ 505/2713-6549). There is an ATM at **Texaco Starmart,** 5 blocks north of the soccer stadium. Money-changers operate along Avenida Principal. Money transfers can be arranged at the **Western Union** outlet (℃ 505/2713-5046), which is 60m (197 ft.) south of the store Super Las Segovias. **Hotel El Mesón,** 1 block north of the plaza (℃ 505/2713-2655), is one of the few places that will change traveler's checks.

A number of Internet cafes are situated north of the plaza. All charge approximately C38 ($1.75) an hour and are open all day every day. You might try **@Gnica,** which is 1 block south of the southwest corner of the plaza. The main ENITEL office is 1 block east of the post office (℃ 505/2713-2222). It's open Monday to Friday from 8am to 8pm and Saturday 8am to 5pm.

El Hospital Regional de Estelí (℃ 505/713-6300) is south of the city on the road to Managua. **Pharmacia Corea,** 1 block north of the market (℃ 505/2713-2609), offers mail services and money transfers in addition to stocking pharmaceutical goods.

In case of emergencies, dial ℃ **101.** For other matters, call the police station at ℃ **505/2713-2615.**

The main post office, **Correos de Nicaragua Estelí,** is at the junction with Calle Transversal and Avenida Central.

SHOPPING

If you're after leather cowboy boots, you need to stop by Estelí. All around avenues 1a N.O. and Avenida Central, you'll find stores selling quality leather goods in the form of belts, hats, saddles, and of course footwear for the discerning *vaquero*. Most shops will carefully measure your feet and rustle up a custom-made pair of boots in less than a week, for around C1,200 ($56).

Artesanía La Esquina, 1 block north of the cathedral (© **505/2713-2229**), and **Artesanía Nicaraguense,** 1 block south of the cathedral (© **505/2713-4456**), have a good selection of local soapstone pieces and Ducualí pottery, as well as general Nicaraguan handicrafts. **Guitarras y Requintas el Arte,** beside INISER (© **505/2713-7555**), sells beautifully crafted guitars and mandolins.

WHAT TO SEE & DO

In addition to the below attractions, check out the **Museo de Historia y Arqueología** (© **505/2713-3753**), which houses a small, mildly interesting collection of pre-Columbian artifacts. It is in the same building as the Casa de Cultura and is open 9am to midday except Wednesdays and weekends.

Iglesia de San Francisco This grand, cream-colored church with its neoclassical facade and elegant twin bell towers stands in front of the town's central plaza (Parque Central). The church has been rebuilt several times, each time getting bigger and more sophisticated. It began as a simple adobe structure in 1823 and was revamped with a baroque facade in 1889. Architecturally, it is the most interesting building in the city.
Parque Central. No phone. Free admission. Daily 5–8pm.

La Casa de Cultura This is Estelí's cultural nucleus, with activities such as dance performances, art classes, and music instruction offered every week. The spacious lobby holds exhibitions by local artists, and there are live events most weekends. A pleasant open-air cafe is out back, serving vegetarian fare and fresh juices. You can't miss the building, as it is completely covered in colorful murals.
Av. Central and Calle Transversal. No phone. Free admission. Mon–Fri 9am–noon and 2–5pm.

La Galería de Héroes y Mártires This simple but touching one-room museum is a tribute to the many young men and women who died in Estelí's darkest days—when it was an urban battleground between the Sandinistas and the National Guard. Curated by 300 women who lost their children in the war, the museum exhibits old photos, weaponry, uniforms, and personal items of the fallen. The building itself used to be a Somoza jailhouse, and you'll often find mothers of the martyrs in attendance to give their personal stories of those awful times. You can ask to see other memorabilia that are not on permanent display.
½ block south of the church. © **505/2713-3753.** Mon–Sat 9am–4pm.

ATTRACTIONS AROUND ESTELI

One of the best area hiking excursions is to the lush green and picturesque **Estanzuela Falls,** a 20m (66-ft.) cascade with a pool that's perfect for swimming and cooling off in. You must take the road to the hamlet of Estanzuela just south of the city (turn right after the hospital) to get to the path. It is only an hour-long walk, but

RESERVA natural MIRAFLOR

Miraflor means "flower view," and the 254-sq.-km (98-sq.-mile) patch of pristine nature that is **Reserva Natural Miraflor** ★★ certainly lives up to its name. It has one of the largest colonies of orchids in the world, with 300 species blooming amid begonias and moss-draped oak trees. Tall pine trees hide toucans and parakeets while armadillos and skunks scurry across the forest floor. Howler moneys jump from branch to branch while sloths just do their thing and hang out. There are over 200 bird species and numerous butterflies all sharing this diverse habitat of tropical savanna, jet black marshy swamp, dry bush, and a cloud forest that peaks at 1,484m (4,870 ft.).

Five thousand people are also scattered across the reserve, some of whom offer homestays where you can sit on a simple veranda and enjoy the view while sipping homegrown chamomile tea or coffee. You can trek or horseback ride to hilltop lookout points, ancient caves, prehistoric mounds, and pre-Columbian settlements. La Chorrera is one of the more ambitious hikes, the destination being a spectacular 60m-high (197-ft.) waterfall.

The reserve is a local initiative, operated and preserved by the community that lives here with little or no government help. They are pioneers in sustainable farming, organic agriculture, fair-trade produce, and ecotourism. The reserve's facilities are rustic and unassuming. There is little or no electricity, nor piped water. This is no five-star jungle hideaway but nature in all its raw glory—it's perfect for birders, horseback riders, artists, and orchid lovers. It is possible to visit the reserve in 1 day, but to truly appreciate it, stick around, stay with a family for a few days, and explore it further.

UCA, 2 blocks north and 1 block west of the Esso station in Estelí (✆ **505/2713-2971;** www.miraflor.org), is one of the main cooperatives that oversee the reserve. They can help with excursions and homestays. The office is open Monday to Friday from 8am to 12:30pm and 2 to 5pm. **Posada La Soñada** (✆ **505/2713-6333** in Estelí) is a well-established lodge that's basic but comfortable, with a large porch stuffed with hammocks and rocking chairs. The owner, Doña Corina, is famous for her vegetarian cooking. **Finca Lindos Ojos** (✆ **505/2713-4041** in Estelí; www.finca-lindos-ojos.com) has 14 comfortable rooms that start at $40 for a double with full board. The lodge is an organic coffee farm with solar-powered lighting, and is operated by a German couple. They also offer tours in the area.

Miraflor is a 45-minute, bone-shaking ride from Estelí in a colorful school bus. There are four buses a day. The earliest leaves from COTRAN Sur at 6am. The rest leave from COTRAN Norte at noon, 2:15pm, and 3:40pm. The UCA (see above) can also help with transport.

take food and water, as there are no stores after the highway junction. **Reserva Tisey** nature reserve is worth visiting just to climb its hill and enjoy its spectacular view. On a clear day, the Pacific lowlands and a line of volcanic peaks as far away as Lake Managua sweep before you. The reserve itself is made up of organic farms and jungle treks. You can go horseback riding or stay at the **Eco Posada Tisey** (✆ **505/2713-6213;** tisey69@latinmail.com), an organic farm that offers simple rooms for $20 and dorm beds for $10. It is 8km (5 miles) southwest of the city, a little beyond Salto Estanzuela on the same road.

Touring the Tobacco Factories

Tobacco will kill you. But in the meantime, why not take advantage of being in the cigar capital of Nicaragua and check out just how they make the world-famous Nicaraguan *puro*. You don't have to be a puffing tycoon to appreciate the rich history and skill that goes into a Churchill or a cohiba. Estelí's plantations were founded by Cuban exiles in search of the perfect spot, and their cigars now rival those from the Caribbean island. Cigar tours are still a novelty and visits to the surrounding factories can be hit-and-miss. Be sure to make an appointment or, better still, arrange a tour with the friendly staff at Hospedaje Luna.

Nic Cigar—Tabacalera Perdomo   The heaps of bicycles outside this industrial building hint at the 500 workers inside, sitting at tables hand-rolling 45,000 cigars a day. Large, cavernous rooms are a hive of activity, with missile-shaped cigars lying wrapped in newspapers and the occasional torpedo hanging from a supervisor's mouth. The factory conducts 15-minute tours explaining the different stages in the process while a nose-tingling acrid smell hangs in the air. On-site, there is a box workshop, where display cases are made from cedar. The Baltimore-based owners display a sign thanking their workers "who do not understand failure." Traded under the Perdomo label, Nic Cigars are exported to Miami, Austria, Mexico, and as far afield as Russia. The leaf is sourced from nearby fields and the skins are imported from Indonesia and Cameroon to give each brand its own particular color and taste. The factory is 5 minutes from town on the northern highway just over the bridge and down a dirt track.

Barrio el Rosario, Km 150 Carretera Panamericano, Estelí. (✆ **505/2713-5486.** www.perdomocigars. com.

Tabacalera Santiago ★   Here, even the security guard has a fat cigar in his mouth. Tabacalera Santiago is one of the more attractive cigar factories, offering a comprehensive tour explaining all the stages that go into making a giant-size, aromatic stogie. A large yellow-and-blue warehouse building surrounds a courtyard with a fountain and palm trees. Piles of leaves dry under the sun, while hundreds of workers mill around and haul bales from trucks. Each room has a specific purpose and a worker from each explains its purpose. There is a fermentation room where piles of leaves sit gathering taste as giant thermometers monitor the temperature. In the skin room, vapor-soaked leaves are imported from all over the world to use as a final wrap that can vary in color from black to beige. In the assembly room, hundreds of human rollers sit at tables sprucing five leaves together to form a tight roll in a matter of seconds and then placing the rolls in molds to give them a uniform shape. The aging room displays giant cigars in a variety of shapes—magnums, Churchills, coronas, and twisters, all of which can be bought at the gift store. Make sure you call ahead to make an appointment. Tours are in Spanish. For an English guide contact Hospedaje Luna.

Km 141 Carretera Panamericano. (✆ **505/2713-2758.** Mon–Fri 7–11:30am and 2–4pm.

WHERE TO STAY

Hospedaje Luna   A clothesline stretches across a plain, central courtyard with tall doors leading to two ample dorms and two private rooms. Hospedaje Luna is the backpackers' choice in Estelí, where travelers find a bunk amid basic decor with local information divulged over free tea and coffee. The helpful owners will set you up with what's possible to do, and there are bikes to help you get around. Across the road is the sister establishment Cafe Luz.

1 block north behind cathedral. (✆ **505/8441-8466.** www.cafeluzyluna.com. 4 units. $20 double; $7 dorm. AE, MC, V. **Amenities:** Dining area; Wi-Fi. *In room:* Fan.

Spanish-Language Schools in Estelí

The Internationalists may have come and gone, but they left behind a large selection of Spanish schools. Estelí is a great place to brush up on your Spanish because it has a number of good schools. **Asociación de Madres de Héroes** (© 505/2713-3753; emayorga70@yahoo.com) is a good place to start. It is in the Galería de Héroes y Mártires, listed earlier in this chapter.

Cenac Spanish School (© 505/2713-2025; www.spanishschoolcenac.com) arranges homestays and offers intensive courses. It is on the Panamericano, close to Calle 7a SE. **Hijos del Maiz** (© 505/2713-4819; www.hijosdelmaiz. net) is a community-based initiative that offers homestays in a village called El Lagartillo 1 hour by bus from Estelí.

Hotel Cuallitlan If you ignore the somewhat scuzzy neighborhood and the 4km (2½-mile) distance from town, the Cuallitlan is one of the most distinctive hotels in the area. It consists of a set of well-appointed chalets surrounding a lush courtyard teeming with plants and animals. A parrot greets you at reception, while a selection of cans and pots hold plants and shrubs, and typewriters sit beside ancient radios with the occasional ceramic hen for ornamentation. There are birdhouses and a garden nursery and a patio restaurant to take it all in. The cabins are handsome and spacious. The beds are a little low but they are surrounded by sturdy rock walls and attractive fittings. The bathrooms are medium size with lots of light. The hotel is down an unpaved road lined with breeze-block huts, but is perfect for those who have their own wheels and can come and go on their own.

2 blocks south and 4 blocks east of COTRAN Sur. © **505/2713-2446.** cuallitlan@zonaxp.com. 14 units. $35–$50 double. AE, MC, V. **Amenities:** Dining area. *In room:* Fan, TV.

Hotel Don Vito Estelí's newest hotel (opened in late 2008) is a small, family-run affair with psychedelic coloring and lots of mirrors. Orange spiral pillars set the tone as you enter a small lobby with white floor tiles and blue-and-white ceilings. The rooms are just as colorful but medium size and immaculate. There is a balcony upstairs with wicker chairs overlooking the street. Popular with business clientele and the occasional family, the Don Vito makes a welcome midrange option in a city that lacks good hotels.

Half-block east of Jardin Infantil. © **505/2713-4318.** www.hoteldonvitoEsteli.com. 25 units. $30 double; $40 with A/C. AE, MC, V. **Amenities:** Dining area; Internet (wireless $2 charge). *In room:* Fan, TV.

Hotel El Mesón ✋ One of Estelí's most established hotels is a rambling, decrepit property with shabby courtyard and dim, rickety rooms. This low, blue corner building is 1 block from the plaza and holds a cafe and travel agent. It's an adequate choice if you can get no better or are watching your córdobas. The hotel also offers a car-rental service and organized tours. It is one of the few places you can cash traveler's checks in town as well.

1 block north of the cathedral. © **505/2713-2655.** 16 units. $15–$20 double. AE, MC, V. **Amenities:** Dining area. *In room:* Fan, TV.

Hotel Los Arcos ★ Hotel Los Arcos is an excellent nonprofit endeavor that meets the needs of tourists while helping the local community. *Familias Unidas* has been training young people since 1997, and their students played a large part in building this hotel. The large mansion-style house, a half-block from the plaza, has a delightful color scheme of blue and orange, and is set amid arched galleries that overlook a gorgeous garden courtyard with a fountain and palm trees. The halls are wide and dotted with potted plants. Out back there is a larger courtyard with a giant mural. The rooms are smallish but have comfy double beds and big fans. The bathrooms are tight but are delightfully decorated with rainbow-colored tiles, and there is a solid half-wall separating the shower. The windows look out onto an internal hall or gallery and they have no lace curtains, meaning you must pull the heavy curtains and lose the light if you want privacy. Also, the corrugated roof can be noisy on a windy night.

1 block north of the cathedral. (℗) **505/2713-3830.** www.familiasunidas.org/arcos/introduction.htm. 32 units. From $45 double; from $55 triple; from $60 quadruple. AE, MC, V. **Amenities:** Restaurant; bar. *In room:* Fan, TV.

WHERE TO DINE
Moderate

Cafe Arte Tipiscayan NICARAGUAN   Sculptor Freddie Moreno has opened a restaurant to display his art and sculptures and share highland culinary delights such as *puyaso* (grilled meat) and *pinol* (a milky corn drink). Leather-backed chairs surround solid round tables held up with rock sculptures. There is a small garden shrine out back, and the owners plan to open a roof terrace as well as refit the facade with a sculpture of the planet. It's an interesting lunch stop, and if Freddie is around, he'll take you on a tour of his nearby workshop.

200m (660 ft.) north of Shell and 150m (490 ft.) west. (℗) **505/2713-7303.** Main courses from C100. Cash only. Tues–Sun midday–10pm.

El Rincon Pinareño INTERNATIONAL   Estelí's most formal restaurant is not so formal considering it has pink plastic seating and paper napkins. It does have a nice arched balcony overlooking the street, and the menu is extensive if unsurprising. Chicken comes in 12 varieties, including smoked, roasted, fried, breaded, and in salad. The garlic prawns are delicious, as are the many juices and cocktails. Try the vanilla flan for dessert.

Beside Enacal, Casa 8. No phone. Main courses C100 ($4.65). Cash only. Mon–Sat 11am–10pm.

Mocha Nana Cafe ★ ☺ COFFEEHOUSE   At last a cafe that does cafe! Mocha Nana offers eight coffee varieties, including macchiato and mocha. This pleasant bungalow has white walls and dark rafters. Chunky wooden seats sit around dark-stained tables with wood place mats. There is a comfy couch in one corner and a small bookshop in the other. The decor is light, elegant, and restrained, and there is a patio out back with a simple garden and child's slide. The menu includes hot bagels, cold shakes, and toasted sandwiches.

3½ blocks east of Casa de Cultura. (℗) **505/2713 3164.** Main courses C80 ($3.70). Cash only. Mon–Fri 9am–7pm; Sat 10am–7pm.

Vuela Vuela NICARAGUAN   This is one of Estelí's more inviting restaurants, with orange-wash walls and tall doors. In a colorful corner town house a block from the plaza, it has wagon-wheel ceiling lamps and primary-colored tablecloths and overall a laid-back, casual atmosphere. A brick bar with stools sits at the back of this smallish establishment that attracts a fairly mixed crowd. The food is pretty standard and won't be getting any Michelin stars soon. Still, it's a convenient stop for steak, pork, and chicken, with a little paella thrown in. The wine list is varied, with 18 labels from Argentina, Chile, Spain, and Italy.

1 block north of cathedral beside Los Arcos. ☎ **505/2713-3830.** Main courses C100 ($4.65). AE, MC, V. Mon–Sat 8am–11pm.

Inexpensive

Cafe Luz ★ 🍴 COFFEEHOUSE/RESTAURANT   This rainbow-colored cafe is more than just a good breakfast stop but also a valuable information point run by Brit Janie Boyd, known as Juanita to the locals. Tall doorways open onto checkered floor tiles, with a small back bar in the corner. Popular with travelers early in the morning or late at night, the kitchen dishes out decent shakes and juices, as well as lasagna and fajitas. The scarlet walls hold a bulletin board with local events and volunteering opportunities, as well as a tiny gift shelf with cigars and beads. Across the road is the sister establishment, **Hospedaje Luna.**

1 block north behind cathedral. ☎ **505/2713-6100.** www.cafeluzyluna.com. Main courses C80 ($3.70). Cash only. Daily 8am–midnight.

El Recanto COFFEEHOUSE   This popular breakfast stop is a small house with two table-jammed rooms that lead to a small courtyard out back next to the noisy kitchen. Tartan tablecloths sit beneath yellow walls with butterfly hangings. It is packed with locals in the early morning, feasting on generous helpings of *gallo pinto*.

1 block south and half a block east of the post office. ☎ **505/2713-2578.** Breakfast C80 ($3.70). Cash only. Mon–Fri 7am–5:30pm; Sat 7am–3pm.

La Casita ★★ ☺ COFFEEHOUSE   An inconspicuous house on the side of the highway is the entrance to a delightful cafe that is also a garden, plant nursery, park, playground, and meeting place. A small wooden bridge crosses a flower-trimmed stream and leads to a rock path that leads to a bamboo grove and a cactus garden. School kids study on the lawn, while people eat fresh bread, cheese, and yogurt beneath a wooden frame topped with ceramic tiles. Its Scottish owner, David Thomson, must be commended for creating a charming refuge popular with both locals and visitors. La Casita is a 5-minute taxi ride from the town center.

Beside the new hospital, opposite La Barranca. ☎ **505/2713-4917.** Main courses C80 ($3.70). Cash only. Tues–Sun 9am–7pm; Mon 2–7pm.

AFTER DARK IN ESTELI

For such a small town, Estelí has a lively night scene if you know where to look. **Cafe Luz** (see above) is a popular pit stop before venturing farther. If you don't know where to go, just follow the crowd.

   Rincon Legal, 1 block west of Textiles Kanan (☎ **505/2714-1871**), appears somewhat illegal with the arsenal of homemade bazookas and shotguns that hang on the wall. This large, ample disco bar is a shrine to all things Sandinista, and the decor could be described as guerrilla chic. It is open from Thursday to Sunday midday to 10pm. **Ixcoteli,** 1 block south of Petronic (☎ **505/2714-2212**), is a courtyard bar with a nice vibe, even if it is rough around the edges. The crowd is a little older than that at Rincon Legal, and they come here to enjoy good old-fashioned ranchero and romantica peppered with '80s rock and pop. It is open daily from 10am to midnight. **Semaforo Rancho Bar** ★, 500m (1,640 ft.) south of the hospital (☎ **505/2813-3814**), is a gigantic frond-thatched barn with a long bar. A stage to the left hosts live music on weekends, attracting an older crowd that sits at the tables tapping their feet to ranchero.

Matagalpa

Enjoy a cup of the finest coffee in the world while admiring this distinctive valley city and its surrounding green hills. The "Pearl of the North" has steep, hilly streets and clean mountain air and is settled by 80,000 Norteños, who occupy themselves mostly with cattle or coffee beans. Though it's not the tidiest of towns, it has a rural charm and is nestled along a narrow stream called the Río Grande de Matagalpa—actually Nicaragua's second-longest river, which flows the whole way to the Caribbean.

Matagalpa was settled by the Nahuatl Indians, and though the Spanish introduced cattle in the 17th century and the Germans introduced coffee in the 19th, the Europeans originally came here looking for gold. They never found it, but the city became a coffee boomtown and important economic center for the country. Such fortune has waned a bit since the drop in the price of beans. This town is also the birthplace of the greatest Sandinista, Carlos Fonseca, and the resting place of the much-loved juggling volunteer Benjamin Linder. In addition to boasting great shops selling local black ceramics and coffee farms primed for visitors, Matagalpa makes a good base for nearby treks in the beautiful tropical forest; it's also the last stop before the famous Selva Negra Mountain Resort.

ESSENTIALS

GETTING THERE   Matagalpa's main bus station, **COTRAN Sur,** 1km (⅔ mile) west of Parque Darío (✆ 505/2782-3809), services routes from Estelí, Jinotega, León, Masaya, and Managua. The Managua buses depart every hour from Mercado Mayoreo in the capital, take 2½ hours, and cost C60 ($2.80).

Small *collectivos* also travel every 30 minutes between Matagalpa and Managua, starting at 5am and ending at 6pm. There are two services daily from León bus station to Matagalpa. They depart at 5am and 3pm, take 3 hours, and cost C50 ($2.35). The reverse service goes to León at 6am and 3pm.

There is a smaller bus station called **COTRAN de Guanaco** (no phone) in the north of the city that serves towns farther in the interior such as San Ramón and Río Blanca. The roads are sometimes impassable in the rainy season, however.

ORIENTATION   The heart of the city stretches along the eastern bank of the river and its epicenter lies between two plazas, **Parque Morazán** and **Parque Rubén Darío,** the former of which is alive with people walking, talking, selling, or admiring the plaza's many trees and birds. There are only two streets with names in the entire city, Avenida José Benito Escobar and Avenida Central Don Bartolomé Martinez.

GETTING AROUND   If your legs are up for it, try to walk everywhere in the city—the steep streets open up its secret charms. Taxis within the town cost C15 (70¢) and there are regular city buses that crisscross the town for C5 (25¢).

The surrounding area has some of the most scenic roads in Nicaragua, especially the curving valley road to Jinotega. I recommend renting a car so that you can pull into coffee plantations and explore beautiful cedar, pine, and hardwood forests. **Budget** (✆ **505/2772-3041;** www.budget.com.ni) has an outlet at La Virgen Shell Station on the southern outskirts of the town. **Autos Economicos de Nicaragua** (✆ **505/2772-2445**) is half a block west of the park on its northern side; **Rent a Car Simo** (✆ **505/2772-6290**) is 1 block west and half a block south of the Banco Mercantil; and **Simo's Rent a Car** (✆ **505/2772-6260**) is on the corner of El Progresso. Rates for all agencies start at C800 ($37) per day.

Mark Your Calendar for Matagalpa's September Festival

If you're in town on or around September 24, get ready to put on your cowboy hat and join the town's annual party. Festivities on this date include a farmer's fair, bullfights, parades, and traditional dancing on the city's principal streets. The party gets going a week beforehand with the local fire brigade parading a statue of the **Virgen de la Merced** through the city streets. It culminates in a grand show of horsemanship on the city streets on the 25th.

Visitor Information

Intur, 1 block north of Parque Rubén Darío (✆ 505/8612-7060), is open Monday to Friday from 8am to noon and 1:30 to 5pm.

Matagalpa Tours, half a block east of Banpro (✆ 505/2772-0108; www.matagalpatours.com), is the trekking expert for the area. They also conduct tours of the coffee farms and arrange overnight stays in nearby ecolodges.

Drop into **Centro Girasol,** 2 blocks south and 1 block west of COTRAN (✆ 505/2772-6030), for information about horseback riding in the area.

FAST FACTS   Most of the city's banks are on the southeast corner of Parque Morazán. **Banpro** is 1 block south of Parque Morazon on Avenida Bartolomé Martinez (✆ 505/2772-2574). There is an ATM at **BAC** (✆ 505/2772-5905), a halfblock east of the southeast corner of Parque Morazán. Casual money-changers operate on all corners in this area, as well. Money transfers can be arranged at the **Western Union outlet** (✆ 505/2778-0069), a half-block north of the Alcaldía.

Internet outlets are available throughout the city, but **CyberCafé Downtown** has the best location, a half-block west of the southwest corner of the Parque Darío. It's open daily from 8:30am to 8pm. All outlets charge approximately C40 ($1.85) an hour. Cheap international calls can be made from most Internet cafes. Public phones are in the post office and a number of card-based booths are dotted around town. The main **ENITEL office** is 1 block east of Parque Morazán. It's open daily from 7am to 9pm.

Matagalpa Hospital (✆ 505/2772-2081) is north of the city on the road to San Ramón. **Pharmacy Matagalpa** (✆ 505/2772-7280) is in front of the restaurant Pescamar. It's open Monday to Saturday from 8am to 6pm and Sunday 8am to noon.

For emergencies, dial ✆ 101. For other matters, call ✆ 505/2772-3870. The fire brigade can be called at ✆ 505/2772-3167.

The main post office, **Correos de Nicaragua Matagalpa** (✆ 505/2772-4317), is 1 block south and 1 block west of Parque Morazán's southeastern corner.

SHOPPING

This area is famous for its black ceramics and you'll find numerous outlets selling such pottery. **Ceramica Negra,** next to Parque Darío Rubén (✆ 505/2772-2464), specializes in this type of ceramics, as does **La Casa de la Carámica Negra,** 2 blocks east of Parque Morazá on the northern side (✆ 505/2772-3349). **Centro Girasol,** in the yellow corner building past the first bridge (✆ 505/2772-6030), has a crafts store and food store with local organic produce.

WHAT TO SEE & DO
In Town
La Iglesia de Molaguina, 2 blocks east and 2 blocks north of Parque Darío (no phone), is a beautiful, simple church. It is popular with locals and nobody can

THE life & times OF BENJAMIN LINDER

Benjamin Linder was a young engineering graduate from California who moved to Nicaragua in the early 1980s. An accomplished juggler and unicyclist, Linder was inspired by the 1979 Sandinista revolution and, like hundreds of other *internacionalistas*, wished to contribute toward helping the country's poor. He moved to the Northern Highlands and helped out in community projects such as vaccination drives. It was there that he put his skills as a juggler to good use. He dressed as a clown and with his unicycle encouraged families to visit the local clinic for measles jabs. He also began work on a small hydroelectric dam with the aim of bringing light to the village of San José de Bocay. While working there, the 27-year-old was ambushed and killed by Contra rebels, along with two Nicaraguan companions.

His death in 1987 made world headlines. It came amid an intense debate in the United States over the government's support of counterrevolutionary rebels.

The Contras were trained and funded by a Reagan administration that feared that the Sandinista government was a communist threat in Central America. Linder's death shone light on a conflict that had killed 30,000 Nicaraguans. It contributed to Congress finally withdrawing support a year later.

Linder is now revered in Nicaragua and celebrated in countless murals as a juggling ambassador. You can visit the Benjamin Linder Café in León and see one such mural celebrating his life. He is held up by many as an American who made a positive contribution, and his efforts have now been duplicated by countless Americans doing good works in Nicaragua, whether they are Peace Corps volunteers or hotel owners funding public libraries. Benjamin Linder's grave can be visited in the Northern city of Matagalpa. Hundreds of mourners attended his funeral and he had a most poignant guard of honor—a line of children dressed as clowns.

remember when exactly it was built. East of the city, in the local cemetery, you'll find the final resting place of **Benjamin Linder,** an American volunteer killed during the war (see the box above). His simple gravestone reflects his passion for juggling and unicycling.

Casa Cuna Carlos Fonseca   This adobe building is the birthplace of Carlos Fonseca, founder of the FSLN and martyr of the revolution, Matagalpa's most famous son. The building exhibits artifacts from the commandant's life, such as his typewriter, uniforms, and other memorabilia.

1 block east of Parque Darío's south side. (📞 **505/2772-3665.** Free admission. Mon–Fri 8am–noon and 2–5pm.

El Templo de San José de Laborio   One of the earliest church sites in the city, El Templo is historically significant, as it was used as a base by the indigenous tribes during an uprising in 1881. The current baroque-style church was built in 1917 but rests on the foundations of ruins that date from 1751.

Parque Darío. No phone. Free admission. Daily 5–8pm.

La Cathedral de San Pedro   Undoubtedly Matagalpa's most imposing building, the city cathedral seems like many Nicaraguan churches—out of proportion to the size and importance of the city. Built in 1874, this third-largest church in all of

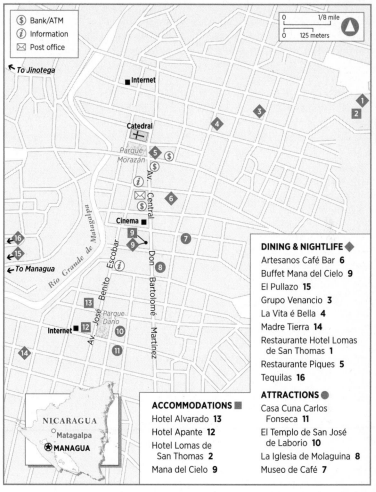

Map Legend:
- ⑤ Bank/ATM
- ⓘ Information
- ✉ Post office

0 — 1/8 mile
0 — 125 meters

To Jinotega

Internet

Catedral

Parque Morazán

Av. Central

Cinema

Av. José Benito Escobar

Don Bartolomé Martínez

Río Grande de Matagalpa

To Managua

Parque Darío

Internet

NICARAGUA
Matagalpa
★ MANAGUA

DINING & NIGHTLIFE ◆
Artesanos Café Bar **6**
Buffet Mana del Cielo **9**
El Pullazo **15**
Grupo Venancio **3**
La Vita é Bella **4**
Madre Tierra **14**
Restaurante Hotel Lomas de San Thomas **1**
Restaurante Piques **5**
Tequilas **16**

ATTRACTIONS ●
Casa Cuna Carlos Fonseca **11**
El Templo de San José de Laborio **10**
La Iglesia de Molaguina **8**
Museo de Café **7**

ACCOMMODATIONS ■
Hotel Alvarado **13**
Hotel Apante **12**
Hotel Lomas de San Thomas **2**
Mana del Cielo **9**

Nicaragua has a white exterior and a huge, cavernous nave guarded by two bell towers. It is decorated in a simple baroque style with some beautiful woodcarvings and paintings. Though the church dominates the entire city skyline, it's best viewed from the city's northern hillside.

North side of Parque Morazán. No phone. Free admission. Daily 5–8pm.

Museo de Cafe More a local history museum than an homage to coffee, this building displays murals and photographs and a small selection of indigenous artifacts. You can buy a bag of local coffee here, and it is a good meeting point to hook up with other travelers in the area.

On Main St., 2 blocks east of the mayor's office. ☎ **505/2772-4608.** Free admission. Mon–Fri 8am–noon and 2–5pm.

Around Matagalpa

Cerro Apante is a 1,442m-high (4,730-ft.) hill that dominates the town from its southeastern location. It makes for a good half-day hike, and has splendid views at the top. Start at the northeastern corner of Parque Darío and walk southeast down Calle Principal. You'll eventually begin to leave the city, walking through the neighborhood of Apante. (If you get lost, just ask for "*el cerro.*") The actual summit is off-limits, but if you follow the ridgeline north, you'll find a footpath that takes you back down to the town another way.

Castillo Cacao ★   This boutique chocolate factory is the real deal and makes genuine "almost organic" chocolate from sacks of beans that go through a roasting machine, then a crusher, then a grinder to produce rich, dark fudge. The Dutch-Chilean owners have set up a showroom in a villa-style home while the factory itself is a little workshop out back designed like a minicastle. Giggling girls with chocolate-covered hands greet you in the kitchen workshop. Neophytes learn that the cacao beans come from a pod, shaped like an American football, in different varietals, and it is important to know where they are grown to determine their quality. (Local beans are grown on the slopes of Volcán Mombacho.) There are no on-site guides so it is wise to call ahead and arrange a visit or book a tour through your hotel or a local tour operator.

1km (⅔ mile) east of Esso Las Marias on Carretera La Dalia. ⓒ **505/2772-2002.** www.elcastillodel cacao.com. Free admission. Mon–Fri 9am–noon and 2–5pm.

WHERE TO STAY
In Town

The choice of hotels is limited in town; I suggest you stay in the surrounding countryside to take full advantage of the area's natural beauty. Many budget hotels have no hot water, so check beforehand if you dislike cold morning dips.

Hotel Alvarado   Somewhat dark and dingy, the Alvarado's main attraction is its great location and friendly owners. A dim hallway takes you from the street to a small lobby that would pass for somebody's living room. In fact, it is somebody's living room; Dr. Noel and Dr. Flor have family photos to admire while you check in or out. Rooms vary in size and light quality with the best options at the back, away from the busy street and with views of the mountains. There's no hot water or breakfast. If you like roughing it amid '70s furniture, this place is for you.

Northwest corner of Parque Darío. ⓒ **505/2772-2830.** 8 units. From $15 double. Rates include breakfast. No credit cards. **Amenities:** Dining area. *In room:* TV.

Hotel Apante   This place is like the Alvarado, but more spruced up and bright (and with hot water). Checkered floors line a long corridor and a small lobby. The rooms are simple, with open wardrobes and bare walls. The lower rooms have no outside windows so are somewhat darker with less privacy. The overall feel is rickety and dated, but it's a bargain price and the hot showers are excellent. Room no. 5 is a good choice as it is large and has a small communal courtyard.

West side of Parque Darío. ⓒ **505/2772-6890.** 18 units. From $11 double. Rates include breakfast. No credit cards. **Amenities:** Dining area. *In room:* TV.

Hotel Lomas de San Thomas ★ 🍴 ☺   This is a beautiful hotel that, like its hilltop location, is way above anything else in town. The mock-colonial style seems almost genuine, with its brick arches resting on thick concrete pillars. A gallery runs around a central courtyard with a long pool-like fountain graced with vegetation and

TOURING THE coffee FARMS AROUND MATAGALPA

While you're in the area, you should take a tour of some coffee farms—it's a great opportunity to meet real Nicaraguans, as well as try some great coffee. Coffee tourism is very much in its infancy, however, with few farms offering set tours in English. It is best to organize a tour through your hotel or lodge. **Finca Esperanza Verde ★★**, Yucul Road, 18km (11 miles) east of San Ramón (℮ **505/2772-5003;** www.finca esperanzaverde.org), is one of the better-known coffee-farm lodges, and it's been lauded for its responsible tourism and sustainable practices. You can see the bean-processing facilities, view the verdant slopes of coffee plantations, and hike some lovely trails with fantastic bird life. See below regarding accommodations at the *finca*. **Selva Negra,** Km 140 Carretera, Matagalpa-Jinotega (℮ **505/8612-3883;** www.selvanegra. com), is Nicaragua's most famous coffee farm and lodge. The 660-hectare (1,600-acre) estate offers day tours of the facilities where you can also do some excellent forest treks through the sprawling property. The coffee factory itself is a large warehouse in front of the family home.

a marvelous view. The rooms are too big and could easily accommodate a family of five, and include a TV, fridge, and walk-in closet. The bathrooms are also massive, with blue marble tops and wooden board ceilings. Each room has a balcony with a communal balcony at the center. Everything is well maintained and immaculate, with nice touches of Spanish tile and dashes of blue. If it had a pool it would be perfect. The San Thomas is several blocks from the town center, up a steep incline that would tax a marathon runner.

Just east of the Guanaca school. ℮ **505/2772-4201.** 25 units. From $45 double; from $60 triple; from $70 family (sleeps 4). AE, DC, MC, V. **Amenities:** Restaurant; bar; Internet; laundry service; room service. *In room:* Cable TV.

Mana del Cielo Mana del Cielo is the best option after San Thomas. It is anything but grand, but it is a nicely decorated medium-size hotel with attractive furnishings and immaculate rooms on a busy street. The lobby is large and airy, with eye-pleasing stone walls and a blue tiled floor. Rocking chairs sit beneath chintzy curtains but there is lots of light. The rooms are medium size and a little dark as the windows face the corridor. The pink walls and flowery bedcovers are a little over-the-top but you'll appreciate the cushioned toilet seats, if not the ruffled curtain showers. Everything is clean and well maintained and there are several spaces to sit back and read, including an upstairs balcony overlooking the street and church.

1½ blocks south of Banco Uno. ℮ **505/2772-5686.** mana01@turbonett.com.ni. 17 units. Double $13. AE, DC, MC, V. **Amenities:** Restaurant; bar; Internet; laundry service; room service. *In room:* Cable TV.

Outside Matagalpa

Finca Esperanza Verde ★★ This "farm of green hope" is a pioneer in responsible tourism and sustainable agriculture. Here you'll find basic, brick cabins and a lodge surrounded by organic coffee plantations, cloud forest, waterfalls, and a butterfly farm. A white picket fence encloses an open, timber-framed dining room. The green-roofed cabins, which can accommodate six, are solar-powered and the drinking water comes from a natural spring. The buildings are constructed from handmade brick and other local materials. The lodge is a leading light on the Ruta del Café, and sets up tours to that route's coffee plantations during harvest time from November to February. The farm is also a nature reserve with hundreds of species of birds and butterflies and orchids. There is also a campsite with a roofed picnic area set amid a coffee and banana grove.

Yucul Rd., 18km (11 miles) east of San Ramón. ℂ **505/2772-5003.** www.fincaesperanzaverde.org. 6 units. $12 dorm; from $45 cabin for 2. Rates include breakfast. AE, DC, MC, V. **Amenities:** Restaurant. *In room:* Fan, no phone.

Selva Negra Mountain Resort ★★ ☺ An old tank marks the entrance to this legendary hotel. The Bavarian-style wooden cabins betray its German ownership (*"selva negra"* means black forest). They are set around a pond in what is a working coffee farm called La Hammonia. Here you can tour the farm, horseback ride, hike, or simply enjoy the peacefulness of this mountain cloud-forest retreat. It has excellent wildlife-watching and there is even a stone chapel for those true romantics who wish to get married amid all this nature. The owners are very friendly and also operate a youth hostel on the grounds. The lodge survived the revolution and war, though guests were required to ration toilet paper. The wood frame and brick and glass-fronted cabins come with porches and private bathrooms and are fairly basic but homey. The farm is also open to day visitors. It's a 20-minute drive from Matagalpa on the scenic road to Jinotega.

Km 140 Carretera, Matagalpa-Jinotega. ℂ **505/8612-3883.** www.selvanegra.com. 34 units. From $30 dorm; $60-$150 bungalow; $100-$150 chalet. AE, DC, MC, V. **Amenities:** Restaurant. *In room:* No phone.

WHERE TO DINE

Some of the best restaurants in the area are outside the city. In fact, if you are staying in any of the *finca* lodges above, you can experience fresh, organic food where it is grown. **Restaurante Lomas de San Thomas** (ℂ **505/2772-4201**) serves an eclectic menu such as fajitas, steaks, and shrimp dishes. The spacious restaurant has lots of natural light and a great view over the valley. **La Vita é Bella,** Colonia Lainez (ℂ **505/2772-5476;** vitabell@ibw.com.ni), is a rare find—a genuine Italian restaurant in the heart of cowboy country. The menu is vegetarian-friendly, with a little chicken Marsala thrown in for die-hard carnivores. They even serve genuine Italian vodka. This pleasant restaurant is open for lunch and dinner. It's on a narrow, high street 2 blocks east and 2 blocks north of the cathedral. **El Pullazo,** on the highway to Managua, is humble in appearance but big at heart. The menu is genuine Nicaraguan, with great beef dishes, *guirila* pancakes, and *cuajada* cheese. It must be one of the few places with a fish tank in the Northern Highlands. The popular **Buffet Mana del Cielo** (ℂ **505/2772-5686**) offers huge meals in which the choice of Nicaraguan food will make your mouth water. The restaurant is 1½ blocks south of Banco Uno and is open daily from 7am to 9pm. **Restaurante Piques** (ℂ **505/2772-2723**) is a laid-back Mexican restaurant, half a block east of the BAC bank, close to Parque Morazán. It is open daily from 10am to midnight. The down-to-earth **El Disparate de Potter** (ℂ **505/8621-3420**) makes a perfect lunch stop while touring the Matagalpa-Jinotega road. The name refers to a rocky outcrop blasted apart by an English landowner while building a road to his coffee farm in the 1920s. The roadside restaurant is popular with locals and serves Nicaraguan fare, in a space with a great view. (There's even a viewing platform nearby.) The restaurant is open daily from 8:30am to 8pm. **Artesanos Cafe Bar ★**, a half-block east of Banpro, in front of Social Club (✆ **505/2772-2444**), is by far the hippest cafe in town, with roomy ambience and a laid-back vibe. The building itself is a nicely restored town house with high ceilings and cornflower-colored walls. The menu is short but decent, with chicken dishes and salads. It attracts a mix of old and young, local and foreign. It is open Tuesday to Sunday, 9am to midnight.

MATAGALPA AFTER DARK

Grupo Venancia ★, 3 blocks north and 4 blocks east of Parque Morazán (✆ **505/2772-3562**), is an excellent cultural space that was started by a volunteer woman's group with the idea of creating a venue for music, dance, and the arts in general. It has a low-key atmosphere with an open-air bar offering live performances and movie screenings. It attracts a good mix of Matagalpa's well-heeled culture vultures and a bohemian crowd, especially on Saturdays. If you have some time on your hands, they are always looking for volunteers to help out as they also organize workshops, publish books, and have a radio show.

Parque Darío ★ is the venue for a festivity called Noches Matagalpinas that runs the last weekend of each month—expect live music, food stands, and a festive atmosphere.

Locals here are fond of scuffing their cowboy boots to ranchera, merengue, and reggaeton. Saturdays nights are the liveliest, with roadhouse discos like **Tequilas,** 3km (1¾ miles) out on the Managua highway, coming alive with revelers. **Madre Tierra ★** goes all week (except Tues) with an open-air bar offering pub grub and hammocks. It is located 1½ blocks west of Texaco Central.

SAN JUAN DEL SUR ★

138km (86 miles) S of Managua; 96km (60 miles) S of Granada; 215km (134 miles) S of León

San Juan del Sur used to be a sleepy little Pacific-coast hamlet, until it was discovered by backpackers and surfers as the perfect spot to hang a hammock and enjoy a rum-colored sunset. It is now Nicaragua's top Pacific-coast destination for foreign visitors and its pioneering blond-haired wave riders have gradually given way to silver-haired property seekers. Retirement homes are beginning to dot the hillsides, and upscale hotels are appearing along the coast. There is even the occasional cruise ship idling in the bay.

Development is happening at a not-too-fast pace and San Juan hasn't lost the laid-back charm that attracted travelers here. The area is perfect for beach wandering, leisure sailing, deep-sea fishing, and scuba diving. And the town still comes alive for holidays, particularly for its delightful religious flotilla on July 17. The lunar cycles between September and April see a beach party of a different kind—the hatching of sea turtles and their spectacular but treacherous rush to the sea. One of Nicaragua's most amazing sights takes place just south of the town.

San Juan del Sur's history is as colorful as its bay-framed sunset. It was discovered in 1523 by sailor Andres Niño, who was trying to find a passage to the Caribbean. It remained a tiny fishing village until the 1850s, when it became the final staging post for Americans heading west to California via the Caribbean on an overland trip from Lake Nicaragua. William Walker used it as a base to invade and eventually flee the region. He was prevented from invading again when the British navy ship the *Vixen* blocked the bay. In the 1970s, the area became the stronghold of legendary rebel

Commandante Zero, who fought off Somoza's National Guard and forced them to flee the port as the Sandinistas advanced from the town of Rivas.

Essentials

GETTING THERE

BY TAXI/SHUTTLE The safest and most convenient way to get to San Juan del Sur is via a shuttle service that picks you up from Managua or Granada. **Adelante Express** (© 505/8850-6070; www.sanjuanvan.com) arranges taxis or vans to Managua, with rates that run from C600 to C800 ($28–$37) depending on group size.

BY BUS Buses leave from **Mercado R. Huembes** in Managua at 10:30am, 4pm, and 5:30pm (3 hr.; C60/$2.80), but it's a long, bumpy ride, with lots of stops. The 4pm is the "Expresso" in name only. Buses going to Managua directly leave from the **San Juan del Sur market** (at calles Central and Market) at 5am and 6am daily. There are buses to Rivas every 45 minutes (1 hr.; C30/$1.40) between 5am and 5:30pm, where you then catch a connection to Managua and elsewhere. **Central Line S.A.,** half a block west of the market (© 505/2568-2573), has direct buses to Managua at 10am, going to the Antiguo Cine Cabrera, on Avenida 27 Mayo. The fare is C40 ($1.85).

ORIENTATION & GETTING AROUND

San Juan del Sur is small and easy to explore on foot. Beaches farther north and south can be accessed by boat, taxi, or shuttle bus. **Rana Tours** (© 505/8877-9255) operates a daily water taxi to Maderas beach at 11am, returning at 5pm. They have a beach kiosk in front of the Hotel Estrella from which the boat departs. A round-trip ticket costs C200 ($9.30). The coastal road to the surrounding beaches is rough and unpaved with little to see. It is best traveled in a four-wheel-drive. Beaches south of the town can be accessed by a regular bus to the southern town of Ostonial that leaves from the market at 1, 4, and 5pm.

> **Fiesta Patronales**
>
> **The entire town comes alive from June 16 to June 24 with fun and frolics such as rodeos, pig chasing, and pole climbing.**

Hostel **Casa Oro,** 1 block west of the plaza (© 505/8458-2415), organizes beach shuttles three times a day to Majagual and Maderas beach at 10am, 12:30pm, and 4pm. The cost is C100 ($4.65) round-trip.

Taxis are easy to catch on any street corner, but always negotiate the price before jumping in.

Alamo (© 505/2277-1117) has an office in front of the restaurant El Velero in the Hotel Colonial. **Bike & Quad Rentals,** beside the Mercado Municipal (© 505/2568-2439), does exactly what they say on the sign. **Elizabeth's Guesthouse,** 75m (246 ft.) east of Mercado Municipal (© 505/8822-7075), rents bicycles for C100 ($4.65) per day, as well as rooms.

VISITOR INFORMATION

The tourism office **Tesorera Cantur** (© 505/8458-2473) is located 1½ blocks west of the market, but is not very helpful (though they will find you a hotel room if pushed). Much better is the hostel **Casa Oro,** 1 block west of the plaza (© 505/8458-2415; www.casaeloro.com), which does a good job of keeping people up to

ACCOMMODATIONS ■
Casa El Oro **13**
El Encanto del Sur **19**
Hostel Pachamama **10**
Hotel Gran Océano **12**
Inn on the Pacific **5**
La Posada Azul **11**
Pelican Eyes Resort **18**
DINING & NIGHTLIFE ◆
Bambu Beach Club **3**
Bar Republika **14**
Barrio Café **9**
Big Wave Daves **6**
Club Sunset **2**
Crazy Crab Beach Club **1**
El Colibrí **16**
El Gato Negro **7**
El Pozo **15**
Iguana Bar **8**
La Cascada **17**
Mercado Municipal **20**
Smokeys **4**

$ Bank/ATM
+ Hospital
✉ Post office

Footbridge
Río San Juan del Sur
NICARAGUA
MANAGUA
San Juan del Sur
Texaco ■
Av. del Mar
Bahía de San Juan del Sur
Internet
Market
Av. del Cine
Bus Stop
Water Taxi
Av. Central
Calle Central
Av. del Mercado
Parque Central
Dock
Police ■
0 200 yds
0 200 m

8

NICARAGUA | San Juan del Sur

date with what is going on, what excursions are available, and the ever-changing bus timetable. The website **www.sanjuandelsur.org.ni** gives limited listings; **www.vianica.com** is a more comprehensive site, with information such as hotel addresses and telephone numbers.

FAST FACTS You can exchange money or withdraw cash from ATMs at **Bancentro,** half a block east of El Timon restaurant (✆ **505/2568-2449**), or at **Procredit,** 1 block west of the market (✆ **505/8853-3433**). There is another ATM at BDF a half-block from the Casa de Cultura.

Traveler's checks can be changed at Casa Oro, 1 block west of the plaza (✆ **505/8458-2415**).

The closest hospital is in Rivas, though there is a clinic known as **Centro de Salud** (no phone) that will take care of minor ailments. It is 20m (66 ft.) southwest of the Texaco station and is open from 7am to 8pm Monday to Saturday and 8am to noon on Sunday.

Cyber Leo's (no phone) is one of the better established Internet cafes, a half-block south of El Gato Negro. There is another one at the **Hotel Costa Azul,** 1½ blocks west of the market on Calle Central. The rate per hour is C30 ($1.40).

What to See & Do

San Juan del Sur has little of historical significance to see except the town's old clapboard houses and its simple wooden church, **Parroquia San Juan,** on the main plaza. The **Lighthouse,** a 1-hour trek south of the town, is also worth a visit. You must follow a trail behind the town dock until you turn right. This site has a spectacular view of the sea and coast. Below it there is a pelican nesting area. On the northern side of town is an excellent **petroglyph** by the river depicting a 1,500-year-old hunting scene. To walk there, take the road to Rivas and turn left after the bridge. Continue walking until you reach a farm where water pipes lead you to the river. Be sure to ask permission as you must cross private land. Otherwise, contact **Da Flying Frog** (𝄢 **505/8611-6214;** tiguacal@ibw.com.ni), which can include a trek to the petroglyph in their canopy excursion. Farther up the river is a small waterfall.

San Juan del Sur's other main attractions are the beaches and sea, though it must be said, this is not the Caribbean. Contradicting what many brochures may advertise, the water here is not turquoise clear and the beaches are not dazzling white and lined with palm trees. There are lots of water activities to be had, though; see "Outdoor Activities," below, for details.

Refugio de Vida Silvestre La Flor ★★★ Eighteen kilometers (11 miles) south of San Juan del Sur is one of Nicaragua's most fascinating beaches—and that's not because of its breaks or palm trees. Playa La Flor is a 1.6km (1-mile) stretch of wildlife preserve and scene of nighttime *arribades,* or mass turtle hatchings. Twenty-thousand olive ridley turtles nest on the beach every year, and 45 days later, their offspring hatch and break for the water. This happens from July to February, though the best time to see the nesting is in August or September. Always go with a reputable guide and be aware of turtle-watching etiquette, like not using the flash on your camera. The reserve also has an abundance of birds in the estuary and the mangroves at the south end of the beach. To the north, you may see hundreds of hermit crabs scuttling up the beach at sunset. Park rangers give talks in Spanish and camping is allowed during the hatching at $25 per night per group. There is a small hut that sells some basic supplies, but it is best to come prepared, especially with insect repellent and a mosquito net. **Hostel Casa Oro,** 1 block west of the plaza (𝄢 **505/8458-2415**), organizes excellent evening excursions, including a brief pretour video explaining the turtle hatching and how to act responsibly while witnessing an unforgettable sight.

Playa El Coco. No phone. www.marena.gob.ni. Admission $10.

The Beaches

Surfers put this once-sleepy village on the map, and it's the string of beaches north and south of the town that continue to attract the most visitors. The town's beach is itself slightly disappointing, as the sand is dark and there is little privacy. Neither is it suitable for surfing. If you want big waves and privacy, you will have to venture farther up or down the coast. A coastal road is coming together, but for the moment much of it is a bumpy dirt track. Facilities on these beaches are usually a few beach-bum campsites and some high-end lodges. New developments are appearing all the time and in danger of denying land access to the beaches. There is little in the way of stores or bars, so be sure to pack some food and refreshments for the day.

NORTH East of the Texaco station a road leads to Chocolata. After 7km (4 miles) turn left at Chocolata. The road to the right goes to Playa Majagual and the road to the left goes to Playa Marsella and Playa Madera. Rides are available from any of the surf shops, or catch a water taxi from in front of the Hotel Estrella on the waterfront.

Playa Marsella is one of the closest to town and popular with day-trippers. On weekends there is a small, casual food stall serving fish and beer. The road comes right up to the beach. **Playa Madera ★** is 30 minutes north by water taxi or car. Here you'll find a lovely, breezy beach with big waves and some good snorkeling opportunities. Popular with surfers and sunset watchers alike, the beach is accessed by road and there is room for parking. Some scruffy-looking surf camps offer cheap bunks and lunches. The more upscale **Buena Vista Surf Club** is located on a hilltop overlooking the beach. **Bahía Majagual** is a beautiful cove a little farther to the north, 12km (7½ miles) from San Juan del Sur.

SOUTH   A bus service leaves from San Juan del Sur to the southern Pacific town of Ostonial, passing close to many beaches on the way, particularly Playa Yanqui and Playa Coco. The buses depart from the market at 1, 4, and 5pm, returning at 5am, 7:30am, and 4pm, and take 2 to 3 hours to reach Ostonial. Be sure to double-check these times as they are subject to change.

Playa Remanso is the first beach to the south. It has a long shore, which is ideal for exploring and rock hopping. Follow the southern road out of town past the stadium and cemetery. Take the road right at a Y junction and you'll find a path to the beach. *Note:* This path has a reputation for robberies, so do not go alone. **Playa Tamarindo** is accessed by walking south for 30 minutes along the rocks. **Playa Hermosa** is a 50-minute walk farther south or a 20-minute stroll from the bus stop at El Carrizal on the main road. **Playa Yanqui** is an expansive beach with powerful waves popular with surfers. It is a 20-minute drive from town. **Playa Coco ★** is 18km (11 miles) south of the town and is the best regarding facilities, with a restaurant, an Internet cafe, and several cabins to rent. Close by is the turtle nesting sanctuary **La Flor Wildlife Refuge.**

Outdoor Activities

CANOPY TOURING ★★   Had enough of surf? Feel like soaring across the treetops at 70kmph (45 mph)? **Da Flying Frog** (✆ **505/8611-6214;** tiguacal@ibw. com.ni) specializes in an epic 3.2km (2-mile) canopy ride through the forest that is the best in the country. It takes place on a ranch a small distance from the town on the Chocolata Road. You get a quick tutorial before riding uphill by jeep (and get a great view of the bay). Sixteen cables connect 17 platforms. The excursion costs $25, including a pickup in town. Trekking and horseback riding are also available.

SAILING ★   San Juan del Sur's surrounding coastland makes the perfect playground for an afternoon on a boat. **Aida Sailing Tours** (✆ **505/2568-2287**) offers 1-day and half-day tours in its yacht. Prices start at $30 per person. **Hotel Piedras y Olas** (✆ **505/2568-2110**) also organizes similar excursions on a 14m (46-ft.) sailboat starting at $40 for a half-day and $80 for a full day. Action Tours (✆ **505/ 8843-8157;** www.actiontoursurfnica.com) combines cruising, fishing, and surfing. A full day trip costs $180.

SURFING ★★★   San Juan del Sur has become San Juan del *Surf,* and you will find many boarders testing the waves on the beaches north and south of what has become the surf center of Nicaragua. You can catch good waves all year, but particularly in the rainy season from March to November. Then, waves can get as high as 4m (13 ft.). The two big inland lakes ensure that there is a constant offshore breeze. The water is warm, averaging 77°F (25°C) but can cool considerably from December to April, when a wet-suit top is a good idea. Beginners are advised to go in the dry season when the weather is more amenable and the waves average between 1 and 2m (3–6½ ft.). Some of the best breaks are accessed by boat only.

Playa Madera to the north has two left and right breaks and an increasing selection of surf camps. It can get crowded on weekends. **Panga Drops** is a reef break just north of Playa Madera that can be accessed only by boat. **Playa Tamarindo** is probably the best of the beaches south of the town, having a long wave with left and right breaks. Hard-core surfers should go farther north to lose the crowds. Here a series of beaches are world famous among surfers, especially **Popoyo.** Beware of surfing etiquette on each beach where certain waves are left to the locals to ride and it is considered bad form to hog, especially if you are a beginner. Boards can be hired in town at **Arena Caliente,** beside the market (*②* **505/8636-1769;** www.arena caliente.com), for C200 ($9.30), and lessons are on offer for C400 ($19). This outfit can also help you with a lift to the beach for $5. **Dale Dagger's Surf Nicaragua,** 1 block inland from the Mercado Municipal (*②* **505/2568-2492;** www.nicasurf. com), is one of the better established surfing outfitters, offering excursions and week-long all-inclusive packages for $1,500 including accommodations. It's best to write or call in advance to ensure your spot.

Other Activities

SPANISH CLASSES   The **Spanish School House Rosa Silva,** 50m (164 ft.) west of market (*②* **505/8682-2938;** www.spanishsilva.com), also offers accommodations and activities. For private lessons, contact **Karla Cruz** (*②* **505/8657-1658;** karlacruzsjds@yahoo.com), who teaches at her house 1½ blocks south of the central plaza.

YOGA   Nica Yoga (*②* **505/8400-0255;** www.nicayoga.com) is Nicaragua's first yoga community, 3km (1¾ miles) north of town on the road to Rivas. Thatched huts surround a hardwood-floored communal space. You can do an all-inclusive yoga retreat with accommodations and surfing excursions provided, starting at $486 per person.

Shopping

Besides some itinerant boys selling ceramics and some tourist shops selling T-shirts and chitzy souvenirs, there is not much to browse in town. **Galeria del Sur Art Gallery** (*②* **505/2568-2453;** galeriadelsur@gmail.com) is the only art store in the area, displaying local art as well as running workshops and art classes. It is located a half-block south of the market and is open weekdays 9am to 7pm, Saturday 9am to 5pm, and Sunday 10am to 3pm.

Where to Stay

Every rickety town house in San Juan del Sur seems to have a HOSPEDAJE sign, indicating that the resident family has some rooms available for budget travelers. The town's more upscale hotels are on the outskirts or at the northern end of the beach.

 Holiday Blackouts

If you like creature comforts, inquire whether your hotel has its own generator; power outages are frequent here and no electricity often means no water as well.

There is an increasing number of surf camps, beach lodges, and gated tourist complexes up and down the coast.

EXPENSIVE

Inn on the Pacific   Its cream-colored, mock-Spanish facade is a touch tacky, but you can't beat this hotel for its beachfront location and comfortable, huge rooms, five of which have large kitchenettes. The lobby is small and uninviting, but get past that, and you'll find that everything is clean and well maintained. Each room has a flatscreen TV and sofa, and bathrooms are large. Spacious balconies offer good views of the bay, though they also overlook a busy street that can be noisy.

Av. Costera, 150m (492 ft.) north of Restaurante El Timón. ✆ **505/8880-8120.** Fax 505/2568-2439. www.innonthepacific.net. 6 units. From $92 twin; from $103 single suite (sleeps 2); from $126 penthouse (sleeps 2); from $126 double suite (sleeps 4). Rates include breakfast. AE, DC, MC, V. **Amenities:** Pool. *In room:* A/C, TV, Internet, kitchenette.

La Posada Azul ★★   This is probably the most delightful boutique hotel in town, and it boasts an authentic charm and a decor that makes you feel like you've stepped back in time. High ceilings grace neat wooden interiors and an old-world living room. Wicker wardrobes match wicker headboards in the generously sized rooms. The bathrooms are small but bright and cheerful. The veranda is spectacular; long and wide, it runs the length of the house alongside a lovely flower garden with a fountain and small pool out back. This atmospheric villa was built in 1910 and everything is now immaculate and top-notch.

Calle Central, 2½ blocks west of Parque Central. ✆ **505/2568-2524.** www.laposadaazul.com. 7 units. From $105 twin; from $105 double. Rates include breakfast. AE, DC, MC, V. **Amenities:** Pool; Wi-Fi. *In room:* A/C.

Palermo Hotel and Resort ★★ ☺   This is a large, five-star gated resort with lots of style, comfort, and panoramic views. Manicured lawns surround 50 boxy, condominium-style villas with tiled roof porches and designer-stained walls. Modern, fully equipped kitchens make it ideal for families. The rooms are spacious and immaculate, decked out in hardwood furnishings and local art. Each has an upstairs balcony with beautiful views. The bedrooms have king-size beds and contemporary furnishings spread out across checkered floors that stretch into walk-in closets. The clubhouse is an elegant mix of marble floors, modern sofas, and classical-style tables contrasting with its palm-thatched roof. Big windows, glass doors, and tall ceilings allow for lots of light. A fabulous pool and excellent international **restaurant** complete the equation. Its only fault is its distance from the beaches and town. It is 10 minutes by taxi on the road to La Virgen but there is a free shuttle service that runs throughout the day.

Lomas de Palermo, San Juan del Sur. ✆ **505/8672-0859.** www.villasdepalermo.com. 50 units. Cabin from $350 (sleeps 5). AE, DC, MC, V. **Amenities:** Restaurant; bar; pool. *In room:* A/C, TV, kitchen.

Pelican Eyes Resort ✋ ☺   This gleaming garden hotel dominates the town's main hillside. Brick steps and white walls rise through the property's gardens and palm trees, passing its restaurant La Cascada to the left, before continuing upward to a complex of guest rooms, villa-like cottages, and private homes. The style is big and clunky, with uneven walls and glass tiles adorning open kitchens and expansive bedrooms. Farther up, there are a series of pools and one restaurant, all set in lush gardens that are open to the public. The view from the gardens is fantastic. Beware of a 50% cancellation fee if you cancel within 7 days of your stay.

Calle Central, 1½ blocks east of Parque Central. ✆ **505/2568-2110.** www.pelicaneyesresort.com. From $207 double; from $224 cabin (sleeps 4); from $195 casita (sleeps 4); from $265 town house casa (sleeps 4); from $282 casa (sleeps 6). Rates include breakfast. AE, DC, MC, V. **Amenities:** Restaurant; bar; Internet in lobby; laundry service; pool. *In room:* A/C, cable TV, kitchenette.

MODERATE

El Encanto del Sur   This simple, no-frills hotel is one of the best budget options in town, with a basic no-nonsense decor and a hard-to-beat price. The modern house has a central salon overlooked by an internal balcony with lots of light. The rooms are simple, clean, and appealing, with en suite bathrooms.

2 blocks south of plaza. ✆ **505/2568-2222.** www.hotelencantodelsur.com. 18 units. From $35 double. AE, DC, MC, V. *In room:* A/C, TV.

Hotel Gran Oceano 🏊   A handsome mansion-style building in the town center boasts a huge pool in a courtyard of brown pillars and garden plants, and a front patio with rocking chairs and beautiful ceramic tile work. However, the standard rooms are not so grand—everything is quite small, including the beds, wardrobes, and bathrooms. Still, rooms are colorful and appealing, and they come at a great price. There are some larger rooms available for more money, as well.

Calle Central, 2½ blocks west of Parque Central. ✆ **505/2568-2219.** www.hotelgranoceano.com.ni. 23 units. From $56 double; from $65 triple. Rates include breakfast. AE, MC, V. **Amenities:** Pool. *In room:* A/C, cable TV.

INEXPENSIVE

Casa el Oro ★   Casa el Oro has that colorful, tumbledown feel that's popular with hostels the world over. This one also serves as San Juan del Sur's unofficial tourism office, dispensing info on everything from bus timetables to Spanish classes. You can change traveler's checks, swap books, and organize beach shuttles and turtle-nesting excursions through the proactive owners. A set of tidy dorms are arranged around a courtyard with an open-air kitchen. There are some private rooms too, which are small and basic (with shared bathrooms) but comfy.

Calle Central, 1 block west of the plaza. ✆ **505/2568-2415.** www.casaeloro.com. 12 units (7 dorms). From $25 double; $7.50 dorms. AE, DC, MC, V. **Amenities:** Restaurant; bar. *In room:* Fan, no phone.

Hostel Pachamama ★   San Juan del Sur's newest hostel is also the town's party center with a busy, fun-loving clientele. The communal areas are modern and spacious and the two private rooms are a bargain, but require booking well in advance. The American owner, Alex, is very helpful and will help set up any excursions required. There is a Ping-Pong table up front and lively bar at the back.

Calle Central, 2 blocks west of the plaza. ✆ **505/2568-2043.** www.hostelpachamama.com. 7 units (5 dorms). From $20 double; $8 dorms. No credit cards. **Amenities:** Bar. *In room:* Fan, no phone.

Where to Stay Outside San Juan del Sur

Buena Vista Surf Club ★ 🧳   This hip lodge with a Zen-like vibe is set on a hill above Playa Madera, with marvelous views of the beach from an impressive open deck of polished wood. Two treehouses and a suite-style room in the main house are held together by dark, tropical woods and thatched roofs with canopy-style mosquito nets over the beds. The dining area and bar is stylish and impressive and invites loafing with a chilled-out vibe. The food is excellent, with fresh, seasonal ingredients. Only nine people can stay at any one time, ensuring that it remains easygoing and intimate.

Playa Madera, San Juan del Sur. ℗ **505/8863-4180.** www.buenavistasurfclub.com. 3 units. From $95 double, minimum 2 nights. No credit cards. **Amenities:** Restaurant; bar; Internet in lobby; laundry service; pool. *In room:* A/C.

Empalme a Las Playas ★

This is a jungle lodge with no frills but lots of fronds, bamboo, and wood. Located 6.4km (4 miles) outside of town on the road that leads to Playas Marsella and Maderas, it is on a hill overlooking the forest. The large, airy cabins sit on stilts and are plain, but attractive and very authentic. Wooden walkways lead to the all-bamboo huts, and wicker seating goes well with solid wooden beds. There are hammocks to roll into and enjoy the jungle sounds of howler monkeys and birds. The English-speaking owners, Roy and Karen, are excellent hosts and an easy introduction into the expat community in the area. They'll encourage you to try your hand at horseshoe throwing. Rustic and basic, the lodge is an enjoyable and very genuine place to stay.

Empalme a las Playas, Chocolata Rd., San Juan del Sur. ℗ **505/8818-3892.** www.playamarsella.com. 5 units. From $65 double. Rates include breakfast. No credit cards. **Amenities:** Restaurant; bar.

Mango Rosa ★ 🍋

The Mango Rosa is an upscale resort on the road to Playa Marsella, 7km (4⅓ miles) from town. The spacious bungalows are a nice arrangement of white walls, cane ceilings, wicker furniture, and hardwood counters. Lime-green cushions, plants, and pink candles add a sense of style. The bathrooms are long and roomy, with designer stone sinks and tall mirrors. The stepped pool is surrounded by multicolored deck chairs and sand-colored walls. There is a lively **bar and grill,** and owner Greg will happily set you up with a sunset booze cruise on the bay. The Mango Rosa is nice mix of beachside informality in stylish surroundings. The hotel is a 10-minute walk from the beach.

Chocolata Rd., San Juan del Sur. ℗ **505/8477-3692.** www.mangorosanicaragua.com. 6 units. From $95 1-bedroom villa; from $135 2-bedroom villa. AE, DC, MC, V. **Amenities:** Restaurant; bar; pool. *In room:* A/C, TV, Wi-Fi.

Morgan's Rock Hacienda and Eco Lodge ★★

San Juan del Sur has attracted its fair share of luxury accommodations in recent years, but none has created quite the same buzz as this place. Eighteen kilometers (11 miles) north of the town you'll find 15 luxury bungalows, accessed by a 100m (328-ft.) suspension bridge over a tropical gorge. Architecturally stunning and with superb attention to detail, the lodge combines luxury and environmentally friendly accommodations and has no phones, Internet, or air-conditioning. You'll just have to make do with the infinity pool and the beautiful, deserted Ocotal beach. The bungalows are quite a hike, with many steps, but they are breezy and open-air. Make sure to request your morning coffee brought to your door in a thermos. The 1,000-hectare (2,471-acre) property includes a nature preserve, shrimp farm, and sugar processing plant that produces its own rum. Kayaking tours are available and the farm produces the dairy products, herbs, and vegetables used in the restaurant.

Majagual, San Juan del Sur. ℗ **505/8670-7676,** or 506/2232-6449 in Costa Rica. www.morgansrock. com. 15 units. From $372 double. Rates include breakfast and dinner. AE, DC, MC, V. **Amenities:** Restaurant; bar; Internet in lobby; laundry service; pool.

Parque Maritimo El Coco

Three modern villas of varying size offer apartments and bungalows for rent. The decor is basic and somewhat old-fashioned, with heavy drapes and little ornamentation. However, lots of light and a large veranda ensure a pleasant stay on this beach compound close to Reserva La Flor, 18km (11 miles) south of San Juan del Sur. The restaurant **Puesta del Sol** is also worth a stop if you are in the area (open Wed–Mon 8am–6pm).

Playa El Coco, 18km (11 miles) south of San Juan del Sur. ✆ **505/8892-0124.** www.playaelcoco.com.ni. 9 units. From $184 double. AE, DC, MC, V. **Amenities:** Restaurant; bar; Internet in lobby; laundry service; pool. *In room:* A/C, cable TV, kitchenette.

Where to Dine

In addition to the restaurants reviewed below, you might want to check out one of the many thatched-roof restaurants that line the beachfront here. They all serve excellent shrimp and lobster dishes ranging from C300 to C400 ($14–$19). The **Mercado Municipal** ★ has a small, cluttered food hall that offers great-value chicken and rice dishes for less than C80 ($3.70) a portion. **Barrio Café,** 1 block west of Market (✆ 505/2568-2294; www.barriocafesanjuan.com), is where everybody goes for morning coffee. The more cerebral traveler hangs out at **El Gato Negro,** 1 block east of Timon (✆ 505/8809-1108), an excellent bookshop and coffeehouse. **Big Wave Daves,** a half-block east of Bancentro (✆ 505/2568-2151), offers hamburgers, pasta, and shrimp and is a lively spot for early-evening drinks.

El Colibri ★★ 📷 INTERNATIONAL   This restaurant is as enchanting as its name implies—*el colibri* is Spanish for hummingbird. Set within a funky clapboard house with a large veranda overlooking a garden, the building is a piece of art put together from recycled materials by its Anglo-Irish owner, Mary O'Hanlon. Mosaic-framed mirrors hang between stained-glass lamps and African masks. Elephant woodcuts are illuminated by candelabras, and there are delightful touches like small colored stones that hold down the place mats, lest the sea breeze carry them away. The menu could best be described as adventurous and organic. Hummus dip complements beef kabobs, and the filet mignon comes in a bacon-and-vodka cream sauce. The homemade pâté is a revelation, made from chicken, bacon, and sherry. Check the chalkboard for specials, as the menu is very much seasonal. Laid-back music adds to the overall relaxing atmosphere.

On the east side of Parque Central, 1 block south of Hotel Villa Isabella. ✆ **505/8863-8612.** Reservations recommended. Main courses C160 ($7.45). AE, MC, V. Daily 6–11pm.

El Pozo ★★ 🍴 MODERN AMERICAN   Californians Christian and Claire opened this gourmet restaurant in 2007 with the intention of bringing some contemporary American-style cuisine to the southwestern coast of Nicaragua. They've succeeded with this small, modern bistro, which has a minimalist design with an open kitchen at the back, hardwood furniture, and a cane ceiling. The menu includes a refreshing watermelon salad and a delicious tamarind pork chop.

El Pozo is also a good stop-off point for a late-night cocktail. The small, inviting bar serves the best martinis in town. The wine list is unusually good, with French champagne and Italian wines, among others.

Av. del Mercado, 10m (33 ft.) south of the market. ✆ **505/8806-5708.** Main courses C160–C260 ($7.45–$12). AE, DC, MC, V. Thurs–Mon 6pm–1am.

La Cascada ★ INTERNATIONAL   La Cascada is much like the hotel Piedras y Olas it belongs to—it's big, impressive, and somewhat over-the-top. The large, open space is the size of a movie set and doubtless will be used some day in a Hollywood blockbuster. The thatched roof encompasses a curved bar, spacious dining area, and terrace with a widescreen view of the bay. There is a pool up front if you fancy a dip between courses. The imaginative menu includes Cajun sausage soup and almond

Peñas Blancas is the main crossing into Costa Rica, and its size and modernity reflect the huge numbers that pass back and forth. Avoid crossing just before major holidays, as crowds of returning Nicaraguans who live in Costa Rica create lengthy delays. Make sure to get your visa or passport stamped on both sides to avoid problems later. If you are traveling with an international bus company, an attendant often collects the passports and fees on the bus and does the processing for you, though you do have to disembark with your bags to be searched at Customs. A C80 ($3.70) fee is charged when you leave Nicaragua and a C180 ($8.35) fee is assessed when you enter. The charges fluctuate slightly (they are higher early in the morning or late at night). Be aware of an extra C20 (95¢) "mayor's tax" as you enter the Customs area. The border crossing is open from 6am to 10pm every day but Sunday, when it closes at 8pm. Make sure to sell all your córdobas before you leave Nicaragua as you will not be able to change them farther south. Buses and taxis are available on both sides if you're not traveling on an express bus.

stir-fry, with the usual delicious mix of lobster and shrimp thrown in. The staff is very friendly and speaks English.

Calle Central, 1½ blocks east of Parque Central. ⓒ **505/2568-2110.** Main courses C160–C280 ($7.45–$13). AE, DC, MC, V. Daily 6:30am–11pm.

San Juan del Sur After Dark

Like any beach town, San Juan del Sur has its fair share of reveling vacationers enjoying rum and doing extensive research into whether they prefer Victoria or Toña beer. Yet the town's nightlife is pretty sedate and civilized, with just a few bars along the beachfront and two all-night discos that come alive on weekends. **Iguana Bar ★**, half a block north of El Velero restaurant (ⓒ **505/2568-2085**), attracts a lively young crowd of locals and visitors. It is on the beachfront and has a bar upstairs and downstairs. **Bar Republika** (no phone) is a small street bar located a half-block west of the Mercado Municipal. **Club Sunset,** in a green clapboard house on the waterfront (no phone), is open for all-night dancing Friday and Saturday. It has outside seating if the mixture of salsa and reggaeton blaring inside gets to be a little too much. There is a cover charge of C50 ($2.35). **Bambu Beach Club ★** (ⓒ **505/2568-2101;** www.thebambubeachclub.com) hosts DJs and bands at its lounge overlooking the beach on the northern end of the bay. Close by is a sports bar called **Smokey's** (no phone) that has bamboo walls, a pool table, and some TV screens to watch the latest game. **Crazy Crab Beach Club** (no phone) is a rancho-style disco at the northern end of the beach that packs in both locals and expats every weekend with DJs and occasional live music.

ISLA DE OMETEPE

The twin peaks of the Concepción and Maderas volcanoes rise out of Lago de Nicaragua, forming a muddy jungle island that sustains 35,000 people, countless bird life, cattle, and howler monkeys. Fireflies dance beneath banana trees as people on old buses, bikes, horses, and even oxen negotiate the rutted roads and countless trails.

Rocks carved into zoomorphic figures and pre-Columbian petroglyphs dot the landscape of tropical forest and patchwork fields. The rich, volcanic soil provides abundant crops of bananas, maize, coffee, avocados, and beef, most of which is crammed on the boats that ply the waterway between the island and the mainland port of San Jorge, 1 hour to the west.

The island here, known as **Isla de Ometepe,** is sacred ground. Legend has it that the Nahuatl tribe fled the Aztecs and went southward in search of a mythical region with two mountains in a lake. There is reason to believe, through the countless artifacts that litter the island, that Nicaragua's pre-Columbian heritage began on the island. In many ways, the islanders remain a people apart from the rest of the country. The turmoil and violence that wracked the mainland for centuries generally bypassed the island, famously referred to by folk singer Luis Enrique Mejia Godoy as "an oasis of peace." The only real drama occurs beneath the ground. In fact, Ometepe used to be two islands before eruptions and lava flow formed the isthmus Istián that now connects both volcanoes. Volcán Concepción is still very much alive, hurling rocks and spewing lava four times in the last century. The last thunderous occasion was in 1957, when the islanders showed their fierce independence and refused to leave after they were ordered to evacuate.

Their reluctance to leave is understandable. The island is an idyllic adventure spot, a rural retreat, and a hiker's paradise. For many visitors, the peaks beckon to be climbed, but be warned: It is a hard slog and can be done only with a guide. Others prefer to wander the volcanoes' lower reaches, bathe on the island's dark beaches, cool off in spring-water pools and waterfalls, or explore the island's many coves and lagoons by foot or kayak.

Essentials

GETTING THERE

BY BOAT San Jorge port just outside Rivas is the main departure point to reach the island. The car/passenger *Ferry Ometepe* (© **505/8459-4284** in Moyogalpa) departs at 7:45am, 10:30am, 2:30pm, and 5:30pm. The fare is C40 ($1.85) per person and C600 ($28) per vehicle, and the crossing takes approximately an hour. Vehicle owners should call well in advance to book (at least 3 days) and reconfirm the day before. Try to get to the dockside office an hour before departure to pay for your tickets and ensure a spot. *Note:* The ferry often leaves as soon as it fills up and before the appointed hour. The ferry returns to the mainland from Moyogalpa at 6am, 9am, 12:30pm, and 4pm.

A handful of other boats cross to Moyogalpa, leaving at 9am, 9:30am, 11:30am, 1:30pm, 3:30pm, and 4:30pm. The fare is C30 ($1.40) and, as on the ferry, the passengers are a colorful mix of locals toting cattle and fruit and whatever else they can get onboard. The water can be choppy; it's best to go early in the morning or late in the afternoon for the smoothest sailing. The smaller boats return to San Jorge from Moyogalpa at 5:30am, 6:30am, 7am, 11:30am, and 1:30pm.

You can also get to Ometepe from Granada on a 4-hour voyage that leaves twice a week. The *Mozorola* leaves every Wednesday and Saturday at 11am and docks at Altagracia on the island. It returns every Tuesday and Friday at 11am. The fare is C40 ($1.85). A ferry called the *EPN* leaves Granada every Monday and Thursday at 3pm, stopping in Altagracia before continuing south to San Miguelito and San Carlos. It returns through Altagracia every Tuesday and Friday at 11pm. Be aware, however, that if the sea is rough, the ferry may skip its stop at Altagracia altogether.

Isla de Ometepe

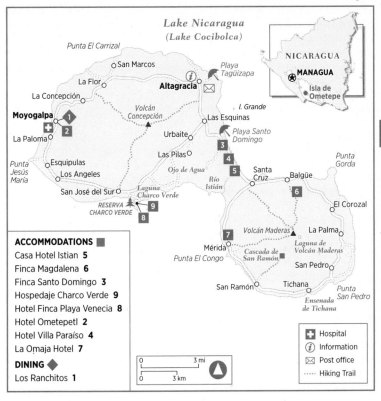

Lake Nicaragua
(Lake Cocibolca)

ACCOMMODATIONS ■
Casa Hotel Istian **5**
Finca Magdalena **6**
Finca Santo Domingo **3**
Hospedaje Charco Verde **9**
Hotel Finca Playa Venecia **8**
Hotel Ometepetl **2**
Hotel Villa Paraíso **4**
La Omaja Hotel **7**
DINING ◆
Los Ranchitos **1**

GETTING AROUND

ON FOOT   The island is a hiker's paradise, with numerous trails, but beware that some of the paths can be rough going, and it is easy to get lost. You will certainly need a guide for any treks up to the volcanoes.

BY CAR/TAXI   If you want to travel around the island on your own, you'll have to get a 4WD vehicle. **Hotel Ometepetl** rents old Toyotas and Suzukis for approximately C760 ($35) for 12 hours. Taxis are plentiful and drivers will swarm you as soon as you step off the boat, as will touts selling rooms and tours.

A pickup taxi from the port to Santo Domingo beach should cost approximately C360 ($17). Two reliable taxi services are **Marvin Arcia** and **Rommel Gómez.**

BY BUS   Old school buses lumber around the island at hourly intervals between Moyogalpa and Altagracia, and they usually travel counterclockwise. The fare for these buses is C6 (30¢). All buses leave from Moyogalpa dock. The journey between the two towns takes about 1 hour, and from Altagracia to Balgue it takes another hour. There are less frequent services to outlying towns like San Ramón and Merida. The bus service on Sunday is much reduced and sometimes nonexistent. *Be warned:* These bus journeys can be slow and uncomfortable, and, if you are traveling across the isthmus, it can seem to take forever.

VISITOR INFORMATION

There is an **Intur** (no phone) office in the plaza of Altagracia. It is open weekdays from 9am to 1pm and 3 to 5pm. Most of the hotels listed below are good sources of local information, too.

FAST FACTS There are no banks on the island. There is a small credit union in Moyogalpa with an ATM, but it is temperamental and does not accept credit cards or debit cards that are linked to the Maestro program. Across from the credit union there is a *"tienda"* that allows you to take money out on a credit card (MasterCard and Visa), but they charge a hefty fee. It is better to get cash in Gada or San Juan de Sur before boarding the boat.

Hospital Moyogalpa (📞 505/2569-4247) is 3 blocks east of the plaza. Altagracia also has a small **Centro de Salud** (📞 505/2552-6089) on the southeast corner of the town plaza.

For Internet access in Moyogalpa, go to **Arcia Cyber Café** on the main street (no phone). It is open daily from 8am to 9pm. In Altagracia, the **Casa Rural,** on the south side of the plaza (no phone), has Internet service, as does the craft store **Tienda Fashion,** 1 block south of the park (no phone).

For phone service, head to **ENITEL** in Moyogalpa, which is 1½ blocks east of the principal street (📞 505/2569-4100), or the Altagracia office, which is in front of the plaza beside Museo Ometepe (no phone).

There is a **post office** in Altagracia, on the corner of the plaza beside the Museo Ometepe (no phone).

Tour Operators

Ometepe Tours ★, in front of the ferry dock in San Jorge (📞 505/2563-4779 in San Jorge, or **2569-4242** in Moyogalpa), runs an excellent 1-day tour of the island, which leaves San Jorge at 9:30am and arrives back on the mainland by 4:30pm. They also arrange multiday package stays with hotels and transport.

On the island, **Bernan Gómez** (📞 505/8836-8360) conducts well-informed tours. If you decide to trek to the volcanoes, make sure you get a reputable guide (known as a *baqueano*) outfitted with a radio and first-aid kit. Guide quality and prices can vary, so ask around before you decide.

What to See & Do

Moyogalpa, on the western side of the island, is a small, quiet town with a sloping main street. The town fountain is a model of the island—it's designed to have water spout from its "volcanoes"—though it has not worked for years. Moyogalpa is the main port that services the island and is a hive of activity when boats arrive. Its pretty hilltop church is at the top of the main street. It has a white facade and attractive wooden doorways and affords a beautiful view from the bell tower. The town museum **Sala Arqueoligica,** 1 block west of the plaza (📞 505/2569-4225; admission C40/$1.85), functions half as an artifact display and half as a handicraft store—it sells local crafts and displays pre-Columbian pieces found by the owner. Both the museum and the shop are open weekdays from 8am to 8pm.

Altagracia is the second-biggest town on the island and a prettier place than Moyogalpa. Its central plaza, known as Parque Central, is a large patch of grass with a shop and playground. The area is famous for its vampire bats, but don't worry, they target only chickens and other small animals. This is where the boats from Granada dock, at a port 3km (1¾ miles) north of the town. **El Museo Ometepe** (1 block from the park; no phone) has some interesting ceramic artifacts. It is open daily from 9am to noon and 2 to 5pm. Admission is C40 ($1.85). **Playa Taguizapa** is a pleasant beach that's a 30-minute walk east of the plaza.

Five kilometers (3 miles) south of Moyogalpa is the long, sandy peninsula of **Punta Jesús Maria,** a tranquil beach that offers the opportunity of beer with a sunset. A cab from Moyogalpa should not cost more than C200 ($9.30) each way. Ten kilometers (6¼ miles) east on the islands' underbelly is **Reserva Charco Verde ★.** Here the jungle rolls down on a black volcanic beach and monkeys howl from the treetops. It is excellent for some bird-watching or kayaking around the bay or through its green lagoon. Be prepared to get your feet wet, as the wooden walkway has collapsed. Some nearby *hospedajes* offer boat trips and horseback-riding excursions. There's a suggested admission fee of C20 (95¢). From the reserve, you can hike through to an isolated cove called **El Tesoro del Pirata ★.** The two volcanoes stand on either side of this serene and peaceful beach.

However, if it is a real beach you want, you must go to **Playa Santo Domingo.** This 4km (2½-mile) stretch of dark sand, with a green jungle backdrop, connects both islands along the Isthmus Istián. The beach can appear a little tatty in parts, but in general is very nice and one of the few in the world that can boast a volcano at either end. It's also where the island's best accommodations are located and a great spot for bathing in the shallow waters—the gray-green waters are choppy yet warm and inviting, and there are thatched parasols if the heat gets to be too much. A 30-minute walk up a dirt track beside Villa Paraíso is a bathing complex called **Ojo del Agua ★,** a series of rock-lined pools fed by a natural spring and surrounded by tall trees. It can get a little crowded, but it's great fun dangling from the swing ropes and watching suicidal divers jump from crazy heights here. The entrance fee is C20 (95¢).

Cascada San Ramón is a spectacular 50m (164-ft.) waterfall on the southern slopes of Volcán Madera. To get there you must go to the small town of San Ramón, 4km (2½ miles) south of Merida. It's a 3-hour hike from there to the falls, but well worth it.

Outdoor Activities

BIKING Volcanic mountains in the area equal lots of slopes, so the island offers some thrilling rides—it is perfect for mountain biking. You can rent bikes from many of the *hospedajes* on the island, including Hotel Hacienda Merida. **Comercial Arcia,** 2 blocks south of Moyogalpa church (no phone), also rents bikes, at a rate of C20 (95¢) an hour.

The east coast of Maderas makes for a particularly good and challenging spin, and along the way, you can stop to see the cave paintings in Tichana and petroglyphs near Corazal. Make sure to get a good bike, as it is tough terrain.

HIKING ★ Besides enabling you to notch a volcanic peak or two into your belt (see "Climbing Ometepe's Volcanoes," above), the island provides ample opportunities for you to go for a wander, trip upon ancient pre-Columbian relics, and admire the stunning sunsets. Just pick a path, but remember that much of what you walk upon is private property and, though the islanders in general have no problem with your traipsing across their lands, you should always ask for permission first. Most hotels and lodges have their own set of circuits and interesting things to see close by, one example being the petroglyphs of Finca Magdalena (p. 533).

HORSEBACK RIDING In many ways, horseback riding is the best way to get around this muddy, steep terrain. Indeed, I'm surprised no independent operator is offering rides yet. Ask at your hotel for what they offer regarding saddleback riding.

CLIMBING OMETEPE'S volcanoes

In Isla de Ometepe, you can stand beside a lake within a volcano. However, it's not that easy! **Volcán Maderas** may be the smaller of the two volcanoes at 1,394m (4,573 ft.), and the most frequently hiked, but it is not a walk in the park, so to speak. Getting there involves an all-day hike up a steep incline, passing coffee plantations and the occasional pre-Columbian carving along the way, and down into its inner rim. This last part requires ropes, so it is imperative that you go with a reputable, fully equipped guide. People who attempt the volcanoes alone can end up lost, injured, or dead. There are two ways of approaching the peak, either through the grounds of **Finca Magdalena** near Balgue (p. 533), which charges a small fee if you are not a guest) or from the other side at **Merida. Hotel Hacienda Merida** (© 505/8868-8973 or 8894-2551; www.hmerida.com) arranges excursions in which trekkers descend at Finca Magdalena and are transported back to the hotel.

Volcán Concepción is the big one—a perfectly formed cone 1,610m (5,280 ft.)

high. It is a long and arduous climb of 10 hours up and down and a different experience from Maderas in the sense that you walk on a live volcano that could erupt at any time. The last time it rattled its bowels was in 1957, and it has done so four times in the past 100 years. Do the math: An eruption is due *soon*. A thick jungle forest with monkeys and birds gives way to rocks and shale the higher you go. A stiff wind helps or hinders until suddenly the hot, sulfurous belch blasts upward from the crater as you reach the rim. This is what forms the almost permanent cloud that clings to the peak. If you are lucky and come on a clear day, you'll be rewarded with the sight of the volcano's chilling stony interior and spectacular views of the island—you'll want to linger and take in its otherworldly atmosphere. La Sabana is the best place to start your climb. You can also approach the volcano from a trail behind Altagracia. Again, you *must* go with a guide, even if you just want to explore the lower reaches, as it is very easy to get lost.

KAYAKING ★ Reserva Charco Verde is a good spot for paddling. You can rent kayaks at **Hospedaje Charcoe Verde** (© **505/8887-9302**) at hourly rates of C100 ($4.65) single and C150 ($7) double. Another great splash is along the coast north of Merida and up the **Istián River.** It can be tough going if you have the wind against you, but once you get on the river, it's worth it. Another less challenging kayak trip is to **Isla el Congo** south of Merida. Ask at your hotel about kayak rentals for the river Istián and Isla el Congo.

Where to Stay

There are no true luxury hotels on the island. What you get are charming, down-to-earth, rustic lodges with slow but friendly service. Moyogalpa has the best concentration of budget options, but my advice is to get out of that town and stay farther out, where there are plenty more places at reasonable rates.

MODERATE

Finca Santo Domingo This large blue bungalow-style hotel is a little rough around the edges, but is surrounded by gorgeous green foliage and boasts roll-out-of-bed access to the beach. It has very basic rooms and you might get some nighttime intruders in the form of snakes and ants. Be prepared for cold-water showers only, and few amenities other than a restaurant and Internet service.

Playa Santo Domingo. ℘ **505/8694-1594.** hotel_santo_domingo@yahoo.com. 15 units. From $25 double; from $35 triple; from $35 cabin (sleeps 2); from $40 cabin (sleeps 3). AE, MC, V. **Amenities:** Restaurant; bike rental; Internet in lobby. *In room:* A/C or fan.

Hotel Villa Paraíso ★   You might have to line up behind a herd of cows on the muddy dirt track leading up to this isolated hotel, but the view from your patio hammock is worth it. Often cited as the best hotel on the island, the Paraiso offers stone and wood cabins perched on a cliff with Volcán Maderas to the right. The rooms are good size, though the two beds are small and low, and surface areas could be cleaner. Each comes with a private, rustic bathroom. The **restaurant** is a mite tacky, with wine barrels set into a concrete bar and a stone mosaic overhead, and service is slow. Still, it offers delicious fresh fish platters, among other dishes.

Playa Santo Domingo. ℘ **505/2563-4675.** www.villaparaiso.com.ni. 25 units. From $29 double; from $73 suite; from $73 quadruple. AE, DC, MC, V. **Amenities:** Restaurant; Internet in lobby; pool. *In room:* A/C, TV.

La Omaja Hotel ☺   Set on a steep hill with great views of Concepción, La Omaja offers spartan cabins amid a lush garden of green lawn, shrubs, and palm trees. The rooms are big, accommodating two good-size double beds. The decor could stand a bit of sprucing up and the furniture is functional, with deck chairs serving as sitting chairs. Only the deluxe and family cabins have private bathrooms. There are no screens on any of the windows, so bring bug repellent.

Merida. ℘ **505/8885-1124.** www.laomaja.com. 6 units. From $40 deluxe cabin (sleeps 4); from $25 family cabin (sleeps 5); $5 per person shared cabin. AE, DC, MC, V. **Amenities:** Restaurant; Internet in lobby; laundry service. *In room:* A/C, fan (in shared cabin), TV.

INEXPENSIVE

Casa Hotel Istiam 🛏   The colorful, two-story property is close to Playo Domingo and has its own private beach. The property is basic but attractive, with large balconies and lots of hammocks. Rooms are large and clean and come with or without a bathroom. Rates are a bargain, starting at $6 per person.

Villa Paraíso, Playa Santo Domingo. ℘ **505/8868-8682** or 8887-9891. 12 units. $20 double with private bathroom. No credit cards. **Amenities:** Restaurant. *In room:* A/C (1 room), fan.

Finca Magdalena 🛏 ☺   What Finca Magdalena lacks in luxury it makes up for in community spirit and heart. It's the confiscated property of rich landowners who found themselves on the wrong side during the revolution. It is now a coffee cooperative of 24 families who offer dorm-style accommodations in a barnlike hacienda, along with some cottages for those who'd like a little more privacy. There are some closet-size double rooms in the main building. Be prepared for cold showers and communal meals, but lots of character and a chance to sample a farming lifestyle. There's easy access to sites like the Volcán Madera and petroglyphs scattered around the wild garden grounds. The downside is that the *finca* is a long haul from Moyogalpa, 2 hours on the bus followed by a 2km (1¼-mile) walk uphill.

Balgue. ℘ **505/8880-2041.** www.fincamagdalena.com. 21 units. From $46 cabin; $11 double; $4 dorm. No credit cards. **Amenities:** Restaurant; communal kitchen. *In room:* Fan, no phone.

Hospedaje Charco Verde   This hotel is right beside the lagoon reserve and offers handsome wooden cabins with lots of light and space. It has a more rural setting than Hotel Ometepetl and is more rustic. The beds are big and the furniture is comfortable, with a veranda and hammock. The owners have a farm nearby and also rent out kayaks and horses. You can arrange short boat trips to Isla de Quiste or along the shoreline. There is also a **restaurant** and **bar** on the premises that is open to the public.

Charco Verde. 🕐 **505/8887-9302.** www.charcoverde.com.ni. 8 units. $40–$50 double. AE, MC, V. **Amenities:** Restaurant; bike rental. *In room:* A/C or fan.

Hotel Finca Playa Venecia ★ 🔥   This large, hacienda-style property has simple cabins with an excellent location close to the green lagoon of Charco Verde. There is a nice lounge area with hammocks, set in a pastoral paradise. The **restaurant** is decent and the owner rents out bikes and horses to explore the area further. Prices range from $7 a night in a triple room with fan, to $17 for double room with fan, through to $57 for a triple cabin with air-conditioning.

San José del Sur, btw. Moyogalpa and Altagracia. 🕐 **505/8887-0191.** www.fincavenecia.com. 8 units. $10 per person or $35 cabana (sleeps 4). No credit cards. **Amenities:** Restaurant; bar. *In room:* A/C or fan.

Hotel Ometepetl   This hotel is one of the better established on the island, with a convenient location in the center of Moyogalpa. It has an attractive courtyard, with an effusion of plant life, a pool, and lounging areas with giant hammocks. Chunky wooden furniture sits on tiled floors that lead to pleasant-size rooms with private bathrooms. The open-air restaurant has lots of light and white tablecloths on the tables. Service can be mixed, and the air-conditioning problematic. The hotel also offers jeep rentals and is the only place on the island that accepts traveler's checks.

Moyogalpa, 50m (164 ft.) uphill from port. 🕐 **505/2569-4276.** 13 units. From $20 double; from $35 triple; from $45 quadruple. AE, DC, MC, V. **Amenities:** Pool. *In room:* A/C or fan.

Where to Dine

The better hotels in town have restaurants, so you should not have to wander too far for a meal. **Restaurant Villa Paraíso,** in the Hotel Villa Paraíso (🕐 **505/2563-4675**), is one of the best. It serves international fare and is open daily from 7am to 9pm, for breakfast, lunch, and dinner. Main courses start at C200 ($9.30). **Restaurante Charco Verde ★**, in the Hospedaje Charco Verde (🕐 **505/8887-9302**), is another pleasant hotel restaurant offering a wide variety, from pasta and steak to a giant filet of fish. The dining area is under a large wooden roof with open walls. It is open daily from 7am to 8pm. Meals start at C190 ($8.85). Finally, you may want to try **Restaurante Ometepetl** (🕐 **505/2569-4132**), in the hotel of the same name. It has a pleasant open front dining area and serves Nicaraguan staples. It's open daily from 6am to 10pm. Meals start at C160 ($7.45).

Los Ranchitos NICARAGUAN   Try this spot in Moyogalpa that offers inexpensive fare in an open-air setting. It is popular with locals and visitors, and the menu includes everything from pizza to fish served in huge portions. The restaurant also offers a taxi service if you're too stuffed to walk home.

4 blocks uphill from the dock and half a block south, Moyogalpa. 🕐 **505/2569-4112.** Main courses from C100 ($4.65). No credit cards. Daily 7am–9pm.

THE RIO SAN JUAN ★★

This is a mighty river; a broad, majestic, expanse of fresh water that pours slowly out of Lake Nicaragua toward the Atlantic Ocean 210km (130 miles) away. It passes rainforests and cattle ranches, stilted shacks on the water, and quiet river lodges. It widens in parts to 350m (1,150 ft.), and in other areas it narrows into treacherous rapids, particularly at the 300-year-old Spanish fort of El Castillo. More than 25 rivers flow into the San Juan from the Nicaraguan and Costa Rican shorelines, and it forms the border between both countries from El Castillo to the Atlantic estuary. The shoreline teems with wildlife, especially at the mammoth Indo-Maiz Biological Reserve on the Nicaraguan side. The ghost town of Greytown lies at the end, as does its rebranded and relocated sister town, San Juan del Norte.

The Rama tribe lived here before the Spanish arrived, and some remain in Indo-Maiz reserve and on a small island in Bluefields Bay. From 16th-century Granada, the Europeans sent down several expeditions, hoping the river led to the sea. The rapids at Río Sábalo thwarted several missions until the Caribbean was reached in 1539 by an intrepid soldier named Alonso Calero. It happened on St. John the Baptist's feast day, thus the name. The river became the main conduit to carry the Spanish Empire's plunder from the Pacific side of its Central American territories. Gold, silver, and indigo were just some of the commodities that sailed east, and Granada became wealthy and prosperous because of its strategic location. It was a prosperity coveted by other nations.

The French and English sent constant raiding parties to take the spoils, and the river's history is a fascinating catalog of pirate raids and colonial sieges. Mark Twain sailed down this "earthly paradise" on his way to New York from San Francisco, a passenger on Vanderbilt's interoceanic steamship service. William Walker made a stand at San Carlos, as did the Contras farther downriver during the counterrevolution in the 1980s. Nicaragua and Costa Rica have had countless diplomatic spats over who owns the river. The waterway also came very close to being the Nicaraguan version of the Panama Canal. Imagine, instead of giant silver tarpon fish we would have giant, rusty oil tankers with not a howler monkey or parrot in sight. Thank goodness for no progress!

How to Get There

The only regular boat service to Castillo is from San Carlos. **San Carlos** is a hot, fetid port town straight out of a Graham Greene novel. It is the sort of place you stay in only if you're waiting for something—usually the next boat downriver or the next plane to Managua. If you find yourself trapped in this grubby place, the best hotels are **Hotel Carelys** (✆ **505/2583-0389**) and **Cabinas Leyko** (✆ **505/2583-0354;** leykou7@yahoo.es). Basic rooms at both range from $13 to $50.

To truly explore the river and its tributaries, you need a private boat with guide, possibly arranged in San Carlos, but best arranged with the expert agencies in Managua, who will provide English-speaking, qualified guides. Access to many tributaries is restricted and you must show written permission from MARENA in Managua to get past the checkpoints and soldiers. Pack the strongest bug repellent you can find and wear clothes that easily dry.

What to See & Do

A BOAT RIDE DOWN THE RIO SAN JUAN ★★

San Carlos is at the mouth of the **Río San Juan** and the departure point for a breathtaking river journey 70km (43 miles) downriver to the old historical fort town of **El Castillo.** The truly adventurous can hire a boat to continue another 140km (87 miles) to the lonely Caribbean port town of **San Juan del Norte,** passing **Reserva Biológica Indio Maiz** on the way. Bird life is abundant along the riverbanks, with large flocks of egrets and cormorants swirling overhead or floating down the mirror-like waters on floating clumps of water hyacinth. Look out for the occasional kingfisher and the large silver fish called a tarpon, which slips through the water like a dolphin, known locally as *sabalo*.

This river journey is interrupted by several stops to pick up and drop off people at small settlements. The occasional boat even pulls up alongside the *collectivo* to sell food and drinks and fresh fish from iceboxes. **Boca de Sábalos** is a muddy little settlement of 1,200 people with two decent hotels and a 2,000-hectare (5,000-acre) palm-oil farm and factory. As the town's name implies, it is an excellent place for fishing sabalo, which can run as long as 2.5m (8¼ ft.). There is also a local version of the snook fish called *robalo*.

Beyond **El Castillo,** the rapids known as **Raudal el Diablo** are easily negotiated by an experienced boatman, and the location is a popular fishing spot with locals. The wild jungle of **Reserva Biológica Indio Maiz** contrasts with bare ranch land on the Costa Rican side. A sunken steamship lies in the mouth of the **Río Samoso,** while crocodiles and turtles sunbathe on the sandbanks. Tiny waterways lead to dark grottoes. Giant palms and drapes of vines hang from gigantic cedar trees. At the **Río Sarapiqui** there is a border checkpoint and small settlement. This was Contra territory in the 1980s. Past several more tributaries the river turns north as it approaches the sea, then meanders through wetlands and swamp. A broad beach appears, separated by a long sandbar known as **La Barra.** Bull sharks lie in the estuary and along the shore feeding on the many fish, meaning this is not a good place to swim.

Local Fauna: Deadly Frogs

The poison used by local indigenous tribes to produce poison darts is taken from a toxin secreted by a frog commonly seen in the forest. Unsurprisingly, the bright green, black-spotted amphibian is now called *poison dart frog.*

A series of connected waterways and estuaries to the north are known as **Bahía de San Juan.** An old dredger lies abandoned in the water, a reminder of human plans to turn this river into a canal. The high-end lodge **Río Indio** is located here, close to a spectacular river of the same name. The blue waters of the waterway are excellent for fishing and exploring. **Greytown** lies abandoned at the edge of a waterway. This ghost town was named after a British governor of Jamaica and had a tumultuous history of English invasion, Nicaraguan possession, and U.S. bombing before it became a steamship boomtown and finally a ragged Contra stronghold. The Sandinistas burned it down in 1982 and the only interesting thing to see is its jungle-covered cemetery. The 19th-century tombs are segregated by race and the graveyard is now a national monument. A new settlement was created upriver, an uninteresting swamp town called **San Juan del Norte.** Here you have finally reached the end of the line, with nothing more but the vast rainforest on one side and the Atlantic on the other.

EL CASTILLO ★

The dark-stained stone remains of the Spanish fort **El Castillo de la Inmaculada Concepción de Maria** remind one of a Maya temple. It's a relic of just how important the river was as a gateway between Europe and Central America. The Spanish built several forts along the river to deter pirates bent on raiding Granada. El Castillo was the biggest, and was constructed between 1673 and 1675. It is Nicaragua's oldest Spanish building still in its original state. The fort is situated on a river bend and sits high over a cluster of stilted houses with red tin roofs and has an excellent view downriver.

In its heyday, it was a formidable obstacle, with 32 cannons trained on any strangers and a well-stocked armory. It was the scene of many skirmishes and sieges, and the British Navy tried several times to take it. In 1762, they laid siege to the fort for 5 days. A captain's daughter, Rafaela Herrera, became a national heroine when she rallied the troops and led the defense, breaking the British attack by sending burning flotsam downstream toward the enemy ships. The British tried again in 1779, when seven warships carrying 1,000 troops gathered at the river mouth. A young, unknown captain named Horatio Nelson decided to attack the fort from the jungle behind and successfully took it. However, the Spanish then laid siege, and disease and desertion forced the British to abandon their prize.

There is now a well-stocked and interesting **Museo** that explains the fort's swashbuckling heritage (in Spanish). Artifacts like cannonballs and old rum bottles add color. It is open daily from 8am to noon and 1 to 5pm. There is an entrance fee of C40 ($1.85). **Centro de Interpretación de la Naturaleza** is another museum behind the fort that showcases the area's flora and fauna. It is open daily from 10am to 4pm.

RESERVA BIOLOGICA INDIO-MAIZ

A rainforest needs a lot of rain, and 500 centimeters (197 in.) fall on this reserve each year, making it one of the wettest places on earth. Not that you'd notice. The 50m-high (164-ft.) trees support an intricate canopy of vines and creepers that crawl up toward the sun, creating a dense umbrella. The abundance of water gives the canopy that lush greenness and provides humidity for fungi to thrive and frogs to flourish. There are 300 species of reptiles and amphibians in this park, which is the second-largest reserve and largest primary rainforest in Central America. The dark slopes of several volcanoes host 200 species of mammals, including tapir, deer, and big cats. There are 600 species of birds, including hummingbirds, kingfishers, toucans, flycatchers, and woodpeckers. Río-Maiz is an ecological blockbuster, but there are zero facilities and it requires a guide to visit. It is bordered by the Río Bartola in the west and the Caribbean in the east. Check at the Managua MARENA office regarding access, or book with a specialist tour agency.

Where to Stay

Lodges are just beginning to pop up along the river, where you can book multiday packages. All have generator-provided electricity that is turned off at night, so make sure to pack a flashlight.

Hotel Albergue El Castillo, El Castillo (✆ **505/8892-0195** or 8924-5608), is a large, two-story structure overlooking the river, a short walk from the fort. The rooms are simple but well appointed. Doubles start at $26. **Hotel Sabalos,** Boca de Sabaloss, Río San Juan (✆ **505/8894-9377** or 8659-0252; www.hotelsabalos. ni) has a beautiful location over the water with sweeping views of the river. Doubles start at $36. **Montecristo River Lodge** (✆ **505/2583-0197;** www.montecristo-river.com) is a rustic resort on a lush green slope several miles before El Castillo. The hotel also organizes river excursions on their small fleet of boats, including tours of local fish and shrimp farms. A double room runs $130, full board, with excursions included. **Río Indio Lodge ★★** Located in the Río Maiz National Park along the San Juan river, near San Juan del North (✆ **506/2296-0095** in Costa Rica; www. therioindiolodge.com), is an American-style lodge that provides the ultimate jungle experience with all the creature comforts. The hotel offers excursions and birding expeditions and is regarded as one of the best jungle lodges in Central America. The lodge charges $250 per person per night, within a minimum 5-day stay; full board and tours are included. Fishing and bird-watching will cost extra. **Sábalos Lodge,** El Toro Rapids, Río San Juan (© **505/8850-7623;** www.sabaloslodge.com), is an attractive collection of bamboo huts with thatched roofs scattered across a riverside property just downriver from Boca de Sábalos. The rooms are simple but charming, with all-wood interiors and lots of light. A 3-day package, all-inclusive, costs $435 per person.

A Side Trip to Archipelago de Solentiname

The Solentiname Archipelago is a scattering of 36 islands in the southern corner of Lago Nicaragua. Geographically it is an isolated, tropical backwater, but historically and culturally it is the nucleus of Nicaragua's world-famous primitive art movement and a hotbed of liberation theology. That's due mainly to poet and priest Ernesto Cardenal, who came here in the late '60s and encouraged ordinary islanders to pick up a paintbrush and paint what they saw. The result was astounding—vibrant renditions in oil and balsa wood of the islands' nature and people. Complete families became artists, and by the early '70s TV crews were coming to make documentaries about the phenomenon. Only 750 people live on the islands today, but they act as hosts to hundreds of tourists every year who come to paint, observe, or study the region's rich natural wonders.

ESSENTIALS
Getting There
BY PLANE & BOAT   Getting to Solentiname is not easy and is particularly grueling if you are on a budget. The fastest, but more expensive, way is to catch a plane from Managua to the river town of San Carlos, and then to catch the 2-hour boat ride to the dock in Mancarrón. **La Costeña** (© **505/2263-1228** in Managua, or 583-0271 in San Carlos; www.lacostena.com.ni) operates a daily "puddle jumper" flight. It leaves Managua at 9am daily except Fridays and Sundays, when it leaves at midday. It departs from San Carlos daily at 10am, except Fridays and Sundays, when it leaves at 1pm. The journey takes 1 hour and costs approximately $116 round-trip. Flights should be booked well in advance and reconfirmed.

The scheduled boat from San Carlos leaves on Saturdays and Tuesdays at 1pm, returning on Mondays and Thursdays. The cost is C95 ($4.40). Private boats can be arranged but expect to pay C2,280 ($106) one-way. You can arrange this with a dockside boat owner (*panguero*) or book in advance through **Intur** in San Carlos, opposite Clínica San Lucas (© **505/2583-0301** or 2583-0363), or **Armando Ortiz's Viajes Turísticos,** by the Western Union (© **505/2583-0039**).

BY BOAT   A ferry called the *EPN* (no phone) leaves Granada every Monday and Thursday at 3pm, stopping in Altagracia on Isla de Ometepe before continuing south to San Miguelito and San Carlos. It arrives in San Carlos at 6am the next day. It is wise to get to the ticket office 2 hours before departure. First-class seats cost C240 ($11) and are on the upstairs deck, which is air-conditioned. Second class is on the lower deck, without air-conditioning, and costs C160 ($7.45). The ferry returns through Altagracia every Tuesday and Friday at 3pm. Be aware, however, that if the sea is rough it may skip its stop at Altagracia altogether. There are also three boats a day that leave from the Costa Rican town of Los Chiles. Departure times are 7am, 1pm, and 3pm but these are liable to frequent changes. The 2-hour trip costs C160 ($7.45).

BY BUS The bus trip to San Carlos is a 300km (186-mile) epic journey and a test of endurance. The road is in a terrible condition for much of the way, and the bus ride is a bone-shaking one that travels at a snail's pace. This is for people on a strict budget with lots of time on their hands. Buses leave from Managua's Mayoreo Market at 8 and 11:45am. The fare is C200 ($9.30). During bad weather, the road closes completely. San Carlos bus station is close to the town center by the main dock. It is actually easier to reach San Carlos from Costa Rica. The 3½-hour bus journey from San José to Los Chiles costs $8. From there you can catch a boat for a 2-hour trip upriver to San Carlos, for which the fare is $10.

GETTING AROUND

Only 2 of the 36 islands have tourist facilities: **Isla Mancarrón** and **Isla Elvis Chavarría** (also known as Isla San Fernando). **Isla Mancarroncito** and Isla **Donald Guevara** (also known as Isla la Venada) are the only two other populated islands. *Collectivo* water taxis run twice a week between these islands, though you can, of course, charter your own *panga,* at a price—in general, gas is much more expensive in this part of the country. There is a definite advantage to arranging a trip with a tour company, including transport, accommodations, and a guide. Independent travelers will need to allot lots of time and adopt a flexible attitude to getting around.

VISITOR INFORMATION

There is no tourist information office on the islands, but lodge owners like Maria Guevara at **Albergue Celentiname** (✆ **505/2276-1910**) are more than happy to help with any queries. Another excellent source of info is **Doña Maria Amelia Gross** (✆ **505/2583-0271**), who runs the La Costeña office in San Carlos. The **San Carlos Intur office,** in front of the Clínica San Lucas (✆ **505/2583-0301** or 2583-0363), has brochures and can help arrange transport. It's open Monday to Saturday from 10am to 6pm. The islanders have their own website, www.solentiname. com, where you can get general information about the islands.

TOUR OPERATORS & TRAVEL AGENCIES

MUSAS (El Museo Archipiélago de Solentiname) organizes 4-day tours of the archipelago, including accommodations and transportation from San Carlos. They can be contacted through ACRA in San Carlos (✆ **505/2583-0095**) or in Managua (✆ **505/2249-6176;** musasni@yahoo.com). Prices depend on group size but expect to pay at least C5,700 ($265) for a 4-day tour.

The operator **Galería Solentiname,** Colonia Centro America, 3 blocks south of Iglesia Fatima, Managua (✆ **505/2252-6262** or 2277-0939; gsolentiname@amnet. com.ni), can organize package tours; it's owned by the same family that operates Don Julio Lodge on La Isla Elvis Chavarría. **Solentiname Tours,** Apartado Postal 1388, Managua (✆ **505/2270-9981;** www.solentinametours.com), offers countrywide tours including several days on the islands and down the Río San Juan. **Tours Nicaragua** (✆ **505/2252-4063;** www.toursnicaragua.com) also offers packages on both islands.

WHAT TO SEE & DO

Solentiname will require you to slow way down. There is not much to do, though there's a lot to see and admire. **Mancarrón** is the main island. Only 200 people live on its 20 sq. km (7¾ sq. miles) of lush green vegetation, with the 260m-high (850-ft.) Cerro Las Cuevas dominating the waterline. Close to the dock there are a collection of houses and the **Iglesia Solentiname ★**, designed by Ernesto Cardenal. This tiny adobe building is one the most colorful and quirky churches you'll see in Nicaragua, with playful images on its white walls and a simple altar with pre-Columbian patterns. Ernesto Cardenal began his project in the 1960s to bring art to the islands here. Close by is the **APDS** complex. This is the local development association and they have a display room holding books, art, and artifacts about the islands, including info on its artists and Ernesto Cardenal.

La Isla Elvis Chavarría is named after a martyr killed during the revolution. Also known as San Fernando, it is the archipelago's second-biggest island and has a sizable community with a school and health clinic. **El Museo Archipiélago de Solentiname,** or MUSA (© **505/2283-0095;** www.manfut.org/museos/solentiname.html), is a museum, art gallery, library, information point, medicine garden, and arboretum. Just follow the butterflies and hummingbirds up the garden path behind the village and you'll find it. The museum is open daily from 7am to noon and 2 to 5pm. Admission is C40 ($1.85).

La Cueva del Duende is an underwater cave of mythological importance to the islanders. They believed it was the path to the other side, and marked on the walls are representations of the dead. It is accessible only in the dry season (Mar and Apr). **Mancarroncito** is one of the archipelago's wilder, untouched islands with a 100m-high (328-ft.) peak shrouded in thick jungle. **Zapote** is a bird sanctuary with a colony of 20,000 birds—it gets noisy, especially during the dry season. **El Padre** is just as noisy, because of its boisterous howler monkey community.

WHERE TO STAY

There are many families on both **Isla Mancarrón** and **Isla Elvis Chavarría** that rent rooms in a homestay fashion. Look around for signs outside these houses. Bear in mind that wherever you choose to stay will also be where you will eat, as the islands have no dining scene. **El Buen Amigo,** the community center, Isla Mancarrón (© **505/8869-6619**), offers basic rooms for $12 per person. **Villa Esperanza,** next to the community center, Isla Mancarrón (© **505/2583-9020**), is a step up in comfort and offers rooms at $25 per person. On Isla Elvis Chavarría a good budget option is **Cabañas Paraiso,** southern shore (© **505/2278-3392;** gsolentiname@amnet. com.ni). Here you can get a room with private bathroom for $35 full board.

Moderate

Hotel Mancarrón　These are by far the plushest accommodations you'll get on the archipelago. The property, made up of homes with red roof tiles and white adobe walls, sits up in a 3-hectare (7½-acre) site that is bordered by forest and lakes. Rooms are simple and spacious, and overlook the dock. A large dining room with a bar is on-site. All water is heated by solar energy, though there is also a backup generator. The hotel organizes excursions to local artists' workshops and will arrange art lessons for those who want to capture the island's colors.

Isla Elvis Chavarría. © **505/2270-9981** or 2277-3495. hotelmancarrun@gmail.com. 12 units. From $35 double; from $45 triple; $50 quadruple. No credit cards. **Amenities:** Bar; restaurant. *In room:* Fan, no phone.

Inexpensive

Albergue Celentiname　On the western edge of La Elvis, this family-run lodge has been in operation since 1984 and provides rustic cabins with shared bathrooms. It has a waterfront setting and great views of the islands, volcanoes, and the Cost Rican border. The cabins are basic and a little dark, but are clean and come with an all-important hammock and small porch. There's an attractive restaurant on the grounds. The hospitality of the hosts is what really makes this place memorable; Doña María Guevara and her family are all painters and are enthusiastic in sharing the delights of the island. You also can't beat the lodge when it comes to providing an ultimate jungle experience—you'll be surrounded by a cacophony of wildlife sounds at most times.

Isla San Fernando. ✆ **505/2276-1910.** celentiname7@yahoo.es. 8 units with shared bathroom. $50 double. No credit cards. **Amenities:** Restaurant. *In room:* Fan, no phone.

THE CARIBBEAN COAST

La Costa is a world apart from the rest of Nicaragua yet it is slowly gaining fame for its authentic Caribbean charm. Tropical paradises such as the **Pearl Lagoon** outside Bluefields and the beautiful **Corn Islands,** 80km (50 miles) off the coast, are becoming more popular, as they offer a postcard-perfect white-beach environment. Another great attraction is the region's rich mix of Miskito Indian culture, pirate heritage, English legacy, and African roots. This means its people are more like West Indians than Nicaraguans, and they generally speak a lilting form of English creole rather than Spanish. They are also the most laid-back population in the country, with a fondness for late-night partying and music. This is all the more evident in May, when cities such as Bluefields rock to the calypso sounds of the Palo de Mayo festival.

The Spanish never got around to conquering this part of Nicaragua. Though Columbus brushed along its shores, the coast's unwelcoming geography and Indian resistance meant the conquistadors did very little conquering, especially when the Miskito tribe killed and ate the first governor in 1545. It was the British who first established a toehold, finding the coves and bays invaluable ports of call during the many wars of the period. They traded with the Miskitos and backed a Miskito king to rule over the neighboring tribes. German Protestant missionaries in the 1800s added to the cultural mix, and their legacy can be seen in the stark Moravian churches that dominate each town. In 1894, Nicaraguan president Zelaya marched his army into Bluefields to finally lay claim to the region.

Bluefields

440km (273 miles) SE of Managua; 465km (289 miles) SE of Granada

In Bluefields, a gritty but colorful port town of 50,000, the Caribbean collides with Latin America. It's a languid and slightly edgy place, perhaps in keeping with a town named after a pirate (a Dutch marauder named Blewfeldt). It was a thriving 19th-century town, living off timber, bananas, and God (in the form of Moravian missionaries whose neat little churches dot the region). The 20th century saw a decline in the region's fortunes, compounded by a confrontational attitude by the Managua government.

Today, an diverse ethnic mix of Miskito Indian, *mestizo,* Spanish, and West Indian locals call the town home. Bluefields is also an important port, with a murky bay and murkier crime image. This image is somewhat unfounded, though the area is becoming famous for abandoned bales of cocaine rolling up on its coast (known as white lobster) and the social problems such a phenomenon causes. Many people choose to skip the town on their way to the Corn Islands, but if you decide to linger, you'll find some of the best nightclubs and party spots in Nicaragua, as well as access to incredible coastal wildlife and landscapes, such as the Pearl Lagoon and the tropical archipelago known as the Pearl Cays.

ESSENTIALS

Getting There

BY PLANE   **Bluefields Airport** (**BEF;** no phone) is a tiny, modern terminal 3km (1¾ miles) south of the town. There are always taxis outside when a plane arrives. **La Costeña** (© **505/2263-1228** in Managua, or 2572-2500 in Bluefields; www.la costena.com.ni) operates daily service between Managua and Bluefields, with a flight that goes to the Corn Islands. The airline has small, turbo-powered airplanes that are not for the fainthearted. Flights start at $164 round-trip from Managua to the islands.

BY BUS & BOAT   **Transportes Vargas Peña** (© **505/2280-4561**) offers a bus-boat package from Managua, leaving Mercado Iván Montenegro at 9pm daily. The journey takes from 12 to 15 hours and is not pleasant, as the road is very bad. **Transportes Aguilar** (© **505/2248-3005**) offers a similar service, leaving from Mayoreo at 9pm. Both trips cost roughly C360 ($17) one-way.

The river town of Rama is the boat departure point from the mainland to Bluefields. A large boat leaves every Tuesday, Thursday, Saturday, and Sunday at noon and takes 4½ hours. The cost is C50 ($2.35). Faster *panga lanchas* run daily from 6am to 4pm, for a 2-hour journey. The cost is C100 ($4.65).

Getting Around

Taxis cost less than C20 (95¢) for most trips within the town, and there are plenty of buses that trundle around. The fare is C5 (25¢). To go farther afield, you'll need a boat or *panga*. **Jipe,** Mercado Municipal (© **505/2572-1871**), is a water-taxi company that provides private excursions to the area's surrounding attractions. Pangas leave for el Bluff and Pearl Lagoon from the town pier and cost between C20 (95¢) and C60 ($2.80). The last boats return at 4pm.

Visitor Information

There is an **Intur office** half a block south of the park (© **505/2572-0221**); it's open Monday to Friday from 9am to 4:30pm. **CIDCA** (no phone), a research and local history organization, is 50m (164 ft.) north of the police station and offers good information on the area. It's open Monday to Friday from 8am to 5:30pm. A good Spanish-language website to check is **www.bluefieldspulse.com**; it offers events listings and local news.

FESTIVALS

Palo de Mayo is the event of the year, when the entire town gets down to some serious Caribbean boogieing throughout the month of May. The festival has English and Dutch origins, dating from when a Maypole was erected in the center of town and the people celebrated the coming of spring by decorating it with ribbons and flowers. The modern version is somewhat racier and erotic, with parades, costumes, and dancing to a soundtrack of tropical calypso music. September 30 is the city's patron saint day, and the locals need little excuse to party, with a repeat festival on October 30 celebrating the region's autonomy. Food, music, and dancing are the order of the day.

WHERE TO STAY

The best places to stay in Bluefields are north of the town pier. I recommend spending a little extra on accommodations here, as some of the budget options are the sort of places that are rented by the hour.

Oasis Hotel Casino ★, 150m (490 ft.) from the bay (© **505/2572-2812;** www. oasiscasinohotel.com), is one of the better moderately priced hotels in town, with large rooms and suites. Beds are big and comfortable and the rooms come with air-conditioning and cable TV. Doubles start at $80. **Hotel Bluefields Bay** (© 505/2572-0120; www.bluefieldsbay.galeon.com), 2 blocks north of the Municipal Dock, is a well-appointed B&B by the shoreline. Rooms start at $28. **Hotel South Atlantic II,** west of the municipal market (© 505/2572-1022), is another good option. Rooms start at $35 and have air-conditioning and TV.

For inexpensive rooms, **Hotel Caribbean Dream,** 20m (66 ft.) south of the Municipal Market (© 505/2572-0107; reyzapata1@yahoo.com), has a nice blue-and-white veranda facing the main street. Rooms start at $32 and come with air-conditioning and private bathrooms. Alternatively, try **Mini Hotel Central,** dockside by the Municipal market (© 505/2572-2362), which is well run and has friendly owners. Rooms start at $25.

WHERE TO DINE

Fresh seafood is the order of the day, and shrimp and lobster are featured on every menu. Take advantage of the relatively cheap prices and try something like yellowfin or snapper with vegetables and coconut curry. While in town, you should also try coco bread, a popular puffed loaf of bread, as well as hot coconut buns. Most formal restaurants in town open for lunch and close at 10pm daily.

Manglares Restaurant ★, in the Hotel Bluefields Bay (© 505/2572-0107), has the best seaside dining in the area, along with a nice location on a dock over the bay. Main courses start at C190 ($8.85). Another seafood restaurant with a great view is **El Flotante,** 4 blocks south of the church (© 505/2572-2988). Main courses start at C220 ($10). **La Loma Rancho** (© 505/2572-2875) is set on a hill overlooking the town and has a pleasant open-air dining area. Main courses start at C190 ($8.85). If you like your meals formal and elegant, go to **Chez Marcel** (© 505/2572-2347), where they do exquisite lunches and dinners. Main courses start at C260 ($12).

The restaurant within the **Hotel South Atlantic II** (© 505/2572-1022) serves excellent seafood and meat dishes that won't bust your budget. Main courses start at C130 ($6). Another good hotel restaurant within the same price range is the **Mini-Hotel Central** (© 505/2572-2362).

BLUEFIELDS AFTER DARK

This so-called "Jamaica of Nicaragua" comes alive at night, and the locals have no inhibitions when it comes to getting down. Bluefields lives and breathes music, and the rough-and-tumble bars and clubs here play an eclectic mix, to say the least. One minute you might be grinding to Daddy Yankee and next weeping into your beer to Tammy Wynette. Whatever you do, dress down and make sure you get a taxi to and from the venues listed below, for safety reasons.

Four Brothers (no phone), 6 blocks south of the park in Barrio Puntafria, is a popular roadhouse disco that gets a good mix of people. It is open Thursday to Sunday

---

Going "Country" in Nicaragua

The popularity of old-fashioned, North American country-and-western music along the Nicaraguan coast surprises many visitors. Apparently the locals' fondness for Kenny Rogers comes from the fact that the only radio station worth listening to during the war years was one out of Houston, Texas, that gave the locals a taste for Kenny Rogers and his country compatriots.

ATTRACTIONS AROUND bluefields

Greenfields Nature Reserve is a private nature reserve that offers excellent jungle excursions and canoeing trips in the pristine wilderness. It can be seen in a 1-day trip from Bluefields that costs approximately $20, or you can choose to stay for 3 nights for $180 full board (price varies with group size). Contact the owners of the reserve at ℂ **505/2278-0589** or 8434-4808 (cell) or visit www.greenfields.com.ni for info.

Pearl Lagoon is a small, peaceful village an hour away from Bluefields by boat and is a lovely, relaxing antidote to Bluefields's shabbiness. Pearl Lagoon has a beautiful church, and a variety of lodgings are springing up. It is often used as a base to explore the amazing archipelago known as the **Pearl Cays ★★**. There is little or no tourist infrastructure, so bring lots of water and food. To arrange tours of the Cays (pronounced *keys*), try the **Casa Blanca Hotelito y Restaurante,**

Barrio May 4, Pearl Lagoon (ℂ **505/2572-0508**). This also has the best accommodations in town, with bright, clean rooms and a decent restaurant. Prices range from $10 to $30. Another good if very basic lodge is **Green Lodge Guesthouse,** 1 block south of the dock, beside Enitel, Pearl Lagoon (ℂ **505/2572-0507**). Here a tiny room goes for $15 and the owner also arranges tours of the area.

Pangas leave for the lake and village each day regularly (as soon as they fill up), but it advisable to go to the dock in Bluefields as early as possible (the first *panga* leaves at 6am with another one soon after). There is much less activity on Sundays. The trip itself is beautiful, since it takes you up the Río Escondido and through a maze of streams and waterways, filled with wildlife. The fare costs C120 ($5.60) one-way.

and the party here goes on all night. **Fresh Point ★** (no phone) is a similar roadhouse disco, but with a slightly livelier scene. It is 2km (1¼ miles) north of the city, northeast of the Municipal Dock, and has a pleasant outdoor area with palm trees and tables overlooking the bay. Saturday night is the best night here. **La Loma Rancho** (ℂ **505/2572-2875;** see "Where to Dine," above), is a restaurant that converts into a happening party spot Thursday through Sunday, with great views overlooking the city. **Cima Club** (no phone), 1 block west of Moravian Church on Avenida Cabezas, is a more laid-back joint, with salsa and Latin beats and a little karaoke, as well as open-air seating.

THE CORN ISLANDS ★★★

"How the Caribbean should be," is how one visitor described one of Nicaragua's unspoiled treasures. The Corn Islands, consisting of 10-sq.-km-long (3¾-sq.-mile) Big Corn and 2.9-sq.-km (1-sq.-mile) Little Corn, are two kernels of Caribbean paradise 83km (52 miles) east of the Nicaraguan coast and perhaps my favorite part of Nicaragua. The islands' luminous coastal bays and shores are ideal for diving, snorkeling, fishing, or sunning. And how could you *not* be happy on islands with names like Coconut Point, Sally Peaches, and Jokeman Bank?

Though the islanders, many of whom have surnames like Morgan and Dixon that call to mind the pirates and adventurers who once landed here, are dependent on fishing and coconut growing for a living, tourism is becoming another economic force here. I hope that this increasing tourism unfolds in a sustainable manner, for these are two true treasure islands, with some of the best beaches I have ever wandered. The laid-back vibe lends itself to some great parties: During Easter, the otherwise deserted beaches get packed with revelers, as they do for the Crab Soup Festival in late August, a traditional festival celebrating slave emancipation.

There is very little happening here in terms of nightlife. Unlike Bluefields, the only thing to do here after dark is stroll along the beach or have a drink in your hotel—so don't come expecting to party.

ESSENTIALS
Getting There
BY PLANE **Corn Island Airport** (**RNI;** no phone) is served by two small airlines that make connections to Bluefields and Managua. **La Costeña** (© 505/2575-5131) and **Atlantic Airlines** (© 505/2270-5355) both depart from Managua at 6:30am and 2pm daily and leave the island at 8am and 3pm. The journey takes 1½ hours; arrive at least 30 minutes before departure and always reconfirm your outward flight on arrival. Expect to fly in small, antiquated prop planes.

The airport is 2km (1¼ miles) from Brig Bay. There are always taxi drivers waiting at the airport when each plane arrives. The fare is C40 ($1.85) per person no matter where you go, though you may be charged a little extra for luggage.

BY BOAT Three boats depart from Bluefields on different days. A 5-hour express called *Río Escondido* departs at 9am every Wednesday, returning at 9am on a Tuesday. The cost is C210 ($9.75). A ferry called *St Nikolas* (© 505/2695-3344) leaves on Friday at 9am and takes 7 hours. It returns on Sunday at midday. The cost one-way is C100 ($4.65). The *Captain D* (© 505/2850-2767) leaves Rama on Wednesday at noon and goes to El Bluff; from there it departs at 5pm for a 10pm arrival to the Corn Islands. The main return boat departs the Corn Islands at midnight on Saturday for Bluefields. The cost one-way from Rama is C350 ($16) and from El Bluff C250 ($12). All boats dock at Brig Bay, Big Corn Island's main port.

Getting Around
A taxi costs C16 (75¢) per person to travel anywhere on the island and C21 ($1) after 10pm or if you have a lot of luggage. There is a minibus that circles the island at a cost of C5 (25¢). Perhaps the most fun way to get around is to rent a golf cart for C200 ($9.30) per hour. Contact **Arenas Beach Hotel** (© 505/2456-2220) to do so.

Orientation
Big Corn has a 12km (7½-mile) road that circles the island, frequented by the occasional car, taxi, and golf cart. This is where you'll find the island's main port, Brig Bay, and the airport. Generally, the best beaches in Big Corn are to the southwest, as it is more sheltered than the eastern side, though the reverse happens in November. The north end has the best spots for snorkeling.

FAST FACTS **Banpro,** on the road to Hotel Puertas del Sol, Brig Bay (© 505/2575-5107), is the only bank and ATM on the island. It's best to bring plenty of cash to the island in case you can't get to the bank. Make sure you are carrying immaculate American dollar notes as the locals can be fussy about what they accept. With a Visa credit card, you can take out money at Banpro at the airport. Money transfers can be arranged at the **Western Union** outlet (© 505/2575-5074) beside the Caribbean Depot, close to the dock.

For emergencies, dial © **101.** For other matters, call © **505/2575-5201.**

Corn Island Hospital (☎ 505/2575-5236) is behind Nautilus and is open every day, all day. For an English-speaking doctor call **Dr. David Somarriba** (☎ 505/2575-5184), or for a dentist call ☎ 505/2575-5236.

Pharmacy Monica (☎ 505/2575-5251) is in front of the government house in the center of the island. It is open Monday to Saturday from 8am to 6pm and Sunday from 8am to noon. **Pharmacy Guadelupe** (☎ 505/2575-5217) is farther east, close to the baseball stadium, and is open Monday to Saturday from 7am to 9pm.

Most of the better hotels on the island have Internet service. **Cyber Café** (no phone), near Nautilus, charges C40 ($1.85) per hour. The **Western Union** outlet (see above) also provides Internet and fax services.

WHAT TO SEE & DO

The first thing you should do is head for the beaches, the best of which is **Picnic Beach ★★★**, in the south bay of Big Corn. This is a long white strand beach, with turquoise waters and not a soul in sight (for now, anyway). Another beautiful Big Corn beach is **Sally Peaches** on the northeastern side of the island. Here you have shallow pools and pink coral sand. It is unsuitable for swimming (because of rocks) but makes for great photo opportunities from the hill, **Mount Pleasant,** upon which is a small watchtower. The watchtower can be accessed by a path in front of Nicos Bar.

OUTDOOR ACTIVITIES

DIVING   Spotted tiger rays, black-tip sharks, stingrays, spider crabs, parrotfish, angelfish, barracuda, and triggerfish—they are all out there in the pristine waters waiting for you to drop in. **Nautilus Dive,** north of Brig Bay (☎ 505/2575-5077; www.bigcornisland.com/nautilus.html), is the most established operator on the island. It offers everything from open-water to advanced courses and allows guests to explore the island's three coral reefs or a volcanic pinnacle known as **Blowing Rock.** Fun dives start at C800 ($37) and a 3-day open-water course costs C5,600 ($260). Nautilus Dive also offers snorkeling tours and glass-bottom boat excursions over reefs and shipwrecks for those who don't want to get their feet wet. The outfit's German and Guatemalan owners, Regina and José, have recently branched out and opened a gift store and restaurant by the same name, close to the dive shop.

SNORKELING & KAYAKING   You can pull your goggles on anywhere and go for a float. However, one of the best places to snorkel is the shallow waters around **Anastasias on the Sea,** North Shore (☎ 505/2575-5001; www.cornislandresort.com). This is a hotel, restaurant, marine park, and fishing outfitter. You can rent snorkeling equipment through them for C200 ($9.30) per hour or kayaks for C280 ($13) per day for use around their amazingly beautiful location, or go on a full-day sport- or fly-fishing excursion, which can cost between C2,800 and C10,000 ($130–$465).

FISHING   The islands provide excellent sportfishing opportunities. Red snapper, kingfish, and barracuda are enticed out of the water. **Blue Runner Charter,** Southend (☎ 505/2847-5745), is run by true blue local fisherman Alwin Taylor and offers sea tours and fishing trips, which cost between C2,800 and C4,600 ($130–$214). **Anastasias on the Sea,** North Shore (☎ 505/2575-5001; www.cornisland resort.com), is also a well-established outfitter.

Where to Stay

Most of the accommodations options on the island are limited to two-star basics with a few memorable exceptions. It is wise to stay in a hotel that has an adjoining

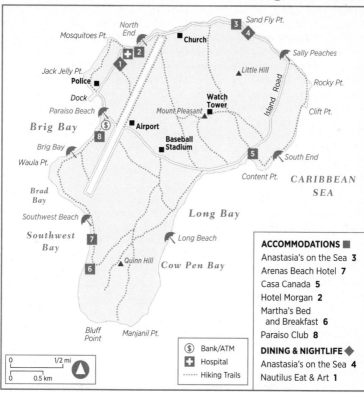

Mosquitoes Pt.

North End

■ **Church**

3

4

Sand Fly Pt.

Sally Peaches

Jack Jelly Pt.

1

2

Police ■

Little Hill

Rocky Pt.

Dock

▲

Watch Tower

Island Road

Paraiso Beach

Mount Pleasant ■

▲

Clift Pt.

Brig Bay

$

■ **Airport**

Baseball Stadium ■

Brig Bay

8

Waula Pt.

5

South End

Brad Bay

Content Pt.

CARIBBEAN SEA

Southwest Beach

Long Bay

Southwest Bay

7

Long Beach

6

▲ Quinn Hill

Cow Pen Bay

Bluff Point

Manjanil Pt.

0 — 1/2 mi

0 — 0.5 km

▲

$ Bank/ATM

✚ Hospital

······ Hiking Trails

ACCOMMODATIONS ■

Anastasia's on the Sea **3**

Arenas Beach Hotel **7**

Casa Canada **5**

Hotel Morgan **2**

Martha's Bed and Breakfast **6**

Paraiso Club **8**

DINING & NIGHTLIFE ◆

Anastasia's on the Sea **4**

Nautilus Eat & Art **1**

restaurant and make sure the hotel has its own generator. Otherwise, when the lights go out, you'll have to be happy with a hammock and a glass of rum. Since tourism is a relatively new phenomenon, service can be slow wherever you go.

EXPENSIVE

Arenas Beach Hotel ★ ☺ Situated on what must be one of the most spectacular beaches in the world (Picnic Beach), the Arenas is a spacious hotel-and-cabin complex. Don't let the exterior colors or decor turn you off. Bright orange-and-blue walls topped with white lattice arches might not be to everybody's taste, but they hide a collection of spacious rooms with great views and a large veranda. The bungalows have a little more style and character, with pine walls and stained-glass lamps. The hotel has no pool but you'll understand why when you step out front onto the white beach—it renders a chlorinated swim obsolete. The hotel also has a very good if expensive **restaurant** and is family-friendly, with a number of rooms that comfortably fit up to six people.

Picnic Beach. ✆ **505/2851-8046.** www.arenasbeachhotel.com. 22 units. From $75 double; from $105 triple; from $120 quadruple. Rates include breakfast. MC, V. **Amenities:** Restaurant; bar; laundry service; room service. *In room:* A/C, TV, Wi-Fi.

Casa Canada ★★   This chunk of oceanside paradise is the most beautiful and well-appointed hotel on the island. The row of cottage-style rooms might look unassuming from the road, but they face a nicely tiled pool and long rock shore of palm trees and small patches of lawn. Rooms are large with every type of modern amenity, including a coffeemaker, kitchenette, and blessedly silent air conditioner. The beds are big and comfortable and the bathrooms are medium size and immaculate. The rooms are lined along a beachfront garden, which features a resident monkey and iguana for entertainment. The hotel's **restaurant** provides excellent seafood and hearty breakfasts.

Canadian owner Larry is a perfect, gregarious host and the staff is equipped to set up many organized tours. The Casa Canada's particular slice of actual sandy beach is rather small, but since this whole island is one big beach, don't let that deter you. The only possible annoyance is the sound of crashing waves a few feet from your doorway—but some would consider that an asset.

South End. ✆ **505/2644-0925.** www.casa-canada.com. 21 units. From $125 double. AE, MC, V. **Amenities:** Restaurant; bar; Internet; infinity pool. *In room:* A/C, TV/DVD, minibar.

Paraiso Club   This cluster of palm-fringed cabins stands a stone's throw from the beach. They look exotic and inviting from the outside but are somewhat disappointing on the inside—cramped, with low ceilings and very basic bathrooms. The beds are hard and the decor could do with renovating. The Paraiso Club is a step down from Casa Canada and attracts a younger, hardier clientele. Its main attractions are its two friendly Dutch owners and a lively restaurant bar with excellent food. Access to the hotel is down an unpaved road close to Brig Bay.

Brig Bay. ✆ **505/2575-5111.** www.paraisoclub.com. 15 units. From $69 double; from $92 triple; from $109 quadruple. Rates include breakfast. MC, V. **Amenities:** Restaurant; bar; free airport transfers; laundry service; room service. *In room:* A/C, TV, Wi-Fi.

MODERATE

Hotel Morgan 🍴   This roadside complex of timber and pink-plaster cottages is a little worn and tired, but still a good value. The small, low beds complement the old-fashioned laminated furniture, and the bland bathrooms are smallish and clean. The purple rocking chair out front adds a touch of color to the drab decor, and, though rooms don't have views, there is a decent seafood **restaurant** in the main building, with a good vista of the sea.

North End, beside Victoria beer warehouse. ✆ **505/2575-5052.** kerrygean.morgan@gmail.com. 10 units. From $15 double with no A/C; $40 double with A/C. AE, DC, MC, V. **Amenities:** Restaurant. *In room:* A/C or fan, TV, fridge.

Martha's Bed and Breakfast   From a distance, this place appears fantastic. A beach entrance leads to a bridge over a lagoon of inky black water, after which you can follow a flowered pathway through a lawn of palm trees until a plantation-style mansion appears, replete with a veranda and wicker rocking chairs. So far, so good. Up close, though, the property's garish red railings smack of bad taste, and the rooms themselves are a little disappointing. They are average size with an overpowering smell of disinfectant; flowered quilts cover low, small beds; and the open wardrobes are oddly placed in the bathrooms. Though it's not perfect, the B&B, which is owned by the English-speaking Martha, does have an ideal location, right in front of Picnic Beach.

South West Bay. ✆ **505/8835-5930.** 8 units. From $58 double; from $69 triple. Rates include breakfast. All-inclusive packages available. No credit cards. **Amenities:** Dining area. *In room:* A/C, TV.

Food for Thought

Never go to a restaurant if you're in a hurry or starving. The easygoing attitude of the locals is as predominant in the kitchen as anywhere else on the coast, and you can wait for hours for your food. Also, don't take the waitstaff's rude, surly attitude too personally; they are like that with everybody.

INEXPENSIVE

Anastasia's on the Sea ★   Anastasia's is shabby, but in an absolutely charming way. This budget hotel practically sits on its beach's turquoise waters, which are perfect for snorkeling amid exotic fish and psychedelic-colored shells. The hotel consists of a long, wide corridor with marine-themed murals and badly done tile mosaics. Blue doors on either side lead to fair-size rooms that have a musty odor and two double beds. The service is lousy but the staff is endearing. What can I say? I loved it. You may hate it. The hotel also offers kayak and fishing rod rental, and has a good **restaurant** (reviewed in the "Where to Dine" section, below).

North End. © **505/2937-0016.** www.cornislandresort.com. 17 units. From $34 double. No credit cards. **Amenities:** Restaurant. *In room:* A/C or fan, TV.

WHERE TO DINE

In addition to the restaurants reviewed below, all hotels listed above have in-house restaurants. Lobster and shrimp appear on nearly every menu. The former is causing some controversy, as overfishing and unsafe conditions for poorly paid lobster divers are compelling many people to say it's unethical to eat lobster. What you should definitely try is the popular local dish *run down,* a delicious mix of vegetables, coconut milk, and seafood, which is so called because it brings you back to life if you feel a little "run down." The **Anastasia's on the Sea** ★ (© **505/2937-0016;** www.corn islandparadise.com) North End restaurant is very much like its hotel—crumbling and charming. A long wooden dock leads to a wide, rickety building on stilts set over brilliant turquoise water. At night, the restaurant shifts somewhat into a country music roadhouse—a beer-swilling, honky-tonking, foot-tapping Caribbean paradise. Daily 7am to 10pm. **Nautilus Eat & Art,** Brig Bay (© **505/2451-7216**), is a rickety old wooden restaurant, laden with psychedelic artwork that exudes a marine theme. The food is wholesome and comes in huge portions, with standout items including the delicious callaloo soup, curry, and mounds of steaming shrimp cooked in lemon juice and tequila. Daily 8am to 10pm.

Little Corn Island

Little Corn is as close as you'll get to a deserted island without being shipwrecked. It's wilder and more untamed than its bigger brother and draws a sturdier traveler who can withstand the 30km (19-mile) boat ride here and the fact that there is no electricity for the entire morning, every morning. There are no cars and the only concrete path is near the tiny dock; the rest is beach trails and dirt paths. How long it will stay like this remains to be seen, but if you have a primitive streak and enjoy being barefoot and surrounded on all sides by coral reef and mango trees, Little Corn is for you.

8

NICARAGUA

The Corn Islands

ESSENTIALS
Getting There

A *panga* leaves daily to Little Corn from the Great Corn Island dock at 10am and 4pm. The journey takes 25 minutes and costs C120 ($5.60) one-way. The boat leaves from Little Corn dock to return to Big Corn at 7am and 2pm daily. There is a charge of 3C (15¢) to enter the dock.

WHERE TO STAY

Choose the location of your hotel carefully, as some are at the end of isolated paths that are easy to get lost in when returning at night, yet offer perfect solitude. Most lodgings are on the lower western shore, but this area can get a little crowded with partying backpackers. Don't forget to pack a flashlight, or candles and waterproof matches for that matter. Make sure your hotel has snorkel gear if you plan on exploring the reefs. Otherwise, bring your own.

Sunshine Hotel ★, a 3-minute walk from the pier, 50m (164 ft.) north of the Fresh Lobster Company (℃ **505/8405-9422;** www.sunshinehotellittlecornisland. com), is a bright yellow establishment with clean and tidy rooms. The owner, Glynis, is famous for her cooking, especially her excellent breakfasts. Prices start at $35 per room. **Hotel Los Delfines** (north of Jokeman Bank; ℃ **505/8820-2241;** www. hotellosdelfines.com.ni) is two charming Caribbean-style bungalows of white wooden pillars and green picket balustrades surrounding verandas and balconies. Its location is central, close to where most of the villagers live and the nearby dock. Its 18 well-appointed rooms start at $40, though kids 11 and under stay free.

Dereks Place, Georges Cay (℃ **505/8419-0600;** www.dereksplacelittlecorn. com), offers basic but romantic "treehouse"-style huts on a green lawn overlooking the shore on the northern tip of the island. Prices start at $50 per room. **Casa Iguana ★**, on the south end of Iguana Beach (no phone; www.casaiguana.net;), is a well-run collection of beach houses with a cliff-top view of a deserted beach on the southern end of the island. Yoga instruction and massage are available, and some fantastic snorkeling reefs are within paddling distance. Doubles start at $35 or $65 with private bathroom. **Ensueños,** north end of the island, east of Otto beach (no phone; www.ensuenoslittlecornisland.com), has *cabanas* that seem to have grown from the ground in a funky, organic form. Inside you'll find carved wood, twisted trunks, and recycled driftwood. Its isolation at the northern end of the island is a factor to consider. Doubles start at $25, or $50 with private bathroom.

WHERE TO DINE

Stand-alone restaurants are few and far between. The best places to eat are attached to the hotels listed under "Where to Stay," above, though there are some exceptions: **Bridget's First Stop Comedor** (no phone), just north of the dock, is popular with locals, who come to eat its shrimp and lobster. **Elsa's** (no phone), on the eastern side of the island, is a beachside restaurant that does hearty grilled dishes. **Habana Libre,** north of the pier (℃ **505/8848-5412**), is a Cuban-owned bar and restaurant that serves excellent veal and of course fresh seafood. The terrace view is delicious, as are the *mojitos* made from homegrown mint. The bar is popular with locals and visitors and has a nice vibe with good music.

COSTA RICA

by Eliot Greenspan

"*Pura Vida!*" ("Pure Life!") is Costa Rica's unofficial national slogan, and in many ways it defines the country. You'll hear it exclaimed, proclaimed, and simply stated by Ticos from all walks of life, from children to octogenarians. It can be used as a cheer after your favorite soccer team scores a goal, or as a descriptive response when someone asks you, "How are you?" ("¿Cómo estás?"). It is symbolic of the easygoing nature of this country's people, politics, and culture.

Costa Rica is the most popular and trendy tourist spot in Central America. To cope with the popularity and demand, the country has undergone massive development over the past 10 years, with the principal tourist towns bursting at the seams with hotels, restaurants, and bars, and large luxury resorts springing up along its long Pacific coast.

Despite this boom, Costa Rica remains rich in natural wonders and biodiversity, a place where you can still find yourself far from the madding crowds. The country boasts a wealth of unsullied beaches that stretch for miles, small lodgings that haven't attracted hordes of tourists, jungle rivers for rafting and kayaking, and spectacular cloud forests and rainforests with ample opportunities for bird-watching, hiking, and wildlife viewing.

With no armed forces, Costa Rica is sometimes called the "Switzerland of Central America," and has historically been an oasis of tranquillity in a region that has been troubled by civil war and armed conflict for centuries.

THE REGIONS IN BRIEF

Bordered by Nicaragua in the north and Panama in the southeast, Costa Rica is slightly larger than Vermont and New Hampshire combined. Much of the country is mountainous, with three major ranges running northwest to southeast. Among these mountains are several volcanic peaks, some of which are still active. Between the mountain ranges are fertile valleys. With the exception of the dry Guanacaste region, much of Costa Rica's coastal area is hot and humid and covered with dense rainforests.

SAN JOSE & THE CENTRAL VALLEY The Central Valley is characterized by rolling green hills that rise to heights between 900 and 1,200m (3,000–4,000 ft.) above sea level. The climate here is mild and springlike year-round. It's Costa Rica's primary agricultural region, with coffee farms making up the majority of landholdings. The rich volcanic soil of this region makes it ideal for farming. The country's earliest settlements were in this area, and today the Central Valley (which includes San

José) is densely populated, crisscrossed by decent roads, and dotted with small towns. Surrounding the Central Valley are high during cycles of activity in the past 2 centuries. Many of the mountainous regions to the north and to the south of the capital of San José have been declared national parks (Tapantí, Juan Castro, and Braulio Carrillo) to protect their virgin rainforests against logging.

GUANACASTE The northwestern corner of the country near the Nicaraguan border is the site of many of Costa Rica's sunniest and most popular **beaches,** including **Playa del Coco, Playa Hermosa, Playa Flamingo, Playa Conchal, Tamarindo,** and the **Papagayo Peninsula.** Because many foreigners have chosen to build beach houses and retirement homes here, Guanacaste has experienced considerable development over the years. You won't find a glut of Cancún-style high-rise hotels, but condos, luxury resorts, and golf courses have sprung up all up and down the coastline here. However, you can still find long stretches of deserted sands.

With about 65 inches of rain a year, this region is by far the driest in the country and has been likened to west Texas. In addition to cattle ranches, inland Guanacaste boasts semiactive volcanoes, several lakes, and one of the last remnants of tropical dry forest left in Central America. (Dry forest once stretched all the way from Costa Rica up to the Mexican state of Chiapas.)

PUNTARENAS & THE NICOYA PENINSULA Just south of Guanacaste lies the Nicoya peninsula. Similar to Guanacaste in many ways, the Nicoya peninsula is nonetheless somewhat more inaccessible, and thus much less developed and crowded. However, this is already starting to change. The neighboring beaches of **Malpaís** and **Santa Teresa** are perhaps the fastest-growing hot spots anywhere along the Costa Rican coast.

While similar in terms of geography, climate, and ecosystems, as you head south from Guanacaste, the region begins to get more humid and moist. The forests are taller and lusher than those found in Guanacaste. The Nicoya peninsula itself juts out to form the Golfo de Nicoya (Nicoya Gulf), a large, protected body of water. **Puntarenas,** a small fishing city, is the main port on this gulf, and a departure point for the regular ferries that connect the Nicoya peninsula to San José and most of mainland Costa Rica.

THE NORTHERN ZONE This inland region lies to the north of San José and includes rainforests, cloud forests, hot springs, the country's two most active volcanoes (**Arenal** and **Rincón de la Vieja**), **Braulio Carrillo National Park,** and numerous remote lodges. Because this is one of the few regions of Costa Rica without any beaches, it primarily attracts people interested in nature and active sports. **Lake Arenal** boasts some of the best windsurfing and kitesurfing in the world, as well as several good mountain biking trails along its shores. The **Monteverde Cloud Forest,** perhaps Costa Rica's most internationally recognized attraction, is another top draw in this region.

THE CENTRAL PACIFIC COAST Because it's the most easily accessible coastline in Costa Rica, the central Pacific coast boasts a vast variety of beach resorts and hotels. **Playa de Jacó,** a beach just an hour or so drive from San José, attracts many sunbirds, charter groups, and a mad rush of Tico tourists every weekend. It is also very popular with young surfers, and has a distinct party vibe to it. **Manuel Antonio,** one of the most emblematic destinations in Costa Rica, is built up around a popular coastal national park, and caters to people looking to blend beach time and fabulous panoramic views with some wildlife viewing and active adventures. This region is also home to the highest peak in Costa Rica—**Mount Chirripó**—a beautiful summit, where frost is common.

THE SOUTHERN ZONE   This hot, humid region is one of Costa Rica's most remote and undeveloped. It is characterized by rainforests, national parks, and rugged coastlines. Much of the area is uninhabited and protected in **Corcovado, Piedras Blancas,** and **La Amistad** national parks. A number of nature lodges are spread around the shores of the **Golfo Dulce** and along the **Osa Peninsula.** There's a lot of solitude to be found here, due in no small part to the fact that it's hard to get here and hard to get around. But if you like your ecotourism authentic and challenging, you'll find the southern zone to your liking.

THE CARIBBEAN COAST   Most of the Caribbean coast is a wide, steamy lowland laced with rivers and blanketed with rainforests and banana plantations. The culture here is predominantly Afro-Caribbean, with many residents speaking an English or Caribbean patois. The northern section of this coast is accessible only by boat or small plane and is the site of **Tortuguero National Park,** which is known for its nesting sea turtles and riverboat trips. The towns of **Cahuita, Puerto Viejo,** and **Manzanillo,** on the southern half of the Caribbean coast, are increasingly popular destinations. The coastline here boasts many beautiful beaches and, as yet, few large hotels. However, this area can be rainy, especially between December and April.

THE BEST OF COSTA RICA IN 1 WEEK

The timing is tight, but this itinerary packs a lot into a weeklong vacation. This route takes you to a trifecta of Costa Rica's primary tourist attractions: Arenal Volcano, Monteverde, and Manuel Antonio. You can explore and enjoy tropical nature, take in some beach time, and experience a few high-adrenaline adventures to boot.

Day 1: Arrive & Settle into San José

Arrive and get settled in **San José.** If your flight gets in early enough and you have time, head downtown and tour the **Museos del Banco Central de Costa Rica (Gold Museum)** ★★ (p. 570). Then head over to the **Teatro Nacional (National Theater;** p. 240). If anything is playing that night, buy tickets for the show. For an elegant and delicious dinner, I recommend **Grano de Oro Restaurant** ★★★ (p. 580), which is a refined restaurant with seating in and around an open-air central courtyard in a beautiful downtown hotel.

Day 2: Hot Rocks ★★

Rent a car and head to the Arenal National Park to see **Arenal Volcano** ★★. Settle into your hotel and spend the afternoon at the **Tabacón Grand Spa Thermal Resort** ★★★ (p. 621). In the evening either sign up for a volcano-watching tour or take one on your own by driving the road to **Arenal National Park** and finding a quiet spot to pull over and wait for the sparks to fly.

Day 3: Adventures Around Arenal, Ending Up in Monteverde ★★

Spend the morning doing something adventurous around Arenal National Park, from white-water rafting to mountain biking to horseback riding and then hiking to the Río Fortuna Waterfall. My favorite is the **canyoning** adventure offered by **Desafío Expeditions** ★★ (p. 619). Allow at least 4 hours of daylight to drive around **Lake Arenal** to **Monteverde.** Once you get to Monteverde, settle into your hotel and head for a drink and dinner at **Sofía** ★★★ (p. 612).

Costa Rica in 1 Week

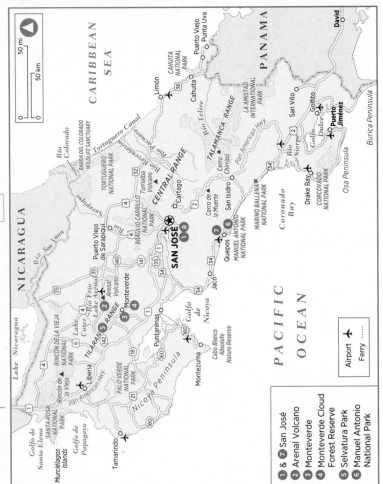

- **1 & 7** San José
- **2** Arenal Volcano
- **3** Monteverde
- **4** Monteverde Cloud Forest Reserve
- **5** Selvatura Park
- **6** Manuel Antonio National Park

Day 4: Monteverde Cloud Forest Biological Reserve ★★★

Wake up early and take a guided tour of the **Monteverde Cloud Forest Biological Reserve** ★★★ (p. 606). Stop in at the **Hummingbird Gallery** ★ (p. 609) next door to the entrance after your tour. There's great shopping, and the scores of brilliant hummingbirds buzzing around your head at this attraction are always fascinating. Spend the afternoon visiting several of the area's attractions, which might include any combination of the following: the **Butterfly Garden** ★, **Orchid Garden** ★★, **Monteverde Serpentarium** ★, **Frog Pond of Monteverde** ★, the **Bat Jungle,** and the **World of Insects** (p. 608).

Day 5: From the Treetops to the Coast ★★★

Use the morning to take one of the **zip-line canopy tours** here. I recommend **Selvatura Park ★★** (p. 607), which has a wonderful canopy tour, as well as other interesting exhibits. Be sure to schedule the tour early enough so that you can hit the road by noon for your drive to **Manuel Antonio National Park.** Settle into your hotel and head for a **sunset drink** at **Agua Azul ★** (p. 633), which offers up spectacular views over the rainforest to the sea. You can drop your car off at any point now and just rely on taxis and tours.

Day 6: Manuel Antonio ★★

In the morning take a boat tour of the mangroves of **Damas Island estuary** (p. 630), and then reward yourself with an afternoon lazing on one of the beautiful beaches inside **Manuel Antonio National Park ★★** (p. 624). If you just can't lie still, be sure to hike the loop trail through the rainforest here and around **Cathedral Point ★★**. Make reservations at the **El Patio Bistro Latino ★★★** (p. 634) for an intimate and relaxed final dinner in Costa Rica.

Day 7: Saying *Adiós*

Fly back to **San José** in time to connect with your flight home. If you have extra time, feel free to head back into Manuel Antonio National Park, do some souvenir shopping, or simply laze around your hotel pool. You've earned it.

PLANNING YOUR TRIP TO COSTA RICA

Visitor Information

In the United States or Canada, you can get basic information on Costa Rica by contacting the **Costa Rican Tourist Board** (**ICT,** or Instituto Costarricense de Turismo; ℂ **866/COSTA-RICA** [267-8274] in the U.S. and Canada, or 2223-1733 in Costa Rica; www.visitcostarica.com). Travelers from the United Kingdom, Australia, and New Zealand will have to rely primarily on this website because the ICT does not have toll-free access in these countries.

In addition to this official site, you'll be able to find a wealth of Web-based information on Costa Rica with a few clicks of your mouse. In fact, you'll be better off surfing, as the ICT site is rather limited and clunky.

You can pick up a map when you arrive at the ICT's information desk at the airport, or at their downtown San José offices. Perhaps the best map to have is the waterproof country map of Costa Rica put out by **International Travel Maps** (www.itmb.com), which can be ordered direct from their website or any major online bookseller, like Amazon.com.

TOUR OPERATORS

If you're not booking your hotel, tours, and transportation by yourself, you might want to consider using a tour agency that has earned high marks in this area. In San José, **Horizontes ★★**, Calle 32 between avenidas 3 and 5 (ℂ **2222-2022;** www.horizontes.com), has garnered particularly high marks from several rating agencies and organizations. Other exemplary operators include **Costa Rica Expeditions ★★** (ℂ2257-0766; www.costaricaexpeditions.com), **Costa Rica Sun Tours ★** (ℂ2296-7757; www.crsuntours.com), and **Swiss Travel Service** (ℂ **2282-4898;** www.swisstravelcr.com).

TELEPHONE dialing INFO AT A GLANCE

To call Costa Rica from abroad:
1. Dial the international access code: 011 from the U.S. and Canada; 00 from the U.K., Ireland, or New Zealand; or 0011 from Australia.
2. Dial the country code 506.
3. Dial the eight-digit number.

To make international calls: To make international calls from Costa Rica, first dial 00 and then the country code (U.S. or Canada 1, U.K. 44, Ireland 353, Australia 61, New Zealand 64). Next you dial the area code and number. For example, if you wanted to call the British Embassy in Washington, D.C., you would dial 00-1-202-588-7800.

For directory assistance: Dial 113 if you're looking for a number inside Costa Rica, and dial 124 for numbers to all other countries.

For operator assistance: If you need operator assistance, dial **116** if you're trying to make an international call and **0** if you want to call a number in Costa Rica.

Toll-free numbers: Numbers beginning with 0800 or 800 within Costa Rica are toll-free, but calling a 1-800 number in the States from Costa Rica is not toll-free. In fact, it costs the same as an overseas call.

Entry Requirements

Citizens of the United States, Canada, Great Britain, and most European nations may visit Costa Rica for a maximum of 90 days. No visa is necessary, but you must have a valid passport, which you should carry with you at all times while you're in Costa Rica. Citizens of Australia, Ireland, and New Zealand can enter the country without a visa and stay for 30 days, although once in the country, visitors can apply for an extension.

If you overstay your visa or original entry stamp, you will have to pay around $45 for an exit visa. If you need to get an exit visa, a travel agent in San José can usually obtain one for a small fee and save you the hassle of dealing with Immigration. If you want to stay longer than the validity of your entry stamp or visa, the easiest thing to do is cross the border into Panama or Nicaragua for 72 hours and then reenter Costa Rica on a new entry stamp or visa. However, be careful: Periodically the Costa Rican government has cracked down on "perpetual tourists"; if it notices a continued pattern of exits and entries designed simply to support an extended stay, it might deny you reentry.

COSTA RICAN EMBASSY LOCATIONS

In the U.S.: 2114 S St. NW, Washington, DC 20008 (✆ **202/234-2945;** www.costarica-embassy.org for consulate locations around the country).

In Canada: 325 Dalhousie St., Ste. 407, Ottawa, Ontario K1N 5TA (✆ **613/562-2855**).

In the U.K.: 14 Lancaster Gate, London, England W2 3LH (✆ **020/7706-8844**). There are no Costa Rican embassies in Australia or New Zealand, but you could try contacting the honorary consul in Sydney, Australia, at Level 11, De La Sala House, 30 Clarence St., Sydney NSW 2000 (✆ **02/9261-1177**).

Customs

Visitors to Costa Rica are permitted to bring in all manner of items for personal use, including cameras, video cameras, tape recorders, personal computers, and music players. Customs officials in Costa Rica seldom check tourists' luggage.

Money

The unit of currency in Costa Rica is the **colón.** Frommer's lists prices in this chapter in U.S. dollars, because the Costa Rican colón is in a constant state of devaluation and fluctuation. More important, almost every hotel in the country, as well as a fair number of restaurants in popular tourist destinations, advertise and list their prices in U.S. dollars. Finally, those hotels and restaurants that don't usually peg their prices to the dollar make periodic adjustments. Airport taxis will all accept U.S. dollars, as will virtually every hotel and many restaurants.

The colón is divided into 100 **céntimos.** Currently, two types of coins are in circulation: gold-hued 5-, 10-, 25-, 50-, 100-, and 500-colón coins, and lightweight silver-colored alloy 5- and 10-colón coins. There are paper notes in denominations of 1,000, 2,000, 5,000, and 10,000 colones. You might also encounter a 5-colón bill, which is a popular gift and souvenir. It is valid currency, although it sells for more than its face value. You might hear people refer to a *rojo* or *tucán,* which are slang terms for the 1,000- and 5,000-colón bills, respectively. One-hundred-colón denominations are called *tejas,* so *cinco tejas* is 500 colones. I've yet to encounter a slang equivalent for the 2,000 and 10,000 bills.

Forged bills are not entirely uncommon. When receiving change in colones, it's a good idea to check the larger-denomination bills, which should have protective bands or hidden images that appear when held up to the light.

CHANGING MONEY You can change money at all banks in Costa Rica. The principal state banks are Banco Nacional and Banco de Costa Rica. However, be forewarned that service at state banks can be slow and tedious. You're almost always better off finding a private bank. Luckily, there are hosts of private banks around San José and in most major tourist destinations.

Since banks handle money exchanges, there are very, very few exchange houses in Costa Rica. One major exception to this is the **Global Exchange** (© **2431-0686;** www.globalexchange.co.cr) office at the airport. However, be forewarned that they exchange at more than 10% below the official exchange rate.

Hotels will often exchange money and cash traveler's checks; there usually isn't much of a line, but they might shave a few colones off the exchange rate. Be careful about exchanging money on the streets; it's quite risky. In addition to forged bills and short counts, street money-changers frequently work in teams that can leave you holding neither colones nor dollars. Also be very careful when leaving a bank. Criminals are often looking for foreigners who have just withdrawn or exchanged cash.

ATMs You'll find ATMs in all but the most remote tourist destinations and isolated nature lodges. It's probably a good idea to change your PIN to a four-digit PIN before you go, as some ATMs in Costa Rica will accept only four-digit PINs.

In 2009, in response to a rash of "express kidnappings" in San José, in which folks were taken at gunpoint to an ATM to clean out their bank accounts, both Banco Nacional and Banco de Costa Rica stopped ATM service between the hours of 10pm and 5am. Other networks still dispense money 24 hours a day.

CREDIT CARDS   MasterCard and Visa are the most widely accepted credit cards in Costa Rica, followed by American Express. Most hotels and restaurants accept all of these, especially in tourist destination areas. Discover and Diners Club are far less commonly accepted.

When to Go

Costa Rica's high season for tourism runs from late November to late April, which coincides almost perfectly with the chill of winter in the United States, Canada, and Great Britain, and includes Christmas, New Year's, Easter, and most school spring breaks. The high season is also the dry season. If you want some unadulterated time on a tropical beach and a little less rain during your rainforest experience, this is the time to come. During this period (and especially around the Christmas holiday), the tourism industry operates at full tilt—prices are higher, attractions are more crowded, and reservations need to be made in advance.

Local tourism operators often call the tropical rainy season (May through mid-Nov) the "green season." The adjective is appropriate. At this time of year, even brown and barren Guanacaste province becomes lush and verdant. I personally love traveling around Costa Rica during the rainy season (but then again, I'm not trying to flee cold snaps in Canada). It's easy to find or at least negotiate reduced rates, there are far fewer fellow travelers, and the rain is often limited to a few hours each afternoon (although you can occasionally get socked in for a week at a time). *A drawback:* Some of the country's rugged roads become downright impassable without a four-wheel-drive during the rainy season.

CLIMATE   Costa Rica is a tropical country and has wet and dry seasons. However, some regions are rainy all year, and others are very dry and sunny for most of the year. Temperatures vary primarily with elevations, not with seasons: On the coasts it's hot all year; in the mountains it can be cool at night any time of year. Frost is common at the highest elevations (3,000–3,600m/9,840–11,800 ft.).

Generally, the **rainy season** (or "green season") is from May to mid-November. Costa Ricans call this wet time of year their winter. The **dry season,** considered summer by Costa Ricans, is from mid-November to April. In Guanacaste, the dry northwestern province, the dry season lasts several weeks longer than in other places. Even in the rainy season, days often start sunny, with rain falling in the afternoon and evening. On the Caribbean coast, especially south of Limón, you can count on rain year-round, although this area gets less rain in September and October than the rest of the country.

In general, the best time of year to visit weather-wise is in December and January, when everything is still green from the rains but the sky is clear.

HOLIDAYS   Because Costa Rica is a Roman Catholic country, most of its holidays are church-related. The biggies are Christmas, New Year's, and Easter, which are all celebrated for several days. Holy Week (Easter week) is the biggest holiday time in Costa Rica, and many families head for the beach. (This is the last holiday before school starts.) There is no public transportation on Holy Thursday or Good Friday. Government offices and banks are closed on official holidays, transportation services are reduced, and stores and markets might also close.

Official holidays in Costa Rica include **January 1** (New Year's Day), **March 19** (St. Joseph's Day), Thursday and Friday of Holy Week, **April 11** (Juan Santamaría's Day), **May 1** (Labor Day), **June 29** (St. Peter and St. Paul Day), **July 25** (annexation of the province of Guanacaste), **August 2** (Virgin of Los Angeles's Day), **August 15** (Mother's Day), **September 15** (Independence Day), **October 12** (Discovery of America/Día de la Raza), **December 8** (Immaculate Conception of the Virgin Mary), **December 24** and **25** (Christmas), and **December 31** (New Year's Eve).

Health Concerns

Staying healthy on a trip to Costa Rica is predominantly a matter of being a little cautious about what you eat and drink, applying sunscreen, and using common sense. Know your physical limits, and don't overexert yourself in the ocean, on hikes, or in athletic activities. Respect the tropical sun and protect yourself from it. See p. 69 in chapter 3 for more info on avoiding and treating illness.

COMMON AILMENTS   Your chance of contracting any serious tropical disease in Costa Rica is slim, especially if you stick to the beaches or traditional spots for visitors. However, malaria, dengue fever, and leptospirosis all exist in Costa Rica, so it's a good idea to educate yourself about these illnesses and their symptoms ahead of time.

DIETARY RED FLAGS   Even though the water in San José and most popular destinations in Costa Rica is generally safe, and even if you're careful to buy bottled water, order *frescos en leche* (fruit shakes made with milk rather than water), and drink your soft drink without ice cubes, you still might encounter some intestinal difficulties. Except in the most established and hygienic of restaurants, it's advisable to avoid ceviche, a raw seafood salad, especially if it has any shellfish in it. It could be home to any number of bacterial critters.

Getting There

BY PLANE

It takes between 3 and 7 hours to fly to Costa Rica from most U.S. cities, from where most direct and connecting flights will depart. Most international flights still land in San José's **Juan Santamaría International Airport** (© **2437-2626** for 24-hr. airport information; airport code SJO). However, more and more direct international flights are touching down in Liberia's **Daniel Oduber International Airport** (© **2668-1010** or 2688-1117; airport code LIR).

Liberia is the gateway to the beaches of the Guanacaste region and the Nicoya Peninsula, and a direct flight here eliminates the need for a separate commuter flight in a small aircraft or roughly 5 hours in a car or bus. If you are planning to spend all, or most, of your vacation time in the Guanacaste region, you'll want to fly in and out of Liberia. However, San José is a much more convenient gateway if you are planning to head to Manuel Antonio, the Central Pacific coast, the Caribbean coast, or the Southern zone.

Numerous airlines fly into Costa Rica. Be warned that the smaller Latin American carriers tend to make several stops (sometimes unscheduled) en route to San José, thus increasing flying time.

FROM NORTH AMERICA   Air Canada, American Airlines, Continental, Delta, Frontier, Grupo Taca, JetBlue, Mexicana, Spirit Air, and US Airways all have regular direct flights to Costa Rica.

FROM EUROPE   **Iberia** is the only airline with regular routes to San José, some direct and others with one connection. Alternatively, you can fly to any major U.S. hub-city and make connections to one of the airlines mentioned above.

Getting Around

It's pretty easy to get around Costa Rica. Your options range from rental cars and commuter flights to public buses and regularly scheduled tourist shuttles.

BY PLANE   Flying is one of the best ways to get around Costa Rica. Because the country is quite small, flights are short and not too expensive. The domestic airlines of Costa Rica are Sansa and Nature Air.

Sansa (℗ **877/767-2672** in the U.S. and Canada, or 2290-4100 in Costa Rica; www.flysansa.com) operates from a separate terminal at San José's **Juan Santamaría International Airport** (see above).

Nature Air (℗ **800/235-9272** in the U.S. and Canada, or 2299-6000; www. natureair.com) operates from **Tobías Bolaños International Airport** (℗ **2232-2820;** airport code SYQ) in Pavas, 6.4km (4 miles) from San José. The ride from downtown to Pavas takes about 10 minutes, and a metered taxi fare should cost $10 to $20.

In the high season (late Nov to late Apr), be sure to book reservations well in advance. Both companies have online booking systems via their websites.

BY BUS   This is by far the most economical way to get around Costa Rica. Buses are inexpensive and relatively well maintained, and they go nearly everywhere. There are two types: Local buses are the cheapest and slowest; they stop frequently and are generally a bit dilapidated. Express buses run between San José and most beach towns and major cities; these tend to be newer units and more comfortable, although very few are so new or modern as to have bathroom facilities, and they sometimes operate only on weekends and holidays.

Two companies run regular, fixed-schedule departures in passenger vans and small buses to most of the major tourist destinations. **Gray Line** (℗ **2220-2126;** www.graylinecostarica.com) is run by Fantasy Tours, and has about 10 departures leaving San José each morning and heading for or connecting to Jacó, Manuel Antonio, Liberia, Playa Hermosa, La Fortuna, Tamarindo, and playas Conchal and Flamingo. There are return trips to San José every day from these destinations and a variety of interconnecting routes. A similar service, **Interbus** (℗ **2283-5573;** www.interbusonline.com), has a slightly more extensive route map and more connections. Fares run between $29 and $45 depending on the destination. Gray Line offers an unlimited weekly pass for all of its shuttle routes for $132.

BY CAR   Driving in Costa Rica is no idle proposition. The roads are riddled with potholes, most rural intersections are unmarked, and, for some reason, sitting behind the wheel of a car seems to turn peaceful Ticos into homicidal maniacs. But unless you want to see the country from the window of a bus or pay exorbitant amounts for private transfers, renting a car might be your best option for independent exploring.

Be forewarned, however: Although rental cars no longer bear special license plates, they are still readily identifiable to thieves and are frequently targeted. (Nothing is ever safe in a car in Costa Rica, although parking in guarded parking lots helps.) Transit police also seem to target tourists; never pay money directly to a police officer who stops you for any traffic violation.

Before driving off with a rental car, be sure that you inspect the exterior and point out to the rental-company representative every tiny scratch, dent, tear, or any other damage. It's a common practice with many Costa Rican car-rental companies to claim that you owe payment for minor dings and dents that the company finds when you return the car. Also, if you get into an accident, be sure that the rental company doesn't try to bill you for a higher amount than the deductible on your rental contract.

Among the major international agencies operating in Costa Rica are **Alamo, Avis, Budget, Hertz, National, Payless,** and **Thrifty.** For a complete list of car-rental agencies and their contact information, see the "Getting Around" sections of major tourist destinations in this chapter.

Keep in mind that four-wheel-drives are particularly useful in the rainy season (May to mid-Nov) and for navigating the bumpy, poorly paved roads year-round.

Note: It's sometimes cheaper to reserve a car in your home country rather than booking when you arrive in Costa Rica. If you know you'll be renting a car, it's always wise to reserve it well in advance for the high season because the rental fleet still can't match demand.

BY TAXI   All city taxis, and some rural cabs, have meters (*marías*), although drivers sometimes refuse to use them, particularly with foreigners. If this is the case, be sure to negotiate the price upfront. Try to get drivers to use the meter first (say, *"Ponga la maría, por favor"*). The official rate at press time is around 80¢ for the first kilometer (⅔ mile) and another 80¢ for each additional kilometer. If you have a rough idea of how far it is to your destination, you can estimate how much it should cost from these figures, or you can ask at your hotel how much a specific ride should cost. After 10pm, taxis are legally allowed to add a 20% surcharge. Some of the meters are programmed to include the extra charge automatically, but be careful: Some drivers will use the evening setting on their meter during the daytime or (at night) to charge an extra 20% on top of the higher meter setting.

Tipping taxi drivers is not common, nor expected.

Tips on Accommodations

When the Costa Rican tourist boom began in the late 1980s, hotels popped up like mushrooms after a heavy rain. By the 1990s the country's first true megaresorts opened, more followed, and still more are under construction or in the planning phase. Except during the few busiest weeks of the year, there's a relative glut of rooms in Costa Rica. Most hotels are small to midsize, and the best ones fill up fast most of the year. Still, in broader terms, the glut of rooms is good news for travelers and bargain hunters. Less popular hotels that want to survive are being forced to reduce their rates and provide better service.

Rates given in this chapter do not include the 16.3% room taxes, unless otherwise specified. These taxes will add considerably to the cost of your room.

Tips on Dining

Costa Rican cuisine is less than memorable. San José remains the gastronomic capital of the country, and you can find many of the cuisines of the world served here at moderate prices. However, the major beach destinations of Tamarindo, Manuel Antonio, and the Papagayo Peninsula are starting to catch up.

Costa Rica is a major producer and exporter of beef; consequently, the country has plenty of steakhouses. Unfortunately, quantity doesn't mean quality. Unless you go to one of the better restaurants or steakhouses, you will probably be served tough steaks, cut thin. With the increase in international tourism, local chefs have created "nouvelle Costa Rican cuisine," updating timeworn recipes and using traditional ingredients in creative ways.

If you're looking for cheap eats, you'll find them in little restaurants known as **sodas,** which are the equivalent of diners in the United States. At a *soda,* you'll have lots of choices: rice and beans with steak, rice and beans with fish, rice and beans

Two words of advice: Buy coffee. Lots of it.

Coffee is the best shopping deal in all of Costa Rica. One pound of coffee sells for around $3 to $6. It makes a great gift and truly is a local product.

Café Britt is the big name in Costa Rican coffee. These folks have the largest export business in the country, and, although high-priced, its blends are very dependable. Café Britt is available at gift shops around the country, and at the souvenir concessions at both international airports. My favorites are the coffees roasted and packaged in Manuel Antonio and Monteverde, by **Café Milagro** and **Café Monteverde.** If you visit either of these places, definitely pick up their beans.

The best place to buy coffee is in any supermarket. (Why pay more at a gift shop?) If you buy prepackaged coffee in a supermarket, the whole beans will be marked either *grano* or *grano entero* (for whole bean), or *molido* (for ground). If you opt for ground, be sure the package is marked *puro;* otherwise, it will likely be mixed with a good amount of sugar, the way Ticos like it.

with chicken, or, for vegetarians, rice and beans. You get the picture. Rice and beans are standard Tico fare and are served at all three daily meals. Also, although plenty of seafood is available, at *sodas,* it's all too often served fried.

Keep in mind that there is an additional 13% sales tax, as well as a 10% service charge. By law, Costa Rican restaurants must show their prices with the 13% sales tax figured in. However, this is often not the case. In addition, Ticos rarely tip, but that doesn't mean that you shouldn't. If the service was particularly good and attentive, you should probably leave a little extra.

Tips on Shopping

Serious shoppers will be disappointed in Costa Rica. Aside from coffee and hand-painted wooden ox carts, there isn't much that's distinctly Costa Rican. To compensate for its relative lack of goods, Costa Rican gift shops do a brisk business selling crafts and clothes from Guatemala, Panama, and Ecuador.

Notable exceptions to the meager crafts offerings include the fine wooden creations of **Barry Biesanz** ★★ (© **2289-4337;** www.biesanz.com). His work is sold in many of the finer gift shops and at his own shop, but beware: Biesanz's work is often imitated, so make sure that what you buy is real (he generally burns his signature into the bottom of the piece). **Lil Mena** is a Costa Rican artist who specializes in working with and painting on handmade papers and rough fibers. You'll find her work in a number of shops around the country.

You might also run across **carved masks** made by the indigenous Boruca people of southern Costa Rica. These full-size balsa-wood masks come in a variety of styles, both painted and unpainted, and run anywhere from $15 to $80, depending on the workmanship. **Cecilia "Pefi" Figueres** ★★ makes ceramic wares that are lively and fun. Look for her brightly colored abstract and figurative bowls, pitchers, and mugs at some of the better gift shops around the city.

[FastFACTS] COSTA RICA

Business Hours Banks are usually open Monday through Friday from 9am to 4pm, although many have begun to offer extended hours. Post offices are generally open Monday through Friday from 8am to 5:30pm, and Saturday from 7:30am to noon. (In small towns, post offices often close on Sat.) Stores are generally open Monday through Saturday from 9am to 6pm (many close for 1 hr. at lunch), but stores in modern malls generally stay open until 8 or 9pm and don't close for lunch. Most bars are open until 1 or 2am, although some go later.

Embassies & Consulates In San José: **United States Embassy,** in front of Centro Commercial, on the road to Pavas (✆ **2519-2000,** or 2220-3127 after hours in case of emergency); **Canadian Consulate,** Oficentro Ejecutivo La Sabana, Edificio 5 (✆ **2242-4400**); and **British Embassy,** Paseo Colón between calles 38 and 40 (✆ **2258-2025**). There are no Australian or New Zealand embassies in San José.

Emergencies In case of any emergency, dial ✆ **911** (which should have an English-speaking operator); for an ambulance, call ✆ **128;** and to report a fire, call ✆ **118.** If 911 doesn't work, you can contact the police at ✆ **2222-1365** or 2221-5337, and hopefully they can find someone who speaks English.

Hospitals In San José try **Clínica Bíblica** (Av. 14 btw. calles Central and 1), which offers emergency services to foreign visitors at reasonable prices (✆ **2522-1000;** www.clinicabiblica.com), or the **Hospital CIMA** (✆ **2208-1000;** www.hospitalsanjose.net), in Escazú, which has the most modern facilities in the country.

Language Spanish is the official language of Costa Rica. However, in most tourist areas, you'll be surprised by how well Costa Ricans speak English.

Newspapers & Magazines There are a half-dozen or so Spanish-language dailies in Costa Rica and one English-language weekly, the *Tico Times.* In addition, you can get *Time, Newsweek,* and several U.S. newspapers at some hotel gift shops and a few of the bookstores in San José. If you understand Spanish, *La Nación* is the paper you'll want. Its "Viva" and "Tiempo Libre" sections list what's going on in the world of music, theater, dance, and more.

Police In most cases, dial ✆ **911** for the police, and you should be able to get someone who speaks English on the line. Other numbers for the **Judicial Police** are ✆ **2222-1365** and 2221-5337. The numbers for the **Traffic Police (Policía de Tránsito)** are ✆ **800/8726-7486** toll-free nationwide, or 2222-9330.

Post Offices & Mail At press time, it costs 350 colones to mail a letter to the United States, and 395 colones to Europe. You can get stamps at post offices and at some gift shops in large hotels. Given the Costa Rican postal service's track record, I recommend paying an extra 600 colones to have anything of any value certified. Better yet, use an international courier service or wait until you get home to post it. **DHL,** on Paseo Colón between calles 30 and 32 (✆ **2209-0000;** www.dhl.com); **EMS Courier,** with desks at most post offices nationwide (✆ **800/900-2000** in Costa Rica; www.correos.go.cr); **FedEx,** which is based in Heredia but will arrange pickup anywhere in the metropolitan area (✆ **800/463-3339;** www.fedex.com); and **United Parcel Service,** in Pavas (✆ **2290-2828;** www.ups.com), all operate in Costa Rica.

Safety Although most of Costa Rica is safe, petty crime and robberies committed against tourists are endemic. San José is known for its pickpockets, so never carry a wallet in your back pocket. A woman should keep a tight grip on her purse (keep it tucked under your arm). Thieves also target gold chains, cameras and video cameras, cellphones, prominent jewelry, and nice sunglasses.

Be sure not to leave valuables unsecured in your hotel room. Given the high rate of stolen passports in Costa Rica, mostly as collateral damage in a typical pickpocketing or room robbery, it is recommended that, whenever possible, you leave your passport in a hotel safe, and travel with a photocopy of the pertinent pages.

Rental cars generally stick out and are easily spotted by thieves. Don't park a car on the street in Costa Rica, especially in San José; plenty of public parking lots are available. Don't leave anything of value in a car parked on the street, not even for a moment. Be wary of solicitous strangers who stop to help you change a tire or take you to a service station. Although most are truly good Samaritans, there have been reports of thieves preying on roadside breakdowns. There have actually been numerous cases of scammers deliberately puncturing tires at a stoplight or parking area and then following the victim until they pull over to change the suddenly flat tire.

Public intercity buses are also frequent targets of stealthy thieves.

Finally, single women should use common sense and take precautions, especially after dark. I don't recommend that single women walk alone anywhere at night, especially on seemingly deserted beaches or dark uncrowded streets.

Taxes There is a national 13% value added tax (often written as i.v.i. in Costa Rica) added to all goods and services. This includes hotel and restaurant bills. Restaurants also add a 10% service charge, for a total of 23% more on your bill. There is an airport departure tax of $26. This tax must be purchased prior to check-in. There are desks at the main terminal of all international airports where you can pay this tax. Some local travel agencies and hotels offer to purchase the departure tax in advance, as a convenience for tourists. You must give them authorization, as well as your passport number, and pay a small service fee.

Tipping Tipping is not necessary in restaurants, where a 10% service charge is always added to your bill (along with a 13% tax). If service was particularly good, you can leave a little at your own discretion, but it's not mandatory. Porters and bellhops get around 75¢ per bag. You don't need to tip a taxi driver unless the service has been superior; a tip is not usually expected.

SAN JOSÉ & THE CENTRAL VALLEY

To most, San José seems little more than a chaotic jumble of cars, buses, buildings, and people. The central downtown section exists in a near-constant state of gridlock. Antiquated buses spewing fumes and a lack of emission controls have created a brown cloud over the city. Sidewalks are poorly maintained and claustrophobic, and street crime is a serious problem. Most visitors seek the sanctuary of their hotel room and the first chance to escape the city.

Still, things have been improving. Mayor Johnny Araya (who was up for reelection in Dec 2010) has led ambitious and controversial campaigns to rid the sidewalks of impromptu and illegal vendors, to reduce the clutter of billboards and overhead signs, and to bury a good share of the city's electrical and phone cables. Moreover, as the country's only major city, San José offers varied and active restaurant and nightlife scenes, several museums and galleries worth visiting, and a steady stream of theater, concerts, and other cultural events that you won't find elsewhere in the country.

At 1,125m (3,690 ft.) above sea level, San José enjoys springlike temperatures year-round. The mild climate, along with views of lush green mountainsides, makes San José a pleasant city to visit. And if the city's offerings aren't enough for you, you'll find that it's extremely easy to get out into the countryside. Within an hour or two, you can climb a volcano, go white-water rafting, hike through a cloud forest, and stroll through a butterfly garden—among many other activities.

Essentials

GETTING THERE

BY PLANE **Juan Santamaría International Airport** (✆ **2437-2626** for 24-hr. airport information; airport code SJO) is near the city of Alajuela, about 20 minutes from downtown San José. A taxi into town costs between $12 and $22, and a bus is only 75¢. The Alajuela–San José buses run frequently and will drop you off anywhere along Paseo Colón or at a station near the Parque de la Merced (downtown, btw. calles 12 and 14 and avs. 2 and 4). There are two separate lines: **Tuasa** (✆ **2442-6900**) buses are red; **Station Wagon** (✆ **8388-9263**) buses are beige/yellow. At the airport you'll find the bus stop in front of the main terminal. Be sure to ask whether the bus is going to San José, or you'll end up in Alajuela. If you have a lot of luggage, take a cab.

In terms of taxis, you should stick with the official airport taxi service, **Taxis Unidos Aeropuerto** (✆ **2221-6865;** www.taxiaeropuerto.com), which operates a fleet of orange vans and sedans. These folks have a kiosk in the no man's land just outside the exit door for arriving passengers. Here they will assign you a cab. These taxis now use meters, and fares to most downtown hotels should run $12 to $22. Despite the fact that Taxis Unidos has an official monopoly at the airport, you will usually find a handful of regular cabs (in traditional red sedans) and "pirate" cabs, driven by free-lancers using their own vehicles. You could use either of these latter options, and "pirate" cabs tend to charge a dollar or two less, but I recommend using the official service for safety and standardized prices.

If you arrive in San José via Nature Air, or another small commuter or charter airline, you might find yourself at the **Tobías Bolaños International Airport** in Pavas (✆ **2232-2820;** airport code SYQ). This small airport is on the western side of downtown San José, about 10 minutes by car from the center. There are no car-rental desks here, so unless you have a car or a driver waiting for you here, you will have to take a cab into town, which should cost between $10 and $20.

BY BUS If you're coming to San José by bus, where you disembark depends on where you're coming from. (The different bus companies have their offices, and thus their drop-off points, all over downtown San José. When you buy your ticket, ask where you'll be let off.) Buses arriving from Panama pass first through Cartago and San Pedro before letting passengers off in downtown San José; buses arriving from Nicaragua generally enter the city on the west end of town, on Paseo Colón. If you're staying here, you can ask to be let off before the final stop.

ORIENTATION

Downtown San José is laid out on a grid. *Avenidas* (avenues) run east and west, while *calles* (streets) run north and south. The center of the city is at **Avenida Central** and **Calle Central.** To the north of Avenida Central, the *avenidas* have odd numbers beginning with Avenida 1; to the south, they have even numbers beginning with Avenida 2. Likewise, *calles* to the east of Calle Central have odd numbers, and those

San José

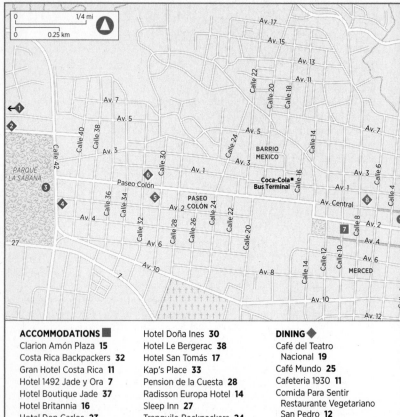

to the west have even numbers. The main downtown artery is **Avenida 2,** which merges with Avenida Central on either side of the downtown area. West of downtown, Avenida Central becomes **Paseo Colón,** which ends at Parque La Sabana and feeds into the highway to Alajuela, the airport, Guanacaste, and the Pacific coast. East of downtown, Avenida Central leads to San Pedro and then to Cartago and the Pan-American Highway (Carretera Panamericana) heading south. **Calle 3** takes you out of town to the north, onto the Guápiles Highway that leads to the Caribbean coast.

GETTING AROUND

BY BUS Bus transportation around San José is cheap—the fare is somewhere around 10¢ to 45¢—although the Alajuela/San José buses that run in from the airport cost 75¢. The most important buses are those running east along Avenida 2 and west along Avenida 3. The **Sabana/Cementerio** bus runs from Parque La Sabana to downtown and is one of the most convenient. You'll find a bus stop for the outbound

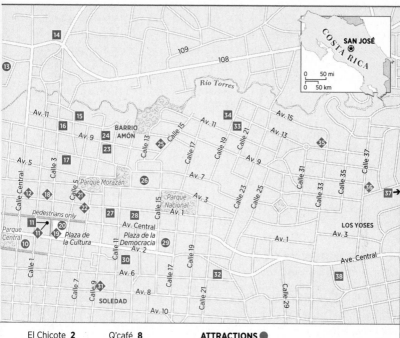

El Chicote **2**
Grano de Oro
  Restaurant **5**
Ichiban **21**
Machu Picchu **6**
Olio **36**
Pane e Vino **22**
Park Café **1**

Q'café **8**
Soda Tapia **4**
Vishnu **18, 31**
Whappin' **35**

ATTRACTIONS ●
Catedral **10**
Centro Nacional de Arte y Cultura **26**
Mercado Central **9**
Museo de Arte Costarricense **3**
Museo de los Niños **13**
Museo Nacional de Costa Rica **29**
Museos del Banco Central de Costa Rica **20**

Sabana/Cementerio bus near the main post office on Avenida 3 near the corner of Calle 2, and another on Calle 11 between avenidas Central and 1. This bus also has stops all along Avenida 2. **San Pedro** buses leave from Avenida Central between calles 9 and 11, in front of the Cine Capri, and take you out of downtown heading east. **Escazú-** and **Santa Ana**–bound buses leave from the Coca-Cola bus station, as well as from Avenida 1 between calles 24 and 28. Alternatively, you can pick up both the Escazú and Santa Ana buses from the busy bus stop on Calle 42, just north of Gimnasio Nacional.

The bus drivers can make change, although they don't like to receive large bills. Be especially mindful of your wallet, purse, or other valuables, because pickpockets often work the crowded buses.

BY TAXI Although taxis in San José have meters (*marías*), the drivers sometimes refuse to use them, particularly with foreigners, so you'll occasionally have to negotiate the price. Always try to get them to use the meter first (say, "*Ponga la maría, por* *favor"*). For information on rates, see "Fast Facts: Costa Rica" in "Planning Your Trip to Costa Rica," at the beginning of this chapter.

Depending on your location, the time of day, and the weather (rain places taxis at a premium), it's easy to hail a cab downtown. You'll always find taxis in front of the Teatro Nacional (albeit at high prices) and around the Parque Central at Avenida Central and Calle Central. Taxis in front of hotels and the El Pueblo tourist complex usually charge more than others, although this is technically illegal. Most hotels will gladly call you a cab, either for a downtown excursion or for a trip back out to the airport. You can also get a cab by calling **Coopetaxi** (© **2235-9966**), **Coopeirazu** (© **2254-3211**), **Coopetico** (© **2224-7979**), or **Coopeguaria** (© **2226-1366**). **Cinco Estrellas Taxi** (© **2228-3159**) is another company that is based in Escazú but services the entire metropolitan area and airport, and claims to always have an English-speaking operator on call.

BY CAR   Most major car-rental agencies have offices at the airport. If not, they will either pick you up or deliver the car to any San José hotel. If you decide to pick up your rental car in downtown San José, be prepared for very congested, chaotic streets. See "Planning Your Trip to Costa Rica," at the beginning of this chapter, for car-rental agency info. *Tip:* You can often save money by reserving your car in advance from home, especially during high season.

VISITOR INFORMATION

There's an **Instituto Costarricense de Turismo** (**ICT;** © **2443-1535;** www.visit costarica.com) desk at the Juan Santamaría International Airport, in the baggage claims area, just before Customs. You can pick up maps and browse brochures, and they might lend you a phone to make or confirm a reservation. It's open daily from 9am to 9:30pm. If you're looking for the **main ICT visitor information center** in San José, it's below the Plaza de la Cultura, at the entrance to the Museos del Banco Central de Costa Rica, on Calle 5 between avenidas Central and 2 (© **2222-1090**). The people here are friendly, although the information is rather limited. This office is open Monday through Saturday from 9am to 5pm.

FAST FACTS   In case of an **emergency,** call © **911.** You can reach the **Red Cross** and request an **ambulance** at © **2233-7033;** for **police assistance** call © **2222-1365.**

Clínica Bíblica, Avenida 14 between calles Central and 1 (© **2522-1000;** www. clinicabiblica.com), is located close to downtown and has several English-speaking doctors. The **Hospital CIMA** (© **2208-1000;** www.hospitalcima.com), in Escazú on the Próspero Fernández Highway, which connects San José and the western suburb of Santa Ana, has the most modern facilities in the country.

American Express Travel Services is represented in Costa Rica by **ASV Olympia,** Oficentro La Sabana, Sabana Sur (© **2242-8585;** www.asvolympia.com), which can issue traveler's checks and replacement cards and provide other standard services. To report lost or stolen Amex traveler's checks within Costa Rica, call the number above or © **2295-9000,** or call collect to 336/393-1111 in the U.S.

Internet cafes are all over San José. Rates run between 50¢ and $2 per hour. Many hotels have their own Internet cafe or allow guests to send and receive e-mail. And many have added wireless access, either free or for a small charge. You can also try **Racsa,** Avenida 5 and Calle 1 (© **2287-0087;** www.racsa.co.cr), the state Internet monopoly, which sells prepaid cards in 5-, 10-, and 15-hour denominations for connecting your laptop to the Web via a local phone call. Some knowledge of configuring your computer's dial-up connection is necessary, and you'll want to factor in the phone-call charge if calling from a hotel.

The main **post office** *(correo)* is on Calle 2 between avenidas 1 and 3 (② **2202-2900;** www.correos.go.cr).

What to See & Do

Most visitors to Costa Rica try to get out of the city as fast as possible so they can spend more time on the beach or in the rainforests. But there are a few attractions in San José to keep you busy. Some of the best and most modern museums in Central America are here, with a wealth of fascinating pre-Columbian artifacts.

ORGANIZED TOURS   There really isn't much reason to take a tour of San José. It's so compact that you can visit all the major sights on your own. However, if you want to take a city tour, which will run between $20 and $50, here are some companies you can use: **Horizontes Travel ★★**, Calle 32 between avenidas 3 and 5 (② **2222-2022;** www.horizontes.com); **Gray Line Tours,** Avenida 7 between calles 6 and 8, with additional offices at the Hampton Inn and Best Western Irazú (② **2220-2126;** www.graylinecostarica.com); and **Swiss Travel Service** (② **2282-4898;** www.swisstravelcr.com). These companies also offer a range of day trips out of San José. Almost all of the major hotels have tour desks, and most of the smaller hotels will also help arrange tours and day trips.

THE TOP ATTRACTIONS
In addition to the attractions listed below, you might consider a quick stop at San José's main **cathedral.** The church and its interior are largely unspectacular. How-ever, you'll see a pretty garden, as well as a massive marble statue of Pope Juan Pablo II, with a woman and child, carved by celebrated Costa Rican sculptor Jorge Jiménez Deredia. Deredia also has a work at the Vatican. The cathedral is located at the corner of Avenida 2 and Calle Central.

The **Museo Nacional de Costa Rica ★** (② **2257-1433;** www.museocostarica. go.cr/index.php?lang=en_en), located on Calle 17 between avenidas Central and 2 on the Plaza de la Democracia, is arguably Costa Rica's most important historical museum. You might also want to visit the **Centro Nacional de Arte y Cultura** (**National Center of Art and Culture;** ② **2255-3376;** www.madc.ac.cr), a full-city-block complex that houses the offices of the Cultural Ministry, several perform-ing arts centers, and the Museum of Contemporary Art and Design. It's located on Calle 13 between avenidas 3 and 5.

Museo de Arte Costarricense (Costa Rican Art Museum) ★★   This small museum at the end of Paseo Colón in Parque La Sabana was originally the country's principal airport terminal. Today it houses a collection of works in all mediums by Costa Rica's most celebrated artists. On display are some beautiful pieces in a wide range of styles, demonstrating how Costa Rican artists have interpreted and imitated the major European movements over the years. In addition to the permanent collec-tion, there are rotating temporary exhibits. Be sure to visit the outdoor sculpture garden, which features works by José Sancho, Jorge Jiménez Deredia, Max Jiménez, and Francisco Zuñiga. You can easily spend an hour or two at this museum—more if you take a stroll through the neighboring park.

Calle 42 and Paseo Colón, Parque La Sabana Este. ② **2222-7155.** www.musarco.go.cr. Admission $5 adults, $3 students with valid ID, free for children and seniors, free for everyone Sun. Tues–Fri 9am–5pm; Sat–Sun 10am–4pm.

Museo de Los Niños (Children's Museum) ☺ If you're traveling with children, you'll want to come here, and maybe even if you aren't. A former barracks and then a prison, this museum houses an extensive collection of exhibits designed to edify and entertain children of all ages. Experience a simulated earthquake or make music by dancing across the floor. Many exhibits encourage hands-on play. The museum sometimes features limited shows of "serious" art and is also the home of the National Auditorium. Be careful, though: The museum is large and spread out, so it's easy to lose track of a family member or friend.

This museum is a few blocks north of downtown, but the walk is through the worst part of the red-light district, so you might want to take a cab.

Calle 4 and Av. 9. ⓒ **2258-4929.** www.museocr.org. Admission $2.50 adults, $1.25 students and children 17 and under. Tues–Fri 8am–4:30pm; Sat–Sun 9:30am–5pm.

Museos del Banco Central de Costa Rica (Gold Museum) ★★ Directly beneath the Plaza de la Cultura, this underground museum houses one of the largest collections of pre-Columbian gold in the Americas. On display are more than 20,000 troy ounces of gold in more than 2,000 objects, spread over three floors. The number of pieces can be overwhelming, but the unusual display cases and complex lighting systems show off every piece to its utmost. This complex also includes a gallery for temporary art exhibits, numismatic and philatelic museums (coins and stamps, for us regular folks), a modest gift shop, and a branch of the Costa Rican Tourist Institute's info center. Plan to spend an hour or two here.

Calle 5, btw. avs. Central and 2, underneath the Plaza de la Cultura. ⓒ **2243-4202.** www.museosdel bancocentral.org. Admission $9 adults, $5 students, free for children 11 and under. Daily 9am–5pm.

OUTSIDE SAN JOSE

A host of excellent attractions and adventures await visitors just outside of San José. The following are some of my favorites:

Café Britt Farm ★ Although bananas are the main export of Costa Rica, most people are far more interested in the country's second-most-important export crop: coffee. Café Britt is one of the leading brands, and the company has put together an interesting tour and stage production at its farm, 20 minutes outside of San José. Here, you'll see how coffee is grown and visit the roasting and processing plant to learn how a coffee "cherry" is turned into a roasted bean. Tasting sessions are offered for visitors to experience the different qualities of coffee. There is also a restaurant and store where you can buy coffee and coffee-related gift items. The entire tour, including transportation, takes about 3 to 4 hours. Allow some extra time and an extra $10 for a visit to their nearby working plantation and mill. You can even strap on a basket and go out coffee picking during harvest time.

North of Heredia on the road to Barva. ⓒ **2277-1600.** www.coffeetour.com. Admission $20 adults, $16 children 6–11; $37 adults, $33 children, including transportation from downtown San José and a coffee drink. Add $15 for a full buffet lunch. Tour daily at 11am (additional tour at 3pm during high season). Store and restaurant daily 8am–5pm year-round.

INBio Park ★★ ☺ Run by the National Biodiversity Institute (Instituto Nacional de Biodiversidad, or INBio), this place is part museum, part educational center, and part nature park. In addition to watching a 15-minute video, visitors can tour two large pavilions explaining Costa Rica's biodiversity and natural wonders, and hike on trails that re-create the ecosystems of a tropical rainforest, dry forest, and premontane forest. A 2-hour guided hike is included in the fee, and self-guided-tour booklets are also available. There's a good-size butterfly garden, as well as a Plexiglas viewing window into the small lagoon. One of my favorite attractions here is the series of animal sculptures donated by one of Costa Rica's premier artists, José Sancho. There's a simple cafeteria-style restaurant for lunch, as well as a coffee shop and gift shop. You can easily spend 2 to 3 hours here.

400m (1,300 ft./4 blocks) north and 250m (820 ft./2½ blocks) west of the Shell station in Santo Domingo de Heredia. © **2507-8107.** www.inbio.ac.cr. Admission $23 adults, $13 children 12 and under. Packages that include transportation, entrance, and lunch $44. Tues–Fri 8:30am–4:30pm (admission closes at 2pm); Sat–Sun 9am–3:30pm.

La Paz Waterfall Gardens ★★ ☺ The original attraction here is a series of trails through primary and secondary forests alongside the La Paz River, with lookouts over a series of falls, including the namesake La Paz Fall. In addition to their orchid garden and a hummingbird garden, you must visit their huge butterfly garden, which is easily the largest in Costa Rica. A small serpentarium, featuring a mix of venomous and nonvenomous native snakes, and several terrariums containing various frogs and lizards are also parts of the attraction. There's even a man-made trout pond where you can cast for trout, or just take a swim with them. While the admission fee is a little steep, everything is wonderfully done and the trails and waterfalls are beautiful. A buffet lunch at the large cafeteria-style restaurant costs an extra $12 for adults, or $6 for kids. This is a good stop after a morning visit to the Poás Volcano. Plan to spend 2 to 4 hours here.

6km (3¾ miles) north of Varablanca on the road to San Miguel. © **2225-0643.** www.waterfallgardens. com. Admission $35 adults, $20 children and students with valid ID. Daily 8am–5pm. There is no bus service here, so you will need to come in a rental car or taxi, or arrange transport with the gardens.

Outdoor & Wellness Activities

Due to the chaos and pollution, you'll probably want to get out of the city before undertaking anything too strenuous. But if you want to brave the elements, there are a few outdoor activities in and around San José.

Parque La Sabana (at the western end of Paseo Colón), formerly San José's international airport, is the city's center for active sports and recreation. Here you'll find everything from jogging trails, soccer fields, and a few public tennis courts to the National Stadium. All the facilities are free and open to the public. Families gather for picnics, people fly kites, and there's even an outdoor sculpture garden. If you really want to experience the local culture, try getting into a pickup soccer game here. However, be careful in this park, especially at dusk or after dark, when it becomes a favorite haunt for youth gangs and muggers.

BIRD-WATCHING Serious birders will certainly want to head out of San José, but it is possible to see quite a few species in the metropolitan area. Two of the best spots for urban bird-watching are the campus at the **University of Costa Rica,** in the eastern suburb of San Pedro, and **Parque del Este** ★, located a little farther east on the road to San Ramón de Tres Ríos. You'll see a mix of urban species and, if you're lucky, a couple of hummingbirds or even a blue-crowned motmot. To get to the university, take any San Pedro bus from Avenida Central between calles 9 and 11. To get to Parque del Este, take the San Ramón/Parque del Este bus from Calle 9 between avenidas Central and 1. To find fellow birders, e-mail the **Birding Club of Costa Rica** ★★ (costaricabirding@hotmail.com), which organizes expeditions around the Central Valley and beyond.

GOLF & TENNIS   If you want to play tennis or golf in San José, your options are limited. If you're looking for a local experience on some rough concrete courts, you can take a racket and some balls down to **Parque La Sabana.** The best facilities for visiting golfers and tennis players are found at **Parque Valle del Sol ★** (© **2282-9222;** www.vallesol.com), in the western suburb of Santa Ana. The 18-hole course here is open to the general public. Greens fees are $94 per golfer per day, including the cart and unlimited playing on both the course and the driving range. The tennis courts here cost $8 per hour. Reservations are essential. The golf course at the Cariari Country Club is not open to the general public.

JOGGING   Try **Parque La Sabana,** or head to **Parque del Este,** which is east of town in the foothills above San Pedro. Take the San Ramón/Parque del Este bus from Calle 9 between avenidas Central and 1. It's never a good idea to jog at night, on busy streets, or alone. Women should be particularly careful about jogging alone. And remember, Tico drivers are not accustomed to joggers on residential streets, so don't expect drivers to give you much berth.

SOCCER (FUTBOL)   Ticos take their *fútbol* seriously. Costa Rican soccer is some of the best in Central America, and the national team, or *Sele* (*selección nacional*), qualified for the World Cup in 2002 and 2006, although they failed to qualify for the 2010 World Cup. The soccer season runs from September to June, with the finals spread out over several weeks in late June and early July.

You don't need to buy tickets in advance. Tickets generally run between $2 and $15. It's worth paying a little extra for *sombra numerado* (reserved seats in the shade). This will protect you from both the sun and the more rowdy aficionados. Costa Rican soccer fans take the sport seriously, and periodic violent incidents, both inside and outside the stadiums, have marred the sport, so be careful. Other options include *sombra* (general admission in the shade), *palco* and *palco numerado* (general admission and reserved mezzanine), and *sol general* (general admission in full sun).

The main San José team is Saprissa (affectionately called El Monstruo, or "The Monster"). **Saprissa's stadium** is in Tibás (© **2240-4034;** www.saprissa.co.cr; take any Tibás bus from Calle 2 and Av. 5). Games are often held on Sunday at 11am, but occasionally they are scheduled for Saturday afternoon or Wednesday evening. Check the local newspapers for game times and locations.

Shopping

THE SHOPPING SCENE   San José's central shopping corridor is bounded by avenidas 1 and 2, from about Calle 14 in the west to Calle 13 in the east. For several blocks west of the Plaza de la Cultura, **Avenida Central** is a pedestrian-only street mall where you'll find store after store of inexpensive clothes for men, women, and children. Depending on the mood of the police that day, you might find a lot of street vendors as well. Some shops close for lunch, while others remain open (it's just the luck of the draw for shoppers). You'll be happy to find that the sales and import taxes have already been figured into the display price.

MARKETS   There are several markets near downtown, but by far the largest is the **Mercado Central,** between avenidas Central and 1 and calles 6 and 8. Although this dark maze of stalls is primarily a food market, inside you'll find all manner of vendors, including a few selling Costa Rican souvenirs, crude leather goods, and musical instruments. Be careful about your wallet or purse and any prominent jewelry because skilled pickpockets frequent this area. All the streets surrounding the

Mercado Central are jammed with produce vendors selling from small carts or loading and unloading trucks. It's always a hive of activity, with crowds of people jostling for space on the streets. Street markets tend to operate roughly from around 7am to 5 or 6pm. Your best bet is to visit on Sunday or on weekdays; Saturday is particularly busy. In the hot days of the dry season, the aromas can get quite heady.

There is also a daily street market on the west side of the **Plaza de la Democracia.** Here you'll find two long rows of outdoor stalls selling T-shirts, Guatemalan and Ecuadorian handicrafts and clothing, small ceramic *ocarinas* (a small musical wind instrument), and handmade jewelry. The atmosphere here is much more open than at the Mercado Central, which I find just a bit too claustrophobic. You might be able to bargain prices down a little bit, but bargaining is not a traditional part of the vendor culture here, so you'll have to work hard to save a few dollars.

MODERN MALLS With globalization and modernization taking hold in Costa Rica, much of the local shopping scene has shifted to large megamalls. Modern multilevel affairs with cineplexes, food courts, and international brand-name stores are becoming more ubiquitous. The biggest and most modern of these malls include the **Mall San Pedro, Multiplaza, Terra Mall,** and **Mall Real Cariari.** Although they lack the charm of small shops found around San José, they are a reasonable option for one-stop shopping; most contain at least one or two local galleries and crafts shops, along with a large supermarket, which is always the best place to stock up on local coffee, hot sauces, liquors, and other nonperishable foodstuffs.

SHOPPING A TO Z

Boutique Annemarie Occupying two floors at the Hotel Don Carlos, this shop has an amazing array of wood products, leather goods, papier-mâché figurines, paintings, books, cards, posters, and jewelry. You'll see most of this stuff at the other shops, but not in such quantities or in such a relaxed and pressure-free environment. At the Hotel Don Carlos, Calle 9, btw. avs. 7 and 9. ✆ **2221-6063.**

Boutique Kiosco ★★ 🎒 This place features a range of original and one-off pieces of functional, wearable, and practical pieces made by contemporary Costa Rican and regional artists and designers. While the offerings are regularly changing, you'll usually find a mix of jewelry, handbags, shoes, dolls, furniture, and knickknacks. Often the pieces are made with recycled or sustainable materials. Calle 7 and Av. 11, Barrio Amón. ✆ 2258-1829. www.kioscosjo.com.

Galería 11–12 ★★★ This outstanding gallery deals mainly in high-end Costa Rican art, from neoclassical painters such as Teodorico Quirós to modern masters such as Francisco Amighetti and Paco Zuñiga, to current stars such as Rafa Fernández, Rodolfo Stanley, Fernando Carballo, and Fabio Herrera. Plaza Itzkatzu, off the Próspero Fernández Hwy., Escazú. ✆ **2288-1975.** www.galeria11-12.com.

Galería Namu ★★★ Galería Namu has some very high-quality arts and crafts, specializing in truly high-end indigenous works, including excellent Boruca and Huetar carved masks and "primitive" paintings. It also carries a good selection of more modern arts and craft pieces, including the ceramic work of Cecilia "Pefi" Figueres. This place organizes tours to visit various indigenous tribes and artisans as well. Av. 7 btw. calles 5 and 7. ✆ **2256-3412.** www.galerianamu.com.

Where to Stay

San José offers up a broad range of hotel choices, from large plush resorts and luxurious boutique inns to budget pensions charging only a few dollars a night. However, these two extremes are the exceptions, not the norm. The vast number of accommodations, and the best deals, are in the $80 to $160 price range. Within this relatively moderate bracket, you'll find restored homes that have been turned into small hotels and bed-and-breakfasts, modern hotels with pools and exercise rooms, and well-equipped downtown business hotels.

While, in general, there are plenty of rooms to go around in San José, the small boutique hotels and better-run establishments (including those recommended here) are often booked well in advance during the high season.

CHOOSING WHERE TO STAY   **Downtown hotels** are convenient to museums, restaurants, and shopping, but can be noisy. Many people are also bothered by the exhaust fumes that permeate downtown. Moreover, because the streets of downtown are not especially safe, particularly at night, you should plan on taking taxis whether you stay downtown or in a nearby neighborhood or suburb. **Barrio Amón** is the downtown neighborhood with the most character and remnants of colonial architecture. If you want clean air and a peaceful night's sleep, consider staying in the suburbs. **Escazú** and **Santa Ana** are quiet yet modern suburbs, and many of the hotels have great views. Heading east from downtown, **Los Yoses** is fairly close to the center of the action yet is still quiet. If you've rented a car, make sure your hotel provides secure parking or you'll have to find (and pay for) a nearby lot. If you plan to take some day tours, you can just as easily arrange these from a hotel situated outside the downtown area.

If you're heading out to Guanacaste, the central Pacific, or the northern zone, you might consider a hotel or bed-and-breakfast either near or beyond the airport. Sure, you give up proximity to downtown, but you can cut as much as an hour off your travel time to any of these destinations. Many car-rental companies will even deliver to or pick up cars from these establishments.

DOWNTOWN SAN JOSE/BARRIO AMON
Expensive
In addition to the hotel listed below, **Clarion Amón Plaza** (Av. 11 and Calle 3 bis; ℂ 877/424-6423 in the U.S. and Canada, or 2523-4600 in Costa Rica) is a dependable business-class option.

Radisson Europa Hotel ★★   This hotel is geared mainly to business travelers, but is a good choice for anyone wanting a big, dependable hotel near downtown San José. Angular window nooks and other small architectural details give these rooms an edge over those in the Clarion Amón Plaza, although it's not as convenient for walking around downtown. It is, however, particularly well located if you are driving to or from the Caribbean coast, as it is set right off the main downtown entrance to the highway to Guápiles.

Calle Blancos, behind La República building, San José. ℂ **800/395-7046** the U.S., or 2257-3257. Fax 2257-8221. www.radisson.com. 210 units. $190 double; $230 executive room; $280 junior suite. Rates include continental breakfast. AE, DC, MC, V. Free parking. **Amenities:** 2 restaurants; bar; lounge; casino; executive-level rooms; extensive health club; outdoor pool; room service; smoke-free rooms. *In room:* A/C, TV, hair dryer, minibar, free Wi-Fi.

Moderate
In addition to the hotels listed below, the **Sleep Inn** (Av. 3 btw. calles 9 and 11; ℂ **2222-0101;** www.sleepinnsanjose.com) is a modern, American-style chain hotel in the heart of downtown. The **Hotel Britannia** (Calle 3 and Av. 11; ℂ **800/263-2618** in the U.S., or 2223-6667; www.hotelbritanniacostarica.com) is the most

elegant of the many small hotels in downtown that have been created from restored old houses. **Hotel Doña Inés** (✆ 2222-7443; www.donaines.com), on Calle 11 between avenidas 2 and 6, and **Hotel Santo Tomás** (✆ 877/446-0658 in the U.S., or 2255-0448 in Costa Rica; www.hotelsantotomas.com), on Avenida 7, between calles 3 and 5, are two little boutique hotels that are also good options. The **Gran Hotel Costa Rica** (✆ 800/949-0592 in the U.S., or 2221-4000; www.grandhotel costarica.com) is arguably the best located of any downtown hotel, near the Teatro Nacional and the Plaza de la Cultura.

Hotel Don Carlos ★★ 🎁 If you're looking for a small downtown hotel that is unmistakably Costa Rican and hints at the days of the planters and coffee barons, this is the place for you. Located in an old residential neighborhood, only blocks from the business district, the Don Carlos was a former president's mansion. Inside you'll find a slew of arts-and-crafts works and archaeological reproductions, as well as orchids, ferns, palms, and parrots. The rooms are all distinct and vary greatly in size, so be specific when you reserve, or ask if it's possible to see a few when you check in. Breakfast is served in an outdoor orchid garden and atrium. The gift shop here is one of the largest in the country.

779 Calle 9, btw. avs. 7 and 9, San José. ✆ **2221-6707.** Fax 2221-9678. www.doncarloshotel.com. 33 units. $80–$90 double. Rates include continental breakfast. AE, MC, V. Free parking. **Amenities:** Restaurant; bar; Jacuzzi; room service. *In room:* TV, hair dryer, free Wi-Fi.

Inexpensive

In addition to the place listed below, **Kap's Place** (✆ 2221-1169; www.kapsplace. com), located across from the Hotel Aranjuez on Calle 19 between avenidas 11 and 13, is another good choice, while real budget hounds might want to try **Tranquilo Backpackers** (✆ 2222-2493; www.tranquilobackpackers.com), on Calle 7 between avenidas 9 and 11; **Pensión de la Cuesta** (✆ 2256-7946; www.pension delacuesta.com), at 1332 Cuesta de Núñez, Avenida 1 between calles 11 and 15; or **Costa Rica Backpackers** (✆ 2221-6191; www.costaricabackpackers.com), on Avenida 6 between calles 21 and 23.

Hotel Aranjuez ★ 🍃 This is probably the best and deservedly most popular budget option close to downtown. On a quiet and safe street in the Barrio Amón neighborhood, this humble hotel is made up of five contiguous houses. Rooms and bathrooms vary greatly in size, so ask when reserving, or try to see a few rooms when you arrive. The nicest features here, aside from the convivial hostel-like atmosphere, are the lush and shady gardens; the hanging orchids, bromeliads, and ferns decorating the hallways and nooks; and the numerous open lounge areas furnished with chairs, tables, and couches—great for lazing around and sharing travel tales with your fellow guests. The hotel has a couple of computers, as well as a free Wi-Fi network, and provides free local calling.

Calle 19, btw. avs. 11 and 13, San José. ✆ **2256-1825.** Fax 2223-3528. www.hotelaranjuez.com. 35 units, 6 with shared bathroom. $25 double with shared bathroom; $42–$56 double with private bathroom. Rates include breakfast buffet and taxes. AE, MC, V. Free parking. **Amenities:** Restaurant; bar; several lounge areas. *In room:* TV, free Wi-Fi.

LA SABANA/PASEO COLON
Moderate

Hotel Grano de Oro ★★ 🎁 San José boasts dozens of old homes that have been converted into hotels, but the Grano de Oro tops them all in terms of design, comfort, and service. On a quiet side street off Paseo Colón, it offers a variety of room types to fit a range of budgets and tastes. I favor the patio rooms, which have French doors opening onto private patios. The Vista de Oro suite is the hotel's crown jewel, with its own private staircase and wonderful views of the city and surrounding mountains. If you don't grab one of the suites (which have whirlpool tubs), you still have access to the hotel's two rooftop Jacuzzis. The **restaurant** serves excellent international cuisine and some of the city's best desserts. The hotel owners support a noble shelter for young, unwed mothers, Casa Luz. Feel free to inquire as to how you can help.

Calle 30, no. 251, btw. avs. 2 and 4, 150m (492 ft./1½ blocks) south of Paseo Colón, San José. © **2255-3322.** Fax 2221-2782. www.hotelgranodeoro.com. 40 units. $123 double; $186 suite. AE, MC, V. Free parking. **Amenities:** Restaurant; bar; lounge; concierge; 2 rooftop Jacuzzis; room service; all rooms smoke-free. *In room:* TV, minibar, free Wi-Fi.

SAN PEDRO/LOS YOSES
Moderate

In addition to the places below, the **Hotel Boutique Jade** (© **2224-2455;** www.hotelboutiquejade.com) is a business-class hotel with an excellent restaurant, while the **Hotel 1492 Jade y Oro** (© **2256-5913;** www.hotel1492.com) is a good option in a converted home, with interesting artwork.

Hôtel Le Bergerac ★★ 👜 With charm and sophistication, the Hôtel Le Bergerac has ingratiated itself over the years with business travelers and members of various diplomatic missions. Still, you don't have to be a diplomat or business traveler to enjoy this hotel's charms. Le Bergerac is composed of three houses with courtyard gardens in between. Almost all the rooms are fairly large, and each is a little different. I favor those with private patio gardens. In the evenings candlelight and classical music set a relaxing and romantic mood.

Calle 35 no. 50, San José. © **2234-7850.** Fax 2225-9103. www.bergerachotel.com. 25 units. $90–$145 double. Rates include full breakfast. AE, DC, MC, V. Free parking. **Amenities:** Restaurant; lounge; concierge. *In room:* TV, hair dryer.

ESCAZU & SANTA ANA

About 15 minutes west of San José and about the same distance from the international airport, these affluent suburbs have experienced rapid growth in recent years. Both Escazú and Santa Ana are popular with the Costa Rican professional class and North American retirees and expatriates, and quite a few hotels have sprung up to cater to their needs. It's relatively easy to commute between Escazú or Santa Ana and downtown via bus or taxi.

The **Real InterContinental San José** (© **2208-2100;** www.interconti.com) is a large, upscale resort hotel just off the highway, adjacent to a major shopping mall. The **Hotel Milvia** (© **2225-4543;** www.hotelmilvia.com) is an offbeat small hotel with bright, airy rooms.

Expensive

Alta Hotel ★★ This small boutique hotel is infused with old-world charm. Curves and high arches abound. My favorite touch is the winding interior alleyway that snakes down from the reception through the hotel. Most of the rooms here have wonderful views of the Central Valley from private balconies; the others have pleasant garden patios. The rooms are all up to modern resort standards, although some have slightly cramped bathrooms. The suites are considerably larger, each with a separate sitting room with its own television, as well as large Jacuzzi-style tubs in spacious bathrooms. If you opt to rent the entire upper floor, the penthouse becomes a three-bedroom, full-floor extravaganza, with a massive living room and open-air rooftop patio. The hotel's **La Luz** restaurant is one of the more elegant and creative dining spots in the Central Valley.

Alto de las Palomas, old road to Santa Ana. © **888/388-2582** in the U.S. and Canada, or 2282-4160. Fax 2282-4162. www.thealtahotel.com. 23 units. $149 double; $179 junior suite; $199 master suite; $820 penthouse. Rates include continental breakfast. AE, DC, MC, V. Free parking. **Amenities:** Restaurant; bar; concierge; small exercise room; Jacuzzi; midsize outdoor pool; room service; sauna. *In room:* A/C, TV, hair dryer, minibar, free Wi-Fi.

Moderate

In addition to the hotels listed below, the **Courtyard San José** (© **888/236-2427** in the U.S. and Canada, or 2208-3000; www.marriott.com) and **Quality Hotel Santa Ana** (© **877/424-6423** in the U.S. and Canada, or 2204-6700; www.choice hotels.com) are both modern business-class hotels a few miles from each other, right on the western Próspero Fernández Highway connecting Santa Ana and Escazú with San José. **Casa de las Tías** (© **2289-5517**; www.hotels.co.cr/casatias.html) is a quaint, family-run hotel in downtown Escazú.

Hotel Casa Alegre 🗱   Housed in a converted home on a residential side street just a couple of blocks from Santa Ana's central square and church, this hotel offers spacious, comfortable rooms. The decor leans heavily on Southwest American artwork and design touches, combined with Guatemalan textiles and locally made heavy wooden furniture. My favorite rooms are the upstairs units. Room nos. 3 and 4 even have skylights in their bathrooms. A midsize outdoor pool, which is good for lap swimming, takes up much of the backyard, but there's also a shady lounge area out back.

Santa Ana. © **2203-7467.** Fax 2241-2906. www.hotelcasaalegre.com. 8 units. $70–$87 double. Rates include full breakfast. MC, V. **Amenities:** Pool. *In room:* TV, free Wi-Fi.

HEREDIA & ALAJUELA (AIRPORT AREA)

Alajuela and Heredia, two colonial-era cities that lie much closer to the airport than San José, are great places to find small, distinct, and charming hotels. If you plan to get yourself to a remote beach or rainforest lodge and to use San José and the Central Valley as a transportation hub, or if you just detest urban clutter, noise, and pollution, you might do well to choose one of the hotels listed below.

Very Expensive

In addition to the places below, the **Doubletree Cariari by Hilton** (© **800/222-8733** in the U.S. and Canada, or 2239-0022; www.cariarisanjose.doubletree.com) is a modern resort hotel near the airport, while **Xandari Resort & Spa** ★★ (© **866/363-3212** in the U.S., or 2443-2020 in Costa Rica; www.xandari.com) and **Vista del Valle Plantation Inn** ★★ (© **2450-0800** or ©/fax 2451-1165; www.vistadel valle.com) are two more luxury boutique hotels worth considering. Part of the La Paz Waterfall Gardens (p. 571), **Peace Lodge** is another good option in this category (© **954/727-3997** in the U.S., or 2482-2720 or 2482-5100 in Costa Rica; www. waterfallgardens.com).

Finca Rosa Blanca Coffee Plantation & Inn ★★★ 🗱   Finca Rosa Blanca is an architectural gem set amid the lush, green hillsides of a coffee plantation. There's a turret atop the main building, walls of glass, arched windows, and curves instead of corners at almost every turn. If breathtaking bathrooms are your idea of luxury, consider splurging on the Rosa Blanca suite, which has a stone waterfall that cascades into a tub in front of a huge picture window, and a spiral staircase that leads to the top of the turret. All of the suites and villas have the same sense of eclectic luxury, with beautiful tile work, fabulous views, and creative design touches. The restaurant and spa here are top-notch, and the owners have a real and noticeable dedication to sustainable practices. The hotel has 14 hectares (35 acres) of organic coffee under cultivation, and their in-house coffee tour is not to be missed.

Santa Bárbara de Heredia. ✆ **2269-9392.** Fax 2269-9555. www.fincarosablanca.com. 13 units. $290–$490 double. Rates include breakfast. AE, MC, V. Free parking. **Amenities:** Restaurant; bar; lounge; babysitting; concierge; small free-form pool set in the hillside; room service; all rooms smoke-free; full-service spa. *In room:* Minibar, free Wi-Fi.

Marriott Costa Rica Hotel ★★★   For my money, the Marriott remains the best large luxury resort hotel in the San José metropolitan area. The hotel is designed in a mixed colonial style, with hand-painted Mexican tiles, antique red-clay roof tiles, weathered columns, and heavy wooden doors, lintels, and trim. The centerpiece is a large open-air interior patio that somewhat replicates Old Havana's Plaza de Armas. All rooms are plush and well-appointed, with either a king-size or two double beds, a working desk, an elegant wooden armoire, plenty of closet space, a comfortable sitting chair and ottoman, and a small "Juliet" balcony. The casual **Antigua** restaurant serves well-prepared Costa Rican and international dishes, and there's a more upscale Spanish restaurant and tapas bar. The large lobby-level bar features daily piano music and weekend jazz nights, with both indoor and patio seating.

San Antonio de Belén. ✆ **888/236-2427** in the U.S. and Canada, or 2298-0844 in Costa Rica. Fax 2298-0011. www.marriott.com. 299 units. $260 double; $315 executive level; $600 master suite; $1,000 presidential suite. AE, DC, MC, V. Free valet parking. **Amenities:** 3 restaurants; bar; lounge; free airport transfers; babysitting; concierge; golf driving range; small but well-appointed health club; Jacuzzi; 2 outdoor pools; room service; sauna; smoke-free rooms; 2 tennis courts. *In room:* A/C, TV, hair dryer, minibar, Wi-Fi.

Moderate

In addition to the place listed below, **Viña Romantica** (✆ **2430-7621;** www.vinaromantica.com) is a cozy new bed-and-breakfast in the hills just above Alajuela, which is earning strong praise for its amiable hosts and excellent restaurant. **Pura Vida Hotel** (✆ **2441-1157;** www.puravidahotel.com) and **Orquídeas Inn** (✆ **2433-7128;** www.orquideasinn.com) are popular Alajuela options convenient to the airport as well.

However, if you want to be right next to the airport, check out the **Hampton Inn & Suites** (✆ **800/426-7866** in the U.S., or 2436-0000 in Costa Rica; www.hamptoninn.com).

Hotel Bougainvillea ★ 🖋   The Hotel Bougainvillea is an excellent choice—a great value if you're looking for a hotel in a quiet residential neighborhood not far from downtown. It offers most of the amenities of the more expensive resort hotels around the Central Valley, but it charges considerably less. Rooms are carpeted and have small triangular balconies oriented to the wonderful views across the valley. The hillside property's gardens are beautifully designed and well tended, with pretty good bird-watching. The hotel has an extensive recycling program and is working hard to implement sustainable tourism practices.

In Santo Tomás de Santo Domingo de Heredia, 100m (328 ft./1 block) west of the Escuela de Santo Tomás, San José. ✆ **2244-1414.** Fax 2244-1313. www.hb.co.cr. 81 units. $110–$125 double; $140 suite. AE, DC, MC, V. Free parking. **Amenities:** Restaurant; bar; babysitting; midsize pool in attractive garden; room service; sauna; smoke-free rooms; 2 lighted tennis courts. *In room:* TV, hair dryer, Wi-Fi for small fee.

Where to Dine

DOWNTOWN SAN JOSE

Moderate

Café Mundo ★ 🍴 INTERNATIONAL   This place mixes contemporary cuisine with an ambience of casual elegance. Wood tables and Art Deco wrought-iron chairs are spread spaciously around several rooms in this former colonial mansion. Additional seating can be had on the open-air front veranda and in the small gardens both in front and out back. The appetizers include vegetable tempura, crab cakes, and chicken satay alongside more traditional Tico standards such as *patacones* (fried plantain chips) and fried yuca. There's a long list of pastas and pizzas, as well as more substantial main courses, nightly specials, and delicious desserts. One room here boasts colorful wall murals by Costa Rican artist Miguel Casafont. This place is almost always packed to the gills with a broad mix of San José's gay, bohemian, theater, arts, and university crowds.

Calle 15 and Av. 9, 200m (656 ft./2 blocks) east and 100m (328 ft./1 block) north of the INS building. ✆ **2222-6190.** Reservations recommended. Main courses $6–$28. AE, MC, V. Mon–Thurs 11am–11:30pm; Fri 11am–midnight; Sat 5–11:30pm.

Cafeteria 1930 📷 INTERNATIONAL   With veranda and patio seating directly fronting the Plaza de la Cultura, this is one of the most atmospheric spots for a casual bite and some good people-watching. A wrought-iron railing, white columns, and arches create an old-world atmosphere; on the plaza in front of the cafe, a marimba band performs and vendors sell handicrafts. Stop by for the breakfast and watch the plaza vendors set up their booths, or peruse the *Tico Times* over coffee while you have your shoes polished. The menu covers a lot of ground, and the food is respectable, if unspectacular, but there isn't a better place downtown to bask in the tropical sunshine while you sip a beer or have a light lunch, and it's a great place to come before or after a show at the Teatro Nacional.

At the Gran Hotel Costa Rica, Av. 2, btw. calles 1 and 3. ✆ **2221-4011.** Sandwiches $6.50–$12; main courses $7–$32. AE, DC, MC, V. Daily 6am–10pm.

Inexpensive

In addition to the places listed below, the **Q'Café** (✆ **2221-0707**) is a delightful little European-style cafe with a pretty perch above the busy corner of Avenida Central and Calle 2. Try to grab a seat overlooking the action on the street below. Vegetarians might want to head to one of several **Vishnu** (✆ **2256-6063**) restaurants located around downtown and the central valley.

Café del Teatro Nacional ★ CAFE/COFFEEHOUSE   Even if there's no show during your visit, you can enjoy a light meal, sandwich, dessert, or a coffee here, while soaking up the neoclassical atmosphere. The theater was built in the 1890s from the designs of European architects, and the Art Nouveau chandeliers, ceiling murals, and marble floors and tables are pure Parisian. The ambience is French-cafe chic, but the marimba music drifting in from outside the open window and the changing art exhibits by local artists will remind you that you're still in Costa Rica. On sunny days, there's outdoor seating at wrought-iron tables on the side of the theater. In addition to the regular hours of operation listed below, the cafe is open until 8pm any evening that there is a performance in the theater.

In the Teatro Nacional, Av. 2 btw. calles 3 and 5. ✆ **2221-1329.** Sandwiches $4–$7; main courses $5–$12. AE, MC, V. Mon–Sat 9am–4:30pm.

DINING UNDER THE stars ON A MOUNTAIN'S EDGE

Although there are myriad unique experiences to be had in Costa Rica, one of my favorites is dining on the side of a volcano with the lights of San José shimmering below. These hanging restaurants, called *miradores,* are a resourceful response to the city's topography. Because San José is set in a broad valley surrounded on all sides by volcanic mountains, people who live in these mountainous areas have no place to go but up—so they do, building roadside cafes vertically up the sides of the volcanoes.

The food at most of these establishments is not spectacular, but the views often are, particularly at night, when the wide valley sparkles in a wash of lights. While the town of **Aserri,** 10km (6¼ miles) south of downtown San José, is the king of *miradores,* there are also *miradores* in the hills above Escazú and

in San Ramón de Tres Ríos and Heredia. The most popular is **Le Monestère** (✆ **2289-4404;** www.monastere-restaurant.com; closed Sun), an elegant converted church serving somewhat overrated French and Belgian cuisine in a spectacular setting above the hills of Escazú. I recommend coming here just for the less formal **La Cava Grill ★,** which often features live music, mostly folk-pop but sometimes jazz. I also like **Mirador Tiquicia ★** (✆ **2289-5839;** www.miradortiquicia.com), which occupies several rooms in a sprawling old Costa Rican home and has live folkloric dance shows on Thursday. This latter place offers a free shuttle Tuesday through Friday, which you can reserve, at least 1 day in advance, at ✆ **8381-3141** (tiquicia.shuttle.service@gmail. com).

LA SABANA/PASEO COLON
Expensive

Grano de Oro Restaurant ★★★ INTERNATIONAL   Set around the lovely interior courtyard of the Hotel Grano de Oro (p. 575), this restaurant manages to have an atmosphere that's intimate, relaxed, and refined, all at the same time. The menu features a wide range of meat and fish dishes. The *lomito piemontes* is two medallions of filet mignon stuffed with Gorgonzola cheese in a sherry sauce, while the lamb chops come with an herbs de Provence, pistachio, and macadamia nut crust. Be sure to save room for the "Grano de Oro pie," a decadent dessert with various layers of chocolate and coffee mousses and creams. This place also has a good wine list, including a range of options by the glass.

Calle 30, no. 251, btw. avs. 2 and 4, 150m (492 ft./1½ blocks) south of Paseo Colón. ✆ **2255-3322.** Reservations recommended. Main courses $14–$44. AE, MC, V. Daily 6am–10pm.

Park Café ★★★ FUSION   Having opened and run a Michelin two-star restaurant in London and another one-star joint in Cannes, Richard Neat now finds himself turning out his fusion cuisine in an intimate space spread around the interior patio courtyard of a stately old downtown mansion, which doubles as an antiques and furniture store. The menu changes regularly but might feature roasted scallops with ricotta tortellini in a pumpkin jus, or some expertly grilled quail on a vegetable purée bed, topped with poached quail egg. Presentations are artfully done, and often served in such a way as to encourage sharing. The well-thought-out and fairly priced wine list is a perfect complement to the cuisine.

Sabana Norte, 1 block north of Rostipollos. ⓒ **2290-6324.** Reservations recommended. Main courses $13-$25. AE, MC, V. Tues-Sat 12:15-2:15pm and 7:15-9:15pm.

Moderate

Meat aficionados should head to **El Chicote ★** (Av. Las Américas; ⓒ **2232-0936** or 2232-3777; www.elchicote.com), one of San José's most venerable and popular steakhouses.

Machu Picchu ★ PERUVIAN/INTERNATIONAL   Machu Picchu is an unpretentious little restaurant that is perennially one of the most popular places in San José. The menu is classic Peruvian. One of my favorite entrees is the *causa limeña,* lemon-flavored mashed potatoes stuffed with shrimp. The ceviche here is excellent, as is the *ají de gallina,* a dish of shredded chicken in a fragrant cream sauce, and octopus with garlic butter. For main dishes, I recommend *corvina a lo macho,* sea bass in a slightly spicy tomato-based seafood sauce. Be sure to ask for a pisco sour, a classic Peruvian drink made from pisco, a grape liquor. These folks have a sister restaurant over in San Pedro (ⓒ **2283-3679**).

Calle 32, btw. avs. 1 and 3, 150m (492 ft./1½ blocks) north of the KFC on Paseo Colón. ⓒ **2222-7384.** www.restaurantemachupicchu.com. Reservations recommended. Main courses $8-$16. AE, DC, MC, V. Mon-Sat 11am-10pm; Sun 11am-6pm.

Inexpensive

Soda Tapia COSTA RICAN   The food is unspectacular, dependable, and quite inexpensive at this very popular local diner. There's seating inside the brightly lit dining room, as well as on the sidewalk-style patio fronting the parking area. Dour but efficient waitstaff take the order you mark down on your combination menu/bill. This is a great place for late-night eats or for before or after a visit to Parque La Sabana or the Museo de Arte Costarricense. These folks also have another site in a small strip mall in Santa Ana (ⓒ **2203-7174**).

Calle 42 and Av. 2, across from the Museo de Arte Costarricense. ⓒ **2222-6734.** Sandwiches $2-$4; main dishes $4.50-$9. AE, MC, V. Daily 2-9pm.

SAN PEDRO/LOS YOSES

In addition to the restaurants listed below, local and visiting vegetarians swear by the little **Comida Para Sentir Restaurante Vegetariano San Pedro** (ⓒ **2224-1163**), located 125m (410 ft./1¼ blocks) north of the San Pedro Church. Despite the massive size and popularity of the nearby **Il Pomodoro,** I prefer **Pane E Vino** (ⓒ **2280-2869;** www.paneevino.co.cr), an excellent pasta-and-pizza joint on the eastern edge of San Pedro, with other outlets around town, as well.

If you want to experience an excellent Argentine-style steakhouse, head to **Donde Carlos** (ⓒ **2225-0819;** www.dondecarlos.com) in Los Yoses. Finally, if you're hankering for sushi, try **Ichiban ★** (ⓒ **2253-8012;** www.ichibanrestaurante.com), in San Pedro, or **Matsuri ★** (ⓒ **2280-5522**), a little farther east in Curridabat.

Moderate

Olio ★ ⚐ MEDITERRANEAN   Exposed brick walls, dark-wood wainscoting, and stained-glass lamps imbue this place with character and romance. Couples will want to grab a table in a quiet nook, since groups tend to dominate the large main room or crowd the bar. The extensive tapas menu features traditional Spanish fare, as well as bruschetta, antipasti, and a Greek *mezza* plate. For a main dish, I recommend the chicken Vesuvio, which is marinated first in a balsamic vinegar reduction and finished with a creamy herb sauce; or the *arrollado siciliano,* a thin filet of steak rolled around spinach, sun-dried tomatoes, and mozzarella cheese and topped with a pomodoro sauce. The midsize wine list features reasonably priced wines from Italy, France, Spain, Germany, Chile, Greece, and even Bulgaria. *Nonsmokers, be forewarned:* The bar and dining areas here are often tightly packed and smoke-filled.

Barrio California, 200m (656 ft./2 blocks) north of Bagelman's. 🕐 **2281-0541.** Reservations recommended. Main courses $5–$12. AE, DC, MC, V. Mon–Wed noon–11pm; Thurs–Fri noon–midnight; Sat 6pm–midnight.

Inexpensive

Whappin' ★ 🍴 COSTA RICAN/CARIBBEAN   You don't have to go to Limón or Cahuita to get good home-cooked Caribbean food. In addition to *rondon,* a coconut milk–based stew or soup, you can also get the classic rice and beans cooked in coconut milk, as well as a range of fish and chicken dishes from the coastal region. I like the whole red snapper in a spicy sauce of sautéed onions. There's a small bar at the entrance and some tables spread around the restaurant, with an alcove here and there. Everything is simple, and prices are reasonable. After a dinner of fresh fish, with rice, beans, and *patacones,* the only letdown is that the beach is 4 hours away.

Barrio Escalante, 200m (656 ft./2 blocks) east of El Farolito. 🕐 **2283-1480.** www.whapin.com. Main courses $9–$26. AE, MC, V. Mon–Sat 8am–2:30pm and 6–10pm.

ESCAZU & SANTA ANA

These two suburbs on the western side of town have the most vibrant restaurant scenes in San José. A good one-stop option to consider is the Plaza Itskatzu shopping center, just off the highway and sharing a parking lot with the Courtyard San José. Here you'll find a wide variety of moderately priced restaurant options, including **Tutti Li** (🕐 **2588-2405**), a good Italian restaurant and pizzeria; **Chancay** (🕐 **2288-2327**), which serves Peruvian and Peruvian/Chinese cuisine; and **Las Tapas de Manuel** ★ (🕐 **2288-5700**), a Spanish-style tapas restaurant. In addition, **Il Panino** ★ (🕐 **2228-3126**) is an upscale sandwich shop and cafe, located in the Centro Comercial El Paco. Barbecue Los Anonos ★ (🕐 **2228-0180**), 600m (1,970 ft.) west of the Los Anonos bridge in San Rafael de Escazú, offers good steaks and well-prepared Costa Rican cuisine, making this homey restaurant something of an institution.

Expensive

Bacchus ★★★ 🍴 ITALIAN   My favorite Italian restaurant in the San José metropolitan area, this place is housed in a historic home that is over a century old. Nevertheless, this place somehow seamlessly blends the old with the new in an elegant atmosphere. The best tables are on the covered back patio, where you can watch the open kitchen and wood-burning pizza oven in action. The regularly changing menu features a range of antipasti, pastas, pizzas, and main dishes. Everything is perfectly prepared and beautifully presented. The desserts are also excellent, and the wine list is extensive and fairly priced.

Downtown Santa Ana. 🕐 **2282-5441.** Reservations required. Main courses $8–$24. AE, MC, V. Mon–Sat noon–3pm and 6–11pm; Sun noon–9pm.

Moderate

La Cava Grill ★ 🍴 COSTA RICAN/STEAK   This place is a cozy and warm spot built underneath the popular yet overpriced and overrated Le Monestère restaurant. While the decor is much less ornate, the service much less formal, and the menu much less French, the view is just as spectacular. Grab a window seat on a clear night and enjoy the sparkle of the lights below. The menu features a range of simply prepared meat, poultry, and fish. More adventurous diners can try the *tepezquintle* (a large rodent, also called a *paca*), which is actually quite tasty. There's live music and a festive party most weekend nights in the attached bar. My big complaint here is that the wine list is borrowed from the upstairs restaurant, and is pretentious and overpriced.

1.5km (1 mile) south of Centro Comercial Paco; follow the signs to Le Monestère. ☏ **2228-8515.** Reservations recommended. Main courses $6–$25. AE, MC, V. Mon–Sat 6pm–1:30am.

San José After Dark

Catering to a mix of tourists, students, and party-loving Ticos, San José has a host of options. You'll find plenty of interesting clubs and bars, a wide range of theaters, and some very lively discos and dance salons.

To find out what's going on in San José while you're in town, pick up a copy of the *Tico Times* (English) or *La Nación* (Spanish). The former is a good place to find out where local expatriates are hanging out; the latter's "Viva" and "Tiempo Libre" sections have extensive listings of discos, movie theaters, and live music.

THE BAR SCENE Lounge lizards will be happy in most hotel bars in the downtown area, while students and the young at heart will have no problem mixing in at the livelier spots around town. Sports fans can find plenty of places to catch the most important games, and there are even a couple of brewpubs.

The best part of the bar scene in San José is something called a *boca,* the equivalent of a tapa in Spain: a little dish of snacks that arrives at your table when you order a drink. Although this is a somewhat dying tradition, especially in the younger, hipper bars, you will still find *bocas* in the older, more traditional San José drinking establishments. In most, the *bocas* are free, but in some, where the dishes are more sophisticated, you'll have to pay. You'll find drinks reasonably priced, with beer around $2 to $3 a bottle, and mixed drinks costing $2 to $5.

The funky 2-block stretch of **San Pedro ★★** just south of the University of Costa Rica has been dubbed La Calle de Amargura, or the "Street of Bitterness," and it's the heart and soul of the college and youth scene. Bars and cafes are mixed in with bookstores and copy shops. After dark the streets are packed with teens, punks, students, and professors barhopping and just hanging around. You can walk the strip until someplace strikes your fancy—you don't need a travel guide to find **Omar Khayyám** (☏ **2253-8455**), **Marrakech Pool & Pizza** (☏ **2253-2049**), **Tavarua Surf & Skate Bar** (☏ **2225-7249**), or **Caccio's** (☏ **2224-3261**), which lie at the heart of this district. *Note:* La Calle de Amargura attracts a certain unsavory element. Use

---

El Pueblo: A One-Stop Shop

A good place to sample a range of San José's nightlife is in **El Pueblo**, a shopping, dining, and entertainment complex done up like an old Spanish village. It's just across the river to the north of town. The best way to get there is by taxi; all the drivers know El Pueblo well. Within the alleyways that wind through El Pueblo are a dozen or more bars, clubs, and discos—there's even an indoor soccer playing field. **Fiesta Latina** (☏ **2222-8782**), **Twister** (☏ **2222-5746**), and **Friends** (☏ **2233-5283**) are happening party spots. For a mellower option, inside El Pueblo, try **Café Art Boruca** (☏ **2221-3615**).

caution here. Try to visit with a group, and try not to carry large amounts of cash or wear flashy jewelry.

Other good options include **El Observatorio** ★ (Calle 23 btw. avs. Central and 1; ✆ **2223-0725**) and **El Cuartel de la Boca del Monte** ★★ (Av. 1 btw. calles 21 and 23; 50m/164 ft./½ block west of the Cine Magaly; ✆ **2221-0327**). The latter is a local institution and packed to the gills most nights Wednesday through Saturday.

If you want a taste of old San José, check out **Chelles** ★ (Av. Central and Calle 9; ✆ **2221-1369**), a bare-bones 24-hour joint in the heart of downtown.

THE GAY & LESBIAN SCENE Because Costa Rica is such a conservative Catholic country, the GLBT communities here are rather discreet. Homosexuality is not generally under attack, but many gay and lesbian organizations guard their privacy, and the club scene is changeable and not well publicized.

The most established bar and dance club is **La Avispa** ★, Calle 1 between avenidas 8 and 10 (✆ **2223-5343**; www.laavispa.co.cr). It is popular with both men and women, although it sometimes sets aside certain nights of the week or month for specific persuasions. There's also **Club Oh** (✆ **2221-9341**), on Calle 2 between avenidas 14 and 16; **Pucho's Bar** (✆ **2256-1147**), on Calle 11 and Avenida 8; and **El Bochinche** (✆ **2221-0500**; www.bochinchesanjose.com), on Calle 11 between avenidas 10 and 12.

DANCE CLUBS To mix with locals, head to **Castro's** ★ (✆ **2256-8789**; Av. 13 and Calle 22, Barrio Mexico), which has several dance and lounge areas spread over several floors, or **El Tobogán** ★★ (✆ **2223-8920**; 200m/656 ft./2 blocks north and 100m/328 ft./1 block east of the La República main office, off the Guápiles Hwy.), where the dance floor seems to be as big as a football field.

For a younger, more contemporary scene, try **Club Blu** (✆ **2233-3814**; Calle 3 btw. avs. 1 and 3) or **Vértigo** (✆ **2257-8424**; Edificio Colón, Paseo Colón).

Most places charge a nominal cover; sometimes it includes a drink or two.

LIVE MUSIC The daily "Viva" and Friday's "Tiempo Libre" sections of *La Nación* newspaper have weekly performance schedules.

Perhaps the most dependable club to catch live music is the **Jazz Café** ★ (✆ **2253-8933**; www.jazzcafecostarica.com) in San Pedro, or its sister club **Jazz Café Escazú** (✆ **2288-4740**), just off the highway between San José and Escazú.

Visiting artists stop in Costa Rica on a regular basis. Recent concerts have featured Guns 'N Roses, Metallica and Korn, Argentine pop star Fito Páez, Colombian cumbia sensation Carlos Vives, and Spanish rocker Joaquin Sabina. Many of these performances take place in San José's two historic theaters, the **Teatro Nacional** (see below) and the **Teatro Melico Salazar,** Avenida 2 between calles Central and 2 (✆ **2233-5424** or 2257-6005; www.teatromelico.go.cr), as well as at the **Auditorio Nacional** (see below). Really large shows are usually held at soccer stadiums or large, natural amphitheaters.

PERFORMING ARTS Theater is very popular in Costa Rica, and downtown San José is studded with small theaters. However, tastes tend toward the burlesque. The **National Theater Company** (✆ **2221-1273**) is an exception, tackling works from Lope de Vega to Lorca to Mamet. Similarly, the small independent group **Abya Yala** (✆ **2240-6071**; www.teatro-abyayala.org) also puts on several cutting-edge avant-garde shows each year. Almost all of the theater offerings are in Spanish, although the **Little Theater Group** (✆ **8858-1446**; www.littletheatregroup.org) is a long-standing amateur group that stages works in English. Finally, **Britt Expresivo**

(© 2277-1600) has been staging regular works ranging from original pieces to Shakespeare to Beckett, in English and Spanish, at the small theater up at **Café Britt** (p. 570) in the hills above Heredia. Check the *Tico Times* to see if anything is running during your stay.

The **National Symphony Orchestra's** season runs March through November, with concerts roughly every other weekend at the **Teatro Nacional,** Avenida 2 between calles 3 and 5 (© 2221-5341; www.teatronacional.go.cr), and the **Auditorio Nacional** (© 2256-5876), at the Museo de Los Niños (p. 570). Tickets cost between $3 and $30 and can be purchased at the box office.

Costa Rica's cultural panorama changes drastically every November when the country hosts large arts festivals. In odd-numbered years, **El Festival Nacional de las Artes** reigns supreme, featuring local talent. In even-numbered years, the month-long fete is **El Festival Internacional de las Artes,** with a nightly smorgasbord of dance, theater, and music from around the world. Most nights offer between 4 and 10 shows. Many are free, and the most expensive ticket is usually around $5. For exact dates and details, you can contact the **Ministry of Youth, Culture, and Sports** (© 2255-3188; www.mcjdcr.go.cr), although you might have trouble getting any information if you don't speak Spanish.

Side Trips & Adventure Tours from San José

San José makes an excellent base for exploring the beautiful Central Valley and the surrounding mountains. For first-time visitors, the best way to make the most of these excursions is usually to take a guided tour, but if you rent a car, you'll have greater independence. Some day trips also can be done by public bus.

A number of companies offer a wide variety of primarily nature-related day tours out of San José. The most reputable include **Costa Rica Expeditions** ★★ (© 2257-0766; www.costaricaexpeditions.com), **Costa Rica Sun Tours** ★ (© 2296-7757; www.crsuntours.com), **Horizontes Tours** ★★ (© 2222-2022; www.horizontes.com), and **Swiss Travel Service** (© 2282-4898; www.swisstravel cr.com).

Before signing on for a tour of any sort, find out how many fellow travelers will be accompanying you, how much time will be spent in transit and eating lunch, and how much time will actually be spent doing the primary activity. I've had complaints about tours that were rushed, that spent too much time in a bus or on secondary activities, or that had a cattle-car, assembly-line feel to them.

BUNGEE JUMPING   There's nothing unique about bungee jumping in Costa Rica, but the site here is quite beautiful. **Tropical Bungee** ★ (© 2248-2212; www.bungee.co.cr) will let you jump off an 80m (262-ft.) bridge for $65; two jumps cost $95. Transportation is provided free from San José twice daily. Someone should be there from 9am to 3pm every day. They prefer for you to have a reservation, but if you show up, they'll probably let you jump, unless huge groups are booked ahead of you. These folks also offer paragliding tours.

CANOPY TOURS & AERIAL TRAMS   Getting off the ground and up into the treetops is a big trend in Costa Rican tourism, and there are scores of such tours around the country. You have several options relatively close to San José.

The **Rain Forest Aerial Tram Atlantic** ★ (© 2257-5961; www.rainforesttram. com) is built on a private reserve bordering Braulio Carrillo National Park. This tramway takes visitors on a 90-minute ride through the treetops, where they have the chance to glimpse the complex web of life that makes these forests unique. There's

HOLY SMOKE! CHOOSING THE volcano TRIP THAT'S RIGHT FOR YOU

Poás, Irazú, and Arenal volcanoes are three of Costa Rica's most popular destinations, and the first two are easy day trips from San José (see below). Although numerous companies offer day trips to Arenal, I don't recommend them because there's at least 3½ hours of travel time in each direction. You usually arrive when the volcano is hidden by clouds and leave before the night's darkness shows off its glowing eruptions. For more information on Arenal Volcano, see p. 613.

Tour companies offering trips to Poás and Irazú include **Costa Rica Expeditions** ★★ (© 2257-0766), **Costa Rica Sun Tours** ★ (© 2296-7757), **Horizontes** ★★ (© 2222-2022), and **Swiss Travel Service** (© 2282-4898). Prices range from $30 to $50 for a half-day trip, and from $50 to $120 for a full-day trip.

The 3,378m (11,080-ft.) **Irazú Volcano** ★ (© 2200-5615) is historically one of Costa Rica's more active volcanoes, although it's relatively quiet these days. It last erupted on March 19, 1963, the day that President John F. Kennedy arrived in Costa Rica. There's a paved road right to the rim of the crater, where a desolate expanse of gray sand nurtures few plants and the air smells of sulfur. The landscape here is often compared to that of the moon. There are magnificent views of the Meseta Central and Orosi Valley as you drive up from Cartago, and if you're very lucky, you might be able to see both the Pacific Ocean and the Caribbean Sea. Clouds usually descend by noon, so get here as early in the day as possible.

The visitor center up here has information on the volcano and natural history. A short trail leads to the rim of the volcano's two craters, their walls a maze of eroded gullies feeding onto the flat floor far below. This is a national park, with an admission fee of $10 charged at the gate. Dress in layers; this might be the Tropics, but it can be cold up at the top if the sun's not out. The park restaurant, at an elevation of 3,022m (9,915 ft.), with walls of windows looking out over the valley far below, claims to be the highest restaurant in Central America.

If you don't want an organized tour, buses leave for Irazú Volcano daily at 8am from Avenida 2 between calles 1 and 3 (across the street from the entrance to the Gran Hotel Costa Rica).

also a zip-line canopy tour, and the grounds feature trails through the rainforest, a butterfly garden, a serpentarium, a frog collection, and a restaurant—a trip here can easily take up a full day. The cost for a full-day tour, including both the aerial tram and the canopy tour, all the park's other attractions, and transportation from San José and either breakfast or lunch, is $90. Alternatively, you can drive or take one of the frequent Guápiles buses—they leave every half-hour throughout the day and cost $2—from the Caribbean bus terminal (Gran Terminal del Caribe) on Calle Central, 1 block north of Avenida 11. For walk-ins, the entrance fee is $55; students and anyone 17 and under pay $28. Because this is a popular tour for groups, I highly recommend that you get an advance reservation in the high season and, if possible, a ticket; otherwise, you could wait a long time for your tram ride or even be shut out. If you want to spend the night, there are 10 simple but clean and comfortable bungalows, which cost $150 per person per day (double occupancy), including three meals, three guided tours, taxes, two tram rides, and unlimited use of the rest of the facilities.

The fare is $7 round-trip, with the bus leaving the volcano at 12:30pm. This company is particularly fickle; to make sure that the buses are running, call ☏ **2530-1064,** although that might not help much, since they often don't answer their phone and speak Spanish only. If you're driving, head northeast out of Cartago toward San Rafael, and then continue driving uphill toward the volcano, passing the turnoffs for Cot and Tierra Blanca en route.

Poás Volcano ★★ (☏ **2482-2424**) is 37km (23 miles) from San José on narrow roads that wind through a landscape of fertile farms and dark forests. As at Irazú, there's a paved road right to the top, although you'll have to hike in about 1km (⅔ mile) to reach the crater. The volcano stands 2,640m (8,660 ft.) tall and is located within a national park, which preserves not only the volcano but also dense stands of virgin forest. Poás's crater, said to be the second largest in the world, is more than a mile across. Geysers in the crater sometimes spew steam and muddy water 180m (590 ft.) into the air, making this the largest geyser in the world. There's an information center where you can see a slide show about the volcano, and there are well-groomed and marked hiking trails through the cloud forest that rings the crater. About 15 minutes from the parking area, along a forest trail, is an overlook onto beautiful Botos Lake, which has formed in one of the volcano's extinct craters.

Be prepared when you come to Poás: This volcano is often enveloped in dense clouds. If you want to see the crater, it's best to come early and during the dry season. Moreover, it can get cool up here, especially when the sun isn't shining, so dress appropriately. Admission to the national park is $10.

In case you don't want to go on a tour, there's a daily bus (☏ **2442-6900** or 2222-5325) from Avenida 2 between calles 12 and 14 that leaves at 8:30am and returns at 2pm. The fare is $6 round-trip. The bus is often crowded, so arrive early. If you're driving, head for Alajuela and continue on the main road through town and follow signs for Fraijanes. Just beyond Fraijanes you will connect with the road between San Pedro de Poás and Poasito; turn right toward Poasito and continue to the rim of the volcano.

Turu BaRi Tropical Park (☏ **2250-0705** or 2428-6070; www.turubari.com) is another attraction that aims to cover as many bases as possible. About 90 minutes outside San José, this park features a series of gardens, trails, and exhibits set in a valley that you can reach by means of a gondola-style ski lift, by cable and zip-line canopy tour, or on horseback. Down in the valley, you can wander around the botanical gardens, orchid gardens, and butterfly gardens; grab a bite at the typical Costa Rican restaurant; or even take a turn on their massive climbing wall. The basic fee admission is $60 for adults, and $40 for children; all the various adventure and activity options cost extra. However, various combination package tours, with or without transportation and meals, are available.

DAY CRUISES Several companies offer cruises to lovely Tortuga Island in the Gulf of Nicoya. These full-day tours generally entail an early departure for the 1½-hour chartered bus ride to Puntarenas, where you board your vessel for a 1½-hour cruise to Tortuga Island. Then you get several hours on the uninhabited island, where you can swim, lie on the beach, play volleyball, or try a canopy tour, followed by the return journey.

The original and most dependable company running these trips is **Calypso Tours ★** (© 2256-2727; www.calypsotours.com). The tour costs $119 per person and includes round-trip transportation from San José, a basic continental breakfast during the bus ride to the boat, all drinks on the cruise, and an excellent buffet lunch on the beach at the island. The Calypso Tours main vessel is a massive motor-powered catamaran. They also run a separate tour to a private nature reserve at **Punta Coral ★**. The beach is much nicer at Tortuga Island, but the tour to Punta Coral is more intimate, and the restaurant, hiking, and kayaking are all superior here. These folks provide daily pickups from San José, Manuel Antonio, Jacó, and Monteverde, and you can use the day trip on the boat as your transfer or transportation option between any of these towns and destinations.

HIKING   Most of the tour agencies listed above offer 1-day guided hikes to a variety of destinations. In general, I recommend taking guided hikes to really see and learn about the local flora and fauna.

RAFTING, KAYAKING & RIVER TRIPS   Cascading down Costa Rica's mountain ranges are dozens of tumultuous rivers, several of which are popular for white-water rafting and kayaking. If I had to choose just one day trip, it would be a white-water rafting trip. For between $75 and $120, you can spend a day rafting through tropical forests; multiday trips are also available. Some of the most reliable companies are **Costa Rica Nature Adventures ★★** (© 800/321-8410 in the U.S., or 2225-3939; www.toenjoynature.com), **Exploradores Outdoors ★** (© 2222-6262; www.exploradoresoutdoors.com), and **Ríos Tropicales ★★** (© 866/722-8273 in the U.S. and Canada, or 2233-6455 in Costa Rica; www.rios tropicales.com). These companies all ply a number of rivers of varying difficulties, including the popular Pacuare and Reventazón rivers.

Perhaps the best-known river tours are those that go up to **Tortuguero National Park ★★**. It's possible to do this tour as a day trip out of San José, but it's a long, tiring, expensive day. You're better off doing it as a 1- or 2-night trip.

CARTAGO & THE OROSI VALLEY

These two regions southeast of San José can easily be combined into a day trip. You might also squeeze in a visit to the Irazú Volcano (see box above for details).

Cartago

Located about 24km (15 miles) southeast of San José, **Cartago ★** is the former capital of Costa Rica. Founded in 1563, it was Costa Rica's first city—and was, in fact, its *only* city for almost 150 years. Irazú Volcano rises up from the edge of town, and although it's quiet these days, it has not always been so peaceful. Earthquakes have damaged Cartago over the years, so today few of the old colonial buildings are left standing. In the center of the city, a public park winds through the ruins of a large church that was destroyed in 1910 before it could be finished. Construction was abandoned after the quake, and today the ruins sit at the heart of a neatly manicured park, with quiet paths and plenty of benches. The ruins themselves are closed off, but the park itself is lovely. (The park is a free Wi-Fi hot spot as well.)

Cartago's most famous building is the **Basílica de Nuestra Señora de los Angeles (Basilica of Our Lady of the Angels) ★**, which is dedicated to the patron saint of Costa Rica and stands on the east side of town. Within the walls of this Byzantine-style church is a shrine containing the tiny carved figure of **La Negrita**, the Black

Virgin, which is nearly lost amid its ornate altar. Legend has it that La Negrita first revealed herself on this site to a peasant girl in 1635. Miraculous healing powers have been attributed to La Negrita, and, over the years, a parade of pilgrims have come to the shrine seeking cures for their illnesses and difficulties. August 2 is her patron saint's day. Each year, on this date, tens of thousands of Costa Ricans and foreign pilgrims walk to Cartago from San José and elsewhere in the country in devotion to this powerful statue. The walls of the shrine are covered with a fascinating array of tiny silver images left as thanks for cures affected by La Negrita. Amid the plethora of diminutive silver arms and legs, there are also hands, feet, hearts, lungs, kidneys, eyes, torsos, breasts, and—peculiarly—guns, trucks, beds, and planes. Outside, vendors sell a wide selection of these trinkets, as well as little candle replicas of La Negrita.

More than 1km (⅔ mile) east of Cartago, on the road to Paraíso, you'll find **Lankester Gardens** ★ (© 2552-3247), a beautiful botanical garden known for its orchid collection.

GETTING THERE **Lumaca** buses (© 2537-0347) for Cartago leave San José every 3 to 5 minutes between 4:30am and 9pm, with slightly less frequent service until midnight, from Calle 3 and Avenida 2. You can also pick up one en route at any of the little covered bus stops along Avenida Central in Los Yoses and San Pedro. The length of the trip is 45 minutes; the fare is about 70¢.

Orosi Valley

The Orosi Valley, southeast of Cartago and visible from the top of Irazú on a clear day, is generally considered one of the most beautiful valleys in Costa Rica. The Reventazón River meanders through this steep-sided valley until it collects in the lake formed by the Cachí Dam. There are scenic overlooks near the town of Orosi, which is at the head of the valley, and in Ujarrás, which is on the banks of the lake. Near **Ujarrás** are the ruins of Costa Rica's oldest church (built in 1693), whose tranquil gardens are a great place to sit and gaze at the surrounding mountains. In the town of Orosi itself, there is yet another colonial church and convent, built in 1743. A small museum here displays religious artifacts.

Near the town of Cachí, you'll find **La Casa del Soñador (House of the Dreamer)** ★ (© 2577-1186), the home and gallery of the late sculptor Macedonio Quesada and his sons, who carry on the family tradition. Quesada earned fame with his primitive sculptures of La Negrita (p. 588) and other religious and secular characters carved on coffee tree roots and trunks. You can see some of Macedonio's original work here, including his version of *The Last Supper* carved onto one of the walls of the main building. You can also shop among their current collection of small sculptures, carved religious icons, and ornate walking sticks.

From the Orosi Valley, it's a quick shot to the entrance to the **Tapantí National Park** ★ (© 2206-5615), where you'll find some gentle and beautiful hiking trails, as well as riverside picnic areas. The park is open daily from 8am to 4pm; admission is $10.

If you're interested in staying out here, check out the charming little **Orosi Lodge** (© 2533-3578; www.orosilodge.com), which is right next to some simple hot spring pools.

GETTING THERE If you're driving, take the road to Paraíso from Cartago, head toward Ujarrás, continue around the lake, and then pass through Cachí and on to Orosi. From Orosi, the road leads back to Paraíso. It is difficult to explore this area by public bus because this is not a densely populated region and connections are often infrequent or unreliable. However, there are buses from Cartago to the town of Orosi. These buses run roughly every half-hour and leave the main bus terminal in Cartago. The trip takes 30 minutes, and the fare is 60¢.

HEREDIA & SARCHÍ

You can combine visits to Heredia and Sarchí, located northwest of San José, into a long day trip (if you have a car), perhaps in conjunction with a visit to Poás Volcano and/or the Waterfall Gardens. The scenery here is rich and verdant, and the small towns and scattered farming communities are truly representative of Costa Rica's agricultural heartland and *campesino* tradition. This is a great area to explore on your own in a rental car, if you don't mind getting lost a bit (roads are narrow, winding, and poorly marked). If you're relying on buses, you'll be able to visit either town, but probably just one a day.

The road to Heredia turns north off the highway from San José to the airport. If you're going to Sarchí, take the highway west toward Puntarenas.

Heredia

Set on the flanks of the impressive Barva Volcano, this city was founded in 1706. Heredia is affectionately known as "The City of Flowers." A colonial church inaugurated in 1763 stands in the central park—the stone facade leaves no questions as to the age of the church. The altar inside is decorated with neon stars and a crescent moon surrounding a statue of the Virgin Mary. In the middle of the palm-shaded park is a music temple, and across the street, beside several tile-roofed municipal buildings, is the tower of an old Spanish fort. Of all the cities in the Meseta Central, Heredia has the most colonial feel to it—you'll still see adobe buildings with Spanish tile roofs along narrow streets. Heredia is also the site of the **National Autonomous University,** and you'll find some nice coffee shops and bookstores near the school.

Surrounding Heredia is an intricate maze of picturesque villages and towns, including Santa Bárbara, Santo Domingo, Barva, and San Joaquín de Flores. San Isidro de Heredia has a lovely, large church with an ornate facade. However, the biggest attraction up here is **INBio Park ★★** (© **2507-8107;** p. 570). Located on 5 hectares (12 acres) in Santo Domingo de Heredia, this place is part museum, part educational center, and part nature park. This is also where you'll find the **Café Britt Farm ★** (© **2277-1600;** p. 570). On the road to Barva, you'll find the small **Museo de Cultura Popular** (© **2260-1619;** www.museo.una.ac.cr), which is open Monday through Friday from 8am to 4pm and Sunday from 10am to 5pm; admission is $2. Anyone with an interest in medicinal herbs should plan a visit to the **Ark Herb Farm ★** (© **8922-7599** or 2269-4847; www.arkherbfarm.com). These folks offer guided tours of their gardens, which feature more than 300 types of medicinal plants. The tour costs $12 per person, and includes a light snack and refreshments. Reservations are required.

If you make your way to San Pedro de Barva de Heredia, stop in at **La Lluna de Valencia ★★** (© **2269-6665;** www.lallunadevalencia.com), a delightful rustic Spanish restaurant with amazing paella, delicious sangria, and a very amiable host. And if you're looking to overnight, high in the hills of Heredia, near the Barva volcano, check out the high-end B&B the **Orchid Lodge** (© **2260-2744;** www.theorchid lodge.com).

GETTING THERE   Buses leave for Heredia every 5 minutes between 5am and 11pm from Calle 1 between avenidas 7 and 9, or from Avenida 2 between calles 12 and 14. Bus fare is 65¢ (© **2233-8392**).

Sarchí ★

Sarchí is Costa Rica's main artisan town. The colorfully painted miniature **ox carts** that you see all over the country are made here. Ox carts such as these were once used to haul coffee beans to market. Today, although you might occasionally see ox carts in use, most are purely decorative. However, they remain a well-known symbol of Costa Rica. In addition to miniature ox carts, many carved wooden souvenirs are made here with rare hardwoods from the nation's forests. There are dozens of shops in town, and all have similar prices. Perhaps your best one-stop shop in Sarchí is the large and long-standing **Chaverri Oxcart Factory ★** (✆ **2454-4411;** www.sarchi costarica.net), which is right in the center of things, but it never hurts to shop around and visit several of the stores.

Aside from handicrafts, there are other reasons to visit Sarchí. Built between 1950 and 1958, the town's main **church ★** is pink with aquamarine trim and looks strangely like a child's birthday cake. But my favorite attraction in Sarchí is the **Else Kientzler Botanical Garden ★★** (✆ **2454-2070**), which features an extensive collection of several thousand types of plants, flowers, and trees.

While there are no noteworthy accommodations in Sarchí itself, the plush **El Silencio Lodge & Spa** (✆ **2291-3044;** www.elsilenciolodge.com) is about a 35-minute drive away in a beautiful mountain setting.

GETTING THERE Tuan (✆ **2258-2004**) buses leave San José about five times throughout the day for Sarchí from Calle 18 between avenidas 3 and 5. The fare is $1.25. Alternatively, you can take any Grecia bus from this same station. In Grecia they connect with the Alajuela-Sarchí buses, leaving every 30 minutes from Calle 8 between avenidas Central and 1 in Alajuela.

GUANACASTE: THE GOLD COAST ★★

Liberia: 217km (135 miles) NW of San José, 132km (82 miles) NW of Puntarenas; Playa Hermosa/Papagayo: 258km (160 miles) NW of San José, 40km (25 miles) SW of Liberia; Playa del Coco: 253km (157 miles) NW of San José, 35km (22 miles) W of Liberia; Tamarindo: 295km (183 miles) NW of San José, 73km (45 miles) SW of Liberia

Guanacaste is indeed Costa Rica's "Gold Coast," and not just because this is where the Spanish conquistadors found vast quantities of the brilliant metal ore. Beautiful beaches abound along this coastline: from long, broad sections of sand stretching on for miles, to tiny pocket coves bordered by rocky headlands. Several are packed with a mix of hotels and resorts, some are still pristine and deserted, and others are backed by small fishing villages.

This is Costa Rica's most coveted vacation destination and the site of its greatest tourism development. It's also Costa Rica's driest region. The rainy season starts later and ends earlier, and overall it's more dependably sunny here than in other parts of the country. Combine this climate with a coastline that stretches south for hundreds of miles, from the Nicaraguan border all the way to the Nicoya Peninsula, and you have an equation that yields beach bliss.

There is one caveat: During the dry season (mid-Nov to Apr), when sunshine is most reliable, the hillsides in Guanacaste turn browner than the chaparral of Southern California. Dust from dirt roads blankets the trees in many areas, and driving these dirt roads without air-conditioning and the windows rolled up tight can be extremely unpleasant. On the other hand, if you happen to visit this area in the rainy season (particularly May–Aug), the hillsides are a beautiful, rich green, and the sun usually shines all morning, giving way to an afternoon shower—just in time for a nice siesta.

Inland from the beaches, Guanacaste remains Costa Rica's "Wild West," a land of dry plains populated with cattle ranches and cowboys, who are known here as *sabaneros,* a name that derives from the Spanish word for "savanna" or "grassland." If it weren't for those rainforest-clad volcanoes in the distance, you might swear you were in Texas.

Guanacaste is home to several active volcanoes and some beautiful national parks, including **Santa Rosa National Park** ★, the home to massive sea turtle nestings and the site of a major battle to maintain independence, and **Rincón de la Vieja National Park** ★★, which features hot springs and bubbling mud pots, pristine waterfalls, and an active volcanic crater.

Essentials

GETTING THERE

BY PLANE The **Daniel Oduber International Airport** (② 2668-1010 or 2688-1117; airport code LIR) in Liberia receives a steady stream of scheduled commercial and charter flights throughout the year. **Delta** (② 800/241-4141; www.delta.com) has daily direct flights between its Atlanta hub and Liberia; **American Airlines** (② 800/433-7300; www.aa.com) offers daily direct flights between Miami and Liberia, and twice-weekly flights between Dallas–Ft. Worth and Liberia; **Continental** (② 800/231-0856; www.continental.com) has daily direct flights between Houston and Liberia, and one weekly direct flight between Newark and Liberia; and **US Airways** (② 800/622-1015; www.usairways.com) has one weekly direct flight between Charlotte and Liberia. In addition, there are numerous commercial charter flights from various North American cities throughout the high season. Check with your travel agent.

Sansa (② 877/767-2672 in the U.S. and Canada, or 2290-4100 in Costa Rica; www.flysansa.com) has two daily flights to Liberia, at 7am and noon, from San José's Juan Santamaría International Airport (p. 559). Return flights depart for San José at 8am and 1:15pm. During the high season, one late-afternoon flight is added. The fare for the 50-minute flight is $114 each way.

Nature Air (② 800/235-9272 in the U.S. and Canada, or 2299-6000; www.natureair.com) has four flights daily to Liberia at 6:30 and 11:45am, and 3:20pm from Tobías Bolaños International Airport in Pavas (p. 560). Return flights leave Liberia at 7:20am and 12:40 and 4:45pm. Fares run between $91 and $131 each way. Nature Air also has direct flights between Liberia and Arenal, Quepos, Tamarindo, and Tambor, as well as connections to just about every major destination in Costa Rica.

From Liberia, a taxi to most of the beaches mentioned in this section will take about 25 minutes and cost $35 to $50. A taxi to Tamarindo will take slightly longer and cost around $50 to $70. Alternatively, you can use **Tamarindo Shuttle** (② 2653-4444; www.tamarindoshuttle.com), which charges $18 per person one-way. These folks also offer a variety of tours and transfer services.

BY CAR To get to Playa Hermosa, Playa Panamá, or Papagayo from Liberia, take a left at the main intersection in Liberia onto CR21, which heads toward Santa Cruz and the beaches of Guanacaste. The turnoff for the Papagayo Peninsula is prominently marked 8km (5 miles) south of the Liberia airport.

Guanacaste & the Nicoya Peninsula

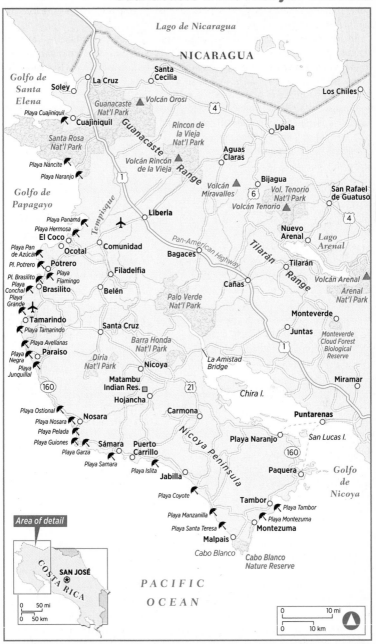

Lago de Nicaragua

NICARAGUA

Golfo de Santa Elena

Soley
La Cruz
Santa Cecilia
Los Chiles

Playa Cuajiniquil
Cuajiniquil
Guanacaste Nat'l Park
Volcán Orosi
Rincon de la Vieja Nat'l Park
Upala

Santa Rosa Nat'l Park
Volcán Rincón de la Vieja
Aguas Claras

Playa Nancite
Playa Naranjo
Volcán Miravalles
Bijagua
Vol. Tenorio Nat'l Park
San Rafael de Guatuso

Golfo de Papagayo
Volcán Tenorio

Liberia

Playa Panamá
Playa Hermosa
El Coco
Ocotal
Comunidad
Bagaces
Nuevo Arenal
Lago Arenal

Tempisque
Pan-American Highway
Tilarán
Tilarán Range

Playa Pan de Azúcar
Pl. Potrero
Potrero
Playa Flamingo
Filadelfia
Cañas
Volcán Arenal
Arenal Nat'l Park

Pl. Brasilito
Playa Conchal
Brasilito
Belén
Palo Verde Nat'l Park

Playa Grande
Tamarindo
Playa Tamarindo
Santa Cruz
Barra Honda Nat'l Park
La Amistad Bridge
Monteverde
Juntas
Monteverde Cloud Forest Biological Reserve

Playa Avellanas
Paraiso
Díria Nat'l Park
Nicoya
Chira I.
Miramar

Playa Negra
Playa Junquillal
Matambu Indian Res.
Hojancha

Playa Ostional
Nosara
Carmona
Puntarenas

Playa Nosara
Playa Pelada
Playa Guiones
Sámara
Puerto Carrillo
Playa Naranjo
San Lucas I.

Playa Garza
Playa Samara
Playa Islita
Jabilla
Paquera
Golfo de Nicoya

Playa Coyote
Nicoya Peninsula

Playa Manzanilla
Tambor
Playa Tambor

Playa Santa Teresa
Playa Montezuma
Montezuma

Malpais

Cabo Blanco
Cabo Blanco Nature Reserve

PACIFIC OCEAN

Area of detail

COSTA RICA
SAN JOSÉ

0   50 mi
0   50 km

0   10 mi
0   10 km

To get to Playa del Coco or Playa Ocotal from Liberia, head west on CR21 toward Santa Cruz. Just past the village of Comunidad, turn right. In about 11km (6¾ miles) you'll come to a fork in the road. Take the left fork. The right fork goes to Playa Hermosa. The drive takes about 4 hours from San José.

To get to playas Flamingo, Portrero, Brasilito, or Conchal from Liberia, head west on CR21 toward Santa Cruz. Just past the village of Comunidad, turn right. In about 11km (6¾ miles) you'll come to a fork in the road. Take the left fork. The drive takes about 4 hours from San José.

To get to Tamarindo and Playa Grande from San José, you can either take the Interamerican Highway, which is what the Pan-American Highway is often called in Costa Rica, (CR1) north from downtown San José, or first head west out of the city on the new San José–Caldera Highway (CR27). The trip should take around 4 hours.

BY BUS   Gray Line (© 2220-2126; www.graylinecostarica.com) and **Interbus** (© 2283-5573; www.interbusonline.com) have daily buses from San José to all of the beaches in this section. **Tralapa** express buses (© 2221-7202) leave San José daily for Playa Hermosa, Playa Panamá, Playa del Coco, Playa Ocotal, and Tamarindo. **Alfaro** express buses (© 2222-2666 in San José, or 2653-0268 in Tamarindo; www.empresaalfaro.com) leave San José daily for Tamarindo.

GETTING AROUND

The best way to get around Guanacaste is by taxi or rental car, or as part of an organized tour. For information on the many available tour options, ask at your hotel, or see below.

BY TAXI   Taxis are available at the airport and in all the major beach towns. Any hotel in the area can call you a taxi, or you can call © **2670-0408.** Rates range from $3 to $6 for short rides, to $20 to $45 for longer jaunts between more-distant towns and destinations.

BY CAR   If you're looking to rent a car after arriving in the region, **Adobe** (© 2667-0608), **Alamo** (© 2668-1111), **Avis** (© 2668-1138), **Budget** (© 2668-1118), **Dollar** (© 2668-1061), **Economy** (© 2666-2816), **Hertz** (© 2668-1048), **Payless** (© 2667-0511), **Sol** (© 2666-2222), **Thrifty** (© 2665-0787), and **Toyota** (© 2668-1212) all have local offices at the Liberia airport, and in some cases at the various destination beaches.

BY BUS   Public buses are not a practical means for most tourists to get around Guanacaste. Although regular local buses connect most of the major beach towns and destinations with Liberia, you'll find virtually no connections among the different beach towns and destinations.

VISITOR INFORMATION & FAST FACTS

If you need to contact the **police,** dial © **911,** and for an **ambulance** dial © **128.** The Liberia Hospital (© **2666-0011**) is the best hospital in the area. A smaller hospital lies in the city of Santa Cruz. Most of the beach towns have some sort of health clinic.

Banks and ATMs are in Playa del Coco, Playa Hermosa, Playa Flamingo, and Tamarindo. You'll find easy access to the Web and plenty of Internet cafes in all of the major beach towns and destinations of this region.

A small information kiosk is at the Liberia airport, but your best bet for information will be your hotel front desk, concierge, or tour desk. Tour desks are available at almost every hotel, as well as tour offices in most major beach towns.

Introducing the Beaches & Attractions

The beaches of Guanacaste come in various shapes and sizes. Some are protected and calm, while others feature strong surf. Some are quite developed, while others are home to just a few hotels and small resorts.

Here's a quick rundown of the principal beach destinations, running (more or less) from north to south.

PLAYA HERMOSA, PLAYA PANAMA & PAPAGAYO   While most of Costa Rica's coast is highly coveted by surfers, the beaches here are mostly protected and calm, making them good destinations for families with kids. **Playa Hermosa ★** means "beautiful beach," which is an apt moniker for this pretty crescent of sand. Surrounded by steep forested hills, this curving gray-sand beach is long and wide and the surf is usually quite gentle. Fringing the beach is a swath of trees that stays surprisingly green even during the dry season. The shade provided by these trees, along with the calm protected waters, is a big part of the beach's appeal. Rocky headlands jut out into the surf at both ends of the beach, and at the base of these rocks, you'll find fun tide pools to explore. Beyond Playa Hermosa you'll find **Playa Panamá ★** and, farther on, the calm waters of **Bahía Culebra ★**, a large protected bay dotted with small, private patches of beach and ringed with mostly intact dry forest. Around the north end of Bahía Culebra is the **Papagayo Peninsula ★**, which has a half-dozen or so small to midsize beaches, along with two large all-inclusive resorts and one championship golf course.

PLAYA DEL COCO & PLAYA OCOTAL   Playa Ocotal is a tiny pocket cove featuring a small salt-and-pepper beach bordered by high bluffs. It's quite beautiful. When the water is calm, you'll find good snorkeling around some rocky islands close to shore. You'll see a fair amount of residential development here, as well as a couple of small hotels and resorts.

More interesting still, in my opinion, is **Playa Ocotal ★**, which is a couple of kilometers to the south. This tiny pocket cove features a small salt-and-pepper beach bordered by high bluffs and is quite beautiful. When it's calm there's good snorkeling around some rocky islands close to shore here.

PLAYAS CONCHAL, BRASILITO & FLAMINGO   Playa Conchal ★★ is the first in a string of beaches stretching north along this coast. This beach is almost entirely backed by the massive Paradisus Playa Conchal resort and Reserva Conchal condominium complex. The beach here was once made up primarily of soft crushed shells. Nearly everyplace you could walk, turn, or lay down your towel was a shell-collectors' heaven. Unfortunately, as Conchal has developed and its popularity spread, builders have brought in dump trucks to haul away the namesake seashells for landscaping and construction, and the impact is noticeable.

Just beyond Playa Conchal to the north, you'll come to **Playa Brasilito,** a tiny beach town and one of the few real villages in the area. The soccer field is the center of the village, and around its edges you'll find a couple of little *pulperías* (general stores). There's a long stretch of beach, and though it's of gray sand, it still has a quiet, undiscovered feel to it.

Playa Flamingo ★★ is in my opinion the prettiest beach in the region. A long, broad stretch of pinkish white sand, it is on a long spit of land that forms part of Potrero Bay. At the northern end of the beach is a high rock outcropping upon which most of Playa Flamingo's hotels and vacation homes are built. There are great views from this rocky hill.

If you continue along the road from Brasilito without taking the turn for Playa Flamingo, you'll come to **Playa Potrero.** The sand here is a brownish gray, but the beach is long, clean, deserted, and very protected for swimming. You can see the hotels of Playa Flamingo across the bay. Drive a little farther north and you'll find the still-underdeveloped beaches of **Playa La Penca ★** and, finally, **Playa Pan de Azúcar ★,** or **Sugar Beach.**

PLAYAS TAMARINDO & GRANDE   Tamarindo is the biggest boomtown in Guanacaste—and in some ways, I think the boom went a bit too far, a bit too fast. The main road into Tamarindo is a helter-skelter jumble of strip malls, surf shops, hotels, and restaurants, and ongoing development is spreading up the hills inland from the beach and south beyond Punta Langosta. Still, the wide range of accommodations, abundant restaurants, and active nightlife, along with very dependable surf, have established Tamarindo as one of the most popular beaches on this coast. The beautiful beach here is a long, wide swath of white sand that curves gently from one rocky headland to another. Fishing boats bob at their moorings and brown pelicans fish just beyond the breakers. A sandy islet off the southern end of the beach makes a great destination if you're a strong swimmer; if you're not, it makes a great foreground for sunsets. Tamarindo is very popular with surfers, who ply the break right here or use the town as a jumping-off place for beach and point breaks at playas Grande, Langosta, Avellanas, and Negra.

Just to the north of Tamarindo lies **Playa Grande,** one of the principal nesting sites for the giant leatherback turtle. This beach is often too rough for swimming, but the well-formed and consistent beach break is very popular with surfers. I almost hate to mention places to stay in Playa Grande because the steady influx of tourists and development has apparently doomed it as a turtle-nesting site.

What to See & Do

Nearly all the hotels and resorts in Guanacaste have a tour desk or can help you arrange a variety of day tours and activities. Prices range from $35 to $120 per person, depending on the length of the tour and the activity or activities involved.

EXPLORING THE REGION

RINCON DE LA VIEJA NATIONAL PARK ★★   This national park begins on the flanks of the Rincón de la Vieja Volcano and includes this volcano's active crater. Down lower you'll find an area of geothermal activity similar to that of Yellowstone National Park in the United States. Fumaroles, geysers, and hot pools cover this small area, creating a bizarre, otherworldly landscape. In addition to hot springs and mud pots, you can explore waterfalls, a lake, and volcanic craters. The bird-watching here is excellent, and the views across the pasturelands to the Pacific Ocean are stunning.

Several excellent trails run inside the Rincón de la Vieja National Park. More energetic hikers can tackle the 8km (5 miles) up to the **summit** and explore the several craters and beautiful lakes up here. On a clear day you'll be rewarded with a fabulous view of the plains of Guanacaste and the Pacific Ocean below. The easiest hiking is the gentle **Las Pailas loop ★**. This 3km (1.8-mile) trail is just off the Las Espuelas park entrance and passes by several bubbling mud pots and steaming fumaroles. Don't get too close, or you could get scalded. Happily, the strong sulfur smell given off by these formations works well as a natural deterrent. This gentle trail crosses a river, so you'll have to either take off your shoes or get them wet. The loop is 3.2km (2 miles) and takes around 2 hours at a leisurely pace.

My favorite hike here is to the **Blue Lake** and **La Cangrejo Waterfall ★★**. This 9.6km (6-mile) round-trip trail passes through several different life zones, including dry forest, transitional moist forest, and open savanna. While not requiring any great climbs or descents, the hike is nonetheless arduous. A variety of birds and mammals are commonly sighted. Pack a lunch; at the end of your 2-hour hike in, you can picnic at the aptly named Blue Lake, where a 30m (98-ft.) waterfall empties into a small pond whose crystal-blue hues are amazing.

SANTA ROSA NATIONAL PARK   Known for its remote, pristine beaches (reached by several kilometers of hiking trails or a 4WD vehicle), **Santa Rosa National Park ★ (© 2666-5051)** is a great place to camp on the beach, surf, or (if you're lucky) watch sea turtles nest. Located 30km (19 miles) north of Liberia and 21km (13 miles) south of La Cruz on the Interamerican Highway, Costa Rica's first national park blankets the Santa Elena Peninsula. Unlike other national parks, it was founded not to preserve the land but to save a building, known as **La Casona,** which played an important role in Costa Rican independence. It was here, in 1856, that Costa Rican forces fought the decisive Battle of Santa Rosa, forcing the U.S.-backed soldier of fortune William Walker and his men to flee into Nicaragua. La Casona was completely destroyed by arson in 2001, but it has been rebuilt, very accurately mimicking the original building, and now houses a small museum, detailing the political history of the ranch house and housing rotating temporary art exhibits. The museum descriptions are in Spanish only.

There are a few hiking trails near La Casona. The best for most visitors is the **Indio Desnudo (Naked Indian) trail.** This 2.6km (1.6-mile) loop trail should take you about 45 minutes. It leads through a small patch of tropical dry forest and into overgrown former pastureland. If you're lucky, you might spot a white-tailed deer, coatimundi, black guan, or mantled howler monkey along the way.

It costs $10 per person to enter the park; day visitors can access the park daily from 7am to 5pm. Camping is allowed at several sites. A campsite costs $2 per person per day. There's camping near the entrance and principal ranger station, as well as near La Casona and down by playas Naranjo and Nancite.

OUTDOOR & WELLNESS ACTIVITIES

There's a host of adventure, sport, and outdoor activities to keep you busy, from surfing and sailing to horseback riding and hiking. There are several golf courses in the area, as well as various zip-line canopy tours. Again, your hotel tour desk and local tour agencies will be your best bet for seeing what's available near you.

CANOPY TOURS   If you want to try one of the zip-line canopy tours, your best option in this area is the **Canyon Tour** operation at **Hacienda Guachipelin** (see below). This tour has a little bit of everything, with treetop platforms as well as cables crisscrossing a deep mountain canyon, some suspended bridges, a couple of pendulum swings, and two rappels.

However, if you don't want to head that far afield, there are a few other options near some of the beach towns mentioned above: **Santa Rosa Canopy Tour (© 2653-0926)** and **Cartagena Canopy Tour (© 2675-0801)** just outside of Tamarindo, and **Witch's Rock Canopy Tour (© 2667-0661;** www.witchsrock canopytour.com) out on the Papagayo peninsula.

FISHING   The waters off Guanacaste's coast are teeming with fish and world-class sportfishing opportunities. Anglers can land marlin and sailfish, as well as tuna, dorado, roosterfish, and more.

A half-day of fishing, with boat, captain, food, and tackle, should cost between $200 and $600 for two to four passengers; a full day, between $400 and $1,600. The range in prices reflects a wide range in the size of the boats, equipment, and distance traveled.

Although fishing is good all year, the peak season for billfish is between mid-April and August.

A host of boats and captains dot the Guanacaste coast. Some of the better operators are **Capullo Sportfishing** (✆ 2653-0048; www.capullo.com) in Tamarindo; **Oso Viejo** (✆ 8827-5533 or 2653-8437; www.flamingobeachcr.com) in Playa Flamingo; and **Tranquilamar** (✆ 8814-0994; www.tranquilamar.com) in Playa del Coco.

FOUR-WHEELING **Hightide Adventures** (✆ 2653-0108; www.tamarindo adventures.net) in Tamarindo offers a variety of guided ATV tours that range in duration from 1 to 3 hours and in price from $75 to $150 per person. Similar ATV tours are offered by **Fourtrax Adventures** (✆ 2670-1071 or 2653-4040; www.fourtrax adventure.com) in Playa del Coco and Tamarindo. The 2-hour outing costs $85. You can also combine their ATV tour with a canopy tour, for $145 per person.

GOLFING Golf is just beginning to take off in Costa Rica, but you'll find some of the country's best courses in Guanacaste.

The **Paradisus Playa Conchal ★★** (✆ 2654-4123) is home to the **Garra de León (The Lion's Claw)** golf course. This Robert Trent Jones–designed resort course features broad open fairways, fast greens, and a few wonderful views of the ocean. It is open to the walk-in public from neighboring hotels and resorts. It costs $200 in greens fees for as many rounds as you can squeeze into 1 day, including a cart. If you tee off after 1pm, the price drops to $160.

South of Tamarindo, **Hacienda Pinilla ★★** (✆ 2680-7000; www.hacienda pinilla.com) is a beautiful 18-hole links-style course. The course is currently accepting golfers staying at hotels around the area, with advance reservations. Greens fees run around $165 for 18 holes, including a cart.

About 10km (6¼ miles) outside Playa del Coco, the **Papagayo Golf & Country Club ★** (✆ 2697-0169; www.papagayo-golf.com) offers up a full 18-hole course, with a pro shop, driving range, and rental equipment. It costs $95 in greens fees, including a cart and access to the pool. Tee-time reservations are necessary on weekends. The course is closed on Mondays.

Finally, the most impressive course in the country is the Arnold Palmer–designed course at the **Four Seasons Resort** (p. 600; ✆ 800/819-5053 in the U.S., or 2696-0000 in Costa Rica; www.fourseasons.com). This stunning course features ocean views from 15 of its 18 holes. It is open only to hotel guests.

HORSEBACK RIDING In addition to a trot down one of the beaches in the area, there's plenty of stunning scenery in the hillsides, forests, and farmlands around Guanacaste, making for a pleasant horseback ride.

Be careful; many of the folks offering riding in this area, especially those plying the beaches themselves, are using poorly trained and poorly kept animals. Be sure you feel comfortable with the condition and training of your mount.

If your hotel tour desk can't arrange this for you, the following companies are all reputable, with good horses: **Casagua Horses** (✆ 2653-8041); **Brasilito Excursions** (✆ 2654-4237); **Flamingo Equestrian Center** (✆ 8846-7878; www. equestriancostarica.com); and **Finca Los Caballos** (✆ 2642-0124; www.nature lodge.net).

Hacienda Guachipelin (© 2665-3303 or 2666-8075; www.guachipelin.com) offers up a range of adventure tour options, including horseback riding, hiking, white-water river inner-tubing, a waterfall canyoning and rappel tour, and a more traditional zip-line canopy tour. The most popular is the hacienda's **1-Day Adventure pass** ★★, which allows you to choose as many of the hotel's tour options as you want and fit them into 1 adventure-packed day. The price for this is $80, including a buffet lunch and transportation. Almost all of the beach hotels and resorts of Guanacaste offer day trips here, or you can book directly with the lodge. *Be forewarned:* During the high season, there's a bit of a cattle-car feel to the whole operation, with busloads of day-trippers coming in from the beach. Also, I have found the inner-tube adventure to be fairly dangerous when the river is high, particularly during or just after the rainy season.

While here, you can take advantage of the hot spring pools, and hot mud pools at the hacienda's **Simbiosis Spa** (© 2666-8075; www.simbiosis-spa.com). A $20 entrance fee gets you a stint in a sauna, self-application of the hot volcanic mud, and free run of the pools. *Be forewarned:* The pools are better described as warm, not hot, mud pools, and mud is the operative word here. A wide range of massages, mud wraps, facials, and other treatments are available at reasonable prices.

SAILING   The winds off Costa Rica's Pacific coast are somewhat fickle and can often be slight to nonexistent. However, December through March, they can be quite strong, with impressive gusts. Still, plenty of sailing options abound if you want to head to sea here.

A host of different boats take out day charters ranging from a few hours to a full day. Many include some food and drinks, as well as a break or two for some swimming or snorkeling. Some will take you to a deserted beach, and others let you throw a line overboard for fishing.

Rates run around $50 to $75 per person for a few hours or a sunset cruise, and $80 to $130 per person for longer outings.

If your hotel can't line up a sail for you, check out the *Blue Dolphin* ★ (© 8842-3204 or 2653-0867; www.sailbluedolphin.com), a 40-foot catamaran based in Tamarindo, or the *Samonique III* (© 8388-7870; www.costarica-sailing.com), a 52-foot ketch sailing out of Playa Flamingo.

SCUBA DIVING   Some of Costa Rica's best diving can be had around the offshore islands and underwater rock formations of Guanacaste. Most hotel and tour desks can arrange a dive trip for you. Many also offer certification courses or shorter resort courses, the latter of which will get you some basic instruction and a controlled dive in the shortest amount of time.

A two-tank dive should run between $70 and $130 per person, depending primarily on the distance traveled to the dive sites.

If you don't set up your dive trip through your hotel, several reputable dive operations are **Diving Safaris de Costa Rica** ★ (© 2672-1259; www.costaricadiving.net), in Playa Hermosa; **Rich Coast Diving** (© 800/434-8464 in the U.S. and Canada, or 2670-0176 in Costa Rica; www.richcoastdiving.com), in Playa del Coco;

9

COSTA RICA

Guanacaste: The Gold Coast

and **Resort Divers** (© 2672-0106; www.resortdivers-cr.com), which has set up shop at the **Hilton Papagayo Resort** (below).

SURFING The Guanacaste coast is home to some of Costa Rica's best and most consistent surf breaks. Whether you're already a pro or you're looking to get your feet wet, you'll find beaches and breaks that are just right for you.

For beginners, Tamarindo is your best bet, with consistent shore breaks and numerous surf shops renting boards and giving lessons.

More experienced surfers will want to explore the coast more, looking for lesser known and more remote breaks, like Playa Grande, Play Negra, and Playa Avellanas. For a more remote spot, try booking a boat out of Playas del Coco to take you to Witch's Rock or Ollie's Point, inside the Santa Rosa National Park. Most of the above-mentioned sportfishing and dive operations also offer trips to ferry surfers up to these two isolated surf breaks. Alternatively, you can contact **Roca Bruja Surf Operations** (© 2670-1020). A boat that carries six surfers for a full day, including lunch and beer, should run around $300 to $350. *Tip:* Both Witch's Rock and Ollie's Point are technically within Santa Rosa National Park. Permits are sometimes required, and boats without permits are sometimes turned away. If you decide to go, be sure your boat captain is licensed and has cleared access to the park. You may also have to pay the park's $10 entrance fee.

Where to Stay
VERY EXPENSIVE
In addition to the hotel listed below, **Hilton Papagayo Resort** (© 800/445-8667 in the U.S. and Canada, or 2672-0000 in Costa Rica; www.hilton.com) is a good family-friendly option in Playa Panamá.

Four Seasons Resort Costa Rica ★★★ ☺ Set on a narrow spit of land between two stunning white-sand beaches, this is the most luxurious and impressive resort in Costa Rica. The architecture is unique, with most buildings featuring flowing roof designs and other touches imitating the forms of turtles, armadillos, and butterflies. Rooms are very spacious, with beautiful furnishings, fixtures, and decorations from around the world, and marble bathrooms with deep tubs and separate showers. Each has a large private balcony with a sofa, a table, and a couple of chairs. Rooms on the third and fourth floors have the best views and are priced accordingly. Suites and villas have even more space and a private pool, a Jacuzzi, or an open-air gazebo for soaking in the views. The resort features the Four Seasons' renowned service (including family-friendly amenities such as kid-size bathrobes and childproof rooms), one of the best-equipped spas in the country, and a spectacular golf course that offers ocean views from 15 of its 18 holes. Despite being such a large resort, these folks have been granted "4 Leaves" by the CST Sustainable Tourism program.

Papagayo Peninsula, Guanacaste. © **800/819-5053** in the U.S., or 2696-0000. Fax 2696-0500. www.fourseasons.com/costarica. 153 units. $450–$1,240 double; $895–$13,500 suites and villas. Children stay free in parent's room. AE, DC, DISC, MC, V. **Amenities:** 4 restaurants; 2 bars; lounge; babysitting; children's programs; concierge; championship 18-hole golf course; 3 free-form pools; room service; smoke-free rooms; full-service spa; 2 tennis courts; watersports equipment. *In room:* A/C, TV/DVD, hair dryer, MP3 docking station, Wi-Fi.

EXPENSIVE
Other good options in this category include **Villa Alegre** (© 2653-0270; www.villaalegrecostarica.com) in Playa Langosta and **El Ocotal Beach Resort** (© 2670-0321; www.ocotalresort.com) in Ocotal.

Hotel Capitán Suizo ★★ ☺   This well-appointed beachfront hotel sits on the quiet southern end of Tamarindo. The rooms are housed in a series of two-story buildings. The lower rooms have air-conditioning and private patios; the upper units have plenty of cross ventilation, ceiling fans, and cozy balconies. All have large bathrooms and sitting rooms with fold-down futon couches, and there's a lovely little beachfront spa. The spacious bungalows are spread around the shady grounds; these all come with a tub in the bathroom and an inviting outdoor shower among the trees. The best room is the beachfront honeymoon suite. The hotel's free-form pool is a delight, with tall shade trees all around. The shallow end slopes in gradually, imitating a beach, and there's also a separate children's pool. Perhaps the greatest attribute here is that it's just steps from one of the calmer and more isolated sections of Playa Tamarindo.

Playa Tamarindo, Guanacaste. ⓒ **2653-0353** or 2653-0075. Fax 2653-0292. www.hotelcapitansuizo. com. 29 units, 7 bungalows. $165–$285 double; $220–$325 bungalow; $325–$385 suite. Rates include breakfast buffet. AE, MC, V. **Amenities:** Restaurant; bar; babysitting; small exercise room; midsize pool and children's pool; spa; free Wi-Fi. *In room:* A/C (in some), hair dryer, minifridge.

MODERATE

In addition to the hotels listed below, you could look into **El Velero Hotel** (ⓒ **2672-1017;** www.costaricahotel.net) and **Villa del Sueño Hotel ★** (ⓒ **800/378-8599** in the U.S. and Canada or 2672-0026 in Costa Rica; www.villadelsueno.com) in Playa Hermosa; **Hotel Villa Casa Blanca** (ⓒ **2670-0518;** www.hotelvillacasa blanca.com) in Ocotal; and **Hotel Sugar Beach ★★** (ⓒ **2654-4242;** www.sugarbeach.com) in Playa Pan de Azúcar.

Hotel Playa Hermosa Bosque del Mar ★★★   Following a major rebuild, this has emerged as the premier beachfront boutique hotel in the area. The oceanfront suites here are plush, and feature outdoor Jacuzzis. The gardenview suites are very similar but an indoor sauna replaces the Jacuzzi. In both cases, second-floor units have better views and higher ceilings. The junior suites are all cozy and well equipped. The whole complex was built around and among the lush existing gardens and trees, and employs sustainable practices wherever possible. Trees come up and through the main lobby and restaurant, and through some of the decks off the rooms. Three of the suites are handicapped accessible. The second-floor bar and lounge has great views through the trees to the sea.

Playa Hermosa, Guanacaste. ⓒ **2672-0046.** Fax 2672-0019. www.hotelplayahermosa.com. 32 units. $175 junior suite; $225–$275 suite. AE, MC, V. **Amenities:** Restaurant; bar; Jacuzzi; pretty outdoor pool w/sculpted waterfall; free Wi-Fi. *In room:* A/C, TV, hair dryer, minifridge.

INEXPENSIVE

In addition to the places below, **Hostal La Botella de Leche** (ⓒ **2653-2061;** www.labotelladeleche.com) is a popular Tamarindo budget option. In Brasilito, I recommend **Hotel Brasilito** (ⓒ **2654-4237;** www.brasilito.com).

Hotel Zully Mar   The Zully Mar has long been a favorite of budget travelers, although they've upgraded their rooms and upped their prices over the years. The best rooms here are in a two-story white-stucco building with a wide, curving staircase on the outside. They have air-conditioning, tile floors, long verandas or balconies, overhead or standing fans, large bathrooms, and doors that are hand-carved with pre-Columbian motifs. The less expensive rooms are smaller and darker and have ceiling fans. There is a small pool that's refreshing if you don't want to walk across the street to the beach. This place is set on the busiest intersection in Tamarindo, and noise can be a problem at times.

Playa Tamarindo, Guanacaste. ☎ **2653-0140.** Fax 2653-0028. www.zullymar.com. 25 units. $46–$69 double. AE, MC, V. **Amenities:** Restaurant; small pool. *In room:* A/C (in some), minifridge, no phone.

Where to Dine

In most of the beach destinations in this region, your best bet is to find a simple, and sanitary, restaurant close to the water serving basic Tico fare and fresh seafood. I especially like **Camarón Dorado** (☎ **2654-4028**) in Brasilito.

VERY EXPENSIVE

Mar y Sol ★★ 🍴 INTERNATIONAL/SEAFOOD   French chef Alain Taulere has prepared food for regular folk and royalty. For visitors to his hilltop restaurant in Flamingo Beach, he offers a small, well-executed, and pricey selection of fresh seafood and meats. The ambience is casually formal, with the open-air main dining room dimly lit by old-fashioned lampposts and covered by a thatch roof. Along with a surf-and-turf combo featuring filet mignon and either lobster tails or jumbo shrimp, menu highlights include a Peking-style duck served with maple-hoisin sauce. For starters, try the escargot in puff pastry, or the refreshing Gazpacho, which is a family recipe that's been passed down for generations. Call in advance for free transportation from and back to your hotel.

Playa Flamingo. ☎ **2654-4151.** www.marysolflamingo.com. Reservations recommended for dinner in high season. Main courses $12–$25. AE, DC, MC, V. Nov–Apr daily 10am–3:30pm and 5–10pm; May–Aug daily 2–10pm. Closed Sept–Oct.

MODERATE

While in Tamarindo, check out what's shaking at **Dragonfly Bar & Grill ★★** (☎ **2653-1506**), which has a creative fusion menu and huge servings, or **Café de Playa** (☎ **2670-1621**), which is the hippest place in town, with a broad fusion menu and chill Euro-chic ambience.

Ginger ★★ 🍴 INTERNATIONAL/TAPAS   In this most creative restaurant in the area, the architecture and decor are stylish and modern, with sharp angles and loads of chrome and glass. The food is an eclectic mix of modern takes on wide-ranging international fare, all served as tapas, meant to be shared while sampling some of the many cocktails and wines served here. Still, it's easy to make a full meal. Order the house-special ginger-glazed chicken wings, along with some spring rolls, and a plate of fresh mahimahi marinated in vodka and Asian spices. There are also more traditional Mediterranean and Spanish-style tapas, as well as delicious desserts.

On the main road, Playa Hermosa. ☎ **2672-0041.** Tapas $4.50–$8. MC, V. Tues–Sun 5–10pm.

INEXPENSIVE

Marie's ★ COSTA RICAN/SEAFOOD   This long-standing local restaurant is a large open-air affair, with a soaring thatch roof and tall, thick columns all around. The menu has grown steadily over the years, although the best option here is always some simply prepared fresh fish, chicken, or meat. Check the blackboard for the daily specials, which usually highlight the freshest catch, such as mahimahi (*dorado*), marlin, and red snapper. You'll also find such Tico favorites as *casados* (a rice-and-bean dish), rotisserie chicken, and ceviche, as well as burritos and quesadillas.

Playa Flamingo. ☎ **2654-4136.** www.mariesrestaurantincostarica.com. Reservations recommended for dinner during the high season. Main courses $6.50–$23. V. Daily 6:30am–9:30pm.

Guanacaste After Dark

Nightlife varies from beach town to beach town. Tamarindo and Playa del Coco are probably the two rocking-est towns, while Flamingo, Brasilito, and Playa Hermosa are pretty quiet in comparison.

Some of my favorite bars in the area include the **Lizard Lounge** ★ (© 2670-0307) and **Zouk Santana** ★ (© 2670-1798; www.zouksantana.com) in Playa del Coco, and **Aqua** ★ (© 2653-2782; www.aquadiscoteque.com) and **Bar 1** ★★ (© 2653-2686) in Tamarindo.

For those looking for some gaming, there are two casinos in Tamarindo: the **Jazz Casino** (© 2653-0406), across from the El Diriá hotel, and the casino at the **Barceló Playa Langosta** resort (© 2653-0363). There's also one in Playa del Coco at the **Coco Beach Hotel & Casino** (© 2670-0494; www.cocobeachhotelandcasino. com), and another in Playa Flamingo at **Amberes** (© 2654-4001), just up the hill off the beach at Amberes.

MONTEVERDE

167km (104 miles) NW of San José; 82km (51 miles) NW of Puntarenas

Monteverde translates as "green mountain," and that's exactly what you'll find at the end of the steep and windy rutted dirt road that leads here. Next to Manuel Antonio, this is Costa Rica's most internationally recognized ecotourism destination. The fame, rapid growth, and accompanying traffic have led some to dub it the Monteverde Crowd Forest. Nevertheless, the reserve itself and the extensive network of private reserves around it are incredibly rich in biodiversity, and a well-organized infrastructure helps guarantee a rewarding experience for both first-time and experienced ecoadventurers.

The village of Monteverde was founded in 1951 by Quakers from the United States who wanted to leave behind a constant fear of war as well as an obligation to support continued militarism through paying U.S. taxes. They chose Costa Rica primarily because it had no standing army. Although Monteverde's founders came here to farm the land, they recognized the need to preserve the cloud forest that covered the mountain slopes above their fields, and dedicated the largest adjacent tract of cloud forest as the **Monteverde Biological Cloud Forest Reserve.**

Cloud forests are a mountaintop phenomenon. Moist, warm air sweeping in off the ocean is forced upward by mountain slopes, and as this moist air rises, it cools, forming clouds. This constant level of moisture has given rise to an incredible diversity of innovative life forms and a forest in which nearly every square inch of space has some sort of plant growing. Within the cloud forest, the branches of huge trees are draped with epiphytic plants: orchids, ferns, and bromeliads. This intense botanic competition has created an almost equally diverse population of insects, birds, and other wildlife.

 Today's Forecast: Misty & Cool

Make sure you understand that the climatic conditions that make Monteverde such a biological hot spot can leave many tourists feeling chilled. More than a few visitors are unprepared for a cool, windy, and wet stay, and can find Monteverde a bit inhospitable, especially from August to November.

Essentials

GETTING THERE

BY CAR From San José, take the Pan-American Highway north. About 20km (12 miles) past the turnoff for Puntarenas, there will be a marked turnoff for Sardinal, Santa Elena, and Monteverde. From this turnoff, the road is paved almost as far as the tiny town of Guacimal. From here it's another 20km (12 miles) to Santa Elena. It should take you a little over 2 hours to reach the turnoff and another 1 hour or so from there.

The final going is slow because the roads into Santa Elena are rough, unpaved dirt and gravel affairs. However, once you arrive, the roads in and around Santa Elena are paved, including all the way to Cerro Plano, and about halfway to the Cloud Forest Preserve.

BY BUS **Transmonteverde** express buses (© **2222-3854** in San José, or 2645-5159 in Santa Elena) leave San José daily at 6:30am and 2:30pm from Calle 12 between avenidas 7 and 9. The trip takes around 4 hours; the fare is $4.45. Buses arrive at and depart from Santa Elena. If you're staying at one of the hotels or lodges toward the reserve, you'll want to arrange pickup if possible, or take a taxi or local bus. Departing buses follow the same schedule.

Gray Line (© **2220-2126;** www.graylinecostarica.com) has a daily bus that leaves San José for Monteverde at 8am; the fare is $35. **Interbus** (© **2283-5573;** www.interbusonline.com) has two daily buses that leave San José for Monteverde at 8:15am and 2:30pm; the fare is $35 to $39. Either company will pick you up and drop you off at most San José and Monteverde area hotels.

ORIENTATION

As you approach Santa Elena, take the right fork in the road if you're heading directly to Monteverde. If you continue straight, you'll come into the little town center of tiny **Santa Elena,** which has a bus stop, a health clinic, a bank, a supermarket and a few general stores, and a collection of simple restaurants, budget hotels, souvenir shops, and tour offices. Heading just out of town, toward Monteverde, there's a new strip mall, with a large and prominent Megasuper supermarket. **Monteverde,** on the other hand, is not a village in the traditional sense of the word. There's no center of town—only dirt lanes leading off from the main road to various farms. This main road has signs for all the hotels and restaurants mentioned here, and it dead-ends at the reserve entrance.

GETTING AROUND

There are some six buses daily between the town of Santa Elena and the Monteverde Cloud Forest Biological Reserve. The first bus leaves Santa Elena for the reserve at 6am, and the last bus from the reserve leaves there at 4pm. The fare is $1.50. There's also periodic van transportation between the town of Santa Elena and the Santa Elena Cloud Forest Reserve. Ask around town and you should be able to find the current schedule and book a ride for around $2 per person. A **taxi** (© **2645-6969** or 2645-6666) between Santa Elena and either the Monteverde Reserve or the Santa Elena Cloud Forest Reserve costs around $8 to $10 for up to four people. Count on paying between $3 and $8 for the ride from Santa Elena to your lodge in Monteverde. Finally, several places around town rent **ATVs,** or all-terrain vehicles, for around $50 to $75 per day. Hourly rates and guided tours are also available. If this is up your alley, try **Aventura** (© **2645-6959;** www.cienporcientoaventura.com).

Monteverde

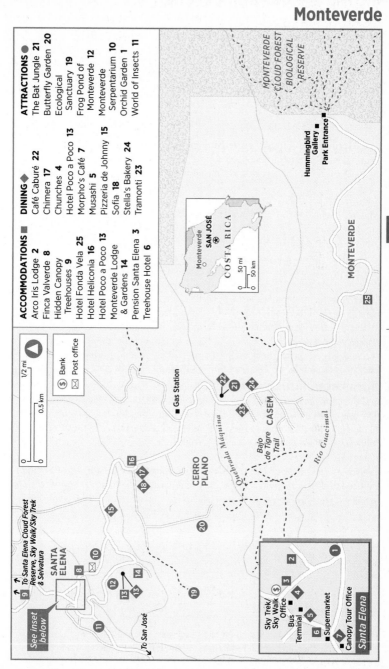

ACCOMMODATIONS ■
Arco Iris Lodge **2**
Finca Valverde **8**
Hidden Canopy Treehouses **9**
Hotel Fonda Vela **25**
Hotel Heliconia **16**
Hotel Poco a Poco **13**
Monteverde Lodge & Gardens **14**
Pension Santa Elena **3**
Treehouse Hotel **6**

DINING ◆
Café Caburé **22**
Chimera **17**
Chunches **4**
Hotel Poco a Poco **13**
Morpho's Café **7**
Musashi **5**
Pizzeria de Johnny **15**
Sofia **18**
Stella's Bakery **24**
Tramonti **23**

ATTRACTIONS ●
The Bat Jungle **21**
Butterfly Garden **20**
Ecological Sanctuary **19**
Frog Pond of Monteverde **12**
Monteverde Serpentarium **10**
Orchid Garden **1**
World of Insects **11**

ⓢ Bank
⊠ Post office

0 ½ mi
0 0.5 km

*To Santa Elena Cloud Forest
Reserve, Sky Walk/Sky Trek
& Selvatura*

SANTA ELENA

See inset below

To San José

CERRO PLANO

Quebrada Máquina

Gas Station ■

Bajo de Tigre Trail

CASEM

Río Guacimal

MONTEVERDE CLOUD FOREST BIOLOGICAL RESERVE

Hummingbird Gallery ■
Park Entrance ■

MONTEVERDE

Monteverde
SAN JOSÉ ✴

COSTA RICA

0 50 mi
0 50 km

Santa Elena

Sky Trek/ Sky Walk Office
Bus Terminal
Supermarket ■
Canopy Tour Office

9

COSTA RICA | Monteverde

VISITOR INFORMATION & FAST FACTS

The telephone number for the **local clinic** is ℂ 2645-5076; for the **Red Cross,** ℂ 2645-6128; and for the **local police,** ℂ **911** or 2645-6248. There's a 24-hour gas station about halfway between the town of Santa Elena and the Monteverde Cloud Forest Biological Reserve. The **Farmacia Monteverde** (ℂ 2645-7110) is right downtown. There's a **Banco Nacional** (ℂ 2645-5610) in downtown Santa Elena and a **Coopemex** (ℂ 2645-6948) on the road out to Santa Elena, near Finca Valverde; both have 24-hour ATMs.

What to See & Do

The **Monteverde Cloud Forest Biological Reserve** (ℂ 2645-5122; www.cct. or.cr) is one of the most developed and well-maintained natural attractions in Costa Rica. The trails are clearly marked, regularly traveled, and generally gentle in terms of ascents and descents. The cloud forest here is lush and largely untouched. Still, keep in mind that most of the birds and mammals are rare, elusive, and nocturnal. Moreover, to all but the most trained of eyes, those thousands of exotic ferns, orchids, and bromeliads tend to blend into one large mass of indistinguishable green. However, with a guide hired through your hotel, or on one of the reserve's official guided 2- to 3-hour hikes, you can see and learn far more than you could on your own. At $17 per person, the reserve's tours might seem like a splurge, especially after you pay the entrance fee, but I strongly recommend that you go with a guide.

Perhaps the most famous resident of the cloud forests of Costa Rica is the quetzal, a robin-size bird with iridescent green wings and a ruby-red breast, which has become extremely rare due to habitat destruction. The male quetzal also has two long tail feathers that can reach nearly .6m (2 ft.) in length, making it one of the most spectacular birds on earth. The best time to see quetzals is early morning to midmorning, and the best months are February through April (mating season).

ADMISSION, HOURS & TOURS   The reserve is open daily from 7am to 4pm, and the entrance fee is $17 for adults and $9 for students and children. Because only 160 people are allowed into the reserve at any one time, you might be forced to wait for a while. Most hotels can reserve a guided walk and entrance to the reserve for the following day for you, or you can get tickets in advance directly at the reserve entrance.

Some of the trails can be very muddy, depending on the season, so ask about current conditions. If the mud is heavy, you can rent rubber boots at the reserve entrance for $2 per day. They might make your hike much more pleasant. Before venturing into the forest, have a look around the information center. There are several guidebooks

Seeing the Forest for the Trees, Bromeliads, Monkeys, Hummingbirds . . .

Because the entrance fee to Monteverde is valid for a full day, I recommend taking an early-morning walk with a guide and then heading off on your own either after that hike or after lunch. A guide will point out and explain a lot, but there's also much to be said for walking quietly through the forest on your own or in very small groups. This will also allow you to stray from the well-traveled paths in the park.

available, as well as posters and postcards of some of the reserve's more famous animal inhabitants.

Night tours of the reserve leave every evening at 6:15pm. The cost is $17, including admission to the reserve, a 2-hour hike, and, most important, a guide with a high-powered searchlight. For an extra $3, they'll throw in round-trip transportation to and from your area hotel.

ACTIVE ADVENTURES OUTSIDE THE RESERVE

CANOPY TOURS & MORE   There's a glut of canopy tours in the Monteverde area, but I can recommend only those mentioned below. Anybody in average physical condition can do any of the adventure tours in Monteverde, but they're not for the fainthearted or acrophobic. Beware of touts on the streets of Monteverde, who make a small commission and frequently try to steer tourists to the operator paying the highest percentage.

One of the most complete attractions in the area is **Selvatura Park ★★** (© **2645-5929;** www.selvatura.com). Located close to the Santa Elena Cloud Forest Reserve, it is the best one-stop shop for various adventures and attractions in the area. In addition to an extensive canopy tour, with 13 cables connecting 15 platforms, they also have a network of trails and suspended bridges, a huge butterfly garden, a hummingbird garden, a snake exhibit, and a wonderful insect display and museum. Prices vary depending on how much you want to see and do. Individually, the canopy tour costs $45; the walkways and bridges, $25; the snake and reptile exhibit, $12; and the butterfly garden and the insect museum, $12 each. Packages to combine the various exhibits are available, although it's definitely confusing, and somewhat annoying, to pick the perfect package. For $121, you get the run of the entire joint, including the tours, lunch, and round-trip transportation from your Monteverde hotel. It's open daily from 7am to 4:30pm.

Another popular option is offered by the folks at **Sky Trek ★★** (© **2645-5238;** www.skyadventures.travel), which is part of a large complex of aerial adventures and hiking trails. This is one of the more extensive canopy tours in the country, and begins with a cable car ride (or **Sky Tram**) up into the cloud forest, where their zip-line canopy tour commences. This tour features 10 zip-line cables. The longest of these is some 770m (2,525 ft.) long, high above the forest floor. There are no rappel descents here, and you brake using the pulley system for friction. This tour costs $60.

One of the oldest canopy tours in the country is run by the **Original Canopy Tour ★** (© **2645-5243;** www.canopytour.com). This is one of the more interesting canopy tours in Costa Rica because the initial ascent is made by climbing up the hollowed-out interior of a giant strangler fig. The tour has 13 platforms and one rappel. The 2- to 2½-hour tours run four times daily and cost $45 for adults, $35 for students, and $25 for children 11 and under.

BIRD-WATCHING & HIKING   You can also find ample bird-watching and hiking opportunities outside the reserve boundaries. Avoid the crowds at Monteverde by heading 5km (3 miles) north from the village of Santa Elena to the **Santa Elena Cloud Forest Reserve ★★** (© **2645-5390;** www.reservasantaelena.org). This 310-hectare (766-acre) reserve has a maximum elevation of 1,680m (5,510 ft.), making it the highest cloud forest in the Monteverde area. There are 13km (8 miles) of hiking trails, as well as an information center. Because it borders the Monteverde Reserve, a similar richness of flora and fauna is found here, although quetzals are not nearly as common. The $14 entry fee at this reserve goes directly to support local schools. The reserve is open daily from 7am to 4pm. Three-hour guided tours are available for $15 per person, not including the entrance fee. (Call the number above to make a reservation for the tour.)

Sky Walk ★★ ((C) **2645-5238;** www.skyadventures.travel) is a network of forest paths and suspension bridges that provides visitors with a view previously reserved for birds, monkeys, and the much more adventurous traveler. The bridges reach 39m (128 ft.) above the ground at their highest point, so acrophobia could be an issue. The Sky Walk and its sister attraction, **Sky Trek** (see "Canopy Tours & More," above), are about 3.5km (2¼ miles) outside the town of Santa Elena, on the road to the Santa Elena Cloud Forest Reserve. The Sky Walk is open daily from 7am to 4pm; admission is $30, which includes a knowledgeable guide. For $60 per person, you can do the Sky Trek canopy tour and then walk the trails and bridges of the Sky Walk. Reservations are recommended for the Sky Trek; round-trip transportation from Santa Elena is just $5 per person.

Finally, you can walk the trails and grounds of the **Ecological Sanctuary ★** ((C) **2645-5869**), a family-run wildlife refuge and private reserve located down the Cerro Plano road. This place has four main trails through a variety of ecosystems, and wildlife viewing is often quite good here. There are a couple of pretty waterfalls off the trails. It's open daily from 7am to 5:30pm; admission is $10 for self-guided hiking on the trails; $25 during the day for a 2-hour guided tour; and $22 for the 2-hour guided night tour that leaves at 5:30pm.

HORSEBACK RIDING　There's excellent terrain for horseback riding all around Monteverde. **La Estrella Stables** ((C) **2645-5075**), **Palomina Horse Tours** ((C) **2645-5479**), and **Sabine's Smiling Horses** ((C) **2645-6894;** www.smiling horses.com) are the more established operators, offering guided rides for around $15 to $20 per hour.

OTHER ATTRACTIONS IN & AROUND MONTEVERDE

It seems as if Monteverde has an exhibit or attraction dedicated to almost every type of tropical fauna. I wish these folks would band together and offer some sort of general pass. However, as it stands, you'll have to shell out for each attraction.

Butterflies abound here, and the **Butterfly Garden ★** ((C) **2645-5512;** www. monteverdebutterflygarden.com), near the Pensión Monteverde Inn, displays many of Costa Rica's most beautiful species. Besides the hundreds of preserved and mounted butterflies, there are a garden and a greenhouse where you can watch live butterflies. The garden is open daily from 9am to 4pm, and admission is $12 for adults, $9 for students, and $4 for children, including a guided tour. The best time to visit is between 9:30am and 1pm, when the butterflies are most active.

If your taste runs toward the slithery, you can check out the informative displays at the **Monteverde Serpentarium ★** ((C) **2645-5238;** www.snaketour.com), on the road to the reserve. It's open daily from 9am to 8pm and charges $8 for admission. The **Frog Pond of Monteverde ★** ((C) **2645-6320**), a couple of hundred meters north of the Monteverde Lodge, is probably a better bet. The $12 entrance gets you a 45-minute guided tour, and your ticket is good for 2 days. A variety of amphibian species populate a series of glass terrariums. In addition, these folks have a butterfly garden. It's open daily from 9am to 8:30pm. I especially recommend that you stop by at least once after dark, when the tree frogs are active.

Fans of invertebrates will want to head to **World of Insects** ((C) **2645-6859**), which features more than 30 terrariums filled with some of the area's more interesting creepy-crawlies. My favorites are the giant horned beetles. This place is 300m (984 ft.) west of the supermarket in Santa Elena. It's open daily from 9am to 7pm; admission is $10.

Finally, don't go running from the **Bat Jungle** (© 2645-6566; www.batjungle. com), which provides an in-depth look into the life and habits of these odd flying mammals. A visit here includes several types of exhibits, from skeletal remains to a large enclosure where you get to see various live species in action—the enclosure and room are kept dark, and the bats have had their biological clocks tricked into thinking that it's night. It's quite an interesting experience. The Bat Jungle is open daily from 9am to 7:30pm. Admission is $10. In addition, there's a good gift shop and separate coffee shop, where they make homemade chocolate.

If you've had your fill of birds, snakes, bugs, butterflies, and bats, you might want to stop at the **Orchid Garden ★★** (© 2645-5308; www.monteverdeorchidgarden. com), in Santa Elena across from the Pension El Tucano. This botanical garden boasts more than 450 species of orchids. The tour is fascinating, especially the fact that you need (and are given) a magnifying glass to see some of the flowers in bloom. Admission is $10 for adults and $7 for students. It's open daily from 8am to 5pm.

Almost all of the area hotels can arrange a wide variety of other tours and activities, including guided night tours of the cloud forest and night trips to the Arenal Volcano (a tedious 4-hr. ride each way).

Shopping

The best-stocked gift shop in Monteverde is the **Hummingbird Gallery ★** (© 2645-5030). You'll find the gallery just outside the reserve entrance. Hanging from trees around it are several hummingbird feeders that attract more than seven species of these tiny birds. At any given moment, there might be several dozen hummingbirds buzzing and chattering around the building and your head. Inside you will find many beautiful color prints of hummingbirds and other local flora and fauna, as well as a wide range of craft items, T-shirts, and other gifts. The Hummingbird Gallery is open daily from 8am to 6pm.

Another good option is **CASEM ★** (© 2645-5190), on the right side of the main road, just across from Stella's Bakery. This crafts cooperative sells embroidered clothing, T-shirts, posters, and postcards with photos of the local flora and fauna, Boruca weavings, locally grown and roasted coffee, and many other items to remind you of your visit to Monteverde. CASEM is open Monday through Saturday from 8am to 5pm and Sunday from 10am to 4pm (closed Sun May–Oct). There is also a **gift shop** at the entrance to the Monteverde Cloud Forest Biological Reserve. You'll find plenty of T-shirts, postcards, and assorted crafts here, as well as a selection of science and natural history books.

Over the years, Monteverde has developed a nice little community of artists. Around town you'll see paintings by local artists such as Paul Smith and Meg Wallace, whose works are displayed at the Fonda Vela Hotel and Stella's Bakery, respectively. You should also check out **Casa de Arte ★★** (© 2645-5275), which has a mix of arts and crafts in many mediums.

Finally, it's also worth stopping by the **Monteverde Cheese Factory** (© 2645-5150; www.monteverde.net) to pick up some of the best cheese in Costa Rica. (You can even watch it being processed and get homemade ice cream.) The cheese factory is right on the main road about midway between Santa Elena and the reserve. They offer 1-hour tours at 9am and 2pm, at a cost of $10.

Where to Stay

When choosing a place to stay in Monteverde, be sure to check whether the rates include a meal plan. In the past almost all the lodges included three meals a day in their prices, but this practice is waning. Check before you assume anything.

EXPENSIVE

Hidden Canopy Treehouses ★★ 🏠 The individual villas here are the most unique accommodations in the area. All are built at treetop level on stilts, making them feel at one with the surrounding forest. All also feature tons of varnished hardwood, custom furniture, and a sculpted waterfall shower. Most have a four-poster handmade bed and some sort of canopy-level balcony or outdoor deck area. My favorite is "Eden," a two-level unit, with a sitting area and large deck upstairs, and bedroom, fireplace, and glassed in two-person Jacuzzi surrounded by forest below. Breakfast and sunset tea are served in the main lodge, which has spectacular views—especially at sunset—of the Nicoya gulf. This is also where you'll find two more economical room options.

On the road to the Santa Elena Cloud Forest Reserve. ℂ **2645-5447,** or 8888-7514. Fax 2645-9952. www.hiddencanopy.com. 8 units. $165 double; $245–$295 double treehouse. Rates include breakfast, afternoon tea, and taxes. Extra person $25. AE, MC, V. No children 7 and under. **Amenities:** Lounge; free Wi-Fi. *In room:* Hair dryer, minibar.

Hotel Fonda Vela ★★ Although it's one of the older hotels here, Fonda Vela remains one of my top choices. Moreover, this is one of the closer lodges to the Cloud Forest Reserve, a relatively easy 15-minute walk away. Guest rooms are in a series of separate buildings scattered among the forests and pastures of this former farm, and most have views of the Nicoya Gulf. The junior suites all come with cable television. The newer block of junior suites, some of which have excellent views, are the best rooms in the house, and I prefer them to the older and larger junior suites. The dining room has great sunset views, and it sometimes even features live music. Throughout the hotel, you'll see paintings by co-owner Paul Smith, who also handcrafts violins and cellos and is a musician himself.

On the road to the Monteverde Cloud Forest Reserve. ℂ **2645-5125.** Fax 2645-5119. www.fondavela. com. 40 units. $124 double; $146 junior suite. Extra person $10. AE, MC, V. **Amenities:** Restaurant; bar. *In room:* TV, hair dryer, minibar.

MODERATE

In addition to the hotels listed below, **Finca Valverde** (ℂ **2645-5157;** www. monteverde.co.cr), **Hotel Heliconia** (ℂ **2240-7311** for reservations or 2645-5109 at the hotel; www.hotelheliconia.com), and **Hotel Poco A Poco** (ℂ **2645-6000;** www.hotelpocoapoco.com) are other good options in this price range.

Arco Iris Lodge ★★ 🌿 This is my favorite hotel in the town of Santa Elena and an excellent value to boot. The rooms are spread out in a variety of separate buildings, including several individual cabins. All have wood or tile floors and plenty of wood accents. My favorite is the "honeymoon cabin," which has a Jacuzzi tub and its own private balcony with a forest view and good bird-watching, although room nos. 16 and 17 are good choices, also with their own small private balconies. The management here is helpful, speaks five languages, and can arrange a wide variety of tours. Although they don't serve lunch or dinner, breakfast is offered in a spacious and airy dining and lounge building, where refreshments are available throughout the day and evening.

Santa Elena. ✆ **2645-5067.** Fax 2645-5022. www.arcoirislodge.com. 20 units. $80 double; $195 honeymoon cabin. AE, MC, V. **Amenities:** Lounge. *In room:* No phone, free Wi-Fi.

Monteverde Lodge & Gardens ★★ ☺   This was one of the first ecolodges in Monteverde, and it remains one of the best. Rooms are large and cozy. Most feature angled walls of glass with chairs and a table placed so that avid bird-watchers can do a bit of birding without leaving their rooms. The gardens and secondary forest surrounding the lodge have some gentle groomed trails and are home to quite a few species of birds. Perhaps the lodge's most popular attraction is the large hot tub in a big atrium garden just off the lobby. The dining room offers great views, excellent food, and attentive service. The adjacent bar is a popular gathering spot, and there are regular evening slide shows focusing on the cloud forest. Scheduled bus service to and from San José is available, as is a shuttle to the reserve, horseback riding, and a variety of optional tours.

Santa Elena. ✆ **2257-0766** reservations office in San José, or 2645-5057 at the lodge. Fax 2257-1665. www.monteverdelodge.com. 28 units. $100–$224 double. Rates slightly lower in the off season, higher during peak periods. AE, MC, V. **Amenities:** Restaurant; bar; Jacuzzi; free Wi-Fi.

INEXPENSIVE

In addition to the hotels listed below, there are *pensiones* and backpacker specials in Santa Elena and spread out along the road to the reserve. The best of these is the **Pensión Santa Elena** (✆ **2645-5051;** www.pensionsantaelena.com).

It's also possible to stay in a room at the **Monteverde Cloud Forest Biological Reserve** (✆ **2645-5122;** www.cct.or.cr). A bunk bed, shared bathroom, and three meals per day here run $53 per person. For an extra $11 you can get a room with a private bathroom. Admission to the reserve is included in the price.

Treehouse Hotel   Housed in Santa Elena's first, and only, high-rise building, this hotel offers clean and spacious rooms in the center of town. Taking up the third—and highest—floor of this building, the rooms vary in size and the number of beds they feature. The best rooms come with small balconies overlooking the town, although these are also susceptible to street noise, particularly early in the morning and on weekend nights. All rooms feature bright-white tile floors, colorful bedspreads, and sparse furnishings. Although the building is modern, it is built around a massive old fig tree, hence the hotel's name.

Santa Elena. ✆ **2645-5751.** Fax 2257-6418. www.treehouse.cr. 7 units. $45 double. AE, MC, V. **Amenities:** Restaurant. *In room:* TV, hair dryer, no phone.

Where to Dine

Most lodges in Monteverde have their own dining rooms, and these are the most convenient places to eat, especially if you don't have a car. Because most visitors want to get an early start, they usually grab breakfast at their hotel. It's also common for people to have their lodge pack them a lunch to take to the reserve, although there's now a *soda* at the reserve entrance, and another coffee shop next to the **Hummingbird Gallery** (see above), just before the reserve entrance.

In addition to the places listed below, you can get good pizzas and pastas at **Tramonti** (✆ **2645-6120**) and **Pizzeria de Johnny** (✆ **2645-5066**), both out along the road to the reserve, and passable sushi and Japanese fare at **Musashi** (✆ **2645-7160**) in downtown Santa Elena. The restaurant at the **Hotel Poco a Poco** (✆ **2645-6000**) gets good marks for its wide range of international dishes. A popular choice for lunch is **Stella's Bakery** (✆ **2645-5560**), across from the CASEM gift

If all of the activities in Monteverde have worn you out, stop in at **Chunches** (☎ **2645-5147**), a bookstore with a small coffee shop and espresso bar that also doubles as a laundromat.

shop. The selection changes regularly but might include vegetarian quiche, eggplant parmigiana, and different salads, in addition to the daily supply of decadent baked goods. Finally, **Chimera** (☎ **2645-6081**) is a creative yet casual tapas restaurant, owned and run by the folks behind **Sofía** (see below).

EXPENSIVE

Sofía ★★★ 🎁 COSTA RICAN/FUSION This restaurant serves top-notch eclectic cuisine in a beautiful setting. Start everything off with a mango-ginger mojito and then try one of their colorful and abundant salads. Main courses range from seafood *chimichangas* to chicken breast served in a guava reduction. The tenderloin comes with a chipotle butter sauce, or in a roasted red-pepper and cashew sauce, either way served over a bed of mashed sweet potatoes. Everything is very well prepared and reasonably priced. There are two good-size dining rooms here; the best seats are close to the large arched picture windows overlooking the neighboring forest and gardens.

Cerro Plano, just past the turnoff to the Butterfly Farm, on your left. ☎ **2645-7017**. Reservations recommended during high season. Main courses $13–$17. AE, DC, DISC, MC, V. Daily 11:30am–9:30pm.

MODERATE

Café Caburé ★★ DESSERT/ARGENTINE Specializing in homemade artisanal truffles and other organic chocolate creations, this cozy spot is a good call for breakfast, lunch, dinner, or a sinfully sweet coffee break. Although they advertise themselves as an Argentine restaurant, I find that description lacking. The menu includes excellent curries and chicken mole, as well as an Argentine-style breaded steak, and fresh baked empanadas. A large, simple space, this place is located on the second floor of the Bat Jungle (p. 609). Be sure to save room for some chocolates for dessert, or their chocolate-walnut soufflé.

On the road btw. Santa Elena and the reserve, at the Bat Jungle. ☎ **2645-5020**. www.cabure.net. Reservations recommended during high season. Main courses $6–$14. AE, MC, V. Mon–Sat 8am–8:30pm.

INEXPENSIVE

Morpho's Café 🍃 COSTA RICAN/INTERNATIONAL Probably the best and definitely the most popular restaurant in the town of Santa Elena, this simple second-floor affair serves up hearty and economical meals. There are soups, sandwiches, and *casados* (plates of the day) for lunch and dinner, and delicious fresh-fruit juices, ice-cream shakes, and home-baked desserts throughout the day. The tables and chairs are made from rough-hewed lumber and whole branches and trunks, and the place brims with a light, convivial atmosphere. Morpho's is a very popular hangout for backpackers.

In downtown Santa Elena, across from the supermarket. ☎ **2645-5607**. Main courses $4.50–$16. AE, MC, V. Daily 11am–9pm.

Monteverde After Dark

The most popular after-dark activities in Monteverde are night hikes in one of the reserves and a natural-history slide show. However, if you want a taste of the local party scene, head to **Mata 'e Caña ★★** (**☎ 2645-5883**), which is just outside of downtown Santa Elena next to the entrance to Finca Valverde. With a contemporary club vibe, this place attracts a mix of locals and tourists, cranks its music loud, often gets people dancing, and occasionally has live bands. Alternatively, **Bromelias ★** (**☎ 2645-6272;** www.bromelias-cafe.com), located up a steep driveway from Stella's Bakery, sometimes features live music, theater, or open-mic jam sessions. These folks also run the neighboring **Monteverde Amphitheater,** a beautiful open-air performance space, which is the site of regular performances by acts visiting from San José and beyond.

THE ARENAL VOLCANO & ENVIRONS

140km (87 miles) NW of San José; 61km (38 miles) E of Tilarán

I've visited scores of times, and I never tire of watching red lava rocks tumble down the flanks of **Arenal Volcano,** and listening to its deep rumbling. If you've never experienced them firsthand, the sights and sounds of an active volcano are awe-inspiring. Arenal is one of the world's most regularly active volcanoes. In July 1968, the volcano, which had lain dormant for hundreds of years, surprised everybody by erupting with sudden violence. The nearby village of Tabacón was destroyed, and nearly 80 of its inhabitants were killed. Since that eruption, 1,607m (5,270-ft.) Arenal has been Costa Rica's most active volcano. Frequent powerful explosions send cascades of red-hot lava rocks down the volcano's steep slopes. During the day these lava flows smoke and rumble. However, at night the volcano puts on its most mesmerizing show. If you are lucky enough to be here on a clear and active night—not necessarily a guaranteed occurrence—you'll see the night sky turned red by lava spewing from Arenal's crater.

Lying at the eastern foot of this natural spectacle is the farming community of **La Fortuna.** This town has become a magnet for volcano-watchers, adventure tourists, and travelers from around the world. A host of budget and moderately priced hotels are in and near La Fortuna, and from here you can arrange night tours to the best volcano-viewing spots, which are 17km (11 miles) away on the western slope, on the road to and beyond the Tabacón Grand Spa Thermal Resort.

Essentials

GETTING THERE

BY PLANE   **Nature Air** (**☎ 800/235-9272** in the U.S. and Canada, or 2299-6000; www.natureair.com) flies to Arenal/La Fortuna daily at 12:20am from Tobías Bolaños International Airport in Pavas. The flight duration is 30 minutes. Return flights depart for San José at 12:50pm. One-way fares are $98. Nature Air also has connecting flights between Arenal and other destinations in the country.

Taxis are sometimes waiting for all arriving flights. If not, you can call one at **☎ 2479-9605** or 2479-8522. The fare to La Fortuna runs around $7. Nature Air can also arrange to have a van waiting for you, for $57 for up to four people.

BY CAR There are several routes to La Fortuna from San José. The most popular is to head west on the Interamerican Highway (CR1) and then turn north at Naranjo, continuing north through Zarcero to Ciudad Quesada on CR141. From Ciudad Quesada, CR141 passes through Florencia, Jabillos, and Tanque on its way to La Fortuna. This route offers wonderful views of the San Carlos valley as you come down from Ciudad Quesada; Zarcero, with its topiary gardens and church, makes a good place to stop, stretch your legs, and snap a few photos.

You can also stay on the Interamerican Highway (CR1) until San Ramón (west of Naranjo) and then head north through La Tigra on CR142. This route is also very scenic and passes the Villa Blanca Cloud Forest & Spa. The travel time on any of the above routes is roughly 3 to 3½ hours.

BY BUS Buses (© **2255-0567**) leave San José for La Fortuna at 6:15, 8:40, and 11:30am from the **Atlántico del Norte** bus station at Avenida 9 and Calle 12. The trip lasts 4 hours; the fare is $3.70. The bus you take might be labeled TILARAN. Make sure it passes through Ciudad Quesada. If so, it passes through La Fortuna; if not, you'll end up in Tilarán via the Interamerican Highway, passing through the Guanacaste town of Cañas, a long way from La Fortuna.

Or, you can take a bus from the same station to Ciudad Quesada and transfer there to another bus to La Fortuna. These buses depart roughly every 30 minutes between 5am and 7:30pm. The fare for the 2½-hour trip is $3. Local buses between Ciudad Quesada and La Fortuna run regularly through the day, although the schedule changes frequently, depending on demand. The trip lasts an hour; the fare is $1.50.

 ## BOATS, HORSES & taxis

You can travel between La Fortuna and Monteverde by boat and taxi, or on a combination boat, horseback, and taxi trip. A 10- to 20-minute boat ride across Lake Arenal cuts out hours of driving around its shores. From La Fortuna to the put-in point is about a 25-minute taxi ride. It's about a 1½-hour four-wheel-drive taxi ride between the Río Chiquito dock on the other side of Lake Arenal and Santa Elena. These trips can be arranged in either direction for between $25 and $50 per person, all-inclusive.

You can also add on a horseback ride on the Santa Elena/Monteverde side of the lake. There are several routes and rides offered. The steepest heads up the mountains and through the forest to the town of San Gerardo, which is only a 30-minute car ride from Santa Elena. Other routes throw in shorter sections of horseback riding along the lakeside

lowlands. With the horseback ride, this trip runs around $50 to $75 per person.

Warning: The riding is often rainy, muddy, and steep. Many find it much more arduous than awe-inspiring. Moreover, I've received numerous complaints about the condition of the trails and the treatment of the horses, so be very careful and demanding before signing on for this trip. Find out what route you will be taking, as well as the condition of the horses if possible. **Desafío Expeditions** (© **2479-9464;** www.desafio costarica.com) is one of the more reputable operators. They will even drive your car around for you while you take the scenic (and sore) route.

If you're looking to make the ride just by taxi and boat, check in with **Jeep Boat Jeep** (© **2479-9955**), which has two daily fixed departures in each direction at 7am and 4pm for $25 per person.

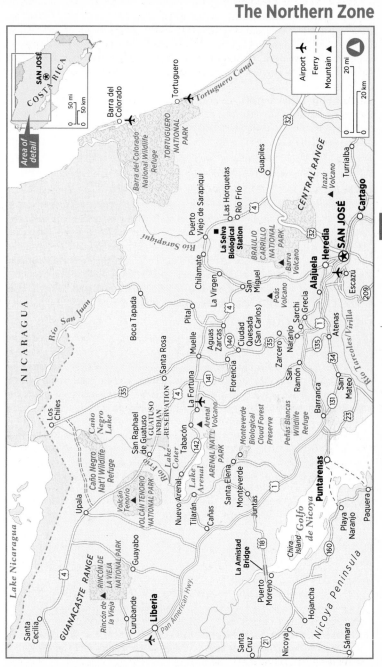

Buses depart **Monteverde/Santa Elena** for Tilarán every day at 7am. This is a journey of only 35km (22 miles), but the trip lasts 2½ hours because the road is in such horrendous condition. People with bad backs should think twice about making the trip, especially by bus. The return bus from Tilarán to Santa Elena leaves at 12:30pm. The fare is $2.30. Buses from Tilarán to La Fortuna depart daily at 8am and 4:30pm, and make the return trip at 7am and 12:30pm. The trip is 3 to 4 hours; the fare is $2.75.

Gray Line (© **2220-2126;** www.graylinecostarica.com) has a bus that leaves from San José to La Fortuna daily at 8am. The fare is $35. **Interbus** (© **2283-5573;** www.interbusonline.com) also has two buses daily leaving San José for La Fortuna at 8:15am and 2:30pm. The fare is $39. Both companies will pick you up at most San José–area hotels. And both companies also run routes from La Fortuna with connections to most other major destinations in Costa Rica.

ORIENTATION & FAST FACTS

As you enter La Fortuna, you'll see the massive volcano directly in front of you. La Fortuna is only a few streets wide, with almost all the hotels, restaurants, and shops clustered along the main road that leads out of town toward Tabacón and the volcano. There are several information and tour-booking offices and Internet cafes, as well as a couple of pharmacies, general stores, and laundromats on the streets that surround the small central park that fronts the Catholic church. There's a Banco de Costa Rica as you enter La Fortuna, just over the Río Burío bridge, and a Banco Nacional in the center of town, across the park from the church. Both have ATMs.

GETTING AROUND

If you don't have a car, you'll need to either take a cab or go on an organized tour if you want to visit the hot springs or view the volcano eruption. There are tons of taxis in La Fortuna (you can flag one down practically anywhere), and there is always a line of them ready and waiting along the main road beside the central park. A taxi between La Fortuna and Tabacón should cost around $6 to $7. Another alternative is to rent a car when you get here. **Alamo** (© **2479-9090;** www.alamocostarica.com) has an office in downtown La Fortuna.

There are also several places to rent scooters and ATVs around town. I like **Moto Rental** (© **2479-7376**), which rents ATVs, scooters, and off-road motorcycles. Provided it's not raining too heavily, this is a good way to get around. Rates run around $35 to $50 per day for a scooter, and $50 to $90 for an ATV or a dirt bike.

What to See & Do

EXPERIENCING THE VOLCANO ★★

The first thing you should know is that Arenal Volcano borders a region of cloud forests and rainforests, and the volcano's cone is often socked in by clouds and fog. Many people come to Arenal and never get to see the exposed cone. Moreover, the volcano does go through periods when it is relatively quiet.

The second thing you should know is that you can't climb Arenal Volcano—it's not safe due to the constant activity. Several foolish people who have ignored this warning have lost their lives, and others have been severely injured. The most recent fatalities occurred in August 2000.

Still, waiting for and watching Arenal's regular eruptions is the main activity in La Fortuna and is best done at night when the orange lava glows against the starry sky. Although it's sometimes possible simply to look up from the middle of town and see

TAKING A SOOTHING soak IN HOT SPRINGS

Arenal Volcano has bestowed a terrific fringe benefit on the area around it: several naturally heated thermal springs.

At the site of the former village that was destroyed by the 1968 eruption, **Tabacón Grand Spa Thermal Resort ★★★** (⌀ **2519-1900;** www.tabacon.com) is the most extensive, luxurious, and expensive spot to soak your tired bones. A series of pools, fed by natural springs, are spread out among lush gardens. At the center is a large, warm, spring-fed swimming pool with a slide, a swim-up bar, and a perfect view of the volcano. One of the stronger streams flows over a sculpted waterfall, with a rock ledge underneath that provides a perfect place to sit and receive a free hydraulic shoulder massage. The grounds here are extensive and worth exploring. The pools and springs closest to the volcano are some of the hottest—makes sense, doesn't it? The resort also has an excellent spa on the grounds offering professional massages, mud masks, and other treatments, as well as yoga classes (appointments required). Most of the treatments are conducted in lovely open-air gazebos surrounded by the rich tropical flora. The spa here even has several permanent sweat lodges, based on a Native American traditional design. A full-service restaurant, a garden grill, and a couple of bars are available for those seeking sustenance.

Entrance fees are $85 for adults and $40 for children 11 and under. This rate includes a buffet lunch or dinner, and allows admission for a full day. After 6pm, you can enter for $45, not including meals. The hot springs are open daily from noon to 10pm (spa treatments can be scheduled as early as 8am, and hotel guests can enter at 10am). The pools are busiest between 2 and 6pm. Management enforces a policy of limiting visitors, so reservations (which can be made online or by phone) are recommended. Spa treatments must be purchased separately, and reservations are required.

Baldi Hot Springs (⌀ **2479-2190;** www.baldihotsprings.cr), next to the Volcano Look Disco, are the first hot springs you'll come to as you drive from La Fortuna toward Tabacón. This place has grown substantially over the years, with many different pools, slides, and bars and restaurants spread around the expansive grounds. However, I find this place far less attractive than the other options mentioned here. There's much more of a party vibe at Baldi, with loud music often blaring at some of the swim-up bars. Admission is $26.

Just across the street from Baldi Hot Springs is the unmarked entrance of my current favorite local hot spring, **Eco Termales ★★** (⌀ **2479-8484**). Smaller and more intimate than Tabacón, this series of pools set amid lush forest and gardens is almost as picturesque and luxurious, although there are far fewer pools, the spa services are much less extensive, and there is no view of the volcano. Reservations are absolutely necessary here, and total admissions are limited so that it is never crowded. Admission is $29. These folks have added a restaurant serving basic local fare, but I recommend just coming for the springs.

Finally, there's **Tikokú ★** (⌀ **2479-1700**), which is located right beside Baldi, and run by the folks at Arenal Kioro (p. 621). This spot features a row of eight descending sculpted pools. Admission is $21.

Arenal erupting, the view is usually best from the north and west sides of the volcano along the road to Tabacón and toward the national park entrance. In fact, the best angle for volcano viewing often changes, as the activity shifts around the cone and side vents. If you have a car, you can ask at your hotel and around town for the best current spot to view the action and drive there. If you've arrived by bus, you will need to take a taxi or tour.

Arenal National Park ★★ (*②* **2461-8499**) constitutes an area of more than 2,880 hectares (7,117 acres), which includes the viewing and parking areas closest to the volcano. The park is open daily from 8am to 3:30pm and charges $10 admission per person. The trails through forest and over old lava flows inside the park are gorgeous and fun. (Be careful climbing on those volcanic boulders.)

Every hotel in town and several tour offices offer night tours to the volcano. (They don't actually enter the park; they stop on the road that runs btw. the park entrance and the Arenal Observatory Lodge.) Often these volcano-viewing tours include a stop at one of the local hot springs, and the price varies accordingly.

Note: Although it's counterintuitive, the rainy season is often a better time to see the exposed cone of Arenal Volcano, especially at night. I don't know why this is, but I've had excellent volcano-viewing sessions at various points during the rainy season; during the dry season the volcano can often be socked in solid for days at a time. The bottom line is that catching a glimpse of the volcano's cone is never a sure thing.

OTHER ADVENTUROUS PURSUITS IN THE AREA

Aside from the impressive volcanic activity, the area around Arenal Volcano is packed with other natural wonders.

ATV   Fourtrax Adventures (*②* **2479-8444;** www.fourtraxadventure.com) offers a 3-hour adventure through the forests and farmlands around La Fortuna. The tour includes a stop at a jungle swimming hole, where you can cool off. You get good views of the volcano, as well as the La Fortuna Waterfall. The cost is $85 per ATV. A second rider on the same ATV costs $25.

CANOPY TOURS & CANYONING   There are numerous ways to get up into the forest canopy here. Perhaps the simplest way is to hike the trails and bridges of **Arenal Hanging Bridges** (*②* **2290-0469;** www.hangingbridges.com). Located just over the Lake Arenal dam, this attraction is a complex of gentle trails and suspension bridges through a beautiful tract of primary forest. It's open daily from 7:30am to 4:30pm; admission is $22.

Another option is the **Sky Tram ★★** (*②* **2479-9944;** www.skyadventures. travel), an open gondola-style ride that begins near the shores of Lake Arenal and rises up, providing excellent views of the lake and volcano. From here you can hike their series of trails and suspended bridges. In the end you can hike down, take the gondola, or strap on a harness and ride their zip-line canopy tour down to the bottom. The zip-line tour here features several very long and very fast sections, with some impressive views of the lake and volcano. The cost is $66 for the combined tram ride up and zip-line down tour. It's $55 to ride the tram round-trip. The tram runs daily from 7:30am to 3pm. These folks also have a butterfly garden exhibit on-site.

There are several other zip-line canopy tours in the area, including the **Arenal Canopy Tour** (*②* **2479-9769**) and **Ecoglide ★** (*②* **2479-7120;** www.arenal ecoglide.com). The hotel **Montaña de Fuego** (p. 621) even has its own zip-line tour set up.

If you'd like a bigger rush than the canopy tours offer, you could go "canyoning" with **Pure Trek Canyoning ★★** (© **866/569-5723** in the U.S. and Canada, or 2479-1313; www.puretrekcostarica.com) and **Desafío Expeditions ★★** (© **2479-9464;** www.desafiocostarica.com); both offer canyoning adventures. This adventure sport is a mix of hiking through and alongside a jungle river, punctuated with periodic rappels through and alongside the faces of rushing waterfalls. Pure Trek's trip is probably better for first-timers and families with kids, while Desafío's tour is just a bit more rugged and adventurous. Both charge $90. Both of these companies offer various combination full-day excursions, mixing canyoning with other adventure tours, and tend to have two to three daily departures, including one in the morning and one in the afternoon.

You can take a bungee jump in La Fortuna at **Arenal Bungee** (© **2479-7440;** www.arenalbungee.com). The bungee jump here is a 40m (130-ft.) fall from a steel tower constructed on the outskirts of downtown La Fortuna. You can even try a water landing, as well as a "rocket launch," which is kind of the equivalent of becoming a human slingshot. Jumps, falls, and rocket shots cost $50 each, with various packages available. This attraction is open 9:30am to 6:30pm daily.

HIKING & HORSEBACK RIDING Horseback riding is a popular activity in this area, and there are scores of good rides on dirt back roads and through open fields and dense rainforest. Volcano and lake views come with the terrain on most rides. Horseback trips to the Río Fortuna waterfall are perhaps the most popular tours sold, but remember, the horse will get you only to the entrance; from there, you'll have to hike a bit. A horseback ride to the falls should cost between $20 and $45, including the entrance fee.

One popular and strenuous hike is to **Cerro Chato,** a dormant volcanic cone on the flank of Arenal. There's a pretty little lake up here. **Desafío Expeditions ★** (© **2479-9464;** www.desafiocostarica.com) leads a 5- to 6-hour hike for $75, including lunch.

Aventuras Arenal (© **2479-9133;** www.arenaladventures.com), **Desafío Expeditions ★★** (© **2479-9464;** www.desafiocostarica.com), **Jacamar Tours** (© **2479-9767;** www.arenaltours.com), and **Sunset Tours** (© **866/417-7352** in the U.S. and Canada, or 2479-9800 in Costa Rica; www.sunsettourcr.com) are the main tour operators. In addition to the above tours, each of these companies offers most of the tours listed in this section, as well as fishing trips and excursions on the lake, and transfers to other destinations around Costa Rica.

LA FORTUNA FALLS Leading the list of side attractions in the area is the impressive **Río Fortuna Waterfall ★** (© **2479-8338;** www.arenaladifort.com), located about 5.5km (3½ miles) outside of town in a lush jungle setting. There's a sign in town to indicate the road that leads out to the falls. You can drive or hike to just within viewing distance. When you get to the entrance to the lookout, you'll have to pay a $9 entrance fee to actually check out the falls. It's another 15- to 20-minute hike down a steep and often muddy path to the pool formed by the waterfall. The hike back up will take slightly longer. You can swim, but stay away from the turbulent water at the base of the falls—several people have drowned here. Instead, check out and enjoy the calm pool just around the bend, or join the locals at the popular swimming hole under the bridge on the paved road, just after the turnoff for the road up to the falls. The trail to the falls is open daily from 8am to 4pm.

MOUNTAIN BIKING This region is well suited for mountain biking. Rides range in difficulty from moderate to extremely challenging. You can combine a day on a mountain bike with a visit to one or more of the popular attractions here. **Bike Arenal ★** (📞 **866/465-4114** in the U.S. and Canada, or 2479-7150; www.bikearenal. com) offers up an excellent collection of top-notch bikes and equipment and a wide range of tour possibilities.

WHITE-WATER RAFTING & CANOEING   For adventurous tours of the area, check out **Desafío Expeditions ★★** (📞 **2479-9464;** www.desafiocostarica.com) or **Wave Expeditions ★★** (📞 **2479-7262;** www.waveexpeditions.com). Both companies offer daily raft rides of Class 1 to , 3, and 4 to 5 on different sections of the Toro, Peñas Blancas, and Sarapiquí rivers. A half-day float trip on a nearby river costs around $65 per person; a full day of rafting on some rougher water costs $85 per person, depending on what section of what river you ride. Both companies also offer mountain biking and most of the standard local guided trips. If you want a wet and personal ride, try Desafío's tour in inflatable kayaks, or "duckies."

A more laid-back alternative is to take a canoe tour with **Canoa Aventura** (📞 **2479-8200;** www.canoa-aventura.com), which offers half-, full-, and multiday excursions on a variety of rivers in the region, which range from $55 to $150 per person.

A similar option, although in a kayak, is offered up by **Rios Tropicales ★★** (📞 **2233-6455;** www.riostropicales.com), which offers a 4-hour paddle on the lake, with drinks and a snack, for $60.

SIDE TRIPS FROM LA FORTUNA

La Fortuna is a great place from which to make a day trip to the **Caño Negro National Wildlife Refuge ★**. This vast network of marshes and rivers (particularly the Río Frío) is 100km (62 miles) north of La Fortuna near the town of Los Chiles. This refuge is best known for its amazing abundance of bird life, including roseate spoonbills, jabiru storks, herons, and egrets, but you can also see caimans and crocodiles. Bird-watchers should not miss this refuge, although keep in mind that the main lake dries up in the dry season (mid-Apr to Nov), which reduces the number of wading birds. Full-day tours to Caño Negro average between $55 and $65 per person. However, most of the tours run out of La Fortuna that are billed as Caño Negro never really enter the refuge but instead ply sections of the nearby Río Frío, which features similar wildlife and ecosystems. If you're interested in staying in this area and really visiting the refuge, check out the **Caño Negro Natural Lodge** (📞 **2265-3302** for reservations in San José, or 2471-1426 at the lodge; www.canonegrolodge.com).

You can also visit the **Venado Caverns,** a 45-minute drive away. In addition to plenty of stalactites, stalagmites, and other limestone formations, you'll see bats and cave fish. Tours here cost around $45. All of the tour agencies and hotel tour desks can arrange or directly offer trips to Caño Negro and Venado Caverns.

Shopping

La Fortuna is chock-full of souvenir shops selling standard tourist fare. However, you'll find one of my favorite craft shops here. As you leave the town of La Fortuna toward Tabacón, keep your eye on the right-hand side of the road. When you see a massive collection of wood sculptures and a building called **Original Grand Gallery** (no phone), slow down and pull over. This local artisan and his family produce works in a variety of styles and sizes. They specialize in faces, many of them larger than a typical home's front door. You can also find a host of animal figures, ranging in style from purely representational to rather abstract. Another good shop, which features original oil paintings and acrylics, as well as other one-off jewelry and jade pieces, is **Art Shop Onirica** (✆ 2479-7589), located next to the La Fortuna post office.

Where to Stay

While La Fortuna is the major gateway town to Arenal Volcano, the best places to stay are located on the road between La Fortuna and the National Park.

VERY EXPENSIVE

In addition to the hotel reviewed below, another good upscale choice is **Arenal Kioro** ★★ (✆ 888/866-5027 in the U.S. and Canada, or 2461-1700; www.hotel arenalkioro.com).

Tabacón Grand Spa Thermal Resort ★★★   This is the most popular resort in the Arenal area—and for good reason. Many rooms have excellent, direct views of the volcano. Rooms on the upper floors of the 300-block building have the best vistas. Still, some have obstructed, or no, views. Be sure to specify in advance if you want a view room. Nine of the rooms are accessible to travelers with disabilities. Guests enjoy privileges at the spectacular hot-springs complex and spa across the street (see "Taking a Soothing Soak in Hot Springs," on p. 617), including slightly extended hours. When you consider the included entrance fee to the hot springs, the rates here are actually rather reasonable. This hotel has shown a committed and innovative approach to sustainable tourism. Guests are encouraged to make their stay carbon neutral, and the hotel is actively involved in a range of local development and conservation programs.

On the main road btw. La Fortuna and Lake Arenal, Tabacón. ✆ 877/277-8291 in the U.S. and Canada, or 2519-1999 reservations in San José, or 2479-2020 at the resort. Fax 2519-1940. www.tabacon.com. 114 units. $245–$390 double; $450 suite. Rates higher during peak periods. AE, DC, MC, V. **Amenities:** 2 restaurants; 2 bars; exercise room; Jacuzzi; large pool w/swim-up bar; all rooms smoke-free; access to nearby spa and hot springs. *In room:* A/C, TV, hair dryer, Wi-Fi.

EXPENSIVE

Montaña de Fuego Inn ★   This resort is a collection of individual and duplex cabins spread over hilly grounds. Most have marvelous volcano views from their spacious glass-enclosed porches. Some rooms even have back balconies overlooking a forested ravine, in addition to the volcano-facing front porch. The suites and junior suites all have a Jacuzzi tub. I actually prefer the juniors over the full suites, since the Jacuzzis in the juniors are set in front of a volcano-view picture window. Behind the hotel are some rolling hills that lead down to a small river surrounded by patches of gallery forest, where they conduct an adventurous horseback, hiking, and a zip-line canopy tour.

La Palma de la Fortuna, San Carlos. ✆ 2479-1220. Fax 2479-1240. www.montanafuegohotel.com. 69 units. $128 double; $174–$198 suite. Rates include buffet breakfast and taxes. AE, MC, V. **Amenities:** Restaurant; 2 bars; 2 Jacuzzis; outdoor pool; room service; full-service spa. *In room:* A/C, TV, hair dryer, minibar.

MODERATE

Other good options in this price range include **Volcano Lodge** (✆ 800/649-5913 in the U.S. and Canada, or 2479-1717; www.volcanolodge.com), on the road between town and Tabacón; **Hotel La Fortuna** (✆ 2479-9197; www.fortunainn.com); and **Hotel San Bosco** (✆ 2479-9050; www.hotelsanboscocr.com), in the town of La Fortuna proper.

Arenal Observatory Lodge ★★ This place is built on a high ridge very close to the volcano, with a spectacular view of the cone. The best rooms here are the junior suites below the restaurant and main lodge, as well as the four rooms in the Observatory Block, and the White Hawk villa. The "Smithsonian" rooms feature massive picture windows with a direct view of the volcano. The lodge offers a number of guided and unguided hiking options, including a free morning guided hike through their trails and gardens, as well as a wide range of other tours. Five rooms are truly equipped for wheelchair access, and a paved path extends almost 1km (⅔ mile) into the rainforest. When you're not hiking or touring the region, you can hang by the volcano-view swimming pool and Jacuzzi. The hotel maintains much of its land as part of a private nature reserve and is committed to sustainable and green tourism practices. If you're getting there on your own, keep in mind that while four-wheel-drive vehicle is not essential, you'll always be better off with the clearance afforded by a 4WD.

On the flanks of Arenal Volcano. To get here, head to the national park entrance, stay on the dirt road past the entrance, and follow the signs to the Observatory Lodge. ℭ **2290-7011** reservations number in San José, or 2479-1070 at the lodge. Fax 2290-8427. www.arenalobservatorylodge.com. 42 units. $87 La Casona double; $118 standard double; $153 Smithsonian; $175 junior suite. Rates include breakfast buffet and taxes and are lower in the off season. AE, MC, V. **Amenities:** Restaurant; bar; Jacuzzi; midsize outdoor pool; smoke-free rooms. *In room:* No phone.

INEXPENSIVE

La Fortuna is a tourist boomtown; basic hotels have been popping up here at a phenomenal rate for several years running. Right in La Fortuna you'll find a score of budget options. If you have time, it's worth walking around and checking out a couple. One of the better options is **Arenal Backpackers Resort** (ℭ **2479-7000;** www.arenalbackpackersresort.com), which bills itself as a five-star hostel. It has both shared-bathroom dorm rooms, and more upscale private rooms, but even backpackers get to enjoy the large pool, Wi-Fi, and volcano views.

There are a couple places both in town and right on the outskirts of La Fortuna that allow camping, with access to basic bathroom facilities, for around $5 to $10 per person per night. If you have a car, drive a bit out of town toward Tabacón and you'll find several more basic cabins and camping sites, some that even offer views of the volcano.

Hotel Las Colinas ★ 🍴 Las Colinas sits as the centerpiece of a mini-mall, which features some shops and a small spa. The rooms range from budget accommodations to spiffy junior suites with a volcano-view balcony and Jacuzzi. The budget rooms come with televisions, but lack the other amenities found in the rest of the rooms. The best feature of the hotel is its ample rooftop terrace, where breakfasts are served. Ecofriendly touches include solar-heated water.

La Fortuna, San Carlos. ℭ **2479-9305.** Fax 2479-9160. www.lascolinasarenal.com. 19 units. $45 budget room double; $66 double; $78 junior suite. Rates include breakfast and taxes. MC, V (5% surcharge). **Amenities:** Restaurant. *In room:* A/C, TV, minifridge, free Wi-Fi.

Where to Dine

The favorite meeting places in town are the **El Jardín Restaurant** (ℭ **2479-9360**) and **Lava Rocks** (ℭ **2479-8039**); both are on the main road, right in the center of La Fortuna. Other choices include **Rancho La Cascada** (ℭ **2479-9145**) and **Restaurante Nene's** (ℭ **2479-9192**) for Tico fare, and **Las Brasitas** (ℭ **2479-9819**) for a Mexican food fix. For good pizza and Italian cuisine, try either **Anch'io**

SUSTAINABLE volunteer PROJECTS IN COSTA RICA

Below are some institutions and organizations that are working on ecology and sustainable development projects in Costa Rica.

APREFLOFAS (Association for the Preservation of the Wild Flora and Fauna; © **2240-6087;** www.apreflofas. or.cr) is a pioneering conservation organization that accepts volunteers and runs educational tours around the country.

Asociación de Voluntarios para el Servicio en las Areas Protegidas (ASVO) ★ (© **2258-4430;** www.asvocr. org) organizes volunteers to work in Costa Rican national parks. A 2-week minimum commitment is required, as is a basic ability to converse in Spanish. Housing is provided at a basic ranger station, and there is an $18 daily fee to cover food, which is basic Tico fare.

Caribbean Conservation Corporation (© **800/676-2018** in the U.S., or 2278-6058; www.cccturtle.org) is a nonprofit organization dedicated to sea turtle research, protection, and advocacy. Their main operation in Costa Rica is headquartered in Tortuguero, where volunteers can aid in various scientific studies, as well as nightly patrols of the beach during nesting seasons to prevent poaching.

Costa Rica Rainforest Outward Bound School (© **800/676-2018** in the U.S., or 2278-6062; www.crrobs.org) is the local branch of this international adventure-based outdoor-education organization. Courses range from 2 weeks to a full semester, and offerings include surfing, kayaking, tree climbing, and learning Spanish.

Eco Teach (© **800/626-8992** in the U.S.; www.ecoteach.com) works primarily in facilitating educational trips for high-school and college student groups. Trips focus on Costa Rican ecology and culture. Costs run around $1,500 to $1,800 (not including airfare) per person for a 10-day trip, including lodging, meals, classes, and travel within the country.

Global Volunteers (© **800/487-1074** in the U.S. and Canada; www.global volunteers.org) is a U.S.-based organization that offers a unique opportunity to travelers who've always wanted a Peace Corps–like experience but can't make a 2-year commitment. For 2 to 3 weeks, you can join one of its working vacations in Costa Rica. A certain set of skills, such as engineering or agricultural knowledge, is helpful but not necessary. Each trip is undertaken at a particular community's request, to complete a specific project. *However, be warned:* These "volunteer" experiences do not come cheap. You must pay for your transportation as well as a hefty program fee, around $2,395 for a 2-week program.

Habitat for Humanity International (© **2296-3436;** www.habitatcostarica. org) has several chapters in Costa Rica and sometimes runs organized Global Village programs here.

The **Institute for Central American Development Studies** ★ (© **2225-0508;** www.icads.org) offers internship and research opportunities in the areas of environment, agriculture, human rights, and women's studies. An intensive Spanish-language program can be combined with work-study or volunteer opportunities.

The **Monteverde Institute** (© **2645-5053;** www.mvinstitute.org) offers study programs in Monteverde and also has a volunteer center that helps in placement and training of volunteers.

(*(© 2479-7560), near the heart of town, or **El Vagabundo** ★ (*(© 2479-9565), just on the outskirts.

For some fine and fancy dining, you can try **Los Tucanes** ★★ (*(© 2460-2020) restaurant at the Tabacón Grand Spa resort.

Don Rufino ★ COSTA RICAN/INTERNATIONAL   On a busy corner in the heart of town, this is easily the best—and the busiest—option right in town. The front wall and bar area open onto the street and are often filled with local tour guides and tourists. Try the *pollo al estilo de la abuela* (Grandma's chicken), which is baked and served wrapped in banana leaves, or one of the excellent cuts of meat. The chateaubriand and imported top sirloin steaks are huge and are meant to be shared by two. The bar stays open most nights until 2am or so.

Downtown La Fortuna. (*(© **2479-9997.** www.donrufino.com. Main courses $6–$40. Reservations recommended during the high season. AE, MC, V. Daily 11am–11pm.

Lava Lounge ★ 🎁 INTERNATIONAL   This humble downtown La Fortuna open-air restaurant combines a very simple setting with a sleek and somewhat eclectic menu. Healthy and hearty sandwiches, wraps, and salads are the main offerings here. You can get a traditional burger or one made with fresh grilled tuna. For more substantial fare, there's traditional Costa Rican *arroz con pollo*, and a *casado*, built around a thick pork chop. You can also get several different pasta dishes, and every evening there are dinner specials, which may include some coconut-battered shrimp with a mango salsa, or a prime sirloin steak in a green pepper or red-wine sauce. The decor consists of a series of rustic wooden tables with mostly bench seats.

Downtown La Fortuna, on the main road. (*(© **2479-7365.** Main courses $4.50–$20. AE, MC, V. Daily 11am–11pm.

La Fortuna After Dark

La Fortuna's biggest after-dark attraction is the volcano, but the **Volcano Look Disco** (*(© 2479-6961) is trying to compete. If you get bored of the eruptions and seismic rumbling, head here for heavy dance beats and mirrored disco balls. In town the folks at Luigi's Hotel have a midsize **casino** (*(© 2479-9898) next door to their hotel and restaurant, while the open-to-the-street bar at **Don Rufino** (see above) is a popular spot for a drink. Finally, there's a cozy sports bar with a pool table and flatscreen televisions on the second floor at the **Hotel Magic Mountain.**

MANUEL ANTONIO

140km (87 miles) SW of San José; 69km (43 miles) S of Playa de Jacó

Manuel Antonio was Costa Rica's first major ecotourist destination and remains one of its most popular. The views from the hills overlooking Manuel Antonio are spectacular, the beaches (especially those inside the national park) are idyllic, and its rainforests are crawling with howler, white-faced, and squirrel monkeys, among other forms of exotic wildlife. The downside is that you'll have to pay more to see it, and you'll have to share it with more fellow travelers than you would at other rainforest destinations around the country. Moreover, development has begun to destroy what makes this place so special. What was once a smattering of small hotels tucked into the forested hillside has become a long string of lodgings along the 7km (4⅓ miles) of road between Quepos and the national park entrance. Hotel roofs now break the tree line, and there seems to be no control over zoning and unchecked construction.

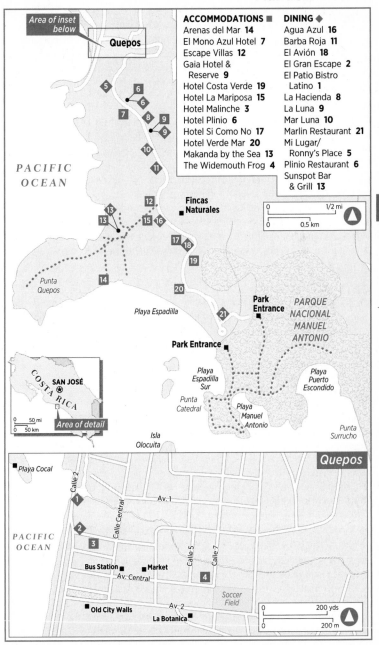

ACCOMMODATIONS ■

Arenas del Mar **14**
El Mono Azul Hotel **7**
Escape Villas **12**
Gaia Hotel &
  Reserve **9**
Hotel Costa Verde **19**
Hotel La Mariposa **15**
Hotel Malinche **3**
Hotel Plinio **6**
Hotel Si Como No **17**
Hotel Verde Mar **20**
Makanda by the Sea **13**
The Widemouth Frog **4**

DINING ◆

Agua Azul **16**
Barba Roja **11**
El Avión **18**
El Gran Escape **2**
El Patio Bistro
  Latino **1**
La Hacienda **8**
La Luna **9**
Mar Luna **10**
Marlin Restaurant **21**
Mi Lugar/
  Ronny's Place **5**
Plinio Restaurant **6**
Sunspot Bar
  & Grill **13**

Area of inset below

Quepos

PACIFIC OCEAN

Fincas Naturales

Punta Quepos

Playa Espadilla

Park Entrance

PARQUE NACIONAL MANUEL ANTONIO

Park Entrance

Playa Espadilla Sur

Punta Catedral

Playa Manuel Antonio

Playa Puerto Escondido

Punta Surrucho

COSTA RICA

SAN JOSÉ

Area of detail

Isla Olocuita

Quepos

Playa Cocal

PACIFIC OCEAN

Calle 2
Calle Central
Av. 1
Calle 5
Calle 7
Bus Station
Market
Av. Central
Soccer Field
Old City Walls
Av. 2
La Botanica

9

COSTA RICA | Manuel Antonio

A jumble of snack shacks, souvenir stands, and makeshift parking lots choke the beach road just outside the park, making the entrance road look more like a shanty than a national park.

Still, this remains a beautiful destination, with a wide range of attractions and activities. Gazing down on the blue Pacific from high on the hillsides of Manuel Antonio, it's almost impossible to hold back a gasp of delight. Offshore, rocky islands dot the vast expanse of blue, and in the foreground, the rich, deep green of the rainforest sweeps down to the water. Even cheap disposable cameras regularly produce postcard-perfect snapshots. It's this superb view that keeps people transfixed on decks, patios, and balconies throughout the area.

Those views that are so bewitching also have their own set of drawbacks. If you want a great view, you aren't going to be staying on the beach—in fact, you probably won't be able to walk to the beach. This means that you'll be driving back and forth, taking taxis, or riding the public bus. Also keep in mind that it's hot and humid here, and it rains a lot. However, the rain is what keeps Manuel Antonio lush and green, and this wouldn't be the Tropics if things were otherwise.

If you're traveling on a rock-bottom budget or are mainly interested in sportfishing, you might end up staying in the nearby town of **Quepos,** which was once a quiet banana port and now features a wide variety of restaurants, shops, and lively bars; the land to the north was used by Chiquita to grow its bananas.

Essentials

GETTING THERE

BY PLANE   **Sansa** (© 877/767-2672 in the U.S. and Canada, or 2290-4100 in Costa Rica; www.flysansa.com) has eight daily flights to the **Quepos airport** (XQP; no phone) beginning at 6am, with the final flight departing at 3:30pm from San José's Juan Santamaría International Airport (p. 559). The flight's duration is 30 minutes; the fare is $75 each way.

Nature Air (© 800/235-9272 in the U.S. and Canada, or 2299-6000; www. natureair.com) flies to Quepos daily at 9am and 2 and 4:20pm from Tobías Bolaños International Airport in Pavas (p. 560). The flight duration is 30 minutes; the fare runs $70 to $83 each way.

Both Sansa and Nature Air provide minivan airport-transfer service coordinated with their arriving flights. The service costs around $8 per person each way, depending on how many passengers are traveling. Speak to your airline's agent when you arrive to confirm your return flight and coordinate a pickup at your hotel for that day if necessary. Taxis meet incoming flights as well. Expect to be charged between $10 and $15 per car for up to four people, depending on the distance to your hotel.

When you're ready to depart, **Sansa** (© 2777-1912 in Quepos) flights begin departing at 6:44am, with the final flight leaving at 4:14pm. **Nature Air** (© 2777-2548 in Quepos) flights leave for San José daily at 7:40 and 10:45am and 2:35 and 5pm.

BY CAR   From San José, take the new San José–Caldera Highway (CR27) west to Orotina. Just past the tollbooth at Pavón, this road connects with the Costanera Sur (CR34), or Southern Coastal Highway. The exit is marked for Jacó and CR34. From here it's a straight and flat shot down the coast to Quepos and Manuel Antonio.

If you're coming from Guanacaste or any point north, take the Interamerican Highway to the Puntarenas turnoff and follow signs to the San José–Caldera Highway (CR27). Take this east toward Orotina, where it connects with the Costanera Sur (CR34). It's about a 4½-hour drive from Liberia to Quepos and Manuel Antonio.

BY BUS   **Express buses** (☎ 2223-5567) to Manuel Antonio leave San José daily at 6 and 9am, noon, and 2:30 and 7:30pm from the Coca-Cola bus terminal at Calle 16 between avenidas 1 and 3. Trip duration is 3 hours; the fare is $5.50. These buses go all the way to the park entrance and will drop you off at any of the hotels along the way.

Regular buses (☎ 2223-5567) to Quepos leave San José daily at 4 and 9:30am, noon, and 2, 4, and 6pm. Trip duration is 4 hours; the fare is $4.40. These buses stop in Quepos. From here, if you're staying at one of the hotels on the road to Manuel Antonio, you must take a local bus or taxi to your hotel.

Gray Line (☎ 2220-2126; www.graylinecostarica.com) has two daily buses that leave San José for Quepos and Manuel Antonio at 6:30am and 3pm; the fare is $35. The return bus leaves at 9:25am and 12:25pm for San José. **Interbus** (☎ 2283-5573; www.interbusonline.com) has two daily buses that leave San José for Quepos and Manuel Antonio at 8am and 2pm; the fare is $39. Return buses leave at 8:30am and 1:30pm. Both companies will pick you up at most San José—and Manuel Antonio—area hotels and also offer connections to various other popular destinations around Costa Rica.

In the busy winter months, tickets sell out well in advance, especially on weekends; if you can, purchase your ticket several days in advance. However, you must buy your Quepos-bound tickets in San José and your San José return tickets in Quepos. If you're staying in Manuel Antonio, you can buy your return ticket for a direct bus in advance in Quepos and then wait along the road to be picked up.

GETTING AROUND

A taxi between Quepos and Manuel Antonio (or any hotel along the road toward the park) costs between $4 and $6, depending on the distance. At night or if the taxi must leave the main road (for hotels such as La Mariposa, Parador, Makanda, and Arenas del Mar), the charge is a little higher. If you need to call a taxi, dial ☎ 2777-3080 or 2777-0425. Taxis are supposed to use meters, although this isn't always the case. If your taxi doesn't have a meter, or the driver won't use it, try to negotiate in advance. Ask your hotel desk what a specific ride should cost, and use that as your guide.

The bus between Quepos and Manuel Antonio takes 15 minutes each way and runs roughly every half-hour from 6am to 7pm daily, with one late bus leaving Quepos at 10pm and returning from Manuel Antonio at 10:30pm. The buses, which leave from the main bus terminal in Quepos, near the market, go all the way to the national park entrance before turning around and returning. You can flag down these buses from any point on the side of the road. The fare is 30¢.

You can also rent a car from **Adobe** (☎ 2777-4242), **Alamo/National** (☎ 2777-3344), **Economy** (☎ 2777-5260), **Hertz** (☎ 2777-3365), or **Payless Rent-a-Car** (☎ 2777-0115 or 8855-3540) for around $45 to $90 a day. All have offices in downtown Quepos, but with advance notice, someone will meet you at the airport with your car for no extra charge.

If you rent a car, never leave anything of value in it unless you intend to stay within sight of the car at all times. Car break-ins are common here. There are now a couple of parking lots just outside the park entrance that cost around $3 for the entire day. You should definitely keep your car in one of these while exploring the park or soaking up sun on the beach. And although these lots do offer a modicum of protection and safety, you should still not leave anything of value exposed in the car. The trunk is probably safe, though.

To rent a scooter, try **Fast Eddie's Scooter Rental** (☎ 2777-4127).

VISITOR INFORMATION & FAST FACTS

There's no real tourism information office in Quepos or Manuel Antonio. Your best source of information will be your hotel desk. The various tour operators around town are also a good bet.

FAST FACTS The telephone number of the **Quepos Hospital** is ℂ **2777-0922.** In the event of an emergency, you can also call the **Cruz Roja** (**Red Cross;** ℂ **2777-0116**). For the **local police,** call ℂ **2777-1511** or 2777-2117.

The **post office** (ℂ **2777-1471**) is in downtown Quepos. There are several pharmacies in Quepos, as well as a pharmacy at the hospital, and another close to the park entrance. There are also a half-dozen or so laundromats and laundry services in town.

Several major Costa Rican banks have branches and ATMs in downtown Quepos, and a couple of ATMs have sprung up along the road to the national park. An ample array of **Internet cafes** can be found around Quepos and along the road to Manuel Antonio, and many hotels have them as well.

What to See & Do

EXPLORING THE NATIONAL PARK

One of the most popular national parks in the country, Manuel Antonio is also one of the smallest, covering fewer than 680 hectares (1,680 acres). Its several nearly perfect small beaches are connected by trails that meander through the rainforest. The mountains surrounding the beaches quickly rise as you head inland from the water; however, the park was created to preserve not its beautiful beaches but its forests, home to endangered squirrel monkeys, three-toed sloths, purple-and-orange crabs, and hundreds of other species of birds, mammals, and plants. Once, this entire stretch of coast was a rainforest teeming with wildlife, but now only this small rocky outcrop of forest remains.

A guide is not essential here, but unless you're experienced in rainforest hiking, you'll see and learn a lot more with one. A 2- or 3-hour guided hike should cost between $25 and $45 per person. Almost any of the hotels in town can help you set up a tour of the park. Bird-watchers might want to book a tour with **Ave Natura** (ℂ **2777-0973;** www.avenatura.com), a local tour agency that specializes in birding. If you decide to explore the park on your own, a basic map is usually available at the park entrances for $1.

ENTRY POINT, FEES & REGULATIONS The park (ℂ **2777-5155**) is closed on Monday but is open Tuesday through Sunday from 8am to 4pm year-round. The entrance fee is $10 per person. The principal park entrance is at **Playa Espadilla,** the beach at the end of the road from Quepos. To reach the park station, you must cross a small, sometimes polluted stream that's little more than ankle-deep at low tide but that can be knee- or even waist-deep at high tide. It's even reputed to be home to a crocodile or two. For years there has been talk of building a bridge over this stream; in the meantime you'll have to either wade it or pay a boatman a small voluntary tip for the very quick crossing. Just over the stream and over a small rise, you'll find a small ranger station. Another ranger station is located inland at the end of the side road that leads off perpendicular to **Playa Espadilla** just beyond Marlin Restaurant. **Note:** The Parks Service allows only 600 visitors to enter each day, which could mean that you won't get in if you arrive in midafternoon during the high season.

THE BEACHES **Playa Espadilla Sur** (as opposed to Playa Espadilla, which is just outside the park; see "Hitting the Water," below) is the first beach within the actual park boundaries. It's usually the least crowded and one of the best places to find a quiet shade tree to plant yourself under. However, if there's any surf, this is also the roughest beach in the park. If you want to explore further, you can walk along this soft-sand beach or follow a trail through the rainforest parallel to the beach. **Playa Manuel Antonio,** which is the most popular beach inside the park, is a short, deep crescent of white sand backed by lush rainforest. The water here is sometimes clear enough to offer good snorkeling along the rocks at either end, and it's usually fairly calm. At low tide, Playa Manuel Antonio shows a very interesting relic: a circular stone turtle trap left by its pre-Columbian residents. From Playa Manuel Antonio, there's another slightly longer trail to **Puerto Escondido,** where a blowhole sends up plumes of spray at high tide.

THE HIKING TRAILS From either Playa Espadilla Sur or Playa Manuel Antonio, you can take a circular loop trail (1.4km/.9 mile) around a high promontory bluff. The highest point on this hike, which takes about 25 to 30 minutes round-trip, is **Punta Catedral ★★**, where the view is spectacular. The trail is a little steep in places, but anybody in average shape can do it. I have done it in sturdy sandals, but you might want to wear good hiking shoes. This is a good place to spot monkeys, although you're more likely to see a white-faced monkey than a rare squirrel monkey. Another good place to see monkeys is the **trail inland** from Playa Manuel Antonio. This is a linear trail and mostly uphill, but it's not too taxing. It's great to spend hours exploring the steamy jungle and then take a refreshing dip in the ocean.

Finally, there's a trail that leads first to Puerto Escondido (see above) and **Punta Surrucho,** where there are some sea caves. Be careful when hiking beyond Puerto Escondido: What seems like easy beach hiking at low tide becomes treacherous to impassable at high tide. Don't get trapped.

Hitting the Water

BEACHES OUTSIDE THE PARK **Playa Espadilla,** the gray-sand beach just outside the park boundary, is often perfect for board surfing and bodysurfing. At times it's a bit rough for casual swimming, but with no entrance fee, it's the most popular beach with locals and visiting Ticos. Some shops by the water rent boogie boards and beach chairs and umbrellas. A full-day rental of a beach umbrella and two chaise longues costs around $10. (These are not available inside the park.) This beach is actually a great spot to learn how to surf, because there are several open-air shops renting surfboards and boogie boards along the road fronting the beach. Rates run between $5 and $10 per hour, and around $20 to $40 per day. If you want a lesson, check in with the **Manuel Antonio Surf School** (© 2777-4842; www.masurf school.com), which has a roadside kiosk on the road to Manuel Antonio.

BOATING, KAYAKING, RAFTING & SPORTFISHING TOURS **Iguana Tours** (© 2777-2052; www.iguanatours.com) is the most established and dependable tour operator in the area, offering river rafting, sea kayaking, mangrove tours, and guided hikes.

The above company, as well as **Rios Tropicales** (© 2777-4092; www.aventuras h2o.com), offers full-day rafting trips for around $85 to $110. Large multiperson rafts are used during the rainy season, and single-person "duckies" are broken out when the water levels drop. Both of the above companies also offer half-day rafting adventures and sea-kayaking trips for around $65. Depending on rainfall and demand, they will run either the Naranjo or Savegre rivers. I very much prefer the **Savegre River ★★** for its stunning scenery.

Another of my favorite tours in the area is a mangrove tour of the **Damas Island estuary.** These trips generally include lunch, a stop on Damas Island, and roughly 3 to 4 hours of cruising the waterways. You'll see loads of wildlife. The cost is usually around $60 to $80.

Among the other boating options around Quepos/Manuel Antonio are excursions in search of dolphins and sunset cruises. **Iguana Tours** (see above) and **Planet Dolphin ★** (✆/fax **2777-1647;** www.planetdolphin.com) offer these tours for $75 per person, depending on the size of the group and the length of the cruise. Most tours include a snorkel break and, if lucky, dolphin sightings. **Jungle Coast Jets** (✆ **2777-1706;** www.junglecoastjets.com) offers 2-hour jet-ski tours for $105 per person. This tour plies the same waters and includes some snorkeling and the possibility of a dolphin encounter.

Quepos is one of Costa Rica's billfish centers, and sailfish, marlin, and tuna are all common in these waters. In the past year or so, fresh and brackish water fishing in the mangroves and estuaries has also become popular. If you're into sportfishing, try hooking up with **Blue Fin Sportfishing** (✆ **2777-0000;** www.bluefinsportfishing. com) or **Luna Tours Sportfishing** (✆ **2777-0725;** www.lunatours.net). A full day of fishing should cost between $400 and $1,800, depending on the size of the boat, distance traveled, tackle provided, and amenities. There's a lot of competition here, so shop around.

SCUBA DIVING & SNORKELING   Oceans Unlimited ★ (✆ 2777-3171; www.oceansunlimitedcr.com) offers both scuba diving and snorkel outings, as well as certification and resort courses. Because of river runoff and often less-than-stellar visibility close to Quepos, the best trips involve some travel time. Tours around Manuel Antonio run $65 to snorkel, and $95 for a two-tank scuba dive.

However, **Isla del Caño** (p. 639) is only about a 90-minute ride (each way). This is one of the best dive sites in Costa Rica, and I highly recommend it. Trips to Isla del Cano are $150 for snorkeling and $220 for two-tank scuba diving.

OTHER ACTIVITIES IN THE AREA

ATV   If you want to try riding a four-wheel ATV (all-terrain vehicle), check in with the folks at **Fourtrax Adventures** (✆ 2777-1829; www.fourtraxadventure.com). Their principal tour is a 3-hour adventure through African palm plantations, rural towns, and secondary forest to a jungle waterfall, where you stop for a dip. You cross several rivers and a long suspension bridge. Either breakfast or lunch is served, depending on the timing. The cost is $95 per ATV. A second rider on the same ATV costs $30.

BIKING   If you want to do some mountain biking while you're here, contact **Estrella Tour** (✆ 2777-1286) in downtown Quepos. These folks offer a number of different guided tours according to skill level for between $45 and $75 per day, as well as multiday expeditions.

BUTTERFLY GARDEN   Fincas Naturales/The Nature Farm Reserve ★ (✆ 2777-1043; www.wildliferefugecr.com) is just across from (and run by) Hotel Sí Como No (p. 632). A lovely bi-level **butterfly garden ★** is the centerpiece attraction here, but there is also a private reserve and a small network of well-groomed trails through the forest. A 1-hour guided tour of the butterfly garden costs $20 per person, or $35 when combined with a 1-hour guided hike through the forest. This is also a good place to do a night tour ($35).

CANOPY ADVENTURES   There are several canopy tours in the area. The most adventurous is offered by **Canopy Safari ★** (✆ 2777-0100; www.canopysafari. com), which features 18 platforms connected by a series of cables and suspension bridges. Adventurers use a harness-and-pulley system to "zip" between platforms, using a leather-gloved hand as their only brake. The **Titi Canopy Tour** (✆ 2777-3130; www.titicanopytours.com) is a similar but mellower setup. A canopy tour should run you between $50 and $70 per person.

About 20 minutes outside of Quepos is **Rainmaker Nature Refuge** (✆ 2777-3565; www.rainmakercostarica.org). The main attraction here is a system of connected suspension bridges strung through the forest canopy, crisscrossing a deep ravine. There are six bridges; the longest is 90m (295 ft.) across. There's also a small network of trails and some great swimming holes. The refuge is open daily from 7am to 4pm. The entrance fee is $15 and it's $30 for a guided tour.

HORSEBACK RIDING   While you can still sometimes find locals renting horses on the beaches outside the national park, I discourage this, as there are just too many crowds, the beach is too short, and the droppings are a problem. Better yet, head back into the hills and forests. Both **Finca Valmy** (✆ 2779-1118; www.valmytours.com) and **Brisas del Nara** (✆ 2779-1235; www.horsebacktour.com) offer horseback excursions that pass through both primary and secondary forest and feature a swimming stop or two at a jungle waterfall. Full-day tours, including breakfast and lunch, cost between $55 and $90 per person. Finca Valmy also offers an overnight tour for serious riders, with accommodations in rustic, but cozy, cabins in the Santa Maria de Dota mountains.

SPAS & WELLNESS CENTERS   There are quite a few massage therapists around Manuel Antonio and a couple of day spas. The best of these are **Raindrop Spa** (✆ 2777-2880; www.raindropspa.com), **Spa Uno ★** (✆ 2777-2607; www. spauno.com), and **Serenity Spa ★** at the Hotel Sí Como No. A wide range of treatments, wraps, and facials are available at all of the above. **Sivana Yoga** (✆ 2777-3899 or 8899-2987; www.sivanayoga.com) has open classes ($12) Monday through Friday at 7 and 8:15am above the Anaconda restaurant, across from the Hotel Costa Verde. Private classes are also offered.

Shopping

If you're looking for souvenirs, you'll find plenty of beach towels, beachwear, and handmade jewelry in a variety of small shops in Quepos and at impromptu stalls down near the national park.

For higher-end gifts, check out Hotel Sí Como No's **Regálame** (www.regalameart. com) gift shop, which has a wide variety of craft works, clothing, and original paintings and prints. Finally, one of my favorite shops from Jacóhas has a branch in Manuel Antonio. Look for handmade batik and tie-dye clothing at **Guacamole ★** (✆ 2777-2071) in the small Plaza Yara shopping center, along the road between Quepos and Manuel Antonio.

Where to Stay

Take care when choosing your accommodations in Quepos/Manuel Antonio. There are very few true beachfront hotels in Manuel Antonio, so you won't have much luck finding a hotel where you can walk directly out of your room and onto the beach. In fact, most of the nicer hotels here are 1km (⅔ mile) or so away from the beach, high on the hill overlooking the ocean.

VERY EXPENSIVE

In addition to the places listed below, **Gaia Hotel & Reserve ★★** (✆ 800/226-2515 in the U.S., or 2777-9797; www.gaiahr.com), **Hotel La Mariposa ★** (✆ 800/572-6440 in the U.S. and Canada, or 2777-0355; www.lamariposa.com), and **Makanda by the Sea ★★** (✆ 888/625-2632 in the U.S., or 2777-0442; www.makanda.com) are also all good choices.

If you're coming for an extended stay with your family or a large group, look into **Escape Villas ★★** (✆ 800/969-5806 in the U.S., or 2777-5258 in Costa Rica; www.escapevillas.com), which rents a broad selection of very large and luxurious private villas with all the amenities and some of the best views in Manuel Antonio.

Arenas del Mar ★★★ 🛎 This place has it all—direct beach access, a rainforest setting, fabulous views, and luxurious accommodations. Designed and built by the folks behind Finca Rosa Blanca (p. 577), Arenas del Mar is deeply committed to sustainability. Not all rooms have ocean views, so be sure to specify if you want one. However, all are spacious, with cool tile floors and stylish decorative accents. Most have outdoor Jacuzzi tubs on private balconies. The apartments are immense two-bedroom, three-bathroom affairs with a kitchenette, perfect for families and longer stays. The restaurant, lobby, and main pool are set on the highest point of land here, and several spots have fabulous views of Manuel Antonio's Punta Catedral. *Note:* The beautiful patch of beach right in front of Arenas has for decades been the town's de facto nude beach. Those who might find this offensive can walk farther down the beach or stick to the pools.

Manuel Antonio. ✆/fax **2777-2777.** www.arenasdelmar.com. 38 units. $290 double; $450 suite; $740 2-bedroom apt. Rates include full breakfast. AE, MC, V. **Amenities:** 2 restaurants; bar; snack bar; babysitting; concierge; 2 small outdoor pools; room service; spa. *In room:* A/C, TV, minibar, free Wi-Fi.

EXPENSIVE

Hotel Sí Como No ★★ 😊 🛎 This local favorite is a lively, upscale, midsize resort that blends in with and respects the rainforests and natural wonders of Manuel Antonio. The hotel is equally suited to families traveling with children and to couples looking for a romantic getaway. All the wood used is farm-grown, and while the rooms have energy-efficient air-conditioning units, guests are urged to use them only when necessary. The standard rooms are quite acceptable, but it's worth the splurge for a superior or deluxe room or a suite. Most of these are on the top floors of the two- to three-story villas, with spectacular treetop views out over the forest and onto the Pacific. There are a series of deluxe suites with lots of space and large garden bathrooms, some of which have private Jacuzzis. This hotel has earned "5 Leaves" in the CST Sustainable Tourism program, and the parent organization, Green Hotels of Costa Rica, was honored in 2009 as a corporate leader in sustainability by the Rainforest Alliance.

Manuel Antonio. ✆ **2777-0777.** Fax 2777-1093. www.sicomono.com. 52 units. $210–$265 double; $305–$340 suite. Extra person $30. Rates include breakfast buffet. Children 5 and under stay free in parent's room. AE, MC, V. **Amenities:** 2 restaurants; 2 bars; babysitting; concierge; 2 Jacuzzis; 2 midsize pools, including 1 w/small water slide; all rooms smoke-free; modest spa; free Wi-Fi. *In room:* A/C, hair dryer, minibar.

MODERATE

In addition to the hotels below, **El Mono Azul Hotel** (✆ 800/381-3578 in the U.S., or 2777-2572; www.monoazul.com), **Hotel Costa Verde** (✆ 866/854-7958 in the U.S. and Canada, or 2777-0584; www.costaverde.com), and **Hotel Plinio** (✆ 2777-0055; www.hotelplinio.com) are other options in this category.

Hotel Verde Mar ★   This hotel is a great choice for proximity to the national park and the beach, and I recommend it much more than the similarly priced hotel Karahé. From your room it's just a short walk to the beach (Playa Espadilla) via a raised wooden walkway. All the rooms here have plenty of space, nice wrought-iron queen-size beds, tile floors, a desk and chair, a fan, and a small porch. All but two of the rooms come with a basic kitchenette. Some of the larger rooms even have two queen-size beds. The hotel has no restaurant, but plenty are within walking distance. There's also a small pool here, for when the surf is too rough.

Manuel Antonio. © **877/872-0459** in the U.S. and Canada, or 2777-1805 in Costa Rica. Fax 2777-1311. www.verdemar.com. 24 units. $100 double; $110 suite. MC, V. **Amenities:** Small pool; free Wi-Fi. *In room:* A/C, kitchenette (in some), no phone.

INEXPENSIVE

In addition to the place listed below, the **Widemouth Frog** (© **2777-2798;** www. widemouthfrog.org) is a hostel option in downtown Quepos, which even has its own swimming pool.

Hotel Malinche   A good choice for budget travelers, the Hotel Malinche has consistently been my top choice in this category right in Quepos. The standard rooms are small but have hardwood or tile floors and clean bathrooms. Some of those on the second floor even have small private balconies that open onto a small interior courtyard. The more expensive rooms are larger and have air-conditioning, TVs, and carpets.

Half-block west of downtown bus terminal, Quepos. © **2777-3723.** Fax 2777-0093. hotelmalinche@ racsa.co.cr. 24 units. $30–$60 double. AE, MC, V. *In room:* No phone, free Wi-Fi.

Where to Dine

Scores of dining options are available around Manuel Antonio and Quepos, and almost every hotel has some sort of restaurant. For the cheapest meals around, try a simple *soda* in Quepos, or head to one of the open-air joints on the beach road before the national park entrance. The standard Tico menu prevails, with prices in the $4-to-$8 range. Of these, **Marlin Restaurant** (© **2777-1134**), right in front of Playa Espadilla, and **Mar Luna** (© **2777-5107**), on the main road just beyond Hotel La Colina, are your best bets. For simple pasta, pizzas, and Italian gelato, head to **Pizza de Marco** (© **2777-9400;** in the Plaza Yara shopping center). In addition to the places listed below, another good option, on the outskirts of Quepos, is **Mi Lugar,** or **"Ronny's Place"** (© **2777-5120;** www.ronnysplace.com).

For a taste of the high life, head to the **La Luna** ★ restaurant at Gaia Hotel & Reserve (see above) for their sunset tapas menu. The views are great and the creative tapas are very reasonably priced. **Barba Roja** ★ (© **2777-0331**) is another good choice on the road between Quepos and Manuel Antonio, with a creative fusion menu and sushi bar, as well as great sunset views and a lively bar scene. Other good and worthwhile options include **Agua Azul** ★ (© **2777-5280**), **El Avión** (© **2777-3378**), **La Hacienda** (© **2777-3473**), and **Plinio Restaurant** (© **2777-0055**), all located along the road between Quepos and the National Park.

El Gran Escape ★★ SEAFOOD   This Quepos landmark is consistently one of the top restaurants in the area. The fish is fresh and expertly prepared, portions are generous, and the prices are reasonable. If that's not enough of a recommendation, the atmosphere is lively, the locals seem to keep coming back, and the service is darn good for a beach town in Costa Rica. Sturdy wooden tables and chairs take up the large indoor dining room, and sportfishing photos and an exotic collection of masks fill up the walls. If you venture away from the fish, the menu features hearty steaks and giant burgers; there's also a wide assortment of delicious appetizers, including fresh tuna sashimi, and an excellent breakfast menu. El Gran Escape's **Fish Head Bar** is usually crowded and spirited, and if there's a game going on, it will be on the television here.

On the main road into Quepos, on your left just after the bridge. © **2777-0395.** www.elgranescape. com. Main courses $15–$33. AE, MC, V. Daily 7am–10pm.

El Patio Bistro Latino ★★★ NUEVO LATINO/FUSION   This small bistro-style restaurant is an outgrowth of the popular coffeehouse and roasting company Café Milagro. The same attention to detail and focus on quality carries over here. By day you can get a wide range of coffee drinks and specialties, as well as full breakfasts, fresh-baked sweets, and a variety of salads, sandwiches, wraps, and light lunch dishes. By night, things get more interesting. The menu features inventive main dishes that take advantage of local ingredients and various regional culinary traditions. Fresh mahimahi comes steamed in a banana leaf with a spicy *mojo*, and the tenderloin features a tamarind glaze and is served over roasted local yuca purée. There are nightly specials, and you may even find some of their home-roasted coffee used as an ingredient in a glaze, sauce, or dessert.

On the road btw. Quepos and Manuel Antonio. © **2777-0794.** www.elpatiobistrolatino.com. Reservations recommended. Main courses $8–$22. AE, MC, V. Daily 6:30am–10pm.

Sunspot Bar & Grill ★ 🍴 INTERNATIONAL   Dining by candlelight under a purple canvas tent at one of the few poolside tables here is one of the most romantic dining experiences to be had in Manuel Antonio. The menu changes regularly but features prime meats and poultry and fresh fish, excellently prepared. The rack of lamb might get a light jalapeño-mint or mango chutney, and the chicken breast might be stuffed with feta cheese, kalamata olives, and roasted red peppers and topped with a blackberry sauce. There are nightly specials and a good selection of salads, appetizers, and desserts.

At Makanda by the Sea (p. 632). © **2777-0442.** Reservations recommended. Main courses $10–$30. MC, V. Daily 11am–10pm.

Manuel Antonio After Dark

The bars at the **Barba Roja** restaurant, about midway along the road between Quepos and Manuel Antonio, and the **Hotel Sí Como No** (p. 632) are good places to hang out and meet people in the evenings. To shoot some pool, I head to the **Billfish Sportbar & Grill** ★ at the Byblos Resort (on the main road btw. Quepos and the park entrance). For tapas and local *bocas*, try **Salsipuedes** (roughly midway along the road btw. Quepos and the National Park entrance), which translates as "get out if you can." If you want live music, **Bambu Jam** ★ (along the road btw. Quepos and the park entrance) and **Dos Locos** (in the heart of downtown) are your best bets. In downtown Quepos, **Los Pescadores, Sargento Garcia's, Wacky Wanda's,** and the **Fish Head Bar** at El Gran Escape (see above) are all popular hangouts.

Night owls and dancing fools have several choices here, although the bulldozing of Mar y Sombra down by the beach has really hurt the scene. The live music at **Bambu Jam** is often salsa and merengue, perfect for dancing. For real late-night action, the local favorite appears to be the **Arco Iris,** which is located just before the bridge heading into town. Admission is usually around $3.

THE SOUTHERN ZONE

Golfito: 87km (54 miles) S of Palmar Norte, 337km (209 miles) S of San José; Drake Bay: 145km (90 miles) S of San José, 32km (20 miles) SW of Palmar; Puerto Jiménez: 35km (22 miles) W of Golfito by water (90km/56 miles by road), 85km (53 miles) S of Palmar Norte.

Costa Rica's southern zone is an area of jaw-dropping beauty, with vast expanses of virgin lowland rainforest, loads of wildlife, and few cities, towns, or settlements. Lushly forested mountains tumble into the sea, streams still run clear and clean, scarlet macaws squawk raucously in the treetops, and dolphins frolic in the **Golfo Dulce.** The **Osa Peninsula** is the most popular attraction in this region and one of the premier ecotourism destinations in the world. It's home to **Corcovado National Park ★★★**, the largest single expanse of lowland tropical rainforest in Central America, and its sister, **Piedras Blancas National Park ★★**. Scattered around the edges of these national parks and along the shores of the Golfo Dulce are some of the country's finest nature lodges. These lodges, in general, offer comfortable to nearly luxurious accommodations, attentive service, knowledgeable guides, and a wide range of activities and tours, all close to the area's many natural wonders.

But this beauty doesn't come easy. You must have plenty of time (or plenty of money—or, preferably, both) and a desire for adventure. It's a long way from San José, and many of the most fascinating spots can be reached only by small plane or boat—although hiking and four-wheeling will get you into some memorable surroundings as well. In many ways, this is Costa Rica's final frontier, and the cities of Golfito and Puerto Jiménez are nearly as wild as the jungles that surround them. Tourism is still underdeveloped here; there are no large resorts in this neck of the woods. Moreover, the heat and humidity are more than some people can stand. So it's best to put some forethought into planning a vacation down here, and it's usually wise to book your rooms and transportation in advance.

The best of these nature lodges are located around Drake Bay, Puerto Jiménez, and along the shores of the Golfo Dulce, or "Sweet Gulf." Despite being the largest and most important city in Costa Rica's southern zone, Golfito, in and of itself, is neither a popular nor a particularly inviting tourist destination. However, Golfito is still a major sportfishing center and a popular gateway to some of the lodges along the Golfo Dulce, as well as the isolated beach towns of Playa Zancudo and Pavones, farther south.

Although most of the lodges listed are quite cozy, and some are even spectacular, remember, none of these has an in-room television, telephone, or air-conditioning. Although this region is noted for its hot and steamy weather, most of these nature lodges are built with cool tile or wood floors and plenty of shade and ventilation. I never find it uncomfortable, and hordes of satisfied visitors seem to agree. However, if you are particularly sensitive to the heat, or particularly fond of air-conditioning, be sure to book a hotel with in-room air-conditioning.

Essentials

GETTING THERE

BY PLANE   Most travelers fly to the southern zone. **Sansa** (© 877/767-2672 in the U.S. and Canada, or 2290-4100 in Costa Rica; www.flysansa.com) and **Nature Air** (© 800/235-9272 in the U.S. and Canada, or 2299-6000; www.natureair.com) both have daily flights to Drake Bay, Golfito, and Puerto Jiménez. All of the lodges listed below will work with you to coordinate your transportation to their remote locations.

BY CAR   Take the San José–Caldera Highway (CR27) to the first exit past the Pozón tollbooth, where you will pick up the Southern Highway or Costanera Sur (CR34). Take this south through Jacó, Quepos, and Dominical to Palmar Norte, where you'll meet up with the Interamerican Highway (CR2). Take this south to the turnoff for La Palma, Rincón, and Puerto Jiménez.

If you're heading to Golfito, pass the turnoff and continue to Río Claro, where you'll notice a couple of gas stations and a bit of activity. Turn right here and follow the signs to Golfito. If you end up at the Panama border, you've missed the turnoff by about 32km (20 miles). The complete drive takes about 6 hours.

If you're heading to Puerto Jiménez, take the turnoff for La Palma, Rincón, and Puerto Jiménez. This road is paved at first, but at Rincón it turns to gravel. The last 35km (22 miles) are slow and rough, and, if it's the rainy season (mid-Apr to Nov), it'll be too muddy for anything but a four-wheel-drive vehicle.

BY BUS   Express buses leave San José daily at 7am and 3:30pm from the **Tracopa** bus station (© **2221-4214** or 2258-8939; www.tracopacr.com) on the Plaza Viquez at Calle 5 between avenidas 18 and 20. The trip takes 7 hours; the fare is $8. Buses depart Golfito for San José daily at 5am and 1:30pm from the bus station near the municipal dock.

Transportes Blanco-Lobo express buses (© **2257-4121** in San José, or 2771-4744 in Puerto Jiménez) leave San José daily at 8am and noon from Calle 12 between avenidas 7 and 9. The trip takes 7 to 8 hours; the fare is $10. Buses depart Puerto Jiménez for San José daily at 5 and 9am.

BY BOAT   There are speedboats working as boat taxis between Puerto Jiménez and Golfito. The fare is $5, and the ride takes a little under 30 minutes. These boats leave five or six times throughout the day, beginning at around 5am and finishing up at around 5pm. Ask at the *muellecito* (public dock) for schedules.

There is also a daily passenger launch. This slower boat takes 1½ hours, and the fare is $3. The ferry leaves the public dock in Golfito at 6am for Puerto Jiménez. The return trip leaves Puerto Jiménez's municipal dock at 11:30am.

It's also possible to charter a water taxi in Golfito for the trip across to Puerto Jiménez. You'll have to pay between $40 and $80 for an entire launch, some of which can carry up to 12 people.

GETTING AROUND

Most of the lodges listed are very isolated. All will work with you to coordinate your transportation to and from the destination, as well as during your stay.

What to See & Do

All lodges in the area also offer a host of half- and full-day tours and activities, including hikes in Corcovado National Park, horseback rides, and sportfishing. In some cases, tours are included in your room rate or package; in others, they must be bought a la carte. Other options include mountain biking and sea kayaking. Most of these tours run between $60 and $120, depending on the activity, with scuba diving ($90–$125 for a two-tank dive) and sportfishing ($450–$1,500, depending on the size of the boat and other amenities) costing a bit more.

EXPLORING CORCOVADO NATIONAL PARK ★★★

Exploring Corcovado National Park is not something to be undertaken lightly, but neither is it the expedition that some people make it out to be. The weather is the biggest obstacle to overnight backpacking trips through the park. Within a couple of

Trail Distances in Corcovado National Park

It's 14km (8⅔ miles) from La Leona to Sirena. From Sirena to San Pedrillo, it's 23km (14 miles) along the beach. From San Pedrillo, it's 20km (12 miles) to Drake Bay. It's 19km (12 miles) between Sirena and Los Patos.

hours of Puerto Jiménez (by 4WD vehicle) are several entrances to the park; however, there are no roads in the park, so once you reach any of the entrances, you'll have to start hiking. The heat and humidity are often quite extreme, and frequent rainstorms can make trails fairly muddy. If you choose the alternative—hiking on the beach—you'll have to plan your hiking around the tides when often there is no beach at all and some rivers are impassable.

Because of its size and remoteness, Corcovado National Park is best explored over several days; however, it is possible to enter and hike a bit of it on day trips. The best way to do this is to book a tour with your lodge on the Osa Peninsula, from a tour company in Puerto Jiménez, or through a lodge in Drake Bay.

GETTING THERE & ENTRY POINTS   The park has four primary entrances, which are really just ranger stations reached by rough dirt roads. When you've reached them, you'll have to strap on a backpack and hike. Perhaps the easiest one to reach from Puerto Jiménez is **La Leona ranger station,** accessible by car, bus, or taxi. If you choose to drive, take the dirt road from Puerto Jiménez to Carate (Carate is at the end of the road). From Carate, it's a 3km (1¾-mile) hike to La Leona. To travel there by "public transportation," pick up one of the collective buses (actually, a 4WD pickup truck with a tarpaulin cover and slat seats in the back) that leave Puerto Jiménez for Carate daily at 6am and 1:30pm, returning at 9am and 4pm. Remember, these "buses" are very informal and change their schedules regularly to meet demand or avoid bad weather, so always ask in town. The one-way fare is around $9. A small fleet of these pickups leaves just south of the bus terminal, and will stop to pick up anyone who flags them down along the way. Your other option is to hire a taxi to suit your schedule, which will charge approximately $70 to $90 each way to or from Carate.

You can also travel to **El Tigre,** about 14km (8⅔ miles) by dirt road from Puerto Jiménez, where there's another ranger station. But note that trails from El Tigre go only a short distance into the park.

The third entrance is in **Los Patos,** which is reached from the town of La Palma, northwest of Puerto Jiménez. From here, there's a 19km (12-mile) trail through the center of the park to **Sirena,** a ranger station and research facility (see "Beach Treks & Rainforest Hikes," below). Sirena has a landing strip that is used by charter flights.

The northern entrance to the park is **San Pedrillo,** which you can reach by hiking from Sirena or by taking a boat from Drake Bay or Sierpe (see "Beach Treks & Rainforest Hikes," below). It's 14km (8⅔ miles) from Drake Bay.

If you're not into hiking in the heat, you can charter a plane in Puerto Jiménez to take you to Carate or Sirena. A five-passenger plane costs between $200 and $400 one-way, depending on your destination. Contact **Alfa Romeo Air Charters** (© **2735-5353** or 2735-5112; www.alfaromeoair.com) for details.

FEES & REGULATIONS   Park admission is $10 per person per day. Only the Sirena station is equipped with dormitory-style lodgings and a simple *soda,* but the others have basic campsites and toilet facilities. All must be reserved in advance by contacting the **ACOSA** (Area de Conservación de Osa) in Puerto Jiménez (© **2735-5036;** fax 2735-5276; pncorcovado@hotmail.com). For a good overview of the park and logistics, check out **www.corcovado.org**. Its offices are adjacent to the airstrip. Only a limited number of people are allowed to camp at each ranger station, so make your reservations well in advance.

BEACH TREKS & RAINFOREST HIKES   The park has quite a few good hiking trails. Two of the better-known ones are the beach routes, starting at either the La Leona or San Pedrillo ranger stations. Between any two ranger stations, the hiking is arduous and takes all or most of a day, so it's best to rest for a day or so between hikes if possible. Remember, this is quite a wild area. Never hike alone, and take all the standard precautions for hiking in a rainforest. In addition, be especially careful about crossing or swimming in any isolated rivers or river mouths. Most rivers in Corcovado are home to crocodiles; moreover, at high tide, some are frequented by bull sharks. For this reason, river crossings must be coordinated with low tides. During the wet months (July–Nov) parts of the park may be closed. One of the longest and most popular hikes, between San Pedrillo and La Sirena, can be undertaken only during the dry season.

Sirena is a fascinating destination. As a research facility and ranger station, it's frequented primarily by scientists studying the rainforest. There's a network of trails that can easily keep you busy for several days. Just north of the station lies the mouth of the Río Sirena. Most days at high tide, bull sharks swarm and feed in this river mouth. There are also large crocodiles, so swimming is seriously discouraged. Still, it's quite a spectacle. The **Claro Trail** will bring you to the mouth of the Río Claro. A bit smaller, this river also houses a crocodile population, although allegedly fewer bull sharks. However, if you follow the Claro trail upstream, you can find several safe and appropriate swimming spots.

WHERE TO STAY & DINE IN THE PARK: CAMPSITES, CABINS & CANTINAS   Reservations are essential at the various ranger stations if you plan to eat or sleep inside the park (see "Fees & Regulations," above). **Sirena** has a modern research facility with dormitory-style accommodations for 28 persons, as well as a campground, *soda,* and landing strip for charter flights. There is also camping at the **La Leona, Los Patos,** and **San Pedrillo** ranger stations. Every ranger station has potable water, but it's advisable to pack in your own; whatever you do, don't drink stream water. Campsites in the park are $4 per person per night. A dorm bed at the Sirena station will run you $8—you must bring your own sheets, and a mosquito net is highly recommended—and meals here are another $40 per day. Everything must be reserved in advance.

AROUND PUERTO JIMENEZ

Kayaking trips around the estuary and up into the mangroves and out into the gulf are popular. Contact **Escondido Trex** ★ (© **2735-5210;** www.escondidotrex. com). There are daily paddles through the mangroves, as well as sunset trips where you can sometimes see dolphins. These folks also do guided rainforest hikes and can have you rappelling down the face of a jungle waterfall. More adventurous multiday kayak and camping trips are also available, in price and comfort ranges from budget to luxury (staying at various lodges around the Golfo Dulce and Matapalo).

For a real adventure, check in with **Psycho Tours** ★★ (© **8353-8619;** www. psychotours.com). These folks, who also call themselves Everyday Adventures, run a variety of adventure tours, but their signature combo trip features a free climb up (with a safety rope attached) the roots and trunks of a 60m-tall (200-ft.) strangler fig. You can climb as high as your ability allows, but most try to reach a natural platform at around 18m (60 ft.), where you take a leap of faith into space and are belayed down by your guide. This is preceded by an informative hike through primary rainforest, often wading through a small river, and followed by a couple of rappels down jungle waterfalls, the highest of which is around 30m (100 ft.). You can do either one of the above adventures separately, but I recommend the 5- to 6-hour combo tour, which costs $120.

If you want to learn to surf, contact **Pollo's Surf School ★** (© **8366-6559;** rhoades_gretchen@hotmail.com), which is near some excellent learning waves on Pan Dulce beach. A 2-hour lesson runs $55 per person.

AROUND DRAKE BAY

One of the most popular excursions from Drake Bay is a trip out to **Isla del Caño** and the **Caño Island Biological Reserve ★★** for a bit of exploring and snorkeling or scuba diving. The island is about 19km (12 miles) offshore from Drake Bay and was once home to a pre-Columbian culture about which little is known. A trip to the island will include a visit to an ancient cemetery, and you'll also be able to see some of the stone spheres believed to have been carved by this area's ancient inhabitants. Few animals or birds live on the island, but the coral reefs just offshore teem with life and are the main reason most people come here. This is one of Costa Rica's prime **scuba spots ★★**. Visibility is often quite good, and there's even easily accessible snorkeling from the beach. All of the lodges listed below offer trips to Isla del Caño.

One of the most interesting tour options in Drake Bay is a 2-hour **night tour ★★** (© **8382-1619;** www.thenighttour.com; $35 per person) offered by Tracie Stice, who is affectionately known as the "Bug Lady." Equipped with flashlights, participants get a bug's-eye view of the forest at night. You might see reflections of some larger forest dwellers, but most of the tour is a fascinating exploration of the nocturnal insect and arachnid world. Consider yourself lucky if she finds the burrow of a trapdoor spider or tarantula. Any hotel in Drake Bay can book the tour for you. However, the travel distance makes it impossible for those staying at hotels outside of walking distance of the town.

Where to Stay & Dine

In addition to the places listed below, the following lodges are all excellent options: **El Remanso ★★** (© **2735-5569;** www.elremanso.com); **Lapa Ríos ★★** (© **2735-5130;** www.laparios.com); **Playa Nicuesa Rainforest Lodge ★★** (© **866/504-8116** in the U.S.; www.nicuesalodge.com); and **Hotel Jinetes de Osa** (© **866/553-7073** in the U.S. and Canada; www.drakebayhotel.com).

Bosque del Cabo Rainforest Lodge ★★★ 🎁 This lodge is my favorite spot in this neck of the woods. The large individual cabins are attractively furnished, have wooden decks or verandas to catch the ocean views, and are set amid beautiful gardens. The deluxe cabins come with king-size beds and more deck space. The Congo cabin is my choice for its spectacular view of the sunrise from your bed. All cabins have indoor bathrooms, while tiled showers are set outdoors amid flowering heliconia and ginger. About half of the units also have outdoor bathtubs.

One trail leads to a jungle waterfall, and several others wind through the rainforests of the lodge's 260-hectare (642-acre) private reserve. If you're too lazy to hike down to the beach, there's a beautiful pool by the main lodge. Other attractions include a canopy platform 36m (118 ft.) up a Manu tree, reached along a 90m (295-ft.) zip line, as well as a bird- and wildlife-watching rancho set beside a little lake. If you have a mind to surf, they will rent you a board. These folks also rent out four separate, fully equipped houses that are quite popular, along with a couple of cabins set inland by their gardens. In addition to conservation and reforestation efforts, the owners here are actively involved in a host of local environmental and educational causes, and the lodge has been awarded "4 Leaves" by the CST Sustainable Tourism program.

Osa Peninsula. (✆)/fax **2735-5206** or 8389-2846. www.bosquedelcabo.com. 10 units. $310–$460 double. Rates include 3 meals daily and taxes. $30 per person round-trip transportation from Puerto Jiménez. MC, V. **Amenities:** Restaurant; bar; midsize pool. *In room:* No phone.

La Paloma Lodge ★★★ 🏠   On a steep hill overlooking the Pacific, with Isla del Caño in the distance, the luxurious bungalows at La Paloma offer expansive ocean views that make this my top choice in Drake Bay. All of the bungalows feature private verandas, and are set among lush foliage facing the Pacific. The large two-story Sunset Ranchos are the choice rooms here, with fabulous panoramic views. The other cabins are a tad smaller, but all are plenty spacious, beautifully appointed, and feature luxurious bathrooms and pretty good ocean views as well. Standard rooms, located in one long building, are smaller and less private than the cabins, but they're still attractive and have good views from their hammock-equipped balcony. The beach is about a 7-minute hike down a winding jungle path. Hearty and delicious meals are served family style in the restaurant. The owners are committed environmentalists and actively work on conservation and local development issues.

Drake Bay. (✆) **2293-7502** or (✆)/fax 2239-0954. www.lapalomalodge.com. 11 units. $1,115–$1,470 per person for 4 days/3 nights with 2 tours; $1,310–$1,700 per person for 5 days/4 nights with 2 tours. Rates are based on double occupancy and include round-trip transportation from San José, all meals, park fees, indicated tours, and taxes. Rates slightly lower in off season. AE, MC, V. **Amenities:** Restaurant; bar; small tile pool w/spectacular view; free Wi-Fi around the main lodge. *In room:* Minibar, no phone.

CARIBBEAN COAST BEACHES: CAHUITA & PUERTO VIEJO

213km (132 miles) E of San José, 55km (34 miles) S of Limón; Cahuita: 200km (124 miles) E of San José, 42km (26 miles) S of Limón, 13km (8 miles) N of Puerto Viejo; Tortuguero: 250km (155 miles) NE of San José, 79km (49 miles) N of Limón

Costa Rica's Caribbean coast is a world apart from the rest of the country. The pace is slower, the food is spicier, the tropical heat is more palpable, and the rhythmic lilt of patois and reggae music fills the air. Much of this coast was settled by Afro-Caribbean fishermen and laborers who came to this region in the mid-1800s to work on the railroad and banana plantations here. Today the population is still in large part made up of English-speaking blacks, whose culture and language set them apart from other Costa Ricans.

This remains one of Costa Rica's least discovered and explored regions. More than half of the coastline here is still inaccessible except by boat or small plane. Aside from the jungle canals, rainforests, and turtles of **Tortuguero National Park** (which is covered separately on p. 646), two small and atmospheric beach towns, **Cahuita** and **Puerto Viejo,** are the main attractions here. Cahuita is the quieter of the two, with a small and pretty national park backing its beaches and coral reefs, while Puerto Viejo is much more lively, with a strong surfer culture. Both boast some of the prettiest stretches of beach in the country.

Essentials

GETTING THERE

BY BUS **MEPE** express buses (📞 2257-8129) to Cahuita and Puerto Viejo leave San José daily at 6 and 10am, noon, and 2 and 4pm from the Caribbean terminal (Gran Terminal del Caribe) on Calle Central, 1 block north of Avenida 11. The trip to Cahuita takes about 4 hours; Puerto Viejo is a half-hour past Cahuita. Buses leave Puerto Viejo for San José daily at 9 and 11am and 4pm, stopping in Cahuita about a half-hour later.

Gray Line (📞 2220-2126; www.graylinecostarica.com) and **Interbus** (📞 2283-5573; www.interbusonline.com) also each have a daily bus from San José to both Cahuita and Puerto Viejo.

BY CAR The Guápiles Highway heads north out of San José on Calle 3 before turning east and passing close to Barva Volcano and through the rainforests of Braulio Carrillo National Park en route to Limón. The drive takes about 2½ hours and is quite beautiful. As you enter Limón, about 5 blocks before the busiest section of downtown, watch for a paved road to the right, just before the railroad tracks. Take this road south to Cahuita and Puerto Viejo. Alternatively, there's a turnoff with signs for Sixaola and La Bomba several miles before Limón. This winding shortcut skirts the city and puts you on the coastal road several miles south of town. From Limón it's roughly another 30 minutes to Cahuita, and 45 minutes to Puerto Viejo.

GETTING AROUND

Both Cahuita and Puerto Viejo are tiny little towns, and you can easily walk anywhere in the "downtown" section of each. To get to hotels and destinations a little farther afield, you'll find taxis in both towns. Your best bet is to ask your hotel to call you one, or call **Alejandro** (📞 8875-3209), **Wayne** (📞 2755-0078), or **Dino** (📞 2755-0012) in Cahuita, or **Bull** (📞 2750-0112 or 8836-8219) or **Taxi Kale** (📞 8340-2338) in Puerto Viejo.

VISITOR INFORMATION

Your hotel and the small local tourist agencies will be your best sources of information, especially in Cahuita. In Puerto Viejo, you can stop in at the **Asociación Talamanqueña de Ecoturismo y Conservación (ATEC; Talamancan Association of Ecotourism and Conservation)** ★★ (📞 2750-0398 or 📞/fax 2750-0191; www.ateccr.org), across the street from the Soda Tamara, a local nonprofit that runs excellent tours, has an Internet cafe, and serves as the de facto information center for the town.

FAST FACTS Tony Facio Hospital (📞 2758-0580), located just outside of downtown Limón, is the closest hospital. In Cahuita, there's a **Banco de Costa Rica** and ATM in the small strip mall in front the bus station; in Puerto Viejo, there's one on the main road in town, as well as a **Banco Nacional** in **Bribri,** about 10km (6 miles) away. To contact the police in Cahuita, dial 📞 2755-0217; in Puerto Viejo, dial 📞 2750-0230.

There are Internet cafes and small laundromats in both towns.

What to See & Do

CAHUITA NATIONAL PARK ★★

This little gem of a national park sits at the southern edge of the town of Cahuita. Although the pristine white sand beach, with its picture-perfect line of coconut palms and lush coastal forest backing it, is the main draw here, the park was actually created to preserve the 240-hectare (593-acre) **coral reef** that lies just offshore. The reef contains 35 species of coral and provides a haven for hundreds of brightly colored tropical fish. You can walk on the beach itself or follow the trail that runs through the forest just behind the beach to check out the reef.

One of the best places to swim is just before or beyond the **Río Perezoso (Lazy River),** several hundred meters inside Cahuita National Park. The trail behind the beach is great for bird-watching, and if you're lucky, you might see some monkeys or a sloth. The loud grunting sounds you'll hear off in the distance are the calls of howler monkeys, which can be heard from more than a kilometer away. Nearer at hand, you're likely to hear crabs scuttling amid the dry leaves on the forest floor—a half-dozen or so species of land crabs live in this region—my favorites are the bright orange-and-purple ones.

The trail behind the beach stretches a little more than 9km (5.6 miles) to the southern end of the park at **Puerto Vargas,** where you'll find a beautiful white-sand beach, the park headquarters, and a rustic campground with showers and outhouses. The best section of reef is off the point at Punta Cahuita, and you can snorkel here. If you don't dawdle, the 3.8km (2.4-mile) hike to Punta Cahuita should take a little over an hour each way, although I'd allow plenty of extra time to marvel at the flora and fauna, and take a dip or two in the sea. Bring plenty of mosquito repellent because this area can be buggy.

Although there's snorkeling from the shore at Punta Cahuita, the nicest coral heads are several hundred meters offshore, and it's best to have a boat take you out. A 3-hour **snorkel trip** costs between $15 and $30 per person with equipment. You can arrange one with any of the local tour companies below. *Note:* These trips are best taken when the seas are calm—for safety, visibility, and comfort.

The **in-town park entrance** is just over a footbridge at the end of the village's main street. It has bathroom facilities, changing rooms, and storage lockers. This is the best place to enter if you just want to spend the day on the beach and maybe take a little hike in the bordering forest. The alternate park entrance is at the southern end of the park in **Puerto Vargas.** This is where you should come if you plan to camp at the park or if you don't feel up to hiking a couple of hours to reach the good snorkeling spots. The road to Puerto Vargas is approximately 5km (3 miles) south of Cahuita on the left.

Officially, **admission** is $10 per person per day, but this is collected only at the Puerto Vargas entrance. You can enter the park from Cahuita for free or with a voluntary contribution. The park is open from dawn to dusk for day visitors. **Camping** is an extra $2 per person. Fifty campsites at Puerto Vargas stretch along for several kilometers and are either right on or just a few steps from the beach.

THE MANZANILLO-GANDOCA WILDLIFE REFUGE ★★

The Manzanillo-Gandoca Wildlife Refuge, 15km (9⅓ miles) south of Puerto Viejo, encompasses the tiny village of Manzanillo, and extends all the way to the Panamanian border. Manatees, crocodiles, and more than 350 species of birds live within the boundaries of the reserve. The reserve also includes the coral reef offshore—when the seas are calm, this is the best **snorkeling** and **diving** spot on this entire coast. Four species of **sea turtles** nest on one 8.9km (5½-mile) stretch of beach within the reserve between March and July. Three species of dolphins also inhabit and frolic in the waters just off Manzanillo. The waters here are home to Atlantic spotted, bottlenose, and the rare tucuxi. This latter species favors the brackish estuary waters, but has actually been observed in mixed species mating with local bottlenose dolphins. Many local tour guides and operators offer boat trips out to spot them.

If you want to explore the refuge, you can easily find the single, well-maintained trail by walking along the beach just south of town until you have to wade across a small river. On the other side, you'll pick up the trail head. Otherwise, you can ask around the village for local guides. For organized sportfishing excursions or dolphin-sighting tours around Manzanillo, check in with the folks at **Bacalao Tours** (© **2759-9116;** bacalaomanzanillo@yahoo.com).

Buses run periodically between Puerto Viejo and Manzanillo throughout the day, or you can hire a cab for around $7 to Punta Uva or $12 to Manzanillo. Alternatively, it's about 1½ hours each way by bicycle, with only two relatively small hills to contend with. Although the road is paved all the way to Manzanillo, between the near-constant potholes and washed-out sections, it's almost like riding an off-road trail. It's also possible to walk along the beach all the way from Puerto Viejo to Manzanillo, with a couple of short and well-worn detours inland around rocky points. However, I recommend you catch a ride down to Manzanillo and save your energies for the trails and beaches inside the refuge.

CULTURAL & ADVENTURE TOURS   A host of local tour agencies offer a range of tour and adventure options, including snorkeling trips, jungle tours, white-water rafting trips, bird-watching outings, zip-line canopy adventures, and tours to the Bribri reservation. Rates run from $20 to $110 depending on the activity, group size, and length of the tour.

In Cahuita, I recommend **Cahuita Tours and Adventure Center** (© **2755-0000;** www.cahuitatours.com). While in Puerto Viejo, you should check in with the **Asociación Talamanqueña de Ecoturismo y Conservación (ATEC; Talamancan Association of Ecotourism and Conservation)** ★★ (© **2750-0398** or ©/fax 2750-0191; www.ateccr.org), **Aventuras Bravas** ★★ (© **2750-2000** or 8849-7600; www.braveadventure.net), **Exploradores Outdoors** ★★ (© **2750-2020;** www.exploradoresoutdoors.com), and **Terraventuras** ★ (© **2750-0750;** www.terraventuras.com).

Several operators and makeshift roadside stands in both towns offer bicycles, scooters, boogie boards, surfboards, and snorkel gear for rent. Shop around and compare prices and the quality of the equipment before settling on any one.

SURFING   Surfers will want to head to Puerto Viejo. Just offshore from the tiny village park is a shallow reef where powerful storm-generated waves sometimes reach 6m (20 ft.). **Salsa Brava,** as it's known, is the prime surf break on the Caribbean coast. Even when the waves are small, this spot is recommended only for very experienced surfers because of the danger of the reef. Other popular beach breaks are south of town on Playa Cocles. If you're interested in surf lessons or want to rent a board, check in with **Aventuras Bravas** (see above).

WILDLIFE VIEWING UP CLOSE & PERSONAL   Bird-watchers and sloth lovers should head north 9km (5½ miles) to **Aviarios Sloth Sanctuary of Costa Rica** ★★ (©/fax **2750-0775;** www.slothrescue.org). Their signature tour features an informative visit to their sloth rehabilitation project and learning center, as well as a 1-hour canoe tour through the surrounding estuary and river system. More than 330 species of birds have been spotted here. You'll get an up-close look at a range of rescued wild sloths, both adults and babies, as well as several bred in captivity. Afterward, you can hike their trail system and look for sloths in the wild. Tours begin at 7am, with the last tour of the day leaving at 2:30pm. It's best to make reservations in advance.

NOT YOUR EVERYDAY GARDENS There are several interesting botanical, butterfly, and multipurpose gardens in this area. On the main highway, just north of the main entrance to Cahuita, is the **Mariposario Cahuita** (© **2755-0361**), a large, informative butterfly-farm attraction that charges $8 and is open daily from 8:30am to 3:30pm. It's best to come in the early morning on a sunny day, when the butterflies are most active.

In Puerto Viejo, be sure to visit the **Finca La Isla Botanical Gardens ★★** (© **2750-0046** or 8886-8530; www.costaricacaribbean.com), a couple hundred meters inland from the Black Sand Beach on a side road just north of El Pizote lodge. Peter Kring and his late wife Lindy poured time and love into the creation of this meandering collection of native and imported tropical flora. You'll see medicinal, commercial, and just plain wild flowering plants, fruit, herbs, trees, and bushes. Visitors get to gorge on whatever is ripe at the moment. There's also a rigorous rainforest loop trail leaving from the grounds. The gardens are generally open Friday through Monday from 10am to 4pm, but visits at other times can sometimes be arranged in advance. Entrance to the garden is $5 per person for a self-guided tour of the trails (you can buy their trail map for an extra $1), or $10 for a 2½-hour guided tour.

Cacao Trails ★ (© **2751-8186**) is a one-stop attraction featuring botanical gardens, a small serpentarium, an open-air museum demonstrating the tools and techniques of cacao cultivation and processing, and a series of trails. There's also a large open-air restaurant, and a swimming pool for cooling off. You can take canoe rides on the bordering Carbon River, and even watch leatherback sea turtles lay their eggs during the nesting season (see p. 647 for info). Admission to the attraction is $25, including a guided tour. A full-day tour, including lunch and a canoe trip, as well as the guided tour, costs $47. During turtle nesting season, they do night tours to watch sea turtles lay their eggs.

Where to Stay
IN CAHUITA

In addition to the places listed below, **Magellan Inn** (©/fax **2755-0035**; www.magellaninn.com) and **Alby Lodge** (©/fax **2755-0031**; www.albylodge.com) are both excellent, intimate, long-standing local options.

El Encanto Bed and Breakfast ★★ The individual bungalows at this little bed-and-breakfast are set in from the road on spacious and well-kept grounds. The bungalows are also spacious and have attractive touches that include wooden bed frames, arched windows, Mexican-tile floors, Guatemalan bedspreads, and framed Panamanian *molas* (paintings on cloth) hanging on the walls. There is a separate two-story, three-bedroom, two-bathroom house with a full kitchen. Hearty breakfasts are served in the small open dining room surrounded by lush gardens. The hotel also has a small kidney-shaped pool, a wood-floored meditation and yoga hall, a covered garden gazebo, and an open-air massage room.

Cahuita (just outside of town on the road to Playa Negra). © **2755-0113.** Fax 2755-0432. www.el encantobedandbreakfast.com. 7 units. $70–$90 double; $185 house. Rates include full breakfast. Rates slightly lower in off season, higher during peak weeks. MC, V. **Amenities:** Small pool; free Wi-Fi. *In room:* No phone.

IN & AROUND PUERTO VIEJO

There are tons of lodging options in and around Puerto Viejo. **Banana Azul Guest House** (© **2750-2035** or 8351-4582; www.bananaazul.com) is an economical option just north of town on Black Sand Beach, while down south of town you might also consider **Cariblue Bungalows** (© 2750-0035; www.cariblue.com) or **Playa Chiquita Lodge** (© 2750-0062; www.playachiquitalodge.com).

For some serious luxury, check out the **Tree House Lodge ★★★** (© 2750-0706; www.costaricatreehouse.com), whose four individual houses are architectural and artistic marvels.

La Costa de Papito ★ 🏖 This small collection of individual and duplex cabins is across from Playa Cocles, about 1.6km (1 mile) south of Puerto Viejo. The wooden bungalows come with one or two double beds, tiled bathrooms, and an inviting private porch with a table and chairs and either a hammock or a swing chair. There's also a larger, two-bedroom unit. There's an excellent restaurant in-house, and the **Pure Jungle Spa** is on the grounds, as well.

Playa Cocles, Puerto Viejo, Limón. © **2750-0704** or ©/fax 2750-0080. www.lacostadepapito.com. 13 units. $54–$89 double. AE, DISC, MC, V. **Amenities:** Restaurant; bar; bike rental; small spa; watersports equipment rental. *In room:* No phone.

Playa Negra Guesthouse ★★ 😊 Expansive gardens and grounds, a beautiful pool, attentive owners, cozy accommodations, and direct beach access make this my top choice in Cahuita. Rooms are immaculate and well lit and most come with a wet bar, in addition to the coffeemaker and minifridge. My favorite option for couples is the two private cabins, while the two independent two-bedroom cottages are perfect for families, with a full kitchen and large veranda. The hotel is located just across the road from a wonderful section of Playa Negra.

On Playa Negra (about 1.5km/1 mile north of town), Cahuita. © **2755-0127.** Fax 2755-0481. www.playanegra.cr. 7 units. $70–$80 double room; $80–$120 cabin; $120–$140 cottage. AE, MC, V. **Amenities:** Small pool. *In room:* Minifridge, no phone, free Wi-Fi.

Where to Dine

IN CAHUITA

In addition to the place listed below, I recommend **Cha Cha Cha ★** (© 8368-1725) for its excellent seafood and inspired fusion cuisine, and **Sobre Las Olas** (© 2755-0109) for its fabulous setting and view.

Restaurant Edith CREOLE/SEAFOOD This place is a local institution. Miss Edith's daughters do most of the cooking and serving, but you will often find the restaurant's namesake matriarch on hand. The menu is long, with lots of local seafood dishes and creole combinations such as yuca in coconut milk with meat or vegetables. The sauces have spice and zest and are a welcome change from the typically bland fare served up elsewhere. It's often crowded, so don't be bashful about sitting down with strangers. Hours can be erratic; it sometimes closes without warning, and service can be slow and gruff at times. After you've ordered, it's usually no more than 45 minutes until your meal arrives.

By the police station, Cahuita. © **2755-0248.** Reservations not accepted. Main courses $3–$22. No credit cards. Mon–Sat 11:30am–10pm.

IN & AROUND PUERTO VIEJO

To really sample the local cuisine, you need to look up a few local women. Ask around for **Miss Dolly, Miss Sam, Miss Isma,** and **Miss Irma,** who all serve sit-down meals in their modest little *sodas* in downtown Puerto Viejo. **Soda Tamara** (© 2750-0148) is one excellent option.

El Loco Natural ★★ 🎒 INTERNATIONAL A friendly, hippie vibe pervades this open-air restaurant. Seating is at wooden tables, and if the few smaller, more private tables are taken, you can take any empty seat at one of the larger communal tables. The short menu features several vegetarian items, as well as fresh fish and some chicken and meat dishes, prepared in curry, Thai, and Mexican sauces. There's often live music here, ranging from reggae to jazz to Latin American folk.

On the main road just south of downtown, about 1 block beyond Stanford's. ⓒ **2750-0530.** Main courses $4–$13. No credit cards. Thurs–Mon 6–10pm.

La Pecora Nera ★★★ ⓜ ITALIAN   This open-air joint on the jungle's edge has a deserved reputation as the finest Italian restaurant in the region, if not the country. Owner Ilario Giannoni is a whirlwind of enthusiasm and activity, switching hats all night long from maitre d' to chef to waiter to busboy in an entertaining blur. Sure, he's got some help, including his grandmother, who makes gnocchi, but it sometimes seems like he's doing it single-handedly. The menu has a broad selection of pizzas and pastas, but your best bet is to just ask Ilario what's fresh and special for that day, and to trust his instincts and inventions. I've had fabulous fresh pasta dishes and top-notch appetizers every time I've visited. The various carpaccios are fabulous, and the gnocchi here is light and mouthwatering. These folks also run **Gatta Ci Cova,** a less formal pizzeria and trattoria on the main road, near the entrance to La Pecora Nera.

50m (164 ft.) inland from a well-marked turnoff on the main road south just beyond the soccer field in Cocles. ⓒ **2750-0490.** Reservations recommended. Main courses $10–$24. AE, MC, V. Tues–Sun 5:30–11pm.

CAHUITA & PUERTO VIEJO AFTER DARK

As I said before, Cahuita is the quieter of the two towns. Here folks tend to gather in the evenings at either **Coco's Bar ★**, a classic Caribbean watering hole, or the **National Park Restaurant,** which has a popular bar and disco on most nights during the high season and on weekends during the off season.

Down in Puerto Viejo there are two main dance spots, **Johnny's Place ★★** (ⓒ **2750-0623**) and **Stanford's** (ⓒ **2750-0016**). Both have small dance floors with ground-shaking reggae, dub, and rap rhythms blaring. Other popular places in town include the **Tex Mex** (ⓒ **2750-0525**) restaurant and bar, right where the main road hits the water, and the **Sunset Bar** (ⓒ **8341-8163**), also near the water and sometimes featuring live music. For a more sophisticated ambience, try the downtown **Baba Yaga ★** (ⓒ **8388-4359**) or the oceanside **E-Z Times** (ⓒ **2750-0663**). Finally, for a more local scene, check out **Bar Maritza's** (ⓒ **2750-0003**) in the center of town, which really seems to go off on Sunday nights.

JUNGLE CANALS & TURTLE NESTING IN TORTUGUERO ★

Sometimes dubbed "the Venice of Costa Rica," Tortuguero is connected to Limón, and the rest of mainland Costa Rica, by a series of rivers and canals. This aquatic highway is lined almost entirely with a dense tropical rainforest that is home to howler and spider monkeys, three-toed sloths, toucans, and great green macaws. A trip through the canals is nothing like touring around Venice in a gondola, but it is a lot like cruising the Amazon basin—on a much smaller scale.

"Tortuguero" comes from the Spanish name for the giant sea turtles *(tortugas)* that nest on the beaches of this region every year from early March to mid-October (prime season is July–Oct, and peak months are Aug and Sept). The chance to see this nesting attracts many people to this remote region, but just as many come to explore the intricate network of jungle canals that serve as the region's main transportation arteries.

Essentials
GETTING THERE
There are no roads into Tortuguero. The only way to get here is by boat or small plane. Flying to Tortuguero is convenient if you don't have much time, but a boat trip through the canals and rivers of this region is often the highlight of any visit to Tortuguero. **However, be forewarned:** Although this trip can be stunning and exciting, it can also be long, tiring, and uncomfortable. You'll first have to ride by bus or minivan from San José; then it's 2 to 3 hours on the water, usually on hard wooden benches or plastic seats.

All of the lodges listed in this section offer transportation along with their lodging and tour packages. The transportation can be by either air or boat, or a mixture of the two (one-way by air, one-way by water).

Budget travelers can do it on their own, with a mix of public buses and private water taxis. If you want info on the current state of this method, check out the site www.tortuguerovillage.com, which has detailed directions about how to get to Tortuguero by a variety of routes.

ORIENTATION
Tortuguero is one of the most remote locations in Costa Rica. There are no roads into this area and no cars in the village, so all transportation is by boat or foot. Most of the lodges are spread out over several kilometers to the north of the village on either side of the main canal; the small airstrip is at the north end of the beachside spit of land. At the far northern end of the main canal, you'll see the **Cerro de Tortuguero (Turtle Hill),** which, at some 119m (390 ft.), towers over the area. The hike to the top of this hill is a popular half-day tour and offers some good views of the Tortuguero canals and village, as well as the Caribbean Sea.

Tortuguero Village is a small collection of houses connected by footpaths. The village is spread out on a thin spit of land, bordered on one side by the Caribbean Sea and on the other by the main canal. At most points, it's less than 300m (984 ft.) wide. If you stay at a hotel on the ocean side of the canal, you'll be able to walk into and explore the village; if you're across the canal, you'll be dependent on the lodge's boat transportation. However, some of the lodges across the canal have their own network of jungle trails that might appeal to naturalists.

VISITOR INFORMATION & FAST FACTS
There are no banks, ATMs, or currency-exchange houses in Tortuguero, so be sure to bring sufficient cash in colones to cover any expenses and incidental charges. The local hotels and shops generally charge a hefty commission to exchange dollars. There's an Internet cafe (no phone) right across from the main dock in town, although I prefer the one found at **La Casona** (© 2709-8092), a small restaurant and budget hotel in the heart of the village.

Exploring the National Park
Four different species of sea turtles nest in Tortuguero National Park: the green turtle, the hawksbill, the loggerhead, and the giant leatherback. The prime nesting period is from **July to mid-October** (Aug and Sept are peak months). The park's

beaches are excellent places to watch sea turtles nest, especially at night. The beaches are not great for swimming. The surf is usually very rough, and the river mouths attract sharks that feed on the turtle hatchlings and fish that live here.

Green turtles are perhaps the most common turtle found in Tortuguero, so you're more likely to see one of them than any other species if you visit during the prime nesting season. **Loggerheads** are very rare, so don't be disappointed if you don't see one. The **giant leatherback** is perhaps the most spectacular sea turtle to watch laying eggs. The largest of all turtle species, the leatherback can grow to 2m (6½ ft.) long and weigh well over 1,000 pounds. It nests from early March to mid-April, predominantly in the southern part of the park.

You can explore the park's rainforest, either by foot or by boat, and look for some of the incredible varieties of wildlife that live here: jaguars, anteaters, howler monkeys, collared and white-lipped peccaries, some 350 species of birds, and countless butterflies, among others. Some of the more colorful and common bird species you might see in this area include the rufescent and tiger herons, keel-billed toucan, northern jaçana, red-lored parrot, and ringed kingfisher. Boat tours are far and away the most popular way to visit this park, although one frequently very muddy trail starts at the park entrance and runs for about 2km (1.2 miles) through the coastal rainforest and along the beach.

ENTRY POINT, FEES & REGULATIONS The Tortuguero National Park entrance and ranger station are at the south end of Tortuguero Village. The ranger station is housed inside a landlocked old patrol boat, and there's a small, informative open-air kiosk explaining a bit about the park and its environs. Admission to the park is $10. However, most people visit Tortuguero as part of a package tour. Be sure to confirm whether the park entrance is included in the price. Only certain canals and trails leaving from the park station are within the park. Many hotels and private guides take their tours to a series of canals that border the park and are similar in terms of flora and fauna but don't require a park entrance. When turtles are nesting, you will have to arrange a night tour with your hotel or one of the private guides in town. These guided tours generally run between $10 and $15. Flashlights and flash cameras are not permitted on the beach at night because the lights discourage the turtles from nesting.

ORGANIZED TOURS   Most visitors come to Tortuguero on an organized tour. All of the lodges listed below, with the exception of the most inexpensive accommodations in Tortuguero Village, offer package tours that include various hikes and river tours; this is generally the best way to visit the area.

In addition, several San José–based tour companies offer budget 2-day/1-night excursions to Tortuguero, including transportation, all meals, and limited tours around the region. Prices for these trips range between $100 and $220 per person, and—depending on price—guests are lodged in either one of the basic hotels in Tortuguero Village or one of the nicer lodges below. Reputable companies offering these include **Exploradores Outdoors ★★** (© **2222-6262;** www.exploradores outdoors.com), **Jungle Tom Safaris** (© **2221-7878;** www.jungletomsafaris.com), and **Iguana Verde Tours** (© **2231-6803;** www.iguanaverdetours.com). There are 1-day trips that spend almost all their time coming and going but that do allow for a quick tour of the canals and lunch in Tortuguero. These trips are good for travelers who like to be able to say, "Been there, done that," and they run between $80 and $100 per person. However, these trips spend most of their time traveling to and from

Tortuguero. If you really want to experience Tortuguero, I recommend staying for at least 2 nights.

Or you could go with **Fran and Modesto Watson ★** (𝒞 **2226-0986;** www. tortuguerocanals.com), who are pioneering guides in this region and operate their own boat. The couple offers a range of overnight and multiday packages to Tortuguero, with lodging options at most of the major lodges here.

Exploring the Village

The most popular attraction in town is the **Caribbean Conservation Corporation's Visitors' Center and Museum ★** (𝒞 **2709-8091;** www.cccturtle.org). The museum has information and exhibits on a whole range of native flora and fauna, but its primary focus is on the life and natural history of the sea turtles. There's a small gift shop, and all the proceeds go toward conservation and turtle protection. The museum is open Monday through Saturday from 10am to noon and 2 to 5:30pm, and Sunday from 2 to 5pm. There's a $1 admission charge, but more generous donations are encouraged.

In the village you can also rent dugout canoes, known in Costa Rica as *cayucos* or *pangas*. Be careful before renting and taking off in one of these; they tend to be heavy, slow, and hard to maneuver, and you might be getting more than you bargained for. **Miss Junie** (𝒞 **2709-8102**) rents lighter and more modern fiberglass canoes for around $5 for 3 hours.

You'll find a handful of souvenir shops spread around the center of the village. The **Paraíso Tropical Gift Shop** has the largest selection of gifts and souvenirs. But I prefer the **Jungle Shop,** which has a higher-end selection of wares and donates 10% of its profits to local schools.

Where to Stay & Dine

My favorites are **Manatus Hotel ★★** (𝒞 **2239-4854** for reservations, or 2709-8197 at the hotel; www.manatushotel.com), **Laguna Lodge ★** (𝒞 **2272-4943** for reservations, or 2709-8082 at the lodge; www.lagunatortuguero.com), and **Tortuga Lodge** (𝒞 **800/886-2609** in the U.S. and Canada, or 2257-0766 reservations in San José or 2709-8034 at the lodge; www.tortugalodge.com). Budget travelers should check out **Casa Marbella** (𝒞/fax **2709-8011;** http://casamarbella.tripod.com).

PANAMA

by Jisel Perilla

For such a thin squiggle of land, Panama offers a surprisingly diverse selection of landscapes, cultures, and experiences. In Panama City, modern skyscrapers contrast with 18th-century architecture, and a 10-minute cab ride from downtown puts you deep in rainforest teeming with wildlife. From the cool, fertile highlands in the Chiriquí region to the thick lowland jungle and white-sand beaches of Panama's tropical islands, this tiny nation allows you to pack a lot of fun and adventure into a short period of time. Also, Panama boasts a rich history and a melting pot of cultures, including seven indigenous groups, many of whom maintain their customs today. Best of all, the country is mostly free of tourists—but get here soon because Panama is far too attractive to stay a secret for long. Panama claims a history rich with Spanish conquistadores and colonists, pirates, gold miners and adventurers, canal engineering, international trade, and mass immigration from countries as close as Jamaica and as far away as China. The pastiche of European and African cultures blended with the country's seven indigenous groups has had a tangible effect on Panama's architecture, cuisine, language, and folklore.

Given Panama's compact size and diversity, visitors here can take part in wildly different experiences without having to travel very far.

THE REGIONS IN BRIEF

Panama, an S-shaped **isthmus** that measures little more than 77,700 sq. km (30,000 sq. miles), is just slightly smaller than South Carolina—yet there is a huge diversity of landscapes and microclimates within this tiny nation. Costa Rica borders Panama to the west, Colombia to the east, and, in what can be vexing to the traveler with no sense of direction, the Pacific Ocean to the south and the Caribbean Sea to the north. Because Panama City faces southeast, travelers are presented with the uncommon view of the sun rising over the Pacific. At its narrowest point, Panama measures just 50km (31 miles) wide.

Besides the isthmus, Panama is made up of more than 1,500 **islands,** many of them uninhabited and cloaked in thick vegetation. These islands are grouped into four regions. In the Caribbean Sea there are the Bocas del Toro and San Blas archipelagos; in the Pacific Ocean, Las Perlas

Archipelago in the Gulf of Panama, and Coiba Island and its accompanying tiny islands in the Gulf of Chiriquí.

Panama is home to two **mountain ranges,** the Serranía del Darién in the east, and the Cordillera Central in the west, the latter of which is home to the highest peak in the country, the dormant Volcán Barú, at 3,475m (11,400 ft.). This is the only place in Panama where you are likely to experience brisk temperatures—the rest of the country averages 75° to 85°F (24°–29°C) year-round.

Panama is a centralized nation, with about a third of its population of three million living in Panama City; in comparison, the population of the second-largest city, Colón, is just under 200,000 residents. The country is divided into nine *provincias,* or provinces, three provincial-level indigenous territories called comarcas, and two subprovincial comarcas.

PANAMA CITY, THE CANAL & SURROUNDINGS Beyond the streets of Panama City, the Canal Zone is characterized by a species-rich, dense tropical rainforest, hundreds of rivers, mangrove swamps, the Pacific Ocean coastline, and Las Perlas Archipelago in the Gulf of Panama. Thanks to the Panama Canal and its reliance on the local watershed, the rainforest in this area is protected as a series of national parks and reserves (Chagres, Soberanía, Sherman, and Camino de Cruces, for example). Visitors to Panama City are often surprised by how quickly they can reach these parks and surround themselves in steamy jungle, and view a dazzling array of both North and South American birds and other wildlife. Near the city, the shore consists mostly of mud flats; visitors seeking beaches must head to the islands, or drive about 1 hour southwest.

CENTRAL PANAMA Considered the country's cultural heartland, Central Panama covers Panama City beaches, the Coclé Province, and the Azuero Peninsula. In Coclé, city dwellers flock to popular El Valle de Antón, a verdant mountain hideaway in the crater of an extinct volcano (1,173m/3,850 ft. at its highest peak). The area is blessed with a mild climate that is a respite from the humid lowlands. The Pacific coast southwest of the city is another popular weekend getaway for its beaches and a few all-inclusive resorts. Farther southwest, the Azuero Peninsula has been largely deforested, but it is still a popular destination for its traditional festivals, handicrafts, and Spanish villages whose architecture dates back to the medieval era. The beaches along the peninsula are blissfully uncrowded any time of year.

BOCAS DEL TORO ARCHIPELAGO Bocas del Toro is in the northwest corner of the country, near the border with Costa Rica, and it's one of the more popular and easily accessed Caribbean destinations, with a wide variety of hotels and amenities. The region is characterized by an eclectic mix of indigenous groups, Spanish descendants, Afro-Caribbeans, and, more recently, American expats; it is also one of the wettest areas of Panama. Outside of brief dry seasons in September/October and February/March, the rain is constant, so bring an umbrella or waterproof gear. Although there are a few beautiful beaches here, there are also riptides, and visitors come more to scuba dive, snorkel, boat, see wildlife, or just soak in the bohemian vibe of Bocas Town, the capital city.

THE WESTERN HIGHLANDS & GULF OF CHIRIQUI The Western Highlands—so-called for the region's location and its Cordillera Central range—is a paradise of fertile peaks and valleys, crystal-clear rivers, mild temperatures, and fresh air. The region is undergoing a palpable growth spurt as hundreds of North Americans

10

PANAMA

The Regions in Brief

continue to buy second and retirement homes here, so expect to hear a lot of English. The region centers around the skirt of Volcán Barú, a dormant volcano capped by a moist cloud forest. Farther south are the humid lowlands, the capital city David, and the wondrous coast and islands of the Gulf of Chiriquí. This is Panama's up-and-coming beach/ocean destination, with its highlight being Coiba National Park, one of the most diverse and pristine islands for scuba diving and snorkeling in the world.

THE DARIÉN   The easternmost region of Panama is the Darién Province, a swath of impenetrable rainforest and swampland that is undeveloped, save for a handful of tiny villages and indigenous settlements. It is Panama's wildest region and the most difficult to reach: This is the famous "missing link" of the Pan-American Highway that runs from Alaska to Puerto Montt, Chile. The interior of the Darién can be reached only by foot, boat, or small plane—and herein lies the allure of adventure for travelers. Within the province lies the Darién National Park, most of it inaccessible except for the Cana Research Station, an area revered by birders worldwide for the abundance of endemic and "show-bird" species such as macaws and harpy eagles, the largest predator in the world. Along the Pacific shore is the famous Tropic Star Lodge, but otherwise, lodging in the Darién is in rustic shelters and tents.

THE COMARCA KUNA YALA (THE SAN BLAS ARCHIPELAGO)   Though commonly referred to as the San Blas Archipelago, this semiautonomous region, or comarca, is named for the Kuna Yala, perhaps Panama's most well-known indigenous group. The Kuna are recognized for their tightly knit culture, colorful clothing, and handicrafts such as mola tapestries. More than 300 lovely, palm-studded islands in turquoise Caribbean waters make up the archipelago in what is truly an unspoiled paradise. The San Blas is a very popular cruise stop. However, staying on the islands requires a sense of adventure because they can be reached only by a small plane or boat. Lodging is alfresco with rustic accommodations and little in the way of activities other than swimming and swaying in a hammock.

THE BEST OF PANAMA IN 1 WEEK

Given Panama's compact size, and the short flights that quickly connect you to other destinations, travelers can pack a lot into a week here—but the timing is tight. This itinerary includes a 2-day visit to Bocas del Toro, but you might opt instead to spend 2 nights in Boca Chica, near David, and to visit Isla Coiba the first day (a long day trip, but worth it), then head out to the Gulf of Chiriquí National Marine Park the next day for sportfishing or lounging on the beach of an uninhabited island.

Day 1: Getting to Know Panama City

Arrive and get settled in **Panama City** ★★. If your flight arrives early, visit **Panama Viejo** ★★★ (p. 670) to get your historical bearings, then head across town for a walking tour of **Casco Viejo** ★★★. Travelers with little time will want to head straight to Casco Viejo, where they can dine on Panamanian food at **S'cena** ★★★ (p. 685) or **Manolo Caracol** ★★ (p. 684).

Day 2: Getting Deep in the Jungle

One of Panama's top parks for birding and hiking is just 45 minutes from Panama City: **Soberanía National Park** ★★★ (p. 694). Leave early and bring your binoculars to view hundreds of birds on a walk or mountain bike ride along

Pipeline Road ★★; join a **jungle cruise** to see monkeys, crocodiles, and transiting ships on the Panama Canal; ride a dugout canoe up the Chagres River to visit an **Emberá village** (p. 698). In the afternoon, pay a visit to the country's star attraction, the **Panama Canal** ★★★, at the **Miraflores Locks** (p. 692), where you can have lunch and tour their visitor center. Head back to Panama City and cool off with a stroll or bike ride along the **Amador Causeway** ★★ (p. 673).

Days 3 & 4: To the Highlands

Fly to **David** and grab a taxi or rent a car for the 45-minute drive to **Boquete** ★★★. Spend the afternoon getting to know the town on foot or by bike, visiting the town's public gardens and other sights. Another option is to dive into an adventurous afternoon activity such as a canopy ride on the **Boquete Tree Trek** (p. 707) or a low-key booked visit to the coffee farm **Café Kotowa** ★★ (p. 708). The following day, spend the day **rafting** (p. 698) on a Class 2 to Class 5 river. You can also book a bird-watching tour that includes **Finca Lérida** ★★★ (p. 708) and **Volcán Barú National Park** ★ (p. 704).

Days 5 & 6: From the Highlands to the Lowlands

Catch an early-morning flight from David to **Bocas del Toro** ★, and settle in to a hotel in **Bocas Town** ★, on Isla Colón. Preplan an afternoon tour with your hotel or an outfitter to visit **Swan's Cay** and **Boca del Drago** beach ★★ (p. 716) and rent a bicycle and pedal out to **Bluff Beach,** or take another hop over to **Isla Bastimentos** ★★★ (p. 717).

Day 7: Leaving Bocas del Toro

Spend the morning wandering around town and soaking up the Caribbean vibe, architecture, and culture. There are quite a few **souvenir shops** in Bocas where you can pick up gifts before your flight back to Panama City.

PLANNING YOUR TRIP TO PANAMA

Visitor Information

The **Panama Tourist Board,** known as the Autoridad de Turismo de Panama (ATP), has a website at www.visitpanama.com, which offers versions in Spanish, English, and Portuguese. The website is relatively unhelpful, but it offers more information than can be gotten from any ATP representative on the phone (and in person, for the most part). Make sure to check out **www.panamainfo.com** as well; it's probably the best travel site currently available on Panama, and they also publish a quarterly magazine with tourist, real estate, and restaurant information. The quarterly magazine *Panama 980* (www.panama980.com) provides English-language tourist information and in-depth hotel and restaurant reviews. *980* can be purchased at the airport and is available at some hotels and restaurants.

ATP centers in major tourist destinations such as Panama City, Boquete, and Bocas del Toros also generally provide regional maps, though hotels are sometimes incorrectly marked. The best country and regional maps can be found in **El Hombre de la Mancha** bookstores in Panama City (p. 677). Maps are available online at **www.panama-maps.com**.

Panama in 1 Week

Legend:

1 & 7 Panama City
2 Soberanía National Park
3 & 4 Boquete
5 & 6 Bocas del Toro Archipelago

TOUR OPERATORS

Local travel agencies are another good source of information and are generally cheaper than international tour operators. **Ancon Expeditions** (℅ **269-9415;** www.anconexpeditions.com) is the foremost tour operator in Panama, with a full-time staff of degreed naturalists and bird-watching experts, a handful of remote lodges, and offerings of day excursions and preset and custom-planned journeys to all corners of Panama. **Ecocircuitos** (℅ **314-0068;** www.ecocircuitos.com) is run by a young, dynamic group of travel professionals who specialize in small groups (minimum four and maximum eight people), and who focus heavily on sustainable tourism with a low impact on the environment. **Adventures in Panama** (℅ **315/849-5144** in the U.S., or 260-0044; www.adventuresinpanama.com), whose slogan is "No Tours, Just Adventures," is the operator to go to for active sports such as kayaking, rafting, mountain biking, and rock climbing around Panama, and day adventures around Panama City. **Advantage Panama** (℅ **6676-2466;** www.advantagepanama.com) specializes in bird-watching trips but also does day trips to Emberá villages, the Canal Zone, and Lake Gatún. In addition, non-birding custom tours can be arranged to just about anywhere in Panama, and prices are more affordable than those of better-known Ancon Expeditions. **Futura Tours** (℅ **360-2030** or 6674-6050; www.panamatravel tours.com) offers half-day, full-day, and overnight tours in the Panama City area. **Margo Tours** (℅ **263-8888;** www.margotours.com) is a relative newcomer to the tour scene and offers day and overnight tours, as well as fishing excursions and a unique real estate and lifestyle tour for travelers thinking about a move to Panama. **Pesantez Tours** (℅ **366-9100;** www.pesantez-tours.com) is an established company that can do all your booking for you if you're not looking to join a set tour.

Entry Requirements

The Terrorism Prevention Act of 2004 requires U.S. citizens traveling to Panama to present a valid passport.

Important: When entering the country, travelers must be able to demonstrate proof of sufficient funds if requested, and they must present an onward or return ticket. However, I've never been asked to present proof of either, and I've been to Panama eight times in the past 3 years.

Citizens of the United States, Canada, Great Britain, and most European nations may visit Panama for a maximum of 90 consecutive days. No visa is necessary. Carry your passport with you at all times. Police will sometimes ask for your documents, particularly on long bus rides on routine checks.

PANAMANIAN EMBASSY LOCATIONS

In the U.S.: 2862 McGill Terrace NW, Washington, DC 20008; ℅ **202/483-1407;** info@embassyofpanama.org.

In Canada: 130 Albert St., Ste. 300, Ottawa, ON K1P 5G4; ℅ **613/236-7177;** info@panama-embassy.ca.

In the U.K.: 40 Hertford St., London W1Y 7TG; ℅ **44171/409-2255.**

Customs

Visitors to Panama may bring with them personal items such as jewelry, and professional equipment including cameras, computers, and electronics, as well as fishing and diving gear for personal use—all of which are permitted duty-free. Customs officials in Panama seldom check arriving tourists' luggage.

Money

The unit of currency in Panama is the U.S. dollar, but the Panamanian **balboa,** which is pegged to the dollar at a 1:1 ratio, also circulates in denominations of 5¢, 10¢, 25¢, and 50¢ coins. (U.S. coins are in circulation as well.) Balboa coins are sized similarly to their U.S. counterparts, and travelers will have no trouble identifying their value.

EXCHANGING MONEY

Travelers with pounds or euros may exchange money at **Banco Nacional,** which has branches across the nation. To save time, you may want to convert your money into dollars before arriving in Panama. Note that there is nowhere to exchange money at the airport.

ATMS

The easiest and best way to get cash in Panama is from an ATM, available throughout Panama in banks and supermarkets, and identifiable by a red SISTEMA CLAVE sign with a white key. ATMs, called *cajeros automáticos,* can be found in larger towns only, so if you're visiting out-of-the-way destinations such as an offshore island, plan to bring extra cash.

Note that some ATMs in Panama limit withdrawals to $200 per day, others to $500.

CREDIT CARDS

Credit cards are widely accepted in Panama City, and most chain hotels, resorts, B&Bs, moderate-to-upscale restaurants, and malls, as well as most travel agencies, take MasterCard and Visa. American Express and Discover are becoming increasingly popular. Diners Club is not widely accepted. In rural areas and smaller towns, make sure to bring enough cash, as few businesses are likely to take credit cards.

In the event of a lost or stolen card, **Visa**'s emergency number is © **800/847-2911** toll-free in the U.S., or call 410/902-8022 collect from Panama. **American Express** cardholders and traveler's check holders should call © **207-1100** in Panama, or its 24-hour service in the United States at 800/111-0006. **MasterCard** holders should call © **800/307-7309,** or make a collect call to 636/722-7111.

TRAVELER'S CHECKS

Traveler's checks are readily accepted at major hotels, but less so at budget hotels and many restaurants. Other than that, you'll mostly get blank stares if you try to use traveler's checks.

When to Go

PEAK SEASON The best time to visit Panama is during the **dry season** between mid-December and mid-April. Keep in mind that this is also the most expensive time to visit, and hotels jack up their rates by up to 50%. Destinations such as the Chiriquí Highlands, el Valle de Antón, and Bocas del Toro see more rain than the rest of the country, though mornings are usually bright and sunny. If you are unable to visit during the dry season, keep in mind that the early months (Apr–July) are characterized by sudden, heavy thunderstorms in the afternoon that are short in duration, and can happen every few days. Often, the skies are sunny in the morning or afternoon.

CLIMATE Panama lies between 7 degrees and 9 degrees above the Equator, which places it firmly within the Tropics. Accordingly, average year-round temperatures are

TELEPHONE dialing INFO AT A GLANCE

Panama has a seven-digit phone numbering system, and there are no city or area codes. The country code for Panama is 507, which you use only when dialing from outside the country. Cellphones are prefixed by 6; in this chapter, telephone numbers include this prefix because most businesses' published phone numbers include the prefix. **For directory assistance,** dial ℂ **102;** for assistance with finding an international number, dial ℂ **106** for an operator who can connect you with international directory assistance. **For operator assistance** dial ℂ **106.** For an international operator in the U.S., dial ℂ **109** (AT&T), **108** (MCI), or **115** (Sprint). **To call Panama from outside**

the country: First dial the international access code—**011** from the U.S.; **00** from the U.K., Ireland, or New Zealand; or **0011** from Australia. Then dial the country code **(507)** followed by the number. **To make international calls from within Panama,** first dial **00** and then the country code (U.S. or Canada 1, U.K. 44, Ireland 353, Australia 61, and New Zealand 64). Next dial the area code and number. For example, if you want to call the British Embassy in Washington, D.C., dial ℂ **00-1-202-588-7800. Toll-free numbers** in Panama begin with 800, but calling an "800" number in the States from Panama is not toll-free. In fact, it costs the same as an overseas call.

a balmy 75° to 85°F (24°–29°C), varying only with altitude. The average temperature in the Chiriquí Highlands, for example, is 60°F (16°C), and is the only area in Panama where you will likely feel cold.

Humidity is always high in Panama, and rainfall varies noticeably between the Pacific and Caribbean sides of the country, with some areas in the Caribbean receiving almost twice the yearly rainfall of Panama City. The Chiriquí Highlands experiences a variety of microclimates that can change drastically, sometimes even within a few miles. In Boquete, high winds and a peculiar misting rain called *bajareque* are common from mid-December to mid-February; January sees the occasional thunderstorm; and March to May are the sunniest months.

PUBLIC HOLIDAYS Like any respectable Latin American country, Panama has many religious and nonreligious holidays. Most are celebrated on Mondays to allow for 3-day weekends. Official holidays in Panama include January 1 (New Year's Day), January 9 (Martyr's Day), Good Friday, Easter Sunday, May 1 (Labor Day), August 15 (Founding of Old Panama—observed in Panama City only), October 12 (Hispanic Day), November 2 (All Souls' Day), November 3 (Independence Day), November 4 (Flag Day), November 5 (Colón Day—observed in the city of Colón only), November 10 (First Call for Independence), November 28 (Independence from Spain), December 8 (Mother's Day), and December 25 (Christmas Day).

Health Concerns

Travelers have a low risk of contracting a tropical disease while in Panama. Cases of **malaria** are not common and mostly afflict rural citizens who live in remote areas, such as Ngöbe-Buglé Indian tribes in Bocas del Toro, the Darién, and the San Blas Archipelago. More common than malaria is **dengue fever,** an infectious disease caused by an arbovirus transmitted by daytime mosquitoes. **Hepatitis A** can occur

CELLPHONES BY THE numbers IN PANAMA

I strongly recommend buying a cellphone in Panama. It's expensive to call cellphones from land lines, meaning reaching taxi drivers, some restaurants, and even hotels can be difficult without a cellphone. Luckily, a cellphone in Panama can be obtained for as little as $10. You can buy calling cards starting at $5.

There are no phone-rental kiosks in the Panama City airport, and travelers who need to make a lot of local calls and receive international calls are better off **buying a phone.** Cellphones that accept prepaid phone cards are as cheap as $30 in electronics stores in Panama City (and come with a bonus of $20 in calls), and phone-card companies have nonstop promotions that double or triple the value of phone cards. Local calls are as low as 10¢ per minute, and

incoming calls are free. While some higher-end hotels rent cellphones, it's probably cheaper to buy a new one. Prepaid phone cards can be purchased in just about any grocery store or pharmacy, and instructions for how to add credit are listed on the back of each card. The instructions are in Spanish, but whoever sells you the card can credit your account if you ask.

The major cellphone providers in Panama are **Movistar** and **Cable & Wireless.** Note that calling cards are service-provider-specific, so you'll have to buy a different card depending on whether you have a Movistar or Cable & Wireless phone. If you are unsure what kind of phone you have, a salesperson can help you. Calling cards generally come in denominations of $5, $10, and $12.

in impoverished areas with poor sanitation, but visitors can and should get vaccinated at home. See "Health" in chapter 3 for more info.

Panama is also home to many ticks and sand flies, as well as poisonous snakes such as the pit viper, the fer-de-lance, and the patoca, but bites are rare, and can easily be avoided by wearing long pants or good boots while hiking.

More common illnesses that affect tourists are TD, or **traveler's diarrhea,** caused by microbes in food and water, and sunstroke. See p. 70 in chapter 3 for info on how to prevent and treat these illnesses.

Getting There
BY PLANE
All international flights land at **Tocumen International Airport** (PTY; ✆ 238-2700). Air Panama flights from Costa Rica to Panama City land at the **Marcos A. Gelabert Airport** (PAC), which is commonly referred to as **Albrook Airport.** There is also direct service from San José, Costa Rica, to the David and Bocas del Toro airports. TACA Airlines (see below) has service from Costa Rica, arriving at Tocumen. An expansion of the David airport was recently approved, so flights from Florida and other international destinations will eventually be able to land in David, meaning travelers going directly to Bocas and Boquete won't have to fly into Panama City. However, this project is in the early stages and likely won't be finished for at least a couple years.

The following airlines serve Panama City from the United States, using the gateway cities listed. **American Airlines** (✆ 800/433-7300 in the U.S., or 269-6022 in Panama; www.aa.com) has two daily flights from Miami; **Copa Airlines** (✆ 800/359-2672 in the U.S., or 227-0116 in Panama; www.copaair.com) has two daily flights from Miami, and one daily flight from Orlando, New York, Los Angeles, and Washington, D.C. **Delta Airlines** (© 800/241-4141 in the U.S., or 214-8118 in Panama; www.delta.com) offers one daily flight from Atlanta; **TACA** (© 800/400-8222 in the U.S., or 360-2093 in Panama; www.taca.com) has one daily flight from all major U.S. hubs, but with a stopover in El Salvador or Costa Rica. **Mexicana** (© 800/531-7921 in the U.S., or 264-9855 in Panama; www.mexicana.com) offers daily flights from Miami, Dallas, and Los Angeles; however, they connect with Copa Air in Mexico City, so you're better off with a direct flight with Copa. From Canada, flights to Panama City are available through American Airlines, with a connection in Miami. **Spirit Airlines** (© 800/772-7117; www.spiritair.com) offers nonstop service to Panama City from Fort Lauderdale.

From London, **Iberia** (© 0870/609-0500 in the U.K., or 227-3966 in Panama; www.iberia.com) has daily flights to Panama City that connect in either Madrid or Costa Rica; **American Airlines** and **British Airways** have daily flights that connect in Miami; **Continental Airlines** has daily flights that connect in Orlando or Houston; and **Delta** has a daily flight that connects in Atlanta or Newark.

From Australia, **Qantas** (© 9691-3636; www.qantas.com) has daily flights in conjunction with Copa Air from Sydney, connecting in Honolulu or Los Angeles; **Air New Zealand** (© 507-264-8756 in New Zealand; www.airnewzealand.com) also works in conjunction with Copa Air with one daily flight from Auckland, connecting in Los Angeles.

BY BUS

Buses from Costa Rica arrive in cities throughout Panama, and all major carriers have their final stop in Panama City. Remember, if you're crossing into Panama from Costa Rica by bus or car, you'll have to go through Customs, which can take up to 2 hours, and you'll have to buy a $10 visitor stamp for your passport. There are no buses between Colombia and Panama.

Two companies offer service to and from Costa Rica: **Tica Bus** (© 314-6385; www.ticabus.com) and **Panaline** (© 227-8648). Both companies have large, air-conditioned coaches. Tica Bus leaves for San José at 11am, and Panaline leaves at 12:30pm; the cost is $50 round-trip.

Getting Around
BY PLANE

Air travel is a safe and quick way to get around Panama. Because of rising fuel costs, however, note that prices are rapidly increasing. **Aero Perlas** (© 378-6000; www.aeroperlas.com) and **Air Panama** (© 316-9000; www.flyairpanama.com) are Panama's two air carriers, servicing major destinations in the country. More-remote destinations in Panama can be reached by scheduled or charter flights aboard a small plane, which touches down on a dirt airstrip. Airlines charge a 5% tax on all flights. See "Getting Around" in the separate sections below for more info.

BY CAR

Driving in Panama allows you the most flexibility if you can afford it. Renting a car costs about as much as in the U.S., and gas is a little more expensive, so while this isn't the cheapest option, it allows you to enjoy the scenery, adhere to your own schedule, make pit stops, and visit destinations away from your hotel. Generally speaking, speed limits in Panama are about 60 to 80kmph (37–50 mph) on major roadways and slower on secondary roads. You'll want to stick to this limit, as police speed traps are common.

There are car-rental kiosks at both the Tocumen and Albrook airports (car-rental agencies at Tocumen are open 24 hr.; Albrook rental agencies are open 8am–6:30pm), and each agency has a few locations in town. Tocumen Airport car-rental agency phone numbers are as follows: **Alamo** (© 238-4142; www.alamopanama.com), **Avis** (© 238-4056; www.avis.com), **Budget** (© 263-8777; www.budgetpanama.com), **Dollar** (© 270-0355; www.dollarpanama.com), **Hertz** (© 238-4081; www.hertz.com), **National** (© 238-4144; www.nationalpanama.com), and **Thrifty** (© 264-2613; www. thrifty.com).

When renting a car in Panama, you must purchase two kinds of basic insurance. The agency will also offer a variety of other full-coverage options, but generally, your credit card rental insurance should cover you, and you really need only the obligatory insurance.

Keep in mind that, depending on your destination, it's sometimes better to get a four-wheel-drive vehicle, as some of Panama's roads are unpaved and rocky, but you should be fine if you're sticking to the Pan-American Highway.

Although most Panamanians drive stick shift vehicles, automatics are readily available at all car-rental agencies, though you should expect to pay a bit more. Generally speaking, renting a car in Panama should cost you between $40 and $100 a day, depending on the kind of car and how you reserve. Some distances are as follows:

- Panama City to Colón: 1 hour
- Panama City to Gamboa: 25 minutes
- Panama City to Portobelo: 1½ hours
- Panama City to Carti: 3 hours
- Panama City to Boquete: 7 hours
- Panama City to the Azuero Peninsula: 7 hours

There are also car-rental agencies in David, Colón, and other popular tourist destinations.

BY BUS

Bus routes between major and minor destinations in Panama are frequent and relatively inexpensive. Expect to pay about $2 to $4 per hour, depending on your destination. Panama City's bus terminal is adjacent to Albrook Airport. It's not necessary to reserve your tickets ahead of time unless you are traveling on a holiday weekend or during December or Easter week. Be sure to arrive at the terminal at least 45 minutes ahead of time. You'll need a nickel to get on the bus, so make sure you have change. Long-distance buses are air-conditioned, are comfortable, have an onboard bathroom, and usually show movies. Shorter routes tend to use smaller, less comfortable buses, but are usually air-conditioned. If your route is 4 or more hours, the driver will make a pit stop about halfway through for lunch or dinner.

BY TAXI

Some taxis work directly for a hotel, and rip off guests by charging up to three times the going fare, and they're not going to budge when you contest the fare. These are the taxis that await guests directly at the front door. Simply walk out to the street and flag a taxi down for cheaper fare. In Panama City, David, Colón, and Boquete, taxis can be hailed off the street relatively easily, though calling ahead will cost you only

$1 or $2 more. This is an especially good option in Colón, where it's not particularly smart to walk around too much. In small towns and more remote destinations, you'll probably have to have your hotel or restaurant call a taxi for you.

Tips on Accommodations

High season in Panama is the dry season, roughly between mid-December and mid-April. While hotels in Panama City keep their rates consistent throughout the year, hotels in popular tourist destinations such as Bocas del Toro and the Chiriquí Highlands increase their prices by as much as 30% to 50% during the dry season. Price ranges listed in hotel reviews reflect a range encompassing low and high season; for example, $50 to $75 for a double would mean $50 from May to November and $75 from December to April. Precise start and end dates for high season may vary from hotel to hotel. Some hotels on the coast close during rainy season, so call ahead.

Tips on Dining

Panama is a melting pot of cultures and ethnic groups, and the dining scene here reflects this, especially in Panama City. International restaurants such as Italian, Swiss, Chinese, Middle Eastern, and creative fusion-style eateries please more sophisticated palates and are plentiful. There are a lot of solid choices for cheap dining, too, and the usual fast-food chains abound.

In general, **Panamanian food** is tasty, but a lot of it is fried—especially breakfast items like empanadas, *hojaldras* (fried bread), and tortillas. Outside of major cities and tourist destinations, travelers will find mostly traditional Panamanian food that is heavy on seafood—primarily *pargo* (red snapper), *corvina* (sea bass), *langostina* (jumbo shrimp), calamari, and *pulpo* (octopus). Though Panamanian fare is quite good, there isn't much diversity, and meat and seafood are always paired with the ubiquitous coconut rice and beans, a small cabbage salad, and *patacones* (fried green plantains).

For inexpensive dining, Panama has diner-like *cafeterías* that serve a set meal called *comida corriente,* which consists of an appetizer or soup, a main course, and usually a beverage; these generally cost from $3 to $5. *Panaderías* are bakeries and a good bet for a breakfast of a pastry and coffee; some even have tables.

Tipping is a customary 10% of the total bill. **Note:** Avoid overtipping and check the breakdown of charges on your bill, because many restaurants automatically charge a 10% service fee as a tip. The tax on restaurant bills is 5%.

Tips on Shopping

Shoppers will feel quite at home in Panama. Handicrafts are relatively cheap and easy to find. Most destinations, even small towns, will have at least one store selling handicrafts, and weekend markets are often the most colorful and exciting way to get your hands on traditional Panamanian arts, though don't forget to bargain!

There are modern shopping malls in Panama City on par with those found in the U.S. Outside major cities, however, clothing and jewelry shopping is limited to small shops, and quality isn't exceptional. Though Colón's free trade zone is famous all over Latin America for its "deals and steals," the reality is that, unless you're shopping in bulk, you're not going to get any great deals here, and the hassle of getting to Colón simply isn't worth the trip.

[Fast FACTS] PANAMA

American Express American Express Travel Services has emergency card pickup at Agencia de Viajes Fidanque in Centro Comercial La Galeria on Avenida Ricard J Alfaro in Panama City (☎ 265-2444) but you're better off calling their U.S.-based 24-hour number at ☎ 800/528-4800.

Business Hours Hours for service-oriented businesses in Panama are generally 8am to 1pm and 2 to 5pm on weekdays, and 8am to noon on Saturdays. Businesses in Panama City usually don't close for lunch. Shops open at 9 or 10am and close at 6 or 7pm; shopping malls close around 8pm. Grocery stores are open 24 hours or 8am to 8pm.

Electricity Electrical plugs are the same as in the U.S., as is Panama's voltage, 110 AC.

Embassies & Consulates The **United States Embassy** is in Panama City on Demetrio Basilio Lakas Avenue in Clayton (☎ 207-7000). The **Canadian Embassy** is at Torres de las Americas Tower A, 11th floor, in Punta Pacifica (☎ 294-2500),

The **British Embassy** is at Calle 53 Este and Nicanor de Obarrio, Panama City (☎ 269-0866). **Australia** and **New Zealand** do not have an embassy or a consulate in Panama; however, the British Embassy can provide consular assistance to citizens of those countries.

Emergencies For fire or ambulance dial ☎ 103. For police dial 103.

Etiquette & Customs Panama City professionals dress well in spite of the heat, meaning no flip-flops, shorts, or tank tops—so bring at least one nice outfit with you. Many better restaurants will not serve patrons in shorts, women included. In resort or beach areas, and in smaller towns with a large expat presence like Boquete, casual wear is okay.

In the San Blas Islands, Kuna Indians frequently request money to have their photo taken.

Gasoline (Petrol) Gas is slightly more expensive than in the U.S. At press time, 1 gallon of gas in Panama cost about $3. In more remote locations, such as Bocas del Toro and the Kuna Yala Islands, gas can cost almost twice as much. Taxes are already included in the printed price. One Panama gallon equals 3.8 liters or .85 imperial gallons.

Internet Access Internet access is plentiful in Panama, except in more remote areas. Nearly every hotel has at least one computer with Internet access; some have data-ports or Wi-Fi (usually in the hotel lobby or business center). Most Internet cafes charge between $2 and $3 per hour.

Language Spanish is the official language in Panama, though English is widely spoken in the tourism industry, and many hotel owners are native English-speakers themselves. Panama's seven indigenous groups speak their own languages in their communities, and in some isolated areas indigenous groups do not speak Spanish fluently. On the Caribbean coast, creoles speak a patois called Guari-Guari or Wari-Wari, a mix of English, Spanish, and Ngöbe-Buglé.

Mail Panama has no stamp vending machines or post boxes, so you'll have to head to the post office to send a postcard, or ask your hotel if they can do it for you. A letter sent regular mail to the U.S. will arrive in 5 to 10 days; the cost, at press time, is 35¢ for a letter and 25¢ for a postcard. For quick service, send a package via a courier.

Newspapers & Magazines Panama's principal daily newspaper is *La Prensa;* the five other dailies include *La Panamá América, Crítica Libre, El Universal,* and *La Estrella. La Prensa* publishes a weekend guide supplement on Thursdays, and is the best paper for event listings. The English-language *Panama News,* once available in print, is available online at **www.thepanamanews.com**. *The Panama Visitor* is in Spanish and English and is a free, bimonthly publication for tourists. You can find copies of the *Miami Herald* in English at supermarkets and at the Gran Morrison chain.

Police   For police, dial ✆ **104.**

Restrooms   It's rare to find a public restroom in Panama—you'll generally have to rely on hotel lobbies or restaurants. For the most part, they are clean, with modern septic systems. In some remote areas or beach locations, an outhouse-style restroom or a toilet that requires flushing with a bucket of water is more the norm. Restrooms are called *baños,* and are marked *hombres* or *caballeros* for men, and *damas* or *mujeres* for women.

Smoking   All restaurants, bars, and dance clubs have recently gone nonsmoking, so smokers will have to take it outside.

Smoking isn't even allowed in outside dining areas or balconies.

Taxes   All hotels charge 10% tax. Restaurants charge 5% on the total cost of the bill, and often sneak in an automatic 10% for service—check your bill carefully to avoid overtipping.

Telephones   The cheapest way to phone is to use a prepaid phone card, available in kiosks, supermarkets, and pharmacies in quantities of $5, $10, and $20—however, these cards have a life span of 15 to 30 days. **ClaroCOM** has the best rates, with 5¢ per minute for national and international calls to the U.S. and the U.K., and 35¢ per minute to cellular phones. Cable and wireless **Telechip** cards are less value at 15¢ per minute for national calls and 25¢ per minute for international calls. The cards have an access phone number and a scratch-off code, as well as bilingual service. Remember that hotels charge a connection fee even if the connection number is a toll-free number.

Time Zone   Panama is 5 hours behind Greenwich Mean Time (GMT), and 1 hour ahead of Costa Rica. Panama does not observe daylight saving, so from the first Sunday in November to the second Sunday in March, the time in Panama is the same as that in the U.S. Eastern Time Zone (New York, Miami, and others); from mid-March to early November, it's the same as that in the U.S. Central Time zone (Chicago, Houston, and others).

Tipping   Tipping in Panama at restaurants is 10% (see "Taxes," above). Taxi drivers do not expect tips, but you might consider it if you've rented a taxi for the day. Porters and bellhops should be tipped $2 to $5 depending on the caliber of the hotel.

Water   The water in most of Panama's major cities and tourist destinations is safe to drink, except in Bocas del Toro. Many travelers' stomachs react adversely to water in foreign countries, however, so it might be a good idea to drink bottled water outside of major hotels and restaurants.

PANAMA CITY ★★

Long overshadowed by the Panama Canal and with a reputation as a hub for drug running, Panama City is not only reinventing itself as the thriving commercial and financial hub of the Americas, but becoming a burgeoning tourist destination. Panama City (commonly referred to simply as "Panama") is one of those rare Central American capitals that has it all: a relatively high standard of living, a seemingly endless supply of investment from abroad, a surplus of natural beauty, and a rich cultural brew of ethnicities and religions. There is a sizable expat presence in the city, as well as a growing Asian community, both of which continue to change the face of Panama City.

Panama City

To Colón

To Gamboa

To El Dorado

Avenida Arnulfo Arias Madrid

Avenida Omar Torríjos Herrera

Av. Diógenes De La Rosa

Calle 7

Calle 6

Calle 5

Calle 4

Calle 3

Calle 2

Calle 1

Avenida Ascanio Villalaz

Av. Juan Pablo II

Albrook
(Marcos Gelabert)
Airport

Ferrocarril
de Panamá

1 Albrook
Mall

ALTOS DE
CURUNDÚ

METROPOLITANO
NATIONAL
PARK

To Colón

Corredor Norte

Avenida Ascanio Villalaz

Calle Rubén Darío

Av. M. Sosa

Av. Transístmica

BALBOA

Mercado de
Abastos

Av. Gaillard

Av. Roosevelt

Av. Santa Cruz

Av. Juan D. Arosemena

CURUNDÚ

Avenida Frangipani

Avenida Simón Bolívar

LA
CRESTA

Cerro
Ancón

Luis. F. Clement

Avenida Nacional

Av. 1 Norte

Central

National
Archives **2**

Avenida

Central España

Calle 43 Este

Calle 44 Este

ANCÓN

3 Museo Antropológico
Reina Torres de Araúz

Museo de
Ciencias Naturales

Av. Perú

Parque
Porras

CALIDONIA

Cuba

Av.

Calle 42 Este

To Amador
Causeway

Avenida de los Mártires

del Estudiante

Museo
Afroantillano

Calle 26 Este

Calle 28 Este

Calle 30 Este

Calle 32 Este

Avenida

Justo

Arosemena

México

Calle 37 Este

Calle 39 Este

Calle 41 Este

Parque
Urracá

EL CHORRILLO

SANTA
ANA

Calle 25 Este

Avenida Balboa

10 Balboa
Monument

Parque
Anayansi

Marina
Miramar

Av. A

Calle 21 Oeste

Calle 18 Oeste

Calle 16 Oeste

Calle 12 Oeste

Avenida Central

Avenida B

4

Av. Eloy Alfaro

Bahía de Panamá

Presidential
Palace

Calle Av.

Av. B

Av. Central

Teatro
Nacional

CASCO VIEJO
(SAN FELIPE)

See "Casco Viejo"
inset map

Casco Viejo

Museo de
Historia

Plaza de la
Independencia

Museo del
Canal de Panamá

Plaza
Bolívar

Calle 4

9

Iglesia
San Francisco
de Asís

5

Iglesia de
Santo Domingo
(Arco Chato)

Av. Central

8

Teatro
Nacional

7

CASCO VIEJO
(SAN FELIPE)

*Bahía de
Panama*

Av. A

Calle 2

6

Plaza
de Francia

Paseo de
Las Bóvedas

0   50 m

0   50 yds

ACCOMMODATIONS ■

Best Western Las Huacas Hotel & Suites **19**
The Bristol Panama **13**
The Canal House **5**
Hotel la Casa de Carmen **22**
Hotel Marbella **28**
Hotel Milan **26**
La Estancia **3**
The Panama Marriott Hotel **14**
Radisson Decapolis Hotel **18**
Veneto Hotel & Casino **31**

DINING ◆

Beirut **17**
Café Rene **2**
Cafeteria Manolog's **2**
Casa Vegeteriana **30**
Costa Azul **16**
Ego y Narciso **9**
El Trapiche **21**
Eurasia **11**
Fusion **18**
Granclement **6**
La Posta **12**
Las Barandas **13**
Limoncillo Pony Club **33**
Machu Picchu **25**
Manolo Caracol **8**
Martin Fierro **27**
Matsui **24**
Monsoon **34**
Napoli **23**
New York Bagel **20**
Nikos Café **1, 10, 28**
Restaurante Mercado Mariscos **4**
S'cena **7**
Ten Bistro **15**

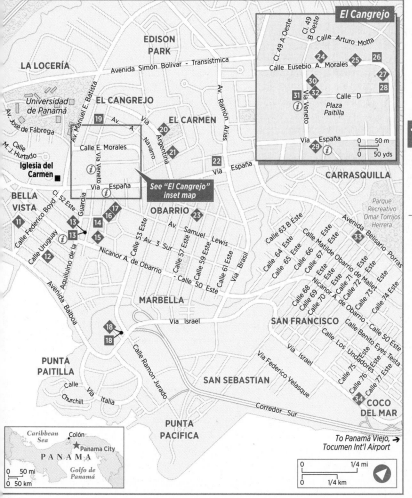

10

PANAMA | Panama City

Signs of Panama City's reinvention are everywhere. The Amador Causeway, formerly a U.S. military base, is the site of several multimillion-dollar condominium and commercial-center developments, such as the new Biodiversity Museum designed by Frank Gehry. The run-down 19th-century buildings of Casco Viejo have been revitalized with private and public funds and declared a World Heritage Site by UNESCO. Along the coast, swiftly rising skyscrapers, spurred by an irresistible 20-year tax exemption, portend a megalopolis in the making:

But Panama City's visitors need not venture far from their air-conditioned hotels to immerse themselves in the wild tropical jungle characteristic of this region. Even the city's Metropolitan Park is the protected home of more than 200 species of birds, mammals, and reptiles. Dozens of remarkable destinations outside the city limits can be reached in less than 2 hours, meaning travelers can spend the day exploring but head back to the city and be well fed and rested for the next day's adventure.

Essentials

GETTING THERE

BY PLANE   All international flights, except those from Costa Rica, land at **Tocumen International Airport** (PTY; ✆ **238-2700**), 21km (13 miles) from Panama City. Flights from Costa Rica to Panama City land at Albrook Airport (see below), and there is direct service from San José to David and Bocas del Toro airports.

There are **ATP visitors' kiosks** inside Tocumen's arrival terminal (one in baggage claim and another through the Customs gate), with information about Panama City and some brochures; it's recommended, though, that travelers research accommodations and make reservations before their arrival because hotels are often booked.

The unit of currency in Panama is the balboa, but U.S. dollars are accepted everywhere at a 1:1 rate, so for those coming from the United States there is no need to exchange money. If you are coming from elsewhere, there is nowhere to exchange currency at Tocumen Airport, so be sure to bring your debit card or exchange at least $30 before arriving to cover the cost of your taxi before exchanging in the city center.

A licensed taxi from Tocumen to Panama City costs $20 to $25, plus toll fees for a total of about $25 to $30. Many hotels offer free pickup and drop-off service, or they will arrange transportation for you—inquire when booking at your hotel.

All rental-car agencies have desks in the arrival terminal and are open 24 hours a day. See "Getting Around," below, for more information.

Domestic flights, flights to Costa Rica, and charter flights to the 150 or so airstrips located on Panama's islands and remote jungle areas leave from **Marcos A. Gelabert Airport** (PAC), which is more commonly referred to as **Albrook Airport** (✆ **501-9271**).

Albrook is northwest of Cerro Ancón (Ancón Hill) off Avenue Omar Torrijos Herrera, near the canal. A taxi costs $2.25 to $3 to downtown Panama City and takes about 20 minutes. There are usually taxis waiting at the airport, although you can also cross the street and hail a taxi for a shorter wait. Rental-car agencies here are generally open from 8am to 6:30pm. Each company offers a key drop box for customers who need to return a vehicle when rental desks aren't open.

Tip: Travelers who arrive at Tocumen Airport and plan to head directly to another destination in Panama via a domestic flight must transfer to Albrook Airport, about a 45-minute drive (or longer during rush hour) from Tocumen. A taxi costs about $30.

BY BUS

If arriving by bus, you'll be dropped off at the Albrook bus terminal near the Albrook airport and shopping center. A taxi to town costs $2.25 to $3 and takes 10 to 15 minutes. A taxi to the Gamboa area costs $25 and takes 30 minutes.

BY CAR

Travelers arriving in Panama City by car will do so via the **Pan-American Highway** from the west, first crossing the canal on the Puente de las Américas (Bridge of the Americas) and arriving in the Balboa district of the city. Follow signs to Avenida Balboa to reach downtown. Drivers headed to Panama City from the west may also use the new Puente Centenario (Centennial Bridge), which crosses the canal near Paraíso, and avoid traffic congestion on the Bridge of the Americas. The road that crosses this bridge is also known as Vía Benedicto XVI, named after Pope Benedict XVI. There are currently plans to build an underground tunnel to Puente de la Americas, which would make leaving Panama City much quicker, but there's no telling how long this project will take or when it will even get underway.

The Pan-American Highway continues east toward Colombia and ends in Yaviza, in the Darién Region. It is not possible to reach Colombia by car, and at this book's publication there were no ferries for vehicles to Colombia, although there is talk that this service might be reinstated soon.

ORIENTATION

Panama City lies on the eastern shore of the Panama Canal, and is bordered by the Pacific Ocean to the southeast, which can disorient first-time visitors unaccustomed to seeing the sun rise over the Pacific Ocean. Throw in a mesh of looping avenues and streets with two different names, or no name at all, and prepare to feel hopelessly lost during your first few days in Panama City. I lived in Panama City for over a year, but still can't make sense of the city layout—or lack of layout. Visitors rely on taxis, which are safe and cheap, about $1.50 to $3 for most locations in the city. Taxis from the city center to the Amador Causeway usually run about $5.

In very general terms, Panama City can be divided into **four areas:** Old Panama (the ruins of the first settlement here); Casco Viejo, the city center during the late 19th and early 20th centuries; the former Canal Zone; and modern Panama, with its wide boulevards, glittering skyscrapers, and impoverished slums.

At the southwest end of the city lie the Amador Causeway, Casco Viejo, Cerro Ancón (Ancón Hill), and the former Canal Zone. As a visitor, you'll probably spend most of your time here. From here, three principal avenues branch out across the city. Avenida Central, which begins in Casco Viejo as a thriving shopping center hawking cheap, imported goods, changes its name to Avenida Central España as it passes through Calidonia, and then becomes Vía España as it runs through the commercial area and financial district of El Cangrejo. Avenida Balboa extends the length of the coast, then forks into Vía Israel, later called Cincuentenario as it heads out to Old Panama. Corredor Sur, a fast-moving toll expressway, connects the city with Tocumen Airport. Avenida Simón Bolivar (also known as Av. 2da. Norte Transístmica) heads north to Colón; however, a new toll expressway, called the Corredor Norte, provides a faster route to Colón, eventually connecting with the Transístmica around Chilibre.

There are no beaches in the immediate area of the city—only mud flats—and visitors will need to travel northeast to the Caribbean or southwest to the Pacific beaches, about a 1- to 1½-hour drive from the city.

GETTING AROUND

BY TAXI Taxis are inexpensive, safe, and plentiful—except when it is raining during rush hour and it seems that every worker heading to, or leaving, work is trying to flag one down. Quite often, a taxi will stop for another passenger if he or she is headed in your general direction, but the driver will usually deliver you to your destination first. Taxis charge $1.25 to $2 for most destinations within Panama City, but confirm the price beforehand as the "zones" that taxi drivers use for price reference are vague. Taxis from the city center to the Amador Causeway will run you about $5. Unscrupulous drivers may try to charge you more, especially to and from the Amador Causeway.

ON FOOT Panama City is not easy to navigate on foot because of its interweaving streets, lack of street signs, and few recognizable landmarks for visitors. Also, many neighborhoods aren't within walking distance of each other. To get around without a fuss, take a cab; that said, the Casco Viejo neighborhood is best explored on foot.

BY BUS You'll feel more comfortable getting around Panama City by taxi than by bus.

BY CAR You won't need or want a rental car while visiting just Panama City, considering how economical taxis are and how difficult and chaotic driving can be. If you do decide to rent a car, there are car-rental kiosks for most major car-rental agencies at both the Tocumen and Albrook airports (car-rental agencies at Tocumen are open 24 hr.; Albrook rental agencies are open 8am–6:30pm), and each agency has a few locations in town. If you are renting a car to visit outlying areas such as the canal, Portobelo, or the Panamanian interior, have your rental agency show you, in detail, the quickest and most efficient route to your destination.

Visitor Information

The **Autoridad de Turismo de Panama (ATP)** main office is on Calle Samuel Lewis on the first floor of Edificio Central, across from the Camosa; although open to the public, it does not have a proper information center (✆ **526-7000** or 526-7100; www.visitpanama.com). ATP has visitor centers at Vía España and Ricardo Arias (✆ **269-8011**), though they won't do much except give you a few brochures.

FAST FACTS American Express Travel Services has an emergency card pickup at Agencia de Viajes Fidanque in Centro Comercial Via Pacifica, local 9, in Punta Paitilla (✆ **265-2444**).

Called *farmacias* in Spanish, **drugstores** are plentiful in Panama City. For 24-hour service, visit a branch of **El Rey** supermarket, the most central of which is on Vía España (✆ **223-1243**). Another reliable pharmacy is **Farmacias Arrocha** (✆ **360-4000**), with locations at Vía España in front of El Panama Hotel, Vía Argentina, and Punta Paitilla. You will probably be able to get most of your medication without a prescription, but bring an empty prescription container; medications often go by different names and an official prescription or prescription container can help the pharmacist figure out what medicine you're asking for.

For fire, dial ✆ **103;** for police, dial **104;** for an ambulance, dial **Seguro Social** at ✆ **502-2532,** or **Cruz Roja** at ✆ **228-2187.**

Postal service is scarce in Panama City; your best bet is to ask your hotel to mail something for you, or try Mail Boxes Etc. or another international courier service. The central post office (Correos y Telégrafos) is open Monday through Friday 8am to 4pm

and 6:30pm, has been installed. *Tip:* Visit the tower in the afternoon, when the morning tour buses have gone. Otherwise, you might find yourself waiting up to 20 minutes to enter. Spanish-speaking guides offer free tours of the tower. If you skip the museum, the cost to get in the area around the tower is $4 for adults, $3 for seniors, and $2 for students; it's open Tuesday to Sunday, 8:30am to 6pm. The cathedral is a good 15-minute walk from the museum.

One of the city's best **handicrafts markets** is at Panama Viejo, and has recently been relocated to the visitor center (no phone; call the visitor center for information; approximately 9am–5 or 6pm). *Note:* Even though the Cathedral Tower and museum are closed on Monday, you can still visit the ruins and walking paths.

CASCO VIEJO ★★★

Casco Viejo, the Old Quarter, is also referred to as Casco Antiguo or by its original and formal name, San Felipe. No trip to Panama City would be complete without a visit to this charming neighborhood, with its narrow streets; its turn-of-the-19th-century Spanish-, Italian-, and French-influenced architecture; its bougainvillea-filled plazas; and its breezy promenade that juts out into the sea. Visitors often compare Casco Viejo to Havana or Cartagena. The neighborhood's historical importance and antique beauty spurred UNESCO, in 1997, to declare it a World Heritage Site. For the past century, Casco Viejo was a run-down neighborhood whose antique mansions were left to rot after wealthy residents moved to other parts of Panama City. With the drop in land value, squatters and low-income families moved in, many of whom continue to live here but are being pushed out by a public and privately funded large-scale gentrification project. This is most evident along the southeastern tip of the neighborhood, where lovingly restored mansions line the streets; renovation isn't happening as fast elsewhere as was hoped when the project began more than 10 years ago. To combat the housing shortage, the government is offering funds to help resettle poor residents. Foundations such as the Oficina Casco Antiguo are working on a plan that will invest heavily in tourism, expanding services and even reinstalling the old streetcar that once ran along the city streets.

Safety note: In spite of Casco Viejo's renovation projects and the fact that both the mayor's *and* the president's offices are located here, tourists should stay alert and protect themselves from theft. Generally speaking, the peninsula of Casco Viejo, starting at Calle 11 Este and heading east and away from the Santa Ana neighborhood, is safe. There are two principal entryways into Casco Viejo but both pass through poor ghettos, so always take a **taxi** to get here. Taxis for a trip out of Casco Viejo can usually be found around the Plaza de la Independencia, or if you are dining here, have the restaurant call one for you. The Estación de Policía de Turismo (Tourism Police Station) is on Avenida Central at Calle 3a Este; the office is open 24 hours, and from Monday to Friday, 8am to 5pm, there is an English-speaking attendant. Generally, they do a good job of patrolling Casco Viejo and are relatively helpful if you run into any problems.

Most important in this area is to tone down the "gringo look" if possible, meaning no shorts with a zillion pockets or ostentatious clothing like Hawaiian shirts. Also, do not wear flashy jewelry or walk the streets brandishing your top-of-the-line camera.

CERRO ANCON ★★

This conspicuous forested hill that rises 198m (650 ft.) above the city is another "reverted" property from the canal days that is now open to the public. The hill is bordered in the north by Heights and Culebra streets, and avenidas Arías and de los Mártires in the south. At the entrance to the office of the environmental organization ANCON, at Calle Quarry Heights, a winding, pedestrian-only road provides for a brisk uphill walk to a **lookout point ★★★**, with 360-degree views of the city center, Casco Viejo, and the canal. The hill is home to tiny Geoffrey's tamarins, *ñeques* (agoutis), and migratory birds. The **Museo de Arte Contemporáneo** is here (see "Other Museums in Panama City," below).

Mi Pueblito 👋 Located at the southeastern foot of Cerro Ancón, Mi Pueblito is a mock village depicting three Panamanian cultures: Afro-Caribbean, the interior region, and indigenous groups. At the main entrance is a colonial Spanish hacienda–style building with displays of polleras, both antique and new, plus roped-off interiors with various and sundry antique household items placed to give visitors an idea of life during the 19th century. Here, at the entrance, one of several guides will approach you and offer to explain the historical and cultural significance of each display. Across the street are a few typical Caribbean-style homes, as well as the thatched-roof huts of Kuna and Emberá Indians. Altogether Mi Pueblito is a touristy, uninspiring attraction whose purpose seems less to educate travelers and more to hawk clothing and crafts at high prices. However, travelers who only plan to visit Panama City and are in the Cerro Ancón area might find it interesting to view the sharply contrasting cultural fabric of Panama displayed in the architectural design of the center's buildings.

Entrance at Cerro Ancón from Av. de los Mártires. 📞 **506-5725.** Free admission. Tues–Sun 9am–7pm. Reached by tour or taxi.

Panama Canal Murals ★ High on a grassy slope, the **Canal Administration Building,** built by the U.S. in 1914, houses the offices of the Autoridad del Canal de Panamá (Panama Canal Authority). At the bottom of the slope is the formidable Goethals Monument, dedicated to the chief canal engineer, George W. Goethals, who initiated construction of the Canal Building. Entering the building, visitors are taken aback by the beauty of the glass cupola, the focal point of the lobby. The cupola is encircled with handsome murals that narrate the heroism and relentless struggle to build the canal. The murals were done by William B. Van Ingen, a painter from New York who also did murals for the Library of Congress in Washington and the U.S. Mint in Philadelphia. There are four murals here. The first depicts the excavation of the Gaillard Cut; the second shows the construction of the Gatún Dam; the third, the construction of the Gatún Locks; and, finally, the last is an impressive depiction of the building of the Miraflores Locks. Visitors may visit only this wing of the building, and entrance is free.

To put the Canal Zone in perspective, head out to the back of the building, facing the Goethals Monument. The flagpole here once displayed ensigns from both Panama and the United States, but today the only flag proudly flapping in the wind is Panamanian. There is a broad view of the Balboa neighborhood and the Bridge of the Americas beyond it. This area was a residential zone for American canal employees before the handover. Today, the buildings have been converted into residences for Panamanians, most of whom have no connection to the canal.

You may wish to visit the Canal Building before heading up to the top of Cerro Ancón because the road (via Quarry Heights) leads up from here.

PARQUE NATURAL METROPOLITANO ★

The Natural Metropolitan Park is the only protected tropical forest within the city limits of a major urban area in the Americas. In other words, one 5- to 10-minute taxi ride and you can delve into the earthy environs of thick jungle with a surprising array of fauna, more than 200 species of birds, and 40 species of mammals. Expect to see mostly birds and the occasional blue Morpho butterfly fluttering by. The park, roughly 265 hectares (655 acres), is located on the northern edge of Panama City, hemmed in by a few rather busy roads, including the new and noisy Corredor Norte, which runs the eastern flank of the park. The park is overseen by the Smithsonian Tropical Research Institute, which carries out scientific studies here, and by the city, which maintains an administration center with maps, educational exhibits, and a bookstore. If you're planning to visit any regional national parks such as Soberanía, skip this attraction; if your visit to the country is limited to Panama City, this park is a must-see.

Three short trails give visitors a chance to get out and stretch their legs. **Los Momótides** trail is the shortest (30 min.) and therefore the most appropriate trail for young children and visitors in a hurry. It begins at the administration center, but you must cross busy Avenida Juan Pablo II, so be careful. **Mono Tití Road** heads up to Cedro Hill and a lookout point with sweeping views of the city; alert hikers occasionally catch sight of Geoffrey's tamarins, a pint-size primate, along this trail. The most difficult trail, and the longest at 2 hours round-trip, is **Cienequita Trail,** which begins just up the road from the center. It is possible to connect with Mono Tití Road after reaching the lookout point. If you'd prefer something more adventurous, **Ancon Expeditions** recently launched their **Metropolitan Nature Park and Smithsonian Rainforest Canopy Crane** tour, perfect for nature lovers and bird-watchers alike, especially if you won't be venturing far from the city. The tour consists of a 50-minute ride on the Smithsonian's 42m-high (138-ft.) research crane plus 2 hours of nature observation at Parque Metropolitano Natural's hiking trails. The guided tour is limited to groups of four, costs $99 per person, and includes transportation to and from any hotel in Panama City plus an English-speaking guide. For more information, e-mail canopycrane@anconexpeditions.com. **Advantage Panama** (www.advantage panama.com) also does guided tours of the park.

The park is open daily from 6am to 6pm; the visitor center is open Monday to Friday 6:30am to 4:30pm and Saturday 8am to 1pm. Adult entrance is $2 per person, children 50¢. English-language tours are $10 per person with a reservation made at least 24 hours in advance (© **232-5516** or 232-5552; www.parquemetropolitano. org). There are also trail maps available for a small fee.

CALZADA DE AMADOR (AMADOR CAUSEWAY) ★★

The Amador Causeway is a series of three small islands—Naos, Perico, and Flamenco—connected by a road and pedestrian walkway that projects out into the Panama Bay, offering spectacular views of the glittering city skyline and a consistent breeze. The islands, once the haunt of pirates, were connected in the early 1900s with rock and dirt excavated from the Culebra Cut in the Panama Canal to form a breakwater for a protective harbor for ships waiting to enter the canal, and to prevent the buildup of sediment. Later, the United States militarized the promontory and fortified it with ordnance for protection during the two world wars. The causeway

OTHER museums IN PANAMA CITY

Museums across Panama are under-funded and poorly staffed, and the story here in the capital isn't any different just because it's a metropolitan city. Things could change when the Museo Antroologico Reina Torres (Av. Ascanio Villalaz, Natural Metropolitan Park; (*℗* 501-4743) finally fully reopens at its new location on the edge of Parque Natural Metropolitano, but the project is far behind schedule and there is cur-rently only one exhibition open to the public.

The **Museo Afroantillano** ★ (*℗* 501-4130; Calle 24 Oeste and Av. Justo Arosemana; Tues–Sat 8:30am–3:30pm; admission $1) is a small museum housed in the 1910-era Iglesia de la Misión Cristi-ana. The Museo Afroantillano (Afro-Antillian Museum) pays tribute to the more than 30,000 West Indians who represented 85% of all foreign laborers during the building of the canal.

Museo de Arte Contemporáneo ★ (*℗* 262-8012; www.macpanama.org; Av. de los Mártires at Calle San Blas; Tues–Sun 9am–5pm; admission $1), the city's Contemporary Art Museum, has improved over the years, but it is still

erratic when it comes to the quality of temporary exhibitions. Their permanent collection features a selection of mostly watercolor and oil paintings by well-known and up-and-coming Panamani-ans and other Latin Americans.

Museo de Arte Religioso Colonial ★ (*℗* 501-4127; Av. A at Calle 3a, Casco Viejo; Tues–Sat 8am–4pm, Sun 1–5pm; admission $1) exhibits a small but vivid collection of 220 religious art pieces and is housed in the old Santo Domingo convent, famous for the Arco Chato. The religious pieces are the last vestiges from the height of colonial baroque art in the Americas.

The **Museo del Canal Interoceánico de Panamá** ★★★ (*℗* 211-1649; www.museodelcanal.com; Av. Central at Plaza Independencia; Tues–Sun 9am–5pm; admission $2) is one of the best muse-ums in Panama City and an obligatory stop for every traveler. The museum is a study of the Panama isthmus—from pre-Columbian times, to the arrival of the Spanish, to the French and the Ameri-can canal-building efforts, through the present day.

remained off-limits to Panamanians until 1999, when the canal handover opened this prime spot of real estate, much to the delight of walkers, joggers, bike riders, and diners. There is nothing like jogging or walking along the causeway early in the morn-ing with the sun rising over the Pacific and casting its pastel hues on the glittering high-rises of downtown Panama City. The causeway is packed on Sundays.

Large-scale, multimillion-dollar real estate projects are on the horizon for the causeway, including a grand hotel, a casino, condo development, and new marinas.

By any measure, Panamanians are most excited about the opening of the new **Bridge of Life Biodiversity Museum,** designed by renowned architect Frank Gehry (who is married to a Panamanian), which features high-concept exhibitions about the relation-ship between nature and man. Check the website, **www.biomuseopanama.org**, for more information. The museum wasn't quite ready at press time, and although I was told repeatedly it would open later in 2010, I wouldn't cross my fingers.

Punta Culebra Marine Exhibition Center ★★ ☺ Spread across a patch of dry forest on the tiny island of Naos, a former U.S. defense site during the two world wars, Punta Culebra is a kid-friendly attraction run by the Smithsonian Tropical

Research Institute. It's a well-designed but small exhibition, with a short path that offers sweeping views and mounted telescopes that you can use to scan the horizon and get up-close views of ships waiting to transit the canal. The center will take a back seat to the Biodiversity Museum (once it opens). Really, if you're an adult without kids and you're having lunch at Mi Ranchito or riding a bike around, it makes sense to swing through here quickly—otherwise, don't go out of your way to visit the center when there are so many other attractions in and around Panama City.

Within the center's grounds are a "touching pool" that allows kids to handle and closely examine aquatic life such as sea cucumbers, sea urchins, and starfish; an aquarium with tropical fish and a comparison between coral reefs of the Pacific and Atlantic; and an information center with videos. An interpretive trail winds through dry forest, which long ago was common up and down the Central American Pacific coast; if you're lucky, you will catch sight of a sloth or an iguana. Call ahead for a guided tour. You'll see the Marine Exhibitions Center sign just before Mi Ranchito.

Isla Naos. © **212-8793.** www.stri.org. Admission $2 adults, 50¢ kids 11 and under, $1 seniors. Tues-Fri 1-6pm; Sat-Sun 10am-6pm. Around late Dec to Mar, the center opens for summer vacation daily 10am-6pm, but call ahead to confirm.

Outdoors, Spectator Sports & Wellness Activities

Soccer never cast its spell over Panama as it has with the rest of Latin America—here baseball is king, yet stadium crowds and big-league games are not common. Games are mostly by national and local teams vying for regional championships. For spectator sports, check out the horse races for a lively show and lots of colorful Panamanian characters. Walking and bicycling are best on the Amador Causeway, especially early in the morning with the sunrise.

BIRD-WATCHING   Serious birders will want to visit renowned sites such as Pipeline Road (p. 695). Within the city limits, **Natural Metropolitan Park** (p. 673) is a fine spot for glimpsing some of the more than 200 species found here. Check the Panama Audubon Society's website, **www.panamaaudubon.org**, for upcoming field trips to the park and destinations around the city. **Ancon Expeditions** (© **269-9415**) and **Advantage Panama** (www.advantagepanama.com) both offer guided birding tours around the city.

HORSE RACING   The **Hipódromo Presidente Remón** (© **217-6060;** www.hipodromo.com), inaugurated more than a half-century ago, is a prestigious venue and a fun place to spend an afternoon. Races are held on Thursday, Saturday, Sunday, and holidays. To get here, take a taxi to Vía José Agustín Arango, on the way out to the airport. The Hipódromo can be reached via the Corredor Sur or by following Vía España until it turns into Vía Arango.

HOTEL SPAS & WORKOUT FACILITIES   Nearly every moderate to high-end hotel has a fitness center, and major hotels have full-service spas, which are the best in the city. Especially noteworthy are the spas at the **Veneto, Decapolis Radisson,** and **Marriott.** These hotels allow you to book a session even if you're not lodging there. **Vita Luxury Spa & Holistic Wellness Center** (© **390-9919** or 6677-6616; www.altavitaspa.com), located diagonally across from Multiplaza Shopping Center, offers chemical-free services and is one of the few high-quality stand-alone spas in Panama City.

Shopping

You'll hear a lot of talk about duty-free shopping in Panama, but it is exaggerated. Really, the only place you can duty-free shop is at the plethora of stores at the Tocumen Airport. Shopping complexes such as the **Flamingo Center** on the Amador Causeway limit duty-free purchases to cruise ships in port. Even the duty-free zone in Colón is overrated, as most wholesalers do not sell to independent travelers. The major shopping malls offer excellent quality and national and international brands, though prices are comparable to those in the United States. A principal shopping avenue is **Vía España,** where both high- and low-end shops vie for business, as well as grocery stores and pharmacies. Designer stores are located around Calle 53 in Marbella and in the nearby World Trade Center's Centro de Comercio. Also try Plaza Paitilla in the Paitilla neighborhood. You'll find electronics shops around Vía Estronga, in the Financial District.

Modern Shopping Malls

Globalization and the rising demand for high-quality products have shifted the shopping scene to spacious megamalls that house international brands, cinemas, and a food court. **Multiplaza Pacific** (✆ 302-5380) offers the most in terms of selection and quality, yet it is the most expensive in town. Colombian-owned **Multicentro** (✆ 208-2500), conveniently located across from the Radisson on Avenida Balboa, has a number of Latin-diva-style boutiques; there's also a cinema and a casino. **Albrook Mall** (✆ 303-6333) is an air-conditioned shrine to low-cost outlet shopping, but you'll have to do a lot of digging around to find a gem. Because it is next to the bus terminal, it is busy with families who arrive from the interior of Panama, ready to shop. There is a cinema at Albrook Mall, too. **Metro Mall,** located on Avenida Domingo Diaz on Via Tocumen, is a brand-new mall located near the airport. You'll find designer and nondesigner shops here, and because the mall always seems to be empty, most stores usually have 20%- to 75%-off sales.

MARKETS

The **Mercado de Mariscos ★★★**, located on Avenida Balboa and Calle 15 Este, is distribution headquarters for fresh seafood pulled from the Pacific and Caribbean. It's a vibrant market with lots of action as fishmongers shout while they deftly fillet corvina, tuna, octopus, and more. You can dine here at their upstairs restaurant. Several food stands sell seafood snacks like ceviche. Next door is the brand-new **Mercado Público ★★**, the covered farmer's market of Panama City, with exotic fruit and vegetables, meats, dried spices and nuts, and a food court of *fondas,* or cheap food stands serving Panamanian fare. Don't forget to bring your camera.

Artesanía, or indigenous handicrafts, are the number-one buy here in Panama (with the exception of real estate). Molas, the reversed appliqué panels made by Kuna Indian women, rank high on the list of popularity for souvenirs and gifts, sewn onto a beach bag, as a shirt, or sold individually for you to frame or stitch onto anything you'd like (pillowcases are an ideally sized canvas). Other popular handicrafts, such as *tagua* nuts or vegetable ivory carved into tiny figurines, Ngöbe-Buglé dresses, and Emberá Indian baskets and masks, can be found at the following markets. These markets do not have phones, and all are open daily with the general hours 8 or 9am to 5 or 6pm (until about 2pm Sun). The **Mercado Nacional de Artesanías ★★★**, in Panama Viejo next to the visitor center, is expansive and sells handicrafts from around the country. In Balboa, on Avenida Arnulfo Arias Madrid and Amador, is a small **YMCA Handicrafts Market** ★, with mostly Kuna and Emberá indigenous arts and crafts, and clothing. A little farther east and up Avenida Arnulfo Arias Madrid is the **Kuna Cooperative** ★★, featuring Kuna handicrafts. This market is fun for kids because Kuna women offer to affix their traditional beaded bands onto the arms and legs of tourists, just as they themselves wear them.

You can also find plenty of high-quality molas and handicrafts on Paseo Esteban Huertas in Casco Viejo, an unofficial Kuna market area.

BOOKSTORES

Exedra Books, on the corner of Vía Brasil and Vía España (✆ **264-4252;** www. exedrabooks.com; Mon–Fri 9am–8:30pm, Sat 10am–7pm) is the top resource for English-language books, with dozens of titles, a cafe, a reading area, a children's corner, and Internet access. The Smithsonian's small but excellent **Corotu Bookstore,** at the Earl S. Tupper Research and Conference Center on Roosevelt Avenue in Ancón (✆ **212-8029;** www.stri.org; Mon–Fri 10am–4:30pm) offers a comprehensive collection of books about Panama's flora, fauna, history, and culture, including large-format photo books, maps, and gifts. **El Hombre de la Mancha** (www.books hombredelamancha.com) is a bookstore cafe with a small selection of English-language fiction and the best Panama City map in town. They have locations in the Multiplaza, Multicentro, Albrook Mall, and the Centro Comercial Camino de Crucez Boulevar El Dorado, though the selection isn't exactly impressive. The **Gran Morrison** chain (Vía España at Calle 51 Este, ✆ **269-2211;** Punta Paitilla, ✆ **264-5266**) has a limited English-language book section and a variety of U.S. magazines such as *People* and *Time.*

JEWELRY

During the centuries before the arrival of the Spanish, indigenous groups produced decorative gold pieces called *huacas,* which they laid to rest with the dead to protect their souls in the afterlife. The word comes from the Incas, meaning something that is revered, such as an ancestor or a god. Spurred by the theft of *huacas* from the national anthropology museum, an American living in Panama during the 1970s set up **Reprosa,** which makes elaborate and stunning jewelry casts using the "lost wax" process of the ancient indigenous groups. If you're searching for a one-of-a-kind, luxury gift for someone special, come here. Reprosa has several more demure collections that include orchids, treasures from the sea, and so forth.

Reprosa also offers a popular factory tour to demonstrate the casting and assembly process. The factory can be found just off the Costa del Este exit near Panama Vieja, and just after turning left on the first street next to the Felipe Motta shop. English-language tours cost $10 per person and must be booked at least 1 day in advance; call Monica at ✆ **271-0033.**

OUTDOOR GEAR & CLOTHING

It's best to buy your outdoor gear and equipment before your trip—there isn't a wide selection of outdoor products in Panama and you won't pay any less than you would at home. The chain store **Outdoors** (✆ **302-4828** or 208-2647) represents the brands Columbia and Caterpillar, and their stores carry clothing and footwear, sleeping bags, and accessories for biking, fishing, bird-watching, and other adventure sports. Outdoors has stores in the Multicentro, Multiplaza, and a low-cost outlet store in the Albrook Mall. **Sportline** at Albrook Mall also sells outdoor gear and equipment.

10

PANAMA

Panama City

Where to Stay

Most hotels are concentrated in **El Cangrejo** and the **Area Bancaria (Financial District),** home to banking institutions, commercial services, shopping malls, and many of the city's best restaurants. For charm, you can't beat the cobblestone streets and renovated antique homes in **Casco Viejo,** which has apartment-style lodging units with kitchens. Cab hailing, however, can be arduous in this neighborhood, especially at night, when raining, or during holidays, and walking to El Cangrejo or Bella Vista from here is out of the question. If you're staying in Casco Viejo, have your hotel provide you with the number of a radio taxi. This area also tends to get a bit seedy at night.

Elsewhere, there are excellent hotels scattered about the city in the **Marbella/Coastal** area, on the slope of leafy **Cerro Ancón** hill, and near the **Amador Causeway.** If cities aren't for you, you may want to consider staying in the comparatively quiet **Ancón** or **Amador** neighborhoods.

Although Panama City is best known for its high-end lodging options, there are some budget gems for those turned off by the prospect of spending a couple hundred dollars a night on a hotel. **Hostal La Casa de Carmen,** Calle 1a between Vía Porras and Vía Brasil, El Carmen (✆ **263-4366;** www.lacasadecarmen.net), is a pleasant eight-room guesthouse on a quiet residential street just 1 block from the Vía España. Rooms vary between hostel and B&B quality. Dorm rooms cost $15 a night and doubles with private bathroom run $55 a night. All credit cards are accepted. Another good option, **Hostal Amador Familiar,** is housed in an older reverted canal home. There are dorm rooms and doubles available, ranging between $15 for a dorm room and $40 for a double with A/C. The Hostal Amador Familiar is a good option for families, the only drawback being that you'll have to take a taxi just about everywhere.

Tip: When booking a reservation at a local hotel (meaning not a chain hotel), always ask for the **corporate rate,** even if you're not on corporate business. A hotel may ask for the name of the company you work for, but most do not require any other identification or proof. Corporate rates are $20 to $30 cheaper than rack rates. Also, hotels listed below as "expensive" offer much cheaper rates for travelers booking through their websites. All hotels recommended in this chapter have **free parking** and at least one computer with an **Internet connection.** And if you're in town on a weekend, be sure to ask about weekend discount rates. Hotels in Panama City fill up during the week and empty out a bit on the weekends, and hotels are sometimes willing to negotiate weekend rates. Keep in mind that you'll probably get better rates when booking online than calling in person.

EL CANGREJO/AREA BANCARIA/MARBELLA (FINANCIAL DISTRICT)
Very Expensive

The Bristol Panama ★★★   This boutique hotel is an excellent choice for business travelers and those seeking quiet, centrally located accommodations. The decor, uncharacteristic of tropical Panama City, is done in conservative, richly textured hues with mahogany furnishings—very English in style, and guest rooms have carpeted floors. The on-site restaurant is one of the best in town (see "Where to Dine," below). The eager-to-please staff can accommodate any need, including pressing a shirt or arranging a tour, and they issue all guests a set of business cards printed with their name and the hotel's info. The downsides: There's no pool, and the lobby is tiny (though the cozy bar serves 72 kinds of rum).

Aquilino de la Guardia at Obarrio. ℰ **265-7844.** www.thebristol.com. 56 units. $265 double; $395 junior suite. AE, DC, MC, V. **Amenities:** Restaurant; bar; piano bar; concierge; fitness center; room service. *In room:* A/C, TV/DVD/VHS, CD player, fax, hair dryer, minibar, Wi-Fi.

The Panama Marriott Hotel ★★   The Panama Marriott is the overall best grand hotel in the city. It's within walking distance of top restaurants and Internet cafes. Their high-tech fitness center is enormous, and the spa is extensive and reasonably priced. There are amenities galore, and the staff provides courteous, helpful service. The handsome, oversize lobby is generously appointed with huge bouquets of fresh flowers, and an ample, comfortable lounge is the perfect spot for reading the paper. The guest rooms are spacious and attractive; standard doubles have a couch and large bathroom. Executive rooms are higher up and nearly identical to standard rooms, but come with upgraded amenities such as a private lounge on the 19th floor with a dynamite view. The Marriott also has a casino for a little gaming action and disco nightlife, but one big word of caution: Rooms that end in even numbers suffer from the pounding of DJ music and partying on weekends.

Calle 52 at Ricardo Arias. ℰ **800/228-9290** toll-free in the U.S. and Canada, or 210-9100. www.marriott.com/PTYPA. 295 units. $275 double; $296 executive. AE, DC, MC, V. **Amenities:** Restaurant; deli; sports bar; babysitting; outdoor pool; spa and 24-hr. fitness center w/whirlpool, steam room, and sauna; room service. *In room:* A/C, TV, hair dryer, high-speed Internet, minibar.

Radisson Decapolis Hotel ★★   Trendy 30-somethings will find their home at the deliciously fresh and fun Decapolis Radisson. Think glass and steel, a sleek martini-and-sushi bar, stark decoration, and hallways filled with a rainbow of ambient light. This is not a true luxury hotel, but it provides excellent value with its fashionable decor and wide range of amenities, including one of the city's best spas, full business services such as cellphone rental, chic restaurants, and a casino and shopping mall connected by a walkway. Bright, spacious guest rooms (with walk-in closets and big bathrooms) are mostly white with wood-grain paneling and touches of whimsical lime, orange, and leopard print. On weekends, there is a throbbing party atmosphere in the lobby-level lounge and fourth-floor pool, which draws the young glitterati of Panama City. If you're looking for quiet (and a view), book anything from the 10th floor up, or consider a different hotel. Check the website for deals.

Av. Balboa at the Multicentro Mall. ℰ **888/201-1718** in the U.S., or 215-5000. www.radisson.com. 240 units. $274 double standard; $295 executive double; $340 executive suite. AE, MC, V. **Amenities:** Restaurant; martini/sushi bar and pub-style bar; babysitting; concierge; fitness center; room service; full-service spa. *In room:* A/C, TV, CD player, high-speed Internet, hair dryer, minibar.

EXPENSIVE

Veneto Hotel & Casino ★   The Veneto likens itself to a Las Vegas–style hotel/casino, and from the garish exterior it's easy to see why—but step inside the wide, low-slung lobby and enter a hotel with a lot of style. During the day, their elegant casino on the mezzanine level is hardly noticeable unless you head up the escalator and pay a visit; but at night, the music pumps and the lobby takes on a very festive atmosphere. Strangely, the rooms here are all business, with conservative furniture and cool tones of blue; the beds are ultracomfortable, with crisp linens, duvets, and orthopedic mattresses, and there are luxurious marble-inlaid bathrooms. The pool here hints at resort glamour, and their spa is one of the most complete in Panama, but there are a few slight defects here and there that prevent it from feeling like a five-star hotel. Some doubles are an odd rectangular shape and feel a little claustrophobic; they vary in size so you might ask to see more than one.

Av. Eusebio A. Morales at Vía Veneto. © **877/999-3223** in the U.S., or 340-8888. www.vwgrand.com. 301 units. $200 double; $245 junior suite. AE, DC, MC, V. **Amenities:** 3 restaurants; pool bar and 24-hr. sports bar; babysitting; concierge; outdoor pool; room service; state-of-the-art spa and fitness center w/whirlpool, steam room, and sauna. *In room:* A/C, TV, minibar, Wi-Fi.

MODERATE/INEXPENSIVE

Best Western Las Huacas Hotel and Suites ☺   This small Best Western franchise hotel, a converted apartment building, is centrally located and features a playful, Panamanian-folklore decor and guest rooms with kitchenettes. It's not luxurious in any sense; indeed, you'll feel as if you're subletting someone's kooky apartment. Las Huacas probably most appeals to a young teen who thinks that the leopard-print-and-bamboo tropical style is cool, as well as to someone seeking a venue for a margarita-fueled bachelor party. On the other hand, this hotel doesn't have the mass-produced feel of chains; the accommodations are spacious and the service is friendly. When choosing a room, keep in mind that the lower floors facing the street can be noisy, and that those accommodations abutting the next-door apartment put you uncomfortably face-to-face with your neighbors. Buffet breakfast is included in rates.

49 A. Oeste, near Av. Eusebio Morales. © **213-2222.** www.lashuacashotel.com. 33 units. $88 junior suite; $90–$130 suite. AE, DC, MC, V. **Amenities:** Restaurant; fitness center; room service. *In room:* A/C, TV, kitchenette, minibar.

Hotel Marbella ★   Because of its price and location, the Marbella is a popular hotel with budget travelers. It offers clean rooms that are in good shape if a bit on the small side—all are fitted with a double and twin bed that take up most of the space. Also, because there is no pool, this is an ideal hotel for travelers who plan to spend their days out and about, and simply need a comfortable place to sleep at night. The bathrooms are on the small side, too, but have large walk-in showers. The front desk staff is courteous and bilingual; there is a (slightly pricey) restaurant for breakfast. If you're staying for a few nights, ask for one of the small refrigerators in storage. Taxes are included in rates.

Calle D at Eusebio A. Morales. © **263-2220.** hmarbella@cableonda.net. 84 units. $55 double. MC, V. **Amenities:** Restaurant; room service. *In room:* A/C, TV.

Hotel Milan ⬧   This is a no-frills hotel, but it's relatively new and everything is fresh and works properly. For the price, you'd have a hard time finding a better deal when looking for a downtown hotel close to restaurants and shops. Rooms are plain, but the frilly bedspreads and aqua-blue guest-room walls add a touch of character. The "suite" is a large double with a minifridge and whirlpool bath (situated incongruously in a room behind a small bar), and not worth the extra cash. The lighting in guest rooms is awfully dim, so order a proper nightstand lamp from the front desk. Economy doubles are slightly smaller versions of doubles. The hotel is safe, clean, and a good lodging option if you're just looking for a place to sleep and ambience isn't high on your list of priorities. A 55-room addition is in the works, something to keep in mind if you're easily bothered by noise. Service is a bit lackluster and slow. You get a significant discount if you pay with cash.

Av. Eusebio A. Morales 31. © **263-6130.** hotelmilan@cwpanama.net. 53 units. $57–$77 economy double; $77–$90 suite. AE, MC, V. **Amenities:** Restaurant; bar; room service. *In room:* A/C, TV, high-speed Internet (in top 2 floors and all new rooms).

OTHER AREAS

Country Inn & Suites—Panama Canal ★ ☺ Located near the Amador Causeway and fronting Miraflores Locks of the Panama Canal, this hotel is worth considering if you have kids, seek quiet accommodations, and/or want plenty of space to walk, jog, or ride a bike. The hotel has a view that sweeps from the Bridge of the Americas to the Causeway, overlooking bobbing sailboats and ships awaiting the canal crossing. The decor is country-style and guest rooms look like any cookie-cutter hotel room, but with tile flooring. They all have terraces and kitchenettes, though, and there is an irresistible outdoor pool and a 3.2km (2-mile) walkway along the coast. You'll need a taxi to get anywhere ($3–$5; if you can, flag a regular taxi on the periphery of the hotel rather than taking the hotel's taxi), or you can rent a bike and pedal out to the Amador Causeway for a meal. Insist on an oceanview room—it costs only $25 more, and the sparkling nighttime view of the bridge is the unique perk of this hotel.

Av. Amador at Av. Pelícano, Balboa. (2) **800/456-4000** in the U.S., or 211-4500. www.panama canalcountry.com/amador. 98 units. $135–$160 deluxe standard; $145–$180 junior suite; $215 master suite. AE, MC, V. **Amenities:** Restaurant; bar; bikes; children's play area; gym; outdoor pool; room service; spa; tennis courts. *In room:* A/C, TV, fridge, Wi-Fi.

La Estancia ★ 🔥 Located on the forested slope of Cerro Ancón in a renovated 1960s Canal Zone home, La Estancia is a quiet refuge from the hustle and bustle of Panama City. You're likely to see plenty of birds, sloths, and even monkeys from one of the hotel's many balconies as you read the morning paper. The B&B has spotless, bright accommodations and personalized service that includes an on-site, reputable travel agency. There's nothing within walking distance, except the winding road up to the top of the hill, so you'll need a cab for sightseeing or dining out. Doubles are either en suite or have a bathroom just outside the door. (Choose the latter—the bathroom is for your use only, and these rooms have terraces.) The two suites are enormous, and have sleek kitchens and long outdoor terraces. The intimacy of La Estancia encourages socializing among guests—those seeking absolute privacy will be happiest in a suite or a second-floor room, which has its own common area. Rooms can be a bit musty.

Quarry Heights, Cerro Ancón. (2) **314-1417.** www.bedandbreakfastpanama.com. 10 units. $83 double; $99 suite. MC, V. **Amenities:** Snack bar. *In room:* Wi-Fi, hair dryer.

CASCO VIEJO

Casco Viejo offers travelers some lovingly restored apartments that can be rented nightly or weekly by **Arco Properties,** Calle 2A Oeste, Galería San Felipe ((2) **211-2548;** www.arcoproperties.com). Rental properties are on a space-available basis (most owners live outside Panama City and visit for short periods during the year), and they feature daily maid service but limited parking. The cost for a one- to two-bedroom apartment ranges, per night, from $100 to $200 May to November, and $150 to $250 December to April. Check out the Arco Properties website for photos (some rentals are fancier than others), or e-mail for availability at clara@arco properties.com or patrizia@arcoproperties.com. **Los Cuatro Tulipanes ★★★** ((2) **211-0877;** www.loscuatrotulipanes.com) offers 10 apartments housed in fully restored mansions and buildings scattered throughout Casco Viejo, and is a top-notch option in the old quarter for those seeking a memorable lodging experience.

The Canal House ★★★ 🎁 This brand-new hotel in a 115-year-old renovated Spanish-style mansion offers the most unique accommodations in Panama City. Each room is different from the next, but all are elegant, with tasteful tropical decor, orthopedic beds, and stylish furniture. The best room is the expansive downstairs Mira Flores Suite, which feels more like an apartment than a hotel room, complete with separate sleeping, living, and work areas. The two upstairs bedrooms, the Gatún and San Miguel rooms, are comfortable and attractive but a bit dim. There is a large dining area with capacity for up to 14, perfect for business meetings or social gatherings. Perhaps the best thing about the Canal House is the service: Whether you want complete privacy or a more hands-on experience, the staff will accommodate your needs.

Calle 5ta. Ave. A. (✆ **228-1907.** www.canalhousepanama.com. 3 units. $155–$325, depending on room. MC, V. **Amenities:** Concierge; access to nearby gym; spa. *In room:* A/C, TV, MP3 docking station, Wi-Fi.

Where to Dine

Like any port city worth its salt, Panama City has a gastronomic scene influenced by a melting pot of immigrants from around the world, and by its regional neighbors Colombia, Mexico, and Peru. Foodies will be overjoyed by what's on offer in this metropolitan city: Chinese food ranked by gourmets as some of the best on this side of the Pacific, fine European cuisine, Middle Eastern eateries, Argentine steakhouses, English-style pubs, and, of course, Panamanian restaurants influenced by Afro-Caribbeans, indigenous groups, and Spanish descendants. Panamanian food is tasty, but a lot of it is fried—especially breakfast items like empanadas, *hojaldras* (fried bread), and tortillas. Most main courses are accompanied by a rice-beans-plantain combo that can become repetitive. In other words, if you're planning to visit other destinations in Panama, I say sample the rich variety of international and fusion-style restaurants here and savor Panamanian fare later.

Don't overlook hotel restaurants. The Hotel Deville's trendy **Ten Bistro** serves contemporary, French-influenced food where each main course costs—you guessed it—$10. **Monsoon,** the Sheraton Panama's Asian restaurant, has been honored with international culinary awards. Monsoon offers a sushi night on Tuesday, and shellfish specials on Friday. The Decapolis Radisson's **Fusion** restaurant and its hip sushi lounge is the trendiest see-and-be-seen venue in town for dining. Fusion has a reasonably priced menu and often features a fixed-price buffet lunch for under $20. The **Hotel Executive** serves breakfast 24 hours a day, as well as some of the best burgers in town. See below for a review of the Bristol Panama's restaurant, **Las Barandas;** it offers some of the best Panamanian food in the city and is overseen by Panama's most famous chef. Limoncillo, one of Panama City's traditionally best restaurants, has moved and reopened in San Francisco under the name **Limoncillo Pony Club,** Calle 69 Este (✆ **270-0807;** www.limoncillo.com).

For cheap Panamanian food you can't beat the 24-hour chain **Niko's Café,** which, in addition to basic sandwiches, serves 100 snacks and items, such as a tamale or fried egg, for less than 90¢ each. Niko's is at Vía España and Calle Gerardo Ortega (Calle 51B Este, near the Continental Hotel), at the Albrook Bus Terminal, or on Calle 50 (Nicanor Obarrio). There are many holes-in-the-wall and cafeterias that serve what's called *comida corriente,* or the cheap daily special that might include a beverage. One of the best spots for cheap food is **Casa Vegeteriana** with locations off of Via Veneto on Calle D and in El Dorado. Portions of anything cost 50¢, meaning you can eat to your heart's desire for $1.50 to $3. American fast-food chains, such as Dunkin' Donuts, Bennigan's, McDonald's, T.G.I. Friday's, and Subway, are everywhere. The Bennigan's on the Amador Causeway is particularly hopping on Friday and Saturday nights. Fast-food chains are clustered next to the Veneto Hotel and the Multicentro Mall. *Note:* All Panamanian restaurants and bars recently became smoke-free, so smokers will have to take it outside. Restaurants come and go in Panama with relative frequency, so you may want to call ahead to make sure newer restaurants are still open. Also, restaurants tend to come in and out of fashion quickly, so a place that was hopping a year ago may be empty most weeknights now.

GROCERY & SPECIALTY STORES   The supermarket chain **El Rey** is Panama's largest, and most branches are open 24 hours a day. You can find national products plus a large selection of imported brands from the U.S. The most convenient location is on Vía España, near the Continental Riande; there is another in the Albrook area, on Avenida Omar Torrijos on the way to Gamboa. Another option is the Super 99 supermarket with many locations scattered all over the city, some open 24 hours a day. For more upscale shopping, head to the **Riva-Smith grocery store** in Bella Vista. Riva-Smith carries many organic and alternative products, though it's a bit more expensive than El Rey or Super 99. The premier wine store **Felipe Motta,** in Marbella on Calle 53 (© **302-5555**), is the most complete in Central America, and their prices are reasonable. For organic groceries and health products, try **Orgánica** in Marbella, at the Plaza Paitilla mall on Ramón H. Jurado (© **215-2400**) or **Super Gourmet** (© **212-3487**) behind the Canal Museum in the Casco Viejo neighborhood (Av. A and 6th St.), which offers many organic and healthy choices as a well as a deli serving up tasty sandwiches and lunch options. **Foodie** is the most upscale place in town to buy fruit and vegetables and is located in the Bal Harbour Plaza in Punta Paitilla, across from Multicentro.

BELLA VISTA/AREA BANCARIA & MARBELLA/BELLA VISTA AREA
Expensive

Eurasia ★★★ FUSION   One of Panama City's tonier restaurants, Eurasia is the only restaurant in Central America to receive a five-diamond rating from the American Academy of Hospitality, and continues to be a favorite among tourists and wealthier Panamanians looking for a unique dining experience. As the name implies, Eurasia's dishes are European with dashes of Asian flavors, stylishly presented. Daring and delicious, the food truly reflects the immigrant melting pot that is Panama City. The ambience is elegant, with papaya-colored walls, lavish art, heavy Spanish ironwork, and checkered marble floors; there is a slightly more casual dining area near the bar. Waiters in starched white shirts and shiny cummerbunds provide some of the best service in all of Panama. You can expect to find classics such as prawns in tamarind and coconut sauce with pilaf Eurasia, or grilled chateaubriand Indochine with petit potatoes and fine herbs. In addition, Eurasia offers a variety of mouthwatering desserts.

Edificio La Trona, Calle 48 btw. Parque Urraca and Federico Boyd Av., Bella Vista. © **264-7859.** eurasia_restaurant@hotmail.com. Reservations recommended for dinner. Main courses $7–$29. AE, MC, V. Mon–Fri noon–3pm and 7–10:30pm; Sat 7–11pm.

Moderate

La Posta ★★ 🎁 INTERNATIONAL   The long-term popularity of this restaurant derives from the lively, 1950s Havana-style ambience, as well as the tasty creations of its American-trained chef. La Posta has a gorgeous tropical decor, wicker ceiling fans, and plantation-style architecture. Although elegant, the restaurant does not feel pretentious. During the day, floor-to-ceiling windows separate the dining area from an outdoor patio (with outdoor seating), filled with vegetation, which provides for a bright and cheerful lunchtime setting. La Posta is inexpensive for such a lovely atmosphere but you'll definitely want to make reservations to avoid a long wait. Try the starters (there are more than a dozen, so you might consider ordering an assortment of these rather than an entree): yellowfin tuna seviche with capers; *mero* (a high-quality grouper) carpaccio; or fried polenta with Gorgonzola and portobello mushrooms. The thin-crust pizzas are delicious, as are the risottos. Seafood dishes are tasty but simple, such as jumbo prawns with passion fruit and rice pilaf.

Calle 49 at Calle Uruguay. ✆ **269-1076.** www.lapostapanama.com. Reservations recommended. Main courses $9.75–$16; pizzas $6.50–$9. AE, DC, MC, V. Daily noon–3pm and 7–10:30pm.

Napoli ☺ ITALIAN   This bustling, casual Italian eatery in the Obarrio neighborhood is a longtime favorite with Panamanian families. The place lacks ambience and feels a bit like a cafeteria, but the smartly dressed staff is polite and helpful, and parents won't have to worry that their children are disturbing other diners as it can get pretty loud here. Dishes are tasty and hearty, particularly the spaghetti *al pescatore* (seafood spaghetti in tomato sauce) and the many pizza selections. The tiramisu is also good, and there's a decent selection of Italian and international wines.

Calle 57 Obarrio. ✆ **263-8800.** napoli@liberty-tech.net. Main courses $5–$11. AE, MC, V. Tues–Sun 11am–11pm.

CASCO VIEJO

Once shrugged off as a dying, forgotten quarter, Casco Viejo is quickly becoming one of Panama City's most important dining scenes, and in my opinion, boasts the city's most colorful restaurants. In addition to the options listed below, **Café Rene,** Calle Pedro J. Sossa (✆ **262-3487**), follows the same concept as Manolo Caracol—no ordering and a different menu every day—and in fact, Rene used to run Manolo Caracol. Café Rene is a bit cheaper than Manolo's but the dishes are just as good. **Puerta de la Tierra,** Avenida Central and Calle 9, serves Argentine-style steaks and offers excellent service. **Pony Rosso Café,** Avenida A between calles 7 and 8, is another good lunchtime option serving mostly light fare. The cafe is located in the Diablo Rosso Art Gallery, and is a testament to Casco Viejo's growing art scene.

Expensive

Manolo Caracol ★★ INTERNATIONAL   This artistic eatery may not appeal to every diner, but I say give it a try. Manolo, the Spanish chef, professes "cooking with love," and his adventurous and creative daily menu embraces fresh, in-season products he finds every morning in the local market. There's no ordering here: Customers pay $15 for lunch and $20 for dinner (not including drinks), and sit back and wait for a vibrantly composed parade of up to 12 courses to be slowly ushered to their table. A day's offering might include sole carpaccio, green mango seviche, pork loin with pineapple, and gingery prawns. Meals range from delicious to mediocre depending on the menu and who's cooking, and service can be regular to shabby, accounting for the mixed reviews among customers. However, Manolo Caracol's modern, fixed-menu concept and the fact that it's been around for a while in Casco Viejo, where restaurants open and close with frequency, is a testament to its popularity among Panamanians and tourists alike. The dining area is within an antique colonial building, and is casual and warm, with wood tables, white stucco walls, and plenty of religious artifacts and local art.

Calle 3 at Av. Central Sur (in front of the National Theater). © **228-4640** or 228-9479. www.manolo caracol.net. Reservations recommended for dinner. Fixed-price lunch $15; fixed-price dinner $20. AE, MC, V. Mon–Sat noon–3pm and 7-10:30pm.

S'cena ★★★ INTERNATIONAL   This sexy, sophisticated jazz club/upscale restaurant is the perfect spot for an all-in-one night out and is one of my favorite dining spots in Casco Viejo. The jazz club, Platea, is on the first floor, the restaurant on the second. The bar in Platea is a good place to start or end a meal, and they serve appetizers for less-hungry patrons. Upstairs, S'cena is casual elegance, with a New York vibe, with white table linens and exposed brick walls. The cuisine is very good and Mediterranean influenced, crafted by a talented young chef on loan from Spain. The meal begins with a complimentary *amuse-bouche*. Order a bottle of wine from the well-chosen, and reasonably priced, wine list, and follow it with shellfish sautéed in Pernod or octopus caramelized in white wine. Main courses include fish and meat dishes, and a few pasta highlights such as "Grandmother's Catalan Cannellonis."

In front of old Club Union. © **228-4011.** Reservations recommended. Main courses $9–$18. AE, MC, V. Tues–Sun noon–4pm and 7:30-11pm (bar until 1am on weekends).

Moderate

Ego y Narcisco ★ TAPAS   Ego is a cosmopolitan bar/cafe, on a quiet corner of Plaza Bolívar, specializing in tapas. Make a meal out of hot chili seviche; a salad of arugula, fig, and Camembert cheese; and cilantro beef skewers. Nicely mixed cocktails, a long swooshing bar, and outdoor seating are a few of Ego's perks. (There's air-conditioned seating indoors.) Large, cold pitchers of sangria are also a treat.

Calle Antonio J. de Sucre, on the corner of Plaza Bolívar. © **262-2045.** Tapas $4–$8.50. AE, DC, MC, V. Mon–Sat 5-11:30pm.

EL CANGREJO
Expensive

In addition to the places listed below, **Costa Azul,** by the Marriott, specializes in seafood and Panamanian dishes, and is popular with business folks on their lunch breaks. **New York Bagel,** off Via Argentina near La Cabeza de Einstein, is a popular expat hangout serving, as the name implies, bagel breakfasts, bagel sandwiches, bagel chips, and other breakfast and light lunch items. It feels a bit like a converted warehouse on the inside and is one of my favorite spots to go when I want to get work done. (For those traveling alone, New York Bagel is also a good spot to meet fellow travelers. You must purchase at least $4.25 to be able to connect to the Wi-Fi network.) **Machu Picchu,** Calle Eusebio A. Morales no. 16 (© 264-9308), serves up some of the best Peruvian food in Panama City and has been a longtime favorite among Panamanians and expats alike. **Matsui** (© **264-9562;** Calle Eusebio A.

Restaurant Mercado del Marisco

To find the freshest seafood in Panama City, you have to visit the Mercado del Marisco (Fish Market) at Avenida Balboa and its unassuming little eatery on the second floor (📞 **212-3898**). This market restaurant serves quite possibly the best seviche in town, perhaps because the owner is Peruvian and lends his special flavor to such an emblematic Latin American dish. The portions are hearty, the price is reasonable, and, best of all, you can see below in the market what your catch looked like before it got to your plate. It's open daily from 11am to 7pm, but come before 1pm or after 2pm because this place gets packed during the lunch hour. *A word of caution:* Fresh seafood means fresh seafood, so if you can't stand the smell of fish, this place is definitely not for you. *Tip:* If the restaurant is full or you are on the run, buy a $1-to-$2 generous portion of seviche from Shiela (you can identify her by her gold tooth).

Morales no. 12-A) is, in my opinion, the best sushi place in town, proved by its 30-year longevity on the Panama City dining scene.

Las Barandas ★★★ CONTEMPORARY PANAMANIAN   Cuquita, the chef at Las Barandas, is nationally famous as the Martha Stewart of Panama, producing her own line of culinary magazines in addition to a weekly cooking show. At Las Barandas, Cuquita is the creator of the restaurant's gourmet Panamanian food and oversees the kitchen staff. The restaurant, located inside the Bristol Panama, is a sleek and chic dining area with just a handful of tables—so book ahead. At Las Barandas, traditional recipes are updated to appeal to modern gourmet tastes, with dishes such as maize soup, plantain won tons, grouper in ginger, sea bass in tamarind, and chicken breast roasted with pumpkinseeds, all bursting with flavor yet not too over-the-top so as to appeal to more conservative tastes. In addition to an extensive menu, there is a special "South Beach" menu for dieters watching their waistlines. Of special note is Las Barandas's Sunday brunch from 10am to 3pm.

Aquilino de la Guardia at Obarrio, in the Bristol Panama Hotel. 📞 **265-7844.** Reservations recommended. Main courses $12–$25. AE, MC, V. Daily 6–10am, noon–3pm, and 6:30–11pm.

Moderate

Beirut ★ LEBANESE   Beirut is always busy and enjoys popularity among Panamanians, expats, and vacationers. This is an excellent spot for a couple or a larger group because it serves reasonably priced combo plates and appetizer platters. Combos come with dozens of little dishes and finger foods such as hummus, baba ghanouj, fried kibbe, almond rice, and so on, offering a filling meal and varied sample of flavors. There are also salads, falafel and other sandwiches, and kabobs. Beirut's low ceilings, molded banquet seating, and exotic decor make you feel as if you've actually stepped into Lebanon. Additionally, the food is light and fresh, and powerful air-conditioning provides a refreshing escape from the hot Panama City streets. The chef, a Lebanese immigrant, patrols the dining room for quality control, sometimes refilling the occasional guest's hookah pipe, which is *de rigueur* in this establishment. A Lebanese Table, with a selection of dishes, for four guests is $58; a special combo large enough to feed two is just $10.

Ricardo Arias at Calle 52, near the Marriott Hotel. ⒸⓉ **214-3815.** Main courses $6.50–$15. MC, V. Daily 11am–2pm.

Martín Fierro ★★ STEAKHOUSE   Named after Argentina's epic literary hero, a gaucho who wandered the pampa, this restaurant, accordingly, serves thick slabs of beef and other meats that would satisfy a gaucho or any weary traveler who's had a hard day and longs for a hearty, satisfying meal. Martín Fierro features meats cut Argentine-style, but the price differs between domestic meat and that imported from the U.S. You'll find pastas and fish on the menu, but if you're not a carnivore there's really no reason to eat here. (They boast about their salad bar, but it's insubstantial and won't do much more than decorate your plate.) Martín Fierro strives to be an elegant eating establishment, but the bright lights and decor keep it decidedly casual.

Eusebio Morales, in front of Bonavel. ⒸⓉ **264-1927.** Main courses $8–$25. AE, MC, V. Mon–Sat noon–3pm and 6–11pm; Sun noon–9:30pm.

Inexpensive

Cafetería Manolo's PANAMANIAN   This neighborhood standby is a plain-as-Jane diner with uniformed waitresses and a long list of Panamanian dishes of varying quality. It's the kind of place you go for a quick, no-frills meal, or to kill time with a cold beer while sitting on the outdoor terrace. It therefore draws as many locals as tourists who can't be bothered with a serious sit-down restaurant. Manolo's sandwiches are your best bet here, but there are also quick-fry steaks, grilled fish, and local dishes such as *sancocho* (chicken stew). Try the sugary *churros* (a cornmeal pastry with gooey filling) for dessert. For breakfast try the Panamanian eggs and tortillas. There are two locations, but I like the Vía Veneto diner the best.

Calle 49B Oeste, in front of the Veneto Hotel. ⒸⓉ **269-4514** (another location at Vía Argentina and Av. 2B Norte; ⒸⓉ **264-3965**). Reservations not accepted. Main courses $6–$9; sandwiches $2.50–$4.50. AE, MC. Both locations daily 6am–1am.

El Trapiche PANAMANIAN   Ask anyone in Panama City where to savor great Panamanian food, and chances are the first place they say is El Trapiche. There's nothing palatial about it, but you can cool off in the air-conditioned dining room or people-watch from the outdoor sidewalk cafe. Newcomers to Panama should not miss the house specialty, the "Panamanian Fiesta" combination plate, which offers a taste of eight different local dishes. This is also where you'll want to try the hefty Panamanian breakfast—order tasajo entomatado (beef jerky) with eggs and fried-bread hojaldras. The old-world sugar-mill decor comes from the name, El Trapiche, which refers to a press used to extract juice from sugar cane. Main courses, such as broiled sea bass or smoked pork chops with rice, beans, and fried plantains, are hearty and satisfy big appetites. Their fresh fruit juice blends are perfect on a hot day.

Vía Argentina at Av. 2a B Norte. ⒸⓉ **269-4353.** Main courses $3–$11. AE, MC, V. Sun–Thurs 7am–11pm; Fri–Sat 7am–midnight.

AMADOR CAUSEWAY

In general, the food quality is not the highest on the Amador Causeway, but the places below serve pretty decent food.

Expensive

Bucanero ★ SEAFOOD   Bucanero, with its kitschy maritime decor, serves some of the area's best food. The restaurant is seriously overpriced, but the portions are hearty and the cuisine is a step above that of its neighbors. There are meats on the menu (including *parrilladas,* or barbecue meat platters), but the specialty is seafood. Start with a tangy seviche, and then have the stuffed sea bass, a rich Parmesan-cheese crab gratin, or jumbo shrimp in a vodka sauce. There are shared platters for groups. Dining is on a breezy veranda overlooking a parking lot and the Flamenco Shopping Plaza. Because the cruise-ship dock is nearby, some passengers stop at the Bucanero for meals. One caveat here has to do with the waiters, who are attentive but try to rip off guests by suggesting a higher quality seafood (jumbo shrimp, for example, as opposed to shrimp), thereby doubling the cost of the dish without warning the diner. Alas, the Flamenco area is a tourist trap anyway. Live jazz is featured on Wednesday, and salsa music on Thursday and Friday.

Flamenco Shopping area (end of the Amador Causeway). (C) **314-1774.** Main courses $14–$26. AE, MC, V. Daily 11:30am–midnight.

Inexpensive

Mi Ranchito ★★ PANAMANIAN   This is certainly not the best Panamanian food in the city (El Trapiche, Las Barandas, Al Tambar de la Alegría, and Las Tinajas fill that bill), but nevertheless the great view of the Panama City skyline and the almost constant cool breeze that blows through account for its crazy popularity among tourists and Panamanians alike. And, to be quite honest, I love this place. The restaurant is open-air and under a massive thatched-roof *bohio* on Isla Naos, near the Smithsonian Museum. You'll find typical Panamanian dishes here such as grilled meat, prawns, sea bass, and snapper served in a garlic or tomato-and-onion sauce and paired with coconut rice and fried plantains. Mi Ranchito has an appetizer mix of Panamanian specialties such as empanadas, *patacones* (fried plantains), and *carimañolas* (yucca root stuffed with meat), but they are so deep-fried they almost all look and taste the same. Stick with the fresh fish and shellfish dishes, and an ice-cold beer. After lunch, you can rent a bike next door and go burn off all those calories.

Isla Naos. (C) **228-4909.** Reservations not accepted. Main courses $7–$10. MC, V. Mon–Sat 9:30am–12:30am; Sun 9:30am–11pm.

Panama City After Dark
THE PERFORMING ARTS
Theater, Ballet & Classical Music

Theater tickets can be purchased by calling the theater directly, or you can buy tickets at **Blockbuster** locations and at the bookstore **El Hombre de la Mancha** or **Exedra Books** (see "Bookstores" on p. 677). All theater productions are in Spanish, with the exception of the **Ancón Theater Guild** ((C) **212-0060;** www.tga-panama. com; admission donation around $10). The well-respected guild has been around for more than a half-century, first opening its doors in Colón to provide entertainment to U.S. troops during World War II. The guild normally produces contemporary dramas and comedy with a mix of native English speakers and Panamanian actors trained in English-language schools.

Classical music productions, plays, and ballet take place at Panama City's turn-of-the-20th-century **National Theater,** on Avenida B in Casco Viejo, but shows are infrequent. The best Spanish-language theater productions can be found at **Teatro la Quadra,** on Calle D in El Cangrejo ((C) **214-3695;** www.teatroquadra.com; tickets average $10). This cultural center was founded to promote and develop the art of theater in Panama, and they receive acclaim for their nightly performances of well-known plays and children's theater. **Teatro ABA** at Avenida Simon Bolívar (Transístmica), near

Avenida de los Periodistas in front of the Riba Smith supermarket (© **260-6316;** tickets cost an average of $5), produces half its own shows and rents out its 200-person theater to independent groups; productions are mostly comedy, drama, and well-established plays. Check www.prensa.com for theater listings here. **Teatro en Círculo,** on Avenida 6C Norte at Vía Brasil (© **261-5375;** www.teatroencirculo.com), is an esteemed playhouse with original Panamanian productions and classic international productions. The historic **Teatro Anita Villalaz** (© **501-5020;** tickets average $10), on Plaza Francia in Casco Viejo, is administered by the National Cultural Institute (INAC); the intimate theater is home to folkloric productions, concerts, and plays, some of which are produced by the University of Panama students.

The Club & Music Scene

The nightclubs listed below open at 10pm but don't really get going until midnight or later; during the first hours of operation, however, nightclubs typically offer drink specials. Nightclub partyers tend to dress smartly for the occasion, so don your slinkiest or sharpest outfit or risk being refused entry (or just feeling out of place).

For folkloric presentations in a less-trendy environment, try **Las Tinajas** or **Al Tambor a la Alegría.** Most clubs in Panama City are located in Casco Viejo, Calle Uruguay, or the new "Zona Viva." Because of local residents tired of loud, all-night partyers on Calle Uruguay, many clubs have moved to the Zona Viva, located just before the Amador Causeway.

For Salsa, head to **Habana Panama** (Calle Eloy Alfaro y Calle 12 Este, Barrio San Felipe, Casco Antiguo; © **6780-2183;** www.habanapanama.com), which hosts live bands every Thursday, Friday, and Saturday and is, in my opinion, the best and most authentic place to listen to and dance salsa in Panama City. This area can be a bit dodgy at night, so be sure to have the club call a cab if you're leaving unaccompanied. **Bar Platea** ★★ (© **228-4011**) is another Casco Viejo Spot with plenty of soul; jazz is alive and well at this new sophisticated bar/club, on the ground floor of a colonial town house in Casco Viejo. The club shares the building with its partner, S'cena restaurant (p. 685). Platea is cozy and classy, and appeals to a diverse crowd of Panamanians and foreigners young and old. Platea is known for its Jazz Thursdays and Salsa Saturdays and is located in front of the Old Club Union in Casco Viejo. **Oz Bar and Lounge** (Calle 53 Este, Marbella; © **265-2805**) draws Panama City's elite 20-somethings for its chic decor, live DJ music (mostly house and chill-out), and popular Tuesday karaoke nights. On Friday from 9 to 11pm it's ladies' night with free shots, and Saturday "Cocktail" Night means free sangria for women until midnight. **Wasabi Sushi Lounge** (Calle 54 at Calle 50, Marbella; © **264-1863**) is characterized by '60s pop-retro, low-to-the-ground white tulip chairs, mosaic walls, and orange transparent acrylic furniture. It's trendy and lively, especially on Wednesdays, when women drink free sangria until midnight and snack on sushi. There are several different salons, each with individual music. DJs spin house music and reggae.

BARS

The Amador Causeway is an up-and-coming nightlife spot, with new bars and restaurants opening monthly. Many bars on Calle Uruguay and in other locations are moving to the new Zona Viva, as it's called. As a nightspot, the area tends to draw groups of friends, and an upscale, older crowd. Most sit-down full-service restaurants in Casco Viejo—and most of Panama City, for that matter—turn into bars in the evening.

Decapolis Radisson Sushi Bar & Martini Lounge   This popular upscale bar is located on the lobby level of the Decapolis Hotel. The ultrachic ambience draws an upscale crowd that spans a range of ages, making this a good bet for travelers seeking a refined, hip bar without the post-teen crowd. Live DJ music, and a second, poolside bar, keep the party going well into the night. The scene gets started a little earlier here than in other city bars and nightclubs. Av. Balboa at the Multicentro Mall. ✆ **215-5000.**

THE GAY & LESBIAN SCENE

Panama is a mostly Catholic country and although the GLBT scene here is not underground, it is discreet. There are a couple of clubs in the city that operate without much fanfare, and attacks, raids, harassment, and so on are thankfully not very common. For a calendar of events, check out **www.farraurbana.com**. There are few, if any, venues or events directed at the lesbian-only scene, though lesbians are welcome at gay venues. Clubs are open at 10pm Wednesday through Sunday; weeknight cover charges are around $3 to $5, $8 to $10 on weekends. Early arrivals can take advantage of happy-hour drink specials.

The most established gay clubs are **BLG,** at Calle 49 and Calle Uruguay (✆ **265-1624**), with dancing to top DJ music Thursday to Saturday, and other special events like Gay Pride Nights on weekdays; and **Lips** (no phone), at Avenida Manuel Espinoza Batista, next to Café Duran, with nightly drag shows on weeknights and dancing on Fridays and Saturdays. The largest gay dance club is called **Glam: The Club** (✆ **265-1624**), which features nightly drag shows, fashion shows, and more, followed by late-night dancing until dawn (the best nights are Fri and Sat). To get here, you need a taxi; the club is at Tumba Muerto (in the Urb. Industrial La Esperanza neighborhood) on Vía Ricardo J. Alfaro. **Punta G,** at Calle D in El Cangrejo (next to Ginza Teppanyaki; ✆ **265-1624**), has barmen in spandex, DJ music, and a dance floor.

CASINOS

Gambling is legal in Panama, and virtually every major hotel in the city has an adjoining casino. You'll find slot machines, video poker, gaming tables, sports betting, and special shows and parties. The hottest casino at the moment is at the **Veneto Hotel & Casino.** The Veneto has a sophisticated gaming area and often hosts over-the-top parties such as E! Entertainment's *Wild On*. There is a sushi bar here, too. The **Marriott's Fiesta Casino** is popular with foreigners and expats thanks to its convenient central location, and **El Panama Hotel** has one of the newer centrally located casinos, which offers cheap drink specials for women. The **Sheraton Hotel and Convention Center** hotel has a large, elegant casino, but its out-of-the-way location means it's really visited only by guests. The bar here, though, is popular with young Panamanians.

THE PANAMA CANAL & THE CANAL ZONE ★★★

77km (48 miles) long from Panama City to Colón

The construction of the Panama Canal was one of the grandest engineering feats in history, an epic tale of ingenuity and courage but one marked by episodes of tragedy. When it was finally completed in 1914, the canal cut travel distances by more than half for ships that previously had had to round South America's Cape Horn. Today,

the canal is one of the world's most traveled waterways, annually handling around 13,000 ships that represent 5% of global trade.

The history of the canal dates back to the 16th century, when Vasco Núñez de Balboa discovered that Panama was a narrow strip of land separating the Caribbean from the Pacific. In 1539, King Charles I of Spain dispatched a survey team to study the feasibility of building a waterway connecting the two oceans, but the team deemed such a pursuit impossible.

The first real attempt to construct a canal was begun by the French in 1880, led by Ferdinand de Lesseps, the charismatic architect of the Suez Canal. The Gallic endeavor failed miserably, however, as few had anticipated the enormous challenge presented by the Panamanian jungle, with its mucky swamps, torrential downpours, landslides, floods, and, most debilitating of all, mosquito-borne diseases such as malaria and yellow fever. In the end, more than 20,000 perished.

In 1903, the United States bought out the French and backed Panama in its secession from Colombia in exchange for control of the Canal Zone. For the next 10 years, the U.S., having essentially eradicated tropical disease, pulled off what seemed impossible in terms of engineering: It carved out a 14km (8⅔-mile) path through the Continental Divide and constructed an elevated canal system and a series of locks to lift ships from sea level up to 26m (85 ft.) at Lake Gatún. The lake, created after construction crews dammed the Chagres River near the Gatún Locks, was at the time the largest man-made lake in the world.

In 1977, U.S. President Jimmy Carter and President Omar Torrijos of Panama signed a treaty that would hand over control of the canal to the Panamanians on December 31, 1999. It was a controversial move, because most Americans did not believe that Panama was up to the task—but those concerns have proved to be unfounded. As an autonomous corporation, the Panama Canal Authority has reduced safety problems and improved maintenance and productivity to the point where the canal basically runs itself.

It takes between 8 and 10 hours to transit the entire canal. There are three locks, the **Miraflores, Pedro Miguel,** and **Gatún,** whose maximum size is 320m (1,050 ft.) in length and 34m (112 ft.) in width. Ships built to fit through these locks are referred to as **Panamax** ships, which set the size standard until the 1990s, with the building of post-Panamax ships (mostly oil tankers) that are up to 49m (160 ft.) wide. The Panama Canal Authority, seeking to avoid becoming obsolete, is currently constructing two multibillion-dollar three-chamber locks to increase traffic and allow for wider ships.

Seeing the Panama Canal in Action

MIRAFLORES LOCKS ★★★

The best land-based platform from which to see the Panama Canal at work is at **Miraflores Visitors Center** (✆ 276-8325; www.pancanal.com), located a 15-minute drive from the heart of the city. The center is an absorbing attraction for both kids and adults, with four floors of exhibitions and interactive displays—and a theater—providing information about the canal's history and its impact on world trade, plus explanations of how the region's natural environment is crucial to the function of the canal. Ships can also be viewed from an observation deck. In fact, it's probably Panama's best museum. *Tip:* You'll have better luck catching sight of enormous Panamax ships around 11am or 3pm. I recommend calling the Visitors Center ahead of time to find out what time large ships are expected to cross.

As you view ships in the locks, a monologue (in Spanish and English) piped through a loudspeaker indicates what a ship is carrying, where it is registered, where it is going, and how much it paid; the speaker is cheerleader-like and tends to qualify the experience by saying such things as, "Can you *believe* they spent $200,000 to transit the canal, man?" There are also a snack bar and a gift shop. The center is open daily from 9am to 5pm (ticket office closes at 4pm). Admission to the center's exhibitions and observation terrace is $8 adults, $5 children and students with ID, and free for children 4 and under; or $5 adults, $3 children to visit only the restaurant and gift shop.

Best of all, there is the **Miraflores Visitors Center Restaurant ★★★** (daily 11am–11pm; main courses $7–$20), which gets three stars because of its extremely unique location; the food is not particularly memorable, but you can dine while watching colossal ships transit the locks just 30m (100 ft.) away. Lunch is the most popular time to eat here, so arrive early or make a reservation, and try to get a table as close to the railing as possible. At night, the locks are well lit and provide clear views of the ships.

Getting There

BY ORGANIZED TOUR   City tours of Panama usually include a 2-hour stop at Miraflores, or you can take a taxi for $25 to $30 round-trip for a 45-minute to 1-hour visit. However, keep in mind that the increasing price of gas is making transportation more and more expensive in Panama, so prices are subject to change. Agree on a price with the driver beforehand.

BY BUS   Buses headed to Gamboa and the Canal Zone leave from the SACA station at the Palacio Legislativo at Plaza Cinco de Mayo, near Avenida Central, not from the main terminal in Albrook. The cost is 65¢ adults, 35¢ children. This bus drops passengers off at stops along the Gaillard Highway and Gamboa Road, including at the Miraflores Locks. However, the stop for Miraflores is an 8- to 10-minute walk from the visitor center. Buses leave weekdays at 5, 5:45, 6:30, 8, and 10am, noon, 1, 2, 3, 4:30, 6:30, 8, and 10:30pm; on Saturday and Sunday buses leave at 6, 7, 8, and 10am, noon, 2, 4:30, 6:30, 8, and 10:30pm. I really don't recommend this option; I tried it once and waited for a bus outside the Miraflores Visitor Center for nearly an hour and a half, not a particularly enjoyable wait in 90-degree weather.

BY CAR   To get to Gamboa and the Canal Zone, head out of Panama City toward Albrook to the **Gaillard Highway,** which runs along the canal and passes the Miraflores Locks. The road continues on past the Pedro Miguel locks and the Summit Golf Course until it forks at the ANAM ranger station just after you pass under a railway bridge. To get to Gamboa, the Gamboa Resort, Barro Colorado Island, the Canopy Tower, El Charco Trail, or Pipeline Road, take a left here on Gamboa Road. To get to the Camino de Cruces trail, continue straight on a lovely, jungle-fringed road that cuts through Soberanía National Park and eventually connects with the road to Colón. The sign for the Cruces trail is clearly marked at an off-road picnic site.

TRANSITING THE PANAMA CANAL ★★★

Visitors to Panama who are not part of a long-haul cruise can still transit the canal by boat on a journey from Panama City to Colón, or they can do a partial transit from Gamboa to the Pacific or vice versa. Beyond the thrill of transiting locks is the opportunity to get close to colossal Panamax-size ships en route from one ocean to the other. Partial tours are by far the most popular because they pass through the Pedro Miguel and Miraflores locks, and sail under the grand span of the Bridge of the Americas, which is enough for most visitors. The companies below are all reputable and offer excellent partial and full transit tours of the canal.

Panama Marine Adventures (✆ 226-8917; www.pmatours.net) offers partial canal transit with a shuttle leaving from the Flamenco Resort and Marina on the Amador Causeway at 10am and going to their *Pacific Queen,* docked at Gamboa. Trips leave every Saturday year-round, and every Thursday and Friday from January to April. The company offers full transit of the canal one Saturday every month (check the website for dates) leaving at 7:30am, first passing through the Miraflores locks and finishing at the Gatún Locks; the company provides transportation by vehicle back to Panama City. Partial transit, which lasts 4 to 6 hours depending on traffic, costs $115 for adults and $65 for kids 11 and under; full transit costs $165 for adults and $75 kids 11 and under; it lasts 10 to 12 hours. The price includes all transportation, a bilingual guide, and lunch and soft drinks. The *Pacific Queen* has a capacity of 300 passengers.

Canal & Bay Tours ★★★ (© 209-2009 or 209-2010; www.canalandbaytours. com) is a pioneer in canal tourism, offering transit aboard one of two boats, the refurbished *Isla Morada,* a wooden boat with a capacity of 100 guests, or the *Fantasía del Mar,* a steel boat with a capacity of 500. The company offers full-day transit of the canal the first Saturday of every month for $165 adults, $75 children 11 and under, and partial transit every Saturday for $115 adults, $60 children 11 and under. Canal & Bay has full transit and partial transit (you pick) the third Tuesday of every month from January to April. Tours leave at 7:30am from the Flamenco Marina, docking in Gamboa or Gatún, depending on the tour. They also offer Saturday-evening **"Rumba in the Bay"** tours of the Bay of Panama, leaving at 9:30pm from their pier, with live music and an open bar.

Ancon Expeditions (© **269-9415;** www.anconexpeditions.com) also offers full and partial transits of the canal. Ancon offers early-morning hotel pickup to the Port of Balboa, where you'll board a passenger ferry. Partial transits cost $95 for adults and full transits cost $150. Full transits are offered the first and third Saturday of every month with one additional Thursday departure in January, and partial transits depart every Thursday and Friday January through March and every Saturday year-round. After transiting, a bus will take you back to your hotel. **Margo Tours** (© **264-8888;** www.margotours.com) also offers partial and complete canal transits. Partial transits cost $115 and leave every Saturday from La Playita de Amador on the Causeway. Complete transit costs $165, but they happen only once a month, so call ahead and find out when the next scheduled transit is. Complimentary hotel pickup is available.

More Highlights Around Panama City

SOBERANIA NATIONAL PARK ★★★

Soberanía National Park comprises 19,425 hectares (48,000 acres) of undulating, pristine tropical rainforest on the eastern shore of the Panama Canal. It is Panama's most important national park in terms of tourism and economics: Not only is Soberanía one of the most accessible, species-rich parks in the Americas, but it also is part of the watershed that provides hundreds of millions of gallons of water to keep the Panama Canal in operation and the cogs of international commerce greased and moving. The park is just 40 minutes from Panama City.

Wildlife from North and South America, including migratory birds, meets here in Soberanía, creating a diverse natural wonderland. The park has 105 species of mammals and a staggering number of bird species—525 at last count. There are jaguars, yes, and collared peccaries and night monkeys too, but you're more likely to catch sight of a coatimundi, three-toed sloth, or diminutive tamarin monkey. Bring binoculars even if you're not an avid birder.

There are several ways to see the park. ANAM, the park ranger service, has several excellent hiking trails for day excursions that range from easy to difficult; there are a full-scale resort, a birder's ecolodge, a recreational park and zoo, and the Pipeline Road, a site revered for its abundant diversity of birds. Soberanía National Park is open daily from 6am to 5pm, and costs $3 per person to enter (free for kids 11 and under). Paying is tricky; they ask that you stop at the ranger station to pay because there isn't anyone to collect money at the trail head—but it's unlikely that every visitor does this. Play it safe, though, and stop to pay; the pass permits you to use any trails within the space of a day.

The park can be accessed by rental vehicle or taxi, or by joining a tour. If you take a taxi, plan a time for the driver to pick you up or have the driver wait. For more information, call the park's office at © **232-4192;** the website, www.anam.gob.pa, has limited park info in Spanish. The park office is open from 7am to 7pm daily, but if no one is inside, check around out back.

HIKING & BIRD-WATCHING TRAILS Sendero El Plantación (Plantation Trail), located at the turnoff for the Canopy Tower lodge on the road to Gamboa, is a moderate, 6.4km (4-mile) trail that ends at the intersection for the Camino de Cruces trail. This is not a loop trail, so hikers will need to either return via the same trail or, with a little preplanning, arrange to be dropped off at the Camino de Cruces trail on the road to Colón, hike northwest and connect with the Plantation Trail, and finish near the Canopy Tower, or vice versa (see Camino de Cruces, below). The Plantation Trail follows a road built in the 1910s by La Cascadas Plantation, the largest in the old Canal Zone during that period, producing cacao, coffee, and rubber. Alert hikers will spot remnants of these crops, especially the cacao plant. This trail is popular with bird-watchers, but mammals such as tamarins are frequently seen, too.

Continuing on the road to Gamboa, and to the right, is the trail head for **Sendero Charco (Pond Trail),** an ultraeasy, 20-minute loop that follows the Sardinilla River. The trail gives even the most reluctant walkers a brilliant opportunity to immerse themselves in thick tropical rainforest.

A little more than a mile past the bridge and turnoff to Gamboa Resort is **Camino de Oleoducto,** better known as **Pipeline Road,** the celebrity trail for bird-watching in Panama, renowned worldwide as a record-setting site for 24-hour bird counts. Even nonbirders can't help getting caught up in the action with so many colorful show birds fluttering about, such as motmots, trogons, toucans, antbirds, a rainbow of tanagers, and flycatchers. Bird-watching starts at the crack of dawn, when the avian world is at its busiest, so try to make it here at least before 9am, if not earlier. In spite of the name, the Pipeline Road is not drivable. More than half of the bird-watchers who visit here walk only a mile or so, but if you like to hike or mountain bike (see below), push on because the chances of spotting rare birds and wildlife increase the farther you go. To get here by vehicle, pass the Gamboa Resort turnoff, and continue until you reach a fork. Turn left here onto a gravel road and continue until you see the Pipeline Road sign.

Soberanía's other prime attraction is historic **Camino de Cruces (Las Cruces Trail).** Before the railway and the canal existed, the only path from the Caribbean to the Pacific was the Chagres River to what's now called Venta de Cruces, followed by a treacherous walk along Las Cruces Trail. The Spanish used this route during the 16th century to transport looted treasure to the Caribbean and onward to Spain. In some areas, the cobblestone remains of the trail still exist or have been restored, and can be seen even if you walk just 10 or 20 minutes from the picnic area and trail head off Madden Road. The trail is moderate to difficult, and is about 9.7km (6 miles) to its terminus at Venta de Cruces. From here, a local boat can pick you up and drop you off at the Gamboa Resort, but you'll need a guide (a tour or your hotel can arrange this for you). Also, hikers may lose their way because the trail becomes somewhat indecipherable the closer you get to Venta las Cruces, another reason to have a guide. Backpackers can camp along the trail, but must pay a $5 fee at the park-ranger station beforehand.

If this trail really piques your interest, check out Ancon Expeditions' 8-day "Camino Real Tour," which gives travelers a taste of what it was like to cross the isthmus by foot during the Gold Rush era, and includes tent lodging in the rainforest and at an Emberá Indian village. Ancon Expeditions (see above), Advantage Panama (p. 697), and **Panama Pete Adventures** (✆ 888/726-6222; www.panamapete adventures.com) all offer bird-watching, hiking, and Emberá village day tours, as does **Adventures Panama Canal** (✆ 6636-4647).

The second alternative is to hike the trail and turn into the Plantation Trail, which finishes near Canopy Tower and the road to Gamboa. This hike takes around 5 hours to complete and is a moderately difficult trek. To get to the trail head, continue straight at the fork in the road to Gamboa on what's known as Madden Road (but not signed as such). The road presents a lovely drive through the park along a road flanked with towering rainforest canopy. About 6km (3¾ miles) past the fork there are covered picnic tables and the trail head.

MOUNTAIN BIKING   The tour company **Adventures in Panama** offers a half-day mountain bike trip on the Pipeline Road, leaving Panama City at 8am and returning at 1:30pm (cost averages $95 per person, and includes transportation, equipment, and a box lunch). The bike terrain is sand, pavement, packed dirt, and mud, and is classified as moderate to difficult. Your group can bike up to 29km (18 miles) round-trip or less depending on your appetite for riding. The minimum age for this bike trip is 8 years old.

Panama Pete Adventures (see above) offers a similar mountain bike trip for $76 per person, including transportation, equipment, box lunch, and bilingual guide. This day trip is for experienced bikers only and children must be at least 12 years old to participate.

LAGO GATÚN

Engineers understood that the only feasible way to build the Panama Canal was to employ a system of locks to lift ships up and over higher altitudes on the isthmus, and central to this was the creation of Gatún Lake. The lake was formed in 1913 with the completion of the Gatún Dam, which staunched the powerful Chagres River—a tremendous feat considering that Gatún Dam and Gatún Lake were the largest earth dam and largest man-made lake of their time. The lake flooded roughly 425 sq. km (164 sq. miles), an area slightly larger than Detroit, creating islands out of hilltops and submerging entire forests and villages.

The thick rainforest that cloaks the shoreline provides water for Gatún Lake, which in turn provides water for the canal locks, and therefore the Canal Authority is keen to keep deforestation at bay. This is good news for ecotravelers—wildlife sightings are common. Ships traverse 38km (24 miles) across the lake from the Gatún Locks to the Gaillard Cut, and travelers can take part in this experience with a partial canal transit, or take part in a jungle cruise on the lake. There is also fishing, or you can visit Barro Colorado Island. Getting on the lake provides a more intimate view of the canal than a visit to the Miraflores Locks does.

JUNGLE CRUISES ★★★ ☺   Half-day jungle cruises in Lake Gatún are mini-adventures that are as fun for kids as for adults, and they are dependable ways to catch sight of monkeys such as white-faced capuchins, howler monkeys, and Geoffrey's tamarins up close and in their natural habitat. Expect also to see sloths, crocodiles, caimans, turtles, and even capybaras, the world's largest rodents. The boat ride also allows passengers to get unusually close to monster tankers and ships transiting the canal. The **Gamboa Resort** offers a jungle cruise as part of their in-house excursions; others leave from the Gamboa pier and provide land transportation to and from Panama City. Guides provide passengers with an entertaining account of the history of the canal, the mechanisms that operate the canal, and fun anecdotes, while ducking in and out of island passageways searching for birds and wildlife. **Ancon Expeditions** (✆ **269-9415;** www.anconexpeditions.com) has the best guides and service, not to mention the most experience in the area. Their Panama Canal Rainforest Boat Adventure leaves early from Panama City and returns in the midafternoon; the cost is $110 adults, $65 kids 12 and under, which includes lunch, naturalist guides, and all transportation. **Advantage Panama** (www.advantagepanama.com) also offers a rainforest land-and-water tour including a stroll through Soberanía National Park before boarding their aquatic vessel. The tour lasts about 6 hours, includes drinks and snacks, and costs $87.

Jungle Land Explorers, part of Panama City Tours (✆ **209-5657;** www.gatun explorer.com), offers an interesting motorboat tour of Gatún Lake and a stop at their anchored, double-decker *Gatún Explorer* houseboat, where guests have lunch and kick back in the middle of the jungle; kayaking and fishing are also options. They have a library with educational videos and books, too. The tour leaves from La Represa dock on the west side of the canal; however, round-trip transportation from Panama City is included, leaving at 8am and returning at 4:30pm. Tours cost $95 per person. Call ahead for tour days and availability.

FISHING ★★★   I give this three stars because in Gatún Lake you're guaranteed a fish—or your money back. The lake is packed with peacock bass, and all you need to do is just casually throw a line in and you'll easily snag one, sometimes within minutes. Fishermen tell stories of catching not dozens but hundreds of peacock bass and tarpon, which also reside here. Also, as on a jungle cruise, you can get relatively close to ships on the canal and enjoy wild surroundings. **Panama Canal Fishing** (✆ **315-1905** or 6678-2653; www.panamacanalfishing.com; info@panamacanal fishing.com) has a 5.5m (18-ft.) Fun Deck with a 115-horsepower motor, live bait box, and fishing rods. The cost is $395 a day for two people plus $20 each additional angler, with lures, rods, snacks, and beer included. They recently began offering ocean boats for inshore fishing. The operation is run by Richard Cahill, a Panamanian-American who knows the lake inside and out. Rich recently added fishing tours to the Bayana River for snook and tarpon fishing ($550 all-inclusive), which is located about 1½ hours from Panama City. If you're looking for something cheaper, he can put you in touch with a local boat operator who will charge $80 a day for a 4.9m (16-ft.) boat, but rods and food are extra (and local guides speak limited English). Local boat operators charge about $120 a day. **Adventures Panama Canal** (✆ **6636-4614**) can also organize fishing excursions. **Gamboa Tours** (www.gamboatours.com) at the Gamboa Resort can charter private fishing excursions, though you should expect to pay a bit more.

RIO CHAGRES & EMBERA VILLAGES

The Chagres River flows from the San Blas Cordillera down into Gatún Lake near Gamboa—on the other side of the lake, the river is blocked by the Gatún Dam, which created its namesake lake. Travelers visit this river for two reasons: cultural tours of Emberá Indian villages, or intermediate-level white-water rafting. Along the way, the jungle-draped riverbanks teem with birds, animals, and fluttering butterflies, providing an exciting sense of adventure without an investment of a lot of time or money.

EMBERA INDIANS VILLAGE TOUR ★★ ☺ Emberá Indians are native to the Darién Province, but many groups have resettled on the banks of the Chagres River. For the most part, they continue to live life much as they have for centuries, traveling by dugout canoe, wearing a skirt or sheath, and sleeping under thatched-roof huts. To earn income, the Emberá villages **Parara Puru, Emberá Puru,** and **Emberá Drua,** which are close to the mouth of the Chagres River, have opened to tourism, allowing visitors to share in their culture and see how they live. In the true sense, the villages are not pristine examples of Emberá life, and I can't help but feel that they exist as a sort of "Disney World" of indigenous culture; but the chance to travel by dugout canoe, interact with this culture, and, yes, buy a few of their intricately woven baskets and other handicrafts can be both informative and delightful. For a few bucks, you can have an Emberá hand-paint a traditional "tattoo" with *jagua* vegetable dye on a part of your body (it takes 10–14 days for the stain to wear off). Part of the tour includes a typical Emberá lunch and watching a folkloric dance show; like most folkloric shows, these are demonstrations of rituals long gone, but the music and dancing are still entertaining. Bring your swimsuit because tours include a walk to a cascade for a dip in cool water. All Panamanian tour operators offer this Emberá trip, though prices vary. **Ancon Expeditions** (p. 655) charges $130 for this half-day trip, while **Advantage Panama** (p. 655) charges $81. **Panama Pete Adventures** (p. 696) charges $95, and **Margo Tours** (p. 655) charges $85.

RAFTING AND KAYAKING ★★ The tour company **Aventuras Panama** (© 260-0044; www.aventuraspanama.com) specializes in what it calls the "Chagres Challenge," with a hiking and rafting trip down the Class 2 and 3 river. It's a long float but technically not difficult, and it starts early, leaving Panama City at 5am by 4WD and going to the village San Cristóbal. From here you hike for more than an hour to the put-in site on the Chagres. The rafting portion lasts about 5 hours, but included in that is a picnic lunch on the river. Travelers pass by Emberá villages but do not spend much time there. Expect to arrive back in Panama City around 7pm. The cost is $165 per person, and includes transportation, breakfast and lunch, and all equipment. You must be between the ages of 12 and 70 to participate.

Aventuras Panama and **Panama Pete Adventures** both offer kayaking adventures. Aventuras Panama offers guided excursions of the Chagres River and Lake Gatún for $150 per person, and Panama Pete offers Lake Gatún excursions at $76 per person. Both tours leave Panama around 8am and return around 3:30pm.

SUMMIT GARDENS PARK & ZOO ★★

Summit Gardens Park & Zoo is a good introduction to the flora and fauna native to the country. For kids, there are a lot of wide, grassy areas on which to run around, and enough animals on view to delight all ages. It isn't a fancy, state-of-the-art zoo by U.S. standards; however, Summit recently hired a new director to refocus and revamp the zoo and gardens and to create a cohesive exhibition that illustrates biodiversity using animals, birds, and reptile displays.

The zoo has a wonderful display of "showcase" wildlife, including tapirs, white-faced capuchins and spider monkeys, ocelots, a jaguar, puma, collared peccaries, and more, some of which have been rescued from unscrupulous wildlife poachers (the young tapir "Lucia" was saved during a sting operation that nabbed two Panamanians trying to sell her on the Internet). But without a doubt the **harpy eagle** takes center stage here. The harpy is Panama's national bird and the largest eagle in the world, about half the size of an average human.

Summit began as a botanical garden in 1923, created by the U.S. in an effort to reproduce and distribute tropical plants from around the world. It is now home to the world's leading collection of palms, among other exotic species. Because Panama City has few green spaces for a picnic or a chance to let the kids run free, Summit is popular with families on weekends. The grassy picnic area and park are free, or you can pay $8 for a covered eating area and barbecue pit. The zoo costs $1 for adults and teens, kids 12 and under get in free, and it's open daily from 9am to 5pm. Call ✆ 232-4854 for more information.

WHERE TO STAY & DINE

Canopy Tower ★★ ☐ Canopy Tower is an ex-U.S.-military radar station that has been converted into a fantasy lodge for bird-watchers—something like a cross between a stylish B&B and a scientific research center. There is a 360-degree observation deck that provides stunning views and serves as a platform for observing the 400-plus species of birds; there's also a comfy social lounge with wraparound windows that are flush with the trees. In the morning, the spooky roar of howler monkeys serves as a wake-up call. The best room here is the Blue Cotinga Suite, one of two "suites," which are really large doubles with a hammock and private bathroom. Doubles on the second floor are comfortably spaced; however, the pie-slice single rooms are tiny and noisy in the morning (starting at 5:30am). No rooms have curtains; single rooms have shared bathrooms. The prices include meals, but tours—with the exception of bird-watching around the lodge—are an additional cost.

Road to Gamboa. ✆ **264-5720,** 263-2784, or 6613-7220. www.canopytower.com. 12 units. $100–$130 single; $125–$175 per person double; $145–$200 per person suite. AE, MC, V. **Amenities:** Restaurant; bar. *In room:* No phone, Wi-Fi.

Gamboa Rainforest Resort ★★ ☺ Sprawled along the shore of the Chagres River in Soberanía National Park, the Gamboa Rainforest Resort is an ideal destination for families with kids, given the resort's jungle boat cruises, aerial tram ride through the rainforest, and minizoo of reptile, butterfly, and marine species exhibits. Every amenity under the tropical sun is offered here, such as a full-service spa, guided tours, and several restaurants. Spacious double rooms have garden or river views (with private balconies) and a pleasant chainlike decor; attractive suites have Indonesian furniture and large living areas. The bathrooms are elegant and spacious. The 1930s-era clapboard homes at the resort's entrance have one- and two-bedroom apartments with kitchenettes. The apartments are quite appealing in a historical sense, with their hardwood floors and wicker furniture, but they are the cheapest lodging options because they do not have a view and are a short walk or minivan transfer from the main hotel. Book one of the newly renovated units in no. 253, 255, 256, or 258.

Gamboa. ✆ **877/800-1690** in the U.S., or 314-5000. www.gamboaresort.com. 107 units. $175–$250 double with garden view; $195–$285 double with river view; $290–$350 junior suite; $150–$215 1-bedroom apt. AE, MC, V. **Amenities:** 3 restaurants; 2 bars; bike and kayak rental; concierge; outdoor pool; room service; spa and fitness center w/whirlpool, steam, and massage; tennis courts. *In room:* A/C, TV, hair dryer, minibar.

BOQUETE ★★★

40km (25 miles) from David; 473km (294 miles) from Panama City

This is the destination of choice for most tourists visiting the Chiriquí Highlands, and with nearly 25% of the population hailing from the United States, Canada, or Europe,

Boquete

ACCOMMODATIONS ◼
The Coffee Estate Inn **4**
Hotel Oasis **11**
Hotel Petit Mozart **7**
Isla Verde Hotel **10**
Los Establos **5**
Panamonte Inn & Spa **6**
The Riverside Inn **2**
Villa Marita **1**

DINING ◆
Art Café du Crepe **9**
Il Pianista **3**
La Casona Mexicana **15**
Machu Picchu **12**
Panamonte Inn
  Restaurant **6**
The Rock **2**
Roxanne's Grill **13**
Sabroson **9**
Tammy's **14**

ARCO IRIS

ALTO LINO

PALO ALTO

HORQUETA

Río Palo Alto

LOS NARANJOS

Río Caldera

BAJO LINO

To Sendero Los Quetzales

LOS CABEZOS

Quebrada La Zumbona

To Volcán Barú (peak)

JARAMILLO ARRIBA

Quebrada Grande

See inset map

BOQUETE

Volcán Barú
3, 475 m
(11, 400 ft)

JARAMILLO CENTRO

VOLCANCITO

Iglesia San Juan Bautista
Feria de las Flores

Calle Central

Av. A Oeste

Av. A Este

Av. B Este

Av. Central

Calle 1 Sur

Calle 2 Sur

Av. B Oeste

Parque D. Médica

Calle 4 Sur

Avenida

Police

Calle 5 Sur

Río Caldera

Av. A Este

Av. B Porras

Gas Station

ATP Visitor Center

JARAMILLO ABAJO

Río Caldera

ALTO BOQUETE

To La Estrella

43

To David & to Caldera Hot Springs

Caribbean Sea · Colón
Boquete · ⊗PANAMA CITY
PANAMA
Golfo de Panamá
0   50 mi
0   50 km

it feels somewhat like a tropical colony—you'll find plenty of foreign-owned, international restaurants here, and you'll get along just fine even if you don't speak a word of Spanish. Boquete is one of the fastest-changing destinations in Panama, with new restaurants, hotels, and real estate agencies opening left and right. It is located in a steep-walled, green, and flower-filled valley on the flank of the Barú Volcano and at the shore of the Caldera River.

Despite Boquete's somewhat utilitarian downtown, on the whole, it oozes charm and offers a bounty of activities. Recently, Boquete became one of the top-five retirement destinations in the world, and large-scale gated communities have begun their spread on the city's outskirts. Boquete has taken on a more international feel than its counterpart Cerro Punta on the other side of the volcano. But, given the bounty of services, tours, attractions, restaurants, and lodging options, Boquete makes an ideal base for exploring the Chiriquí Highlands.

Essentials
GETTING THERE
Most hotels either provide transportation from the David airport or can arrange for you to be picked up by a taxi for the 45-minute drive to Boquete.

BY BUS & TAXI   Buses for Boquete leave from the David bus terminal every 25 minutes, take approximately 1 hour, and cost $1.45 one-way. You can catch a bus from Boquete to David from the north side of the main plaza. If you're coming from Bocas del Toro or from Panama City, you'll need to transfer in David. It takes 7 hours by bus from Panama City, and costs $13. A taxi from David to Boquete costs approximately $15 to $20 one-way, or you can contact **Boquete Shuttle Services** (© **720-0570**), which charges $15 each way.

BY CAR   If you're driving from Panama City, you'll turn right on the signed turnoff for Boquete before entering David, at the intersection next to the Shell gas station.

The road to Boquete is well paved; there are two side roads that provide shortcuts if you're driving from the Bocas del Toro area.

GETTING AROUND   If you're a do-it-yourself traveler who likes to explore at your own pace, you'll want to rent a vehicle to get around—but you'll have to do it at the David airport; some hotels can arrange for a rental car to be delivered to you in Boquete for an additional $30. I recommend renting a car in Boquete, as it's the best way to explore the countryside.

Taxis around town cost $1 to $3; unless your hotel is located in the town center, you'll need one to get back and forth. If you're looking for a fluent English-speaking taxi driver for a half- or full-day tour around Boquete, try **Daniel Higgins** (© **6617-0570**); he charges $15 per hour.

Local buses cruise Avenida Central and the hilly roads around Boquete, but taxis are so cheap that you'll invariably end up hailing a cab before taking a bus.

ORIENTATION
Boquete's **CEFATI visitor center** (© **720-4060;** daily 9am–4:30pm) is the large building on your right just before you enter town. Call ahead about weekend hours. With its location high above the Río Caldera, the visitor center provides sweeping views of town. You'll find **Café Kotowa** here, too, with a small shop. On the center's second floor is an interpretive display (in Spanish) of the history and anthropology of the region. Ask for a representative here to give you a quick tour and translate the

ISLA coiba

Once the haunt of pirates, and in recent times an island feared by convicted criminals who were sent there, **Isla Coiba ★★★** (© **998-4271**; www.coibanationalpark.com) is now a national park, UNESCO World Heritage Site, and nature lover's, fisherman's, and scuba diver's dream destination. Given Isla Coiba's natural diversity, rich sea life, and rare species, it is frequently referred to as the Galápagos of Central America. Isla Coiba is the largest island in Panama, but the national park spreads beyond the main island, encompassing 38 islands and islets and marine waters for a total of 270,128 hectares (667,500 acres). The area is home to the second-largest coral reef in the eastern Pacific, at Bahía Damas, and its waters teem with schools of colorful fish, hammerhead and nurse sharks, dolphins, manta rays, tuna, turtles, whales, and other gigantic marine species. Onshore, there are 36 species of mammals and 39 species of reptiles, including saltwater crocodiles. Coiba is also one of the last places on earth where it is possible to see a scarlet macaw in the wild. Indeed, few places in the Americas are as wild, remote, and full of life as Isla Coiba National Park.

Hiking, fishing, snorkeling, and diving opportunities abound here, which might make roughing the park's rustic cabins worthwhile. ANAM allows only catch-and-release fishing within a mile of the boundary of the national park–protected area, so you'll have to go a little farther if you'd like to keep what you catch. Most of the tour operators listed on p. 655 offer fishing excursions of Isla Coiba, but you may also want to check out the following: **Coiba Adventure** (© **800/800-0907** in the U.S., or 999-8108; www.coibadventure.com), the **M/V Coral Star** (© **866/924-2837** in the U.S.; www.coralstar.com), and **Pesca Panama** (© **800/946-3474** in the U.S.; www.pescapanama.com). Those looking for snorkeling and diving opportunities should book an excursion with **Panama Divers** (© **314-0817** or 6613-4405; www.panamadivers.com), the country's most respected diving and snorkeling outfitter.

The park is administered by ANAM, which has a **ranger station** (© **998-0615**) and the only lodging on the island, consisting of several basic air-conditioned cabins on a glorious white-sand and turquoise-water beach. The cost to visit Coiba National Park is $10 per person.

displays. The center isn't within walking distance from downtown, so you'll need to take a cab ($1) or a local bus (25¢).

Boquete sits in a fertile valley below the Barú Volcano, and is bisected by the Caldera River. A recent flood redirected the river, and when I was in town, there was currently construction going on to avoid future flooding. The main street, Avenida Central, runs the length of town from north to south, and businesses and transportation services are clustered around the main plaza on streets that run east-west. From downtown, a series of paved and gravel roads climb the hilly terrain surrounding Boquete.

FAST FACTS   For the **police,** dial © 104; for the **fire department,** dial © 720-1224. The **Centro Médico San Juan Bautista,** located on Avenida Central, 2 blocks up the road past the Hotel Panamonte, has English-speaking doctors; for serious health problems, you'll need to head to the hospital in David. The **post office** is located on the plaza, and is open Monday to Friday 8am to 5:45pm, and Saturday

8am to 4:45pm; for fast service go to **Mailboxes Etc.** (© **720-2684**) on Avenida Central, in front of the Almacén Reina.

Twenty-four-hour ATMs can be found at **Banco Nacional** and **Global Bank,** which lie across from each other on Avenida Central and Calle 5 Sur (Mon–Fri 8am–3pm; Sat 9am–noon). There is also an ATM in **Los Establos Plaza** in downtown. Most hotels have a computer with Internet access or Wi-Fi for their guests, or try **Java Juice** on Avenida Central.

What to See & Do

There's no shortage of things to see and do in Boquete: adrenaline-pumping outdoor adventures, quiet forays in the rainforest seeking the elusive quetzal, and walks among perfume-scented flowers at public gardens; you can learn how to make a good cup of joe and about the local Ngöbe-Buglé tribe . . . and the list goes on. As mentioned throughout this chapter, a lot of visitors opt to rent a car—the area offers so many beautiful scenic drives. Here are a few:

The **Bajo Mono Loop** takes you high above the town along a newly asphalted road for panoramic vistas and beautiful forest scenery. This is a good drive from which to get your bearings and see why everyone's gone wild about living in Boquete. To get here, follow the main road past the church and head left at the fork, passing Café Ruiz and staying left until you see the sign for BAJO MONO. Just as pretty is the **Volcancito Loop**—to get here, follow the main road out of town and when you see the CEFATI visitor center, turn right and follow the loop until you arrive back at town. You can bike these loops as well. (See "Biking," below.)

One of the most beautiful drives in Panama heads to **Finca Suiza** on the main road to the Atlantic Coast, in the Bocas del Toro Province. The scenic drive winds through mountain forests and open fields with sweeping views, and farther down to the lush lowlands and rainforest of Bocas Province. Take the left turn to Caldera 16km (10 miles) south of Boquete and continue along paved/gravel road, until you hit the major road to Bocas. You can also take a completely paved, easier-to-follow road by heading toward David and turning left toward Gualaca.

Boquete Mountain Safari Tours (© **6627-8829** or 6742-6614; www.boquetemountainsafaritours.com) is a company well known for their bilingual, open-air yellow jeep tours. They offer wildlife tours ($80 full day), as well as half-day tours to the Caldera Hot Springs ($35) and the Boquete Mountains ($35) among others. Their latest offering is called the Grand Coffee Adventure, in which you travel through the lush cloud forest and mountainsides to visit various boutique coffee estates for tastings, as well as a horseback-riding tour and there's also a tour that combines riding and coffee-tasting tour for $60. Boquete Mountain Safari Tours is a professional operation, and all tour guides speak English. Check their website for a listing of full- and half-day excursions.

HIKING & BIRD-WATCHING OUTFITTERS/GUIDES

The following tour outfitters and local guides offer hiking, bird-watching, and other general excursions to destinations and attractions listed below in this section. With their new office in Boquete, the reputable Panama City–based adventure company **Ecocircuitos** recently closed their Boquete office, but their Boquete representative can be reached at **6617-6566.** Ecocircuitos is a one-stop shop for short adventures in the Chiriquí area; they offer kayaking, hiking, family adventures, and bird-watching day trips; and they focus on green tourism that promotes local communities. Another company, **Coffee Adventures** (✆ **720-3852;** www.coffeeadventures.net), offers guided excursions around Boquete and their bird-watching tours are particularly good. Coffee Adventures offers cultural excursions to a Ngöbe-Buglé community near the Caribbean coast, guided hikes on Los Quetzales Trail from Boquete to Cerro Punta (or vice versa), and low-key excursions like bird-watching and trips to the Caldera Hot Springs. **Feliciano González** is a local guide with more than 20 years' experience in the Boquete area (✆ **6632-8645** or 6624-9940). He has a 4WD vehicle, speaks basic English, and can customize tours of Boquete as well as day hikes on the Quetzales Trail, the Pianista Trail, and the full-day hike to the summit of Volcano Barú ($100 for up to four people). Based in Volcán, **Nariño Aizpurua** (✆ **771-5049** or 6775-0118; westernwindnature@yahoo.com or nature_tour@yahoo. com) is a fun and friendly guide who specializes in bird-watching; he is a recommended guide for Los Quetzales Trail if you plan to start on that side. Half-day tours start at $60. Transportation isn't included in prices.

For birding, you can't beat local guide **Santiago "Chago" Caballero** (✆ **6626-2200;** santiagochagotours@hotmail.com) or one of his protégés. Want to see a quetzal? If you're here from December to May, Santiago can guarantee you will—the reason he is such a valued guide in the region. Santiago typically takes birders to Finca Lérida but can customize tours, including searches for wild orchids in the rainforest. Terry from Coffee Adventures offers private bird-watching tours, and her knowledge is unbeaten in Boquete.

EXPLORING EL PARQUE NACIONAL VOLCAN BARU

This national park is centered around the 3,475m (11,400-ft.) extinct **Barú Volcano,** the highest point in the country and the center of adventurous outdoor pursuits for bird-watchers, hikers, rafters, and nature lovers. The park is on the Pacific-facing side of the Talamanca Mountain Range, and encompasses 14,000 hectares (34,600 acres) of rugged topography cloaked in primary and secondary rainforest. This rainforest provides a home to nearly 250 species of birds, the most notable of which is the **resplendent quetzal,** whose extraordinary beauty puts the bird in the number-one spot on many a bird-watching list.

Owing to the volcano's height and isolation, this area is considered a "bioclimatic island." Its forest is home to unique species of orchids and uncommon flora such as magnolia and giant oak trees, some of which are between 600 and 900 years old. You'll also see wild bamboo gardens and gigantic, gnarled trees dripping with vines and sprouting prehistoric-looking bromeliads from their trunks. In higher reaches, an intermittent cloud forest provokes an eerie ambience. Come prepared with waterproof outerwear and shoes and a dry change of clothes. In this national park, temperatures average 50° to 60°F (10°–16°C).

Natural beauty aside, the park is economically important because it protects the headwaters that provide irrigation to the country's prime agricultural region, concentrated in the fertile areas of the volcano's skirt. These rivers are also revered by rafters and kayakers for their Class 3 to Class 5 rapids, which provide thrills and a sense of remote solitude—a sure recipe for adventure. For more information about rafting, see below.

Volcán Barú National Park ★ is administered by ANAM, which has ranger stations at the Los Quetzales trail heads in both Boquete (Alto Chiquero) and Cerro Punta (El Respingo), and charges a $3-per-person entrance fee. Both ranger stations have a handful of truly rustic bunks with shared bathrooms, which cost $5 per bed.

There's not much ambience at the Boquete station to encourage even the hardiest of nature lovers to lodge there, however. A taxi to the ranger station, about 8km (5 miles) from Boquete, costs $3. Volcán Barú is a tough hike, and unfortunately, the views are not as fantastic as one would hope; however, fit hikers who want to challenge themselves will enjoy the hike.

HIKING   By any measure, the most popular trail is **Sendero Los Quetzales ★★★**, a superb, short-haul day hike—regarded as the best in Panama. The rainforest here is thick and lush and dazzling with its array of colorful birds, panoramic lookout points, and crystalline streams rushing across velvety moss-covered rocks. The trail connects Cerro Punta (and Guadalupe) with Boquete, allowing hikers to have their baggage sent from one town to the other, and to arrive by foot at their next destination. If you're physically up to it, I recommend the entire trek as one of the region's highlights—but remember: Cerro Punta's altitude is 1,981m (6,500 ft.), while Boquete's is 975m (3,200 ft.)—so the trail is mostly downhill from Cerro Punta. A lot of Boquete residents and tour guides will pooh-pooh the level of difficulty and stamina needed, but every hiker I saw doing the trail uphill looked frazzled. If you're fit and looking for a workout, walk Boquete to Cerro Punta; if not, plan your trip so that you visit the western region of the volcano first and then Boquete, or, if you only plan to walk the trail for the day, leave early and drive to Cerro Punta. For those who want to just get out and hike around a little, you'll be okay because the first couple of kilometers from the Boquete ranger station are relatively flat, offer outstanding opportunities to see birds (especially the quetzal), and put you in the middle of a stream-lined forest. You can walk as little or as much as you like and then turn around and head back.

The Quetzales Trail from Boquete begins with a 45-minute walk from the ranger station on a semipaved road. After the sign for the trail head, the trail continues for about 2 hours before heading up into a steep ascent. Midway up the ascent is a picnic area with tables. Farther up, about halfway along the trail, is a sweeping lookout point, with a roofed eating area and a couple of campsites.

From the Cerro Punta ranger station, a rutted road requiring a 4WD heads downhill for almost 3km (1¾ miles) until it reaches the paved road to Cerro Punta. Tour operators and taxis with 4WD traction can make it up and down this road, but few seem willing—so prepare yourself to walk this portion. The total number of trail miles is anyone's guess, as park signs, rangers, and tour guides all disagree on the distance; it's estimated that the trail is about 9.7km (6 miles). From station to station, plan on 6 to 7 hours if walking uphill, and 4½ hours if walking downhill, plus another 45 minutes to 1 hour for the last leg of the Cerro Punta ranger station to the road.

Keen adventurers might be interested in the trail to the **volcano's summit,** a very arduous climb that puts visitors at the highest point in Panama and offers views from the Caribbean Sea to the Pacific Ocean. Although this trail can be reached from the Cerro Punta side, the trail from the Boquete side is far easier and better marked. You don't want to get lost on the volcano. This is one of the serious considerations you must make when attempting to summit the volcano. The trail, an old service road, is ragged and rough, and even the most agile hikers often slip and fall on the slick downhill trip. Second, the trail is confusing in some areas, so it's highly recommended that you hire a guide. Lastly, the peak is shrouded in thick clouds with such frequency that the chances of seeing the view are not particularly good; but even on good-weather days you'll want to begin the hike at the crack of dawn to increase your chances of clear skies. The trail takes between 5 and 6 hours to climb, and about 4 to 5 hours to descend.

Keep in mind that the Quetzal trail hasn't been all that well maintained, meaning hiking can be difficult in some areas where the vegetation is thicker and the trail less visible.

RIVER RAFTING & KAYAKING

The translucent rivers that pour down the Talamanca Mountain Range in the Chiriquí Highlands provide for Class 3 to 5 white-water kayaking and rafting, and gentler floats for the whole family. What's special about the area is that relatively few paddlers have discovered it, so rafters and kayakers have the crystalline river and pristine mountain scenery—replete with birds and wild animals—to themselves. The variety and number of rivers in this area provide fanatics with enough white-water options to fill a week with rafting or kayaking.

Technical rides that are 2 to 5 hours in duration with Class 3 to Class 5 conditions are principally on the **Chiriquí River** east of Volcán Barú and close to Boquete, and the **Chiriquí Viejo River** west of the volcano, near the Costa Rica border. The Chiriquí Viejo River is revered by rafters for its challenging rapids and scenery, but it is a full-day trip that requires a drive to the other side of the volcano. (Visitors to Volcán or Cerro Punta are closer to the put-in site for this river.) Unfortunately, the Chiriquí Viejo is being threatened by a series of dams for a hydroelectric project—but for now it's pristine and fun to ride. There are tamer floats, such as the **Esti River,** a Class 2 that is perfect for young rafters, families, and beginners; there's the **Gariche River,** with Class 2 and 3 rapids that are suitable for beginners but a bit more adrenaline-charged than an easy float. Many rivers can be rafted year-round, but others, like the Chiriquí and the Gariche, are rafted from July to November when the rivers are full.

Two reputable rafting companies in Boquete have years of experience and knowledge of the region. **Chiriquí River Rafting,** on Avenida Central (© **720-1505** or 6618-0846; www.panama-rafting.com), is run by Héctor Sanchez, a pioneer in the Chiriquí Highlands, with more than 2 decades of experience and an excellent safety record. Héctor and his guides are fluent in English. Depending on the river and logistics, rafting trips cost between $85 and $105, and require a minimum of four guests (a few trips require only three guests); trips include all gear, transportation, and lunch. Héctor can also plan multiple-day packages that include rafting, hiking, fishing, and more. Note that Chiriquí River Rafting offers accommodations at **El Bajareque Lodge,** a hostel-like spot with dynamite views, simple bunks, and communal meals; Héctor also offers more upscale rooms in his private home.

Boquete Outdoor Adventures (© **720-2284** or 6630-1453; www.boquete outdooradventures.com) is run by the friendly and enthusiastic Jim Omer and specializes in white-water kayaking trips, and offers a number of different excursions in the Chiriquí Highlands as well as the Boca Chica Region. Some of their sea kayak excursions include Boca Brava and the 1-day white-water kayak sampler, which serves as an introduction to white-water kayaking. There are motorboat excursions to the Laguna de Chiriquí and the Golfo de Chiriquí, as well as excellent excursions to Isla Coiba. Trips range from $60 to $80 per person.

OTHER OUTDOOR ACTIVITIES IN THE AREA

BIKING Boquete provides visitors with kilometers of picturesque, winding roads; moderate terrain; and pastoral views. Bicyclists on main paved roads will need to keep an eye open for speeding motorists, as there are virtually no shoulders and lots of blind curves. For bike rental, check out **Boquete Tree Trek** (see "Canopy Tours," below). The cost to rent is $3 per hour. A half-day bike tour around Boquete is offered by **Aventurist** (© **720-1635** or 6615-3300; www.aventurist.com). Tours begin by traveling by vehicle to the scenic heights at Alto Quiel, where bicyclists and their guide descend for 2 hours for a total of 26km (16 miles) until they reach town. Tours leave at 7am and 1pm, and cost $25 per person.

CANOPY TOURS   Canopy tours, where you zip through the treetops suspended by a harness attached to a cable, are available through **Boquete Tree Trek** at Avenida Central (© **720-1635;** www.aventurist.com). This exhilarating ride is appropriate for kids as young as 3, and the weight limit for each rider is 113 kilograms (249 lb.) for men, and 77 kilograms (170 lb.) for women. The zip line is 3km (1¾ miles) long, with a drop of 351m (1,150 ft.), and is located in the upper reaches of the Palo Alto valley, about 45 minutes from town. A 2½- to 3-hour canopy adventure costs $60. Women should avoid wearing skirts because of the harness seat. The best attire is long pants or shorts that do not ride up too high and closed-toe shoes like sneakers or hiking boots.

HORSEBACK RIDING   Eduardo Caño (© **720-1750** or 6629-0814), a guide from Boquete, is the man to go to for horseback riding tours of 2 to 5 hours, along trails on the outskirts of Boquete in areas such as Volcancito and Jaramillo. The views of Boquete and the surrounding area are splendid, but Eduardo speaks limited English, so unless you know Spanish, you'll need your hotel to call and make arrangements. Sample prices for two are $5 per person per hour. Also, contact **Ecocircuitos** (see "Hiking & Bird-Watching Outfitters/Guides," above) for horseback riding or to hire an English-speaking nature guide to accompany you and Eduardo on your ride. Boquete Mountain Safari tours offer $40 horseback rides around town, $60 for horseback riding and coffee tasting.

HOT SPRINGS   The **Caldera Hot Springs** are four undeveloped pools in natural surroundings, with mineral water in varying temperatures. It's worth a stop if you're a fan of hot springs, are in the area, or are looking for a pretty low-key activity—otherwise, I can't figure out what the big to-do is, especially considering that it's a half-hour drive from Boquete. The hot springs are next to the Caldera River, which you can bathe in as well. To get here, you'll need to be part of a tour, or have a 4WD. Head south from Boquete, and 11km (7 miles) later, turn left at the sign for Caldera; once you arrive in Caldera, keep driving until you see a sign for the hot springs. Follow a rather brutal dirt road to the end and then walk about 10 minutes to the hot springs.

COFFEE TOURS

Panama produces some of the most flavorful coffee in the world. A relatively new player on the gourmet-coffee market, the country produces traditional shade-grown coffee varieties that are considered to be more complex and distinctive than those produced by its more famous neighbor, Costa Rica. Most coffee plantations in Panama are centered around Boquete because of the high altitude required for prime coffee growing, and because of the region's fertile volcanic soil. Coffee tours are available and recommended. Even coffee snobs will glean insight into the meticulous growing process and the economics of the local Ngöbe-Buglé indigenous labor and culture, the "shade-grown" theory to protect the environment and to grow a better bean, the effect coffee has on the world, and what coffee producers really think about Starbucks. Tours are capped off with a "cupping," which, much like a wine tasting (and *almost* as fun), gives you a chance to sample different flavors, strengths, and roasts. In addition to the following companies, see Finca Lérida's tours, below.

Café Ruiz, S.A. ★★ (📞 720-1000 or 6672-3786; www.caferuiz-boquete.com) is one of the oldest and most respected coffee producers in the country and a top-quality coffee-roasting organization. A visit entails a three-stop visit to the plantation, the processing plant, and the roasting-and-packaging facility. Visits, led by a jovial and bilingual local Ngöbe-Buglé descendant Indian guide, are offered Monday through Saturday from 9am to noon, or from 1 to 4pm; the cost is $30 per person. Or you can visit the roasting facility for a 45-minute informational general session on high-end quality coffee; the cost is $9 per person. Casa Ruiz, S.A. is the largest specialty green coffee exporter of Panama.

Café Kotowa ★★ (📞 720-1430; www.kotowacoffee.com) is a boutique coffee farm founded nearly a century ago by a Scottish immigrant, and still run by the same family. Kotowa, the indigenous word for "mountain," has earned a reputation for award-winning coffee beans, and though they've moved on to modern production means, the farm's antique, water-powered mill still exists and is part of their tour. Visits to Kotowa are one-stop—first you amble through the coffee plantation, then you tour the production-and-roasting facility, and finally you have a cupping in the old mill. The tour is led by Hans and Terry of **Coffee Adventures** (📞 720-3852; www.coffeeadventures.net), who pioneered coffee tours in Boquete and who are animated and amusing. Tours are Monday through Saturday at 2pm and cost $20 per person, which includes transportation from Boquete to their farm in Palo Alto. Children must be 10 or older, unless they're part of a private tour. Private tours cost $45 per person but can be scheduled at any time, including Sundays. This is the best coffee tour in Boquete.

Finca Lérida ★★★ (see below) also offers coffee tours.

VISITING FINCA LERIDA

Finca Lérida ★★★ (📞 720-2285; www.fincalerida.com; open daily sunrise–sunset) is a 324-hectare (800-acre) coffee plantation and nature reserve 10 minutes from Boquete in the alpine setting of Alto Quiel. The *finca* is regarded as one of the most important bird-watching sites in Panama, not only because of the sheer numbers of species, but also because it is a hot spot for seeing the resplendent quetzal, among other rare birds. The Finca Lérida has stepped up operations lately, building an 11-room ecolodge on their property and has also added a new exhibit showcasing their highly rated coffee and growing process, and giving information about the bio-diversity of their property and the surrounding region.

Finca Lérida has three nature trails (one easy, two moderate) that offer a chance to put yourself in the middle of pristine primary and secondary forest. Independent visitors are charged $10 per person for access to the trails, and though they're marked, there are no maps or interpretive information available. The *finca* works with the best local birding and naturalist guides, if you need one (highly recommended); the cost is an additional $25. Or you can book a 2-hour coffee tour for $16 per person, and take to the trails following the tour. For the complete (and somewhat pricey) package, a full-day tour includes a guide, bird-watching, coffee tour, gourmet lunch, transportation to and from Boquete, and access to trails for $310 for two guests.

Shopping

Bagged coffee beans are sold all around town in cafes and grocery stores. **Café Kotowam,** at the visitor center, sells top-rated blends and souvenir and gift packs. The **Harmony Gift Shop** on Avenida Central has arts and crafts, jewelry, and other gift items for sale. **Souvenir El Cacique,** on Avenida Central at the plaza, has indigenous handicrafts made by the Ngöbe-Buglé, Kuna, and Emberá indigenous groups, plus handicrafts from indigenous groups around Central America. **Ingana Art Shop** (✆ 720-1699) sells ethnic handicrafts and art from all over the world, and the **Galeria de Arte** (✆ 6769-6090), adjacent to Art Café La Crepe, 150m (490 ft.) north of the church, sells jewelry, molas, ceramics, and paintings by international artists. **Boquete Mountain Safari Tours** (p. 703) recently opened a store in Los Establos Plaza (✆ 720-1147) that sells Panama-made handicrafts, Boquete maps, souvenirs, and coffee.

Where to Stay

Travelers can opt to stay in town and be close to services and restaurants, or outside of the center in a more forested setting. It's a good idea to book ahead of time in Boquete. Besides the places listed below, **Los Establos** (✆ 720-2685; Jaramillo Arriba) and the historic **Panamonte Inn and Spa** (✆ 720-1327; www.panamonte innandspa.com) also offer excellent, high-end accommodations.

For budget options, check out **Hotel Oasis** (✆ 720-1586) or **Hotel Petit Mozart** (✆ 6487-7042). You'll need a taxi from both to get into town.

EXPENSIVE

The Coffee Estate Inn ★★★ 📷   Cozy yet spacious accommodations with all the trimmings, gorgeous views of Volcán Barú, and truly personalized service are the hallmarks of the Coffee Estate Inn, which is my favorite place to stay in Boquete and is located 2.5km (1½ miles) from downtown Boquete, on a steep slope overlooking the valley below. Owners Jane and Barry go out of their way to help guests feel welcome and relaxed; if you're looking for a real treat, request Barry's "no-frills" and "date night" dinners, beautifully presented on a flower-strewn table on your balcony. Three contemporary and cheery cabins contain a bedroom for two guests, a living area, a fully stocked kitchen, and an outdoor terrace. The cabins are enveloped in native forest, fruit trees, and flowers that attract myriad birds. The owners recommend that guests rent a vehicle (they'll set this up for you), and they'll provide maps, directions, contacts for the best guides in the area, and anything else you need for a day of adventure. There are 1.5km (1 mile) of hiking trails on the property. Daily breakfast consists of homemade breads, and estate fresh-roasted coffee and fruit, and you can also have an on-site coffee tour with Barry.

Jaramillo Arriba. ✆ **720-2211.** www.coffeeestateinn.com. 3 units. $145 double. Extra person $50. MC, V. Children 14 and under not accepted. **Amenities:** Wi-Fi. *In room:* TV/DVD, CD player, hair dryer, kitchenette.

Riverside Inn ★★   This boutique hotel is sophisticated and gives discriminating travelers the highest level of accommodations available in Boquete—but you wouldn't know it from the exterior, which looks a like a country-style inn. On the shore of the Palo Alto River, the hotel is next to the **Rock,** its gourmet restaurant. There are only six guest rooms, the best of which are in back, overlooking the river. A bit of color has recently been added to the once-neutral rooms, giving the inn a well-done mini-face-lift. Standard decor consists of exposed wooden beams, stark walls, Indonesian teak furniture, and luxurious bathrooms. All rooms have king-size beds with Egyptian cotton sheets. Guest rooms feature lots of amenities, including a whirlpool tub in the master suite. My favorite thing about the Palo Alto is the common areas where guests can sit and read or converse.

Palo Alto. ✆ **720-1076.** www.riversideinnboquete.com. 6 units. Low season $80 suite, $105 master suite; high season $165 suite, $195 master suite. MC, V. **Amenities:** Restaurant; bar; spa; Wi-Fi. *In room:* TV/DVD, minibar.

MODERATE

Isla Verde Hotel ★ ☺   This is the best hotel walking distance from town. Located in a residential area about a 3-minute walk from Boquete, the German-owned Isla Verde features six cheery cabins, called "roundhouses." Half the cabins are for four guests, and half are quite spacious, with a capacity for up to six guests (though they're ideal for a group of just four). There is a queen-size bed on the ground floor (but not separate from the living area), and a loft with a double bed; the additional "beds" for the six-person units are comfortable sleeper sofas. Isla Verde recently added four fetching suites for couples, each with a terrific outdoor patio that offers forest views, especially from the second-floor units, which are more expensive. The suites have a bedroom and independent living area, and kitchenettes; the cabins as well as all the roundhouses have full kitchens.

Calle 2 Sur Bajo Boquete. ✆ **720-2533** or 6677-4009. www.islaverdepanama.com. 10 units. Prices based on double occupancy: $100 big roundhouse; $80 small roundhouse; $80–$100 suite. Children 4 and under stay for free; children 5–18 $10; extra adult $20. MC, V. **Amenities:** Internet service. *In room:* Cable TV, kitchen or kitchenette, no phone, Wi-Fi.

Villa Marita ★   High on a plateau above a twisting road 3.5km (2¼ miles) from town, this hotel is strong in panoramic views of Volcán Barú and the river valley below. It's too far to walk to town, so if you don't mind taking a taxi or driving, the reasonably priced cabins here are an attractive option. There are six mustard-colored cabins, for up to four guests (one bedroom and a sofa bed), which are outfitted with a fridge. French doors open onto a roofed terrace with the dynamite view. There are also three newer and comfortable hotel rooms in a new wing adjacent to the main building, which is a converted home with a lived-in and homey ambience. Families might be interested in their "Big House" unit that sleeps six to eight guests and has a kitchen but no view. The friendly, knowledgeable host and his wife will gladly serve you a home-cooked meal with ingredients from their on-site organic greenhouse. The owners have lived in this area for 40 years and can help with tours and information about the area.

Alto Lino. ✆ **720-2165.** www.villamarita.com. 10 units. $50 double hotel room; $80 cabin; $130 family house. AE, MC, V. **Amenities:** Restaurant; Wi-Fi. *In room:* TV, fridge (in cabins), no phone.

Where to Dine

Given that many of Boquete's residents are retired folks who tend to dine in or not stay out too late, the restaurants mentioned below can unexpectedly close early or for the night during the low season, from May to November. Also, keep in mind that most restaurants are closed on Monday.

   Machu Picchu ★★ (✆ 264-9308; Av. Belisario Porras) is one of the best restaurants in town. Try the sea bass with black butter and capers or the creamy jumbo

CENTRAL PANAMA IN brief

Central Panama is not yet on the radar for most foreign travelers. There are a few destinations worth mentioning. The easiest way to get to and around Central Panama is by renting a car, but if you don't wish to rent a car, **Pesantez Tours** (𝄞 **366-9106;** www.pesantez-tours.com) offers rides to all the Pacific beaches as well as the Valle de Antón, or you can hire a taxi to Valle de Antón or the Pacific beaches. (This will cost you $60–$180 round-trip depending on where you are going.)

The Pacific beaches are popular with Panama City dwellers looking for a bit of weekend relaxation. These are not the most attractive beaches in Panama, and are really worth a visit only if your travels to Panama won't take you to any of the better beaches or you're part of an all-inclusive resort package. The **Inter-Continental Playa Bonita Resort and Spa** (Playa Kobbe, Punta Bruja; 𝄞 **211-8600,** or 800/424-6835 in the U.S.; www.ichotelsgroup.com), a half-hour away, is the closest beach resort from Panama City. The **Coronado Gulf and Beach Resort** (Av. Punta Prieta, Coronado; 𝄞 **264-3164** or 240-4444; www.coronadoresort.com) on Playa Coronado is the oldest resort on the Pacific, and a longtime favorite with golfers. **Playa Blanca Resort** (𝄞 **264-6444;** www.playablancaresort.com) and the gargantuan **Royal Decameron Beach Resort, Golf, Spa & Casino** (Playa Blanca; 𝄞 **206-5324;** www.decameron.com) offer all-inclusive packages if you wish to stay on Playa Blanca, about a 2-hour drive from Panama City.

Valle de Antón, a picturesque mountain village 2 hours from Panama City, is also popular with wealthy Panamanians because of its cooler weather. El Valle, as it is popularly known, offers a number of canopy, hiking, and bird-watching activities, and is worth a stop if you don't have a chance to visit Boquete or the Chiriquí highlands. Some of my favorite hotels here are **Los Mandarinos** (Calle El Ciclo; 𝄞 **983-6645;** www.losmandarinos.com) and the **Park Eden Bed and Breakfast** (Calle Espavé; 𝄞 **983-6167** or 6695-6190; www.parkeden.com).

Finally, the Peninsula de Azuero is Panama's most traditional province and home to a number of picturesque colonial-style towns, the most notable being Pedasi, a quiet place where life hasn't changed much in the past hundred years. The Azuero peninsula is famous for its beautiful, ornate Carnaval processions, making these pre-Lent festivities the most popular and expensive time to visit. I recommend renting a car if you decide to visit, as most attractions are spread out, and bus service is sporadic at best. The best hotels here are **Los Guayacanes** (𝄞 **996-9758;** www.losguayacanes.com) in Chitre, the capital of the Azuero peninsula; **Hotel la Villa** (𝄞 **966-8201**) in La Villa de los Santos; and the basic but comfortable **Dim's Hostal** (𝄞 **995-2303;** mirely@iname.com) in charming Pedasi.

If you are looking for something a bit more luxurious, head to the coast and check out **Posada los Destiladores** (Los Destiladores; 𝄞 **6675-9715**); **Villa Camilla** (Los Destiladores; 𝄞 **232-6721**) on Playa los Destiladores; or **Villa Marina** (Playa Venado; 𝄞 **211-2277**) on Playa Venado, all of which are consistently rated among the best small resort hotels in Panama.

prawns. The **Rock,** at the Riverside Inn ★★ (𝄞 **720-1076;** road to Palo Alto) is a refined place for upscale international fare.

The **Panamonte Inn Restaurant ★★★** (𝄐 720-1324; Av. Central) is hands down the best restaurant in Boquete. Try the wild-mushroom polenta, pork chops with onion ragout, and veal stock wine sauce or seafood stew. **Tammy's** (𝄐 6524-1013) serves the best vegetarian Mediterranean platter in Panama and is behind **Roxanne's Grill** (no phone). **Art Café la Crepe** (𝄐 6769-6789) is a good spot for crepes and light French fare and is located adjacent to a well-put-together art gallery. One of my personal favorites, **Il Pianista** (𝄐 720-2728), serves up Sicilian specialties created by Chef Giovanni Sotorno.

For cheaper dining options, head to **La Casona Mexicana** (𝄐 720-1274; Av. Central). There are hearty burritos, fajitas, and chimichangas here. **Sabroson** (𝄐 720-2147; Av. Central near the church) is as typical as it gets in Boquete. The cafeteria-style restaurant is far from fancy, but the food is filling and tasty.

Boquete After Dark

Most Boquete residents are tucked into bed by 11pm, but there are a couple of places for a nightcap or a night out. **Zanzíbar,** located on Avenida Central on the right side past the church, is an attractively decorated bar with African odds and ends. It's a cozy place for a cocktail (open Tues–Sun until midnight), and my favorite nightspot in Boquete. **Las Cabanas Lounge,** located 3.2km (2 miles) outside of town on the road to the Coffee Estate Inn, is a newer bar/dance club popular with Boquete's younger crowd. It gets crowded Friday and Saturday nights after Zanzíbar closes.

BOCAS DEL TORO ARCHIPELAGO ★

The Bocas del Toro Archipelago is a scattering of seven islands and more than 200 islets off the northwestern coast of Panama, near the border with Costa Rica. The region has all the trappings of a Caribbean fantasy: dreamy beaches, thatched-roof huts, aquamarine sea, thick rainforest, and soft ocean breeze. Add to that a funky, carefree ambience and a large English-speaking population, and it's easy to see why Bocas del Toro is emerging as an ecotourism hot spot faster than any other part of Panama.

The principal island is Isla Colón, 62 sq. km (24 sq. miles) and home to **Bocas Town,** the regional capital and the center of activity in the archipelago.

Bocas can hold its own against nearby Costa Rica when it comes to adventure travel in the Caribbean. The diving and snorkeling are outstanding—Bocas is home to some of the best-preserved hard and soft coral on the planet—but make sure your tour operator is willing to take you to the finest examples instead of bleached-out coral in "typical" tourist spots. Your options include sailing tours, boat tours to deserted islands and visits to Indian communities, hiking through luxuriant rainforest in Isla Bastimentos Park, and riding waves in what is largely considered the surfing epicenter of the southwest Caribbean.

Historically there has always been a rough, end-of-the-line feel to Bocas del Toro, which is perceptible even today. But underneath this are the rumblings of an upcoming boom in tourism, with multimillion-dollar hotels, gated communities, and waterfront condominiums either in the works or already breaking ground. Still, the laid-back friendliness that characterizes Bocas del Toro endures.

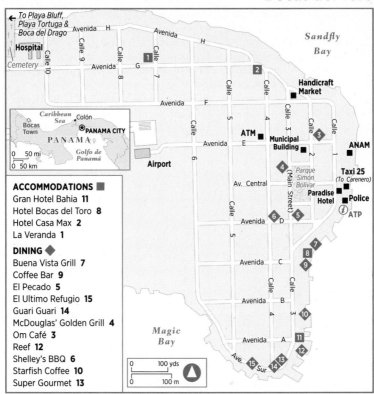

Bocas del Toro

To Playa Bluff,
Playa Tortuga &
Boca del Drago

Sandfly Bay

Hospital

Cemetery

Caribbean Sea
Colón
Bocas Town
PANAMA CITY
PANAMA
Golfo de Panamá

0   50 mi
0   50 km

Handicraft Market

ATM

Municipal Building

ANAM

Airport

Av. Central

Parque Simón Bolívar

Taxi 25
(To Carenero)

Paradise Hotel

Police

ATP

ACCOMMODATIONS ■
Gran Hotel Bahia **11**
Hotel Bocas del Toro **8**
Hotel Casa Max **2**
La Veranda **1**

DINING ◆
Buena Vista Grill **7**
Coffee Bar **9**
El Pecado **5**
El Ultimo Refugio **15**
Guari Guari **14**
McDouglas' Golden Grill **4**
Om Café **3**
Reef **12**
Shelley's BBQ **6**
Starfish Coffee **10**
Super Gourmet **13**

Magic Bay

0   100 yds
0   100 m

10

PANAMA

Bocas del Toro Archipelago

Isla Colón: Bocas Town ★

30 min. by boat from Almirante; 1 hr. by boat from Changuinola; 1 hr. by plane from Panama City

ESSENTIALS
Getting There
GETTING THERE & DEPARTING   There are two ways to get to Bocas del Toro: via a land/sea combination, or by air. Considering the short flight (1 hr. from Panama City), most travelers opt to fly. If crossing into Bocas del Toro from Costa Rica by land, travelers head to Changuinola, where they can grab a boat shuttle to Bocas (1 hr.) or hop over on a small plane from Changuinola (10 min.). *Tip:* If traveling from Costa Rica, remember that Costa Rica is **1 hour ahead** of Panama.

BY PLANE   The basic but spruce **Bocas International Airport** (☎ **757-9208**) is serviced by daily flights from Panama City, David, Changuinola, and Costa Rica. Both Air Panama and Aeroperlas charge about $180 (including taxes) for a round-trip ticket from Panama City to Bocas Town, but rising gas prices mean is the price is likely to go up by the time you read this.

Air Panama (℡ 316-9000; www.flyairpanama.com) has service to Bocas del Toro from Panama City, David, and San José, Costa Rica (for Costa Rica flights, see From Costa Rica by Plane, below). From Panama City, there are two daily flights leaving at 6:30am and 6:30pm, though flights are added when demand is high. Return flights from Bocas to Panama City leave at 8am (Mon–Sat), 9:15am (Sun), 1:45pm (Mon, Wed, Fri), and 4:30pm (daily), but call ahead to confirm times.

Aeroperlas (℡ 378-6000; www.aeroperlas.com) offers two daily flights from **Panama City** to Bocas, weekdays at 3:45 and 4pm; the return trip to Panama City leaves at 9am and 5:20pm. From **David,** flights leave once daily, on Mondays, Wednesdays, and Fridays only at 11:20am; the flight from Bocas is at noon.

BY BOAT **Bocas Marine & Tours** (℡ 757-9033 in Bocas, 758-4085 in Almirante; www.bocasmarinetours.com) has daily boat service between Almirante and Bocas every 30 to 40 minutes, from 6am to 6:30pm (6:30am–6:30pm from Bocas to Almirante). *Note:* Owing to the increase in fuel costs, Bocas Marine & Tours operates with a minimum of six passengers; this means that when business is slow they might not leave on schedule.

Taxi 25 (℡ 757-9028) operates between Almirante and Bocas, leaving every half-hour from 6am to 6:30pm. Both charge $4 per person, one-way, and leave from the Almirante dock; Bocas Marine & Tours is on Main Street in Bocas, and Taxi 25 can be found next to the ATP office. If you have a vehicle, there is parking for $3 a day at the lot at the Almirante boat dock. To get to the Almirante bus station for the 4-hour bus ride to David, take a $1 taxi that waits at the port.

FROM COSTA RICA BY PLANE **Nature Air,** a Costa Rican airline (℡ **506/ 2299-6000** in Costa Rica, or 800/235-9272 in the U.S. and Canada; www.natureair. com), has one flight to Bocas from San José (with connections from Quepos, Liberia, and Puerto Jiménez) on Sunday, Wednesday, and Friday, leaving at 11am and returning from Bocas at 1:30pm; the flight costs $111 to $139 one-way, $222 to $278 round-trip. Note that Nature Air is known to increase prices during the high season (Dec 1–Apr 20).

FROM COSTA RICA BY ROAD Travelers entering Panama from Costa Rica by road at the Sixaola-Guabito border can take a taxi (about $15) to **Changuinola,** then a boat to Bocas del Toro with **Taxi 25** (see above). Have your taxi driver take you to the dock at Finca 60, just outside of Changuinola. The boat journey passes through the San San Pond Sak wetlands and an old banana plantation canal, and is so scenic it could be considered a low-price tour. From Changuinola, boats leave daily at 8am, 9:30am, 11am, 12:30pm, 2pm, 3:30pm, and 5pm. From Bocas Town to Changuinola, boats leave at 7am, 8am, 9:30am, 11am, 12:30pm, 2pm, 3:30pm, and 4:30pm. The cost is $5 per person one-way. Remember, if you're crossing into Panama from Costa Rica, you'll have to go through Immigration. This can take a long time on a 50-passenger bus, so be prepared for a 1- to 2-hour process. If you're arriving by car, Immigration should take only 15 to 20 minutes.

Orientation

Bocas is the only town on Isla Colón, centered around a bustling Main Street (Calle 3) and Simon Bolívar Plaza. There are fewer than two dozen streets in Bocas, and most are unpaved. The airport is a couple of blocks away from the main plaza, meaning you could walk to your hotel if you felt like it. Calles 1 through 10 run west-east and avenidas A to H run north-south. There is no "downtown," but most hotels and restaurants are concentrated on the south end where Calle 1 meets Main Street. Internet cafes and shops are along Main Street between avenidas E and D.

Getting Around

Everything in Bocas Town is within walking distance, but shared-ride taxis are plentiful if you need one. Most hotels arrange pickup and drop-off for guests arriving by air, but there are also taxis waiting for every arrival at the airport. If arriving by boat, find out where your hotel is in relation to the dock—you may already be close enough to walk. Taxis cost between 50¢ and $1. There are two principal roads on the island: One runs along the coast and ends at Playa Bluff; the other crosses the island to Boca del Drago.

There are **bicycle** rentals on Main Street across from the plaza; all charge $1 an hour, or $5 to $8 a day. Informal **water taxis** are available at the dock next to the ATP office, with service to neighboring Isla Carenero ($1 one-way) and Isla Bastimentos ($7 one-way to Red Frog Beach). Hours are irregular, with service generally running from 7am to 9pm. Most people visit Isla Bastimentos as part of a day tour; resorts on that island include round-trip transportation in the price and an extra charge for additional trips.

For beaches outside of Bocas Town, see "What to See & Do," below.

Visitor Information

There is an **ATP visitor center** (© **757-9642;** Mon–Fri 9am–12:45pm and 1:45–4pm) in a yellow building on the waterfront at Calle 1, near the police station. It appears that ATP blew its budget on this sparkling new office, because English-speaking, trained information officers, maps, and brochures are all in short supply. Around lunchtime, you'll be lucky to find anyone staffing the desk, though on the second floor you'll find a display on the natural history of Bocas, and there are public bathrooms too. For additional information about Bocas, try the Web portal **www. bocas.com**, which has links to hotels, tourism services, transportation information, and more.

Note: Though not dangerous by any means, there has been a slight increase in theft in Bocas Town, mostly due to the lack of economic opportunity for the native Afro-Caribbean population paired with the comparative affluence of expats and tourists. Just keep an eye on your personal belongings as you would anywhere else; you are highly unlikely to be violently assaulted, but if you're careless with your wallet or camera, you may not find it where you left it.

FAST FACTS   For an ambulance, call © **757-9814;** for fire, dial © **103;** for police, dial © **104** or 757-9217. There is a basic **hospital clinic** in Bocas, located at Calle 10 and Avenida G (© **757-9201**), with a 24-hour emergency room. However, service is limited and those with more serious health problems will need to seek medical care in Panama City or David. There are multiple **Internet cafes** on Bocas's main street and many hotels also offer free Wi-Fi. The **post office** is at Calle A and Avenida 2 (no phone). It's run by a no-nonsense woman who maintains hours Monday through Friday from 8am to noon and 2 to 4pm (some days 3–4pm "when I feel like taking a long lunch"), and Saturday 8am to noon.

What to See & Do

Despite its location in the warm Caribbean Sea, Bocas offers poor swimming conditions because of strong riptides. The closest decent beach to Bocas Town (**Bluff**

Beach) is an 8km (5-mile) bike or taxi ride away, and the beaches on Isla Bastimentos can be reached only by boat, followed by a short to medium-long walk. During the calm-water months (early Sept to early Nov), it's possible to arrive directly by boat at the beaches of Isla Bastimentos.

If you don't have an all-inclusive package, or if your hotel does not offer trips, there are plenty of tour agencies to fulfill your excursion needs. Bocas is a good base for exploring the archipelago—nearly every kind of excursion and destination can be reached from here, including spots for watersports and cultural visits. Trips to Isla Bastimentos and the Zapatilla Cays are better, with fast boats that offer flexible itineraries. If you have a group or can afford a private-boat rental, do so because it offers you the freedom to plan your own itinerary.

Beaches & Other Natural Attractions

BOCA DEL DRAGO BEACH & SWAN'S CAY ★★   Boca del Drago is the best beach on Isla Colón for swimming, and when the sea is calm, visitors can snorkel from the shore here. Though often there isn't much beach to speak of—just a couple of feet or so for throwing down a towel or beach chair—it's still a lovely spot. The beach is on the north shore of Isla Colón. Tour companies include Boca del Drago as part of their standard day tour, including a visit to nearby **Swan's Cay,** a picturesque rocky outcrop and bird sanctuary that attracts nesting boobies, frigates, and the magnificent red-billed tropic bird. You can also get to Boca del Drago from Bocas Town by road in a taxi, which costs $25 round-trip and takes 30 minutes.

BLUFF BEACH ★   This gorgeous, golden-sand beach would be perfect if it weren't for a light sprinkling of trash. It's still the prettiest beach close to town for catching some rays—but don't plan on getting more than your feet wet here because the ocean is fraught with riptides. The beach is about 8km (5 miles) from the city center and can be reached by taxi for $10 one-way. Some drivers are willing to hang around if you plan on staying an hour or two; if not, you'll need to arrange for pickup later. In this case, negotiate to pay when the driver returns (to make sure that he comes back). You can also rent a bicycle and pedal there, which is quite a pleasant ride if you're up to it. Rain can wreak havoc on the road, so be prepared for lots of puddles.

SAN SAN POND SAK WETLANDS ★★★   The San San Pond Sak Wetlands, covering nearly 16,187 hectares (40,000 acres), are on the coast about 4.8km (3 miles) north of Changuinola. The wetlands are home to sloths, white-faced capuchin monkeys, and caimans, but more important, San San is the natural habitat of the manatee, an aquatic, elephant-like mammal that weighs between 363 and 544 kilograms. Previously it was difficult to visit San San, but **Starfleet Scuba** (see "Scuba Diving & Snorkeling," below) now offers a full-day excursion (7am–5pm) that provides for an out-of-the-ordinary experience. Because there is so little human traffic in this region, your chances of spotting a manatee are good, but please note that manatees are protected animals. Do not chase, pet, or harass these magnificent creatures—and report anyone who does. The Starfleet tour takes visitors to the coast, where they are transported by minibus to the put-in site for the *cayuco* (dugout canoe) to paddle quietly through the wetlands. There is also an easy nature trail for getting out and stretching your legs. The cost includes a full lunch, park entrance fees, guides, and transportation; contact Starfleet for prices.

ISLA bastimentos

Those looking for a more exotic beach experience may want to consider **Isla Bastimentos ★★★**, which is perfect for honeymooners, offering dense jungles and lovely beaches—it's perhaps the best beach in Bocas del Toro, and only 30 minutes by boat from Isla Colón. Hotels here tend to offer packages including lodging, three meals a day, transportation to and from the Isla Colón airport, and some excursions. Getting such a package deal is your best option since you will have a hard time finding food or arranging transport on your own. Most of the tour companies listed under Bocas del Toro also offer day trips to the beaches and national parks of Isla Bastimentos, and you can find out more about these tours by visiting individual companies during your stay on Isla Colón.

One of the best hotels on the Isla is **Tranquilo Bay** (*℅* **713/589-6952** in the U.S., or 380-0721 in Panama; www.tranquilobay.com). This beautiful ecolodge offers modern, brightly decorated cottages with air-conditioning, and the American expat owners offer serious personal attention. Another great option if you are looking for something a little bit more rustic is **La Loma Jungle Lodge** (*℅* **6619-5364;** www.thejunglelodge.com), which is set against a backdrop of pristine tropical forest. The Jungle Lodge also functions as a chocolate farm, and although the three cabins are not air-conditioned, the lack of such an amenity is part of the experience—there is no better place to feel at one with nature.

Fun in the Water

SCUBA DIVING & SNORKELING   Scuba diving and snorkeling are among the most popular activities in Bocas del Toro, owing to well-preserved displays of hard and soft coral, mangrove swamps, volcanic-rock walls, and underwater caves. You might also see colorful sponges, and there is even an underwater landing craft that was sunk to create an artificial reef. Recommended snorkeling and diving sites are **Crawl Cay** (or Coral Cay), with shallow waters and some of the best coral formations in the area; **Hospital Point,** just a 10-minute boat ride from Bocas and easy to reach by water taxi; **Polo Beach,** a shallow system of caves suitable for snorkelers but reachable only 6 months of the year; **Swan's Cay,** with interesting rock formations created by battering waves and also a migratory-bird site; and **Cayos Zapatillas,** two delicate islands with white-sand beaches surrounded by an extensive reef system that attracts lots of tropical fish. Cayos Zapatillas, it should be noted, has currents and is for strong swimmers only.

Divers also head to **Buoy Line** near Isla Solarte, which is a deepwater channel where pelagic and larger marine species can be seen; the same is true of **Tiger Rock,** an offshore site and rocky outcrop whose distance from Bocas Town keeps the crowds away. Adventurous divers and snorkelers really looking to get away from other travelers might consider visiting **Isla Escudo de Veraguas,** which is a full-day trip and a fairly large undertaking (usually available only Sept–Oct). The beaches here are generally considered to be the loveliest in the entire region.

The principal shortcoming of Bocas del Toro as a diving and snorkeling destination is the **unpredictability of the weather,** with spontaneous downpours and wind gusts that can churn up the sea and cloud visibility. If the focus of your trip is diving and snorkeling, come from September to early November, when the sea is tranquil and flat. Other months with better visibility are March and April, but rain and wind can occur at any time during these months. Dive sites with deeper water and larger species (mostly offshore sites such as Tiger Rock) can be visited only during these more tranquil months.

Bocas Water Sports on Main Street (✆ 757-9541; www.bocaswatersports. com) is the oldest operation in town, and has been taken over by new American owners. Dive trips include all gear; a two-dive trip is $60 per person, a one-dive trip $35 per person. Trips last 3 hours and depart at 9am and 2:30pm. Dives to Tiger Rock and Cayos Zapatillas are $75 per person and are available only during calm months. Night dives from 6:30 to 8:30pm are $50 per person. Snorkeling tours are $17 to $20 for a full day, not including lunch.

Starfleet Scuba, at Calle 1A (✆ 757-9630; www.starfleetscuba.com), has a spotless record. Starfleet has three boats plus a new 80kmph (50-mph) inflatable Zodiac boat that gives the company the edge in terms of more quickly getting to remote destinations like Tiger Rock ($90 for minimum of four people; lunch included). Two-tank dives cost $50, a one-tank dive $35; snorkeling tours are $20 per person. Starfleet works in conjunction with the U.K.-based **Ocean Pulse,** a marine-research group that offers 2-week "eco-ventures" to travelers with advanced diving experience. Participants accompany marine biologists exploring new dive sites to monitor for conservation, and are treated to lectures and presentations about species and habitats throughout the day. Packages vary depending on accommodations requirements, so it's best to contact them for prices (✆ 0175/220-2101 in the U.K.; www.oceanpulse.co.uk).

La Buga Dive and Surf (next to Farmacia Rosa Blanco; ✆ 757-9534; www. labugapanama.com) offers PADI certification as well as dive excursions. A two-tank half-day dive costs $60 and night dives cost $50. A 3-day PADI-certification course will cost you $235; however, Bocas Water Sports and Starfleet are a bit more reputable. In addition to diving, La Buga offers surfing, snorkeling, and kayaking excursions.

Several companies offer snorkeling and diving trips in addition to the two mentioned above. Day trips include equipment; lunch is extra, so bring cash for a local restaurant, or bring your own food. There are plenty of operators along the waterfront; **J & J Transparente Boat Tours** offers trips to all the islands, but they're garden-variety. Tours cost $17 to $22 per person, and suffer from a "get-em-in and get-em-out" mentality. However, J & J is the company to call for charter-boat rentals, which cost $200 for a full day, not including lunch.

Catamaran Sailing Adventures at Main Street (✆ 757-9710 or 6637-9064; www.bocassailing.com) has a 12m (40-ft.) catamaran for laid-back and enjoyable full-day snorkeling trips to Bocas del Drago or around Isla Bastimentos for $30 per person (4-person minimum, 18 maximum), including a sack lunch. Charter rentals cost $250 a day. The catamaran has little protection from the sun, so bring sunscreen and a hat.

WATERSPORTS **Bocas Water Sports** (see above) offers water-skiing for $45 for 1 hour, gear included, using their 7.6m (25-ft.) tour boat (maximum four people). There are many mangrove-fringed canals in the area that provide for glassy water year-round. Full-day water-skiing trips can be arranged; contact the company for price information. Bocas Water Sports also rents one-person kayaks that cost $3 per hour, or $10 for a half-day. During bad-weather days, you'll only be able to navigate around mangrove swamps and the coast, but on calm days experienced kayakers can make it all the way to Hospital Point.

BOATING & SAILING   For catamaran tours, see **Catamaran Sailing Adventures,** under "Scuba Diving & Snorkeling," above. **Boteros Bocatoreños** (© 757-9760; boterosbocas@yahoo.com) is a group of local boatmen who have banded together in the face of encroaching competition—they can provide custom tours at slightly lower prices than outfitters. Most speak at least some English and have local knowledge, and they can be found on the Via Principal by the ATP office. **Boteros Nuestra Señora del Carmen** (© 757-9039) is another group of local operators. They require a minimum of five people and tours usually cost $3 to $20 per person, though Cayos Zapatilla costs $25 per person. You can find them at Calle 3 next to Catamaran Tours. They have snorkeling equipment. Another good source for local boatmen is **Ancon Expeditions** (© 507/269-9415; www.anconexpeditions.com).

SURFING   Bocas experiences the largest and most consistent swells from December to March, and during June and July, with reef point breaks, beach breaks, and huge, challenging waves recommended only for experienced surfers. The waves in Bocas are more suitable for shortboarding and bodyboarding; if you're bringing your own board, check with your airline about requirements because some smaller planes may not accept a long board. **Del Toro Surf** (© 6570-8277; deltorosurf@yahoo.com.ar) offers surf lessons and board rentals to clients participating in lessons. To rent a surfboard, try **Tropix,** located on Main Street across from the plaza, or **Flow** surf shop (no phone) on Avenida H below the Om Restaurant. All offer tips and maps to the best surf spots in the area, as well as information on how to get there. **La Buga** (see "Scuba Diving & Snorkeling," above) offers surf trips from $10 to $20 for those who already know how to surf, half-day surf trips for $49, and full-day surf trips for $99 for those interested in learning. The **Best of Both Adventures for Women** (see "Spas," below) offers women-only surf tours. **Bocas Surf School** (© 6852-5291 or 757-9057; www.bocassurfschool.com) is owned and operated by Bryan and Jana Hudson, who offer beginner through advanced surfing courses and surfing excursions.

Other Activities in Bocas Town
SCIENTIFIC VISITS   The **Smithsonian Tropical Research Institute** has a base in Bocas del Toro, and is open to the public every Friday from 3 to 5pm. If you're lucky, you'll be around for one of their monthly chats led by a scientist who highlights the center's work and discoveries in the region. Contact the institute at © 212-8000, or visit their site, www.stri.org, for information about upcoming lectures.

Local Events
The **Fería Internaciónal del Mar (International Festival of the Sea),** which takes place around the second week of September, is a 5-day event featuring handicrafts booths, food stands serving local cuisine, and exhibits by the Smithsonian Institute and ANAM (the park service), with displays of animals and natural history information. Nightly events include folkloric presentations and dances, all culminating with the crowning of the Sea Fair Queen. Contact the ATP office for exact dates. The **Fundación de la Provincia de Bocas del Toro (Founding Day of Bocas del Toro)** takes place on November 16, and is celebrated with parades and other events; on November 23, residents of Isla Bastimentos celebrate **Bastimentos Day,**

with parades and live music. There is a maypole dance in Bocas and on Isla Basti-mentos for **Palo de Mayo,** which takes place on May 1. Lastly, on July 16 is the **Día de la Virgen del Carmen,** which honors the patron saint of Bocas with a parade; the following Sunday hundreds make the pilgrimage across the island to visit the shrine of the virgin at La Gruta.

Spas

If you're winding down from a day of activity, try Donna at **Spa Flora Bella** (✆ **6591-3814;** islagirly@yahoo.com), which offers deep-tissue massages, reflexology, and hot-stone treatments, as well as an assortment of beauty services. Donna has two locations, but give her a call or send her an e-mail to set up an appointment. Several massage therapists provide in-hotel services; try **Holistic Alternative Therapy** (✆ **6686-0235**), which has Zen Shiatsu massage and Thai foot massages. **Starfleet Scuba** (✆ **757-9630;** see "Scuba Diving & Snorkeling," above) now has a low-key day spa above their in-town office. Thirty-minute massages cost $40, and 1-hour massages $60. Pedicures, manicures, and waxing are also available, or you can head to **Danuta's Holistic Therapy** (✆ **757-9308** or 6676-0235). The **Best of Both Adventures for Women** (www.bestofbothadventures.com) offers women-only adventures throughout Panama (and Latin America), which feature yoga, spa, and massage treatment. For more information, call Dez Bartelt at ✆ **787/823-0610** or check out the website.

WHERE TO STAY

Easygoing travelers enjoy the laid-back Caribbean vibe in Bocas Town, and its prox-imity to restaurants, bars, and shopping. But loud music and other street noise is a factor, and travelers seeking peaceful isolation will do better lodging elsewhere. Neighboring Isla Carenero is close enough that you can occasionally hear music on loud party nights in Bocas, but it still gives travelers an option for being near Bocas without actually staying in it.

Very Expensive

Playa Tortuga Resort ★ ☺   The Playa Tortuga resort is really more a medium-size hotel with lots of amenities and services. Located about 3.2km (2 miles) from Bocas town, the resort fronts a small, relatively calm beach and is perfect for families and those looking for comfort and convenience. The lobby is a bit dim and unwel-coming, but the cheerful, friendly (and bilingual) staff makes up for this. Rooms have a familiar, chainlike decor, but all have their own balcony, complete with a hammock and sitting area, many with great ocean views. The best thing about the Playa Tortuga Resort is its impressive, cascading pool, complete with a pool bar and restaurant. The hotel's service desk offers snorkeling, fishing, and wildlife excursions for those looking for a little bit of adventure and is especially great for kids. Though it may not provide a world-class resort experience, there's really nothing else like it on the island, and it will suffice for those used to more upscale accommodations.

Playa Big Creek. ✆ **302-5424** or 757-9050. www.hotelplayatortuga.com. 118 units. $135 double; $150 1-bedroom suite; $300 grand master suite; $600 Almirante suite. Rates include breakfast. AE, MC, V. **Amenities:** Restaurant; 2 bars; room service. *In room:* A/C, TV, minibar, Wi-Fi.

MODERATE

Gran Hotel Bahía ★   This is the town's most historic hotel, located in the old United Fruit Company headquarters. Although it is not located on the waterfront, nor does it have ocean views, it's a lovely example of Caribbean architecture, with breeze-swept verandas, built in 1905. Vestiges of the building's original purpose remain, such as the front desk's barred windows and an enormous steel safe; and the long hall with polished pine floors is antique splendor. Superior doubles are better than standards because they have been recently renovated, but even the standards were recently painted colors and country-style teak furniture was added. Nevertheless, the superiors are comfortable and have a lot of amenities. The Hotel Bahía has very friendly service. Note that the hotel closes in June. Steep discounts are available in low season.

South end of Main St. ✆ 757-9626. www.ghbahia.com. 18 units. $80 double; $90 superior double. MC, V. **Amenities:** Restaurant. *In room:* A/C, TV, Wi-Fi (additional cost).

Hotel Bocas del Toro ★   With its full-service restaurant and dock furnished with lounge chairs, this place is one of the best places to stay on Isla Colón, and the staff here is a bit more attentive than in other similarly priced hotels. Hotel Bocas del Toro features beautiful wood craftsmanship and a fresh, nautical decor, but some of the standard doubles that do not face the water or the street are dark and small; "premium" rooms have balconies. The third-floor "Luxury Room" is one of the best rooms in town for its ample size, long balcony, and water view; and it has a queen-size and a double bed for up to three guests. If you have a laptop, you'll enjoy the free Wi-Fi service in their restaurant. Like the Limbo, this is not a particularly loud hotel, but a lot of action in the area means it's not whisper-quiet, either.

Calle 1 at Main St. ✆ **757-9018** or 757-9771. www.hotelbocasdeltoro.com. 11 units. $126–$145 double with street view; $140–$195 double with ocean view; $270 luxury room. AE, MC, V. **Amenities:** Restaurant; bar; massage. *In room:* A/C, TV.

INEXPENSIVE

Hotel Casa Max   This Dutch-owned hostel is housed in a Caribbean-style, two-story turquoise wooden building, with a barlike common area spread across the ground floor. On the whole, Casa Max offers good value for low-budget travelers, with tasteful but small rooms that are kept very clean. Five more rooms with A/C, TV, and minibar have been added above the relatively new Indonesian/international restaurant. The service is accommodating and friendly. My only caveat is that Casa Max is in front of the surf bar Mondo Taitu, and light sleepers may be disturbed by late-night music.

Av. G. ✆ **757-9120.** casamax1@hotmail.com. 16 units. $30–$40 double with fan; $45–$60 double with A/C. No credit cards. *In room:* No phone.

La Veranda ★   Housed in a lovely converted home built in 1910, this is one of the best economy hotels in Bocas. It's about a 5-minute walk on a paved road to the main strip, but there's an open-air, communal kitchen if you'd like to cook and dine in. The rooms are mostly simple, with mosquito nets, pastel-colored walls, and polished floors. Rooms with a private bathroom cost more, but they are well worth the investment because they are larger and brighter than room nos. 4 and 5. The perk at this hotel is its spacious, pleasant veranda, for which the hotel is named. It's a very relaxing place, giving travelers on a shoestring a place to just sleep, while they do their unwinding elsewhere.

Calle G. ✆ **757-9211.** http://laverandapanama.tripod.com. 7 units. $30–$49 double with shared bathroom; $30–$59 double with private bathroom. Extra person $10. No credit cards. **Amenities:** Communal kitchen. *In room:* A/C (some units), no phone, Wi-Fi.

THE SAN BLAS islands

The adventurous will not want to miss out on the rustic and wonderfully undiscovered **San Blas Islands ★★★** on the Caribbean coast bordering Colombia. Home to the Kuna Indians, who have not allowed foreign or even Panamanian investment or megaresorts to infringe upon the islands, this is the perfect kind of place to spend a couple of days sleeping in a hammock and swimming in the clear blue sea. There is not much else to do, but you will have the opportunity to interact with the Kuna community and eat tasty if simple Kuna meals. The hotels in this region are all-inclusive, and are quite a bit cheaper than those found on Isla Bastimentos (see earlier in this chapter), mostly due to the rustic accommodations.

For a customized tour of the Kuna Yala Islands, contact guide Gilberto Alemancia, director of local communities at the **ATP** (② **6948-0525;** gilbert04@yahoo.com). Gilberto has coordinated expeditions for *National Geographic,* Photo Safari, PhotoAdventure, Discovery Channel Adventure, and the BBC, and is the go-to guy for all things Kuna. Fully bilingual and U.S. educated, Gilberto is himself a Kuna, and extremely knowledgeable about that culture's history and customs. He can organize specialized tours, set up boat transportation to and from different islands, organize camping trips, or even accompany visitors to the comarca, which can include a stay at a traditional Kuna hut on his home island. Call for prices and information. Other recommended outfitters are listed below. Before embarking on a tour to Kuna Yala, be sure that your outfitter is permitted to give tours; Kuna Yala is an autonomous region of Panama and tourism rules and regulations are set by the Kuna Council.

KAYAKING There is no outfitter with more experience operating in the comarca, or more dedicated to preserving the Kuna Yala culture, than **Xtrop ★★★** (② **317-1279;** www.xtrop.com), which is short for Expediciones Tropicales. The Panama City–based company is highly respected, specializing in sea-kayak tours with an emphasis on nature and culture, and employing only local Kuna guides. Xtrop, which works with companies like

WHERE TO DINE

Believe it or not, tiny Bocas is home to one of the few gourmet supermarkets in the country, **Super Gourmet** (② 757-9357; Mon–Sat 9am–7pm), with imported foods, vegetarian and organic products, and very expensive produce. Super Gourmet, which has a full-service delicatessen, is next to the Hotel Bahía on the south end of Main Street. You'll find good coffee drinks and lots of reading material at **Starfish Coffee** on Main Street next to El Encanto bar, and good breakfasts on a waterfront dock at the **Coffee Bar** inside Hotel El Limbo on the Sea (Calle Primera; ② 507/757-9062). For cheap, tourist-style fast food, try **McDouglas' Golden Grill** (daily 7:30am–11pm) on Main Street across from the plaza. **Guari Guari ★★★** (② 6575-5513), just outside of town, is conceptually similar to Manolo Caracol in Panama City. It's open for dinner only, and reservations are required. For $16, you get a 6- to 12-course meal including whatever the chef feels like serving that day. **El Ultimo Refugio** (② 6568-8927), also just outside town, is one of the area's most atmospheric places to dine, with dishes such as grilled tuna and Cajun-style chicken. Reservations are recommended here too.

Mountain Travel Sobek in the U.S., has received permission from Kuna chiefs to operate in some of the areas that are richest in marine life (they call them "aquatic trails"), and they have access to areas no one else can go, including forested coastal areas. Best of all, Xtrop is very active in developing programs in the region for sustainable tourism, so you can feel good about how your money is spent. Xtrop has over 15 years of experience in the comarca and is one of the few companies officially allowed to take tours and excursions to Kuna Yala. Trips are from 3 nights to a week long, and lodging is in tents or huts. Xtrop can also book just lodging for you, if that's the only service you need.

HIKING & GENERAL TOURS   Ecocircuitos ★★ (✆ **314-0068** or 314-0698; www.ecocircuitos.com) has guided walks through PEMASKY (Project for the Study and Management of Wilderness Areas of Kuna Yala), a protected coastal jungle in the comarca around the road to Cartí Suitupo, which is ranked as one of the best trails in the world for spotting birds and diverse flora. Ecocircuitos

also offers multiday trips around Panama that include a couple of days visiting islands in the comarca. **Adventures in Panama** (✆ **877/726-6222** in the U.S.; www.adventuresinpanama.com) can also book lodges for travelers having a hard time doing it on their own.

SAILING   San Blas Sailing ★ (✆ **314-1800**; www.sanblassailing.com) is a French-owned company that has a fleet of monohull and multihull sailboats; their largest boat can hold eight passengers. They've been based in the comarca since 1997 and know the area intimately. Trips, which run from 3 to 14 nights and include meals, drinks, tours, and onboard accommodations, involve sailing around the islands, snorkeling, kayaking, and visiting Kuna villages. If you are looking for fine accommodations in the comarca, this is your best bet, but of course you'll spend all your nights onboard. There have been customer complaints about poor communication and dangerous road conditions on the Llanos-Cartí road, however, which is something you may want to keep in mind.

Right in town, **El Pecado** (✆ **6852-3600;** Main St. at the Plaza) serves Thai, Mexican, Lebanese, and Panamanian food, but while the food is good, the building itself feels like it's on the verge of collapse. **Om Café** ★★ (✆ **6624-0898**) is considered one of the top in-town dining options, and serves up delicious Indian food and a funky, mellow vibe that is pure Bocas.

The **Buena Vista Grill** (✆ **757-9336;** Calle 1 at Calle 2) offers typical American fare such as BLT and hot Reuben sandwiches. **Reef** (Main St. on the south end of town) is a local dive serving ultrafresh Panamanian seafood in a rough-and-tumble, saltwater ambience. **Shelley's BBQ** (✆ **6710-1200;** corner of Calle 4 and Av. D) is a hole-in-the-wall Mexican rotisserie, but a delicious one at that. Try their outstanding tacos and quesadillas.

BOCAS TOWN AFTER DARK

Bocas Town is Party Central for the archipelago, but there are plenty of low-key venues for a quiet drink, and the town's friendly atmosphere creates an environment that encourages meeting fellow travelers and locals. **Iguana Bar and Surf Club,** on

Calle 1, is the best all-around bar, with a surfer theme and a wood-hewn, comfy ambience that's good for conversation and suitable for all ages, though the party can pick up late in the evening. **Buena Vista** (see above) is an old-school expat hangout, with a wooden bar, lapping seafront, and decent cocktails. The open-air waterfront bar **Barco Hundido (Shipwreck Bar),** on Calle 1, is the party zone with late nights and dancing that culminates with one or two drunk guys jumping into the water on a dare. The bar often has live DJs or bands with a cover charge. **Mondo Taitu,** on Avenida G, caters to 20-something surfers and backpackers, and has cheap drinks and good music late into the night.

FAST FACTS: CENTRAL AMERICA

Area Codes See individual chapters for info.

Business Hours See individual chapters for info.

Car Rentals See "Toll-Free Numbers & Websites," p. 728.

Drinking Laws The legal drinking age throughout Central America is 18 (except in Honduras, where you must be 21 to drink, but 18 to purchase alcohol), although it is often not enforced. Beer, wine, and liquor are sold in most supermarkets and convenience stores Monday through Saturday. No liquor is sold on Good Friday or Easter Sunday or election days. Possessing, using, or trafficking drugs anywhere in the region brings severe penalties, including long jail sentences and large fines.

Driving Rules See "Getting There" and "Getting Around" info throughout this book.

Electricity Central American countries run on 110 volts, 60 Hz, the same as the United States and Canada. However, three-prong grounded outlets are not universally available. It's helpful to bring a three-to-two-prong adapter. European and Asian travelers should bring adapters with any accompanying appliances. Be prepared for frequent blackouts, and bring surge protectors.

Embassies & Consulates See individual chapters for info.

Emergencies See individual chapters for info.

Holidays See "Calendar of Events," p. 56.

Insurance **Medical Insurance** For travel overseas, most U.S. health plans (including Medicare and Medicaid) do not provide coverage, and the ones that do often require you to pay for services upfront and reimburse you only after you return home.

As a safety net, you may want to buy travel medical insurance, particularly if you're traveling to a remote or high-risk area where emergency evacuation might be necessary. If you require additional medical insurance, try **MEDEX Assistance** (© **410/453-6300;** www.medexassist.com) or **Travel Assistance International** (© **800/821-2828;** www.travelassistance.com); for general information on services, call the company's **Worldwide Assistance Services, Inc.,** at © **800/777-8710.**

Canadians should check with their provincial health plan offices or call **Health Canada** (© **866/225-0709;** www.hc-sc.gc.ca) to find out the extent of their coverage and what documentation they must take home if they are treated overseas.

Travelers from the U.K. should carry their **European Health Insurance Card (EHIC),** which replaced the E111 form as proof of entitlement to free/reduced-cost medical treatment abroad (© **0845/606-2030;** www.ehic.org.uk). Note, however, that the EHIC covers only "necessary medical treatment," and for repatriation costs, lost money, baggage, or cancellation, travel insurance from a reputable company should always be sought (www.travelinsurance web.com).

Travel Insurance   The cost of travel insurance varies, depending on the destination, the cost and length of your trip, your age and health, and the type of trip you're taking, but expect to pay between 5% and 8% of the price of the vacation. You can get estimates from various providers through **InsureMyTrip.com.** Enter your trip cost and dates, your age, and other information, for prices from more than a dozen companies.

U.K. citizens and their families who make more than one trip abroad per year may find that an annual travel insurance policy works out cheaper. Check **www.money supermarket.com**, which compares prices across a range of providers. Most big travel agents offer their own insurance and will probably try to sell you their package when you book a holiday. Think before you sign. **Britain's Consumers' Association** recommends that you insist on seeing the policy and reading the fine print before buying travel insurance. The **Association of British Insurers** (© 020/7600-3333; www.abi.org.uk) gives advice by phone and publishes *Holiday Insurance,* a free guide to policy provisions and prices. You might also shop around for better deals; try **Columbus Direct** (© 0870/033-9988; www.columbusdirect.net).

Trip-Cancellation Insurance   Trip-cancellation insurance will help retrieve your money if you have to back out of a trip or depart early, or if your travel supplier goes bankrupt. Trip cancellation traditionally covers such events as sickness, natural disasters, and State Department advisories. The latest news in trip-cancellation insurance is the availability of **expanded hurricane coverage** and the **"any reason"** cancellation coverage—which costs more but covers cancellations made for any reason. You won't get back 100% of your prepaid trip cost, but you'll be refunded a substantial portion. **TravelSafe** (© 888/885-7233; www.travelsafe.com) offers both types of coverage. Expedia also offers any-reason cancellation coverage for its air-hotel packages. For details, contact one of the following recommended insurers: **Access America** (© 866/807-3982; www.accessamerica.com); **Travel Guard International** (© 800/826-4919; www.travelguard.com); **Travel Insured International** (© 800/243-3174; www.travelinsured.com); and **Travelex Insurance Services** (© 888/457-4602; www.travelex-insurance.com).

Internet Access   Internet access is easy to find in the region, as even the smallest towns usually have at least one Internet center. Access usually costs 50¢ to $1 per hour. Nearly every hotel has at least one computer with Internet access; some have dataports or Wi-Fi (usually in the hotel lobby or business center). See "Fast Facts" sections throughout the country chapters for specific locations.

Language   Spanish is by far the dominant language in the region, except in Belize, where English is spoken. You will also hear English spoken in the Bay Islands in Honduras, the Canal Zone in Panama, and more touristy destinations. The Caribbean coast has its own form of lilting creole that has West Indian roots. A number of indigenous languages have survived, most notably Mayan. See the individual destination chapters throughout this book for more info. It is also advisable to learn some basic Spanish before you travel here; we recommend picking up a copy of *Frommer's Spanish PhraseFinder & Dictionary.* We've also included a short list of useful Spanish terms and a pronunciation guide in the chapter following this one.

Lost & Found   Be sure to tell all of your credit card companies the minute you discover that your wallet has been lost or stolen, and file a report at the nearest police precinct. See individual chapters for more info.

If you need emergency cash, you can have money wired to you via **Western Union** (© 800/325-6000; www.westernunion.com).

Mail Every country in Central America varies regarding the price, efficiency, and speed of its mail service (known as *correo*). In general, expect it to take 2 weeks for your letter or postcard to reach home. If you're sending a parcel, a Customs officer may have to inspect it first. Theft is a common problem. Always try to send mail from a main post office and insist that the envelope be stamped in front of you. It's wise to send things via registered post, though often the letter can be tracked as far as the border and no more. Private courier services are everywhere but most are expensive. See the individual chapters throughout this book for specifics.

Measurements See the chart on the inside front cover of this book for details on converting metric measurements to nonmetric equivalents.

Newspapers & Magazines *The Miami Herald* (www.miamiherald.com) is probably the most widely available English-language paper about the region. The Costa Rican–based *Tico Times* (www.ticotimes.net) is another. You can find both in most capital-city downtown kiosks and airport newsstands. See individual chapters for each country's major newspapers.

Passports The websites listed provide downloadable passport applications as well as the current fees for processing applications. For an up-to-date, country-by-country listing of passport requirements around the world, go to the "International Travel" tab of the U.S. State Department site at **http://travel.state.gov**.

Allow plenty of time before your trip to apply for a passport; processing normally takes 3 weeks but can take longer during busy periods (especially spring). And keep in mind that if you need a passport in a hurry, you'll pay a higher processing fee.

For Residents of Australia You can pick up an application from your local post office or any branch of Passports Australia, but you must schedule an interview at the passport office to present your application materials. Call the **Australian Passport Information Service** at (C) **131-232,** or visit the website at www.passports.gov.au.

For Residents of Canada Passport applications are available at travel agencies throughout Canada or from the central **Passport Office,** Department of Foreign Affairs and International Trade, Ottawa, ON K1A 0G3 ((C) **800/567-6868;** www.ppt.gc.ca). *Note:* Canadian children who travel must have their own passport.

For Residents of Ireland You can apply for a 10-year passport at the **Passport Office,** Setanta Centre, Molesworth Street, Dublin 2 ((C) **01/671-1633;** www.irlgov.ie/iveagh). Those 17 and under, or 66 and older, must apply for a 3-year passport. You can also apply at 1A South Mall, Cork ((C) **21/494-4700**), or at most main post offices.

For Residents of New Zealand You can pick up a passport application at any New Zealand Passports Office or download it from their website. Contact the **Passports Office** at (C) **0800/225-050** in New Zealand, or 04/474-8100, or log on to www.passports.govt.nz.

For Residents of the United Kingdom To pick up an application for a standard 10-year passport (5-year passport for children 15 and under), visit your nearest passport office, major post office, or travel agency, or contact the **United Kingdom Passport Service** at (C) **0870/521-0410,** or search its website at www.ukpa.gov.uk.

For Residents of the United States Whether you're applying in person or by mail, you can download passport applications from the U.S. State Department website at **http://travel.state.gov**. To find your regional passport office, either check the U.S. State Department website or call the **National Passport Information Center** toll-free number ((C) **877/487-2778**) for automated information.

Police See individual chapters for information.

Smoking Except for Panama, which recently banned smoking in all restaurants and bars, there are no government smoking bans in Central America at the moment. Private companies do not allow smoking in places like cinemas or long-distance buses, however. The region's better hotels and restaurants have nonsmoking rooms and areas, but in general you can still puff wherever you want.

Taxes VAT and Customs duties differ from country to country. See individual chapters for info.

Telephones See p. 80 in chapter 3, along with the "Telephone Dialing Info at a Glance" boxes throughout this guide, for info.

Time Zone Central America is 6 hours behind Greenwich Mean Time, except Panama, which is 5 hours behind. No countries observe daylight saving time.

Tipping Ten percent is the general rule for tipping in restaurants, though tips are sometimes included in bills. In hotels, tip **bellhops** at least $1 per bag ($2–$3 if you have a lot of luggage) and tip the **chamber staff** $1 to $2 per day. See individual chapters for more info.

Toilets These are known as *sanitarios, servicios sanitarios,* or *baños.* They are marked *damas* or *mujeres* (women) and *hombres* or *caballeros* (men). Throughout Central America, public restrooms are hard to come by. One must count on the generosity of some hotel or restaurant. Same goes for most beaches. Most restaurants, and, to a lesser degree, hotels, will let you use their facilities, especially if you make a small purchase. Bus and gas stations often have restrooms, but many are pretty grim. Don't flush toilet paper; put it in the trash bin.

Water The water in most major cities and tourist destinations throughout Central America is ostensibly safe to drink. However, many travelers react adversely to water in foreign countries, and it is probably best to drink bottled water and avoid ice or food washed with tap water throughout your visit to the region. See p. 70 in chapter 3 for more info.

TOLL-FREE NUMBERS & WEBSITES

MAJOR INTERNATIONAL AIRLINES

Aeroméxico
✆ 800/237-6639 (in the U.S.)
www.aeromexico.com

Aero Perlas
✆ 378-6000 (in Panama)
www.aeroperlas.com

Air Canada
✆ 888/247-2262 (in the U.S. and Canada)
www.aircanada.com

Air Panama
✆ 316-9000 (in Panama)
www.flyairpanama.com

American Airlines
✆ 800/433-7300 (in the U.S. and Canada)
✆ 0844/4997-3000 (in the U.K.)
www.aa.com

British Airways
✆ 800/247-9297 (in the U.S. and Canada)
✆ 0844/493-0787 (in the U.K.)
www.britishairways.com

Continental Airlines
✆ 800/523-3273 (in the U.S. and Canada)
✆ 084/5607-6760 (in the U.K.)
www.continental.com

Copa Air
📞 800/359-2672 (in the U.S. and Canada)
📞 0871/1744-0335 (in the U.K.)
www.copaair.com

Delta Air Lines
📞 800/221-1212 (in the U.S. and Canada)
📞 084/5600-0950 (in the U.K.)
www.delta.com

Frontier Airlines
📞 800/432-1359 (in the U.S. and Canada)
www.frontierairlines.com

Iberia Airlines
📞 800/722-4642 (in the U.S. and Canada)
📞 087/0609-0500 (in the U.K.)
www.iberia.com

Lan Airlines
📞 866/435-9526 (in the U.S.)
📞 305/670-9999 (in other countries)
www.lan.com

Martin Air
📞 305/704-9800 (in the U.S.)
www.martinair.com

Spirit Airlines
📞 800/772-7117 (in the U.S.)
www.spiritair.com

TACA
📞 800/535-8780 (in the U.S.)
📞 800/722-TACA (8222; in Canada)
📞 087/1744-0337 (in the U.K.)

United Airlines
📞 800/864-8331 (in the U.S. and Canada)
📞 084/5844-4777 (in the U.K.)
www.united.com

US Airways
📞 800/428-4322 (in the U.S. and Canada)
📞 084/5600-3300 (in the U.K.)
www.usairways.com

CAR-RENTAL AGENCIES

Alamo
📞 800/462-5266 (in the U.S. and Canada)
www.alamo.com

Avis
📞 800/331-1212 (in the U.S. and Canada)
📞 084/4581-8181 (in the U.K.)
www.avis.com

Budget
📞 800/527-0700 (in the U.S.)
📞 800/268-8900 (in Canada)
📞 084/4544-4444 (in the U.K.)
www.budget.com

Dollar
📞 800/800-4000 (in the U.S.)
📞 800/848-8268 (in Canada)
📞 080/823-42474 (in the U.K.)
www.dollar.com

Hertz
📞 800/645-3131 (in the U.S. and Canada)
📞 800/654-3001 (for international reservations)
www.hertz.com

National
📞 800/CAR-RENT (227-7368; in the U.S. and Canada)
www.nationalcar.com

Thrifty
📞 800/367-2277 (in the U.S. and Canada)
📞 918/669-2168 (international)
www.thrifty.com

MAJOR HOTEL & MOTEL CHAINS

Best Western International
📞 800/780-7234 (in the U.S. and Canada)
📞 0800/393-130 (in the U.K.)
www.bestwestern.com

Clarion Hotels
📞 800/252-7466 or 877/424-6423 (in the U.S. and Canada)
📞 0800/444-444 (in the U.K.)
www.choicehotels.com

Comfort Inns
📞 800/228-5150
📞 0800/444-444 (in the U.K.)
www.comfortinn.com

Courtyard by Marriott
📞 888/236-2427 (in the U.S.)
📞 0800/221-222 (in the U.K.)
www.marriott.com/courtyard

Crowne Plaza Hotels
📞 888/303-1746 (in the U.S. and Canada)
www.ichotelsgroup.com/crowneplaza

Days Inn
📞 800/329-7466 (in the U.S.)
📞 0800/280-400 (in the U.K.)
www.daysinn.com

Doubletree Hotels
✆ 800/222-TREE (8733; in the U.S. and Canada)
✆ 087/0590-9090 (in the U.K.)
www.doubletree.com

Econo Lodges
✆ 800/55-ECONO (552-3666)
www.choicehotels.com

Embassy Suites
✆ 800/EMBASSY (362-2779)
www.embassysuites.hilton.com

Four Seasons
✆ 800/819-5053 (in the U.S. and Canada)
✆ 0800/6488-6488 (in the U.K.)
www.fourseasons.com

Hilton Hotels
✆ 800/HILTONS (445-8667; in the U.S. and Canada)
✆ 087/0590-9090 (in the U.K.)
www.hilton.com

Holiday Inn
✆ 800/315-2621 (in the U.S. and Canada)
✆ 0800/405-060 (in the U.K.)
www.holidayinn.com

InterContinental Hotels & Resorts
✆ 800/424-6835 (in the U.S. and Canada)
✆ 0800/1800-1800 (in the U.K.)
www.ichotelsgroup.com

Marriott
✆ 888/236-2427 (in the U.S. and Canada)
✆ 0800/221-222 (in the U.K.)
www.marriott.com

Quality
✆ 877/424-6423 (in the U.S. and Canada)
✆ 0800/444-444 (in the U.K.)
www.QualityInn.ChoiceHotels.com

Radisson Hotels & Resorts
✆ 888/201-1718 (in the U.S. and Canada)
✆ 0800/374-411 (in the U.K.)
www.radisson.com

Ramada Worldwide
✆ 888/2-RAMADA (272-6232; in the U.S. and Canada)
✆ 080/8100-0783 (in the U.K.)
www.ramada.com

Residence Inn by Marriott
✆ 800/331-3131
✆ 800/221-222 (in the U.K.)
www.marriott.com

Sheraton Hotels & Resorts
✆ 800/325-3535 (in the U.S.)
✆ 800/543-4300 (in Canada)
✆ 0800/3253-5353 (in the U.K.)
www.starwoodhotels.com/sheraton

Westin Hotels & Resorts
✆ 800/937-8461 (in the U.S. and Canada)
www.starwoodhotels.com/westin

Wyndham Hotels & Resorts
✆ 877/999-3223 (in the U.S. and Canada)
www.wyndham.com

HELPFUL SPANISH PHRASES

Throughout this book, we've noted the places where English is widely spoken, but it's a good idea to carry a good phrase book (like *Frommer's Spanish PhraseFinder & Dictionary*) or download an app on your smartphone with you if you aren't fluent. We've also included some useful "survival Spanish" phrases below. Note that there's a fairly wide range of accents throughout Central America, with the Guatemalan accent said to be one of the cleanest and easiest Spanish accents to master. Costa Rica's accent is unique and sometimes gets made fun of by other Central America Spanish speakers for its "rr"s. We've included information on opportunities to study Spanish in each of the country chapters in this book.

BASIC SPANISH PHRASES

English	Spanish	Pronunciation
Good day	**Buen día**	Bwehn *dee*-ah
Good morning	**Buenos días**	*Bweh*-nohs *dee*-ahs
How are you?	**¿Cómo está?**	*Koh*-moh eh-*stah*
Very well	**Muy bien**	Mwee byehn
Thank you	**Gracias**	*Grah*-syahs
You're welcome	**De nada**	Deh *nah*-dah
Goodbye	**Adiós**	Ah-*dyohs*
Please	**Por favor**	Pohr fah-*bohr*
Yes	**Sí**	See
No	**No**	Noh
Excuse me	**Perdóneme**	Pehr-*doh*-neh-meh
Give me	**Déme**	*Deh*-meh
Where is . . . ?	**¿Dónde está . . . ?**	*Dohn*-deh eh-*stah*
the station	**la estación**	lah eh-stah-*syohn*
a hotel	**un hotel**	oon oh-*tehl*
a gas station	**una gasolinera**	*oo*-nah gah-soh-lee-*neh*-rah
a restaurant	**un restaurante**	oon res-tow-*rahn*-teh
the toilet	**el baño**	el *bah*-nyoh
a good doctor	**un buen médico**	oon bwehn *meh*-dee-coh
the road to . . .	**el camino a/hacia**	el cah-*mee*-noh ah/*ah*-syah

English	Spanish	Pronunciation
To the right	**A la derecha**	Ah lah deh-*reh*-chah
To the left	**A la izquierda**	Ah lah ees-*kyehr*-dah
Straight ahead	**Derecho**	Deh-*reh*-choh
I would like	**Quisiera**	Key-*syeh*-rah
I want . . .	**Quiero**	*Kyeh*-roh
to eat	**comer**	koh-*mehr*
a room	**una habitación**	*oo*-nah ah-bee-tah-*syohn*
Do you have . . . ?	**¿Tiene usted . . . ?**	Tyeh-neh oo-*sted*
a book	**un libro**	oon *lee*-broh
a dictionary	**un diccionario**	oon deek-syoh-*nah*-ryoh
How much is it?	**¿Cuánto cuesta?**	*Kwahn*-toh *kweh*-stah
When?	**¿Cuándo?**	*Kwahn*-doh
What?	**¿Qué?**	Keh
There is (Is there . . . ?)	**(¿)Hay (. . . ?)**	Eye
What is there?	**¿Qué hay?**	Keh eye
Yesterday	**Ayer**	Ah-*yer*
Today	**Hoy**	Oy
Tomorrow	**Mañana**	Mah-*nyah*-nah
Good	**Bueno**	*Bweh*-noh
Bad	**Malo**	*Mah*-loh
Better (best)	**(Lo) Mejor**	(Loh) Meh-*hohr*
More	**Más**	Mahs
Less	**Menos**	*Meh*-nohs
No smoking	**Se prohibe fumar**	Seh proh-*ee*-beh foo-*mahr*
Postcard	**Tarjeta postal**	Tar-*heh*-tah poh-*stahl*
Insect repellent	**Repelente contra insectos**	Reh-peh-*lehn*-teh *cohn*-trah een-*sehk*-tohs

MORE USEFUL PHRASES

English	Spanish	Pronunciation
Do you speak English?	**¿Habla usted inglés?**	*Ah*-blah oo-*sted* een-*glehs*
Is there anyone here who speaks English?	**¿Hay alguien aquí que hable inglés?**	Eye *ahl*-gyehn ah-*kee* keh *ah*-bleh een-*glehs*
I speak a little Spanish.	**Hablo un poco de español.**	*Ah*-bloh oon *poh*-koh deh eh-spah-*nyohl*
I don't understand Spanish very well.	**No (lo) entiendo muy bien el español.**	Noh (loh) ehn-*tyehn*-doh mwee byehn el eh-spah-*nyohl*
The meal is good.	**Me gusta la comida.**	Meh *goo*-stah lah koh-*mee*-dah
What time is it?	**¿Qué hora es?**	Keh *oh*-rah ehs
May I see your menu?	**¿Puedo ver el menú (la carta)?**	*Pweh*-doh vehr el meh-*noo* (lah *car*-tah)
The check, please.	**La cuenta, por favor.**	Lah *kwehn*-tah pohr fa-*borh*

English	Spanish	Pronunciation
What do I owe you?	**¿Cuánto le debo?**	*Kwahn*-toh leh *deh*-boh
What did you say?	**¿Mande?** (formal)	*Mahn*-deh
	¿Cómo? (informal)	*Koh*-moh
I want (to see) . . .	**Quiero (ver)** . . .	*kyeh*-roh (vehr)
a room	**un cuarto** or **una habitación**	oon *kwar*-toh, *oo*-nah ah-bee-tah-*syohn*
for two persons	**para dos personas**	*pah*-rah dohs pehr-*soh*-nahs
with (without) bathroom	**con (sin) baño**	kohn (seen) *bah*-nyoh
We are staying here only . . .	**Nos quedamos aquí solamente** . . .	Nohs keh-*dah*-mohs ah-*kee* soh-lah-*mehn*-teh
one night.	**una noche.**	*oo*-nah *noh*-cheh
one week.	**una semana.**	*oo*-nah seh-*mah*-nah
We are leaving . . .	**Partimos (Salimos)** . . .	Pahr-*tee*-mohs (sah-*lee*-mohs)
tomorrow.	**mañana.**	mah-*nya*-nah
Do you accept . . . ?	**¿Acepta usted . . . ?**	Ah-*sehp*-tah oo-*sted*
traveler's checks?	**cheques de viajero?**	*cheh*-kehs deh byah-*heh*-roh
credit cards	**¿ . . . tarjetas de crédito**	tar-heh-tas deh creh-dee-to

NUMBERS

1	uno (ooh-noh)	12	doce (doh-seh)	50	cuenta (seen-kwen-tah)
2	dos (dohs)	13	trece (treh-seh)	60	sesenta (seh-sehn-tah)
3	tres (trehs)	14	catorce (kah-tohr-seh)	70	setenta (seh-tehn-tah)
4	cuatro (kwah-troh)	15	quince (keen-seh)	80	ochenta (oh-chehn-tah)
5	cinco (seen-koh)	16	dieciséis (dyeh-see-sayes)	90	noventa (noh-behn-tah)
6	seis (sayes)	17	diecisiete (dyeh-see-syeh-teh)	100	cien (syehn)
7	siete (syeh-teh)	18	dieciocho (dyeh-syoh-choh)	200	doscientos (do-syehn-tohs)
8	ocho (oh-choh)	19	diecinueve (dyeh-see-nweh-beh)	500	quinientos (kee-nyehn-tohs)
9	nueve (nweh-beh)	20	veinte (bayn-teh)	1,000	mil (meel)
10	diez (dyehs)	30	treinta (trayn-tah)		
11	once (ohn-seh)	40	cuarenta (kwah-ren-tah)		

TRANSPORTATION TERMS

English	Spanish	Pronunciation
airport	**Aeropuerto**	Ah-eh-roh-*pwehr*-toh
flight	**Vuelo**	*Bweh*-loh
rental car agency	**Arrendadora de autos**	Ah-*rehn*-da-doh-rah deh *ow*-tohs
bus	**Autobús**	Ow-toh-*boos*
bus or truck	**Camión**	Ka-*myohn*

English	Spanish	Pronunciation
lane	**Carril**	Kah-*reel*
nonstop (bus)	**Directo**	Dee-*rehk*-toh
baggage (claim area)	**Equipajes**	Eh-kee-*pah*-hehss
intercity	**Foraneo**	Foh-rah-*neh*-oh
luggage storage area	**Guarda equipaje**	*Gwar*-dah eh-kee-*pah*-heh
arrival gates	**Llegadas**	Yeh-*gah*-dahss
originates at this station	**Local**	Loh-*kahl*
originates elsewhere	**De paso**	Deh *pah*-soh
Are seats available?	**Hay lugares disponibles?**	Eye loo-*gah*-rehs dis-pohn-ee-blehss
first class	**Primera**	Pree-*meh*-rah
second class	**Segunda**	Seh-*goon*-dah
nonstop (flight)	**Sin escala**	Seen ess-*kah*-lah
baggage claim area	**Recibo de equipajes**	Reh-*see*-boh deh eh-kee-*pah*-hehss
waiting room	**Sala de espera**	*Sah*-lah deh ehss-*peh*-rah
toilets	**Sanitarios**	Sah-nee-*tah*-ryohss
ticket window	**Taquilla**	Tah-*kee*-yah

DINING TERMINOLOGY
Menu Reader

Latin American cuisine varies broadly from region to region, but we've tried to make our list of classic dishes as encompassing as possible. In this category, we're listing the Spanish name first (as you might see it on your menu) then the English equivalent.

APPETIZERS/TAPAS

Spanish	English	Pronunciation
aceitunas	olives	ah-seh-ee-*too*-nahs
albóndigas	meatballs in sauce	ahl-*bohn*-dee-gahs
bacalao	dried salt cod	bah-kah-*lah*-oh
conejo	braised rabbit	koh-*neh*-ho
croquetas	croquettes	kroh-*keh*-tahs
gambas	broiled shrimp with garlic	*gahm*-bahs
jamón	ham	hah-*mohn*
pescados fritos	fried fish	pehs-*kah*-dohs *free*-tohs
quesos	cheeses	*keh*-sohs
de leche de cabra	goat's milk	deh *leh*-cheh deh *kah*-brah
rallado	grated	rah-*yah*-doh
tortilla española	omelet with potato	tohr-*tee*-yah ehs-pah-*nyoh*-lah

SALADS

Spanish	English	Pronunciation
chonta	hearts-of-palm salad	*chohn*-tah
ensalada mixta	salad with lettuce, tomatoes, olives, tuna	ehn-sah-*lah*-dah *mees*-tah
ensalada de verdures	green salad	ehn-sah-*lah*-dah deh vehr-*doo*-rahs
ensalada de espinacas	spinach salad	ehn-sah-*lah*-dah deh ehs-pee-*nah*-kahs

SAUCES/SEASONING BASES

Spanish	English	Pronunciation
adobo	mixture of crushed peppercorns, salt, oregano, garlic, olive oil, and lime juice or vinegar	ah-*doh*-boh
mole	sauce of unsweetened chocolate, chilies, and spices	*moh*-leh
sofrito	mixture of onions, cilantro, garlic, and chilies	soh-*free*-tohs

SOUPS AND STEWS

Spanish	English	Pronunciation
buseca	stew with sausages	boo-*seh*-kah
caldo gallego	soup with salt pork, white beans, chorizo, ham, and turnip/collard greens	*kahl*-doh gah-*yeh*-goh
gazpacho	cold vegetable soup	gahs-*pah*-cho
locro de papas	creamy potato soup	*loh*-kroh deh *pah*-pahs
sancocho, sancochado	thick soup with meats, vegetables, and corn on the cob, served with rice	sahn-*koh*-choh, sahn-koh-*chah*-doh
sancocho de gallina	chicken soup	sahn-*koh*-choh deh gah-*yee*-nah
sopa de ajo	garlic soup	*soh*-pah deh *ah*-hoh
sopa de chiles poblanos	green chili soup	*soh*-pah deh *chee*-lehs poh-*blah*-nohs
sopa negra/frijoles negros	black bean soup	*soh*-pah *neh*-grah/free-*hoh*-lehs *neh*-grohs

RICE DISHES

Spanish	English	Pronunciation
Arroz con pollo	chicken and rice	ah-*rrohs* kohn poy-yo
arroz con gandules	yellow rice with pigeon peas	. . . gahn-*doo*-lehs
arroz negro	rice stew with octopus in its own ink	ah-*rrohs* *neh*-groh

SIDE/VEGETABLE DISHES

Spanish	English	Pronunciation
papas fritas	french fries	pah-pas free-tas
choclo	Andean corn	choc-lo
chiles rellenos	poblano peppers stuffed with cheese or ground meat, battered and fried	*chee*-lehs rreh-*yeh*-nohs
tostones	fried plantain slices	tohs-*toh*-nehs
yuca frita	fried yucca	*yoo*-kah *free*-tah

BEEF

Spanish	English	Pronunciation
bife de lomo	filet mignon	*bee*-feh deh *loh*-moh
carne en polvo	seasoned ground beef	*kahr*-neh ehn *pohl*-voh
locro criollo	beef stew with potatoes	*loh*-kroh kree-*oh*-yoh
olla de carne	beef stew with yucca, squash, and pumpkin	*oh*-yah deh *kahr*-neh
ropa vieja	stewed shredded beef	*roh*-pah *vyeh*-hah

GOAT

Spanish	English	Pronunciation
cabrito asado	oven-roasted kid	kah-*bree*-toh ah-*sah*-doh
seco de chivo	goat stew in wine sauce	*seh*-koh deh *chee*-voh

PORK

Spanish	English	Pronunciation
carnitas	slow-cooked pork served with corn tortillas	kahr-*nee*-tahs
chicharrón	deep-fried pork skin	chee-chah-*rrohn*
cochinillo/lechón	asado roast suckling pig	koh-chee-*nee*-yoh/leh-*chohn* ah-SAH-doh
costillas	pork ribs	kohs-*tee*-yahs
puerco en adobo	pork in chili sauce	*pwehr*-koh ehn ah-*doh*-boh
seco de chancho	pork stew	*seh*-koh deh *chahn*-cho

POULTRY

Spanish	English	Pronunciation
ají de gallina	creamed chicken with green chilies	ah-*hee* deh gah-*yee*-nah
arroz con pollo	rice with chicken and vegetables	ah-*rrohs* kohn *poh*-yoh
chilaquiles	chicken/cheese/tortilla casserole	chee-lah-*kee*-lehs

Spanish	English	Pronunciation
mole poblano	chicken with bitter chocolate/chili sauce	*moh*-leh poh-*blah*-noh
pollo a la brasa	spit-roasted chicken	*poh*-yoh ah lah *brah*-sah
pollo al jerez	chicken in sherry	*poh*-yoh ahl heh-*rehs*
pollo frito	fried chicken	*poh*-yoh *free*-toh
empanadas de pavo	turkey meat pies	ehm-pah-*nah*-dahs deh *pah*-voh
patas de pavo rellenas	stuffed turkey legs	*pah*-tahs deh *pah*-voh reh-YEH-nahs
sopa de pavo	turkey soup	*soh*-pah deh *pah*-voh

FISH AND SEAFOOD

Spanish	English	Pronunciation
ceviche	seafood marinated with lemon or lime, along with cilantro, garlic, red pepper, and onion; served cold	seh-*vee*-cheh
escabeche	spicy fish stew	ehs-kah-*beh*-cheh
zarzuela	mixed fish and seafood soup with tomatoes, saffron, garlic, and wine served over bread	sahr-*sweh*-lah
jueyes hervidos	boiled crab	*hweh*-yehs ehr-*vee*-dohs
camarones en cerveza	shrimp in beer	kah-mah-*roh*-nehs ehn sehr-*veh*-sah
bacalao guisado	cod marinated in herbs	bah-kah-*lah*-oh gee-*sah*-doh
camarones al ajillo	garlic shrimp stew	kah-mah-*roh*-nehs ahl ah-*hee*-yoh
chupin de camarones	spicy shrimp stew	*choo*-peen deh kah-mah-*roh*-nehs
salmorejo de jueyes	crab in tomato and garlic sauce	sahl-moh-*reh*-hoh deh *hweh*-yehs
taquitos de pescado	grilled shark in tomato sauce on tacos	tah-*kee*-tohs deh pehs-*kah*-doh

DESSERTS

Spanish	English	Pronunciation
arroz con leche/arroz con	dulce rice pudding	ah-*rrohs* kohn *leh*-cheh/ah-*rrohs* kohn *dool*-seh
buñuelos	round, thin fritters dipped in sugar (may also be savory)	boon-yoo-*eh*-lohs
dulce de plátano	ripe yellow plantains cooked in wine and spices	*dool*-seh deh *plah*-tah-noh
flan	custard	flahn
helado	ice cream	eh-*lah*-doh
panqueques	dessert crepes with caramel and whipped cream	pahn-*keh*-kehs

Spanish	English	Pronunciation
sopapillas	puffed-up crisps of a pie crust like dough, drizzled with honey and sprinkled with powdered sugar	soh-pah-*pee*-yahs
tembleque	coconut milk custard	tehm-*bleh*-keh
pastel tres leches	three-milk cake	pahs-*tehl* trehs *leh*-chehs

STREET FOOD

Spanish	English	Pronunciation
arepas	savory stuffed cornmeal patties	ah-*reh*-pahs
caña	raw sugar cane	*kah*-nyah
chalupas	corn tortillas filled with meat and cheese	chah-*loo*-pahs
chicha	fermented (alcoholic) corn drink	*chee*-chah
chorreados	corn pancakes with sour cream	choh-rreh-*ah*-dohs
churros	breakfast/dessert fritters	*choo*-rrohs
coco verde	green coconut	*koh*-koh *vehr*-deh
cuchifrito	deep-fried pork pieces (ears, tail, and so on)	koo-chee-*free*-toh
empañadas/ empanadas	turnovers filled with meat and/or cheese, beans, potatoes	ehm-pah-*nyah*-dahs/ehm-pah-*nah*-dahs
empanadas chilenas	turnovers filled with meat, boiled onion and raisins, an olive, and part of a hard-boiled egg	ehm-pah-*nah*-dahs chee-*leh*-nahs
enchiladas	pastries stuffed with cheese, meat, or potatoes	ehn-chee-*lah*-dahs
gorditas	thick, fried corn tortillas stuffed with cheese, beans, and/or meat	gohr-*dee*-tahs
juanes	rice tamales with chicken or fish	*hwah*-nehs
pupusas	corn pancakes with cheese	poo-*poo*-sahs
quesadillas	tortillas with cheese	keh-sah-*dee*-yahs
rellenos	bits of meat or cheese breaded with yucca or potato paste and deep-fried	rreh-*yeh*-nohs
salteñas (aka empanadas chilenas)	chicken or beef with onions and raisins wrapped in pastry	sahl-*teh*-nyahs

Street food is generally inexpensive. Keep a supply of small-denomination bills and change on you because vendors generally won't be able to change large bills.

Spanish	English	Pronunciation
tacos	corn/flour tortillas with beef/ chicken/pork	*tah*-kohs
tamales	chicken, pork, or potatoes with chilies in cornmeal steamed inside a banana leaf or corn husk	tah-*mah*-lehs
tortas	sandwiches with meat and/or cheese, garnished with vegetables	*tohr*-tahs

Index